On-line support for
BEHAVIOR IN ORGANIZATIONS SEVENTH EDITION

What is PHLIP? Prentice Hall Learning on the Internet Partnership (PHLIP) is a content-rich, multidisciplinary business education Web site created by professors for professors and their students. Developed by Professor Dan Cooper at Marist College, PHLIP provides academic support for faculty and students using this text.

For Students

- **STUDENT STUDY HALL**
  - ◆ **Ask the Tutor** offers Virtual Office Hours.
  - ◆ **Writing Center** provides links to on-line resources.
  - ◆ **Study Skills Center** provides study-skills tips and resources.
  - ◆ **Career Center** offers tips, sample resumes and on-line job applications.
  - ◆ **Research Center** provides resources for using the Internet as a research tool.
- **CURRENT EVENTS** summarize and link to current news articles. Each article is fully supported by group activities, critical thinking exercises, discussion questions, reference resources, key topics, and more.
- **INTERACTIVE STUDY GUIDE** offers multiple-choice and true/false questions for every chapter. Students submit responses to the PHLIP server for scoring and receive immediate feedback, including page references linked to the text. Students can e-mail their scores to the instructor and/or teaching assistant.
- **INTERNET RESOURCES** provide links to related Web sites, complete with an "Info" button that offers professors and students a helpful description of each site.

For Instructors

- **TEXT-SPECIFIC RESOURCES**
  - ◆ Downloadable supplements
  - ◆ On-line faculty support
- **FACULTY LOUNGE**
  - ◆ **Talk to the Team** is a password-protected conference and chat room system.
  - ◆ **Teaching Archive** includes sample syllabi.
  - ◆ **Help with Computers** provides tips and links to on-line tutorials.
  - ◆ **Internet Skills** offers advice, tips, and tutorials for using the Internet.

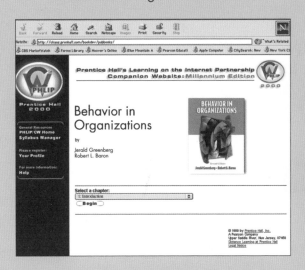

For more information on PHLIP resources, please see the preface of this book, or visit our Web site at

www.prenhall.com/greenberg

Cristina Colwell

Cristina Colwell

BEHAVIOR IN ORGANIZATIONS

Understanding and Managing
the Human Side of Work

SEVENTH EDITION

BEHAVIOR IN ORGANIZATIONS

Understanding and Managing the Human Side of Work

Jerald Greenberg
The Ohio State University

Robert A. Baron
Rensselaer Polytechnic Institute

Prentice Hall, Upper Saddle River, New Jersey 07458

Senior Acquisitions Editor: Stephanie Johnson
Editor-in-Chief: Natalie Anderson
Assistant Editor: Hersch Doby
Managing Editor (editorial): Jennifer Glennon
Marketing Manager: Michael Campbell
Associate Managing Editor (production): Judith Leale
Manufacturing Supervisor: Arnold Vila
Senior Manufacturing Manager: Vincent Scelta
Senior Designer: Cheryl Asherman
Design Manager: Patricia Smythe
Interior Design: Donna Wickes
Line Art: Electra Graphics
Infographics: Batelman Illustration
Cover painting: Alain Reno
Cover Design: Robin Hoffman
Composition: York Graphic Services

Library of Congress Cataloging-in-Publication Data
Greenberg, Jerald.
    Behavior in organizations : understanding and managing the human
side of work / Jerald Greenberg, Robert A. Baron. — 7th ed.
      p. cm.
    ISBN 0-13-085026-8
    1. Organizational behavior.   2. Personnel management.   i. Baron,
Robert A.   II. Title.
HD58.7.B37   1999
658.3—dc21

99-14674
CIP

Prentice-Hall International (UK) Limited, London
Prentice-Hall of Australia Pty. Limited, Sydney
Prentice-Hall Canada, Inc., Toronto
Prentice-Hall Hispanoamericana, S.A., Mexico
Prentice-Hall of India Private Limited, New Delhi
Prentice-Hall of Japan, Inc., Tokyo
Prentice-Hall (Singapore) Pte. Ltd.
Editora Prentice-Hall do Brasil, Ltda., Rio de Janeiro

Printed in the United States of America

10 9 8 7 6 5 4 3 2

BRIEF CONTENTS

CONTENTS

Ushering Organizational Behavior into the Twenty-First Century

It is a new century—a new millennium, in fact—and you hold in your hands a new edition of this book. Although these facts are merely coincidental, the dawning of a new era cannot help but force us to consider how the field of organizational behavior (OB) has changed in recent years—and how these changes are reflected in this text. After all, as the seventh edition launches this book into its third decade of publication, the field of OB clearly has changed dramatically.

In preparing this edition of *Behavior in Organizations*, we have chronicled these various twists and turns to provide the most up-to-date coverage of the field to be found in any text. Some changes have been revolutionary and others merely evolutionary. We have seen changes that are truly substantial and others that border on the cosmetic. Topics have waxed and waned in popularity, albeit with neither the speed nor the deliberateness of the fashion designer. The balance of attention to research and theory relative to practical application in the field also has shifted. None of these changes escaped our attention as we updated this book.

Frankly, it would be impossible to ignore them. After all, these trends confront both of us daily in all our professional activities (away from the glamorous world of authoring textbooks). We both teach very demanding and sophisticated college students with work experience who know what is going on in the business world—and who do not hesitate to tell us whenever we may appear misguided. The same goes for the employees at all levels whom we train, and with whom we consult, in companies both large and small throughout the country. They not only care intimately about the latest developments in OB, they live with them daily on their jobs and in their lives. Such individuals—from highly paid executives to minimum-wage laborers—keep us focused on reality. They deny us the simplistic luxury of offering the ivory tower–only view of OB toward which we might lean based on our professional training—and more than a half century of combined experience—as social scientists.

At the same time, we also are active researchers in universities where scholarly contributions not only are valued but demanded. We are proud of the body of knowledge our field's research has generated—not just our own work but also that of our many colleagues. After all, without such scholarly contributions, we would have no basis for knowing—let alone teaching—anything about OB that went beyond mere speculation based on personal experience. Of course, as a field, OB is firmly grounded in science, and these scientific underpinnings also are squarely highlighted in this book.

As you read this, you may be left with the impression this book is a blend of many things. If so, we would not have misled you. In fact, that conclusion would be correct not only regarding this text but also regarding the field itself. And that is precisely our point: Because the field of OB is a blend of many things, so, too, and quite deliberately, is this book.

A CAREFULLY BALANCED APPROACH TO THE FIELD

It helps to think of our coverage as taking a carefully balanced approach to OB. Some competing textbooks focus a great deal on one topic or another. Others invest all their intellectual capital in a particular conceptual or pedagogical approach. These presentations then are justified as selling points. We do not take this approach. Yes, such books are unique, but their uniqueness comes at a cost: Skewed approaches do not reflect what today's field of OB is really like. To us, it is crucial to characterize the field as it is, and it is a responsibility we do not take lightly. For this reason, we focus on representing OB as the balanced, integrated field it is.

To illustrate this point, let us consider how our balanced approach comes across in four major respects: topic coverage, mix of theory and practice, company examples, and pedagogical focus.

Topic Coverage: Old and New

You would not have a serious OB book without attention to Weber's concept of bureaucracy, Maslow's need hierarchy, Woodward's research linking technology and organizational structure, and dozens of other classical theories and studies. Such works are to be found in these pages.

Competing for space are an equal number of more contemporary approaches to OB. Consider, for example, just a few of the many new topics covered in this book:

- Employee support policies (chapter 1)
- Innovative reward systems (chapter 2)
- Practical, emotional, and cognitive intelligence (chapter 3)
- Procedural justice (chapter 4)
- Dispositional model of job satisfaction (chapter 5)
- Entrepreneurship (chapter 6)
- High-performance teams (chapter 7)
- Video-mediated communication (chapter 8)
- Goal-framing effects (chapter 9)
- Deviant organizational behavior (chapter 10)
- Issue selling (chapter 11)
- Autocratic-delegation continuum model (chapter 12)
- Double S cube model of organizational culture (chapter 13)
- Autonomous and systemic change (chapter 14)
- Machine vision (chapter 15)
- Strategic planning (chapter 16)

Theory? Research? Practice? Yes, Yes, and Yes!

In an old TV commercial, two people are arguing whether the product in question is a candy mint or a breath mint. Shortly into the debate (albeit not quick enough for our tastes), someone proposes a resolution: "Stop," she says, "you're both right." We are reminded of this drama whenever we hear similar discussions about OB. To those who argue "OB is a theoretical field" or "OB is an applied field," we issue the same admonishment: "Stop, you're both right."

Indeed, our image of the field of OB is of an applied science—that is, science undertaken with practical applications in mind. Those of us who are involved in OB think of ourselves as scientist-practitioners. We conduct "pure" scientific research to understand fundamental individual, group, and organizational processes. We then put this knowledge to use in organizations, and based on what we learn, we go back to the drawing board, revise our underlying theories as dictated, and conduct more research. This leads to more application, and so the cycle continues. This, we believe, makes the field of OB so special, so unique, and so important.

We have gone out of our way in this book to capture the process of moving from theory to research to application and back to theory. This is a broad and a dynamic approach, thus making it difficult to capture, but we believe we have done so—at least wherever the various pieces of the puzzle are identifiable. For example, in chapter 2, we cover both theories of learning and how these theories are involved in such organizational practices as training and OB modification. We design parallels between theory and practice in chapter 4, where we consider the practical implications of each of the theories of motivation we discuss, and we do the same in chapter 5, where we consider theories of job satisfaction and organizational commitment as well as how these approaches may be applied to improving these important organizational attitudes.

More than simply indicating how various theories *may be* applied, we identify precisely how they *are being* applied in today's organizations. For example, in chapter 6, we not only describe the mentorship process but also precisely the forms it is taking today. Similarly, our discussion of diversity management programs in chapter 5 not only analyzes the various forms they take but brings these abstractions to life by identifying exactly what certain companies are doing in diversity management. These are just a few examples. We systematically discuss actual organizational practices throughout this book, and our reasons for doing so are straightforward: It brings the theoretical material to life, and it illustrates the simple truth that the practice of OB is crucial in today's organizations. To talk only about theory, research, or practical application (potential or actual) would be misleading, because the field of OB is all these things. So, too, have we tried to incorporate all these elements into this book.

Company Examples: "Varied" Is the Operative Word

In keeping with our interest in presenting the field of OB as it really is, we went out of our way to describe organizations as they really are. Because today's organizations are so varied, this is no simple task.

Monoliths like GM and Exxon are still on the scene, but clearly they are not the same companies that they were only a few years ago—a fact that has not escaped our attention. Today, we find many people going to work for small upstarts—companies that give employees the opportunity to get in on the ground floor of ventures, which in a few years may become very big, or might not exist at all. Beyond those who opt to work for small companies rather than large ones, there are others who prefer to venture out on their own. Such entrepreneurial ventures are a key part of the work scene and they too are identified in this book. Coverage of a wide variety of organizations is an important feature of this book, because for OB to be a viable field, it must be relevant to the many different kinds of organizations that exist.

If we are guilty of skewing our coverage of organizational examples in any particular way, the evidence may be found in two areas. First, we deliberately paid attention to new forms of business that have been emerging rapidly due to technological advances such as Internet-based organizations (e.g, Yahoo!). Because these types of enterprises have been revolutionizing the world of business, we believe they deserve special attention. This is not to say that we have ignored more traditional, low-tech organizations; indeed, we have plenty to say about them as well. However, given how cyber-businesses are taking over so many forms of commerce (just ask your local bookstore owner about Amazon.com), we felt it was worthwhile to spotlight them wherever appropriate.

We also went out of our way to describe organizations based outside the United States. We highlight the global nature of today's business world in the form of several special features. However, our awareness of the international nature of organizations goes beyond these features to the examples we use to illustrate key points about organizational behavior. Examples of foreign companies and multinational firms based throughout the world are used throughout the book. For example, we launch chapter 1 with a case about Kikkoman, a Japanese company that manufactures soy sauce using an ancient recipe in a modern manufacturing plant located in rural Wisconsin. We like this case—and are pleased to begin the book with it—precisely because of the way it juxtaposes old and new, big and small, and foreign and domestic. In short, it is the embodiment of the "anything goes" approach that is so typical of today's organizations.

Pedagogical Focus: Knowledge and Skills

Educators say there is a fundamental distinction between teaching people about something—that is, providing *knowledge*—and showing them how to do something—that is, developing *skills*. In the field of OB, this distinction becomes blurred. After all, to appreciate fully how to do something, you must have the requisite knowledge. Thus, we pay attention in this book to both knowledge and skills.

As an illustration, consider how the two orientations come together in chapter 13. We describe how the process of creativity works, and we provide tools for developing one's own creativity. The same duality also may be seen in chapter 8. In the course of describing organizational communication, we discuss the process of listening; then, to help readers become effective listeners, we present an exercise designed to promote active listening skills. By doing this—not only in these two examples but throughout this book—we intend to enable readers not only to understand OB but to be in a better position to practice it in their own lives.

Taken together, our coverage of classic and cutting-edge topics; attention to the blend between theory, research, and practice; and dual emphasis on knowledge and skills reflects what we consider to be a balanced and realistic orientation to OB. This is the essence of the field as we know it—and of this book as we present it to you here.

NEW CHAPTERS AND SPECIAL FEATURES

In the course of revising this book, we made many changes. Some came in the process of seeking that balance to which we just referred; others were necessitated by the latest advances in the field. Many of the changes are subtle, affecting only how a topic was framed relative to others. Many other changes, however, are more noticeable and involve the shifting of major topics into new places and the addition of new topics. Doing this required the creation of several new chapters and the addition of several new features.

New and Newly Organized Chapters

Readers who already are familiar with this book will immediately note some new and newly organized chapters. For example:

- *Chapter 6: "Managing Your Own Behavior: Careers and Stress."* This chapter brings together material that provides personal guidance and suggestions for readers. Here, the emphasis shifts from how to manage others to the more basic issue how to manage oneself.
- *Chapter 10: "Working With—and Against—Others: Prosocial and Deviant Behavior in Organizations."* By highlighting both the positive and the negative sides of human nature, this chapter juxtaposes two opposing themes in the field of OB. It provides an opportunity to expand our coverage of the growing literature on deviant behavior in organizations and to contrast it with a more established literature on helping and cooperating with others.

- *Chapter 13: "Culture, Creativity, and Innovation."* This chapter expands our coverage of organizational culture in keeping with growing interest in this topic. It also combines it with a new topic to this book—that is, creativity and innovation. Our orientation is both on individual and team creativity and on what it takes to turn such creativity into highly innovative organizations.
- *Chapter 15: "Technology in Organizations."* Previously, our coverage of technology was spread throughout the book. Here, however, this chapter brings these matters together, which we believe more thoroughly and effectively captures the essence of this important element of OB.

New Special Features

Several new features of this book are designed to make it easier than ever for readers to access material of special, applied interest. In addition to many in-text examples, each chapter also contains two special sections:

- *Trends: What Today's Companies Are Doing.* These sections provide close looks at OB in practice, with extended examples of current organizational practices illustrating key concepts from the book. This brings the material to life and makes it more relevant to students. Some examples include:

  - *Designing a Better Mailbag: Reducing Back Injuries Among Employees of the U.S. Postal System (chapter 3)*
  - *Videoconferencing: Groups in Cyberspace (chapter 7)*
  - *Meeting Consultants Are Making Meetings Work (chapter 8)*
  - *Naval Officers Use Decision Support Systems to Make Combat Decisions (chapter 9)*
  - *Coaching: From Locker Room to Board Room (chapter 12)*

- *Tips: Doing It Right.* These sections are a "how-to" guide to putting OB into practice, providing an overview of practical suggestions following directly from text material. Some highlights include:

  - *Making Telecommuting Work: Some Considerations (chapter 1)*
  - *How to Fire Someone Without Lighting a Fire (chapter 6)*
  - *How to Blow the Whistle Effectively (chapter 10)*
  - *When Should an Organization Go Virtual? (chapter 14)*
  - *Making Changes Stick: Three Not-So-Simple Suggestions from Sears, Shell, and the U.S. Army (chapter 16)*

There also are two new features that highlight the international focus of the field. These are:

- *OB Around the World.* Material in these special sections highlights the international nature of OB today. The emphasis is on how OB practices differ in various nations and how international factors influence the field. Here are just a few selected examples:

  - *Integrated Training at Petroleos de Venezuela's Corporate University, Centro Internacional de Educacion y Desarrolo (chapter 2).*
  - *What Motivates Eastern European Job Recruits? (chapter 4)*
  - *Absenteeism: Same Behavior, Different Meanings in Different Cultures (chapter 5)*
  - *The Organizational Politics of Selecting Women for Overseas Assignments (chapter 11)*
  - *U.S. Firms Lag Behind Japanese Firms in Innovation (chapter 13)*
  - *National Defense: A Concern When Exporting Technology (chapter 15)*

- *Global Matters.* Several of these brief sections "pop-up" throughout each chapter. They contain some combination of international-based facts and discussion points bearing on the text itself.

Another new feature focuses attention on the various ethical issues involved in the field of OB:

- *Ethics Matters.* Paralleling the Global Matters "pop-up boxes," several of these brief sections also appear in each chapter. They contain questions that challenge readers to recognize the ethical issues associated with the text. These, too, are positioned where relevant.

RETURN OF YOUR FAVORITE SPECIAL FEATURES

Fans of the sixth edition of this book need not worry about the whereabouts of the book's most popular special features. These are back—and better than ever. They include:

- *You Be the Consultant.* Special sections asking readers how they would use the material in each chapter to solve organizational problems.
- *Skills Bank.* Each chapter contains a *Skills Bank* consisting of two experiential exercises, one focusing on individual insight and assessment (i.e., "Experiencing Organizational Behavior") and another focusing on group-level experiences (i.e., "Working in Groups"). Many of these exercises are new to this edition.
- *Cases.* Each chapter contains two cases, most of which are completely new or updated. One at the beginning of the chapter (i.e., "Preview Case") is designed to put the material that follows in the context of a real organizational event. The chapter-end case, (i.e., "Case in Point"), is designed to review the material already covered and to bring that material to life. Specific tie-ins are made by use of discussion questions appearing after each "Case in Point" feature.
- *Talking Graphics.* All data presented in graphs come complete with labeled boxes literally pointing at the major idea it contains. Between the highly descriptive in-text material, detailed captions, and these talking graphics, students will continue to find this book to be approachable and easy to understand.

UPDATED SUPPLEMENTS PACKAGE

The changes outlined above constitute the key alterations we have made in the text itself. Other changes, however, involve the materials that accompany *Behavior in Organizations* (7th edition). Foremost among these are:

PHLIP/CW Web Site
(www.prenhall.com/greenberg)

At last, you can now bring the Internet into the OB classroom in a meaningful fashion. PHLIP (Prentice Hall Learning on the Internet Partnership) was developed by Professor Dan Cooper at Marist College, and it provides academic support for faculty and students using this text. PHLIP is divided into a **Student Page** and a **Faculty Page.** The Faculty Page helps professors prepare lectures, integrate technology into the classroom, and enhance in- and out-of-class learning with industry examples as current as today's world news. The Student Page supports students through an Interactive Study Guide, current events cases and exercises, study skills, and writing and research assistance. Features include:

For Instructors (Faculty Page)
- Text-specific **Faculty Resources** including downloadable supplements (Instructor's Manual, Technology Resource Manual, and PowerPoint presentations) and on-line faculty support for the Student Page (including additional cases, articles, links, and suggested answers to the questions posted on the Student Page).
- **Faculty Lounge** featuring generic faculty resources:

  - Talk to the Team *is a moderated and password-protected conference and chat room system designed to allow faculty the opportunity to ask questions, make suggestions, and explore new teaching ideas.*
  - Teaching Archive *features teaching resources submitted by instructors throughout the world, and includes tips, techniques, academic papers, and* **Sample Syllabi** *for traditional classroom presentations and for integrating technology in and out of the classroom.*
  - Help with Computers *provides tips and links to tutorials to help you master spreadsheets, word processing, and/or presentation software.*
  - Internet Skills *offers beginner and advanced advice, tips, and tutorials for using the Internet.*

For Students (Student Page)
- **Student Study Hall** helps develop students' study skills through the following resources:

  - Ask the Tutor *serves as Virtual Office Hours—allowing students to post questions or comments to the threaded message board and receive responses from both the PHLIP faculty and the entire learning community. This feature is monitored by Professor Dan Cooper to maintain quality.*
  - Writing Center *provides links to on-line dictionaries, writing tutors, style and grammar guides, and additional tools to help students develop their writing skills.*
  - Study Skills Center *helps students develop better study skills.*
  - Career Center *encourages students to investigate potential employers, get career information and advice, view sample résumés, and even apply for jobs on-line.*
  - Research Center *provides tips and resources that make it easy to harness the power of the Internet as a research tool through tutorials and descriptive links to virtual libraries and a wealth of search engines.*

- **Current Events Articles and Exercises** Each chapter offers numerous current events to keep your class up to date. Each current event is a summary and analysis of a current news event written by our PHLIP faculty provider and supported with links to the text, discussion questions, group activities, background/historical information, a glossary, a bibliography, and links to related news sources. Whenever possible, there is a link to the original article itself. New current events are added every two weeks (past current events remain on the site until they are no longer useful or valid).
- **Interactive Study Guide** offers multiple-choice and true/false questions for every chapter of this text. Students submit responses to the server, which scores them and provides immediate feedback, including additional help and page references linked to the text. Test scores can be sent to as many as four e-mail addresses.

- **Internet Resources** provide links to helpful Web sites, complete with an "Info" button that offers the professors and students a description of each site.

Revised Color Transparencies and Electronic Transparencies Package

We have revised and expanded the transparency package. A set of 100 full-color transparencies is available, consisting of art adapted from graphic material appearing in the book but redrawn for clearer classroom use. Lecture notes accompany each transparency. Over 200 electronic transparencies also are available on 3½" disk using Microsoft PowerPoint files for the IBM.

Test Item File

A thoroughly revised and expanded **Test Bank** is available to instructors. It contains 100 items per chapter, including multiple choice, scenario-based multiple choice, and essay questions. The Test Bank is designed for use with the Prentice Hall Custom Test program. This computerized package is available in a Windows format.

Extensive Instructor's Manual

The **Instructor's Manual** contains a variety of useful features for instructors using this book in their classes. Among these are: chapter outlines, chapter synopses, answers to all questions within boxed material, answers to end-of-chapter discussion questions, answers/suggestions for Case-in-Point critical thinking questions, and answers/suggestions to Skills Portfolio exercises.

Prentice Hall Organizational Behavior Video Library

A feature that truly brings OB to life is a set of videotapes containing clips and interviews with business leaders taken from the acclaimed public television series *Small Business 2000*. There are 16 video segments. All of these videos are coordinated with the video cases appearing at the end of each chapter of the book. Notes for the cases and the videos appear in the Video User's Guide found inside the *Instructor's Manual*.

ACKNOWLEDGMENTS: SOME WORDS OF THANKS

Writing is a solitary task. However, turning millions of bytes of information stored on a handful of plastic disks into a book is a magical process that requires an army of talented folks. In preparing this text, we have been fortunate enough to be assisted by many dedicated and talented people. Although we cannot possibly thank all of them here, we wish to express our appreciation to those whose help has been most valuable.

First, our sincere thanks to our colleagues who read and commented on various portions of the manuscript for this and earlier editions of this book. Their suggestions were invaluable, and helped us in many ways. These include:

Royce L. Abrahamson, Southwest Texas State University
Rabi S. Bhagat, Memphis State University
Ralph R. Braithwaite, University of Hartford
Stephen C. Buschardt, University of Southern Mississippi
Dawn Carlson, University of Utah

Roy A. Cook, Fort Lewis College
Cynthis Cordes, State University of New York at Binghamton
Patricia Feltes, Southwest Missouri State University
Olene L. Fuller, San Jacinto College North
Richard Grover, University of Southern Maine
Courtney Hunt, University of Delaware
Ralph Katerberg, University of Cincinnati
Paul N. Keaton, University of Wisconsin at LaCrosse
Mary Kernan, University of Delaware
Daniel Levi, California Polytechnic State University
Jeffrey Lewis, Pitzer College
Rodney Lim, Tulane University
Charles W. Mattox, Jr., St. Mary's University
James McElroy, Iowa State University
Richard McKinney, Southern Illinois University
Linda Morable, Richland College
Paula Morrow, Iowa State University
Audry Murrell, University of Pittsburgh
William D. Patzig, James Madison University
Shirley Rickert, Indiana University—Purdue University at Fort Wayne
David W. Roach, Arkansas Tech University
Terri A. Scandura, University of Miami, Coral Gables
Marc Siegall, California State University, Chico
Taggart Smith, Purdue University
Patrick C. Stubbleine, Indiana University—Purdue University at Fort Wayne
Paul Sweeney, Marquette University
Carol Watson, Rider University
Philip A. Weatherford, Embry-Riddle Aeronautical University
Richard M. Weiss, University of Delaware

Second, we wish to express our appreciation to our editor, Stephanie Johnson, who saw us through this project. Her enthusiasm was contagious, and her constant support and good humor helped us bring this book to completion in a timely and enjoyable manner. Stephanie's assistant, Hersch Doby was always there to help, as was the associate editor, Shane Gemza. Our managing editor, Jennifer Glennon, did a terrific job of keeping us focused on all the many details that go into writing a book like this. And, of course, we would be remiss in not thanking Sandy Steiner, Jim Boyd, and Brian Kibby, key members of the PH management team, for their steadfast support of this book.

Third, our sincere thanks go out to Prentice Hall's top-notch production team for making this book so beautiful—Judy Leale, production editor; Cheryl Asherman, senior designer; and Mary Jo Gregory of York Production Services. Their diligence and skill with matters of design, permissions, and illustrations—not to mention constant refinements—helped us immeasurably throughout the process of preparing this work. It was a pleasure to work with such kind and understanding professionals, and we are greatly indebted to them for their contributions.

Finally, we wish to thank our colleagues who have provided expert assistance in preparing various features for this book. Rob Panco diligently researched and wrote the very interesting *Video Cases* that end each chapter. James V. Dupree did a terrific job on the *Test Bank* and *Instructor's Manual*.

Finally, Jerald Greenberg wishes to acknowledge the family of the late Irving Abramowitz for their generous endowment to the Ohio State University, which provided invaluable support during the writing of this book.

To all these truly outstanding people, and to many others too, our warm personal regards.

IN CONCLUSION: AN INVITATION FOR FEEDBACK

Looking back, we can honestly say that we have spared no effort in preparing a book that reflects the current character of the field of OB regarding both scientific inquiry and practical application. Of course, whether and to what extent we have reached this goal, however, can only be judged by you, our colleagues and students. So, as always, we sincerely invite your input. Feel free to e-mail us or to leave a message at our publisher's Web site (http://www.prenhall.com).

Please let us know what you like about the book and what features need improvement. Such feedback is always welcomed, and it will not fall on deaf ears. We promise faithfully to take your comments and suggestions to heart and to incorporate them into the next edition of this book.

Jerald Greenberg
The Ohio State University
GREENBERG1.@OSU.EDU

Robert A. Baron
Rensselaer Polytechnic Institute
BARON@RPI.EDU

PART ONE

Organizational Behavior:
An Introduction

THE FIELD OF ORGANIZATIONAL BEHAVIOR

LEARNING OBJECTIVES

After reading this chapter, you should be able to

1. Define the concepts of *organization* and *organizational behavior*.
2. Describe the field of organizational behavior's commitment to the *scientific method* and the *three levels of analysis* it uses.
3. Trace the historical developments and schools of thought leading up to the field of organizational behavior today.
4. Identify the fundamental characteristics of the field of organizational behavior.
5. Describe how the *global economy* is shaping the field of organizational behavior today.
6. Explain how the workforce is becoming increasingly diversified and how this has led to the development of *flexible working arrangements*.
7. Describe how *technology* has led to the development of new organizational forms.
8. Explain how rising expectations about *quality* and *ethical behavior* have influenced the field of organizational behavior.

PREVIEW CASE

There's No Business Like Shoyu Business

How many companies can you think of that have been in continuous operation since 1630? How about companies with manufacturing plants in both urban Tokyo and rural Wisconsin? Not getting any easier? Here's a hint: It manufactures the world's oldest condiment from fermented soy beans and wheat. Give up? It's Kikkoman — one of Japan's oldest and largest companies and known worldwide for its soy sauce (called *shoyu* in Japanese).

Kikkoman soy sauce holds a commanding 50 percent share of the market for Oriental bottle sauces in North America and a 30 percent share in Japan. To meet worldwide demand (soy sauce is sold in 100 countries around the world), production at Kikkoman has increased tenfold during the past 20 years. In 1997 alone, Kikkoman produced and sold some 116 million gallons of the ebony-colored liquid — an enormous quantity considering that soy sauce is sprinkled sparingly onto foods to help bring out their natural flavors, not gulped like a soft drink. Another reason this statistic is so impressive is that Kikkoman makes its soy sauce using a method that dates back to the seventeenth century and requires several months of brewing time.

Although it relies on traditional, natural ingredients (including a proprietary microorganism to create a culture called *koji*) instead of the chemical substitutes used by competitors, Kikkoman is far from ancient in its manufacturing processes. Its state-of-the-art manufacturing plants in Walworth, Wisconsin, and the Netherlands use the most modern technology available. In fact, outside of the soy sauce business, Kikkoman is regarded as a world leader in genetic engineering, biotechnology, and biochemistry. Using cell-fusion technology,

Kikkoman has even developed an entirely new species of citrus fruit — hardly what you might expect from a company pushing 400 years old.

Actually, Kikkoman is unusual in several ways. First, its founder was a woman — incredibly rare for the 1600s. Also, unlike most Japanese companies, which produce goods that originated in the United States (e.g., cars and electronic goods), Kikkoman has turned its uniquely Japanese product into a staple found in kitchens around the world. Still, the company adheres to the strongly held Japanese tradition of being loyal to its employees — an ideal most Western companies have abandoned. In fact, Kikkoman's commitment to treating individual workers like family permeates all aspects of the company's operations. Interestingly, it was Kikkoman's adherence to the honored Asian traditions of harmony and loyalty that made it an attractive partner for U.S.-based companies (e.g., Xerox) expanding into the Japanese and Chinese markets. Today, in large part because of such partnerships, Kikkoman is considered a key player in the world of international business.

Despite its long, international reach, Kikkoman is faithful to the countries in which it does business. In the Walworth, Wisconsin, plant, for example, the only items — including both ingredients (mostly soy, wheat, salt, and water) and equipment — that are not procured locally are the specialized items needed to make soy sauce. In addition, Kikkoman has been a generous contributor to the local community, not only in terms of expanding its tax base but also in making contributions to everything from 4-H projects to college scholarships for high-school students.

It is obvious that Kikkoman, with roots going back to feudal Japan but also poised on the cutting edge of biotechnology, has taken more than its share of risks over the years. As the ancient Japanese saying goes, "A frog in the well does not know the ocean." Clearly, Kikkoman left the well long ago to explore many different oceans.

T he more closely you examine this preview case, the clearer it becomes that success involves several factors. At the root of the company's success is an excellent product, but this is only the beginning. The road to failure is littered with many good products made by poorly managed companies that, as a result, are no longer with us. Kikkoman, however, has been around for such a long time and has had such great financial success because of its commitment to people — its employees, its suppliers, and its neighbors in the community. In addition, the company has been actively involved in new ventures, pushing the edge of technology and its own influence to the farthest reaches of the globe.

This blend of old and new makes Kikkoman a unique and interesting organization in the history of business. Yet, in many ways, at the base of this company's success lies a key ingredient (not soy!) that is responsible for success in all organizations — people. No matter how good a company's product or service may be, no matter how far a company's equipment pushes the cutting edge of technology, there can be no company without people. From the founder to the loyal employees, it's all about people. In fact, if you've ever managed a business, you know that "people problems" can bring down an organization very rapidly. Hence, it makes sense to realize that "the human side of work" (not coincidentally part of the subtitle of this book) is a critical element in the effective functioning — and even basic existence — of organizations. This people-centered orientation forms the basis of the field of *organizational behavior* (or *OB* for short), which specializes in the study of human behavior in organizations (Figure 1.1).

Scientists and practitioners of OB both study and attempt to solve problems using knowledge derived from research in the **behavioral sciences** (e.g., psychology and sociology). In other words, the field of OB is firmly rooted in science. It relies on research to derive valuable information about organizations and the complex processes that operate within them. Such knowledge is used as the basis for helping to solve a wide range of organizational problems. For example, what can be done to make people more productive and more satisfied on their jobs? When and how should people be organized into teams? How should jobs and organizations be designed to help people best adapt to changes in their work environment? These are just a few of the many important questions the field of OB addresses.

Specialists in OB have studied a variety of issues involving people in organizations. In fact, during the past few decades, OB has developed into a field so diverse that its scientists have examined nearly every conceivable aspect of behavior in organizations.[1] The fruits of this labor have already been enjoyed by people interested in making organizations not only more productive but also more pleasant for those within them.

The remainder of this chapter provides the background information needed to understand the scope of OB and its potential value. It is designed to introduce you formally to the field of OB by focusing on its history and fundamental characteristics. We begin by formally defining OB and describing exactly what it is and what it seeks to accomplish. We then summarize the history of the field, from its origins to its emergence as a modern science. Finally, we discuss the many factors that make OB the vibrant, ever-changing field it is today. After studying this chapter, you will be ready to face the primary goal of this book: To enhance your understanding of the human side of work by giving you a comprehensive overview of the field of OB.

behavioral sciences

Fields such as psychology and sociology that seek knowledge of human behavior and society through the scientific method.

ORGANIZATIONAL BEHAVIOR: A WORKING DEFINITION

Obviously, OB deals with organizations, but what exactly is an organization? Although you probably have a good idea of the answer, the concept of an organization can be difficult to define. Therefore, to avoid ambiguity, we offer the following definition: An

"You know what I think, folks? Improving technology isn't important. Increased profits aren't important. What's important is to be warm, decent human beings."

FIGURE 1.1

People: The Key Ingredient in Organizational Success

If the speaker had read this book, he would be aware that how people behave on the job is, in fact, closely associated with innovations in technology and profitability.

(*Source*: The New Yorker Collection 1987. J.B. Handelsman from cartoonbank.com. All Rights Reserved.)

organization

A structured social system consisting of groups of individuals working together to meet some agreed-on objectives.

organizational behavior

The field that seeks knowledge of all aspects of behaviors in organizational settings by the use of the scientific method.

organization is a structured social system consisting of groups and individuals working together to meet some agreed-on objectives. In other words, organizations consist of structured social units, such as people or work groups, that strive to attain a common goal, such as to produce and sell a product at a profit. This definition is rather abstract, but it will take on more meaning as you read this book.

Now that you know what we mean by an organization, we can define the field of OB formally and describe its basic characteristics. Specifically, **organizational behavior** is the field that seeks knowledge about the behaviors in organizational settings by systematically studying individual, group, and organizational processes. This knowledge is used both as an end in itself by scientists interested in basic human behavior and by practitioners interested in enhancing organizational effectiveness and individual well-being.

To bring this definition to life, we now take a closer look at the defining characteristics of the field itself. In other words, what is the essential nature of the field of OB? The answer lies in two major themes: commitment to the scientific method, and reliance on three levels of analysis.

Applying the Scientific Method to Practical Managerial Problems

Our definition of OB refers to seeking knowledge and studying behavioral processes. This should not be surprising, because as we noted earlier, knowledge in OB is based on the behavioral sciences. Although not as sophisticated or mature as the study of physics or chemistry, the orientation of OB remains scientific in nature. Thus, like other scientific fields, OB seeks to develop a base of knowledge using an empirical, research-based approach. In other words, it is based on systematic observation and measurement of the behavior or phenomenon of interest. As described in an appendix to this chapter, research into OB is neither easy nor foolproof, yet it is widely agreed that the scientific method is the best way to learn about such behavior. Therefore, the scientific orientation should be acknowledged as a hallmark of the field of OB.

Why is it so important to learn about behavior in organizational settings? The answer depends on who you ask. To social scientists, learning about human behavior on the job — "what makes people tick" in organizations — is valuable for its own sake. After all, scientists are interested in generating knowledge — in this case, insight into the effects of organizations on people and the effects of people on organizations. This is not to say, however, that such knowledge has no value outside of scientific circles. Far from it! Specialists in OB also work hard at applying knowledge gained from scientific studies, putting it to good, practical use. They seek to improve organizational functioning and the quality of life for the people working in organizations, and they rely heavily on knowledge derived from OB research. For example, these researchers have shed light on such practical questions as:

- How can goals be set to enhance employees' job performance?
- How can jobs be designed to enhance employees' feelings of satisfaction?
- Under what conditions do individuals make better decisions than groups?
- How can the quality of organizational communication be improved?
- What steps can be taken to alleviate work-related stress?
- What can leaders do to enhance the effectiveness of their teams?

We will explain the scientific research and theory regarding these — and dozens of other — practical questions throughout this book. It is safe to say that the scientific and applied facets of OB not only co-exist but complement each other. Just as knowledge about the properties of physics may be used by engineers and engineering data used to test basic theories of physics, so too are knowledge and practical applications closely intertwined in the field of OB.

Not only may specialists in OB use their knowledge about behavior in organizations to suggest ways of improving organizational problems in general, they also may conduct research designed specifically to solve problems in a particular organization. In other words, specialists in OB use the scientific method to derive both general knowledge about behavior in organizations and specific knowledge to solve problems in a given organization.[2] The underlying reason for conducting the research may differ in each case, but both approaches have something in common — namely, their reliance on the scientific method. Therefore, regardless of one's goals for learning about behavior in organizations — be it deriving theoretical or practical knowledge of organizational behavior in general or insight into a specific organization — the scientific approach is a central, defining characteristic of the modern field of OB.

Three Levels of Analysis: Individuals, Groups, and Organizations

To appreciate behavior in organizations, specialists in OB cannot focus exclusively on individuals acting alone. After all, in organizational settings, people frequently work together in groups. Furthermore, people — whether alone or in groups — both influence and are influenced by their work environment. Therefore, OB focuses on three distinct levels of analysis: individuals, groups, and organizations.

The field of OB recognizes that *all three levels of analysis* must be used to comprehend fully the complex dynamics of behavior in organizations (Figure 1.2). Careful attention to all three levels of analysis is a central theme in modern OB and is fully reflected throughout this text. For example, at the individual level, we describe how specialists in OB are concerned with individual perceptions, attitudes, and motives. At the group level, we describe how people communicate with each other and coordinate their activities in work groups. Finally, at the organizational level, we describe organizations as a whole — the way they are structured and operate in their environments, and the effects of their operations on the individuals and groups within them. We're optimistic that you will come to appreciate the value of all three approaches by the time you finish this book.

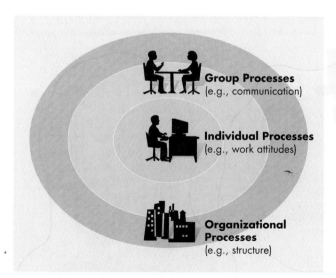

Group Processes
(e.g., communication)

Individual Processes
(e.g., work attitudes)

Organizational
Processes
(e.g., structure)

FIGURE 1.2

The Three Levels of Analysis Used in Organizational Behavior

To understand behavior in organizations fully, we must consider three levels of analysis: processes occurring within individuals, groups, and organizations.

AN HISTORICAL OVERVIEW OF THE FIELD

Although today we take for granted the importance of understanding the functioning of organizations and the behavior of people at work, this was not always the case. In fact, it was not until the early twentieth century that the idea even developed, and only during the last few decades has it gained widespread acceptance.[3] Therefore, to appreciate how the field of OB got to where it is today, we now briefly outline its history and describe some of the most influential forces in its development.

Scientific Management: The Roots of Organizational Behavior

The earliest attempts to study behavior in organizations came out of a desire by experts in industrial efficiency to improve worker productivity. Their central question was straightforward: What could be done to get people to do more work in less time? It is not particularly surprising that attempts to answer this question were made at the dawn of the twentieth century. This was a period of rapid industrialization and technological change in the United States. As engineers attempted to make machines more efficient, extending their efforts to work on the human side of the equation — making people more productive — was only natural. Given this history, it should not be surprising that the earliest people to receive credit for their contributions to OB were actually industrial engineers.

Frederick Winslow Taylor worked for most of his life in steel mills, starting as a laborer and eventually reaching the position of chief engineer (Figure 1.3).[4] In the 1880s, while a foreman at Philadelphia's Midvale Steel Company, Taylor became aware of some inefficient practices by the employees. For example, laborers wasted movements when shifting pig iron, so Taylor studied the individual components of this task and established what he believed was the best way — motion by motion — to perform it. A few years later, while a consulting engineer at Pittsburgh's Bethlehem Steel, Taylor similarly redesigned the job of loading and unloading rail cars to be as efficient as possible. On the heels of these experiences, Taylor published his groundbreaking book *Scientific Management*. In this work, Taylor argued that the objective of management is "to secure the maximum prosperity for the employer, coupled with the maximum prosperity of each employee."[5]

Beyond identifying ways in which manual labor could be performed more efficiently, Taylor's **scientific management** approach was unique in its focus on the role of employees as individuals. Taylor advocated two ideas that hardly seem special today but were quite new almost a century ago. First, he recommended that employees

scientific management
An early approach to management and organizational behavior emphasizing the importance of designing jobs as efficiently as possible.

FIGURE 1.3

Frederick Winslow Taylor (1856–1917): The Father of Scientific Management

The scientific management approach, advanced by Frederick Winslow Taylor, was directed at finding the most efficient ways for people to perform their jobs. Taylor is regarded as among the first to pioneer the scientific study of people at work.

be carefully selected and trained to perform their jobs—helping them become, in his own words, "first-class" at some task. Second, he believed that increasing workers' wages would raise their motivation and, in turn, their productivity. Although this idea is unsophisticated by today's standards—and also is not completely accurate—Taylor may be credited with recognizing the important role of motivation in job performance. Contributions like these stimulated further study of behavior in organizations, and they created an intellectual climate that eventually paved the way for the modern field of OB. Acknowledging these contributions, management theorist Peter Drucker described Taylor as "the first man in history who did not take work for granted, but who looked at it and studied it."[6]

Scientific Management stimulated several other scientists to expand on Taylor's ideas. For example, the psychologist Hugo Münsterberg worked to "humanize" jobs by explaining how the concepts of learning and motivation related to the behavior of people at work.[7] Similarly, management writer Mary Parker Follet claimed that organizations could benefit by recognizing the needs of employees.[8] The scientists most closely influenced by Taylor, however, were the industrial psychologists Frank and Lillian Gilbreth. This husband-and-wife team pioneered an approach known as **time-and-motion study**, which is a type of applied research designed to classify and streamline the individual movements needed to perform jobs—with the intent of finding "the one best way" to perform them.[9] At first glance, this approach appears to be highly mechanical and dehumanizing, but the Gilbreths, who also were the parents of 12 children, practiced Taylorism with a human face in their personal lives. You may even recall the story of how the Gilbreths applied the principles of scientific management to the operation of their own household as told in the classic film and book, *Cheaper by the Dozen*.

> **time-and-motion study**
> A type of applied research designed to classify and streamline the individual movements needed to perform a job so as to find the "one best way" to perform it.

ETHICS MATTERS

Recognizing the value of helping people who are physically disabled to fulfill themselves through work, the Gilbreths designed tools and methods that enable such individuals to find gainful employment.[10] Although considered radical almost a century ago, this practice is commonplace today. What particular accommodations are made today to help people with physical handicaps perform their jobs effectively? ▪

The Human Relations Movement: Elton Mayo and the Hawthorne Studies

Despite its important contributions, scientific management did not go far enough in directing our attention to the many factors that might influence behavior in work settings. Efficient performance of jobs and monetary incentives are important, to be sure, but emphasizing these factors makes people feel like cogs in a machine. In fact, many employees and theorists rejected Taylorism, favoring instead an approach that focused on the employees' own views and emphasized a respect for individuals.

At the forefront of this new approach was Elton W. Mayo, an organizational scientist and consultant widely regarded as being the founder of the **human relations movement**.[11] This brand of management philosophy rejects the primarily economic orientation of scientific management and instead focuses on the noneconomic, social factors operating in the workplace. Mayo and other proponents of the human relations movement *were* concerned with task performance, but they also realized that it was greatly influenced by the social conditions in organizations—the way employees were treated by management and the relationships they had with each other.

In 1927, what became known as the Hawthorne studies began at Western Electric's Hawthorne Works near Chicago. Inspired by scientific management, these researchers were interested in determining, among other things, the effect of

> **human relations movement**
> A perspective on organizational behavior that rejects the primarily economic orientation of scientific management and instead recognizes the importance of social processes in work settings.

illumination on work productivity. In other words, how brightly or dimly lit should the work environment be for people to produce at their maximum level? Two groups of female employees took part in the study. One group, the control room condition, worked without any changes in lighting; the other group, the test room condition, worked while the lighting was systematically varied, sometimes getting brighter and sometimes getting dimmer. The results were baffling: Productivity increased in *both* groups. Just as surprising, there was no clear connection between illumination and performance. In fact, output in the test room remained high even when the level of illumination was so low that workers could barely see what they were doing!

In response to these puzzling findings, Western Electric officials called in a team of experts headed by Elton Mayo. Attempting to replicate these results, Mayo and his colleagues examined the effects of many different variables, including length of rest pauses, duration of the work day and work week, and presence or absence of a free midmorning lunch, on productivity. Female employees working in the company's Relay Room took part in the study. As Figure 1.4 shows, the results were again quite surprising: Productivity improved following almost every change in working conditions.[12] In fact, performance remained extremely high even when the conditions were returned to normal — the way they were before the study began.

Not all of Mayo's studies showed that Hawthorne employees were highly productive, however. In another study conducted at the company's Bank Wiring Room, male members of various work groups were observed during regular working conditions and interviewed at length after work. In this investigation, no attempts were made to alter the work environment. What Mayo found here was surprising as well. Instead of improving their performance, employees deliberately restricted their output. Not only did the researchers actually see the men stopping work long before quitting time, the men admitted in the interviews that they could do more if they desired.

Why did this occur, especially in view of the increased performance noted in the Relay Room studies? Eventually, Mayo and his associates recognized the

FIGURE 1.4

The Hawthorne Studies: Some Puzzling Results

In one part of the Hawthorne studies, female employees were exposed to several changes in working conditions. Surprisingly, however, almost every one of these alterations resulted in increased productivity.

(*Source*: Based on data from Roethlisberger & Dickson, 1939; see note 12.)

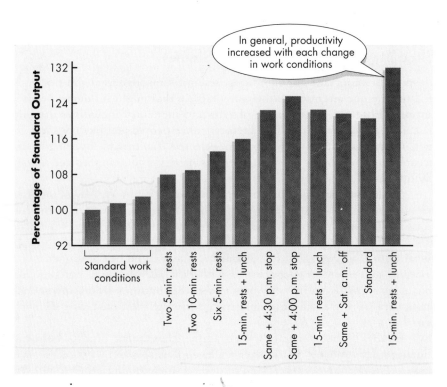

answer — that organizations are *social systems*. How effectively people worked depended in great part not only on the physical aspects of the working conditions but also on the social conditions they encountered. In the Relay Room studies, productivity rose simply because people responded favorably to the special attention they received. Knowing they were being studied made them feel special and motivated them to do their best. Hence, it was these social factors more than the physical factors that had such profound effects on job performance. The same explanation applied in the Bank Wiring Room study as well. These employees feared that because they were being studied, the company eventually would raise the amount of work they were expected to do each day. Therefore, to guard against the imposition of unreasonable standards — and, hopefully, to keep their jobs! — the men agreed among themselves to keep their output low. In other words, informal rules were established about what constituted acceptable job performance, and the social forces at work in this setting proved to be much more potent determinants of job performance than the physical factors studied.

This conclusion, based on the surprising findings of the Hawthorne studies, is important, because it produced a new way of thinking about behavior at work. It suggests that to understand behavior on the job, we must fully appreciate the employees' attitudes and how they communicate with each other. This way of thinking, which is so fundamental to the modern field of OB, may be traced back to Elton Mayo's pioneering Hawthorne studies. Considering the scientific management views prevailing at the time, this perspective was quite novel.

This is not to say that the Hawthorne studies were perfect. Indeed, by modern standards, the research was seriously flawed. As we describe later in this chapter, the research violated several important rules. For example, no effort was made to assure the rooms used were identical in every way except for the variables studied (i.e., level of illumination, scheduling and duration of the rest pauses), thus making it possible for factors other than those being studied to influence the results. (Interestingly, research on the topic of illumination is still being conducted today — although in a far more careful and sophisticated manner.[13]) Furthermore, because no attempt was made to ensure the employees chosen for study were representative of all those in their factory (or of all manufacturing personnel in general), it is difficult to generalize the results of the study beyond those individuals actually involved.

Clearly, however, the impact of the Hawthorne studies on the field of OB is considerable. The contribution has nothing to do with what the research revealed about the effects of illumination, but it has everything to do with what it revealed indirectly about the importance of human needs, attitudes, motives, and relationships in the work place. In this respect, the work established a close link between the newly emerging field of OB and the behavioral sciences of psychology and sociology — a connection that persists today. Although the human relations approach was gradually replaced by more sophisticated views, several of its ideas and concepts contributed greatly to the development of the field of OB. Little would those workers in that long-vanished plant outside of Chicago have guessed that their contribution to the social science of OB would be so enduring.

Classical Organizational Theory

During the same time that proponents of scientific management got people thinking about the interrelationships between workers and their jobs, another approach to managing people emerged. Known as **classical organizational theory**, this perspective focused on the efficient structuring of overall organizations. This is in contrast, of course, to scientific management, which sought to organize effectively the work of individuals.

Several different theorists have been identified with classical organizational theory. Among the first was Henri Fayol, a French industrialist who attributed his

classical organizational theory

An early approach to the study of management that focused on the most efficient way of structuring organizations.

managerial success to various principles that he developed.[14] These included the following:

know these steps

- A *division of labor* should be used, because it allows people to specialize and do only what they do best.
- Managers should have *authority* over their subordinates, which means the right to order them to do what's necessary for the organization.
- Lines of authority should be uninterrupted; in other words, a *scalar chain* should exist that connects the top management with the lower-level employees.
- A clearly defined *unity of command*, such that employees receive directions from only one person, should exist to avoid confusion.
- Subordinates should be given *initiative* to formulate and implement their own plans.

Although many of these principles are still accepted today, it now is recognized that they should not always be applied in exactly the same way. For example, some organizations thrive on being structured according to a unity of command, but others require that some employees take directions from several different superiors. This topic is discussed in more detail in chapter 14. For now, however, suffice it to say that current organizational theorists owe a debt of gratitude to Fayol for his pioneering and far-reaching ideas.

Probably the best-known classical organizational theorist is the German sociologist Max Weber.[15] Among other things, Weber proposed a form of organizational structure that is well-known today — the **bureaucracy**. Much as proponents of scientific management searched for the ideal way to perform a job, Weber believed this was the one best way to organize work in all organizations efficiently. The elements of an ideal bureaucracy are summarized in Table 1.1. When you think about bureaucracies, negative images probably come to mind, involving lots of inflexible people getting bogged down in red tape. (By the way, the phrase *red tape* is said to have become popular during World War I, when red tape was used on documents from the British government.[16] Given the tendency for national governments to be bureaucratic in structure, it is not surprising this term came to refer to bureaucracies of all types.) Weber's "universal" view of bureaucratic structure contrasts with the more modern

bureaucracy

An organizational design developed by Max Weber that attempts to make organizations operate efficiently through clear hierarchy of authority in which people perform well-defined jobs.

Weber - becam with the beurocracy

TABLE 1.1

Characteristics of an Ideal Bureaucracy

According to Max Weber, bureaucracies are the ideal organizational form. To function effectively, however, they must possess the characteristics identified here.

CHARACTERISTICS	DESCRIPTION
Formal rules and regulations	Written guidelines are used to control all employees' behaviors.
Impersonal treatment	Favoritism is to be avoided, and all work relationships are to be based on objective standards.
Division of labor	All duties are divided into specialized tasks and are performed by individuals with the appropriate skills.
Hierarchical structure	Positions are ranked by authority level in clear fashion from lower-level to upper-level ones.
Authority structure	The making of decisions is determined by one's position in the hierarchy; higher-ranking people have authority over those in lower-ranking positions.
Lifelong career commitment	Employment is viewed as a permanent, lifelong obligation on the part of the organization and its employees.
Rationality	The organization is committed to achieving its ends (e.g., profitability) in the most efficient manner possible.

approaches to organizational design (see chapter 14), which recognize that different forms of organizational structure may be more or less appropriate under different situations. Although the bureaucracy may not actually be the perfect structure for organizing all work, organizational theorists owe a great deal to Weber, many of whose ideas are still considered viable today.

Organizational Behavior in the Modern Era

Based on the pioneering contributions noted thus far, the realization that behavior in work settings is shaped by many individual, group, and organizational factors set the stage for the science of OB. By the 1940s, there were clear signs that an independent field had emerged. For example, in 1941, the first doctoral degree in OB was granted (to George Lombard at the Harvard Business School).[17] Only four years later, the first textbook in this field appeared.[18] By the late 1950s and early 1960s, OB was clearly a going concern. By that time, there were active programs of research into such key processes as motivation and leadership and the impact of organizational structure.[19]

Unfortunately—but not unexpectedly for a new field—the development of scientific investigations into managerial and organizational issues was uneven and unsystematic in the 1940s and 1950s. In response to this state of affairs, the Ford Foundation sponsored a project in which economists R. A. Gordon and J. E. Howell carefully analyzed the nature of business education in the United States. Published in 1959, their findings became a very influential work known as the Gordon and Howell Report.[20] Gordon and Howell recommended that the study of management pay greater attention to basic academic disciplines, especially the social sciences. This advice influenced business school curricula enormously during the 1960s, and it promoted the development of the field of OB. After all, OB draws heavily on the basic social science disciplines recommended for incorporation into business curricula by Gordon and Howell.

Stimulated by this work, the field of OB rapidly grew into one that borrowed heavily from other disciplines. In fact, OB as we know it today may be characterized as a hybrid science that draws from many of the social sciences. For example, studies of personality, learning, and perception draw on psychology. Similarly, studies of group dynamics and leadership rely heavily on sociology. Studies of organizational communication networks draw on research in the field of communication. Studies of power and politics draw on political science, and studies of cross-cultural themes draw on anthropology. Researchers in OB even look to the field of management science to understand ways to manage quality in organizations. Taken together, modern OB is truly a multidisciplinary field (Figure 1.5).

Now that we know what the field of OB is all about and how it has gotten where it is today, we can turn our attention to another basic question: What are the field's fundamental assumptions? By calling attention to the underlying assumptions in OB about human behavior, we can understand how the field operates and the kinds of questions it asks.

FUNDAMENTAL ASSUMPTIONS OF CONTEMPORARY ORGANIZATIONAL BEHAVIOR

This section focuses on three fundamental assumptions of OB:

1. Organizations can be made more productive while also improving the quality of people's work life.
2. There is no one best approach to studying behavior in organizations.
3. Organizations are dynamic and ever-changing.

FIGURE 1.5

OB: A Hybrid Science

The field of OB may be characterized by the fact that it draws on several different disciplines of the social sciences.

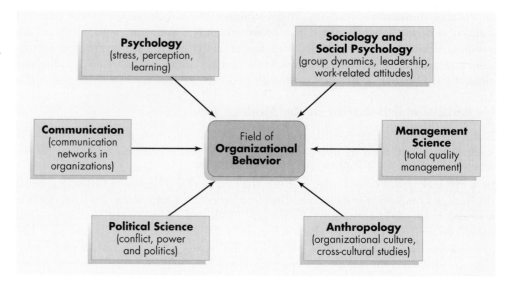

Work Can Be Both Productive and Pleasant

Early in the twentieth century, as railroads opened up the western portion of the United States and the nation's population rapidly grew (doubling from 1880 to 1920!), the demand for manufactured products was great. New factories were built and attracted waves of immigrants searching for a living wage. Laborers were lured off farms by the employment prospects such factories offered. These men and women found that factories were gigantic, noisy, hot, and highly regimented—in short, factories were brutal places in which to work (Figure 1.6). Bosses demanded more and more of their employees and treated them like disposable machines, replacing those who quit or died from accidents with still others who waited outside the factory gates.[21]

Obviously, the managers of 100 years ago held very negative views of their employees. They assumed that people were basically lazy and irresponsible, and they treated workers with disrespect. This negativistic approach, which has been with us for many years, reflects the traditional view of management—what McGregor called a **Theory X** orientation.[22] This philosophy assumes that people are basically lazy, dislike work, need direction, and work hard only when pushed and goaded into performing (i.e., because there is a carrot at the end of the stick).

Theory X

A traditional philosophy of management suggesting that most people are lazy, irresponsible, and work hard only when forced to do so.

FIGURE 1.6

Factory Work: Then and Now

Unlike the relatively safe and comfortable conditions in today's factories (*left*), manufacturing plants at the beginning of the twentieth century (*right*) were highly unpleasant places in which to work. The field of OB assumes that work can be both productive and pleasant.

Today, however, if you asked a diverse group of corporate officials to describe their basic views of human nature, you would probably find some more optimistic thoughts. Although some of today's managers still believe that people are basically lazy, most would disagree, arguing that it is just not that simple. They would claim the vast majority are at least as capable of working hard as they are of "goofing off." If employees are recognized for their efforts (e.g., by being appropriately paid) and given an opportunity to succeed (e.g., by being well trained), they may be expected to work very hard without being pushed. Thus, employees may put forth great effort simply because they want to. The job of management, therefore, is to create those conditions that make people want to perform as desired.

The approach that assumes people are not intrinsically lazy but are willing to work hard under the right conditions is known as the **Theory Y** orientation. This philosophy assumes that people have a psychological need to work and to seek achievement and responsibility. In contrast to the Theory X philosophy, which essentially demonstrates distrust of employees, the Theory Y approach is strongly associated with promoting the betterment of human resources. For a summary of these differences, see Figure 1.7.

As you might suspect, the Theory Y perspective currently prevails among those interested in OB. This approach assumes that people are highly responsive to their work environments and that how they are treated influences how they will act. Specialists in OB are interested in learning exactly what conditions lead people to behave in the most positive ways. Conditions in which employees are treated favorably help them to become more committed to their organizations and to go above and beyond the call of duty. In contrast, employees who are exploited act more negatively, such as by slacking off, behaving antisocially (e.g., stealing), or even quitting. In short, modern OB assumes there are no intrinsic reasons why work settings cannot be made both pleasant and productive.

There Is No "One Best Approach" to Managing People

What is the most effective way to motivate people? What style of leadership works best? Should teams be used to make important organizational decisions? Questions such as these appear to be quite reasonable, but there is a basic problem with all of them: They all assume there is one simple answer. That is, they suggest there is one best approach — one best way to motivate, one best way to lead, and one best way to make decisions.

Modern specialists in OB agree that no one approach is best when it comes to such complex phenomena. To assume otherwise is not only overly simplistic and naive

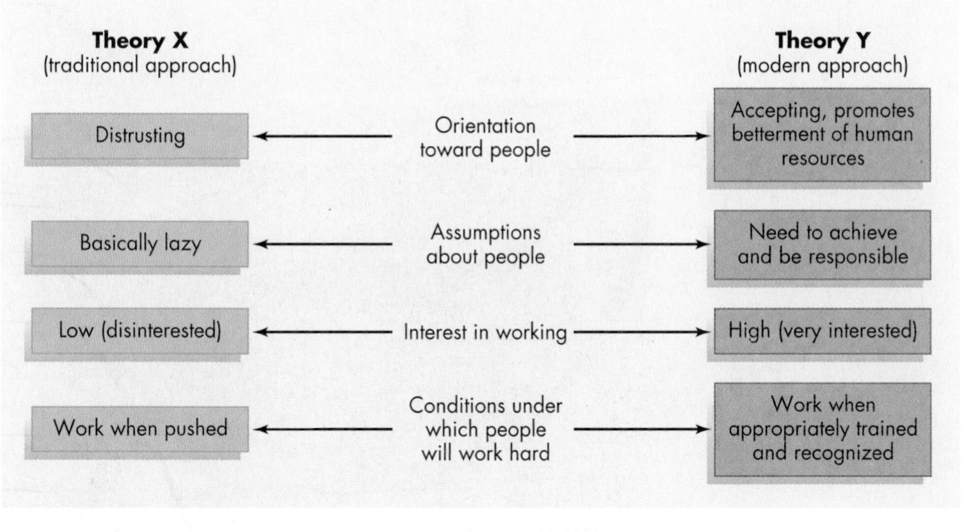

Theory Y

A philosophy of management suggesting that under the right circumstances, people are fully capable of working productively and accepting responsibility for their work.

FIGURE 1.7

Theory X Versus Theory Y: A Summary

The traditional Theory X orientation toward people is far more negativistic than the more contemporary Theory Y approach that is widely accepted today. Some of the key differences between these management philosophies are summarized here.

Theory X (traditional approach)		Theory Y (modern approach)
Distrusting	Orientation toward people	Accepting, promotes betterment of human resources
Basically lazy	Assumptions about people	Need to achieve and be responsible
Low (disinterested)	Interest in working	High (very interested)
Work when pushed	Conditions under which people will work hard	Work when appropriately trained and recognized

but, as you will see, it is also grossly inaccurate. When studying human behavior in organizations, there are no simple answers; the processes involved are too complex to permit such a luxury. Instead, scholars of OB recognize that behavior in work settings is the complex result of many interacting forces. This fact is recognized in what has become known as the **contingency approach**, an orientation that is a hallmark of modern OB.[23]

Consider, for example, the broad array of factors that may determine how productive someone is on the job. Various personal characteristics, such as an individual's work values, skills, and motives to work hard, clearly are important, but these factors only tell part of the story. We also must consider various situational factors, such as the nature of the organization (e.g., the social relations between coworkers). And, we also must consider numerous characteristics of the environmental context in which the work is done. For example, how strong is the economy? How competitive is the industry in which the organization operates? These variables all may play separate roles when it comes to influencing how a particular individual behaves on the job, but they also may combine to paint a very complicated picture. Such complexities are in the forefront of the contingency approach to OB (Figure 1.8).

When we teach OB to our students, we often find ourselves answering their questions by saying "It depends." As our knowledge of behavior on the job becomes more and more complex, it becomes increasingly difficult — if not impossible — to give "straight answers." Rather, it usually is necessary to report that people do certain things "under some conditions" or "when all factors are equal." Such phrases clearly indicate that the contingency approach is being used. They tell us that a certain behavior is *contingent on* the existence of certain conditions — hence, the name.

This approach may frustrate and disappoint some people, because it makes impossible the use of simple cookbook formulas to predict and to explain behavior. We believe that such a complaint is unjustified, however. After all, *accuracy* and not *simplicity* is the ultimate goal of our studies. The chapters that follow show how this approach prevails regarding various aspects of the field. In presenting this material to you, we attempt to walk the fine line between being so complex as to be incomprehensible and being so simplistic as to be misleading.

contingency approach

A perspective suggesting that organizational behavior is affected by many interacting factors. How someone will behave is said to be contingent on many different variables at once.

FIGURE 1.8

The Contingency Approach to Organizational Behavior

By adopting a contingency approach, the field of OB recognizes that a wide variety of factors, all in combination with each other, influence behavior in organizations.

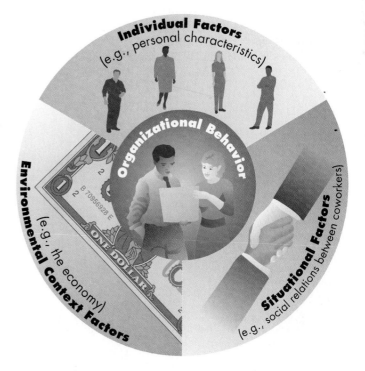

Do you think that national culture is a variable on which all forms of organizational behavior are contingent? In other words, is it overly simplistic to expect universal principles of organizational behavior to exist? ■

Organizations Are Dynamic and Ever-Changing

In studying organizations, specialists in OB recognize that organizations are not static. Instead, they are dynamic and ever-changing entities. In other words, they recognize that organizations are **open systems** — that is, self-sustaining systems that use energy to transform resources from the environment (e.g., raw materials) into some form of output (e.g., a finished product).[24] Figure 1.9 summarizes some of the key properties of open systems. As the diagram makes clear, organizations receive input from their environments and continuously transform that input into output. This output is then transformed back into input, and the cyclical operation continues.

Consider, for example, how organizations may tap human resources in the community by hiring and training people to do jobs. These individuals may work to provide a product in exchange for wages. They then spend these wages, putting money back into the community and allowing more people to afford the company's products. In turn, this creates the need for still more employees, and so on. If you think about it this way, it is easy to realize that organizations are dynamic and constantly changing. Viewed this way, they also are like the operations of the human body. As people breathe, they take in oxygen and transform it into carbon dioxide, which in turn sustains the life of green plants, which in turn emit oxygen for people to breathe. The continuous nature of an open system characterizes not only human life but the existence of organizations as well.

In keeping with the idea that the field of OB is carefully attuned to the dynamic nature of organizations, it is important to note that OB is being shaped continuously by forces in the environment as well. These forces include social trends, economic changes, technological advances, and the like. In short, organizations must be viewed as constantly changing entities. As a result, so too must the field of OB be recognized as one that is in constant transition. With this in mind, we now turn our attention to several of the dynamic forces shaping this field.

Forces Shaping Organizational Behavior Today

To appreciate fully the nature of OB as a contemporary field, it is important to recognize its connection to a variety of forces. In particular, the field of OB is highly related to several economic, social, and cultural trends in today's society. These include:

1. The globalization of the economy.
2. The diversification of the workforce.
3. The development of flexible, new working arrangements.

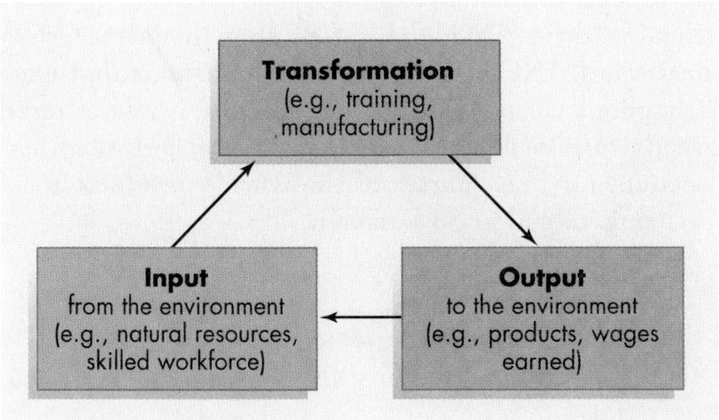

open systems
Self-sustaining systems that transform input from the external environment into output, which the system then returns to the environment.

FIGURE 1.9

Organizations as Open Systems

The open systems approach assumes that organizations are self-sustaining — that is, that they transform inputs to outputs in a continuous fashion.

(*Source*: Based on suggestions by Katz & Kahn, 1978; see note 24.)

4. Technological advances creating new organizational forms.
5. The quality revolution.
6. Expectations of socially responsible behavior.

International Business and the Global Economy

Chances are good that the car you drive is constructed of parts made in several different countries. It may even have been assembled in many countries as well. The bank on the nearest corner may be owned by a large Japanese conglomerate headquartered halfway around the world, and your personal computer with the well-known U.S. brand-name may be assembled in Mexico using chips made in Korea. Your clothes may be sewn by people in Taiwan using fabric woven in India. We could go on and on, but our point is clear: Today's world of business is an international one.

As you might imagine, this has important implications for the study of OB. With this in mind, we examine two important—and highly interrelated—issues: the international nature of today's organizations and the important role of culture in organizations.

Organizations in the Global Arena   To understand fully behavior in organizations, you must appreciate that organizations operate within an economic system in which resources (e.g., information, goods, and money) are constantly flowing. In recent decades, economic transactions have not been restricted to those occurring within a single country. With growing frequency, economic transactions have occurred between countries as well. As one expert put it, "By a wide margin . . . global competition is the single most powerful economic fact of life in the 1990s."[25] Consider these facts:

- Whereas only seven percent of U.S. companies were influenced by foreign competition in the 1960s, the comparable figure stands at more than 70 percent today.[26]
- Either directly or indirectly, international trade accounts for approximately 20 percent of all U.S. jobs.[27]
- For every $1 billion exported by U.S. companies, approximately 20,000 new jobs are created.[28]

Indeed, trade between nations has grown from $308 billion in 1950 to $3.8 trillion in 1993.[29] Several factors account for this dramatic growth. First, technology has lowered the cost of transportation and communication drastically, thereby enhancing opportunities for international commerce. Second, laws restricting trade have, in general, become liberalized throughout the world (e.g., in the United States and other heavily industrialized countries, free trade policies have been advocated). Third, developing nations have sought to expand their economies by promoting exports and opening their doors to foreign companies seeking investments, and this has expanded opportunities for economic growth and competition throughout the world. These factors all contribute to the growing trend toward **globalization**, which is the process of interconnecting the world's people with respect to the cultural, economic, political, technological, and environmental aspects of their lives.[30]

If international trade is the major "driver" of globalization, then the primary "vehicles" are **multinational corporations (MNCs)**. MNCs are organizations that have significant operations spread throughout various nations but that are headquartered in a single nation. MNCs are greatly responsible for direct investment in foreign nations: The 300 largest MNCs account for one-quarter of the world's productive assets, with the 100 largest MNCs being valued at $3.1 trillion.

globalization

The process of interconnecting the world's people regarding the cultural, economic, political, technological, and environmental aspects of their lives.

multinational corporations (MNCs)

Organizations with significant operations spread throughout various nations but headquartered in a single nation.

GLOBAL MATTERS

Many MNCs consistently call the same few countries home. In fact, approximately half of all MNCs are headquartered in only four nations: the United States, Japan, Germany, and Switzerland.[31] ∎

There are approximately 35,000 MNCs throughout the world at present, and their numbers are growing — particularly in high-tech fields.[32] MNCs generally have very large proportions of their total assets invested in foreign countries (more than 50 percent is not uncommon). This also applies to the distribution of human resources within MNCs. For example, at Matsushita Electric, the large Japan-based MNC, more than half of the employees live and work in other countries.[33] People who are citizens of one country but who are living and working in another are known as **expatriates**. With today's MNCs having more than 170,000 foreign affiliates (including branch offices or other companies owned by the parent company), this type of organization is greatly responsible for the existence of expatriates throughout the world.

Clearly, the trend toward globalization has complex and widespread effects on the lives of people throughout the world, and this fact has not escaped the attention of specialists in OB. In fact, the management of human resources is widely acknowledged as being an integral aspect of competitiveness in the global arena. As one expert put it:

> *Virtually any type of international problem, in the final analysis, is either created by people or must be solved by people. Hence, having the right people in the right place at the right time emerges as the key to a company's international growth.*[34]

Culture and Its Impact   When it comes to the globalization of organizations, the field of OB is primarily interested in the influence of culture on people's attitudes and behaviors at work.[35] The general question of interest is: Do people in various cultures behave similarly or differently regarding their behavior in organizations?

To examine this question, we first must clarify what is meant by **culture**. Most social scientists agree this term may be defined as the set of values, customs, and beliefs that people have in common with other members of a social unit (e.g., a nation).[36] So, for example, to the extent that citizens of a specific country share a set of values, customs, and beliefs, they may be said to have a distinct culture. It would be erroneous, however, to assume that a given country has one culture that is shared by everyone. Although a set of widely accepted values may be shared by most Americans, for example, it would be misleading to claim that there is a single culture within the United States. Indeed, the United States is a **multicultural society** — one with many different racial, ethnic, socioeconomic, and generational groups, each with its own culture. Recognizing this, scientists use the term **subculture** to describe smaller cultural groups within larger, primary cultural groups, each of which may have its own well-defined culture.

The effects of culture on people often occur without their awareness. In fact, people often must be confronted with different cultures before they become conscious of their own. In fact, when people such as expatriates working for MNCs are faced with new cultures, it is not unusual for them to become confused and disoriented, which is a phenomenon known as **culture shock**.[37] People also experience culture shock when they return to their native culture after spending time away from it, which is a process of readjustment known as **repatriation**. In general, culture shock results from people's recognition that others may be different from them in ways they never imagined, and this takes some getting used to.

Specifically, scientists have observed that the process of adjusting to a foreign culture generally follows a U-shaped curve (Figure 1.10).[38] At first, people are optimistic and excited about learning a new culture; this usually lasts about a month or so. Then, for the next several months, they become frustrated and confused as they struggle to learn the new culture (i.e., culture shock occurs). Finally, after about six months, they adjust to their new culture and become more accepting of and satisfied with it. These observations imply that feelings of culture shock are inevitable. Some degree of frustration may be expected when you first enter a new country, but the

expatriates
People who are citizens of one country but who live and work in another.

culture
The set of values, customs, and beliefs people have in common with other members of a social unit (e.g., a nation).

multicultural society
A society with many different racial, ethnic, socioeconomic, and generational subgroups, each with its own culture.

subculture
A smaller cultural subgroup, having its own well-defined culture, operating within larger, primary culture.

culture shock
The tendency for people to become confused and disoriented when adjusting to a new culture.

repatriation
The process of readjusting to one's own culture after spending time away from it.

FIGURE 1.10

Adjusting to Foreign Culture: The General Stages

People's adjustment to a new culture generally follows the U-shaped curve illustrated here. After an initial period of excitement, culture shock often occurs. After this period of adjustment (approximately six months), however, the more time spent in the new culture, the better it is accepted.

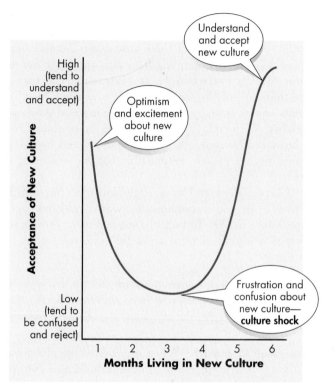

more time you spend learning its ways, the better you will come to understand and to accept it.[39]

In general, culture shock results from the tendency for people to be highly *parochial* in their assumptions about others—taking a narrow view of the world by believing there is one best way of doing things. Such people also tend to be highly *ethnocentric*—believing their way of doings things is best. For example, Americans tend to be highly parochial by speaking only English, whereas most Europeans generally speak several languages. Americans also tend to be ethnocentric by believing that everyone else in the world should learn their language. As we just explained, however, over time, exposure to other cultures teaches people that there may be many different ways of doing the same thing—thus making them less parochial—and that these different ways may be equally good, if not better—thus making them less ethnocentric. These biases may have been reasonable 50 years ago, when the United States was the world's dominant economic power (producing three-quarters of its wealth), but they are extremely costly today. Indeed, because the world's economy is now global in nature, highly parochial and ethnocentric views cannot be tolerated.

It also may be said that highly narrow and biased views about the management of people in organizations may severely limit our understanding about OB. During the 1950s and 1960s, management scholars tended to overlook the importance of cultural differences in organizations. Instead, they made two key assumptions: that principles of good management are universal, and that the best management practices are those that work well in the United States.[40] This highly inflexible approach is known as the **convergence hypothesis**. Such a biased orientation reflects the fact that the study of behavior in organizations first emerged at a time when the United States was the world's predominant economic power.

With the ever-growing global economy, an American-oriented approach may be highly misleading when it comes to understanding which practices work best in various countries. In fact, there may be many possible ways to manage people effectively, all of which depend greatly on the individual culture involved. This alternative ap-

convergence hypothesis

A biased approach to the study of management that assumes principles of good management are universal and ones that work well in the United States apply equally well in other nations.

proach, which is widely accepted today, is known as the **divergence hypothesis**. Following this orientation, understanding the behavior of people at work requires carefully appreciating the cultural context in which they operate. For example, U.S. cultural norms suggest it would not be inappropriate for an employee to question a superior, but this would be taboo for a worker in Japan. Thus, today's organizational scholars are increasingly sensitive to the ways in which culture influences OB.

The Shifting Demographics of the Workforce: Trends Toward Diversity

Thus far, we have discussed cultural differences between people from companies in different nations. However, widespread cultural differences also may be found *within* organizations. A broad range of people from both sexes as well as from different races, ethnicities, nationalities, and ages can be found throughout U.S. organizations. Therefore, this section chronicles the highly diverse nature of today's workforce and shares projections about diversity in the future. We also outline some of the things that modern organizations do to accommodate—and to capitalize on—growing levels of diversity within the workforce. Before getting to these matters, however, we distinguish between two approaches to diversity that have been taken in American society.

The Melting Pot and Cultural Pluralism   For most of the twentieth century, the "melting pot" analogy was used to describe how new immigrants were assimilated into the American way of life: They would hit U.S. soil and "melt" into a common culture. Formally, the **melting pot** refers to the principle that people from different racial, ethnic, and religious backgrounds are transformed into a common American culture. Although this analogy implied that American culture would be altered somewhat by the addition of new people into the mix, it did not work that way in reality. Instead, because immigration was relatively low in the decades following World War II and more than 95 percent of Americans were native born, until the mid-1960s the stew consisted primarily of people who were white, Anglo-Saxon, and Protestant.[41] Practically speaking, it was implied that by jumping into the melting pot, foreigners would conform to the socioeconomic and cultural ways of mainstream America.

Things changed in the mid-1960s, however, as the civil rights movement caught on and people began to challenge the dominant hold of the majority on society. Traditional societal ideals were questioned and respect for differences was nurtured. As this occurred, the melting pot philosophy fell into disrepute. Supplanting it was the

divergence hypothesis

The approach to the study of management that recognizes knowing how to manage most effectively requires a clear understanding of the culture in which people work.

melting pot

The principle that people from different racial, ethnic, and religious backgrounds are transformed into a common American culture.

YOU BE THE CONSULTANT

Your U.S.-based company is setting up a new division in Chile, which requires three top executives to move to Santiago for several years. Given the lengthy stay, they will be moving their families along with them and setting up new households.

1. What problems would you anticipate these executives will have as they adjust to their new surroundings?

2. What specific measures could be taken to help these individuals avoid the effects of culture shock?

3. What difficulties might these individuals have when they return to their own country at the end of their assignments? What could be done to minimize these problems?

cultural pluralism

The idea that social harmony does not require people from various cultures to assimilate or "melt" together into one but that people's separate identities should be maintained and accepted by others.

notion of **cultural pluralism** — the idea that social harmony does not require people from various cultures to assimilate (or melt) together into one. Rather, people's separate identities should be maintained and accepted by others. Cultural pluralists would have people from many cultures work beside each other and not expect them to become the same but to recognize, accept, and appreciate each other's differences. For a summary of the distinction between the melting pot and cultural pluralism, see Figure 1.11.

GLOBAL MATTERS   Some countries are more prone to cultural pluralism than others. Traditionally, for example, the United States has been far more pluralistic than Australia. Changes in immigration laws, however, have now made Australia a more diverse place. What other countries can you think of that embrace cultural pluralism? ■

valuing diversity

The practice of encouraging awareness of and respect for different people in the workplace.

The cultural pluralism approach that is popular today is frequently reflected in the movement toward **valuing diversity** — that is, encouraging awareness of and respect for different people in the workplace. Chapter 5 examines the factors affecting attitudes toward other people and ways to manage diversity in the workforce effectively. Here, however, we focus on the demographic trends themselves.

The Diverse Workforce   During the late 1950s and early 1960s, several popular TV situation comedies portrayed the typical American family as a middle-aged, white male head of the household who worked from 9:00 to 5:00 each day and earned enough money to support several children and a wife who stayed at home and took care of the household. This picture is quite far from today's reality, however. Consider the following trends:

- *More women are in the workforce than ever before.* More than half of all women are employed today, and just under half of all people in the workplace are women — and these figures have been rising steadily over the years.[42] This trend stems from several factors, including the growing social acceptance of women working outside the home as well as its economic necessity. (As women who traditionally worked inside the home have moved to working outside the home, companies have found it beneficial — and even necessary, in some cases — to help make this possible. For a look at some of the most popular practices in this regard, see the "Trends" section on page 22.

- *Racial and ethnic diversity is reality.* Just as yesterday's workers were primarily men, they also were primarily white. Just as growing numbers of women have made men less of a majority, however, so too have growing numbers of different racial and ethnic groups made whites a smaller majority. Specifically, although

FIGURE 1.11

The Melting Pot Versus Cultural Pluralism: A Comparison

The melting pot philosophy asserts that a main culture is created by combining various subcultures (here, shown as *Culture "A-B-C-D"*) that "melt" into a mix representing all of the subcultures. In contrast, the cultural pluralism philosophy asserts that people from various subcultures live together in a common society that maintains and recognizes their individual cultural identities.

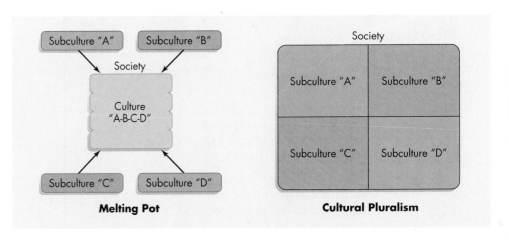

Baby Boom Started after World War II 60's [handwritten annotation]

white, non-Hispanic workers are currently the dominant group, this proportion is dropping (Figure 1.12). At the same time, the numbers of African Americans, Hispanics, and Asians in the workforce will increase in large part because of liberal immigration policies. Between 1990 and 2005, minorities will enter the workforce at a greater rate than the majority, thus making them even more prevalent. In fact, by 2050, it is estimated that racial and ethnic minorities will comprise 47 percent of the U.S. population—making obsolete the current term *minority*.[43]

- *People are living—and working—longer than ever before.* In the years after World War II, the peacetime economy flourished in the United States, and with it came a large increase in population as soldiers returned home and began families. The generation of children born during this period is widely referred to as the **baby boom generation**. Today, the first of these baby boomers are turning 55 years old and are considered to be "older workers" by labor economists, and only a few years from now, the number of older people in the workplace will swell dramatically. Living during a period in which retirement is no longer automatic at age 65, aged baby boomers will comprise a growing segment of the population in the years to come. In fact, people older than 85 years already are the fastest-growing segment of the U.S. population.[44] Clearly, this trend has profound implications on the traditional patterns of work and retirement that have developed in the United States.

Baby Boom: After War World II up to the 60's [handwritten annotation]

baby boom generation
The generation of children born in the economic boom period following World War II.

FIGURE 1.12

Minorities in the Workplace: Their Numbers Are Rising

Statistics show that the relative percentage of whites in the U.S. workforce, although currently still the highest of any group, is dropping. The relative percentage of African Americans, Hispanics, and Asians, however, is rising. As this trend continues, the term *minority group* will lose its meaning.

(*Source*: Based on estimates and projections reported in 1999, by the U.S. Census Bureau.)

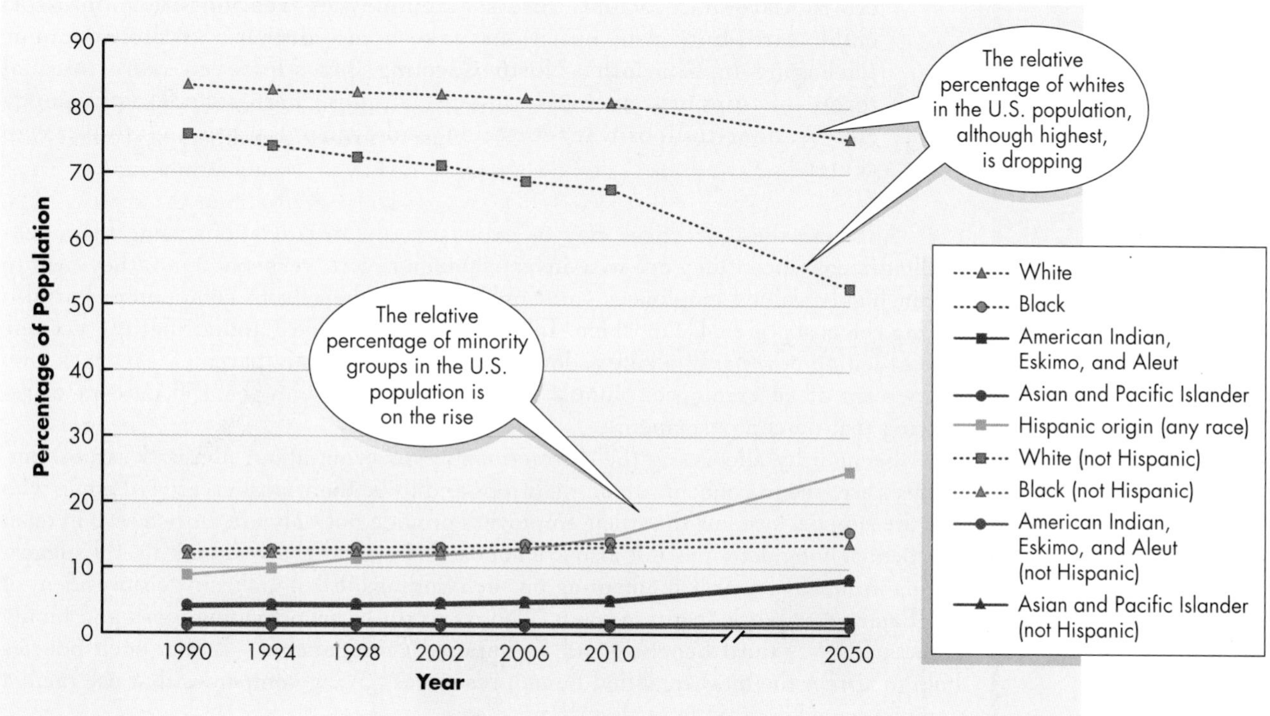

The relative percentage of whites in the U.S. population, although highest, is dropping

The relative percentage of minority groups in the U.S. population is on the rise

Legend:
- White
- Black
- American Indian, Eskimo, and Aleut
- Asian and Pacific Islander
- Hispanic origin (any race)
- White (not Hispanic)
- Black (not Hispanic)
- American Indian, Eskimo, and Aleut (not Hispanic)
- Asian and Pacific Islander (not Hispanic)

TRENDS: WHAT TODAY'S COMPANIES ARE DOING

■ Employee Support Policies

With increasing frequency, companies are taking proactive steps to help employees meet their personal needs and family obligations. In so doing, they make it possible for employees to satisfy the demands imposed by their nonwork lives, which in turn allows companies to draw on a diverse group of prospective employees who otherwise might not be able to lend their talents to the organization. Three practices have been especially useful in this regard.

child-care facilities

Sites either at or near company locations where parents can leave their children during work.

elder-care facilities

Facilities where employees can leave elderly relatives for whom they are responsible (e.g., parents and grandparents) during work.

personal support policies

Widely varied practices that help employees to meet the demands of their family lives, thus freeing them to concentrate on their work.

- **Child-care facilities.** These are sites either at or near company locations where parents can leave their children while they work. America West, for example, believes so strongly in the importance of providing child care that it offers these services 24 hours a day. The company even maintained these benefits during bankruptcy proceedings in 1991.[45]

- **Elder-care facilities.** Just as companies are making facilities available to employees to care for their children, with increasing frequency, companies also are making facilities available to care for elderly relatives such as parents and grandparents.[46] For example, Lancaster Laboratories in Lancaster, Pennsylvania, provides a place where its employees can bring adult family members who need care during working hours.[47] The *St. Petersburg Times* advises its employees about ways to help meet the needs of elderly family members.[48] Given the projections that multigenerational families will become increasingly common during the next few decades, we can expect elder-care facilities to grow in popularity.

- **Personal support policies.** These are widely varied practices that help employees to meet the demands of their family lives, thus freeing them to concentrate on their work. For example, the SAS Institute in Cary, North Carolina, not only offers its employees free, on-site Montessori child care but also nutritious take-home dinners. Wilton Connor Packaging in Charlotte, North Carolina, provides even more unusual forms of support, such as on-site laundry, high-school equivalency classes, door-to-door transportation, and even a children's clothing swap center.[49]

Although these practices may be expensive, the organizations using them generally are convinced they are wise investments in several respects. First, they help to retain highly valued employees—not only keeping them from competitors but also saving the costs of replacing them. In fact, officials at AT&T found that the average cost of letting new parents take as long as one year of unpaid parental leave was only 32 percent of an employee's annual salary—compared with the 150 percent of replacing that person permanently.[50]

Second, by alleviating the distractions of worrying about nonwork issues, employees are free to concentrate on their jobs and to be their most creative. People who use the support systems that their employers provide not only are more active in team problem-solving activities but also are almost twice as likely to submit useful suggestions for improvement. Commenting on such findings, Ellen Galinsky, co-president of the Families & Work Institute, said, "There's a cost to *not* providing work and family assistance."[51] A third benefit—and an important one, at that—is that such policies help to attract the most qualified human resources, giving companies that use them a competitive edge over those that do not.[52] ■

Flexible, New Working Arrangements

Half a century ago, when husbands worked outside the home and wives stayed in the home with the children, the standard 9-to-5 working hours were fine. Today, however, with two-income families, single-parent households, and people taking care of elderly relatives, greater flexibility is needed. The new diversity of lifestyles demands a new diversity of working arrangements. Fortunately, several practices have gained popularity in recent years.

Flextime Programs **Flextime programs** are policies that give employees some discretion over when they can arrive and leave work, thereby making it easier to adapt their work schedules to the demands of their personal lives. Typically, employees must work a common core of hours, such as 9:00 A.M. to 12 noon and 1:00 P.M. to 3:00 P.M. Scheduling of the remaining hours within certain spans, such as 6:00 A.M. to 9:00 A.M.. and 3:00 P.M. to 6:00 P.M., is then left to the employees themselves.

Generally, such programs have been well-received and linked to improvements in performance and job satisfaction as well as to drops in employee turnover and absenteeism.[53] Recently, companies such as Pacific Bell and Duke Power have found that flexible work scheduling has helped their employees to meet the demands of juggling both work and family lives (Figure 1.13).[54]

flextime programs

Policies that give employees some discretion over when they can arrive and leave work, thereby making it easier to adapt their work schedules to the demands of their personal lives.

Compressed Workweeks Instead of working five days of eight hours each, growing numbers of people are enjoying **compressed workweeks** — the practice of working fewer days each week but longer hours each day (e.g., four 10-hour days). The popular practice among firefighters of being on duty for 24 hours and then off duty for 48 hours is a good example of a compressed workweek. Shell Canada has found that compressed workweeks helped to make more efficient use of its manufacturing plant in Sarnia, Ontario. The Royal Bank of Canada, which is headquartered in Montreal, has found that compressed workweek options greatly help its recruitment efforts by offering prospective employees the choice of schedules based on either compressed workweeks (four 9.5-hour days) or standard five-day workweeks.[55]

compressed workweeks

The practice of working fewer days each week but longer hours each day (e.g., four 10-hour days).

Job Sharing **Job sharing** is a form of regular, part-time work in which pairs of employees assume the duties of a single job, thus splitting its responsibilities, salary, and benefits in proportion to the time each works. Job sharing is rapidly growing in popularity as people enjoy the kind of work that full-time jobs allow but require the flexibility of part-time work. Often, job-sharing arrangements are temporary.

job sharing

A form of regular part-time work in which pairs of employees assume the duties of a single job, thus splitting its responsibilities, salary, and benefits in proportion to the time each works.

FIGURE 1.13

Pacific Bell Employees Enjoy Flextime

These employees of Pacific Bell are among a growing number of workers using *flextime* programs, which allow them to determine (within certain limits) their own working hours. This practice helps people to balance the demands of their job with their personal lives.

At Xerox, for example, several sets of employees share jobs, including two female employees who were once sales rivals but have now joined forces to share one job when each needed to reduce their working hours so they could devote time to their new families.[56] At Pella, the Iowa-based manufacturer of windows, job sharing has been successful in reducing absenteeism among its production and clerical employees.[57]

voluntary reduced work time (V-time) programs

Programs that allow employees to reduce the amount of time they work by a certain amount (typically 10 or 20 percent) with a proportional reduction in pay.

Voluntary Reduced Work Time (V-time) Programs   Programs known as **voluntary reduced work time (V-time) programs** allow employees to reduce the amount of time they work by a certain amount (typically 10 or 20 percent) with a proportional reduction in pay. During the past few years, these programs have become popular among various state agencies in the United States. For example, various employees of the New York state government have enjoyed having professional careers with hours that also make it possible to meet their family obligations. Not only does the state benefit from the money that it saves, the employees also enjoy the extra time they gain for nonwork pursuits.

telecommuting

The practice of using communications technology to perform work from remote locations (e.g., the home).

Telecommuting   In recent years, the practice of **telecommuting** has been growing in popularity. Telecommuting is the practice of using communication technology to enable work to be performed from remote locations, such as the home. Also known as *flexplace* programs, it is used at such companies as J.C. Penney and Pacific Bell and makes it possible for employees to avoid the hassle of daily commuting.[58] It also allows companies to comply with governmental regulations (e.g., the Federal Clean Air Act of 1990) requiring them to reduce the number of trips made by employees. Statistics indicate that telecommuting is in full swing today.[59] For example:

- There are estimated to be approximately 25 million telecommuters.
- Among employees of *Fortune* 500 firms, 78 percent perform significant amounts of work off-site.
- Telecommuting is most prevalent among smaller firms—77 percent of telecommuters work for organizations employing fewer than 100 people.

Given its technological advantage, it should not be too surprising that IBM was one of the first companies to use telecommuting. Although IBM's midwest division is headquartered in Chicago, few of its 4,000 employees, including salespeople and customer service technicians, show up more than once or twice a week (Figure 1.14). Instead, they have "gone mobile," using the company's ThinkPad computers, fax-

FIGURE 1.14

Telecommuting in Action: Is This Man at Work?

Employees at IBM's midwest division use their portable computers to work from remote locations. As technology makes telecommuting easier and less expensive, more companies have been adopting this trend.

modems, e-mail, and cellular phones to do their work from remote locations. In just a few years, the company has slashed its real estate space by 55 percent, cut the number of fixed computer terminals required, and better satisfied its customers' needs. At the same time, telecommuting has done well for IBM employees: 83 percent report not wanting to return to a traditional office environment.

Companies such as Great Plains Software, Traveler's Insurance Co., U.S. West Communications, and the NPD Group have reported similar benefits with respect to savings in office expenses, gains in productivity, and satisfaction among employees.[60] As you might imagine, however, telecommuting is not for everyone and has its limitations.[61] Therefore, making telecommuting work requires several careful adjustments in the way work is done. For a closer look at these considerations, see the "Tips" section below.

New Organizational Forms Created by Technology

Since the Industrial Revolution, people have performed carefully prescribed sets of tasks—known as *jobs*—within large, hierarchical networks of people who answered to those above them—arrangements known as *organizations*. Although highly simplistic, this picture still characterizes the working arrangements that most people have had during much of the twentieth century. As this era draws to a close, however, the essential nature of jobs and organizations as we have known them is changing. Many factors certainly are responsible for such change, but the major catalyst is rapidly advancing computer technology. Currently, the computing power of microprocessors doubles approximately every 18 months, and as more work shifts to digital brains, some that was once performed by human brains becomes obsolete. Simultaneously, new opportunities arise as people scurry to find their footing amidst the shifting terrain of the high-tech revolution.

As you might imagine, this state of affairs has important implications for the field of OB. We now consider some of the most prominent trends in the workplace that have been identified in recent years.

■ Making Telecommuting Work: Some Considerations

TIPS: DOING IT RIGHT

When people who ordinarily have contact with each other on their jobs no longer have that social contact, several things may happen. For example, when employees do not see each other regularly, it is difficult to build the team spirit that is needed to provide quality goods and services in some organizations. As a result, telecommuting does not lend itself to all jobs. It works best for those that involve information handling, significant amounts of automation, and relatively little face-to-face contact. Sales representatives, computer programmers, word-processing technicians, insurance agents, and securities traders are all good candidates for telecommuting.

This is not to say that everyone in these jobs should be issued a laptop and sent packing. Good candidates for telecommuting also must have the emotional maturity and self-discipline to work without direct supervision. To assist those who have difficulty adjusting to telecommuting, IBM carefully monitors the work of its telecommuters and offers counseling to those having trouble.

To function effectively, telecommuters must be thoroughly trained in the technologies required for them to do their work off-site as well as in the proper conditions for working safely (e.g., avoiding physical problems from staring into video terminals for hours on end and from overusing wrist muscles). They also must be trained in ways to function independently, such as how to manage their time effectively and how to avoid interference from their families while working.

continued

Companies also face the issue of establishing fair wages for telecommuters. For workers who are paid by the amount of work produced, such as the number of insurance claims processed, this is not a problem. Clear criteria for measuring performance, such as specific goals for quantity and quality, are enormously helpful when paying telecommuters. For salaried employees doing jobs in which clear performance criteria are difficult to come by, however, policies must be established regarding what telecommuters should do, for example, when they complete their work in less than the time allotted. At the office, they would pitch in and help others, but at home, they may be tempted to goof off. The key task is to resolve all potentially thorny policy issues regarding pay and performance expectations *before* employees begin telecommuting—and to ensure that these goals are understood and accepted.

Clearly, telecommuting has its limits, but it also has a special role in today's workplace. Given that technology is making it increasingly easier and less expensive for people to telecommute—and traffic congestion is making it increasingly difficult for them to do otherwise—companies would be wise to consider the points outlined here and to respond accordingly. ■

Leaner Organizations   Technology has made it possible for fewer people to do more work than ever before. Of course, automation, which is the process of replacing people with machines, is not new. It has occurred slowly and steadily for centuries. Today, however, because manipulation of digital data rather than large mechanical devices is responsible, scientists have referred instead to the "informating" of the workplace.

The term **informate** describes the process by which workers manipulate objects by "inserting data" between themselves and those objects.[62] When jobs are informated, information technology is used to change a formerly physical task into one that involves manipulation of a sequence of digital commands. For example, a modern factory worker now can move large sheets of steel by pressing a few buttons on a keypad. Likewise, with the right programming, a salesperson can enter an order into a laptop computer and trigger a chain of events involving everything associated with the job: placing an order for supplies, manufacturing the product to exact specifications, delivering the final product, sending out the bill, and even crediting the proper commission to the salesperson's payroll check.

Unlike the gradual process of automation, today's technology is advancing—and the process of informating is occurring—so rapidly that the very nature of work is changing as fast as we can implement those changes. With this, many jobs are disappearing, leaving organizations—at least the most successful ones!—smaller than before.[63] For example, whereas Ford employs some 400 people in its accounts payable department, Mazda's highly computerized system does the same work with only five people! Mazda itself is considerably smaller than Ford, but this difference is still quite striking.

In addition to services, product manufacturing has been informated as well. At GE's Faunc Automation plant in Charlottesville, Virginia, for example, circuit boards are manufactured by half the employees required before informating the facility.[64] Not only blue-collar, manual labor jobs are being eliminated, however. White-collar, "mental labor" jobs are disappearing as well. In many places, middle managers are no longer needed to make decisions that can now be made by computers. In fact, although middle managers comprise only 10 percent of the workforce, they account for 20 percent of recent layoffs.

Another way in which organizations are restructuring is by completely eliminating those parts of themselves that focus on noncore sectors of the business (i.e., tasks peripheral to the organization) and then hiring outside firms to perform these functions instead—a practice known as **outsourcing**.[65] By outsourcing secondary activities, an organization can focus on what it does best—its key capability, which is known as its **core competency**. Companies like ServiceMaster, which provides janitorial services, and ADP, which provides payroll-processing services, make it possible for their clients

informate

The process by which workers manipulate objects through "inserting data" between themselves and those objects.

outsourcing

The process of eliminating those parts of organizations that focus on noncore sectors of the business (i.e., tasks peripheral to the organization) and hiring outside firms to perform these functions instead.

core competency

An organization's key capability (i.e., what it does best).

to concentrate on the business functions most central to their missions. For example, by outsourcing its maintenance work or payroll processing, a manufacturing company may grow smaller and focus its resources on what it does best—manufacturing.

Some critics fear that outsourcing represents a "hollowing out" of companies—a reduction of functions that weakens organizations by making them more dependent on others.[66] Proponents counter that outsourcing makes sense when the work affected is not highly critical to competitive success (e.g., janitorial services) or is so highly critical it can succeed only with outside assistance.[67] For example, among companies selling personal computers today, outsourcing the manufacturing of various components (e.g., hard drives, CD-ROMs, and chips) to other companies is a widespread practice.[68] This may sound atypical compared with what occurs in most manufacturing companies, but it actually is not. In fact, one industry analyst has estimated that 30 percent of the largest U.S. industrial firms outsource more than half their manufacturing.[69]

The Contingent Workforce: "Permanent Temporary" Employees   Instead of eliminating entire organizational functions and buying them back through outside providers, organizations sometimes eliminate individual jobs and then hire people to perform them on an ad hoc basis. Such individuals comprise the **contingent workforce**—people hired temporarily by organizations to work as needed for finite periods of time.[70] The contingent workforce includes not only traditional part-time employees (e.g., department store Santas) but also freelancers, subcontractors, and independent professionals. As Figure 1.15 shows, the specific jobs that contingent workers do most frequently are in the clerical fields.[71] Such highly flexible arrangements make it possible for organizations to grow or shrink as needed and to have access to experts with specialized knowledge when required.

contingent workforce
People hired temporarily by organizations to work as needed for finite periods of time.

The trend toward corporate restructuring has caused many U.S. companies to keep their staff sizes so small they must frequently draw on the services of Manpower or another of the nation's 7,000 temporary-employment firms for help.[72] In fact, some analysts predict that in just a few years, half of all working Americans—some 60 million people—will be working on a part-time or freelance basis.

The Virtual Corporation: A Network of Temporary Organizations   As more and more companies outsource various organizational functions and pare down to their core competencies, they might not be able to perform all the tasks required to complete a project. They can certainly perform their own highly specialized part of it very well however. Therefore, if you take several organizations whose core competencies complement each other and have them work together on a special project, you have a very

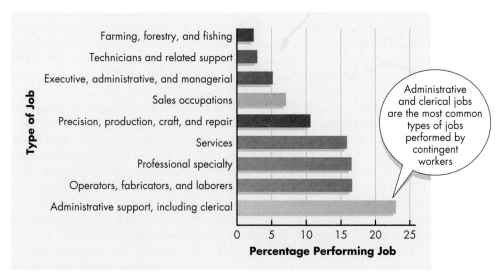

FIGURE 1.15

Contingent Workers: What Kinds of Jobs Do They Do?

Of those people in the contingent workforce, the greatest proportion perform administrative and clerical jobs.

(*Source:* Based on data reported in 1999, from the Bureau of Labor Statistics.)

virtual corporation

A highly flexible, temporary organization formed by a group of companies to exploit a specific opportunity.

strong group of collaborators. This is the idea behind an organizational arrangement that recently has been growing in popularity — the **virtual corporation**. A virtual corporation is a highly flexible, temporary organization formed by a group of companies that join forces to exploit a specific opportunity.[73] (We will discuss this type of organization in more detail in chapter 14.)

Various companies, for example, often come together for special projects in the entertainment industry (e.g., to produce a motion picture) and in the field of construction (e.g., to build a shopping center). After all, technologies are changing so rapidly and skills are becoming so specialized that no one company can do everything itself today. Therefore, companies join forces temporarily to form virtual corporations — not permanent organizations, but temporary ones without their own offices or organizational charts. Virtual corporations are not yet common, but experts expect them to grow in numbers during the years ahead.[74] As one consultant put it, "It's not just a good idea; it's inevitable."[75]

The Quality Revolution

For many years, people complained but could do little when goods they purchased fell apart or a service they received was second-rate. After all, if everything in the market is shoddy, what are the alternatives? Then, for example, Japanese companies such as Toyota and Nissan entered the U.S. auto market. Their cars were more reliable, less expensive, and better designed than cars from Ford, General Motors, and Chrysler, which had grown complacent about offering value to their customers. When Japanese automakers began capturing record shares of the U.S. auto market, American companies were forced to rethink their strategies — and to change their ways.

Today's companies operate quite differently from the U.S. auto companies of decades past. The watchword now is not "getting by" but "making things better" — what has been referred to as the *quality revolution*. The best organizations are ones that strive to deliver better goods and services at lower prices than ever before. Those that do so flourish; and those that do not fade away.

total quality management (TQM)

An organizational strategy of commitment to improving customer satisfaction by developing techniques to carefully manage output quality.

Total Quality Management to the Rescue   One of the most popular approaches to establishing quality is known as **total quality management (TQM)** — an organizational strategy of improving customer satisfaction by developing techniques to carefully manage output quality. TQM is not so much a special technique as a well-ingrained set of corporate values. TQM is a way of life demonstrating a strong commitment to improving quality in everything that is done.

According to W. Edwards Deming, the best-known advocate of TQM, successful TQM requires that everyone in the organization — from the lowest-level employee to the CEO — be fully committed to making whatever innovations are necessary to improve quality. This involves both carefully measuring quality through elaborate statistical procedures and taking whatever steps are necessary to improve it. Typically, this requires continuously improving the manufacturing process to result in ever-higher quality.

In developing the Lexus LS 400, for example, Toyota purchased competing cars from Mercedes and BMW, disassembled them, examined their parts, and then developed ways of building an even better car. (This process of comparing one's own products or services with the best from one's competitors is known as **benchmarking**.) Spending some $500 million in this process, Toyota was clearly dedicated to creating a superior product, and given the recognition that Lexus has received among customers for its high quality, it appears that Toyota's TQM efforts were successful.

benchmarking

The process of comparing one's own products or services with the best from one's competitors.

Another key ingredient of TQM is incorporating a concern for quality into all aspects of organizational culture (a concept we discuss more fully in chapter 13).[76] At Rubbermaid, for example, concern for quality is emphasized in the company's manufacturing process but also in its concern for cost, service, speed, and innovation. To ensure that quality standards are met, many companies conduct **quality control audits** — careful examinations of how well the company meets its own standards. For example, companies such as Pepsi Cola and FedEx regularly interview their clients to find out what problems may be occurring, and these responses are taken very seriously in deciding what improvements are necessary to avoid such problems in the future.

quality control audits

Careful examinations of how well a company meets its standards.

The Baldrige Award   Some companies have been so successful at achieving high quality in all respects they have been honored for their accomplishments. In 1987, the U.S. Congress established the **Malcolm Baldrige Quality Award** (named after President Reagan's late Secretary of Commerce) to recognize American companies that practice effective quality management and make significant improvements in the quality of their goods and services.[77] As many as two companies are given the award each year in each of three categories: manufacturing, service, and small business (any independent company with less than 500 full-time employees). For a listing of each year's winners by category, see Table 1.2.

Malcolm Baldrige Quality Award

An award given annually to U.S. companies that practice effective quality management and significantly improve the quality of their goods and services.

TABLE 1.2

Baldrige Award Winners

The Malcolm Baldrige Quality Award has been given each year since 1988 to U.S. companies whose practices reflect the highest standards of quality in all aspects of their operations. Here is a list of winners in each category: manufacturing, small business, and service. (In 1999, two new categories were added: health care and education.)

YEAR	MANUFACTURING CATEGORY	SMALL BUSINESS CATEGORY	SERVICE CATEGORY
1988	• Motorola, Inc. • Commercial Nuclear Fuel Division of Westinghouse Electric	• Globe Metallurgical, Inc.	[none]
1989	• Miliken & Company • Xerox Business Products and Systems	[none]	[none]
1990	• Cadillac Motor Car Company	• Wallace Co., Inc.	• Federal Express Corporation
1991	• Solectron Corporation	• Marlowe Industries	[none]
1992	• AT&T Network Systems Group • Texas Instruments, Inc.	• Granite Rock Co.	• AT&T Universal Card Services • The Ritz-Carlton Hotel Co.
1993	• Eastman Chemical Company	• Ames Rubber Company	[none]
1994	[none]	• Wainwright Industries	• AT&T Consumer Communication Services • GTE Directories Corp.
1995	• Armstrong World Industries' Building Products Operation • Corning Telecommunications Products Division	[none]	[none]
1996	• ADAC Laboratories	• Trident Precision Manufacturing	• Custom Research • Dana Commercial Credit
1997	• 3M Dental Products Division	• Solectron Corp.	• Merrill Lynch Credit Corp. • Xerox Business Services
1998	• Boeing Airlift and Tanker Programs • Solar Turbines	• Texas Nameplate Co.	[none]

Source: National Institute of Standards and Technology, 1999.

Companies interested in being considered for the award complete a detailed application (as long as 75 pages) in which they thoroughly document their quality achievements. Winners are determined by a board of examiners (currently composed of approximately 250 quality experts) at the National Institute of Standards and Technology. The board reviews each written application and then visits the companies that score high enough to be in contention. Applicants are judged on several criteria, including evidence of customer satisfaction, evidence of improvements in operations, and the extent to which they tap the potential of their employees.

The major goal of the award is to promote quality achievement by recognizing those companies that deliver continually improving value while maximizing overall productivity and effectiveness. To ensure that all companies can benefit, winners are expected to share their successful strategies for quality with other U.S. firms. This has been done in the form of personal presentations, books, and videotapes.[78] In the case of IBM, preparing its application for the Baldrige Award caused it to examine itself so carefully that benefits came not only from the recognition it received by winning (in 1990) but from the detailed process of preparing the application itself as well.[79]

Corporate Social Responsibility: The Ethical Organization

The history of U.S. business is riddled with sordid tales of magnates who went to any length in their quest for success—and in the process destroying not only the country's natural resources and the public's trust but also the hopes and dreams of millions of people. For example, John D. Rockefeller, founder of Standard Oil, regularly bribed politicians and stepped over others in his quest to monopolize the oil industry.

Of course, unsavory business practices are not some relic of the past. Indeed, as you probably know only too well, they tend to be quite common today. For example, recent reports of bribes and kickbacks have tarnished the reputation of the International Olympic Organizing Committee, and accusations of fraudulent practices in its auto-repair business have raised ethical questions about the venerable retailing giant Sears.[80] Clearly, human greed has not faded from the business scene. Something, however, *has* changed—the public's acceptance of unethical behavior by organizations. Consider this statement by a leading expert on business ethics:

> *Ethical standards, whether formal or informal, have changed tremendously in the last century. Boldly stated, no one can make the case that ethical standards have fallen in the latter decades of the twentieth century. The reverse is true. Standards are considerably higher. Businesspeople themselves, as well as the public, expect more sensitive behavior in the conduct of economic enterprise. The issue is not just having the standards, however. It is living up to them.*[81]

To the extent that people are increasingly intolerant of unethical business activity, it makes sense for specialists in OB to examine the factors encouraging unethical practices. Even more important, we need to develop strategies for promoting ethical conduct.

Why Does Unethical Organizational Behavior Occur?   As you might imagine, no one factor accounts for all the unethical things that people do. Rather, a wide variety of forces encourage ethically questionable behavior. Table 1.3 summarizes some of these factors.

Why Should Companies Care About Ethical Behavior?   Obviously, companies *should* promote ethical behavior among employees—simply because this is the right thing to do. Regardless, as suggested by Table 1.3, many potent forces deter people from always doing the right thing. Corporate leaders need to be concerned about this, however, if not for moral reasons then for the simple business reason that good ethics pay off in the long run.

TABLE 1.3

Ethically Questionable Business Practices: Why Do They Occur?

People behave unethically for many reasons. Some of the key determinants of such behavior are listed here.

REASON	COMMENT
Society places a high value on economic success.	People adopting a "bottom-line mentality" strive for financial success at any cost.
Some corporate mission statements emphasize profit as the sole objective.	In organizations cultures develop that encourage people to do whatever is necessary to be profitable.
Intense competition occurs between people, departments, or companies.	In the face of competition, people may lose sight of any goal other than winning, such as behaving ethically.
Management is concerned with "the letter of the law" rather than with "the spirit of the law."	Generally, laws dictate only what is permissible — not what is morally appropriate. As such, laws represent the minimum acceptable standards that people should follow.
Corporate policies regarding ethical behavior are ambiguous.	Many codes of ethics are vague and provide little guidance regarding appropriate and inappropriate behavior.
Inadequate controls allow people to "get away with" behaving unethically.	Lax accounting systems and the absence of security procedures make behaving unethically all too easy for some people.
Business leaders fail to comprehend the public's ethical concerns.	Some people forget the public at large is increasingly intolerant of unethical behavior by business leaders.
The "let the buyer beware" custom prevails.	People sometimes believe it is acceptable to behave unethically because others expect them to do so (e.g., in buyer–seller relationships).

As evidence of this, consider a recent study that showed a strong link between a corporation's financial performance and its commitment to ethics.[82] The researcher conducting the study gathered the 1996 annual reports of the 500 largest public corporations in the United States, as identified by *Business Week* magazine. These companies were then carefully analyzed for statements demonstrating a corporate commitment toward ethical behavior. Some examples include:

- Johnson & Johnson:
  "It has always been the policy and practice of the Company to conduct its affairs ethically and in a socially responsible manner."
- Campbell Soup:
  "The company believes that its long-standing emphasis on the highest standards of conduct and business ethics . . . serves to reinforce its system of internal accounting control."
- DuPont:
  "The company's business ethics policy . . . sets forth management's commitment to conduct business worldwide with the highest ethical standards. . . ."[83]

Such statements were found in 134 of the 500 annual reports that were examined. The researcher then compared the financial performance of these same 500 firms using a variety of standard measures (e.g., sales growth and profit growth) for 1997. These findings were striking: Companies that expressed a commitment to ethics performed better, on average, than those with no such expressed commitment. In other words, the more ethically oriented companies were more financially successful.

Why might this be? A key answer: Companies that behave in a socially responsible manner have a long and financially profitable life because they are supported by the public, which rewards their social consciousness by doing business with it. Indeed, some companies — Ben & Jerry's Homemade and the Body Shop are two good examples — have promoted the socially conscious things they do for the community specifically to court customers who share their values.[84]

ETHICS MATTERS

Ironically, some claim that companies act unethically when they actively promote their socially responsible ways for the sake of gaining business. Do you agree or disagree with this position? In other words, is it unethical to center business promotions on ethical actions? Besides those already mentioned, what other companies have done this? ■

What Can Be Done to Promote Ethical Behavior in Organizations? As you might imagine, getting people to behave ethically is not a simple matter. Because "good ethics" is also "good business," however, it is worth considering tactics for discouraging unethical behavior. Here are some worthwhile suggestions:

- *Test the ethics of any decision you are contemplating.* In this regard, there are four main questions to ask yourself:

  1. Is it right? Although it is not always easy to judge whether a certain action is right, certain universally accepted principles of right and wrong should not be violated. For example, it is widely considered wrong to steal.

  2. Is it fair? Fairness demands treating "likes" as "likes." So, for example, two equally qualified people should be paid the same wages for doing the same job.

  3. Is it purely selfish? If the results of your actions benefit only yourself, then your actions may be unethical. Morally acceptable behaviors are ones that benefit the greatest number and harm the fewest.

  4. How would you feel if others found out? If you think you might be embarrassed by having your actions described on the front page of your local newspaper, then those actions may be ethically dubious.[85]

- *Develop a code of ethics.* A **code of ethics** is a document describing what an organization stands for and the general rules of conduct it expects of its employees (e.g., to avoid conflicts of interest, to be honest, and so on).[86] Some codes are highly specific. For example, some state the maximum size of gifts that can be accepted and exactly how people will be punished for violating the rules. Codes of ethics are especially effective when used in conjunction with training programs that reinforce the company's values.[87] In the absence of such training, however, codes are often seen as "window dressing" and are ignored — if they are even read at all. (For an example of an internationally established code of business ethics, see the OB Around the World box in this chapter.)

- *Conduct an ethics audit.* Just as companies regularly audit their books to identify irregularities in their finances, they also should regularly assess the mortality of their employees' behavior to identify irregularities in this realm as well. Specifically, an **ethics audit** involves actively investigating and documenting incidents of dubious ethical value. These unethical practices should then be discussed in an open and honest fashion, and a concrete plan should be developed to avoid such actions in the future.

- *Challenge your rationalizations about ethical behavior.* We all tend to rationalize things we do so that we can convince ourselves they are right — even though they really may be wrong. Some of the most common rationalizations include:

code of ethics
A document describing what an organization stands for and the general rules of conduct it expects from employees (e.g., to avoid conflicts of interest, to be honest, and so on).

ethics audit
The process of actively investigating and documenting incidents of dubious ethical value within a company.

1. *Convincing yourself something is morally acceptable just because it is legally acceptable.* Think of the law as the minimum standard of acceptable behavior and strive for higher moral standards.

2. *Convincing yourself something is right just because it benefits you.* It may be easy to talk yourself into accepting a bribe because you feel underpaid. Regardless, it is still wrong.

3. *Convincing yourself something is right because you will never get caught.* Something that is wrong is wrong — even if you don't stand a chance of getting caught!

4. *Convincing yourself something is right because it helps the company.* Do not expect the company to condone your immoral actions — even if doing so gives your company an edge. The best companies want to succeed because they have taken the moral high road, not because of the unacceptable practices of its employees.

As you might imagine, avoiding these rationalizations is not always easy. Still, try do your best to catch yourself in the act of rationalizing your actions. To the extent that you are rationalizing, you may be covering up unethical behavior.

THE CAUX ROUND TABLE'S ETHICAL PRINCIPLES OF INTERNATIONAL BUSINESS

OB AROUND THE WORLD

On several occasions between 1992 and 1994, the world's top business leaders (including those from such well-known companies as Philips Electronics, Ciba-Geigy, Cummins, Matsushita, 3M, and Honeywell) met in Caux-sur-Montreaux, Switzerland, to undertake an ambitious project: To draft the first international code of business ethics.[88] Their goal was to set a world standard against which business behavior could be measured, a yardstick that individual companies could use to develop their own codes of ethics.

The document that resulted, *The Caux Round Table Principles for Business*, was not easy to create. The major challenge was to identify those ethical values that cut across all cultures. Naturally, the process of doing so brought into the open quite a few fundamental disagreements between people from various nations. Experts agree, however, that the final product, which was presented in July 1994, was well worth the effort. Indeed, the Caux principles are considered to be a unique blend of ideals from Asian nations (e.g., Japan's concept of *kyosei*, which involves working together for the common good) and from Western nations (e.g., the idea of preserving human dignity). Paraphrasing, the Caux principles are as follows:

1. By sharing the wealth they have created, businesses are responsible for improving the lives of their customers, employees, and shareholders.

2. Businesses should contribute to the economic development of the foreign countries in which they conduct business.

3. Leaders are expected to be sincere, candid, and truthful in all business dealings.

4. Both international and domestic laws should be followed when conducting business in foreign nations.

5. All agreements regarding multilateral trade should be honored.

6. Businesses should protect — and, if possible, enhance — the physical environment.

7. Illicit practices such as bribery, money laundering, and drug trafficking should not be followed.

The Caux principles have been in place for several years, they clearly have been accepted well. In fact, the principles have even been presented and discussed at a United Nations World Summit. This is all well and good, but the real question now is: How, precisely, will the principles help to guide companies conducting international business? To state a principle is one thing; to follow it is quite another. For a principle to guide complex human behavior in the international arena, it certainly must be widely accepted as being valuable. Will the principles adopted at the Caux Round Table ever be so described? Only time will tell. For now, however, one thing is certain: Following these principles will be even more challenging than stating them.

We invite you to visit the Greenberg page on the Prentice Hall Web site at: **www.prenhall.com/greenberg** for the monthly Greenberg update and for this chapter's World Wide Web exercise.

SUMMARY AND REVIEW
OF LEARNING OBJECTIVES

1. **Define the concepts of *organization* and *organizational behavior*.**
   An **organization** is a structured social system consisting of groups and individuals working together to meet some agreed-on objectives. **Organizational behavior** is the field that seeks knowledge of behavior in organizational settings by systematically studying individual, group, and organizational processes.

2. **Describe the field of organizational behavior's commitment to the *scientific method* and the *three levels of analysis* it uses.**
   The field of OB seeks to develop a base of knowledge about behavior in organizations using an empirical, research-based approach. As such, it is based on systematic observation and measuring the behavior or phenomenon of interest. The field of OB uses three levels of analysis: individuals, work groups, and entire organizations—all relying on the scientific method.

3. **Trace the historical developments and schools of thought leading up to the field of organizational behavior today.**
   The earliest approaches to OB relied on the **scientific management** approach, which essentially treated people like machines and emphasized what it took to get the most out of them. For example, this approach relied on **time-and-motion study**, a type of applied research that was designed to find the most efficient way for people to perform their jobs. As this approach grew unpopular, however, it was supplanted by the **human relations movement**, which emphasized the importance of noneconomic, social forces in the workplace and remains popular as an approach today. Such factors were demonstrated in the Hawthorne studies, the first large-scale research project conducted in a work organization that demonstrated the importance of social forces in determining productivity. In contrast with scientific management's orientation toward organizing the work of individuals, proponents of **classical organizational theory** developed ways of efficiently structuring the way that work is done. Weber's concept of **bureaucracy** is a prime example of this approach. Contemporary OB is characterized not by one best approach to management, however, but by systematic scientific research inspired from several fields of social science. Modern OB uses a **contingency approach**, recognizing that behavior may be influenced by many different forces at once and thereby rejecting the idea of any single most effective approach to managing behavior in organizations.

4. **Identify the fundamental characteristics of the field of organizational behavior.**
   The field of OB assumes: that organization can be made more productive while also improving the quality of people's work life, that no one approach to studying behavior in organizations is best, and that organizations are dynamic and ever-changing.

5. **Describe how the *global economy* is shaping the field of organizational behavior today.**
   The world's economy is becoming increasingly global, which affects the field of OB in several distinct ways. For example, organizations are expanding overseas, thus requiring people to live and work in different countries, which involves considerable adjustment. As this occurs, much of what we thought we knew about managing people is shown to be limited by the culture in which that knowledge was developed (the U.S. culture, in most cases).

6. **Explain how the workforce is becoming increasingly diversified and how this has led to the development of *flexible working arrangements*.**

Diversification of the workplace, in large part, is the result of shifting patterns of immigration, which have brought more foreign nationals into the workforce. It also is the result of changes in social values and the economy, which have made women common in today's workforce. Also, thanks to modern medicine, people are living longer and retiring from work later than ever before. In response to the work–family problems that arise when both adult members of a household work outside the home, organizations have instituted a variety of programs that enable employees to meet the conflicting demands of work and family. These include **flextime programs, compressed workweeks, job sharing, voluntary reduced work time (V-time) programs**, and **telecommuting**.

7. **Describe how *technology* has led to the development of new organizational forms.**

As technology becomes increasingly specialized, organizations have found it useful to hire other companies to do nonessential aspects of their operations they once performed themselves—a process known as *outsourcing*. Because the nature of work changes so rapidly today, many people—who are known collectively as the **contingent workforce**—are opting to work on a part-time basis for several companies rather than on a full-time basis for a single company. This is in keeping with the trend toward **virtual corporations**, in which companies temporarily join forces to compete special projects.

8. **Explain how rising expectations about *quality* and *ethical behavior* have influenced the field of organizational behavior.**

Today's consumers demand high-quality products and services, which encourages companies to develop ways of meeting these demands—thereby remaining in existence and possibly even staying ahead of competitors. The popular policy of continuously improving products and services, which is referred to as **total quality management (TQM)**, is a response to this trend. The public at large also appears to be growing tired of unethical practices by individuals and by companies as a whole. As a result, many companies are adopting policies that enhance the ethical nature of their behavior (e.g., conducting **ethics audits** and developing **codes of ethics**), which have a positive influence on the bottom line.

QUESTIONS FOR DISCUSSION

1. How can the field of OB contribute to the effective functioning of organizations *and* to the well-being of individuals? Are these goals inconsistent? Why, or why not?

2. Explain the following statement: People influence organizations, and organizations influence people.

3. What is the *contingency approach*, and why is it so popular in the field of OB today?

4. Explain how the field of OB stands to benefit from a global perspective. What are the major challenges associated with such a perspective?

5. How has your own life—and the lives of your own family members—changed because of the flexible, new working arrangements that have developed in recent years?

6. How has the growing quest for quality products and services affected your own work?

7. Describe a work situation in which you found yourself torn between behaving in an ethical and an unethical manner. What forces pulled you in each direction? What did you finally do? What might have led you to behave differently?

LSG Sky Chefs Adjusts the Standard Recipe for International Management Success

As countries become more interdependent and the life cycles of products and services even shorter, managers in global companies need new skills to succeed. The old view of the expatriate manager — happily and perhaps even royally ensconced in an exotic locale and adrift from headquarters — is fading fast. Today, global managers must react quickly to shifting market and political conditions and always keep an eye on events at headquarters so their local unit is in synch with performance expectations.

Responding to changing conditions may be a new challenge for some managers. That is the case at LSG Sky Chefs, an Arlington, Texas–based airline caterer with more than 200 kitchens worldwide and one-third of a $9 billion global market. "Most of our younger managers grew up in boom times, and they are scared to death now," says Michael Kay, CEO of Sky Chefs. "The more seasoned ones have learned to read and react to good and lousy business conditions."

Kay and his top executives encourage global managers to move quickly to inculcate the corporate culture. "We have worked very hard to standardize our operations, whether the kitchen is in Auckland, Chicago, or Brazil. We have a clear, well-documented way of communicating and doing things, and that helps us enormously in difficult times," says Kay.

This strategy is reflected in the way Sky Chefs now deploys managers on global assignments. In lieu of multi-year expatriate assignments, they go abroad for 90, 120, or another specified number of days to ac-complish a specific task. For example, a manager in Manchester, England, with an $18 million budget and 12 airline customers might be placed in a smaller kitchen in Boston, Massachusetts for four months to master cycle time and variable costs.

"Basically we ran out of appetite for traditional expat[riate] assignments," Kay explains. "We were spending too much money sending people and their families overseas, with all the accoutrements like upscale housing, private schools and chauffeurs that an expat lifestyle required. We now focus on global managers gaining specific skills, short-term, then placing them wherever they are most needed within the company."

CRITICAL THINKING QUESTIONS

1. What changes has LSG Sky Chefs been forced to make because of the global economy?

2. What challenges would you expect the company's employees to face because of these changes?

3. How might flexible working arrangements be used at LSG Sky Chefs?

4. What ethical issues might employees of LSG Sky Chefs be expected to confront as they take on their assignments in new countries?

5. How do you think you might adjust to the new system for overseas assignments used at LSG Sky Chefs? Do you think you would like it more or less than the old system?

VIDEO CASE

The Field of Organizational Behavior

SMALL BUSINESS 2000

The study of organizations is not new, but how we study them — and what we find out when we do — is a lot different today than it used to be. Fortunately, scholars and managers of businesses understand that companies, just like people, change.

Change often occurs for various reasons and in various ways. Thus, it is useful to look at how change affects individuals, groups, and entire companies. In this case, we meet three individuals who initiated changes that affected their lives and the ways they earn a living.

Greg Stickler hung up his tools after 18 years in

(continued)

the log-home construction industry to start a design company. What makes this so interesting? Greg's own life changed dramatically. He gave up being on the road, involvement in heavy labor, and the responsibility for managing several employees. What he got in return is a home-based company nestled on 45 acres, with an office facing a lake and a snow-capped mountain. What did he give up? To hear Greg tell it, not much.

Sue Kauffman was a college professor of English. Her career was pretty typical of someone with a Ph.D. in that field, and as she put it, "I was just another English professor." After 30 years, Sue made a major change. You might expect a professor in a business school to chuck it all and start a company, but an English professor? Sue found a market that saw her skills as something special. She was no longer just another English professor.

Finally, we meet Brett Lascarella. Brett takes the concept of global business and flexibility to the extreme. Not only does he use computer technology and the World Wide Web to reach customers around the world, he uses it to reach customers "from" around the world. Brett is not a guy who likes to sit still. His company is structured in a way that allows him to be flexible in meeting his customers' needs and also allows him to be flexible. Flexible for Brett is not just "flextime," it's also "flex-location."

The three companies we see in this case represent a trend in business today. Having a job does not necessarily mean leaving the house to go to work anymore. This workstyle and lifestyle is not for everyone, but it is one way of building a satisfying career. Look at it from a customer's perspective. Large companies employ many people with varied skills. Sometimes, all those skills are not needed at all times. The problem is that a company might have jobs they need three people to do sometimes, but these people may not be needed at all other times. This can be a dilemma. Companies like the three in this case allow their customers (usually larger companies) the ability to hire them only when needed. Technology makes it easy for them to communicate; they don't even need to be located near each other. In fact, as Sue Kauffman pointed out, sometimes they never even meet in person!

Flexible work arrangements, just like anything else, have their good points and their bad points. While watching this case, think about how you might like to work in a company such as any of the ones in this video. Also, consider what it would be like to manage a group or a company that does business with cyberpartners.

QUESTIONS FOR DISCUSSION

1. In this case, you met three individuals who started home-based businesses as a career alternative. Each started his or her business for different reasons. Discuss these reasons for each. What do you think each gained?

2. The home-based business owners we met had one thing in common: They all had several years of professional experience before starting their companies. Using the information in the case and your own ideas, discuss things that you think are important in considering a career option like the ones Greg, Sue, and Brett have chosen.

3. From the case, we get the idea that working alone may be a great thing. Perhaps it is, but it may have some downsides, too. What do you think are the disadvantages of home-based businesses?

4. All three of the people we met use technology in some way to make their businesses work. Do you think home-based businesses were an option before people had easy access to faxes, PCs, or the World Wide Web? If you were working from home today, what other technology or capability could you dream up that would make your life easier?

SKILLS BANK

EXPERIENCING ORGANIZATIONAL BEHAVIOR

Testing Your Ethical IQ

Ethical dilemmas can be very troubling. In the time-honored metaphor known as "being caught on the horns of a dilemma," you face a charging bull. You are certain to be gored, and as the "moment of truth" approaches, your choice usually comes down to which horn you most wish to avoid. There are two implicit assumptions in dilemmas: that you must choose, and that you have the power to choose. Not choosing is itself a choice, however. This exercise demonstrates how you make choices in situations involving ethical dilemmas.

Directions

What follows are 10 true-life dilemmas from business. Each requires a choice. Give your first-reaction answer to each question by circling either NO, DEPENDS, or YES. Your answers should reflect what you believe you would actually do in the situation, *not* what you think you should do or believe is the best or most ethical answer.

Ethical IQ Test

1. Your are a newly hired junior executive in a large manufacturing firm. The business conference you've been attending on behalf of your firm for the last two days is over. You had planned to fly home, but a couple of friends you've made at the conference are driving back by car and have invited you to ride with them. It would be a five-hour drive instead of a two-hour flight, but they would drop you at your doorstep. It would be stimulating to ride back with your new friends, and it might benefit the company. You reason that the additional travel time would be out of your pocket, so to speak, not the firm's. You decide to drive back with your new colleagues. You toss $10 into the refueling kitty during the midpoint pit stop.

   Q. *Would you cash in the return flight ticket and keep the money?*

    NO   DEPENDS   YES

2. You have a strict code of ethics in your office regarding employee appropriation of office supplies. The most competent and longest-tenured secretary is caught by you, the secretary's boss, taking typewriter ribbons and erasure tapes home in a briefcase. There is a rule against this as well as a clearly established procedure for providing employees with supplies if they do company work at home. The code requires you to fire the secretary on the spot.

   Q. *Would you make an exception for this loyal worker?*

   NO   DEPENDS   YES

3. A friend at work asks whether you'd like a take-home copy of an expensive computer software program. You known it is protected by copyright.

   Q. *Would you let your friend make a copy for you?*

   NO   DEPENDS   YES

4. You are the senior vice president for public responsibility in a large multinational corporation. One of your long-time friends in the marketing department confides to you that the boss is subtly suggesting that sales representatives give misleading information to prospective clients about a particular product. Your friend is very upset about it and wants your advice.

   Q. *Would you encourage your friend to follow the boss's suggestion?*

   NO   DEPENDS   YES

5. You are a public relations professional in a medium-sized midwestern city. Three months ago, you set up your own company. Your first big client wants to promote throughout your region a passive exercise machine. The home office in Texas claims the device is "scientifically proven to take off pounds easily and quickly." The manufacturing firm does not have a national reputation and, despite your repeated requests, has been unable to provide you with any scientific proof of its claims.

   Q. *Would you continue serving this firm as a client without the scientific proof?*

   NO   DEPENDS   YES

6. You are the director of research and development in your firm. The personnel office has found two candidates for a vacant position in new product testing in your department. The better-qualified candidate with more potential for promotion and future contribution to the organization appears to be rather cold and aloof and will likely clash with your personality. The less-qualified candidate is your personal choice even though the company will not be as well served.

   Q. *Would you choose the less-qualified candidate?*

   NO   **DEPENDS**   **YES**

7. You are the product manager for one of your firm's largest dollar-volume brands. You known that your product will soon be challenged by an improved version from a strong, well-financed competitor. One of your venders offers to provide you with a confidential copy of the competitor's strategic marketing plan. No price for the copy is mentioned.

   Q. *Would you use this vital information to help your brand?*

   NO   **DEPENDS**   **YES**

8. You recently accepted the top marketing position at a new company. One of your first assignments is to approve an all-expenses-paid trip for the senior purchasing officer of one of your largest client firms. The four-day seminar in the Caribbean, which is sponsored solely by your company, would include first-class airline tickets for client and spouse, a three-day cruise following the seminar, plus a $500 honorarium. You known that this particular company does not have a written conflict-of-interest policy. You also know that your new boss is very eager to have this purchasing officer at the seminar.

   Q. *Would you authorize the expenditures for this client?*

   NO   **DEPENDS**   **YES**

9. You serve as an outside member on the audit committee of the board of directors of a major pharmaceutical company that markets new drugs through practicing physicians. You have secretly learned that your research department has developed an abortion pill that appears to be 100 percent safe and effective. It has been repeatedly rumored, however, that your chief executive officer will not let this product be brought to market because of deep religious convictions. Millions of dollars of potential revenue and profits will be lost.

   Q. *Would you let this secret decision of your CEO go unchallenged?*

   NO   **DEPENDS**   **YES**

10. You happen to overhear a couple of engineers in your company discussing a radically new product that your colleagues in upper management are anxious to see hit the market on schedule. You accidentally learn that the engineers are also quite concerned about some design flaws that could be harmful to the product's users, although the probabilities are very remote.

    Q. *Since you are not directly responsible for this product, would you completely ignore their comments?*

    NO   **DEPENDS**   **YES**

TOTAL SCORE: ____   ____   ____

Scoring and Interpretation

1. In the spaces provided, total the number of times you circled each NO, DE-PENDS, or YES.

2. Take the highest number from your scores in the three categories, multiply it by 100, and then divide the results by 5. This is your *ethical IQ*. The average is 100; a perfect score is 200.

3. If you scored *higher than 160* in any of the three categories, you are a person with a strong and consistent ethical decision-making pattern. Your colleagues will experience you as being predictable. If your high score is in the NO column, for example, they likely will think of you as a paragon of virtue. Some of your ethical decisions might attract considerable attention, however, because they will seem unfashionable or unpopular. If your high score is in the YES column, your willingness to make exceptions to the rules on a regular basis might earn you the reputation of being unprincipled. You and some of your decisions may be very popular, however, either because they are adventurous or because you don't "stand on ceremony." If your high score is in the DEPENDS column, you likely will be perceived as being indecisive. The popularity of your decisions will rise and fall on a case-by-case basis.

4. If you scored *between 100 and 140* in your highest category, you are probably a very thoughtful person as well as a product of our times. You have scattered your responses among the three alternatives. This pattern reflects the high degree of ethical ambiguity in the marketplace today. The most ethical course of action is not always crystal clear. In fact, we are surfeited with significant choices at every turn. The ethical consequence is a growing number of DE-PENDS or YES responses. It is not as easy to "just say no." What's more, it is often very rewarding to say yes, which can bring excitement and money.

5. If you scored around 110 — which for any given group tends to be the mean — you probably sense that principles from the past cannot be applied rigidly and religiously to many contemporary situations. People who are the most well-adjusted — and sometimes the most prosperous — are those whose ethical IQ scores are nearer this mean. They are more willing, evidently, to make the necessary compromises between unyielding principles and harmful impact on people. Maybe there is more to be said for mediocrity than we thought.

6. If you scored *less than 100* in your highest category, you could be either extraordinarily sensitive or insensitive to ethical issues. You may be aware of dimensions to the questions that others overlook or deliberately ignore as being irrelevant. At the other extreme, you may not have been aware that there was an ethical issue at all. In either case, there is no strong pattern to your answers, so each must be analyzed separately for clues.

Source: Adapted from Verne Henderson. *What's Ethical in Business?* © 1992. New York: McGraw-Hill. Reprinted with permission of the author.

Questions for Discussion

1. What did this ethical IQ test reveal about yourself? Was this something you already suspected, or did it come as a surprise?

2. Into what category did most of your answers fall: YES, DEPENDS, or NO? What do you think this means?

3. Do you think there are any "perfect" answers to the questions in this test? In other words, do you think there are responses that suggest you are completely ethical? Why, or why not?

4. How might different situations — or a person's culture — influence his or her responses to the questions in this test? Explain.

WORKING IN GROUPS

Common Sense About Behavior in Organizations: Putting It to the Test

Even if you already have a good intuitive sense about behavior in organizations, some of what you think may be inconsistent with established research findings (many of which are noted in this book). So that you don't have to rely on your own judgments alone, which may be idiosyncratic, working with others in this exercise gives you a good idea of what our collective common sense has to say about behavior in organizations. You just may be enlightened.

Directions

Divide the class into groups of approximately five. Then, within these groups, discuss the following statements, reaching a consensus as to whether each is true or false. Spend approximately 30 minutes on the entire discussion.

1. People who are satisfied with one job tend to be satisfied with other jobs as well.
2. Because "two heads are better than one," groups make better decisions than individuals.
3. The best leaders always act the same, regardless of the situations they face.
4. Specific goals make people nervous; people work better when asked simply to do their best.
5. People get bored easily, so they welcome organizational change.
6. Money is the best motivator.
7. Today's organizations are more rigidly structured than ever before.
8. People generally shy away from challenges on the job.
9. Using multiple channels of communication (e.g., written and spoken) tends to add confusion.
10. Conflict in organizations is always highly disruptive.

Scoring

Give your group one point for each item you scored as follows: 1 = true, 2 = false, 3 = false, 4 = false, 5 = false, 6 = false, 7 = false, 8 = false, 9 = false, and 10 = false. (Should you have questions about these answers, information bearing on them appears in this book as follows: 1 = chapter 5, 2 = chapter 9, 3 = chapter 12, 4 = chapter 4, 5 = chapter 16, 6 = chapter 4, 7 = chapter 14, 8 = chapter 4, 9 = chapter 8, and 10 = chapter 10.)

Questions for Discussion

1. How well did your group do? Were you stumped on a few?
2. Comparing your experiences with those of other groups, did you find that some questions were trickier than others (i.e., ones where the scientific findings were more counterintuitive)? If you did poorly, don't be frustrated. These statements are a bit simplistic and need to be qualified to be fully understood. Have your instructor explain the statements the class found most challenging.
3. Did this exercise give you a better understanding of the sometimes surprising—and complex—nature of behavior in organizations?

41

THEORY AND RESEARCH: TOOLS FOR LEARNING ABOUT BEHAVIOR IN ORGANIZATIONS

As noted in chapter 1, OB is a science, so it should not be surprising that the field relies heavily on the scientific method. As with other scientific fields, OB uses the tools of science to achieve its goals — in this case, to learn about organizations and the behavior of people working in them. Thus, understanding the basic tools scientists use to learn about behavior in organizations is essential. In this appendix, we briefly describe some of these techniques. Our goal is not to make you an expert in scientific methodology but to give you a solid understanding of the techniques involved with the study of OB.

ISN'T IT ALL JUST COMMON SENSE?

You may not be the top executive of a large business with decades of experience, but you doubtlessly know *something* about the behavior of people on the job. After all, you probably learned quite a bit from whatever jobs you have had or from talking to other people about their own experiences. We also can observe a great deal about people's behavior in organizational settings just by paying casual attention. Thus, whether you are the CEO of a *Fortune* 500 firm or a part-time pizza delivery driver, chances are you already have a few ideas about how people behave on the job. There probably are some things about behavior in organizations that you even take for granted.

Would you say, for example, that happier employees tend to be more productive? You probably would say, "Yes, of course." This is only logical, right? Despite what you may believe, however, this generally is *not* true. In fact, as we see in chapter 5, people who are satisfied with their jobs generally are no more productive than those who are dissatisfied with their jobs. This contradiction of common sense is not an isolated example, either. This book is full of phenomena studied in the field of OB that you might find surprising. To see how good you may be at predicting human behavior in organizations, take the brief quiz in the "Working in Groups" section at the end of chapter 1. If you don't do very well, don't despair. This is just our way of demonstrating there is more to understanding the complexities of OB than meets the eye.

So, if we cannot trust our common sense, on what can we rely instead? This is where the scientific method enters the picture. Social science research is far from perfect, but the techniques used to study OB still can tell us a great deal. Naturally, not everything revealed by scientific research contradicts our common sense. In fact, much research confirms things we already believe to be true. If this occurs, however, is the research then useless? The answer is — emphatically — *no*! After all, scientific evidence often provides great insight into the subtle conditions under which various events occur. Such complexities would not have been apparent from only casual, unsystematic observation—or from common sense. In other words, the field of OB is solidly based on carefully conducted, logically analyzed research. Common sense may provide a useful starting point, but is no substitute for scientific research when it comes to really understanding both what happens and why.

Now that you understand the important role of the scientific method, you can appreciate the specific approaches used to conduct scientific research in the field of OB. We begin our presentation of these techniques with one of the best-accepted sources of ideas for OB research—that is, *theory*.

THEORY: AN INDISPENSABLE GUIDE TO ORGANIZATIONAL RESEARCH

What image comes to mind when you think of a scientist at work? Someone wearing a white lab coat and surrounded by microscopes and test tubes as he or she busily tests theories? Scientists in the field of OB typically do not wear lab coats or use microscopes and test tubes, but they do make use of theories, even though OB is, in part, an applied science. Simply because a field is characterized as being "theoretical," however, does not imply it is impractical or out of touch with reality. To the contrary, a theory simply is a way of describing the relationship between concepts. Thus, theories help our understanding of practical situations.

What Is a Theory, and Why Are Theories Important?

Formally, we define a **theory** as being a set of statements about the interrelationships between concepts that allow us to predict and to explain various processes and events. As you might imagine, such statements may be of interest to practitioners and to scientists alike. As you read this book, you will come to appreciate the valuable role theories play in understanding behavior in organizations—and in putting that knowledge to practical use.

theory

A set of statements about the interrelationships between concepts that allow us to predict and to explain various processes and events.

To demonstrate the value of theory in OB, consider an example based on a phenomenon we describe in more detail in chapter 4—that is, the effects of task goals on performance. Imagine you observe that word-processing operators type faster when given a specific goal (e.g., 75 words per minute) than when they are told simply to do their best. Imagine you also observe that salespeople make more sales when given quotas than when they are not. These are useful observations, because they allow us to predict what will happen when goals are introduced. In addition, they suggest how to change conditions to improve performance among these groups. These two accomplishments—*prediction* and *control*—are major goals of science.

Something is missing, however. Knowing that specific goals improve performance fails to tell us *why* this is so. This observation was made in two different settings and with two different groups of people, but why are people so productive in response to specific goals? This is where theory enters the picture. In contrast to fields such as physics and chemistry, in which theories often take the form of mathematical equations, theories in OB generally involve verbal assumptions. For example, in the present case, it might be theorized as follows that:

- When people are given specific goals, they know exactly what is expected of them.
- When people know what is expected of them, they are motivated to work hard to find ways to succeed.
- When people work hard to succeed, they perform at high levels.

This simple theory—like all others—consists of two basic elements: *concepts* (i.e., goals and motives), and *assertions about how they relate*.

Developing and Testing Theories

hypotheses

Logically derived, testable statements about the relationships between variables that follow from a theory.

In science, forming a theory is only the beginning. Once a theory is proposed, it is used to introduce **hypotheses** — that is, logically derived statements that follow from a theory. In our example, it may be hypothesized that specific goals improve performance only when they can be attained. Next, such predictions are tested in actual research to see if they are confirmed. If such research confirms our hypotheses, we can be more confident about the accuracy of our theory. If our hypotheses are not confirmed after several well-conducted studies, however, we should be less confident about our theory. When this happens, we need to revise the theory and then generate new, testable hypotheses from it. As you might imagine, given the complexities of human behavior in organizations, theories rarely — if ever — are fully confirmed. In fact, many of the field's most popular and useful theories are being constantly refined and tested. (We have summarized the cyclical nature of the scientific endeavor in Figure A.1.)

It probably comes as no surprise that the process of theory development and testing is very laborious, so why do scientists bother constantly fine-tuning their theories? The answer lies in the very useful purposes that theories serve. Specifically, theories serve three important functions: organizing, summarizing, and guiding. First, given the complexities of human behavior, theories provide a way of *organizing* large amounts of data into meaningful propositions. In other words, they help us to combine information so diverse that understanding might be difficult without a theory. Second, theories help us to *summarize* this knowledge by making sense out of bits and pieces of information that otherwise would be difficult — if not impossible — to grasp. Third, theories provide an important *guiding* function — that is, they help scientists to identify important areas of needed research that would not have been apparent without theories to guide their thinking.

Many different theories attempt to explain various aspects of behavior in organizations. We think you will appreciate the useful organizing, summarizing, and guiding roles these theories play — in short, how theories help to provide meaningful explanations of behavior. In all cases, however, the usefulness of any theory is based on the extent to which it can be confirmed or disconfirmed. In other words, theories must be *testable*. A theory that cannot be tested serves no real purpose. A theory (or at least

FIGURE A.1

Theory Testing: The Research Process

Once a theory is formulated, hypotheses derived from it are tested through direct research. If these hypotheses are confirmed, confidence in the theory is increased. If these hypotheses are disconfirmed, confidence in the theory is diminished. At this point, the theory is either modified and retested, or it is rejected completely.

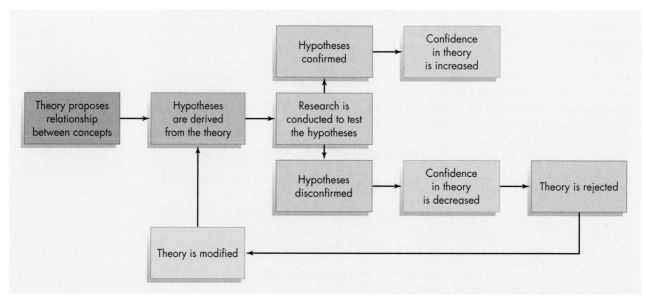

part of it) must be confirmed for it to be considered an accurate account of human behavior—and that, of course, is what the field of OB is all about.

How are theories tested? By conducting *research*. Unless we conduct research, we cannot test theories, and unless we test theories, we are greatly limited in what we can learn about behavior in organizations.[1] This is why research is such a major concern of specialists in OB. Thus, for you to appreciate fully the field of OB, you must understand something about the techniques it uses—that is, how we come to know about the behavior of people at work. As a result, we not only explain throughout this book *what* is known about OB but also *how* that knowledge is derived. We are confident that the better you understand its "tools of the trade," the more you will appreciate the value of OB as a field. Therefore, we now describe some of the major research techniques used to learn about behavior in organizations.

SURVEY RESEARCH: THE CORRELATIONAL METHOD

The most popular approach to conducting research in OB involves giving people questionnaires to report how they feel about various aspects of themselves, their jobs, and their organizations. Known as **surveys**, such questionnaires make it possible for organizational scientists to delve into a broad range of issues, which is why this technique is so popular. After all, you can learn a great deal about how people feel simply by asking them a systematic series of carefully worded questions. Moreover, questionnaires are relatively easy to administer (be it by mail, phone, or in person), and they also are readily quantifiable and lend themselves to powerful statistical analyses. These features make survey research a very appealing option; not surprisingly, we describe quite a few survey studies throughout this text.

surveys

Questionnaires in which people report how they feel about various aspects of themselves, their jobs, and their organizations.

Conducting Surveys

The survey approach consists of three major steps. First, the researcher must identify the variables of interest. These may be various aspects of people (e.g., attitudes toward work), organizations (e.g., pay plans), or the environment in general (e.g., how competitive the industry is). They may be suggested from many different sources, such as a theory, previous research, or even hunches based on casual observations.

Second, these variables are measured as precisely as possible. It is not always easy to tap people's exact feelings about things—especially if they are uncertain about these feelings or reluctant to share them. As a result, researchers must pay great attention to the wording of their questions. (For some examples of questions designed to measure various work-related attitudes, see Table A.1.)

TABLE A.1

Survey Questions Designed to Measure Work Attitudes

Items such as these might be used to measure attitudes toward various aspects of work. People completing the survey are asked to circle the number that corresponds to the point along the scale that best reflects their feelings about the attitude in question.

Overall, how fairly are you paid?
            Not at all fairly 1   2   3   4   5   6   7 Extremely fairly

Imagine one of your officemates needs to stay late to complete an important project. How likely or unlikely would you be to volunteer to help that person, even if you would not receive any special recognition for your efforts?
            Not at all likely 1   2   3   4   5   6   7 Extremely likely

How interested are you in quitting your present job?
            Not at all interested 1   2   3   4   5   6   7 Extremely interested

Finally, after the variables have been identified and measured, scientists must determine how — if at all — these variables relate to each other. With this in mind, scientists analyze their survey findings using a variety of statistical procedures.

Scientists conducting survey research typically are interested in determining how variables interrelate — that is, how changes in one variable are associated with changes in another. For example, suppose a researcher is interested in learning the relationship between how fairly people believe they are paid and various work-related attitudes, such as their willingness to help coworkers and their interest in quitting. Based on various theories and previous research, a researcher may suspect that the more people believe they are unfairly paid, the less likely they are to help coworkers and the more likely they are to desire new jobs. These predictions constitute the researcher's *hypothesis* (i.e., the as-yet-untested prediction based on the theory the researcher wishes to investigate). After devising an appropriate questionnaire to measure these variables, the researcher administers it to a large number of people so that the hypothesis can be tested.

Analyzing Survey Results: Using Correlations

Once the data are collected, the investigator must analyze them statistically to compare the results with the hypothesis. Generally, researchers are interested in seeing how the variables relate to each other — that is, if they are "co-related" (i.e., that there exists a meaningful **correlation** between them). Variables correlate to the extent the level of one variable is associated with the level of another.

Suppose, for example, a researcher obtains results like those shown on the left side of Figure A.2. In this case, the more fairly employees believe they are paid, the more willing they are to help their coworkers. In other words, the variables relate so that the more one variable increases, the more the other increases as well. Any variables described in this way are said to have a **positive correlation**.

Now, imagine the researcher compares the sample's perceptions of pay fairness with employees' interest in quitting their jobs. If the hypothesis is correct, the results will look like those shown on the right side of Figure A.2. In other words, the more people believe their pay is fair, the less interested they are in looking for a new job. Thus, the more one variable increases, the more the other decreases. Such variables are said to have a **negative correlation**.

Scientists are interested not only in the direction of the relationship between variables — that is, whether the association is positive or negative — but also in how strong that relationship is. To gauge this, researchers rely on a statistic known as the

correlation

The extent to which two variables relate to each other.

positive correlation

A relationship between two variables such that more of one is associated with more of the other.

negative correlation

A relationship between two variables such that more of one is associated with less of the other.

FIGURE A.2

Positive and Negative Correlations: What They Mean

Positive correlations (*left*) exist when more of one variable is associated with more of another. Negative correlations (*right*) exist when more of one variable is associated with less of another.

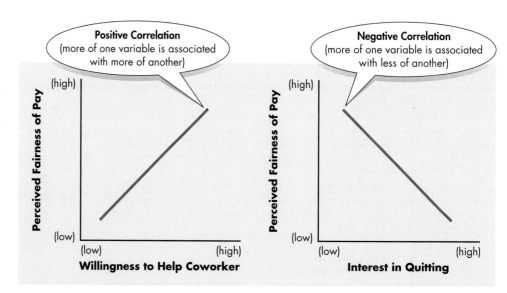

correlation coefficient. This is a number between −1.00 and +1.00, which is used to express the strength of the relationship between variables studied. The closer this number is to 1.00 (either −1.00 or +1.00), the stronger the relationship—that is, the more closely the variables relate to each other. The closer the correlation coefficient is to zero, however, the weaker the relationship between the variables—that is, the less strongly they relate.

When interpreting correlation coefficients, there are two things to remember: its *sign* (in keeping with algebraic traditions, positive correlations usually are expressed without any sign), and its *absolute value* (i.e., the size of the number regardless of its sign). For example, a correlation coefficient of −.92 reflects a much stronger relationship between variables than one of .22. The minus sign simply reveals that the relationship between the variables is negative (i.e., more of one variable is associated with less of another variable). That the absolute value of this correlation coefficient is greater reveals that the relationship between the variables is stronger.

When variables correlate strongly, scientists can make more accurate predictions about how they relate to each other. Using our example of a negative correlation between perceptions of pay fairness and intent to quit, we may expect that in general, those who believe they are unfairly paid are more likely to quit their jobs than those who believe they are fairly paid. If the correlation coefficient is high (e.g., over −.80), we can be more confident that this will occur than if the correlation is low (e.g., under −.20). In fact, as a correlation coefficient approaches zero, it becomes impossible to make any accurate predictions whatsoever. In such cases, knowing one variable does not allow us to predict anything about the other. As you might imagine, organizational scientists are extremely interested in discovering the relationships between variables, and the correlation coefficients tell them a great deal.

The examples we have used involve the relationship between only two variables at a time, but researchers in OB frequently are interested in the interrelationships between many variables at once. For example, an employee's intent to quit may relate to several variables in addition to the perceived fairness of one's pay, including satisfaction with the job itself and liking for one's immediate supervisor. Researchers can make predictions using several variables at once using a technique known as **multiple regression**. Using this approach, researchers are able to tell the extent to which each of several different variables contributes to predicting the behavior in question. In our example, researchers could learn the degree to which the several variables studied—both together and individually—relate to the intent to quit one's job. Given the complex nature of human behavior on the job and the wide range of variables likely to influence it, researchers in OB use the multiple regression technique a great deal.

An Important Limitation of Correlations

Analysis of surveys using correlational techniques such as multiple regression can be very valuable, but conclusions drawn from correlations are limited in a very important way: *Correlations do not reveal anything about causation.* In other words, correlations tell us how variables relate to each other, but they do not provide any insight into their cause-and-effect relationships.

In our example, we learn that the less employees feel they are fairly paid, the more interested they are in quitting—but we do not learn *why* this is the case. In other words, we cannot tell if employees want to quit *because* they believe they are unfairly paid. This might be the case. It also might be the case that people who believe they are unfairly paid tend to dislike the work they do, and this dislike may be what encourages them to find a new job. Another possibility is that people believe they are unfairly paid because their supervisors are too demanding, and this belief may raise their interest in quitting (Figure A.3). All these possibilities are reasonable, but knowing only that variables correlate does *not* permit us to determine what causes what. Establishing the causal relationships between the variables is important, so researchers frequently turn to another technique that *does* permit such conclusions to be drawn—that is, the *experiment*.

correlation coefficient

A statistical index indicating the nature and extent to which two variables relate to each other.

multiple regression

A statistical technique used to determine the extent to which each of several different variables contributes to predicting another variable (typically where the variable being predicted is the behavior in question).

FIGURE A.3

Correlations: What They *Don't* Reveal about Causation

Just because a strong negative correlation may exist between pay fairness and the desire to leave one's job, we cannot tell why this relationship exists. As shown here, there are many possible underlying reasons not identified by knowledge of the correlation alone.

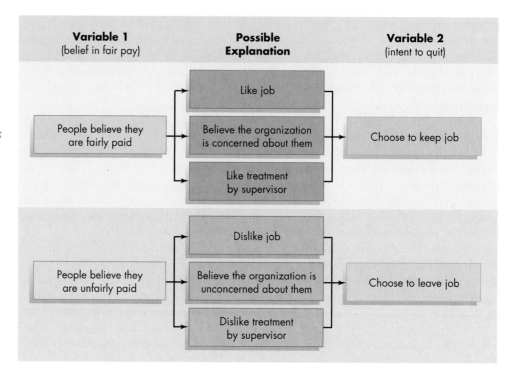

EXPERIMENTAL RESEARCH: THE LOGIC OF CAUSE AND EFFECT

experimental method

A research technique used to determine cause-and-effect relationships between the variables of interest (i.e., the extent to which one variable causes another).

Both scientists and practitioners want to know not only the degree to which variables relate but also how much one variable causes another. Thus, the **experimental method** is popular in the field of OB. The more we know about the causal connections between variables, the better we can explain the underlying causes of behavior—and this, after all, is one of the major goals of OB.

A Hypothetical Experiment

To illustrate how experiments work, suppose we are interested in determining the effects of social density (i.e., the number of people per unit of space) on the job performance of clerical employees. In other words, we are interested in the degree to which crowded working conditions influence the accuracy of word-processing operators.

This topic can be studied in many different ways, but imagine we do the following: First, we select at random a large group of word-processing operators who work in a variety of different organizations (i.e., the participants in our study). Next, we prepare a specially designed office (i.e., the setting for the experiment). Throughout the study, we keep the design of the office and the working conditions (e.g., temperature, light, noise levels) alike, but we systematically vary the number of people working in the office at any given time.

We could, for example, have one condition—the "high-density" condition—in which 50 people are put in a 500-square-foot room at once, thus allowing 10 square feet per person. In another condition—the "low-density" condition—we could put five people into a 500-square-foot room at once, thus allowing 100 square feet per person. Finally—in the "moderate-density" condition—we could put 25 people into a 500-square-foot room, thus allowing 20 square feet per person.

Suppose we have several hundred people participating in the study and we assign them at random to each of these conditions. Each word-processing operator then is given the same passage of text to type for two hours. After this time, the typists are

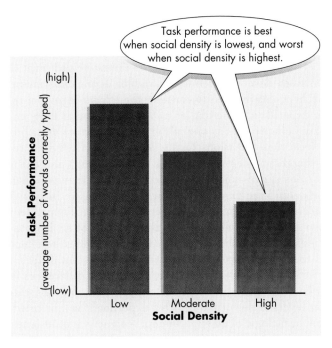

FIGURE A.4

Example of Simple Experimental Results

In our example, word-processing operators are put into rooms that differ only regarding one variable: social density (i.e., the number of people per unit of space). The hypothetical results summarized here show that people perform best under conditions of lowest density and worst under conditions of highest density.

dismissed. The researcher then counts the number of words accurately typed by each typist and notes any possible differences between the performance in the various conditions. Now, suppose we obtain the results summarized in Figure A.4.

Experimental Logic

We now analyze what was done in this simple, hypothetical experiment to help explain the basic elements of the experimental method and its underlying logic. First, recall that participants were selected from the population of interest and assigned to conditions on a *random* basis. Thus, each participant had an equal chance of being assigned to any of the three conditions. This is critical, because differences between conditions could result from having many very good operators in one condition and many unproductive ones in another. Therefore, to safeguard against this possibility, it is important to assign people to the various conditions at random. When this is done, we can assume the effects of any possible differences between people would equalize over all the conditions.

By assigning people to the conditions at random, we can be assured there are as many fast operators and slow operators in each. As a result, there is no reason to believe any differences in productivity between the conditions result from systematic differences in the skills of the participants. Given "the luck of the draw," such differences can be discounted, thereby enhancing our confidence that any differences noted result solely from the social density of the room. This is the logic behind random assignment. It is not always feasible to use random assignment when conducting experiments in organizations, of course, but it is highly desirable to do so whenever possible.

Recall the word-processing operators were assigned to conditions that differed only in the variable of interest — that is, in social density. We can say the experimenter *manipulated* this aspect of the work environment, systematically changing it from condition to condition. A variable altered in this way is called an **independent variable** — that is, a variable systematically manipulated by the experimenter to determine its effects on the behavior of interest. In our example, the independent variable is social density. Specifically, this variable may be said to have three different *levels* (i.e., degrees of the independent variable): high, moderate, and low.

The variable that is being measured (i.e., the one influenced by the independent variable) is known as the **dependent variable**. A dependent variable is the behavior

independent variable

A variable that is systematically manipulated by the researcher to determine its effects on behavior (i.e., the *dependent variable*).

dependent variable

The behavior that is being measured by a researcher; it is dependent on the *independent variable*.

of interest to the researcher—that is, the behavior that is dependent on the independent variable. In this case, the dependent variable is word-processing performance, or the quantity of words accurately typed. We also could have studied other dependent variables, however, such as satisfaction with the work or the perceived level of stress. In fact, researchers often study several dependent variables in one experiment.

By the same token, researchers also frequently consider the effects of several independent variables in a given experiment. The matter of which particular independent and dependent variables are being studied is one of the most important decisions researchers make. They often base these decisions on suggestions from previous research (i.e., other experiments suggesting certain variables are important) and existing theories (i.e., conceptualizations suggesting certain variables may be important).

In general, the basic logic behind the experimental method is simple. In fact, it involves only two major steps. First, some variable of interest (i.e., the independent variable) must be varied systematically. Second, the effects—if any—of such variations must be measured. The idea is that if the independent variable does influence behavior, then people exposed to different amounts of it should behave in different ways. In our example, we can be certain that social density causes any differences in word-processing performance, because when all other factors are held constant, different densities lead to different levels of performance. Our experiment is fabricated, of course, but it follows the same basic logic of all experiments—namely, it is designed to reveal the effects of independent variables on dependent variables.

Drawing Valid Conclusions from Experiments

For the conclusions of experiments to be valid, all factors other than the independent variable must be held constant. Then, if differences in the dependent variable occur, we can assume they result from the effects of the independent variable. In our example, assigning participants to conditions at random is an important step toward ensuring that one key factor—that is, differences in the ability of the participants—is equalized.

As you might imagine, other factors also may affect the results. For example, environmental conditions that might influence word-processing speed also must be held constant. In this case, more people would generate more heat, so to ensure the results are influenced only by density, it would be necessary to air condition the room so that all conditions maintained the same temperatures at all times.

If you think about it, our simple experiment really is not that simple at all—especially if conducted with all the care needed to permit valid conclusions to be drawn. Thus, experiments require all experimental conditions to be kept identical regarding all variables—except for the independent variable—so that the independent variable's effects can be determined unambiguously. As you might imagine, this often is easier said than done.

Where Experiments Are Conducted: Laboratory and Field Settings

How simple controlling the effects of extraneous variables (i.e., factors not of interest to the experimenter) is depends largely on where the experiment is being conducted. In the field of OB, two options generally are available: naturalistic organizational settings, which are referred to as the *field*; or settings specially created for the study itself, which are referred to as the *laboratory* (or *lab* for short). As summarized in Figure A.5, there are trade-offs involved with each setting.

In our example, the study is a lab experiment. In other words, it is conducted in carefully controlled conditions specially created for the research. The great amount of control such settings allow improves the chances of creating the conditions needed to permit valid conclusions to be drawn. At the same time, however, lab studies suffer from a lack of realism. The working conditions can be carefully controlled, but they may be relatively unrealistic (i.e., not carefully simulating the conditions found in actual organizations). As a result, it may be difficult to generalize the findings of lab studies to settings outside the lab (e.g., the workplace).

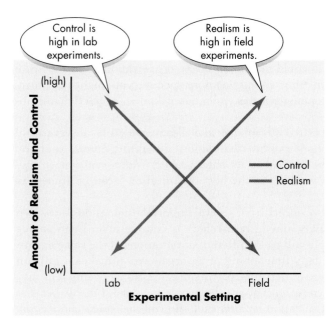

FIGURE A.5

Trade-offs between Lab and Field Experimentation
Researchers in OB may conduct experiments in laboratory or field settings, each of which has advantages and disadvantages. Generally, the lab offers more control but less realism, whereas the field offers less control but more realism.

If we conduct our study in an actual organization, however, there would be many unknowns, many uncontrollable factors, at work. To conduct such a study, we would need to distinguish between those who worked in offices with differing social densities and later compare people's performance. If we did this, we could be sure the conditions studied were realistic, but we would have so little control over the setting that many different factors could be operating. For example, because people would not be assigned to conditions at random, people might work in those settings they most desire. Furthermore, there would be no control over factors such as distractions and differences in environmental conditions (e.g., noise, temperature).

In short, field experiments, though strong in realism, are weak in the level of control they provide. In contrast, lab experiments permit a great deal of control but tend to be unrealistic. Considering these complementary strengths and weaknesses, experiments clearly should be conducted in *both* types of sites. As more researchers do so, our confidence increases that valid conclusions can be drawn about behavior in organizations.

QUALITATIVE RESEARCH METHODS

Compared with the highly empirical approaches to research described thus far, we also should note that researchers sometimes use a less empirical approach. After all, the most obvious way to learn about behavior in organizations is to observe and describe it. Organizational scientists have a long tradition of studying behavior using these nonempirical, descriptive techniques—that is, of relying on what is known as **qualitative research**.[2] The qualitative approach preserves the natural qualities of the situation being studied, and its attempts to capture the richness of the context while disturbing the naturalistic conditions only minimally—if at all. The two major qualitative methods used by OB scientists are *naturalistic observation* and the *case method*.

qualitative research
A nonempirical type of research that relies on preserving the natural qualities of the situation being studied.

Naturalistic Observation

There probably is no more fundamental way of learning how people act in organizations than simply to observe them, which is a technique known as **naturalistic observation**. For example, suppose you want to learn how employees behave in response

naturalistic observation
A research technique in which people are systematically observed in situations of interest to the researcher.

participant observation

A qualitative research technique in which people systematically observe what occurs in a setting by becoming an insider (i.e., part of that setting itself).

to layoffs. One option is to visit an organization in which layoffs are occurring and then systematically observe what the employees do and say, both before and after the layoffs occur. Making comparisons of this type may provide useful insights. As a variation on this technique, you also could take a job in the organization and then make your observations as an "insider," thus giving you a perspective you might not otherwise gain. Often used by anthropologists, this technique is known as **participant observation**.

It is not difficult to think of the advantages and disadvantages of observational research. The major advantage is it can be used without disrupting normal routines, thereby allowing behavior to be studied in its natural state. Moreover, almost anyone—including people already working in the host organization—can be trained to use it.

Observational research also suffers from several important limitations, however. First, the potential for subjectivity among researchers is considerable. Even among the most diligent, different people will make different observations of the same events. Second, being involved in the daily functioning of an organization makes it difficult for observers to be impartial; researchers interpreting organizational events thus may be subject to bias from their own feelings about the people involved. Finally, because most of what goes on in an organization is fairly dull and routine, researchers easily can place great emphasis on unusual or unexpected events, possibly leading to inaccurate conclusions.

Given these limitations, most OB scientists consider observational research to be more useful as a starting point. In other words, they see this method more as a tool for providing basic insight into behavior than for acquiring definitive knowledge about behavior.

The Case Method

case method

A research technique in which a particular organization is thoroughly described and analyzed to understand what occurred in that setting.

Suppose we conducted our hypothetical study of reactions to layoffs in a different manner. For example, instead of observing behavior directly, we might describe the company's history leading up to the event and some statistics summarizing its aftermath (e.g., how long people were unemployed, how the company was restructured after downsizing). We might even include some interviews with people affected by the event and quote them directly. This approach is known as the **case method**. More often than not, the rationale behind the case method is *not* to teach us about a specific organization but to learn what happened in that organization as a means of providing clues regarding what may be going on in other organizations.

The case method is similar to naturalistic observation in that it relies on descriptive accounts of events. It is different, however, in that it often involves using post hoc accounts of events from those involved as opposed to first-hand observations by scientists.

As you might imagine, a great deal can be learned by detailed accounts of events in organizations, summarized in the form of written cases. When these cases are supplemented by careful interviews (in which case the method would be considered quantitative rather than qualitative in nature), cases can paint a particularly detailed picture of events as they unfolded in a particular organization.

To the extent the organization being studied is unique, however, it may not be possible to generalize what is learned. To get around this limitation, some researchers recommend that multiple (as opposed to single) cases be used to test theories.[3] Another problem with this method—and a limitation it shares with naturalistic observation—is that the relatively high potential for bias. As a result, many scientists believe that while the case method may provide a valuable source of hypotheses about behavior on the job, testing those hypotheses requires more rigorous methods.[4]

PART TWO

Basic Human Processes

PERCEPTION AND LEARNING: UNDERSTANDING AND ADAPTING TO THE WORK ENVIRONMENT

LEARNING OBJECTIVES

After reading this chapter, you should be able to

1. Distinguish between the concepts of *perception* and *social perception*.
2. Explain how the *attribution* process works and how it helps us to understand the causes of others' behavior.
3. Describe the various sources of *bias in social perception* and how they may be overcome.
4. Understand how the process of social perception operates in the context of *performance appraisals, employment interviews,* and the cultivation of *corporate images*.
5. Define *learning*.
6. Describe the concepts of *operant conditioning* and *observational learning*.
7. Describe how principles of learning are involved in organizational *training* and *innovative reward systems*.
8. Compare how organizations can use reward in *organizational behavior management* programs and can use punishment most effectively when administering *discipline*.

PREVIEW CASE

Staying Atop the Education Biz

Neither Douglas L. Becker nor R. Christopher Hoen-Saric graduated from college. Becker dropped out of Johns Hopkins, and Hoen-Saric was accepted into Harvard but never attended classes. When you think of tutors, images of people with more impressive educational backgrounds than this probably come to mind. Then again, strictly speaking, Becker and Hoen-Saric are not educators themselves. Rather, these two thirtysomethings are co-CEOs of one of the fastest-growing companies in the education business: Sylvan Learning Systems.

If you were to visit any of the 670 Sylvan Learning Centers, you would not find Becker or Hoen-Saric doing the tutoring themselves — at least, not in the traditional "three R's." However, they probably could teach anyone a thing or two about building their skills (both are admitted computer geeks), working hard, and following their business dreams. This is just what they did in 1982, when as clerks at a Computerland store in Baltimore, they invented an identification card containing an embedded computer chip that could store a person's medical history. Neither Becker nor Hoen-Saric was sure the device would work — but they gladly took the millions of dollars paid to them by Blue Cross and Blue Shield of Maryland, which bought the idea in 1985.

A few years later, they used these funds to buy a 50-percent share of Sylvan, which was owned at the time by the financially unstable day-care operator KinderCare. Then, in 1993, just as Sylvan began to grow, they purchased the remaining 50 percent. Becker and Hoen-Saric did not leave well enough alone, either. They developed a slew of new services. For example, they now administer computerized versions of some of the Educational Testing Service's most popular tests, including the GMAT (i.e., the exam you take to be considered for admission to an MBA program). In fact, their contract with the Educational Testing Service generates approximately 10 percent of Sylvan's revenue stream.

Soon after Becker and Hoen-Saric took complete control of Sylvan, they expanded their private services to public schools. Recognizing that Sylvan's method of helping students to sharpen their reading and math skills was effective, educators from Baltimore opened Sylvan Learning Centers inside some of that city's public schools. Today, funded largely by federal money earmarked to help disadvantaged students, Sylvan operates some 600 centers in public schools — with more on the way. Their objective is not to replace what schools are already doing but to add an additional service — one-on-one tutoring — that most schools are hard-pressed to provide on their own.

Despite Sylvan's success, Becker and Hoen-Saric are well-aware of competition from well-financed upstarts such as Kaplan Educational Centers and others. To stay ahead of the pack, they are working harder than ever. In fact, they hired three new executives just to run daily operations, thereby freeing themselves to go out and drum up new business, and if Becker and Hoen-Saric have their way, there will be lots of it. (They'll need it to fill the 50 new centers they plan on opening each year!) They also are working on cracking the already-crowded market of offering tests for professional certification (e.g., for pilots and computer systems trainers) and on expanding the number of tests the Educational Testing Service offers through Sylvan's facilities — including the popular SAT for college admission. How ironic it is that two young men who never graduated college (one of whom never even got past the SAT!) are now making their fortunes by providing services to people hoping to get into college themselves.

As you read the previous case, you probably cannot help but think of how fortunate Becker and Hoen-Saric are to be at the helm of a multimillion-dollar company. True, their formal education might not have reached the levels of their colleagues in the corporate elite. Clearly, however, they have learned a great deal — not only about applying computers to business problems but also about business itself — from trial and error in the "school of hard knocks." Curiously, their own informal training contrasts with the highly formal, one-on-one training their company offers. In fact, if you think about it, nearly all organizational activities are based on some kind of *learning*. After all, we learn how to do our jobs, please the boss, and make a profit for the company. With this in mind, we carefully describe the process of learning in this chapter.

Although you might not recognize it yet, this case also illustrates another equally fundamental topic that we cover in this chapter: *perception*. Ask yourself the following questions: Was your assessment of Becker and Hoen-Saric influenced by the fact that they didn't graduate from college? How about by the fact they are highly successful entrepreneurs? For most people, the answers would be "Definitely, yes." After all, people tend to believe certain things about successful entrepreneurs who never graduated college—for example, that they are very talented, hard-working, and highly dedicated to their goals. Perhaps this image is colored by what we think about other, similar people, such as Microsoft's Bill Gates (himself a highly successful college dropout). Until we get to know Becker and Hoen-Saric better, it's easy to understand how we might come to think of them as being similar to Gates.

Obviously, there is a subtle yet powerful perceptual process going on here—a process by which people come to judge and understand the people and things with which they come in contact. Like learning, perception is a basic psychological process involved in many aspects of behavior in organizations, so we closely examine this topic here as well.

Specifically, our journey begins by describing the basic processes involved in perception, including the many perceptual errors that people make. Then, armed with this background, we consider several specific organizational situations, such as performance appraisals and job interviews, in which these processes are used (and misused). We follow the same theory-followed-by-practice approach in our coverage of learning. In particular, we begin by describing the basic processes of learning that operate in organizations. Then, we move on to how these processes can be—and are—applied on the job (e.g., through training programs and disciplinary techniques).

SOCIAL PERCEPTION: THE PROCESS OF UNDERSTANDING OTHERS

Without a doubt, the world around us is a very complex place. At any given moment, we are flooded with input from our various senses, yet we do not respond to the world as a random collection of sights, sounds, smells, and tastes. Rather, we notice order and patterns everywhere. Making sense of the vast array of sensory inputs involves the active processing of information—the process of **perception**. Formally, we define perception as the process through which people select, organize, and interpret information.[1]

perception

The process through which people select, organize, and interpret information.

To illustrate this process, consider an example. Suppose you meet your new boss for the first time. You know her general reputation as a manager, see the way she looks, hear the words she says, and read the memos she writes. In no time at all, you're trying to figure her out. Will she be easy to work with as a boss? Will she like me? Will she do a good job for the company? Using whatever information you have available, even if it's very little, you will try to understand her and how you will be affected by her (Figure 2.1). In other words, you will attempt to combine the various

FIGURE 2.1

Meeting New People: An Opportunity for Social Perception

Meeting new people presents many opportunities to combine, integrate, and interpret a great deal of information about them. This is the process of *social perception*.

things you learn about her into a meaningful picture. Interestingly, this process is so automatic we almost never realize it's happening, yet it happens all the time. Clearly, when it comes to understanding the objects and people in our environment, there's a lot more going on than may be obvious.

The process of perception is especially important in the field of organizational behavior (OB). Indeed, other people — whether bosses, coworkers, subordinates, family, or friends — can have profound effects on us. To understand the people around us, to figure out who they are and why they do what they do, may be very helpful to us. After all, you would not want to ask your boss for a raise when you believe he or she is in a bad mood! Clearly, **social perception** — the process of combining, integrating, and interpreting information about others to gain an accurate understanding of them — is very important in organizations.[2]

social perception

The process of combining, integrating, and interpreting information about others to gain an accurate understanding of them.

GLOBAL MATTERS

Because people from some cultures have more exposure to particular objects in their environments (e.g., tall buildings) than people from other cultures, they tend to perceive these objects differently. As you read about social perception in this chapter, ask yourself how the perception of people also may be affected by differences in national culture. ■

attribution

The process through which individuals attempt to determine the causes behind others' behavior.

The sections that follow explore various aspects of social perception. To begin, we summarize the **attribution** process — that is, how people come to judge the underlying causes of others' behavior. Then, we note various imperfections in this process (i.e., errors and sources of bias that contribute to inaccurate judgments of others) as well as ways of overcoming them. Finally, we highlight specific ways the attribution process is used in organizations.

THE ATTRIBUTION PROCESS: JUDGING THE CAUSES OF OTHERS' BEHAVIOR

A question we often ask about others is "Why?" Why did Tonya not return my call? Why did John goof up the order? Why did the company president make the policy she did? When we ask such questions, we are attempting to get at two different types of information: what is someone really like (i.e., what traits and characteristics does he or she possess), and what made that person behave as he or she did (i.e., what accounted for his or her actions)? People attempt to answer these questions in different ways.[3]

Making Correspondent Inferences: Using Acts to Judge Dispositions

In organizations, situations frequently arise in which we want to know what someone is like. Is your opponent a tough negotiator? Are your coworkers punctual? The more you know about what people are like, the better equipped you are to know what to expect — and how to deal with them. How then, precisely, do we go about identifying another person's traits?

Generally, the answer is that we learn about others by observing their behavior and then inferring their traits from this information. The judgments we make about what someone is like based on what we observe about him or her are known as **correspondent inferences**.[4] Simply put, correspondent inferences are judgments about people's dispositions (i.e., their traits and characteristics) that correspond to what we have observed of their actions (Figure 2.2).

correspondent inferences

Judgments about people's dispositions, traits, and characteristics that correspond to what we have observed of their actions.

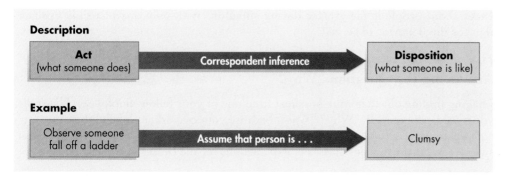

FIGURE 2.2

Correspondent Inferences: Judging Dispositions Based on Behavior

One way that we come to judge what others are like is by making inferences that follow from our observations of their behavior. Known as *correspondent inferences*, such judgments frequently are misleading. How might the inference summarized here be inaccurate?

Challenges in Judging Others Accurately   At first, inferring what people are like based on their behavior seems to be a simple matter. A person with a disorganized desk may be perceived as being sloppy. Someone who slips on the shop floor may be considered to be clumsy. Such judgments might — or might not — be accurate. After all, the messy desk actually may be the result of a coworker rummaging through it to find an important report. Similarly, the person who slipped could have encountered oily conditions under which anyone, even the least clumsy individual, would have fallen. In other words, it is important to recognize that the judgments we make about someone may be inaccurate because there are many possible causes of his or her behavior. A person's underlying characteristics certainly may play a role in determining what they do, but as the next section explains, behavior also can be shaped by external forces. (In our examples, these external factors would be the coworker's actions and the oily floor.) For this reason, correspondent inferences may not always be accurate.

Correspondent inferences also might not be accurate because people on the job tend to conceal some of their traits, especially those likely to be viewed as being negative. So, for example, a sloppy individual may work hard in public to appear to be organized. Likewise, an unprincipled person may talk a good show about the importance of being ethical. In other words, people often do their best to disguise their basic traits. Therefore, because behavior is complex and has many different causes, and people sometimes purposely disguise their true characteristics, forming correspondent inferences is a risky business.

Making Accurate Inferences About Others   Despite such difficulties, several techniques can help to make more accurate correspondent inferences.

First, we can focus on someone's behavior during situations in which he or she doesn't need behave in a pleasant or socially acceptable manner. For example, anyone would behave in a courteous manner toward the president of the company, so when people do so, we don't learn much about them. Only those who are *really* courteous, however, would behave politely toward someone of much lower rank — that is, someone toward whom they *don't* need to behave politely. In other words, someone who is polite toward the company president but condescending toward a secretary probably really is arrogant. The way people behave in situations when a certain behavior clearly is not expected of them may reveal a great deal about their basic traits and motives.

Similarly, we can learn a great deal about someone by focusing on behavior for which there is only a single logical explanation. For example, imagine finding out that a friend has accepted a new job. On questioning him, you learn the position has a very high salary, involves interesting work, and is in a desirable location. What have you learned about what is important to your friend? Not too much. After all, these are all good reasons to consider taking a position. Now, imagine finding out that the work is very demanding, the job is in an undesirable location, but the salary is very high. In this case, you are more prone to learn something about your friend — that he highly values money. Clearly, the opportunity to make accurate correspondent inferences about people is far greater during situations with only one plausible explanation for the behavior observed.

Causal Attribution of Responsibility: Answering the Question "Why?"

Imaging finding out that your boss just fired one of your fellow employees. Naturally, you would ask yourself, "Why?" Was it because your coworker violated the company's code of conduct? Was it because the boss is a cruel and heartless person? These answers represent two major classes of explanations for the causes of someone's behavior:

- **Internal causes of behavior**, which are explanations based on actions for which the individual is responsible.
- **External causes of behavior**, which are explanations based on situations over which the individual has no control.

In our example, the internal cause would be the person's violation of the rules, and the external cause would be the boss's cruel and arbitrary behavior.

Generally, being able to determine whether an internal or an external cause is responsible for someone's behavior is very important. Knowing why something happened to someone else might better help you to prepare for what might happen to you. For example, if you believe that your colleague was fired because of something for which she was responsible, such as violating a company rule, then you might not feel as vulnerable as you would if you thought she was fired because of the boss' arbitrary, spiteful nature. In the latter case, you might decide to take some precautionary actions to protect yourself from your boss, such as staying on his good side, or you might even give up and find a new job—before you are forced to do so.

Kelley's Theory of Causal Attribution   When it comes to social perception, the question of interest to social scientists is: How do people judge whether someone's actions are caused by internal or external causes? One answer is provided by **Kelley's theory of causal attribution**. According to this conceptualization, we base our judgments of internal and external causality on observations we make with respect to three types of information.[5] These are:

- **Consensus**, which is the extent to which other people behave in the same manner as the person who we're judging. If others behave similarly, consensus is considered to be high; if others do not, consensus is considered to be low.
- **Consistency**, which is the extent to which the person who we're judging acts the same way at other times. If the person acts the same at other times, consistency is high; if the person does not, consistency is low.
- **Distinctiveness**, which is the extent to which a person behaves the same way in other contexts. If the person behaves the same way in other situations, distinctiveness is low; if the person behaves differently, distinctiveness is high.

According to this theory, after collecting this information, we combine what we have learned to make our attributions of causality. If we learn that other people act like the person who we're judging (i.e., consensus is high), the person behaves in the same manner at other times (i.e., consistency is high), and the person does not act in the same manner in other situations (i.e., distinctiveness is high), we are likely to conclude the behavior stemmed from *external* causes. In contrast, imaging learning that other people do not act like the person who we're judging (i.e., consensus is low), the person behaves in the same manner at other times (i.e., consistency is high), and the person acts in the same manner in other situations (i.e., distinctiveness is low). In this case, we are likely to conclude the person's behavior stemmed from *internal* causes.

---

internal causes of behavior

Explanations based on actions for which the individual is responsible.

external causes of behavior

Explanations based on situations over which the individual has no control.

Kelley's theory of causal attribution

The approach suggesting that people will believe others' actions to be caused by internal or external factors based on three types of information: consensus, consistency, and distinctiveness.

consensus

In Kelley's theory of causal attribution, information regarding the extent to which other people behave in the same manner as the person who we're judging.

consistency

In Kelley's theory of causal attribution, information regarding the extent to which the person who we're judging acts the same way at other times.

distinctiveness

In Kelley's theory of causal attribution, information regarding the extent to which a person behaves in the same manner in other contexts.

An Example   Because the previous explanation is highly abstract, consider an example that helps to illustrate how this process works. Imagine you're at a business lunch with several of your company's sales representatives when the sales manager makes some critical remarks about the restaurant's food and service. Also imagine that no one else in your party acts this way (i.e., consensus is low), you've heard this person say the same things during other visits to the restaurant (i.e., consistency is high), and you've seen this person act critically in other settings, such as the regional sales meeting (i.e., distinctiveness is low). What would you conclude in this situation? Probably that the sales manager is a "picky" person—someone who is difficult to please. In other words, the behavior stemmed from internal causes.

Now, imagine the same setting but with different observations. Suppose several other members of your group also complain about the restaurant (i.e., consensus is high), you've seen the sales manager complain in the same restaurant at other times (i.e., consistency is high), but you've never seen the sales manager complain about anything else before (i.e., distinctiveness is high). In contrast, this time you probably would conclude that the restaurant really *is* inferior. In this case, the sales manager's behavior stemmed from external causes. For a summary of these contrasting conclusions see Figure 2.3.

THE IMPERFECT NATURE OF SOCIAL PERCEPTION

As you might imagine, people are far from perfect when it comes to judging others. In fact, several systematic biases interfere with making completely accurate judgments of others. In this section, we describe some of these errors—and, of course, ways to overcome them.

How might inaccurate perceptions about people on the job lead us to make potentially unethical decisions? Give an example that illustrates your point. ■

ETHICS MATTERS

FIGURE 2.3

Kelley's Theory of Causal Attribution: A Summary

In determining whether others' behavior stems mainly from internal or external causes, we focus on three types of information: *consensus*, *consistency*, and *distinctiveness*.

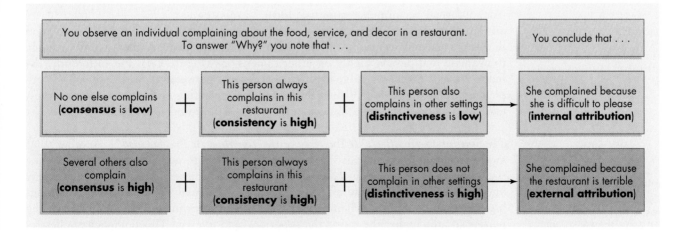

Perceptual Biases: Systematic Errors in Perceiving Others

Some of the errors people make in judging others reflect systematic biases in how we think about other people in general. These are referred to as **perceptual biases**. We now consider five such biases: The fundamental attribution error, the halo effect, the similar-to-me effect, first-impression error, and selective perception.

perceptual biases

Predispositions that people have to misperceive others in various ways. Types include the fundamental attribution error, halo effect, similar-to-me effect, first-impression error, and selective perception.

The Fundamental Attribution Error   Despite what Kelley's theory may imply, people are *not* equally predisposed to reach judgments regarding internal and external causality. Rather, they are more likely to explain someone's actions in terms of internal rather than external causes. In other words, we are prone to assume that people's behavior results from the way they are, from their traits and dispositions (e.g., "She's just that kind of person."). So, for example, we are more likely to assume that someone who shows up for work late does so because he or she is lazy rather than because traffic was heavy. This perceptual bias is so strong it has been referred to as the **fundamental attribution error**.[6]

fundamental attribution error

The tendency to attribute others' actions to internal causes (e.g., their traits) while largely ignoring external factors.

This particular bias results because it is far simpler to explain someone's actions in terms of his or her traits than to recognize the complex pattern of situational factors that may have influenced those actions. As you might imagine, this tendency can be quite damaging in organizations. Specifically, it can lead us to assume prematurely that people are responsible for the negative things that happen to them (e.g., "He wrecked the company car because he was careless.") without considering external alternatives that may be less damning (e.g., "Another driver hit the car."). This can lead to inaccurate judgments about people.

GLOBAL MATTERS   How universal do you believe the fundamental attribution error really is? Would you assume, for example, it is more likely to occur in Western cultures than in Asian cultures? ■

halo effect

The tendency for our overall impressions of others to affect objective evaluations of their specific traits, such as perceiving high correlations between characteristics that may be unrelated.

The Halo Effect: Keeping Perceptions Consistent   Have you ever heard someone say something like "she's very smart, so she also must be hard-working"? Or "he's not too bright, so I guess he's lazy"? If so, then you are already aware of a common perceptual bias known as the **halo effect**.[7] Once we form a positive impression of someone, we tend to view what that person does—even things about which we have no knowledge—in favorable terms. Similarly, a generally negative impression of someone is likely to be associated with negative evaluations of that person's behavior. Both tendencies (even the negative case) are referred to as halo effects despite the word *halo* having positive connotations.

In organizations, the halo effect often occurs when superiors rate subordinates using a formal performance appraisal form. In this context, a manager who evaluates an employee highly on some dimensions may assume that an individual who is so good in this particular area also must be good at others. The manager then would be likely to evaluate that person highly on other dimensions (Figure 2.4). Put differently, the halo effect may be responsible for high correlations between the ratings given to people on various dimensions. When this occurs, the resulting evaluations lack accuracy, and the quality of the resulting evaluations is compromised.

similar-to-me effect

The tendency for people to perceive in a positive light others who they believe are similar to themselves in any of several different ways.

The Similar-to-Me Effect: "If You're Like Me, You Must Be Pretty Good"   Another common perceptual bias involves the tendency for people to perceive those who are like themselves more favorably than those who are dissimilar. This tendency, which is known as the **similar-to-me effect**, constitutes a potential source of bias when judging other people. In fact, when superiors rate their subordinates, the more similar the parties are, the higher the rating the superiors tend to give.[8] This tendency applies re-

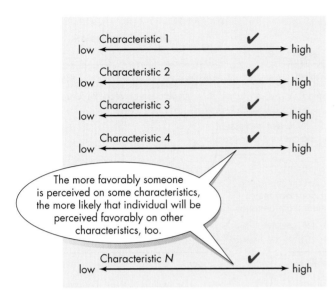

low ◄———— Characteristic 1 ✔ ————► high

low ◄———— Characteristic 2 ✔ ————► high

low ◄———— Characteristic 3 ✔ ————► high

low ◄———— Characteristic 4 ✔ ————► high

The more favorably someone is perceived on some characteristics, the more likely that individual will be perceived favorably on other characteristics, too.

low ◄———— Characteristic N ✔ ————► high

FIGURE 2.4

The Halo Effect: A Demonstration

One manifestation of the *halo effect* is the tendency for people, when rating others, to give either consistently high ratings (if the individual generally is perceived in a positive manner) or consistently low ratings (if the individual generally is perceived in a negative manner). Because each rating dimension is not considered independently, inaccurate evaluations may result.

garding several different dimensions of similarity, such as similarity of work values and habits, similarity of beliefs about how things should be at work, and similarity in demographic variables (e.g., age, race, gender, and work experience).

This effect appears to result partly from the tendency of people to be able to empathize and relate better to—and to be more lenient toward—others who are similar. It also appears, however, that subordinates tend to be more trusting and confident in supervisors they perceive as being similar than those they perceive as being dissimilar.[9] As a result, they may have a more positive relationship with such individuals, and this may lead superiors to judge similar subordinates more favorably. Regardless of the underlying explanation for the similar-to-me effect, it is important to recognize its implications: How people are perceived is based, in large part, on the similarities between the perceiver and the individual being perceived.

First-Impression Error: Confirming One's Expectations   Often, the way we judge someone is not based solely on how well that person performs now but on our initial judgments of that individual—that is, our *first impressions*. To the extent that initial impressions guide our subsequent impressions, we have all been victimized by **first-impression error**.

As you might imagine, this error can be especially problematic in organizations, in which accurately judging the performance of others is a crucial managerial task. When a subordinate's performance improves, that must be recognized, but to the extent that current evaluations are based on poor first impressions, recognizing such improvement is impossible. Likewise, inaccurate assessments of performance result when initially good performers leave positive impressions that linger even when that person's performance has dropped. For a summary of the first-impression error, see Figure 2.5.

Research suggests that first-impression error may take very subtle forms.[10] For example, in one study, corporate interviewers evaluated job applicants by viewing the application blanks and test scores of those prospective employees. The more highly the interviewers judged applicants based on these two criteria alone, the more positively the applicants were treated during the interview process. In fact, candidates who made positive impressions initially were treated more positively during the interview (e.g., they were spoken to in a more pleasant interpersonal style). Thus, instead of using the interviews to gather additional unbiased information, the recruiters appeared to use the interviews simply to confirm their first impressions developed on

first-impression error
The tendency to base judgments of others on our earlier impressions of them.

FIGURE 2.5

First-Impression Error: A Summary

When a *first-impression error* is made, the way we evaluate someone is influenced more by our initial impression of that person than by his or her current performance. In this example, someone who initially was perceived as performing well continues to be rated highly despite a downturn in performance.

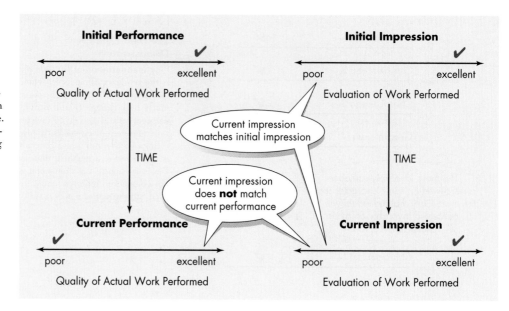

selective perception

The tendency to focus on some aspects of the environment and to ignore others.

stereotypes

Beliefs that all members of specific groups share similar traits and are prone to behave in the same way.

the basis of the test scores and application blanks. This study provides clear evidence of the first-impression error in action.

Selective Perception: Focusing on Some Things While Ignoring Others   Another perceptual bias known as **selective perception** involves the tendency for individuals to focus on certain aspects of the environment while ignoring others.[11] Insofar as we operate in complex environments, in which many stimuli demand our attention, it makes sense that we tend to be selective, thus narrowing our perceptual fields. This constitutes a bias, however, when it limits our attention to some stimuli while heightening our attention to others.

As you might imagine, this process occurs in organizations. In fact, when top executives were asked to indicate which functions of their organizations contributed most strongly to its effectiveness, they tended to cite functional areas that matched their own backgrounds.[12] For example, executives with backgrounds in sales and marketing perceived changes in a company's products and services as being the most important. Similarly, those with backgrounds in research and development focused their perceptions of the business environment more on product designs than on other issues. In other words, executives tend to be affected by selective perception — they give greatest attention to those aspects of the business environment that match their background experiences. Keeping this tendency in mind, it is easy to understand why different people may perceive the same situations very differently.

Stereotypes: Fitting Others into Categories

What comes to mind when you think about people who wear glasses? Are they studious? Are they eggheads? Although there is no evidence of such a connection, it is interesting that such an image lingers in the minds of many people. Of course, this is only one example. You can probably think of many other commonly held beliefs about the characteristics of people belonging to specific groups. Such statements usually take the form of "people from group X possess characteristic Y," and in most cases, the characteristics described tend to be negative. Assumptions of this type are referred to as **stereotypes** — beliefs that members of specific groups tend to share similar traits and behaviors.

Deep down, of course, many of us know that not all people from a specific group possess the negative characteristics we associate with them. In other words, most of us accept that any stereotypes we use are at least partially inaccurate. After all, not *all X's* are *Y*; there are exceptions (maybe even quite a few!). If so, however, why are stereotypes so prevalent? Why do we use them?

GLOBAL MATTERS

Those various jokes about "How many *X's* does it take to screw in a light bulb?" are based on stereotypes about people from group *X*. Interestingly, many of the same jokes told about a particular group *X* in one part of a diverse country (e.g., the United States) may be told about a different group *Y* in another part of the country. What does this phenomenon reveal about stereotypes? What have your own experiences been? ■

Why Do We Rely on Stereotypes?   To a great extent, the answer to this question is that people tend to do as little cognitive work as possible when it comes to thinking about others.[13] That is, we tend to rely on mental shortcuts. If assigning people to groups allows us to assume we know what they are like and how they may act, then we can save all the tedious work of learning about them as individuals. After all, we come into contact with so many people that it's impractical—if not impossible—to learn everything about them we need to know. Therefore, we rely on readily available information such as someone's age, race, gender, or job type as the basis for organizing our perceptions in a coherent way.

For example, if you believe that members of group *X* (e.g., those who wear glasses) tend to possess trait *Y* (e.g., studiousness), then simply observing that someone falls into category *X* becomes the basis for your belief that he or she possesses trait *Y*. To the extent the stereotype applies in this case, then the perception is accurate. Such mental shorthand, however, often leads to inaccurate judgments about people. This is the price we pay for using stereotypes.

The problem with our tendency to rely on stereotypes, of course, is that it leads us to judge people prematurely, without the benefit of learning more about them than just the categories into which they fit (Figure 2.6). Still, we all rely on stereotypes—at least sometimes. Their temptation is far too great to resist.

The Dangers of Using Stereotypes in Organizations   It is easy to imagine how stereotypes can have powerful effects on the judgments people make in organizations. For example, if a personnel officer believes that members of certain groups are lazy, then

FIGURE 2.6

What Are These People Like?

If you have formed some image of what these individuals are like just from this figure, you may be relying on *stereotypes*, which are judgments of others based on their membership in various groups. Stereotypes may lead to inaccurate judgments, which might differ if we took the time to learn about the people we're perceiving.

he or she may purposely avoid hiring or promoting individuals in those groups. This personnel officer may firmly believe that he or she is using good judgment, gathering all the necessary information and listening to the candidate carefully. Still, without being aware of it, these stereotypes may influence how the personnel officer judges certain individuals. The result, of course, is that the fate of the individual in question is sealed in advance — not necessarily because of anything that person may have done or said but by the mere fact that he or she belongs to a certain group. In other words, even people who might not intend to act in a bigoted fashion still may be influenced by the stereotypes they hold.

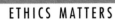

ETHICS MATTERS | Consider how stereotypes about people from various ethnic, national, and religious groups have served as the basis for unethical treatment throughout history. Give some examples of this phenomenon in action throughout the years. ■

We realize, of course, that the effects of stereotyping others are not always as profound as in our example (in which someone is not hired or promoted). Referring to accountants as "bean counters" and professors as "absent-minded" are observations that also reflect stereotypes that appear to be only mildly negative. Still, it must be cautioned that holding stereotypes of people in various groups runs the risk of causing miscommunication and conflict (as we will see in chapter 10).

**TIPS:
DOING IT RIGHT**   ■ **How to Overcome Bias in Social Perception**

For the most part, people's biased perceptions of others do not result from any malicious intent to inflict harm. Instead, biases in social perception tend to occur because we, as perceivers, are imperfect processors of information. We assume that people are internally responsible for their behavior, because we cannot be aware of all the possible situational factors that may be involved — hence, we make the fundamental attribution error. Furthermore, it is highly impractical to learn everything about someone that may guide our reactions — hence, we use stereotypes.

We can, however, minimize the impact of these and other biases. Indeed, several steps can be taken to promote the accurate perception of others in the workplace. The following recommendations are useful in this regard:

- *Do not overlook external causes of others' behavior.* The fundamental attribution error leads us to discount the possibility that people's poor performance may result from conditions beyond their control. Therefore, we may ignore legitimate explanations for poor performance. Ask yourself if anyone else may have performed just as poorly under the same conditions. If the answer is yes, then you should not automatically assume the poor performer is to blame. Good managers need to make such judgments accurately so that they can decide whether to focus their efforts on developing employees or on changing work conditions.

- *Identify and confront your stereotypes.* We all rely on stereotypes — especially when it comes to dealing with new people. Although this is natural, erroneous perceptions — quite possibly at the expense of someone else — are bound to result. Therefore, it is good to identify the stereotypes you hold. Doing so helps you become more aware of them, thus taking a giant step toward minimizing their impact on your behavior. After all, unless you are aware of your stereotypes, you may never be able to counter them.

- *Evaluate people based on objective factors.* The more objective the information you use to judge others, the less your judgments are subjected to perceptual distortion. People tend to bias subjective judgments in self-serving ways, such as positively evaluating the work of those we like and negatively evaluating the work of those we dislike. To the extent that evaluations are based on objective information, however, this is less likely to occur.
- *Avoid making rash judgments.* It is human nature to jump to conclusions about what people are like—even when we know very little about them. Get to know people better before convincing yourself you already know all you need to about them. What you learn may make a big difference in your opinion.

We realize many of these tactics are far easier to say than to do. To the extent that we conscientiously *try* to apply these suggestions to our everyday interactions with others in the workplace, however, we stand a good chance of perceiving people more accurately, and this is a fundamental ingredient in the recipe for managerial success. ■

PERCEIVING OTHERS: ORGANIZATIONAL APPLICATIONS

Thus far, we have identified some basic processes of social perception and have alluded to how they are involved in organizational behavior. In this section, we make these connections more explicit. Specifically, we describe the role of perception in three organizational activities: the *employee performance appraisal*, the *employment interview*, and the organization's development of its *corporate image*.

Performance Appraisal: Formal Judgments About Job Performance

An obvious instance in which social perception occurs is when someone formally evaluates the job performance of another. Known as **performance appraisal**, this process may be defined as the process by which people evaluate the performance of others, often on an annual or a semiannual basis and usually for determining raises, promotions, and training needs.[14]

performance appraisal

The process of evaluating employees on various work-related dimensions.

An Inherently Biased Process   Ideally, a performance appraisal should be a completely rational process, leading to unbiased and objective judgments about how well each employee has performed and how he or she should be treated. Based on our discussion of perception thus far, however, you can probably guess that the performance evaluation process is far from objective. Indeed, people have a limited capacity to process, store, and retrieve information, thus making them prone to bias when evaluating others.[15]

Several such biases have been observed by researchers. For example, people's ratings of others' performance depend on the extent to which that performance is consistent with the raters' initial expectations. Researchers in one study, for example, asked bank managers to indicate how well they expected their newest tellers to perform their jobs.[16] Four months later, they were asked to rate the actual job performance of those tellers. The managers gave higher ratings to those tellers whose performance matched their earlier expectations than to those who either did better or worse than predicted. These effects are unsettling, because they suggest that improved performance by some employees may go unrecognized or, worse yet, be downgraded! Of course, to the extent that human resource management decisions are based on several sources of information, not just judgments by a single superior, such biased judgments are likely to go uncorrected. Nonetheless, these findings clearly underscore a key point: Perceptions are based on the characteristics of the person being perceived and on the characteristics of the perceiver as well.

Research showing several different attribution biases in evaluations of job performance supports this conclusion. Consider, for example, research illustrating how the similar-to-me effect operates in a performance appraisal. Research conducted at a bank has shown that the more tellers cultivate positive impressions by their superiors (e.g., do favors for them, agree with their opinions), the more those superiors view the tellers as being similar to themselves. And the more similar the tellers are believed to be, the more highly the superiors evaluate their work.[17]

As you might imagine, employees often attempt to make themselves look good to their superiors by offering explanations of their work that focus on the internal reasons underlying their good performance and the external reasons underlying their poor performance. Indeed, two equally good performers are unlikely to receive the same performance ratings when different attributions are made by the reviewer about the underlying causes of their performance. Managers tend to rate individuals whose poor performance is attributed to factors outside their control (e.g., someone who is trying hard but is too inexperienced to succeed) higher than they do individuals whose poor performance is attributed to internal factors (e.g., those who are believed to be capable but are just lazy and holding back). In other words, our evaluations of others' performance are qualified by the nature of the attributions we make about that performance.

Findings such as these illustrate that organizational performance evaluations are far from the unbiased, rational procedure one would hope to find. Instead, they represent a complex mix of perceptual biases—effects that must be appreciated and understood if we are ultimately to improve the performance evaluation process.

Cultural Differences in Performance Evaluations   As noted, individual biases in processing information make performance evaluation a less-than-precise process, but cultural differences are involved as well. In other words, the way people tend to evaluate others' work is likely to be influenced by the nations from which they come.[18] This should not be surprising considering that people from various countries differ regarding several key variables in the performance appraisal process, such as how willing people are to be direct with others and how sensitive they are to differences in status. Figure 2.7 summarizes some key differences in performance appraisal practices in the United States and Japan.

Impression Management in the Employment Interview: Looking Good to Prospective Employers

The desire to make a favorable impression on others is universal. In one way or another, we all attempt to control how other people see us, and we often attempt to get them to think of us in the best light possible. This process is known as **impression management**.[19] Generally, individuals devote considerable attention to the impressions they create in others—especially when these others are important, such as prospective employers.

The impressions prospective employers form of us may be based on subtle behaviors, such as how we dress and speak, or on more elaborate acts, such as our announcing our accomplishments.[20] They may result from calculated efforts to get others to think of us in a certain way, or they may be passive, unintended effects of our actions.

impression management
Efforts by individuals to improve how they appear to others.

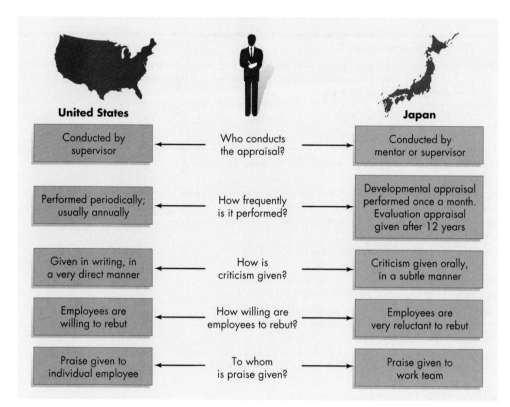

FIGURE 2.7

Cross-Cultural Differences in Performance Appraisals: An Example

Because societies in different countries have different norms and values, differences in how performance appraisals are used in those countries are not surprising. Differences in key aspects of performance appraisals between the United States and Japan illustrate this point.

GLOBAL MATTERS

Impression management is so important in Japan that people sometimes hire actors to assume roles at various social functions (e.g., mourners at a funeral, guests at a wedding). Only the customer knows these people are really only "rented acquaintances" and only there to help them look good.[21] What is it about Japanese culture that makes these "face-saving" antics so popular? Do you believe such services would be popular in our own culture? Why, or why not? ■

When it comes to the employment interview, for example, job candidates commonly do several things to enhance the impressions they make. In one recent study, researchers audiotaped the interviews between college students looking for jobs and representatives of companies that posted openings at the campus job placement center.[22] The various statements made by the candidates were categorized regarding the impression management techniques they used, and several tactics were common. Table 2.1 lists these specific tactics, provides an example of each, and shows the percentage of candidates who used them. Interestingly, the most common technique was *self-promotion*, which is flatly asserting that one has desirable characteristics. In this case, candidates commonly described themselves as being hard-working, interpersonally skilled, goal-oriented, and effective leaders.

The study also found that candidates used these impression management techniques with great success. The more the candidates relied on these tactics, the more positively they were viewed by the interviewer along several important dimensions (e.g., fit with the organization). This study not only confirms that job candidates indeed rely on impression management techniques during job interviews but that such techniques tend to cultivate the positive impressions desired. With this in mind, the job interview may be seen as an ongoing effort by candidates to present themselves as favorably as possible and by interviewers to see through those attempts and to judge candidates accurately. As the evidence suggests, this task may not be as simple as it seems.

TABLE 2.1

How Do Job Applicants Present Themselves Favorably?

Researchers have systematically recorded and categorized what job applicants say to present themselves favorably to recruiters interviewing them. Here is a list of techniques found during one recent study along with the frequencies with which they were used. Descriptions and examples of each technique are given as well.

IMPRESSION MANAGEMENT TECHNIQUE	DESCRIPTION	FREQUENCY USING TECHNIQUE (%)
Self-promotion	Directly describing oneself in a positive manner for the situation at hand (e.g., "I am a hard worker").	100
Personal stories	Describing past events that make oneself look good (e.g., "In my old job, I worked late anytime it was needed").	96
Opinion conformity	Expressing beliefs that are assumed to be held by the target (e.g., agreeing with something the interviewer says).	54
Entitlements	Claiming responsibility for successful past events (e.g., "I was responsible for the 90 percent sales increase that resulted").	50
Other enhancement	Making statements that flatter, praise, or compliment the target (e.g., "I am very impressed with your company's growth in recent years").	46
Enhancements	Claiming that a positive event was more positive than it really was (e.g., "Not only did our department improve, it was the best in the entire company").	42
Overcoming obstacles	Describing how one succeeded despite obstacles that should have lowered performance (e.g., "I managed to get a 3.8 average although I worked two part-time jobs").	33
Justifications	Accepting responsibility for one's poor performance but denying the negative implications of it (e.g., "Our team didn't win a lot, but it's just how you play the game that really matters").	17
Excuses	Denying responsibility for one's actions (e.g., "I didn't complete the application form because the placement center ran out of them").	13

Source: Based on information in Stevens & Kristof, 1995; see note 22.

Corporate Image: Impression Management by Organizations

corporate image
The impressions that people have of an organization.

Not only do individuals desire to cultivate positive impressions of themselves, entire organizations do as well. This has been termed **corporate image**.[23] As you might imagine, the impression an organization makes on people can have a considerable effect on the way these individuals relate to it. Extending our discussion of the job recruitment setting, individual candidates want to make good impressions on prospective employers, but employers also want their job offers to be accepted by the best candidates.

A company's image strongly relates to people's interest in seeking employment with it.[24] Specifically, the more favorable a company's reputation is considered to be (based on a *Fortune* survey), the more interested prospective employees are in working there.[25] (Table 2.2 lists some of the most admired companies identified in the *Fortune* survey.) This relationship is important, because organizations must successfully recruit prospective employees to function effectively. Given this important point, it seems worthwhile to consider exactly what factors contribute to corporate image.

One thing influencing a company's image is the amount of information people have about it from *recruitment ads*. Generally, longer ads are associated with more positive images. This may be because of what is said in the ad—but also because of the sheer length of the ad itself. Specifically, because recruitment ads emphasize the benefits of employment with a firm, longer ads describe more benefits than shorter ones, thereby creating even stronger positive images. Moreover, to the extent that people believe longer ads reflect a company's commitment to obtaining good employees (e.g.,

TABLE 2.2

America's Most Admired Companies

According to a recent survey by *Fortune* magazine, the following companies are the most admired in the United States based on ratings on eight important characteristics. Positive corporate images are important, because they help to attract qualified job candidates.

RANK	COMPANY	PRINCIPLE PRODUCT OR SERVICE
1	General Electric	Broadcasting, electrical appliances
2	Coca-Cola	Soft drinks
3	Microsoft	Computer software
4	Dell Computer	Personal computers
5	Berkshire Hathaway	Investments
6	Wal-Mart Stores	Retail sites of discounted merchandise
7	Southwest Airlines	Air transportation
8	Intel	Computer chips
9	Merck	Pharmaceuticals
10	Walt Disney	Entertainment productions

Source: Based on Brown, 1999; see note 25.

by their willingness to invest in a large ad), they may be more impressed with that company as a prospective place to work.

Another mechanism organizations use to promote their corporate images is their *annual report*, which is a company's official statement to its stockholders regarding its activities and financial state. These booklets contain such things as letters from CEOs as well as descriptions of projects and future plans—in short, information that helps to shape the image of the company in the minds of both employees and stockholders (Figure 2.8).

Traditionally, annual reports have been strikingly beautiful, glossy booklets with elaborate photography, glitzy images, and trappings of success designed to instill confidence among investors. Recently, however, many companies, such as St. Paul Companies, Avery Dennison, General Dynamics, and others, have spared such ex-

FIGURE 2.8

Annual Reports: An Important Determinant of Corporate Image

Many of us—and apparently even the creatures shown here—form impressions of companies by examining their annual reports.

(*Source*: © The New Yorker Collection 1973. Donald Reilly from cartoonbank.com. All Rights Reserved.)

penses, issuing bare-bones annual reports instead.[26] The reason: To promote an image of austerity. Today's investors are looking for value, so companies are going out of their way to cultivate the impression they are not wasting money. Looking *too* successful by squandering money on elaborate annual reports may raise questions about where the profits are going.

Whether these publications are elaborate or simple, annual reports are designed to cultivate the "right" corporate image—whatever that may be. Clearly, just like individuals, organizations also stand to benefit from making positive impressions on others, and they work hard to do so.

LEARNING: ADAPTING TO THE WORLD AROUND US

Thus far, we have focused on perception, which is one of the basic human psychological processes most actively involved with explaining behavior in organizations. Another process, however, is equally important—*learning*. After all, learning is involved in a broad range of organizational behaviors, from developing new vocational skills to changing how people do their jobs to managing employees in ways that foster the greatest productivity. Not surprisingly, the more a company fosters an environment in which employees can learn, the more productive and profitable that organization is likely to be.[27] Naturally, scientists in the field of OB are extremely interested in understanding the process of learning, both how it occurs and how it may be applied to the effective functioning of organizations.

learning
A relatively permanent change in behavior resulting from experience.

Before turning our attention to these matters, we should first explain exactly what we mean by learning. Specifically we define **learning** as a relatively permanent change in behavior occurring as a result of experience.[28] Despite its simplicity, several aspects of this definition bear mentioning. First, learning requires that some kind of change occur. Second, this change must be more than just temporary. Finally, this change must result from experience—that is, from continued contact with the world around us. Given this definition, we cannot say that short-lived performance changes on the job, such as those resulting from illness or fatigue, are the result of learning. Like so many concepts in the social sciences, learning is difficult for scientists to understand, because it cannot be observed directly. Instead, it must be inferred based on relatively permanent changes in behavior.

There are several different kinds of learning, but here we examine the two that occur most often in organizations. These are *operant conditioning* and *observational learning*.

Operant Conditioning: Learning Through Rewards and Punishments

Imagine you are a chef at a catering company and are planning a special menu for a fussy client. If your dinner menu is accepted and the meal is a hit, the company stands a good chance of landing a huge new account. You work hard at doing the best job possible, and you present your culinary creation to the skeptical client. Now, how does the story end? If the client loves your meal, your grateful boss gives you a huge raise and a promotion. If the client hates your meal, however, your boss asks you to turn in your chef's hat. Regardless of which outcome occurs, one thing is certain: Whatever you do in this situation, you will do it again if it is successful and avoid doing it again if it is a failure.

operant conditioning
The form of learning in which people associate the consequences of their actions with the actions themselves. Behaviors with positive consequences are acquired; behaviors with negative consequences are eliminated.

instrumental conditioning
See *operant conditioning*.

This situation nicely illustrates an important principle of **operant conditioning** (also known as **instrumental conditioning**)—namely, that our behavior produces consequences, and how we behave in the future depends on what those consequences are. If our actions have pleasant effects, we likely will repeat them in the future. If our actions have unpleasant effects, however, we will be less likely to repeat them. This phenomenon, which is known as the **Law of Effect**, is fundamental to operant conditioning. Our knowledge of this phenomenon comes from the famous social scientist B. F. Skinner.[29] Skinner's pioneering research showed that we learn to behave in certain ways through the connections between our actions and their consequences. Figure 2.9 summarizes this process.

Reinforcement Contingencies Operant conditioning is based on the idea that behavior is learned because of the pleasurable outcomes associated with it. In organizations, for example, people usually find receiving monetary bonuses, paid vacations, and various forms of recognition both pleasant and desirable. The process by which people learn to perform acts leading to such desirable outcomes is known as **positive reinforcement**. Whatever behavior led to the positive outcome is likely to occur again, thereby strengthening that behavior. For a reward to serve as a positive reinforcer, however, it must be contingent on the specific behavior being sought. For example, if a sales representative is given a bonus after landing a huge account, that bonus will reinforce the person's actions only if he or she associates it with landing the account. When this occurs, the sales representative will be more inclined in the future to do whatever it was that helped to get that account.

Sometimes, we also learn to perform acts because they permit us to avoid undesirable consequences. Unpleasant events such as reprimands, rejection, probation, and termination are some of the consequences faced for negative actions in the workplace. The process by which people learn to perform acts that help to avoid such undesirable consequences is known as **negative reinforcement**, or simply **avoidance**. Whatever response led to the termination of these undesirable events is likely to occur again, thereby strengthening that response. For example, you may stay late at the office one evening to revise a sales presentation, because you believe the boss will "chew you out" if it is not ready in the morning. At some point, you learned how to avoid this type of aversive situation, and you behaved accordingly in this instance.

Thus far, we have identified responses that are strengthened, either because they lead to positive consequences or avoid negative consequences. The connection between a behavior and its consequences is not always strengthened, however. Such links also may be weakened, and this is what happens in the case of **punishment**. Punishment involves presenting an undesirable or aversive consequence in response to an unwanted behavior. A behavior accompanied by an undesirable outcome is less likely to occur again if the person associates the negative consequences with that behavior. For example, if your boss chastises you for taking excessively long coffee breaks, you consider this as being punished for that action. As a result, you are less likely to take long coffee breaks again.

The link between a behavior and its consequences also may be weakened by withholding a reward, which is a process known as **extinction**. When a previously

Law of Effect
The tendency for behaviors leading to desirable consequences to be strengthened and for behaviors leading to undesirable consequences to be weakened.

positive reinforcement
The process through which people learn to perform behavior that leads to the presentation of desired outcomes.

negative reinforcement
The process through which people learn to perform acts that lead to the removal of undesired events.

avoidance
See *negative reinforcement*.

punishment
Decreasing undesirable behavior by following it with undesirable consequences.

extinction
The process through which responses that are no longer reinforced tend to gradually diminish in strength.

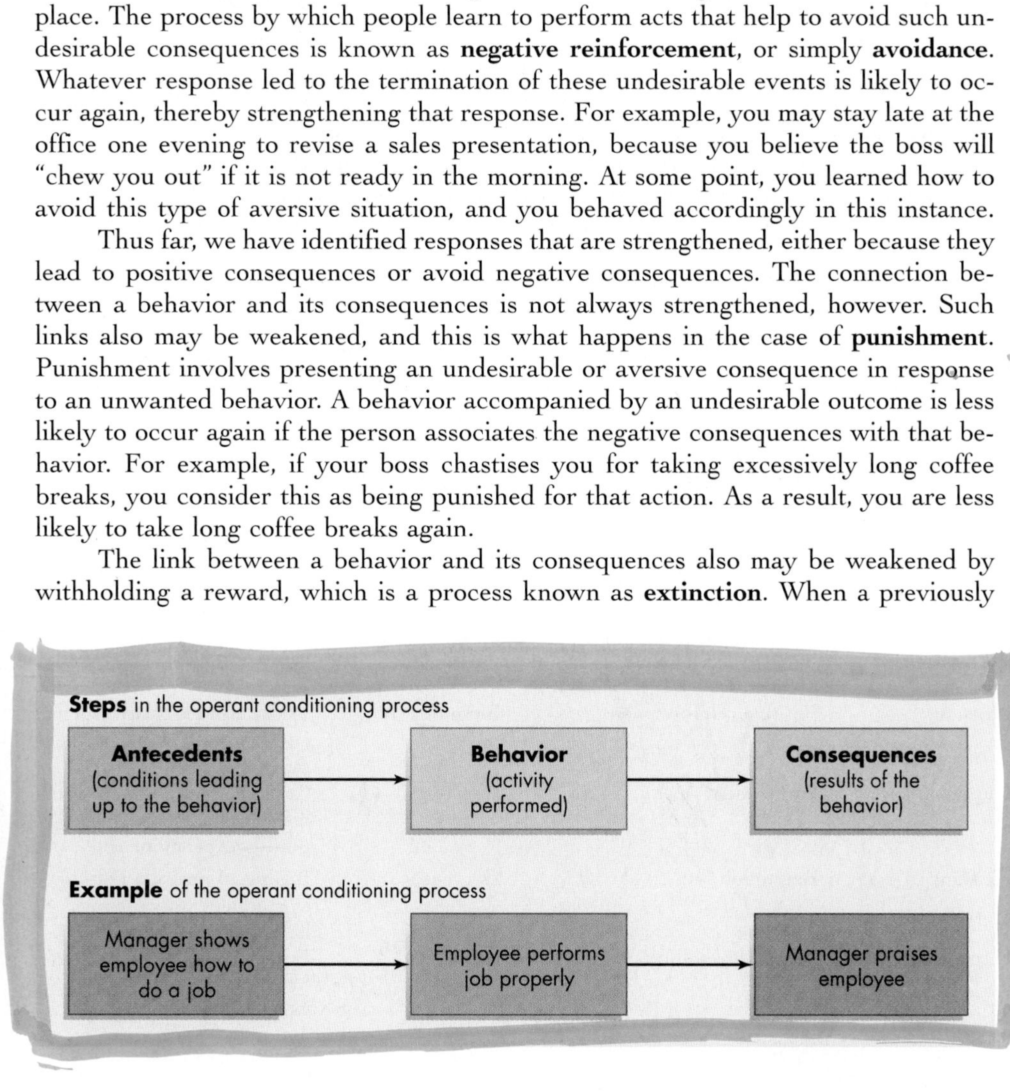

Steps in the operant conditioning process

Antecedents (conditions leading up to the behavior) → **Behavior** (activity performed) → **Consequences** (results of the behavior)

Example of the operant conditioning process

Manager shows employee how to do a job → Employee performs job properly → Manager praises employee

FIGURE 2.9

The Operant Conditioning Process: An Overview

The basic premise of *operant conditioning* is that people learn by connecting the consequences of their behavior with the behavior itself. In this example, the manager's praise increases the subordinate's tendency to perform the job properly. Thus, learning occurs by providing the appropriate antecedents and consequences.

rewarded response is no longer rewarded, that response tends to weaken and, eventually, to die out—in other words, to be *extinguished*. For example, suppose that for many months you brought boxes of donuts to your weekly staff meetings. Your colleagues always thanked you as they gobbled them down. Thus, you were positively reinforced by their approval, so you continued bringing the donuts. Now, after several months, your colleagues have begun dieting, and although they are tempting, your donuts go uneaten. After several months of no longer being praised for your generosity, you will be unlikely to continue bringing donuts. Your once-rewarded behavior will die out, having been extinguished.

The various relationships between a person's behavior and the consequences resulting from it—*positive reinforcement*, *negative reinforcement*, *punishment*, and *extinction*—are known collectively as **contingencies of reinforcement**. They represent the conditions under which rewards and punishments are given or taken away. Table 2.3 summarizes the four contingencies, and as we will see later in this chapter, administering these contingencies can be an effective tool for managing behavior in organizations.

Schedules of Reinforcement: Patterns of Administering Rewards   Thus far, our discussion of whether a reward is presented or withdrawn has assumed that the presentation or withdrawal follows each occurrence of the behavior in question. It is not always practical—even advisable—to do this, however. Reinforcement may be administered according to various rules governing its timing and frequency, collectively referred to as **schedules of reinforcement**. Rewarding *every* desired response is called **continuous reinforcement**, but unlike animals performing tricks in a circus, people on the job are rarely reinforced continuously. Instead, organizational rewards tend to be administered following **partial reinforcement** (also known as **intermittent reinforcement**) schedules. Under these schedules, rewards are administered intermittently, with some desired responses being reinforced and others not. Four varieties of partial reinforcement schedules have direct application to organizations.[30] These are:

1. **Fixed interval schedules**, which are those in which reinforcement is administered the first time the desired behavior occurs after a specific amount of time has passed. The practice of issuing paychecks each Friday at 3:00 P.M. is an example of a fixed interval schedule, because the rewards are administered at regular times. Fixed interval schedules are not especially ef-

---

contingencies of reinforcement

The various relationships between one's behavior and the consequences of that behavior (e.g., positive reinforcement, negative reinforcement, punishment, and extinction).

schedules of reinforcement

Rules governing the timing and frequency of administering reinforcement.

continuous reinforcement

A schedule of reinforcement in which all desired behaviors are reinforced.

partial reinforcement

A schedule of reinforcement in which only some desired behaviors are reinforced. Types include fixed interval, variable interval, fixed ratio, and variable ratio.

intermittent reinforcement

See *partial reinforcement*.

fixed interval schedule

Schedules of reinforcement in which a fixed period of time must elapse between reinforcements.

TABLE 2.3

Contingencies of Reinforcement: A Summary

The four contingencies of reinforcement may be distinguished by the presentation or withdrawal of a pleasant or an unpleasant stimulus. Positively or negatively reinforced behaviors are strengthened, whereas punished or extinguished behaviors are weakened.

STIMULUS PRESENTED OR WITHDRAWN	DESIRABILITY OF STIMULUS	NAME OF CONTINGENCY	STRENGTH OF RESPONSE	EXAMPLE
Presented	Pleasant	Positive reinforcement	Increases	Praise from a supervisor encourages continuing the praised behavior
	Unpleasant	Punishment	Decreases	Criticism from a supervisor discourages enacting the punished behavior
Withdrawn	Pleasant	Extinction	Decreases	Failing to praise a helpful act reduces the odds of helping in the future
	Unpleasant	Negative reinforcement	Increases	Future criticism is avoided by doing whatever the supervisor wants

fective at maintaining a desired behavior, however. For example, employees who know their boss will pass by their desks every day at 11:30 A.M. make sure they are working hard at that time. Without the boss around to praise them, they may take an early lunch or otherwise work less hard, because they know there will be no positive reinforcement for their efforts or punishment for their not working.

2. **Variable interval schedules**, which are those in which a variable amount of time (based on some average amount) must elapse between administrations of reinforcement. For example, consider a bank auditor who pays surprise visits to the branch offices an average of every six weeks (e.g., visits may be four weeks apart at one time and eight weeks apart at another). The auditor is using a variable interval schedule. Because the bank managers cannot tell exactly when their branch may be audited, they cannot afford to slack off. (Another inspection may be closer than they think!) Not surprisingly, variable interval schedules tend to be more effective than fixed interval schedules.

variable interval schedules
Schedules of reinforcement in which a variable period of time (based on some average) must elapse between reinforcements.

3. **Fixed ratio schedules**, which are those in which reinforcement is administered the first time the desired behavior occurs after a specified number of such actions have been performed. For example, suppose members of a sales staff know they will receive a bonus for each $1,000 worth of goods they sell. Immediately after receiving the first award, performance may slack off, but as their sales begin to approach $2,000 — the next level at which a reward is expected — performance improves.

fixed ratio schedule
Schedules of reinforcement in which a fixed number of responses must occur between reinforcements.

4. **Variable ratio schedules**, which are those in which a variable number of desired responses (based on some average amount) must elapse between administrations of reinforcement. A classic example is people playing slot machines. Most of the time, when people put a coin in the slot, they lose. After some unknown number of plays, however, the machine pays off. Because gamblers can never tell which pull of the handle will win the jackpot, they are likely to keep on playing for a long time. As you might imagine, variable ratio schedules tend to be more effective than fixed ratio schedules.

variable ratio schedules
Schedules of reinforcement in which a variable number of responses (based on some average) must occur between reinforcements.

Do you consider it to be unethical for casinos to "prey" on the weaknesses of gamblers by programming slot machines to pay off on variable ratio schedules? Why, or why not? ■

ETHICS MATTERS

These various schedules of reinforcement have several important similarities and differences, which are summarized in Figure 2.10. As you review this figure remember that these schedules represent "pure" forms. In practice, several different reinforcement schedules may be combined, thus making complex new schedules. Whether they operate separately or in conjunction with one another, however, it is important to recognize the strong influences that schedules of reinforcement can have on behavior in organizations.

Observational Learning:
Learning by Imitating Others

Operant conditioning is based on the idea that we engage in behaviors for which we are directly reinforced, but many things we learn on the job are *not* directly reinforced. For example, suppose that you see a fellow sales representative on your new job developing a potentially valuable lead by joining a local civic organization. Soon thereafter, while talking to people around the office, you learn yet another one of your colleagues has picked up a lucrative lead from a civic group to which he belongs. After

FIGURE 2.10

Schedules of Reinforcement: A Summary
The four schedules of reinforcement represent different ways of administering reward intermittently.

observational learning

The form of learning in which people acquire new behaviors by systematically observing the rewards and punishments given to others.

modeling

See *observational learning*.

observing this several times, chances are that you will eventually make the connection between joining such groups and getting sales leads as well. Although you may not have made any useful contacts from such groups in the past yourself, you would come to expect these leads to pan out based on what you observed from others. This is an example of what is known as **observational learning,** or **modeling.**[31] It occurs when someone acquires new knowledge *vicariously*—that is, by observing what happens to others. The person whose behavior is imitated is referred to as the *model*.

Steps in the Observational Learning Process   To learn from observing models, several processes must occur. Figure 2.11 summarizes these processes.

First, the learner must pay careful *attention* to the model—the greater the attention, the more effective the learning. To facilitate learning, models sometimes call attention to themselves. This is what happens when supervisors admonish their subordinates to "pay close attention" to what they are doing.

Second, people must have good *retention* of the model's behavior. Developing a verbal description or mental image of someone's actions helps a person to remember them. After all, we cannot learn from observing behavior we cannot remember.

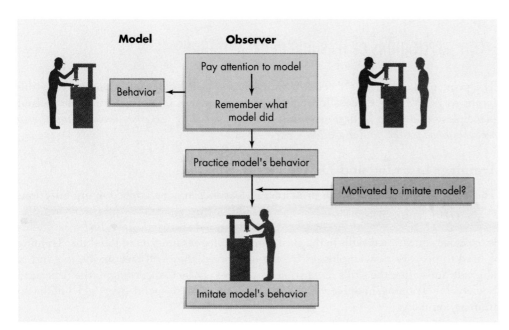

FIGURE 2.11

Observational Learning: An Overview

The process of *observational learning* requires that an observer pay attention to and remember a model's behavior. By observing what the model did and then rehearsing those actions, the observer may learn to imitate the model—but only if the observer is motivated to do so (i.e., if the model was rewarded for behaving as observed).

Third, there must be some *behavioral reproduction* of the model's behavior. Unless people can do exactly what the models do, they cannot learn from observing them. Naturally, this ability may be limited at first, but it should improve with practice.

Finally, people must have some *motivation* to learn from the model. We do not emulate every behavior we see. Instead, we focus on those we have some reason or incentive to match, such as actions for which others are rewarded.

Examples of Observational Learning in Organizations   Much of what is learned about how to behave in organizations can be explained by the process of observational learning.[32] For example, observational learning is a key part of many formal job training programs.[33] As we explain in the next section, trainees who are given a chance to observe experts doing their jobs, which is followed by an opportunity to practice the desired skills, and then are given feedback on their work tend to learn new job skills quite effectively.

Observational learning also occurs in a very informal, uncalculated manner. For example, people who experience the norms and traditions of their organizations and subsequently incorporate these into their own behavior may be recognized as having learned through observation. Indeed, people tend to learn the culture of their organizations (a topic that we discuss in chapter 13) through organizational learning.

People learn not only what to do by observing others but also what *not* to do. Specifically, people who see their coworkers getting punished for behaving inappropriately on the job tend to refrain from engaging in those same actions themselves.[34] As you might imagine, this is a very effective way for people to learn how to behave — and without experiencing any displeasure themselves.

- FORMAL JOB TRAINING
- ABSORBTION OF NORMS AND TRADITIONS

Unfortunately, employees may learn various unethical behaviors, such as how to steal from the company and how to get away with sexual harassment, by observing others. What concrete steps can managers take to minimize this? ■

ETHICS MATTERS

The principles of learning discussed thus far are used by organizations in many different ways. We now discuss four systematic approaches to incorporating the various principles of learning in organizations: *training, innovative reward systems, organizational behavior management*, and *discipline*.

Training: Learning and Developing Job Skills

training

The process of systematically teaching employees to acquire and improve job-related skills and knowledge.

The most obvious use to which principles of learning may be applied in organizations is **training**—the process through which people systematically acquire and improve the skills and knowledge they need to better their job performance. Just as students learn basic educational skills in the classroom, employees must learn job skills. Training is used to prepare new employees for the challenges they will face on the job and to upgrade and refine the skills of existing employees. In fact, according to the American Society for Training and Development, U.S. companies spend over $44 billion on training annually.[35]

Varieties of Training   Training can take many forms. Some training is quite informal in nature, consisting of experienced employees taking new personnel under their wings to show them how to do the job in question. Training also may involve formal classroom instruction, in which instructors describe the various requirements of the job and provide tips on how to meet them. Typically, people learning new skills in the classroom are given an opportunity to practice these skills, either in a simulated work setting or on the job itself.

For example, consider how people are trained as account representatives at Payco, a collection agency in Columbus, Ohio. Account representatives are those individuals who call consumers to arrange payment on seriously delinquent accounts. These reps receive ten days of intensive classroom training that covers such things as approaches to take in getting people to pay, procedures to follow for sending payment, payment programs available to the consumer, and the laws that bill collectors must follow. This classroom training is supplemented by simulated practice calls, in which the budding reps can practice their new skills. Following this training, the reps are allowed to make actual calls, but these early calls are closely monitored by experienced personnel who stand ready to guide the trainee as needed.

apprenticeship programs

Formal training programs, often used in the skilled trades, involving both on-the-job and classroom training, usually over a long period.

Growing in popularity today are formal **apprenticeship programs**, in which classroom training is systematically combined with a long period of on-the-job instruction (often several years in the case of skilled tradespeople such as carpenters, electricians, and masons). Recognizing the importance of such programs in developing human resources, the U.S. federal government has invested hundreds of millions of dollars in apprenticeship programs and encouraged training partnerships between government and private industry.[36] Apprenticeship programs often are designed and regulated by professional trade associations. The American Culinary Federation, for example, has a program that certifies apprentice chefs, who are required to complete a specific course of study and to demonstrate specific competencies while working in restaurant kitchens over a three-year period.

Given the increasing globalization of the workplace, today's companies often need to send their employees to work abroad. A growing number of such companies are discovering that employees are more likely to succeed in their overseas assignments when they have been thoroughly trained in the culture of the country in which they will live. Of course, it helps to know the language of the host country, but this is only the beginning. If you have ever lived in another country—or even *visited* one, for that matter—then you can appreciate how vital it is to understand fully the culture of any country in which you are doing business. With this in mind, many companies have invested in **cross-cultural training (CCT),** which is a systematic way of preparing employees to live and work in another country.[37] CCT is not a single method, however. It is a variety of specific, effective training techniques. Table 2.4 summarizes some of the most effective CCT methods.

Another popular form of training is **executive training programs** — sessions in which companies systematically attempt to develop the skills of their top leaders. The skills involved in these programs can range from how to use computer software to more general skills, such as how to get along with others.[38] This is accomplished by bringing in outside experts to train personnel in-house or by sending the personnel to specialized programs conducted by private consulting firms, colleges, or universities.[39]

Some companies (e.g., Apple Computer, the Tennessee Valley Authority, Motorola, and Sprint) are so serious about training they have developed their own **corporate universities** — centers devoted to handling a company's training needs on a full-time basis. Among the best-known is McDonald's "Hamburger University," where franchisees from all over the world learn and polish the skills they need to successfully operate a McDonald's restaurant.

Most organizational training is not as formal as the approaches described here. Still, training is involved in everyday job instruction, in which employees simply are told about the job, shown how to do it, and allowed to practice as a more experienced coworker watches and offers suggestions. Informal though it may be, this is training, and it requires every bit as much attention to the principles of learning to be successful as any other, more formal method.

As you might imagine, no one approach to training is ideal. Some techniques are better suited than others to learning certain skills because they incorporate more principles of learning than others. Not surprisingly, the best training programs often use many different approaches, thereby assuring that several different learning principles are incorporated in the training.[40]

Keys to Effective Training   If you recall how you learned skills such as how to study, drive, or use a word processor, you probably can appreciate some of the

cross-cultural training (CCT)
A systematic way of preparing employees to live and work in another country.

executive training programs
Sessions in which companies systematically develop their top leaders, either in specific skills or in general managerial skills.

corporate universities
Centers devoted to handling a company's training needs on a full-time basis.

TABLE 2.4

Summary of Techniques Used in Cross-Cultural Training (CCT)

People working overseas often have been trained for their assignments using one or more of the techniques described here.

Cultural briefings	Explain the major aspects of the host country culture, including customs, traditions, everyday behaviors.
Area briefings	Explain the history, geography, economy, politics, and other general information about the host country and region.
Cases	Portray a real-life situation in business or personal life to illustrate some aspect of living or working in the host culture.
Role playing	Allows the trainee to act out a situation that he or she might face in living or working in the host country.
Culture assimilator	Provides a written set of situations that the trainee might encounter in living or working in the host country. Trainee selects from a set of responses to the situation and is given feedback as to whether it is appropriate and why.
Field experiences	Provide an opportunity for the trainee to go to the host country or another unfamiliar culture to experience living and working for a short time.

Source: INTERNATIONAL ORGANIZATIONAL BEHAVIOR by Francesco/Gold, © 1998. Reprinted by permission of Prentice-Hall, Inc., Upper Saddle River, NJ.

OB AROUND THE WORLD

INTEGRATED TRAINING AT PETROLEOS DE VENEZUELA'S
CORPORATE UNIVERSITY, CENTRO INTERNACIONAL DE EDUCACIÓN Y DESARROLO

Few businesses are as subject to fluctuations in both supply and demand as those involving petroleum exploration, refining, and manufacturing. When prices dip on the world market, oil companies must tighten their belts, and when opportunities abound, they must seize them. Riding the crest of this wave requires basic knowledge of the oil-refining business itself and sound skills in basic business management. This idea has not been lost on Petroleos de Venezuela, S. A. (PDVSA), the world's second-largest oil company, which operates a corporate university, Centro Internacional de Educación y Desarrollo (CIED), headquartered in Caracas but operating in 14 locations throughout Venezuela.[41]

The CIED is divided into three separate institutes: one dealing with industrial training, another focusing on professional and technical development, and a third devoted to managerial development. Through these institutes, PDVSA offers a tightly focused, carefully designed curriculum that goes beyond traditional education to instill values consistent with PDVSA's corporate mission. The objective is to provide employees with the skills required to work in the complicated and volatile economic environment in which the company operates.

The Management Development Institute (MDI) provides a good example of this approach. A key aspect of MDI training involves instilling a sense of PDVSA's vision and history as well as the strategies of the overall organization and its subsidiaries, which in the United States includes CITGO. Because the company is large, with more than 20 international subsidiaries and some 2.35 trillion bolivars (4.5 billion U.S. dollars) in net earnings, employees can easily lose track of the big picture. To help meet the company's business plan, which includes the goal of doubling oil production by 2004, the MDI provides training in leadership and negotiation skills in addition to the topics covered in standard business courses, including finance, marketing, accounting, and the like. Furthermore, to supplement training in these areas, the CIED has developed alliances with U.S. business schools, including those at Harvard, Cornell, and MIT, to provide customized executive training.

Company president Luis E. Giusti is confident the CIED has played a significant role in PDVSA's record-breaking earnings during recent years. Broad-based corporate training also plays a large role in helping the company meet its ambitious objectives, including increased sales throughout the Americas (CITGO is currently the third-largest gasoline supplier in the United States — and the largest in terms of the number of sales outlets) and further joint ventures in Europe, where, for example, it has developed partnerships with Ruhr Oel GmbH, Veba Oel AG, and AB Nynäs.

Interestingly, PDVSA has contributed extensively to social development programs in Venezuela, particularly those in education. For example, the company has supported the mathematics, chemistry, and physics "olympics" organized by the Centro Nacional para el Mejoramiento de la Enseñanza de la Ciencia, in which 110,000 high-school students from across that country participated. In so doing, PDVSA clearly is investing some of its profits in the long-term education of its future employees, thereby planting the seeds of its own success in the years ahead. The company has adopted a strategy that works: Training leads to success, which leads to more training, which leads to even more success. This is something to consider the next time you fill your gas tank.

principles that help to make training effective. Four major principles are most relevant:

participation

Active involvement in the process of learning (more active participation leads to more effective learning).

repetition

The process of repeatedly performing a task so that it may be learned.

1. **Participation**. People not only learn more quickly but retain skills longer when they actively participate in the learning process. This applies to learning motor tasks as well as cognitive skills. For example, when learning to swim, there is no substitute for actually getting in the water and moving your arms and legs. In the classroom, students who listen attentively to lectures, think about the material, and involve themselves in discussions tend to learn more effectively than those who just sit passively.

2. **Repetition**. If you know the old adage "practice makes perfect," you already are aware of the benefits from repetition when learning. Perhaps you learned the multiplication table, a poem, or a phrase in a foreign language by going over it repeatedly. Indeed, mentally "rehearsing" such cognitive tasks increases our effectiveness at performing them.[42] Scientists have established the benefits of repetition — and that these effects are even greater when prac-

tice is spread out over time than when it is all lumped together. After all, when practice periods are too long, learning can suffer because of fatigue, whereas learning a little bit at a time allows the material to sink in.

3. **Transfer of training**. As you might imagine, training is most effective when what is learned during the training session must be applied to the job. In general, the more closely a training program matches the demands and conditions on a job, the more effective that training is. A good example is the elaborate simulation devices used to train pilots and astronauts. Another is the equipment used by many technical schools for people to learn skilled trades such as welding, computer repair, and radiation technology. By closely simulating the actual job conditions and equipment, the learned skills are expected to transfer to the job.

   The same may be said of training on supervisory skills. In this context, the benefits of training are best realized when the trainees apply their newly learned skills in organizations that accept the forms of supervision they learned.[43] Learning to supervise others in ways that may be resisted on the job, however, may be a waste of time as well as potentially disruptive.

4. **Feedback**. It is extremely difficult for learning to occur in the absence of feedback—that is, knowledge about the results of one's actions. Feedback provides information about the effectiveness of one's training.[44] Unless you learn what you are doing well and what behaviors you need to correct, you probably will be unable to improve your skills. For example, for people being trained as word-processing operators, it is critical to know exactly how many words they enter correctly per minute if they are to gauge their improvement.

   One type of feedback that has become popular in recent years is known as **360° feedback**—the process of using multiple sources from around the organization to evaluate the work of a single individual. This goes beyond simply collecting feedback from superiors (as is customary). It extends the gathering of feedback to other sources, such as one's peers, direct reports (i.e., immediate subordinates), customers, and even oneself (Figure 2.12).[45] Many companies, including General Electric, AT&T, Monsanto, Florida Power and Light, DuPont, Westinghouse, Motorola, Fidelity Bank, FedEx, Nabisco, and Warner-Lambert, have used 360° feedback to give more complete performance information to their employees, thus greatly improving not only their own work but overall corporate productivity as well.[46] To get a feel for how some companies use this technique, see the "Trends" section below.

transfer of training
The degree to which skills learned during training sessions may be applied to performance of one's job.

feedback
Knowledge of the results of one's behavior.

360° feedback
The practice of collecting performance feedback from multiple sources at various organizational levels.

TRENDS: WHAT TODAY'S COMPANIES ARE DOING

■ **Using 360° Feedback: Three Profiles**

Giving questionnaires to various people in an organization to assess how large groups of its members feel about each other can serve a lot of purposes. The survey findings can be used to help assess job performance and for many other purposes as well. For example, 360° feedback can be used to assess training needs systematically, to determine new products and services desired by customers, to gauge team members' reactions to each other, and to learn about many potential human resource problems.[47] To understand these and other uses of this popular tool, we now consider three specific examples of 360° feedback in action.[48] These are:

- *Changing organizational culture at the Landmark Stock Exchange.* The Landmark Stock Exchange is one of several smaller stock exchanges in the United States. Eclipsed by the "giants," such as the New York Stock Exchange and NASDAQ, Landmark

continued

has strived to become the best marketplace in the world by providing faster and more accurate movement of stocks than its well-known competitors. Meeting this objective requires a culture that supports rapid change and innovation. To see how it was doing in this regard, Landmark implemented a 360° feedback program that provided employees with feedback in such key areas as consulting others, inspiring others, team-building, and networking. This feedback was then used as the basis for systematic training in ways to change any specific behaviors found to be lacking. Given how important these behaviors are to developing an open culture at Landmark, they have been incorporated into the employees' formal performance appraisals.

- *Promoting individual development at Leher McGovern Bovis.* You probably never heard of Leher McGovern Bovis (LMB), but you certainly are familiar with some of the construction projects it has managed through the years, including the renovation and restoration of such New York City landmarks as the Statue of Liberty and Grand Central Station. LMB is unique in the construction industry in the attention it pays to not just meeting but *anticipating* its customers' needs and to working proactively to develop its employees' leadership skills, thus preparing them for senior positions in the company. Toward these ends, LMB implemented a 360° feedback program that helped to identify employee readiness for advancement to leadership positions within the company and the best candidates for management training. The 360° feedback program helped to reduce turnover among project managers from 12 percent to only 2 percent. Moreover, everyone in the company benefited from the positive feelings created by LMB's major investment in its employees by making them feel special.

- *Identifying training and selection requirements at Northwestern Mutual Life Insurance Company.* From its ads, you probably recognize Northwestern Mutual Life (NML) as "the quiet company." Indeed, this 140-year-old firm prides itself on the quality rather than the quantity of its accounts. Recently, however, competition has put pressure on the company's financial performance, thus making it necessary for its "general agency offices," which are similar to regional offices, to work harder at developing new business. Because of the company's structure, as many as 100 individual agencies are managed by general agency offices. This makes it important for the right people to serve as "general agents"—and for these individuals to be ready to meet the leadership challenges that confront them. With this in mind, NML introduced a 360° feedback program that taps the potential of individual agents to be promoted to general agents. The program then uses this information to provide the most-needed forms of management training. NML's selection of general agents has been more effective than ever, in great part because of the 360° feedback program.

As these examples illustrate, 360° feedback can be a very successful tool in meeting a wide variety of organizational objectives. Clearly, its use is a trend that can be expected to continue. ■

In sum, these four principles—*participation, repetition, transfer of training,* and *feedback*—are key to the effectiveness of any training program. The most effective training programs are those that incorporate as many of these principles as possible.

Innovative Reward Systems: Going Beyond Merit Pay

When we talk about "reward" in organizations, we mostly tend to focus on pay and fringe benefits, which are based on standards such as merit (i.e., how well one performs) or seniority (i.e., how long one has remained on the job). Recently, however,

FIGURE 2.12

360° Feedback: An Overview
Many companies today have begun using *360° feedback*, which is the process of using multiple sources of feedback to improve performance.

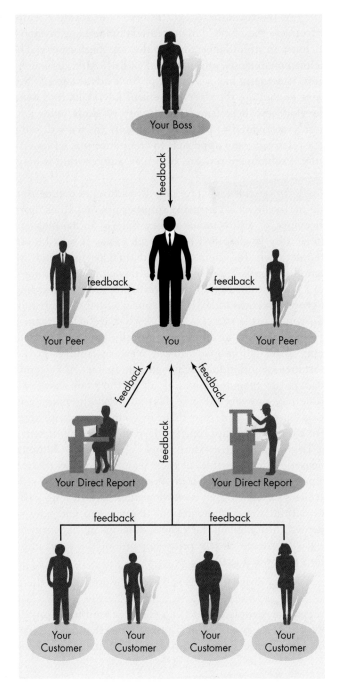

organizations have begun using far more innovative approaches. Because these are based on various principles of learning, it makes sense to identify them here.

Skill-Based Pay   Traditionally, employees are paid based on the jobs they perform, and some jobs mean more pay than others. In **skill-based pay**, however, people are paid based on the number of different skills they have learned — skills that eventually may prove useful to the organization. Under a skill-based pay system, an employee must demonstrate the ability to perform a new skill relevant to performing one or more jobs to get a raise. This contrasts with traditional pay systems, in which raises are given based on meritorious performance of a job or seniority in the company.

skill-based pay

An innovative reward system in which people are paid based on the number of different skills they have learned relevant to performing one or more jobs in the organization.

At the toymaker Lego Systems, for example, employees are paid based on how effectively they have demonstrated competence in each of three areas that were found to exist in abundance among the top performers. These are technical skills, team achievement skills, and personal skills.[49] Although such a system may seem strange at first, it actually has several important advantages.[50] Specifically, skill-based pay systems encourage the development of key skills that help the company to grow and to develop, and because of the variety of skills involved, employees stand to be more highly motivated to perform their jobs (as we will see in chapter 4). Skill-based pay is a relatively new approach to compensation, so its effectiveness has not been tested fully. Preliminary reports, however, suggest that it may be very promising.[51]

Team-Based Rewards   As noted, traditional compensation systems focus on individual performance. A growing number of companies, however, now emphasize the performance of entire teams rather than of individual employees (a trend we describe more fully in chapter 7).[52] In such cases, it may be potentially disruptive to reward people solely for their own individual performance while ignoring their team's accomplishments. After all, a basic principle of learning is that people perform behaviors that are positively reinforced. Therefore, rewarding behaviors that contribute to a group's success today will encourage further contributions to the group's success tomorrow. This is the idea behind what are called **team-based rewards** (Figure 2.13).

Employees at all levels naturally have concerns about team-based reward systems. After all, people in most Western cultures grow up learning to value the importance of individual achievement. In fact, they tend to be afraid of having "freeloaders" on their team who don't do their fair share of the work but who receive the same pay as everyone else. Not surprisingly, many companies that have introduced team-based rewards use them in conjunction with traditional, individual-based pay. For example, this approach is used at a Unisys office in Bismarck, North Dakota, and at Trigon Blue Cross–Blue Shield of Virginia.[53] Although these companies have been pleased with the results of their team-based reward systems, most companies are still experimenting with such methods. Until systematic studies have evaluated the effectiveness of team-based reward systems over a long period of time, it is difficult to offer definitive recommendations about when and how such systems should be implemented.[54] Still, given the growth of teams in the workplace (see chapter 7) team-based reward systems clearly represent one of the most important and promising innovations in reward systems.

team-based rewards

Innovative reward systems in which employees are paid based on their team's performance.

GLOBAL MATTERS   In general, people from Asian cultures tend to be more collaborative in their orientation (i.e., they focus primarily on others) than people from Western cultures, who tend to have a more individualistic orientation (i.e., they focus primarily on themselves).

FIGURE 2.13

Team-Based Rewards: A Growing Trend

Because more people today are working together in teams, companies are changing compensation systems to reward team successes instead of individual performance alone. For example, part of the compensation received by these Unisys workers from Bismarck, North Dakota, is based on their team's accomplishments.

Not surprisingly, employees of Japanese companies tend to be more accepting of teams than employees of U.S. companies — and more likely to experience success with team-based reward systems. ■

Organizational Behavior Management: Positively Reinforcing Desirable Organizational Behaviors

In describing operant conditioning, we noted that the consequences of our behavior determines whether we repeat that behavior or abandon it. Behaviors that are rewarded tend to be strengthened and to be repeated in the future. With this in mind, it is possible to administer rewards selectively to reinforce behaviors that we wish to be repeated in the future. This is the basic principle behind **organizational behavior management** (also known as **organizational behavior modification**, or **OB Mod** for short), which may be defined as the systematic application of positive reinforcement principles in organizational settings to raise the incidence of desirable organizational behaviors.

organizational behavior management
The practice of altering behavior in organizations by systematically administering rewards.

organizational behavior modification (OB Mod)
See *organizational behavior management.*

Basic Steps in OB Mod   To use organizational behavior management programs effectively, managers should follow certain steps.[55] These are:

1. *Pinpoint the desired behaviors.* Managers should specify exactly what they want to be done differently (e.g., saying they want to answer customers' inquiries 50 percent quicker instead of saying they want to improve customer service).

2. *Perform a baseline audit.* Managers should determine exactly how well people perform the behavior they wish to change (e.g., how quickly they currently answer calls).

3. *Define a criterion standard.* Managers should define exactly what performance goal is being sought (e.g., all calls should be answered within the first 30 seconds).

4. *Choose a reinforcer.* Managers should choose exactly how the desired behavior will be rewarded. Will service agents be given a bonus for answering within 30 seconds all calls received in a month? If so, what form will the bonus take? Today, many companies have been using nonmonetary incentives, in part because they serve as reminders of one's accomplishments. A $100 check, for example, can be gone in no time flat, but the reward value of a trophy on the mantle persists for a long time.[56] Some nonmonetary incentives have been quite exotic, such as the hot-air balloon trip over the Napa Valley and the mountain-climbing expedition to the Swiss Alps offered by MCI Communications.[57] Incentives need not be so elaborate, however. Praise is a highly effective reinforcer in organizations — and an inexpensive one at that!

5. *Selectively reward desired behaviors that approximate the criterion standard.* The learning process may be facilitated by rewarding behaviors that come close to the desired level. For example, if agents are answering calls within 60 seconds, their progress should be rewarded a little. After a while, however, the reward should be given only after the 50-second level is reached, and then the 40-second level, and so on. The process of selectively reinforcing behavior that approaches a goal is known as **shaping**. Frequently used in training animals to perform tricks, this technique applies equally well in teaching human beings to perform a desired behavior.

shaping
The process of selectively reinforcing behaviors that approach a desired goal behavior.

6. Periodically re-evaluate the program. Is the goal behavior still performed? Are the rewards still working? Changes in these events over time should be expected. Therefore, administrators of behavior management programs should monitor carefully the behaviors they worked so hard to develop.

An Example of OB Mod in Action   OB Mod programs have successfully stimulated a variety of behaviors in many different organizations.[58] A particularly interesting and effective program was used at Diamond International, the Palmer, Massachusetts, company of 325 employees that manufactures Styrofoam egg cartons. In response to sluggish productivity, a simple but elegant reinforcement was instituted: Any employee working a full year without an industrial accident is given 20 points. Perfect attendance is given 25 points. Once a year, the points are totaled. When employees reach 100 points, they get a blue nylon jacket with the company's logo on it and a patch identifying their membership in the "100 Club." Those earning still more points receive extra awards. For example, at 500 points, employees can select from a number of small household appliances. These inexpensive prizes go a long way toward symbolizing to the employees the company's appreciation for their good work.

This program has helped to improve productivity dramatically at Diamond International. Compared with before the OB Mod program began, output has improved 16.5 percent, quality-related errors have dropped 40 percent, grievances have decreased 72 percent, and time lost because of accidents has been lowered by 43.7 percent. The overall result has been more than $1 million in gross financial benefits from the company—and a much happier workforce. Needless to say, this has been a very simple and effective OB Mod program. Although not all such programs are equally successful, evidence suggests they generally are quite beneficial. For example, highly successful OB Mod programs have been used at companies such as General Electric, Weyerhauser, and General Mills.

Discipline: Eliminating Undesirable Organizational Behaviors

Just as organizations use rewards systematically to encourage desirable behavior, they also use punishment to discourage undesirable behavior. Problems such as absenteeism, lateness, theft, and substance abuse cost companies vast sums of money, and many companies attempt to manage these situations using **discipline**—the systematic administration of punishment.

By administering an unpleasant outcome (e.g., suspension without pay) in response to an undesirable behavior (e.g., excessive tardiness), companies seek to minimize that behavior. In one form or another, using discipline is a relatively common practice. In fact, 83 percent of companies use some form of discipline—or at least the threat of discipline—in response to undesirable behaviors.[59] As you might imagine, however, disciplinary actions taken in organizations vary greatly. At one extreme, they may be formal, such as written warnings that become part of the employee's permanent record. At the other, they may be informal and low key, such as friendly reminders and off-the-record discussions between supervisors and problem subordinates.

In one survey, nursing supervisors were asked to list the disciplinary actions they used most often and to rank them by their severity.[60] Table 2.5 shows the resulting list and reveals that a broad range of disciplinary measures are used. Although the sample size in this study was limited, these results probably are typical of what would be found across a wide variety of jobs.

Disciplinary Practices in Organizations   One common practice involves using punishment *progressively*—that is, starting mildly and then increasing in severity with each successive infraction. This is the idea behind **progressive discipline**—the practice of basing punishment on the frequency and severity of the infraction.[61]

Consider an example of how progressive discipline might work for a common problem such as chronic absenteeism or tardiness. First, the supervisor gives the employee an informal, oral warning. Then, if the problem persists, there is an official

discipline

The process of systematically administering punishment.

progressive discipline

The practice of gradually increasing the severity of punishments for employees who exhibit unacceptable job behavior.

TABLE 2.5

A Continuum of Disciplinary Measures

Ranked from mildest to most severe, these are the most commonly used disciplinary tactics among a recent sample of nursing supervisors.

RANK	DISCIPLINARY MEASURE
1	Talk to or counsel the employee about the problem
2	Oral warning
3	Written warning or letter of reprimand
4	Coach the employee about the problem
5	Provide special in-house services to help the employee
6	Send the employee to formal program designed to help with the problem
7	Transfer the employee to a different part of the company
8	Intervene in the situation
9	Put the employee on probation
10	Withhold a portion of the merit raise earned
11	Suspend without pay
12	Terminate

Source: Based on findings reported by Trahan & Steiner, 1994; see note 60.

meeting with the supervisor and a formal oral warning issued. The next offense results in a formal, written warning that becomes part of the employee's personnel record. Subsequent offenses result in suspension without pay, and finally, if all else fails, the employee is terminated. In the case of more serious offenses such as gambling, some of the preliminary steps would be dropped, and a formal, written warning would be given at the start. For the most serious offenses, such as stealing or intentionally damaging company property, officials would move immediately to the most severe step; immediate dismissal.

Companies with the most effective disciplinary programs tend to *make the contingencies clear* (e.g., by publicizing punishment rules in the company handbook). When this is done, employees know exactly what behaviors the company will not tolerate, which often minimizes the need for discipline at all.

It probably comes as no surprise that supervisors do not always punish all inappropriate behaviors they encounter.[62] A key reason for this is that the supervisors may feel constrained by limitations imposed through labor unions or by their own lack of formal authority. In addition, without clear company policy regarding how to use discipline, supervisors may fear strong, negative emotional reactions from the punished individual and even revenge and retaliation. Therefore, many supervisors may look the other way and simply do nothing when employees behave inappropriately. Doing nothing may be easy in the long run, of course, but ignoring chronic problems is a way of informally approving of them, thus leading to increasingly serious problems in the future.

With this in mind, companies with the best disciplinary programs make it a practice to *take immediate action*. At Honda of America, for example, human resource specialist Tim Garrett notes the company pays close attention to all infractions of the rules, including ones "that other companies wouldn't think of paying attention to" so that "if there's a problem, we'll pay attention to it right away."[63]

Is it generally unethical for organizations to discipline their employees? What specific forms of disciplines may be ethical or unethical to use? ■   **ETHICS MATTERS**

YOU BE THE CONSULTANT

Employees at a corporate call center have not been spending enough time at their cubicles answering the phones, as required. Instead, they have been walking throughout the facility and talking with each other about personal matters. Customer service problems have resulted.

1. What types of attributions would you be prone to make about these employees, and how would these relate to the performance evaluations you give them?

2. What types of errors would you be prone to in making these judgments, and what might you do to overcome them so that you can make more accurate judgments?

3. How might you use training, innovative reward systems, organizational behavior management problems, and discipline to address the problem?

Keys to Using Punishment Effectively   Obviously, it is not easy to know exactly when and how to administer punishment or how it can be administered in a way that is considered to be fair and reasonable. Fortunately, research and theory have pointed to some effective principles that maximize the effectiveness of discipline in organizations.[64] We now consider several of these key principles:

1. *Deliver punishment immediately after the undesirable response occurs.* The less time between the occurrence of an undesirable behavior and the administration of a negative consequence, the more strongly people make the connection between them. When people make this association, the negative consequence is likely to serve as a punishment, thereby reducing the probability of the unwanted behavior occurring again. With this in mind, it is best for managers to talk to their subordinates about their undesirable behaviors immediately after the subordinate commits them (or at least as soon thereafter as practical). Expressing disapproval after several days or weeks have passed is less effective, since the passage of time weakens the association between the behavior and its consequences.

2. *Give moderate levels of punishment — nothing too high or too low.* If the consequences of an undesirable action are not severe (e.g., rolling one's eyes as a show of disapproval), those consequences are unlikely to operate as a punishment. After all, living with such a mild response is easy. In contrast, however, consequences that are overly severe might be perceived as being unfair and inhumane.[65] When this occurs, the individual might resign and a strong signal is sent to others about the unreasonableness of the company's actions. In either case, the company risks losing its most valuable assets: its human resources.

3. *Punish the undesirable behavior, not the person.* Good punishment is impersonal in nature, and it focuses on the individual's actions rather than on his or her personality. For example, when addressing an employee repeatedly caught taking excessively long breaks, it is unwise to say, "You're lazy and have a bad attitude." Instead, it is better to say, "By not being at your desk when expected, you're making it more difficult for all of us to get our work done on time." Responding in this manner is less humiliating for the individual, thus making the discussion far less unpleasant.

   In addition, focusing on exactly what someone can do to avoid such disapproval (i.e., taking shorter breaks in this example) increases the likelihood that individual will attempt to alter his or her behavior in the desired fashion. In contrast, the person who feels personally attacked might not only "tune out" the message but also not know exactly how to improve.

4. *Use punishment consistently — all the time, for all employees.* Sometimes, managers attempting to be lenient turn a blind eye toward infractions of company rules. Doing this may cause more harm than good, however, because it inadvertently reinforces the undesirable behavior by demonstrating that employees can get away with breaking the rules. Therefore, it is most effective to administer punishment after each occurrence of an undesirable behavior.

   Similarly, it is important for managers to show consistency in their treatment of all employees. In other words, everyone who commits the same infraction should be punished in the same way, regardless of the person administering the punishment. When this occurs, supervisors are unlikely to be accused of showing favoritism. In addition, if one supervisor is perceived to be very lenient and another to be very harsh, subordinates may learn to avoid the harsh supervisor rather than to avoid the undesirable behavior!

5. *Clearly communicate reasons for the punishment.* Making clear exactly what behaviors lead to what disciplinary actions greatly facilitates the effectiveness of punishment. Clearly communicated expectations also help to strengthen the perceived connection between behavior and its consequences. Wise managers use their opportunities to communicate with subordinates to make clear that punishments do not constitute revenge but are an attempt to eliminate unwanted behavior (which, of course, they are). Communicating information about poor performance in a personal interview is a good idea, but doing so is not easy. To make such interviews as effective as possible, managers should conduct them systematically, following the steps outlined in Figure 2.14.[66]

6. *Do not follow punishment with noncontingent rewards.* Imagine you are a supervisor and have just written a formal letter of discipline because of a serious infraction by a particular subordinate. The disciplined employee is feeling very low, which makes you feel remorseful. You reduce your guilt by telling the employee he can take the rest of the day off with pay. This may make you feel better, but it poses a serious problem: You inadvertently reward the person for the unwanted behavior. The serious infraction was punished by the letter but rewarded by the time off. Consequently, the effect of the punishment may be greatly diminished. Such an action also sends the wrong message to the other employees, who soon learn that you will give them time off if they display the proper degree of dejection. The advice is clear: For

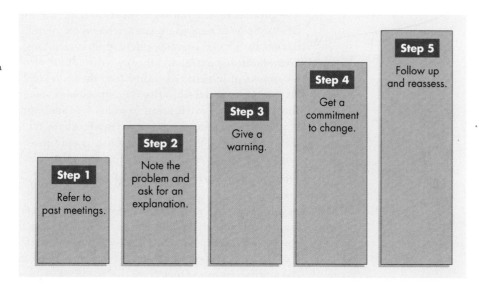

FIGURE 2.14

Conducting a Disciplinary Interview: Key Steps

It is never easy to communicate a performance problem. Following the steps listed here, however, helps to ensure the problem is identified and the consequences for failing to improve are made clear.

(*Source*: Based on suggestions by Lussier, 1990; see note 66.)

Step 1
Refer to past meetings.

Step 2
Note the problem and ask for an explanation.

Step 3
Give a warning.

Step 4
Get a commitment to change.

Step 5
Follow up and reassess.

punishment to be most effective, supervisors should refrain from inadvertently rewarding undesirable behaviors.

As obvious as this suggestion may be, it is not always followed.[67] In fact, top executives recognize that today's organizations frequently reward behaviors *opposite* those they really desire.[68] For example, although organizations hope for teamwork and collaboration, they tend to reward the best individual member of the team. Similarly, although organizations hope for high achievement, they tend to reward merely putting in another year of service. Thus, it cannot be said that organizations do a good job of rewarding desirable behaviors. In fact, they often do just the opposite!

If after reading all this you think it is truly difficult to administer rewards and punishments properly in organizations, you have reached the same conclusion as experts in the field of OB. Indeed, one key skill that makes some managers so effective is their ability to influence others by properly administering rewards and punishments.

We invite you to visit the Greenberg page on the Prentice Hall Web site at: **www.prenhall.com/greenberg** for the monthly Greenberg update and for this chapter's World Wide Web exercise.

SUMMARY AND REVIEW OF LEARNING OBJECTIVES

1. **Distinguish between the concepts of *perception* and *social perception*.**
   Perception is the process through which people select, organize, and interpret the information around them. When this process focuses on the interpretation of information about people, it is referred to as **social performance**.

2. **Explain how the *attribution* process works and how it helps us to understand the causes of others' behavior.**
   The process of **attribution** involves judging the underlying reasons for people's behavior. Some of our judgments are based on inferences made by observing others' behavior. Known as **correspondent inferences**, these judgments often are inaccurate. Our search for explanations about the causes of others' behavior leads us to make judgments of **internal causality** (i.e., the individual is responsible for his or her own actions) or **external causality** (i.e., someone or something else is responsible). **Kelley's theory of causal attribution** explains that such judgments are based on three types of information: **consensus** (i.e., whether others act in a similar manner), **consistency** (i.e., whether the individual previously acted this way in the same situation), and **distinctiveness** (i.e., whether this person acted similarly in different situations).

3. **Describe the various sources of *bias in social perception* and how they may be overcome.**
   Several types of systematic errors, which are known as **perceptual biases**, limit the accuracy of social perception. These include the **fundamental attribution error** (i.e., the tendency to attribute others' actions to internal causes), the **halo effect** (i.e., the tendency to perceive others in consistently positive or negative terms), the **similar-to-me effect** (i.e., the tendency to perceive similar others in a favor-

able light), **first-impression error** (i.e., the tendency for initial impressions to guide subsequent ones), and **selective perception** (i.e., the tendency for people to focus on only certain aspects of the environment). Perceptual inaccuracies also result from the tendency of people to rely on **stereotypes** (i.e., judgments of others based on the categories to which they belong). Perceptual biases are not overcome easily, but attempts at doing so can be made. Such attempts can include considering the external causes of others' behavior, identifying and confronting one's stereotypes, evaluating others objectively, and avoiding rash judgments.

4. **Understand how the process of social perception operates in the context of *performance appraisals, employment interviews*, and the cultivation of *corporate images*.**
   Biased judgments about others sometimes occur during the process of **performance appraisal**. In this context, people judge as being superior those individuals whose performance matches their expectations, those whose good performance is attributed to internal sources, and those whose poor performance is attributed to external sources. People generally are interested in getting others to perceive them favorably, and their efforts in this regard are known as **impression management**. This process is particularly important during employment interviews, but it sometimes interferes with the accuracy of information being presented about the individuals or companies. An organization's overall impression on people — its **corporate image** — is a determinant of its ability to attract qualified job applicants.

5. **Define *learning*.**
   Learning refers to relatively permanent changes in behavior that result from experience.

6. **Describe the concepts of *operant conditioning* and *observational learning*.**
   In **operant conditioning**, individuals learn to behave in certain ways based on the consequences of those actions. Reinforcement may be either *positive* (i.e., based on presentation of a desirable outcome) or *negative* (i.e., based on withdrawal of an unwanted outcome). The probability of certain responses can be decreased if an unpleasant outcome results (i.e., **punishment**) or if a pleasant outcome is withdrawn (i.e., **extinction**). **Observational learning** involves learning through modeling the behavior of others. By paying attention to and rehearsing such behavior, we can learn vicariously (i.e., through the model's experiences).

7. **Describe how principles of learning are involved in organizational *training* and *innovative reward systems*.**
   Learning is directly involved in efforts to teach people new job skills, which is the process of **training**. Training is most effective when people actively participate in the learning process, repeat the desired behaviors, receive feedback on their performance, and learn under conditions closely resembling those on the job. Today, companies are experimenting with innovative reward systems that include **skill-based pay** (i.e., paying people for the various skills they have demonstrated on the job) and **team-based rewards** (i.e., paying people for their contributions to team performance).

8. **Compare how organizations can use reward in *organizational behavior management* programs and can use punishment most effectively when administering *discipline*.**
   Organizational behavior management is a systematic attempt to apply the principles of reinforcement to the workplace to improve organizational functioning. Reinforcing desired behaviors can greatly improve organizational functioning. **Discipline**, in contrast, is the systematic application of punishments to minimize undesirable organizational behaviors. Discipline is most effective when punishment is applied immediately after the undesirable activity, is moderately severe, focuses on the activity rather than on the individual, is applied consistently over time, is clearly explained and communicated, and is not weakened by inadvertent rewards.

QUESTIONS FOR DISCUSSION

1. Describe an organizational situation in which it is important to judge whether someone's behavior stems primarily from internal or from external causes.

2. How do stereotypes influence the way we judge others in organizations? How may stereotypical judgments be overcome?

3. What can people do to leave positive impressions on others in organizations?

4. How can you learn important things about life in an organization through operant conditioning? How about through observational learning?

5. How might each of the four different schedules of reinforcement be used on your own job, on a job you've had, or on a job you would like to have in the future?

6. What types of training are organizations using today, and what could be done to make them more effective?

7. What types of innovative reward systems are organizations using today, and what could be done to make them more effective?

8. How can you enhance the quality of an organization's disciplinary program?

Case in Point

Finding a Safe Way to Smile at Safeway

Any training course on the essentials of customer service will always advise you to smile at and to make eye contact with customers. In fact, this seems to be so obvious as to not need repeating. Little would you imagine, therefore, that doing precisely this would actually cause problems for some supermarket clerks! A dozen employees at a Safeway store in California recently claimed their eye contact and smiles have elicited unwanted attention from shoppers—who have mistaken these friendly gestures as flirting. Some clerks have had to resort to hiding in the store to escape customers who were hungry for "services" that weren't for sale. A produce clerk at one northern California store was even followed to her car and propositioned by a supermarket shopper who got the wrong idea.

The root of the problem, argue the 12 clerks who filed grievances with their union in the summer of 1998, is Safeway's "Superior Service" policy, which explicitly requires them to smile at customers and to maintain three seconds of eye contact with each one. It also requires clerks to anticipate their customers' needs, help them find items for which they're looking, and call them by name if they're paying by check or credit card.

This policy was in place for five years before Safeway officials began enforcing it using undercover shoppers to spot violators. These violators were sent letters warning them of the negative evaluations and disciplinary measures (even firing!) that could result from failing to comply. Soon thereafter, the incidents of customer harassment began. The union is seeking a modified policy that gives workers some discretion in the matter, allowing them to chose whether to maintain eye contact or to refuse to carry a customer's bags to his or her car at night.

From its headquarters in Pleasanton, California, Safeway officials are quick to acknowledge that although some customers get out of hand, their policy is not the cause. They also add that not one of the 150,000 employees have ever been fired for failing to be friendly. Even so, 100 employees have been sent to a daylong, remedial training class on friendliness—what they call "Smile School." This, says Safeway spokesperson Debra Lambert, "is not about discipline. It's about treating customers well and training employees to do that."

The next time you're in your local supermarket looking for laundry detergent—and that surly clerk doesn't even look up to acknowledge you, think about this when you complain.

CRITICAL THINKING QUESTIONS

1. How, specifically, does this case illustrate the process of attribution?

2. What do you suppose is being done to help train people to be more friendly toward customers? In other words, what do you imagine goes on in Safeway's "Smile School"?

3. What do you think of sending undercover shoppers into stores to spot violators of the customer service policy? In your opinion, is this ethical?

4. Describe what you believe might be the progressive disciplinary steps outlined in the warning letter sent to unfriendly Safeway clerks.

5. Do you believe the union's complaints about the "Superior Service" policy are warranted? What, if anything, should be done to change this policy?

Perception and Learning: Understanding and Adapting to the Work Environment

SMALL BUSINESS 2000

You may have heard the phrase "work can be fun." Angelo DeLusia and his team at Del's Lemonade show us that fun can be work. Based in Rhode Island, Del's Lemonade has more than 60 stores. There's even one in Tokyo. This is a thriving company that continues to look for ways to be more efficient, to be more "tuned in" to its customers, and to continue to grow.

To hear DeLusia tell the story, it sounds like the success of the business just happened. He tells us about hard work and dedication, both his own and that of those who work with him, but he doesn't seem to think there is much more to it. This is what DeLusia tells us, but from listening to him and others tell the Del's story, we begin to understand that DeLusia knows there is more to it — there is just only so much that he wants to share.

Fortunately, we can figure out a lot just by listening to Angelo, his employees, and his franchisers. This business certainly was built on hard work. It also has a unique style and personality, molded from what DeLusia believes is the right way to treat people and to approach work. Most people involved in major roles at Del's have worked their way up through the business, many of them starting out by sweeping the parking lot or working the counter. They also are loyal customers. DeLusia tells us there is something magic about his lemonade that hooks people — they keep coming back for more. It seems that Angelo has a way of hooking people when it comes to working for Del's, too.

This company is successful because it follows a formula — Angelo DeLusia's formula. People are not selected for key jobs just because they know Angelo, but because of *how* they know him and how he knows them. In many franchise businesses, people are evaluated on financial criteria and selected to be owners based primarily on their ability to make an initial investment. At Del's, however, people come first. If DeLusia thinks you have the right stuff, you're in. If not, it doesn't matter what your bank balance is.

QUESTIONS FOR DISCUSSION

1. DeLusia tells an interesting story about how he got his first loan. The banker referred to Angelo and his wife "as two good, hard-working, Italian people." What do you think the lender meant by that statement? What do you think DeLusia might have said to give the lender this impression? What does this say about how the lender made his decision to lend Angelo the money he needed?

2. DeLusia offered the first Del's franchise to one of his employees. He probably did this for a reason. From what you have read in this chapter, what aspects of learning and training do you think may have influenced Angelo's decision to select an employee to run the first franchise?

3. The top management group at Del's is made up mostly of people who have worked with Angelo, usually as employees of Del's Lemonade, for quite some time. As a result, we might expect the management group to include people who are a lot like DeLusia. Do you think this is a good thing? Describe some of the advantages and limitations of a management team whose members are selected because they are alike.

EXPERIENCING ORGANIZATIONAL BEHAVIOR

Identifying Occupational Stereotypes

Although we usually reserve concern over stereotypes to those involving women and members of racial or ethnic minorities, people can hold stereotypes toward members of *any* group. In organizations, people are likely to hold stereotypes about others based on a variable whose importance cannot be downplayed — the occupational groups to which they belong. What we expect of people — and the way we treat them — is likely to be affected by stereotypes about their professions. This exercise helps you to understand this phenomenon better.

Directions

Using the following scale, rate each of the occupational groups listed here regarding how much of each characteristic the people in these groups tend to show:

1 = not at all
2 = a slight amount
3 = a moderate amount
4 = a great amount
5 = an extreme amount

Accountants

_____ interesting
_____ generous
_____ intelligent
_____ conservative
_____ shy
_____ ambitious

Professors

_____ interesting
_____ generous
_____ intelligent
_____ conservative
_____ shy
_____ ambitious

Lawyers

_____ interesting
_____ generous
_____ intelligent
_____ conservative
_____ shy
_____ ambitious

Clergy

_____ interesting
_____ generous
_____ intelligent
_____ conservative
_____ shy
_____ ambitious

Physicians

_____ interesting
_____ generous
_____ intelligent
_____ conservative
_____ shy
_____ ambitious

Plumbers

_____ interesting
_____ generous
_____ intelligent
_____ conservative
_____ shy
_____ ambitious

Questions for Discussion

1. Did your ratings of the various groups differ? If so, which groups were perceived most positively and which were perceived most negatively?
2. On what characteristics, if any, did you find no differences among the various groups? What do you think this means?

3. To what extent did your ratings agree with those of others? Was there general agreement about the stereotypical nature of people in various occupational groups?

4. To what extent were your responses based on specific people you know? How did specific knowledge—or lack of knowledge—regarding members of the various occupational groups influence your ratings?

5. By becoming aware of these stereotypes, do you believe that you will perpetuate them in the future or that you will refrain from behaving in accord with them? Explain.

WORKING IN GROUPS

Role Play: Conducting a Disciplinary Interview

Knowing how to discipline employees who behave inappropriately is an important managerial skill. The trick, however, is to change the bad behavior into good behavior *permanently* by getting people to accept their mistakes and to understand how to correct them. As you might imagine, this is often far more difficult than it sounds. After all, people generally are reluctant to admit their errors, and they may have developed bad work habits that must be overcome. In addition, they tend to resist being chastised—and simply do not like listening to criticism. With this in mind, disciplining others represents quite a challenge for managers, thus making it a skill worth developing.

Directions

1. Select four students from the class, and divide them into two pairs. One person from each pair should read only the role sheet for Andy F., a machine operator, and the other person from each pair should read only the role sheet for Barry B., his supervisor. Send both pairs outside the room until you call for them.

2. Members of the class will serve as observers and should read both role sheets.

3. Call in the first pair of role players, and ask them to spend approximately 10 to 15 minutes playing their roles—that is, acting as they would if they were the characters in the role sheets. They should feel free to assume any additional facts not described in those sheets.

4. Members of the class should observe the role play closely and take careful notes. The class should *not* get involved in what the actors are saying, however.

5. Repeat steps 3 and 4 with the second pair of role players.

Role Sheets

Andy F., Machine Operator

You have worked at Acme Manufacturing for six years and have a good record. Because you do your job so well, you sometimes take liberties and horse around with your buddies. For example, one Friday afternoon you were caught dancing around the shop floor when a good song came on the radio, and Barry B., your supervisor, called you on the carpet for leaving your station. You think he has it in for you and is trying to run you off the job. Although you know you were acting silly, you are convinced it doesn't matter, because you were getting your job done. Now Barry B. has called you in to discuss the situation.

Barry B., Supervisor

After several years of experience in other shops, you were hired by Acme Manufacturing to be its new shop supervisor — a job you've had for only four months. Things have gone well during that time, but you've been having trouble with one machine operator, Andy F., who seems to do an acceptable job but is not giving it his all. Part of the problem is that he goofs around a lot. You have spoken to him about this informally a few times on the floor, but nothing seems to change. One Friday afternoon, you even caught him away from his station, dancing around the shop floor. Not only was he not doing his own job, he was distracting the other workers. You have just called Andy in to discuss the situation.

Questions for Discussion

1. Did the supervisor, Barry B., define the problem in a nonthreatening way?
2. Did each party listen to the other, or did each party shut the other out and merely explain his own side of the story?
3. Did Barry B. suggest specific things Andy F. could do to improve? Were the specific punishments associated with future bad acts spelled out explicitly?
4. Were the discussions impersonal in nature, or did they focus on each other's personality?
5. Considering all these questions, which supervisor (among the role players) did a better job of administering discipline? What could be done to improve the way each supervisor conducted the disciplinary meeting?

INDIVIDUAL DIFFERENCES: PERSONALITY AND ABILITIES

LEARNING OBJECTIVES

After reading this chapter, you will be able to

1. Define *personality,* and describe its role in the study of OB.

2. Distinguish between a test's *reliability* and its *validity.*

3. Identify the *big five dimensions of personality,* and explain how they relate to several aspects of OB.

4. Explain *positive and negative affectivity* and how they affect behavior in organizations.

5. Distinguish between *Type A* and *Type B behavior patterns* and how they influence behavior in organizations.

6. Describe the nature of *self-efficacy,* and explain how this differs from *self-monitoring.*

7. Describe *Machiavellianism* and the conditions under which individuals possessing high amounts of this trait tend to be most successful.

8. Explain *achievement motivation* (or *need for achievement*) and the performance differences between people showing high and low amounts of this characteristic.

9. Describe the difference between *morning* and *evening persons* and the relevance of this individual difference to on-the-job behavior.

10. Describe *practical intelligence, emotional intelligence,* and the roles each plays in career success relative to *cognitive intelligence.*

PREVIEW CASE

"Fast Eddie" Strikes Again!

It's hard to imagine a CEO being known affectionately as "Fast Eddie" by the employees of his multibillion dollar bank. Well, meet Edward E. Crutchfield, CEO of First Union Corp., the sixth-largest bank in the United States. Starting in the mid-1980s, Crutchfield revolutionized his bank through more than 70 acquisitions and by developing and implementing an entirely new concept for what a bank could — and, perhaps, should — be.

Dissatisfied with First Union's traditional, low-key approach to banking, Crutchfield developed a more proactive approach to seeking and satisfying customers known as "future bank." The idea is simple: Rather than simply waiting for customers, First Union should aggressively market their financial products and services and develop new ones to fend off growing competition from brokerage houses and mutual funds. Crutchfield did several things to help make future bank a reality. For example, he set up a huge call center that contacted new and existing customers about the bank's services. Then, rather than leave customers wandering around when they entered the bank, he introduced "greeters," who asked customers why they came to the bank and then directed them to the appropriate individuals (or to ATMs) for their transactions.

What kind of person is behind these initiatives? Crutchfield is a native southerner whose veneer of politeness and "folksy" sayings of-ten conceal his intense competitive spirit. Beneath his outward charm and relaxed style beats the heart of a real go-getter, someone who truly is driven to succeed. Signs of Crutchfield's special nature showed up early in his career as well. For example, when he graduated from college, Crutchfield did not simply accept a job at one of the three big banks that recruited him. Instead, he spent a day at each, and while there, he prowled the halls so he could measure the people with whom he eventually would compete for promotions. It appears he made a wise choice, because the person who hired him — Clifford Cameron — soon took over First Union and, liking what he saw in young Crutchfield, immediately began grooming him for the top position.

Shortly, however, a problem emerged: Crutchfield did not get along well with others. To counter this, Cameron assigned him to revamp the human resources department. The skills Crutchfield acquired in that position have served him well ever since. Today, for example, he runs his giant organization through a "town-hall" format: He spends half his time in meetings with employees, answering their questions and listening to their reactions, and though quite unusual for a top executive, is involved intimately in the bank's day-to-day operations — even to the point of personally approving new voice-mail systems.

Can a "sell, sell, sell!" approach really work in the formerly staid and traditional banking industry? So far, the results suggest Crutchfield's plan is right on target. In fact, First Union's earnings have risen to record high levels. Whatever tale the numbers eventually may tell, however, "Fast Eddie" will remain a unique character in the banking world — an industry in which his flexibility and openness to change continue to earn him his nickname.

Years ago, when the authors (and Eddie Crutchfield) were children, all banks looked very much the same: large, solid buildings with pillars, impressive doorways, and polished marble floors. In other words, they were designed to inspire confidence in their stability among the customers. Today, the situation is totally different. Banks can look like almost anything, and as our preview case illustrates, they are taking on many new initiatives. Few in the banking industry, however, have moved as aggressively to change the nature of banking as Edward Crutchfield. The practices and approaches he introduced at First Union have spread throughout the industry and now are being imitated by many other banks.

Many of Crutchfield's banking innovations are standard marketing practices today, but we cannot overlook that there's something special about Edward Crutchfield himself, something unique that allowed him to break free of the traditional, cast-in-stone image of banks. Many factors — everything from the Information Revolution to the increasing globalization of the world's economy — probably played a role. We believe, however, that part of the answer lies in two key aspects of Crutchfield's being: his *personality*, or the traits and characteristics that make him unique; and his *abilities*, or the tasks he can perform. In other words, it took a special kind of person with an unusual combination of personal traits to recognize the need for a new approach to banking and then to convert these ideas into a thriving reality — the "new" First Union Corp.

In short, we believe that what have been termed *individual differences* — that is, differences between individuals along a large number of dimensions — matter a great deal, and that these differences often play a key role in many aspects of OB, including career success. The remainder of this chapter provides evidence supporting this view — one that has a long history in the field of OB.

To provide an overview of what organizational researchers have learned about the nature and effect of individual differences, we define personality more precisely and examine its role in organizational behavior. Next, we consider several specific aspects of personality that have important effects on organizational processes. We then turn our attention to other aspects of individual differences — *abilities*, or the mental and physical capacities to perform various tasks — and the role of such abilities in work-related behavior. Finally, we examine various methods of measuring individual differences. These techniques are essential for comparing individuals regarding various traits or abilities and for using this information to make practical decisions, such as whom to hire for a specific job or whom to promote.

PERSONALITY: ITS BASIC NATURE AND KEY ISSUES

To set the stage, we undertake two key tasks: formally defining personally, and discussing the special role that personality plays in understanding behavior in organizations.

Defining Personality

If we learn any one thing from our experiences with other people, surely it is that they are all *unique* in some ways, and all, to a degree, *consistent* in their behavior. In other words, all human beings possess a distinct pattern of traits and characteristics that no other person fully duplicates, and many of these characteristics are quite stable over time. Thus, if you know someone who is optimistic, confident, and friendly today, chances are this person also showed these same traits in the past and will continue showing them in the future. Moreover, this individual probably also demonstrates such traits in many different situations. This person probably is optimistic, friendly, and confident when making a presentation at work or when meeting people for the first time in a local club.

Together, these two features form the basis for a useful working definition of **personality** — *the unique and relatively stable pattern of behaviors, thoughts, and emotions shown by individuals*.[1] Such stable patterns are important, because they help us to understand how people likely will behave in various situations. Whether we're talking about the best way to bring up a work-related problem to the boss or simply chatting with a friend about a football game, that other individual's personality is likely to affect not only how we approach him or her but also the general nature of the interaction (Figure 3.1).

> **personality**
> The unique and relatively stable pattern of behaviors, thoughts, and emotions shown by an individual.

The Role of Personality in Organizational Behavior

Ask one of your coworkers *why* Joe always makes the morning coffee for the office or Mary always comes to the rescue when the copy machine jams. As straightforward as these questions may appear, the answers probably are based on several important observations.

First, at the most basic level, you may note these individuals possess the appropriate *knowledge, abilities*, and *skills* to perform the tasks in question. In other words, they *know how to perform the task* (i.e., knowledge), they *possess the capacity to perform the task* (i.e., abilities), and they have *developed the capacity to perform those tasks well* (i.e., skills).[2] Joe and Mary *can* perform the tasks in question, because they *have* what it takes to do so.

Your answer to the question of why Joe and Mary actually do these things likely goes beyond the mere fact that they *can* and ventures into the possibility that they actually *want* to, thus leading you to say something like "That's the way they are," or "They're very kind and helpful people." Statements like these highlight your second observation: Joe and Mary possess the kinds of personality traits likely to lead them to perform the behaviors in question. Thus, at least part of your answer probably is based on the characteristics of the individuals in question—their knowledge, ability, skills, and personality.

To say, however, that people—be they Joe and Mary, or anyone else for that matter—behave as they do solely because of "who they are" (i.e., their knowledge, ability, skills, and personality) is misleading. Doing so ignores an important determinant of human behavior—the *situation* a person faces, or the *setting* in which that behavior occurs. This is especially important for managers, who are trained to create conditions that bring out the best in people. Not surprisingly, various situational variables are discussed in detail throughout this book. (For example, for the rewards people are given on the job, see chapters 2 and 4; for superiors' styles of leadership, see chapter 12; and for the way that organizations are designed and structured, see chapter 14.)

Interestingly, situational variables have become so popular that some social scientists now reject the notion of personality altogether, arguing instead that behavior is determined mainly by external conditions.[3] Still, most social scientists believe that stable personality traits *do* exist, and that these traits lead people to behave consistently over time as well as in different settings. In fact, most experts in the field of OB believe that *both* the person and the situation play roles in determining behavior in organizations. In other words, *behavior usually results both from the characteristics of an individual (i.e., his or her knowledge, abilities, skills, and personality) and the nature of the situation* (Figure 3.2). Known as the **interactionist perspective**, this approach is dominant among today's organizational scientists.

As an example of this approach, consider someone who is known to all his acquaintances as "a hothead," someone with "a very short fuse" who loses his temper frequently, even in response to fairly mild provocations. Now, imagine that one day, this person is questioned by his boss about some errors in his work. Will he "blow up" when the boss approaches him? Perhaps. More likely, however, he will restrain this tendency—at least somewhat—and behave more politely. After all, the cost of losing one's temper in this situation is obvious—and considerable!

Another implication of this approach is that some people may be better suited than others for certain jobs. This notion is referred to as **person-job fit**, which for-

interactionist perspective
The view that behavior results from a complex interplay between personality and situational factors.

person-job fit
The extent to which individuals possess the traits and competencies required for specific jobs.

FIGURE 3.1

Consistency: A Key Element of Personality

People tend to be consistent in how they approach others, both between situations and over time. Such consistency is an important element of *personality*.

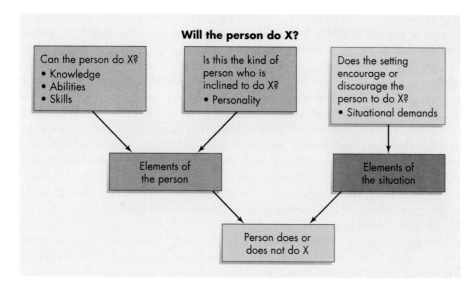

FIGURE 3.2

The Interactionist Perspective

According to the *interactionist perspective*, behavior usually is determined by a complex interplay between individual differences — in knowledge, abilities, skills, and personality — and a host of situational factors.

mally is defined as *the extent to which the traits and abilities of individuals match the requirements of the jobs they must perform.*[4] Indeed, much evidence indicates that the more closely individual's personality, traits, and abilities match those required by a given job, the more productive and satisfied he or she tends to be.[5] (For a more detailed discussion of career success, see chapter 6.)

How Do We Measure Personality?

Now that we know what personality is and the role that it plays in organizations, we can recognize the importance of tools to measure personality. As you might imagine, this is not so easy; however, scientists have developed good ways of systematicallyassessing people's personalities. We do not describe these techniques in detail, but getting a sense of how we measure personality traits before we discuss them is important.

Physical traits, such as height and weight, can be measured readily with simple tools. Various aspects of personality, however, cannot be assessed so easily. There are no rulers or thermometers that we can put to the task. How, then, can we quantify differences between individuals regarding their various personality characteristics? Several methods exist. In this section, we describe the two that are most important and then consider some of the essential requirements of all procedures for measuring individual differences.

Objective Tests: Indicating with Paper and Pencil Who We Are   Have you ever completed a questionnaire that asked you to indicate whether a set of statements is true or false about yourself, the extent to which you agree or disagree with various sentences, or which of a pair of named activities you prefer? If so, chances are good that you completed an **objective test**, which is a paper-and-pencil inventory that asks people to respond to a series of questions designed to measure one or more aspects of their personality. Objective tests are the most widely used method of measuring both personality and mental abilities (e.g., intelligence). (For some examples of objective tests of personality, see the "Experiencing Organizational Behavior" section at the end of this chapter.)

Answers to questions on objective tests are scored by means of special keys, and the score obtained by a specific person is then compared with those obtained by hundreds — or even thousands — of other people. In this way, an individual's relative standing on the trait or ability being measured can be determined. Scores then can be used

objective tests

Questionnaires and inventories designed to measure various aspects of personality.

to predict various aspects of behavior. These tests are considered to be "objective" in that they can be scored directly, simply by counting responses that fall into various categories and then comparing them with the scores of others.

Essential Requirements of Personality Tests   Imagine a tailor is measuring you for a new pair of pants and stretches a tape measure around your waist. Suppose, however, that it is not a very good tape measure, being made of elastic and stretching when used. As a result, each measurement yields a different value. One time, your waist measures 38 inches; another time, it measures only 30 inches. Assuming that your waist really has not changed on each occasion, the resulting measurements clearly are no good. Scientists would say these measures are not *reliable*, and if we are to have confidence in something that we measure—be it waists or personalities—we must be able to measure it reliably. The **reliability** of a measure refers to the extent to which it is stable and consistent over time.

As you might imagine, a measure of personality must have a high degree of reliability for any conclusions to be based on it. Scientists measure a test's reliability by subjecting it to rigorous statistical analyses (that lie beyond the scope of this book). These procedures result in a number reflecting the degree to which a test measures something consistently, both over time and from one part of the test to another. Only those tests with high degrees of reliability are used in scientific research in the field of OB—or at least, in the research reported in this book. After all, tests that do not yield reliable results may tell us little—or even worse, be misleading.

A test must be reliable, but this alone is not sufficient for scientists to consider it as being a useful source of information. After all, just because we can measure something reliably does not mean those measures are meaningful. For example, to measure your intelligence, suppose that we record the dimensions of your skull and then use this to estimate the size of your brain. Such measurements could be highly reliable— each time we took them, we would get very much the same physical readings. Would they actually tell us anything about your intelligence, however? Definitely not. The notion that brain size is directly linked to intelligence has been discredited through scientific research. The point is that in addition to being reliable, a test also must really measure whatever it claims to be measuring—that is, it must be *valid*. Scientists refer to a test's **validity** to describe the degree to which that test actually measures what it purports to measure.

Establishing the validity of any tests of personality we use is very important, but how do we go about doing so? Social scientists follow an arduous process that requires many systematic, empirical steps and uses many sophisticated statistical techniques. Sparing the details, validity is established by relating scores on the test to various aspects of behavior already assumed to reflect the trait being measured. Conceptually, a test of a personality trait is valid to the extent that what it measures closely relates to the "true" measure of that trait as measured by other established tests (Figure 3.3). For a test of a personality characteristic to be considered valid, scores on that test must be highly associated with scores on other tests purporting to measure that same characteristic.

Validity is especially important when measuring various aspects of personality and mental aptitudes. For example, if scores on an intelligence test closely relate to grades in school or scores on tests like the GMAT (the Graduate Management Aptitude Test, which many schools use in selecting MBA students), this provides some evidence of the test's validity. Although other means of establishing the validity of a test exist, this is the most straightforward and convincing.

Before concluding, we should note that all traits and abilities considered in this chapter are measured by tests that are known to be both reliable and valid. Thus, you can be confident the findings discussed do, in fact, relate to important aspects of personality—and to ones that have significant implications for various forms of OB.

reliability
The extent to which a test yields consistent scores on various occasions and to which all its items measure the same underlying construct.

Know the difference!

validity
The extent to which a test actually measures what it claims to measure.

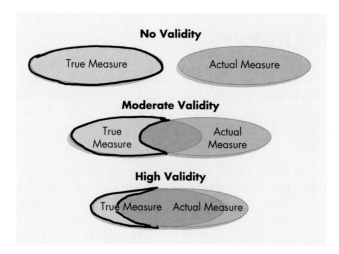

FIGURE 3.3

Validity: An Important Characteristic of Any Personality Test

For a personality test to yield useful information, it must be *valid*. A test of any characteristic is valid to the extent that what it measures is highly associated with a "true" measure of that same characteristic.

ETHICS MATTERS

Some managers have been known to administer personality tests whose reliability and validity have not been assessed carefully — or even tests that were faulty. They justify this practice by claiming no medical diagnoses are made and the tests are used only for initiating discussions and making people think about various aspects of their work. In your opinion, is this practice justifiable on ethical grounds? Why, or why not? ■

To conclude, then, personality is an important determinant of behavior in organizations, but along with several aspects of the environment, it is one of many factors that may be involved. Moreover, measuring personality presents several difficult challenges. Still, to understand behavior in organizations fully, it is important to recognize — and to acknowledge — differences in people's personalities. With this in mind, we now turn our attention to the important task of examining those aspects of personality that are most influential in OB.

YOU BE THE CONSULTANT

A large insurance company has been having difficulty attracting and retaining sales agents. On advice of consultants, personality tests have been used to identify individuals with the greatest potential for success in these jobs. Unfortunately, however, these tests have helped little.

1. Why do you think this may be so?
2. How might problems with the reliability and validity of these tests be involved?
3. What would the interactionist perspective suggest about the role of personality tests in predicting job success?
4. In view of these considerations, what steps may be taken to improve the situation?

WORK-RELATED ASPECTS OF PERSONALITY

Now that we have established the role of personality in OB, we examine those several aspects of personality that relate most closely to behavior in organizations.

The Big Five Dimensions of Personality: Our Most Fundamental Traits

How many different words can you think of that describe others' personalities? Would you believe *17,953*? That is the number of personality-related words found during a search of an English-language dictionary in a study conducted more than 60 years ago.[6] Even after combining words with similar meanings, the list still contained 171 distinct traits. Does this mean we must consider all these characteristics to understand fully the role of personality in OB?

Fortunately, a growing body of evidence points to only five key dimensions. Because these same five dimensions have emerged in so many different studies, which were conducted in so many different ways, they are often referred to as the **big five dimensions of personality**.[7] These are:

big five dimensions of personality
Five basic dimensions of personality assumed to underlie many specific traits.

- *Conscientiousness*: The extent to which individuals are hardworking, organized, dependable, and persevering versus lazy, disorganized, and unreliable.
- *Extraversion-Introversion*: The degree to which individuals are gregarious, assertive, and sociable versus reserved, timid, and quiet.
- *Agreeableness*: The extent to which individuals are cooperative, warm, and agreeable versus belligerent, cold, and disagreeable.
- *Emotional Stability*: The degree to which individuals are insecure, anxious, and depressed versus secure, calm, and happy.
- *Openness to Experience*: The extent to which individuals are creative, curious, and cultured versus practical and having narrow interests.

Scientists measure these personality dimensions as they do most others — using objective tests (described earlier) in which people answer various questions about themselves using paper and pencil. You can learn a great deal about a personality characteristic by examining some of the items used to measure it. Table 3.1 lists some sample items similar to those used to assess an individual's standing on each of the big five dimensions. (By completing these items, you stand to gain some insight into just where *you* stand regarding these important traits.)

GLOBAL MATTERS   People in many different cultures use the big five dimensions of personality when describing themselves.[8] What does this suggest about the universality of these dimensions? ■

How important are the big five dimensions of personality? Research suggests they are very important. One ambitious investigation reviewed many previous studies, involving tens of thousands of participants overall, that examined the relationship between standing on the big five dimensions and job performance.[9] Many different occupational groups (e.g., professionals, police, managers, salespersons, skilled laborers) were included, and several kinds of performance measures (e.g., ratings of an individual's performance by managers or others, performance during training programs, personnel records) were examined. In addition, participants came from several different countries within the European Economic Community. Despite these differences,

TABLE 3.1

The "Big Five" Dimensions of Personality
The items listed here are similar to ones used to measure each of the *big five dimensions of personality*. Answering them may give you some insight into key aspects of your personality.

Directions: Indicate the extent to which you agree or disagree with each item by entering a number in the space beside it. Enter 5 if you agree strongly with the item, 4 if you agree, 3 if you neither agree nor disagree, 2 if you disagree, and 1 if you disagree strongly.

Conscientiousness:
_____ I keep my room neat and clean.
_____ People generally find me to be extremely reliable.

Extraversion?
_____ I like lots of excitement in my life.
_____ I usually am very cheerful.

Agreeableness:
_____ I generally am quite courteous to other people.
_____ People never think I am cold and sly.

Emotional Stability:
_____ I often worry about things that are out of my control.
_____ I usually feel sad or "down."

Openness to Experience:
_____ I have a lot of curiosity.
_____ I enjoy the challenge of change.

Scoring: Add your scores for each item. Higher scores reflect greater degrees of the personality characteristic being measured.

---

however, the results were clear: High degrees of *conscientiousness* and *emotional stability* were associated with high degrees of performance across all occupational groups and all measures of performance (Figure 3.4). Other differences emerged as well. For example, as might be expected, individuals with high degrees of conscientiousness were less likely to be absent from the job than those with low degrees of this dimension, whereas the opposite was true among individuals with high degrees of extra-

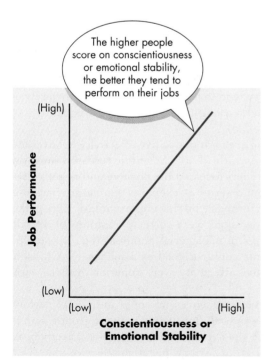

The higher people score on conscientiousness or emotional stability, the better they tend to perform on their jobs

Job Performance
(High)
(Low)

(Low) **Conscientiousness or Emotional Stability** (High)

FIGURE 3.4

The Impact of Two Key Personality Variables

Two of the *big five dimensions of personality* — *conscientiousness* and *emotional stability* — are positively associated with many different aspects of job performance among people in many occupational groups.

(*Source*: Based on suggestions by Salgado, 1997; see Note 9.)

version.[10] (Apparently, these people have so much fun away from work, they are more likely to miss a day now and then!)

Interestingly, the other personality dimensions also related to job performance, only in a more limited manner.[11] For example, openness to experience was strongly linked to success during job training. In addition, extraversion related to job performance among individuals who are required to interact with many other people during the course of the day and who, as a result, tend to confront situations in which being friendly and sociable comes in handy (e.g., managers and police officers). It is especially noteworthy that an individual's standing on several of the big five dimensions also related to the performance of teams to which he or she belonged. Specifically, the higher the average scores of team members on conscientiousness, agreeableness, extraversion, and emotional stability, the higher their teams performed (as rated by managers).[12] Overall, the big five dimensions of personality clearly are highly relevant to several important aspects of OB.

Positive and Negative Affectivity: Tendencies Toward Feeling Good or Bad

People's moods often fluctuate rapidly—and sometimes widely—during the course of a day. An e-mail message containing good news may leave us smiling, whereas an unpleasant conversation with a coworker may leave us feeling dejected. Such temporary feelings are known as *mood states*, and they are likely to affect anyone at any time. Mood states are only part of the total picture, however, when considering how we feel at work.

In addition to these rapidly changing reactions are more stable *traits*, which are consistent differences in the overall tendency to experience positive or negative feelings.[13] Some people tend to be "up" most of the time, whereas others tend to be more subdued or even depressed. These tendencies are apparent in a wide range of contexts, as well. In other words, people's moods—or what scientists call *affect*—are based on temporary conditions (i.e., mood states) that can influence anyone at any time and also on relatively stable differences in people's dispositions (i.e., personality traits).

Scientists are aware of these differences in people's predispositions toward positive and negative moods, and researchers consider them to be an important aspect of people's personalities. In fact, such differences relate to how people approach things in their lives—and on their jobs. Specifically, individuals with high degrees of **positive affectivity** tend to have an overall sense of well-being, see people and events in a positive light, and experience positive emotional states. In contrast, those individuals with high degrees of **negative affectivity** tend to hold negative views of themselves and others, interpret ambiguous situations in a negative manner, and frequently experience negative emotional states (Figure 3.5).[14]

When it comes to OB, do people who are high in positive affectivity behave differently than people who are high in negative affectivity? Scientific research suggests they do. For example, in one study, researchers assessed the positive and negative affectivity of people who also participated in a series of exercises simulating business decision making.[15] Several measures of performance on this important task were gathered, including accuracy (i.e., how often decisions were correct), rankings of overall performance by other students, and ratings of managerial potential (i.e., ratings by experts of the degree to which participants could succeed as a manager). On each measure, people with high levels of positive affectivity were superior to those with high levels of negative affectivity.

Research also indicates that affectivity influences not only individual performance but the performance of work teams as well. For example, work groups with a positive affective tone (i.e., those in which the average level of positive affectivity is high) function more effectively than work groups with a negative affective tone (i.e., those in which the average level of negative affectivity is high).[16] In sum, a growing

positive affectivity

The tendency to experience positive moods and feelings in many settings and under many different conditions.

negative affectivity

The tendency to experience negative moods in many settings and under many different conditions.

body of evidence suggests that stable tendencies to experience positive or negative moods at work have important implications, not only for the personal happiness and well-being of individuals but for their organizations as well.

The Type A Behavior Pattern: Being in a Hurry Can Be Costly to Your Health

Think about the people you know. Can you name one person who is always in a hurry, extremely competitive, and often irritable? Can you name one who shows the opposite pattern, someone who usually is relaxed, not very competitive, and easy-going? The people you have in mind represent the extremes on one key dimension of personality. The first person demonstrates the **Type A behavior pattern**; the second represents the **Type B behavior pattern**.[17] People who are classified as "Type A's" show high levels of competitiveness, irritability, and time urgency. In other words, they are always in a hurry. In contrast, people who are classified as "Type B's" show the opposite pattern; they are much more calm and laid back.

As you might guess, Type A's and Type B's tend to behave very differently on the job.[18] These differences fall into three categories: personal health, task performance, and relations with others.[19] Because we examine the effect of the Type A behavior pattern on health in connection with our discussion of stress in chapter 6, here we consider the Type A behavior pattern in connection with task performance and interpersonal relations.

Type A's and Task Performance   First, do Type A's and Type B's differ regarding job performance? Given their high level of competitiveness, it seems reasonable to expect that Type A's work harder than Type B's at various tasks—and as a result, perform at higher levels. In fact, however, the situation is more complex. Type A's *do* tend to work faster than Type B's on many tasks, even when no pressure or deadline is involved. Similarly, Type A's can get more done in the presence of distractions,[20] and they tend to seek more difficult and challenging work than Type B's.[21]

Type A's are not always superior to Type B's, however. Indeed, Type A's frequently perform poorly on certain kinds of tasks, including those requiring patience or careful judgment. They are simply in too much of a hurry to complete such work effectively.[22]

> **Type A behavior pattern**
> A pattern of behavior involving high levels of competitiveness, time urgency, and irritability.
>
> **Type B behavior pattern**
> A pattern of behavior characterized by a casual, laid-back style; the opposite of the Type A behavior pattern.

FIGURE 3.5

Positive and Negative Affectivity: An Important Personality Trait

Anyone might be happy or sad at any given time, but some people—those possessing the trait of *positive affectivity*—tend to see things in a generally positive way and to have an overall sense of well being. Other people—those possessing the trait of *negative affectivity*—tend to hold negative views of people and situations.

Consistent with this idea are surveys revealing that most top executives are Type B's rather than Type A's.[23] Several factors probably contribute to this pattern. First, Type A's simply may not last long enough to rise to the highest management levels. (As we see in chapter 6, the health risks of their "always-in-a-hurry" lifestyle are too great!) Second, the irritability or hostility Type A's often show may have negative effects on their careers, thus preventing them from rising to the top of their organizations. In fact, Type A's do appear to have very "short fuses"—that is, they often become angry and behave aggressively in situations that others may be inclined simply to ignore.[24] Finally, the impatience of Type A's often is incompatible with the deliberate, carefully considered decisions required from top-level managers (Figure 3.6).

A seemingly perfect example of a top executive who appears to be Type B is Jack Smith, the CEO of General Motors. Smith is described by those who know him as someone who remains calm in almost every situation and who rarely loses his temper. He certainly works hard to assure GM's success, but he is *not* in a hurry. He also does not like to make waves. In fact, outsiders even have criticized him for showing too much loyalty to subordinates, treating them with "velvet gloves" even when they fail at important tasks. Similarly, he has remained above the fray, refusing to take vigorous action to stop costly squabbling between GM's various divisions. Of course, Jack Smith also saved GM from what seemed like certain bankruptcy in the early 1990s, so his calm, "one-step-at-a-time" approach *can* work—and work well. Indeed, that most top executives appear to be Type B's suggests this kind of approach often may be more effective than the irritable, perfection-seeking, always-in-a-hurry style of Type A's.

GLOBAL MATTERS   In Asian and African cultures, the link between executive success and the calmer, Type B behavior pattern is even stronger than in Western cultures.[25] In those cultures, top executives are *supposed* to show a calm, cautious style—and they often do. What other personality variables do you think are likely to be different among executives from different cultures? ■

In summary, neither pattern—Type A or Type B—has the overall edge when it comes to task performance. Type A's may excel at tasks involving time pressure or solitary work, but Type B's have the advantage in tasks involving complex judgments

FIGURE 3.6

Type A's: Why They Often Don't Make It to the Top

Contrary to what you might expect, more top executives are *Type B's* than *Type A's*. The factors shown here indicate some of the key reasons why this is so.

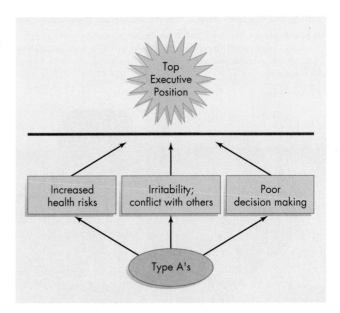

Handwritten margin notes:

Type A works better under pressure

Type B - more Advanced

Know bout crutchfield

and accuracy as opposed to speed. So, the question of whether Type A's or Type B's make more productive employees boils down to the issue of person-job fit; productivity is enhanced when people perform the "right" kind of jobs for them.

ETHICS MATTERS

Beyond selecting individuals for jobs that match their personalities, it should be possible—logically, at least—to achieve person-job fit by changing people's personalities to fit the jobs they already have. Can you think of when this might occur? Do you believe this practice is ethical? If so, why? If not, why not? ■

Type A's and Interpersonal Relations   A key aspect of success in many jobs involves getting along with others. Your intuition may suggest the more relaxed style of Type B's would make them better suited to those jobs in which interpersonal skills are important.

Indeed, research has confirmed this prediction. Because of their impatience and irritability, Type A's tend to annoy their coworkers. Moreover, they also are more likely to lose their tempers and to lash out at others. As a result, Type A's tend to have more conflicts than Type B's at work.[26] In fact, recent evidence suggests Type A's also may be more likely than Type B's to engage in various forms of aggressive and counterproductive behavior (e.g., saying negative things about one's coworkers and the company itself). This is an important form of behavior that we examine more closely in chapter 11.

In conclusion, Type A's often seem to be "cyclones of activity" and may move large volumes of work across their desks very quickly, but there is definitely a downside to this pattern—both for the Type A's themselves and for their coworkers and organizations.

Self-Efficacy: The "Can Do" Facet of Personality

Suppose two individuals are assigned the same task by their supervisor. One is confident of her ability to perform this task successfully, but the other has some serious doubts. Which person is more likely to succeed?

The first person may be said to be higher in a personality characteristic known as **self-efficacy**—that is, the belief in one's own capacity to execute courses of action required to reach specific levels of performance.[27] Simply put, self-efficacy refers to an individual's confidence in his or her capacity to perform a specific task.[28] Judgments of self-efficacy consist of three basic components:

self-efficacy
An individual's beliefs concerning his or her ability to perform specific tasks successfully.

1. *Magnitude*: The level at which an individual believes she or he can perform.
2. *Strength*: The person's confidence that she or he can perform at that level.
3. *Generality*: The extent to which self-efficacy in one situation or for one task extends to other situations and other tasks.[29]

When considered in the context of any given task, self-efficacy is not, strictly speaking, an aspect of personality.[30] People also seem, however, to acquire general expectations about their abilities to mobilize the motivation, cognitive resources, and strategies they need to control the events in their lives.[31] Such generalized beliefs about task-related capabilities are stable over time, and these beliefs can be viewed as an important aspect of personality.

How do beliefs about self-efficacy develop? Two major factors are involved: *direct experience*, or feedback from performing similar tasks in the past; and *vicarious experience*, or observations of others performing these tasks.[32] Based on information from these sources, people reach initial conclusions about the skills and abilities a task requires, whether they possess these skills and abilities, whether other factors or conditions may interfere with their performance, and so on. Together, these conclusions shape their current beliefs regarding self-efficacy. In turn, these beliefs then are adjusted in the light of new information, such as that from further experience with actually performing the task.

What are the effects of such generalized beliefs about one's self-efficacy? First, such judgments can strongly influence many critical aspects of OB. For example, people who expect to do well—that is, those who believe they "have what it takes"—often really *do* succeed. At the very least, they do better than individuals who are more skeptical about their ability to perform adequately.[33] After all, when we feel optimistic about our capacity to succeed, we are willing to intensify our efforts and to persist despite long odds and setbacks. When we feel we have little chance of success, however, we are unlikely to rise to the occasion—and often simply give up. Not surprisingly, people with higher levels of self-efficacy also tend to be happier with their work—and with their lives in general.[34]

Fortunately, generalized self-efficacy—unlike several other aspects of personality—can be changed. In other words, people who, based on life experiences, have reached the conclusion they are not very competent or effective can, in fact, learn to see themselves and their abilities in a more positive light under certain conditions. Furthermore, such changes can have dramatic effects on their lives.

To demonstrate this, one team of researchers helped to raise the self-efficacy of a group of unemployed Israeli vocational workers in two ways: by teaching them how to search for jobs more effectively (e.g., how to present their skills to prospective employers), and by sharing the success stories of others who found jobs.[35] (In other words, these workers received both the direct and the vicarious experiences discussed earlier.) This occurred as part of a series of intensive workshops conducted over 2.5 weeks in which the unemployed workers were given critical feedback designed to help them carefully hone their skills as job-seekers, thereby boosting beliefs about their capacities to succeed. Shortly thereafter, the workers' feelings of self-efficacy were boosted dramatically, and these feelings translated into success: People whose self-efficacy had been low before training developed higher self-efficacy during training—and these individuals were as successful in finding jobs as those who began with high levels of self-efficacy (Figure 3.7).

These findings are important for several reasons. From a scientific perspective, they suggest that a fundamental aspect of people's personality can be changed—and in a way that benefits their own well-being as well as society. From a practical perspective, they suggest that concrete steps can be taken to help unemployed people become re-employed. Systematic training in self-efficacy appears to help those individuals who suffer from low self-efficacy to take more control over their lives. In short, it helps them to help themselves.

FIGURE 3.7

Self-Efficacy and Job Loss

A person's sense of *self-efficacy* tends to suffer when he or she loses a job. When people are trained in job-searching skills, however, they find new jobs—and their self-efficacy beliefs rise as well.

During 1998, an economic crisis occurred in several Asian and European countries (e.g., Russia). Given that self-efficacy is influenced by life experience, do you think these events may affect the self-efficacy of people in these countries? If so, what effect, do you believe this may have on the economies of these regions? ■

GLOBAL MATTERS

Self-Monitoring: Self-Image Versus Private Reality

Imagine you are a first-level supervisor. Would you behave differently with your subordinates than you would with your boss, or with your boss' boss? Interestingly, different people are likely to answer this question very differently. Some people readily change their behavior to match each situation they encounter, and they strive to make the best possible impression on others. As a result, they adopt one style when dealing with subordinates and another—perhaps more respectful—style when dealing with their boss. In contrast, other individuals are less willing to change their personal style in this manner; with them, "what you see is what you get" across a wide range of contexts. Such people are unlikely to behave differently toward members of different groups with whom they interact.

This aspect of personality is known as *self-monitoring*, and it, too, has important implications for OB.[36] Formally, **self-monitoring** may be defined as the varying tendency for people to change how they behave to suit the situation in which they are acting. As this definition suggests, people who are high self-monitors may have a distinct edge in situations when making an impression on others is important (refer to the discussion of *impression management* in chapter 2). Because they will change their behavior to suit the situation, high self-monitors are inclined to do whatever it takes to generate positive reactions from others. As you might imagine, this can lead to important differences between high and low self-monitors regarding important factors such as task performance, career success, and relationships with others.

Just know the def-

self-monitoring
A personality trait involving the extent to which individuals adapt their behavior to specific situations, primarily to make the best possible impression on others.

Self-Monitoring and Work Performance If people differ regarding self-monitoring, do they also differ regarding how well they perform their jobs? Simply put, yes—at least for certain kind of jobs. Specifically, high self-monitors tend to do better than low self-monitors in jobs requiring what are known as *boundary-spanning* activities. These are tasks that involve communicating and interacting with people from contrasting professional or occupational groups (see chapter 8). For example, the chairperson of an academic department in your college or university may be seen as a boundary spanner, because he or she interacts with faculty members as well as with administrators and may be considered a member of both groups. Metaphorically, he or she "spans the boundary" between these groups.

Successful boundary spanners are required to adjust their actions to the norms, expectations, and styles of each group. Therefore, high self-monitors are particularly well-equipped to interact with both groups, and they tend to do so successfully.[37] Low self-monitors, in contrast, are more poorly equipped to perform boundary-spanning roles, and they generally are not as adept at handling them, either. Given how important boundary-spanning roles can be in most organizations, it makes sense to consider assigning people who are high in self-monitoring to such positions.

Self-Monitoring and Career Success Self-monitoring has an important effect on one's career success. Specifically, high self-monitors tend to obtain more promotions than low self-monitors, especially when these promotions involve movement from one company to another.[38] Why is this? One likely answer is that their greater willingness to adapt their behavior to the situation and to act in ways that please others helps them to get over the all-important first round of promotion contests.[39] High self-monitors seem to approach various situations by asking, "What kind of person does this situation require, and how can I best be that person?" Low self-monitors, however, seem to ask, "How can I best be *me* in this situation?" The result? High self-monitors make a better impression on others, thus gaining the edge in early promotions. Once they do, they are on the road to success, and their careers often prosper.

Another reason behind the success of many high self-monitors may be their ability to empathize with others—that is, to "walk in their shoes" or to "see the world through their eyes." For example, several observers attribute the outstanding success of Orit Gadiesh, who is the head of Bain & Co., a highly successful management consulting firm, to her tendency to engage in self-monitoring.[40] Ms. Gadiesh often is noticed first for her flamboyant personal style, marked in part by her multi-hued hairdo, but her ability to look at things from others' perspectives is what truly impresses her clients. Says James Morgan, CEO of Philip Morris USA, "Orit has that talent for making you feel you're the most important person in the room. She bleeds your blood." This high degree of empathy—a characteristic commonly found among high self-monitors—keeps her clients impressed and coming back for more. Interestingly, although Ms. Gadiesh is clearly unique, her high level of empathy is typical of a difference between women and men along this dimension: Women generally tend to be more empathic than men. (Because this issue is so interesting, we again discuss the potential value of empathy when we look at emotional intelligence later in this chapter.)

Interpersonal Relationships: The Potential Liability of Self-Monitoring   Before you conclude that being a high self-monitor is a true blessing for your working life, we must caution that this trait also has a downside. Namely, because high self-monitors are so changeable, they have been referred to as "social chameleons"—that is, people who risk being viewed as unreliable, inconsistent, or even manipulative.[41] Given such perceptions, high self-monitors not surprisingly tend to form less stable and more shallow personal relationships with others compared to low self-monitors.[42]

In addition, because high self-monitors tend to change their behavior across situations, they generally seek different friends for different settings. In contrast, low self-monitors remain much the same, and as a result, they form fewer—but deeper—relationships. In short, like most other dimensions of personality, self-monitoring has complex effects, and any assessment of the relative costs and benefits from being high or low on this dimension must account carefully for such complexity. For a summary of the positive and negative aspects of high self-monitoring, see Figure 3.8.

Machiavellianism: Using Others to Get Ahead

In 1513, the Italian philosopher Niccolo Machiavelli published a book entitled *The Prince*. In it, he outlined a ruthless strategy for seizing and holding political power.

FIGURE 3.8

High Self-Monitoring: A Mixed Bag

People who are high in *self-monitoring* behave in ways that are aimed at pleasing others. When these actions are perceived as being positive (e.g., a sign of empathy), these people tend to form close relationships with others and get promoted. When these same actions, however, are perceived negatively (e.g., being ingenuine), these people tend to form only shallow relationships with others and to be held back in their careers.

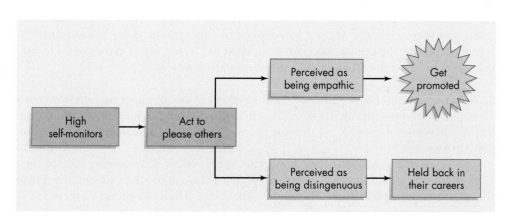

The essence of his approach was *expediency*: Do whatever is required to get ahead of another. Among the guiding principles he recommended were:

- Never show humility. Arrogance is far more effective when dealing with others.
- Morality and ethics are for the weak. Powerful people feel free to lie, cheat, and deceive whenever it suits their purpose.
- It is much better to be feared than to be loved.

In short, Machiavelli urged those who desired power to adopt an approach based solely on expediency or usefulness. Let others be swayed by friendship, loyalty, or beliefs about decency and fair play, he suggested, because a truly successful leader should always be above these things. He or she should be willing to do *whatever it takes to win*.

Clearly—and fortunately!—most people with whom we interact have not adopted Machiavelli's philosophy. As you probably have experienced, however, some do seem to embrace many of these principles. This led researchers to propose that acceptance of this ruthless creed involves yet another dimension of personality, one that is known—appropriately—as **Machiavellianism**.

Persons who are high on this dimension (i.e., high Machs) accept Machiavelli's suggestions and seek to manipulate others in a ruthless manner.[43] In contrast, persons who are low on this dimension (i.e., low Machs), reject this approach and *do* care about fair play, loyalty, and other principles that Machiavelli rejected. Machiavellianism is measured by means of a relatively brief questionnaire. Sample items similar to those used on the *Mach Scale* are shown in Table 3.2.

The Characteristics of High Machs   What are people who score high in the Machiavellianism scale like? Recent research suggests they are very much like those individuals described by psychologists as being *psychopaths*.[44] Such persons are glib and charming, lie easily, have no qualms about manipulating or conning others, have little remorse or guilt about harming others, are callous, and show little empathy. In addition, they also tend to be impulsive, irresponsible, and prone to feeling bored. If this description sounds to you like the "con artists" we often read about in the news, you are correct: Recent evidence suggests that persons scoring high in Machiavellianism show precisely these characteristics.[45]

Machiavellianism

A personality trait involving a willingness to manipulate others for one's own purposes.

TABLE 3.2

Measuring Machiavellianism

The items listed here are similar to those included in one of the most widely used measures of Machiavellianism.

Directions: In the space next to each item enter a number that characterizes your own feelings about that statement. If you disagree strongly, enter 1; if you disagree, enter 2; if you neither agree nor disagree, enter 3; if you agree, enter 4; if you strongly agree, enter 5.

_____ 1. The best way to handle people is telling them what they want to hear.

_____ 2. When you ask someone to do something for you, it is best to give the real reasons for wanting it rather than giving reasons that might carry more weight.

_____ 3. Anyone who completely trusts anyone else is asking for trouble.

_____ 4. It is hard to get ahead without cutting corners and bending the rules.

_____ 5. It is safest to assume that all people have a vicious streak—and that it will come out when given a chance.

_____ 6. It is never right to lie to someone else.

_____ 7. Most people are basically good and kind.

_____ 8. Most people work hard only when they are forced to do so.

Scoring: The more strongly you agree with items 1, 3, 4, 5, and 8 but disagree with items 2, 6, and 7, the more Machiavellian you tend to be.

Test questions About Percentages

Given that high Machs may be backstabbers, spotting such people is especially important on the job. What specific tactics are signs that someone is a high Mach? Among other things, high Machs may be expected to do the following:

1. Neglect to share important information (e.g., claiming to have "forgotten" to tell you about key meetings and assignments).

2. Find subtle ways of making you look bad to management (e.g., damning you with faint praise).

3. Fail to meet their obligations (e.g., not holding up their end on joint projects and thereby making you look bad).

4. Spread false rumors about you (e.g., making up things that embarrass you in front of others).

Machiavellianism and Success   If high Machs are willing to do whatever it takes to succeed, you might expect they would tend to be successful. This is not always the case, however. How well they do tends to be associated with two important factors: the kind of jobs they have, and the nature of the organizations in which they work.

For example, Machiavellianism is not closely related to success in jobs where people operate with a great deal of autonomy, such as a salesperson, marketing executive, and university professor. These employees have a great deal of freedom to act as they wish, thus giving them good opportunities to free themselves from a high Mach's clutches—or to avoid interacting with a high Mach altogether![46] For much the same reason, high Machs tend to be much more successful in organizations that are *loosely structured* (i.e., those with few established rules) than in organizations that are *tightly structured* (i.e., those with clear and explicit rules regarding expected behavior).[47] The reasoning is simple: When rules are vague and unclear, it is far easier for high Machs to "do their thing," whereas when rules are strict and binding, high Machs are far more limited in what they can do.

This raises an interesting question: How can we protect ourselves from high Machs? For some intriguing answers to this question, refer to the "Tips" section below.

TIPS: DOING IT RIGHT

■ Handling High Machs: Three Defensive Strategies

Because high Machs are quite merciless and seem to have little concern with anyone's welfare but their own, they can be potentially dangerous in organizational settings. Also, because they are attracted to situations in which they can use their devious skills, they can be tough adversaries. You cannot always restructure work situations to neutralize high Machs, but you can protect yourself from them. Here are a few methods that may be effective:

1. *Expose them to others.* One reason high Machs often get away with breaking promises, lying, and using "dirty tricks" is that their victims remain silent. This is hardly surprising, because few people wish to call attention to their having been cheated or manipulated. This understandable desire to protect one's ego, however, plays directly into the high Machs' hands, thus leaving them free to repeat such actions. One means of blocking them, therefore, is to make their actions public.[48] In other words, publicly confront them with their actions and the false statements they have made. The high Machs probably won't be able to back them up and, as a result, will lose face—and the potential to weave their evil web of deception and betrayal again.

(continued)

2. *Pay attention to what others do, not what they say.* High Machs often are masters of deception. They convince other people they have their interests at heart, and often are most persuasive when busily cutting the ground out from under their unsuspecting victims! How can you protect yourself against such tactics? It helps to focus on what others do rather than on what they say. If their actions suggest they are cold-bloodedly manipulating the people around them, disregard even fervent claims about any commitment to principles of loyalty and fair play; these are just camouflage to mislead you.

3. *Avoid situations that give high Machs an edge.* To assure their success, high Machs prefer to operate in situations where other people's emotions run high and the persons they wish to manipulate are unsure of how to proceed. High Machs realize that under such conditions, many people are distracted and less likely to recognize they are being manipulated. It usually is wise, therefore, to avoid such situations whenever you can. If this is not possible, at least refrain from making important decisions or commitments during such situations. Such restraint may make it harder for high Machs to use you for their own benefit.

Together, these suggestions may help you to avoid falling under the spell—and into the clutches—of unprincipled high Machs. Given the presence of at least some high Machs in most organizations and the dangers they pose to the unwary, these suggestions should be kept firmly in mind. ■

Achievement Motivation: The Quest for Excellence

Can you recall the person in your high school who was named "Most likely to succeed"? If so, you probably are thinking of someone who was truly competitive, an individual who wanted to win in every situation—or at least in the important ones. As you think about this question, you are acknowledging an important difference between people: the tendency for some to be more concerned than others about coming out on top and achieving success. Indeed, this key personality variable is known as **achievement motivation** (or **need for achievement**)—that is, the strength of an individual's desire to excel, to succeed at difficult tasks, and to do them better than others.

achievement motivation

The strength of an individual's desire to excel, to succeed at difficult tasks, and to do them better than others.

need for achievement

See *achievement motivation.*

Need for Achievement and Attraction to Difficult Tasks   Perhaps the most interesting distinguishing factors between people who are high and who are low in need for achievement involve their pattern of preferences for tasks of varying difficulty. These differences may have profound effects on managerial success as well.

Because high need achievers so strongly desire success, they tend to steer away from certain kinds of tasks, such as those that are very easy or very difficult. After all, especially simple tasks are not challenging enough to attract high need achievers, and especially difficult ones are certain to result in failure—an unacceptable outcome. Not surprisingly, high need achievers are most strongly attracted to moderately challenging tasks and, thereby, prefer tasks of intermediate difficulty.[49]

The opposite pattern occurs among people who are low in achievement motivation. These people much prefer very easy and very difficult tasks to ones that are moderately difficult. The reasoning is simple: People with low achievement motivation like to perform easy tasks, because success is virtually certain and, therefore, not threatening to how they perceive themselves. At the same time, because failure is certain on difficult tasks, it can be dismissed readily as not indicating anything unflattering about themselves. After all, anyone would fail on a difficult task. Because failure on a moderately difficult task, however, may be the basis for unflattering attributions about oneself (see chapter 2), low need achievers may shy away from them. (For a summary of these tendencies, see Figure 3.9.)

FIGURE 3.9

Achievement Motivation and Task Preference

People who are low in *need achievement* prefer tasks of low difficulty (because they are likely to succeed) and of high difficulty (because they may readily excuse their failures). People who are high in need achievement, however, prefer tasks of intermediate difficulty, because tasks that are too easy are not challenging enough to be desirable and tasks that are too difficult are certain to result in failure (which is unacceptable).

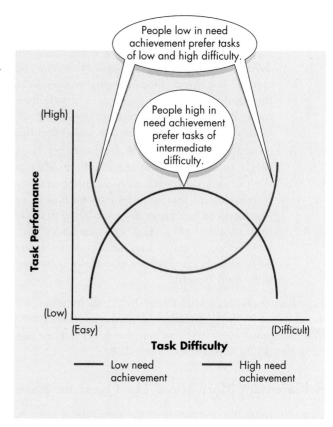

These differences between high and low need achievers are interesting by themselves. Their real value, however, becomes most evident when considering the role they play in success for managers.

Are High Need Achievers Successful Managers?   We have characterized people with high achievement motivation as having a highly task-oriented outlook. They are concerned with getting things done, which encourages them to work hard and to strive for success. Do these people always succeed, however, especially in managerial positions? As with so many other questions in the field of OB, the answer is not straightforward.

Given their strong desire to excel, you might expect people high in achievement motivation to attain greater success than others in their careers. This is true—to a limited extent. People who are high in achievement motivation tend to gain promotions more rapidly than those who are low in achievement motivation, at least early in their careers.[50] The interest in attaining success "jump starts" their careers, but as those careers progress, their unwillingness to tackle difficult challenges interferes with further success.

Moreover, these people tend to be so focused on their own success they sometimes refrain from delegating authority to others, thereby failing to give subordinates the tools they need to make the best possible decisions for their organization. Indeed, CEOs who are high in achievement motivation tend to keep organizational power concentrated in just a few people. (This is the concept of centralization of power, which we discuss in chapters 8, 11, and 14.) This fails to empower their team members as needed, which often proves to be an ineffective strategy for management.[51]

At the same time, people with high achievement motivation have an important characteristic going for them: They have a strong desire for feedback regarding their performance. In other words, because they so greatly want to succeed, they have a

ACHIEVEMENT MOTIVATION AND ECONOMIC GROWTH

A wide variety of factors — including, for example, the price and availability of natural resources, labor costs, and government policies — contribute to national differences in economic growth and development. These factors do not tell the whole story, however. Indeed, an important social factor also is involved as well; national differences in achievement motivation.

Although achievement motivation, strictly speaking, is a dimension of personality — and as such relates primarily to differences between individuals — considerable evidence suggests it also varies between different cultures. In addition, these differences relate to important economic variables.

This point was illustrated dramatically by a classic study in which researchers analyzed children's stories from 22 different cultures regarding themes of achievement motivation.[52] (For example, the story "The Little Engine That Could," which was read by millions of children in the United States, reflects a great deal of achievement motivation.) The investigators then related these levels of achievement motivation to key measures of economic development, such as per capita income and per capita electrical production. The findings were remarkable: The greater the emphasis placed on achievement in the children's stories of a given nation, the more rapid the economic growth in that nation as the children grew up!

These findings are not just a fluke; similar results have been found repeatedly.[53] For example, a massive study involving more than 12,000 participants in 41 different countries also confirmed the idea that national differences in achievement motivation can be quite real and relate to differences in economic growth.[54] Specifically, various attitudes toward work, such as competitiveness, were found to be different across countries, and those countries whose citizens were most competitive tended to be those with higher rates of economic growth.

How can this be so? How can achievement motivation, which is a characteristic of individuals, influence economic activity? Perhaps because economic trends reflect the actions of many individuals. So to the extent this is true it should not be surprising that factors such as achievement motivation might play a role in shaping the destiny of national economies. The economic whole, after all, is indeed the sum of its parts — and these "parts" consist of thinking, feeling, and behaving human beings!

---

strong interest in knowing how well they are doing so they can adjust their goals accordingly (see chapter 4). Not surprisingly, people who are high in need achievement strongly prefer merit-based pay systems (i.e., those in which pay is based on performance), because these systems recognize individual achievements. At the same time, they tend to dislike seniority-based pay systems (i.e., those in which pay is based on how long one has worked in the company), because these systems fail to recognize differences between people's job-based achievements — aside from merely staying on the job, that is.[55]

Our discussion thus far has focused on the success of individuals based on their achievement motivation. This prompts a larger-scale question: Does achievement motivation play a role in the economic fortunes of entire countries?

Morning Persons and Evening Persons: "Oh, How I Hate to Get Up in the . . ."

At present, approximately 20 percent of the total U.S. labor force work at night or on rotating shifts.[56] This figure has increased in recent years, and as more and more businesses choose to operate around the clock, this figure likely will continue its upward course.[57] Unfortunately, the health and well-being of many individuals suffer when they work at night, so this trend can be costly.[58] As you probably know from experience, however, some people thrive on "the graveyard shift" — and actually prefer it. (In fact, if you are up late at night reading this, you may well be one of them!)

The idea of individual differences in the times of day when people feel most alert and energetic is supported by evidence showing that such differences not only exist but are stable over time. Specifically, most people fall into one of two categories: **morning persons**, who feel most energetic early in the day; or **evening persons**, who feel most energetic at night.

morning persons
Individuals who feel most energetic and alert early in the day.

evening persons
Individuals who feel most energetic and alert late in the day.

Presumably, evening persons find the task of adapting to night work less stressful than morning persons and, consequently, do better work in such conditions. Consider one recent study involving a population with which most readers are familiar: college students. The students in this study were asked to keep diaries, in which they reported the times each day when they slept and when they studied.[59] Information also was obtained from university records concerning the students' class schedules and academic performance. In addition, all participants completed a brief questionnaire designed to measure the tendency to be a morning or an evening person.

The results revealed intriguing differences between participants who were classified as being high in the tendency to be a morning person or in the tendency to be an evening person. As you might expect, morning persons reported sleeping primarily at night and studying in the morning, whereas evening persons reported the opposite pattern. Similarly, class schedules for the two groups also differed: Morning persons tended to schedule their classes earlier in the day than evening persons. Perhaps most interesting of all, morning persons did better in their early classes than they did in their later ones, whereas the opposite was true for evening persons (Figure 3.10).

These findings—and those of many other studies—suggest that individual differences in preferences for various times of day are both real and are very important when it comes to job performance.[60] Ideally, only individuals who are at their best late in the day should be assigned to night work. The results of this policy might well be better performance, better health, and fewer accidents for employees, which are beneficial outcomes for them as well as for their organizations.

FIGURE 3.10

Time of Day and Academic Performance

In this study, students who felt most alert and energetic early in the day (i.e., *morning persons*) did better in early classes than in late classes. In contrast, students who felt most alert and energetic late in the day (i.e., *evening persons*) did better in late classes than in early classes.

(*Source*: Based on data from Guthrie, Ash, & Bandapudi, 1995; see note 56.)

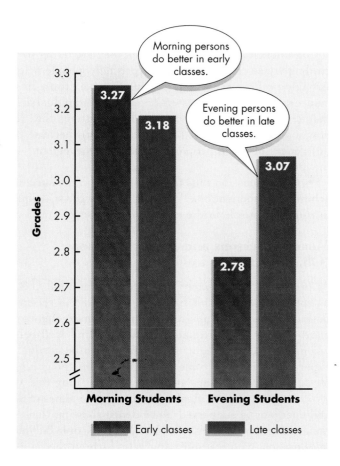

ABILITIES: HAVING WHAT IT TAKES

"We hold these truths to be self-evident, that all men [i.e., people] are created equal. . . ." This statement from the Declaration of Independence is a noble one and, indeed, one with which most of us are very familiar. We need to be careful, however, about interpreting this famous proclamation. It does *not* mean that all people are born with equal abilities to perform all tasks. It does mean that all people are endowed with equal rights to use the abilities we do have in a wide range of situations.

We all know from experience that human beings are definitely *not* created equal regarding various **abilities**—that is, the capacity to perform various tasks.[61] For example, no matter how hard we might have tried, neither author of this book could have succeeded as a professional basketball player. We are neither tall enough nor co-ordinated enough to succeed. We do have other abilities, however, including ones that some of the most famous athletes may not possess. Our point is simple: People not only have a very large number of abilities, but they differ widely in them. Despite the many abilities we may identify, these tend to fall into one of two different categories: *intellectual abilities*, which involve the capacity to perform various cognitive tasks; and *physical abilities*, which involve the capacity to perform various physical actions.

abilities
Mental and physical capacities to perform various tasks.

Intellectual Abilities: Cognitive, Practical, and Emotional Intelligence

Traditionally, when people speak about someone's "intelligence," they are referring to a specific form that psychologists call **cognitive intelligence**, which is the ability to understand complex ideas, to adapt effectively to the environment, to learn from experience, to engage in various forms of reasoning, and to overcome obstacles by careful thought.[62] People possess different amounts of this type of intelligence, and different jobs place different demands on people regarding to the amount of cognitive intelligence they need to succeed. Success in some jobs, such as top executive positions, requires high levels of *information processing*—that is, cognitive effort involving the combination, integration, and use of complex information. In contrast, other jobs are far less demanding of such abilities. They are largely routine, and they do not require careful thought or analysis of information.

cognitive intelligence
The ability to understand complex ideas, adapt effectively to the environment, learn from experience, engage in various forms of reasoning, and overcome obstacles by careful thought.

This approach to intelligence has been around for more than 100 years, but today's scientists see that it may be very limited. Instead, they recognize that intelligence is not simply a matter of "how much?" but also of "what kind?" It is widely acknowledged that intelligence is not a single, unitary ability; rather, it is a group of different abilities.[63] Several different forms of intelligence have been identified, but two have been linked most closely to various forms of behavior in organizations. One of these is *practical intelligence*, or what we commonly refer to as "street smarts." Like the young woman shown in Figure 3.11, people with high amounts of practical intelligence are adept at solving the problems of everyday life. Another form, *emotional intelligence*, refers to someone's abilities to be sensitive to people's emotions. As you might imagine, both forms of intelligence are important in OB, so we now describe them in more detail.

Practical Intelligence: "Doing Smarts" Let's begin with an example of practical intelligence in operation. The city of Tallahassee, Florida, provides trash containers to all residents. For many years, sanitation workers would retrieve containers of refuse from the citizens' backyards, bring them to the truck, empty them, and then return the containers to their original locations. This system continued until a newly

FIGURE 3.11

Practical Intelligence in Operation

The woman shown here has demonstrated a high level of practical intelligence: She managed to keep her job, whereas the others lost theirs!

(*Source*: © The New Yorker Collection 1996. Ed Fisher, from cartoonbank.com. All Rights Reserved.)

"Pam here is the winner of our 'How small a salary can I live on?' essay contest. The rest of you are fired."

practical intelligence

Adeptness at solving the practical problems of everyday life.

tacit knowledge

Knowledge about how to get things done.

hired employee realized the amount of work involved could be cut almost in half through one simple, ingenious change: After each trash can was emptied, it would be brought to the next yard instead of being returned to its original location. There, it would replace the full container that would be carried to the truck. Because all the trash cans were identical, it made no difference to each resident which can they received back; however, this simple step saved one entire trip to each backyard for the trash collectors. The employee who came up with this scheme appears to have a great deal of **practical intelligence**—that is, the ability to devise effective ways of getting things done. Growing evidence suggests that practical intelligence is, indeed, different from that measured by IQ tests, and that it is especially important in business settings.[64]

How, precisely, do people with high amounts of practical intelligence go about solving problems? The secret to their success appears to lie in **tacit knowledge**—that is, knowledge about how to get things done. In contrast with *formal academic knowledge*, which as you know often involves memorizing definitions, formulas, and other information, tacit knowledge is far more practical in nature. Specifically, tacit knowledge has three major characteristics:

1. *Tacit knowledge is action-oriented.* It involves knowledge about "knowing how" to do something as opposed to "knowing that" something is the case. For example, a locksmith may have a high amount of tacit knowledge about how locks are assembled. This same locksmith, however, may not know facts and figures about the lock company or the chemical composition of the alloys of which the lock is made.

2. *Tacit knowledge allows individuals to achieve goals they personally value.* As such, it is practically useful, focusing on knowledge that is relevant to them (a concern voiced by any student who ever complained about academic course content by saying, "This stuff is not relevant; I can't use it for anything in my life!").

3. *Tacit knowledge usually is acquired without direct help from others.* In fact, such knowledge often is acquired on one's own, largely because it often is unspoken. As such, people must recognize it—and its value—for themselves. For example, no one actually may tell an employee that getting help from a

more senior person will aid his or her career, but this person still may recognize this fact — and act on it.

In sum, growing evidence suggests there is more to intelligence than the verbal, mathematical, and reasoning abilities often associated with academic success. Practical intelligence also is important, and it contributes to success in many areas of life.

GLOBAL MATTERS

Cultures vary greatly regarding the amount of status they confer on individuals with high levels of "cognitive intelligence" — that is, the kind that produces high grades in school. Do you think these differences also might influence the level of practical intelligence in these cultures? If so, do you believe this in turn might affect their economies as well? ■

Emotional Intelligence: "Feeling Smarts"   All the aspects of intelligence considered thus far relate to what might be termed the *cognitive* side of intelligence, or the ability to process various forms of information. According to Daniel Goleman, however, there is another important kind of intelligence — one that he describes as **emotional intelligence** (or **EQ**),[65] which refers to a cluster of abilities relating to the emotional or "feeling" side of life. Specifically, emotional intelligence involves several major components:

emotional intelligence (EQ)
A cluster of skills relating to the emotional side of life (e.g., the ability to recognize and regulate our own emotions, to influence those of others, to self-motivate).

1. *The ability to recognize and regulate our own emotions.* People with a high EQ can recognize they may be growing angry but still manage to hold their tempers in check.

2. *The ability to recognize and influence other people's emotions.* Those with a high EQ can gauge the degree to which other people are interested in what they have to say — and can make others enthusiastic about their own ideas.

3. *Self-motivation.* Individuals with a high EQ can motivate themselves to work long and hard on various tasks and to resist the temptation to quit or give up.

4. *The ability to form effective long-term relationships with others.* Those with a high EQ can keep many different relationships going over long periods of time and often many life changes as well. As part of this, they tend to be proficient in skills such as co-ordinating efforts with people, negotiating solutions to complex interpersonal problems, and getting others to like as well as trust them.

Is emotional intelligence valuable in organizational settings? Growing evidence indicates it is. For example, several aspects of emotional intelligence (e.g., accuracy in "reading" others) highly relate to the financial success of entrepreneurs.[66] Likewise, scientists who are adept at accurately "reading others" and who, partly because of this ability, tend to be liked by their colleagues are more productive than scientists who are lower in this aspect of emotional intelligence. The highly liked scientists are included in informal e-mail networks and get the latest word on what is happening in their field. Their less emotionally intelligent associates are less liked and, as a result, tend to be cut out of such networks. In short, being high in various aspects of emotional intelligence can be an important "plus" in one's career (Figure 3.12).

Other Cognitive Abilities   Although various types of intelligence are important, they are not the only types of cognitive abilities that matter in OB. Several more specific aspects of cognitive functioning also relate to job performance. These include:

- *Perceptual speed*: The ability to recognize quickly similarities and differences in visual stimuli (e.g., a designer recognizing irregular patterns in a fabric).
- *Number aptitude*: The ability to work with numbers both quickly and accurately (e.g., an accountant spotting an error in a financial report).
- *Spatial visualization*: The ability to imagine how various objects look when rotated or moved in space (e.g., an architect planning a change in a building design).

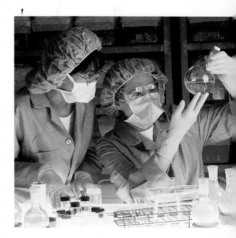

FIGURE 3.12

Emotional Intelligence: An Important Ability on the Job

Having a high amount of *emotional intelligence* (i.e., having a high *EQ*) is an important element of success for many jobs. Among other characteristics, individuals with high EQs are particularly adept at "reading others" accurately. As a result, they tend to be included in informal interactions with their colleagues, which often helps to further their own careers.

Obviously, matching people to jobs that best suit their abilities is essential. Air traffic controllers must have good perceptual speeds. Comptrollers must have good number aptitude. Engineers must be adept at spatial visualization. People who lack the basic abilities to perform their jobs usually recognize this early in their careers—if not on their own, then because others, often insensitively, point it out to them—and shift their careers toward jobs that better match the abilities they do have.

Physical Abilities

physical abilities

The capacity to engage in the physical tasks required to perform a job.

When we speak of **physical abilities**, we refer to the capacity to engage in the physical tasks required to perform a job.[67] Different jobs require different physical abilities, but several types are common to many jobs. These include:

- *Strength*: The capacity to exert physical force against various objects.
- *Flexibility*: The capacity to move one's body in an agile manner.
- *Stamina*: The capacity to endure physical activity for prolonged periods.
- *Speed*: The ability to move quickly.

If we considered all the jobs that people perform, we might be able to identify those that require primarily intellectual abilities and those that require primarily physical abilities. This exercise may not be as simple as it seems, however, and the results may be misleading. In fact, many jobs traditionally regarded as requiring more physical abilities than intellectual abilities actually call for a blend of both. Consider, for example, a bridge painter—someone who hangs from bridge trestles high above roadways and waterways while sanding the metal and applying fresh paint. This person may not need a high level of emotional intelligence to succeed, but he or she must possess other intellectual abilities, including high amounts of practical intelligence (e.g., how to navigate dangerous spans). In addition, unlike some executives—whose greatest physical exertion is walking from house to car to office—our bridge painter must have considerable physical skills to climb spans and carry equipment while maintaining his or her balance. The same is true for other professions as well. Professional football players, for example, need incredible physical prowess as well as several types of intellectual intelligence (e.g., perceptual speed) and emotional intelligence (e.g., to not say anything unprofessional about one's teammates, coaches, or opponents) (Figure 3.13).

FIGURE 3.13

Some Jobs Require Many Types of Intelligence and Many Different Abilities

What forms of intelligence and what specific abilities are required of these football players? As with many jobs, almost all forms of intelligence and ability are required to perform this job successfully.

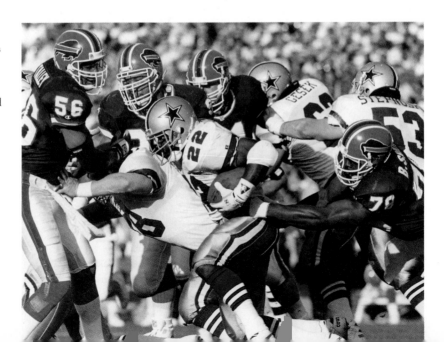

Although we have no difficulty recognizing the physical demands placed on football players, we should not ignore the physical demands in other jobs that might not be as obvious at first glance. For example, administrative assistants (and office workers of all types) often must sit in specific postures, enter text or numbers at a computer keyboard, and stoop over files for hours at a stretch. Considerable flexibility is needed for such jobs, but training in this important area only rarely is provided. Not surprisingly, engaging in such tasks for prolonged periods can affect a person's health adversely (especially when done improperly).[68] Thus, it is not surprising that more and more companies are introducing measures to promote the health and well-being of employees performing physical tasks. For a look at how one large organization is doing this, see the "Trends" section below.

■ Designing a Better Mailbag: Reducing Back Injuries Among Employees of the U.S. Postal Service

The sight of a letter carrier strolling down the street with a leather mailbag slung over her or his shoulder is familiar to many people.

In fact, the design of mailbags has not changed much in centuries. "Why should it?" you may be wondering.

Any mail carrier probably can answer this question for you. Sadly letter carriers throughout the world report these mailbags cause considerable discomfort. They are designed to carry heavy loads—a minimum of 35 pounds and often much more. In addition, because they rest on one shoulder, they also cause many muscle and back injuries.[69]

This led the U.S. Postal Service (USPS) to fund research on designing a better mailbag—one that is less likely to cause back strain and other injuries. With this in mind, the USPS compared two new-and-improved designs with the traditional mailbag.[70] One of the new designs involved having the mailbag supported at the waist by a belt. The other mailbag had two pouches and was supported by both shoulders. These three designs (i.e., the original design and the two new ones) were compared by measuring muscle fatigue among male volunteers both before and after using each mailbag for an hour.

The results were clear: All three bags produced some fatigue, but the standard bag produced significantly *more* fatigue than the other two designs. The conclusion? The standard mailbag can definitely be improved.

As a result, the USPS currently is considering a change to the improved designs. It seems likely that if this shift is made, the incidence of back strain and injuries among employees will drop dramatically. Whether the change is implemented, of course, is up to the USPS. We cannot resist the temptation, however, to point out that this is a compelling illustration of how careful research can inform company policy—and improve outcomes that are important to employees, including their job satisfaction, performance, and health. ■

We invite you to visit the Greenberg page on the Prentice Hall Web site at: **www.prenhall.com/greenberg** for the monthly Greenberg update and for this chapter's World Wide Web exercise.

SUMMARY AND REVIEW
OF LEARNING OBJECTIVES

1. **Define *personality*, and describe its role in the study of OB.**
   Personality is the unique and relatively stable pattern of behaviors, thoughts, and emotions shown by individuals. Along with abilities (i.e., the capacity to perform various tasks) and various situational factors, it determines behavior in organizations. This idea is reflected by **interactionist perspective**, which is widely accepted in the field of OB today.

2. **Distinguish between a test's *reliability* and its *validity*.**
   To be useful, any measure of individual differences must be **reliable** — that is, it must yield consistent measurements over time. In addition, all such tests must be **valid** — that is, they must, in fact, measure what they claim to measure.

3. **Identify the *big five dimensions of personality*, and explain how they relate to several aspects of OB.**
   The **big five dimensions of personality** — so named because they appear to be very basic aspects of personality — seem to play roles in the successful performance of many jobs. These dimensions are: *conscientiousness, extroversion-introversion, agreeableness, emotional stability*, and *openness to experience*. Two of these — conscientiousness and emotional stability — are good predictors of success in many different jobs. This is especially true under conditions in which job autonomy is high.

4. **Explain *positive and negative affectivity* and how they affect behavior in organizations.**
   Positive affectivity and **negative affectivity** refer to the stable tendencies of people to experience positive or negative moods at work, respectively. Compared with people scoring high in negative affectivity, those scoring high in positive affectivity tend to make higher-quality individual decisions and to be more willing to help others.

5. **Distinguish between *Type A* and *Type B behavior patterns* and how they influence behavior in organizations.**
   People showing the **Type A behavior pattern** are highly competitive, irritable, and always in a hurry. Such persons tend to perform better than those with the opposite pattern — **Type B** — on tasks requiring speed; however, they may perform less well than Type B's on tasks requiring considered judgment. Type A's experience more conflict with others and may become involved in more instances of workplace aggression. They also experience serious health problems more frequently than Type B's, and this may prevent them from reaching the top in many organizations.

6. **Describe the nature of *self-efficacy*, and explain how this differs from *self-monitoring*.**
   Individuals who believe they possess the capability to perform many different tasks are high in generalized **self-efficacy**, and they often achieve higher levels of performance than people who lack such confidence in their abilities. People who are high in **self-monitoring** are concerned with making good impressions on others, and they readily adapt their behavior to match the requirements of a given situation. In contrast, low self-monitors remain much the same person across many different contexts. Compared with low self-monitors, high self-monitors are more successful at getting promoted but sometimes are recognized as being unreliable.

7. **Describe *Machiavellianism* and the conditions under which individuals possessing high amounts of this trait tend to be most successful.**
   People who adopt a manipulative approach to their relations with others are described as being high in **Machiavellianism** (and are known as high Machs). They are not influenced by considerations of loyalty, friendship, or ethics.

Instead, they do whatever is needed to achieve their own way. High Machs tend to be most successful in situations where people cannot avoid them and in organizations with few established rules.

8. **Explain** *achievement motivation* (or *need for achievement*) **and the performance differences between people showing high and low amounts of this characteristic.**

    Achievement motivation (or **need for achievement**) refers to the strength of an individual's desire to excel, to succeed at difficult tasks, and to do them better than others. People with high achievement motivation tend to avoid tasks that are extremely simple (because these offer little challenge) and that are extremely difficult (because these are likely to result in failure). The opposite pattern occurs among those with low achievement motivation. People with high achievement motivation tend to be promoted rapidly at first, but their avoidance of challenging situations sometimes holds them back over the long run.

9. **Describe the difference between** *morning* **and** *evening persons* **and the relevance of this individual difference to on-the-job behavior.**

    Morning persons feel most energetic early in the day, whereas **evening persons** feel most energetic at night. People tend to do their best work during that portion of the day they prefer — and during which they feel most energetic.

10. **Describe** *practical intelligence, emotional intelligence,* **and the roles each plays in career success relative to** *cognitive intelligence.*

    Cognitive intelligence is the ability to understand complex ideas, to adapt effectively to the environment, to learn from experience, to engage in various forms of reasoning, and to overcome obstacles by careful thought. It is what we traditionally mean when we refer to intelligence. Other forms of intelligence have been recognized as well, however, and these play important roles in organizational functioning. These other forms include **practical intelligence**, which is the ability to devise effective ways of getting things done, and **emotional intelligence**, which is a cluster of abilities relating to the emotional (or "feeling") side of life.

QUESTIONS FOR DISCUSSION

1. Why might two individuals with very similar personalities behave differently in a given situation?

2. How does a close *person-job fit* contribute to good performance?

3. What is the difference between being in a good mood and having the characteristic of *positive affectivity*?

4. Suppose you were hiring someone to perform a job that required very fast performance. Would you prefer a *Type A* or a *Type B* person? Why?

5. How does having low *self-efficacy* interfere with task performance?

6. Why are persons high in self-monitoring so effective in *boundary-spanning* positions? Can you think of jobs in which they would *not* be so effective?

7. If you suspect that someone you are dealing with is high in *Machiavellianism*, how can you protect yourself from this person?

8. Can you think of cultures that induce a low level of *need for achievement* among the persons living in them? Are these cultures high or low in economic development?

9. Suppose you are a *morning person* — that is, you feel most alert and energetic early in the day. How can you make this characteristics a plus for your personal productivity?

10. Suppose you were hiring someone for a job in sales. Would you prefer someone high in *cognitive intelligence* or high in *emotional intelligence*? Why?

Bob Kierlin's Nuts-and-Bolts Approach to Business

If you bought stock in Fastenal a few years ago, you probably have done quite well. In fact, this company's profits have risen more than 38 percent per year in each of the past five years — far more than venerable, blue-chip companies such as Coca-Cola, Microsoft, and General Electric. Unlike these corporate icons, however, Fastenal's product line is, shall we say, a bit less glamorous. This company peddles nuts and bolts — 49,000 different kinds in all — from 620 stores, mostly in small towns across the United States and Canada.

The man behind Fastenal's success is CEO Bob Kierlin, a 58-year-old engineer who founded the company in 1967 along with four card-playing buddies. By age seven, while sweeping the floor in his father's auto-parts store, Kierlin knew he wanted to run a factory. Instead of dreaming about being a baseball player or going to college like other boys his age, the young Kierlin just wanted to make and sell things. So, after studying engineering, he ended up working at IBM. Big corporate life was not for him, however. All he wanted was to get back to his home in Winona, Minnesota — the riverside town where Fastenal remains to this day.

Winona is not exactly the kind of place you expect to find a company posting $25 billion in annual sales, but neither is Bob Kierlin the kind of individual you expect to be running such a large firm. If you're looking for any of the trappings of success, forget it; they're not to be found. Kierlin — or "BK" as he's affectionately called around the company — is known for his ultrathrifty ways. For example, when business recently required him to be in California, he didn't fly. Instead, he took the company minivan on the 5,000-mile round trip, stopping in inexpensive hotels and fast-food restaurants along the way. Not only wouldn't most top CEO's do that, they also wouldn't dress like BK, either, who always wears second-hand suits and short-sleeve shirts. Neither would they take only $120,000 in annual salary. As you might imagine, he is no more generous to his employees, who receive scant perks and no pension whatsoever.

So, what does Kierlin offer his employees? Responsibility — and lots of it. Unlike many other companies, where the path to the top is far steeper, salespeople are likely to become store managers after only three years. For example, the manager of the Hackensack, New Jersey, branch is only 24 years old, yet he, along with his even-younger assistant manager, have considerable opportunities to make decisions on everything for their local branch, ranging from the mundane (e.g., arranging to get used office furniture free in exchange for helping a friend move) to the more sophisticated (e.g., solving a thorny inventory distribution problem that was holding back sales). The reason why these managers work so hard to do well while saving the company money is simple: Half their compensation is based on bonus pay, so the better the company does, the better they do — and recently, all have done quite well.

Although remarkably laid back, Kierlin is always hard at work. Not resting on his laurels, he shows up at the office before 6:00 A.M. each morning and promptly gets down to work managing what he sees as the company's most important asset: its people. For example, if a new store takes in more than $5,000 on any day, Kierlin spots it on a printout and call that store's manager to offer his congratulations. In addition, while touring the country on business trips, he always stops by the local stores to see how everything is going.

Giving people responsibility, Kierlin emphasizes, is what business is really all about — not product lines or gross margins. People are the real "nuts and bolts" of the business to him. "Just believe in people, given them a chance to make decisions, take risks, and work hard," he urges, adding, "We could have made this work selling cabbages."

CRITICAL THINKING QUESTIONS

1. How do you think Bob Kierlin's personality has contributed to Fastenal's amazing growth in recent years? What specific personality variables seem to be important in this case?

2. Fastenal insiders say that Kierlin will never retire, but suppose he does. Do you think Fastenal would change? Would it remain largely the same type of company?

3. What role do you think emotional, practical, and intellectual intelligence have played in how Bob Kierlin has run his business?

Individual Differences: Personality and Abilities

SMALL BUSINESS 2000

If you have brothers or sisters, you know that even though you are related, you are different. Think about how you get along, deal with disagreements, and how much you are alike or different. Sometimes, you might wish that people were more alike—and perhaps even more like you. Think about that for a minute. Do you think others would be easier or harder to deal with if they all were like you?

Now imagine owning and running a business with your brothers and sisters. You may be frightened by the thought, but the Calise brothers do just that. They bought an existing business and have been running it together for more than 30 years. Interestingly, they bought the business from their father and their uncles. As the brothers tell it, the business was in bad shape when they bought it because their father and uncles didn't get along.

In a work setting, people need to be able to work together, but this does not mean they need to be friends. One thing that affects how well individuals work together is their personalities. The Calise brothers share a common goal: to run a successful whole-sale bakery that is recognized as one of the best in its industry. Even so, each has his own unique ideas about how to achieve this goal, has certain skills and limitations in working toward this goal, and probably has different knowledge to bring to the table. Before we focus our attention on how members of groups and teams work together, it is important to understand in-

dividuals. As you watch the Calise brothers talk about their business, think about what each brings to the table. Pay attention to what they have in common and to the differences among them. Try to understand what makes each of them tick and how they might satisfy their individual needs while making a contribution that benefits the company as a whole.

QUESTIONS FOR DISCUSSION

1. Mike, Joe, and Bob Calise talk a bit about the household they grew up in and the advice they received from their mother. How do you think this may have helped shape their personalities? What do you think they learned from their parents?

2. Pick one of the brothers, and discuss what you have learned about him. Focus specifically on the three types of intelligence you have learned about in this chapter.

3. You have learned about Machiavellianism in this chapter. What do you think would happen at the Calise Brothers Bakery if one of the brothers left the company and was replaced by somebody high in Machiavellianism?

4. Affectivity is presented as a way to understand an individual's personality. Do you think the Calise brothers possess positive or negative affectivity? Using examples from the video, build a case to support your answer.

SKILLS BANK

EXPERIENCING ORGANIZATIONAL BEHAVIOR

Measuring Your Own Self-Monitoring

As you read about the personality characteristic of self-monitoring, did you suspect you were high or low on this trait? In other words, can you be very different people in different situations? If so, you may be a high self-monitor. To see where you stand on this important dimension, complete and score the following questionnaire using the directions below.

Directions

Indicate whether each of the following statements is true (or mostly true) or false (or mostly false) about yourself. If a statement is true (or mostly true), enter the letter *T* in the blank space to the left. If a statement is false (or mostly false), enter the letter *F*.

_____ 1. It is difficult for me to imitate the actions of other people.

_____ 2. My behavior usually reflects my true feelings, attitude, or beliefs.

_____ 3. At parties and social gatherings, I always try to say and do things that others will like.

_____ 4. I can give a speech on almost any topic — even ones about which I know very little.

_____ 5. I would probably make a very poor actor.

_____ 6. Sometimes I put on a show to impress or entertain people.

_____ 7. I find it difficult to argue for ideas in which I do not believe.

_____ 8. In different situations and with different people, I often act in very different ways.

_____ 9. I would not change my attitudes or actions to please other people or to win their approval.

_____ 10. Sometimes other people think I am experiencing stronger emotions than I really am.

_____ 11. I am not especially good at making other people like me.

_____ 12. If I have a strong reason for doing so, I can look others in the eye and lie with a straight face.

_____ 13. I make up my own mind about movies, books, or music; I don't rely on the advice of friends in these respects.

_____ 14. At a party, I usually let others keep the jokes and stories going.

_____ 15. I am not always the person I seem to be.

Scoring

1. To obtain your score, give yourself one point for each of your answers that agrees with the following key: 1. F; 2. F; 3. T; 4. T; 5. F; 6. T; 7. F; 8. T; 9. F; 10. T; 11. F; 12. T; 13. F; 14. F; 15. T.

2. Add the number of items you answered according to the key (i.e., your total points).

3. If your total is eight or higher, you probably are high in self-monitoring. If your total is four or lower, you are relatively low on this dimension.

Questions for Discussion

1. How did you score? How did your score compare with others in your class?

2. Is being a high self-monitor always a "plus?" Are there situations in which being high on this trait might affect one's career or job performance negatively.

3. Would you prefer people who are high or low in self-monitoring for each of these positions?

   a. Salesperson

   b. Engineer

   c. Accountant

   d. Human resources manager

WORKING IN GROUPS

Machiavellianism in Action: The $10 Game

Because they are true pragmatists, people who are high in Machiavellianism (i.e., high Machs) often come out ahead when dealing with others. In other words, they tend to be willing to do or say whatever it takes to win or get their way. Several questionnaires exist for measuring Machiavellianism as a personality trait; however, tendencies in this direction can be observed in many face-to-face situations as well. This exercise offers one useful means for observing individual differences regarding Machiavellianism.

Directions

1. The class is divided into groups of three.
2. The three people in each group are handed a sheet with the following instructions:

    Imagine I have placed a stack of ten $1 bills on the table before you. This money will belong to *any two of you* who can decide how to divide it.

3. Groups are allowed 10 minutes to reach a decision on this task.
4. Each group is then asked whether they reached a decision, and if so, what it was. In each group, two people probably have, in fact, agreed on how to divide the money, thus leaving the third "out in the cold."

Questions for Discussion

1. How did the two-person groups form? Was there a particular person in each group who was largely responsible for creating the winning coalition?
2. Why was the third person left out of the agreement? What did this person say or do—or fail to say or do—that led to his or her being omitted from the two-person coalition that divided the money?
3. Do you think that actions in this situation relate to Machiavellianism? If so, how? In other words, what particular things did anyone do that you see as being an indicator of a high Mach?
4. How can people who are low in Machiavellianism protect themselves from being left "out in the cold" during such situations?

4

MOTIVATION IN ORGANIZATIONS

LEARNING OBJECTIVES

After reading this chapter, you should be able to

1. Define *motivation*, and explain its importance in the field of organizational behavior.
2. Describe *need hierarchy theory* and what it recommends about improving motivation in organizations.
3. Identify and explain the conditions through which *goal setting* can be used to improve job performance.
4. Describe *equity theory* and *procedural justice*, and explain how they may be applied to motivating people in organizations.
5. Describe *expectancy theory* and how it may be applied in organizations.
6. Distinguish between *job enlargement* and *job enrichment* as techniques for motivating employees.
7. Describe the *job characteristics model* and its implications for redesigning jobs to enhance motivation.

PREVIEW CASE

Information Technology with a Human Touch: The Magic Mix that Keeps Wal-Mart Going Strong

When Sam Walton died in 1992, some industry insiders doubted that the Wal-Mart chain he founded some 30 years earlier would retain its prominence as a discount retailer. Lost for good, they feared, would be the "magic spark" that Walton used to light fires under the chain's 720,000 employees. Wal-Mart stock also failed to enjoy the bull-market growth of many other companies during the mid-1990s, so the pundits appeared to be correct. Today, however, Wal-Mart has rebounded. Not only does it have stores in all 50 U.S. states and eight other countries, it leads the pack of discount stores with record earnings.

Many believe that one key to Wal-Mart's success is how it energizes its sales force. For example, employee meetings at Wal-Mart stores are the same pep rally–type affairs that Walton himself organized years ago. Cries of "Give me a W, give me an A, give me an L . . ." are led by store managers, who whip sales clerks into selling frenzies as they prepare for the day's onslaught of customers. Those clerks also know just what their customers want and how many are buying their merchandise. Just to make sure, however, the clerks are given thorough sales figures to show exactly how their particular store is doing. How much money did they take in compared with the previous day, or week, or year? What items are hot sellers, and what is their markup?

Representatives of the various departments proudly announce the answers, but not in the dry tone used at most business meetings. At Wal-Mart, they make it fun for everyone. For example, if you were a Wal-Mart employee in Pasadena, Texas, not too long ago, you could have won a package of Oreo cookies for correctly guessing the store sold 15,850 packages during the previous four weeks. Granted, the prize does more for the winner's waistline than for his or her net worth, but such events promote the camaraderie and sense of fun that define the working experience at Wal-Mart.

As you might imagine, the sales figures quoted come from the company's computers. What you probably never would imagine, however, is that Wal-Mart's information technology is so advanced that it provides up-to-the-minute detail on every sales figure throughout the chain. In fact, Wal-Mart spends some $500 million each year on the latest information technology, and it is second only to the U.S. government in the amount of information storage capacity at its disposal (a whopping 24 terabytes!). No other retail establishment even comes close.

This technology gives Wal-Mart employees complete information on the status of every item it sells. With the stroke of a simple, hand-held scanning wand over an item's bar code, a store manager can get detailed information about that item's past, present, and projected sales. (Did you know, for example, that Wal-Mart sells a Barbie doll every 20 seconds?) If a Wal-Mart employee finds a competing store advertising a lower price on any item that Wal-Mart also sells, his or her store manager can immediately match that price and send the new, lower price to all 2,400 Wal-Mart stores via the company's satellite system. The price reduction then is trumpeted on in-store bulletin boards.

Wal-Mart officials view this whiz-bang technology not only as a useful merchandising tool but as a high-tech counterpart to their other employee-energizing tactics, such as its decidedly low-tech pep rallies. Company officials contend that Wal-Mart employees, armed with information on how well they are doing, will be inspired to rise to the occasion to do their very best. If the company's recent $3 billion profit is any indication, this strategy seems to be working just fine, too.

Wal-Mart's success, which has earned it the status of being "the world's largest retailer," is certainly impressive. That it sells quality products at attractive prices certainly is central to this success, but the same also can be said of many other far less successful discount chains. What, then, makes Wal-Mart so special? One key ingredient appears to be how it acts toward its employees. After all, sales clerks at Wal-Mart are made to feel special by giving and receiving information about the products that they sell, and they are energized into becoming enthusiastic boosters of those products through in-store pep rallies. In addition, they receive up-to-the-minute information on the effectiveness of their promotional efforts. Put it all together, and you have the special managerial tactics that make Wal-Mart the retail titan it is today.

This raises some interesting questions, of course. Specifically, what about those pep rallies stimulates people into action? How does the feedback that sales clerks receive encourage them to work hard? And why does making the job both fun and interesting help so much? Combining these into one basic question that reflects the

FIGURE 4.1

How *not* to Motivate Employees

Surely, even the worst managers recognize that poor Mr. Pendleton will not be motivated to "keep up the good work" as requested. Unless they thoroughly understand the complexities of the motivation process, however, even the most well-meaning bosses risk stumbling into pitfalls that keep their own subordinates from doing their best.

(*Source*: © The New Yorker Collection 1992. Robert Mankoff from Cartoonbank.com. All Rights Reserved.)

"*Pendleton, as of noon today your services will no longer be required. Meanwhile, keep up the good work.*"

theme of this chapter, we may ask: How do you go about motivating people to work? Thus, with an eye toward answering this question, we examine the process of *motivation* in this chapter.

People in business may have many interesting ideas about how to motivate employees, but these ideas are not always effective (Figure 4.1). The approach of OB toward understanding, however, is based not on intuition but on science. This is not to say that we are interested only in research and theory—far from it! We also are extremely interested in what these efforts tells us about how to motivate people on the job. In other words, in keeping with the orientation of the field of OB, our approach is based on conducting and applying sound, scientific research to issues faced by managers in attempting to motivate their employees. With this in mind, we are interested in asking both theoretical questions (e.g., "*What* motivates people, and *why*?") as well as applied questions (e.g., "*How* can this knowledge be put to practical use?"). This dual focus will be apparent throughout this chapter.

The theories we consider here represent the major approaches to the topic of motivation as currently studied.[1] Our look at each major approach will focus on what that theory says, the research bearing on it, and its practical implications. This orientation should help you to develop a solid understanding about the importance of motivation as a topic of interest to organizational scientists and practitioners. Before turning to these theories and applications, however, we begin by taking a closer look at the concept of motivation itself.

MOTIVATION IN ORGANIZATIONS: ITS BASIC NATURE

motivation

The set of processes that arouse, direct, and maintain human behavior toward attaining some goal.

Motivation is a broad and complex concept, but organizational scientists agree on its basic characteristics.[2] We define **motivation** as *the set of processes that arouse, direct, and maintain human behavior toward attaining some goal.* The diagram in Figure 4.2 will guide our explanation as we elaborate on this definition.

Components of Motivation

The first part of our definition deals with *arousal*, which has to do with the drive or energy behind our actions. For example, people may be guided by their interest in making a good impression on others, in doing interesting work, in being successful at

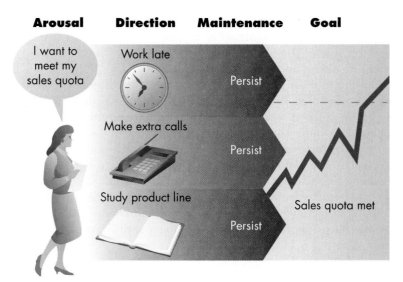

FIGURE 4.2

Motivation: Its Basic Components

Motivation involves the arousal, direction, and maintenance of behavior toward a goal.

what they do, and so on. Their interest in fulfilling these motives stimulates them to engage in behaviors that are designed to fulfill these motives.

What will people do to satisfy their motives, however? Motivation also is concerned with the choices that people make, with the *direction* their behavior takes. For example, employees who are interested in cultivating a favorable impression among their supervisors may do many different things, such as compliment their

WHAT MOTIVATES EASTERN EUROPEAN JOB RECRUITS?

OB AROUND THE WORLD

Eastern Europe is an area in which rapidly changing social and political environments have produced rocky economic conditions. To get this once-thriving region back on its feet requires knowing how to motivate people, especially young people seeking their first jobs. Specifically, what attracts young people to various jobs, and what gets them to perform these jobs well? A recent survey of 1,100 students graduating from business and engineering programs in Poland, the Czech Republic, and Hungary provides some insight.[3]

As you might imagine, money was important. Indeed, 43 percent indicated that they sought competitive salaries. This makes sense considering that the students live in a newly emerging market. Even more, some 52 percent, however, said that they wanted a working environment of people with whom they could enjoy socializing. Approximately one-fifth to one-quarter of the students surveyed indicated that they were motivated to

find jobs that would enhance their careers. Notably, they expressed interest in jobs that enabled them to specialize in their area of interest (26 percent), jobs that would serve as good references for their future careers (22 percent), and jobs that offered good training programs (21 percent). The opportunity to perform a wide variety of tasks was of interest to 20 percent. The exact numbers and statistics may vary from country to country, but the relative importance of the various factors appears to be remarkably consistent.

These findings illustrate two important points. First, many of the same things that motivate employees in one part of the world also motivate people in other parts of the world. Second, money is only one of several motivating factors — and not necessarily the most important one. The fact that money is not head-and-shoulders above all other factors, even in an emerging market where it is key to success, helps to make our point.

good work, do special favors, work extra hard on an important project, and the like. Each of these options may be recognized as a path toward meeting that employee's goal.

The final part of our definition deals with *maintaining* behavior. How long will people continue attempting to meet their goal? To give up before a goal is attained means not to satisfy the need that stimulated that very behavior in the first place. Obviously, people who do not persist at meeting their goals (e.g., salespeople who give up before reaching their quotas) cannot be called highly motivated.

To summarize, motivation requires all three components of goal-directed behavior: arousal, direction, and maintenance. An analogy may help to tie these components together: Imagine that you are driving down a road on your way home. The arousal part of motivation is like the energy created by the car's engine. The direction component is like the steering wheel, taking you along your chosen path. Finally, the maintenance aspect is the persistence that keeps you going until you arrive home — and reach your goal.

Three Key Points About Motivation

Now that we have defined motivation, we consider three important points that may change how you think about motivation on the job.

Motivation and Job Performance Are Not Synonymous   Rather, motivation is one of several possible determinants of job performance. Just because someone performs a task well does not mean that he or she is highly motivated. This person actually may be very skilled but not putting forth much effort at all. For example, if you are a mathematical genius, you may breeze through your calculus class without much effort. Someone who performs poorly, however, may be putting forth a great deal of effort but falls short of a desired goal because he or she lacks the skill to succeed. (If you ever tried to learn a new sport but just could not get the hang of it no matter how hard you tried, then you know what we mean.)

Motivation Is Multifaceted   People may have several different motives operating at once, and sometimes, these motives may conflict. For example, a word-processing operator might be motivated to please his or her boss by being as productive as possible. Being too productive, however, may antagonize coworkers, who fear being made to look bad. The result is that these two motives may pull the individual in different directions, and the one that wins is the one that is strongest in that situation. Clearly, motivation is a complex and important concept in the field of OB.

People Are Motivated by More than Just Money   Surveys show that most Americans would continue to work even if they did not need the money.[4] Of course, money is important to people, but they are motivated to attain many other goals on the job as well. Because of technological advances that took the drudgery out of many jobs, today's workers are motivated by the prospect of performing interesting and challenging — not just well-paying — jobs (Figure 4.3). They also seek jobs that actively involve them in the success of the business and that reward them for this success (e.g., through stock ownership, bonuses, and so on). The field of OB considers a wide variety of factors that motivate people on the job, and our discussion of the various theories will highlight these variables. (For a look at some of the factors that motivate workers in one developing part of the world, see "OB Around the World" in this chapter.)

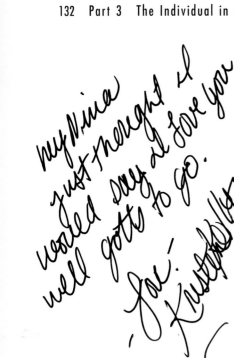

FIGURE 4.3

Work: An Important Source of Life Fulfillment

John Jarrell, of Westerville, Ohio, won millions of dollars in a national lottery but kept his job at a machine shop. The reason why, he explains, is that the job — and the people with whom he works — are an important part of his life.

MOTIVATING BY MEETING NEEDS

Thus far, our discussion has indicated that a wide variety of factors are responsible for motivating people on the job. However, we have not yet explained exactly how these factors work in conjunction with each other.

The theories we examine here explain motivation in terms of satisfying basic human needs. Indeed, organizational scholars have paid great attention to the idea that people are motivated to use their jobs as mechanisms for satisfying their needs. We will describe two such theories: Maslow's *need hierarchy theory*, and Alderfer's *ERG theory*.

Maslow's Need Hierarchy Theory

Probably the best-known conceptualization of human needs in organizations was proposed by Abraham Maslow.[5] Maslow was a clinical psychologist who introduced a theory of personal adjustment, the **need hierarchy theory**, based on his observations of patients throughout the years. His premise was that if people grow up in an environment where their needs are not met, they will be unlikely to function as healthy, well-adjusted individuals. Much of the popularity of Maslow's approach is based on applying the same idea to organizations. In other words, unless people get their needs met on the job they will not function as effectively as possible.

Specifically, Maslow theorized that people have five types of needs and that these are activated in a *hierarchical* manner. Thus, the needs are aroused in a specific order, from lowest to highest, and the lowest-order need must be fulfilled before the next-higher-order need is triggered, and so on. The five major categories of needs are listed on the left side of Figure 4.4; please refer to this diagram as a summary of the needs as we describe them here.

need hierarchy theory

Maslow's theory specifying there are five human needs (physiological, safety, social, esteem, and self-actualization) that are arranged so that lower-level, more basic needs must be satisfied before higher-level needs become activated.

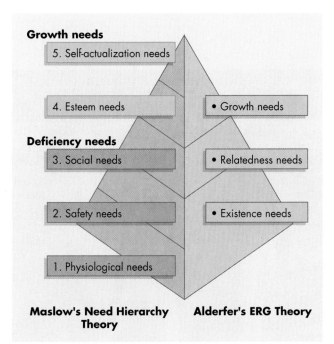

Growth needs
5. Self-actualization needs
4. Esteem needs

Deficiency needs
3. Social needs
2. Safety needs
1. Physiological needs

• Growth needs
• Relatedness needs
• Existence needs

Maslow's Need Hierarchy Theory   **Alderfer's ERG Theory**

FIGURE 4.4

Need Theories: A Comparison
The five needs identified by Maslow's *need hierarchy theory* (*left*) correspond with the three needs of Alderfer's *ERG theory* (*right*). Whereas Maslow's theory specifies that these needs are activated in order from lowest level to highest level, Alderfer's theory specifies that needs can be activated in any order.

physiological needs

The lowest-order, most basic needs in Maslow's *need hierarchy theory*, including fundamental biological drives such as the need for food, air, water, and shelter.

Physiological Needs   At the bottom of the hierarchy are **physiological needs**. These are the lowest-order, most basic needs specified by Maslow, and they refer to satisfying fundamental biological drives (e.g., the need for food, air, water, and shelter). To satisfy such needs, organizations must provide employees with a salary that affords them adequate living conditions. Similarly, sufficient opportunities to rest (e.g., coffee breaks) and to engage in physical activity (e.g., fitness and exercise facilities) also are important for people to meet these needs. With increasing frequency, companies are now providing exercise and physical fitness programs for their employees to help them stay healthy (Figure 4.5).[6] The rationale is simple: People who are too hungry or too ill to work can hardly make much of a contribution to their companies.

ETHICS MATTERS

Sadly, millions go hungry because they don't get enough nutritious food in their diets. Targeting this problem, volunteer chefs have launched *Operation Frontline* to teach people with limited incomes how to budget and plan meals to provide maximum nutritional value with minimum expense.[7] By learning cooking skills, ways of stretching grocery budgets, and ideas for making inexpensive but nutritious recipes, participants in *Operation Frontline* come away knowing how to improve their diets — and from this, their health. By satisfying this physiological need, these people are put on the path to becoming productive, employable members of society as well. ∎

safety needs

In Maslow's *need hierarchy theory*, the need for a secure environment, free from threats of physical or psychological harm.

Safety Needs   The second level of need in Maslow's hierarchy, **safety needs**, are activated after the physiological needs are met. Safety needs refer to the need for a secure environment that is free from threats of physical or psychological harm. Organizations can do many things to help satisfy safety needs. For example, they may provide employees with safety equipment (e.g., hard hats and goggles), life and health insurance, and security forces (e.g., police and fire protection). Similarly, jobs that provide tenure (e.g., teaching) and no-layoff agreements provide a psychological security blanket that helps to satisfy safety needs. All these practices enable people to do their jobs without fear of harm and in a safe and secure atmosphere.

FIGURE 4.5

Exercise: One Route to Satisfying People's Physiological Needs

At its 74-acre corporate campus in Beaverton, Oregon, Nike provides a wide array of fitness facilities to satisfy their employees' physiological needs (by keeping them healthy) as well as their social needs (by keeping them interacting with each other in a friendly manner).

Social Needs Maslow's third level of need, **social needs**, are activated after the safety needs are met. Social needs refer to the need to be affiliative (e.g., to have friends, to be loved and accepted by other people). To help meet the social needs of employees, organizations may encourage participation in social events (e.g., office picnics or parties). Company bowling or softball leagues as well as country club memberships also provide good opportunities for meeting social needs. Not only do such activities help to promote physical fitness—helping to satisfy physiological needs, as noted earlier—but they also give employees a chance to socialize and to develop friendships.

As a group, physiological needs, safety needs, and social needs are known as **deficiency needs**. Maslow's idea was that if these needs are not met, an individual will not develop into a healthy person, both physically and psychologically. In contrast, the two highest-order needs, the ones at the very top of the hierarchy, are known as **growth needs**. Gratification of these needs is said to help a person to grow and to develop to his or her fullest potential.

Esteem Needs The fourth level of need, **esteem needs**, are a person's need to develop self-respect and to gain the approval of others. The desire to achieve success, have prestige, and be recognized by others falls into this category. Companies do many things to satisfy their employees' esteem needs. For example, they may have awards banquets to recognize distinguished achievements. Giving monetary bonuses—even small ones—in recognition of employees' suggestions for improvement also helps to promote their esteem. Nonmonetary awards (e.g., trophies and plaques) provide reminders of an employee's important contributions as well and continuously fulfill esteem needs.[8] Including articles in company newsletters that describe an employee's success, giving keys to the executive washroom, assigning private parking spaces, and posting signs identifying the "employee of the month" also are examples of things that can satisfy esteem needs.

Self-Actualization Needs At top of Maslow's hierarchy is a need that is aroused only after all the lower-order needs are met—the need for **self-actualization**. This refers to the need to become all that one can be, to develop one's fullest potential. By working at their maximum creative potential, self-actualized employees can be extremely valuable assets to their organizations. Individuals who have self-actualized are working at their peak, and they represent the most effective use of an organization's human resources.

Research has supported Maslow's distinction between deficiency needs and growth needs. Unfortunately, however, research also has shown that not all people can satisfy their higher-order needs on the job. For example, Porter found that whereas lower-level managers could satisfy only their deficiency needs on the job, higher-level managers could satisfy both their deficiency and their growth needs.[9] In general, Maslow's theory has not received a great deal of support regarding the specific notions it proposes—namely, the exact needs that exist and the order in which they are activated.[10] Many researchers have failed to confirm that only five basic categories of need exist and that these needs are activated in the exact order specified by Maslow.

social needs

In Maslow's *need hierarchy theory*, the need to be affiliative—that is, to have friends and to be loved and accepted by other people.

deficiency needs

The group of physiological needs, safety needs, and social needs in Maslow's *need hierarchy theory*. If these needs go unmet, people will fail to develop in a healthy fashion.

growth needs

In Maslow's *need hierarchy theory*, esteem needs and the need for self-actualization condensed as a group. Gratification of these needs helps a person to reach his or her full potential.

esteem needs

In Maslow's *need hierarchy theory*, the need to develop self-respect and to gain the approval of others.

self-actualization

In Maslow's *need hierarchy theory*, the need to discover who we are and to develop ourselves to our fullest potential.

GLOBAL MATTERS

Do you think that Maslow's theory, which was developed by studying Americans, would have been different if he had examined people from different nations? On what do you base these beliefs? ■

Alderfer's ERG Theory

ERG theory

An alternative to Maslow's need hierarchy theory proposed by Alderfer that asserts there are three basic human needs: existence, relatedness, and growth.

In response to the criticisms of Maslow's theory, an alternative formulation has been proposed by Alderfer.[11] Known as **ERG theory**, his approach is much simpler. Alderfer specifies only three types of needs instead of five, but he also holds these are not necessarily activated in any specific order. In fact, Alderfer postulates that any need may be activated at any time. The three needs as specified by ERG theory are the needs for *existence*, *relatedness*, and *growth*. *Existence* needs correspond to Maslow's physiological and safety needs. *Relatedness* needs correspond to Maslow's social needs, *growth* needs correspond to Maslow's esteem and self-actualization needs. A summary of Alderfer's ERG theory is shown on the right side of Figure 4.4 (along with the corresponding needs as proposed by Maslow).

Clearly, ERG theory is much less restrictive than need hierarchy theory. The advantage is that ERG theory fits better with research evidence suggesting that although basic needs exist, they are not exactly as specified by Maslow.[12] The two need theories do not agree completely about the precise number of needs and the relationships between them, but they do agree that satisfying human needs is an important part of motivating behavior on the job.

Managerial Applications of Need Theories

Probably the greatest value of need theories is their practical implications for management. In particular, these theories are important because they suggest specific ways managers can help their subordinates to become self-actualized. Self-actualized employees are likely to work at their maximum creative potential, so it makes sense to help people attain this state by helping them to meet their needs. Therefore, with this in mind, it is worthwhile to consider what organizations may do to help satisfy their employees' needs.

Promote a Healthy Workforce   Some companies help to satisfy their employees' physiological needs by providing incentives to stay healthy. For example, Hershey Foods Corporation and Southern California Edison Company, among others, give insurance rebates to employees with healthy lifestyles and charge extra premiums to employees whose habits (e.g., smoking) put them at greater risk for health problems.[13] To the extent these incentives encourage employees to adopt healthier lifestyles, the likelihood of satisfying their physiological needs is increased.[14]

Companies also are interested in promoting their employees' mental health as well. Visits to psychotherapists can be very expensive, however, and mental health professionals are not always available in remote locations. To meet this need, the psychological services company Wilson Banwell, which is based in Vancouver, British Columbia, Canada, provides a World Wide Web–based counseling service, PROACT.[15] For a fee to subscribing companies, Wilson Banwell provides live, on-line "cybertherapy" sessions with one of 68 staff psychologists. It may not be the same as face-to-face therapy, but patients generally like the service and their employers welcome the unique opportunities it affords.

Provide Financial Security   Financial security is an important type of safety need, and some companies are going beyond the more traditional forms of payroll savings and profit-sharing plans. Notably, Com-Corp Industries, which is an auto-parts manufacturer based in Cleveland, Ohio, found that its employees had serious financial difficulties when faced with sending children to college — leading the company to offer employees very low interest loans (only three percent annually for 10 years) for this purpose.[16]

outplacement services

Assistance in finding new jobs that companies provide to employees they lay off.

Financial security is a key aspect of job security, particularly in troubled economic times. To help soften the blow of layoffs, more and more organizations are providing **outplacement services** — that is, assistance with securing new employment. In the most extensive of such programs, AT&T and Wang have provided extensive career counseling and job-search assistance to its laid-off employees.[17] It certainly is more desirable not to be laid off at all, but knowing that such assistance is available, if needed, helps to reduce the negative emotional aspects of job insecurity.

It certainly is kind and pleasant of companies to make outplacement services available, but it also may be argued it is unethical to do so because such programs come at great financial cost and thereby weaken stockholders' investments. How do you feel about this argument? ■

Provide Opportunities to Socialize   To help satisfy its employees' social needs, IBM holds a "Family Day" picnic each spring near its Armonk, New York, headquarters.[18] Some other companies also have incorporated social activities deep into the fabric of their cultures. For example, Odetics, Inc., the Anaheim, California, manufacturer of intelligent machine systems, not only has its own repertory theater troupe but also regular "theme" days (e.g., a "sock hop" in the company's cafeteria) and a standing "fun committee," which has organized events such as a lunch-hour "employee Olympics," complete with goofy games.[19]

Recognize Employees' Accomplishments   Recognizing employees accomplishments is an important way to satisfy their esteem needs (Figure 4.6). In this connection, GTE Data Services of Temple Terrace, Florida, gives awards to employees who develop ways of improving customer satisfaction or business performance.[20] The big award is a four-day, first-class vacation as well as $500, a plaque, and recognition in the company magazine. Not all such awards are equally extravagant, however. Companies such as American Airlines, Shell Oil, Campbell Soup Company, AT&T, and each of the big-three automakers (i.e., General Motors, Ford, and Chrysler) all offer relatively small nonmonetary gifts (e.g., dinner certificates, VCRs, and computers) to employees in recognition of their accomplishments.[21]

Whatever form they take, awards enhance esteem only when they are clearly linked to desired behaviors. Awards that are too general (e.g., a trophy for "best attitude") may not only fail to satisfy esteem needs but also minimize the impact of awards that truly are deserved. (Several of today's companies, however, have recognized that one particular reward—time off the job—can be valuable for all employees, because it helps to satisfy a variety of different needs. For a closer look at this practice, see the "Trends" box on page 138.)

FIGURE 4.6

Recognizing Meritorious Service: An Effective Way to Satisfy Esteem Needs

After working for 41 years at Draper Labs in Cambridge, Massachusetts, Norm Sears was recognized for a career of outstanding service. The awards given to employees at company banquets typically have little monetary value, but they go a long way toward satisfying esteem needs.

TRENDS:
WHAT TODAY'S
COMPANIES ARE DOING

■ Time Off for Good Behavior

In addition to satisfying employees' needs on the job, many companies have been satisfying employees' needs by giving them time *off* their jobs. This may take the form of vacations or leaves of absence known as *sabbaticals*.

Once reserved for teachers, who were recognized to derive professional benefit from being given time off to update their skills and to develop new ones, sabbaticals have found their way into growing numbers of private companies, including giants such as American Express, DuPont, McDonald's, and Xerox.[22] In fact, it has been estimated that various types of corporate leave are being offered by 14 to 24 percent of U.S. companies today. The idea behind sabbaticals is that they help to satisfy employees' basic physiological needs by giving them a chance to earn a well-deserved rest and recharge. Officials at several companies have recognized this explicitly, noting that opportunities for rejuvenation are vital in industries that change so rapidly that people often are run ragged and burn out. For example, all of Apple Computer's employees get a six-week sabbatical program every five years, during which time they can do whatever they want to refresh themselves.

Sabbaticals provide yet another important benefit: They reward faithful service, thereby satisfying esteem needs. According to Apple spokesman Frank O'Mahoney, their sabbatical program *Restart* "is a symbol that Apple cares for you as a well-balanced person; you're not just a drone."[23]

Not all employees expect sabbatical leaves, but growing numbers expect increases in vacation time. In fact, according to Marilyn Moats Kennedy, a career-planning strategist, job hunters are not shy about negotiating as much time off their jobs as possible. The trend, she notes, is finding more people "who will change jobs solely for increased vacation time, or more lenient leave policies, even if there's no appreciable increase in pay."[24]

At the very least, today's employees demand more opportunities to get even unpaid time off their jobs so they can fulfill their nonwork-related interests. This has led to some very creative practices, particularly at small companies. For example, any of the 65 employees of Autumn-Harper, the Bristol, Vermont, manufacturer of skin-care products, can donate unused vacation days to other employees who need them for one reason or another.[25] This does not cost the company a thing, but it helps to satisfy employees' social needs and esteem needs by leading them to understand that their coworkers have contributed to their well-being.

Experts caution that people who take large amounts of time off their jobs may be seen as weak and undedicated to their companies, but for some, it's worth it. This is not a problem in some organizations, however, where employees are *required* to take sabbaticals. As consultant Joan Kofodimos explains, "growing people is good for the company. Companies have to say, 'Go get a life. That's what we reward around here.'"[26] Indeed, as companies take steps to satisfy their employees' needs, such as by offering them time off the job, need theories lead us to expect that both employees and their organizations will reap the benefits. ■

MOTIVATING BY SETTING GOALS

Just as people are motivated to satisfy their needs on the job, they also are motivated to strive for and to attain goals. In fact, setting goals is one of the most important motivational forces in organizations.[27] With this in mind, we now describe a prominent theory of **goal setting** and identify some practical suggestions for setting goals effectively.

goal setting
The process of determining specific levels of performance for workers to attain.

Locke and Latham's Goal-Setting Theory

Suppose you are doing a task, such as word processing, when a performance goal is assigned. You now are expected, for example, to type 70 words per minute (wpm) instead of the 60 wpm you have been doing. Would you work hard to meet this goal, or would you simply give up? Some insight into how people respond to assigned goals is provided by Locke and Latham.[28] These theorists claim that an assigned goal influences people's beliefs about their ability to perform the task in question (i.e., the personality variable of **self-efficacy**, as described in chapter 3) as well as their personal goals. In turn, both of these factors influence performance.

self-efficacy
An individual's beliefs concerning his or her ability to perform specific tasks successfully.

The basic idea behind Locke and Latham's theory is that a goal serves as a motivator because it causes people to compare their present capacity to perform with that required to succeed at the goal. To the extent people believe they will fall short of the goal, they will feel dissatisfied and work harder to attain it — so long as they believe it is possible to do so. When they succeed at meeting a goal, they feel competent and successful.[29] Having a goal enhances performance largely because the goal makes clear exactly what type and level of performance is expected.

This model also claims that assigned goals lead to acceptance of those goals as personal goals. In other words, assigned goals will become accepted as one's own. This is the idea of **goal commitment**, which is the extent to which people invest themselves in meeting a goal.[30] Indeed, people will become more committed to a goal to the extent they desire to attain that goal and also believe they have a reasonable chance of doing so.[31] Likewise, the more strongly that people believe they can meet a goal, the more strongly they accept it as their own. In contrast, workers who perceive themselves as being physically incapable of meeting performance goals, for example, generally are not committed to meeting those goals — and do not strive to do so.[32]

goal commitment
The degree to which people accept and strive to attain goals.

Finally, this model claims that beliefs about both self-efficacy and goal commitment influence task performance. This makes sense, because people will exert greater effort when they believe they will succeed than when they believe their efforts will be in vain.[33] Moreover, goals that are not personally accepted have little capacity to guide behavior. In fact, the more strongly people are committed to meeting goals, the better they will perform.[34] In general, Locke and Latham's model of goal setting has been supported by several studies, which suggests it is a valuable source of insight regarding how the goal-setting process works (Figure 4.7).[35]

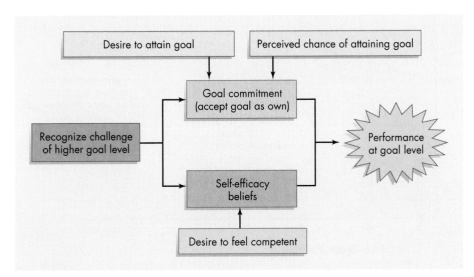

FIGURE 4.7

A Cognitive Summary of the Goal Setting Process

When people are challenged to meet higher goals, several things happen. First, they assess their desire to attain the goal as well as their chances of attaining the goal, which jointly affects their *goal commitment*. Second, they assess the extent to which meeting the goal will enhance their beliefs in their own *self-efficacy*. When levels of goal commitment and self-efficacy are high, people are motivated to perform at the goal level.

GLOBAL MATTERS   Do you believe that striving to obtain goals is a basic human characteristic or that it differs between people from different nations? In other words, are people from some countries likely to be more concerned about meeting goals than people from other countries? ▒

Managers' Guidelines for Setting Effective Performance Goals

Because researchers have been studying the goal-setting process for many years, their findings can be summarized in the form of principles. These represent practical suggestions that managers can use to enhance motivation.

Assign Specific Goals   Probably the best-established finding on goal setting is that *people perform at higher levels when asked to meet a specific, high-performance goal than when asked simply to "do your best" or when no goal at all is assigned.*[36] People tend to find specific goals as being quite challenging and are motivated to meet them — not only to fulfill management's expectations but also to convince themselves they have performed well.

One classic study conducted at an Oklahoma lumber camp dramatically demonstrated this principle.[37] The participants were lumber-camp crews who hauled logs from forests to their company's nearby sawmill. During a three-month period before the study began, the crew loaded trucks only to approximately 60 percent of their legal capacity, thus wasting trips and costing the company money. Then a specific goal was set that challenged the loggers to load the trucks to 94 percent of capacity before returning to the mill. How effective was this goal in raising performance? As summarized in Figure 4.8, the results show that the goal was extremely effective. In fact, not only was this specific goal effective in raising performance in just a few weeks, the effects were long-lasting as well. The loggers even sustained this level of performance as long as seven years later! The resulting savings for the company were considerable.

This is just one of many studies that clearly demonstrate the effectiveness of setting specific, challenging performance goals. Specific goals also are helpful in bringing about other desirable organizational goals (e.g., reducing absenteeism and industrial accidents).[38] Naturally, to reap such beneficial effects, goals must not only be highly specific but challenging as well.

FIGURE 4.8

Goal Setting: Some Impressive Effects

The performance of loggers loading timber onto trucks markedly improved after a specific, difficult goal was set. The percentage of the maximum possible weight loaded onto the trucks rose from approximately 60 percent before any goal was set to approximately 94 percent — the goal level — after the goal was set. Performance remained at this level as long as seven years.

(*Source*: Adapted from Latham & Baldes, 1975; see note 37.)

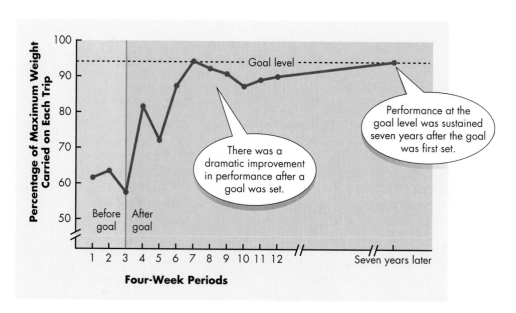

Assign Difficult — but Acceptable — Performance Goals The goal set at the logging camp was successful because it was specific, but it also was successful because it pushed crew members to a higher standard. Obviously, however, a goal that is too easy to attain will *not* bring about the desired performance increase. For example, if you already type 70 wpm, a goal of 60 wpm—although specific—probably would *lower* your performance. The key point is that *a goal must be difficult as well as specific for it to raise performance.* At the same time, however, people will work hard to reach challenging goals so long as these goals are within the limits of their capability. As goals become too difficult, performance suffers, because people reject those goals as being unrealistic and unattainable.[39]

For example, as a student, you may work harder in a challenging class than in a very easy one. At the same time, you probably would give up trying if the only way to pass the class was to get perfect scores on all exams—a standard you would reject as being unacceptable. In short, specific goals are most effective when they are set neither too low nor too high.

This same phenomenon occurs in organizations. For example, Bell Canada's telephone operators are required to handle calls within 23 seconds, and FedEx's customer service agents are expected to answer questions within 140 seconds.[40] Initially, both were considered to be difficult goals, but the employees of both companies eventually met—or even exceeded—these goals and enjoyed the satisfaction of knowing they succeeded. At a General Electric manufacturing plant, specific goals were set for productivity and cost reduction, and those goals that were perceived as being challenging but possible led to improved performance. Those goals that were thought to be unattainable, however, led to decreased performance.[41] How, then, should goals be set in a manner that strengthens the commitment of employees' to them?

One obvious way of enhancing goal acceptance is to *involve employees in the goal-setting process.* People better accept goals they were involved in setting than they do goals assigned by their supervisors—and they work harder as a result.[42] In other words, participation in the goal-setting process tends to enhance goal commitment. Not only does participation help them to better understand and appreciate the goals they had a hand in setting, it also helps to ensure the goals that were set are not unreasonable.

Provide Feedback Concerning Goal Attainment The final principle of goal setting appears to be glaringly obvious but often is not followed in practice: Feedback helps people to attain their performance goals. Just as golfers who are interested in improving their swings need feedback about where their balls are going, workers need feedback about how closely they are approaching their performance goals if they are to meet them.

The importance of using feedback in conjunction with goal setting was demonstrated by a study of people in a vital yet underinvestigated profession—pizza delivery drivers.[43] These individuals must deliver their customers' pizzas quickly, but of course, they also must do so safely and in compliance with all traffic laws. All too often, however, in the interest of keeping their pizzas hot, some delivery people's driving styles are even hotter (and "saucier"). To speed delivery, for example, some even have been known to fail to stop completely at intersections.

With an eye toward curbing this behavior, officials of pizza shops in two different towns participated in a study that systematically observed their deliverers' driving behavior during a nine-month period. Trained observers hidden from view recorded various aspects of the deliverers' driving behavior during prime-time hours, particularly the percentage of times they came to complete stops at intersections. Over a six-week period, drivers from both locations came to complete stops, on average, just less than half the time. Because this was unacceptable, the drivers in one location—the experimental group—were asked to come to a complete stop 75 percent of the time, and over a four-week period, they were given regular performance appraisals on how

FIGURE 4.9

Feedback: An Essential Element of Goal Setting

Pizza delivery drivers came very close to reaching a goal — coming to a complete stop at intersections 75 percent of the time — during the period in which they were given regular feedback on goal performance. Several months later, however, after such feedback was no longer given, their performance returned to previous levels.

(*Source*: Based on data reported by Ludwig & Geller, 1997; see note 43.)

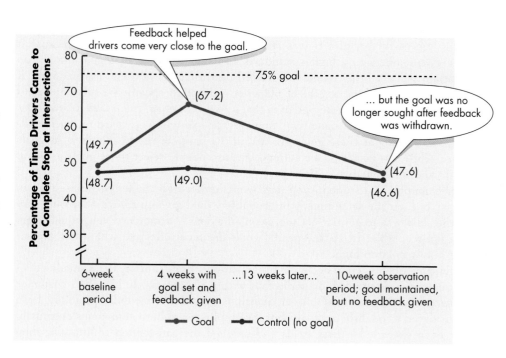

organizational justice

People's perceptions of fairness in organizations, consisting of perceptions regarding how decisions are made concerning the distribution of outcomes (*procedural justice*) and the perceived fairness of those outcomes themselves (as studied in *equity theory*).

successful they were in meeting this goal. Drivers in the control group were not asked to meet any goals, however, and they were not given any feedback on their driving. Following this feedback period, drivers in the experimental group were asked to maintain the 75-percent goal but stopped receiving feedback. Observations of their driving behavior as well as that of the control group continued during this six-month period.

How did the drivers do? The results of the study, as summarized in Figure 4.9, show that goal setting in conjunction with feedback was highly successful. Specifically, it led those drivers to come very close to the assigned goal of stopping completely at intersections three-quarters of the time. Once that feedback was withdrawn, however, these drivers returned to stopping only half the time — as often as they did before the study began, and just as often as drivers in the control group (who received neither goals nor feedback). These findings clearly demonstrate the importance of accompanying specific, difficult goals with clear feedback about the extent to which those goals are being met. Setting goals without providing such feedback effectively forces workers to do their jobs blindly. Providing feedback, however, shines a spotlight on task performance that is essential to success.

In sum, goal setting is an effective tool that managers can use to motivate people. Setting a specific, acceptably difficult goal and then providing feedback about progress toward that goal greatly enhances job performance.

MOTIVATING BY BEING FAIR

The theories described thus far are based on completely individual processes — the activation of needs and the responses to goals. The next approach to motivation that we consider, **organizational justice**, also is an individual-based theory, but this one adds a social component.[44] Specifically, various conceptualizations of organizational justice view motivation from the perspective of the *social comparisons* people make — that is, what they see when they compare themselves with others and with the prevailing standards.[45] In this section, we describe two major approaches to organizational justice: *equity theory*, which focuses on how organizational resources are distributed; and *pro-

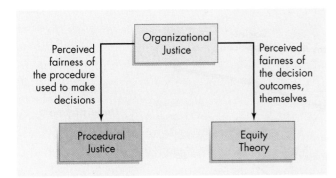

FIGURE 4.10

Two Types of Organizational Justice

People's perceptions of fairness in organizations (*organizational justice*) are based on their beliefs about the fairness of the procedures used to determine outcomes (*procedural justice*) as well as on what those outcomes are (*equity theory*).

cedural justice, which focuses on the processes used to make those resource-allocation decisions (Figure 4.10).[46] After describing these approaches to organizational justice, we then summarize their implications for motivating people on the job.

Adams' Equity Theory

One major approach to organizational justice, known as **equity theory**, proposes that individuals are motivated to maintain fair — or *equitable* — relationships among themselves and to avoid those relationships that are unfair — or *inequitable*.[47] The ways in which this is done has been a topic of considerable interest in the field of organizational behavior.

Specifically, equity theory holds that people comparing themselves with others focus on two variables: *outcomes* and *inputs*.[48] **Outcomes** are things we get out of our jobs and include pay, fringe benefits, and prestige. **Inputs** are things we contribute, such as the amount of time worked, amount of effort expended, number of units produced, and the qualifications we bring to the job. Equity theory is concerned with outcomes and inputs as they are *perceived* by the people involved, which may or may not be accurate. Not surprisingly, therefore, people sometimes disagree about what constitutes equitable treatment on the job.

Equity theory states that people compare their outcomes and inputs with those of others and then judge the equitableness of these relationships in the form of a ratio. Specifically, people compare the ratios of their own outcomes/inputs with the ratios of other's outcomes/inputs. This "other" who serves as the basis for comparison may be someone else in the work group, another employee in the organization, an individual in the same field, or even oneself at some earlier point in time — in short, almost anyone against whom we can compare ourselves. As shown in Figure 4.11, these comparisons can result in any of three different states: *overpayment inequity*, *underpayment inequity*, or *equitable payment*.

To illustrate these concepts, consider an example. Imagine that Jack and Ray work alongside each other on an assembly line. Both men do the same job and have equal amounts of experience, training, and education. In addition, both work equally long and hard at their jobs. In short, their inputs are equivalent. Suppose, however, that Jack is paid a salary of $500 per week but that Ray is paid only $350 per week. In this case, Jack's ratio of outcomes/inputs is higher than Ray's, thus creating a state of **overpayment inequity** for Jack and of **underpayment inequity** for Ray (because the ratio of his outcomes/inputs is lower). According to equity theory, when Jack realizes he is being paid more than an equally qualified person doing the same work, he will feel *guilty* in response to his overpayment. In contrast, when Ray realizes he is being paid less than an equally qualified person doing the same work, he will feel *angry* in response to his underpayment. Feeling guilty or angry are negative emotional states that people are motivated to change. Specifically, they will seek to create a state

equity theory

The theory stating that people strive to maintain a ratio of their own outcomes (rewards) to their own inputs (contributions) equal to the outcome/input ratios of others with whom they compare themselves.

outcomes

The rewards, such as salary and recognition, that employees receive from their jobs.

inputs

People's contributions to their jobs, such as their experience, qualifications, or amount of time worked.

overpayment inequity

The condition, resulting in feelings of guilt, in which the ratio of one's outcomes to one's inputs is more than the corresponding ratio of another, comparison person.

underpayment inequity

The condition, resulting in feelings of anger, in which the ratio of one's outcomes to one's inputs is less than the corresponding ratio of another, comparison person.

FIGURE 4.11

Equity Theory: An Overview

To judge equity or inequity, people compare the ratios of their own outcomes to inputs with the corresponding ratios of others (or of themselves at earlier points in time). The resulting states—*overpayment inequity, underpayment inequity,* and *equitable payment*—and their associated emotional responses are summarized here.

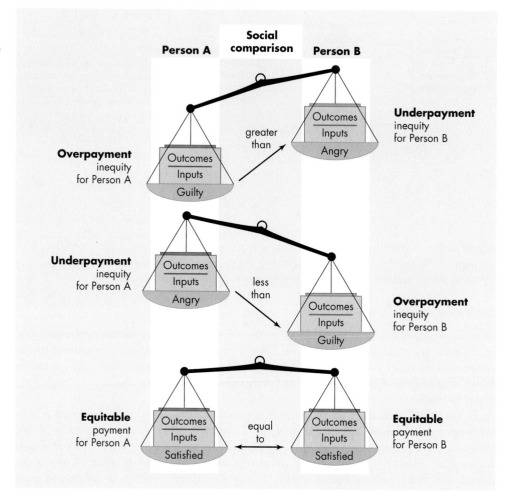

equitable payment

The state in which one person's outcome/input ratio is equivalent to that of another, comparison person.

of **equitable payment** in which their outcome/input ratios are equal, thus leading them to feel *satisfied*.

How can people change inequitable states to equitable ones? Equity theory suggests several possible courses of action (Table 4.1). In general, people who are underpaid may lower their inputs or raise their outcomes. Either action would effectively bring the underpaid individual's outcome/input ratio into line with that of the comparison person. In our example, the underpaid Ray might lower his inputs by slacking off, arriving late, leaving early, taking longer breaks, doing less work, or doing lower-quality work. In an extreme case, Ray even might quit his job. He also may attempt to raise his outcomes, however, such as by asking for a raise or even by taking home company property (e.g., tools or office supplies). In contrast, the overpaid Jack might do the opposite and either raise his inputs or lower his outcomes. For example, Jack might put forth more effort, work longer hours, and make a greater contribution to the company. He also might lower his outcomes by working through a paid vacation or not taking advantage of fringe benefits the company offers. These are all specific *behavioral* reactions to inequitable conditions—that is, things that people *do* to change inequitable states to equitable ones.

As you might imagine, however, people may be unwilling to do some of the things that are necessary to respond behaviorally to inequities. In particular, they may be unwilling to restrict their productivity (in fear of getting caught "goofing off") or be uncomfortable with asking their boss for a raise. As a result, they may resort to resolving the inequity not by changing their behavior but by changing how they think about the situation. Because equity theory deals with perceptions of fairness or un-

TABLE 4.1

Possible Reactions to Inequity: A Summary
People can respond to overpayment and underpayment inequities in behavioral and/or psychological ways. A few of these are summarized here. These reactions help change the perceived inequities into a state of perceived equity.

	TYPE OF REACTION	
TYPE OF INEQUITY	**BEHAVIORAL** (WHAT YOU CAN DO IS . . .)	**PSYCHOLOGICAL** (WHAT YOU CAN THINK IS . . .)
Overpayment inequity	Raise your inputs (e.g., work harder), or lower your outcomes (e.g., work through a paid vacation).	Convince yourself that your outcomes are deserved based on your inputs (e.g., rationalize that you work harder than others and so you deserve more pay).
Underpayment inequity	Lower your inputs (e.g., reduce effort), or raise your outcomes (e.g., get raise in pay).	Convince yourself that others' inputs are really higher than your own (e.g., rationalize that the comparison worker is really more qualified and so deserves higher outcomes).

fairness, it is reasonable to expect that inequitable states may be redressed simply by altering one's thinking about the circumstances. For example, underpaid people may rationalize that others' inputs really are higher than their own (e.g., "I suppose she really *is* more qualified than me"), thereby convincing themselves that the higher outcomes are justified. Similarly, overpaid people may convince themselves that they really *are* better, thereby deserving their relatively higher pay. So by changing how they see things, people may come to perceive inequitable situations as being equitable, thus effectively reducing their distress over the inequity.[49]

A great deal of evidence suggests that people are motivated to redress inequities at work and that they respond much as equity theory suggests. For example, professional basketball players who are underpaid (i.e., ones who are paid less than others who perform equally well or better) score fewer points than those who are equitably paid.[50] In other words, they lower their inputs. In addition, people who have their pay cut tend to steal from their employers much more than those who receive their regular pay.[51] From the perspective of equity theory, these individuals may be seen as raising their outcomes. Indeed, it is not unusual for people to retaliate against their employers for treating them unfairly.[52]

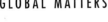

GLOBAL MATTERS

Dividing rewards equitably sometimes results in giving one person a greater share than another. This makes sense in countries such as the United States, where people have an individualistic orientation toward work. People from Asian countries, however, which generally have a collectivistic orientation, tend to favor equal distributions of reward. ■

Procedural Justice: Making Decisions Fairly

The idea of *procedural justice* originally came from the legal arena, where it has long been understood that for the outcome of a trial to be fair, the procedures used in that trial (e.g., rules regarding the nature of evidence) must be fair.[53] More recently, specialists in OB have recognized that this same basic idea applies to decisions made on the job as well.[54] Hence, we refer to **procedural justice** as the perceived fairness of the processes by which organizational decisions are made. People in organizations are

procedural justice
Perceptions regarding the fairness of procedures used to determine outcomes.

greatly concerned about making decisions fairly, and they are motivated to get others to accept these decisions as being fair. The reason is simple: Both individual employees and entire organizations benefit when the organization is thought to follow fair procedures.

Scientists have recognized two sides to procedural justice: a structural side (i.e., procedural justice based on how decisions are structured), and a social side (i.e., procedural justice based on how people are treated in the course of making decisions). Let's examine each one in turn.

The Structural Side of Procedural Justice   The structural side of procedural justice deals with determining how decisions need to be made for them to be considered fair. (It is important to remember we are *not* talking about *what* those decisions are. We are talking about *how* those decisions are made.) Several things can be done to make organizational decisions seem fair. These include:

1. *Give people a say in how decisions are made.* Having a *voice* — that is, a say in decision-making procedures — is key to procedural justice. For example, people believe their performance appraisals are more fair when they have an opportunity to provide information regarding their performance than they do when no such input is solicited.[55]

2. *Provide an opportunity for errors to be corrected.* Just as fairness demands that court decisions can be appealed, organizational decisions should afford the same opportunity. In fact, for drug-screening procedures to be considered as being fair, the people tested must have an opportunity to request a re-test.[56] (For other examples, see Figure 4.12).

3. *Apply rules and policies consistently.* Suppose an organization has a policy regarding how vacation time is selected. People with the greatest seniority pick first, which leaves the remaining times for more junior staff members. This policy may be fair on its own, but the organization would not be fair if it only applied this policy to some people and not to others. Clearly, *consistency* is key to establishing procedural justice.

4. *Make decisions in an unbiased manner.* For an organizational decision to be considered as being procedurally fair, the decision-maker must be unbiased. Suppose, for example, a human resources manager holds prejudicial attitudes against a certain racial group, thus leading him or her to systematically reject potential hires from that group (such biases are discussed in

FIGURE 4.12

Enhancing Procedural Justice by Correcting Erroneous Judgments: Two Examples
The National Football League allows officials to correct their judgments by reviewing plays as needed (*left*). This procedure enhances procedural justice, but its use is restricted because it slows down the game. In contrast, society tolerates delays in legal decisions created by the opportunities to appeal judgments (*right*). We do so because knowing that poor decisions can be corrected enhances our perceptions of the procedural fairness of the legal system.

chapter 5). In this case, we would say that procedurally fair decisions could not be made.[57]

The Social Side of Procedural Justice   The structural factors just identified are very important, but they do not tell the whole story regarding procedural justice. There also is a social side. In other words, when considering the fairness of procedures, people also take into account the quality of the interpersonal treatment they receive at the hands of decision-makers. This idea has been referred to as **interactional justice**.

Two major factors contribute to the fairness of interpersonal treatment: *informational justification*, which is the thoroughness of the information received about a decision; and *social sensitivity*, which is the amount of dignity and respect demonstrated when presenting an undesirable outcome (e.g., a pay cut or loss of a job). People respond much more favorably to negative outcomes when these are presented in a very thorough and informative manner—and with a great deal of interpersonal sensitivity—than they do when these are presented in a less informative and more insensitive manner.[58] By "more favorably," we mean a variety of things. For example, high levels of interactional justice facilitate the acceptance of smoking bans among smokers and even of extreme outcomes such as pay cuts and layoffs. People might not like these things, but they are more likely to accept them if they are presented in an interpersonally fair manner.

Organizational Justice: Some Motivational Tips for Managers

Equity theory has some important implications for motivating people.

Avoid Underpayment   Companies that attempt to save money by reducing employees' salaries may find that employees "even the score" in many different ways. For example, they may steal, shave a few minutes off their work days, or otherwise withhold production.

Employees also may express their feelings of extreme underpayment inequity by going on strike. This is exactly what happened in August 1997, when 185,000 members of the Teamsters Union went on strike against UPS, the world's largest package-distribution company (Figure 4.13). The employees claimed the company had hired many part-time workers who were paid less than full-time workers doing the same jobs. After a 16-day strike that cost UPS millions in lost revenue and crippled package shipments throughout the world, a settlement the Teamsters believed would result in more equitable treatment for their members was reached. This included limiting the use of part-time employees and increasing hourly wages by $3.10 for full-time and $4.10 for part-time employees over five years. This is only one example of employees who believe they are underpaid going on strike.

Over the past few years, a particularly unsettling form of institutionalizing underpayment has materialized in the form of **two-tier wage structures**. Under these payment systems, newer employees are paid less than those who were hired to do the same work at an earlier point in time. Not surprisingly, such systems are considered to be highly unfair, particularly by those in the lower tier.[59] When such a plan was instituted at the Giant Food supermarket chain, two-thirds of the lower-tier employees quit their jobs during the first three months. "It stinks," said a clerk at one store in Los Angeles. "They're paying us lower wages for the same work."[60] Not surprisingly, proposals to introduce two-tier wage systems have met considerable resistance among employees and, when applicable, the unions representing them.

Avoid Overpayment   Because overpaid employees work hard to feel they deserve their pay, you may think paying people more than they merit would be a useful motivational technique. There are several reasons why this would not work, however. First,

interactional justice
The perceived fairness of the interpersonal treatment used to determine organizational outcomes.

FIGURE 4.13

A Striking Response to Feelings of Inequity

In August 1997, UPS drivers complained the company was hiring part-time workers at lower wages than full-time workers to do the same work. They also went on strike to express their feelings of underpayment inequity, an action that cost the company millions of dollars.

two-tier wage structures
Payment systems in which newer employees are paid less than employees hired at earlier times who do the same work.

the increases in performance resulting from overpayment inequity tend to be temporary. As time goes on, people begin to believe they actually deserve the higher pay they receive and then lower their work level to normal. Second, when you overpay one employee, you are underpaying all the others. In turn, when most employees feel underpaid, they will lower their performance, thus resulting in a net *decrease* in productivity — and widespread employee dissatisfaction. Hence, the conclusion is clear: *managers should strive to treat all employees equitably.*

We realize, of course, that this may be easier said than done. Part of the difficulty is because feelings of equity and inequity are based on perceptions, and perceptions are not always easy to control. One approach that may help is to *be open and honest about outcomes and inputs.* People tend to overestimate how much their superiors are paid and, therefore, to feel their own pay is not as high as it should be.[61] If information about pay is shared, however, inequitable feelings may not result.

Give People a Voice in Decisions That Affect Them   People are likely to believe that decisions have been made fairly to the extent they have a chance to influence those decisions — that is, to the extent they are given a "say in the matter." For example, people consider election results to be fair so long as all those who are eligible were given an opportunity to participate in the process (whether or not they chose to do so). When people are denied a voice they believe they should have, they respond negatively — even if the resulting decision is the *same* as it would have been if they had participated.

As a case in point, consider the work slowdown among New York City taxicab drivers that caused serious traffic problems (more serious than usual!) during a week in 1998. These drivers were protesting the mayor's decision to impose certain rules, which they resented. Interestingly, the drivers did not object to the rules themselves — in fact, most drivers gladly accepted them. Rather, they were upset that the mayor had imposed these rules without consulting them on the matter.

Present Information About Outcomes in a Thorough, Socially Sensitive Manner
People's assessments of fairness on the job go beyond what their outcomes and inputs are. These assessments also involve their knowledge of *how* these outcomes and inputs were determined. For example, even negative outcomes such as layoffs, pay freezes, and pay cuts can be accepted and recognized as being fair to the extent that people understand the procedures involved in making those decisions. When such procedures appear to be unbiased and carefully enacted and the negative outcomes are presented in a highly sensitive and caring manner, the sting is taken out of the undesirable outcomes.[62]

Illustrating this point, consider what it must be like to live through a long pay freeze. This is likely to be painful, but people may be more accepting of a pay freeze as being fair if the procedure used to determine the need is believed to have been both thorough and careful — that is, if "a fair explanation" can be provided. This was precisely the finding in a recent study of manufacturing workers' reactions to a pay freeze.[63] Specifically, the researchers compared two groups of workers: those who received a thorough explanation of the procedures necessitating the pay freeze (e.g., information about the organization's economic problems), and those who received no such information. All workers were adversely affected by the freeze, but those who received an explanation better accepted it. In particular, the explanation reduced their interest in looking for a new job. These findings suggest that even if managers cannot do anything to eliminate workplace inequities, they might be able to ease the sting by explaining why these unfortunate conditions are necessary.

MOTIVATING BY ALTERING EXPECTATIONS

Instead of focusing on individual needs, goals, or social comparisons, **expectancy theory** takes a broader approach. It looks at the role of motivation in the overall work environment. In essence, expectancy theory asserts that people are motivated to work when they expect they will achieve the things that they want from their jobs. Expectancy theory characterizes people as rational beings who think about what they must do to be rewarded and how much that reward means to them before they actually perform their jobs. This theory does not focus only on what people think, however. It also recognizes that these thoughts combine with other aspects of the organizational environment to influence job performance.

expectancy theory

The theory that asserts motivation is based on people's beliefs about the probability that their effort will lead to performance (*expectancy*), multiplied by the probability that performance will lead to reward (*instrumentality*), multiplied by the perceived value of that reward (*valence*).

Basic Elements of Expectancy Theory

[handwritten: know these theory's]

Several different versions of expectancy theory have been proposed, but expectancy theorists agree that motivation results from three different types of beliefs that people have.[64] These are: **expectancy**, which is the belief that one's effort will result in performance; **instrumentality**, which is the belief that one's performance will be rewarded; and **valence**, which is the perceived value of the rewards to the recipient.

Expectancy People sometimes believe that by putting forth a great effort, they will get a lot accomplished. In other cases, however, people do not expect their efforts to have much effect on how well they do. For example, an employee operating a faulty piece of equipment may have a very low *expectancy* that his or her efforts will lead to high levels of performance. Naturally, someone working under such conditions probably will not exert much effort.

expectancy

The belief that one's efforts will influence one's performance positively.

instrumentality

An individual's beliefs regarding the likelihood of being rewarded according to his or her own level of performance.

valence

The value a person places on the rewards he or she expects to receive from an organization.

Instrumentality Even if an employee works hard and performs at a high level, his or her motivation may falter if that performance is not suitably rewarded—that is, if the performance is not perceived as *instrumental* to bringing about the rewards. For example, an extremely productive worker may be poorly motivated to perform if he or she has already reached the top level of pay in a company.

Valence Even if employees believe that hard work will lead to good performance *and* that their reward will be commensurate with their performance, they still may be poorly motivated if those rewards have a low *valence* to them. In other words, someone who does not care about the rewards offered by an organization is not motivated to attain them. For example, a reward of $100 would not be likely to motivate a multimillionaire, whereas it might be a very desirable reward for someone of more modest means. Only those rewards with a high positive valence to their recipients will motivate behavior.

GLOBAL MATTERS

Considering the valence of a reward is especially important when it comes to motivating people from different nations. After all, the national culture may play a large role in determining someone's preferences for different types of rewards. Can you identify any examples of this? ▪

Combining All Three Components Expectancy theory claims that motivation is a multiplicative function of all three components. In other words, higher levels of motivation result when expectancy, instrumentality, and valence are all high than result when they are all low. The multiplicative assumption of this theory also implies that if any one component is zero, then the overall level of motivation also is zero. For example, even if an employee believes that her effort will result in performance, which will result in reward, her motivation will be zero if the valence of the reward she expects is zero. Figure 4.14 summarizes the definitions of these components and shows their relationships with one another.

Other Determinants of Job Performance   Figure 4.14 also highlights a point in our opening remarks about motivation—that motivation is not equivalent to job performance. Expectancy theory recognizes that motivation is only one of several important determinants in job performance.

For example, expectancy theory assumes that both *skills* and *abilities* also contribute to a person's job performance. Some people are better suited than others to performing their jobs by virtue of their unique characteristics, special skills, and abilities. For example, a tall, strong, well-coordinated person is likely to make a better professional basketball player than a very short, weak, uncoordinated one—even if that shorter person is highly motivated to succeed.

Expectancy theory also recognizes that job performance is influenced by people's *role perceptions*—that is, what they believe is expected of them on the job. To the extent that disagreements arise about what one's job duties are, performance may suffer. For example, an assistant manager who believes her primary duty is to train new employees may find that her performance is downgraded by a supervisor who believes she should be spending more time on routine paperwork instead. In this case, the person's performance does not suffer because of any deficit in motivation but because of misunderstandings regarding what the job entails.

Finally, expectancy theory also recognizes the role of *opportunities to perform* one's job. Even the best employees may perform at low levels if their opportunities are limited. For example, a highly motivated salesperson may perform poorly if the territory is having a financial downturn or the available inventory is limited (i.e., if opportunities are restricted).

It is important to recognize that expectancy theory views motivation as one of several determinants of job performance. Motivation combined with a person's skills and abilities, role perceptions, and opportunities influence job performance.

Expectancy theory has generated much research and been applied successfully to understanding behavior in many different organizational settings.[65] Although the theory has received only mixed support regarding some of its specific aspects (e.g., the multiplicative assumption), it remains one of the dominant approaches to the study of motivation in organizations. Probably the main reason for this popularity is the many useful suggestions the theory makes for practicing managers. We now describe some of the most essential applications of expectancy theory and provide examples from organizations in which they have been implemented.

FIGURE 4.14

Expectancy Theory: An Overview

According to *expectancy theory*, motivation is produced by three types of beliefs: *expectancy* (the belief that one's effort will influence performance), *instrumentality* (the belief that one will be rewarded for one's performance), and *valence* (the perceived value of the rewards expected). The theory also recognizes that motivation is only one of several factors responsible for job performance.

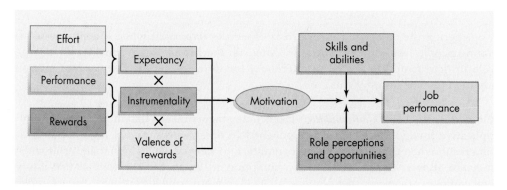

Managerial Applications of Expectancy Theory

Expectancy theory is a very practical approach to motivation. In fact, it suggests several important ways to motivate employees.

Clarify People's Expectancies That Their Effort Will Lead to Performance   Motivation may be enhanced by training employees to do their jobs more efficiently, thereby achieving higher levels of performance from their efforts. Effort–performance expectancies also may be enhanced by following employees' suggestions about ways to change their jobs. To the extent that employees are aware of problems that interfere with their performance, attempting to alleviate these problems may help them to perform more effectively. In essence, *make the desired performance attainable*. Good supervisors make it clear to people what is expected of them and also help them to attain that level of performance.

Administer Rewards with a Positive Valence to Employees   In other words, the carrot at the end of the stick must be tasty for it to be a motivator. These days, with a highly diverse workforce, it would be misleading to assume that all employees care about having the same rewards. Some might recognize the incentive value of a pay raise; others might prefer additional vacation days, improved insurance benefits, and day-care or elder-care facilities. Thus, many companies have introduced **cafeteria-style benefit plans** — that is, incentive systems allowing employees to select their fringe benefits from a menu of available alternatives. Given that fringe benefits represent almost 40 percent of payroll costs, more and more companies are recognizing the value of administering these benefits flexibly.[66] For example, Primerica has used a flexible benefit plan since 1978 — and almost 95 percent of the company's 8,000 salaried employees believe it is extremely beneficial to them.[67]

cafeteria-style benefit plans
Incentive systems in which employees can select the fringe benefits they want from a menu of available alternatives.

Clearly Link Valued Rewards and Performance   Unfortunately, not all incentive plans do as good a job as they should in rewarding desired performance. A recent survey found that only 25 percent of employees see a clear link between good job performance and pay raises. Obviously, many organizations have a long way to go in raising their employees' instrumentality beliefs.[68] In other words, managers should enhance their subordinates' beliefs about instrumentality by specifying exactly what job behaviors lead to what rewards.

How can they do this? To the extent that employees can be paid in ways directly linked to their performance — such as through piece-rate incentive systems, sales commission plans, or bonuses — expectancy theory specifies it would be effective to do so. Some companies even give their employees a small piece of the company in exchange for their contributions — a practice sure to link performance with rewards in their minds.[69] Indeed, performance increases can result from carefully implemented merit systems, which frequently are referred to as **pay-for-performance** plans.[70]

pay-for-performance
A payment system in which employees are paid differentially based on the quantity and quality of their performance. Pay-for-performance plans strengthen *instrumentality* beliefs.

ETHICS MATTERS

Several years ago, Sears auto mechanics were paid in proportion to the volume of their repairs. This policy allegedly encouraged them to make unnecessary repairs on customers' cars.[71] Sears has since eliminated this method of paying its auto mechanics, but the message is clear: When you pay people for their performance, be careful; you just might get what you're paying for! ▪

To illustrate the importance of selecting only the most desired performance to reward, consider the pay plan IBM uses for its 30,000 sales representatives. Previously, most of the pay these reps received was based on a flat salary; their compensation was not linked to how well they did. Now, however, their pay is carefully tied to two essential factors in the company's success: profitability, and customer satisfaction. So, instead of receiving commissions on the amount of the sale — as so many other salespeople do — 60 percent of IBM sales reps' commissions are tied to the company's profit on that sale. As a result, the more the company makes, the more the reps make. To make sure the reps do not push only high-profit items that customers might not need, the remaining 40 percent of their commissions are based on customer satisfaction, which is assessed in regular surveys. Since introducing this plan in late 1993, IBM has effectively reversed its unprofitable trend. There certainly are many factors responsible for this turnaround, but experts are confident that this practice of clearly linking desired performance to individual rewards is a key one.

Another example is Continental Airlines. In 1994, this air carrier was ranked dead last in on-time performance, and this problem was costing the company $6 million per month.[72] To combat this problem, management started paying bonuses to employees to reward on-time performance: $100 per employee for a top ranking, and $65 per employee for a number-two or number-three ranking. Since initiating this plan, Continental has placed consistently among the industry's on-time leaders, earning each employee some $700 in one recent year.

Of course, rewards need not be monetary in nature. Even symbolic and verbal recognition for a job well done can be very effective. Some companies help to recognize their employees organizational contributions by acknowledging them on the pages of their corporate newsletter. For example, employees of Merck, the large pharmaceutical company, enjoyed the recognition they received for developing Proscar, a highly successful drug treatment for prostate enlargement, when they saw their pictures in the company newsletter. This example illustrates the important point that employee recognition need not be lavish or expensive. It can be nothing more than a heart-felt "thank you." As Mark Twain put it, "I can live for two months on a good compliment." With this in mind, some companies have taken very creative measures; for some examples, see Table 4.2.[73]

TABLE 4.2

Nonmonetary Recognition: Some Creative Examples from Small Companies
Recognition can be one of the most effective types of reward, and because it can be so inexpensive, it is popular among small companies. The small companies identified here recognize their employees in some particularly creative ways. The companies involved also have found these techniques to be useful in attracting new employees.

COMPANY	NATURE OF BUSINESS	FORM OF RECOGNITION
Kendle	Designs clinical tests for drugs	Photos of all 288 employees, posed engaging in their favorite outside activity, line the hallways.
Leonhardt Plating Company	Manufactures steel plating	Employees of the polishing department are allowed to manage themselves.
50 small businesses in the vicinity of the Cincinnati/ Northern Kentucky Airport	Miscellaneous	These companies banded together to offer free transportation services to their employees who don't live nearby.
Payne Firm, Inc.	Environmental consulting firm	Set up telecommuting facilities that make it easy for some employees to work while staying at home.

Source: Based on information in Schafer, 1997; see note 73.

MOTIVATING BY STRUCTURING JOBS TO MAKE THEM INTERESTING

The final approach to motivation that we consider is the largest in scope, because it aims to improve the nature of the work performed. The idea behind **job design** is that by making jobs more appealing to people, motivation can be enhanced. Recall from chapter 1 Frederick W. Taylor's principle of *scientific management*, which attempted to stimulate performance by designing jobs in the most efficient fashion. Treating people like machines, however, often meant having them engage in repetitive movements, which they found to be highly routine and monotonous. Not surprisingly, people became bored with such jobs and frequently quit.[74] Fortunately, today's organizational scientists have found several ways of designing jobs that can not only be performed very efficiently but are highly pleasant and enjoyable as well.

Job Enlargement and Job Enrichment

Imagine you have a highly routine job, such as tightening the lugs on the left rear wheel of a car as it rolls down the assembly line. Naturally, such a highly repetitive task can be monotonous and not very pleasant. One of the first modern approaches to redesigning jobs suggested that such consequences could be minimized if people perform an increased number of different tasks all at the same level. This approach is known as **job enlargement**. To enlarge the jobs in our example, workers could be required to tighten the lugs on all four wheels. As a result, employees have no more responsibility nor use any greater skills, but they do perform a wider variety of different tasks at the same level. Adding tasks in this fashion is said to increase the *horizontal job loading* of the position.

A few years ago, American Greetings Corp. of Cleveland, Ohio, enlarged some 400 jobs in its creative division.[75] Now, rather than always working exclusively on Christmas cards, for example, employees can move back and forth between different teams, such as those working on birthday ribbons, humorous mugs, and Valentine's Day gift bags. Employees at American Greetings reportedly enjoy the variety, as do those at RJR Nabisco, Corning, Eastman Kodak, and other companies that recently have allowed employees to make such lateral moves.

Most reports on the effectiveness of job enlargement have been anecdotal, but a few carefully conducted empirical studies have examined their impact as well. For example, one group studied the effects of a job enlargement program at a large financial services company.[76] The unenlarged jobs had different employees perform separate paperwork tasks, such as preparing, sorting, coding, and keypunching various forms. In the enlarged jobs, however, these various functions were combined into larger jobs performed by the same people. Although it was more difficult and expensive to train people for the enlarged than for the separate jobs, important benefits resulted. In particular, employees with enlarged jobs expressed greater job satisfaction and less boredom, and because one person followed the job all the way through, greater opportunities to correct errors existed. Not surprisingly, customers were satisfied with the result as well.

Unfortunately, a follow-up investigation of the same company conducted two years later found that not all the beneficial effects had continued.[77] Notably, employee satisfaction had leveled off, and the rate of errors had risen, thus suggesting that as employees got used to their enlarged jobs, they found them to be less interesting and stopped paying attention to all the details. Hence, job enlargement may help to improve job performance, but its effects may not be lasting.

In contrast to job enlargement, **job enrichment** gives employees not only more jobs to do but more tasks to perform at a higher level of skill and responsibility

job design
An approach to motivation suggesting that jobs can be designed to enhance people's interest in doing them (see *job enlargement, job enrichment,* and the *job characteristics model*).

job enlargement
The practice of expanding the content of a job to include more variety and more tasks at the same level.

job enrichment
The practice of giving employees a high degree of control over their work, from planning and organization through implementation and evaluating the results.

(Figure 4.15). Job enrichment provides the opportunity for employees to take greater control over how to do their jobs. Because people performing enriched jobs have increased opportunities to work at higher levels, the job enrichment process is said to increase a job's *vertical job loading*.

GLOBAL MATTERS

Among the oldest job enrichment programs is that developed by Volvo, the Swedish auto manufacturer. Instead of producing cars on an assembly line, Volvos are assembled by 25 groups of approximately 20 workers, who are each responsible for one part of the car's assembly (e.g., engine, electrical system).[78] Some American auto workers do not like this approach, but others do. Why do you suppose this is? ▪

Evidence suggests that job enrichment programs have been successful at other organizations as well, but several factors limit their popularity.[79] Most obvious is the *difficulty of implementation*. To redesign existing facilities so that jobs can be enriched often is prohibitively expensive, and the technology needed to perform certain jobs can make it impractical for them to be redesigned. Another impediment is the *lack of employee acceptance*. Many employees relish this change, but some may *not* desire the additional responsibility associated with enriched jobs. In particular, individuals with low achievement motivation are especially frustrated with enriched jobs.[80] Similarly, people may get used to doing their jobs in certain ways and not like having to change them. In fact, when a group of U.S. auto workers went to Sweden to work in a Saab engine-assembly plant—where jobs were highly enriched—five out of six indicated that they preferred their traditional assembly line jobs.[81] As one union leader put it; "If you want to enrich the job, enrich the paycheck."[82] Clearly, enriched jobs are not for everyone.

Thus far, we have failed to specify precisely *how* to enrich a job. What elements of a job must be enriched for it to be effective? An attempt to expand on the idea of job enrichment, known as the *job characteristics model*, provides an answer to this important question.

The Job Characteristics Model

The **job characteristics model** assumes that jobs can be designed to help people get enjoyment from them and to make them feel they are doing meaningful and valuable work. In particular, this approach specifies that enriching certain elements of jobs alters people's psychological states in a manner that enhances their work effectiveness.[83] Specifically, the model identifies five *core job dimensions* that help to create three *critical psychological states*, which in turn lead to several beneficial *personal and work outcomes* (Figure 4.16 on page 156).

job characteristics model

An approach to job enrichment that specifies that five core job dimensions (skill variety, task identity, task significance, autonomy, and job feedback) that produce critical psychological states that, in turn, lead to beneficial outcomes for individuals (e.g., high job satisfaction) and the organization (e.g., reduced turnover).

Components of the Model   The five critical job dimensions in this model are *skill variety, task identity, task significance, autonomy*, and *feedback*. Let's take a closer look at each:

- *Skill variety* is the extent to which a job requires a number of different activities using several of the employee's skills and talents. For example, an office manager in a job with high skill variety may have to perform many different tasks (e.g., do word processing, answer the telephone, greet visitors, and file records).
- *Task identity* is the extent to which a job requires completing an entire piece of work from beginning to end. For example, tailors have high task identity if

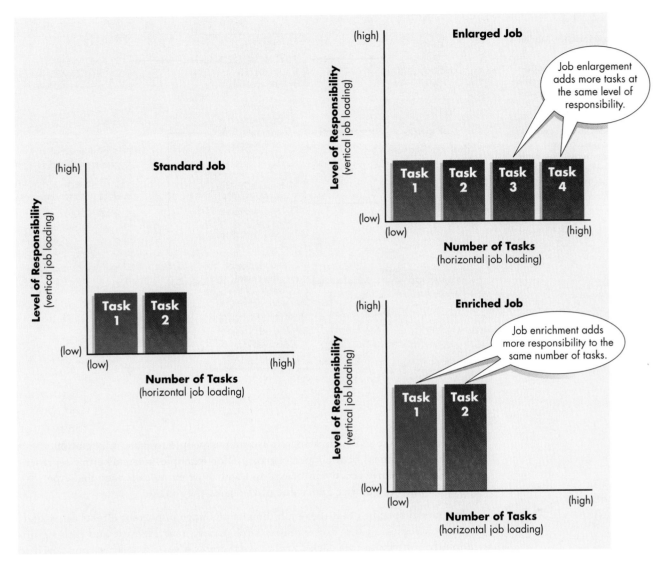

FIGURE 4.15

Job Enlargement and Job Enrichment: A Comparison

Redesigning jobs by increasing the number of tasks performed at the same level (*horizontal job loading*) is referred to as *job enlargement*. Redesigning jobs by increasing the employees' level of responsibility and control (*vertical job loading*) is referred to as *job enrichment*.

they do everything related to making an entire suit (e.g., measuring the client, selecting the fabric, cutting and sewing it, and altering it to fit).

- *Task significance* is the degree of impact the job is believed to have on others. For example, medical researchers working on a cure for a deadly disease probably recognize the importance of this work to the world at large. Even more modest contributions, however, can be recognized as being significant to the extent that employees understand the role of their jobs in the overall mission of the organization.

- *Autonomy* is the extent to which employees have the freedom and discretion to plan, schedule, and perform their jobs as desired. For example, a furniture repair person may act highly autonomously by scheduling his or her day's work and deciding how to tackle each repair job that he or she confronts.

FIGURE 4.16

**The Job Characteristics Model:
Basic Components**

The *job characteristics model* stipu-
lates that certain *core job dimensions*
lead to certain *critical psychological
states*, which in turn lead to several beneficial *personal and work outcomes*. The model also recognizes
that these relationships are
strongest among individuals with
high levels of *growth need strength*.

(*Source*: Adapted from Hackman & Oldham,
1980; see note 83.)

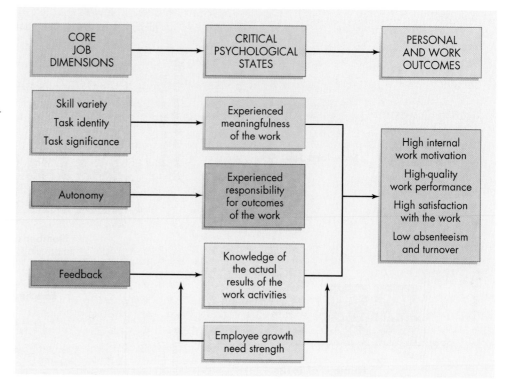

• *Feedback* is the extent to which a job allows people to have information about
the effectiveness of their performance. For example, telemarketing representatives regularly receive information about how many calls they make per day
and both the number and value of the sales they make.

The model specifies that these job dimensions have important effects on various
critical psychological states. For example, skill variety, task identity, and task significance jointly contribute to a task's *experienced meaningfulness*. A task is considered to
be meaningful to the extent that someone experiences it as being highly important,
valuable, and worthwhile. Jobs that provide a great deal of autonomy are said to make
people feel *personally responsible and accountable for their work*. When people are free to
decide what to do and how to do it, they feel more responsible for the results—whether
good or bad. Finally, effective feedback gives employees *knowledge of the results of their
work*. When a job provides people with information about the effects of their actions,
these people are better able to develop an understanding of how effectively they have
performed. In turn, such knowledge improves their effectiveness.

The job characteristics model specifies that the three critical psychological states
affect various personal and work outcomes—namely, people's feelings of motivation;
the quality of work performed; satisfaction with work, absenteeism, and turnover. The
higher the experienced meaningfulness of the work, the responsibility for the work
performed, and the knowledge of results, the more positive the personal and work
benefits will be. When people perform jobs that incorporate high levels of the five
core job dimensions, they should feel highly motivated, perform high-quality work,
be highly satisfied with their jobs, be absent infrequently, and be unlikely to resign.

Does the Model Apply to Everyone?   We should note the model is theorized to be especially effective in describing the behavior of individuals who are high in **growth
need strength**—that is, people with a high need for personal growth and development. People who are not particularly interested in improving themselves on the job

growth need strength

The personality variable describing the extent
to which people have a high need for personal
growth and development on the job. The *job
characteristics model* best describes people with
a high growth need strength.

cannot be expected to experience the theorized psychological reactions to the core job dimensions or, consequently, to enjoy the beneficial personal and work outcomes predicted by the model.[84] By introducing this variable, the job characteristic model recognizes the important limitation of job enrichment noted earlier — not everyone wants and benefits from enriched jobs.

Putting It All Together Based on the proposed relationship between the core job dimensions and their associated psychological reactions, job motivation should be highest when the jobs being performed rate high on the various dimensions. To assess this idea, a questionnaire known as the Job Diagnostic Survey (JDS) has been developed to measure the degree to which various job characteristics are present in a given job.[85] Based on responses to the JDS, we can predict the degree to which a job motivates the people who perform it. This is done using an index known as the **motivating potential score (MPS)**, which is computed as follows:

$$MPS = \frac{\text{Skill variety} + \text{Task identity} + \text{Task significance}}{3} \times \text{Autonomy} \times \text{Feedback}$$

motivating potential score (MPS)
A mathematical index describing the degree to which a job is designed to motivate people, as suggested by the *job characteristics model*. It is computed based on the Job Diagnostic Survey (JDS) questionnaire.

The MPS is a summary index of a job's potential for motivating people. The higher the score for a given job, the greater the likelihood of experiencing the personal and work outcomes as specified by the model. Knowing a job's MPS helps one to identify jobs that might benefit from being redesigned.

Evidence for the Model The job characteristics model has been the focus of many empirical tests, most of which have supported many aspects of the model.[86] One study conducted among a group of South African clerical workers found particularly strong support.[87] In some of the offices in this company, jobs were enriched according to the techniques specified by the job characteristics model. Specifically, employees performing enriched jobs were given opportunities to choose what kinds of tasks they performed (high skill variety), to do the entire job (high task identity), to receive instructions regarding how their job fit into the organization as a whole (high task significance), to set their own schedules and to inspect their own work (high autonomy), and to keep records of their daily productivity (high feedback). Another group of employees, who were equivalent in all respects except that their jobs were not enriched, served as a control group.

After employees performed the newly designed jobs for 6 months, they were compared with their counterparts in the control group. For most of the outcomes specified by the model, individuals performing redesigned jobs showed superior results. Specifically, these employees reported feeling more internally motivated and more satisfied with their jobs. They also had lower rates of absenteeism and turnover. The only outcome predicted by the model that was not found to differ was the actual work performance: People performed equally well in enriched and unenriched jobs. Considering the many factors responsible for job performance (as discussed in connection with expectancy theory), this finding should not be too surprising.

Techniques for Designing Jobs that Motivate: Some Managerial Guidelines

The job characteristics model specifies several ways that jobs can be designed to enhance their motivating potential.[88] Table 4.3 presents these in the form of general principles.

Combine Tasks Instead of having several workers perform separate parts of a whole job, have each person perform the entire job. This provides greater skill variety and task identity. For example, Corning Glass Works in Medford, Massachusetts,

TABLE 4.3

Enriching Jobs: Some Suggestions from the Job Characteristics Model

The job characteristics model specifies several ways jobs can be designed to incorporate the core job dimensions responsible for enhancing motivation and performance. A few are listed here.

PRINCIPLES OF JOB DESIGN	CORE JOB DIMENSIONS INCORPORATED
1. Combine jobs, enabling workers to perform the entire job	Skill variety Task identity
2. Establish client relationships, allowing providers of a service to meet the recipients	Skill variety Autonomy Feedback
3. Load jobs vertically, allowing greater responsibility and control over work	Autonomy
4. Open feedback channels, giving workers knowledge of the results of their work	Feedback

Source: Based on information in Hackman, 1976; see note 88.

redesigned jobs so that people who assembled laboratory hot plates put together entire units instead of contributing a single part to the assembly process.[89]

Open Feedback Channels   Jobs should be designed to give employees as much feedback as possible. The more people know about how well they do (be it from customers, supervisors, or coworkers), the better equipped they are to take appropriate corrective action. (We already noted the importance of feedback in the learning process in chapter 2). Sometimes, cues about job performance can be clearly identified as people perform their jobs (as we noted in conjunction with goal setting). In the best cases, open lines of communication between employees and managers are so strongly incorporated into the corporate culture — as is the case at Boise Cascade's paper products group — that feedback flows without hesitation.[90]

Establish Client Relationships   The job characteristic model suggests that jobs should be designed so that the person performing a service (e.g., an auto mechanic) comes into contact with the recipient of that service (e.g., the car owner). Jobs designed in this manner not only help the employee by providing feedback, they also provide skill variety (e.g., by talking to customers in addition to fixing cars) and enhance autonomy (e.g., by giving people the freedom to manage their own relationships with clients) (Figure 4.17).

This suggestion has been implemented at Sea-Land Service, the large, containerized ocean-shipping company.[91] Once this company's mechanics, clerks, and crane operators started meeting with customers, their productivity increased. Having faces to associate with the once-abstract jobs they did clearly helped them take those jobs more seriously.

Load Jobs Vertically   As described earlier, loading a job vertically involves giving people greater responsibility for that job. Taking responsibility and control over performance away from managers and then giving it to their subordinates increases the level of autonomy these jobs offer the lower-level employees. According to a recent poll, autonomy is among the most important things people look for in their jobs — even more important than high pay.[92] Therefore, a growing number of companies are yielding control and giving employees increased freedom to do their jobs as they wish (within limits, at least).

FIGURE 4.17

Establishing Client Relationships: An Example

Ernie Garcia spends his mornings delivering shirts for Cadet Uniform Service. To improve customer service, he now spends his afternoons responding to customers' special requests and complaints. Both Ernie and the customers on his route are quite satisfied with the result.

YOU BE THE CONSULTANT

Absenteeism has been so chronically high at a manufacturing plant that some days not enough crew are present at the start of a shift to staff all the stations of the assembly line. The company is suffering as a result and turns to you for advice.

1. How can the job be made more interesting to encourage employees to show up for work?

2. How can rewards help to alleviate this problem? What are the theoretical bases for these suggestions?

3. How would equity theory explain this situation? What recommendations would it offer as a solution?

Consider, for example, Childress Buick, an auto dealership in Phoenix, Arizona. This company suffered serious customer dissatisfaction and employee retention problems before the owner, Rusty Childress, began encouraging his employees to use their own judgment and initiative. Sometimes, previously autocratic managers are shocked when they see how hard people work once they are allowed to make their own decisions. Bob Freese, the CEO of Alphatronix, Inc., in Research Triangle Park, North Carolina, is among the newly converted. "We let employees tell us when they can accomplish a project and what resources they need," he says. "Virtually always they set higher goals than we would ever set for them."[93] (For suggestions on how, exactly, to make autonomy work, see the "Tips" section below.)

■ **Three Not-So-Simple Rules for Making Autonomy Work**

TIPS: DOING IT RIGHT

Naturally, autonomy is not a panacea. If it *always* were effective in motivating people, then all companies would be using it all the time. There are, however, some commonalties between organizations that use autonomy effectively. By understanding these, we can recognize ways of using autonomy effectively in our own organizations. That said, we ask what, exactly, do companies do to make autonomy work?

First, companies that have successfully given employees autonomy tend to invest both time and effort in ensuring they hire people who can do their jobs properly without close supervision. Giving people autonomy without making sure they want it is a sure path to disaster.

Second, once employees who are interested in autonomy are selected (e.g., those who are high in growth need strength), they must be trained to do their jobs effectively. After all, they need to know what they are doing very, very well before they are left to do that job on their own.

Third, autonomy works in organizations in which high-quality performance is always expected—and even demanded. As you know, some companies are more tolerant of marginal performance—and even of average performance—than others. No one ever likes to see questionable work, but it tends to be accepted without question in some places more than in others. Employees should not be given a great deal of autonomy in any such organization. In fact, among those organizations in which autonomy works effectively, it does so *because* everyone involved strongly believes in the importance of performing at exceptionally high levels.

In closing, we acknowledge that the three guidelines identified here are far easier to describe than to implement. After all, personnel selection rarely is perfect, and people who are wrong for the job sometimes do slip in. By the same token, even the most highly trained people can make poor decisions when left on their own. Finally, even the strongest organizational norms embracing high-quality work may not always lead to such. Despite these concerns, we believe the potential benefits associated with giving workers job autonomy makes any efforts at tackling these challenges head-on worthwhile. ■

We invite you to visit the Greenberg page on the Prentice Hall Web site at: **www.prenhall.com/greenberg** for the monthly Greenberg update and for this chapter's World Wide Web exercise.

SUMMARY AND REVIEW
OF LEARNING OBJECTIVES

1. **Define *motivation*, and explain its importance in the field of organizational behavior.**
   Motivation is concerned with the set of processes that arouse, direct, and maintain behavior toward a goal. It is not equivalent to job performance, but it is one of several determinants in job performance. Today's work ethic motivates people to seek interesting and challenging jobs instead of simply money.

2. **Describe *need hierarchy theory* and what it recommends about improving motivation in organizations.**
   Maslow's **need hierarchy theory** postulates that people have five basic needs. These needs are activated in a specific order from the most basic, lowest-level need (i.e., physiological needs) to the highest-level need (i.e., need for self-actualization). This theory has not been supported by rigorous research studies, but it has been quite useful in suggesting several ways of satisfying employees' needs on the job. A less restrictive conceptualization, Alderfer's **ERG theory**, proposes

that people have only three basic needs: existence, relatedness, and growth. Following from these theories, companies can do several things to motivate their employees. Notably, they should promote a healthy workforce, provide financial security, provide opportunities to socialize, and recognize their employees' accomplishments.

3. **Identify and explain the conditions through which *goal setting* can be used to improve job performance.**

Locke and Latham's **goal setting** theory claims that an assigned goal influences a person's beliefs about being able to perform a task (referred to as **self-efficacy**) as well as his or her personal goals. In turn these factors, influence performance. People will improve their performance when specific, acceptably difficult goals are set and feedback about task performance is provided. The task of selecting goals that are acceptable to employees is facilitated by allowing employees to participate in the goal-setting process.

4. **Describe *equity theory* and *procedural justice*, and explain how they may be applied to motivating people in organizations.**

Adams' **equity theory** claims that people desire to attain an equitable balance between the ratio of their work rewards (i.e., outcomes) and their job contributions (i.e., inputs) and the corresponding ratios of others. Inequitable states of **overpayment inequity** and of **underpayment inequity** are undesirable, thus motivating people to attain equitable conditions. Responses to inequity may be either behavioral (e.g., raising or lowering one's performance) or psychological (e.g., thinking differently about work contributions). People are concerned about establishing equitable relationships and about **procedural justice** — that is, having organizational decisions made using fair processes both in structural terms (e.g., having a voice in decision-making procedures) and in interpersonal terms (e.g., by being treated with dignity and respect). These theories, which are known collectively as theories of organizational justice, suggest that companies should avoid intentionally underpaying or overpaying their employees and that managers should thoroughly explain the basis for outcomes in a socially sensitive manner.

5. **Describe *expectancy theory* and how it may be applied in organizations.**

Expectancy theory recognizes that motivation is the product of a person's beliefs about **expectancy** (i.e., that effort will lead to performance), **instrumentality** (i.e., that performance will result in reward), and **valence** (i.e., the perceived value of the rewards). In conjunction with skills, abilities, role perceptions, and opportunities, motivation contributes to job performance. Expectancy theory suggests that motivation may be enhanced by linking rewards to performance (as in **pay-for-performance plans**) and by administering rewards that are highly valued (as in **cafeteria-style benefit plans**).

6. **Distinguish between *job enlargement* and *job enrichment* as techniques for motivating employees.**

An effective, organizational-level technique for motivating people is designing or redesigning jobs. **Job design** techniques include **job enlargement** (i.e., performing more tasks at the same level) and **job enrichment** (i.e., giving people greater responsibility and control over their jobs).

7. **Describe the *job characteristics model* and its implications for redesigning jobs to enhance motivation.**

The **job characteristics model** identifies the specific job dimensions that should be enriched (i.e., skill variety, task identity, task significance, autonomy, and feedback) and relates these to the critical psychological states that are influenced by including these dimensions on a job. In turn, these psychological states will lead to certain beneficial outcomes for both individual employees (e.g., job satisfaction) and the organization (e.g., reduced absenteeism and turnover). Jobs may be designed to enhance motivation by combining tasks, opening feedback channels, establishing client relationships, and loading jobs vertically (i.e., enhancing responsibility for one's work).

QUESTIONS FOR DISCUSSION

1. Based on Maslow's need hierarchy theory, what specific things can be done to enhance an employee's motivation?

2. Why might setting goals be an effective way of motivating people on the job? What steps can be taken to ensure the effectiveness of goal setting in practice?

3. Suppose an employee feels underpaid relative to his or her coworkers. What conditions may have led to these feelings, and how might you expect such an individual to behave on the job?

4. Imagine you are devising a policy for determining the order in which vacation times are selected in your department. How can you do so in a manner

the people involved will believe is procedurally fair?

5. Consider a poor-performing employee who explains to his boss that he is trying very hard. According to expectancy theory, what factors would contribute to such effort? What additional factors (besides motivation) contribute to task performance?

6. According to the job characteristics model, what steps might be taken to enhance the motivation of someone performing a sales job?

7. Explain the role that money plays as a motivator in all theories of motivation as presented in this chapter.

Case in Point

Innovative Compensation Plans Motivate Employees of Three Small Firms

Times have been tough in the plastic knob business. Ask Ed Rogan, the owner of Rogan in Northbrook, Illinois, and he'll tell you how the introduction of electronic controls on calibrating instruments has lost him many of his customers. A declining market made pay raises for his 107 employees out of the question, which in turn made it tough to keep them from bailing out — let alone motivate them. Rogan's solution was to give his employees an incentive to find ways of cutting costs by giving them a share of the savings. The hundreds of ideas he received not only helped the company to

stay afloat but earned the employees an extra 17 percent of their annual salaries in recent years.

The key to the success of Rogan's approach is that sharing improvements encourages employees to take responsibility for their own work. A similar idea is used at Aspect Communications, a communications equipment manufacturer in San Jose, California, where instead of pegging bonuses to savings, pay is linked to two key aspects of customer service: the amount of time the company's product is operational, and measures of customer satisfaction. The basic idea, explains CEO

Jim Carreker, is that for the company to be profitable, employees must demonstrate a long-term commitment to customer service. This approach has kept all of Aspect's 400 employees carefully watching the two measures on which their pay (and their customers' satisfaction) is based — and, we add, has kept them quite happy with their paychecks.

Paychecks also have been full of pleasant surprises for the 190 employees of the Calvert Group, a financial-management company based in Bethesda, Maryland. These checks include bonuses for outstanding performers and regular distributions of the company's profits. The better the employees perform, the better the company does — and the more the employees make. Says Butler Perkins, a microcomputer-support analyst, "We all know the things we have to do to make more money." And, it appears, Calvert employees are doing those things.

This is only part of what the Calvert Group does to show appreciation for its employees, however. In a very unusual move, the company also reimburses its employees' commuting expenses. If you walk to work,

the company will even give you running shoes. To save on other expenses (e.g., dry cleaning) still further, Calvert has dropped its dress code, thus allowing employees to come to work in casual clothes — a feature they all like very much.

CRITICAL THINKING QUESTIONS

1. Explain how concepts of organizational justice may be used to explain the success of the incentive programs described here.

2. Effective incentives involve more than just money. Explain what these three firms are doing in recognition of this fact.

3. What basic tenets of expectancy theory are illustrated by the innovative incentive systems described here?

4. Do you think these same incentive programs would work as effectively at larger companies? Why, or why not?

Motivation in Organizations

People work for many reasons. For most, it has something to do with earning money, but money itself often is not reason enough to hold a particular job with a particular company. There usually is something more to it. The issue becomes even more interesting when you consider why people often stay in the same job for a long time — and enjoy it.

The Harbor Marine Corporation might be a good place to get a better understanding of work motivation. One thing is clear: Everyone who works at Harbor Marine enjoys the water. As one employee put it, "It's a lot of fun, and I get paid for doing what I like doing, working on the water." A love of the water probably is not the only thing that gets these people excited about coming to work.

Another place to better understand the excitement about this company is its owner, Ray DiSanto. DiSanto has been in the construction business for more than 30 years and has owned Harbor Marine for about

17 years. DiSanto has owned his own business since he was 19 years old. There is an obvious pattern in how he has moved from his one-person operation to what he has today. DiSanto loves to work, and he loves the career he has built for himself. Importantly, DiSanto realizes that he has not reached his goals alone. He talks about the importance of what the company stands for in the eyes of its customers. Interestingly, he seems as concerned — if not more concerned — about what the company stands for in the eyes of his employees.

As you watch this video, pay attention to what DiSanto says about why he is proud to own his own business. Consider those things that might help you better understand what makes DiSanto tick. Next, consider DiSanto's comments about running a company and his ideas about how to treat employees. You get to meet some employees of the Harbor Marine Corporation on this video, and as you listen to them talk, think about how what they are saying relates to what you have learned about motivation.

(continued)

1. You have learned a lot about the evolution of Ray DiSanto's career in the construction industry. He does not appear to be a guy who sits still. What do you think motivates DiSanto to keep trying new things?

2. Do you think the excitement that DiSanto brings to the job does anything to motivate his employees? What do you think it is about DiSanto that is important to his employees?

3. You have met a few employees of the Harbor Marine Corporation. Using Alderfer's ERG model, discuss how basic needs are addressed through employment at Harbor Marine.

4. DiSanto talks about the importance of keeping the equipment in good working order; he likes to keep things working smoothly. Do you think this approach affects the motivation of his employees? Why, or why not?

SKILLS BANK

EXPERIENCING ORGANIZATIONAL BEHAVIOR

Do You Receive Fair Interpersonal Treatment on the Job?

A key element of procedural justice focuses on how fairly people believe they are treated by others, including coworkers, bosses, and the company as a whole. The following questionnaire is designed to provide insight into these beliefs.

Directions

Think about what your organization is like most of the time. Then, for each of the 18 items, select *Yes* if the statement describes your organization, *No* if it does not, and *?* if you cannot decide.

In this organization . . .

1. Employees are praised for good work.	Yes	?	No
2. Supervisors yell at employees.	Yes	?	No
3. Supervisors play favorites.	Yes	?	No
4. Employees are trusted.	Yes	?	No
5. Employees' complaints are dealt with effectively.	Yes	?	No
6. Employees are treated like children.	Yes	?	No
7. Employees are treated with respect.	Yes	?	No
8. Employees' questions and problems are responded to quickly.	Yes	?	No
9. Employees are told lies.	Yes	?	No
10. Employees' suggestions are ignored.	Yes	?	No
11. Supervisors swear at employees.	Yes	?	No
12. Employees' hard work is appreciated.	Yes	?	No
13. Supervisors threaten to fire or to lay off employees.	Yes	?	No
14. Employees are treated fairly.	Yes	?	No
15. Coworkers help each other.	Yes	?	No
16. Coworkers argue with each other.	Yes	?	No
17. Coworkers put each other down.	Yes	?	No
18. Coworkers treat each other with respect.	Yes	?	No

Source Questionnaire: Copyright © 1997 by Michelle A. Donovan, Fritz Drasgow, and Liberty J. Munson, University of Illinois at Urbana-Champaign.

Scoring

1. Give yourself one point each time you answer *Yes* to the following questions: 1, 4, 5, 7, 8, 12, 14, 15, and 18.

2. Give yourself one point each time you answer *No* to the following questions: 2, 3, 6, 9, 10, 11, 13, 16, and 17.

3. Add up the number of points that you scored to find your *fair interpersonal treatment score.* Your score may range from 0 to 18, with higher scores representing more positive interpersonal treatment in your organization.

Questions for Discussion

1. What did your score reveal about the degree of interpersonal treatment in your organization? Is this what you would have guessed in advance?

2. Do you think other people in your organization would agree or disagree with how you answered these questions? Why?

3. Is there any one person (e.g., a particular boss) who, in your estimation, is mostly responsible for how you answered the questions? If so, how would you have answered the questions if the organization did not include this individual?

4. What could be done to improve the fairness of the interpersonal treatment you receive in your organization?

SKILLS BANK

WORKING IN GROUPS

Does Goal Setting Really Work? Demonstrate It for Yourself

Specific, difficult goals tend to enhance task performance. The following exercise is designed to help you demonstrate this effect for yourself. All you need is a class of students willing to participate and a few simple supplies.

Directions

1. Select a page of text from a book, and make several photocopies. Carefully count the words, and number each word on one of the copies. This will be your score sheet.

2. Find another class of 30 or more students who do not know anything about goal setting. (We do not want their knowledge of the phenomenon to bias the results.) On a random basis, divide the students into three equal-size groups.

3. Ask the students in the first group — the "baseline" group — to copy as much of the text as they can onto another piece of paper, and give them exactly one minute to do so. Direct them to work quickly. Using the score sheet created in step 1, identify the highest number of words copied by any one of the students, and then multiply this number by 2. This will be the specific, difficult goal level.

4. Ask the students in the second group — the "specific goal" group — to copy the number of words on the same printed page for exactly one minute. Tell them to try to reach the specific goal number identified in step 3.

5. Repeat this process with the third group — the "do your best" group — but instead of giving them a specific goal, direct them to "try to do your best at this task."

6. Compute the average number of words copied in the "difficult goal" group and the "do your best" group. Have your instructor compute the appropriate statistical test (a *t*-test, in this case) to determine the statistical significance of this difference in performance levels.

Questions for Discussion

1. Was there a statistically significant difference between the performance levels of the two groups? If so, did students in the "specific goal" group outperform those in the "do your best" group, as expected? What does this reveal about the effectiveness of goal setting?

2. If the predicted findings were not supported, why do you suppose this happened? What was it about the procedure that may have led to this failure? Was the specific goal (i.e., twice the fastest speed in the "baseline" group) too high, thus making the goal unreachable? Alternatively, was it too low, thus making the specific goal too easy?

3. What do you think would happen if the goal was lowered, thus making it easier, or raised, thus making it more difficult?

4. Do you think that providing feedback about goal attainment (e.g., someone counting the number of words copied and calling this out to the performers as they worked) would have helped?

5. For what other kinds of tasks do you believe goal setting may be effective? Specifically, do you believe that goal setting can improve your own performance on something? Explain this possibility.

WORK-RELATED ATTITUDES: FEELINGS ABOUT JOBS, ORGANIZATIONS, AND PEOPLE

LEARNING OBJECTIVES

After reading this chapter, you should be able to

1. Define *attitudes*, and understand their basic components.
2. Describe the concept of *job satisfaction*, and outline the techniques for measuring it.
3. Summarize two major theories of job satisfaction.
4. Explain the major consequences of job dissatisfaction and how to overcome them.
5. Define *organizational commitment*, and describe the three major types.
6. Describe the major consequences from low levels of organizational commitment and how to overcome them.
7. Distinguish *prejudice* from *discrimination*, and identify victims of prejudice in organizations.
8. Describe how organizations today manage *diversity* in the workforce.
9. Describe the effectiveness of *diversity management programs*.

PREVIEW CASE

Denny's and Shoney's Add Racial Equality to Their Menus

During the early 1990s, if you predicted two of the most popular casual family restaurant chains in the United States — Shoney's and Denny's — would appear on *Fortune* magazine's 1998 list of the best 50 companies for Asians, African Americans, and Hispanics, you would not have been taken seriously. After all, in 1992, Shoney's paid $132.8 million to settle a class-action discrimination suit filed by thousands of minority employees. In 1994, Denny's paid $54.4 million to African-American customers who claimed they were refused service. Only a few years later, however, Shoney's parent company — Advantica — ranked second on *Fortune*'s list, and Denny's ranked thirteenth.

Obviously, things have changed — and quite radically. How could two corporate pariahs transform their treatment of minority customers and employees so dramatically? Officials from both restaurants admit the lawsuits were eye-openers, leading them to find ways to redeem themselves.

Shoney's previously filled high-level positions from outside the company, thus neglecting talented minorities. Today, all openings are posted, and minority employees are seeking — and getting — these positions.

Advantica's CEO, Jim Adamson, is taking an even more proactive stance at Shoney's. Acknowledging that minority candidates tend not to have equal chances in the corporate world, he is taking the initiative at finding such individuals to fill top slots. Today, as a result of these efforts, one-third of the company's directors are Asians, African Americans, and Hispanics — more than any other company on *Fortune*'s list. In 1992, no one from these groups was included among the Shoney's top corporate managers. In addition, direct purchases from minority-owned suppliers have zoomed from $0 to $125 million during the past five years alone.

To ensure Advantica's attention to giving everyone a chance is more than superficial, managers are evaluated on 10 basic competencies, one of which is "valuing diversity." Any manager who falls short on this measure can find one-quarter of his or her bonus pay withheld — and anyone who misses the point completely is dismissed. At Denny's, attention to diversity extends beyond the workforce and to franchise ownership. In fact, minorities now own 35 percent of the company's 737 franchised restaurants.

Admittedly, some critics scoff at these corporate initiatives, claiming their motives are not genuine because the courts are looking over their shoulders. Others countered it is results — not motives — that matter. Given the benefits likely to result from diversifying the workforce — as well as the damage from not doing so — their commitment to minorities probably will continue.

D enny's and Shoney's changed their ways because they had to, but we suspect they eventually will realize the same benefits other companies have enjoyed without being under the gun. In other words, an ethnically diverse group of employees has a great deal to offer, and by giving these individuals equal opportunities, Denny's and Shoney's now can draw on this human capital to improve performance. In turn, this should keep all employees feeling good about working there, thereby keeping them on the job. Obviously, such feelings can have a strong effect on how we behave in organizations. Indeed, such feelings — or *attitudes*, as they are called — represent an important part of people's lives, particularly on the job. Not only may our attitudes toward jobs and organizations, which are referred to as *work-related attitudes* — have profound effects on how we perform, they also may affect the quality of life we experience while at work.

We begin by describing the general nature of attitudes, and then we take a closer look at several specific types of work-related attitudes. We start with *job satisfaction*, which essentially is a person's positive or negative feelings about their job.[1] Specifically, we describe some of the major factors contributing to feelings of satisfaction and dissatisfaction with one's work, and we consider the consequences of such reactions on OB.

Building on this, we then turn to another important work-related attitude: *organizational commitment*. This involves people's feelings about the organizations for which they work — that is, the degree to which they identify with the organizations that employ them.[2] Finally, we turn to a special type of attitude with which you probably are all too familiar: *prejudice*. This involves negative views about others who fall in certain categories, such as women and ethnic minorities (to mention just a few).[3] Such attitudes can seriously disrupt the lives of individuals and the effective functioning of the organizations that employ them.

ATTITUDES: WHAT ARE THEY?

If we asked how you felt about your job, we probably would find you to be very opinionated. For example, you might say you really like it and think it is very interesting. Perhaps you might complain about it bitterly and say it bores you out of your mind. Maybe you would hold views that are more complex, liking some things (e.g., "My boss is great.") and disliking others (e.g., "The pay is terrible.").

Three Essential Components of Attitudes

The attitudes we all express, no matter what they may be, consist of three major components: an *evaluative*, a *cognitive*, and a *behavioral* component.[4] These represent the basic building blocks of our definition of attitudes (Figure 5.1).

Thus far, we have suggested that attitudes greatly affect how we feel about something. Indeed, this aspect of an attitude—that is, its **evaluative component**—refers to our liking or disliking of any particular person, item, or event (what might be called the *attitude object*, or the focus of our attitude). For example, you may feel positively or negatively toward your boss, the sculpture in the lobby, or the fact that your company just landed a large contract.

Attitudes involve more than feelings, however. They also involve knowledge—that is, what you believe about an attitude object. For example, you might believe that a coworker is paid more than you or that your supervisor does not know much about the job. Whether completely accurate or totally false, these beliefs, comprise the **cognitive component** of attitudes.

As you might imagine, what you believe about something (e.g., "My boss is embezzling company funds.") and how you feel about it (e.g., "I can't stand working for him.") may affect how you are predisposed to behave (e.g., "I'm going to look for a new job."). In other words, attitudes also have a **behavioral component**—that is, a

evaluative component
Our liking or disliking of any particular person, item, or event.

cognitive component
What we believe, whether true or false, about an attitude object.

behavioral component
Our predisposition to behave in a way consistent with our beliefs and feelings about an attitude object.

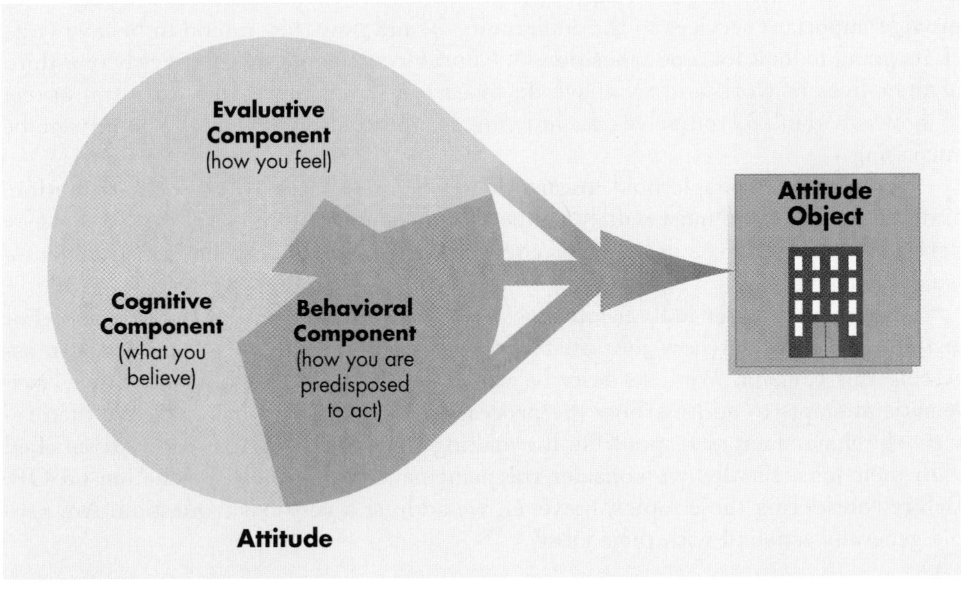

FIGURE 5.1

Three Basic Components of Attitudes

Attitudes are composed of three fundamental components: an *evaluative component*, a *cognitive component*, and a *behavioral component*.

Evaluative Component (how you feel)

Cognitive Component (what you believe)

Behavioral Component (how you are predisposed to act)

Attitude Object

Attitude

predisposition to act a certain way. Such a predisposition may not actually be predictive of one's behavior, however. For example, you may be interested in taking a new job, but you might not actually take one if a better position is not available or if other aspects of the job compensate for your negative feelings. In other words, your intention to behave a certain way may — or may not — dictate how you actually do.

GLOBAL MATTERS

People do not always behave in ways that are consistent with their attitudes. For example, workers from Western countries may hold negative attitudes toward their coworkers and treat them poorly as a result. In Asian cultures, however, treatment of others is more deeply rooted in tradition, which may take precedence over personal feelings. ▪

Basic Definitions

attitudes

Relatively stable clusters of feelings, beliefs, and behavioral intentions toward specific objects, people, or institutions.

Combining these various components, we can define **attitudes** as relatively stable clusters of feelings, beliefs, and behavioral predispositions (i.e., intentions toward some specific object). By including the phrase "relatively stable," we are referring to something that is not fleeting. In other words, once formed, it tends to persist. Indeed, as we explain in throughout this chapter (and also in chapter 16), changing attitudes may require considerable effort.

work-related attitudes

Attitudes relating to any aspect of work or work settings.

When we speak about **work-related attitudes**, we refer to those lasting feelings, beliefs, and behavioral tendencies toward various aspects of the job itself, the setting in which the work is conducted, and the people involved. Work-related attitudes are associated with many important aspects of OB, including job performance, absence from work, and voluntary turnover.

Now that we have identified the basic nature of attitudes, we turn our attention to specific work-related attitudes. We begin by describing a fundamental work-related attitude: *job satisfaction* (i.e., attitudes toward one's job).

JOB SATISFACTION: ATTITUDES TOWARD ONE'S JOB

If you asked people about their jobs, you likely would find they have strong opinions about how they feel (e.g., "I really dislike what I do."), what they believe (e.g., "We provide important services to the community."), and how they intend to behave (e.g., "I am going to look for a new position."). Considering people spend roughly one-third of their lives at work and what we do to earn a living represents a central aspect of how we think of ourselves as individuals, these strong feelings should not be surprising.

job satisfaction

Positive or negative attitudes held by individuals toward their jobs.

The attitudes people hold toward their jobs are referred to as **job satisfaction**, and this is one of the most widely studied work-related attitudes. Formally, we may define job satisfaction as individuals' cognitive, affective, and evaluative reactions toward their jobs.[5]

In taking a closer look at job satisfaction, we address several major issues. For example, we consider how job satisfaction is measured, which is a key issue in assessing this concept. We also describe various theories of job satisfaction (i.e., systematic attempts to address how the process of job satisfaction works). We then review the major factors responsible for making people either satisfied or dissatisfied with their jobs. Finally, we consider the principal effects of job satisfaction on OB. Before considering these topics, however, we address a very basic question: Are people generally satisfied with their jobs?

Are People Generally Satisfied with Their Jobs?

If you were to make assumptions about people's general levels of job satisfaction from stories in newspapers of disgruntled workers going on strike or even killing their supervisors, you probably would think people generally are very dissatisfied with their jobs.[6] These are extreme examples, however. Overall, evidence suggests most people actually are quite satisfied with their jobs.

Demonstrating this, a survey in the United States, Mexico, and Spain had workers indicate their levels of satisfaction with their work and the behavior of their supervisors.[7] As shown in Figure 5.2, the mean response to both questions was quite high—and uniformly so in all three countries. When considered together with other surveys (conducted over several decades) showing that 80 to 90 percent of people are relatively satisfied with their jobs, a much more optimistic picture emerges.[8]

Certain Groups of People Are More Satisfied with Their Jobs than Others   As you might imagine, the complete picture is more complex. Not everyone doing every type of job is equally satisfied. Specific patterns of job satisfaction or dissatisfaction have been clearly established in certain groups. So, then, who tends to be most satisfied with their jobs? Here are some key findings:

- White-collar personnel (e.g., managerial and professional people) tend to be more satisfied than blue-collar personnel (e.g., physical laborers, factory workers).[9]
- Older people generally are more satisfied with their jobs than younger people. Interestingly, however, satisfaction does not increase at an even pace. People become more satisfied with their jobs during their thirties (as they become more successful), level off during their forties (as they become disenchanted), and become more satisfied again during their late fifties (as they resign themselves to their lot in life).[10]

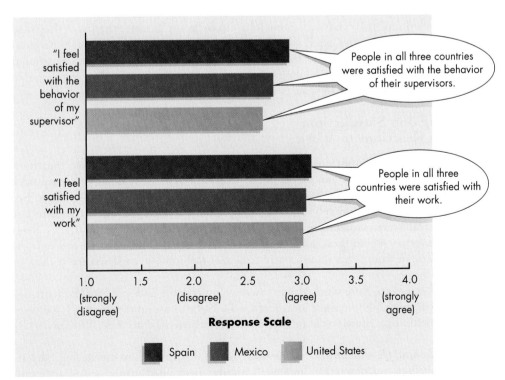

Response Scale

Spain   Mexico   United States

FIGURE 5.2

Are People Satisfied with Their Jobs: A Three-Nation Comparison

When people in Spain, Mexico, and the United States were asked how satisfied they were with their work and the behavior of their supervisors, all responded very positively.

(*Source*: Based on data reported by Page & Wiseman, 1993; see note 7.)

- People who are more experienced on their jobs are more highly satisfied than those who are less experienced.[11] This should not be surprising, because people who are highly dissatisfied with their jobs may be expected to find new ones when they can. Moreover, the longer someone stays on a job, the more strongly that employee rationalizes his or her tenure by perceiving the job in a positive light.

- Women and members of minority groups tend to be more dissatisfied with their jobs than men and members of majority groups.[12] This appears to result from the tendency for victims of discrimination to be channeled into lower-level jobs and positions with limited opportunities for advancement.

GLOBAL MATTERS   Are people from some countries more satisfied with their jobs than those from other countries? Despite some limited evidence of this effect, there appear to be no stable differences in overall job satisfaction throughout the world. ∎

Some Individuals Are Always More Satisfied with Their Jobs than Others: Job Satisfaction As a Personal Disposition   Not only may certain groups of people be more satisfied with their jobs than others, but also it appears some individuals are likely to be either consistently satisfied or dissatisfied with their jobs. This is the basic idea behind the **dispositional model of job satisfaction**. The main idea is that job satisfaction is a relatively stable individual disposition—that is, a characteristic that stays with people across situations. According to this conceptualization, people who like whatever jobs they are doing at one point in time can be expected to like the jobs they are doing at another point in time—even if the jobs are different.

dispositional model of job satisfaction

The conceptualization proposing that job satisfaction is a relatively stable, individual disposition—that is, a characteristic that stays with people across situations.

This is exactly what researchers have found. For example, consider a fascinating study of more than 5,000 men who changed jobs between 1969 and 1971.[13] In this investigation, expressions of job satisfaction were relatively stable. In other words, despite having different jobs, men who were satisfied or dissatisfied in 1969 tended to be equally satisfied or dissatisfied in 1971. More recent research has found these effects last even longer—10 years in one study.[14] Specifically, the more people reported feeling satisfied and involved with their jobs at one point in time, the more they also felt this same way 10 years later, when many things may have changed. (For a general overview of these effects, see Figure 5.3.) Such findings support the dispositional model of job satisfaction, thus leading us to conclude, quite simply, that some people tend to be more satisfied with whatever jobs they have than others.

Measuring Job Satisfaction: Assessing Reactions to Work

People have many different attitudes toward various aspects of their jobs, but these are not as easy to assess as you might think. You cannot directly observe an attitude, after all, and you cannot accurately infer its existence based on people's behavior. So, for the most part, we must rely on what people tell us to determine their attitudes. People generally are not entirely open about this subject, however, and they keep much of what they feel to themselves. Moreover, sometimes our attitudes are so complex it is difficult to express them in any coherent fashion—even if we are willing to do so.

Social scientists have worked hard to develop reliable and valid instruments designed to systematically measure job satisfaction. Several useful techniques have been developed, including *rating scales* or *questionnaires*, *critical incidents*, and *interviews*.

Rating Scales and Questionnaires   The most common approach to measuring job satisfaction involves questionnaires in which highly specialized rating scales are completed. Using this method, people answer questions, thereby allowing them to report

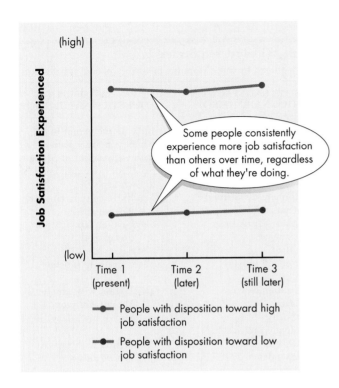

FIGURE 5.3

Some People Are Always More Satisfied with Their Jobs than Others

Results supporting the *dispositional model of job satisfaction* tend to take the form summarized here: Some people are consistently more satisfied with their jobs than others, even when they have held different jobs over long periods of time.

their reactions to their jobs. Several different scales have been developed for this purpose, and these vary greatly in form and scope (Table 5.1 on page 174).

One of the most popular questionnaires is the **Job Descriptive Index (JDI)**, in which people indicate whether each of several adjectives describes a particular aspect of their work.[15] Questions on the JDI deal with five distinct aspects of jobs: the work itself, pay, promotional opportunities, supervision, and people (i.e., coworkers).

Another widely used measure, the **Minnesota Satisfaction Questionnaire (MSQ)**, uses a different approach.[16] In this scale, people rate the extent to which they are satisfied or dissatisfied with various aspects of their jobs (e.g., pay, chances for advancement). Higher scores reflect higher degrees of job satisfaction.

The JDI and the MSQ measure many aspects of job satisfaction, but other scales focus on specific facets of satisfaction. For example, the **Pay Satisfaction Questionnaire (PSQ)** primarily is concerned with attitudes toward various aspects of pay.[17] More specifically, the PSQ provides valid measures of critical aspects such as satisfaction with pay level, pay raises, fringe benefits, and the structure and administration of the pay system.[18]

One important advantage of rating scales is that they can be completed quickly and efficiently by many people. Another benefit is that when the same questionnaire already has been administered to thousands of individuals, average scores for people in many kinds of jobs and types of organizations become available. This allows the scores of people in a given company to be compared with these averages and measures of *relative* satisfaction to be obtained. This may be useful information for scientists interested in studying job satisfaction as well as for companies interested in learning about trends in the feelings of employees.

Critical Incidents Technique   A second procedure for assessing job satisfaction is the **critical incidents technique**, in which individuals describe events relating to their work they found to be especially satisfying or dissatisfying. Their replies then are examined to uncover underlying themes. For example, if many employees mention on-the-job situations in which supervisors treated them rudely or praised supervisors for sensitivity

Job Descriptive Index (JDI)

A rating scale for assessing job satisfaction; individuals respond to this questionnaire by indicating whether various adjectives describe aspects of their work.

Minnesota Satisfaction Questionnaire (MSQ)

A rating scale for assessing job satisfaction in which people indicate the extent to which they are satisfied with various aspects of their jobs.

Pay Satisfaction Questionnaire (PSQ)

A questionnaire to assess employees' satisfaction with various aspects of their pay (e.g., its overall level, raises, benefits).

critical incidents technique

A procedure for measuring job satisfaction in which employees describe incidents relating to their work they found especially satisfying or dissatisfying.

T A B L E   5 . 1

Measures of Job Satisfaction: Some Widely Used Scales

The items shown here are similar to those used in three popular measures of job satisfaction.

JOB DESCRIPTIVE INDEX (JDI)	MINNESOTA SATISFACTION QUESTIONNAIRE (MSQ)	PAY SATISFACTION QUESTIONNAIRE (PSQ)
Enter "Yes," "No," or "?" for each description or word below. Work itself: ___ Routine ___ Satisfactory ___ Good Promotions: ___ Dead-end job ___ Few promotions ___ Good opportunity for promotion	Indicate the extent to which you are satisfied with each aspect of your present job. Enter one number next to each aspect. 1 = Extremely dissatisfied 2 = Not satisfied 3 = Neither satisfied nor dissatisfied 4 = Satisfied 5 = Extremely satisfied ___ Utilization of your abilities ___ Authority ___ Company policies and practices ___ Independence ___ Supervision-human relations	Indicate the extent to which you are satisfied with each aspect of present pay. Enter one number next to each aspect. 1 = Extremely dissatisfied 2 = Not satisfied 3 = Neither satisfied nor dissatisfied 4 = Satisfied 5 = Extremely satisfied Satisfaction with pay level: ___ My current pay ___ Size of my salary Satisfaction with raises: ___ Typical raises ___ How raises are determined

Source: Based on items from the JDI, MSQ, and PSQ; see notes 15, 16, and 17.

during a difficult period, this suggests that supervisory style plays an important role in their job satisfaction.

Interviews   A third procedure for assessing job satisfaction involves careful, face-to-face interviews with employees. By questioning people in person about their attitudes, it often is possible to explore more deeply than by using highly structured questionnaires. By carefully posing questions to employees and systematically recording their answers, it is possible to learn about the causes of various work-related attitudes. For example, one team of researchers relied on face-to-face meetings with employees to learn their feelings about their company's recent bankruptcy filing.[19] This highly personal approach to data collection is particularly effective in gathering reactions to such complex and difficult situations.

ETHICS MATTERS   To avoid jeopardizing respondents' jobs and to ensure valid responses, researchers who collect information about job satisfaction must keep all responses completely confidential and clearly assure the respondents of this. In fact, it is useful to keep the respondents' identities themselves anonymous, thereby making it impossible to identify anything that any one respondent may have said. ■

Theories of Job Satisfaction

What makes some people more satisfied with their jobs than others? What underlying processes account for people's feelings of job satisfaction? We now describe two of the most influential theories of job satisfaction: *two-factor theory*, and *value theory*.

Two-Factor Theory   Think about some things that may have happened on the job that made you feel especially satisfied or dissatisfied. What were these events? (This is an example of the *critical incidents technique* described earlier.) More than 30 years ago, an organizational scientist posed this question to more than 200 accountants and engineers and then carefully analyzed their responses.[20] What that scientist found was somewhat surprising: Different factors accounted for job satisfaction and dissatisfaction. This is known as the **two-factor theory**.

You might have expected certain factors to lead to satisfaction when they are present and to dissatisfaction when they are absent, but this was *not* the case. Job satisfaction and dissatisfaction stemmed from different sources (Figure 5.4). In particular, dissatisfaction was associated with conditions surrounding the job (e.g., working conditions, pay, security, quality of supervision, relations with others) rather than with the work itself. Because these factors prevent negative reactions, they are referred to as *hygiene* (or *maintenance*) *factors*. In contrast, satisfaction was associated with factors associated with the work itself or to outcomes directly derived from it (e.g., nature of the job, achievement in the work, promotion opportunities, chance for personal growth and recognition). Because such factors are associated with high levels of job satisfaction, they are called *motivators*. Because motivators and hygiene factors are the major components of two-factor theory, it sometimes is referred to as **motivator-hygiene theory**.

Research testing this theory has yielded mixed results. Some studies have found job satisfaction and dissatisfaction to be based on different factors, which is in keeping with the distinction between motivators and hygiene factors.[21] Other studies, however, have found factors labeled as hygienes and motivators to exert strong effects on both satisfaction and dissatisfaction, thereby casting doubt on the two-factor theory.[22] Considering such equivocal evidence, we must label two-factor theory as an intriguing—but unverified—framework for understanding job satisfaction.

Two-factor theory still has important implications for managing organizations. Specifically, managers are well advised to focus their attention on factors known to promote job satisfaction, such as opportunities for personal growth. Indeed, several of today's companies have realized that satisfaction within their workforce is enhanced when opportunities are provided for employees to develop their repertoire of professional skills on the job. For example, front-line service workers at Marriott Hotels, who are known as "guest services associates," are hired to perform a variety of tasks, including checking guests in and out, carrying their bags, and so on.[23] Instead of doing just one job, this approach enables Marriott employees to call on and to develop many talents, thereby adding to their level of job satisfaction.

Two-factor theory also implies that conditions that help to avoid dissatisfaction should be created—and it specifies the kinds of variables required to do so (i.e., hy-

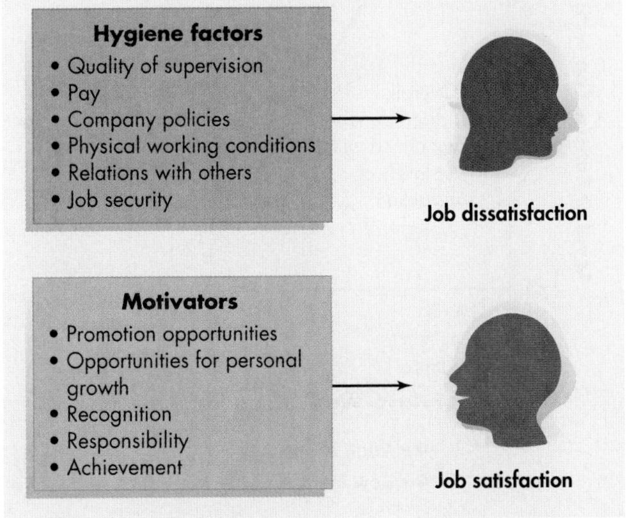

two-factor theory
A theory of job satisfaction suggesting that satisfaction and dissatisfaction stem from different groups of variables (i.e., *motivators* and *hygiene*, respectively).

motivator-hygiene theory
See *two-factor theory*.

Hygiene factors
- Quality of supervision
- Pay
- Company policies
- Physical working conditions
- Relations with others
- Job security

Job dissatisfaction

Motivators
- Promotion opportunities
- Opportunities for personal growth
- Recognition
- Responsibility
- Achievement

Job satisfaction

FIGURE 5.4

The Two-Factor Theory of Job Satisfaction

According to the *two-factor theory*, job satisfaction results from a set of factors referred to as *motivators*, whereas job dissatisfaction results from a different set of factors, which are known as *hygiene factors*. Some common motivators and hygiene factors are shown here.

giene factors). For example, pleasant working conditions may help to avoid job dis-satisfaction. Specifically, dissatisfaction is great under conditions that are highly over-crowded, dark, noisy, extreme in temperature, and poor in air quality.[24] These fac-tors, which are associated with the conditions under which work is performed but are not linked directly to the work itself, contribute much to the levels of job dissatisfac-tion encountered.

value theory

A theory suggesting that job satisfaction depends primarily on the match between the outcomes individuals value in their jobs and their perceptions about the availability of such outcomes.

Value Theory   A second important theory of job satisfaction is **value theory**.[25] This conceptualization claims job satisfaction exists to the extent the job outcomes (e.g., rewards) an individual receives match those that are desired. The more people receive outcomes they value, the more satisfied they are. Likewise, the less people receive out-comes they value, the less satisfied they are. Value theory focuses on *any* outcome that people value. The key to satisfaction in this approach is the *discrepancy* between those aspects of the job one has and those one wants; the greater the discrepancy, the less people are satisfied.

Recent research provides good support for value theory. Using a questionnaire, one team of investigators measured the level of various job facets (e.g., freedom to work one's own way, learning opportunities, promotion opportunities, pay level) that a diverse group of workers wanted as well as how much they felt they already had.[26] These investigators also measured how satisfied respondents were with each facet and how important each was to them. As shown in Figure 5.5, those aspects of the job about which respondents experienced the greatest discrepancies were the ones with which they were most dissatisfied, and those aspects with which they experienced the smallest discrepancies were the ones with which they were most satisfied. Interestingly, this relationship was greater among individuals who placed a high amount of satis-faction on a particular facet. In other words, the more important a particular facet of the job was believed to be, the less satisfied people were when they failed to get as much as they wanted.

FIGURE 5.5

Job Satisfaction: The Result of Getting What We Want

The larger the discrepancy be-tween what people have and what they want regarding various facets of their jobs (e.g., pay, learning opportunities), the more dissatis-fied they are with those jobs. This relationship is greater among those who place great importance on the facet than among those who con-sider it to be less important.

(*Source*: Adapted from McFarlin & Rice, 1992; see note 26.)

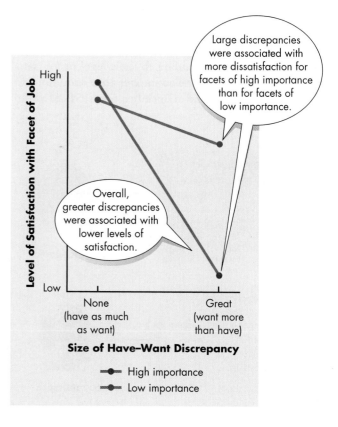

An interesting implication of value theory is that it calls attention to aspects that must be changed for job satisfaction to result. Specifically, this theory suggests these aspects might not be the same for everyone, but any valued aspects about which people perceive serious discrepancies. By emphasizing values, this theory suggests job satisfaction may derive from many factors. Thus, an effective way to satisfy employees is to find out what they want and—to the extent possible—to give it to them.

Believe it or not, this is sometimes easier said than done. In fact, organizations sometimes go through great pain finding out how to satisfy their employees. Thus, a growing number of companies (particularly big ones) have been surveying their employees systematically. For example, FedEx is so interested in tracking employee attitudes it now uses a fully automated, on-line survey. The company relies on information gained from surveys of its U.S.-based employees to identify sources of dissatisfaction among them.

Consequences of Job Dissatisfaction

People talk a great deal about the importance of building employee satisfaction; they assume morale is critical to the functioning of organizations. Job satisfaction does influence organizations, but its effect is not always as strong as one might expect. Thus, what are the consequences of job dissatisfaction? Here, we focus on two main variables: employee withdrawal (i.e., absenteeism and turnover), and job performance.

Job Satisfaction and Employee Withdrawal   When employees are dissatisfied with their jobs, they find ways of reducing their exposure to them. In other words, they stay away from their jobs, which is a phenomenon known as **employee withdrawal**. Two main forms of employee withdrawal are *absenteeism* and *voluntary turnover*.[27] By not showing up to work or by quitting to take a new job, people may be expressing job dissatisfaction or attempting to escape from unpleasant aspects they may be experiencing.

employee withdrawal
Actions such as chronic absenteeism and voluntary turnover (i.e., quitting one's job) that enable employees to escape adverse organizational situations.

The less people are satisfied with their jobs, the more likely they are to be absent.[28] The strength of this relationship, however, is only modest. Job dissatisfaction is likely to be just one of many factors influencing people's decisions to report—or not to report—for work. For example, even people who really dislike their jobs may not be absent if they believe their presence is necessary to complete an important project. Other employees, however, might dislike their jobs so much they will "play hooky," showing no concern for how the company is affected. Thus, absenteeism, though not a perfectly reliable reaction to job dissatisfaction, is one of its most important consequences.

Another costly form of withdrawal is voluntary turnover. The lower people's satisfaction with their jobs, the more likely they are to consider resigning—and to do so. As with absenteeism, this relationship is modest for similar reasons.[29] Many factors relating to individuals, their jobs, and economic conditions shape decisions to move from one job to another. As you might imagine, many more variables are involved in making turnover decisions, many of which are described in Figure 5.6.[30] According to this conceptualization, job dissatisfaction leads employees to think about quitting. In turn, this leads to the decision to search for another job. If the search is successful, the individual develops definite intentions either to quit or to remain on the job. Finally, these intentions are reflected in concrete actions.

The suggestion that economic conditions and, hence, the success of an initial search for alternative jobs strongly affect voluntary turnover is supported by research. For example, consider one interesting study in which researchers examined many previous studies concerned with turnover.[31] They contacted the scientists who originally conducted these studies and determined the precise dates when data had been collected. These researchers then obtained data on unemployment rates at those times. They predicted the relationship between job satisfaction and turnover would be

FIGURE 5.6

Voluntary Turnover: A Model
Scientists conceive of voluntary turnover as a complex process triggered by low job satisfaction. This leads people to think about quitting and, then, to search for another job. Finally, they form intentions to quit or to remain on their present jobs. At several steps in this process, the probability of finding an acceptable alternative plays a role.

(*Source*: Based on suggestions by Mobley, Horner, & Hollingsworth, 1978; see note 30.)

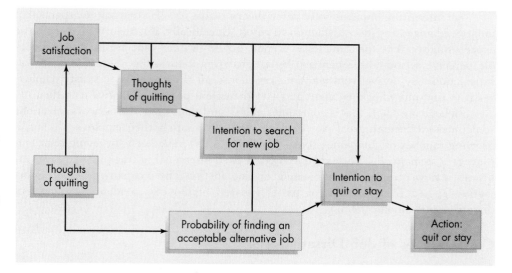

stronger when the unemployment rate was low than when it was high. When unemployment is low, they reasoned, people recognize they have many other job opportunities and are prone to take one when highly dissatisfied with their present jobs. In contrast, high unemployment limits alternative job options, thereby leading people to stay with their present jobs despite their dissatisfaction. This is precisely what they found: The higher the unemployment rates, the lower the correlation between job satisfaction and turnover.

Organizations are highly concerned about withdrawal, because it generally is very costly. The expenses of selecting and training employees to replace those who resign can be considerable. Even unscheduled absences can be expensive, averaging as high as $757 annually per employee by one recent estimate.[32] In fact, for the average large company, losses from absenteeism in 1998 were approximately $4 million — a figure that has been rising steadily over the years. Although voluntary turnover is permanent whereas absenteeism is a short-term reaction, both are effective ways of withdrawing from dissatisfying jobs.

Job Satisfaction and Task Performance Many people believe that happy workers are productive workers, but is this really the case? In other words, is job satisfaction directly linked to task performance or to organizational productivity? Overall, research suggests this relationship is positive but not especially strong. In fact, a review of hundreds of studies on this topic found that the mean correlation between job satisfaction and performance is extremely modest — only .17, which, as explained in the appendix to chapter 1, is quite small.[33] Why does job satisfaction have such a limited relationship to performance? There are several explanations.

First, many work settings have little room for large changes in performance. Some jobs are structured so that employees *must* maintain at least some minimum level of performance just to remain on their jobs. For others, there may be very little leeway for exceeding minimum standards. Thus, the range of possible performance in many jobs is highly restricted. Moreover, the rate at which many employees work is closely linked to the work of others or to the speed of various machines. As such, performance may have such little room to fluctuate it may not be highly responsive to changes in employee attitudes.

Second, job satisfaction and performance actually may not be directly linked. Any apparent relationship between them may stem from both being related to a third factor: receipt of various rewards. Some scientists suggest the relationship works as

follows:[34] Past levels of performance lead to the receipt of both extrinsic rewards (e.g., pay, promotions) and intrinsic rewards (e.g., feelings of accomplishment). If employees judge these rewards to be fair, they eventually may recognize a link between their performance and these outcomes. In turn, this may have two effects. First, it may encourage high levels of effort and, thus, good performance. Second, it may lead to high levels of job satisfaction. In short, high productivity and high satisfaction both may stem from the same conditions; however, these two factors themselves may not be directly linked. Thus, job satisfaction may not relate directly to performance in many contexts.

Job performance might not be closely affected by job dissatisfaction, but the concept of job satisfaction is very important. Naturally, we all want to be satisfied with our jobs. This keeps us from withdrawing from them, and it also makes them more pleasant and enjoyable. This is an important end in itself. (For some specific measures that can promote job satisfaction, see the "Tips" section on page 181.)

Guidelines for Promoting Job Satisfaction

Considering the negative consequences of job dissatisfaction, it makes sense to raise satisfaction and, thus, to prevent dissatisfaction on the job. An employee's dissatisfaction might not account for all aspects of his or her performance, but it is important to promote satisfaction — if for no other reason than to make people happy. After all, satisfaction is a desirable end in itself. Thus, what can be done to promote it? Based on what scientists know, we can offer several suggestions:

1. *Make jobs fun.* People are more satisfied with jobs they enjoy doing than with those they find dull and boring. Some jobs are intrinsically boring, of course, but some level of fun can be infused into almost any job. Creative techniques used in various companies include passing bouquets of flowers from one person's desk to another's every half hour, taking fun pictures of others on the job and posting them on the bulletin board, and organizing a contest in which people submit jokes (with judging conducted during the lunch break).[35] These tactics might not make the jobs themselves more satisfying, but they might reduce dissatisfaction by making the workplace more pleasant. For an example of how one entrepreneur is doing this, see Figure 5.7.

2. *Pay people fairly.* People who believe their organization's pay system is inherently unfair tend to be dissatisfied with their jobs. This applies not only to salary and hourly pay but to fringe benefits as well. In fact, when

FIGURE 5.7

He Can Get Job Satisfaction: Yeah, Yeah, Yeah

Skip Maggioria, owner of Skip's Music in Sacramento, California, is satisfied with his job — because he has fun while helping others have fun. His approach is simple. He organizes rock bands composed of aging baby boomers who come together to relive the musical experience of their youth. This creative tactic not only promotes business at his store, it also creates a sense of fun and importance for Skip and all who work with him.

know these four points

people can select the fringe benefits they most desire, their job satisfaction tends to rise, which is consistent with value theory. After all, given the opportunity to receive the fringe benefits they most desire, employees may have little or no discrepancies between those they want and those they actually have.

3. *Match people to jobs that fit their interests.* People have many interests, which only sometimes are satisfied on the job. The more people find they can fulfill their interests on the job, however, the more satisfied they are with those jobs. This is why career counselors frequently identify people's nonvocational interests. For example, several companies (e.g., AT&T, IBM, Ford Motor Company, Shell Oil, and Kodak) systematically test and counsel their employees so they can match their skills and interests with those positions for which they are best suited. Other companies (e.g., Coca Cola, Disney) even offer individualized counseling to employees so their personal and professional interests can be identified and matched.

4. *Avoid boring, repetitive jobs.* Most people find little satisfaction in highly boring, repetitive jobs (Figure 5.8). In keeping with two-factor theory, people are far more satisfied with jobs that allow them to succeed by taking control over how they do things. (This is the idea of job enlargement discussed in chapter 4.)

In conclusion, there is good news for managers interested in promoting satisfaction—and, thus, in avoiding dissatisfaction—among employees. It might not be easy to promote job satisfaction, especially considering the hectic pace of everyday work, but the benefits of keeping employees satisfied with their jobs suggests this effort may be extremely worthwhile. (Some of what we learn about how to improve job satisfaction comes from companies with dissatisfied employees who changed their attitudes dramatically in response to various things the company did. For an example of such a case, see the "Tips" section on page 181.)

FIGURE 5.8

Boring, Repetitive Jobs: A Common Cause of Dissatisfaction

Most people tend to be dissatisfied with jobs that require highly repetitive, boring work. Fortunately for this patient, these surgeons are unlikely to be using this occasion to make their jobs more interesting!

(*Source*: From *Harvard Business Review*, Jan.–Feb. 1996. © Sidney Harris.)

■ Once Burned from Half-Baked Management, Safeway Bakery Makes Dough Again—And Employee Satisfaction Rises

Not long ago, there was a serious problem at the Safeway market in Clackamas, Oregon. The 130 bakery workers were so upset with their jobs they frequently were absent, quit, and had on-the-job accidents. These were not minor problems. In one year alone, accidents resulted in 1,740 lost workdays—a very expensive problem. Accidents only occurred, of course, when employees bothered to show up. At unpopular times such as Saturday night, it was not unusual for as many as eight percent of workers to call in sick. Almost no one stayed on the job for more than a year. Clearly, withdrawal was a very disruptive response to dissatisfaction in this organization.

What made these workers so dissatisfied? Oddly, it was something that did not have to be a problem: the disrespectful and uncaring way they were treated by management. The bosses were highly intimidating and controlling, thus leaving employees feeling powerless and discouraged. (Little wonder these workers were dissatisfied.)

Once questionnaire responses and interviews identified the problem, however, managers realized they could turn things around—and that they did, by completely changing their management style. Acknowledging the problems caused by their iron-fisted style, managers began loosening their highly autocratic ways and to replace them with a new openness and freedom. Employees were allowed to work together toward solving problems of sanitation and safety, and they were encouraged to suggest improvements.

The results were dramatic: Workdays lost to accidents dropped from 1,740 a year down to only two, absenteeism fell from 8.0 to 0.2 percent, and voluntary turnover was reduced from almost 100 to less than 10 percent per year. Clearly, improving the quality of supervision went a long way toward reversing the negative effects of satisfaction at this Safeway bakery.

In general terms, what, precisely, did the Safeway managers do? First, they clearly treated their employees with respect, showing they had those employees' best interests in mind. They also decentralized the power to make decisions. In other words, instead of making all the decisions for their employees, the managers allowed them to make many of the decisions themselves. When people are allowed to participate freely in decision making, it contributes to their feelings of satisfaction, because it leads them to believe they can affect their organizations. In contrast, when the power to make decisions is concentrated in just a few, employees are likely to feel powerless and ineffective, thereby contributing to their feelings of dissatisfaction.

The changes in supervision made at the Safeway bakery illustrate that job satisfaction is under managers' control. This case also provides a valuable tip: By treating people with respect and allowing them to make decisions bearing on how to do their jobs, satisfaction can be improved. ■

ORGANIZATIONAL COMMITMENT: FEELINGS OF ATTACHMENT TOWARD ORGANIZATIONS

Thus far, our discussion has centered on people's attitudes toward their jobs. To understand work-related attitudes fully, however, we also must focus on people's attitudes toward the organizations in which they work—that is, on their **organizational commitment**. The concept of organizational commitment concerns the degree to which people are involved with their organizations and are interested in remaining within them.

organizational commitment
The extent to which an individual identifies and is involved with his or her organization or is unwilling to leave it (see *affective commitment* and *continuance commitment*).

This important attitude may be completely unrelated to job satisfaction. For example, nurses may like the work they do but dislike the hospitals in which they do it, thus leading them to seek similar jobs elsewhere. By the same token, waiters may have positive feelings about the restaurants in which they work but dislike waiting on tables. These complexities illustrate the importance of studying organizational commitment. We begin by examining the different dimensions of organizational commitment, and we then review the impact of organizational commitment on organizational functioning. We conclude by presenting ways of enhancing commitment.

Varieties of Organizational Commitment

Being committed to an organization is not only a matter of "yes or no"—or even of "how much." Distinctions also can be made regarding "what kind" of commitment is involved. Specifically, scientists have distinguished three forms of commitment (Figure 5.9).

Continuance Commitment   Have you ever stayed on a job because you just did not want to bother finding a new one? If so, you already are familiar with the concept of **continuance commitment**, which refers to the strength of a person's desire to remain working for an organization because of his or her belief it may be costly to leave.

The longer people remain in their organizations, the more they stand to lose what they have invested in them over the years (e.g., retirement plans, close friendships).

continuance commitment

The strength of a person's desire to continue working for an organization because he or she needs to and cannot afford to do otherwise.

FIGURE 5.9

Organizational Commitment: Three Different Forms

Organizational commitment consists of three forms: *continuance commitment, normative commitment,* and *affective commitment.*

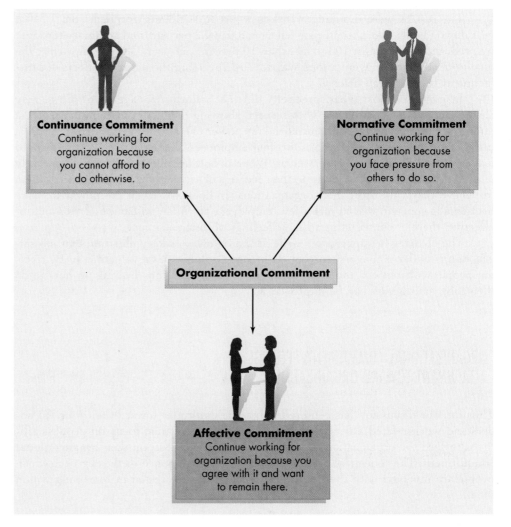

Continuance Commitment
Continue working for organization because you cannot afford to do otherwise.

Normative Commitment
Continue working for organization because you face pressure from others to do so.

Organizational Commitment

Affective Commitment
Continue working for organization because you agree with it and want to remain there.

Many people are committed to staying on their jobs simply because they are unwilling to lose these things. Such individuals may be said to have a high degree of continuance commitment.

Today, however, signs suggest continuance commitment is not as high as it used to be. Traditionally, people sought jobs that offered lifetime employment; many employees would stay on their jobs their whole working lives, starting at the bottom and working their way to the top. That scenario no longer is readily found, however. The unspoken pact of job security in exchange for loyalty has all but faded from the organizational scene. In the words of a young project manager at a New Jersey location of Prudential, "If the economy picked up, I'd consider a job elsewhere much sooner than before. I wouldn't bat an eye."[36] This expression of willingness to leave one's job reflects a low degree of continuance commitment.

Affective Commitment   A second type of organizational commitment is **affective commitment** — that is, the strength of people's desires to continue working for an organization because they agree with its underlying goals and values. People with high degrees of affective commitment desire to remain in their organizations because they endorse what the organization stands for and are willing to help in its mission.

affective commitment
The strength of a person's desire to work for an organization because he or she agrees with its goals and wants to do so.

Sometimes, particularly when an organization is undergoing change, employees may wonder if their personal values continue to match those of the organization in which they work. When this happens, they may question whether they still belong and, if they believe they do not, resign.

Several years ago, Ryder Truck Company successfully avoided losing employees by publicly reaffirming its corporate values. Ryder faced a situation in which the company was expanding beyond its core truck-leasing business and also dealing with changes from deregulation (e.g., routes, tariffs, taxes). To guide employees through this tumultuous time, chief executive Tony Burns went out of his way to reinforce the company's core values: support, trust, respect, and striving. He spread this message far and wide, throughout the company, using videotaped interviews, articles in the company magazine, plaques, posters, and even laminated wallet-size cards printed with the company's core values. Along with other Ryder officials, Mr. Burns is convinced reiterating the company's values was responsible for the high level of affective commitment the company enjoyed during this turbulent period.

Normative Commitment   A third type of organizational commitment is **normative commitment**, which refers to an employee's feelings of obligation to stay with the organization because of pressure from others. People with high degrees of normative commitment are greatly concerned about what others would think of them for leaving. They are reluctant to disappoint their employers, and they worry their fellow employees may think poorly of them for resigning.

normative commitment
The strength of a person's desire to continue working for an organization because he or she feels obligations from others to remain.

GLOBAL MATTERS

Research has found that the same three types of organizational commitment studied in North America — continuance, affective, and normative — also operate in South Korea.[37] ■

Like the other forms, normative commitment, typically is assessed using a paper-and-pencil questionnaire. (For questions measuring organizational commitment and to assess your own degree of organizational commitment, see the "Experiencing Organizational Behavior" section at the end of this chapter.)

Why Strive for a Committed Workforce?

As you might imagine, people who feel deeply committed to their organizations behave differently than those who do not. Specifically, several key aspects of work behavior are linked to organizational commitment.

YOU BE THE CONSULTANT

You are called upon by the president of a financial services company to help address its terrible turnover problem: Almost nobody is staying on the job for longer than four months. This is costing the company not only in terms of lost sales, but also astonomical training costs for new employees.

1. What would you suspect is the problem with respect to job satisfication? How would you assess this problem? Then, what would you consider doing to solve it?

2. What types of organizational commitment may be to blame? What can be done to raise this level of commitment within the organization?

3. What factors do you suspect may be responsible for the low levels of job satisfaction and organizational commitment that exist?

Committed Employees Are Less Likely to Withdraw   The more highly committed employees are to their organizations, the less likely they are to resign or to be absent (i.e., employee withdrawal). Being committed leads people to stay on their jobs and to show up when they are supposed to be there. (High rates of absenteeism may be good signs of low organizational commitment, but people's willingness to be absent from work is likely based, in part, on their national background. For a look at this possibility, see the "OB Around the World" section in this chapter.)

This phenomenon was demonstrated in a large-scale survey study tracing dropout rates among U.S. Air Force cadets during the four years required to get a degree. The more strongly committed to the service cadets were on entering the program, the less likely they were to drop out.[38] That commitment levels could predict behavior so far into the future is a good indication of the importance of organizational commitment as a work-related attitude.

Committed Employees Are Willing to Sacrifice for the Organization   Beyond remaining in their organizations, highly committed employees demonstrate a great willingness to share and to make sacrifices required for the organization to thrive. For example, when Chrysler was in serious financial trouble, CEO Lee Iacocca demonstrated his commitment to the company by reducing his annual salary to only $1. This move clearly was symbolic of the sacrifices the company wanted all its employees to make, but Iacocca's actions no doubt cost him a great deal of real money. Had he been less committed to saving Chrysler — a company that now is highly successful — there would have been little incentive for him to be so generous. In fact, a less strongly committed CEO might have bailed out altogether.

This does not mean only highly magnanimous gestures result from commitment. In fact, small acts of good organizational citizenship also are likely to occur among highly committed people. This makes sense if you consider that it takes being highly committed to an organization for people to be willing to give of themselves for the good of the company.

Not surprisingly, a study in Singapore found that regular employees (i.e., those with on-going employment relationships) are more committed to their jobs and engage in good organizational citizenship more often than contingent employees (i.e., those with no on-going employment relationship and who are called to work only when needed).[39] After all, if employers are not committed to them, employees have little reason to feel committed in return — and to demonstrate that commitment by doing the little things that make life at work more pleasant.

Considering these benefits of organizational commitment, it makes sense for organizations to enhance commitment among its employees. We now describe various ways of doing this.

ABSENTEEISM: SAME BEHAVIOR, DIFFERENT MEANINGS IN DIFFERENT COUNTRIES

It is easy to understand why people who are uncommitted to their jobs may want to stay away, thus potentially resulting in high rates of absenteeism. The degree to which people actually express their low commitment by staying away from their jobs, however, may depend on their national culture. This idea was tested recently by an interesting study in which large groups of employees from Canada and the People's Republic of China were surveyed about their attitudes toward being absent from work.[40]

In general, Chinese managers paid far more attention than their Canadian counterparts to absenteeism. For the most part, absence was very strongly discouraged — so much so that even an uncommitted Chinese worker was unlikely to stay home from work. The Chinese also frowned on absence based on illness, whereas the Canadians generally accepted illness as a valid excuse. This is in keeping with the idea that in Chinese culture, a person of good character is expected to maintain self-control, and taking time off work because of illness is considered to indicate lack of control.[41]

There was an interesting exception, however, to this general tendency for the Chinese to frown on absenteeism.

Specifically, compared with the Canadians, the Chinese were more likely to take time off work to deal with personal, domestic issues. They also believed it was much more appropriate to do so. There are two reasons for this. First, unlike their Canadian counterparts, the Chinese are not paid when they do not go to work; therefore, they do not receive pay for work they did not do, thus avoiding the potential guilt of overpayment inequity (see chapter 4). Furthermore, during the time of this study, it became possible for Chinese citizens to own private homes. Recognizing this, employers generally considered employees taking time off work to attend to household maintenance to be acceptable.

These findings underscore a key point: Lack of commitment may encourage absenteeism (by promoting an attitude in favor of it), but lack of commitment alone may not dictate whether someone actually will be absent. Determining this requires an understanding of the values regarding absenteeism within an employee's culture.

Approaches to Developing Organizational Commitment

Some determinants of organizational commitment fall outside the managers' spheres of control, thus giving them few opportunities to enhance these feelings. For example, commitment tends to be lower when employment opportunities are plentiful. An abundance of job options surely lowers continuance commitment, and there is not much a company can do about it. After all, managers cannot control the external economy, but they can make employees want to stay working for their company — that is, they can enhance affective commitment.

Enrich Jobs   People tend to be highly committed to their organizations to the extent they have a good chance to control how they do their jobs and are recognized for making important contributions. Recall from chapter 4 that enriching jobs involves giving people more interesting work as well as responsibility over their work.

This approach worked well at Ford Motor Company. During the early 1980s, Ford confronted a crisis of organizational commitment in the face of budget cuts, layoffs, plant closings, lowered product quality, and other threats. In the words of Ernst J. Savoie, the director of Ford's Employee Development Office,

> [t]he only solution for Ford, we determined, was a total transformation of our company . . . to accomplish it, we had to earn the commitment of all Ford people. And to acquire that commitment, we had to change the way we managed people.[42]

With this in mind, Ford instituted its *Employee Involvement* program, which was a systematic way of involving employees in many aspects of corporate decision making. Employees not only performed a wide variety of tasks but also enjoyed considerable autonomy in doing them (e.g., freedom to schedule work and to stop the assembly line if needed). By 1985, Ford employees were more committed to their jobs—so much so, in fact, that the usual acrimony at contract-renewal time had all but vanished. Employee involvement may not be the cure for all commitment ills, but it clearly was effective in this case.

Align the Interests of the Company with Those of the Employees   When making something good for the company also makes something good for employees, those employees are likely to be highly committed to that company. Many companies do this directly, such as by introducing **profit-sharing plans**—that is, incentive plans in which employees receive bonuses in proportion to the company's profitability. Such plans often are quite effective in enhancing organizational commitment—especially when they are perceived to be administered fairly.

The Holland, Michigan, auto-parts manufacturer Prince Corporation, for example, gives its employees yearly bonuses based on several indices, including the company's overall profitability, the employee's unit's profitability, and each individual's performance. Similarly, workers at Allied Plywood Corporation, a wholesaler of building materials in Alexandria, Virginia, receive cash bonuses based on company profits, but in this company, these bonuses are distributed monthly as well as yearly. The monthly bonuses are the same size for everyone, whereas the annual bonuses are in proportion to each employee's individual contributions to total profit, days worked, and performance.

These plans are good examples of how companies enhance commitment. The plans themselves differ, but their underlying rationale is the same: When employees share in the company's profitability, they are more likely to see their own interests as being consistent with those of the company. When these interests are aligned, commitment is high.

Recruit and Select New Employees Whose Values Closely Match Those of the Organization   Recruiting new employees is important, both because it provides opportunities to find people whose values match those of the organization and because of the dynamics of the recruitment process itself. Specifically, the more an organization invests in someone (by working hard to lure him or her to the company), the more that individual is likely to return the same investment of energy (by expressing commitment toward the organization). In other words, companies that show employees they care enough to work hard to attract them are likely to find these individuals are strongly committed to the company.

In conclusion, it is useful to think of organizational commitment as being an attitude that managerial actions may influence. Not only might people who are predisposed to be committed to the organization be selected, but various measures also can enhance commitment in the face of indications it is suffering. (For an example of one company that appears to have done several things to promote organizational commitment, see Figure 5.10).

profit-sharing plans

Incentive plans in which employees receive bonuses in proportion to the company's profitability.

PREJUDICE: NEGATIVE ATTITUDES TOWARD OTHERS

"Don't jump to conclusions." This is advice we often hear, but when it comes to forming attitudes about others, it also is advice we often ignore. Instead, people frequently *do* jump to conclusions about others—and on the basis of very limited information. If you have ever made a judgment about someone based on his or her ethnic background, age, gender, sexual orientation, or physical condition, you are well aware of this ten-

FIGURE 5.10

Organizational Commitment: Getting It Right

TDIndustries, a plumbing and air-conditioning contractor in Dallas, Texas, ranked second in *Fortune* magazine's 1999 listing of the 100 best companies for which to work. Its low, 13-percent rate of voluntary turnover is a good indication that employees are highly committed to the company. This makes sense considering that management respects and heeds the preferences of all 994 employees. In fact, lower-level employees own 75 percent of this company's stock.

dency. As we discussed in conjunction with *stereotypes* (see chapter 2), such judgments frequently are negative in nature.

Prejudice and Discrimination: A Key Distinction

A negative attitude toward another based on his or her membership in a particular group is referred to as **prejudice**.[43] Not only might people holding prejudicial attitudes have negative beliefs and feelings, they may be predisposed to behave in ways consistent with those attitudes. For example, an employment interviewer holding negative stereotypes toward a certain minority group may evaluate negatively a candidate belonging to that group and be disinterested in hiring that individual.

     If this prejudicial attitude actually leads the interviewer to not hire the candidate, this is an act of **discrimination**. In other words, the interviewer acted consistently with his or her negative attitude, thereby not giving the candidate a fair chance and treating different people in different ways. The key thing to remember is this: Prejudice is a negative attitude, whereas discrimination is the behavior that follows from it (i.e., the behavioral expression of that attitude). For a summary of this idea, see Figure 5.11.

prejudice

Negative attitudes toward the members of specific groups based solely on their membership in those groups (e.g., age, race, sexual orientation).

discrimination

The behavior consistent with a prejudicial attitude; the act of treating someone negatively because of his or her membership in a specific group.

The Reality of Diversity and the Problems of Prejudice

One reason why organizational leaders must be concerned about prejudice in the workplace is that such views cannot be tolerated. In today's workplace, ethnic and cultural diversity is the rule (see chapter 1).

The Reality of Diversity   The United States is an ethnically diverse nation—and it is getting increasingly more diverse. For example, by 2040, it is estimated that half the U.S. population will be composed of people of African, Latin, Native American, or Asian descent. In addition, women, who for many years only infrequently worked outside the home, currently fill 65 percent of all new jobs, and in just a few years, approximately half the civilian workforce will be composed of women.[44] For some companies, diversity already is a reality. For example, at the Solectron Corporation, a computer-assembly company in Milpitas, California, 30 nationalities and 40 different languages and dialects can be found among the 3,200 employees.[45]

FIGURE 5.11

Prejudice and Discrimination: A Key Distinction

Prejudice is an attitude, and as such, it consists of the three basic components of attitudes. *Discrimination* refers to behavior based on that attitude.

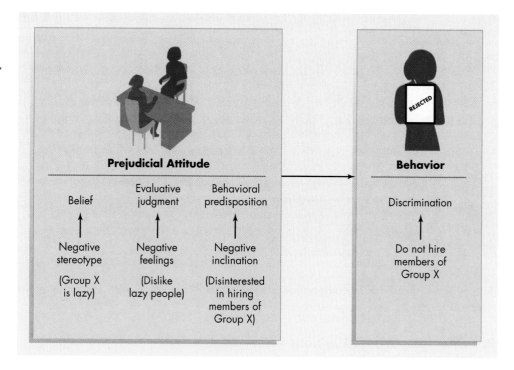

GLOBAL MATTERS   Resulting largely from relaxed immigration restrictions and the availability of inexpensive transportation, the trend toward diversity in the workplace is international in scope. Even nations that traditionally have had few immigrants (e.g., Australia) now have a more diversified workforce than ever. ■

As this picture of the highly diverse U.S. workforce unfolds, prejudices against various groups still exist, and these prejudices are likely to have serious consequences. Before describing the nature of such prejudicial attitudes, however, we first outline some of the general problems they create.

Problems Stemming from Prejudice in the Workplace   First, prejudice can produce *serious friction or conflict* between people. A highly diverse workforce potentially can provide the advantage of differing opinions and perspectives, but this may turn into a disadvantage if individuals hold prejudicial attitudes. Indeed, if one's group membership causes an underlying current of distrust, the resulting conflict may disrupt the organization as people fail to cooperate to get their jobs done. In extreme cases, the discriminatory actions that follow from prejudicial attitudes culminate in legal action, such as employees charging their employer with unfair discrimination[46] and customers charging companies with discriminatory actions.[47]

Second, prejudice may have *adverse effects on the careers of people targeted by such attitudes.* Affected individuals may encounter various forms of discrimination—some very subtle but others quite overt—regarding hiring, promotion, and pay. For example, there are more women than ever in the workforce, and they are doing higher-level work than ever before. Even so, they remain highly underrepresented in the upper echelons of organizations. In fact, only 3.0 percent of senior managers and 5.7 percent of corporate directors of *Fortune* 500 companies are women (Figure 5.12).[48] Because the discrimination is quite real but is not admitted openly, it frequently is referred to as the *glass ceiling* (i.e., a barrier that cannot be seen).

FIGURE 5.12

Women Have Come a Long Way in the Workplace
During World War II, women worked in factories that manufactured products supporting male troops abroad. More than a half-century later, today's women are not relegated to supporting roles in the world of work, but discrimination against women in the workplace still exists, thus creating a barrier that keeps them from attaining top positions.

ETHICS MATTERS

Most people consider the glass ceiling to be unethical, because it denies women equal opportunities to attain top positions. Such equality of opportunity is fundamental to the ethical treatment of people. ■

Third, we cannot overlook the devastating psychological effect on victims of discrimination. Not only is the victim penalized, but so are others with the same background (i.e., *covictimization*).[49] To the extent talented individuals are passed over because of their membership in certain groups, their self-esteem suffers. This, of course, is in addition to the loss to the organization by overlooking talented individuals simply because they are not white males. In today's highly competitive, global economy, this is a mistake no company can afford.

VARIOUS "GROUPISMS": EVERYONE CAN BE A VICTIM OF PREJUDICE

If there is any truly "equal opportunity" for people in today's workplace, it is that we *all* stand a chance of being the victim of prejudice. Indeed, there are many different forms of *groupism*—that is, prejudices based on membership in certain groups—and no one is immune.[50]

Prejudice Based on Age

All of us eventually get older (if we're lucky), and as people live longer and the birth rate holds steady, the median age of Americans is rising.[51] Clearly, however, prejudice based on age remains all too common. Laws in the United States and elsewhere have done much to counter employment discrimination against older workers, but these prejudices continue.

Part of the problem resides in stereotypes that older workers are too set in their ways to train and tend to be sick or accident-prone. As with many attitudes, these prejudices are not founded on accurate information. In fact, survey findings paint just the opposite picture. Organizations tend to have extremely positive experiences with older workers: They have good skills, are highly committed to doing their jobs well, and have outstanding safety records.[52]

Younger workers also find themselves to be victims of prejudice. For them, part of the problem is that as the average age of the workforce advances (from 29 years in 1976 to 39 years in 2000), a gap develops in the expectations of the more experienced, older workers who are in charge and of the younger employees just entering the workforce. Specifically, today's under-30 employees view the world differently compared with older workers. They are more prone to question how things are done, to not see the government as being an ally, and to not expect loyalty. They are likely to consider self-development to be their main interest, and they are willing to learn whatever skills are necessary to make themselves marketable. These differing perspectives may lead older employees to feel uncomfortable with their younger colleagues. This is especially problematic as the nature of work continues shifting so that people with different skills are brought together to work in teams.

There is encouraging news, however. A survey of employees' attitudes toward older workers found that even younger workers hold generally positive views of older workers—though these views were not quite as positive as those the older workers hold toward themselves.[53] Interestingly, this same study found that the more time younger people spend working with their older colleagues, the more positive—and the less stereotypical—their attitudes were toward them. The implications of this are that simply bringing younger and older workers together may chip away at age-based stereotypes (Figure 5.13).

Prejudice Based on Physical Condition

We all have some physical feature that keeps us from doing certain kinds of work. Some people are not strong enough to load heavy packages onto trucks. Others are not athletic enough to play professional sports. Still others lack the agility and stamina needed to be a firefighter. Thus, everyone may be handicapped in some way, but certain physical conditions tend to be the focus of widely held prejudicial attitudes. Such conditions (e.g., blindness, disfigurement, physical paralysis) are said to be *stigmas*—that is, to be negative aspects of one's identity.[54]

During the early 1990s, the Americans with Disabilities Act (ADA) was enacted in the United States to safeguard the rights of people with physical and mental disabilities. The rationale behind this law is simple: Just because an employee is limited in some way, it does not mean that accommodations cannot be made to help this individual perform his or her job. Companies that do not comply are subject to legal damages. In fact, the first award under the ADA—$572,000—was presented to an employee fired after missing work while recovering from cancer, and as many as 15,000 discrimination claims were filed under this law during the first year alone.[55]

Many companies find they can meet the needs of disabled employees quite easily—and with little expense. For example, Greiner Engineering, Inc., of Irving, Texas, accommodated its employees in wheelchairs simply by substituting a lighter-weight door on its restrooms and by raising a drafting table with some bricks under its legs.[56] Not all accommodations are made so easily, of course, but experts are confident the ADA will minimize discrimination against employees based on their physical condition.[57]

Prejudice Based on Race and National Origin

The history of the United States is marked by struggles for acceptance by various racial and ethnic groups. As documented, the U.S. workplace is more diverse today than ever, but prejudicial attitudes clearly linger. The results of a large survey of U.S. workers, as summarized in Figure 5.14, illustrate this point.[58]

Members of various minority groups not only believe they are victims of prejudice and discrimination, they are taking action. For example, complaints of discrimination based on national origin filed at the Equal Employment Opportunity Commission (EEOC) between 1989 and 1991 increased by 30 percent. Moreover,

FIGURE 5.13

Meet "Mr. Adult Education"

We tend to think of young people as being involved in the education business, but John Sperling, 78, shatters this stereotype. His company, the Apollo Group, runs the for-profit University of Phoenix, with 74,500 students (all of whom are older than 23).

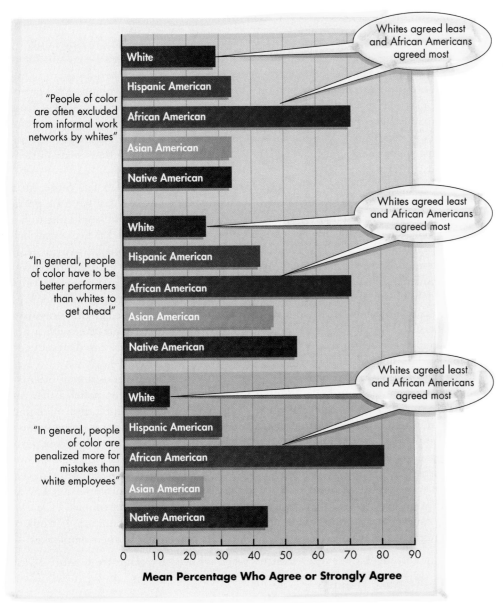

Mean Percentage Who Agree or Strongly Agree

FIGURE 5.14

Does Racial Discrimination Exist? It Depends on Who You Ask

A survey of U.S. workers showed racial discrimination is believed to be prevalent in many forms. Its main victims, African Americans, tend to be more aware of discrimination than those who are least affected by it (i.e., White Americans).

(*Source*: Based on data reported by Fernandez & Barr, 1993; see note 44.)

victims of discrimination have been winning such cases. For example, in 1993, the Supreme Court of the state of Washington upheld a $389,000 judgment against a Seattle bank brought by a Cambodian-American employee who was fired because of his accent.[59] Outside the courtroom, companies that discriminate pay in other ways as well, most notably in lost talent and productivity. According to EEOC Commissioner Joy Cherian, employees who feel victimized "may not take the initiative to introduce inventions and other innovations," and she adds that "every day, American employers are losing millions of dollars because these talents are frozen."[60]

To help minimize these problems, some companies are taking concrete steps. For example, AT&T Bell Labs in Murray Hill, New Jersey, is working with managers to help the company's minority employees get promoted more rapidly. Similarly, Hughes Aircraft of Los Angeles has been assigning mentors to minority employees to teach them the company's culture as well as the skills needed to succeed.[61] Both examples are only modest steps, but they represent encouraging trends that should help to reduce this long-standing problem.

Prejudice Based on Sexual Orientation

Unlike people with physical disabilities, who are protected against discrimination by federal law, no such protection currently exists for another group whose members frequently are victims of prejudice — that is, homosexuals. More people than ever are tolerant of nontraditional sexual orientations, but unfortunately, anti-homosexual prejudice still exists in the workplace. Indeed, approximately two-thirds of CEOs from major companies note they are reluctant to put homosexuals on top management committees.[62] Not surprisingly, without laws to protect them and with widespread prejudices against them, many gays and lesbians are reluctant to make their sexual orientations known.[63]

Fears of being "discovered" (i.e., exposed as being a homosexual) represent a considerable source of stress among such individuals. For example, a gay vice president of a large office-equipment manufacturer in Chicago admits he would like to become the company's CEO, but he fears his chances will be ruined if his sexual orientation becomes known.[64] The pressure of having to go through life — or at least through an important part of it — with a disguised identity must be extreme, but imagine the cumulative effect of such efforts on organizations with several homosexual employees. Such misdirected energy can be a serious productivity issue. In the words of consultant Mark Kaplan, "gay and lesbian employees use a lot of time and stress trying to conceal a big part of their identity."[65] To work in an organization with a homophobic culture, to endure jokes slurring gays and lesbians, easily can distract even the most highly focused employee.

To help avoid these problems — and out of respect for diverse sexual orientations — many organizations have adopted internal fair employment policies that include sexual orientation. In addition, some companies actively prohibit discrimination based on sexual orientation. Extending this idea, still other companies now extend fringe benefits, which traditionally have been offered exclusively to opposite-sex partners, to same-sex domestic partners as well. Russ Campanello, vice president of human resources for Lotus Development Corp., the Cambridge, Massachusetts, developer of software products, notes that having such a program is an important key to his organization's success in attracting highly talented technical personnel.[66] Clearly, some companies are passively discouraging diversity in sexual orientation, but others are encouraging such diversity and using it to their own — and to their employees' — advantage.

Prejudice Against Women

There can be no mistaking the widespread — and ever-growing — presence of women in today's workforce. In 1991, women composed 46 percent of the U.S. workplace, up from 43 percent in 1981. Also in 1991, 41 percent of managers were women, compared with only 27 percent in 1981. Still, female senior executives (i.e., individuals reporting directly to the CEO) are relatively rare — only three percent are women.[67] Is this likely to change during the next 10 years? When executives completing a recent *BusinessWeek*/Harris poll were asked how likely their company is to have a female CEO within 10 years, 82 percent said it was not likely.[68] They were a bit more optimistic, however, about the longer-term prospects. Thus, whereas women regularly populate corporations, only rarely do they run them. Equality for women in the workplace is improving, but it is a slow victory.

Why is this the case? Sufficient time may not have passed for more women to work their way into the top echelons of organizations, but there appear to be more formidable barriers. Most notably, powerful *sex-role stereotypes* — that is, narrow-minded beliefs about the kinds of tasks for which women are most appropriately suited — clearly still persist. For example, eight percent of respondents to the *Business-Week*/Harris survey indicated women are not aggressive or determined enough to make it to the top. This number is small, yes, but it provides good evidence for the persistence of a nagging — and highly limiting — stereotype.

Such stereotypes have kept women from important organizational positions, including that innermost circle of corporate power: the board of directors. The number of women gaining admission to this special group may be growing, but evidence exists that their roles still may be limited by stereotypes. Boards of directors provide important direction to organizations, and they typically are composed of committees dedicated to specific areas of responsibility (e.g., finance, compensation, public affairs). One recent study, however, found that membership in these committees generally followed gender stereotypes.[69] Specifically, women generally were equally qualified to hold memberships in all committees, but they typically were kept off committees closely linked to basic corporate governance (e.g., compensation, finance). Women were favored for membership only in committees with more peripheral functions (e.g., public affairs). Clearly, sex-role stereotypes remain alive and well in this one bastion of organizational power.

MANAGING A DIVERSE WORKFORCE: CURRENT PRACTICES

Having established that prejudices abound and may be harmful in the workplace, a question arises as to what, precisely, organizations can do about this state of affairs. To begin answering this question, it is important to get a sense of the importance of diversity in today's organizations.

Do Companies Care about Diversity?

First, we must ask if companies do care about diversity. Specifically, is it of concern to them, and if so, why?

Is Diversity on Today's Corporate Agenda?   Several years ago, the American Society for Training and Development surveyed a sample of Fortune 1000 companies regarding their stance on diversity issues. The results suggested that diversity management was *not* at the top of their agenda. Only 11 percent reported it was a high priority, but 33 percent indicated they were only beginning to look at it. In fact, one-quarter of the companies surveyed indicated they were not doing anything at all.[70]

An encouraging sign, however, is that the trend clearly is toward more activity, not less. Additional survey results have found that 55 percent of employees believe their company's management has become more strongly supportive of diversity programs during the past two years, and only four percent indicate decreased attention to diversity management efforts.[71] In fact, 91 percent indicate their company's senior management considers the treatment of people to be the "make-or-break corporate resource" of the day.[72] So, to answer the question at the beginning of this section, concern about diversity issues *is* rapidly growing.

 **GLOBAL MATTERS**

The trend toward diversity management is strongest in the United States and Canada and only now is beginning to catch on in other nations. In other words, ethnic diversity is a fact of life in international business, but diversity management practices are not. ■

Why Do Companies Engage in Diversity Management?   You may believe that companies pay attention to diversity management only because of government pressure. In one survey, however, this was identified as being a contributing factor by only 29 percent of respondents.[73] In contrast, this same survey found the two major factors are:

- Awareness by senior managers of the importance of diversity management programs (identified as a contributing factor by 95 percent of respondents).
- Recognition of the need to attract and to retain a skilled workforce (identified as a contributing factor by 90 percent of respondents).

What Are Today's Companies Doing about Diversity?

Identify prejudicial attitudes is one thing. Eliminating them is quite another. Two major approaches have been taken to doing precisely this: *affirmative action plans*, and *diversity management programs*.

affirmative action laws

Legislation to give employment opportunities to groups that have been underrepresented in the workforce (e.g., women, minorities).

Affirmative Action Plans   Traditionally, **affirmative action laws** have been used to promote the ethical treatment of women and minorities in U.S. organizations. Derived from the civil rights initiatives of the 1960s, these laws generally involve efforts to give employment opportunities to groups who traditionally have been disadvantaged. The rationale is quite reasonable: By encouraging the hiring of women and minorities into positions where they traditionally have been underrepresented, more people will be exposed to them, thereby forcing them to see that their negative stereotypes were misguided. Then, as these stereotypes crumble, prejudice—and the discrimination on which it is based—will be reduced.

After some 30 years of affirmative action programs, there can be little doubt that, despite problems, they have been effective at bringing women and minorities into the workforce.

Diversity Management Programs   Many of today's organizations are interested in going beyond affirmative action, not just by hiring a wider variety of different people but also by creating an atmosphere in which diverse groups can flourish. These organizations are not merely obeying the law or being socially responsible. They recognize that diversity is a business issue (Figure 5.15).

As one consultant put it, "A corporation's success will increasingly be determined by its managers' ability to naturally tap the full potential of a diverse workforce."[74]

FIGURE 5.15

Diploma Today, Job Tomorrow
Members of this recent Florida A&M University graduating class have something to cheer about. These talented African Americans are typical of many who today are well trained and are being offered excellent jobs by companies interested in promoting diversity within its ranks.

Thus, many organizations are adopting **diversity management programs** — that is, efforts to celebrate diversity by creating supportive, not just neutral, work environments for women and minorities.[75] Simply put, the underlying philosophy of diversity management programs is that cracking the glass ceiling requires women and minorities be valued, not just tolerated.[76] In this section, we identify various types of diversity management programs, and we describe some examples of successful diversity management efforts.

diversity management programs
Programs in which employees are taught to celebrate the differences between people and in which organizations create supportive work environments for women and minorities.

How Are Companies Fostering Workforce Diversity?   A large survey by the Society for Human Resource Management and the Commerce Clearing House found that several diversity management practices are widespread.[77] These include:

- Promoting policies that discourage sexual harassment (93 percent of organizations surveyed).
- Providing physical access for employees with physical disabilities (76 percent).
- Offering flexible work schedules (66 percent).
- Allowing days off for religious holidays that may not be recognized widely (58 percent).
- Offering parental leaves (57 percent).

This same survey, however, found that organizations did not always follow up on their diversity efforts. Among companies that conducted some type of diversity traning, only 30 percent gathered any formal data to see if it is working, and only 20 percent formally rewarded managers for promoting diversity in the workplace.

The bottom line is clear: There generally is more talk about diversity than action in today's organizations. Still, there are encouraging signs of improvement. Given the growing awareness about the importance of diversity management activities, we suspect more companies will enhance their competitiveness by capitalizing on the diversity of their workforces. (For a closer look at one particular company in this regard, see the "Trends" section below.) With this in mind, we now summarize some of the specific tactics used to manage workplace diversity.

TRENDS: WHAT TODAY'S COMPANIES ARE DOING

■ **Pacific Enterprises Tops the "Diversity Elite"**

Most companies express commitment to a diverse workforce and make some effort at promoting diversity, but a few have gone to great lengths to show how serious they are when it comes to hiring, promoting, and retaining minorities. With the goal of identifying such exemplary organizations — that is, the "diversity elite" — *Fortune* magazine recently evaluated the largest U.S.-based companies regarding their commitment to racial and ethnic diversity.[78] Categories in which companies were scored included representation by minority group members (especially in top-paid, key executive positions and on boards of directors) and the variety of diversity management programs in force.

Making the Top 24 were such highly recognizable corporate icons as BankAmerica, Marriott, Pitney Bowes, Allstate, FedEx, Du Pont, Xerox, Anheuser-Busch, and Nike — all of which have been actively promoting diversity within their ranks. Heading the list, however, was Pacific Enterprises (PE), the Los Angeles–based, energy services holding company whose Southern California Gas Co. is the

continued

largest natural-gas utility in the United States. This $2.8-billion-a-year company (along with BankAmerica) is unusual in that it made virtually all its charitable contributions to organizations that benefit minorities.

What really vaulted PE to the top was its tremendous successes in retaining minority employees and in promoting them to top positions. In fact, one-quarter of all PE's board members, one-third of its corporate officials and managers, and more than half of its 7,100-employee workforce are members of racial and ethnic minorities. That these numbers are higher than those of any other company surveyed—and considerably higher than the national averages for all companies—reflects PE's strategy of providing excellent service by having employees who are similar to its customers. Given what PE's treasurer Dennis Arriola refers to as the company's "smorgasbord of customers," it is no surprise that PE goes out of its way to maintain a "smorgasbord of employees" to serve them.[79]

As with most companies today, keeping talented employees on the payroll has been an on-going challange for PE. Among the company's tactics for winning the retention battle has been an especially potent weapon known as the Readiness for Management (RFM) program, which is a systematic effort to train and promote minority employees before other companies lure them away. The RFM program allows employees to nominate themselves for the managerial fast-track by giving them a series of self-assessment tests to determine how they most need to improve their managerial skills and then guiding them in developing these skills.

Over the years, the RFM program has identified some of PE's most talented minority employees—who otherwise might have been overlooked as prospects for management positions. This program has helped PE to retain its large base of minority employees by convincing them PE is a great company in which to work. Patricia Wallace is a good case in point. An African-American graduate of the RFM program, she has worked her way from an entry-level position to manager of the company's call centers. Although she admits to having "gotten restless from time to time," Ms. Wallace readily acknowledges the company's commitment to continuous learning and has remained at PE because, as she puts it, "working here is probably as good as it gets."[80] Ms. Wallace probably did not realize it when she spoke those words, but the *Fortune* study bears out her observation.

To demonstrate just how good employees have it at PE, the company also does something quite unusual: It actively encourages them to explore jobs elsewhere! In fact, PE even teaches its people the skills of résumé writing and interviewing that would make them more attractive to the competition. Even when flirting with other companies, however, most PE employees have followed Patricia Wallace's example: electing to stay put. The more they look around, the better they appreciate the quality of life at PE. We suspect few other companies would be as secure when it comes to tolerating their employees' notions of resigning—let alone encouraging them to leave by showing them the door! Then again, no other company ranks number one on the list of the diversity elite. ∎

Varieties of Diversity Management Programs

In general, diversity management programs fall into two categories: *awareness-based diversity training*, and *skill-based diversity training*.[81]

awareness-based diversity training
A type of diversity management program to make people more aware of diversity issues in the workplace and get them to recognize the underlying assumptions they make about people.

Awareness-Based Diversity Training   Specifically, **awareness-based diversity training** is designed to raise people's awareness of diversity issues in the workplace and to help them recognize the underlying assumptions they make about people. It is a very basic orientation—and one that takes a cognitive approach. Typically, it involves teaching people about the business necessity of valuing diversity, and it makes them sensitive to their own cultural assumptions and biases. This may involve various experiential

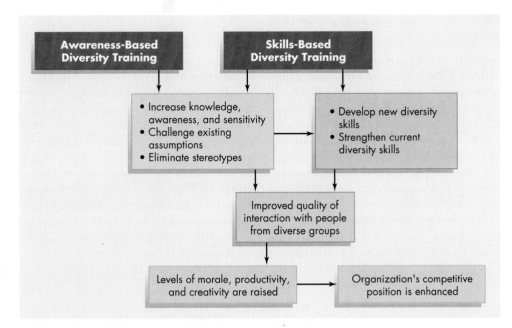

FIGURE 5.16

Diversity Management: Two Major Approaches to Training

Skills-based diversity training builds on the approach taken by *awareness-based diversity training*. Both approaches, however, strive toward achieving the same goals.

(*Source*: Adapted from material in Carnevale & Stone, 1995; see note 81.)

exercises that help people to view others as being individuals, not stereotyped members of groups.

Skills-Based Diversity Training   Building on the awareness approach is **skills-based diversity training**. This orientation is designed to develop people's skills in managing diversity. As such, it goes beyond raising awareness. It develops the tools needed to interact effectively with others. Four main tools are involved in this process.[82] These include:

1. *Cross-cultural understanding*: Understanding the cultural differences responsible for why different coworkers behave differently on the job.
2. *Intercultural communication*: Learning to overcome verbal and nonverbal barriers to communication across cultures.
3. *Facilitation skills*: Training in helping others to alleviate misunderstandings that may result from cultural differences.
4. *Flexibility and adaptability*: Cultivating the ability to patiently take new and different approaches when dealing with others who are different.

Both approaches to diversity training have the same long-term goals, which are summarized in Figure 5.16. They strive to make interaction between diverse groups of people easier and more effective. Once people are paying attention to each other, the road is paved for morale to improve, productivity to be enhanced, and people to focus their creative energies.

With all these benefits in hand, organizations are positioned to attain their ultimate goal: to improve their economic position. Does this, in fact, happen? In other words, are diversity management efforts effective?

skills-based diversity training

An approach to diversity management that goes beyond *awareness-based diversity training* to develop people's skills in managing diversity.

IS DIVERSITY MANAGEMENT EFFECTIVE?

Clearly, companies that invest resources in diverse employees and in bringing out the best in those individuals are interested in getting a return on their investment. Therefore, does diversity management work? The answer is "yes"—but under certain conditions.

Diversity Management: It Works!

Recent evidence paints a convincing picture of the ultimate effectiveness of diversity management efforts. Researchers reasoned that when companies use their human resources effectively, they can lower their costs and, thereby, perform better than their competition.[83] To test this notion, they compared two groups of companies from 1986 through 1992. One group included organizations that received awards from the U.S. Department of Labor for their exemplary efforts at managing diversity. The other group included companies that had settled large claims filed against them for employment discrimination.

To compare the performance of these organizations, the researchers relied on a key index of economic success: stock returns. The findings were striking: Companies that made special efforts to use their diverse human resources were considerably more profitable than those that discriminated against employees. As the researchers explained, organizations that capitalize on the diversity of their workforce are better able to attract and to retain the talented people needed for organizations to thrive. Clearly, managing diversity makes sense not only because it is the right way to treat people, but also because it is good business!

Successful Diversity Management: Some Notes of Caution

Most companies have been pleased with how their diversity management efforts have promoted harmony between employees, but some have encountered problems. In the most serious cases, diversity management efforts have backfired, leaving race and gender divisions even greater.[84]

Focus on Differences Between People, Not Stereotypes   The most serious problems have stemmed from the practice of focusing on stereotypes — even positive ones. Thinking of people in stereotypical ways can create barriers that interfere with looking at people as individuals. Therefore, instead of looking at the *average* differences between people, which may reinforce stereotypes, experts recommend looking at a *range* of differences between people — a range that promises to become even greater in the years ahead.[85]

Managers thus are advised not to treat someone as being special because he or she is a member of a certain group but because of the unique skills or abilities he or she brings to the job. To the extent managers are trained to seek, to recognize, and to develop the talents of employees — regardless of the groups to which they belong — they help to break down the barriers that made diversity training necessary in the first place.

Several other important notes of caution need to be identified, however. These are caveats that must be carefully considered when it comes to successful diversity training.[86] For a summary of several such concerns, see Table 5.2.

Managing Diversity Requires Total Managerial Support   Perhaps the main key to effective diversity management is *complete managerial support*. Indeed, you cannot do something as complex as celebrating diversity with a one-time effort. Successful diversity management requires sustained attention to diversity in all organizational activities. For example, companies with successful diversity management training programs also tend to require everyone to be trained, to define diversity very broadly (i.e., they do not limit it to only one or two groups), and to reward managers for special efforts at increasing diversity.[87] Without "going the extra mile," without completely supporting diversity activities, organizations may find themselves quite disappointed with their efforts.

In conclusion, although mistakes have been made in some diversity management programs, such programs in many cases have greatly helped organizations find ways of tapping the rich pool of talent in a highly diverse workforce.

This will be a test question → (managing diversity requires total managerial support)

TABLE 5.2

Potential Problems in Diversity Training

For diversity training efforts to succeed, they must avoid the potential problems outlined here.

PROBLEM	DESCRIPTION AND SOLUTION
Emotional tension is heightened.	Talking about prejudices is likely to make people feel uneasy. Training needs to be conducted in a "safe," comfortable environment.
Possibility of polarization.	Avoid discussions that have yes or no answers (e.g., "Should gays be allowed in the military?"). Instead, encourage consideration of a broad range of options.
Some people may have personal "axes to grind."	Training sessions should not provide platforms for people who want to vent about past problems. Facilitators should keep the group on target.
Personal attacks may occur.	Strong opinions on diversity issues may box people into corners. Treat everyone with respect and dignity.
Reactions to training will be varied.	Some may welcome the training, whereas others may resent having to go through it. Addressing these feelings should be made a part of training sessions.
White males tend to be blamed.	It is tempting to blame the dominant group, white males, for diversity problems, but no one group has a monopoly on prejudice and discrimination. White males should discuss their difficulties adjusting to a changing world.
Timing may be problematic.	Avoid adding to stress by not scheduling sessions during periods in which other sensitive events (e.g., layoffs, contract negotiations) are occurring.
Reasons for training may be ingenuine.	Diversity training works best when part of a strategic effort by management to change policies to make a more "inclusive" organization. Training conducted because "everyone's doing it," however, is likely to fail—and maybe even backfire.

Source: Adapted from Gardenswartz & Rowe, 1994; see note 86.

We invite you to visit the Greenberg page on the Prentice Hall Web site at: **www.prenhall.com/greenberg** for the monthly Greenberg update and for this chapter's World Wide Web exercise.

SUMMARY AND REVIEW OF LEARNING OBJECTIVES

1. **Define *attitudes*, and understand their basic components.**
    Attitudes are the stable clusters of feelings, beliefs, and behavioral tendencies directed toward some aspect of the external world. **Work-related attitudes** involve

such reactions toward various aspects of work settings or to the people within them. All attitudes consist of a **cognitive component** (i.e., what you believe), an **evaluative component** (i.e., how you feel), and a **behavioral component** (i.e., the tendency to behave a certain way).

2. **Describe the concept of *job satisfaction*, and outline the techniques for measuring it.**

    Job satisfaction involves positive or negative attitudes toward one's work. Such attitudes can be measured by completing *rating scales* (e.g., the JDI, the MSQ), conducting interviews, recounting *critical incidents* (i.e., instances found to be especially pleasing or displeasing), and conducting *interviews*.

3. **Summarize two major theories of job satisfaction.**

    According to the **two-factor theory**, job satisfaction and dissatisfaction stem from different factors. Specifically, this theory claims that job satisfaction stems from factors associated with the work itself (i.e., *motivators*) and that job dissatisfaction stems from the conditions surrounding jobs (e.g., the work environment). **Value theory** suggests that job satisfaction reflects the apparent match between the outcomes individuals desire (i.e., what they *value*) and what they believe they are actually receiving.

4. **Explain the major consequences of job dissatisfaction and how to overcome them.**

    When people are dissatisfied with their jobs, they tend to withdraw. In other words, they frequently are absent and are likely to quit their jobs. Evidence suggests, however, that job performance is only weakly associated with job dissatisfaction. Levels of job satisfaction can be raised by paying people fairly, improving the quality of supervision, decentralizing control of organizational power, and assigning people to jobs that match their interests.

5. **Define *organizational commitment*, and describe the three major types.**

    Organizational commitment focuses on people's attitudes toward their organizations, and there are three major types. **Continuance commitment** is the strength of a person's tendency to continue working for an organization because he or she cannot afford to do otherwise. **Affective commitment** is the strength of a person's tendency to continue working for an organization because he or she agrees with its goals and values and desires to stay. **Normative commitment** is the commitment to remain in an organization because of social obligations to do so.

6. **Describe the major consequences from low levels of organizational commitment and how to overcome them.**

    Low organizational commitment has been linked to high absenteeism and voluntary turnover, the unwillingness to share and make sacrifices for the company, and negative personal consequences for employees. Organizational commitment may be enhanced, however, by enriching jobs, aligning the interests of employees with those of the company, and recruiting newcomers whose values closely match those of the organization.

7. **Distinguish *prejudice* from *discrimination*, and identify victims of prejudice in organizations.**

    Prejudice refers to negative attitudes toward members of specific groups, and **discrimination** refers to treating people differently because of those prejudices. Today's workforce is characterized by high diversity, with many groups finding themselves the victims of prejudicial attitudes and discriminatory behaviors based on many different factors, including age, sexual orientation, physical condition, racial or ethnic group membership, and gender. People are becoming more tolerant of individuals from diverse groups, but prejudicial attitudes persist.

8. **Describe how organizations today manage *diversity* in the workforce.**

    To tap the rich pool of resources available in today's highly diverse workforce, many companies are using **diversity management programs** — that is, techniques for systematically teaching employees to celebrate the differences between people. Typically, these programs go beyond efforts to recruit and hire women and minorities. They create supportive work environments for them as well. The most effective programs not only focus on enhancing awareness of the benefits from a diverse workforce but on developing skills that help employees to embrace diversity.

9. **Describe the effectiveness of** *diversity management programs.*
Implementing diversity management programs is potentially difficult, but the benefits — both organizational and personal — are considerable. For example, companies with employees who systematically embrace diversity tend to be more profitable than those that allow discrimination to occur.

QUESTIONS FOR DISCUSSION

1. Someone tells you that people in general do not like their jobs. Would you agree or disagree with this statement? Why?

2. As a manager, you want to enhance job satisfaction among your subordinates. How might you accomplish this goal?

3. "Happy workers are productive workers." Do you agree or disagree with this statement? Why?

4. Absenteeism and voluntary turnover are costly problems for many companies. How can the incidence of these forms of employee withdrawal be reduced?

5. Suppose an employee is highly dissatisfied with his or her job and organization but does not look for a new one. How would you explain this person's behavior?

6. "Sexism and racism are things of the past." Do you agree or disagree with this statement? Why?

7. How are today's organizations managing diversity in their workforces? Give an example.

Case in Point

Workplace Equality Yields High Interest at the Bank of Montreal

When you're Canada's oldest bank, people probably assume you're stodgy and conservative. Chairman Matthew Barrett and President Tony Comper, however, knew that getting an edge on the competition — and there is lots of it these days — required incorporating new perspectives into the bank's traditional corporate structure. This meant capitalizing on the rich diversity of its workforce, but opportunities for advancement were far from equal. Women held 91 percent of the bank's nonmanagerial jobs, whereas they held only nine percent of executive jobs.

Something had to be done to achieve equality, so Barrett and Comper sprung into action. They formed the Task Force on the Advancement of Women, and they charged this group with identifying barriers to advancement for women and with creating specific plans for breaking them down. The task force conducted extensive research and found the major barrier

(continued)

to advancement was a series of widely held myths about women executives. For example, survey findings revealed that women were assumed to be less committed to their companies because they quit their jobs to raise children. The reality for most jobs at the bank, however, is that women actually have *longer* service records than men — a direct contradiction of conventional wisdom!

According to Johanne M. Totta, vice president of employee programs and workplace equality, one key to turning the situation around was speaking the language best understood within the bank: numbers. Typically, managers were used to getting quarterly reports assessing the effect of their work on the bank's financial picture. Now, managers also receive quarterly feedback telling them how well they are meeting equality goals, such as hiring females and helping those already working for the bank to learn new skills and to advance through the ranks. The managers' own performance evaluations — and their pay — carefully reflect attainment of these goals.

Furthermore, advisory councils have been created in which a diverse sample of employees at various levels meets quarterly with bank officials to discuss progress toward equality. These sessions provide useful feedback, which is channeled to Totta's office. More importantly, perhaps, they provide helpful ideas for prompting equality that people can take back to their workplaces.

The Bank of Montreal has received several awards for its Workplace Equality Program, including the Distinction Award from the YWCA and the Mercury Award from the International Communications Academy of Arts and Sciences. For bank officials, however, the highest accolade will be overcoming the barriers to developing human potential that not only hold back their own female employees but also keep them from better serving their customers. As Totta said, "Banks offer about the same rates; it is people who make the difference — the customer service." With 6,000 branches internationally, there surely are many customers to serve. Thus far, it looks as if the Bank of Montreal's Workplace Equality Program promises to be a high-yield investment.

CRITICAL THINKING QUESTIONS

1. What were the causes of the problem at the Bank of Montreal?
2. How effective will the Workplace Equality Program continue to be in the future?
3. What obstacles will the bank face with this program in the future?
4. How else can the bank promote equality within its workforce?

VIDEO CASE

Work-Related Attitudes: Feelings About Jobs, Organizations, and People

SMALL BUSINESS 2000

Attitudes have a lot to do with how people look at — and live — their lives. Attitudes are not fixed, meaning they can change, but they generally are treated as being relatively stable. We can learn about how people approach work by understanding their attitudes.

Judy Jacobsen, the founder of Madison Park Greeting Card Company, has "a great attitude," but what, exactly, does this mean? Jacobsen comes across as having a very positive outlook on life. This carries over into her attitudes and approaches to work. Jacobsen worries about the bottom line, but we get the idea she is willing to forgo some profit to ensure that she (and others) have a chance to feel good about what they are doing. Jacobsen appreciates the need to

run a strong and financially healthy company; at the same time, she is committed to having a happy, positive, and attitudinally healthy company, too!

In this video, you get the idea that at Madison Park Greeting, people are the greatest asset. Nobody is forced to expose a lot about themselves or to "buy into" things with which they don't agree, but there is an opportunity to be part of a family — as much as to be part of a company — if one chooses. The staff meets daily (yes, daily!) for brief status updates on key projects. These meetings give Jacobsen a chance to see how people are doing, too. It seems like Judy plays a bit of a motherly role.

The environment at Madison Park Greeting Card Company might seem a bit odd to you. It certainly is not what you would expect if you were finishing school and going to work for a large, *Fortune* 100 corporation. It probably is not even what you would expect if you were going to work for many smaller companies. The point is, this approach may not be for everyone. On the other hand, if this is the type of organization within which someone feels comfortable, it could be great for both the company and the individual. Working in a place that makes you feel good and that allows you to be yourself probably influences how well you work — and how committed you are to the company. There are mixed opinions about how much to worry about employee turnover, but good employees are a valuable asset. If we accept that there is a relationship between a feeling of "belongingness" and good work, Judy Jacobsen might be on to something.

QUESTIONS FOR DISCUSSION

1. You have met Judy Jacobsen and learned a bit about how she started and evolved her business. Consider what she says about how she has grown as a business owner and the work environment she has established. How would you describe her attitudes toward work?

2. Think about what you have learned about organizational commitment. What types of commitment issues might exist among various employees at Madison Park Greeting Card Company? Do you think everybody feels the same as Jacobsen about the company and their job?

3. We have learned two interesting things about Jacobsen's approach to employing family: She believes there can be only one leader and has selected one of three children working with her to be the company president, and she has required her children to work somewhere else before coming to work in the company. What do you think about these decisions? Do you agree with what Jacobsen did? Why, or why not?

4. We were introduced to various employment programs for people of various abilities and cultural backgrounds. This small company even has a program to help high-school students earn money toward a college education. Do you think such programs are necessary? Why do you think companies have them?

EXPERIENCING ORGANIZATIONAL BEHAVIOR

Are You Committed to Your Job?

Questionnaires similar to the one presented here, which is based on established instruments, are used to assess three types of organizational commitment: *continuance*, *affective*, and *normative*. Completing this scale (based on Meyer & Allen, 1991; see note 88) will give you a feel both for your own level of job commitment and for how this important construct is measured.

Directions

In the space to the left of each statement below, write the number that best reflects the extent to which you agree with it personally. Express your answers using the following scale: 1 = not at all, 2 = slightly, 3 = moderately, 4 = a great deal, and 5 = extremely.

_____ 1. At this point, I stay on my job more because I have to than because I want to.

_____ 2. I feel I strongly belong to my organization.

_____ 3. I am reluctant to leave a company once I have been working there.

_____ 4. Leaving my job would entail great personal sacrifice.

_____ 5. I feel emotionally connected to the company for which I work.

_____ 6. My employer would be very disappointed if I left my job.

_____ 7. I have no other choice but to stay on my present job.

_____ 8. I feel like I am part of the family at the company in which I work.

_____ 9. I feel a strong obligation to stay on my job.

_____ 10. My life would be greatly disrupted if I left my present job.

_____ 11. I would be quite pleased to spend the rest of my life working for this organization.

_____ 12. I stay on my job because people would think poorly of me for leaving.

Scoring

1. Add the scores for items 1, 4, 7, and 10. This reflects your degree of _continuance commitment_.

2. Add the scores for items 2, 5, 8, and 11. This reflects your degree of _affective commitment_.

3. Add the scores for items 3, 6, 9, and 12. This reflects your degree of _normative commitment_.

Questions to Ask Yourself

1. Which form of commitment does the scale reveal you to have most? Which do you have least? Are these differences great, or are they highly similar?

2. Did the scale reveal something you did not already know about yourself, or did it merely reinforce your intuitive beliefs about your own organizational commitment?

3. To what extent is your organizational commitment, as reflected by this scale, related to your interest in quitting your job and in taking a new position?

4. How do your answers to these questions compare with those of your classmates? Are your responses similar to theirs, or are they different? Why do you think this is?

SKILLS BANK

WORKING IN GROUPS

Recognizing Differences in Cultural Values on the Job

One major barrier to understanding and appreciating people from other cultures is that they may adopt widely different values — especially when it comes to basic organizational activities (e.g., hiring). The following exercise (adapted from Gardenswartz & Rowe, 1994; see note 86) should make you aware of such differences and sensitize you to their effect on life in organizations.

Directions

1. Divide the class into groups of approximately five to 10 students each.
2. Review the differences in values noted in the list that follows.
3. As a group, identify and discuss specific examples, based on your personal experiences, of each cultural distinction noted.

4. As a group, discuss the implications of these differences. For example, note specific problems likely to arise because of such differences.

5. As a class, review the major implications identified by each group in step 4.

In Mainstream American Culture . . .	*But in Many Other Cultures . . .*
People's primary obligation is toward their job.	People's primary obligation is toward their family and friends.
Employment is "at will"; an employee may be terminated at the discretion of the organization.	Employment is for life.
Competition is an accepted way of life.	Cooperation is considered to be better, because it promotes harmony between people.
People strive for personal achievement	Personal ambition is frowned on; group achievement is highly valued.

Questions for Discussion

1. Was your group — or the class as a whole — generally sensitive to the differences in values noted in this exercise?

2. What were the major organizational implications of the cultural differences in values identified by the class?

3. What can be done to help people recognize and accept these cultural differences?

4. Did you come away from this exercise with a better understanding of the way that cultural differences may affect organizational activities?

6

MANAGING YOUR OWN BEHAVIOR: CAREERS AND STRESS

LEARNING OBJECTIVES

After reading this chapter, you should be able to

1. Understand *socialization*, and identify the stages through which it develops.
2. Explain what *mentors* are, what they do, and the benefits as well as costs of mentoring to both mentors and their protégés.
3. Describe how people choose their *careers*, and explain how the nature of careers has changed in recent years.
4. Explain how the careers of women and men differ, including the so-called *glass ceiling*.
5. Define *stress*, and distinguish it from *strain*.
6. Describe the major organizational and personal causes of stress.
7. Describe the adverse effects of stress, including *burnout*, and explain how individual differences play roles in such effects.
8. Describe individual as well as organizational techniques for managing stress.

PREVIEW CASE

Gray Expectations: What To Do When They Change All the Rules

It's 6:45 A.M., and Chris Toal, a mid-level manager at Open Market, Inc., a company specializing in Internet commerce, is working out furiously in a gym near his office. By 8:00 A.M., he'll be behind his desk at the company's Burlington, Massachusetts, headquarters, where he oversees a small staff. His duties vary and include projecting revenue, supervising expenses in the sales division, and resolving disputes over compensation.

At age 55, Toal was born just before the baby boom generation. When he started working more than three decades ago, he expected to have a smooth career, with one or, maybe, just a handful of companies. He also fully expected that when he reached his current age, he could slow down, spend more time with his family, and generally enjoy life more. This was not to be, however, because changes in the business world took their toll on Toal's career.

After several years as a high-school teacher and then (after law school) as a lawyer in a poor Boston neighborhood, Toal took a job with a high-tech start-up firm: LTX, Inc. He quickly rose through the ranks, too, and by 1989, Toal was earning more than $90,000. That's when his troubles began. To remain competitive, LTX began downsizing its workforce, forcing Toal to scramble just to keep his job. He moved from manufacturing to purchasing to sales administration, but these efforts were in vain. At age 50, he found himself a victim of the layoffs. His next job was at Proteon, Inc., another high-tech firm, but it lasted only a few years. Once again, Toal found himself searching for another position. Then, in 1996, he came to Open Market, where he has worked hard to expand his skills — and to keep his job.

Mr. Toal is one of the oldest employees at Open Systems, and he has had to learn many new skills to stay competitive, including computer skills, information management skills, teleconferencing, and more. Sadly, he has realized that his age and experience do not give him the advantages they once conferred: the respect of younger employees, and a high level of job security. On the contrary, as he sees it, his age and experience have become liabilities instead of assets. "The younger folks don't come to you as a mentor or experienced person," Toal remarks. "You are all competing for jobs and the future and success." His boss is considerably younger and often kids him about his conservative dress (Toal is one of the few people who wears a tie to work) and about his new — and still unpolished — computer skills. This only causes Toal to redouble his efforts, and he typically works 12- to 15-hour days.

Every few weeks, he gets together with a group of other fifty-something employees to bemoan how their lives have been altered — usually negatively — by changes in the workplace. "I feel like I've peaked in my career, but I don't think I've peaked as a human being," Toal sighs. Then, somewhat wistfully, he adds, "Things are not what any of us anticipated — that with natural talent, hard work, and good values there would come some sense of stability. In fact, there is no security and no stability."

Although you may never have heard of Chris Toal, you probably know someone just like him — that is, someone who has been forced to spend the years he or she had planned on "coasting to retirement" as a seasoned veteran instead learning new skills and working hard just to keep a job. Long gone are the days when people graduated from school, joined a company, and remained there for decades, gradually rising in status and earnings until, eventually, they reached a level corresponding to their own talents and motivation. Gone, too, are the days when individuals could learn a single set of skills and then use these to guide them through their entire careers. Instead, today's employees generally expect to work for many different companies, and they probably never will enjoy the level of job security experienced by past generations. They already know something that Mr. Toal found out the hard way — that people in today's workforce must continually learn new skills, reinventing themselves as needed, just to maintain their value in the marketplace.

Frustrating as they may be, Mr. Toal's experiences illustrate the complexities of *career management*, which is the process of controlling the range of skills and experiences needed to grow and develop as desired on the job.[1] Indeed, acquiring the range of skills needed to enjoy a satisfying career is a large part of adapting to a rapidly changing world. As you might imagine, however, taking control of your own behavior on the job effectively involves other important considerations as well. Among the most important of these is *managing stress*—that is, doing things to minimize the adverse emotional and physiological reactions to various demands faced both within and outside an organization.[2]

Our discussion of career management and stress management reflects a focus on *managing your own behavior in organizations*. Until now, we have dealt mostly with managing others—an approach that predominates throughout the rest of this book as well. In this chapter, however, we supplement this orientation by focusing on how individuals can manage their own behavior at work. This is not to say, of course, that others are not involved as well in our careers and the stresses we face. Far from it! Rather, unlike some other topics in this book, which focus primarily on things we do either to or for others, here we focus on things we do primarily for ourselves—specifically, managing our own careers and the stresses in our lives.

We begin with career management. Specifically, our discussion focuses on three major topics:

1. *Organizational socialization*, or the process of becoming a member of an organization.[3]
2. *Mentoring*, or a one-on-one form of socialization that helps to advance one's career.[4]
3. *Career development*, or the process of planning and working your way through many jobs over the course of one's working life.[5]

ORGANIZATIONAL SOCIALIZATION: THE PROCESS OF LEARNING THE ROPES

Think of the jobs you have held in recent years. Can you recall your feelings and reactions during the first few days or weeks on each? If so, you probably remember these as being somewhat uncomfortable periods. As a new employee, you were confronted with a work environment that differed in many respects from the one you had left. Most—if not all—of the people around you were strangers, and you had to get to know them—and their personal quirks—from scratch. Unless your job was identical to the one you had before, you also had to learn new procedures, skills, and operations relating to it as well as the policies and practices of your new organization. In short, you had to *learn the ropes* so that you could perform your new job effectively (Figure 6.1).

People accomplish these tasks through a process known as **organizational socialization**, which is defined as *the process through which individuals are transformed from outsiders into participating, effective members of organizations*.[6] In a sense, a career consists of a series of socialization experiences that occur as an individual moves into a succession of new organizations or positions over time. Accordingly, to understand careers, we must understand the process of organizational socialization.

Organizational socialization clearly is a continuous process, beginning before people arrive on the job and continuing for weeks or months after they begin working. Everyone's socialization experiences are different, but organizational socialization progresses in three regular steps: *getting in*, *breaking in*, and *settling in*.[7] We now describe each phase of the socialization process (Figure 6.2).

Getting In: What Happens Before People Are Hired?

Can you think of a specific company you would like to work for in the future? Why would you like to work there? What makes this company such an attractive choice for you? To the extent you can answer these questions, you recognize that you know

organizational socialization
The process through which newcomers to an organization become full-fledged members who share its major values and understand its policies and procedures.

Just know the definition thats all.

quite a bit about an organization even before you start working there. In other words, people often develop expectations about an organization before actually being hired. Therefore, in a sense, organizational socialization begins well before people accept and fill a new job—a period described as the *pre-entry period*.[8]

How Do We Learn About Organizations?   Several sources of information contribute to beliefs about an organization. First, friends or relatives who already work there might describe their experiences. Second, you might acquire information from sources such as professional journals, new stories, and corporate annual reports. These sources of information about an organization are far from perfect, however. They may paint rosier pictures than are justified by the facts, but they still are useful in allowing us to form preliminary ideas about what it might be like to work there.

Another source of information is the organization itself, such as through recruiters or interviewers. Unfortunately, such information can be biased as well. These days, when competition for good employees is fierce, successful recruitment usually involves a skilled combination of salesmanship and diplomacy. Recruiters tend to describe their companies in glowing terms, glossing over internal problems and external threats while emphasizing the positive features. As a result, potential employees often receive unrealistically positive impressions of the organization. Then, when they arrive on the job and find their expectations are not met, they experience disappointment, dissatisfaction, and even resentment about being misled—a combination of reactions known as **entry shock**.

Reducing Entry Shock with Realistic Job Previews   The less that employees' job expectations are met, the less satisfied and committed those employees are to those jobs and the more likely they are to think about quitting—and to actually do so.[9] Clearly, this is a very disruptive and expensive state of affairs. So, to avoid such negative reactions, a growing number of organizations are providing job candidates with accurate information about the organizations in which they seek employment. Known as **realistic job previews**, these descriptions of life on a job provide employees with an accurate picture of what working in the organizational will be like. Growing evidence indicates that realistic job previews are effective. Prospective employees who were given realistic job previews not only are more satisfied with their jobs but also are less likely to leave them voluntarily compared with those who received glowing—but often misleading—information about the conditions they will face.[10]

A study that compared the turnover rates of employees in four different conditions illustrates this conclusion.[11] One condition consisted of employees who, as job

FIGURE 6.1

Learning the Ropes

Have you ever felt lost on your first day at a new job? If so, welcome to the club. Almost everyone has had such experiences.

entry shock
The confusion and disorientation experienced by many newcomers to an organization

realistic job previews
Accurate information concerning the conditions within an organization or job provided to potential employees before their decision to join.

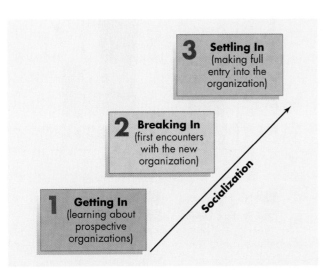

3 Settling In (making full entry into the organization)

2 Breaking In (first encounters with the new organization)

1 Getting In (learning about prospective organizations)

Socialization

FIGURE 6.2

The Three Stages of Organizational Socialization

Organizational socialization generally involves three stages: *getting in*, *breaking in*, and *settling in*.
(*Source*: Based on suggestions by Feldman, 1981; see note 7.)

applicants, received only positive information about the jobs they later took (i.e., the positive information condition). In another condition, applicants received both positive and negative descriptions of the job in question (i.e., the realistic job preview condition). In the third condition, applicants were not given specific information about the job in question (i.e., the expectation-lowering condition); instead, they were warned about the dangers of unrealistically inflated expectations and urged to develop realistic ones on their own. Finally, in the fourth condition, no information was provided at all (i.e., the no-information condition). Which group of employees showed lowest turnover?

As shown in Figure 6.3, the results were clear: Individuals given realistic job previews as well as those exposed to the expectation-lowering treatment later showed more realistic expectations — and lower turnover rates — than those in the other two conditions. In sum, providing employees with realistic expectations about their new jobs — or simply encouraging them to avoid unrealistically high expectations on their own — can yield important practical benefits.

An Important Caution About Realistic Job Previews   Before you conclude that using realistic job previews is always wise, an important qualification is in order. Specifically, the best, most qualified applicants tend to give greater weight than less qualified applicants to negative information about potential jobs.[12] Perhaps because the best applicants can demand the best opportunities, they are most sensitive to the negative features of jobs. Therefore, although providing prospective employees with realistic information about the job can prevent entry shock and make it more likely they will remain on the job, such procedures also could make hiring the best applicants difficult.

Thus it may be wise to carefully balance the information presented to job prospects. You want to provide enough realistic information to prevent unrealistic expectations, but you also should avoid dwelling on the negative aspects of the job for fear of driving away the best applicants.

FIGURE 6.3

Techniques for Preventing "Entry Shock"

New employees who were exposed to realistic job previews or information designed to prevent excessively positive expectations about their new jobs later showed lower turnover than employees who were either given no information about their new jobs or a standard job preview including mainly positive information.

(*Source*: Based on data from Buckley et al., 1998; see note 11).

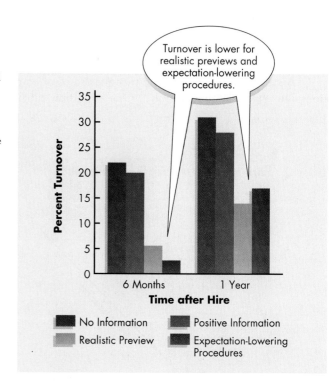

Is it ever appropriate for people to paint an unrealistically "rosy" picture of what working in their organization will be like? Does this constitute lying, or is providing realistic information about the working conditions prospective employees will encounter *always* the ethically correct thing to do? ■

Breaking In: The Encounter Stage

The second stage in organizational socialization begins after individuals are hired, when they actually assume their new duties. During this stage, employees face several challenges. Of course, they need to master the skills required by their new jobs.[13] They also must become oriented to the practices and procedures of the new organization — that is, to the way things are done. They must learn about the *organizational culture*; the shared attitudes, values, and expectations of existing organization members (we discuss this topic more fully in chapter 13).

Learning an organization's culture is an important task. After all, doing so can help new employees to decide if they really belong in that company. In fact, this process is so important that some companies help their employees to assess the organizational culture during key socialization periods. Conrail, for example, did this when it merged with Norfolk Southern. To avoid potential culture clashes from having people work where they feel they do not belong, Conrail hired consultants to help employees make the transition. In deciding whether to stay with the new company or to seek employment elsewhere, employees were encouraged to ask questions about important aspects of the organization: the way it communicates feedback, the dress code, how executives expect to be addressed, openness about company decisions, attention to deadlines, and so on. The idea was straightforward: By focusing on such issues, prospective employees can determine whether there is a good or a poor fit between a company's culture and their own values.[14]

It is during the encounter stage, which sometimes is known as the *accommodation stage*, that newcomers learn what the organization expects from them and how to be a participating member of their work group, and this is when formal *orientation programs* are conducted. These programs teach new employees about their organizations, their day-to-day operations as well as their histories, missions, and traditions. Without such orientation programs, new employees probably would find it harder to fit in and to understand the organization. Much of what these programs cover may be learned informally over time, but when conducted well, such formed programs often are more efficient at transmitting large amounts of information to new employees in a short amount of time.

Settling In: The Metamorphosis Stage

Sometime after an individual enters an organization, she or he attains full member status. Depending on the type and length of the orientation program, this entry may be marked by a formal ceremony, such as dinner or a graduation exercise, or it may be quite informal (Fig. 6.4). Alternatively, new employees may receive a concrete sign of their new status as full members, such as a pass to the executive dining room. In other cases, especially when training has been short or informal, full acceptance may be signaled through informal means, such as being invited to lunch with the group.

In whatever form, the settling-in phase of socialization marks important shifts for individuals and their organizations. Employees make permanent adjustments to their jobs, and organizations now treat them as if they will be long-term members of the work team.

FIGURE 6.4

Marking Entry into an Organization

Formal ceremonies sometimes acknowledge an individual's entry into an organization or profession. Having just completed an extensive training program, these state troopers are participating in such a ceremony.

mentoring like a coach - to train

mentoring

The process of serving as a mentor.

mentor

A more experienced employee who offers advice, assistance, and protection to a younger, less experienced one (i.e., a *protégé*).

protégé

A less experienced (often new) employee whose organizational socialization is facilitated by working with a *mentor*.

MENTORING: ONE-ON-ONE SOCIALIZATION

Consider 50 new college graduates hired by a large corporation for basically the same job. All begin on fairly equal footing, but if you return a year later, you might already note substantial differences. Some would be gone, others would be falling behind, and a few would be on the fast track to success already.

What accounts for these differences? Many factors certainly play a role, but one of the most important is **mentoring**.[15] This is a process in which a more experienced employee — a **mentor** — advises, counsels, and otherwise enhances the personal development (and career) of a new employee — a **protégé**. If you ever had an older, more experienced person take you under her or his wing, then you already know how valuable a mentor can be. In fact, having a mentor early in one's career is an important predictor of success: The more mentoring that people receive, the more promotions they gain and the more highly compensated they are.[16]

We now take a close look at mentoring relationships, examining precisely what mentors do, how such relationships form and change over time, and the role of mentors in career success.

What Do Mentors Do?

Mentors do many things for their protégés.[17] For example, they provide much-needed emotional support and confidence for those just starting out (and likely to be somewhat insecure). Mentors also help to pave the way for their protégés' job success. They nominate protégés for promotions, provide opportunities for them to demonstrate their competence, and generally bring them to the attention of higher management. Mentors also suggest useful strategies for reaching work goals — often ones that protégés might not generate for themselves. Finally, mentors often protect their protégés from the consequences of errors and also help them to avoid situations that may threaten their careers.

Given the potential benefits of mentoring, many companies do not leave the formation of mentor-protégé relationships to chance. Rather, they have formal programs in which newcomers are assigned to more experienced persons, who then are expected to serve as the newcomers' mentors.[18] For a summary of what some companies are doing in this respect, see Table 6.1.

TABLE 6.1

Mentorship Programs: What Some Companies Are Doing

Because the mentoring process is so important, many companies have been unwilling to leave it to chance. Thus, they have developed formal mechanisms to encourage mentoring relationships.

COMPANY	DESCRIPTION
Colgate-Palmolive	All new white-collar employees are assigned individual, higher-ranking employees as mentors.
NYNEX	Mentoring circles, consisting of six lower-ranking and two higher-ranking female employees, meet monthly to discuss work-related issues.
Dow Jones	Groups of four are formed that consist of a high-level mentor and three others: a white male, a woman of any race, and a minority group member of either gender.
Chubb & Son Insurance	In its Sponsorship Program, three protégés are assigned to each of 10 different mentors.

Source: Based on information in Granfield, 1992; see note 18.

How Mentoring Relationships Form and Change

As noted, mentor-protégé relationships do not form at random. Rather, they often are the result of a complex selection process, in which both mentors and potential protégés play active roles. Mentors don't want to waste their time and effort on just anybody, so they seek only the best and most promising newcomers for their protégés. The process by which they do so is not always explicit, but given that potential protégés outnumber potential mentors in most organizations, careful selection of potential protégés does occur.

Protégés engage in selection as well. They generally seek mentors who are older and more experienced than themselves—and ones who are known to be successful in the organization. Once they identify potential mentors, they may take active steps to establish a relationship with these people.[19]

What happens to mentoring relationships once they are formed? Do they remain unchanged over time? No. In fact, most mentor-protégé relationships pass through four distinct phases.[20]

Phase 1: Initiation   The first phase lasts from six months to one year. During this period, the relationships gets started and takes on importance for both parties. The mentor and the protégé get to know one another, and each learns what he or she has to offer—and can expect from—the other.

Phase 2: Cultivation   This stage may last an additional two to five years. During this period, the bond between the mentor and the protégé deepens, and the young individual may make rapid career progress because of the mentor's skilled assistance.

Phase 3: Separation   This period occurs when the protégé feels it is time to assert independence and to strike out on his or her own. It also may result from some externally produced change in their roles, such as when the protégé is promoted or the mentor is transferred. In addition, separation can occur if the mentor feels unable to continue providing support and guidance to the protégé (e.g., if the mentor becomes ill). This stage can be quite stressful if the mentor resents the protégé's growing independence or the protégé feels the mentor has withdrawn his or her support prematurely.

Phase 4: Redefinition   The final phase of the relationship occurs after the separation has been successful. In this stage, both persons perceive their bond as being primarily one of friendship. They come to treat one another as equals, and the roles of mentor and protégé fade away. In other words, as the protégé gains in experience and skill, the need for a mentor-protégé relationship gradually decreases. Even after the relationship ends, however, the mentor may continue taking pride in the accomplishments of the former protégé, and the protégé may continue feeling gratitude toward the former mentor.

Sometimes, however, less desirable reasons also exist. For example, the mentor may feel jealousy of the protégé, or the protégé may feel the mentor is stifling his or her development. On the other hand, protégés may cling to the relationship after it no longer is beneficial, either to the protégé or to the mentor. Such factors may lead to *dysfunctional* terminations of mentor to protégé relationships—that is, ones that may result in considerable bitterness on both sides.[21]

Gender, Race, and Mentoring

In general, people tend to prefer, like, and feel more comfortable around persons who are similar to themselves than around persons who are different. Thus, people tend to form friendships and other personal relationships with persons who are generally similar to themselves in traits, attitudes, or background, not with persons who are opposite to themselves. Does this principle apply to mentoring relationships? Growing evidence suggests that it does. Women and minorities (e.g., African Americans) seem to have more difficulty than white males obtaining mentors in their organizations.[22] There are exceptions to this pattern, of course, but overall, women and minorities appear to be at a distinct disadvantage in obtaining a mentor (Figure 6.5).[23] One reason seems to involve the principle stated earlier: Even today, most managers in the United States as well as in many other countries are white males, and such persons feel most comfortable around those of similar background.

Other factors also play a role, however. In recent surveys, women have reported less willingness to serve as mentors than men.[24] Apparently, women are more concerned than men about the potential negative consequences that may follow if they adopt a protégé who fails.

Test question over ▶

FIGURE 6.5

Gender, Race, and Mentoring
Women and minorities often find it more difficult than white males to find mentors. This largely results from the tendency for potential mentors, who mostly are white males, to select protégés demographically similar to themselves. This problem is expected to lessen, however, as the workforce becomes increasingly diverse.

Do you think it is harder to obtain a mentor in some cultures than in others? If so, why? What effects might this have on the careers of young employees and the competitiveness of organizations in various cultures? ■

On the other hand, many male managers have concerns about mentoring female employees: They fear the close relationships that develop may be misperceived as romantic entanglements! Given that having a mentor early in one's career often is highly beneficial, it seems important for organizations to reduce these barriers and to increase mentoring opportunities for women and minorities. Failing to do so may deny persons in these groups access to a vital ingredient of career success.

With this in mind, many companies have created mentoring programs that intentionally bring together members of majority and minority groups. For example, at DuPont, where a formal mentoring program has been in place since 1985, mentoring has helped minority employees to secure positions that otherwise might have been unattainable.[25] Notably, the proportion of minorities in top positions at DuPont has risen from 10 percent to 30 percent in recent years—even as the overall number of management jobs has dropped. Thus, it would appear that mentoring is a vital tool in the arsenal of those attempting to eliminate prejudicial attitudes and discriminatory behaviors toward minorities (see chapter 5).

CAREERS: NEW FORMS, NEW STRATEGIES

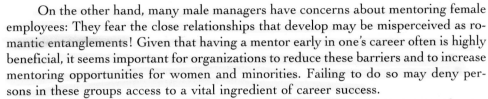

"Where do you want to work when you graduate?" Not long ago, most people gave the same answer: "A big company, like one of the *Fortune* 500 firms."

Until a decade ago, this answer made sense, too. Big companies offered what seemed to be the surest route to the top—a series of steps up the corporate ladder, leading to ever-greater responsibilities and rewards. Today, however, most students—and especially those completing their MBAs—have a different answer. A few recent statistics tell the tale:

- Less than half of all MBA graduates take jobs in large companies. Most take jobs at small companies or consulting firms instead.[26]
- More than 14 million Americans are self-employed, including 8.3 million as independent contractors and 2.3 million with temporary agencies.[27]
- One of every 25 U.S. adults is involved in trying to start a business.[28]
- The number of home-based businesses has risen to record levels and, at present, exceeds more than 27 million![29]

Facts like these suggest something major is in the wind concerning the nature of *careers*. A **career** may be defined simply as *the evolving sequence of a person's work experiences over time*. Common conceptions of what these sequences are—or should be—have altered greatly in recent years, partly because of equally sweeping changes in the business world.[30] In other words, people currently hold different conceptions of what their careers will be like than they held in the past because they are increasingly aware of the tremendous shifts in how companies do business, including how they hire, train, promote, and retain their employees.

In this section, we focus on several important aspects of careers and their changing nature. First, we consider how individuals make vocational choices (i.e., why they choose specific jobs). Next, we examine some major ways in which careers have changed and how individuals can best react to these changes when planning their

career

The evolving sequence of a person's work experience over time.

YOU BE THE CONSULTANT

Female and minority hires, although highly talented and carefully selected, have not been advancing through the ranks as quickly as white males at a large advertising agency. An employee survey reveals this has resulted, in part, from the difficulties of women and minorities in finding mentors.

1. How can these difficulties be explained? In other words, what do you suspect is their underlying cause?
2. What can be done to help women and minorities obtain mentors at this firm?
3. If this initiative fails to produce more rapid advancement for women and minorities, what else can be done to attain this goal?

own careers. Finally, we consider the role of gender in careers, addressing the question of whether women and men have different career experiences and, if so, why this may be.

GLOBAL MATTERS   Although careers are changing around the world, the desire to start one's own business is stronger in the United States than anywhere else. Why do you think this is? Do you think this shift toward entrepreneurial careers will increase in other countries as their economies develop? ▪

Choosing a Job: Making Vocational Choices

How do people end up in specific jobs? Many factors play roles in this process, but we focus here on several that appear to be most important.

Person-Job Fit   Ask yourself this question: What kind of person becomes an attorney, or a professional soldier, or an elementary school teacher? Do your descriptions of these persons differ? If so, they reflect your understanding that persons possessing specific characteristics are attracted to certain kinds of jobs. This is the idea of *person-job fit*, which we discussed in chapter 3—that is, the suggestion that because of their personal characteristics (e.g., traits or abilities), individuals are better suited for some jobs than for others.[31]

Researchers who have studied this relationship believe people generally select jobs that match their personalities, abilities, and values, and study findings tend to confirm this idea.[32] The closer the person-job fit, the greater individuals' job satisfaction.[33] In fact, many people tend to assign greater importance to this kind of fit than to pay or promotional opportunities when choosing a job.[34]

Job Opportunities   Another factor strongly influencing job choice is people's beliefs about the future of these jobs. In other words, we tend to be quite rational in our choice of jobs, focusing on those we believe will offer growing opportunities while avoiding those that seem to be declining in this regard. Most people know there is not much call for blacksmiths or train conductors today, so they tend not to consider these jobs—even if they find them personally appealing.

Many other jobs can be expected to grow in numbers — and in opportunities — in the future, and these tend to capture our attention when considering which job to enter. They also capture the attention of people administering vocational programs in high schools, technical schools, and colleges. To be popular with prospective students, these programs offer training in areas where the jobs are likely to be. The availability of such training opportunities also attracts people to the kinds of jobs that require this training. In other words, the situation appears to be cyclical: Growth in certain areas promotes people's interest in those areas, which in turn encourages the development of training programs in those areas, which in turn provides skilled people to develop those areas, thus further fueling growth.

What careers are likely to prosper in the future? Table 6.2 provides an overview of some jobs that are likely to be "hot" in the years ahead.[35] Specifically, it identifies the fastest-growing occupations projected through 2006 by level of education and training. If you are looking for promising employment opportunities, these careers may be worth considering.

TABLE 6.2

Where Will Tomorrow's Jobs Be?

Certain jobs — summarized here by level of education and training required — are expected to grow most rapidly through the year 2006.

First professional degree
    Chiropractors
    Veterinarians and veterinary inspectors
    Physicians
    Lawyers
    Clergy
Doctoral degree
    Biological scientists
    Medical scientists
    College and university faculty
    Mathematicians and all other mathematical scientists
Master's degree
    Speech-language pathologists and audiologists
    Counselors
    Curators, archivists, museum technicians
    Psychologists
    Operations research analysts
Work experience plus bachelor's or higher degree
    Engineering, science, and computer systems managers
    Marketing, advertising, and public relations managers
    Artists and commercial artists
    Management analysts
    Financial managers
Bachelor's degree
    Database administrators and computer support specialists
    Computer engineers
    Systems analysts
    Physical therapists
    Occupational therapists
Associate degree
    Paralegals
    Health information technicians
    Dental hygienists
    Respiratory therapists
    Cardiology technologists

(continued)

TABLE 6.2 (*continued*)

Postsecondary vocational training
   Data processing equipment repairers
   Emergency medical technicians
   Manicurists
   Surgical technologists
   Medical secretaries
Work experience
   Food service and lodging managers
   Teachers and instructors, vocational education and training
   Lawn service managers
   Instructors, adult education
   Nursery and greenhouse managers
Long-term training and experience (more than 12 months of on-the-job training)
   Desktop publishing specialists
   Flight attendants
   Musicians
   Correction officers
   Producers, directors, actors, and entertainers
Moderate-term training and experience (1 – 12 months of combined on-the-job experience and informal training)
   Physical and corrective therapy assistants and aides
   Medical assistants
   Occupational therapy assistants and aides
   Social and human services assistants
   Instructors and coaches, sports and physical training
Short-term training and experience (up to 1 month of on-the-job experience)
   Personal and home care aides
   Home health aides
   Amusement and recreation attendants
   Adjustment clerks
   Bill and account collectors

Source: Bureau of Labor Statistics, 1997; see note 35

The Changing Nature of Career Plans

Have you ever seen the film or play *How to Succeed in Business Without Really Trying*? It offers a tongue-in-cheek look at how someone lacking any special talent or skills can rise quickly to the top through a combination of impression management, good luck, and ruthless — if humorous! — manipulation. As the story unfolds, the hero moves through a series of jobs, each one higher in pay and status — and also on a higher floor in the company's huge building.

Although single-track career paths like this still exist, they are becoming the exception rather than the rule. Today, careers generally do *not* involve a straightforward climb through a successive series of clearly defined steps. More frequently, they include lateral moves, rotation through several different jobs, geographic relocations, and — increasingly — periods of time spent as an independent contractor or subcontractor rather than as a regular, full-time employee.

Why have these shifts in the nature of careers occurred? Mainly because organizations themselves have changed. For example, as described in chapter 1, many have been reorganized to make themselves "leaner and meaner" (a trend we explain in greater detail in chapter 14). Chris Toal, the individual from our preview case, as well as millions like him (including the people in Figure 6.6) surely can tell you what it's like to be "downsized" out of jobs they thought they never would lose. As organizations change what they do and how they operate, many of the career paths that once

CLOSE TO HOME

(Source: Close To Home © John McPherson.
Reprinted with permission of Universal Press Syndicate. All rights reserved.)

Krepner Industries was notorious for its abrupt lay-offs.

F I G U R E 6 . 6

Lifetime Employment with One Company? Don't Bet On It!

An increasing number of companies respond to increased competition through downsizing and related procedures. *Single-track careers*, in which individuals are employed by one company for their entire working lives, have virtually vanished.

(*Source*: CLOSE TO HOME © John McPherson. Reprinted with permission of Universal Press Syndicate. All rights reserved.)

existed in them have evaporated.[36] Given this radically altered set of conditions, what kind of career goals and paths should individuals seek today?

Career Goals: What Should Employees Seek?   Except for Japan (as noted in the "OB Around the World" section of this chapter), organizations in most countries no longer offer employees lifelong employment. Given this fact of organizational life today, what should individuals seek in return?

Because they no longer can count on job security, employees should focus on each job or assignment as a means of acquiring valuable skills. In short, they should view their careers as a series of opportunities for gaining new proficiencies, each of which increase their value on the job market. The basic idea is simple: As individuals acquire these competencies, they become more desirable as employees, and so the scope of their future career possibilities expands as well. Thus, when contemplating a job, it probably is better to ask "What will I learn from this assignment?" than "How long will it last?" or "What are the possibilities of promotion?" By viewing jobs primarily as learning experiences, we can map out a career strategy that will lead us to what we need to be—a highly desirable commodity in the employment market.

Job Rotation: A Key Ingredient in Career Development   It is one thing to recommend that employees view their jobs as learning experiences, but it is quite another to translate this general principle into concrete steps toward reaching this goal. How precisely can individuals use their jobs as a base for acquiring marketable skills?

One important way is using **job rotation**—that is, the practice of transferring employees laterally between jobs in an organization. The best-performing employees in organizations (i.e., those who receive the highest salaries and are promoted most

job rotation
Lateral transfers of employees between jobs in an organization.

OB AROUND THE WORLD

In many countries, the idea of a permanent job with one company is as dated as families only consisting of a single breadwinner, a stay-at-home spouse, and several children. One country, however, continues to buck this trend: Japan. There, the idea of lifetime employment persists, at least in the largest companies, and this tradition remains largely intact despite Japan's recent economic woes. In fact, strict laws prohibit the firing of full-time employees. So, why does this system work so well in Japan?

Lifetime employment is widely believed to follow from Japan's deep-rooted, paternalistic cultural values, but Japan's lifetime employment system evolved only after the country was rebuilt after World War II.[37] Instead, Japan's inclination toward lifetime employment seems to be based on a far more practical consideration — the enlightened self-interest of Japan's largest organizations. In other words, Japanese companies adopted this policy because for them, it pays — and pays handsomely at that. Consider the following points:

- Japanese companies are famous for their speed in adopting new technologies. One reason they can do so is that employees quickly embrace new technology. They know that it will enhance their company's profitability — and, hence, their own outcomes as well.

- Because employees are hired permanently, money spent on extensive training is a good investment rather than resources down the drain, as in the U.S. system where employees, once let go, may never return. In addition, Japan has laws preventing companies from advertising for labor and from hiring their competitors' employees. Therefore, the lifetime employment policy assures that training increases the value of employees to their organization and not to competitors who steal them away.

- With rules against hiring each others' employees, Japanese companies are assured former employees will not take R&D secrets to competitors. Because they have little fear of losing the fruits of R&D activities to other companies, Japanese corporations spend more on these vital activities — and with excellent results.

Note that in addition to benefiting the employees and the companies involved, lifetime employment also offers advantages to Japanese society at large. By keeping employees on their payrolls even during recessions, downswings in the business cycle are dampened. Most employees still have their jobs (if not their bonuses), so they can purchase goods and services and prevent the snowball effect that deepens and prolongs recession in other countries.

In sum, the Japanese system of lifetime employment persists because it works. Could the same system be adopted in other countries? Perhaps, but doing so would require extensive changes in existing labor laws, involving restrictions on stealing employees from other companies as well as stiff penalties for firing them. Adoption of such laws is unlikely in many countries, however, so Japan probably will remain relatively unique in the commitment to lifetime employment by many of its leading organizations.

rapidly) experience job rotation relatively early in their careers.[38] Not surprisingly, people who rotate through a succession of jobs find it a valuable way for them to acquire the variety of skills they needed to be successful (Figure 6.7). The career implications are evident: If you are offered job rotation, accept it. The benefits of doing so can be substantial.

Entrepreneurship: Should You Start Your Own Business?

Earlier, we shared a fascinating statistic: One of every 25 U.S. adults is (or has been involved in) starting his or her own business. These figures are growing, too.[39] These individuals are referred to as *entrepreneurs*. An **entrepreneur** is an individual who starts his or her own company.

entrepreneur
An individual who starts his or her own business.

The Trend Toward Entrepreneurship   Why is entrepreneurship rapidly becoming the career path of choice for so many people? As with many choices people make, there seems to be a "push" *and* a "pull" involved.

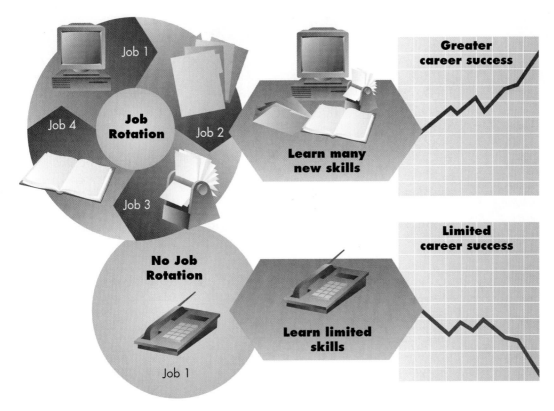

FIGURE 6.7

Job Rotation: A Path to Career Success

The process of rotating through various jobs helps people to pick up valuable skills, which enhance their chances of having successful careers. In contrast, people who remain on a single job tend to develop fewer skills, which limits their chances for success.

(*Source*: Based on suggestions by Campion, Cheraskin, & Stevens, 1994; see note 38.)

Several factors are involved on the "push" side, but perhaps most important is the low degree of job security people face today. Many people realize they cannot count on holding jobs with various organizations forever, even if they perform them quite well. Facing such uncertainty, they reason, why not take the plunge and start their own business? Similarly, the millions who have been "downsized" in recent years are excellent candidates for becoming entrepreneurs. After all, such people suddenly find themselves sitting "high and dry," without a job, and often at an age when other companies are less than eager to hire them. As a result, they take matters into their own hands — by turning to entrepreneurship.

It would be misleading to permit these economic considerations to disguise another, very personal factor also contributing to the recent growth of entrepreneurship: the growing desire for independence and autonomy, especially among young people. In survey after survey, recent business graduates indicate that being in charge of their own lives is extremely important to them.[40] This makes a career as an entrepreneur highly appealing.

On the "pull" side, business news and other media are filled — repeatedly — with the success stories of entrepreneurs who have "made it big." These include people like Bill Gates of Microsoft, Andy Grove of Intel, or Michael Dell of Dell Computers, who all have built huge fortunes from companies they started in a basement or a garage (Figure 6.8). Such examples also enhance the appeal of entrepreneurship as a career choice.

FIGURE 6.8

Some Highly Successful Entrepreneurs

Reports of the vast fortunes accumulated by entrepreneurs such as Michael Dell (left) of Dell Computers, and Andrew Grove (right) of Intel influence many people to start their own businesses.

We also should add there is a pro-social side to entrepreneurship as well. By starting new businesses, entrepreneurs not only build their own fortunes but also contribute tremendously to the wealth of their societies.[41] Indeed, in the early 1990s when large companies were downsizing, start-up companies provided millions of new jobs. Today, start-ups continue to grow, although their popularity has waned in the face of a flourishing economy in which large companies are hiring many employees.

The Risks of Entrepreneurship   Considering all these factors, should *you* start your own company? Only you can make this decision. You should note, however, that although the upside of starting your own business may be high, so may be the downside. Consider a few facts[42]:

- Twenty-four percent of new businesses fail within two years, and 63 percent vanish within six years.
- Few new businesses yield any income to their founders during their first year of operation, and many only become profitable after several years.
- The founders of new businesses often experience a sharp increase in personal workload—that is, they work longer and harder than ever before, and often for less income.

If you feel you can handle these risks, then starting your own business may be for you. If you choose this route, however, we advise you to first get a solid business background and take several courses in entrepreneurship. Not only will you learn a great deal about what this process requires, but you also may be alerted to several readily avoided pitfalls.

The Careers of Women and Men: How Similar Are They?

As you read about careers, it's natural to be asking "What about me? Is this the kind of career I can—or should—have?" Naturally, much of your answer is based on your past experience in different jobs. And although the job experiences of no two people are completely alike, it is interesting to consider the possibility that some of these differences occur in a systematic fashion—especially regarding gender. In this connection, we ask two related questions: *Do* the career experiences of women and men differ, and if they do, *why* is this so?

Contrasting Experiences on the Road to Success   The first question has a straightforward answer: Yes, women and men *do* have somewhat different career experiences. Such differences take many forms, but the most important surround the different paths that women and men choose in their quests for the top. Some of the major differences include[43]:

- Although increased training leads to managerial advancement for men as well as women, these benefits are greater for men.
- Work experience and education increase the training opportunities for both genders, but again, the links between these variables are stronger for men than for women.
- Whereas having a spouse and dependents at home interferes with women's work experiences, it enhances the experiences of men.
- Career encouragement from colleagues relates more closely to managerial advancement for women than for men.

In sum, although the same factors play roles in the career success of women as well as men, these factors operate quite differently regarding the specific roles they play.

Explaining Women's and Men's Career Differences: The Glass Ceiling   One key reason why women and men have such different job experiences is that as a group, women generally face barriers that prevent them from reaching top positions in many companies. Referred to as the **glass ceiling**, the U.S. Department of Labor defines such barriers as *those artificial barriers based on attitudinal or organizational bias that prevent qualified individuals from advancing in their organizations.*[44]

glass ceiling

A barrier preventing females from reaching top positions in many organizations.

During the last 30 years, the proportion of managers who are female has risen dramatically—from 16 percent to more than 42 percent. Even so, the proportion of top managers who are women has increased from three percent to only five percent.[45] Statistics such as these suggest there well may be a glass ceiling. Furthermore, it appears that sex-role stereotypes are key in keeping this ceiling in place (as we describe more fully in chapter 5).

Specifically, the glass ceiling often takes subtle forms rather than conscious efforts by male executives to keep women from their domain. For example, women may receive fewer opportunities than men to develop their skills and competencies—opportunities that prepare them for top-level jobs. Women also report fewer chances than men to take part in projects that increase their visibility or widen the scope of their responsibilities. In short, women are not given work assignments that teach them new skills and, at the same time, permit them to demonstrate their competence.[46] In addition, women report encountering more obstacles overall in their jobs: They note it is harder to find personal support, they often are left out of important networks, and they must fight hard to be recognized for excellent work.[47]

Interestingly, the women holding influential positions report they do *not* act like men at work. On the contrary, they have a uniquely "female" style, which involves less concern with status and hierarchies as well as a willingness to compromise and mediate, rather than the male need to "win." These women also have a warmer, more approachable interpersonal style. As Esther Dyson, the chair of EDventure Holdings, a rapidly growing high-tech company, says, "The men are trying to do all this explicit hierarchical, formal stuff. They follow job titles. Women pay more attention to human factors." Similarly, Amy Pascal, the former president of Columbia Pictures, said, "I manage from a place—how my employees are feeling—and men don't do that. Women are trained in the art of compromise and men aren't . . . I think I am much more attuned to people's feelings . . . I think I can talk to them in a more straightforward way. . . ."[48]

Further evidence of cracks in the glass ceiling comes from a recent study comparing the outcomes and experiences of female and male executives in a large

FIGURE 6.9

The Glass Ceiling: A Barrier to Career Success for Women

Traditionally, greater opportunities for men compared to women have lessened women's chances for obtaining the highest-level promotions. Today, this *glass ceiling* remains in many organizations, but increasing numbers of women are breaking through, at least denting — if not piercing — the glass ceiling.

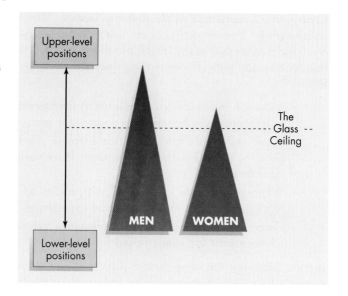

company.[49] Both groups provided information on their salaries and bonuses, how many people they supervised, their past developmental opportunities, obstacles they had encountered, and previous career interruptions. The researchers expected female and male executives would differ in all respects, but very few differences between these groups actually emerged. Females did supervise fewer subordinates, have more career interruptions, and report more obstacles (e.g., trying to influence other people without any authority to support such attempts). They did *not* differ from their male colleagues, however, in terms of salary, bonuses, developmental opportunities, or fitting less well into a male-dominated organizational culture (Figure 6.9).

This study provides evidence for cracks in the glass ceiling, but the research was conducted in a single company. Therefore, these results might not indicate overall trends in society at large. In addition, the executives in this particular research project were very successful and earned very high incomes — their median annual salary was close to $170,000. As a result, their experiences might not be generalizable to those with less exceptional competence (and incomes). Still, the researchers did uncover some vestiges of a glass ceiling. For example, the female executives supervised fewer people than their male counterparts, and they reported encountering more obstacles on their way to the top. Furthermore, when asked to estimate their future career opportunities, the women responded less optimistically than the men.

Thus, although the glass ceiling may have been breached in some careers, a second — and higher — ceiling still may exist and operate against even exceptionally competent women. Only further research can resolve this question, but one point is clear: Major change has occurred in many work settings during recent years, and some of these changes appear to have lessened — if not eliminated — barriers to women's success.

STRESS ON THE JOB: TOO IMPORTANT TO IGNORE

Baltimore (Associated Press). The job was getting to the ambulance attendant. He felt disturbed by the recurring tragedy, isolated by the long shifts. His marriage was in trouble. He was drinking too much.

One night it all blew up.

He rode in the back that night. His partner drove. Their first call was for a man whose leg had been cut off by a train. His screaming and agony were horrifying, but the second call was worse. It was a child beating. As the attendant treated the youngster's bruised body and snapped bones, he thought of his own child. His fury grew.

Immediately after leaving the child at the hospital, the attendants were sent out to help a heart attack victim lying in the street. When they arrived, however, they found not a cardiac patient but a drunk—a wino passed out. As they lifted the man into the ambulance, their frustration and anger came to a head. They decided to give the wino a ride he would remember.

The ambulance vaulted over railroad tracks at high speed. The driver took the corners as fast as he could, flinging the wino from side to side in the back. To the attendants, it was a joke.

Suddenly, the wino began having a real heart attack. The attendant in back leaned over the wino and started shouting. "Die you #@%e3!" he yelled. "Die!"*

He watched as the wino shuddered. He watched as the wino died. By the time they reached the hospital they had their stories straight. Dead on arrival, they said. Nothing they could do.

The attendant talked about that night at a recent counseling session on "professional burnout"—a growing problem in high-stress jobs.[50]

This news report recounts a devastating and tragic event. Sadly, not only is it real, it is all too familiar to the many thousands of people who put their lives on the line and confront the uglier side of life everyday. When reading such a story, most of us may take comfort in being spared such drama in our own working lives. We may enjoy the relative safety of modern offices, but we should not dismiss what this incident reveals about how people respond to *stress*. However reassuring it may be to do so, there is an element of this case that we cannot—and must not—ignore: The characters' reactions resulted from exposure to highly stressful conditions. We might never confront the drama faced by these ambulance attendants, but we all encounter many sources of stress in whatever work we do.

Some Distressing Statistics About Stress

Although not always life-threatening, stress can have devastating effects on nearly all aspects of human behavior and organizational functioning. To make the case about the importance of stress most strongly, consider the following facts and figures[51]:

number three essay question

- Stress-related problems in the United States cost $500 billion annually.
- In California alone, workers' compensation claims for mental stress increased more than 700% in the 1980s.
- Four of every 10 U.S. workers rate their jobs as being very stressful or extremely stressful.
- Half of all workers say their jobs are more stressful now than just a few years ago.
- People experiencing high levels of stress are three times more likely to be ill than those without stress.
- Stress-related illnesses cost U.S. industry 132 million workdays of lost production each year.

You might dismiss our account of the ambulance attendants as being an extreme case, but it is difficult to imagine that statistics like these result exclusively from material fit for the evening news or a television docudrama. Rather, they tell an important tale—namely, that we all are affected by stress in some way. Indeed, stress is an inevitable fact of work as we enter the twenty-first century.

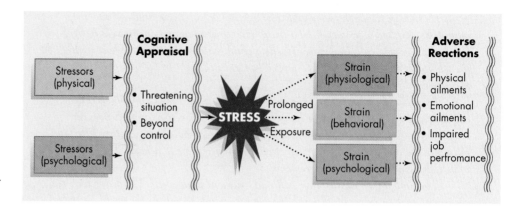

Distinguishing Between Stressors, Stress, and Strain

Stimuli known as *stressors*, which are both physical and psychological in nature, lead to *stress* reactions when they are *cognitively appraised* as being threatening and beyond one's control. The deviations from normal states resulting from stress are known as *strain*; both physical and emotional ailments as well as impaired job performance result from strain.

stress

The pattern of emotional states, cognitions, and physiological reactions resulting from *stressors*.

stressors

Various factors in the external environment that induce stress among people exposed to them.

strain

Deviations from normal states or functioning that result from *stress*.

[handwritten margin notes] Stressors - employee's at home to. Stressors cause Stress. Just know what stress and stressors are

What Is Stress? A Definition

Our discussion of stress thus far has assumed you already know something about it. Indeed, we use the term in everyday life. As you might imagine, however, organizational scientists use the term more precisely. They also carefully distinguish it from several related terms.

Specifically, we define **stress** as *a complex pattern of emotional states, physiological reactions, and related thoughts in response to external demands*. These external demands are referred to as **stressors**.

The related term, **strain**, refers to *the accumulated effects of stress, primarily deviations from normal states or performance resulting from exposure to stressful events*. These effects can involve physical symptoms, reduced performance, and other changes in behavior.

When distinguishing between these terms, it helps to draw an analogy to the physical world—specifically, building a bridge. Civil engineers are concerned with the forces acting on the surface of a bridge at any time. For example, vehicular traffic constitutes one such force. Both we—and the engineers—would refer to these forces as *stressors*. These stressors force the bridge to "give" somewhat, to bend under the weight of the passing cars and trucks. These are *stress reactions*. Then, as the effects of the stressors accumulate over time, they begin taking their toll on the bridge—no pun intended!—and the bridge begins to show *strain reactions*. In particular, the pavement might crack and the girders begin to buckle.

Although we are concerned with people instead of bridges, the same basic idea applies. With human beings, however, the story is made more complicated, because whether something serves as a stressor depends on people's interpretation of what is happening to them—that is, on their *cognitive appraisal* of the stressors they confront.[52] Stress occurs only to the extent that people perceive (1) that the situation they face is somehow threatening to them, and (2) that they cannot cope with these potential dangers or demands—that the situation is, in some sense, beyond their control. For a summary of these concepts, see Figure 6.10.

POTENTIAL SOURCES OF STRESS

What factors contribute to stress in work settings? We called attention to one in our preview case: failure in one's career. Many other factors also influence the level of stress that individuals experience at work, however. Thus, for the sake of clarity, we divide these into two major categories: factors relating to organizations or jobs, and factors relating to other aspects of individuals' lives.

Work-Related Causes of Stress

As anyone who ever held a job knows, work settings often are highly stressful environments, yet they also vary greatly in this respect. Some jobs and organizations expose individuals to high levels of stress, whereas others involve much lower levels. What factors account for these differences?

Occupational Demands: Some Jobs Are More Stressful Than Others   Consider the following jobs: firefighter, actuary, senior executive, accountant, surgeon, technical writer, and air traffic controller. Do these jobs differ in stressfulness? Common sense — and systematic research — suggests they do.[53]

Some jobs, such as firefighters, senior executive, surgeon (and from our example, ambulance attendant), expose workers to high levels of stress. Other jobs, such as actuary, accountant, or technical writer, are far less stressful. Surveys showing that some jobs are much more stressful than others have compared people with hundreds of occupations on a variety of criteria, including overtime, quotas, deadlines, competitiveness, physical demands, environmental conditions, hazards encountered, initiative required, stamina required, win-lose situations, and working in the public eye.[54] Using these criteria, which job headed the list as the most stressful? President of the United States — a fact to which recent holders of this position surely can attest. For a more complete listing of selected jobs and their relative stressfulness, see Table 6.3.

What precisely makes some jobs more stressful than others? Several key factors appear to be involved.[55] Specifically, jobs become increasingly stressful to the extent they meet several requirements:

1. *They require making decisions.* Military leaders have stressful jobs, because they are required to make life-and-death decisions involving thousands of people — and world politics.

TABLE 6.3

What Jobs Are Most — and Least — Stressful?

Using a variety of standards, scientists rated 250 different jobs regarding how stressful they are. Shown here are the rankings and stress scores for selected occupations. (Higher scores reflect greater levels of stress encountered.)

RANK SCORE	STRESS SCORE	RANK SCORE	STRESS SCORE
1. U.S. president	176.6	47. Auto salesperson	56.3
2. Firefighter	110.9	50. College professor	54.2
3. Senior executive	108.6	60. School principal	51.7
6. Surgeon	99.5	103. Market research analyst	42.1
10. Air traffic controller	83.1	104. Personnel recruiter	41.8
12. Public relations executive	78.5	113. Hospital administrator	39.6
16. Advertising account executive	74.6	119. Economist	38.7
17. Real estate agent	73.1	122. Mechanical engineer	38.3
20. Stockbroker	71.7	124. Chiropractor	37.9
22. Pilot	68.7	132. Technical writer	36.5
25. Architect	66.9	149. Retail salesperson	34.9
31. Lawyer	64.3	173. Accountant	31.1
33. General physician	64.0	193. Purchasing agent	28.9
35. Insurance agent	63.3	229. Broadcast technician	24.2
42. Advertising salesperson	59.9	245. Actuary	20.2

Source: Reprinted by permission of the *Wall Street Journal;* © 1997 Dow Jones & Company, Inc. All rights reserved worldwide.

know these six →

2. *They involve constant monitoring of devices or materials.* Air traffic controllers have stressful jobs, because they are required to concentrate on radar screens throughout their shifts.

3. *They require repeated exchange of information with others.* Traders on Wall Street encounter stress when they place buy and sell orders to others on the floor of the stock market.

4. *They occur in unpleasant physical conditions.* As any mine worker knows, being exposed to the dark, dirty, and dangerous environment they face underground is a source of stress.

5. *They involve performing unstructured tasks.* If you ever attempted to compose a song or write a story, you know how stressful facing a blank piece of paper can be.

6. *They involve dealing with the public.* If you ever waited tables at a restaurant, you know how stressful dealing with the public can be. Similarly, recent accounts of misbehavior by airline passengers has added to the stress encountered by flight attendants.[56]

Conflict Between Work and Nonwork: Stress from Competing Demands   As noted previously, both spouses in most of today's families with children work full-time—or at least part-time. The result is a constant juggling of work and family responsibilities, which in turn exposes those involved to another widely recognized cause of stress: **role conflict,** or the incompatibility between the expectations of parties or the aspects of a single role. In this case, the expectations of spouses and children often conflict with the expectations of bosses and coworkers, and conflicts between family and work can be very stressful indeed.[57] Fortunately, such effects can be lessened by high levels of social support in work settings.[58]

role conflict

Incompatible demands on an individual made by different groups or persons.

Role Ambiguity: Stress from Uncertainty   Even if individuals can avoid the stress associated with role conflict, they still may encounter that associated with **role ambiguity.** This occurs when individuals experience uncertainty about what actions they should take to meet the requirements of a job. Most people dislike uncertainty and find it to be quite stressful, but it is difficult to avoid. In fact, role ambiguity is quite common: From 35 to 60 percent of employees in one survey report experiencing it to some degree.[59]

role ambiguity

Uncertainty among employees about the key requirements of their jobs.

Interestingly, the amount of role ambiguity experienced by employees differs sharply from culture to culture. In one study involving participants from 21 countries, role ambiguity was relatively low in countries with large differences in status or power between managers and subordinates (i.e., high power distance countries).[60] Role ambiguity also was relatively low in countries where people preferred to act as members of groups rather than as individuals (i.e., low individualism). Both power distance and individualism are basic dimensions along which many cultures vary.[61] As Figure 6.11 shows, role ambiguity is relatively low in Asian and African countries known to be high in power distance but low in individualism. In contrast, role ambiguity is higher in Western countries, which are low in power distance but high in individualism. Based on findings such as these, we may expect people to encounter higher levels of stress in Western countries than in Asian or African countries.

know quantitative overload and underload →

quantitative overload

A situation requiring individuals to accomplish more work than they actually can in a given period of time.

qualitative overload

The belief among employees that they lack the skills or abilities needed to perform their jobs.

Overload and Underload: Doing Too Much or Too Little   When the phrase "work-related stress" is mentioned, most people think of employees working frantically and doing more than they can handle. Such images relate to *overload,* which can take two different forms. **Quantitative overload** occurs when individuals are asked to do more work than they can complete in a specific period of time. In contrast, **qualitative over-**

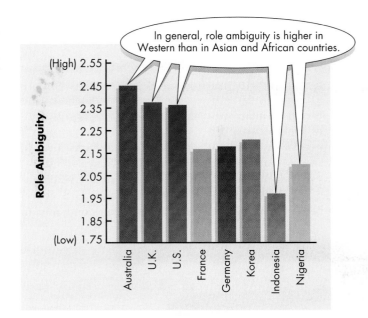

In general, role ambiguity is higher in Western than in Asian and African countries.

(High) 2.55
2.45
2.35
2.25
2.15
2.05
1.95
1.85
(Low) 1.75

Role Ambiguity

Australia | U.K. | U.S. | France | Germany | Korea | Indonesia | Nigeria

FIGURE 6.11

Culture and Role Ambiguity

In a study involving 21 countries, role ambiguity—a key determinant of stress—was lower in Asian and African countries than in many Western countries, apparently because Western countries are lower in power distance and higher in individualism.

(*Source*: Based on data reported by Peterson et al., 1995; see note 60.)

load refers to employees' beliefs that they lack the required skills or abilities to perform a given job. Both types of overload are unpleasant, and both can lead to high levels of stress.[62]

Overload is only part of the total picture, however. Being asked to do too much can be stressful, but so can being asked to do too little. Here again, there are two types of *underload*. **Quantitative underload** refers to the boredom that results from having too little to do. **Qualitative underload** refers to the lack of mental stimulation that accompanies many routine, repetitive jobs. If you have ever experienced such conditions—perhaps because of shifting job responsibilities in your company—you probably know only too well just how stressful underload can be.

Lack of Social Support: The Costs of Isolation   If you think of times when you were troubled or experienced high amounts of stress, you probably recall seeking the company of friends or family to help you feel better. This is quite natural. In fact, seeking the support of others can be a very effective way of coping with stress.

Specifically, people confronted with stressful situations fare much better when they have a network of friends and associates they can turn to for support and counsel than when they must face such situations alone. The same principle applies in the workplace as well. Managers who believe they have the friendship and support of their immediate supervisors and coworkers report fewer physical symptoms when exposed to high levels of stress than those managers who do not enjoy such support.[63] In other words, when it comes to stress, "misery loves company" appears not only to be accurate but to be the basis for wise advise as well.

Sexual Harassment: A Pervasive Problem in Work Settings   Teresa Harris was a manager at Forklift Systems, Inc., in Nashville, Tennessee, when she encountered *sexual harassment* from her boss, Charles Hardy.[64] During her 2.5 years with the company, Hardy often made remarks such as "You're a woman, what do you know?" and "We need a man as the rental manager." In front of other employees, he suggested to her that they go to a nearby motel to "negotiate her raise." Occasionally, he asked Ms. Harris to remove coins from his pants pocket or would drop items on the floor and ask her to pick them up. The last straw came after Harris had negotiated a deal with a customer, when he remarked in front of other employees, "What did you promise

quantitative underload

A situation in which individuals have so little to do that they spend much of their time doing nothing.

qualitative underload

The lack of mental stimulation that accompanies many routine, repetitive jobs.

the guy . . . some sex Saturday night?" At this point, Harris quit her job and filed suit against Hardy and her former company. It took several years, but her case reached the Supreme Court—in 1993, she finally won.

This is certainly an extreme case, but sexual harassment—another major source of stress—is far from rare in today's workplace. Indeed, in one recent poll, fully 31 percent of employed women indicated they had encountered such harassment at least once. In contrast, only seven percent of male respondents to the same survey indicated they had been the victim of such actions.[65]

Because experts cannot agree on what exactly constitutes sexual harassment, it is difficult to define. Based on current legal thinking—in the United States, at least—we define **sexual harassment** as unwelcome sexual advances, requests for sexual favors, and other verbal or physical conduct of a sexual nature. Moreover, U.S. courts have ruled that behaviors may be considered sexual harassment under conditions in which:

- Submission to such conduct is made a term or condition of employment either explicitly or implicitly.
- Submission to or rejection of such conduct by an individual is used as a basis for employment decisions affecting that individual.
- Such conduct has the purpose or effect of unreasonably interfering with an individual's work performance or of creating an intimidating, hostile, or offensive working environment.

Sexual harassment is not restricted to the kind of extreme and unpleasant actions encountered by Ms. Harris, of course. It also consists of other, more subtle but also offensive behaviors. Under this definition, actions such as posting pin-ups, staring at another person's anatomy, or even making repeated remarks about someone's appearance may constitute sexual harassment if they create a hostile work environment, and in 1998, the U.S. Supreme Court ruled that employers can even be sued over acts of harassment about which they knew nothing![66]

Is sexual harassment more common today than in the past? Statistics suggests it may be. For example, the number of complaints filed by employees more than doubled during the 1980s—and has continued to rise dramatically during the 1990s.[67] In addition, considering the widespread media attention given to charges of sexual harassment by high-profile executives (including even the President of the United States!), women are becoming more familiar with what constitutes sexual harassment, which many experts believe will cause these figures to climb even higher. Regardless of any effects by the media, however, for every case of sexual harassment that is reported, many more clearly go unrecorded. In fact, only 10 percent of women who report having experienced sexual harassment indicate they ever reported the incident.[68] Findings such as these suggest that sexual harassment is an important cause of stress for many employees—and that organizations must take strong action to protect employees from such treatment.

sexual harassment
Unwanted contact or communication of a sexual nature.

GLOBAL MATTERS   The concept of sexual harassment is familiar to people in Western countries, but it still is quite unknown in parts of Asia and Africa. Why do you think this is? Do you think awareness of sexual harassment—and efforts to combat it—will increase in these countries? If so, why? ■

Responsibility for Others: A Heavy Burden   In general, people who are responsible for others—people who must motivate them, reward or punish them, and communicate with them—experience higher levels of stress and the physical symptoms accompanying it (e.g., hypertension) than those who handle other organizational functions.[69] This profile closely describes the jobs of various types of executives, accounting for their high ranking in Table 6.3.

This should not be too surprising. After all, executives and managers ultimately must confront the human costs of organizational policies and decisions. For example, they must deliver negative feedback—and then witness the distress it generates. In addition, top managers are responsible for dealing with the many frictions that are a normal part of human relations at work. This involves listening to endless complaints, mediating disputes, promoting cooperation, and exercising leadership. All these tasks are demanding, and each contributes to the total stress experienced by managers. (For an example of the responsibility for others that managers face—and how to make it less stressful—see the "Tips" section below.

■ How to Fire Someone Without Lighting a Fire

What is the most stressful situation managers face? Many identify having to fire an employee as being one of the worst, and this is far from surprising. The person being fired probably will react strongly, showing emotions ranging from anger or resentment to tearful appeals for mercy. Some will use every trick at their disposal to make the manager change her or his mind, including promises, threats, and pleas for sympathy. In addition, a few will not merely threaten revenge—they will actually come back and seek it. (See our discussion of workplace aggression and violence in chapter 10.) As a manager, how can you minimize the adverse effects of this stressful, emotionally charged situation? Here are a few tips from human resources experts:

- *Don't fire someone in an offhand, matter-of-fact manner.* Many managers try to conceal their feelings and adopt a "cool," professional manner. Up to a point, this is fine, but it can be carried too far. What is happening usually is *very* upsetting and *very* stressful for the person involved, so approach the situation with this in mind.
- *Don't fire people by e-mail.* To avoid the angry confrontations that firing usually involves, some managers resort to e-mail messages. This is highly insensitive, and it actually may anger the persons involved more than a face-to-face meeting. After all, most people being fired want to talk about the situation and present their side of it. E-mail messages don't allow this, however, and they suggest the manager is totally insensitive to the human costs involved.
- *Don't fire people in groups.* In today's world of downsizing, entire units sometimes are terminated at once. This may be efficient, but it is highly insensitive. It also can fan resentment. It usually is preferable to speak privately with each person involved rather than to fire several as a group.
- *Check the calendar.* One of the worst things you can do is to fire someone on their birthday, anniversary of service with the company, or other significant date. Firing people just as they leave for the day, for the weekend, or for a holiday makes sense—they won't be back to cause friction the next day—but this should be avoided whenever possible. It only makes an already devastating blow even worse.
- *Do ask people to leave immediately.* Once someone is fired, there is no point in that person hanging around for the rest of the day. They probably won't be able to work, and their emotional upset may readily spread to others.

continued

Therefore, if possible, conduct termination meetings near the end of the day, but in any case, be prepared to ask the person involved to leave immediately once the meeting is over.

- *Explain in a sensitive manner why the decision was made.* People don't like being fired, but they are far more likely to accept such decisions when presented in a way that makes clear the firing is absolutely necessary — and that does so with both dignity and respect. Not only is doing so likely to make the encounter less uncomfortable, it also is likely to discourage former employees from suing for wrongful termination.[70]

- *Never get personal.* True, you should not fire someone in an off-hand, casual manner. On the other hand, you should not let them draw you into angry shouting matches. A professional manner that shows concern but also is firm and reserved usually is best.

- *State the reasons for the firing, but don't debate them.* Explain to employees *why* they are being fired, but do this by simply listing the reason. Avoid getting into a debate about them on these reasons. You cannot win such an argument, and because the decision has been made and will not be changed, there is no point to such discussions.

Following these guidelines, you can lessen the possibility that an inherently difficult situation will turn into a truly ugly one. You also will reduce the stress experienced by both you and the person you fire. ■

Causes of Stress Outside Work

Clearly, work is one of the most important activities in many people's lives, but it is not the only activity. Thus, events occurring outside work settings often generate stress that persists — and is carried back to work. Many factors contribute to stress in this manner. Most, however, fit under two broad categories: *stressful life events*, and *daily hassles*.

Stressful Life Events   The death of a spouse, a divorce, injury to one's child, a stock market crash, an unwanted pregnancy — unless someone leads a truly charmed life, he or she likely will experience traumatic events or changes like these at some point. What are the effects of such events? This question was studied first by physicians, who asked large groups of people to assign arbitrary points (from 1 to 100) to various life events according to how much readjustment each had required.[71] The greater the number of points assigned to a given event, the more stressful it was considered to be for those who had experienced it.

Some of the values assigned to various stressful life events are shown in Table 6.4. The highest numbers were assigned to serious events, such as the death of a spouse, divorce, and being sent to jail. The results of collecting a high level of such "stress points" (as they might be termed) are dramatic: When individuals experience events totaling 300 points or more, they show a much higher incidence of illness during the next several months than persons who score 200 points or lower.

The Hassles of Daily Life   Traumatic life events are very stressful, but they are — thankfully! — relatively rare. Many people live for years or even decades without experiencing one. Does this, however, mean such individuals live a totally tranquil life? Hardly!

Daily life is filled with countless minor irritations that seem to make up for their low intensity by their high frequency of occurrence. These are referred to as **daily hassles,** and they occur in several areas of life: household hassles (e.g., preparing meals, shopping), time pressure hassles (e.g., too many things to do), and financial hassles

daily hassles
Problems of everyday life that are important causes of stress.

TABLE 6.4

The Stressfulness of Various Life Events

Paper-and-pencil inventories often are used to assess the extent of various sources of stress in people's lives. Those completing these surveys select from a list events they have experienced during the past year. Associated with each item (although unknown to the person completing the survey) is a predetermined number of points (from a low of 1 to a high of 100) that reflects the amount of readjustment the life event requires. Some of these events and the number of points associated with them are shown here. The more points people accumulate, the more likely they are to suffer serious illness in the future.

EVENT	RELATIVE STRESSFULNESS
Death of a spouse	100
Divorce	73
Marital separation	65
Jail term	63
Death of a close family member	63
Personal injury or illness	53
Marriage	50
Fired from a job	47
Retirement	45
Pregnancy	40
Death of a close friend	37
Son or daughter leaving home	29
Trouble with in-laws	28
Trouble with boss	23
Change in residence	20
Vacation	13
Christmas	12
Minor violations of the law	11

Source: Based on data from Holmes & Rahe, 1967; see note 71.

(e.g., concerns about owing money). These everyday concerns are an important source of stress, as suggested by several studies. In fact, the more daily hassles people experience, the greater their levels of self-reported stress. Of course, with this also comes the potentially adverse effects of stress on health and other aspects of life. Clearly, even minor daily concerns can be very important, and they should not be overlooked.

To this point, we have been very general about what exactly the effects of stress really are. With this in mind, we now examine these effects more closely.

THE MAJOR EFFECTS OF STRESS

As noted, stress is an unavoidable part of working life. As we also have described, it exerts important effects on persons exposed to it as well. The statistics we reported earlier make this point clear, but we cannot resist the temptation to share one more: The costs from adverse effects of stress are estimated to exceed 10 percent of the U.S. gross national product.[72]

Test question over This

FIGURE 6.12

Exceptional Performance in the Face of Stress

When confronting stressful situations, some people (e.g., top athletes) rise to the occasion and turn in exceptional levels of performance.

Much of this amount stems from health-related effects. Growing evidence, however, indicates that stress also influences us in other ways. Specifically, it can strongly affect our psychological well-being and our performance on many tasks. We now take a closer look at these many different effects of stress.

Stress and Task Performance

In the past, the relationship between stress and performance on many tasks generally was assumed to be *curvilinear* in nature. In other words, low levels of stress were assumed to increase performance, whereas beyond some point, further increments tended to reduce performance. This relationship may be true under some conditions, but more recent evidence suggests that stress exerts mainly negative effects on task performance — even at relatively low levels.[73]

Why is this? Shouldn't the arousal generated by moderate levels of stress increase performance in many cases? This may be true in some situations, but there also are several reasons for expecting that even moderate levels of stress interfere with performance. First, even relatively mild stress can be distracting. In other words, people experiencing it may focus on the unpleasant feelings and emotions the stress involves rather than on the task at hand — with their performance suffering as a result. Second, prolonged or repeated exposure to even mild levels of stress may exert harmful effects on health, which interfere with a person's ability to perform many tasks. Finally, even moderate levels of stress sometimes generate very high levels of arousal, which also interfere with performance. Have you ever "choked under pressure"? In such situations, the very high levels of arousal generated by a stressful condition (e.g., an audience watching you) can interfere with effective performance.

Having said all this, we must note there *are* exceptions to the general rule that stress reduces task performance. First, some individuals do seem to "rise to the occasion" and turn in exceptional performances during times of high stress. They may be truly expert in the tasks being performed, as are skilled athletes (Figure 6.12). Alternatively, the individuals involved may view stress as being a *challenge* rather than a *threat*, and this may lead to positive effects.

Second, large individual differences exist regarding the impact of stress on task performance. As your own experience may suggest, some individuals (e.g., the type A's described in chapter 3) seem to thrive on stress. These people actively seek arousal and high levels of sensation or stimulation. For such persons, stress is exhilarating — and it may improve performance. In contrast, others react in an opposite manner, avoiding arousal and high levels of sensation. These individuals find stress upsetting, and it may interfere with their performance.

So, how do we answer the question about the effects of stress on task performance? In many situations, stress interferes with task performance, but its precise effects depend on the nature of the task being performed, the expertise of the person performing it, and several personality traits. Therefore, generalizations about the effect of stress on task performance should be made with caution.

Stress and Psychological Well-Being: Burnout

Most jobs involve some degree of stress, yet somehow, the people holding them manage to cope. Some individuals, however, are not so fortunate. Over time, they are worn down psychologically by repeated exposure to stress. Such people are described as suffering from **burnout**, which is a syndrome that results from prolonged exposure to stress and consists of three components: emotional exhaustion, depersonalization, and reduced personal accomplishment.[74] Summarized in Figure 6.13, these components may be described as follows:

burnout

A syndrome resulting from prolonged exposure to stress and consisting of physical, emotional, and mental exhaustion as well as feelings of a lack of personal accomplishment.

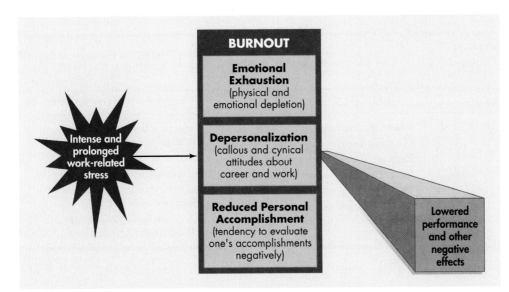

FIGURE 6.13

Major Components of Burnout

As shown, *burnout* results from exposure to intense and prolonged work-related stress, and it consists of three major components: *emotional exhaustion*, *depersonalization*, and *reduced feelings of personal accomplishment*.

- *Emotional exhaustion* is a chronic state of physical and emotional depletion. Persons suffering from it feel drained, fatigued, and no longer able to cope with the demands of their jobs.
- *Depersonalization* involves the development of callous, cynical attitudes about one's career and work. Persons experiencing such attitudes feel that nothing they do has any meaning or value—and that others feel this way, too.
- *Reduced personal accomplishment* refers to a tendency to evaluate oneself negatively regarding your accomplishments at work. People experiencing this reaction feel they have not accomplished much in the past—and that they will not succeed in the future, either.

Some Major Causes   What causes burnout? As already noted, the primary factor seems to be prolonged exposure to stress—that is, to excessive job demands and continuous daily hassles.[75] One key factor in the development of burnout—and especially in emotional exhaustion—is the perception by individuals that they have experienced the *loss of valuable resources* (or are about to do so) or that they will be *unable to cope with work demands*.[76] What resources do people fear losing? Among the most important are social support, participation in decision making, autonomy, and opportunities for job enhancement.

Other variables also pay a role.[77] For example, burnout has been linked to *job conditions suggesting that one's efforts are useless*, ineffective, or unappreciated. Under such conditions, individuals develop feelings of low personal accomplishment, which are an important part of burnout. Similarly, *poor opportunities for promotion* and *inflexible rules and procedures* lead employees to feel they are trapped in an unfair system and contribute to negative views about their jobs. Another important factor is the *leadership style* used by employees' supervisors. The less consideration demonstrated by their supervisors (i.e., the less they are concerned with employees' welfare or with maintaining good relations with them), the higher the employees' levels of burnout.[78] (We discuss various styles of leadership in chapter 12.)

Major Effects   Whatever the precise causes of burnout, it has important consequences for individuals and for the organizations that employ them, as summary in Table 6.5).[79] Clearly, the effects listed as well as others—including job satisfaction, increased

TABLE 6.5

Symptoms of Burnout

The major signs of burnout fall into three categories: physical condition, behavioral changes, and work performance.

PHYSICAL CONDITION	BEHAVIORAL CHANGES	WORK PERFORMANCE
Headaches	Increased irritability	Reduced efficiency (more time spent working but with less productivity)
Sleeplessness	Changing moods	
Weight loss	Reduced tolerance for frustration	Dampened initiative
Gastrointestinal disturbances	Increased suspiciousness	Diminished interest in working
Exhaustion and fatigue	Greater willingness to take risks	Reduced capacity to perform effectively under stress
	Attempts at self-medication (use of alcohol and tranquilizers)	Increased rigidity of thought (closed thinking, inflexible)

Source: Based on material reported by Moss, 1981; see note 79.

voluntary turnover, reduced job performance, and counterproductive work behavior (i.e., behaving in ways that *reduce* productivity) — are very negative.[80]

Can Burnout Be Prevented or Reversed?   The negative effects of burnout raise an important question: Can burnout be prevented or reversed? Fortunately, growing evidence suggests it can.

Regarding prevention, providing individuals with effective ways to cope with stress — techniques we describe later — often can be very helpful. Employees who receive training in such techniques are less likely to experience burnout than those who do not.[81]

In addition, helping employees to cope with *inequity* — that is, the believe they are treated unfairly by their organizations (see chapter 4) — can go a long way toward preventing burnout. In one recent study designed to test this possibility, one group of health-care professionals participated in a program designed to reduce feelings of inequity, and a second group did not.[82] Both groups completed measures of burnout, feelings of inequity, and intention to quit their jobs before the start of the program and twice after the program (six months and one year afterward). Records of employees' absences from work during this period also were obtained.

Results indicated that the intervention program, which involved five weekly group sessions and training in techniques for restoring fairness (e.g., changing their actual outcomes, changing their perceptions of their contributions and outcomes), produced strong, positive effects. Burnout, feelings of inequity, and durations of absence all dropped sharply after this program. Thus, an intervention focused on reducing inequity was quite successful in preventing burnout.

Other techniques have focused on *reversing* burnout. Short breaks, days off from work, and vacations all are effective.[83] Apparently, even short breaks away from stressful conditions at work can help individuals to recover from the emotional exhaustion and depersonalization often resulting from prolonged and unrelenting exposure to high levels of work demands. Such effects appear to be especially beneficial for women, those who are satisfied with their time off from work (e.g., those who enjoy their vacations), and those who also obtain social support from friends, supervisors, or coworkers.[84]

In short, with appropriate help, individuals can escape the dead-end trap of burnout — or even avoid its devastating effects altogether. Procedures for attaining these goals exist; however, their achievement requires active cooperation between employees and their organizations.

Stress and Health: The Silent Killer

Evidence showing a link between stress and personal health is exceptionally strong. In fact, some authorities estimate stress plays a role in between 50 and 70 percent of all forms of physical illness.[85] Moreover, some of the most serious and life-threatening ailments, such as heart disease and stroke, ulcers, headaches, diabetes, and cancer, are included in these figures.[86] In addition to its role in such *degenerative diseases*, stress also may play a key role in *infectious diseases* (e.g., those caused by infectious agents such as bacteria or viruses). Many studies indicate that high levels of stress increase susceptibility to diseases such as upper respiratory infections, herpes virus infections, and various bacterial infections.[87] Thus, in sum, stress often exerts powerful, adverse effects on personal health. Table 6.6 summarizes some of the most serious health-related consequences of stress, including those of a medical, behavioral, and psychological nature.

These findings suggest that stress at work may affect the health of employees adversely, and growing evidence supports this view.[88] For example, factors such as downsizing, lack of control over one's job, and the absence of social support from coworkers and friends — all of which are important causes of work-related stress — are significantly linked to medically certified absences from work.[89] Thus, high levels of work stress can, indeed, exert harmful effects on the health of employees.

ETHICS MATTERS

Suppose an organization becomes aware that working conditions generate high levels of stress among its employees — levels that could aversely effect their health. Is that organization ethically bound to lower these levels of stress? ■

Individual Differences in Resistance to Stress

Earlier, we noted that stress affects most people adversely, but some people seem to thrive on such conditions. We now expand on that point by noting several personal characteristics that seem to play a role in such differences. In other words, to the extent that individuals possess certain traits, they may be more — or less — susceptible to the harmful effects of stress.

We already have mentioned one of these: the Type A behavior pattern. Although Type A's seem to seek out high levels of stress (e.g., by taking on several jobs at once)

TABLE 6.6

Health-Related Consequences of Stress

Stress causes a variety of different health problems, including medical, behavioral, and psychological problems. Listed here are some of the major consequences within each category.

MEDICAL CONSEQUENCES	BEHAVIORAL CONSEQUENCES	PSYCHOLOGICAL CONSEQUENCES
Heart disease and stroke	Smoking	Family conflict
Backache and arthritis	Drug and alcohol abuse	Sleep disturbances
Ulcers	Accident proneness	Sexual dysfunction
Headaches	Violence	Depression
Cancer	Appetite disorders	
Diabetes		
Cirrhosis of the liver		
Lung disease		

Source: Based on material reported by Quick & Quick, 1984; see note 86.

this behavior is somewhat self-destructive. In fact, Type A's are more susceptible than Type B's to the harmful effects of stress.[90] Other personal characteristics (e.g., "optimism" and "hardiness") also influence the effect of stress on personal health. To the extent that individuals possess these traits, they appear to be "buffered" or protected against the harmful effects of stress. Thus, from this important perspective, these traits appear to be adaptive ones.

MANAGING STRESS: SOME EFFECTIVE TECHNIQUES

Stress itself may be unavoidable, but its harmful effects can be countered—or even avoided altogether. In fact, individuals and organizations can take many steps to minimize these adverse effects. We now take a closer look at several of these.

Personal Approaches to Stress Management: Developing Resiliency

resiliency
Learning ways of minimizing the degree to which stressors adversely affect us.

The process of protecting ourselves from stress involves developing **resiliency**—that is, learning ways of minimizing the degree to which stressors adversely affect us. In other words, when we are resilient, we "roll with the punches" instead of getting "knocked out" by them. The concept of resiliency also fits with our bridge-building analogy to describe the concept of stress. We noted that a bridge surface eventually might crack under the strain from years of pressure on the roadway. This is less likely to occur, however, when the bridge surface is made of more pliable material—that is, of material that is resilient and "gives" rather than "cracks" under pressure. This same idea applies to human beings as well. In other words, people are less likely to show serious consequences of stress to the extent they are resilient to its effects. Several strategies are useful in this regard.

Physiological Techniques: Relaxation, Meditation, and . . . Napping! When you think of successful executives at work, what picture comes to mind? Someone trying to speak on three phones at once while also reading a report and speaking to a visitor? This is close to the common conception of how such people live. Someone resting calmly in serene setting—or even sleeping—is definitely *not* part of this image. For a growing number of today's employees, however, this picture is quite common.

For example, at Symmetric—a Lexington, Massachusetts, software developer— many of the company's 125 employees spend as long as 20 minutes a day behind closed office doors relaxing and quietly meditating.[91] Symmetric does not merely tolerate this practice; it encourages it. It even has paid consultants who teach employees how to relax. Many other organizations also have adopted this practice, including Marriott, Polaroid, and The Boston Co. (an investment firm) to name a few.

Similarly, consider Michael K. Lorelli, the president of Tambrands, Inc. He takes short naps during the day and reports they help him greatly. In France, Framatome SA, France's nuclear power company, currently is testing the effects of short naps for employees who must work the night shift. Preliminary findings indicate they awake from these snoozes both refreshed and more alert. Surprisingly, many celebrities take naps as well. For instance, Jim Lehrer, host of public television's *The News Hour*, takes a nap every day at 12:30 P.M. He claims that it greatly increases his alertness.[92]

All these companies make efforts to help their employees become more productive by providing them with techniques for coping with stress. One such technique is napping, and it needs no further explanation. Another is **meditation**—that is, the process by which people learn to clear their minds of external thoughts, often by repeating a single syllable over and over again. Meditation requires sitting quietly in a comfortable position, closing your eyes, relaxing your muscles, and breathing slowly.

meditation
A technique for inducing relaxation in which individuals clear disturbing thoughts from their minds by repeating a single syllable.

The trick is to keep other thoughts, which would break your restful state, from entering your mind. Doing this once or twice a day for 10 to 20 minutes is an effective way of reducing stress—and of increasing your capacity to work and to enjoy life in general (Figure 6.14).[93]

Another technique is **relaxation training**. In this method, people first learn how to tense and then relax their muscles.[94] By becoming familiar with the differences between these states, people can induce relaxation whenever they feel themselves becoming too tense.

relaxation training
Procedures through which individuals learn to relax to reduce anxiety or stress.

Cognitive Techniques: Thinking Yourself Out of Stress Do you worry too much? Almost 90 percent of all people answer "Yes."[95] Moreover, many realize they worry about issues that are unimportant, outside their control, or both. Clearly, worrying about such matters is a waste of effort, and it can contribute to increased stress. By reducing such worrying, many people can boost their psychological resiliency, thus helping to reduce the stress they experience.

Excessive worrying is not the only way we contribute to our own stress, however. Often, we engage in *awfulizing* or *catastrophizing*—that is, patterns of thought in which we magnify the effects of failure, of not being perfect, or of being rejected by others. Such thinking also often adds to our level of stress. Reducing such irrational and self-defeating cognitions, therefore, can be another useful step in combating stress. Doing so avoids stress by focusing on the cognitive appraisal element of stress (described earlier) as a basic component of stress.

The guiding principle in all cognitive techniques for managing stress is straightforward: We cannot always change the world around us, but we *can* change our reactions to it. In other words, we need not worry excessively about things we cannot change. Neither should we strive for absolute perfection or allow irritating—but minor—situations to drive us up the wall. Instead, we can make it our mission to avoid such reactions and, in this manner, reduce the levels of stress that we encounter.

Lifestyle Management One of the most effective ways of coping with stress is to develop physiological resiliency by getting your body into shape; this way, it will not succumb to strain reactions. This may be accomplished in two ways that are easy to describe but often difficult to do: eating a *proper diet*, and engaging in *cardiovascular conditioning*. Today's physicians prescribe a regimen of proper eating and regular, moderate exercise for their patients with the benefits of these lifestyle practices in mind.

Another effective element of lifestyle management involves *balancing life activities*. Typically, people who experience stress in one segment of their lives spend more time in that segment. For example, someone who is under great pressure to complete an important work project may spend more time than usual at the office—and away from

FIGURE 6.14

Relaxation: A Key to Relieving Stress

Employees may be very unproductive while relaxing on the job, but deep relaxation—and even napping—may help to relieve stress, thereby contributing to productivity in the long run.

family activities, cultural activities, social activities, and so on. This may be detrimental, however, because it interferes with the balance in life activities that people require to do their best—at whatever they do. In other words, spending too much time at work actually might interfere with job performance, such as by making people tired and blocking their creativity (see chapter 13). Instead, people can develop resiliency to stress by being well-rounded in their life activities, which help them to approach work fresh, relaxed, and able to take on the challenges they face more effectively.

Time Management: Taking Control of What You Do   Our discussion of balancing life activities suggests it is important that we assume control over how we spend our time. This is especially important on the job, where many events threaten to distract us from doing what's most important. In addition, to the extent we allow distractions to over-run our lives, the resulting pressures we experience—people demanding our attention, deadlines looming large, and crises created by our inattention to things—may bring still more stress to our lives.

The key to managing time effectively—and to avoiding the stresses created by mismanaging time—involves taking control over your own actions. There are several effective ways to go about this[96]:

- *Set priorities and stick to them.* What things are most important for you to do? What things can wait? If something comes up unexpectedly, can it wait? Does it demand our immediate attention? We must answer these questions when setting priorities for ourselves. The things we do should be the ones that meet our goals and objectives. All too often, however, people who do not assign priorities find it too easy to do those things that are easiest, most interesting, or that others want us to do. Setting priorities can be a simple matter of deciding, on a regular basis, what are the most important objectives. Then, of course, the trick is to focus on them until they have been completed.
- *Don't allow others to distract you.* In the name of politeness, we too often allow others to derail us from our priorities, which only adds to the stress we experience later. When someone approaches you with something you think can wait, the trick is to put that person off politely—so that he or she understands why it is necessary to do so. Because the person knocking at your door probably does not understand why you cannot pay attention right then and there, you must take control by doing two things: explaining why you cannot drop what you are doing at this time, and setting a specific time when you can meet with that individual. This may involve saying something as simple as "I'm up against a deadline now. Can we discuss this over lunch, instead?"
- *Delegate responsibility to others.* One of the most effective ways to manage time is by shifting to others the responsibility for some things we may have been expected to do ourselves. This allows you to take control over the things you do. After all, to the extent that others rely less on you, some of the pressure you otherwise might feel is relieved. Of course, this assumes you have delegated wisely—that is, you have given responsibility to others who are ready, willing, and able to perform the task in question. In this connection, it helps to delegate responsibilities to those who have been consulted and have agreed in advance to meet these obligations.

Organization-Wide Strategies for Managing Stress

Thus far, we have focused on what individuals can do to reduce the levels of stress they experience. Organizations, however, also can reduce the levels of stress experienced by their employees. In fact, several organization-based or -initiated tactics can be highly effective in this regard.

Family-Supportive Practices: Reducing the Stress of Work-Family Conflicts As noted earlier, the task of juggling work and family obligations produces stress for many people. Not surprisingly, organizational policies designed to lessen such role conflict (e.g., flexible scheduling) can reduce stress.[97] Such practices appear to help in at least two ways. First, they enhance employees' feelings of personal control, thereby reducing the extent to which they appraise various situations as being stressful. Second, they allow employees to rearrange their lives to eliminate work-family conflicts, thus helping to eliminate this source of stress altogether.

Special Corporate Programs Given how devastating the effects of stress can be, organizations rely on several special programs to help their employees cope with stress. Each takes a somewhat different approach:

- **Stress management programs** involve training in several techniques described earlier (e.g., meditation, relaxation, lifestyle management) as well as in others. For example, the Equitable Life Insurance Company's "Emotional Health Program" offers training in stress management that relies mostly on the physiological techniques described earlier. Company officials estimate that each $33 spent on employees helps to relieve symptoms that would cost the company $100 in lost productivity.[98] Many companies cannot afford to create their own stress management programs, however, so they often rely on prepackaged programs from outside consultants or on off-the-shelf audiovisual programs on videocassettes.

> **stress management programs**
> Systematic efforts by organizations designed to help employees reduce or prevent stress.

- **Wellness programs** help employees to manage stress by keeping them physically and mentally healthy.[99] As such, they are broader in scope than stress management programs. Typically, wellness programs consist of workshops that train employees how to do many of the stress-reducing individual behaviors identified earlier, such as losing weight, exercising, and the like. Although the organizations provide the knowledge in these programs, individual employees are responsible for taking control over their own lives. The underlying assumption is that wellness programs are investments in employees: Stress-free employees are expected to be healthier, thereby saving the company money by reducing dividends for health, disability, and life insurance as well as saving workdays lost because of illness.[100] For a closer look at some of the most successful wellness programs today, see the "Trends" section below.

> **wellness programs**
> A variety of training programs (e.g., exercise, nutritional training) designed to promote healthy employees.

- **Employee assistance programs (EAPs)** provide employees with assistance in meeting various problems (e.g., substance abuse, career planning, financial and legal problems). The Metropolitan Life Insurance Company (MetLife) is one organization whose EAP is actively involved in helping its employees reduce stress.[101] It reaches out to all 42,000 U.S. employees by providing toll-free telephone consultation for those needing help as well as access to on-site and external medical as well as psychological professionals. Few EAPs are as extensive as MetLife's, but the cost-effective nature of such programs makes them an increasingly common form of worker benefit in organizations today.

> **employee assistance programs (EAPs)**
> Plans that provide employees with assistance for various problems (e.g., substance abuse, career planning, financial and legal problems).

TRENDS: WHAT TODAY'S COMPANIES ARE DOING

■ Wellness Programs That Are Doing Well

If you believe the medical economists, today's largest companies pay about as much in employee medical costs as they realize in after-tax profits.[102] To keep such expenses in check, it is not surprising that organizations are introducing wellness

continued

programs. The best such programs do more than offer opportunities for physical exercise, however. They also provide education and counseling in areas such as diet, substance abuse, and body mechanics. Effective wellness programs are not simply one-time offers to get your health checked or attend a seminar; rather, they provide on-going training to help employees meet long-term health and wellness goals.

Wellness programs differ considerably, but the one used by GTE at its Everett, Washington, facility is one of the more thorough in use today. GTE provides strength-training facilities with trainers throughout the day and evening. It also offers several aerobics classes. Look at just a small excerpt from its daily schedule:

- 12 noon to 12:50 P.M.   Step and step/slide interval training
                                Cardiovascular kickboxing
- 2:00 to 2:30 P.M.   Tone and firm training
- 5:20 to 6:10 P.M.   Circuit training

Statistics documenting the effectiveness of corporate wellness programs have been collected by the Wellness Councils of America (WELCOA), a nonprofit organization of 3,000 companies dedicated to promoting health-related activities for people on the job.[103] In existence since 1985, WELCOA's mission is to enhance the health and well-being of employees and, thus, to improve productivity, reduce absenteeism, and contain escalating health-care costs. Have these goals been met? Statistics reported by WELCOA suggests they have. Consider the following examples:

- The *Travelers Corporation* enjoys a return of $3.40 for every $1.00 invested in health promotion, yielding huge savings in benefit costs. In addition, employees who participate in the wellness program are absent from work significantly fewer days than those who do not.
- Employees of *Superior Coffee and Foods*, a subsidiary of *Sara Lee Corp.*, which also has an active wellness program, had 22 percent fewer hospital admissions and 29 percent shorter hospital stays compared with employees of other Sara Lee divisions without such programs in place.
- The wellness program at *Union Pacific Railroad* helps employees lower their risk of high blood pressure, high cholesterol, and obesity. Each $1.00 spent saves the company as much $1.57.
- Absenteeism costs at *Du Pont* have dropped 14 percent at its 41 industrial sites that offer wellness programs, compared with a decline of only 5.8 percent at the 19 sites without such programs.

It is difficult to say whether these results are typical, but the growing number of companies turning to wellness programs suggest they may be one of the most effective—and fun!—ways to help relieve the problems of work-related stress. Given that training programs are now in place to certify personnel working at wellness centers (e.g., at the University of South Florida's Wellness Leadership Program), such wellness should continue to thrive—as will the benefits they provide. ■

We invite you to visit the Greenberg page on the Prentice Hall Web site at: **www.prenhall.com/greenberg** for the monthly Greenberg update and for this chapter's World Wide Web exercise.

1. **Understand *socialization*, and identify the stages through which it develops.**
The process through which newcomers learn the ropes in their organizations and become full-fledged members is known as **organizational socialization**. This process involves three distinct stages: *getting in*, *breaking in*, and *settling in*. **Realistic job previews** given during the recruitment of newcomers help them to avoid unrealistically optimistic or pessimistic expectations, thus reducing **entry shock**.

2. **Explain what *mentors* are, what they do, and the benefits as well as costs of mentoring to both *mentors* and their *protégés*.**
A one-on-one form of socialization known as **mentoring** occurs when an experienced employee (i.e., a **mentor**) advises, counsels, and aids the personal development of a new employee (i.e., a **protégé**). Mentors pave the way for their protégé's job success and also provide a source of emotional support. Mentoring relationships benefit both parties. Because people generally are more comfortable interacting with those who are similar to themselves, women and members of various minorities often have fewer opportunities than other persons to obtain a mentor. Therefore, a growing number of organizations are taking active steps to reduce such barriers, thereby increasing mentoring for women and minorities.

3. **Describe how people choose their *careers*, and explain how the nature of careers has changed in recent years.**
A **career** is the evolving sequence of a person's work experiences over time. Common conceptions of what careers will—or should—be like have changed greatly in recent years, partly because of sweeping changes in the business world. When people make vocational decisions, they often consider how closely their values and attitudes match those of a perspective organization—that is, the **person-job fit**. Today's careers rarely involve movement through a series of steps up the corporate ladder. Instead, growing numbers of people, who are referred to as **entrepreneurs**, start their own businesses.

4. **Explain how the careers of women and men differ, including the so-called *glass ceiling*.**
The careers of women and men are affected by many of the same factors, but some operate differently for the two genders. For example, men's careers often are facilitated by marriage and children, but women's careers sometimes are impaired by these factors—apparently because women still take most of the responsibility for household management and child-rearing. Women also often receive fewer developmental experiences at work, which can adversely affect their careers. In addition, the **glass ceiling** appears to be real—few women are promoted to very high-level jobs. This does not seem to stem from conscious efforts to block advancement by women, however. Rather, it may derive from more subtle factors, such as the belief in the glass ceiling, which keeps many women from applying for high-level jobs. Recent evidence also suggests that the glass ceiling has been breached, if not entirely shattered.

5. **Define *stress*, and distinguish it from *strain*.**
Stress refers to a complex pattern of emotional stages, physiological reactions, and related thoughts in response to external demands (i.e., *stressors*). In contrast, **strain** refers to the effects of stress, primarily deviations from normal states or performance resulting from exposure to stressful events.

6. **Describe the major organizational and personal causes of stress.**
   Stress stems from *work-related* causes and from factors outside of work. One of the most important work-related causes involves **role conflict**, which results from the competing obligations to work and family. Other important work-related causes include occupational demands, overload and underload, responsibility for others, lack of social support, and sexual harassment. Causes of stress outside of work include traumatic life events and the daily hassles of everyday life.

7. **Describe the adverse effects of stress, including *burnout*, and explain how individual differences play roles in such effects.**
   Even relatively low levels of stress adversely influences task performance. In addition, it exerts harmful effects on psychological well-being. Prolonged exposure to stress can lead to **burnout**, which is a syndrome of emotional exhaustion, depersonalization, and feelings of low personal accomplishment. Stress also exerts harmful effects on physical health. It has been linked to various degenerative diseases, such as heart disease, high blood pressure, ulcers, and diabetes, and to infectious diseases as well. Although stress adversely affects the health of employees, some are more resistant to these effects than others; for example, Type B's are more resistant to stress than Type A's.

8. **Describe individual as well as organizational techniques for managing stress.**
   Techniques for managing stress exist at both the personal and the organizational level. Personal techniques include *lifestyle management*, such as good diet and exercise; *physiological techniques*, such as meditation and relaxation; and *cognitive techniques*, which involve changes in how individuals think about stress and the situations that produce it. Organization-based tactics for managing stress include *family-supportive policies*, such as flexible work schedules. Special organizational programs for dealing with stress include **stress management programs** to teach employees various techniques for managing stress, **wellness programs** to help promote health, and **employee-assistance programs** to help employees dealing with important problems (e.g., substance abuse, financial and legal problems). These programs have been very effective.

QUESTIONS FOR DISCUSSION

1. How can organizations reduce *entry shock* among their new hires?

2. How can the availability of mentors to women and minorities be increased?

3. What are the potential benefits of *job rotation*? Are there any potential drawbacks to such experience?

4. Why are more college graduates and new MBAs choosing to start their own companies — that is, to become *entrepreneurs*?

5. Why are people's *cognitive appraisals* of a given situation important in determining the level of stress they experience?

6. Suppose a female manager made several comments about the physique of a male subordinate. Would this constitute sexual harassment? If so, why?

7. Suppose you needed to choose employees for a high-stress job. What personal characteristics would you seek in these individuals? What characteristics would you try to avoid?

8. What steps can individuals take to manage the stress to which they are exposed?

9. What policies can organizations adopt to reduce stress among their employees?

Keeping the Peace Among Palo Alto's Peace Officers

Imagine a job in which you are constantly exposed to danger, deal with the public, face pressure from peers and supervisors, and are frustrated by administrative systems that all-too-frequently undo your hard work. Would you suffer the adverse effects of stress on such a job? Most certainly. Just ask any police officer, who must face these situations daily. Not surprisingly, stress-related disability claims among the half-million U.S. law enforcement officers have been rising steadily.

Fortunately, several communities have made efforts to help these women and men—who play such a vital role in maintaining safety for the rest of us—to stay safe and healthy themselves. Consider, for example, the *Health Resources Coordinator Programs (HRC)*, in the Palo Alto, California, police department, which consists of some 100 sworn officers and 60 civilian employees. As you might expect, this program assists officers in handling stressors such as shootings and SWAT team activities. In addition to providing counseling after signs of distress already are visible, however, the HRC also focuses on prevention. A psychologist is available at the police station—or other locations, as needed—on a full-time basis to discuss the daily pressures officers face and to provide immediate help with them. The program also provides confidential, off-site counseling with therapists as needed for both officers and their families—for whom, as you might imagine, life also can be highly stressful.

The program does more than help people cope with stress. It also coordinates specific activities designed to eliminate potential stressors in the first place. For example, HRC staffers constantly monitor the workplace, searching for specific conditions (e.g., a supervisor with an abrasive style) and more general ones as well (e.g., perceived inequities in the promotion process). In addition, officers are trained in ways to effectively communicate and solve problems with others—skills that may help to avoid potential sources of stress in the future.

Palo Alto's HRC has been effective in managing stress for several reasons. First, its services are highly visible and readily available, thereby avoiding people's concerns about appearing "weak" by using them. Second, it is rooted in the basic structure and operation of the department itself. Third, it is tailored to the special needs of police departments, and finally, it provides immediate assistance to both officers and their families. The Palo Alto police department is not the only one offering such services to its employees, but it clearly is among the leaders regarding organization-wide efforts to manage stress. In an agency where high levels of stress are inevitable, such efforts are well worth making.

CRITICAL THINKING QUESTIONS

1. What special challenges is the HRC likely to face in its efforts to manage stress among police officers?

2. In addition to the measures indicated, what else might the HRC do to manage stress among the agency's employees?

3. How might the HRC's techniques also be used to manage stress among employees in other kinds of organizations?

4. Do you know of any similar programs in use by your local law enforcement agencies? If so, what do they do, and what have their experiences been with these programs?

Managing Your Own Behavior: Career and Success

SMALL BUSINESS 2000

Some people are better than others at taking responsibility for their own success. In this video case, you meet a woman who "grabbed the bull by the horns" and not only found a career that she loves but created it. Lorraine Miller is the founder and owner of Cactus and Tropicals Greenhouse, a Utah-based company that employs more than 45 people, and is also a winner of the Small Business Administration's "Small Business Person of the Year" award. You might guess that Miller has been working in horticulture her entire life and that this business is the result of hard work and a decision to make it on her own. The second half of your guess would be correct. Miller *does* work hard, and she *did* decide that she needed to create her own opportunities.

The facts bearing on the first part of our guess make this case so interesting, however. Miller has *not* been in the plant business her whole life. In fact, she only got into it because her job as a lab technician didn't work out so well. Miller has a lot of energy and a burning desire to learn about new things. She was in a job where her boss was not really interested in teaching her much (other than the tasks he wanted her to complete, of course). For some people, this may be a great job; Just switch into machine mode, and crank out a bunch of work. Not for Miller. She wanted to understand the importance of what she was doing—and how it fit into a bigger picture.

When she started her business, her main motive was to survive. This is true of most new businesses. Miller did some pretty remarkable things and put in some amazingly long hours for this company to blossom into what it is today. She also realized something very important. Eventually, her company became bigger than she alone could handle, and she needed to hire employees. Learning from her own experience as an employee, however, Miller committed to provide a work environment that might be satisfying to others with values like hers. She has created a company that encourages employees both to learn and to speak up. Miller admits the company is not run as a democracy; she still makes the final call on big decisions. She also admits, however, that because of the commitment, enthusiasm, and strong will of her employees, the last final call is usually a "no-brainer."

QUESTIONS FOR DISCUSSION

1. Miller says that "work should not be grueling; it should be enjoyable." Such a statement could be interpreted in many ways. What do you think Miller should do to help new employees understand what she means?

2. You have met some people who work at Cactus and Tropicals and have heard a bit about how much they like working there. From what you heard, why do you thing they left their previous jobs and what about Cactus and Tropicals makes them so happy?

3. Cactus and Tropicals looks like a pretty good place to work. You might think that people are always happy there and that they have very little to get stressed-out about. This may be true. On the other hand, although the stresses might be different than those in other jobs, everything probably is not terrific for all people at Cactus and Tropicals all of the time. What types of things might be sources of stress and strain for the staff at Cactus and Tropicals?

EXPERIENCING ORGANIZATIONAL BEHAVIOR

Your Personal Career Plan

One of the most important things you can do to fulfill your career goals is to develop a **career plan**. Overall, there are five steps in this process, the first three of which you can do right now. (The final two must wait until you're already on the job.)

Directions

To complete the first three steps in the career-planning process, ask yourself the following questions and then record your answers. To achieve the most accurate assessment, answer these questions as honestly as possible.

Step 1: Personal Assessment

    a.   What special skills and aptitudes can you bring to your job?

    b.   What are your most serious weaknesses and limitations?

    c.   What types of jobs do you like?

    d.   To what extent do the jobs you identified in step *c* require the skills you identified in step *a*?

Step 2: Opportunities Analysis

    a.   How has the economy affected your various job prospects?

    b.   Is there an overabundance or a shortage of people to fill the various jobs you might consider?

Step 3: Career Objectives

    a.   What are your long-term goals (i.e., 5–10 years)?

    b.   What are your intermediate goals (i.e., 3–5 years)?

    c.   What are your short-term goals (i.e., 1–3 years)?

Step 4: Implement Your Plan

Step 5: Revise Your Plan as Necessary

    a.   As you work on a job, monitor your progress, solicit feedback, and compare the results to your objectives. Then revise your plan as needed.

    b.   Remember the key to successful career management is *not* necessarily obtaining promotions. Rather, it is building your skills so that you will be a desirable employee for many different companies.

Questions to Consider

1.   How realistic is your career plan? Does it fit your interests and skills?

2.   Is your career plan specific or general? Should it be more precise, or should it be general enough to accommodate adjustments?

3.   How does your career plan compare with those of others who are interested in pursuing the same line of work?

4.   Do you know of others who have followed personal career plans? If so, what advice can they provide?

WORKING IN GROUPS

The Worry Exercise

Everyone worries, and doing so is natural. The trick however, is to worry *constructively*, not *destructively*. In other words, although it often helps to worry about things you can control; worrying about things you cannot control only adds stress to your life. This exercise helps you to move toward the goal of worrying constructively and provides insight into the things about which other people worry.

Directions

1. Individually, list the things about which you most often tend to worry. This should include as many issues, problems, concerns from all aspects of your life as possible.
2. Divide the class into groups of approximately five members each.
3. In each group, one person describes each of his or her worries to the others.
4. The remaining members then discuss each of these worries and determine where, in the following chart, each should be categorized.

CAN THE WORRY BE CONTROLLED?	HOW IMPORTANT IS THE WORRY?	
	IMPORTANT	UNIMPORTANT
Yes, it *can* be controlled	Worthy of concern	Not worth worrying about
No, it *cannot* be controlled	Not worth worrying about	Not worth worrying about

5. Repeat this process until each member in each group has had his or her worries classified.
6. After this activity is completed, each group reports its findings to the class as a whole.

Questions for Discussion

1. How did others classify your worries? Did most of them fall into the "Not worth worrying about" category? Do you agree with their categorizations?
2. Did members of the class admit to worrying about unimportant issues and problems they could not control (i.e., those falling into the "not worth worrying about" category)?

3. Why do you think people worry about things that are not worth worrying about? Does worrying about them make sense? Can doing so produce harmful effects?

4. What do you think people can do to stop worrying about things that are unimportant or beyond their control?

7

GROUP DYNAMICS AND TEAMWORK

LEARNING OBJECTIVES

After reading this chapter, you should be able to

1. Define the term *group*, and explain how this differs from a collection of people.
2. Identify different types of groups operating within organizations as well as how they develop.
3. Describe the importance of *roles*, *norms*, *status*, and *cohesiveness* within organizations.
4. Explain how individual performance in groups is affected by the presence of others (*social facilitation*), the cultural diversity of group membership, and the number of others with whom one works (*social loafing*).
5. Explain what *teams* are, and distinguish them from groups in general.
6. Describe the types of teams that exist in organizations and the steps that should be followed in creating them.
7. Summarize the evidence regarding the effectiveness of teams in organizations.
8. Explain the factors responsible for the failure of some teams to operate as effectively as possible.
9. Identify how successful teams can be built.

PREVIEW CASE

A Team Approach to Selling at Cutler-Hammer

Cutler-Hammer is one of the world's leading suppliers of electrical control products and power distribution equipment. Whether you need a circuit-breaker for your home or apartment or a power transformer for the factory in which you work, this Pittsburgh-based division of Cleveland's Eaton Corp. is sure to make it.

For years, Cutler-Hammer sales reps worked in a very traditional manner: They took orders from customers, who relied on the sales reps' knowledge of the company's products to sell them what they needed. This worked fine until a few years ago, when the product line grew so dramatically in both size and complexity that the sales reps could not keep pace. As a result, they sold whatever products they happed to know — whether or not those products were the best choices.

This was not the only problem, however. Some reps worked hard to land multimillion-dollar contracts, but others goofed off and lived off the fat of their colleagues' successes, contributing little of their own. Naturally, there was considerable resentment, and as you might imagine, the customers were not well served.

Recognizing this was a formula for failure, Bruce Broussard, a manager from Cutler-Hammer's commercial division, introduced a team-selling approach. Instead of individual sales reps struggling to stay abreast of the latest product developments, Broussard composed sales teams — referred to as "pods" — whose individual members specialized in a particular product or service. Now, when a customer has

a problem, a rep can call on the person in his or her pod with the appropriate expertise to solve it. As a result, Cutler-Hammer sales reps now think of themselves as selling solutions rather than products — and their customers appreciate it.

Not surprisingly, this idea generated a great deal of resistance at first, and getting the sales force to accept it took a great deal of training. After all, most sales reps believe they will be called on to know everything there is to know about their company's products — and they expect to be rewarded for doing so. As a result, learning to pass a potential account to someone who was better-equipped to service it did not come easily.

Given the positive effect of this plan, however, it appears the effort was worth it. In fact, the changes have been dramatic. The company now maintains a book of testimonials from satisfied customers, currently numbering 150 — and growing. Not so long ago, any such book would have been empty. This high level of customer satisfaction is reflected on the bottom line as well (much to the delight of company officials). During a recent period in which the market grew only 4 to 7 percent each year, Cutler-Hammer grew at a sustained rate of 18 percent.

Not only has the company's bottom line benefited; the bank accounts of individual sales reps have benefited, too. Although reps may lose by passing along an individual account to a colleague in their pod, they more than make up for it by servicing other accounts with which *they* have greater technical expertise. There also is no fear of someone goofing off under this system: Anyone suspected of doing so is certain not to get any referrals from his or her colleagues. Any Cutler-Hammer reps who were reluctant to give up the old ways now take one look at their paychecks and find themselves among the most ardent supporters of the company's team-based sales approach.

The effectiveness of the team-based sales approach at Cutler-Hammer certainly is impressive. The company's sales reps are more interested than ever in serving the needs of their customers — a situation reflected by a strong base of satisfied customers and a healthy bottom line. Precisely what, however, makes groups of employees like those at Cutler-Hammer so successful? Are all such work teams effective, or is this an unusual case? How should such groups be formed? What problems might be expected, and how can they be overcome? These questions are basic to the topics of *group dynamics* and *teamwork*.

Group dynamics focuses on the nature of groups — that is, the variables governing their formation and development, their structure, and their interrelationships with individuals, other groups, and the parent organizations.[1] **Teamwork** refers to the practice of using teams, or special kinds of groups in which members are mutually committed to some goal and share leadership toward attaining it. Given the prevalence of groups in organizations and the growing popularity of teams, the importance of these topics in the field of OB is obvious.

group dynamics

The social science focusing on the nature of groups, including the factors governing their formation and development, the elements of their structure, and their interrelationships with individuals, other groups, and organizations.

teamwork

The practice of working in teams (see *team*).

Because groups exist in all social settings, the study of group dynamics has a long history in the social sciences, including OB.[2] In this chapter, we describe the nature of groups by defining what they are, identifying various types of groups and why they form, explaining the various stages through which they develop, and describing the dynamics of how groups are structured. We then shift our attention to how effectively groups operate. Specifically, we describe how people are affected by the presence of others, how the cultural diversity of a group affects performance, and the tendency for people to withhold their individual performance under certain conditions. We also describe special kinds of groups known as *teams*. Specifically, we define the concept of teams and distinguish them from groups, describe various types of teams, and identify some basic steps in creating them. Finally, we describe the performance of teams by examining evidence regarding their effectiveness, obstacles that sometimes lead to their failure, and tips for reaching high levels of team performance.

GROUPS AT WORK: THEIR BASIC NATURE

To understand the dynamics of groups and their influence on both individual and organizational functioning, we must raise some basic questions. What is a group? What types of groups exist? Why do people join groups? How do groups come into being, and how are they structured?

What Is a Group? A Working Definition

Imagine three people waiting in line at the supermarket cashier's stand. Now, compare them to the board of directors of a large corporation. Which collection would you consider to be a "group"? In our everyday language, we may refer to the people waiting in line as a group. Clearly, however, they are not a group in the same sense as the board of directors. Obviously, a group is more than simply a collection of people, but what exactly makes a "group" a group?

Social scientists formally define a **group** as a collection of two or more interacting individuals, with a stable pattern of relationships between them, who share common goals and perceive themselves as being a group.[3] To help us examine this definition more closely, Figure 7.1 summarizes the four key characteristics of groups.

group
A collection of two or more interacting individuals who maintain stable patterns of relationships, share common goals, and perceive themselves as being a group.

Social Interaction   One of the most obvious characteristics is that groups are composed of *two or more people in social interaction*. In other words, group members must have some influence on each other. This interaction between the parties may be verbal (e.g., sharing strategies for a corporate takeover) or nonverbal (e.g., exchanging smiles in the hallway), but the parties must affect each other to be considered a group.

Stability   Groups also must possess a *stable structure*. Groups can—and often do—change, but there must be some stable relationships that keep the members together and functioning as a unit. A collection of individuals that constantly changes (e.g., the people inside a waiting room at any given time) cannot be thought of as a group, because a greater level of stability is required.

Common Interests or Goals   A third characteristic of groups is that *members share common interests or goals*. For example, members of a stamp collecting club constitute a group that is sustained by their mutual interest. Other groups form because members with common interests help each other to achieve a mutual goal. For example, the owners and employees of a sewing shop constitute a group formed around a common interest in sewing—and around the common goal of making money.

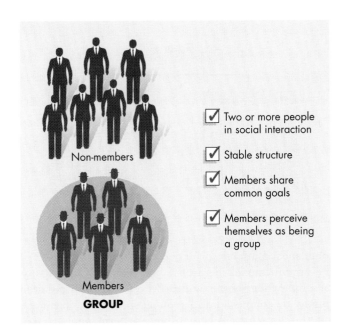

FIGURE 7.1

A Group: Its Defining Characteristics

To be a group, four criteria must be met: there must be two or more people in social interaction, they must share common goals, they must have a stable group structure, and the individuals must perceive themselves as being a group.

Recognition as Being a Group   Finally, to be a group, the individuals involved must *perceive themselves as being a group*. Groups are composed of people who recognize each other as being members of their group and who can distinguish members from non-members. For example, the members of a corporate finance committee or a chess club know who is—and who is not—in their group. In contrast, shoppers in a checkout line probably do not think of each other as being members of a group. They stand physically close to each other and may have passing conversations, but they have little in common—except, perhaps, a shared interest in reaching the end of the line. They also fail to identify themselves with the other people in the line.

By defining groups in terms of these four characteristics, we identify groups as very special collections of individuals. These characteristics are responsible for the important effects groups have on OB. To understand these effects better, we now review the wide variety of groups that operate within organizations.

Types of Groups

What do the following have in common: a military combat unit, three couples getting together for dinner, the board of directors of a large corporation, and the three-person cockpit crew of a commercial airliner? They are all groups. Of course, they also are very different kinds of groups, and ones that people join for different reasons.

Formal and Informal Groups   The most basic way of identifying group types is to distinguish between *formal groups* and *informal groups* (Fig. 7.2). **Formal groups** are created by the parent organization and are intentionally designed to direct members toward some important organizational goal. One type of formal group is referred to as a **command group**—that is, a group determined by the connections between individuals who are formal members of the organization (i.e., those who can legitimately give orders to others). For example, a command group may be formed by the vice president of marketing, who gathers together her regional marketing directors from around the country to hear their ideas about a new advertising campaign. The point is that command groups are determined by the organization's rules regarding who reports to whom, and they usually consist of a supervisor and his or her subordinates.

A formal organizational group also may be formed around some specific task. Such a group is referred to as a **task group**. Unlike command groups, task groups

formal groups

Groups created by the parent organization that are designed intentionally to direct the members toward some organizational goal.

command group

A group determined by the connections between individuals who are formal members of the organization.

task group

A formal organizational group that is formed around some specific task.

FIGURE 7.2

Varieties of Groups in Organizations

Within organizations, one may find formal groups (e.g., *command groups* and *task groups*) as well as informal groups (e.g., *interest groups* and *friendship groups*).

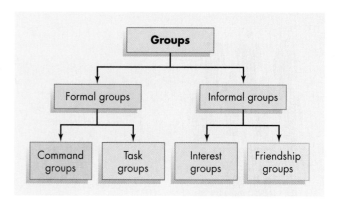

standing committees

Committees that are permanent.

ad hoc committee

A temporary committee formed for a special purpose.

task force

See *ad hoc committee*.

informal groups

Groups that develop naturally among people, without direction from the organization within which they operate.

interest group

A group of employees who come together to satisfy a common interest.

friendship groups

Informal groups that develop because their members are friends and often see each other outside of the organization.

may include individuals with some special interest or expertise in a specific area, regardless of their positions in the organizational hierarchy. For example, a company may have a committee on equal employment opportunities whose members monitor fair hiring practices. This group may be composed of personnel specialists, corporate vice presidents, and workers from the shop floor. Whether they are permanent groups, which are known as **standing committees**, or temporary ones formed for special purposes (e.g., a committee formed to recommend solutions to a parking problem), which are known as **ad hoc committees** or **task forces**, task groups are common in organizations.

As you know, not all groups in organizations are as formal as these. Many are informal in nature as well. **Informal groups** develop naturally among an organization's personnel without any direction from management. One key factor in the formation of informal groups is a common interest shared by its members. For example, a group of employees who band together to seek union representation or who march to protest their company's pollution of the environment may be called an **interest group**. The common goal sought by members of an interest group may unite workers at many different organizational levels. The key factor is that membership is voluntary—it is not created by the organization but is encouraged by the expression of common interests.

Sometimes the interests that bind individuals together are more diffuse. Groups may develop from a common interest in participating in sports, going to the movies, or just getting together to talk. These kinds of informal groups are known as **friendship groups**. For example, a group of coworkers who hang out together during lunch also may bowl or play cards together after work. Friendship groups extend beyond the workplace, because they provide opportunities for satisfying the social needs of workers so important to their well-being.

Informal work groups are an important part of life in organizations, and although, as mentioned, they develop without direct encouragement from management, friendships often originate out of formal organizational contact. For example, three employees working beside each other on an assembly line may start talking and discover their mutual interest in basketball—and then decide to shoot baskets together after work. Such friendships can bind people together, thereby helping them cooperate with each other and producing other beneficial effects on organizational functioning.

Why Do People Join Groups?

As already noted, people often join groups to satisfy their mutual interests and goals. To the extent that getting together with others allows us to achieve ends that would not be possible alone, forming groups makes sense. In fact, organizations themselves can be thought of as collections of groups focused toward achieving the mutual goal of success for the company. There are several additional reasons for joining groups, however, as summarized in Figure 7.3).

Not only do groups form to achieve mutual goals, they also frequently form as a way of seeking protection from other groups. If you ever heard the phrase "there's safety in numbers," you probably already know people join groups for the security of membership. Historically, for example, trade unions such as the AFL/CIO, the UAW, and the Teamsters have been formed by labor for protection against abuses by management. Similarly, professional associations such as the American Medical Association and the American Bar Association were created largely to protect their constituents against undesirable governmental legislation.

This is not to say that groups always are designed to promote some instrumental good. Indeed, they also exist because they appeal to our basic psychological need to be social. As discussed previously in the context of Maslow's need hierarchy theory (see chapter 4), people are social animals. They have a basic need to interact with others. Groups provide good opportunities for friendships to develop and, hence, for social needs to be fulfilled.

Also as suggested by Maslow, people have a basic desire for their self-esteem to be fulfilled, and group memberships can be a very effective way of nurturing self-esteem. For example, if a group to which one belongs is successful (e.g., a sales group that meets its quota), the self-esteem of all members (and supporters) may be boosted. Similarly, election to membership in an exclusive group (e.g., a national honor society) surely raises one's self-esteem.

As shown, people are attracted to groups for many different reasons. People may have different motivations for forming groups, but once formed, groups develop in remarkably similar ways. We now turn our attention to this issue.

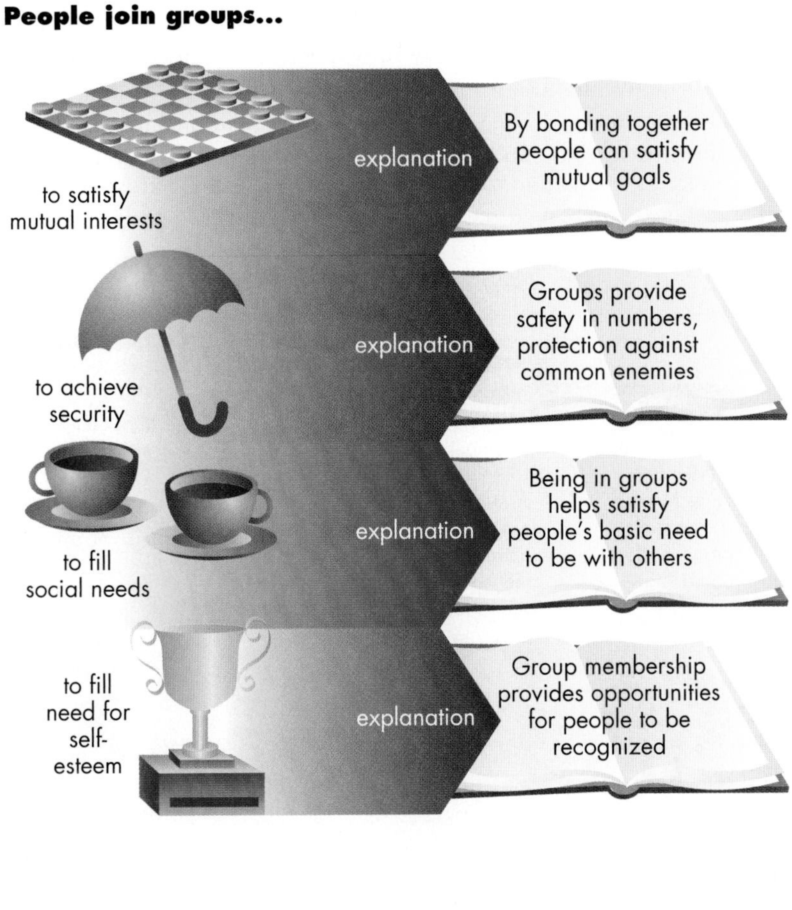

People join groups...

to satisfy mutual interests — explanation → By bonding together people can satisfy mutual goals

to achieve security — explanation → Groups provide safety in numbers, protection against common enemies

to fill social needs — explanation → Being in groups helps satisfy people's basic need to be with others

to fill need for self-esteem — explanation → Group membership provides opportunities for people to be recognized

FIGURE 7.3

Why Do People Join Groups?
People join groups for many different reasons. Four of the most important are identified here.

How Groups Are Formed

Social scientists have long been interested in how people form groups. We cannot predict exactly how all groups form, but two systematic models of group development appear to be most descriptive: the *five-stage model*, and the *punctuated-equilibrium model*.

The Five-Stage Model　Just as infants develop in certain ways during their first months of life, groups also show relatively stable signs of maturation and development.[4] The **five-stage model** identifies five distinct stages through which groups develop.[5] Also summarized Figure 7.4, these five stages are as follow:

five-stage model

The conceptualization claiming that groups develop in five stages—forming, storming, norming, performing, and adjourning.

1. *Forming*: During this stage of group development, the members get acquainted with each other. They also establish the ground rules by finding out what behaviors are acceptable regarding the job (e.g., how productive they are expected to be) and interpersonal relations (e.g., who is really in charge). During the forming stage, people tend to be a bit confused and uncertain about how to act in the group and how beneficial membership will be. Once the individuals come to think of themselves as members of a group, the forming stage is complete.

2. *Storming*: As the name implies, this stage is characterized by a high degree of conflict within the group. Members often resist the control of the group's leaders, and they show hostility toward each other. If these conflicts are not resolved and group members withdraw, the group may disband. Otherwise, as conflicts are resolved and the group's leadership is accepted, the storming stage is complete.

3. *Norming*: During this stage, the group becomes more cohesive, and identification as a member becomes greater. Close relationships develop, and shared feelings become common. A keen interest in finding mutually agreeable solutions also develops. Feelings of camaraderie and shared responsibility for the group's activities are heightened as well. The norming stage is complete when the members accept a common set of expectations constituting an acceptable way of doing things.

4. *Performing*: During this stage, questions about group relationships and leadership have been resolved—and the group is ready to work. Having fully

FIGURE 7.4

The Five-Stage Model of Group Development

In general, groups develop according to the five stages summarized here.

(*Source*: Based on information in Tuckman & Jensen, 1977; see note 5.)

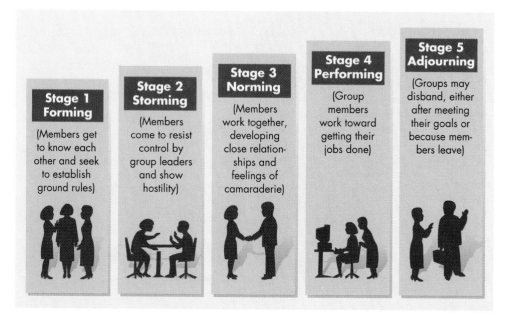

Stage 1 Forming (Members get to know each other and seek to establish ground rules)

Stage 2 Storming (Members come to resist control by group leaders and show hostility)

Stage 3 Norming (Members work together, developing close relationships and feelings of camaraderie)

Stage 4 Performing (Group members work toward getting their jobs done)

Stage 5 Adjourning (Groups may disband, either after meeting their goals or because members leave)

developed, the group may now devote its energy to getting the job done. The members' good relations and acceptance of the leadership helps the group to perform well.

5. *Adjourning*: Groups may cease to exist because they have met their goals and no longer are needed (e.g., an ad hoc group created to raise money for a charity project), in which case the end is abrupt. Other groups may adjourn gradually, as the group disintegrates either because members leave or the norms no longer are effective for the group.

To illustrate these various stages, imagine you have joined several colleagues on your company's newly created budget committee. At first, you and your associates feel each other out: You watch to see who comes up with the best ideas, whose suggestions are most widely accepted, who seems to take charge, and so on (i.e., the forming stage). Then, as members struggle to gain influence, you may see a battle over control of the committee (i.e., the storming stage). This is soon resolved, however, and an accepted leader emerges. At this stage, the members become highly cooperative, working together in harmony and doing things together, such as going out to lunch as a group (i.e., the norming stage). It now becomes possible for committee members to work together at doing their best and giving it their all (i.e., the performing stage). Then, once the budget is created and approved, the group's task is over, and it is disbanded (i.e., the adjourning stage).

It is important to remember that groups can be in any stage of development at any given time. Moreover, the amount of time a group may spend in any given stage varies. In fact, some groups fail before they even have a chance to work together. The boundaries between the various stages may not be clearly distinct, either, and several stages may be combined — especially as deadline pressures force groups to take action.[6] It is best, then, to think of this five-stage model as a general framework of group formation. Many of the stages may be followed, but the dynamic nature of groups makes it unlikely they will progress through these stages in a completely predictable order.

The Punctuated-Equilibrium Model   Not all scientists agree that groups develop in the order identified by the five-stage model. In fact, some argue that there may not be a universal sequence of stages but that there are some remarkable consistencies in how groups form and change. These patterns are described in the **punctuated-equilibrium model**. This approach to group formation recognizes that members working to meet a deadline approach their task differently in the first half of their time together than they do in the second half.[7]

During the first half, or *phase 1*, groups define their task, setting a mission that is unlikely to change until the second half of the group's life. Even if members have new ideas, these generally are not acted on. Interestingly, however, once groups reach the midpoint of their lives (whether this is just a few hours or several months), something curious happens. Almost as if an alarm goes off, groups at this point experience a sort of "midlife crisis" — a time when they recognize they must change how they operate if they are going to meet their goals. This begins *phase 2* of their existence, which is a time when groups drop old ways of thinking and adopt new perspectives. Groups then carry out these missions until they reach the end of phase 2, when they show bursts of activity needed to complete their work. For a summary of these processes, see Figure 7.5.

The idea is straightforward: Groups develop inertia, which keeps them going (i.e., an "equilibrium") until the midpoint, when they realize that deadlines loom. This stimulates them to confront important issues and to initiate changes, beginning (i.e., "punctuation") a new equilibrium phase. This new phase lasts until the group kicks into a final push, just before the deadline.

To illustrate the punctuated-equilibrium model, consider what might happen in a group working to elect a political candidate. When the group first meets in January,

punctuated-equilibrium model
The conceptualization of group development claiming that groups generally plan their activities during the first half of their time and then revise and implement their plans in the second half.

FIGURE 7.5

The Punctuated-Equilibrium
Model

According to the *punctuated-
equilibrium model*, groups go
through two stages marked by the
midpoint of the group's time together. The first half is a period of
equilibrium, in which the group
makes plans but accomplishes little. During the second half, members make changes that lead them
to accomplish the group's task as
the deadline approaches.

(*Source*: Based on suggestions by Gersick,
1989; see note 7.)

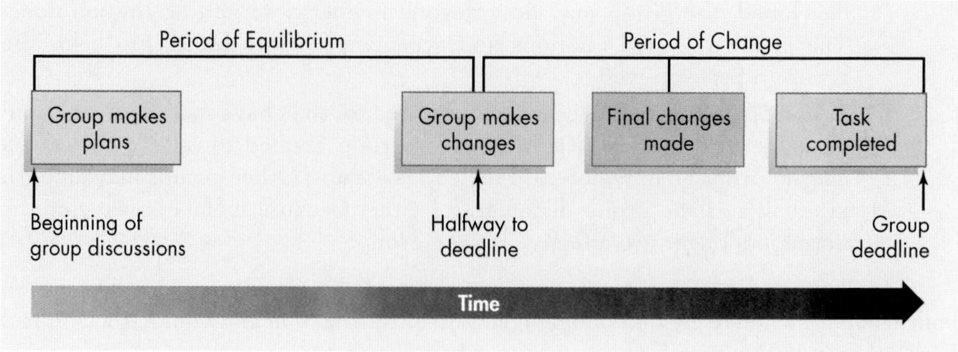

the members get to know each other and plan their campaign strategy. They decide what they need to do in the 10 months that follow to get their candidate into office, and they spring into action. By May or June, however, something happens: It becomes clear there are problems—and that the original plan must be changed. People working on the campaign look critically at what they've been doing, and they take active steps to change things. This continues through October. Then, in the weeks or days right before the November election, the group meets for a long time and makes its final push.

The punctuated-equilibrium is relatively new, but studies suggest it does a good job of describing how groups develop.[8] We think it will make great sense to you if you compare it to your own experience in groups (e.g., on class projects).

The Structural Dynamics of Work Groups

As noted, one key characteristic of a group is its stable structure. As social scientists use the term, **group structure** refers to the interrelationships between the individuals constituting a group and the characteristics that make group functioning both orderly and predictable. In this section, we describe four different aspects of group structure: the various parts played by group members (i.e., *roles*), the rules and expectations within groups (i.e., *norms*), the prestige of group membership (i.e., *status*), and the members' sense of belonging (i.e., *cohesiveness*).

Roles: The Hats We Wear   One primary structural element of groups is the members' tendencies to play specific roles—often more than one—in group interaction. Social scientists use the term *role* much the same as a director would refer to the character in a play. Indeed, the part one plays in the overall group structure is what we mean by a role. More formally, we may define a **role** as the typical behaviors characterizing a person in a social context.[9]

Many roles are assigned based on an individual's position within an organization. For example, a boss may be expected to give orders, and a teacher may be expected to lecture and give exams. These behaviors are expected of individuals in those roles. The person holding the role is a **role incumbent**, and the behaviors expected of that person are **role expectations**. The person holding the office of the president of the United States (i.e., the role incumbent) has certain role expectations simply because he or she currently holds that post. When a new president takes office, that person assumes the same role—and has the same formal powers as the previous president. This is true even though the new president may have very different ideas about issues facing the nation.

The role incumbent's recognition of his or her role expectations helps to avoid the social disorganization that would result without clear role expectations. Sometimes, however, workers may be confused about what is expected of them on the job, such as their level of authority or responsibility (Figure 7.6). Such **role ambiguity** typi-

group structure
The pattern of interrelationships between the individuals constituting a group; the guidelines of group behavior that make group functioning both orderly and predictable.

role
The typical behavior characterizing a person in a specific social context.

role incumbent
A person holding a particular role.

role expectations
The behaviors expected of someone in a particular role.

role ambiguity
The confusion arising from not knowing what one is expected to do as the holder of a role.

FIGURE 7.6

Roles: Our Places in Organizations

Most of us find it far easier than this speaker to identify the roles we play within the organizations in which we work.

(*Source*: © The New Yorker Collection 1994. Eric Teitelbaum, from cartoonbank.com. All Rights Reserved.)

cally is experienced by new members of organizations, who have had little chance to "learn the ropes," and it often results in job dissatisfaction, lack of commitment to the organization, and interest in leaving the job.[10]

As work groups and social groups develop, the various members come to play different roles in the social structure, which is a process referred to as **role differentiation**. The emergence of different roles in groups occurs naturally. Think of committees to which you have belonged. Was there someone who joked and made people feel better, or was there someone who worked hard to focus the group on the issue at hand? These examples of differentiated roles are typical of the role behaviors that emerge in groups. For example, organizations often have their "office comedian" who makes everyone laugh, their "company gossip" who shares others' secrets, or the "grand old man" who tells newcomers stories of the company's "good old days."

Roles tend to be differentiated in some standard ways. For example, in any group, there tends to be one person who, more than anyone else, helps the group to reach its goal.[11] Such a person is said to play the **task-oriented role**. In addition, another member may emerge who is quite supportive and nurturant, someone who makes everyone feel good. This person is said to play a **socioemotional role**. Still others may be recognized by what they do for themselves, often at the expense of the group. These individuals are said to play a **self-oriented role**. Many specific role behaviors fall into one or another of these categories. For a listing of the most common forms these three types of roles may take, see Table 7.1.

Norms: A Group's Unspoken Rules   One feature of groups that enhances their orderly functioning is group norms. **Norms** may be defined as generally agreed-on, informal rules that guide the members' behavior.[12] They represent shared ways of viewing the world. Norms differ from organizational rules as they are not formal and written. In fact, group members may not be aware of the subtle group norms that exist and regulate their behavior. Even so, these norms have profound effects. Norms regulate the behavior of groups in important ways, such as by fostering workers' honesty and loyalty to the company, establishing appropriate ways to dress, and dictating when being late for or absent from work is acceptable.

If you recall the pressure from your peers as you grew up to dress or wear your hair in certain styles, you know the profound normative pressures exerted by groups. Some norms, which are known as **prescriptive norms**, dictate the behaviors that should be performed. Others, which are known as **proscriptive norms**, dictate specific behaviors that should be avoided. For example, groups may develop prescriptive norms to follow their leader or to help a group member in need. They also may develop proscriptive norms to avoid absences or to refrain from telling secrets to the

role differentiation

The tendency for various specialized roles to emerge as groups develop.

task-oriented role

The activities of an individual in a group who, more than anyone else, helps that group to reach its goal.

socioemotional role

The activities of an individual in a group who is supportive and nurturant of other members and who helps them to feel good.

self-oriented role

The activities of an individual in a group who focuses on his or her own good, often at the expense of others.

norms

Generally agreed-on, informal rules that guide the behavior of group members.

prescriptive norms

Expectations within groups regarding what is supposed to be done.

proscriptive norms

Expectations within groups regarding behaviors in which members are not supposed to engage.

TABLE 7.1

Some Roles Commonly Played by Group Members

Organizational roles may be differentiated into task-oriented, relations-oriented (or socioemotional), and self-oriented roles—each of which has several subroles. A number of these are shown here.

TASK-ORIENTED ROLES	RELATIONS-ORIENTED ROLES	SELF-ORIENTED ROLES
Initiator-contributors *Recommend new solutions to group problems*	Harmonizers *Mediate group conflicts*	Blockers *Act stubborn and resistant to the group*
Information seekers *Attempt to obtain the necessary facts*	Compromisers *Shift own opinions to create group harmony*	Recognition seekers *Call attention to their own achievements*
Opinion givers *Share own opinions with others*	Encouragers *Praise and encourage others*	Dominators *Assert authority by manipulating the group*
Energizers *Stimulate the group into action whenever interest drops*	Expediters *Suggest ways the group can operate more smoothly*	Avoiders *Maintain distance, isolate themselves from fellow group members*

Source: Based on Benne & Sheats, 1948; see note 11.

boss. Sometimes the pressure to conform is subtle, as in the dirty looks a manager gives his peers for going to lunch with one of the assembly line workers. Other times, normative pressures may be severe, such as when a production worker sabotages another's work because he is performing at too high a level and, thus, is making his coworkers look bad. Our examples emphasize the underlying social dynamics responsible for how groups develop norms, but this is only one reason. In fact, several factors are responsible for the development of norms.[13] For a summary of these factors, see Table 7.2.

ETHICS MATTERS   Employees of IBM who are caught violating ethical principles are not demoted or transferred—but fired! The norm to take swift and decisive action toward those breaking moral rules developed years ago, when then-president Thomas J. Watson, Jr., was humiliated for going easier on high-level executives than on lower-level employees who also acted improperly.[14] Most companies recognize that dual standards of morality cannot be tolerated. ■

Status: The Prestige of Group Membership   Have you ever been attracted to a group because of the prestige accorded its members? You may have wanted to join a certain fraternity or sorority because it was highly regarded by other students. No doubt, members of championship-winning football teams proudly sport their Super Bowl rings to identify themselves as members of that highly regarded team. Clearly, one potential reward of group membership is the status of being in that group.

Even within social groups, however, different members are accorded different levels of prestige. For example, fraternity and sorority officers as well as committee chairpersons, may be recognized as being more important members of their respective groups. This is the idea behind **status**—that is, the relative social position or rank given to groups or group members by others.[15]

Within most organizations, status can be both formal and informal in nature. **Formal status** refers to attempts to differentiate between the degrees of authority given to employees by an organization. This typically is accomplished through **status symbols**, which are objects reflecting the position of an individual within an organi-

status

The relative prestige, social position, or rank given to groups or individuals by others.

formal status

The prestige one has by virtue of his or her official position in an organization.

status symbols

Objects reflecting the position of an individual within an organization's hierarchy of power.

TABLE 7.2

Norms: How Do They Develop?

This table summarizes four ways in which group norms can develop.

BASIS OF NORM DEVELOPMENT	EXAMPLE
1. Precedents set over time	Seating location of each group member around a table
2. Carryovers from other situations	Professional standards of conduct
3. Explicit statements from others	Working a certain way because you are told "that's how we do it around here"
4. Critical events in group history	After the organization suffers a loss due to one person's divulging company secrets, a norm develops to maintain secrecy

Source: Based on Feldman, 1984; see note 13.

zation's hierarchy. Status symbols include job titles (e.g., Director), perquisites or perks (e.g., a reserved parking space), the opportunity to do desirable and highly regarded work (e.g., serving on important committees), and luxurious working conditions (e.g., a large, private, lavishly decorated office) (Figure 7.7).[16]

Status symbols help groups in many ways.[17] First, they remind members of their relative roles, thereby reducing uncertainty and providing a stable social order (e.g., your small desk reminds you of your lower organizational rank). In addition, they provide assurance of the various rewards available to those who perform at a superior level (e.g., "Maybe one day I'll have a reserved parking spot"). They also provide a sense of identification by reminding members of the group's values (e.g., a gang's jacket may remind its wearer of his or her expected loyalty and boldness). Therefore, organizations do much to reinforce formal status through the use of status symbols.

Symbols of **informal status** within organizations also are widespread. These symbols include the prestige accorded individuals with certain characteristics not formally recognized by the organization. For example, employees who are older and more experienced may be perceived by their coworkers as being higher in status. Those with certain skills (e.g., the home-run hitters on a baseball team) also may be regarded as having higher status than others. In some organizations, the lower value some

informal status

The prestige accorded individuals with certain characteristics not formally recognized by the organization.

FIGURE 7.7

Working Conditions: A Symbol of Organizational Status

A large, elegantly decorated office is a sure symbol of the occupant's high status within this organization.

individuals place on work by women and minorities also can be considered an example of informal status in operation.[18]

As you might expect, higher-status people tend to be more influential than lower-status people. This phenomenon may be seen in a classic study of decision making among three-man bomber crews.[19] After the crews had difficulty solving a problem, the experimenter planted clues to the solution with either a low-status member (i.e., the tail gunner) or a high-status member (i.e., the pilot). The solutions offered by the pilots were far more likely to be adopted than the same solutions offered by the tail gunners. Apparently, the greater status accorded the pilots—because they tended to be more experienced and to hold higher military ranks—was responsible for the greater influence they wielded.

cohesiveness

The strength of the members' desires to remain part of the group.

Cohesiveness: Getting the Team Spirit   One obvious determinant of any group's structure is **cohesiveness**—that is, the strength of members' desires to remain part of their group. Highly cohesive work groups are those in which members are attracted to each other, accept the group's goals, and help each other work toward meeting them. In uncohesive groups, members dislike each other and may even work at cross-purposes.[20] In essence, cohesiveness refers to a *we-feeling*, an *esprit de corps*, and a sense of belonging to a group.

Several important factors influence the extent to which group members "stick together." One involves the severity of initiation into the group: The greater the difficulty of becoming a member, the more cohesive the group.[21] To understand this, consider how highly cohesive certain groups may be that you have worked hard to join. Was it particularly difficult to "make the cut" on your sports team? The rigorous requirements for entry into elite groups (e.g., the most prestigious medical schools and military training schools) may well be responsible for their high degree of camaraderie. Having "passed the test" tends to keep individuals together—and to separate them from those who are unwilling (or unable) to "pay the price" of admission.

FIGURE 7.8

Confronting Common Enemies Breeds Group Cohesiveness

Groups become highly cohesive as they work together to ward off common enemies. This applies to military groups as well as to those in business organizations, whose members face less physical (but equally hostile) battles.

Group cohesion also tends to strengthen under conditions of high external threat or competition. For example, when workers face a "common enemy," they tend to draw together (Figure 7.8). Such cohesion makes workers feel safer and better protected, and it aids the workers by encouraging them to work closely together and to coordinate their efforts toward the common enemy. Under such conditions, petty disagreements that otherwise may cause dissension within the group tend to be put aside.

The cohesiveness of groups is established by several additional factors as well.[22] For one, cohesiveness generally tends to be greater as group members spend more time together. Obviously, limited interaction interferes with opportunities to develop bonds between members. Similarly, cohesiveness tends to be greater in smaller groups. Generally speaking, large groups make it difficult for members to interact and, thus, for cohesiveness to reach a high level. Finally, because "nothing succeeds like success," groups with a history of success also tend to be highly cohesive. It often is said that "everyone loves a winner," and success tends to unite group members as they rally around it. For this reason, employees tend to be loyal to successful companies.

Thus far, our discussion has implied that cohesiveness is a positive thing. For example, people enjoy belonging to highly cohesive groups. In addition, members of closely knit work groups participate more fully in group activities, more readily accept their group's goals, and are absent from their jobs less often than members of less cohesive groups.[23] Not surprisingly, cohesive groups tend to work together quite well, sometimes are exceptionally productive, and have low levels of voluntary turnover.[24]

Highly cohesive groups can be problematic as well, however. For example, if a highly cohesive group's goals are contrary to the parent organization's goals, that group is in a position too harm the organization by working against its interests.[25] Highly cohesive group members who conspire to sabotage their employers are a good illustration. Therefore, it is important to recognize that when it comes to performance, group cohesiveness is a double-edge sword: Its effects can be helpful *and* harmful.

INDIVIDUAL PERFORMANCE IN GROUPS

We now turn to the aspect of group dynamics most relevant to the field of OB: the effects of groups on individual performance. Specifically, we look at three issues in this connection. First, we consider how people's work performance is affected by the presence of others. We then examine how the composition of groups—particularly their racial and ethnic diversity—affects performance. Finally, we describe how performance is affected by group size.

Social Facilitation: Working in the Presence of Others

Imagine you have studied drama for five years and now are ready for your first audition in front of some Hollywood producers. You have rehearsed diligently for months to prepare yourself for the part. Now, however, you no longer are alone at home with your script. Your name is announced, and silence fills the auditorium as you walk onto the stage. How will you perform now that you are in front of an audience? Will you freeze, forgetting the lines you studied so intensely when alone? Will the audience spur you to your best performance yet? In other words, what impact will the presence of the audience have on your behavior?

The answer to this question is not straightforward.[26] Sometimes people perform better in the presence of others than when alone, and sometimes people perform better alone than when in the presence of others. This tendency for the presence of others to enhance an individual's performance at certain times and to impair it at others is known as **social facilitation**. (Although the word *facilitation* implies improvements in task performance, scientists use the term *social facilitation* to refer to both performance improvements and decrements stemming from the present of others.) What accounts for these seemingly contradictory findings?

Explaining Social Facilitation   Many scientists believe the answer boils down to several basic psychological processes.[27] First, social facilitation results from the heightened emotional arousal (e.g., the tension and excitement) people experience in the presence of others. (Wouldn't you feel more tension playing the piano in front of an audience than alone?) Second, when people are aroused, they tend to perform the most dominant response—that is, their most likely behavior in that setting. (Returning the smile of a coworker may be considered a dominant act, because it is a well-learned act to smile at another who smiles at you.) If someone is performing a well-learned act, the dominant response likely would be correct (e.g., speaking the right lines during your fiftieth performance). If the behavior in question is relatively novel and newly learned, however, the dominant response likely would be incorrect (e.g., speaking incorrect lines during an audition).

Together, these ideas are known as the **drive theory of social facilitation**.[28] In this theory, the presence of others increases arousal, which in turn increases the tendency to perform that most dominant responses. If these responses are correct, the resulting performance is enhanced; if these responses are incorrect, the performance is impaired. Based on these processes, performance may be helped (if the task is well-learned) or hindered (if the task is not well-learned). For a summary of this process, see Figure 7.9.

social facilitation
The tendency for the presence of others to enhance an individual's performance at times and to impair it at others.

drive theory of social facilitation
The theory according to which the presence of others increases arousal, which in turn increases people's tendencies to perform the dominant response. If that response is well-learned, performance improves; if that response is novel, performance is impaired.

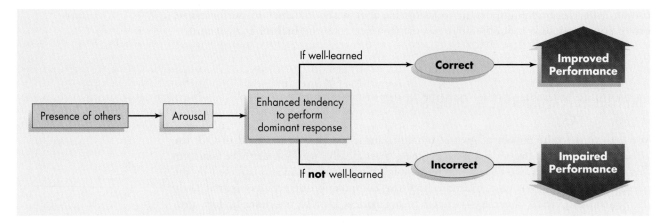

FIGURE 7.9

Social Facilitation: A Drive Theory Approach

Zajonc's *drive theory of social facilitation* states that the presence of others is arousing. In turn, this enhances the tendency to perform the most dominant (i.e., strongest) responses. If these responses are correct (e.g., if the task is well-learned), performance is improved; if these are incorrect (e.g., if the task is novel), performance suffers.

Research has provided considerable support for this theory: People perform better on tasks in the presence of others if that task is well-learned, but they perform more poorly if it is not well-learned. There are several good explanations for this effect, but a key one is based on the idea of **evaluation apprehension** — that is, the fear of being evaluated or judged by another person.[29] Indeed, people may be aroused by performing a task in the presence of others *because* of their concern over what those others might think. For example, lower-level employees may suffer evaluation apprehension when they worry about what their supervisor thinks of their work. Similarly, in the audition example, you may face evaluation apprehension in front of the producers. After all, how well you are received by these producers will go a long way in determining the success of your career. If you know your part well, you probably will perform better in this situation than when rehearsing alone. If the part is new to you, however, and you cannot quite get the hang of it, then fear of what important others may think of you probably will lead you to blow this big opportunity.

evaluation apprehension
The fear of being evaluated or judged by another person.

Social Facilitation via an "Electronic Presence": Computerized Performance Monitoring
If you've read George Orwell's classic novel *1984*, you probably recall "Big Brother," the all-knowing power that monitored your every move. As often occurs, the science fiction of one era eventually becomes the scientific fact of another. In the case of "Big Brother," Orwell was not many years off in his predictions — at least in the workplace. The use of computers to monitor work performance is increasingly common today. **Computerized performance monitoring** already is widely used in the insurance, banking, communications, and transportation industries, and it promises to become even more prevalent in tomorrow's organizations.[30] Thus it is important to learn the effects of monitoring on people's job performance.

One way to understand how computerized monitoring may influence performance is by extending our thinking about social facilitation. Instead of having an individual physically present to watch, this technique provides an indirect computer or "electronic presence." For example, imagine you are entering data into a computer terminal. You can be monitored in a direct, physical way by someone looking over your shoulder — or indirectly by someone checking a computerized record of the speed and accuracy of your every keystroke. If the task being performed is complex, social

computerized performance monitoring
The process of using computers to monitor job performance.

facilitation research suggests the physical presence of an observer leads to reduced performance. Would the same thing occur, however, with an electronic presence?

Research provides an answer.[31] In one study, college students were asked to solve complex anagram puzzles (i.e., unscrambling letters to form words) by entering their responses into a computer terminal. The conditions under which they performed this task were varied systematically by the researchers in several ways. One group of participants (i.e., the control condition) performed the task with no one observing them in any form. A second group (i.e., the person-monitored condition) was monitored by stationing two female observers immediately behind the participants as they performed their task. Finally, a third group (i.e., the computer-monitoring condition) was told their performance would be monitored by people who could see their work on another computer connected to the network. (To make this convincing, participants were shown the other computer equipment.) Participants performed the task for 10 minutes, after which the researchers counted the number of anagrams solved correctly by people in each condition. Figure 7.10 summarizes these findings.

People performed worse when others physically observed them (i.e., the person-monitored group) than when they performed the task alone (i.e., the control group). This is in keeping with both research and theory on social facilitation, according to which performance on complex tasks suffers in the presence of others. Even more interesting, however, was the finding that performance also suffered when it was monitored by computer—that is, even when participants in the study did not have others looking over their shoulders. Apparently, performance can suffer even when the presence of another is imperceptible yet known to exist.

These findings support the idea that social facilitation may result from people's concerns about being evaluated negatively by another—that is, from evaluation apprehension. In this study, participants knew their performance could be just as easily evaluated by watching a remote computer as by watching them directly. Accordingly, opportunities for evaluation existed in both conditions, thus possibly accounting for the apprehension that led to the performance decrements found.

There is an important, applied implication of these results—namely, that the act of monitoring job performance to keep levels high actually may backfire. In other words, instead of improving performance (for fear of being caught doing poorly), monitoring actually might interfere with performance (by providing a distracting source of evaluation). Participants in this study only performed their tasks for brief periods of time, so we cannot tell whether people would get used to the monitoring and improve their performance over time. Until further research addresses this question, we must issue the following caution: Using computers to monitor work performance might

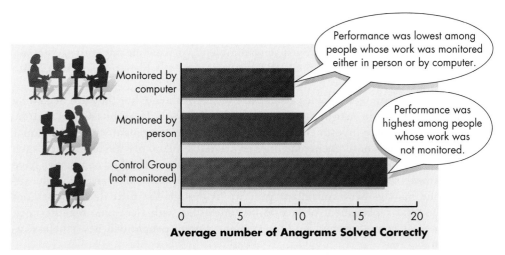

FIGURE 7.10

Computer Monitoring: Evidence of Its Counterproductive Effects

Participants in one recent study performed complex tasks either alone, while being monitored by a computer, or while being monitored by two other people who were physically present. Consistent with other research on *social facilitation*, people performed the complex task worse in the presence of others than when alone. They also performed more poorly when monitored by the "electronic presence" of a computer.

(*Source*: Based on data reported by Aiello & Svec, 1993; see note 31.)

impair the very performance such monitoring is intended to improve. In the end, "Big Brother" might be defeating his own purposes. (A growing trend in today's organizations involves using computers not only for monitoring performance but also for bringing groups together electronically who cannot be together physically. For a closer look at this practice, see the "Trends" section below.)

TRENDS: WHAT TODAY'S COMPANIES ARE DOING

■ Videoconferencing: Groups in Cyberspace

videoconferencing

The practice of using technology to provide audio and video links (either limited or full-motion) between work sites, thus allowing visual communication between people who are not physically present.

If you ever attempted to schedule a group meeting, you know how difficult finding a mutually acceptable time for several busy people can be. This problem is compounded when the meeting involves people in distant locations. In such cases, we must consider not only the time spent on the meeting itself but also the considerable downtime and expenses associated with travel. With an eye toward reducing these obstacles, technology now is bringing people together electronically — in "virtual" space as opposed to physical space. The idea is called **videoconferencing** — that is, the practice of using technology to provide audio and video links (either limited or full-motion) between work sites, thus allowing visual communication between people who are not physically present.

Videoconferencing is less expensive than ever today, thus making it an increasingly common way for groups to meet. If for no other reason, the savings in travel expenses alone may make it cost-effective. One company that has made this investment is BASF's Fibers Division. This firm, which spent $1 million on videoconferencing equipment at 24 worldwide sites, now enjoys an annual savings of $10.4 million on travel expenses.[32] In addition, company officials also find it easier to schedule meetings. Finding a common time when a group of busy professionals can step into their nearest videoconferencing facility is no easy task, but it certainly is much simpler than arranging to bring them together physically. Given the increased ease of co-ordination gained through videoconferencing, some companies have used this technology to gain a competitive advantage as well. For example, Bata Shoes, which has operations in 60 countries, has used videoconferencing to reduce its product-development time by some 90 percent.[33]

shared-screen conferencing

The process of connecting computer workstations to provide concurrent displays of information and interaction between individuals.

A more limited form of multimedia conferencing is **shared-screen conferencing** — that is, connecting computer workstations to provide concurrent displays of information and interaction between several individuals.[34] Using this technology, group members can call up a common document on their desktop computers and work on it simultaneously. This might involve something simple, such as drafting a memo, or something more complex, such as drawing a new design on a blackboard program. Some members of the group can even send completely private messages to each other, without the others knowing it — the high-tech equivalent of whispering something into another's ear.[35]

These emerging technologies clearly are in their infancy, but they are becoming increasingly popular in many organizations. Although only large businesses may be able to afford the huge investment in videoconferencing equipment, small companies can rent public videoconferencing facilities as needed. Several private businesses, such as many Kinko's locations, now offer this service. Given how satisfied companies have been with these services, we should expect to see more videoconferencing in the future. As one management consultant puts it, "Although the next decade does not promise the total replacement of face-to-face meetings with electronic togetherness, new varieties of computer-mediated interactions among people will nevertheless increase."[36] ■

Performance in Culturally Diverse Groups

For many years, the task of composing work groups involved finding individuals with the right blend of skills and then getting them to work together. This alone was challenging enough. Today, however, as the workplace grows increasingly diverse both racially and ethnically, there is a new consideration as well. How does a group's cultural diversity affect task performance?

Considering this question, researchers have reasoned that when a culturally diverse group forms, its members first need time to adjust to their racial and ethnic differences.[37] To the extent that people's differing perspectives and styles interfere with their ability to work together, task performance may suffer. With time, however, group members learn to interact with each other despite their different backgrounds, and these performance differences should disappear.

This idea was tested in a study that assigned college students enrolled in a management class to two types of four-person groups: *homogeneous groups*, which contained members from the same racial and ethnic background; and *diverse groups*, each of which contained one white American, one African-American, one Hispanic-American, and one foreign-national member. After being formed, the groups were asked to analyze business cases—a task with which management students are familiar. The groups worked on four occasions, each scheduled one month apart. Their case analyses then were scored (using several predetermined criteria) by experts who did not know which groups were diverse and which were homogeneous. How did following these two different recipes for group composition influence task performance? The data summarized in Figure 7.11 provide some insight.

Basically, the answer depends on how much time the group spent together. At first, homogeneous groups did considerably better than diverse groups. During the second session, however, these differences grew smaller. By the third session, the differences disappeared almost completely, and by the fourth, the diverse groups did slightly better than the homogeneous groups. All groups improved their performance over time, as you would expect, but the initial advantage of homogeneous groups was a temporary condition and only found in newly created groups. As members gained

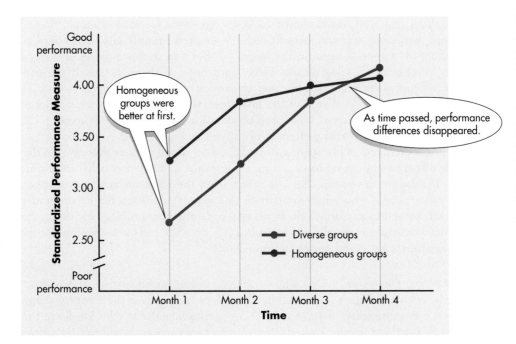

FIGURE 7.11

Task Performance in Culturally Diverse Groups: An Experimental Demonstration

Which performs better—groups that are culturally heterogeneous or culturally homogeneous? According to one experiment, the answer depends on when performance is measured. Specifically, culturally diverse groups performed worse than homogeneous groups at first, but these differences disappear over time.

(*Source:* Based on data reported by Watson, Kumar, & Michaelsen, 1993; see note 37.)

more experience working with each other, the differences between them produced less interference.

Because research on the effects of racial and ethnic composition on group task performance is just beginning, we do not yet know if these results hold for different kinds of tasks as well. We also do not know if diverse groups always eventually perform even better than homogeneous ones. On tasks in which differing perspectives might help a group to do its job, diverse groups may be expected to have an edge. Several key questions about the effects of diversity on group performance remain unanswered, however, but the importance of this variable in group performance is clearly established.

Social Loafing: "Free Riding" When Working with Others

Have you ever helped with several others to move a friend into a new apartment, with each person carrying and transporting part of the load from the old place to the new one? Did you ever sit around a table with others stuffing political campaign letters into envelopes and addressing them to potential donors? These tasks may seem quite different, but they actually share an important common characteristic: Performing each requires only a single individual, but several people's work can be pooled to yield greater outcomes. Because each person's contribution can be added to another's, such tasks have been referred to as **additive tasks**.[38]

additive tasks

Group tasks in which the co-ordinated efforts of several people are added together to form the group's product.

If you ever performed additive tasks such as those described here, you probably found yourself not working quite as hard as you would have alone. Indeed, when several people combine their efforts on additive tasks, each individual contributes less than he or she would when performing that same task alone.[39] As suggested by the old saying "Many hands make light the work," a group of people should be be more productive than any one individual. When several people combine their efforts on additive tasks, however, each individual's contribution tends to be less. Five people working together raking leaves will *not* be five times more productive than a single individual working alone; there are always some who go along for a "free ride." In fact, the more individuals who contribute to an additive task, the less each individual's contribution tends to be, which is a phenomenon known as **social loafing**.[40]

social loafing

The tendency for group members to exert less individual effort on an additive task as the size of the group increases.

This effect was first noted almost 70 years ago by a German scientist, named Ringlemann, who compared the amount of force exerted by different-size groups of people pulling on a rope.[41] Specifically, he found that one person pulling on a rope exerted an average of 63 kilograms of force. In groups of three, however, the per-person force dropped to 53 kilograms, and in groups of eight, it dropped to only 31 kilograms per person — less than half the effort exerted by someone working alone! Social loafing effects of this type have been observed in many different studies.[42] The general form of the social loafing effect is portrayed in Figure 7.12.

social impact theory

The theory that explains social loafing in terms of the diffused responsibility of each group member for doing what is expected (see *social loafing*). The larger the group, the less each member is influenced by the social forces acting on that group.

The phenomenon of social loafing is explained by **social impact theory**.[43] In this theory, the effect of any social force acting on a group is divided equally among its members. The larger the group, the less affect from the force on any one member. Thus, the more people who might contribute to a group's product, the less pressure faced by each person to perform well. In other words, the responsibility for doing the job is diffused over more people. As a result, each member feels less responsible for behaving appropriately — and social loafing occurs.

Is Social Loafing Universal? One way of understanding social loafing is that it occurs because people are more interested in themselves (i.e., getting the most for themselves while doing the least) than in their fellow group members, who are forced to do their work for them. In the United States, this phenomenon should not be particularly surprising considering the tendency for U.S. cultures to be highly individual-

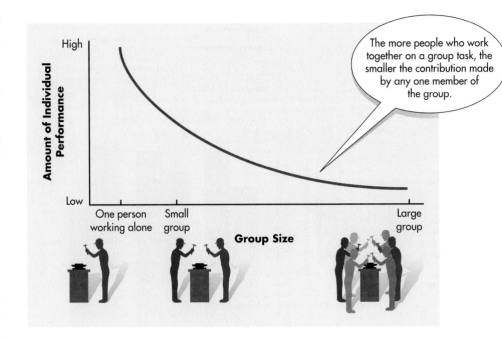

FIGURE 7.12

Social Loafing: Its General Form
According to the *social loafing* effect, when individuals work together on an additive task, the more people contribute to the group's task, the less effort each individual exerts.

istic. In **individualistic cultures**, people value highly individual accomplishments and personal success.

In other countries, however, such as Israel and the People's Republic of China, people value shared responsibility and the collective good of all more highly. Such nations are referred to has having **collectivistic cultures**. In these cultures, people working in groups are not expected to engage in social loafing, because doing so would mean failing in their social responsibility to the group—a responsibility that does not prevail in individualistic cultures. In fact, to the extent that people in collectivistic cultures are strongly motivated to help fellow group members, they can be expected to be *more* productive in groups than when alone. In other words, not only would they not loaf, they would work especially hard!

These ideas were tested in an interesting experiment involving managers from the United States, Israel, and the People's Republic of China.[44] Each manager was asked to complete an "in-basket" exercise. This task simulated the daily activities of managers (e.g., writing memos, filling out forms, rating job applicants) in all three countries. All were asked to perform this task as well as they could for one hour but under one of two different conditions: *alone*, or as part of a *group* of 10 managers. Participants who worked alone were asked simply to write their names on each item they completed and turn it in. Participants who worked in the group condition were told their group's overall performance would be assessed at the end of the hour. Fellow group members were not present physically, but they were described as being highly similar in their family and religious backgrounds as well as in their interests. (The researchers reasoned groups of this type would be ones whose other members people would be especially reluctant to let down by loafing.) To compare the various groups, each participant's in-basket exercises were scored by converting the responses to standardized performance scores.

Did social loafing occur? The results are summarized in Figure 7.13, and they clearly show that social loafing occurred in the United States. In other words, individual performance was significantly lower among people working in groups than among those working alone. The opposite was found in each of the two highly collectivistic cultures (i.e., the People's Republic of China and Israel). In both countries, individuals performed at higher levels when working in groups than when working alone. These people not only failed to loaf in groups, they actually worked *harder* than

individualistic cultures
Cultures whose members place a high value on individual accomplishments and personal success.

collectivistic cultures
Cultures whose members place a high value on shared responsibility and the collective good of all.

FIGURE 7.13

Social Loafing: Not Exactly a Universal Phenomenon

Researchers compared the performance of people from the United States, Israel, and the People's Republic of China who worked alone or in groups on a managerial task. Although individual performance alone was lower than performance as part of a group in the United States (i.e., *social loafing* occurred), the opposite was found in China and Israel. Compared with the more *individualistic* nature of U.S. culture, the highly *collectivistic* nature of Chinese and Israeli cultures discouraged people from letting down their fellow group members.

(*Source*: Based on data reported by Earley, 1993; see note 44.)

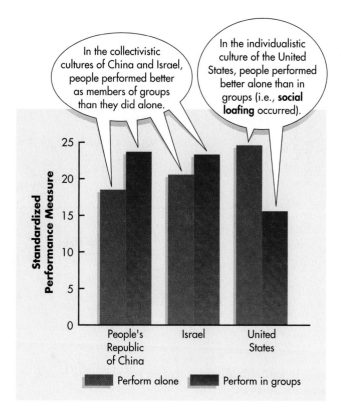

they did alone. Because they strongly identified with their groups and were concerned about the welfare of other members, managers from collectivistic cultures placed their group's interests ahead of their own. (These findings only occurred, however, when people believed they had strong ties to the members of their groups.)

This research suggests that culture plays an important part in determining people's tendencies toward social loafing. It is tempting to think of social loafing as inevitable, but it appears the phenomenon is not as universal as you might think. Instead, loafing appears to be a manifestation of cultural values: Among cultures that stress individualism, individual interests guide performance; among cultures that stress collectivism, group interests guide performance.

Suggestions to Overcome Social Loafing   Obviously, the tendency for people to reduce their effort when working with others is a serious problem in organizations. Fortunately, there are several ways to overcome social loafing.

One possible antidote is to *make each performer identifiable*. Social loafing may occur when people feel they can get away with "taking it easy"—namely, when each individual's contributions cannot be determined. Various studies on the practice of *public posting* support this idea.[45] In other words, when each individual's contribution to a task is displayed for others to see (e.g., weekly sales figures posted on a chart), people are less likely to slack off than when only the overall group (or company-wide) performance is made available. The more one's individual contribution to a group effort is highlighted, the more pressure each person feels to contribute. Thus, social loafing can be overcome if one's contributions to an additive task are identified, because people are not likely to loaf if they fear getting caught.

Another way to overcome social loafing is to *make work tasks more important and interesting*. People are unlikely to go along for a free ride when the task is believed to be vital to the organization.[46] For example, the less meaningful salespeople believe their jobs are, the more they engage in social loafing—especially when they think their supervisors know little about how hard they are working.[47] To help in this regard, corporate officials should make jobs more intrinsically interesting to employees. To the extent that jobs are interesting, people may be less likely to loaf.

In addition, managers can *reward individuals for contributing to their group's performance*—that is, encourage their interest in their group's performance.[48] Doing this, such as by giving all salespeople in a territory a bonus if they jointly exceed their sales goal, may help employees to focus more on collective concerns and less on individualistic concerns, thus increasing their obligations to fellow group members. This is important, because the collective efforts of groups are more likely than the individual contributions of any one member to influence the success of an organization.

Another mechanism for overcoming social loafing is to *use punishment threats*. To the extent that performance decrements may be controlled by threats to punish the individuals slacking off, loafing may be reduced. This effect was demonstrated in a experiment involving members of high-school swim teams who swam either alone or in relay races during practice sessions.[49] In one group, the coach threatened the team, saying that everyone would have to swim "penalty laps" if anyone failed to meet a specified, difficult time for swimming 100 yards freestyle. In a control group, no threats were issued. How did the punishment threats influence task performance? The researchers found that people swam faster alone than as part of relay teams when no punishment was threatened, thereby confirming the social loafing effect. When such threats were made, however, group performance increased, thereby eliminating the social loafing effect.

These findings suggest that social loafing is a potent force—and a serious threat to organizational performance. It can be controlled, however, in several ways that counteract the desire to loaf, such as by making loafing socially embarrassing or harmful to other individual interests.

TEAMS: SPECIAL KINDS OF GROUPS

Now that you understand groups and how they operate, we can compare them to another collection of individuals known as *teams*. In this section, we define teams and how they differ from groups. We then describe various types of teams in organizations. Finally, we present guidelines for creating teams in organizations.

Defining Teams and Distinguishing Them from Groups

If you think about some of the groups described thus far, such as those at Cutler-Hammer (described in our preview case) and the hypothetical budget committee (described in conjunction with the five-stage model), you quickly recognize they are each somehow different. Each is composed of several individuals working together toward common goals, but the connections between employees at Cutler-Hammer appear to be much deeper. The budget committee members may be interested in what they are doing, but the group members at Cutler-Hammer seem more highly committed to their work—and more highly involved in how their jobs are done. This is not to say anything is necessarily wrong with the corporate budget committee. In fact, it would appear to be a rather typical group. Those at Cutler-Hammer, however, are examples of special kinds of groups known as *teams*.

A **team** may be defined as *a group whose members have complementary skills and are committed to a common purpose or set of performance goals for which they hold themselves mutually accountable.*[50] At this point, it probably is not entirely clear exactly how a team

team

A group whose members have complementary skills and are committed to a common purpose or set of performance goals for which they hold themselves mutually accountable.

differs from a group. This confusion probably stems, in part, from people often referring to their groups as teams, even though they really are not.[51] There are several important distinctions between them (Figure 7.14).

First, performance in groups typically depends on the work of individual members. The performance in teams, however, depends on both individual contributions and *collective work products* — that is, the joint outcome of team members working in concert.

A second difference involves accountability for the job. Typically, group members pool their resources to attain a goal, but individual performance is taken into consideration when issuing rewards. Group members usually do not take responsibility for any results other than their own. In contrast, teams focus on both individual and *mutual accountability*. In other words, they work together to produce an outcome (e.g., product, service, decision) that represents their joint contributions, and each member shares responsibility for that outcome. The key difference is that in groups, the supervisor holds individual members accountable for their work, whereas in teams, members hold themselves accountable.

Third, group members may share a common interest goal, but team members also share a *common commitment to purpose*. Moreover, these purposes typically concern winning in some way, such as being first or best at something. For example, a work team in the manufacturing plant of a financially troubled company may be highly committed to making the company top in its industry. A team in a public high school may be committed to preparing all graduates for the outside world better than any other school in the district. Team members focus jointly on such lofty purposes, in conjunction with specific performance goals, and become heavily invested in their activities. In fact, teams are said to establish "ownership" of their purposes and usually spend much time establishing that purpose. Like groups, teams use goals to monitor their progress; however, teams also have a broader purpose, which supplies a source of meaning and emotional energy to the activities performed.

Fourth, in organizations, teams differ from groups by the nature of their connections to management. Work groups typically are required to be responsive to demands regularly placed on them by management. In contrast, once management establishes the mission for a team and the challenge for it to achieve, the team generally is given enough flexibility to do its job without further interference. In other words, to varying degrees, teams are *self-managing* — that is, to some extent, they are

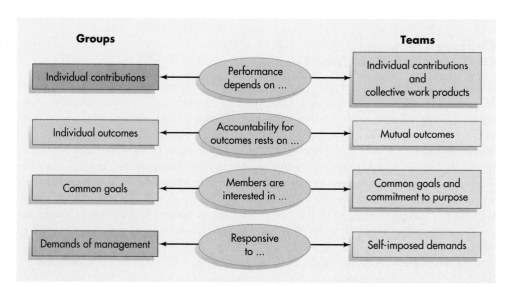

FIGURE 7.14

Groups vs. Teams: A Comparison
Groups may be distinguished from teams by the various characteristics summarized here.

free to set their own goals, timing, and approach, usually without interference by management. Thus, many teams are described as being either *autonomous* or *semiautonomous* in nature. This is not to say teams are completely independent of corporate management and supervision. They still must respond to demands from higher levels — often from higher-level teams known as *top management teams*.

Clearly, teams are special entities. Some even go beyond the characteristics of teams described here and are known as **high-performance teams**. Members of these teams are deeply committed to one another's personal growth and success.[52] Such teams are referred to as *high-performance teams*, because they tend to perform at much higher levels than ordinary teams, whose members lack this additional commitment to others' growth and success.[53] Indeed, the best-performing teams tend to have members who show exceptionally high levels of mutual care, trust, and respect for each other.

high-performance teams
Teams whose members are deeply committed to one another's personal growth and success.

ETHICS MATTERS

Some union leaders argue that teams are unfair, because they lead employees to do extra work without getting the extra pay they deserve. How do you feel about this argument? ■

Types of Teams

Considering their widespread popularity, it should not be surprising that many different kinds of teams exist. To make sense of these, scientists have categorized teams into several commonly found types, which vary along four major dimensions (Figure 7.15).[54]

Purpose or Mission The first dimension deals with a team's major *purpose* or *mission*. In this regard, some teams — known as **work teams** — are concerned primarily with work done by the parent organization, such as developing and manufacturing

work teams
Teams whose members are concerned primarily with using the parent organization's resources to create its results.

FIGURE 7.15

Types of Teams

Teams found in organizations may be distinguished from each other based on the four major dimensions identified here.

(*Source*: Based on suggestions by Mohrman, 1993; see note 54.)

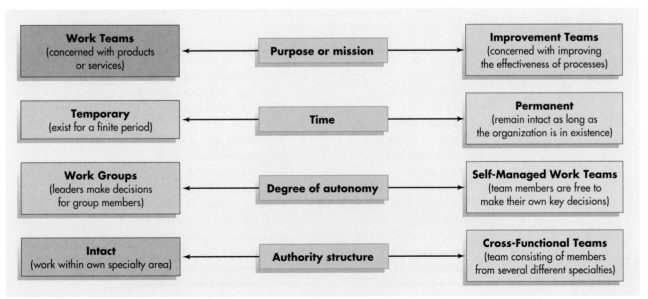

new products, providing services for customers, and so on. Their principal focus is effectively using the organization's resources to create results, be they goods or services. (The teams at Cutler-Hammer described in our preview case appear to be of this type.)

Other teams—known as **improvement teams**—are oriented primarily toward increasing the effectiveness of the processes used by the parent organization. For example, Texas Instruments has relied on teams to help improve the quality of operations at its plant in Malaysia.[55]

Time   A second dimension is *time*. Specifically, some teams are *temporary* and established for a specific project with a finite life. For example, a team created to develop a new product would be considered temporary, because once the job is done, it disbands. Other kinds of teams are *permanent* and stay intact for as long as the parent organization is operating. For example, teams focused on providing effective customer service tend to be permanent parts of many organizations.

Degree of Autonomy   A third distinction deals with the degree to which teams operate autonomously.[56] At one end are *work groups*, in which leaders make decisions on behalf of group members, whose job is to follow the leader's orders. This traditional kind of group is becoming less popular, however, as more organizations are turning to the other end of the scale, where employees are free to make their own key decisions. Such groups commonly are referred to as **self-managed teams** or as **self-directed teams**.

Typically, self-managed teams consist of small numbers of employees (often around 10) who take on duties once performed by their supervisors. These duties likely include making work assignments, deciding on the pace of work, determining how quality is to be assessed, and even deciding who joins the team.[57] A summary of the major distinctions between self-managed teams and traditional work groups is shown in Table 7.3.[58]

improvement teams
Teams whose members are oriented primarily toward increasing the effectiveness of the processes used by the parent organization.

self-managed teams
Teams whose members are permitted to make key decisions about how their work is done.

self-directed teams
See *self-managed teams.*

TABLE 7.3

**Self-Managed Teams vs. Traditional Work Groups:
A Comparison**

As summarized here, self-managed teams differ from traditional work groups in many important ways.

SELF-MANAGED TEAMS	TRADITIONAL WORK GROUPS
Customer-driven	Management-driven
Multiskilled work force	Work force of isolated specialists
Few job descriptions	Many job descriptions
Information shared widely	Information limited
Few levels of management	Many levels of management
Whole-business focus	Function/department focus
Shared goals	Segregated goals
Seemingly chaotic	Seemingly organized
Purpose achievement emphasis	Problem-solving emphasis
High worker commitment	High management commitment
Continuous improvements	Incremental improvements
Self-controlled	Management controlled
Values/principle based	Policy/procedure based

Source: From K. Fisher, *Leading Self-Directed Work Teams,* © 1993. New York: McGraw-Hill. Reprinted with permission of the McGraw-Hill Companies.

Today, self-managed work teams are widespread and still growing in popularity. In fact, it is estimated that 20 percent of U.S. companies now use them — and that this figure is well on the way to 50 percent.[59] Large corporations using such teams include Xerox, Hewlett-Packard, Honeywell, and PepsiCo. In fact, Procter & Gamble, Cummins Engine, and General Motors have used self-managed work teams for more than 30 years.[60]

Authority Structure   The fourth dimension reflects a team's connection to the organization's overall *authority structure* — that is, the connection between various formal job responsibilities. In some organizations, teams remain *intact* regarding their organizational functions. For example, at Ralston-Purina, projects are structured so that people work together on certain products all the time and do not apply their specialty to a wide range of products. Within such organizations, teams can operate without the ambiguities created by straying from one's area of expertise.

With growing frequency, however, teams are crossing over various functional units (e.g., marketing, finance, human resources, and so on). Such teams commonly are referred to as **cross-functional teams** and are composed of employees at identical organizational levels but from different specialty areas. Cross-functional teams are an effective way to bring people together from throughout the organization to co-operate on the diverse tasks needed to complete large projects. In organizations using cross-functional teams, the boundaries between all teams must be considered permeable. Indeed, people frequently are members of more than one team — a situation often required for organizations to function effectively. For example, members of an organization's manufacturing team must co-ordinate carefully their activities with members of the marketing team. To the extent that people are involved in several kinds of teams, they may gain broader perspectives and make more important contributions.

For more than a decade, many automobile manufacturers — including the major U.S. and Japanese companies — have relied on cross-functional teams to create and manufacture new models. For example, the successful Dodge Neon was created completely by cross-functional teams of experts. Similarly, Boeing created cross-functional teams to design and manufacture its latest aircraft, the Boeing 777. In both cases, use of teams has been credited with the record speed in which the products came to market — and with their exceptional quality. As you might imagine, however, cross-functional teams are difficult to manage (Figure 7.16). Specialists in different areas need time to learn how to communicate with each other and to coordinate their

cross-functional teams

Teams that include people from different specialty areas within organizations.

FIGURE 7.16

Cross-Functional Teams at BP Norge

Employees of the Norwegian arm of British Petroleum, BP Norge, have always done grueling, dangerous work on off-shore oil platforms in the North Sea. Now, however, they face a challenge of a different kind — working together in self-managed teams composed of employees representing different organizational functions. The going has not been easy — especially with people speaking languages from different professions as well as different nations — but company officials believe the cross-functional teams have been successful, leading them to consider adopting similar arrangements elsewhere in the company.

efforts. It also takes time to develop the mutual trust and acceptance required for people to work closely together. Considering the great successes of cross-functional teams, however, the effort required appears to be worthwhile.

Creating Teams in Four Stages

Assembling a team is no easy task. It requires the right combination of skilled people and also individuals who are willing to work together with others as a team. When done effectively, designing a work team is a project that involves four distinct stages.[61] Carefully following these steps is a useful way of giving teams a head start on the road to success:

Stage 1: Prework.   Before teams are actually created, a decision must be made whether a team should be formed. A manager may decide to have several individuals working alone answer to him or her or a team may be created if a manager believes it may develop the most creative and insightful ways to get things done. When considering this, it is important to note exactly what work needs to be done. The team's objectives must be established, and an inventory of the skills needed to do the job must be made. In addition, decisions should be made in advance about what authority the team will have. They may be advisory to the manager, or they may be given full responsibility and authority for executing their task (i.e., self-regulating).

Stage 2: Creating performance conditions.   Building on the prework, the organization must ensure the team has the proper resources to perform its work. This involves both material resources (e.g., tools, equipment, money), human resources (e.g., the appropriate blend of skilled professionals), and support from the organization (e.g., willingness to let the team do its own work as it sees fit). Unless managers help to create the proper conditions for team success, they are contributing to its failure.

Stage 3: Forming and building the team.   Three things can help get a team off to a good start. First, managers should form boundaries—that is, clearly establish who is and is not a member of the team. Some teams fail simply because membership is left unclear. Reducing such ambiguity can help to avoid confusion and frustration. Second, members must accept the team's overall mission and purpose. Unless they do, failure is inevitable. Third, organizational officials should clarify the team's mission and responsibilities—that is, make perfectly clear exactly what it is expected to do (but not necessarily *how* to do it). Will team members be responsible for monitoring and planning their own work? If so, such expectations should be explicit.

Stage 4: Providing ongoing assistance.   Finally, once a team is functioning, supervisors may need to help the team to eliminate problems and to perform even better. For example disruptive team members may be counseled or replaced. Similarly, material resources may be replenished or upgraded. It may be unwise for a manger to intervene in a successful team that has taken on its own life, but it also may be unwise to neglect opportunities to help a team do even better.

As you ponder these suggestions, you doubtlessly will recognize the considerable managerial skill and hard work needed to create and manage teams effectively. As managers learn these skills, however, and as individuals gain successful experiences in effective work teams, the deliberate steps outlined here may become second nature to all concerned. In the words of one expert, "When that stage is reached, the considerable investment required to learn how to use work teams well can pay substantial dividends—in work effectiveness and in the quality of the experience of both managers and [team] members."[62] ■

EFFECTIVE TEAM PERFORMANCE

Recently, the popular press has been filled with impressive claims about teams improving quality, customer service, productivity, and the bottom line.[63] For a sampling of these findings, see Table 7.4.[64]

Clearly, we have been led to believe that teams in general can produce impressive results. It is important to consider, however, whether such claims are valid. In this section, we examine evidence bearing on this question. We then focus on several obstacles to team success and some ways to help promote highly successful teams.

TABLE 7.4

A Summary of Team Success Stories

Here are just a few of the organizational successes touted in support of teams.

ORGANIZATION	RESULTS
P&G manufacturing	30–50% lower manufacturing cost.
Federal Express	Cut service glitches (incorrect bills and lost packages) by 13% in one year.
Shenandoah Life Insurance	Case handling time went from 27 to two days. Service complaints "practically eliminated."
Sherwin-Williams Richmond	Costs 45% lower. Returned goods down 75%.
Tektronix Portables	Moved from least profitable to most profitable division within two years.
Rohm and Haas Knoxville	Productivity up 60%.
Tavistock coal mine	Output 25% higher with lower costs than on a comparison face. Accidents, sickness, and absenteeism cut 50%.
Westinghouse Airdrie	Reduced cycle time from 17 weeks to one week.
AT&T Credit Corp.	Teams process 800 lease applications/day vs. 400/day under old system. Growing at 40–50% compound annual rate.
General Electric Salisbury	Productivity improved 250%.
Aid Association for Lutherans (AAL)	Raised productivity by 20% and cut case processing time by 75%.
Cummins Engine Jamestown	Met Japanese $8,000 price for an engine expected to sell for $12,000.
Xerox	Teams at least 30% more productive than conventional operations.
Best Foods Little Rock	Highest quality products at lowest costs of any Best Foods plant.
Volvo Kalmar	Production costs 25% less than Volvo's conventional plants.
Ford Hermosillo	In first year of operation, lower defect rate than in most Japanese automakers.
Weyerhauser Manitowoc	Output increased 33%. Profits doubled.
Northern Telecom Harrisburg	Profits doubled.
General Mills	Productivity 40% higher than traditional factories.
Honeywell Chandler	Output increased 280%. Quality stepped up from 82% to 99.5%.
American Transtech	Reduced costs and processing time by 50%.

Source: From K. Fisher, *Leading Self-Directed Work Teams*, © 1993. New York: McGraw-Hill. Reprinted with permission of The McGraw-Hill Companies.

How Successful Are Teams?

Questions regarding the effectiveness of teams in the workplace are difficult to answer. Not only are many different kinds of teams doing different kinds of jobs in organizations, their effectiveness is influenced by many factors that go well beyond any possible benefits from teams, such as managerial support, the economy, available resources, and the like. As a result, understanding the true effectiveness of teams is tricky at best.

This difficulty has been fueled by recent cover stories in top business periodicals touting the success of teams.[65] How much of this is hype, stemming from the latest management fad, and how much should be accepted as valid evidence for team effectiveness? Fortunately, several types of research investigations have examined this issue.[66]

Survey Evidence   One of the most direct ways of learning about experiences with work teams is to survey the officials of organizations that use them. One large-scale study did just that.[67] Their sample included several hundred of the 1,000 largest U.S. companies. Approximately 47 percent used some work teams, but these typically were in only a few selected sites, not throughout the entire organizations. Where teams were used, however, they generally were highly regarded. Fifty-three percent characterized teams as "successful" or "very successful" in 1987, but this figure grew to 60 percent only three years later. For both years, nearly all other responses fell into the "undecided" category, and "unsuccessful" or "very unsuccessful" responses occurred in only one percent of these cases each year.

Case Study Evidence   In-depth case studies of numerous teams in many different organizations further support their effectiveness.[68] Although difficult to quantify and compare across organizations, research of this type provides some interesting insights into what makes teams successful—and why.

One group of researchers, for example, analyzed the work teams used in the GM battery plant in Fitzgerald, Georgia.[69] The 320 employees at this facility operate in various teams, including managers working together in *support teams*, middle-level teams of *co-ordinators* (i.e., similar to foremen and technicians), and *employee teams* (i.e., natural work units of three to 19 members performing specific tasks). These teams work closely together and co-ordinate their activities, but they function almost as separate businesses.

Because plant employees perform many different tasks in their teams, they are not paid based on their positions but on their knowledge and competence. In fact, the highest-paid employees are those who have demonstrated their competence (usually through highly demanding tests) on all the jobs performed in at least two different teams. This is GM's way of rewarding people for broadening their perspectives—for appreciating "the other guy's problems." By many measures, the Fitzgerald plant has been very effective. Its production costs are lower than comparable units in traditionally run plants, and employee turnover is much lower than the average. Employee surveys also reveal that job satisfaction at this plant is among the highest at any GM facility.

These cases are two examples of different companies that use teams in different ways but with one thing in common—high levels of success (albeit not without some difficulties). There are many more as well.[70] Case studies paint a consistent picture of the effectiveness of teams, but such studies may not be entirely objective. After all, companies may be unwilling to broadcast their failures to the world. This is not to say case studies cannot be trusted. Indeed, when the information is gathered by outside researchers (e.g., those reported here), the stories they tell about how teams are used—and the results of using them—can be quite revealing.[71]

Experimental Evidence   Despite the appeal of case studies, they are, as mentioned, not completely objective. Thus, researchers have begun performing controlled, experimental studies of team effectiveness as well. For example, one such investigation compared various aspects of work performance and the attitudes of two groups of employees at a railroad-car repair facility in Australia.[72] One group (i.e., the autonomous work team) was assembled in which employees could decide freely how to do their jobs. A second group (i.e., the nonautonomous work team) was structured in the more traditional fashion, in which employees were told what to do.

After several months, the two groups were compared. Members of the autonomous work team had significantly fewer accidents as well as lower rates of absenteeism and turnover. Other studies have found that members of work teams in manufacturing plants are more satisfied with their jobs than those in conventional work arrangements (i.e., in which individuals take orders from a supervisor). Thus although workers may not be more productive individually, use of teams has made it possible for several supervisory positions to be eliminated, thereby making an organization more profitable.[73]

Potential Obstacles to Success

We have reported many success stories about teams, but we also have hinted at several problems and difficulties in implementing them. After all, working in a team is demanding, and not everyone may be ready. Fortunately, however, we can learn from these experiences. Analyses of failed attempts at introducing teams into the workplace suggest several avoidable obstacles to team success—if you know about them.[74]

First, some teams fail because their members are *unwilling to co-operate*. This happened a few years ago at Dow Chemical Company's plastics group in Midland, Michigan, where a team was formed to create a new plastic resin.[75] Some members (i.e., those in the research field) wanted to spend several months developing and test-

OB AROUND THE WORLD

COMPARING TEAM EFFECTIVENESS IN JAPAN, THE UNITED STATES, AND GREAT BRITAIN

When your team confronts a problem that requires you to seek advice, where are you most likely to turn: a company policy manual, informal policies, superiors, fellow teammates, or your own experience? In addition, how effective are these various alternatives? The answer to both questions may depend on the national culture of your team. After all, in individualistic cultures (e.g., the United States and Great Britain), people tend to be self-reliant, whereas in collectivistic cultures (e.g., Japan), people tend to be group-oriented. Thus, we would expect people from collectivistic cultures to consult their teammates and people from individualistic cultures to rely on their own experiences.

One recent study found just this.[76] These researchers surveyed team members in the United States, Great Britain, and Japan about the how likely certain actions would be in response to problems confronted by their teams. The findings were clear: In Japan, people were most likely to consult their fellow team members, but in the United States and Great Britain, people were most likely to rely on their own experience and training. These results suggest that national culture influences how team members operate when facing problems.

Which of these strategies, however, is most effective? To answer this question, these same researchers examined the as-

sociation between which strategies teams preferred and how productive their supervisors rated these teams as being. The results were quite interesting. In general, Japanese teams were regarded as being more productive to the extent they relied on company manuals for help. Teams in the United States and Great Britain, however, were rated as being more productive to the extent they relied on their own experiences. These findings are in keeping with the tendency for the Japanese to rely closely on formal procedures (because they represent the collective wisdom of the past) and with the tendency for more individualistic Americans and British to put their faith in their own experiences.[77]

These findings must be interpreted with caution, because they relied on supervisors' ratings of team productivity instead of on objective measures. The supervisors may have given higher ratings to teams because they adhered to culturally endorsed practices, or they may have given higher ratings because these practices really were the most effective. Unfortunately, this research does not tell us which was the case. It does, however, provide good evidence that the effectiveness of team performance likely is closely linked to cultural differences in how teams operate. Therefore, researchers interested in team effectiveness are well-advised to consider the influence of national culture in future studies.

ing new options, whereas others (i.e., those on the manufacturing end) wanted to alter existing products and begin production right away. Neither side budged, and the project eventually stalled. In contrast, when team members share a common vision and are committed to attaining it, they generally are very cooperative, which in turn leads to success.

Some teams also are not effective because they *fail to receive support from management*. For example, consider the experience at the Lenexa, Kansas, plant of the Puritan-Bennett Corporation, a manufacturer of respiratory equipment.[78] After seven years of work to develop improved software for its respirators, product development teams still had not gotten the job done—despite the industry average for such tasks being only three years. According to Roger J. Dolida, the company's director of research and development, the problem was that management never made the project a priority and, thus, refused to free another key person needed to do the job. As he put it, "If top management doesn't buy into the idea . . . teams can go nowhere."[79]

A third—and a relatively common—obstacle to success is that *some managers are unwilling to relinquish control*. Good supervisors work their way up from the plant floor by giving orders and by having those orders followed. Team leaders, however, must build consensus and allow members to make decisions together. As you might expect, letting go of control is not always easy, and this problem emerged at Bausch & Lomb's sunglasses plant in Rochester, New York.[80] In 1989, some 1,400 employees were organized into 38 teams. By 1992, about half the supervisors had not adjusted to this change, despite receiving thorough training in how to work as part of a team. These supervisors argued bitterly when their ideas were not accepted by the team and eventually were reassigned (Figure 7.17). An even tougher approach was taken at the Shelby Die Casting Company, a metal-casting firm in Shelby, Mississippi.[81] When its former supervisors refused to co-operate as equals in their teams, the company eliminated their jobs and let the workers run their own teams. The result? The company saved $250,000 in annual wages, productivity jumped 50 percent, and company profits almost doubled. The message sent by both companies is clear: Those who cannot adjust to teamwork are unwelcome.

Fourth, teams might fail because they *fail to cooperate with other teams*. This problem occurred in General Electric's medical systems division when it assigned two teams of engineers—one in Waukesha, Wisconsin, and another in Hino, Japan—the task of creating software for two new ultrasound devices.[82] These teams pushed features that made their products popular only in their own countries, and they duplicated each other's efforts. When the teams met, language and cultural barriers separated

FIGURE 7.17

Reluctance to Relinquish Control: An Important Barrier to Team Success

Bausch & Lomb met with mixed success when it introduced teams in its sunglasses plant in Rochester, New York. Here—and in many organizations—part of the problem was the reluctance of many managers to give up the control they once wielded.

them, further distancing them from each other. Without close co-operation between teams (as well as within them!), organizations are not likely to reap the benefits they hoped for when creating these teams in the first place.[83]

Building Successful Teams

As described, making teams work effectively is no easy task, and success is not automatic. Rather, teams must be cared for and maintained carefully for them to accomplish their missions. As one expert put it, "Teams are the Ferrari of work design. They're high performance but high maintenance and expensive."[84] What, then, can be done to make teams as effective as possible? Based on analyses of successful teams, we can identify several suggestions[85]:

1. *Diversify team membership.* Teams function most effectively when composed of highly skilled individuals who can bring a variety of different skills and experiences to the task at hand.[86]

GLOBAL MATTERS

Teams sometimes face unique challenges when they include people from different cultural and national groups. Recently, this has been the case within several professional sports teams, whose members come from countries around the world. Can you identify any such teams whose players failed to work well together because of cultural barriers? What has been done — or could be done — to overcome these problems? ■

2. *Keep teams small in size.* Effective teams consist of the smallest number of people needed to do the work. Coordination is difficult when teams are too large, and overload is likely when teams are too small. Generally, 10 to 12 members are ideal.[87]

3. *Select the right team members.* Some individuals enjoy working in teams, and others prefer to work alone. Thus, problems can be eliminated by not forcing loners into teams. Similarly, it is important to select team members based on their skills (or potential skills). Because the success of teams demands the members work together closely on many tasks, it is essential for them to have complementary skills. This includes not only job skills but interpersonal skills as well, especially because getting along with one's teammates is so important.

4. *Train, train, train.* For teams to function effectively, members must have all the technical skills needed for their jobs. This may involve cross-training on key aspects of others' specialty areas. It also is essential for them to be well-trained in the interpersonal skills needed to get along with each other. Given the great responsibilities team members have, they should be trained in the most effective ways to make decisions as well. With these considerations in mind, work teams at Colgate-Palmolive Company's liquid-detergents plant in Cambridge, Ohio, initially receive 120 hours of training in skills such as quality management, problem solving, and team interaction, and they subsequently receive advanced training in these areas, too.

5. *Clarify goals.* When team members have a well-defined mission, they are likely to pull in the same direction and attempt to reach the same goals. Therefore, team goals must be articulated clearly.

6. *Link individual rewards to team performance.* To the extent team members are rewarded for the group's success by getting to share in the financial rewards, they are likely to be highly committed to striving for success.

7. *Use appropriate performance measures.* Teams work best when they develop their own measures of success. Furthermore, these measures should be based on processes rather than on outcomes. For example, instead of

measuring profitability, which is a traditional measure of success, a manufacturing team may concentrate on measures with diagnostic value, such as the average time per service call or the number of late service calls. After all, team members who are aware of these indices may be able to do something about them.

8. *Promote trust.* For teams to operate successfully, members must trust each other to support their mutual interests. People can demonstrate trustworthiness by showing they are concerned for the welfare of the team and all its members.

9. *Encourage participation.* The more team members participate in making decisions, the more likely they are to feel committed to those decisions. Thus, for teams to be committed to their work, all team members must be involved.

10. *Cultivate team spirit and social support.* Teams work most effectively with a "can-do" attitude — that is, when they believe they can succeed. This often is encouraged when team members lend interpersonal and task support to their teammates, but support also must come from top management. To the extent team members suspect management is not fully behind them, they will be unlikely to dedicate themselves to the task at hand.

11. *Foster communication and cooperation.* Naturally, team members must communicate and cooperate with each other so they can coordinate their efforts toward the common goal. At the same time, however, they must communicate and cooperate with other teams as well. Doing so fosters the overall success of the parent organization.

GLOBAL MATTERS   Team leaders from different countries likely take different approaches when communicating with team members. For example, Americans are accustomed to being blunt, but Japanese are accustomed to reaching consensus in a harmonious fashion. Can you identify additional examples of national differences in communication styles within teams? ■

12. *Emphasize the urgency of the team's task.* Team members bend to rally around challenges that compel them to meet high performance standards. For example, several years ago, employees at Ampex Corporation, a manufacturer of professional-quality videotape equipment for broadcast, worked hard to make their teams successful when they recognized the changes necessitated by shifting from analog to digital technology. Unless the company met these challenges, the plug surely would be pulled. Realizing the company's future was at stake, work teams fast-forwarded Ampex into a position of prominence in the industry.

13. *Clarify the rules of behavior.* Effective teams have clear rules about what behaviors are — and are not — expected. For example, at Texas Instruments' Defense System and Electronics Group, rules about good attendance, giving only constructive criticism, and maintaining confidentiality are followed carefully.

14. *Regularly confront teams with new facts.* Fresh approaches are likely to be prompted by fresh information, and introducing new facts may present the challenges teams need to stay innovative. For example, when information about pending cutbacks in defense spending was introduced to teams at Florida's Harris Corporation, an electronics manufacturer, new technologies were developed that positioned the company to land large contracts in nonmilitary government organizations — including a $1.7 billion contract to upgrade the FAA's air traffic control system.

15. *Acknowledge and reward vital contributions to the team.* As indicated in chapter 2, rewarding desired behavior is a way of ensuring that behavior is repeated in the future. Rewards do not have to be large to work, either. For

Officials of a large manufacturing company are concerned about stagnant productivity during the past year. To remedy this situation, they are considering the use of self-managed teams. You have been asked to give your advice on this matter.

1. Do you agree that teams would be effective in this situation? Why, or why not?

2. What potential problems would be associated with the move to teams, and how might these be overcome?

3. If you think teams would work, what advice would you give to help the teams work as effectively as possible?

example, members of Kodak's Team Zebra, its black-and-white film-manufacturing group, are given dinner certificates when they are singled out for making special contributions.[88]

After reading this list, if you are thinking it is no easy matter to make teams work effectively, you have reached the same conclusion as countless practicing managers. Indeed, you do not form teams and then just sit back and watch the amazing results. Teams can be very useful tools, but using them effectively requires work. It also is important to caution that although these suggestions are important, they will not ensure the success of work teams. Many other factors such as the economy, competitors, and the company's financial picture, are important determinants of organizational success as well. In view of the considerable gains found to occur, however, the effort is worth making.

We invite you to visit the Greenberg page on the Prentice Hall Web site at: **www.prenhall.com/greenberg** for the monthly Greenberg update and for this chapter's World Wide Web exercise.

SUMMARY AND REVIEW OF LEARNING OBJECTIVES

1. **Define the term *group*, and explain how this differs from a collection of people.**
   A **group** is a special collection of people that meets certain defining criteria: There must be two or more interacting individuals, with a stable pattern of relationships between them, who share common goals and perceive themselves as being a group.

2. **Identify different types of groups operating within organizations as well as how they develop.**

Within organizations are two major classes of groups: **formal groups**, which include **command groups** and **task groups**; and **informal groups**, which include **interest groups** and **friendship groups**. According to the **five-stage model**, groups develop through five stages: *forming, storming, norming, performing,* and *adjourning.* According to the **punctuated-equilibrium model**, group activity is stable until the midpoint of its time is reached. A flurry of activity then begins and lasts until the group reaches its deadline.

3. **Describe the importance of *roles, norms, status,* and *cohesiveness* within organizations.**

   The structure of groups is determined by four key factors: *roles*, or the typical pattern of behavior in a social context; *norms*, or generally agreed-on, informal rules; *status*, or the prestige accorded group members; and *cohesiveness*, or the pressures faced by members to remain in their groups.

4. **Explain how individual performance in groups is affected by the presence of others (*social facilitation*), the cultural diversity of group membership, and the number of others with whom one works (*social loafing*).**

   Individual productivity is influenced by the presence of other group members. Sometimes a person's performance improves in the presence of others (i.e., when the job they are doing is well-learned), and sometimes performance declines in the presence of others (i.e., when the job is novel). This is known as **social facilitation**. Not only is performance influenced by the presence of others but by the group's racial and ethnic diversity as well. Performance in diverse groups initially is worse than in homogeneous groups, but these differences disappear through members' repeated involvement with the group. On *additive tasks* (i.e., ones in which each member's individual contributions are combined), **social loafing** occurs. According to this phenomenon, the more people who work on a task, the less each group member contributes to it.

5. **Explain what *teams* are, and distinguish them from groups in general.**

   Teams are special kinds of groups whose members focus on collective rather than on individual work products, are mutually accountable to each other, share a common commitment to purpose, and usually are self-managing.

6. **Describe the types of teams that exist in organizations and the steps that should be followed in creating them.**

   Teams differ in several dimensions: their purpose or mission (**work teams** vs. **improvement teams**), time (*temporary teams* vs. *permanent teams*), degree of autonomy (*work groups* vs. **self-managed teams**) and authority structure (*intact teams* vs. **cross-functional teams**). Creating teams involves several basic steps: prework, creating performance conditions, forming and building a team, and providing ongoing assistance.

7. **Summarize the evidence regarding the effectiveness of teams in organizations.**

   In *surveys*, organizational officials report teams operating in their organizations mostly have been successful. Comprehensive *case studies* also find organizational productivity gains (e.g., increased outcome, improved quality, lowered costs) resulting from the use of teams. More objective *experimental research*, however, finds that although employees generally are more satisfied working in teams than under traditional management, they tend to be no more productive at the individual level.

8. **Explain the factors responsible for the failure of some teams to operate as effectively as possible.**

   Despite the evidence of team successes, some teams do fail. This often is because team members are unwilling to co-operate with each other, fail to receive support from management, managers are unwilling to relinquish control, and members fail to co-ordinate their efforts with other teams.

9. **Identify how successful teams can be built.**

With some effort, teams can yield exceptionally high levels of performance. To build successful teams, it helps to do the following: diversify team membership, keep teams small in size, select the right members, train members, clarify goals, link individual rewards to team performance, use appropriate performance measures, promote trust, encourage participation, cultivate team spirit and social support, foster communication and co-operation, emphasize the urgency of the task, clarify the rules of behavior, regularly confront teams with new facts, and acknowledge as well as reward vital contributions to the team.

QUESTIONS FOR DISCUSSION

1. Imagine you are waiting in line with several other people to see a movie. Would you say these people comprise a *group* in the strict sense of the term? Why, or why not?

2. Think of a group in which you have worked. How do the *five-stage model* and the *punctuated-equilibrium model* apply to this experience?

3. How do *norms*, *roles*, and *status* operate within any groups to which you belong? Give at least one example of each.

4. Imagine you are about to go on stage to perform a solo piano recital. How would *social facilitation* affect your performance?

5. Describe an incident of *social loafing* in which you may have been involved (e.g., a class project). What might be done to overcome this effect?

6. What makes a team a special form of group? Is a baseball team really a team, or is it just a group?

7. Based on evidence regarding the effectiveness of teams, would you say today's popularity of teams is well-founded?

8. Suppose you need to compose a work team in your organization. What potential pitfalls would you expect? What would you do to help the team perform at high levels?

Case in Point

SEI Investments: Where Total Teamwork Rules

SEI Investments of Oaks, Pennsylvania, administers $121 billion in assets and handles back-office operations for the trust departments of nearly half the largest banks in the United States. It also sells investment advice to wealthy individuals. Despite what you might think about the starched-collar formality of high finance, SEI does not fit this stereotype. In fact, it does not even come close. The people who work at SEI do not wear suits; they do not have secretaries or even offices.

What they do have is self-managed work teams—approximately 140 of them. In fact, teams are the only unit of operation at SEI. If you're looking for some hierarchy reflected in an organizational chart, forget it. All work is divided among various teams that range in size from two to 30 people. Some teams are permanent, serving important clients or major markets. Others are temporary, however, composed of people coming together as needed to do a job or solve a problem. When finished, those teams disband. According to Al West, SEI's

(continued)

chairman and CEO (titles he holds for legal reasons), "People figure out what they're good at, and that shapes what their roles are. There's not one leader. Different people lead during different parts of the process."

To keep things fluid, there are no walls in SEI's facility. Desks are on wheels, thus allowing them to be repositioned as needed to serve team members. In fact, access to electricity, phone lines, and the Internet is through colorful cables that dangle from the ceiling so that physical barriers cannot keep team members from accessing the resources needed for their work.

In keeping with this ready physical access to others is an absence of the power differences that separate people in traditional organizations. If you want something done at SEI, you must persuade someone to join your team—and if you have a good project idea and can sell others on it, they flock to your team. (Have a poor idea, and it probably will die from lack of support.) For those who thrive on the traditional structure of the investment world, SEI is no place to work. Not surprisingly, the company searches very carefully for new recruits who are receptive to its highly fluid culture. Without a bureaucracy to provide resources or an hierarchy to issue commands, life at SEI is not for everybody.

The numbers, however, suggest that SEI is doing just fine, thank you. In fact, its 1997 revenues—some $300 million—were up more than 30 percent from 1994, and its profits have risen even more. In 1998, shares of SEI traded for as high as $54—up from a low of $18 just a year before. CEO Al West revels in this shining economic picture as well as in how people work at SEI. Compared to the 1980s, when the company operated more like a traditional investment firm, he describes his current job as being "a lot more fun."

CRITICAL THINKING QUESTIONS

1. What kinds of groups or teams are used at SEI?
2. How would you characterize the nature of role differentiation at SEI?
3. Do you think the complete use of self-managed teams as seen at SEI would work as effectively in other kinds of companies? In what kinds of organizations would it be effective? In what kinds of organizations would it be ineffective?
4. What challenges do you think Mr. West faced as he dismantled SEI's traditional organizational structure to pave the way for self-managed work teams?
5. Would you like to work for a company that relies exclusively on self-managed work teams? Why, or why not?

VIDEO CASE

Group Dynamics and Teamwork

People generally do things—at least, important things—for a reason. They may be motivated by something they believe in, by a perceived opportunity, or by a particular need. Whatever the case, we tend to make significant personal investments in the things in which we believe. Jim Morris and the employees of the Jim Morris Environmental T-Shirt Company are people on a mission. They all earn a living, and the company seems to be profitable. Running a good business, however, does not seem to be the only thing that makes these people tick. Something else is going on in this company, too.

Morris trained academically as a mathematician, but when it came to earning a living, he turned to something else. Morris is passionate and committed to doing his part to preserve our natural environment and to protect the animals that live in it. Interestingly, he has used his talents and interests to provide a comfortable workplace for himself and others.

At first glance, you might think this company evolved totally around Morris and his commitment to protecting the environment. On closer observation, however, we find a company made of several individuals, all of whom share some common interests. Everyone at the company is not exactly like Morris, but in his or her own way, each is concerned about the environment.

As you watch this video segment, you will see how a personal interest turned into a job for one man—and eventually into a company. You will see many automated processes within the company, but there is more to it than just Morris and a bunch of machines and computers. Morris employs about 20 people. Some work together, and some work in departments of one. Pay attention to how individuals interact, how they feel about the company, and how Morris, the company's founder, talks about his staff.

QUESTIONS FOR DISCUSSION

1. From what you have learned about Jim Morris, identify a group outside his company to which you think he belongs. Support your answer with information from the video segment and your knowledge of groups.

2. Identify some teams that you believe exist within the Jim Morris Environmental T-Shirt Company. Considering what you have learned about the dimensions of teams (i.e., mission, autonomy, time, and structure), select a team and then briefly analyze it along these dimensions.

3. The people who work at the Jim Morris Environmental T-Shirt Company obviously share many ideals and values. This is a good step toward establishing a good working team. If you were a consultant to Morris, what might you suggest he pay attention to so he can retain a strong and efficient team?

EXPERIENCING ORGANIZATIONAL BEHAVIOR

Are You a Team Player?

Let's face it: Some people find it easier to work in teams than others. Are you a "team player," or have you not yet developed the skills needed to work effectively with others in teams? Knowing where you stand along this dimension may be helpful when considering a new job or planning your next work assignment. The following questionnaire provides insight into this question.

Directions

1. Read each of the following statements, and carefully consider whether it accurately describes you on the job (most of the time).

2. On the line next to each statement, write "Yes" if the statement describes you most of the time or "No" if it does not. If you are uncertain, write a question mark ("?").

3. Do your best to respond to all items as honestly as possible.

Most of the time, on the job, I . . .

_____ 1. Demonstrate high ethical standards.

_____ 2. Deliver on promises I make.

_____ 3. Take the initiative, doing what is needed without being told.

_____ 4. Follow the norms and standards of the groups in which I work.

_____ 5. Put team goals ahead of my own.

_____ 6. Accurately describe my team to others in the organization.

_____ 7. Pitch in to help others learn new skills.

_____ 8. Do at least my share of the work.

_____ 9. Coordinate the work I do with others.

_____ 10. Try to attend all meetings and to arrive on time.

_____ 11. Come to meetings prepared to participate.

_____ 12. Stay focused on the agenda during meetings.

_____ 13. Share with others new knowledge I may have about the job.

_____ 14. Encourage others to raise questions about how things are.

_____ 15. Affirm positive things about others' ideas before noting any concerns.

_____ 16. Listen to others without interrupting.

_____ 17. Ask questions to make certain I understand others.

_____ 18. Make sure I attend to a speaker's nonverbal messages.

_____ 19. Praise others who have performed well.

_____ 20. Give constructive, nonjudgmental feedback.

_____ 21. Receive constructive feedback without acting defensively.

_____ 22. Communicate ideas without threats or ridicule.

_____ 23. Explain the reasoning behind my opinions.

_____ 24. Demonstrate my willingness to change my opinions.

_____ 25. Speak up when I disagree with others.

_____ 26. Show disagreement in a tactful, polite manner.

_____ 27. Discuss possible areas of agreement when I am in conflict with others.

(*Source*: Based on material appearing in McDermott et al., 1998; see note 89.)

Scoring

1. Count the number of times you responded "Yes."
2. Count the number of times you responded "No."
3. Add these two numbers together.
4. To compute your *team player score*, divide the number of times you said "Yes" (step 1) by the total (step 3). Then multiply by 100. Your score will be between 0 and 100. Higher scores reflect greater readiness for working in teams.

Questions for Discussion

1. What was your score, and how did it compare with those of others in your class?
2. What underlying criteria for team success are assessed by this questionnaire?
3. What does this questionnaire reveal about the ways you are best equipped to work in teams?
4. What does this questionnaire reveal about the ways you are most deficient when it comes to working in teams? How could you improve your readiness for working in teams?

WORKING IN GROUPS

Demonstrating the Social Loafing Effect

The social loafing effect is quite strong, and it is likely to occur in many different situations in which people make individual contributions to an additive group task. This exercise demonstrates the effect in your own class.

Directions

1. Divide the class into groups of different sizes. Between five and 10 people should work alone as well. In addition, there should be a group of two, a group of three, a group of four, and so on, until all class members have been assigned to a group. (If the class is small, assign students to groups of vastly different sizes, such as two, seven, and 15.) Form the groups by putting together at tables people from the same group.

2. Each person should be given a page or two from a telephone directory and a stack of index cards. Then have the individuals and the members of each group perform the same additive task — copying entries from the telephone directory onto the index cards. Allow exactly 10 minutes for this task, and encourage everyone to work as hard as they can.

3. When the time is up, count the number of entries copied.

4. For each group and all the individuals, compute the average per-person performance by dividing the total number of entries copied by the number of people in the group.

5. The instructor should graph the results. Along the vertical axis, show the average number of entries copied per person. Along the horizontal axis, show the size of the work groups (i.e., one, two, three, four, and so on). The graph should look like the one in Figure 7.12.

Questions for Discussion

1. Was the social loafing effect demonstrated? What is the basis for this conclusion?

2. If the social loafing effect was not found, why do you think it was not? Could your familiarity with the effect have led you to avoid it? Test this possibility by replicating the exercise using people who do not know about the phenomenon (e.g., another class), and then compare the results.

3. Did members of smaller groups feel more responsible for their group's performance than members of larger groups?

4. How could any "free riding" that may have occurred in this demonstration be countered?

8

COMMUNICATION IN ORGANIZATIONS

LEARNING OBJECTIVES

After reading this chapter, you should be able to

1. Describe the process of communication and its role in organizations.
2. Identify forms of verbal media used in organizations, and explain which are most appropriate for communicating messages of which type.
3. Explain how style of dress and use of time and space are part of nonverbal communication in organizations.
4. Describe individual differences regarding how people communicate.
5. Describe the formal forces responsible for communication in organizations.
6. Describe how informal networks influence communication in organizations.
7. Explain how people can improve the effectiveness of their communication in organizations through clear and simple language, being an active listener, gauging the flow of communication, and giving as well as receiving feedback appropriately.
8. Describe how you can become a supportive communicator and can use technology to become a more efficient communicator.

PREVIEW CASE

What's Going on at Digital?

Although you surely know Compaq Computers, you may have only a passing familiarity with Digital, a subsidiary that Compaq purchased in the summer of 1998. When the upstart Compaq jumped into the personal computer (PC) business during the 1980s to beat the giant IBM at its own game, Digital already was a major player in the business. Its expertise was not in making PCs, however, but in making mainframes and networking products for large businesses. In fact, around the time Compaq was founded Digital already was enjoying major success from Ethernet — the popular local-area network that still connects office computers to this day. Ironically, over the years, these same networks have caused the company serious problems.

On one occasion, an uproar resulted when it became unclear who was next in line to run the company. Everyone believed that Jack Shields, who was then senior vice president, was the heir apparent, but eyebrows rose when president Kenneth Olsen held a "state of the company" meeting in which Shields was conspicuously absent. Curiosity was fueled when Olsen failed to answer questions about Shields' whereabouts in a straightforward manner. The flames were fanned still further when an organizational chart showing new U.S. operations failed to include a box for Shields.

In no time, the story spilled over the company walls and was picked up by the press. With no official announcement in hand, Digital officials denied the rumors. That probably would have put the matter to rest, but a careless TV reporter misread the wire story denying Shields' departure and, instead, aired a story reporting that Shields had, in fact, resigned. Hearing the news on TV, stunned Digital officials repeated this inaccurate story on their own in-house electronic bulletin board. Soon, word reached Wall Street, where the price of Digital stock began dropping.

It was not until Shields set things straight with the press that the matter finally ended. The truth could not have been more simple: Shields had missed the meeting because he was attending another meeting. His absence from the organizational chart was equally innocent as well: The chart didn't go up quite high enough to reach the level of the executive committee, where he held a seat.

Remarkably, this was not the only incident in which Digital suffered from free-floating information. Before its acquisition by Compaq, Digital sold the jewel of its crown — the Network Products unit — to Cabletron Systems. As word got out that Digital was shopping for a buyer, however, many of its top engineers left the company rather than face the uncertainty of a new firm. Any high-tech company's greatest asset is its people, so the Network Products division became less valuable, thus allowing Cabletron to strike a better deal. Before Digital employees could be reassured of their place in the new company — now known as Digital Networks Products Group: A Cabletron Company — the damage had been done.

The more you think about Digital, the more you probably agree that if any one factor is responsible for that company's major accomplishments and problems, it would have to be *communication*. For example, information communicated about the future of the PC business led Digital to ignore that route in favor of mainframes and networking products. Engineers who developed Ethernet systems had to communicate carefully with each other about the technical details that made their project successful. Innocent misunderstandings regarding the whereabouts of one Digital executive sent the stock price downward, and premature leaks about the sale of a unit led talented engineers to leave their jobs, thus lowering the company's value. Each of these situations has its roots in communication, which is the focus of this chapter.

Not surprisingly, experts consider communication to be a key process underlying all aspects of organizational operations.[1] Contemporary scholars variously refer to organizational communication as "the social glue . . . that continues to keep the organization tied together"[2] and as "the essence of organization."[3] Writing many years ago, the well-known management theorist and former New Jersey Bell Telephone president Chester Barnard said, "The structure, extensiveness and scope of the organization are almost entirely determined by communication techniques."[4] This strong statement makes sense considering that supervisors spend as much as 80 percent of their time engaged in some form of communication, such as speaking or listening to others or writing to and reading material from others (Figure 8.1).[5]

FIGURE 8.1

Communication: An Essential Process in Organizations

The basic functioning of organizations depends on the process of communication. Without communication, organizations cannot exist.

messages don't have to be verbal.

Given the importance of communication in organizations, we closely examine the process in this chapter. First, we define the process of communication and characterize its role in organizations. We then describe the two basic forms of communication: verbal, and nonverbal. Next, recognizing that people do not always communicate in the same fashion, we examine several key individual differences regarding communication—differences in personal style, sex differences, and cross-cultural differences. We then distinguish between two major types of communication in which we all engage: formal communication, and informal communication. We conclude this chapter with a series of concrete suggestions for becoming a better communicator. After all, learning the importance of organizational communication makes you appreciate the importance of developing your own communication skills.

COMMUNICATION: ITS BASIC NATURE

Before we can appreciate fully the process of organizational communication, we must address some basic issues. To begin, we formally define *communication*, and then we elaborate on the process by which it occurs. Following this, we describe the important role of communication in organizations.

Communication: A Working Definition and Description of the Process

What do the following situations have in common? The district manager posts a notice that smoking is prohibited on company property. An executive prepares a report about the financial status of a prospect for a corporate takeover. A taxi dispatcher directs Cab 54 to pick up a fare at 1065 Cherry Drive. A foreman smiles at a subordinate and pats him on the back in recognition of a job well done. The answer? Each incident involves some form of communication. You probably have a good idea of what communication entails already, but we can understand communication in organizations better by defining it precisely and then describing the nature of the process itself.

We define **communication** as the process by which a person, group, or organization (i.e., the *sender*) transmits some type of information (i.e., the *message*) to another person, group, or organization (i.e., the *receiver*). To clarify this definition and elaborate on how the process works, we present a summary in Figure 8.2. It may be helpful to follow along with this diagram as we review the various steps.

communication

The process by which a person, group, or organization (i.e., the *sender*) transmits some type of information (i.e., the *message*) to another person, group, or organization (i.e., the *receiver*).

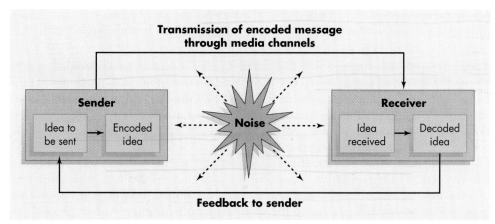

FIGURE 8.2

The Communication Process

Communication generally follows the steps outlined here. Senders *encode* messages and *transmit* them via one or more communication channels to *receivers*, who then *decode* these messages. The process continues as the original receiver sends *feedback* to the original sender. Factors distorting or limiting the flow of information, which are known collectively as *noise*, may enter into the process at any point.

Encoding   The communication process begins when one party has an idea it wishes to transmit to another. (Either party may be an individual, a group, or an entire organization.) The sender's mission is to shape the idea into a form that can be sent to and understood by the receiver. This is the process of **encoding**—i.e., translating an idea into a form (e.g., written or spoken language) that can be recognized by a receiver. We encode information when we select the words used to write a letter or to speak with someone in person. This process is critical to communicating our ideas clearly. Unfortunately, however, people are far from perfect when it comes to encoding their ideas (although this skill can be improved).

> **encoding**
> The process by which an idea is transformed so that it can be transmitted to and recognized by a receiver (e.g., a written or spoken message).

Channels of Communication   An encoded message is ready to be transmitted over one or more **channels of communication**—that is, the pathways along which information travels—to reach the desired receiver. Telephone lines, radio and television signals, fiberoptic cables, mail routes, and even the air waves carrying the vibrations of our voices all represent potential channels of communication. Of course, the form of encoding used largely determines how information is transmitted. Visual information such as pictures and written words may be mailed, delivered in person by a courier, shipped by an express delivery service, or sent electronically (e.g., via modems, fax machines, and satellite dishes). Oral information may be transmitted over the telephone, via radio and television waves, and in person. Whatever channel is used, however, the goal is the same: to send the encoded message accurately to a desired receiver.

> **channels of communication**
> The pathways over which messages are transmitted (e.g., telephone lines, mail, and so on).

Decoding   Once a message is received, the recipient begins the process of **decoding**—that is, of converting the message back into the sender's original ideas. This can involve many different subprocesses, such as comprehending spoken and written words, interpreting facial expressions, and so on. To the extent the receiver accurately decodes the sender's message, the ideas understood by the receiver will be the ones the sender intended. Of course, our ability to comprehend and to interpret information received from others may be imperfect (e.g., restricted by unclear messages or by our own language skills). Thus, as with encoding, limitations in our ability to decode information represent another potential weakness in the communication process (although this skill can be improved as well).

> **decoding**
> The process by which a receiver transforms a message back into the sender's ideas.

Feedback   Once a message is decoded, the receiver can transmit a new message back to the original sender. This is known as **feedback**—that is, knowledge about the effect of messages on receivers. Receiving feedback allows senders to determine whether their messages have been understood properly. At the same time, feedback can help to convince a receiver that the sender really cares about what he or she has to say, because once received, feedback can trigger another idea from the sender, thus

> **feedback**
> Knowledge about the effect of messages on receivers.

beginning another cycle of transferring information. For this reason, we characterize the process of communication summarized in Figure 8.2 as being continuous.

Noise   Despite the apparent simplicity of the communication process, it rarely operates as flawlessly as we describe. There are many potential barriers to effective communication, and the name given to factors distorting the clarity of a message is **noise**. As shown in Figure 8.2, noise can occur at any point in the communication process. For example, messages that are poorly encoded (e.g., written in an unclear way) or poorly decoded (e.g., not comprehended) or channels of communication that are too full of static (e.g., receivers' attentions are diverted from the message) may reduce the effectiveness of communication. These factors as well as others (e.g., time pressure, organizational politics) may contribute to the distortion of information transmitted from one party to another—and to the complexity of the communication process. As you read this chapter, you will appreciate many of the factors that make the process of organizational communication so complex and important.

noise
Factors capable of distorting the clarity of messages.

The Fundamental Role of Communication in Organizations

When you think about people in organizations communicating with each other, what image comes to mind? A typical picture might involve one person telling another what to do. Indeed, a key purpose of organizational communication is to *direct action*— that is, to get others to behave as desired. Communication in organizations, however, often involves not only single efforts but also concerted action. Thus, for an organization to function, individuals and groups must coordinate their efforts and activities carefully.[6] The waiter must take the customer's order and pass it to the chef. The market researcher must collect information about consumer needs and share it with those in charge of manufacturing and advertising. Communication is key in these attempts at coordination. Without it, people would not know what to do, and organizations would not function effectively—if at all. In other words, another key function of communication in organizations is to *achieve co-ordinated action*.

This function is served by the systematic sharing of information. Indeed, *information*—whether data about a product's sales performance, directions to a customer's residence, or instructions on how to perform a task—is the core of all organizational activities. It would be misleading, however, to imply that communication involves only the sharing of facts and data. There is an *interpersonal* facet of organizational communication, a focus on the social relations between people, as well.[7] For example, communication also is highly involved in purposes such as *developing friendships* and *building trust and acceptance*. As you know, what you say—and how you say it—can affect profoundly the extent to which others like you. To the extent people are interested in creating a pleasant interpersonal atmosphere in the workplace, they must be highly concerned about communication.

VERBAL AND NONVERBAL COMMUNICATION: SHARING MESSAGES WITH AND WITHOUT WORDS

verbal communication
The transmission of messages using words, either written or spoken.

Because you are reading this book, we know you are familiar with **verbal communication**—that is, the process of using words to transmit and receive ideas. A face-to-face chat with a coworker, a phone call from a supplier, an e-mail message from the boss, or a memo from company headquarters are all examples of verbal communication. As no doubt you also know, however, people do not communicate only using words. People also engage in **nonverbal communication**—that is, the process of sharing messages without using words. Because both verbal and nonverbal communication occur in organizations, we describe each in this section.

nonverbal communication

The transmission of messages without the use of words (e.g., gestures, use of space).

Verbal Media in Organizations: Oral and Written Messages

When we speak of verbal media, we refer to communication involving words. These words may be transmitted orally or in written form, but both play important roles in organizations.

Richness of Information   Verbal media can be distinguished by their capacity to convey information (Figure 8.3).[8] Some verbal media, such as *face-to-face discussions*, are considered to be especially *rich*, because they provide vast amounts of information, are highly personal in nature, and provide opportunities for immediate feedback. A bit less rich are non–face-to-face interactive media, such as the *telephone*. Not all business communication requires a two-way flow of information, however. For example, toward the *lean* end of the continuum are personal yet static media, such as *memos* (i.e., written messages used for internal communication) and *letters* (i.e., written messages used for external communication).[9] This includes one-way communications sent either physically (e.g., by letter), or electronically (e.g., by fax or e-mail). Finally, at the leanest end of the continuum are highly impersonal and static media, such as *flyers* and *bulletins*. This written information is targeted broadly; it is not aimed at one specific individual.

Two types of written media deserve special mention because of their important role in organizations: *newsletters*, and *employee handbooks*. Although impersonal and aimed at a general audience, **newsletters** serve important functions. They are regularly published, internal documents describing information of interest to employees regarding an array of business and nonbusiness issues.[10] Approximately one-third of all companies rely on newsletters, typically to supplement other means of communicating important information (e.g., group meetings).[11]

Another important internal publication is the **employee handbook**, which is a document that describes basic information about the company. It is a general

newsletters

Regularly published internal documents describing information of interest to employees regarding business and nonbusiness issues affecting them.

employee handbook

A document that describes basic information about a company; a general reference regarding a company's background, the nature of its business, and its rules.

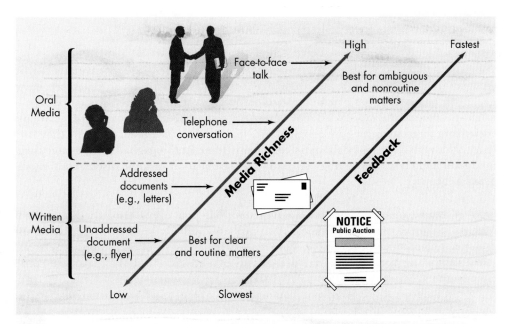

F I G U R E   8 . 3

The Continuum of Verbal Communication Media

Verbal communication media may be characterized along a continuum, ranging from highly rich, interactive media such as face-to-face discussions to lean, static media such as bulletins.

(*Source*: Based on material in Lengel & Daft, 1988; see note 8.)

reference for the company's background, the nature of its business, and its rules.[12] Specifically, the major purposes of an employee handbook are:[13]

1. To explain key aspects of the company's policies.
2. To clarify the expectations of the company and employees toward each other.
3. To express the company's philosophy.

Handbooks are more popular today than ever before. Clarifying company policies may help to prevent lawsuits, and corporate officials also are recognizing that explicitly stating what their company stands for is useful both in socializing new employees and in promoting the company's values.

Matching the Medium to the Message   In general, *communication is most effective when it uses multiple channels, such as both oral and written messages.*[14] Oral messages get people's immediate attention, and a follow-up written portion makes the message more permanent—something that can be referred to in the future. Oral messages also allow for immediate two-way communication, whereas written messages frequently are only one-way or take too long for a response.

Not surprisingly, two-way communications (e.g., face-to-face discussions, telephone conversations) are more common than one-way communications (e.g., memos) in organizations. For example, in a study of civilian U.S. Navy employees, approximately 83 percent of the communications used two-way media.[15] In fact, 55 percent of communications were individual, face-to-face interactions. One-way written communications tended to be reserved for more formal, official messages that might need to be referred to in the future (e.g., official announcements about position openings). Apparently, both written and spoken communications have their place in organizational communication.

A medium's effectiveness depends on how appropriate it is for the message being sent. Specifically, oral media (e.g., telephone conversation, face-to-face meetings) are more effective than written media (e.g., notes, memos) when messages are ambiguous—that is, when people require a great deal of assistance in interpreting them). Written media, however, are more effective when messages are clear.[16] Not surprisingly, managers who match the communications media they use to the message they send are considered to perform their jobs more effectively than those who are not as "media-sensitive."

Nonverbal Communication: Dress, Time, and Space

As you surely know from experience, many of the messages we share with others come from nonverbal cues as well. For example, gestures, distance, and eye contact speak volumes about our relationship with others. As you might imagine, however, precisely *what* these nonverbal cues communicate often varies between countries (Figure 8.4).[17] Even so, some of the most prevalent nonverbal communication cues in organizations come from three sources: how people dress, the way they use time, and how they use space. Nonverbal cues may communicate many different things, but one message they send loud and clear is with one's status in an organization (a topic discussed in more detail in chapter 7).

Style of Dress: Communicating by Appearance   If you ever heard the expression "clothes make the man (or woman)," you probably already know the importance of dress as a communication vehicle. This is especially true in organizations where, as self-styled "wardrobe engineer" John T. Malloy reminds us, the clothing we wear communicates a great deal about ourselves as employees.[18]

Precisely what our wardrobe communicates about us, however, may not be as simple as any "dress for success" guide suggests. We cannot make up for the lack of critical job skills simply by donning the "right" clothing, but qualified people com-

know this chart

When a person from the United States does this	it means . . .	BUT	When the same thing is done by a person from	it means . . .
stands close to another while talking	the speaker is considered pushy		Italy	the speaker is behaving normally
looks away from another	the speaker is shy		Japan	the speaker is showing deference to authority
extends the palm of her hand	the person is extending a greeting, such as a handshake		Greece	the person is being insulted
joins the index finger and thumb to form an "O"	"okay"		Tunisia	"I'll kill you"

FIGURE 8.4

Beware of Nonverbal Miscommunication in Different Countries

Successfully conducting business in another country involves learning that country's spoken language as well as nonverbal mannerisms. As suggested here, even the best-intentioned communicators can unwittingly send the wrong message — some of which can be quite serious.

(*Source*: Based on information in Barnum & Wolniansky, 1989; see note 17.)

municate certain things about themselves by how they dress. For example, women working in a variety of different jobs dress in intentionally different ways to differentiate their status in an organization.[19] Generally speaking, higher status people are less likely to dress in a casual fashion.

This trend is rapidly changing, however. In fact, the style of dress today is more likely than ever to be *business casual* (Figure 8.5). One recent survey revealed that casual dress is the standard at more than one-third of the fastest-growing privately held U.S. companies.[20] Moreover, shedding the pinstriped suit, starched white shirt, and "power" tie — long considered to be the uniform of choice among business leaders — and donning more comfortable business clothing appears to be a worldwide trend.[21] No objective evidence suggests that employees are any more or less productive in standard business attire than in more casual dress, but the trend toward casualization clearly is regarded highly by employees (not to mention the manufacturers of casual clothing) who take it as sign of the organization's interest in treating its employees well.[22]

Time: The Waiting Game   Another important mechanism of nonverbal communication in organizations is the use of time. Have you ever waited in the outer office of a doctor or a dentist? Surely you have — after all, there are special "waiting rooms" just for this purpose! Why do you need to wait for such people? Mainly because they have special skills that create high demands for their services. As a result, their time is organized to be most efficient for them — by keeping others lined up to be seen at their convenience.[23]

High-status individuals in many different organizations communicate the idea that their time is more valuable than others' — and, therefore, that they hold higher-status positions — by making others wait to see them. This is a very subtle yet important form of nonverbal communication. Typically, the longer you must wait to see someone, the higher the organizational status that person has attained.[24] In fact, waiting too long to see a low-status person is a sure sign of disrespect.

The Use of Space: What Does It Say About You?   Like clothing and time, space is another important aspect of nonverbal communication. One's organizational status is communicated by the amount of space at one's disposal. Generally, the more space one commands, the more powerful one is likely to be in an organization. For example, higher-status life insurance underwriters in one organization have larger desks and offices than lower-status underwriter trainees.[25]

GLOBAL MATTERS | People from different cultures prefer different amounts of personal distance. For example, those from northern European countries (e.g., England, Sweden) tend to stand farther apart than those from southern European nations (e.g., Italy, Greece) when conversing. ■

Not only does the amount of space communicate organizational status, so does how that space is arranged. For example, among faculty members at one small college, senior professors were more likely to arrange their offices to separate themselves from visitors with their desks, whereas junior professors were less likely to impose such physical barriers.[26] These various office arrangements systematically communicated different things about the occupants. Specifically, professors who did not distance themselves from students with their desks were seen as being more open and unbiased in their dealings with students than those who used their desks as a physical barrier.

Use of space also has symbolic value in group interactions. For example, consider who usually sits at the head of a rectangular table. In most cases, it is the group leader, and in fact, it is traditional for leaders to do so. At the same time, however, studies have shown that people who emerge as the leaders of groups tend to be ones who just happened to be sitting at the table heads.[27] Apparently, *where* a person sits influences the available communication possibilities, and sitting at the head of a rec-

FIGURE 8.5

Business Casual Dress: A Contemporary Trend

The traditional business dress attire (e.g., business suits) is giving way to a less formal, *business casual* dress standard in many of today's organizations.

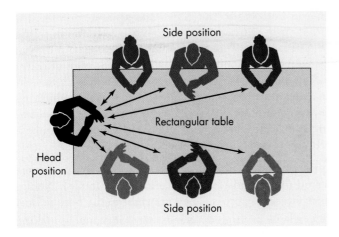

FIGURE 8.6

The Head of the Table: A Good Location for Communication

In part because they can easily see others and be seen by them, people sitting at the heads of rectangular tables enjoy effective communication with those seated at the sides.

tangular table enables a person to see everyone — and to be seen by them (Figure 8.6). That leaders tend to emerge from such positions, therefore, should not be surprising.

Organizations communicate something about themselves by their use of space as well.[28] For example, according to John Sculley, former president of PepsiCo, his company's world headquarters were designed to communicate to visitors they were seeing "the most important company in the world."[29] Similarly, by adding a second office tower to its company headquarters in Cincinnati, Procter & Gamble was said to be creating a gateway-like complex that communicated the company's connection with the community.[30] As these examples suggest, organizations as well as individuals use space to communicate certain aspects of their identities.

In conclusion, we note that the nonverbal mechanisms presented here — as important as they are — represent only a single channel of communication. Both verbal and nonverbal channels are important sources of information when used in conjunction with each other. Thus, although we have isolated the various forms of communication in this presentation, in actual practice they operate together, complementing each other in complex ways.

INDIVIDUAL DIFFERENCES IN COMMUNICATION

As you no doubt know from experience, different people communicate in different ways. Two people saying the same thing might do so very differently, and they might communicate their messages in ways that may have different effects on you. In other words, there are individual differences in how people communicate. We now examine key individual differences in communication, which are based on personal style, gender, and nationality.

Personal Communication Style

Steve and Charlie are two supervisors who are approached by Greg, a subordinate, to discuss the possibility of a salary increase. Both think Greg does not deserve the raise he is requesting, however, Steve and Charlie communicate their feelings quite differently. Steve is direct: "I'll be frank, Greg" he said, "a raise is out of the question." Charlie, however, is far more analytical: "Well, Greg, let's look at the big picture. I see here in your file that we just gave you a raise two months ago, and that you're not scheduled for another salary review for four months. Let me share with you some of the numbers and thoroughly explain why the company will have to stick with that schedule. . . ."

personal communication style

The consistent ways in which people communicate with others (i.e., the *Noble*, the *Socratic*, the *Reflective*, the *Magistrate*, the *Candidate*, and the *Senator*).

[handwritten: know the def. Won't ask about other styles]

The message was the same in both cases, but Steve and Charlie presented it quite differently. In other words, they differed in their **personal communication style**—that is, the consistent ways that people go about communicating with others. As you might imagine, some personal communication styles may be more effective than others, particularly depending on the other person and the situation.

Communication style is learned, so it can change. Before we consider changing how we communicate, however, we first must recognize what style we use. As summarized in Figure 8.7, communications experts have identified six major communication styles, one of which is likely to describe most people[31]:

- *The Noble*. Such individuals tend not to filter what they are thinking; they come right out and say what's on their minds (e.g., Steve in our example). Nobles use few words to get their messages across. They cut right to the bottom line.
- *The Socratic*. These people believe in carefully discussing things before making any decisions. Socratics enjoy the process of arguing their points, and they are

FIGURE 8.7

Personal Communication Styles: A Summary

People tend to communicate using one of six different *personal communication styles*. These styles and their interrelationships are summarized here.

(*Source*: Based on suggestions by McCallister, 1994; see note 31.)

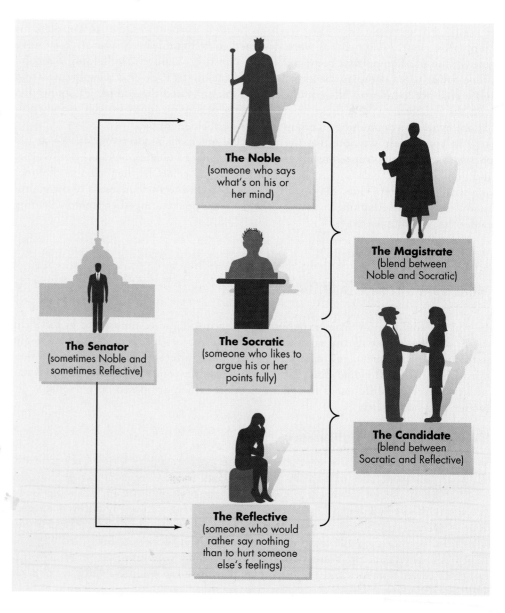

not afraid to engage in long-winded discussions. They have a penchant for details and often "talk in footnotes."

- *The Reflective*. These individuals are concerned with the interpersonal aspects of communication. They do not wish to offend others, and they are great listeners. Reflectives would sooner say nothing—or tell you what you want to hear, even if it might be a "little white lie"—than say something to cause conflict.

- *The Magistrate*. This style is a mix of Noble and Socratic. Magistrates tell you exactly what they think, and they make their cases in great detail (e.g., Charlie in our example). These individuals also tend to have an air of superiority about them, because they tend to dominate the discussion.

- *The Candidate*. This style is a mix between Socratic and Reflective. As such, candidates tend to be warm and supportive while also being analytical and chatty. They base their interactions on a great deal of information, and they do so in a very likable manner.

- *The Senator*. A Senator has developed both the Noble style *and* the Reflective style. They do not mix the two styles, however. Rather, they move back and forth between the two as needed.

We all have the potential to use any of these styles.[32] Generally, however, we tend to rely on one style more than any other. Each has its own strengths and weaknesses, and no one style is better than another. They are simply different. Effective communication begins by understanding your own style (which you can assess in the "Experiencing Organizational Behavior" exercise at the end of this chapter) as well as those used by others. Then, when you first meet someone, it is advisable to match that person's style, because people generally expect others to communicate in the same manner as themselves. The more we get to know and accept another's communication style, however, the more we come to accept how it blends with our own. In either case, the advice is the same: Recognizing and responding to communication styles can enhance communication with one another.

Sex Differences in Communication: Do Women and Men Communicate Differently?

Infuriated and frustrated, Kimberly stormed out of Mike's office. "I explained the problem I was having with the freelancers," she grumbled, "but he just doesn't listen!" Now, if this situation sounds familiar, you probably already are aware of the communication barriers that often exist between women and men. Deborah Tannen, a sociolinguist, recently explained that men and women frequently miscommunicate with each other, because they have learned different ways of using language.[33] In general, what appears to be "natural" to women does not come easily to men, and vice versa.

The basic difference between women and men in communication, Tannen argues, is that men emphasize and reinforce their status when they talk but that women downplay their status. Rather, women focus on creating positive social connections between themselves and others. Thus, whereas men tend to say "I," women tend to say "we." Similarly, whereas men try to exude confidence and boast, thinking of questions as being signs of weakness, women tend to downplay their confidence—even when sure they are correct—and are not afraid to ask questions. (What comes to mind here is the stereotypical image of the couple who gets hopelessly lost—because the man overrules the woman's pleas to ask for directions.)

This difference in style between women and men explains why they respond differently to problems. Women tend to listen and lend social support, but men tend to offer advice. When men do this, they are asserting their power—and contributing to a communication barrier between the sexes. Not surprisingly, whereas men may complain women are "too emotional," women may complain men "do not listen." Similarly, men tend to be more direct and confrontative than women. For example, a man might come right out and say, "I think your sales figures are inaccurate." A woman, however, might ask, "Have you verified your sales figures by comparing them to this morning's daily report?" A man may consider this approach to be sneaky, whereas a woman may believe it to be kinder and gentler than a more direct statement. Likewise, a woman may interpret a man's directness as being unsympathetic.

The implications of these differences surface once we point out another of Tannen's findings: People in powerful positions tend to reward people whose linguistic styles match their own.[34] In most organizations, where men tend to be in charge, the contributions of women therefore often are downplayed, because the things they say tend to be misinterpreted. The woman who politely defers to a dominant male speaker at a meeting may come across—to men, at least—as being passive. As a result, her contributions may never come to the table. The woman who breaks from this pattern and interjects her ideas, however, may come across—again, to men—as being pushy and aggressive. Here, too, her contributions may be discounted. In both cases, the communication barrier has caused a situation in which organizations not only breed conflict but fail to take advantage of the female employees' skills and abilities.

The solution lies in appreciating and accepting the different communication styles that people have. As Tannen puts it, "Talk is the lifeblood of managerial work, and understanding that different people have different ways of saying what they mean will make it possible to take advantage of the talents of people with a broad range of linguistic styles."[35]

Cross-Cultural Differences in Communications

In chapter 1, we noted that the phenomenon of globalization presents many challenges. Clearly, one of the most immediate challenges is communication. After all, when people speak different languages, it only makes sense that communication between them may be imperfect.

Part of the problem is that different words can mean different things to different people.[36] For example, as hard as it might be for people from long-standing capitalist economies to realize, Russians have difficulty understanding words such as *efficiency* and *free market*, which have no direct translation in their language. People who have never known a free-market economy may find it difficult to grasp the very concept. Therefore, basic communication barriers already exist for U.S. executives attempting to conduct business in Russia (Figure 8.8).[37]

In addition to different vocabularies, cross-cultural communication also is difficult because in different languages, even the *same* word can mean different things. For example, imagine how confused a U.S. executive might be when she speaks to her counterpart in Israel, where the same Hebrew word, *shalom*, means "hello," "good-bye," and "peace." The same may be said for cultural differences in the tone of speech used in different settings. For example, whereas Americans might feel free to say the word *you* in both formal and informal situations, the French have different words for each: *tu* for informal speech, and *vous* for formal speech. To confuse these two words may be tantamount to misinterpreting the nature of the social setting—a potentially costly blunder, and all because of a failure to recognize the subtleties of cross-cultural communication. (What can be done to eliminate such blunders caused by the barriers inherent in cross-cultural communication? The "OB Around the World" section in this chapter outlines several key suggestions.)

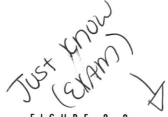

FIGURE 8.8

Russian-American Communication Barriers

Although Russian citizens such as industrialist Giorgi Kovalenko, general director of the Poliplast plastics factory in Rybinsk, are quickly learning capitalist ways, their exposure to many years of communism has left them without a basic business vocabulary, which often hinders communication with those from capitalist nations.

PROMOTING CROSS-CULTURAL COMMUNICATION

As noted, the potential for miscommunication between people from different cultures is considerable. Short of becoming expert in foreign languages and cultures, however, several steps can promote cross-cultural communication.[38]

1. *Observe, but do not evaluate.* Suppose that while touring a foreign factory, you observe several assembly line workers sitting and talking instead of working. Based on your own culture, this would be inappropriate and a sure sign of laziness. Fearing what this means for the plant's productivity, you suddenly develop second thoughts about doing business with this company. As you learn about these workers' national culture, however, you discover they were engaging in a traditional work-break ritual: resting while remaining on the work site. These people were merely doing what was expected of them culturally, so they may not be lazy after all. The point is that you evaluated the situation by applying your own cultural values — and were misled by them. To avoid such problems, simply describe what you observe (i.e., the workers are resting) rather than using these observations as the basis for evaluations (i.e., the workers are lazy). Doing so can help you to avoid serious misinterpretation.

2. *Do not jump to conclusions.* When we perceive various situations, we tend to assume our own judgments are correct. In cross-national settings, however, we should consider our judgments more as educated guesses than as certain conclusions. If you think something is correct (e.g., your interpretation of the lazy workers in the previous example), it is best to compare these to the judgments of experts in the local culture rather than to assume you are correct. By confirming the accuracy of your judgments, misinterpretation is less likely.

3. *Assume people are different from yourself.* Most of us tend to assume that others are similar to ourselves until we learn otherwise. Such an assumption often leads us down the wrong track, however, and seasoned international managers know this. Therefore, they take the opposite stance, assuming that others are different until they learn otherwise. Because these managers "know that they don't know," they are less likely to be surprised by differences which are unexpected yet inevitable.

4. *Take the other person's perspective.* Try to see the situation through the eyes of your foreign colleague. Consider this individual's values and experiences, and ask yourself how he or she might view things differently. To the extent you can switch roles effectively, you can avoid the narrow-mindedness (i.e., "cultural myopia") with which we all tend to make decisions.

These measures may be easier said than done, but with practice, they can be mastered. Given that such practices are key to the success of international managers, the effort involved is worth making.

FORMAL AND INFORMAL COMMUNICATION IN ORGANIZATIONS

Think of the broad range of messages that may be communicated to you in a single workday. Your boss may ask you to complete an important sales report. Another manager from across the hall may hand you a memo regarding the status of a new project. You may read an e-mail message from a coworker regarding who won the office football pool, and the custodian may tell you a joke. Even from these few examples, you can distinguish the two basic types of communication in organizations: **formal communication**, or the sharing of messages regarding the official work of the organization; and **informal communication**, or the sharing of unofficial messages, that go beyond the organization's formal activities. Both formal and informal communication are so widespread in organizations that we describe both here.

formal communication
The sharing of messages regarding the official work of the organization.

informal communication
The sharing of unofficial messages that go beyond the organization's formal activities.

Formal Communication: Up, Down, and Across the Organizational Chart

The basic process of communication described is similar in many different contexts, but one unique feature of organizations profoundly affects this process — namely, their *structure*. Organizations often are organized in ways that dictate who may — and who may not — communicate with whom. Given this, how is the communication process affected by the structure of an organization?

organizational structure

The formally prescribed pattern of interrelationships between the various units of an organization.

organizational chart

A diagram showing the formal structure of an organization and indicating who is to communicate with whom.

Know dif. ?

?

Organizational Structure Influences Communication   **Organizational structure** refers to the formally prescribed pattern of interrelationships between the various units (a topic we return to in chapter 14). An organization's structure may be described using a diagram known as an **organizational chart**, an example of which appears in Figure 8.9. Such a diagram represents an organization's structure graphically. It may be likened to an x-ray film, showing the organization's skeleton — an outline of the planned, formal connections between the various units.[39]

Note the various boxes in the diagram and the lines that connect them. Each box represents a person performing a specific job, and the diagram shows the titles of the individuals performing the various jobs as well as the formally prescribed pattern of communication between them. These patterns are relatively fixed and defined. Each individual is responsible for performing a specified job, so if people in the organization leave, they must be replaced if their jobs are to be done. The key point is that an organization's formal structure does not change because the personnel do.

Connecting the boxes in the organizational chart are lines of *authority* which show who must answer to whom. Each person is responsible to (or answers to) the person at the next-higher level to which he or she is connected. At the same time, each person also is responsible for (or gives orders to) those who are immediately below his or her box. These boxes and lines form a sort of blueprint of an organization, showing what people need to do and with whom they need to communicate for the organization to operate properly.

As you might imagine, the nature and form of communication vary greatly as a function of people's relative positions within an organization. Even a quick look at an organizational chart reveals that information may flow upward (i.e., from lower to higher levels), downward (i.e., from higher to lower levels), or horizontally (i.e., between people at the same level). However, as summarized in Figure 8.9, different types of information typically travel in different directions within a hierarchy.

Downward Communication   Suppose you are a supervisor. What types of messages would you send to your subordinates? Typically, *downward communication* consists of instructions, directions, and orders — that is, messages telling subordinates what they should be doing.[40] Feedback on past performance also typically flows in a downward direction (e.g., when managers tell subordinates how well they have been working). For example, a sales manager might direct members of her sales force to promote a certain product and then congratulate them for being successful.

FIGURE 8.9

The Organizational Chart: An Organization's Formal Communication Network

An organizational chart shows the formally prescribed patterns of communication in an organization. Different types of messages typically flow upward, downward, and horizontally throughout the organization.

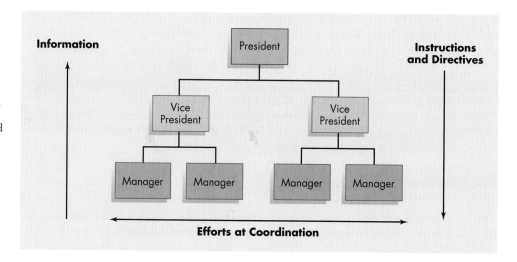

Downward communication flows from one level to the next-lowest one, slowly trickling down to the bottom. As a message passes through the various levels, however, it often becomes less accurate—especially if the information is spoken). Thus, the most effective downward communication techniques are those aimed directly at the people most affected by the messages—namely, small group meetings and organizational publications targeting specific groups.[41] Such methods are being used—and successfully! (One of the most distasteful types of downward communication involves managers telling employees they are fired. The process of communicating a termination decision can be made less unpleasant, however, by following the suggestions outlined in the "Tips" section below.

<table>
<tr><td>■ Saying "You're Fired!" Without Hearing "I'll See You in Court!"</td><td>TIPS:
DOING IT RIGHT</td></tr>
</table>

No manager likes to "drop the ax" on an employee, but doing so is inevitable. The task is more than just unpleasant, however. If done incorrectly, the results can be quite costly. In recent years, courts have awarded millions of dollars to plaintiffs who have won cases against their former employers for "wrongful termination." An alarming number of employees are bringing suit these days as well. According to one recent study, 53 percent of companies have been taken to court by an ex-worker during the past five years.[42] Even when employers prevail, they must spend thousands of dollars to defend themselves, so the trick is to stay out of court in the first place. What can employers do to keep their employees from wanting to sue? Experts recommend several things:[43]

1. *Keep written records of performance problems.* Courts will not force employers to keep inept employees, but proving someone's ineptitude is another matter. Without good documentation of an actual performance problem—and of clear and repeated attempts to fix it—it is all too easy for an employee to claim unfair discrimination (which in some cases may be correct). Employers should maintain careful, written logs that document problems, goals for improvement, and a reasonable timetable for meeting those goals. In addition, employees should be asked to sign all such documents, and they should be given copies as well. Doing this helps employers to defend themselves among employees filing suit against them and may well discourage many employees from even thinking about suing in the first place.

2. *Give fair notice.* If an employee is doing something illegal or that endangers others in the workplace, fire that person on the spot. After all, employers have obligations to create a safe work environment for their employees. In less extreme cases, however, firing without notice only adds insult to injury—and these injured feelings may stimulate aggrieved employees to visit their attorney. How much time constitutes fair notice has no simple answer, but for the most part, it depends on the prevailing practices in the employee's company or industry. Whatever that time is—be it two weeks or one month—employers should provide at least that much notice.

3. *Clearly yet briefly explain the decision.* Too often, people claim that they have no idea why they were fired.[44] Supervisors should explain the problems in clear terms, but they should not talk enough to get themselves in trouble. After explaining the decision and emphasizing it is final, they should move on to practical matters, such as severance pay and continuance of health insurance.

4. *Be sympathetic to the fired worker's feelings.* Because so much of how we define ourselves is based on the work that we do, losing a job is a major threat to
continued

Be able to identify the different ones →

our identity. Naturally, the resulting feelings of uncertainty — both personal and financial — are quite unsettling. Thus, the supervisor should not make the situation worse by being insensitive and uncaring. Compassion is needed at this time. To some extent, demonstrating sympathy and compassion toward the terminated employee can help him or her to accept this unfortunate outcome.

5. *Do the job in person.* However tempting it may be to fire someone in writing (e.g., by e-mail or written letter) or through voice-mail message, don't do it. Not surprisingly, it tends to anger the recipients, who then find some reason to sue.

6. *Reassure the surviving employees.* When someone is fired, word tends to spread quickly, and the surviving employees cannot help but wonder what the future holds for them. Has the boss gone mad? Is the company in financial trouble? To the extent that uncertainty may breed distrust and rumors, people's attentions may be diverted from their jobs. Thus, supervisors should provide appropriate reassurances about the future.

Firing someone is never easy, but these six suggestions can make the task much less distasteful for all concerned. They also can make the termination process less expensive for the company — and less emotionally draining for the ex-employee. ◼

Upward Communication   Information flowing from lower levels to higher levels within an organization (e.g., from subordinate to supervisor) is referred to as *upward communication*. Messages flowing in this direction tend to contain the information managers need, such as data required for decision making and the status of various projects. In short, upward communication keeps managers aware of what is occurring. Types of information that flow upward include suggestions for improvement, status reports, reactions to work-related issues, and new ideas.

Upward communication is not simply the reverse of downward communication. The difference in status between the communicating parties makes for some important distinctions. For example, upward communication occurs much less frequently than downward communication. In fact, one classic study found that 70 percent of assembly line workers initiated communication with their supervisors less than once a month.[45] Further research found that managers directed less than 15 percent of their total communication to their own superiors.[46] When people do communicate upward, their conversations also tend to be shorter than discussions with their peers.[47]

Perhaps even more important, upward communication often suffers from serious inaccuracies. For example, subordinates frequently feel they must highlight their accomplishments — and downplay their mistakes — to be looked on favorably.[48] Similarly, some individuals fear rebuke by their supervisors if they anticipate their remarks will be perceived as threatening.[49] As a result, many people frequently avoid communicating bad news to their supervisors, or they simply "pass the buck" to someone else.[50] This general reluctance to transmit bad news is referred to as the **MUM effect**.[51] As you might imagine, because superiors rely on information when making decisions, keeping silent about important news — even if it is bad — may be one of the worst things a subordinate can do. As one executive put it, "All of us have our share of bonehead ideas. Having someone tell you it's a bonehead idea before you do something about it is really a great blessing."[52]

MUM effect

The reluctance to transmit bad news, which is shown either by not transmitting the message at all or by delegating the task to someone else.

departments on same level

Horizontal Communication   Messages that flow laterally (i.e., at the same organizational level) are characterized by efforts at coordination (i.e., attempts to work together) and are referred to as *horizontal communication*. For example, a vice president of marketing needs to coordinate her efforts to initiate an advertising campaign for a new product with information from the vice president of production about when the first products will come off the assembly line.

Unlike vertical communication, in which the parties are at different levels, horizontal communication involves people at the same level. Therefore, it tends to be easier and friendlier. Communication between peers also tends to be more casual and occurs more quickly, because fewer social barriers exist between the parties. Note, however, that even horizontal communication can be problematic. For example, people in different departments may feel they are competing with others for valued organizational resources and, thereby, substitute an antagonistic, competitive orientation for the friendlier, cooperative one needed to get things done.[53]

Informal Communication Networks: Behind the Organizational Chart

Think about the people you communicate with during an average day. Friends, family members, classmates, and colleagues are among those with whom you may have informal communication—that is, information shared without any formally imposed obligations or restrictions. It is easy to recognize how widespread our informal networks can be: You know someone who knows someone else who knows your best friend, and before long, your informal networks become very far-reaching indeed.

In part because they are so widespread, informal communication networks constitute an important avenue for information in organizations. In fact, middle managers have ranked informal networks as being better sources of organizational information than formal networks.[54] Therefore, if an organization's formal communication represents its skeleton, its informal communication represents its central nervous system.[55]

Organizations' Hidden Pathways   It is easy to imagine how important the flow of informal information may be within an organization. People transmit information to those they come in contact with, thereby providing conduits through which messages can travel. We also tend to communicate most with those who are similar to ourselves in areas such as age and time on the job.[56] Because we are more comfortable with similar than with dissimilar people, we tend to spend more time with them—and to communicate with them more. As a result, many informal, gender-segregated networks tend to form in organizations (e.g., what among men has been referred to the **old-boys network**).

To the extent these associations may isolate people from others in power (who may be different), this practice is limiting.[57] At the same time, however, exposure to similar others with whom people feel comfortable may provide valuable sources of information. For example, many African-American business leaders have created informal networks with others of their race to help share ways of succeeding despite constituting an ethnic minority—alliances that have been helpful to many careers.[58] This informal observation is in keeping with scientific evidence showing that the more involved people are in their organization's communication networks, the more powerful and influential they become.[59]

The idea that people are connected informally also explains an important organizational phenomenon—namely, turnover. Do people resign from their jobs in random and unrelated ways? Research suggests they do not. Rather, turnover relates to the informal communication patterns between people.[60] In fact, voluntary turnover (i.e., employees freely electing to resign) occurs in a kind of **snowball effect**. A snowball does not accumulate snowflakes randomly; it collects those that are in its path. Likewise patterns of voluntary turnover are not independently distributed within a work group. Instead, they result from people's influences on each other. Thus, predicting who will resign may be based, in large part, on knowledge of the informal communication patterns within work groups. In other words, a person who leaves his or her job for a better one in another organization is likely to know someone who already has done so. For a suggestion regarding how this may operate, see Figure 8.10.

old-boys network

A gender-segregated, informal communication network composed of men with similar backgrounds.

snowball effect

The tendency for people to share informal information with others.

FIGURE 8.10

Informal Communication Networks: A Predictor of Turnover Patterns

The informal networks of communication between people (shown here as dotted lines) provide channels to pass along messages about better job opportunities. Patterns of voluntary turnover have been linked to the existence of such informal networks.

(*Source*: Based on suggestions by Krackhardt & Porter, 1986; see note 60.)

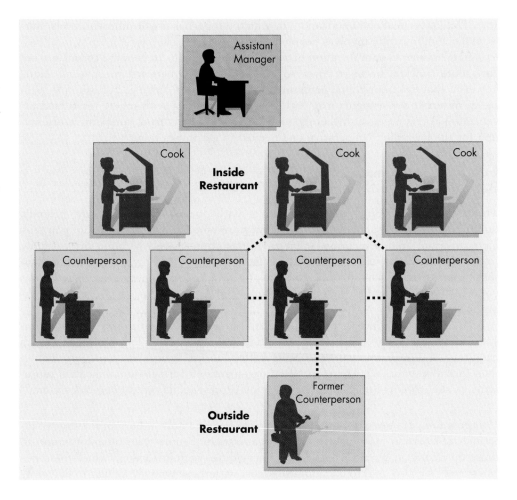

grapevine
An organization's informal channels of communication, which are based mainly on friendship or acquaintance.

Grapevine
Bad part— leads to
rumors

Unlike formal communication networks, informal networks are composed of individuals at different organizational levels. In these groups, people can tell anyone whatever they wish. For example, jokes and funny stories tend to cross organizational boundaries and are shared freely in both the managerial and the nonmanagerial ranks of organizations.[61] On the other hand, it would be quite unlikely — and even considered "out of line" — for a lower-level employee to tell an upper-level employee how to do the job. What flows within the pathways of informal communication networks is informal information — that is, messages not necessarily related to work.

The Grapevine and the Rumor Mill   When anyone can tell something informal to anyone else, it produces a rapid flow of information along what is commonly referred to as the **grapevine** — that is, the pathways along which unofficial, informal information travels. In contrast to a formal organizational message, which might take days to reach its desired audience, informal information traveling along the organizational grapevine tends to reach its audience rapidly, often within hours. This is because informal communication can cross formal organizational boundaries (e.g., you might be able to tell a good joke to anyone, not just to those with whom you are required to communicate) and because informal information tends to be communicated orally.

As noted earlier, oral messages are communicated faster than written ones, but they also may become increasingly inaccurate as they flow from person to person. Because of the confusion grapevines may cause, some people have sought to eliminate them, but grapevines are not necessarily bad. Informally socializing with coworkers can help to make work groups more cohesive and may provide excellent opportunities for desired human contact, thus keeping the work environment stimulating. Grapevines are an inevitable fact of life in organizations.[62]

Most information communicated along the grapevine is accurate as well. In fact, one study found that 82 percent of the information communicated along one company's organizational grapevine on a single occasion was accurate.[63] The problem with interpreting this figure, however, is that the inaccurate portions of some messages may alter their overall meaning. For example, if a story goes around that someone did not get promoted and a lower-ranking employee did, it may cause dissension in the workplace. Now, suppose everything is true except that the first person turned down the promotion because it involved relocation. This important fact completely alters the situation—and the message. Only one fact needs to be wrong for the accuracy of a communication to suffer.

This problem of inaccuracy clearly is what gives the grapevine such a bad reputation. In extreme cases, information may be transmitted that is almost totally without any basis and often is unverifiable. Such messages are known as **rumors**. Typically, rumors are based on speculation, an overactive imagination, and wishful thinking rather than on facts. Rumors race like wildfire through organizations, because the information they present is so interesting—and ambiguous. This ambiguity leaves the rumor open to embellishment as it passes orally from person to person. Before you know it, almost everyone in the organization has heard the rumor, and its inaccurate message becomes taken as a fact. "It must be true, everyone knows it." Hence, even if there once was some truth to a rumor, the message quickly becomes untrue.

If you have ever been the victim of a personal rumor, you know how difficult it can be to crush and how profound its effect can be. This is especially so when organizations are the victims. For example, rumors about the possibility of corporate takeovers not only influence the value of a company's stock but also threaten its employees' feelings of job security. Sometimes, rumors about company products can be very costly as well. For example:

- A rumor about the use of worms in McDonald's hamburgers circulated in the Chicago area during the late 1970s. The rumor was completely untrue, but sales dropped as much as 30 percent in some restaurants.[64]
- In June 1993, stories appeared in the press stating that people across the United States had found syringes in cans of Pepsi-Cola. These stories proved to be completely without fact, but the hoax cost Pepsi a great deal in terms of both investigative and advertising expenses.[65]
- The consumer-products giant Procter & Gamble (P&G) has been subject to consistent, nagging rumors linking it to Satanism.[66] Since 1980, rumors have claimed the company's moon-and-stars trademark is linked to witchcraft. The company has emphatically denied these rumors and even won court judgments against various individuals spreading them—but the rumors still persist.

What can be done to counter the effects of rumors? Unfortunately, evidence suggests that directly refuting a rumor may not always counter its effects. For example, Pepsi officials denied reports about their tainted product. The rumor itself was implausible as well—and also quickly disproven by independent investigators from the U.S. Food and Drug Administration. Sometimes, as the P&G rumor illustrates, rumors are more difficult to disprove and do not die quickly. In such cases, directly refuting the rumor only fuels the fire. When you do (e.g., "I didn't do it."), you actually may help to spread it among those who have not already heard it (e.g., "Oh, I didn't know people thought that.") and even strengthen it among those who have heard it (e.g., "If it weren't true, they wouldn't be protesting so much."). In the case of P&G, the problem is compounded by the allegation that some parties are making a concerted effort to keep the rumor alive. Thus, directing the public's attention away from the rumor may help to minimize its adverse impact. For example, P&G can focus its advertising

rumors

Information with little basis in fact and often transmitted through informal channels (see *grapevine*).

on other, positive things the public already knows about it. With the McDonald's rumor, reminding people of other things they thought about McDonald's (e.g., it is a clean, family-oriented place) helped to counter the negative effects of that rumor.[67]

If you ever become the victim of a rumor, try to refute it immediately with indisputable facts. If it lingers on, try directing people's attention to other, positive things they already believe about you. Rumors may be impossible to stop, but with some effort, their effects can be managed.

Communicating Inside vs. Outside the Organization

All corporate communication can be distinguished by whether it is aimed at people inside the organization (e.g., fellow employees) or outside the organization (e.g., the general public). Do executives say different things when aiming their remarks inside as opposed to outside the company?

Research suggests they do.[68] For example, consider a study in which scientists analyzed comments by CEOs of 10 forest-products companies in their letters to shareholders (i.e., external communications) between 1979 and 1988. Various planning documents (i.e., internal communications) for these same companies also were examined during this period. Instead of looking at exactly what was said, however, the researchers categorized these communications by how they were framed. Specifically, they considered whether the statements focused on threats the company faced (e.g., the rising cost of materials) or on opportunities (e.g., the growth in the housing market).

The results were quite interesting. Because the industry generally improved during the period studied, the proportion of documents framed in terms of threat dropped. The mention of threat, however, was not equally likely to occur in both internal and external statements. For each year studied, a greater proportion of internal documents than external documents referred to threats. Likewise, with few exceptions, a greater proportion of internal documents than external documents focused on opportunities. For a summary of these results, see Figure 8.11.

FIGURE 8.11

Internal vs. External Communications: Is There a Difference?

Executives tend to communicate differently when sending messages inside and outside their organizations. As in one study, internal communications tend to focus on threats more than on opportunities, whereas external communications tend to focus on opportunities more than on threats.

(*Source*: Based on suggestions by Fiol, 1995; see note 68.)

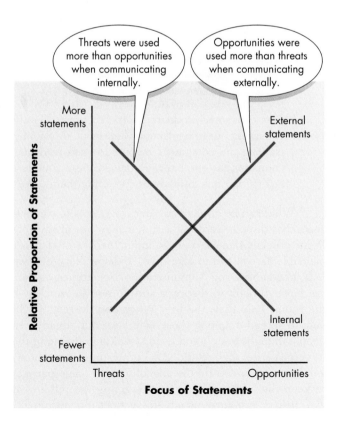

These findings suggest executives were attempting to present their companies in a positive light to the public (e.g., by focusing on opportunities) but were more willing to address threats internally. They may well have been thinking it was important not to frighten the investing public but also to keep employees appraised of any threats so the company could defend itself.

This is the idea behind what is called **strategic communication**—that is, the practice of presenting information about the company to broad, external audiences (e.g., the press). The more effectively companies manage this process, the better the general public receives them, thus yielding considerable benefits (e.g., enhanced customer loyalty, increased sales). Given the importance of clearly and appropriately managing a corporate image through strategic communication, public relations firms often are hired to do this work.

strategic communication

The practice of presenting information about the company to broad, external audiences (e.g., the press).

ETHICS MATTERS

The suggestion that public relations firms are in the business of misleading the public about the organizations they represent is widely considered to be unfair and inaccurate. Rather, these companies "package" information about their clients in ways that best serve the needs of external audiences. Do you generally agree or disagree with this idea? ■

IMPROVING YOUR COMMUNICATION SKILLS

Throughout this chapter, we have noted the central role of communication in organizational functioning. Thus, efforts at improving the communication process may have highly desirable benefits for organizations as well as for the individuals and groups within them. Several steps can be taken to obtain the benefits of effective communication.[69] In this final section, we describe some of these techniques, including measures that can be taken by individuals as well as tactics that involve entire organizations.

Use Simple, Clear Language

Have you ever driven your "previously owned motor vehicle" up to an "ethyl-dispensing device" and been greeted by a "petroleum transfer engineer" who then filled your "fuel-containment module"? Perhaps you have gone to a "home improvement center" looking for a "manually powered impact device." In either case, no one could blame you if you went to another "operating entity" with a better "customer interface capacity." Our point is simple: *Using needlessly formal language may impose a serious barrier to communication.*

Recognize that all organizations, fields, social groups, and professions have their own **jargon**—that is, their own specialized language. Your own college or university may have a "quad," or as a student, you may have a "roomie" who wants to "go Greek" and is interested in "rushing." These are examples of a college student's jargon. No doubt, a lot of language in this book at first sounded strange to you. Our point is that use of jargon is inevitable when people within the same field or social groups communicate.

jargon
The specialized language used by a particular group (e.g., people within a profession).

Some degree of highly specialized language may help communication by providing an easy way for people in the same field to share complex ideas. Jargon also allows professionals to identify others as people in their field, because they "speak the same language." For example, management professors would describe this book as dealing with the "field of OB," but this phrase would have a very different meaning to medical doctors (for whom it refers to the field of obstetrics). Obviously, jargon helps communication within professions, but it can also lead to confusion when used outside the groups within which it has meaning.

K.I.S.S. principle

A basic principle of communication advising that messages should be as short and simple as possible (i.e., *keep it* short and simple).

In addition to avoiding jargon, the clearest communicators also keep their language short, simple, and to the point. Hence, it is wise to adopt the **K.I.S.S. principle** — that is, *keep it short and simple.*[70] People can better understand messages that do not overwhelm them with too much information at once. A wise communicator is sensitive to this and knows how to monitor his or her audience for signs of overloading. Again, although you may know what you are talking about, you may not be able to get your ideas across to others unless you package them in doses that are small and simple enough to be understood. When this is done effectively, even the most complex ideas can be communicated clearly.[71] (You certainly would not want a professor to write an ambiguous message in a letter of recommendation for you.[72] For an example of serious ambiguities that may appear in such important documents, see Table 8.1).

Become an Active, Attentive Listener

Just as you should work at making your ideas understandable to others (i.e., sending messages), you also should work at being a good listener (i.e., receiving messages). People do a great deal of listening, but they pay attention to — and comprehend — only a small percentage of the information directed at them.[73]

Most of us usually think of listening as a passive process, one of taking in information sent out by others, but when done correctly, the process is much more active.[74] For example, good listeners ask questions if they do not understand something, and they nod or otherwise signal when they do. Such cues provide critical feedback to communicators. As a listener, you can help the communication process by letting the sender know if and how his or her messages are coming across to you. *Asking questions* and *putting the speaker's ideas into your own words* are both helpful ways of ensuring you take in all the information presented.

Avoiding distractions in the environment and concentrating on what the other person is saying also are very useful. When listening to others, *avoid jumping to conclusions or evaluating their remarks.* Take in completely what is being said before you respond. Simply dismissing someone because you do not like what he or she said is much too easy, and doing so poses a formidable barrier to effective communication.

TABLE 8.1

The Not-So-Favorable Recommendation

Sometimes, ambiguities in the way letters of recommendation are written disguise truly negative opinions in a highly positive manner. Examples of such statements are shown here. You may need to read these twice to see exactly what the problem is.

TO DESCRIBE SOMEONE WHO IS ...	YOU MIGHT SAY ...
Extremely inept	"I most enthusiastically recommend this candidate with no qualifications whatsoever."
Not particularly industrious	"In my opinion you will be very fortunate to get this person to work for you."
Not worthy of further consideration	"I would urge you to waste no time in making this candidate an offer of employment."
Lacking in credentials	"All in all, I cannot say enough good things about this candidate or recommend him too highly."
An ex-employee who you do not miss	"I am pleased to say that this candidate is a former colleague of mine."
So unproductive as to be worthless	"I can assure you that no person would be better for this job."

Source: Robert J. Thornton, *Lexicon of Intentionally Ambiguous Recommendations (L.I.A.R.),* 2nd edition, 1998, Almus Publications, Central Point, Oregon. Used with permission from the author.

Being a good listener also involves making sure you are aware of others' main points. What is the speaker trying to say? Again, *make sure you understand another's ideas before you reply*. Too often, we interrupt speakers with our own ideas before we have heard theirs fully. If this sounds like something you do, rest assured it not only is quite common but also is correctable.

Although it requires some effort, incorporating these suggestions into your own habits makes you a better listener. Indeed, many organizations seek to help their employees in this way. For example, the corporate giant Unisys for some time has systematically trained thousands of its employees in effective listening skills using both seminars and self-training cassettes. Clearly, Unisys is among those companies acknowledging the importance of good listening skills in promoting effective organizational communication.

The development of listening skills requires you to identify the individual elements of listening—that is, the separate skills that contribute to listening effectiveness. These may be clustered into the six groups of the **HURIER model**.[75] The term *HURIER* stands for the component skills of effective listening: *h*earing, *u*nderstanding, *r*emembering, *i*nterpreting, *e*valuating, and *r*esponding. For a summary of these individual skills, see Figure 8.12. It might seem easy to do the six things needed to be a good listener, but we are all not as good as we may think in this capacity, thus suggesting that listening might not be as easy as it seems.

Management consultant Nancy K. Austin would agree. She explains that when you invite people to talk to you about their problems on the job, you make an implicit promise to listen.[76] Of course, when you do, you may feel hostile and defensive toward the speaker—and become more interested in speaking up and setting the record straight—if you do not like what you hear. This is the challenge of listening. Good listeners resist this temptation and pay careful attention to the speaker. When they cannot, they admit the problem and reschedule another opportunity to get together.

Austin also advises people to "be an equal opportunity listener." In other words, pay attention not only to those with high status but also to those at any level, and make time to hear them all in a democratic fashion. The idea is that people at any level might have something to say—and they may feel good about you as a manager for having shown consideration to them. Austin notes that by listening to an employee, you are saying, "You are smart and have important things to say; you are worth my time."[77] Such a message is critical to establishing the kind of open, two-way communication that is essential for top management.

Research has confirmed the importance of listening as a management skill. In fact, the better listener a person is the more likely he or she is to rise rapidly up the

HURIER model

The conceptualization that describes effective listening as having six components: *h*earing, *u*nderstanding, *r*emembering, *i*nterpreting, *e*valuating, and *r*esponding.

know the six compents in the HURIER model

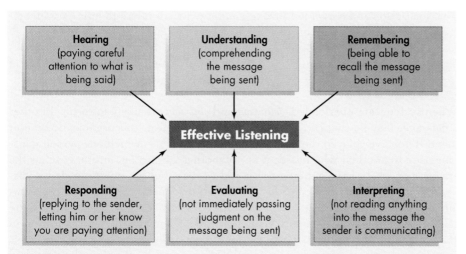

Effective Listening

- **Hearing** (paying careful attention to what is being said)
- **Understanding** (comprehending the message being sent)
- **Remembering** (being able to recall the message being sent)
- **Responding** (replying to the sender, letting him or her know you are paying attention)
- **Evaluating** (not immediately passing judgment on the message being sent)
- **Interpreting** (not reading anything into the message the sender is communicating)

FIGURE 8.12

The HURIER Model: Components of Effective Listening

Six skills contribute greatly to the effectiveness of listening: *h*earing, *u*nderstanding, *r*emembering, *i*nterpreting, *e*valuating, and *r*esponding.

(*Source*: Based on suggestions by Brownell, 1985; see note 75.)

organizational hierarchy[78] and to perform well as a manager.[79] In short, good listening skills are an important aspect of success as a manager. Unfortunately, however, people tend to think they are better listeners than they actually are.[80] Such overconfidence in one's own ability can be a barrier to training in listening skills, because people who believe they already are good listeners may have little motivation to seek such training. When managers do complete formal training programs to enhance their listening skills, however, it generally pays off quite well. (To practice this important management skill, complete the "Working in Groups" exercise at the end of this chapter.)

Gauge the Flow of Information: Avoiding Overload

Imagine a busy manager surrounded by a stack of papers and with a telephone receiver in each ear and a crowd gathered around waiting to talk to her. Obviously, the many demands on this one person can slow down the overall system and make its operations less effective. Likewise, when any part of a communication network becomes bogged down with more information than it can handle, a condition of **overload** exists. For example, consider, the bottleneck in the flow of routine financial information that might result when members of an organization's accounting department are tied up preparing corporate tax returns. Naturally, this state poses a serious threat to effective organizational communication — and things are only getting worse. Because today's managers face more information overload than ever, they tend to ignore a great deal of the information they need to do their jobs. Fortunately, however, several concrete steps can be taken to manage information more effectively.

overload
The condition in which a unit of an organization becomes overburdened with too much incoming information.

GLOBAL MATTERS

Surveys suggest the overload problem exists throughout the world. Half the executives surveyed from the United Kingdom, the United States, Australia, Hong Kong, and Singapore indicated they quite often or very frequently feel unable to handle the volumes of information they receive.[81] No significant differences between countries were found.

First, organizations may employ *gatekeepers* — that is, people whose jobs require them to control the flow of information to potentially overloaded units. For example, administrative assistants are responsible for making sure busy executives are not overloaded by the demands of other people or groups. Newspaper editors and television news directors also may be considered gatekeepers, because such individuals decide what news will — and will not — be shared with the public. It is an essential part of these individuals' jobs to avoid overloading others by gauging the flow of information to them.

Overload also can be avoided through *queuing*, which refers to lining up incoming information so it can be managed in an orderly fashion. "Stacking" jets as they approach a busy airport and making customers take a number (i.e., defining their position in line) at a busy deli counter are both designed to avoid the chaos that may result from too many demands on the system at once. For a summary of these techniques, see Figure 8.13.

When systems are overloaded, *distortion* and *omission* are likely to result. In other words, messages may be changed or left out when passed from one organizational unit to the next. If you ever played the parlor game "telephone" (in which one person whispers a message to another, who passes it on to another, and so on, until it reaches the last person), you likely have experienced — and contributed to — messages being distorted and omitted. When you consider the important messages that often are communicated in organizations, these problems can be serious. They also tend to be quite extreme. For example, in one study tracing the flow of downward communication in more than 100 organizations, the messages communicated downward over five levels lost approximately 80 percent of their original information by the time they reached

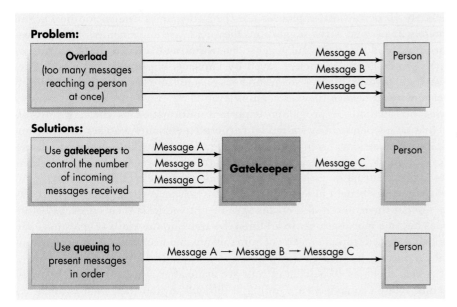

FIGURE 8.13

Overload: A Problem That Can Be Solved

Overload, or receiving too many messages at once, can seriously interfere with organizational functioning. This problem can be minimized, however, by using *gatekeepers* (i.e., individuals who control the flow of information) and *queuing* (i.e., lining up incoming information so it arrives in an orderly fashion).

their destination at the lowest level of the organizational hierarchy.[82] Obviously, something needs to be done.

One effective strategy is *redundancy*. Making messages redundant involves transmitting them again — often in another form or via another channel. For example, in attempting to communicate an important message to her subordinates, a manager may tell them the message and then follow it up with a written memo. In fact, managers frequently encourage this practice.[83]

Another practice that can help is *verification*, which refers to making sure that messages have been received accurately. Pilots use verification when they repeat the messages given by air traffic controllers. Doing so assures both parties that the pilots heard the actual message the controllers sent. Given how busy pilots may be and the interference inherent in radio transmissions — coupled with the vital importance of the messages themselves — the practice of verifying messages is a wise safety measure. This practice may be used by individual communicators as well. Active listeners may wish to verify they understood a speaker correctly and they do so by paraphrasing the speaker's remarks within a question, such as by asking, "If I understood, you were saying . . ."

Give and Receive Feedback: Opening Channels of Communication

To operate effectively, organizations must communicate accurately with those who keep them running (i.e., their employees). Unfortunately, most employees believe the feedback between themselves and their organizations is not as good as it should be.[84] For various reasons, people often are unwilling — or unable — to communicate their ideas to top management. Part of the problem is the lack of available channels for upward communication and people's reluctance to use the ones that do exist. How, then, can organizations obtain information from their employees, thus improving the upward flow of communication?

One means is the use of *suggestion systems*. Too often, employees' good ideas about how to improve organizational functioning fail to make their way up the organizational chart, because the people with the ideas do not know how to reach the people who can implement them. Even worse, employees may feel that even if they can reach the right person, he or she may not listen to them. Suggestion boxes are designed to help avoid these problems and to provide a conduit for employees' ideas.

[handwritten: to u know this percent]

Approximately 15 percent of employees use their companies' suggestion boxes, and approximately 25 percent of the suggestions they made are implemented.[85] Employees usually are rewarded for successful suggestions, either with a flat monetary award or with some percentage of the money saved by implementing the suggestion. It goes without saying, however, that for suggestion systems to have the intended positive effects, everyone must believe they are administered fairly (Figure 8.14).

A second method of providing important information is through *corporate hotlines* — that is, telephone lines staffed by corporate personnel who are ready to answer employees' questions, listen to their comments, and the like.[86] One good example is the "Let's Talk" program developed by AT&T to answer employees' questions during its 1980s antitrust divestiture. By providing personnel with easy access to information, companies benefit in several ways. Doing so shows employees that the company cares about them, and it also encourages them to address their concerns before these issues become more serious. In addition, by tracking the kinds of questions and concerns being voiced, top management gains invaluable insight for improving organizational conditions.

Because as much as 40 percent of calls are made after regular working hours or on weekends, today's companies are finding it difficult to staff their own hotlines. As a result, some organizations have outsourced their hotline services. In fact, several companies — including Pinkerton Services Group, the largest supplier of outsourced hotlines — have emerged in response to this need.[87]

ETHICS MATTERS

Sears uses a toll-free ethics hotline, known as the "Ethics Assist" line, to guide employees in distinguishing between right and wrong.[88] This is part of a focused effort, including a detailed code of ethics and intensive training, that is designed to get employees at all corporate levels to follow high moral standards. ▪

FIGURE 8.14

Suggestion Systems: A Potentially Effective Source of Feedback

The idea behind suggestion systems is straightforward: Invite your employees to recommend ways of improving things. This technique is only effective, however, when employees believe that their ideas will be considered carefully — and that they will be rewarded fairly for offering them.

Source: THE FAR SIDE © FARWORKS, INC. Used by permission. All rights reserved.

A third set of techniques, known as *"brown bag" meetings* and *"skip level" meetings*, are designed to facilitate communication between people who usually do not get together because they work at different organizational levels.[89] Brown bag meetings are informal get-togethers during breakfast or lunch—brought in from home, hence the name "brown bag"—at which people discuss what is going on in the company. The informal nature of these meetings is designed to encourage the open sharing of ideas (eating a sandwich out of a bag is an equalizer!). Skip level meetings do essentially the same thing; these are gatherings of employees with corporate superiors more than one level higher than themselves in the organizational hierarchy. The idea is that new lines of communication can be established by bringing together people who are two or more levels apart and who usually do not come into contact with each other.

Finally, *employee surveys* can gather information about employees' attitudes and opinions regarding key areas of organizational operations. Questionnaires administered at regular intervals may be useful for spotting changes in attitudes as they occur. Such surveys tend to be quite effective when their results are shared with employees, especially when these results form the basis for changing how things are done. Some managers even go so far as to ask their employees to rate them on a "report card."[90]

Be a Supportive Communicator: Enhancing Relationships

To be an effective communicator, you must practice **supportive communication**. By this, we mean any communication that is accurate, honest, and builds and enhances relationships instead of jeopardizing them.

Simply put, how you act toward another influences the nature of your relationship with that person, which in turn influences the quality of communication, which in turn may influence various work-related attitudes (see chapter 5) and job performance. For example, suppose you send someone a very abrasive, insensitive message. That person is likely to become distant, distrustful, and to believe you are uncaring. In turn, this leads the attacked person to become defensive, thus spending more time and energy constructing a good defense rather than listening carefully to your message—a message that is not attended to carefully is not comprehended, thus leading to problematic job performance. For a summary of this process, see Figure 8.15.

This discussion leads to a very important question: How can I become a supportive communicator? Several tried-and-true tactics can be identified.[91]

Focus on the Problem, Not the Person   Referring to an individual's characteristics (e.g., saying "You are lazy.") likely will make that person defensive (e.g., thinking, "No, I'm not."). However, focusing on the problem itself (e.g., saying "We lost the account.") likely will move the conversation toward a solution (e.g., asking "What can we do about it?"). Communication tends to be far more supportive when it focuses on the problem and possible solutions than on any one person's beliefs about the characteristics of another.

Honestly Say What You Mean   Too often, people avoid difficult matters by disguising their true feelings. So, instead of saying everything is fine when everything clearly is not, make clear how you feel. Do not be afraid of saying, "I'm upset by what you did."

supportive communication

Any communication that is accurate and honest and that builds and enhances relationships instead of jeopardizing them.

It is important to caution that what it takes to be a supportive communicator is not the same in all countries. For example, it is deeply engrained in Asian cultures to *not* be direct. ▪

GLOBAL MATTERS

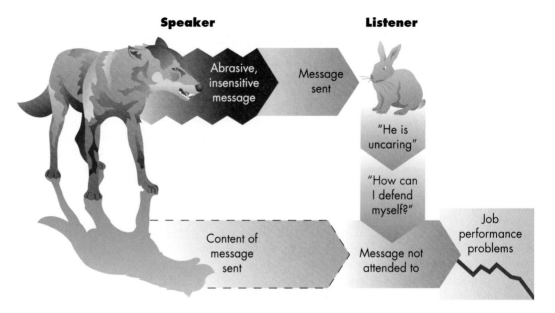

Speaker **Listener**

Abrasive, insensitive message → Message sent

"He is uncaring"

"How can I defend myself?"

Content of message sent → Message not attended to → Job performance problems

FIGURE 8.15

Nonsupportive Communication: A Cause of Performance Problems

As summarized here, communicating with someone in a nonsupportive fashion can interfere with that person's attention to messages needed to perform his or her job properly.

Own Your Decisions Do not hesitate to make clear exactly what you did and how you feel. For example, it is far more supportive to explain to someone precisely why you voted to deny his or her request than to hide behind a general statement (e.g., "The committee saw problems in your proposal."). If you were on the committee, speak for yourself.

Use Validating Language When you do speak your mind, avoid language that arouses negative feelings about someone's self-worth (e.g., "What can you expect from a lawyer?") Statements of this type use what is referred to as **invalidating language**.[92] It is far more effective to state your point in a way that makes people feel recognized and accepted for who they are — that is, to use **validating language**. For example, you might say, "I'm not sure I agree, but I'm interested in hearing your side." This is a far more supportive approach.

invalidating language

Language that arouses negative feelings about one's self-worth.

validating language

Language that makes people feel recognized and accepted for who they are.

YOU BE THE CONSULTANT

The employees in a company's phone center are not paying any attention to new procedures. They also spend so much time bickering with each other that their productivity is suffering. You are called in to handle this situation.

1. How might differences in personal communication styles be at the heart of this situation? What can be done about this?
2. Could sex differences and culture differences be part of the problem?
3. What can be done to make the employees better listeners and more supportive of each other? How do you think these measures would help to address the problem?

Keep the Conversation Going   Saying something like "that's nice, let me tell you about my problems" is a real conversation-stopper. By deflecting the speaker's concerns to your own, you are not being supportive at all. It is far more supportive to probe for additional information (e.g., "Tell me about it.") or by reflecting back what you think the speaker has said (e.g., "If I heard you correctly, you feel . . ."). Another trick for helping conversations to move along is using **conjunctive statements**—that is, comments that connect what you will be saying with the speaker's remarks—instead of using **disjunctive statements**—that is, comments that are disconnected from the speaker's remarks. For example, it is better to say something like "On that same topic, I think . . ." as opposed to something on a completely different subject. Doing so is sure to end the conversation.

conjunctive statements
Statements that keep conversations going by connecting remarks of one speaker with those of another.

disjunctive statements
Statements that are disconnected from a previous statement, thus tending to bring conversations to a close.

Use Technology to Enhance Communication Efficiency

Business communication today is more likely than ever before to rely on advanced technology. After all, more than 100 million people are estimated to be using e-mail, and Internet access is common in most organizations as well as in a significant percentage of private homes.[93] As you might imagine, technology provides wonderful opportunities for people to communicate with each other more effectively. In this regard, several trends are particularly worth noting.

ETHICS MATTERS

Questions have been raised about potential violations of privacy when bosses intercept their employees' e-mail messages. Workers claim this is as inappropriate as going through their desk drawers. Some managers, however, claim that because the equipment belongs to the company, they have a right to make sure employees are not using it for personal purposes. What are your feelings on this matter? ■

Video-Mediated Communications   A particularly promising trend for enhancing communication efficiency is **video-mediated communication (VMC)**.[94] Simply put, VMC involves simultaneously transmitting audio and video between two or more computers. Companies use this technique to link inexpensively employees in distant locations, thus allowing them to have *cybermeetings*. Not only is this much less expensive than air travel in both money and time, it also allows for meetings to be scheduled at the last minute. For example, Boeing uses VMC to connect employees in the Seattle headquarters with those in satellite locations.[95]

video-mediated communication (VMC)
Conferences in which people can hear and see each other using computers.

GLOBAL MATTERS

A primary benefit of VMC is that it allows people from distant nations to come together for cybermeetings very inexpensively. ■

Although meeting others via computer makes it impossible to experience the human touch associated with being there in person, VMC is considered to be much more effective than other, more traditional forms of linking people in distant locations (e.g., phone, e-mail, fax). In fact, in several situations, VMC is preferable to these other communications media.[96] For a summary of these situations, see Table 8.2. As advances in hardware and software continue into the future, VMC should be an increasingly common tool for communication in organizations. (Meanwhile, people in today's organizations make good use of less sophisticated technology to make their meetings more effective. For a look at what some experts are doing in this area, see the "Trends" section on page 320.)

TABLE 8.2

Video-Mediated Communication (VMC): The Next Best Thing to Being There
Although video-mediated conferencing with others is not as intimate as live, in-person meetings, it is useful in a broader range of situations than communication via phone, e-mail, or fax.

MOST APPROPRIATE WHEN . . .	VMC	PHONE	E-MAIL	FAX
Communication is one-way			✓	✓
Communication is two-way	✓	✓		
Information is time-sensitive	✓	✓	✓	✓
Information needs to be in several locations at once	✓	✓	✓	✓
Immediate interaction is desired or required	✓	✓		
Input from several sources is desired or required	✓			
Visual clarification is required	✓			
Several different locations are involved	✓	✓		
Discussion involves materials stored on computer	✓			
Participants have not met before	✓			

Source: Based on suggestions by Diamond & Roberts, 1996; see note 96.

**TRENDS:
WHAT TODAY'S
COMPANIES ARE DOING**

■ **Meeting Consultants Are Making Meetings Work**

Meetings. We've all experienced them—or perhaps we should say endured them. Chances are you only rarely have enjoyed them, and it probably is even less likely you ever have gotten much from them. Not only may they be wastes of time, they may be expensive ones at that. For example, suppose a company holds a two-hour meeting each week attended by 10 people who each are paid $45,000 a year. That company is spending roughly $31,200 annually on these meetings—an amount likely to attract some attention in most corporate budgets.[97] At that price, you would expect to get something out of these sessions. Given how expensive wasted meetings may be, a growing number of companies are finding it cost-effective to invest in the services of a new breed of specialist: the meeting consultant.[98] By taking a page from their books, you should find some useful ways to improve your own meetings.

Take Edith Buhs, for example. Ms. Buhs is national director of the Academy, which teaches companies how to improve their meetings. It was Ms. Buhs who got employees of City Year, a nonprofit service organization based in Boston, to adopt the NOSTUESO rule—that is, "*N*o *O*ne *S*peaks *T*wice *U*ntil *E*verybody *S*peaks *O*nce." With this rule in place, no City Year meeting is likely to be dominated by any one person. Neither are the meetings likely to be boring. To keep things interesting, Ms. Buhs uses a creative exercise of some sort or another. For example, to celebrate City Year's tenth anniversary, she created a four-by-eight-foot magazine cover commemorating the event. Each participant took a turn sharing an idea about what stories the magazine might feature. You might find techniques such as these to be hokey, but they do the trick. Not only did everyone at the meeting get involved, no one fell asleep.

If you have big bucks to burn, you could hire meeting facilitator Douglas Griffen, who for a tidy $5,000 per day will help to bring your group meeting under control. The tool of his trade is the computer. Griffen positions participants around a U-shaped table and places a notebook computer in front of each. Then, when a question is posed to the group—for example, "What new markets can we enter?"—each participant enters his or her own answers on the bottom of the screen and sees other participants' answers at the top. As the responses appear, Griffen scans the screen for prominent themes and summarizes these for all to see. Participants vote on their favorite responses and get instantaneous results after the last vote is cast. This procedure frees participants to discuss the group's best ideas instead of shouting down the others.

Andy Koven, who founded the Institute for Better Meetings, also uses computers to keep product-development meetings moving smoothly at Mattel Media, a division of the giant toy company. Instead of writing ideas on whiteboards, Koven enters everything on a notebook computer, the screen of which is projected onto a large television screen for all to see. Koven does not participate in the meetings themselves, however. His only job is "official notetaker," recording and organizing ideas as the group proceeds. When the meeting is over, everyone gets a hard copy of the notes, and the document is e-mailed wherever it may be needed in the company. Do not think for a second that old notes are just wasted paper; such old notes led to the Hot Wheels Custom Car Designer on CD-ROM.

You might not be able to hire meeting consultants to come to your aid, but you surely can adopt some of their techniques. Although it might not be easy to do these things (old habits die hard!), the effort may be worth it. After all, didn't you say you've never been a fan of meetings? Who knows? Maybe these suggestions will turn things around. ■

Speech Technology You might have inexpensive voice recognition software installed on your computer. If so, you simply speak into a microphone, and what you say — or something like it — appears on the screen. What you may not know is that companies all over the world are using advanced speech recognition technology to do their jobs more effectively. Today's most sophisticated devices are far more accurate than what we use on our personal computers. For example, if you receive a collect call through AT&T, you are asked if you will accept the charges. A computer interprets your "yes" or "no" response, thus saving the company $100 million a year on wages they otherwise would have to pay to operators.[99]

Experts say this is only the beginning. Companies already use voice recognition technology to dial telephones, to allow customers to find telephone numbers, and to help them browse the Internet. There is more to come as well. In not too many years, perhaps you will be able to ask this book to read itself to you — and it will. (Of course, the prospect of getting the book's ideas into your head directly may be a few more years down the line.)

We invite you to visit the Greenberg page on the Prentice Hall Web site at: **www.prenhall.com/greenberg** for the monthly Greenberg update and for this chapter's World Wide Web exercise.

SUMMARY AND REVIEW OF LEARNING OBJECTIVES

1. **Describe the process of communication and its role in organizations.**
   The process of **communication** occurs when a sender of information **encodes** a message and transmits it over communication channels to a receiver, who then

decodes it and then sends **feedback**. Factors interfering with these processes are known as **noise**. Communication in organizations is used to direct individual action and to achieve coordinated action. The heart of communication is information, but communication also is used to develop friendships and to build interpersonal trust and acceptance in organizations.

2. **Identify forms of verbal media used in organizations, and explain which are most appropriate for communicating messages of which type.**
   Communication in both oral and written forms commonly is used in organizations. Verbal media range from those that are *rich* (i.e., highly personal and providing opportunities for immediate feedback), such as face-to-face discussions, to those that are *lean* (i.e., impersonal and one-way), such as flyers. Rich forms are best for communicating ambiguous and nonroutine matters, whereas lean forms are adequate for more routine matters.

3. **Explain how style of dress and use of time and space are part of nonverbal communication in organizations.**
   People tend to have greater self-confidence when they dress appropriately for the jobs they perform. Differences in what constitutes appropriate dress are widespread (e.g., *business casual* dress is rapidly becoming the new standard). People communicate their higher organizational status by requiring lower-ranking individuals to spend more time waiting for them. Status also is communicated nonverbally by use of space: Higher-status people tend to sit at the heads of rectangular tables, for example.

4. **Describe individual differences regarding how people communicate.**
   People tend to have different **personal communication styles**, six of which have been identified: the *Noble*, the *Socratic*, the *Reflective*, the *Magistrate*, the *Candidate*, and the *Senator*. Interpersonal communication is enhanced when people's styles match or when one person anticipates another's style. There also are sex differences in communication. Men tend to communicate to emphasize their status, whereas women tend to focus on making positive social connections. Such differences frequently lead to miscommunication between men and women. Cross-cultural communication is hampered by people from different cultures frequently misunderstanding each other. This may stem from different vocabularies and from subtle differences in the meanings of words that may not be understood outside a particular culture.

5. **Describe the formal forces responsible for communication in organizations.**
   Communication is influenced by **organizational structure**, which is the formally prescribed pattern of interrelationships between people. Structure dictates who must communicate with whom (as reflected in an **organizational chart**, which is a diagram outlining these reporting relationships) and the form that communication takes. Orders flow down an organizational hierarchy, and information flows upward. The upward flow of information often is distorted, however, because people are reluctant to share bad news with their superiors. Attempts at co-ordination characterize horizontal communication, which involve messages between organizational members at the same level.

6. **Describe how informal networks influence communication in organizations.**
   Information flows rapidly along *informal communication networks*. These informal connections between people are responsible for rapidly spreading information, because they transcend formal organizational boundaries. Informal pathways known as the **grapevine** often are responsible for the rapid transmission of partially inaccurate information, or **rumors**. Rumors may be costly to organizations as well as to individuals. Fortunately, however, they can be combated in several ways.

7. **Explain how people can improve the effectiveness of their communication in organizations through clear and simple language, being an active listener, gauging the flow of communication, and giving as well as receiving feedback appropriately.**

   People can become better communicators by keeping their message brief and clear, and by avoiding the use of **jargon** when communicating with those who may not be familiar with such specialized terms. They also may improve their listening skills, such as by learning to listen actively (i.e., thinking about and questioning the speaker) and attentively (i.e., without distraction). The problem of **overload** can be reduced by using *gatekeepers* (i.e., individuals who control the flow of information to others) or *queuing* (i.e., the orderly lining-up of incoming information). *Distortion* and *omission* of messages can be minimized by making messages *redundant* and encouraging their *verification*. At the organizational level, communication may be improved using techniques that open upward channels of communication to employee feedback (e.g., *suggestion systems, corporate hotlines,* and *employee surveys*).

8. **Describe how you can become a supportive communicator and can use technology to become a more efficient communicator.**

   Supportive communicators make an effort to enhance their relationships with others. They do so by focusing attention on the problem and not the person, honestly saying what they mean, owning their decisions, using validating language, and keeping the conversation going. Advances in technology are enhancing the efficiency of communication in several ways; for example, both **video-mediated conferencing** and *speech recognition technology* are being used with growing frequency.

QUESTIONS FOR DISCUSSION

1. Using an example of everyday communication in organization (e.g., a supervisor asking her assistant for the month's production schedule), describe how the communication process operates (e.g., how information is encoded).

2. Imagine you are a district manager explaining a new corporate policy to a group of plant managers. Should you use written communication, spoken communication, or both? Explain your decision.

3. Suppose you are interviewing for a job. Describe how the way you dress and the interviewer's use of time and space can influence what you communicate to each other.

4. Suppose you find yourself having difficulty communicating with a new coworker. Explain how individual differences might be responsible for this and what can be done to overcome them.

5. Imagine your company is being victimized by an untrue rumor about a pending merger. What can you do to put the story to an end? Explain.

6. In Shakespeare's *Hamlet*, Polonius says, "Give every man thine ear, but few thy voice." Discuss the implications of this advice for being an active listener. How else can you enhance the effectiveness of listening?

7. Suppose that whenever you need to talk to a subordinate, you find that they either do not understand or are afraid of you. What can you do to avoid these problems?

Physician Sales & Service: Where Keeping Up with Policies Is More Fun Than Any Policy Manual

At most large companies with different facilities, the challenge of getting things done uniformly is met in straightforward fashion. You have rules, regulations, and procedures, so you write a policy manual. Then you toss it at your managers. All too often, however, those managers toss it right back—to the forsaken recesses of a file drawer.

Acknowledging how useless this practice can be, the founders of Physician Sales & Service (PSS) have taken another approach to corporate communication: They don't write down much. In fact, people in the various branches—86 in the United States and several more in Europe—are only asked to read the first memo sent to them from the corporate office each month. When company officials do share important information in writing, they don't count on any boring policy manuals. For example, when company lawyers insisted PSS have a written nondiscrimination policy, they created a poster using cartoon characters to explain it, and then they hung one in each facility. When company founder Patrick Kelly wanted to get across the company's top 20 core values, he printed them on wallet-size cards for all employees to carry.

None of these tactics means that Kelly and his associates do not get involved in branch operations. Far from it. As Kelly explains, "We certainly want uniformity from one branch to another. PSS's reputation rests on delivering world-class service to its customers, and we have developed systems and methods to ensure that customers get that service. We have our business model, and we don't really want local-branch leaders experimenting with business models of their own."

So, how does PSS maintain uniformity without a policy manual? They use a 100-point checklist known as the Blue Ribbon book. For example: Are the trucks clean? Are there refreshments for guests? Are truck maintenance logs properly maintained. Is there a "Wall of Fame" celebrating employee accomplishments? To ensure these—and the other 96—standards are met, Kelly or another company official makes an unan-

nounced visit to each branch twice a year for a "Blue Ribbon Tour." In true PSS style, however, these are not military-type inspections. Rather, they are fun events in which employees start hooting and hollering as they run around emptying wastebaskets and checking restrooms for toilet paper.

By marking "pass" or "fail" for each of the 100 standards, each branch can score as many as 100 points. Not only does the highest-scoring branch earn bragging rights inside the company, each employee gets a bonus as well. These bonuses range from $3,000 per employee of the top-scoring branch to $500 per employee of the tenth-highest-scoring branch—funds that come from the operating profits of all the other branches. If a branch performs poorly, though, no one gets in trouble. Instead, as Kelly figures, they have plenty of incentive to do better next time. The Blue Ribbon Tour keeps employees following company standards far more stringently than a more standard policy manual.

CRITICAL THINKING QUESTIONS

1. What makes the approach taken at PSS so successful? Would this approach be as effective in the organization in which you work? Why, or why not?

2. What place, if any, do you believe formal policy manuals have in an organization? Explain where they may be most useful.

3. What do you think of rewarding employees for performing well on Blue Ribbon Tours? Do you think this practice will be effective in the long run?

4. What other novel tactics might be used to communicate company policies?

5. How might the various techniques for improving organizational communication described in this chapter be used to communicate organizational policies at PSS?

Communication in Organizations

SMALL BUSINESS 2000

To deliver a message, we must communicate. We communicate in many ways: through our actions, through our words, through our appearance, and even through the company we keep. What is communicated and how it is communicated are important to relationships between individuals, between departments in a company, and between a company and its customers.

Milt Moses, the leader of the Community Insurance Company, understands the importance of good communication in the success or failure of a business. In this video case, Moses talks to us about the importance of communication from various perspectives. In describing how he was motivated to enter the insurance field, we learn about an impression of the industry that he got from his own insurance agent. Moses was not actively recruited; in fact, he sought out the job. Why did he pursue insurance? Through observation, Moses got the idea that insurance could be a lucrative business—and one that might present fewer barriers to him than other careers he had considered. In his own agency, Moses uses many approaches to convey a good image to the community.

Moses also talks about communication within his own agency. We hear about his style of communicating with his staff, his policy toward maintaining an open door, and his belief in the importance of providing top-quality service. His employees do not learn these things about Moses and the company by chance. Everyone who works at Community Insurance does not necessarily get the same message in the same way or at the same time.

One challenge any company faces is to communicate so that the general message gets across. Moses shows us that this can be done in several ways. We see evidence of business planning, job assignment, and an openness to talk with employees. Perhaps most importantly, we get the feeling that Moses walks the talk; not only does he share his beliefs about business, he openly practices them.

QUESTIONS FOR DISCUSSION

1. It seems obvious that at the Community Insurance Company, Milt Moses sets the tone. What do you think Moses is trying to convey to his staff about how the company should operate? Do you think he is successful in conveying this message?

2. You have learned an instance when Moses sent very interesting messages through his actions. For example, listening to music was banned at first but later was allowed as long as employees used headsets. Why do you think Moses changed his mind and allowed something he did not necessarily agree with? What messages do you think this sent to Moses's staff?

3. Moses emphasizes the need to provide superb customer service. In fact, he appears to believe that such service is the key to success in his industry. From what you have learned about the Community Insurance Company and Moses, do you think he is successful in communicating his commitment to providing excellent service? Why, or why not?

EXPERIENCING ORGANIZATIONAL BEHAVIOR

Assessing Your Personal Communication Style

When you read about the six different personal communication styles, did you have some idea of which you tend to use? The following test, which is based on questions similar to those used by scientists to test communication style, should give you a good idea of your own personal communication style.

Directions

Read all 18 of the following statements, and for each one, think of how you *actually* communicate (not of what you think you should do). If you believe the statement describes how you usually communicate, mark "Yes" in the space to the left. If you believe the statement does not describe how you usually communicate, mark "No."

_____ 1. When I talk to others, I tend to be direct and straightforward.

_____ 2. I am a "tell it like it is" kind of person.

_____ 3. I freely share my opinions with others.

_____ 4. I usually say the first thing that comes to mind.

_____ 5. I tend to get impatient when others speak.

_____ 6. I tend to avoid long, detailed discussions.

_____ 7. I very much enjoy chatting with other people.

_____ 8. I tend to give very long, exact directions to others.

_____ 9. I sometimes am accused of being redundant.

_____ 10. I am prone to explain things using anecdotes and examples.

_____ 11. I enjoy arguing and debating things with others.

_____ 12. I have seen people "tune me out" when I speak.

_____ 13. People tend to tell me their problems.

_____ 14. I tend to ignore people who seem angry.

_____ 15. I tend to be soft-spoken.

_____ 16. I may tell another person I agree even if I do not.

_____ 17. People tend to interrupt me when I am speaking.

_____ 18. I tend to be polite and supportive when I talk to people.

Scoring

1. Add the number of "Yes" responses to items 1 through 6. This is your Noble score.

2. Add the number of "Yes" responses to items 7 through 12. This is your Socratic score.

3. Add the number of "Yes" responses to items 13 through 18. This is your Reflective score.

4. To determine your style, compare your scores with each other:

   a. If your Noble score is highest, you are a Noble. If your Socratic score is highest, you are a Socratic. If your Reflective score is highest, you are a Reflective. These are the three dominant styles.

b. If your Noble and Socratic scores are close to each other but far from your Reflective score, you are a Magistrate. If your Socratic and Reflective scores are close to each other but far from your Noble score, you are a Candidate. If your Noble and Reflective scores are close to each other but far from your Socratic score, you are a Senator.

c. If all three scores are close to each other, you might not be aware of how you communicate. Retake the test, concentrating on what you actually do instead of what you think you should do.

Questions for Discussion

1. What style did the test reveal for you? How did this compare with the style you thought you had?

2. Based on the descriptions of the personal communication styles in the text, could you guess in advance which items were indicative of which styles? What additional items might be added to the test to assess each style?

3. How effective do you think you would be in altering your communication style to match another's?

SKILLS BANK

WORKING IN GROUPS

Sharpening Your Listening Skills

Are you a good listener? Are you a *really* good listener—that is, one who understands exactly what someone else is saying? Most of us tend to think we are much better than we really are when it comes to this important skill. After all, we've been listening to others our whole lives, and with that much practice, we certainly must be okay. To gain some insight into your own listening skills, try the following group exercise.

Directions

1. Divide the class into pairs of people who do not already know each other. Arrange the chairs so the people within each pair are facing one another but also are separated from the other pairs.

2. Within each pair, select one person as the speaker and the other as the listener. The speaker should tell the listener about a specific incident on the job during which he or she was harmed (e.g., disappointed by not getting a raise, being embarrassed by another, losing a battle with a coworker, getting fired) and how he or she felt about it. The total discussion should last approximately 10 to 15 minutes.

3. Listeners should attempt to follow the suggestions for good listening summarized in Figure 8.12. To help, the instructor should discuss these suggestions with the class.

4. After the conversations are finished, review the suggestions with your partner. Discuss which ones the listener followed and which the listener ignored. Be as open and honest as possible about assessing strengths and weaknesses. Speakers should consider the extent to which they felt the listeners really paid attention to them.

5. Repeat steps 2 through 4, but this time, change the roles. (Speakers now become listeners, and listeners now become speakers.)

6. As a class, share your experiences as speakers and listeners.

Questions for Discussion

1. What did this exercise teach you about your own skills as a listener?

2. Was there general agreement or disagreement about each listener's strengths and weaknesses? Explain.

3. After the discussion about the first listener's effectiveness, you might expect the second listener to do better. Was this the case in your own group and throughout the class?

4. Which listening skills were easiest and which were most difficult to put into practice? Are there certain conditions under which good listening skills may be difficult to implement?

5. Do you think you will learn something from this exercise that will improve your listening skills in other situations? If so, what? If not, why not?

9

DECISION MAKING IN ORGANIZATIONS

LEARNING OBJECTIVES

After reading this chapter, you should be able to

1. Identify the steps in the *analytical model of decision making*.

2. Distinguish *programmed* from *nonprogrammed* decisions, *certain* from *uncertain* decisions, and *top-down* from *empowered* decisions.

3. Distinguish the various *individual decision styles*.

4. Describe the trade-offs involved in group vs. individual decision making.

5. Identify the various organizational and cultural factors that influence the decision-making process.

6. Distinguish between three approaches to decision making: the *rational-economic model*, the *administrative model*, and *image theory*.

7. Identify the various types of *framing effects* and *heuristics* that potentially limit the effectiveness of decisions.

8. Describe how the bias toward *implicit favorites* and the *escalation of commitment* lead to imperfect decisions.

9. Compare the conditions in which groups make superior decisions with those in which individuals make superior decisions.

10. Describe the various techniques for enhancing the quality of individual as well as group decisions.

PREVIEW CASE

Deere Reinvents Itself to Plow Ahead

During the early 1830s, farming the sticky soil of the U.S. prairie was difficult using the cast-iron plows that worked so well in the looser soil back east. Every few feet, clumps of accumulated soil would need to be scraped from the plow blade, making high-production agriculture impossible. Then, in 1837, things changed. Facing hard times in Vermont, a blacksmith named John Deere moved west and opened a shop in Grand Detour, Illinois. There, he produced the first commercially successful, self-scouring steel plow — which effectively opened the prairie to farming. Needless to say, farm equipment has come a long way in more than 160 years, but one thing has remained constant: Challenging decisions affecting the fate of this business always loom on the horizon.

During the Great Depression of the 1930s, Deere & Co. helped its hard-hit customers by carrying the accounts of debtor farmers. Such generosity built a strong base of incredibly loyal customers, who have served Deere well over three generations. That loyalty provided little support, however, when the "farm depression" of the 1980s hit. Business eroded so much that Deere factories ran at less than half capacity, thereby forcing the company to lay off tens of thousands of employees. Things improved somewhat in the 1990s, but the rollercoaster economy as well as foreign competition have forced Deere executives to make some tough decisions to keep this venerable icon of the American farm plowing ahead for another 160 years.

Much of this challenge has fallen onto the shoulders of Hans W. Bercherer, Deere & Co.'s chairman and CEO. Fortunately, Mr. Bercherer shares the same pioneering spirit of the company's founder and namesake. His seeds, however, are more likely to be sown in fertile fields of management ideas than in Midwestern soil. The terrain is equally rocky, however, especially with formidable competitors like International Harvester.

Even so, Mr. Bercherer and his associates have devised novel ways of luring new customers. Deere's mass-customization program is the centerpiece of this effort. Instead of selling half-million-dollar pieces of equipment and then leaving smaller firms to configure them as required, Deere now does all the customization work for its customers. When a farmer visits his local Deere dealership today, he is asked a series of questions about his farming practices (e.g., the number of rows planted, how tightly spaced they are) so the company can prepare a one-of-a-kind machine to do exactly what the farmer needs. A few months later, the farmer's dream machine is working the fields. Deere can offer more than any small, aftermarket provider can when it comes to tractor attachments, and by providing one-stop shopping, Deere agents makes purchasing a simple matter for busy farmers. Moreover, by establishing an individual relationship with its customers, Deere officials believe the company will fare well even during periods of agricultural decline.

To hedge its bets, however, Deere has branched into businesses its founder never could have imagined. For example, to generate brand awareness, Deere now puts its logo on a line of preschool toys and is sponsoring NASCAR races, and since 1986, Deere has been in the healthcare business as well — extending to client companies the managed-care plan developed for its own employees. John Deere Health Care now provides health-care services to some 1,400 companies.

Such changes were jarring to many long-time Deere employees. Some in the Moline, Illinois, headquarters even broke down and cried as the company discarded many of its old ways. Stockholders, however, have been crying all the way to the bank as Deere & Co. has enjoyed unprecedented earnings, including a record net income of $1 billion in fiscal 1998. Even with this rosy financial picture, however, it would be premature to say Deere is completely out of the woods. Experts caution there still may be more rocky soil to plow through in the years ahead as the company faces challenges brought on by advances in biotechnology. Still, given its executives' willingness to make tough decisions, there seems to be considerable validity to the company's advertising slogan: "Nothing can stop a Deere."

As the world's leading producer of agricultural equipment, Deere & Co., which now does business in 160 countries, has come a long way from its humble beginnings as a company founded on a good idea by an ambitious New England blacksmith. Beneath the obvious success story, however, lies another tale — a parallel account of a string of decisions. Beginning with John Deere's decision to leave Vermont and open a foundry in Illinois through a CEO's decision to change and diversify the company's business, Deere & Co.'s story really is about *decision making*. So, too, is the story of any business, in fact, and of your own personal story as well.

Admittedly, in the grand scheme of things, the decisions you make may be less monumental than those involved in running a large corporation. Still, personal questions about what college to attend, what classes to take, and what company to work for may be difficult to answer—and their answers are important to you. If you consider the difficulties involved with making decisions in your own life, you surely can appreciate how complicated—and important—the process of decision making can be in organizations, where the stakes often are considerable and the effect widespread. In both cases, however, the essential nature of **decision making** is identical: It may be defined as the process of making choices from among several alternatives.

decision making
The process of choosing among several alternatives.

Decision making is one of the most—if not *the* most—important of all managerial activities.[1] Management theorists and researchers agree that decision making represents one of the most common and crucial activities for executives. Everyday, people in organizations make decisions about topics ranging from the mundane to the monumental.[2] Understanding how these decisions are made—and how they can be improved—is an important goal in the field of OB.

In this chapter, we examine theories, research, and practical managerial techniques concerned with decision making in organizations, both by individuals and by groups. Beginning with individuals, we review various perspectives on how people make decisions. We then identify factors that may adversely affect the quality of individual decisions as well as ways of combating them—that is, techniques for improving the quality of decisions. Next, we focus on group decisions and the conditions under which individuals and under which groups are each better suited to making decisions. Finally, we describe factors that make group decisions imperfect and various techniques that can improve their quality. First, however, we examine the general nature of the decision-making process and the variety of decisions made in organizations.

THE NATURE OF DECISION MAKING

We begin by examining the basic nature of the decision-making process. Thus, we present a model describing the general steps by which decisions are made, and then consider the idea that all people do not make decisions in the same manner. Specifically, we discuss individual as well as cultural differences in how people make decisions.

An Analytical Model of the Decision-Making Process

Traditionally, scientists have conceptualized the decision-making process as a series of analytical steps that groups or individuals take to solve problems.[3] A general model of this process, which is known as the **analytical model of decision making**, can help us to understand the complex nature of organizational decision making (Figure 9.1).[4] This approach highlights two important aspects of making decisions: *formulation*, which is the process of understanding a problem and making a decision about it; and *implementation*, which is the process of carrying out that decision.[5] Keep in mind that all decisions might not conform to the neat, eight-step pattern described in this model (e.g., steps may be skipped or combined).[6] To point out how the decision-making process operates, in general, however, this model is quite useful.

analytical model of decision making
A general model that describes the formulation and implementation of decisions occurring in eight steps.

The first step is *problem identification*. To decide how to solve a problem, one first must recognize and identify it. For example, an executive may identify the company not being able to meet its payroll obligations as being a problem. This step is not always as easy as it sounds, however. In fact, people often distort, omit, ignore, and discount information that provides important cues regarding the existence of problems.[7] You may recall from our discussion of social perception (see chapter 2) that people do not always perceive social situations accurately. In turn, someone may fail to recognize a problem if doing so makes him or her uncomfortable. Thus, denying a problem may be the first impediment on the road to solving it.

FIGURE 9.1

The Traditional, Analytical Model of Decision Making

In general, the process of decision making follows the eight steps outlined here. Note how each may be applied to a hypothetical organizational problem, such as having insufficient funds to meet payroll obligations.

(*Source*: Based on information in Wedley & Field, 1983; see note 4.)

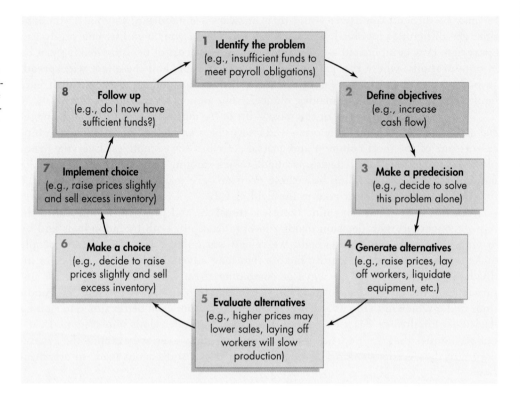

1 **Identify the problem** (e.g., insufficient funds to meet payroll obligations)

2 **Define objectives** (e.g., increase cash flow)

3 **Make a predecision** (e.g., decide to solve this problem alone)

4 **Generate alternatives** (e.g., raise prices, lay off workers, liquidate equipment, etc.)

5 **Evaluate alternatives** (e.g., higher prices may lower sales, laying off workers will slow production)

6 **Make a choice** (e.g., decide to raise prices slightly and sell excess inventory)

7 **Implement choice** (e.g., raise prices slightly and sell excess inventory)

8 **Follow up** (e.g., do I now have sufficient funds?)

ETHICS MATTERS   More often than you might imagine, ethical problems arise when people fail to recognize what they are doing as being inappropriate. For example, if everyone else is taking company property, stealing will not be identified as a problem. How can managers avoid these kinds of problems? ■

After a problem is identified, the next step is to *define the objectives to be met in solving the problem*. It is important to conceive of problems in a way that allows possible solutions to be identified. In our example, the problem identified may be defined as not having enough money — or in business terms, "inadequate cash flow." By looking at the problem this way, the objective becomes clear: increase available cash reserves. Any possible solution to the problem should be evaluated relative to this objective, and a good solution will be one that meets it.

The third step is to *make a predecision*. A **predecision** is a decision about how to make a decision. By assessing the type of problem identified as well as other aspects of the situation, managers may opt to make a decision themselves, to delegate the decision to another, or to have a group make the decision. Predecisions should be based on research into the nature of decisions made under different circumstances, many of which we review later in this chapter.

For many years, managers have relied on their own intuition or empirically based information about OB (contained in books like this) for guidance when making predecisions.[8] Recently, however, computer programs have been developed that summarize much of this information and, thereby, give managers ready access to a wealth of social science information that may help with predecisions.[8] Such **decision support systems (DSS)**, as they are called, can only be as good as the social science information that goes into developing them, but DSS techniques are effective in helping people to make decisions about solving problems.[9] Use of decision-making technology leads to higher-quantity and better quality outcomes than those made without such techniques.[10] (For an example of DSS in a particularly vital application, see the "Trends" section on page 333.)

predecision

A decision about which process to follow in making a decision.

decision support systems (DSS)

Computer programs that present information about OB to decision-makers in a manner that helps them to structure their responses to decisions.

■ Naval Officers Use Decision Support Systems to Make Combat Decisions

The phrase "don't fire until you see the whites of their eyes" may have provided useful guidance to soldiers in the Revolutionary War, but today, the guidelines for military engagements rely on more advanced technology. In particular, sophisticated decision support systems (DSS) assist combat officers in deciding precisely what actions to take in combat situations. For example, in the U.S. Navy, a program known as *Tactical Decision Making Under Stress* (*TADMUS*) was initiated in response to the accidental downing of an Iranian civilian aircraft by the U.S.S. *Vincennes* in 1988.[11]

The technology on which the Navy's DSS is based may be sophisticated, but the basic idea is straightforward: To summarize incoming information and present it in a format that helps officers to take the appropriate action. For example, suppose an unknown object is spotted in the skies. Based on key variables (e.g., where it came from, size, speed, and so on), computers help to identify the degree of threat it poses and to recommend appropriate action — ranging from issuing a warning to shooting it down. Officers then can use this information as the basis for making an appropriate military decision.

Research using experienced military personnel in simulated combat situations found that DSS was helpful in three key ways.[12] Specifically, the Navy's DSS had the following effects:

- It helped officers to identify possible enemy targets both earlier and more accurately.
- It significantly increased the amount of time available to military officers for making vital decisions.
- It helped military personnel track suspicious targets without asking each other as many questions about what they thought they saw.

Given these benefits, the military personnel in this study became strong advocates of DSS. They especially liked that the system did not make crucial military decisions for them but rather simply gave the information they needed to make those decisions themselves. In other words, the computers did not replace the military experts. Instead, they summarized incoming information in a way that helped them to make better decisions, which is precisely what a DSS is all about. ■

The fourth step in the process is *alternative generation*, in which possible solutions are identified. When coming up with solutions, people tend to rely on previously used approaches that might provide ready-made answers.[13] In our example, some possible solutions to the revenue shortage would be reducing the workforce, selling unnecessary equipment and material, and increasing sales.

Because these possibilities may not be equally feasible, the fifth step is *evaluating alternative solutions*. Which solution is best? What is the most effective way of raising the revenue needed to meet the payroll? Some alternatives may be more effective than others, and some may be more difficult to implement than others. For example, increasing sales would help to solve the problem, but this is easier said than done. True, it is a solution, but it is not an immediately practical one.

In the sixth step, *a choice is made*. As we describe later, different approaches to decision making offer different views of how thoroughly people consider their alternatives — and of how optimal their chosen alternative is. Choosing a course of action is the step that most often comes to mind when we think about the decision-making process.

The seventh step calls for *implementation of the chosen alternative*. In other words, the chosen alternative is performed.

The eighth — and final — step is *follow-up*. Monitoring the effectiveness of decisions put into action is important to the success of organizations. Does the problem still exist? Has the solution caused any new problems? In other words, seek feedback about the effectiveness of any attempted solution. This is why the decision-making process is presented as being circular in Figure 9.1. If the solution works, the problem may be considered solved; if not, a new solution must be attempted.

It is important to reiterate this is a very general model of the decision-making process. It may not be followed exactly as specified in all circumstances, but it does paint a good picture of the general nature of this complex set of operations.

The Broad Spectrum of Organizational Decisions

Because decision making is so fundamental to organizations, decisions themselves tend to be of many different kinds. Understanding the variety of decisions that are made in organizations is an important, first step toward understanding the nature of the decision-making process. Therefore, we now distinguish between decisions in three important ways: how routine they are, how much risk is involved, and who in the organization makes them.

programmed decisions

Highly routine decisions made according to pre-established organizational routines and procedures.

nonprogrammed decisions

Decisions made about highly novel problems for which there are no prespecified courses of action.

Programmed and Nonprogrammed Decisions   Think of a decision that is made repeatedly and according to a pre-established set of alternatives. For example, a word-processing operator may decide to make a back-up copy of the day's work on disk, or a manager of a fast-food restaurant may decide to order hamburger buns as the supply begins to get low. Decisions such as these are known as **programmed decisions** — that is, routine decisions by lower-level personnel that rely on predetermined courses of action.

In contrast, we also may identify **nonprogrammed decision** — that is, ones for which no ready-made solutions exist. In these cases, the decision-maker confronts a unique situation, and the solutions are equally novel. For example, a research scientist attempting to cure a rare disease faces a problem that is poorly structured. Unlike an order clerk, whose course of action is clear when the supply of paper clips runs low, the scientist must rely on creativity rather than pre-existing answers to solve the problem at hand.

strategic decisions

Nonprogrammed decisions, typically made by high-level executives, regarding the direction the organization should take to achieve its mission.

Certain types of nonprogrammed decisions are known as **strategic decisions**.[14] Typically, these decisions are made by coalitions of high-level executives and have important, long-term implications for the organization. Strategic decisions reflect a consistent pattern for directing the organization in some specified fashion — that is, according to an underlying organizational philosophy or mission. For example, an organization may make a strategic decision to grow at a specified yearly rate or to be guided by a code of corporate ethics. Both decisions are likely to be considered "strategic," because they guide the future direction of the organization.

Table 9.1 summarizes the differences between programmed and nonprogrammed decisions regarding three important questions. First, *what types of tasks are involved?* Programmed decisions are made on common and routine tasks, whereas nonprogrammed decisions are made on unique and novel tasks. Second, *how much reliance is there on organizational policies?* In making programmed decisions, a decision-maker can count on guidance from statements of organizational policy and procedure. Nonprogrammed decisions, however, require creative solutions that are implemented for the first time; past solutions may provide little guidance. Finally, *who makes the decisions?* Not surprisingly, nonprogrammed decisions typically are made by upper-level

TABLE 9.1

Programmed and Nonprogrammed Decisions: A Comparison

The two major types of organizational decisions—programmed decisions and nonprogrammed decisions—differ regarding the types of task on which they are made, the degree to which solutions may be found in existing organizational policies, and the typical decision-making unit.

	TYPE OF DECISION	
VARIABLE	PROGRAMMED DECISIONS	NONPROGRAMMED DECISIONS
Type of task	Simple, routine	Complex, creative
Reliance on organizational policies	Considerable guidance from past decisions	No guidance from past decisions
Typical decision-maker	Lower-level workers (usually alone)	Upper-level supervisors (usually in groups)

organizational personnel, whereas the more routine, well-structured decisions usually are relegated to lower-level personnel.[15]

Certain and Uncertain Decisions   Just think how easy decisions would be if we knew what the future had in store. Making the best investments in the stock market would be a simple matter of looking up the changes in tomorrow's newspaper. Of course, we never actually know what the future holds, but we can be more certain at some times than at others. Certainty about the factors on which decisions are made is highly desired in organizational decision making.

Degrees of certainty and uncertainty are expressed as statements of *risk*. All organizational decisions involve some degree of risk, which ranges from complete certainty (i.e., no risk) to complete uncertainty or "a stab in the dark" (i.e., high risk). To make the best possible decisions in organizations, people seek to "manage" the risks they take—that is, they try to minimize the riskiness of a decision by gaining access to relevant information.[16]

GLOBAL MATTERS

Because they value tradition and history, Italians are uncomfortable with risk and tend to make rather conservative decisions. Australians, however, are more likely to consider innovative—and much riskier—decisions. ▪

What makes a decision risky is the *probability* of obtaining the desired outcome. Decision-makers try to obtain information about the probabilities (or odds) of certain events occurring given that other events have occurred. For example, a financial analyst may report that when the prime rate has dropped, a certain stock has risen 80 percent of the time, or a meteorologist may report that the probability of precipitation is 50 percent (i.e., in the past it has rained or snowed half the time certain atmospheric conditions existed). These data may be considered to be reports of *objective probabilities*, because they are based on concrete and verifiable data. Many decisions also are based on *subjective probabilities*—that is, personal beliefs or hunches about what will happen (Figure 9.2). For example, a gambler who bets on a horse because its name is similar to one of his children's or a person who suspects it will rain because he just washed his car is basing these judgments on subjective probabilities.

Obviously, uncertainty is an undesirable in decision-making situations. We may view much of what decision-makers do in organizations as attempting to reduce uncertainty (i.e., putting the odds in their favor) so they can make better decisions. How do organizations respond to highly uncertain conditions (i.e., when they do not know

FIGURE 9.2

The Riskiness of a Decision: A Summary

Decisions differ in their degree of riskiness based on how certain (i.e., high probability) or uncertain (i.e., low probability) various outcomes may be. Information—both objective and subjective—is used as the basis for estimating the probability of a decision outcome.

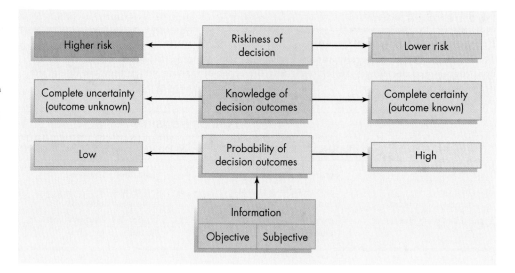

what the future holds)? Decision uncertainty can be reduced by *establishing linkages with other organizations*. The more an organization knows about what another will do, the greater certainty it has in making decisions.[17] This is part of a general tendency for organizational decision-makers to respond to uncertainty by reducing the unpredictability of other organizations in their business environments. Those outside organizations with which managers have the greatest contact are most likely to be those whose actions are copied.[18]

In general, what reduces uncertainty in decision-making situations? The answer is *information*. Knowledge about the past and the present can help when making projections about the future. A modern executive's access to the data needed for important decisions may be as close as the nearest computer. Indeed, computer technology has greatly aided a manager's ability to make decisions quickly by making the most accurate and thorough information available.[19] A variety of on-line information services now provide organizational decision-makers with the latest information relevant to the decisions they are making.

Of course, not all such information comes from computers. Many managerial decisions also are based on the decision-maker's past experiences and intuition.[20] This is not to say top managers rely on subjective information when making decisions—although they might. Rather, their history of past decisions—both the successes and the failures—often is given great weight in the decision-making process. In other words, when making decisions, people often rely on what has worked for them in the past. This strategy often is successful partly because experienced decision-makers tend to make better use of information relevant to the decisions they are making.[21] Individuals with expertise in certain subjects know what information is most relevant as well as how to interpret that information to make the best decisions. Therefore, it should not be surprising that people seek experienced professionals (e.g., doctors and lawyers who are seasoned veterans in their fields) when it comes to making important decisions. With high levels of expertise also comes information relevant to assessing the riskiness of the available alternatives—and to reducing that risk.

Top-down and Empowered Decisions   Traditionally, the job of making all but the most menial decisions in organizations has belonged to managers. In fact, organizational scientist Herbert Simon, who won a Nobel prize for his work on the economics of decision making, has even described decision making as being synonymous with managing.[22] Subordinates collect information and give it to their superiors, who then use it to make decisions. Known as **top-down decision making**, this approach puts the

top-down decision-making

The practice of vesting decision-making power in superiors as opposed to their lower-level employees.

power to make decisions in the hands of managers, thus leaving lower-level workers with little or no opportunity to make decisions. If this sounds familiar, well, it has been the way most organizations have operated.

Today, however, a new approach has come into vogue. The idea of **empowered decision making** allows employees to make the decisions required to do their jobs without seeking supervisory approval. As the name implies, this approach gives employees the power to decide what they must do to do their jobs effectively. The rationale is that the people who actually do the jobs know best, so having someone else make the decision may not make the most sense. In addition, when people are empowered to make their own decisions, they are more likely to accept the consequences of them. If the decision is good, they can feel good about it, and if the decision is bad, they learn a valuable lesson for next time. In either case, people are more committed to actions based on decisions they have made themselves than they are to actions based on decisions others have made. Such commitment can be important in keeping the organization functioning effectively.

Today, many companies are empowering their employees to make a variety of decisions. For example, the Ritz-Carlton hotel chain has empowered each employee to spend as much as $2,000 of the company's money per day to fix whatever needs to be repaired. No longer does a chambermaid who finds a broken lamp need to fill out a form, which then gets passed from one person to the next. He or she is empowered to get the right person to get the job done immediately (Figure 9.3).

Work teams may be empowered as well. For example, employees at the Chesapeake Packaging Company's box plant in Baltimore, Maryland, are organized into eight separate, internal companies.[23] Each such unit is empowered to make its own decisions about key issues, such as ordering, purchasing new equipment, and measuring its own work. Indeed, the concept of self-managed work teams discussed in chapter 7 involves systematically empowering individuals working together with the tools needed to make the most effective decisions possible.

FIGURE   9.3

Empowered Decision Making at "Team Zebra"

Members of Kodak's black-and-white film-manufacturing unit, "Team Zebra," have been highly successful in large part because they are empowered to make decisions about how to perform their jobs.

ETHICS MATTERS

At Maguire Group—a small, professional architecture and engineering firm in Foxborough, Massachusetts—27 employees from various levels worked together for eight months to develop a code of ethics to guide their own behavior.[24] The decisions they made about ethical issues arising in their work (e.g., potential conflicts of interest) are considered to be central to this company's reputation for impeccable integrity. ∎

FACTORS AFFECTING DECISIONS IN ORGANIZATIONS

Given how fundamental the decision-making process is in organizations, this process is influenced by many factors. In fact, organizational decisions are affected by all three levels studied in the field of OB—individuals, groups, and organizations—as well as by national culture. In this section, we consider each of these factors.

Decision Style: Individual Differences in Decision Making

Do all individuals make decisions in the same way? Are there differences in the approaches that people take? In general, there are meaningful differences between people in their orientation toward decisions—that is, in their **decision style**.

empowered decision making
The practice of vesting power for making decisions in the employees.

decision style
Differences between people regarding their orientations toward decisions.

decision-style model

The conceptualization according to which people use one of four predominant decision styles: *directive, analytical, conceptual,* and *behavioral.*

Some people primarily are concerned with achieving success at any cost, but others are more concerned about the effects of their decisions on others. Furthermore, some individuals are more logical and analytical in their approach to problems, whereas others are more intuitive and creative. Clearly, important differences exist in the approaches decision-makers take to problems. The **decision-style model** classifies four major decision styles (Figure 9.4).[25]

The *directive style* is characterized by people who prefer simple, clear solutions. Individuals with this style tend to make decisions rapidly, because they use little information and consider few alternatives. They tend to rely on existing rules to make their decisions, and they aggressively use their status to achieve results.

In contrast, individuals with the *analytical style* are more willing to consider complex solutions based on ambiguous information. People with this style tend to analyze their decisions carefully and to use as much data as possible. Such individuals tend to enjoy solving problems. They want the best possible answers, and they will use innovative methods to achieve them.

Compared to people with the directive or the analytical style, people with the *conceptual style* tend to be more socially oriented in their approach to problems. In other words, their approach is humanistic and artistic. Such individuals consider many broad alternatives and to solve problems creatively. They have a strong future orientation, and they enjoy initiating new ideas.

Individuals with the *behavioral style* have a deep concern for the organizations in which they work and for the personal development of their coworkers. They are highly supportive of others and concerned about others' achievements, and they frequently help others to meet their goals. Such individuals are open to suggestions from others and, therefore, tend to rely on meetings for making decisions.

Although most managers may have one dominant style, they often use many different styles. In fact, those who can shift between styles—that is, those who are most flexible in their approach to decision making—have highly complex, individualistic styles of their own. Even so, a person's dominant style reveals a great deal about how he or she tends to make decisions. Not surprisingly, conflicts often occur between individuals with different styles. For example, a manager with a highly directive style

FIGURE 9.4

Decision-Style Model: A Summary

People tend to adhere to one of the four *decision styles* summarized here.

(*Source*: Based on information in Rowe, Boulgaides, & McGrath, 1984; see note 25.)

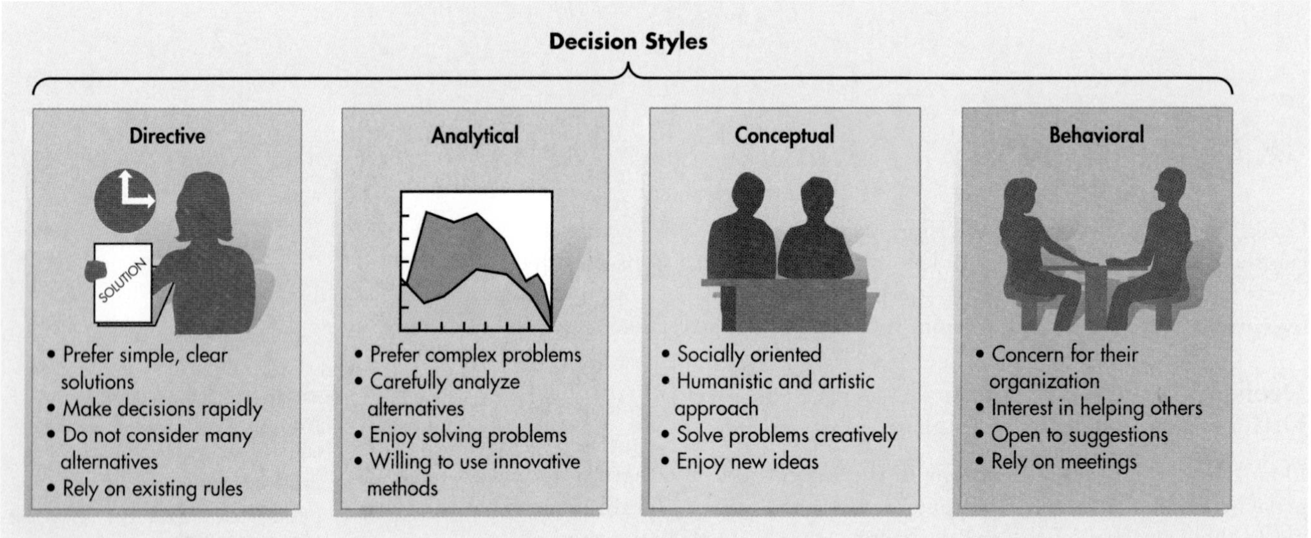

Decision Styles

Directive	Analytical	Conceptual	Behavioral

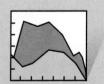

Directive	Analytical	Conceptual	Behavioral
• Prefer simple, clear solutions • Make decisions rapidly • Do not consider many alternatives • Rely on existing rules	• Prefer complex problems • Carefully analyze alternatives • Enjoy solving problems • Willing to use innovative methods	• Socially oriented • Humanistic and artistic approach • Solve problems creatively • Enjoy new ideas	• Concern for their organization • Interest in helping others • Open to suggestions • Rely on meetings

may have difficulty accepting the slow, deliberate actions of a subordinate with an analytical style.

Being aware of people's decision styles is a potentially useful way of understanding social interactions in organizations. With this in mind, scientists have developed the *decision-style inventory*, a questionnaire designed to reveal the relative strength of people's decision styles.[26] The higher an individual scores regarding a given decision style, the more likely that style is to predominate his or her decision making. (To give you a feel for how decision styles are measured—and for your own style—see the "Experiencing Organizational Behavior" exercise at the end of this chapter.)

Research using the decision-style inventory has revealed some interesting findings. For example, when the inventory was given to a sample of corporate presidents, their scores on each of the four categories were approximately equal. Apparently, they had no single dominant style and could switch back and forth between styles with ease. In addition, different groups on average have different styles that dominate their decision making. For example, military leaders tend to have high scores on conceptual style. They were not the domineering individuals that stereotypes suggest; rather, they were highly conceptual and people-oriented in their approach. Such findings paint a far more humanistic and less authoritarian picture of military officers than many would have guessed.

In conclusion, people take very different approaches to the decisions they make. Coupled with their interpersonal skills, their personalities lead them to approach decisions in consistently different ways—that is, using different decision styles. Research on decision styles is relatively new, but understanding such stylistic differences clearly is a key factor in appreciating the potential conflicts between decision-makers.

Group Influences: A Matter of Trade-Offs

Groups influence organizational decisions in many potentially positive and negative ways. We say "potentially," because the variety of factors influencing organizational decisions makes it difficult to predict whether anticipated benefits or problems actually will occur. Still, it is useful to understand some of the major forces with the potential to affect how groups make decisions in organizations.

Potential Benefits of Decision-Making Groups   Undoubtedly, much can be gained from decision-making groups. First, bringing people together may increase the amount of knowledge and information available for making good decisions; in other words, there may be a *pooling of resources*. A related benefit is that in such groups, there also can be a *specialization of labor*. With enough people around to share the work load, individuals then can perform only those tasks at which they are best, thereby potentially improving the quality of the group's efforts.

Another benefit is that group decisions are likely to enjoy *greater acceptance* than individual decisions. People who are involved in making decisions may be expected to understand those decisions better and to be more committed to implementing them than they would be to decisions made by someone else.[27]

Potential Problems of Decision-Making Groups   Of course, some problems also are associated with using decision-making groups. One obvious drawback is that groups are likely to *waste time*. The time spent socializing before getting down to business may be a drain on the group and very costly to organizations.

Another problem is that potential disagreement over important matters may breed ill will and *group conflict*. Constructive disagreement can lead to better group outcomes, but highly disruptive conflict may interfere with group decisions. Indeed, with corporate power and personal pride at stake, lack of agreement often causes bad feelings to develop between group members.

Finally, groups sometimes may be ineffective because of members' *intimidation by group leaders*. A group composed of several "yes" men or women trying to please a dominant leader tends to discourage open and honest discussion of solutions. Considering these problems, it is easy to understand the old adage, "A camel is a horse put together by a committee."

groupthink

The tendency for members of highly cohesive groups to conform so strongly to group pressures regarding a certain decision that they fail to think critically and reject the potentially correcting influences of outsiders.

Groupthink: Too Much Cohesiveness Can Be a Dangerous Thing   As described in chapter 7, sometimes groups members become so concerned about not "rocking the boat" that they become reluctant to challenge the group's decisions. When this happens, group members tend to isolate themselves from outside information, and the process of critical thinking deteriorates. This phenomenon is referred to as **groupthink**.[28]

GLOBAL MATTERS   Because groupthink is based on people's tendencies to adhere to their fellow group members, it may be more likely to occur in nations where people are strongly predisposed to take others' feelings into account (e.g., Japan) than in nations where people tend to be more individualistic in orientation (e.g., the United States). ■

To illustrate groupthink, consider the tragic decision to launch the space shuttle *Challenger* in January 1986. Analyses of conversations between key personnel suggest that NASA officials made the decision to launch while ignoring admonitions from engineers.[29] Given that NASA had such a successful history, the decision-makers operated with a sense of invulnerability. They also worked together so closely and were under such intense pressure to launch without further delay that they all collectively went along with the decision, thus creating the illusion of unanimous agreement. For a more precise description of groupthink and a guide to recognizing its symptoms, see Figure 9.5.

As you might imagine, groupthink occurs in governmental decision making, but it also occurs in the private sector—although in such cases, the failures may be less well publicized. For example, analyses of the business policies of large corporations such as Lockheed and Chrysler have suggested it was the failure of top management teams to respond to changing market conditions that led these firms to the brink of disaster.[30] The problem is that members of very cohesive groups may have considerable confidence in their group's decisions, thereby making them unlikely to raise doubts about these actions (i.e., "The group seems to know what it's doing."). As a result, they may suspend their own critical thinking in favor of conformity. When group

FIGURE 9.5

Groupthink: An Overview

Groupthink occurs when highly cohesive conditions discourage group members from challenging the group's actions. Poor-quality decisions result.

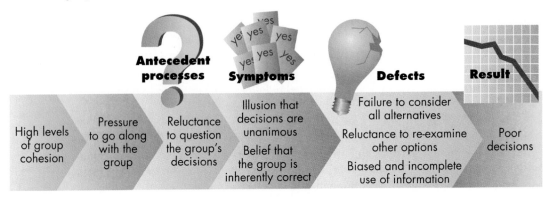

members become fiercely loyal to each other, they may ignore potentially useful information from other sources that challenges the group's decisions. The result? The group's decisions may be uninformed, irrational, and even immoral.[31] (Fortunately, several concrete steps can be taken to avoid groupthink. For some suggestions, see the "Tips" section below.)

■ Strategies for Avoiding Groupthink

Because they have such a good feel for why groupthink occurs, scientists can identify several tactics to weaken the dynamics that make it occur:

1. *Promote open inquiry.* Groupthink arises in response to group members' reluctance to "rock the boat." Thus, group leaders should encourage members to be skeptical of all solutions and to avoid reaching premature agreements. It sometimes helps to play the role of *devil's advocate* — that is, to intentionally find fault with a proposed solution.[32] When this is done, groups make higher-quality decisions.[33] In fact, some corporate executives use exercises in which conflict is intentionally generated just so the negative aspects of a decision can be identified before it is too late.[34] This is not to say leaders should be argumentative. Rather, raising nonthreatening questions to force discussion of both sides of an issue can be very helpful in improving the quality of decisions.

2. *Use subgroups.* Because the decisions made by any one group may result from groupthink, basing decisions on the recommendations of two subgroups is a useful check. If the subgroups disagree, a discussion of their differences is likely to raise important issues. If the subgroups agree, however, you can be relatively confident that their conclusions are not *both* the result of groupthink.

3. *Admit shortcomings.* When groupthink occurs, group members feel confident that they are doing the right thing. Such feelings of perfection discourage them from considering opposing information. If group members acknowledge some of the flaws and limitations of their decisions, however, they may be more open to corrective influences. Remember, no decision is perfect. Asking others to point out their misgivings about a group's decision may help to avoid the illusion of perfection that contributes to groupthink.

4. *Hold second-chance meetings.* Before implementing a decision, hold a *second-chance meeting*, during which group members are asked to express any doubts and to propose any new ideas they may have. Alfred P. Sloan, the former head of General Motors, postponed acting on important matters until any group disagreement was resolved.[35] As people grow tired of working on a problem, they may hastily reach agreement on a solution, so second-chance meetings can be useful devices for seeing if a solution still looks good after "sleeping on it."

Given the extremely adverse effects groupthink can have on organizations, practicing managers would be wise to implement these simple suggestions. The alternative — facing the consequences of groupthink — clearly suggests the need for serious consideration of this issue. ■

Organizational Influences on Decisions

Thus far, we have emphasized the human shortcomings and biases that limit effective decision making. We must not ignore several important organizational factors, however, that also interfere with making rational decisions. Indeed, the situations faced by many organizational decision-makers cannot help but interfere with their capacity to make decisions.

One obvious factor is *time constraints*. Many important organizational decisions are made under severe time pressure, and under such circumstances, it often is impossible for exhaustive decision making to occur. This is particularly true when organizations face a crisis that requires immediate decisions. Under such conditions — when decision-makers feel "rushed" into taking action — they frequently restrict their search for information and their consideration of alternatives that otherwise might help them to make effective decisions.[36]

The quality of many organizational decisions also may be limited by *political "face-saving" pressure*. In other words, people may make decisions that help them to look good to others, even though the resulting decisions might not be in the best interest of their organizations. For example, imagine how an employee might distort the information needed to make a decision if the correct one would jeopardize his or her job. Unfortunately, such misuses of information to support desired decisions are all too common.

GLOBAL MATTERS | Saving face is important to everyone, but it is especially important in Asian societies. What are the implications of this for conducting business in such nations? ▪

One study of political face-saving found that businesspeople working on a group decision-making problem opted for an adequate — but less-than-optimal — decision rather than risk generating serious conflicts with their fellow group members.[37] Furthermore, one proponent of medical inoculation for the flu once was so interested in advancing his pro-inoculation position that he proceeded with the program even though there was only a two-percent chance of an epidemic.[38] Apparently, people often make the decisions needed to cultivate the best impressions even if they may not be the best decisions for their organizations.

Cultural Differences in Decision Making

People are people, and the process of decision making is essentially the same throughout the world — right? Not exactly. Even if people followed the same basic steps when making decisions, there would still be widespread differences in the *way* people from various cultures might go about doing so.[39] Because we often take for granted how we do things in our own countries, especially basic tasks such as making decisions, some of these differences may be quite surprising.

Suppose, for example, you are managing a large construction project and discover your most important supplier will be several months late delivering the necessary materials. What do you do? You probably are thinking, "This is a silly question; I'd simply get another supplier." If you are from the United States, this probably is just what you would do. If you are from Thailand, Indonesia, or Malaysia, however, chances are you simply would accept the situation as fate and allow the project to be delayed. In other words, to an American, Canadian, or Western European manager, the situation is perceived as a problem in need of a decision, whereas Thai, Indonesian, or Malaysian managers perceive no such problem. Thus, even though decision making begins with recognizing that a problem exists, not all people are likely to perceive the same situations as being problems.

Cultures also differ regarding the nature of the decision-making unit they typically employ. For example, in the United States, where people tend to be highly individualist, individual decisions are common. In more collectivist cultures such as Japan, however, it is inconceivable for someone to make a decision without first gaining the acceptance of his or her immediate colleagues.

The idea among the Japanese of building consensus is deeply rooted in their culture. Nothing gets done in Japanese organizations until everyone involved agrees to it, so employees have a strong sense of running the organization. Most Americans, however, probably would find this process to be unnecessary—and agonizingly slow. ▪

Similarly, cultural differences also exist regarding *who* is expected to make decisions. For example, in Sweden, employees at all levels traditionally are involved in making the decisions affecting them. In fact, this is so much the case that Swedes may totally ignore an organizational hierarchy and contact whomever is needed to make a decision, however high-ranking that individual may be. In India, however, where autocratic decision making is expected, a manager consulting a subordinate about a decision is considered to be a sign of weakness.

Yet another cultural difference deals with the amount of time taken to make a decision. For example, in the United States, one mark of a good decision-maker is that he or she is "decisive"—that is, willing to make an important decision without delay. In some other cultures, however, time urgency is downplayed. For example, in Egypt, the more important the matter, the more time the decision-maker is expected to take. Throughout the Middle East, quickly reaching a decision is perceived as being overly hasty.

As these examples illustrate, there are some interesting differences in how people from various countries formulate and implement decisions. Understanding such differences is an important first step toward developing appropriate strategies for conducting business at a global level.[40]

HOW ARE INDIVIDUAL DECISIONS MADE?

Now that we have identified the types of decisions made in organizations, we consider how people go about making them. Perhaps you are thinking, "What do you mean? You just think things over and do what you think is best." This may be true, but there is more to decision making then meets the eye. In fact, scientists have considered several different approaches to how individuals make decisions, and here, we review three of the most important.

The Rational-Economic Model: In Search of the Ideal Decision

All of us like to think we are "rational" people who make the best possible decisions, but what, precisely, does it mean to make a *rational* decision? Organizational scientists view **rational decisions** as being ones that maximize the attainment of goals (whether of a person, a group, or an entire organization).[41] What would be the most rational way for an individual to make a decision? Economists interested in predicting market conditions and prices have relied on a **rational-economic model** of decision making that assumes decisions are optimal in every way. Thus, an economically rational decision-maker attempts to maximize his or her profits by systematically searching for the *optimum* solution to a problem. For this to occur, the decision-maker must have complete and perfect information and then process it in an accurate and unbiased fashion.[42]

In many respects, rational-economic decisions follow the same steps outlined in the analytical model of decision making (see Figure 9.1). What makes the rational-economic approach special, however, is that it calls for decision-makers to recognize *all* alternative courses of action (i.e., step 4) and to evaluate each one accurately and completely (i.e., step 5). This approach views decision-makers as attempting to make *optimal* decisions.

rational decisions

Decisions that maximize the chance of attaining an individual's, group's, or organization's goals.

rational-economic model

The model of decision making according to which decision-makers consider all possible alternatives before selecting the optimal solution.

Of course, the rational-economic approach does not fully appreciate human fallibility. Based on the assumption that people have access to complete and perfect information and then use it to make perfect decisions, this model can be considered a *normative* (or *prescriptive*) approach—that is, one describing how decision-makers ideally *should* behave to make the best possible decisions. It does not describe how decision-makers *actually* behave in most circumstances. This task is undertaken by the next major approach to individual decision making; the *administrative model*.

The Administrative Model: The Limits of Human Rationality

As you know from your own experience, people generally do not act in a completely rational-economic manner. For example, consider how a personnel department might select a new receptionist. After interviewing several applicants, the personnel manager might choose the best one seen and stop interviewing. Had the manager been following a rational-economic model, however, he or she would interview *all* possible candidates before deciding on the best one. By ending the search after finding a candidate who was "good enough," the manager is using a much simpler approach.

administrative model

A model of decision making that recognizes the *bounded rationality* that limits the making of optimally rational-economic decisions.

The process used in this example characterizes an approach to decision making known as the **administrative model**,[43] which recognizes decision-makers may have a limited view of the problems confronting them. In other words, the number of solutions that can be recognized or implemented is limited by the capabilities of the decision-maker and by the available resources of the organization. In addition, decision-makers do not have perfect information about the consequences of their decisions, so they cannot always tell which one is best.

How are decisions made according to the administrative model? Instead of considering all possible solutions, decision-makers consider solutions as they become available, and they decide on the first alternative that meets their criteria. Thus, the decision-maker selects a solution that may be good enough but not optimal. Such decisions are referred to as **satisficing decisions**. Of course, a satisficing decision is easier to make than an optimal decision. In most decision-making situations, satisficing decisions are acceptable and more likely to be made than optimal ones.[44] The following analogy compares the two types of decisions: *Making an optimal decision is like searching a haystack for the sharpest needle, but making a satisficing decision is like searching a haystack for a needle just sharp enough with which to sew*.

satisficing decisions

Decisions made by selecting the first minimally acceptable alternative that becomes available.

As noted, it often is impractical for people to make completely optimal, rational decisions. The administrative model recognizes the **bounded rationality** under which most organizational decision-makers operate. The idea is that people lack the cognitive skills required to formulate and solve highly complex business problems in a completely objective, rational way.[45] In addition, decision-makers limit their actions to those falling within the bounds of current moral and ethical standards—that is, they use **bounded discretion**.[46] So, even though engaging in illegal activities such as stealing may optimize an organization's profits (at least in the short run), ethical considerations strongly discourage such actions.

bounded rationality

The major assumption of the administrative model—that organizational, social, and human limitations lead to making *satisficing* rather than optimal decisions.

bounded discretion

The practice of limiting decision alternatives to those falling within the bounds of current moral and ethical standards.

ETHICS MATTERS   Often, people behave ethically because they are concerned about getting caught behaving unethically. To what extent do you think people would behave unethically if they believed they could not get caught—except by their own consciences, of course? ■

As you might imagine, the administrative model does a better job than the rational-economic model of describing how decision-makers actually behave. This approach is said to be *descriptive* (or *proscriptive*) in nature. An interest in examining the actual, imperfect behavior of decision-makers rather than in specifying the ideal, economically rational behaviors decision-makers should engage in lies at the heart of the administrative model. Our point is not that decision-makers do not want to behave rationally, but that restrictions posed by the innate capabilities of the decision-makers preclude "perfect" decisions.

Image Theory: An Intuitive Approach to Decision Making

Some—but certainly not all—decisions are made following the logical steps of our general model of decision making. Consider Elizabeth Barrett Browning's poetic question, "How do I love thee? Let me count the ways."[47] It is unlikely that anyone ultimately would answer this question by carefully counting what he or she loves about another (though many such characteristics can be enumerated). Instead, a more intuitive decision-making process is likely, not only for matters of the heart but for other important organizational decisions as well.[48]

The point is that selecting the best alternative by weighing all options is not always a major concern when making a decision. People also consider how various alternatives fit with their personal standards, goals, and plans. The best decision for one person might not be the best for someone else. In other words, people may make decisions in a more automatic, *intuitive* fashion than traditionally is recognized. Representative of this approach is Beach and Mitchell's **image theory**, which is summarized in Figure 9.6.[49]

Image theory deals primarily with decisions about adopting a certain course of action (e.g., should the company develop a new product line?) or changing a current course of action (e.g., should the company drop a present product line?). In image theory, people make adoption decisions based on a simple, two-step process. The first step is the *compatibility test*, which is a comparison of the degree to which a particular course of action is consistent with various images—particularly individual principles, current goals, and future plans. If any lack of compatibility exists regarding these considerations, a rejection decision is made. If the compatibility test is passed, however, a *profitability test* then is performed. In other words, people consider the extent to which various alternatives fit with their values, goals, and plans. The decision then is made to accept the best candidate. These tests are used within a certain *decision frame*—that

image theory

A theory of decision making that recognizes decisions are made in an automatic, intuitive fashion. In this theory, people adopt courses of action that best fit their individual principles, current goals, and future plans.

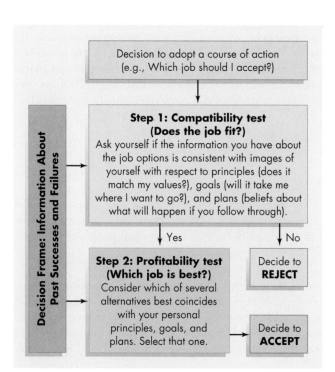

FIGURE 9.6

Image Theory: A Summary and Example

According to *image theory*, decisions are made in a relatively automatic, intuitive fashion following the two steps outlined here.

(*Source*: Adapted from Beach & Mitchell, 1990; see note 49).

is, with consideration of meaningful information about the context of the decision (e.g., past experiences). The basic idea is that we learn from and are guided by the past when making decisions. The example shown in Figure 9.6 highlights this contemporary approach to decision making.

According to image theory, the decision-making process is both rapid and simple. The theory suggests people do not ponder decisions but make them using a smooth, intuitive process—and with minimal cognitive processing. If you ever found yourself saying that something "seemed like the right thing to do" or "didn't feel right," you probably are well aware of the kind of intuitive thinking involved with many decisions. Recent research also suggests that when making relatively simple decisions, people do tend to behave as suggested by image theory.[50] For example, people decide against various options when past evidence suggests these may be incompatible with their images of the future.[51]

To summarize, the rational-economic approach represents the ideal way to make optimal decisions. The administrative model and image theory, however, represent ways that people actually go about making decisions. Both of these approaches have received support, and neither should be seen as a replacement for the other. Instead, several processes may be involved in decision making. In addition, not all decisions are made in the same way: Sometimes decision making might be analytical, and sometimes it might be more intuitive. Modern scholars of OB recognize the value of both approaches, each of which recognizes the fallibility of the human decision-maker. With this in mind, we now turn our attention to the imperfect nature of individual decisions.

IMPERFECTIONS IN INDIVIDUAL DECISIONS

Let's face it; as a whole, people are less than perfect when it comes to making decisions. Mistakes are made all the time. Obviously, people can process only limited amounts of information accurately and thoroughly (much like a computer). For example, we often focus on irrelevant information when making decisions.[52] We also fail to use all the information available, in part because we may forget some of it.[53] Beyond these general limitations, however, we also may note several systematic determinants of imperfect decisions—that is, factors that contribute to the imperfect nature of people's decisions. These variables reside not only within individuals themselves (e.g., biases in how people make decisions) but also within organizations. We now examine five major factors contributing to the imperfect nature of individual decisions.

Framing Effects

framing
The tendency for people to make different decisions based on how the problem is presented.

Have you ever found yourself changing your mind about something because of *how* someone explained it to you? If so, you already are familiar with a well-established decision-making bias known as **framing**—that is, the tendency for people to make different decisions based on how the problem is presented to them. Scientists have identified three different forms of framing effects that occur when people make decisions.[54]

Risky Choice Frames   When problems are framed in a manner emphasizing the positive gains to be received, people tend to shy away from taking risks and go for the sure thing (i.e., decision-makers are said to be *risk-averse*). When problems are framed in a manner emphasizing the potential losses to be suffered, however, people are more willing to take risk to avoid those losses (i.e., decision-makers are said to make *risk-*

seeking decisions).[55] This is known as the **risky choice framing effect**. To illustrate this phenomenon consider the following example:

> *The government is preparing to combat a rare disease expected to take 600 lives. Two alternative programs have been proposed. Program A will save 200 people, if adopted. Program B has a one-third chance of saving all 600 people but a two-thirds chance of saving no one. Which program do you prefer?*

When such a problem was presented to people, 72 percent expressed a preference for Program A and 28 percent for Program B. In other words, they preferred the "sure thing" of saving 200 people over the one-third possibility of saving them all. A curious thing, however, happened when the programs were described in negative terms. For example:

> *Program C will allow 400 people to die if adopted. Program D will allow a one-third probability that no one would die and a two-thirds probability that all 600 would die. Which program do you prefer?*

Compare these four programs. Program C is just another way of stating the outcomes of Program A, and Program D is just another way of stating the outcomes of Program B. Programs C and D, however, are framed in negatives terms, which led to opposite preferences: 22 percent favored Program C, and 78 percent favored Program D. In other words, people tended to avoid risk when the problem was framed in terms of "lives saved" (i.e., in positive terms) but to seek risk when the problem was framed in terms of "lives lost" (i.e., in negative terms). This classic effect has been replicated in several studies.[56]

Attribute Framing   Risky choice frames involve making decisions about a course of action. The same basic idea, however, applies to situations not involving risk but involving evaluations. For example, suppose you are walking down the meat aisle of a supermarket when you spot a package of ground beef labeled "75% lean." Of course, if the same package said "25% fat," you would know exactly the same thing, but you probably would not perceive this to be the case. In fact, consumer marketing research has shown that people rate the same sample of ground beef as tasting better and less greasy when framed with respect to a positive attribute (i.e., "75% lean") than when framed with respect to a negative attribute (i.e., "25% fat").[57]

This example is easy to relate to, but its point can be generalized beyond product evaluation. In fact, the **attribute framing effect** occurs in many organizational settings. In other words, people evaluate the same characteristic more positively when it is described positively than when it is described negatively. For example, consider performance evaluations. In this context, people whose performance is framed in positive terms (e.g., percentage of shots made by a basketball player) tend to be evaluated more positively than those with identical performance framed in negative terms (e.g., percentage of shots missed by that same player).[58]

Goal Framing   A third type of framing—*goal framing*—focuses on one important question: When persuading someone to do something, is it more effective to focus on the positive consequences of doing it or on the negative consequences of not doing it. For example, suppose you are attempting to convince women to perform breast self-examinations to check for signs of cancer. You may frame the desired behavior in positive terms:

> *Research shows that women who do breast self-examinations have an increased chance of finding a tumor in the early, more treatable stages of the disease.*

risky choice framing effect
The tendency for people to avoid risks when situations are presented in a way that emphasizes positive gains and to take risks when presented in a way that emphasizes potential losses.

attribute framing effect
The tendency for people to evaluate a characteristic more positively when it is presented in positive terms than in negative terms.

You also may frame it in negative terms:

> *Research shows that women who* do not *perform breast self-examinations have a decreased chance of finding a tumor in the early, more treatable stages of the disease.*

Which approach is more effective? Research has shown that women are more likely to perform breast self-examinations when they are presented with the consequences of *not* doing it rather than with the benefits of doing it.[59] This is an example of the **goal framing effect** in action. According to this phenomenon, people are persuaded more strongly by negatively framed than by positively framed information.

goal framing effect

The tendency for people to be persuaded more strongly by information framed in negative terms than by information framed in positive terms.

A General Note About Framing   The kinds of framing described here, though similar in several ways, also are quite different. Specifically, they focus on different types of behavior: preferences for risk (i.e., *risky choice framing*), evaluations of characteristics (i.e., *attribute framing*), and taking behavioral action (i.e., *goal framing*). For a summary of these effects, see Figure 9.7.

Scientists believe framing effects result from the tendency of people to perceive equivalent situations framed differently as not really being equivalent.[60] In other words, focusing on the glass as being "half-full" leads people to think about it differently than when focusing on that same glass as being "half-empty"—even though they might recognize intellectually that the two are really the same. Such findings illustrate our point that people are not completely rational decision-makers. Rather, they are systematically biased by the cognitive distortions created by simple differences in how situations are framed.

Reliance on Heuristics

Framing effects are not the only cognitive biases affecting decision-makers. People also often attempt to simplify the complex decisions they face by using **heuristics**—that is, simple rules of thumb that guide them through a complex array of decision alternatives.[61] Heuristics are potentially useful to decision-makers, but they represent potential impediments to decision making as well. Two common types of heuristics may be identified.

heuristics

Simple decision rules (e.g., rules of thumb) used to make quick decisions about complex problems. See *availability heuristic* and *representativeness heuristic*.

availability heuristic

The tendency for people to base their judgments on readily available—though potentially inaccurate—information, thereby adversely affecting decision quality.

The Availability Heuristic   The **availability heuristic** refers to the tendency for people to base their judgments on readily available information—even though that information might not be accurate. For example, suppose an executive needs to know

FIGURE 9.7

Framing Effects: A Summary of Three Types

Information presented (i.e., framed) negatively is perceived differently than the same information presented positively. Framing can be accomplished in three ways: *risky choice framing, attribute framing,* and *goal framing.*

(*Source:* Based on suggestions by Levin et al., 1998; see note 54.)

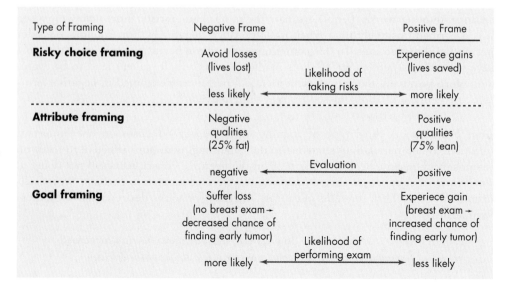

Type of Framing	Negative Frame		Positive Frame
Risky choice framing	Avoid losses (lives lost)	Likelihood of taking risks	Experience gains (lives saved)
	less likely	← →	more likely
Attribute framing	Negative qualities (25% fat)		Positive qualities (75% lean)
	negative	← Evaluation →	positive
Goal framing	Suffer loss (no breast exam → decreased chance of finding early tumor)	Likelihood of performing exam	Experiece gain (breast exam → increased chance of finding early tumor)
	more likely	← →	less likely

the percentage of college freshmen who go on to graduate. There is not enough time to gather the appropriate statistics, however, so she bases her judgments on her own recollections of when she was a student. If the percentage she recalls graduating is higher or lower than the usual number, her estimate will be off accordingly. In other words, basing judgments solely on conveniently available information increases the possibility of inaccurate decisions, yet the availability heuristic often is used.[62]

The Representativeness Heuristic The **representativeness heuristic** refers to the tendency to perceive others in stereotypical ways if they appear to be "typical" representatives of their category. For example, suppose you believe that accountants are bright, mild-mannered individuals whereas salespeople are less intelligent but more extroverted. Furthermore, imagine a party with twice as many salespeople as accountants. At this party, you meet someone who is bright and mild-mannered. Mathematically, the odds are two-to-one this individual is a salesperson rather than an accountant, but chances are, you will guess this individual is an accountant—because he or she possesses the traits you associate with accountants. In other words, you believe this person to be representative of accountants in general, so you knowingly go against the mathematical odds in making your judgment. Research consistently has found that people tend to make this type of error, thereby providing good support for the existence of the representativeness heuristic.[63]

representativeness heuristic
The tendency to perceive others in stereotypical ways if they appear to be typical representatives of the category to which they belong.

ETHICS MATTERS

To what extent do you believe the representativeness heuristic explains some of the biases against people from certain racial and ethnic groups? Give examples to support your answer. ∎

The Helpful Side of Heuristics Heuristics do not always deteriorate the quality of decisions, and in fact, they can be quite helpful. People often use rules of thumb to help simplify the complex decisions they face. For example, management scientists employ many useful heuristics to aid their decisions in matters such as where to locate warehouses or how to compose an investment portfolio.[64] We also use heuristics in our everyday lives, such as when we play chess (e.g., "Control the center of the board.") or blackjack (e.g., "Hit on 16; stick on 17.").

The representativeness heuristic and the availability heuristic, however, may be recognized as impeding to superior decisions, because they discourage people from collecting and processing as much information as they should. Making judgments based on only readily available information or on stereotypical beliefs may make things simple for the decision-maker, but this comes at a potentially high cost—that is, poor decisions. Thus, these systematic biases represent potentially serious impediments to individual decision making.

Bias Toward Implicit Favorites

Consider the following: Don was about to receive his MBA, and this was going to be his big chance to move to San Francisco, the "city by the bay." Don had long dreamed of living there, and he hoped his first "real" job would be his ticket. As the corporate recruiters made their annual migration to campus, Don eagerly signed up for several interviews. One of the first was with Baxter, Marsh, and Hidalgo—a medium-size consulting firm in San Francisco. The salary was right, and the people seemed pleasant. This combination excited Don. Apparently, the interest was mutual, too, because Don soon was offered a position.

Does the story end here? Not quite. It was only March, and Don felt he should not jump at the first job to come along—even though he really wanted it. Therefore, to do the "sensible" thing, he signed up for more interviews. Shortly thereafter, Dixon, Timpkin, and Dinglethorpe—a local firm—made Don a more attractive offer. Not only was the salary higher, but there was every indication this job promised a much brighter future than the one in San Francisco.

What would he do? After thinking it over, Don concluded the work at Dixon, Timpkin, and Dinglethorpe was too low-level (i.e., not enough exciting clients to challenge him). The starting salary was not really all *that* much better than at Baxter, Marsh, and Hidalgo, either. So, the day after graduation, Don was packing for his new office overlooking the Golden Gate Bridge.

Do you think the way Don made his decision was atypical? He seemed to have decided in advance about the job in San Francisco and not to give the other one a real chance. Research suggests people make decisions this way all the time, however — that is, people tend to pick an **implicit favorite** option (i.e., a preferred alternative) early in the decision-making process.[65] Once this occurs, subsequent options are not given serious consideration. Rather, they are used merely to convince oneself the implicit favorite is indeed the best choice. An alternative considered for this purpose is known as a **confirmation candidate**. People often psychologically distort their beliefs about confirmation candidates to justify selecting their implicit favorites. Don did just that when he convinced himself the local job really was not as good as it seemed.

People often make decisions early in the process. For example, in one study of the job recruitment process, investigators found they could predict 87 percent of the jobs that students would take as early as two months before the students actually acknowledged they had made a decision.[66] Apparently, people's decisions are biased by their tendency not to consider all the available relevant information. In fact, they tend to bias their judgments of the strengths and weaknesses of various alternatives to make them fit their already-made decision — that is, their implicit favorite.[67] This phenomenon clearly suggests that people not only fail to consider all possible alternatives when making decisions but even fail to consider all readily available alternatives. Instead, they make up their minds early, and they convince themselves they are right. As you might imagine, this bias toward implicit favorites is likely to limit severely the quality of decisions that are made.

Escalation of Commitment: Throwing Good Money after Bad

Because decisions are always being made in organizations, some inevitably will be unsuccessful. What would you say is the rational thing to do when a poor decision has been made? Obviously, the ineffective action should be stopped or reversed; in other words, it would make sense to "cut your losses and run." People do not always respond in this manner, however. In fact, ineffective decisions sometimes are followed up with still more ineffective decisions.

Imagine, for example, you have invested money in a company that appears to be failing. Rather than lose your initial sum, however, you may invest still more money in the hope of salvaging your first investment. The more you invest, the more you may be tempted to save those earlier investments by making later investments. In other words, people sometimes "throw good money after bad" because they have "too much invested to quit." This is known as the **escalation of commitment phenomenon** — that is, the tendency for people to continue to support previously unsuccessful courses of action because they have sunk costs invested in them.[68]

This might not seem like a rational thing to do, but this strategy frequently is followed. For example, consider how large banks and governments may invest money in foreign governments in the hope of "turning them around" even though such a result becomes increasingly unlikely. Similarly, the organizers of Expo '86 in British Columbia continued pouring money into the fair long after it became apparent it would be a big money-losing proposition.[69]

Why do people do this? Failure to back your own previous courses of action in an organization sometimes can be viewed as an admission of failure — a politically dif-

implicit favorite

One's preferred decision alternative, which is selected even before all the options have been considered.

confirmation candidate

A decision alternative considered only to convince onself of the wisdom of selecting the *implicit favorite*.

escalation of commitment phenomenon

The tendency for individuals to continue supporting previously unsuccessful courses of action.

ficult act in an organization. In other words, people may be concerned about "saving face"—that is, looking good in the eyes of others and oneself.[70] This tendency for *self-justification* primarily is responsible for people's inclination to protect their beliefs about themselves as being rational, competent decision-makers by convincing themselves and others they made the right decision all along—and are willing to back it up.[71] Other reasons for the escalation of commitment phenomenon are possible, but research supports the self-justification explanation.[72] For a summary of the escalation of commitment phenomenon, see Figure 9.8.

People refrain from escalating their commitment to a failing course of action under several conditions.[73] Notably, people stop making failing investments when *available funds for making further investments are limited* and the *threat of failure is overwhelmingly obvious.*[74] For example, when the Long Island Lighting Company decided in 1989 to abandon its plans to operate a nuclear power plant in Shoreham, New York, it did so in the face of 23 years of intense political and financial pressure (i.e., a strong anti-nuclear movement and billions of dollars in cost overruns).[75]

People also refrain from escalating commitment when they can *diffuse their responsibility for the earlier failing actions.* In other words, the more people feel they are just one of several responsible for a failing course of action, the less likely they are to commit to further failing actions.[76] The rationale here is: The less one is responsible for an earlier failure, the less one may be motivated to justify those failures by further investing in them.

In addition, escalation of commitment toward a losing course of action is low in organizations where the people who made the ineffective decisions have left and been replaced by others who are not linked to those decisions. In other words, *turnover* lessens an organization's commitment to a losing course of action. Illustrating this, some banks continue to make bad (i.e., uncollectable) loans to customers they already have loaned money to in the past, but this is less likely in banks where top executives (i.e., individuals considered to be responsible for those loans) have left their posts.[77] Finally, people are unwilling to escalate commitment to a course of action when, clearly, the *total amount invested exceeds the expected gain.*[78] People may wish to invest in projects to recoup their initial investments, but they have little reason to do so when this obviously will be a losing proposition. Under such conditions, further

FIGURE 9.8

Escalation of Commitment: An Overview

According to the *escalation of commitment phenomenon,* people who have repeatedly made poor decisions continue to support those failing courses of action to justify their earlier decisions. Under some conditions, however, as summarized here, this effect will not occur.

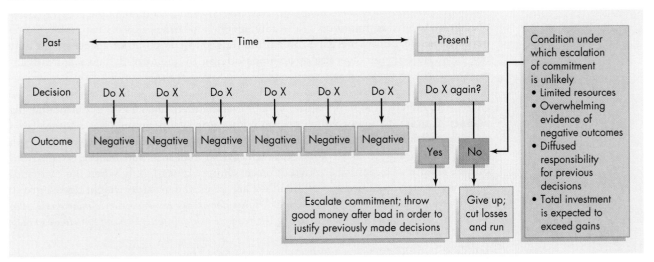

investment is difficult to justify—even if one "hopes against hope" it will work out in the end. Indeed, decision-makers refrain from escalating commitment to decisions when the overall benefit is less than the overall cost.[79] (This finding was more apparent among students with accounting backgrounds than among those without such backgrounds, presumably because their training made them more sensitive to these issues.)

To conclude, the escalation of commitment phenomenon represents a type of irrational decision making. Whether it occurs, however, depends on the various circumstances the decision-makers confront.

GROUP DECISIONS: DO TOO MANY COOKS SPOIL THE BROTH?

Decision-making groups are a well-established fact of modern organizational life. Committees, study teams, task forces, and review panels often are charged with making important business decisions.[80] These groups are so common, in fact, that some administrators spend as much as 80 percent of their time in committee meetings.[81]

In view of this, how well do groups make decisions compared with individuals? Given the several advantages and disadvantages of group decisions we described earlier, this question is particularly important. Specifically, under what conditions might individuals or groups be expected to make superior decisions? Fortunately, research has provided some good answers.[82]

When Are Groups Superior to Individuals?

Whether groups do better or worse than individuals depends on the nature of the task. Specifically, any advantages groups may have over individuals depend on how complex or how simple the task is.

Complex Decision Tasks   Imagine an important decision must be made about a complex problem, such as whether one company should merge with another. This is not the kind of problem about which any one individual working alone could make a good decision. The highly complex nature of this situation may overwhelm even an expert, thereby setting the stage for a group to do a better job. Naturally, groups may excel in such situations.

This does not happen automatically, however. In fact, for groups to outperform individuals, several conditions must exist. First, successful groups tend to be composed of *heterogeneous group members with complementary skills*. For example, a group composed of lawyers, accountants, real-estate agents, and other experts may make much better decisions on the merger problem than a group composed of specialists in only one field. Indeed, the diversity of opinions offered by members is one major advantage of using groups to make decisions.[83]

As you might imagine, it is not enough simply to have skills. For a group to be successful, members must be able to communicate their ideas in an open, nonhostile manner. Conditions under which one individual (or group) intimidates another from contributing his or her expertise can easily negate any potential gain associated with groups of heterogeneous experts. After all, *having* expertise and making a contribution by *using* that expertise are two different things. Indeed, only when the contributions of the most qualified group members are given the greatest weight does a group derive any benefit from their presence.[84] Thus, *for groups to be superior to individuals, they must be a heterogeneous collection of experts with complementary skills who can contribute to their group's product freely and openly.*

Simple Decision Tasks Now imagine a situation in which a decision is required on a simple problem with a readily verifiable answer. For example, suppose you are asked to translate a phrase from a relatively obscure language into English.

Groups might do better than individuals on such a task, but probably only because in a group, the odds are increased that someone knows that language. There is no reason to expect, however, that even a large group could perform this task better than a single individual with the required expertise. In fact, an expert working alone may do even better than a group, because the expert performing a simple task may not be distracted by others or need to convince them of the correctness of his or her solution. Therefore, exceptional individuals tend to outperform entire committees on simple tasks.[85] For groups to benefit from a pooling of resources in such cases, there must be some resources to pool—the pooling of ignorance does not help.

In sum, the question "Are two heads better than one?" can be answered this way: *On simple tasks, two heads may be better than one if at least one of those heads has enough of what it takes to succeed.* Thus, whether groups perform better than individuals depends on the nature of the task and the expertise of the members. For a summary of some key considerations in this area, see Figure 9.9.

When Are Individuals Superior to Groups?

As described thus far, groups may be expected to perform better than average or even exceptional individuals under certain conditions. Under other conditions, however, individuals perform better than groups.

Most of the problems faced by organizations require a great deal of creative thinking. For example, a company deciding how to use a newly developed adhesive in its consumer products faces decisions involving a poorly structured task. You would expect the complexity of such creative problems would give groups a natural advantage, but this is not the case. In fact, *on poorly structured, creative tasks, individuals perform better than groups.*[86]

One approach to solving creative problems commonly used by groups is **brainstorming**, which was developed by advertising executive Alex Osborn as a tool for

brainstorming
A technique to foster group productivity by encouraging interacting members to express their ideas noncritically.

FIGURE 9.9

Group Decisions: When Are They Superior to Individual Decisions?

When performing complex problems, groups are superior to individuals if certain conditions prevail (e.g., members have heterogeneous, complementary skills; they can freely share ideas; and good ideas are accepted). When performing simple problems, however, groups perform only as well as the best individual member, and then only if that person has the correct answer and that response is accepted by the group.

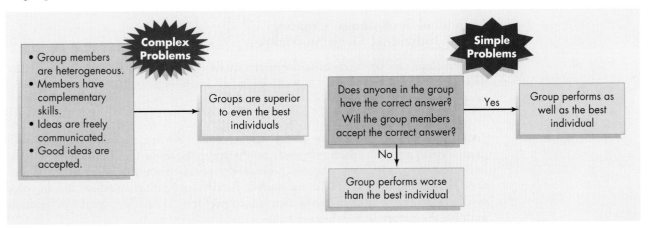

coming up with creative, new ideas.[87] Members of brainstorming groups are encouraged to present their ideas in an uncritical way and to discuss freely and openly all ideas on the floor. Specifically, members are required to follow four main rules:

1. Avoid criticizing others' ideas.
2. Share even far-out suggestions.
3. Offer as many comments as possible.
4. Build on others' ideas to create your own.

Does brainstorming improve the quality of creative decisions? To answer this question, researchers compared the effectiveness of individuals and brainstorming groups working on creative problems.[88] Specifically, participants were given 35 minutes to consider the consequences of situations such as "What if everybody went blind?" or "What if everybody grew an extra thumb on each hand?" Clearly, the novel nature of such problems requires a great deal of creativity. Afterward, the number of solutions generated by groups of four or seven people and a like number of individuals working on the same problems alone were compared. The results were clear: Individuals were significantly more productive than groups.

In summary, groups perform worse than individuals on creative tasks. Some individuals feel inhibited by the presence of others—even though one rule of brainstorming is that even far-out ideas may be shared. To the extent people wish to avoid feeling foolish because of saying silly things, their creativity may be inhibited in groups. Similarly, groups also may inhibit creativity by slowing down the process of bringing ideas to fruition.

TECHNIQUES FOR IMPROVING THE EFFECTIVENESS OF DECISIONS

As made clear in this chapter, certain advantages can be gained from sometimes using individuals and sometimes using groups to make decisions. Thus, a decision-making technique that combines the best features of groups and individuals while minimizing the disadvantages of each would be ideal. Several techniques designed to realize the "best of both worlds" have been widely used in organizations, and these include techniques that involve structuring group discussions in special ways. An even more basic approach to improve the effectiveness of group decisions involves training decision-makers in avoiding some of the pitfalls of group decision making. First, we discuss this training approach to improving group decisions, and we then consider various ways of creating specially structured groups.

Individual Techniques: Creating Better Individual Decision-Makers

Several steps can be taken to improve the quality of decisions made by individuals. These include training people in ways of improving group performance and guiding people toward ethical behavior.

Training Individuals to Improve Group Performance   Earlier, we noted that how well groups solve problems partly depends on the composition of those groups. If at least one member can devise a solution, groups may benefit from that individual's expertise. Thus it follows that the more qualified individual group members are to solve problems, the better their groups as a whole perform. How, then, might individuals improve the nature of the decisions they make?

People tend to make four types of mistakes when attempting creative decisions, and they make better decisions when trained to avoid these errors.[89] Specifically, these mistakes are:

1. *Hypervigilance.* The state of **hypervigilance** involves frantically searching for quick solutions to problems, or going from one idea to another, desperate that one idea is not working and another must be considered before time runs out. Thus, a poor, "last-chance" solution may be adopted simply to relieve anxiety. This problem may be avoided, however, by remembering it is best to stick with one suggestion and then work it out thoroughly. Reassuring the person solving the problem that his or her level of skill and education is adequate to the task at hand also helps. In other words, a little reassurance goes a long way toward keeping individuals on the right track and away from hypervigilance.

2. *Unconflicted adherence.* Many decision-makers stick to the first idea that comes into their heads without evaluating the consequences, which is a mistake known as **unconflicted adherence.** As a result, such people are unlikely to be aware of any problems with their ideas or to consider other possibilities. To avoid unconflicted adherence, decision-makers are urged to think about the difficulties associated with their ideas, to consider different ideas, and to consider the special and unique characteristics of the problem they face — and avoid carrying over assumptions from previous problems.

3. *Unconflicted change.* People sometimes are quick to change their minds and adopt the first new idea to come along, which is a problem known as **unconflicted change.** To avoid unconflicted change, decision-makers are encouraged to ask themselves about the risks and problems of adopting that solution, the good points of the first idea, and the relative strengths and weaknesses of both ideas.

4. *Defensive avoidance.* Too often, decision-makers fail to solve problems effectively because they go out of their way to avoid working on the task at hand. This is known as **defensive avoidance.** People can do three things to minimize this problem. First, *avoid procrastination.* In other words, do not put off the problem indefinitely just because you cannot find a solution right away. Continue budgeting some of your time on even the most frustrating problems. Second, *avoid disowning responsibility.* It is easy to minimize the importance of a problem by saying, "It doesn't matter, so who cares?" Avoid giving up so soon. Finally, *do not ignore potentially corrective information.* It is tempting to put your nagging doubts about the quality of a solution to rest just to be finished with the problem. Good decision-makers, however, do not do this. Rather, they use their doubts to test — and potentially improve — the quality of their ideas.

It is encouraging to note people make better decisions just by *considering* these four pitfalls. How well groups perform depends to a great extent on the problem-solving skills of the individual members. Attempting to avoid the four major pitfalls described here appears to be an effective method of improving individual decision-making skills — and, hence, the quality of group decisions.

Making Ethical Decisions The suggestions just outlined may help individuals to make decisions that are improved in many key ways, but they may not help people to make more ethical decisions. This is an important consideration. After all, the moral scandals making headlines recently (e.g., lies by high-ranking political figures) show how people often have difficulty judging what is right and then behaving accordingly. Unfortunately, as described in chapter 10, cheating and stealing in the workplace are

hypervigilance
The state in which an individual frantically searches for quick solutions and goes from idea to idea from desperation that one is not working and another must be considered before time runs out.

unconflicted adherence
The tendency for decision-makers to stick with the first idea that comes to mind without more deeply evaluating the consequences.

unconflicted change
The tendency for people to change their minds quickly and to adopt the first new idea that comes along.

defensive avoidance
The tendency for decision-makers to fail to solve problems because they avoid working on them.

more common than we would like.[90] The pursuit of quality in organizations, however, demands the highest moral standards.

The problem with this ideal is that even those with high moral values sometimes are tempted to behave unethically. If you are thinking "other people act unethically, but not me," then ask yourself this: Have you ever taken small articles of company property (e.g., pencils, tape) for personal use? Have you ever made personal copies on the company copier or fudged on your expense account?

If the answer is yes, you also may be saying, "Sure, but companies *expect* employees to do these things." Besides, everyone does it. This may be true, but we cannot ignore that people often justify their actions by rationalizing them as not really being unethical. This is especially true when we do something that may be seen as unethical but others with whom we work convince us it really is okay (Figure 9.10). This kind of rationalization makes talking ourselves into unethical decisions possible, because we think they really are "not so bad."

To avoid such situations — and, thereby, to improve ethical decision making — it may be useful to run your contemplated decisions through an ethics test.[91] Ask yourself the following questions:

1. *Does it violate the obvious "shall-nots"?* Many people say they believe "thou shall not lie, or cheat, or steal" but do it anyway. So, instead of thinking of a way around such prohibitions (e.g., by convincing yourself it is acceptable in *this* situation), avoid violating these well-established societal rules altogether.

2. *Will anyone get hurt?* Philosophers consider an action to be ethical to the extent it brings the greatest good to the greatest number. Thus, if someone may be harmed by your actions, think about your decision again, because it probably is unethical.

3. *How would you feel if the newspaper reported your decision on the front page?* If your decision really is ethical, you should have no reason to worry about it being made public. (In fact, you probably would be pleased by the publicity.) If you find yourself uneasy about answering this question, however, the decision you are contemplating may be unethical.

4. *What if you did it 100 times?* Sometimes, an unethical action does not seem so bad because it is done only once. In such a case, the damage might not be so bad, but the action still might not be ethical. If the act appears to be more wrong if it is done 100 times, however, then it probably also is wrong the first time.

FIGURE 9.10

Ethical Decisions: Not Always Clear

When making decisions in groups, people sometimes convince each other that seemingly unethical acts really are not inappropriate. Not surprisingly, unethical decisions are not unusual.

(*Source*: © The New Yorker Collection 1987. Dean Victor, from cartoonbank.com. All Rights Reserved.)

"*This might not be ethical. Is that a problem for anybody?*"

5. *How would you feel if someone did it to you?* If something you plan on doing to another really is ethical, you probably would find it acceptable if your situations were reversed. Thus, if you have any doubts regarding how you would feel being the person affected by your decision, you may wish to reconsider.

6. *What is your gut feeling?* Sometimes things just look bad — and probably because they *are*. If your actions are unethical, you probably can tell by listening to that voice inside your head. The trick is to listen to *that* voice, however, and to silence the one that tells you to do otherwise.

Admittedly, considering these questions will not transform a devil into an angel. Still, they may be useful for judging how ethical the decisions you may be contemplating really are. Your answers to these six questions may help you to avoid rationalizing unethical acts. Once we recognize that the decisions we are considering may not be ethical, we are well on our way to behaving ethically. (National culture also may influence people's perceptions of the ethical appropriateness of a decision. Indeed,

ARE U.S. BUSINESSES OVERLY CONCERNED ABOUT ETHICAL DECISIONS?

As chronicled in chapter 1, today's economy truly is global in nature. Indeed, manufacturing, marketing, and financial operations tend to be similar across the industrialized regions of the world. Interestingly, however, there tend *not* to be equally similar norms regarding ethical and unethical behavior. Rather, ethical standards vary widely among capitalist nations, and Americans appear to be more concerned than their foreign counterparts about ethics—too much so, according to some.

Any U.S. business leader has little difficulty identifying unethical decisions. In fact, incidents of corporate officers and prominent businesspeople in the United States who have behaved unethically (e.g., embezzling funds, offering bribes, fixing elections) and have been jailed or fined for doing so are part of ethical folklore. Such incidents, however, are more likely to be ignored by executives in other countries. By the same token, Americans also are more likely than their foreign counterparts to pay attention to the social responsibility of organizations (e.g., concern about the environment, treatment of employees, animal testing) and to boycott ethically questionable companies. Proud Americans may be tempted to see these things as being evidence of their own high moral standards, but throughout the world, they are taken as signs that the ethical concerns of Americans are overblown.[92]

In many highly industrialized nations, the same acts Americans generally regard as being unethical are widely accepted business practices. For example, in Germany, insider trading is not considered to be so bad, and tax evasion not only is accepted, it is revered as "a gentleman's sport."[93] In Japan, under-the-table favors are such a part of the culture that people who grant them do not think of themselves as doing anything wrong.[94] Many European businesspeople are amused by the attention U.S. companies pay to ethics training and codes

of ethics, leading some to call the United States an "unusually moralizing society" that should "lighten up a little." Also along these lines, in Japan, putting up with the policies of many U.S. companies to not accept gifts is considered to be one of the idiosyncrasies of dealing with them.[95]

Rather than drawing conclusions about whether the American approach is appropriate, it makes more sense to ask *why* these differences exist. To a great extent, the answer seems to be based on the distinction between "us" and "them." Specifically, U.S. society places great emphasis on treating everyone in an arm's-distance manner, and fairness is done when everyone is given an equal chance of success. People in Europe and Japan, however, place less emphasis on equal opportunity. (In fact, the phrases "equal opportunity" and "level playing field" are difficult to translate into Japanese.) Instead, Europeans (especially Southern Europeans) and Japanese pay more attention to fulfilling their obligations to those individuals and institutions with whom they have developed long-term relationships. To individuals from these countries, behaving ethically involves arriving at decisions reflecting the shared values of the company and reaffirming one's obligations to those values.

Despite these long-standing cultural differences, things may be changing. American ethical values are being adopted in businesses throughout the world. In Europe, environmental regulations are being strengthened and legislation banning sexual harassment enacted. People convicted of insider trading also now serve time in jail. The growing global economy and the growth of multinational corporations surely are responsible for this trend, but consider what may happen to distinctive national differences in ethical values as time passes. Will societies change to match the adaptation of businesses to U.S. standards, or will these new business standards wither to the extent they are inconsistent with national norms? Only time will tell.

people from different nations may have different views about ethical and unethical business decisions. For a look at the implications of this, see the "OB Around the World" section in this chapter.)

Group Techniques: Enhancing Group Decision Making

Just as individuals can improve the quality of their decisions, so can groups. The basic idea underlying these techniques is identical: Structure the group experience to experience its benefits without also experiencing its weaknesses.

The Delphi Technique: Decisions by Expert Consensus   According to Greek mythology, to see what fate the future held for them, people could seek the counsel of the Oracle at Delphi. Today, organizational decision-makers sometimes consult experts to help them make the best decisions as well. Developed by the Rand corporation, the **Delphi technique** represents a systematic way of collecting and organizing the opinions of several experts into a single decision.[96] For a summary of the steps in this process, see Figure 9.11.

The Delphi process begins by enlisting the co-operation of experts and presenting the problem to them, usually in a letter. Each expert then proposes what he or she believes is the most appropriate solution. The group leader compiles these individual responses, reproduces them, and shares them with all the other experts in a second mailing. At this point, each expert comments on the other experts' ideas and proposes another solution. These individual solutions are returned to the leader, who then compiles them again and looks for a consensus of opinions. If a consensus is reached, the decision is made; if not, the process of sharing reactions with others is repeated until a consensus eventually is obtained.

The obvious advantage of the Delphi technique is that it allows the collection of expert judgments without the great costs and logistical difficulties of scheduling a face-

Delphi technique

A method of improving group decisions using the opinions of experts, which are solicited by mail and then compiled. The expert consensus of opinions is used to make a decision.

FIGURE 9.11

The Delphi Group: A Summary

The *Delphi technique* allows decisions to be made by several experts while avoiding many of the disadvantages of face-to-face group interaction.

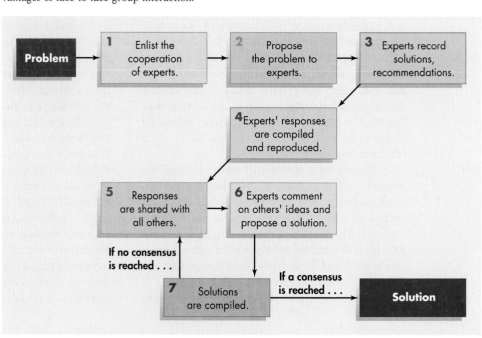

to-face meeting. The technique is not without limitations, however. For example, the Delphi process can be very time-consuming. Mailing letters, waiting for responses, transcribing and disseminating those responses, and then repeating the process until a consensus is reached can take quite some time. In fact, the minimum time required for the Delphi technique is estimated to be more than 44 days. In one case, the process took five months to complete.[97] Obviously, the Delphi approach is not appropriate for crisis situations — or for whenever time is of the essence. The approach has been employed successfully, however, to make decisions such as what items to put on a conference agenda and what the potential effect of implementing new land-use policies would be.[98]

The Nominal Group Technique: A Structured Group Meeting   When only a few hours are available to make a decision, group discussion sessions can be held in which members interact with each other in an orderly, focused fashion. The **nominal group technique (NGT)** brings together a small number of individuals (usually seven to 10) who systematically offer their individual solutions to a problem and share their personal reactions to those solutions.[99] The technique is referred to as *nominal* because the individuals involved form a group in name only. The participants do not attempt to agree on any one solution but rather vote on all the solutions proposed. For an outline of the steps in this process, see Figure 9.12.

The NGT begins by gathering the group members together around a table and identifying the problem at hand. Each member then writes his or her solutions. Next, each member presents his or her solutions to the group, and the leader writes these solutions on a chart. This process continues until all the ideas have been expressed. Each solution then is discussed, clarified, and evaluated by the group. Each member is given a chance to voice his or her reactions to each idea as well. After all the ideas have been evaluated, the group members privately rank-order their preferred solutions. The idea with the highest total rank is taken as the group's decision.

nominal group technique (NGT)

A technique for improving group decisions in which small groups systematically present and discuss their ideas before privately voting on their preferred solution. The most preferred solution then is accepted as the group's decision.

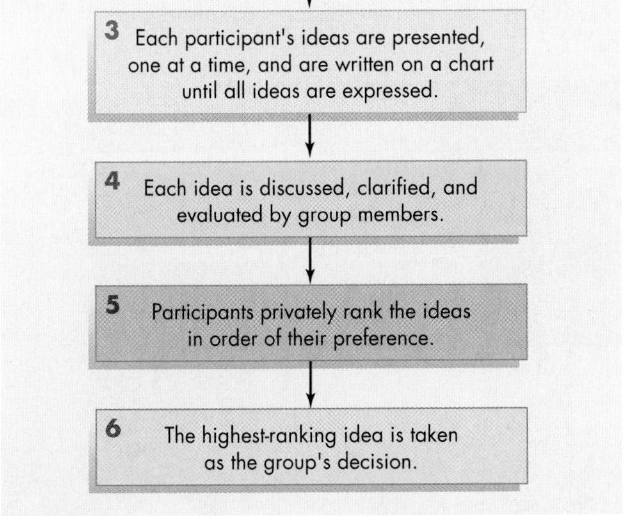

FIGURE 9.12

The Nominal Group Technique: An Overview

The *nominal group technique* structures face-to-face meetings in a way that allows for the open expression and evaluation of ideas.

1. A small group gathers around a table and receives instructions; problem is identified.

2. Participants privately write down ideas about solutions.

3. Each participant's ideas are presented, one at a time, and are written on a chart until all ideas are expressed.

4. Each idea is discussed, clarified, and evaluated by group members.

5. Participants privately rank the ideas in order of their preference.

6. The highest-ranking idea is taken as the group's decision.

The NGT has several advantages and disadvantages.[100] As noted, this approach can arrive at group decisions in only a few hours. It also discourages any pressure to conform to the wishes of a high-status group member, because all ideas are evaluated and all preferences expressed in private balloting. The technique does require a trained group leader, however, and using it successfully requires that only one narrowly defined problem be considered at a time. Thus, for complex problems, many NGT sessions would be needed—and only if the problem under consideration could be broken into smaller parts.

Traditionally, nominal groups meet in face-to-face settings, but modern technology enables such groups to meet even when the members are far away from each other. Specifically, **electronic meeting systems** allow individuals in different locations to participate in group conferences via telephone lines or direct satellite transmissions.[101] Messages may be sent by characters on a computer monitor or by images viewed during a teleconference. Despite their high-tech look, automated decision conferences really are just nominal groups meeting in a manner that approximates face-to-face contact. Because they allow groups to assemble more conveniently than face-to-face meetings, electronic meetings are growing in popularity. Presently, companies such as GE Appliances, US West, and Marriott Corp. (Figure 9.13) rely on electronic meetings.

It is important to consider the relative effectiveness of nominal groups and Delphi groups compared with face-to-face interacting groups. In general, research has shown the superiority of these special approaches to decision making.[102] Overall, members of nominal groups tend to be the most satisfied with their work and to make the best-quality judgments. In addition, both nominal and Delphi groups are more productive than face-to-face interacting groups.

As noted, however, there is one potential benefit from face-to-face interaction that cannot be realized in nominal or Delphi groups: acceptance of the decision. Groups are likely to accept their decisions and be committed to them if the members have been actively involved in making them. Thus, the more detached and impersonal atmosphere of nominal and Delphi groups sometimes makes their members less likely to accept decisions. Thus, there is no one best type of group with which to make decisions. The most appropriate type depends on the trade-offs decision-makers are willing to accept in terms of speed, quality, and commitment.[103]

The Stepladder Technique: Systematically Incorporating New Members   Another way of structuring group interaction is known as the **stepladder technique**.[104] This approach minimizes the tendency for group members to be unwilling to present their ideas. This is accomplished by adding new members one at a time and requiring each to present his or her ideas independently to a group that already has discussed the problem at hand. To begin, each of two people works on a problem independently. Then, they come together to present their ideas and to discuss solutions jointly. While

electronic meeting systems

The practice of bringing individuals from different locations together for a meeting via telephone or satellite transmissions, either on television monitors or shared space on a computer screen.

stepladder technique

A technique for improving the quality of group decisions that minimizes the tendency for members to be unwilling to present their ideas. New members to a group are added one at a time and are required to present their ideas independently to a group that already has discussed the problem at hand.

FIGURE 9.13

An Electronic Meeting in Progress

These employees of GE Appliances are holding a teleconference that allows them to meet and make decisions about important matters without getting together face-to-face.

A large product-distribution company is having trouble during group meetings: One department manager is constantly disrupting meetings while trying to get his own ideas across. He has so consistently intimidated coworkers they now are reluctant to speak. As a result, their ideas are not coming across.

1. Explain how this problem might be avoided.
2. What is your rationale for this advice?
3. What are the advantages and disadvantages of the tactic you identify?

the two-person group is working, a third person working alone also considers the problem. This individual then presents his or her ideas to the two-person group and joins in a three-person discussion of a possible solution. During this period, a fourth person works on the problem alone, then presents his or her ideas to the three-person group, and then joins in a four-person group discussion. After each new person has been added to the group, the entire group works together at finding a solution. For a summary of the steps in this technique, see Figure 9.14.

In following this procedure, each individual must be given enough time to work on the problem before joining the group. Then, each person must be given enough time to present thoroughly his or her ideas to the group. In turn, groups must have sufficient time to discuss the problem and to reach a preliminary decision before the next person is added. The final decision is made only after all individuals have been added to the group.

The rationale is that by forcing each person to present independent ideas—without knowing what the group has decided so far—the new person will not be influenced by the group. In turn, the group is required to consider a constant infusion of new ideas. If this is so, then groups solving problems using the stepladder technique should make better decisions than conventional groups meeting all at once to discuss the same problem. This is exactly what happens too. Moreover, members of stepladder groups report feeling more positive about their group experiences than their counterparts in conventional groups. The stepladder technique is new, but evidence suggests it holds promise for enhancing the decision-making capacity of groups.

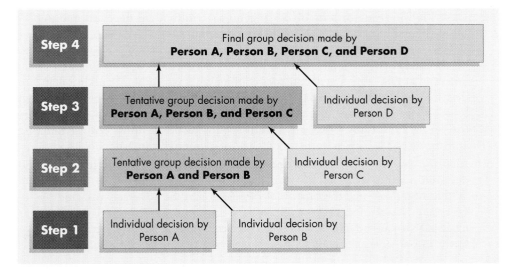

FIGURE 9.14

The Stepladder Technique: A Summary

By systematically adding new individuals into decision-making groups, the *stepladder technique* helps to increase the quality of the decisions made.

(*Source*: Adapted from Rogelberg, Barnes-Farrell, & Lowe, 1992; see note 104.)

We invite you to visit the Greenberg page on the Prentice Hall Web site at:
www.prenhall.com/greenberg for the monthly Greenberg update
and for this chapter's World Wide Web exercise.

SUMMARY AND REVIEW
OF LEARNING OBJECTIVES

1. **Identify the steps in the *analytical model of decision making*.**
   According to the **analytical model of decision making**, the making of decisions is a multistep process. First, a problem is identified. Solution objectives then are defined, and a **predecision** is made (i.e., a decision about how to make a decision). Next, alternatives are generated. These alternatives are evaluated, and one is chosen. The chosen alternative is implemented and then a follow up is done to determine if the problem still exists.

2. **Distinguish *programmed* from *nonprogrammed* decisions, *certain* from *uncertain* decisions, and *top-down* from *empowered* decisions.**
   Decisions made in organizations can be characterized as being either **programmed** (i.e., routine decisions made according to pre-existing guidelines) or **nonprogrammed** (i.e., decisions requiring novel and creative solutions). Decisions also differ regarding the amount of *risk* involved, ranging from those in which the decision outcomes are relatively *certain* to those in which the outcomes are highly *uncertain*. Uncertain situations are expressed as statements of probability based on either objective or subjective information. Decisions also differ regarding whether they are made by high-level organizational officials (i.e., **top-down decisions**) or by employees themselves (i.e., **empowered decisions**).

3. **Distinguish the various *individual decision styles*.**
   There are individual differences in decision making. Generally, people demonstrate one of four dominant decision styles: *directive*, or a preference for simple, clear solutions; *analytical*, or a willingness to consider complex situations based on ambiguous information; *conceptual*, or a humanistic and artistic orientation; and *behavioral*, or a concern for the organization.

4. **Describe the trade-offs involved in group vs. individual decision making.**
   Decision-making groups potentially benefit from the *pooling of resources* and *specialization of labor* that is possible within them. Group decisions also are likely to be accepted more strongly than individual decisions. Groups may waste time, however, and members may confront conflict with each other. In addition, group decisions may suffer because of the tendencies for members to be intimidated by group leaders as well as for **groupthink** to occur. This refers to the tendency for strong conformity pressures within groups to break down critical thinking and to encourage premature acceptance of potentially questionable solutions.

5. **Identify the various organizational and cultural factors that influence the decision-making process.**
   Within organizations, the quality of decisions may be adversely affected by severe time constraints and by political face-saving pressures. Decisions in organizations also are affected by national culture. For example, Americans are more likely to perceive problems as being decisions that need to be made, whereas

Thai's are more likely to accept these problems as they are. Americans also make decisions in a highly individualistic way (i.e., by looking out for themselves), but Asians are more likely to make decisions in a collective manner (i.e., by taking into account the group or organization).

6. **Distinguish between three approaches to decision making: the *rational-economic model*, the *administrative model*, and *image theory*.**
    The **rational-economic model** characterizes decision-makers as thoroughly searching through perfect information to make an optimal decision. This is a *normative* approach, because it describes how decision-makers ideally should behave to make the best possible decisions. In contrast, the **administrative model** is a *descriptive* approach, because it describes how decision-makers actually behave. It recognizes that limitations imposed by people's ability to process the information needed to make complex decisions (i.e., **bounded rationality** and *bounded discretion*) restrict decision-makers to **satisficing decisions** — that is, to solutions that are not optimal but are good enough. An alternative approach, **image theory**, recognizes that decisions are made in an automatic, intuitive fashion; it claims that people adopt a course of action that best fits their individual principles, current goals, and future plans.

7. **Identify the various types of *framing effects* and *heuristics* that potentially limit the effectiveness of decisions.**
    People make imperfect decisions because of cognitive biases. One such bias, **framing**, refers to the tendency for people to make different decisions based on how a problem is presented. For example, when a problem is presented in a way that emphasizes positive gains, people tend to make conservative, risk-averse decisions, whereas when the same problem is presented in a way that emphasizes potential losses, people tend to make riskier decisions. Simple rules of thumb (i.e., **heuristic**) also may bias decisions. For example, according to the **availability heuristic**, people base their judgments only on the information readily available to them, and according to the **representativeness heuristic**, other people are perceived in stereotypical ways if they appear to be representative of the categories to which they belong.

8. **Describe how the bias toward *implicit favorites* and the *escalation of commitment* lead to imperfect decisions.**
    People are biased toward **implicit favorites**, which are alternatives they prefer before considering all their options. Other alternatives, or **confirmation candidates**, are considered only to convince oneself that your implicit favorite actually is the best alternative. According to the **escalation of commitment phenomenon**, people continue to support previously unsuccessful courses of action because they have sunk costs invested in them. This occurs largely because people need to justify their previous actions and wish to avoid admitting their initial decision was a mistake.

9. **Compare the conditions in which groups make superior decisions with those in which individuals make superior decisions.**
    Groups make superior decisions than individuals when they are a heterogeneous mix of experts with complementary skills. Groups may not be any better than their best member, however, when performing a task with a simple, verifiable answer. Individuals make decisions superior to those of face-to-face **brainstorming** groups on creative problems; however, when brainstorming is done

electronically (i.e., using computer terminals to send messages), the quality of group decisions tend to improve.

10. **Describe the various techniques for enhancing the quality of individual as well as group decisions.**

Decision quality may be enhanced in several ways. First, the quality of individual decisions improves after individual training in problem-solving skills. Training in ethics can help people to make more ethical decisions. Group decisions may be improved in three ways. First, in the **Delphi technique**, the judgments of experts are gathered systematically and used to form a single, joint decision. Second, in the **nominal group technique**, group meetings are structured to elicit and evaluate systematically the opinions of all members. Third, in the **stepladder technique**, new individuals are added to decision-making groups one at a time, thus requiring the presentation and discussion of new ideas.

QUESTIONS FOR DISCUSSION

1. Argue pro or con: "All people make decisions in the same manner."
2. Think of a decision you recently made. Would you characterize it as being programmed or nonprogrammed? Highly certain or highly uncertain? Top-down or empowered? Explain your answers.
3. Describe a decision you are likely to make following the administrative model and one you are likely to make following the intuitive approach of image theory.
4. Identify ways in which your own decisions may have been biased by framing, heuristics, implicit favorites, and the escalation of commitment.
5. Imagine you are a manager facing the problem of not attracting enough high-quality personnel to your organization. Would you attempt to solve this problem alone or by committee? Explain your reasoning.
6. Groupthink is a potentially serious impediment to group decision making. Describe this phenomenon, and review what can be done to avoid it.
7. Suppose you were on a committee composed of people from various nations charged with an important decision. How do you think this composition might make a difference in how the group operates?
8. Suppose you learn that a certain important organizational decision must be made by a group but suspect a better one might be made by an individual. Describe three ways you could use groups to make a decision while also avoiding many of the problems associated with groups.

Case in Point

Baby Superstores: Growing, Grown, Gone

If there was one thing Jack Tate learned after graduating from Harvard Law School, it was that he did not want to be a lawyer. Although he hung his shingle in front of an office in Greenville, South Carolina, and practiced law for several years, his heart was never really in it. His consuming passion was a brainstorm that came one day while shopping for his nine-month-old daughter: Instead of going to many different stores to buy items for newborns, why not sell everything under one roof, supermarket-style? Offering diapers, toys, cribs, clothes, and infant formula in a single store would make life so convenient for new parents with hectic schedules they surely would beat a path to your door. Tate's optimism convinced bankers to lend him $200,000 in March 1971, and Carolina Baby was born. A month later, he gave up practicing the law. Tate was now a retailing entrepreneur.

Joining Tate in this venture was Linda Robertson, his former part-time legal secretary, who caught Tate's infectious enthusiasm for Carolina Baby. Business was so good that only two years later, Tate and Robertson opened up a second store in Easley, South Carolina. As their business grew, they narrowed its scope. No longer did they carry lines for all children through the pre-teen years; infants and toddlers were the new focus. Their rationale was clear: First-time parents need to buy a lot of things for their newborns (e.g., strollers, changing tables, car seats) — a market that was estimated at the time to be $13 million annually.

While narrowing their product lines, Tate and Robertson also enlarged their retail spaces. Realizing they were paying premium rent in shopping malls, they moved to less expensive spots in strip centers throughout the Carolinas. By 1987, with 26 stores averaging 6,000 square feet each, their sales hit $14.5 million. That same year, they opened a much larger location — a 20,000-square-foot warehouse store in Marietta, Georgia. When sales jumped 50 percent per square foot, Tate and Robertson knew they were onto something big. They changed the name to match, and Baby Superstore was launched. Shortly thereafter, all stores moved to large warehouse locations as well. Down came the interior walls and ceilings, and up went stacks of merchandise, piled high into the rafters. Modeling Baby Superstore after Home Depot, the successful building-supply chain, Tate and Robertson now offered convenience, huge selection, and low prices.

The formula worked — at least for a while. By 1992, sales had reached $63 million at 26 Baby Superstores. Two years later, the company even went public, and its stock price rose quickly. This took Robertson from being a $55-per-week secretary to a company president with a $50-million stake in the company. Unfortunately, Tate's decision to grow the company to several hundred stores quickly got it into financial trouble. Then, to save the company, Tate made the biggest decision of all in 1996: Baby Superstore would merge with Toys 'R' Us in a stock-swap worth $376 million. The deal resulted in a loss of net worth for Tate, but it made his life far less volatile, thereby allowing him to return to the life he enjoyed in South Carolina.

CRITICAL THINKING QUESTIONS

1. Using the analytical model of decision making, how do you think the process unfolded to develop Baby Superstore?

2. Do you think Tate's decisions would have been better or worse had they been made as part of a group?

3. How might escalation of commitment have been involved in Tate's decisions about the company?

VIDEO CASE

Decision Making in Organizations

SMALL BUSINESS 2000

A company survives or fails based on the quality and outcome of the decisions made by its employees and managers. Some people avoid jobs requiring a lot of decision making; others seek them out. Making sound business decisions is not easy, especially today, when opportunities and markets often change very rapidly. Uncertainty also may complicate decision making for individuals and companies.

In this video segment, we trace the history of a business that faces all these issues and that adds at least one additional twist. Richard Fluker has turned over the management of his business, the Fluker Cricket Farm, to his three children. You read the last sentence correctly; this case takes you on a tour of the Fluker Cricket Farm. You probably are wondering how hard it is to run a cricket farm — and why somebody would even want to. The answer is obvious when you consider the numbers: the Fluker Cricket Farm has annual sales in excess of $5 million dollars, and they ship more than three million live crickets and worms around the world every week.

continued

This company has not always been so successful. When Fluker handed the company to his children a few years ago, its annual sales were about $0.5 million. Since then, the Flukers have implemented many changes, most of them aimed at expanding their product lines and approaching markets they had previously ignored. As you might imagine, none of these initiatives happened on their own. The Flukers had to take action.

In this video case, you will learn what it took to get the company to where it is today. You will hear about some early decisions that influenced the formation of the original Fluker company, and you will learn about decisions now being made that will influence the company both today and in the future. As you watch this case, look for clues as to why certain things were done. You also may want to think about what other options the Flukers may have had—and why they didn't choose them.

QUESTIONS FOR DISCUSSION

1. Richard Fluker talks about a decision he made in 1958 to turn his hobby as a fishing-bait farmer into a full-time job for himself. It's doubtful that this was an easy decision, or one that was made without considerable thought. Using the analytical model, discuss how Richard Fluker might have come to his decision and some of the choices he probably had to make.

2. Howard Fluker shares his ideas about decision making with us. In doing this, he makes a distinction between the "big" things and the "little" things. What do you think of his distinction between the two and of his thoughts on handling them?

3. David Fluker talks about the company's attempts to expand their product line. One in particular, raising mice, didn't work out so well. What do you think about his attempt to enter this area; did he make sound decisions? Also, what do you think he meant when he said, "You've got to know when to say when"?

4. The Fluker Cricket Farm pays its employees above the industry average, and it provides benefits that similar businesses generally don't. Based on what you have learned about heuristics such as availability and representativeness, how might you explain the difference between the Fluker Cricket Farm and other, similar businesses? What do you think motivates the decision to provide above-average compensation?

SKILLS BANK

EXPERIENCING ORGANIZATIONAL BEHAVIOR

What Is Your Personal Decision Style?

As you read about the various personal decision styles, did you put yourself into any of the categories? To get a feel for what the *Decision-Style Inventory* reveals about your own style, complete this exercise. It is based on questions similar to those appearing in the actual instrument (see Rowe, Boulgaides, & McGrath, 1984; see note 25).

Directions

For each of the following questions, select the alternative that best describes how you see yourself in your typical work situation.

1. When performing my job, I usually look for:
   a. Practical results.
   b. The best solutions to problems.
   c. New ideas or approaches.
   d. Pleasant working conditions.

2. When faced with a problem, I usually:
   a. Use approaches that have worked in the past.
   b. Analyze it carefully.
   c. Try to find a creative approach.
   d. Rely on my feelings.
3. When making plans, I usually emphasize:
   a. The problems I currently face.
   b. Attaining objectives.
   c. Future goals.
   d. Developing my career.
4. The kind of information I usually prefer to use is:
   a. Specific facts.
   b. Complete and accurate data.
   c. Broad information covering many options.
   d. Data that are limited and simple to understand.
5. Whenever I am uncertain about what to do, I:
   a. Rely on my intuition.
   b. Look for facts.
   c. Try to find a compromise.
   d. Wait and decide later.
6. The people with whom I work best usually are:
   a. Ambitious and full of energy.
   b. Self-confident.
   c. Open-minded.
   d. Trusting and polite.
7. The decisions I make usually are:
   a. Direct and realistic.
   b. Abstract or systematic.
   c. Broad and flexible.
   d. Sensitive to others' needs.

Scoring

The points reflect the relative strength of your preferences for each decision style.

1. For each *a* you selected, give yourself a point in the *directive* category.
2. For each *b* you selected, give yourself a point in the *analytical* category.
3. For each *c* you selected, give yourself a point in the *conceptual* category.
4. For each *d* you selected, give yourself a point in the *behavioral* category.

Questions for Discussion

1. What style did the test reveal you have? How did this compare with the style you thought you had?

2. Based on the descriptions of the personal decision styles in the text, could you guess in advance which test items were indicative of which style?

3. What additional items may be added to the test to assess each style?

WORKING IN GROUPS

Running a Nominal Group: Try It Yourself

A great deal can be learned about nominal groups by running—or at least by participating in—one yourself. Doing so not only helps to illustrate the procedure but demonstrates how effectively it works.

Directions

1. Select a topic suitable for discussion in a nominal group composed of students in your class. This topic should be narrowly defined and one about which people have many different opinions (these work best in nominal groups). Some possible examples include:

   - What should your school's student leaders do for you?
   - How can the quality of instruction in your institution be improved?
   - How can the quality of jobs your school's students receive when graduating be improved?

2. Divide the class into groups of approximately 10 students. Arrange each group in a circle or around a table, if possible. Then, in each group, select one person to serve as the group facilitator.

3. Following the steps outlined in Figure 9.12, facilitators should guide their groups in discussions regarding the question identified in step 1. Allow approximately 45 minutes to one hour to complete this process.

4. If time allows, select a different question and a different group leader, and then repeat the procedure.

Questions for Discussion

1. Collectively, how did the group answer the question? Do you believe this answer accurately reflected the feelings of the group?

2. How did the various groups' answers compare? Were they similar or different? Why?

3. What were the major problems, if any, associated with the nominal group experience? For example, were any group members reluctant to wait their turns before speaking?

4. If you conducted more than one group discussion, was the process smoother the second time around?

5. How do you think your experiences would have differed with a totally unstructured, traditional, face-to-face group instead of a nominal group?

WORKING WITH—AND AGAINST— OTHERS: PROSOCIAL AND DEVIANT BEHAVIOR IN ORGANIZATIONS

LEARNING OBJECTIVES

After reading this chapter, you should be able to

1. Define *prosocial behavior*, and distinguish it from *altruism*.
2. Describe *organizational citizenship behavior* and the major forms it takes.
3. Explain *whistle-blowing* and the dilemma faced by potential whistle-blowers.
4. Explain the nature of *cooperation*, and identify both individual and organizational factors that influence its occurrence.
5. Define *trust*, and explain its relationship to organizational citizenship behavior and to cooperation.
6. Define *conflict*, and indicate how it can produce positive as well as negative effects.
7. Identify several organizational and interpersonal causes of conflict.
8. Describe various techniques of *managing conflict*.
9. Distinguish *workplace violence* from *workplace aggression*.
10. Describe causes of workplace aggression and techniques for reducing such behavior.
11. Describe the motives behind *employee theft* and techniques for reducing such behavior.

PREVIEW CASE

Bankers with a Heart? Why Japanese Banks Often Lend a Helping Hand to Their Borrowers

Takao Suzuki — the owner of Suzuko Kogyo K.K., a small machine shop in Tokyo — expects to earn less than $150,000 this year, but he owes several large Japanese banks more than $2 million. Are these banks hounding Suzuki for payment or threatening foreclosure? No way! In fact, each bank involved has cut the interest rate on their loans — and even offered new ones to keep Suzuki's business from failing. For example, Johnan Shinkin Bank has reduced the interest rate on its loan from 8 percent in 1992 to 5.6 percent in 1993 and then to 3 percent in 1995. Is that the end of their kindness, however? "They'll lower it again later this year," says Suzuki. "I'm sure they will."

What is going on here — bankers with kind hearts? Hardly! These banks have much to gain from preventing Suzuki's company as well as thousands of other small businesses from failing. Japanese banks recently have experienced large losses from bad debts and, in many cases, may not be able to make additional loans if further losses occur. Making loans is the major business of commercial banks, so this would be equivalent to shutting down their operations.

Corporate debt also does not have the same stigma in Japan as in many other countries. "Japanese businesses run on debt," says Kiyohikio Kawahara, manager of the Johnan Shinkin branch in Tokyo that has lent Suzuki money for three decades. "Debt is the way we do things here."

Suzuki is hardly to blame for his company's current problems. During the boom of the 1980s, banks came to *him*, literally begging him to take their money. When one large bank approached him offering a loan of $1.2 million, Suzuki asked, "What would I use that money for?" "Buy stocks," they told him, which he did — and then experienced large losses when the Tokyo stock market plunged in 1989. In addition, the building owned by his business is located in an area of Tokyo where real estate prices have dropped from 60 to 80 percent during the past 10 years. Therefore, if the banks were to force him out of business and sell the property, which provides collateral for their loans, they would receive very little return.

In short, Suzuki's creditors have strong reasons for their "kindness" toward his company. Driving it out of business would hurt them more than keeping Suzuko Kyogo afloat through reduced interest rates and new loans. So, when Suzuki walks into a branch office and says, "I'm going to need your help today," the loan officers do not react as bankers in many other countries would — by demanding that he pay up first. On the contrary, they roll their eyes, sigh . . . and then lend a helping hand (and a few yen as well).

Banks that reduce interest rates for customers, make new loans on top of old ones, and allow corporate debt to rise to levels fifteen times current earnings sounds like fiction. In modern Japan, however it is current fact. In most cases, banks insist their borrowers repay loans in a timely fashion; if the borrowers do not, the banks seize the collateral, impose penalties, or raise interest rates. In Japan, however, banks have chosen a sharply different strategy: they actively *help* debtors such as Suzuki to survive. What accounts for this strategy? Not, we believe, the "benevolence" of Japanese bankers. On the contrary, this strategy stems from what might be described as "enlightened self-interest." By making more loans and various concessions to Suzuki, the banks help him to remain in business and, in so doing, to keep his loans out of their "bad debt" column. Both sides gain as a result — although here, the borrowers seem to enjoy most of the advantages.

In this situation as well as many others, a choice exists: The parties involved can adopt one of two basic — and in some ways opposite — strategies. First, they can work *against* each other, with each side focused on maximizing its own gains regardless of the costs to the "opponent." On the other hand, they can work *with* each other to attain shared goals and to maximize *joint* rather than individual gains.

Why do individuals, groups, or organizations choose one approach over the other? What are the consequences of each option? These questions are the focus of this chapter, which concentrates on several processes relating to this dimension of working with or against others (Figure 10.1).

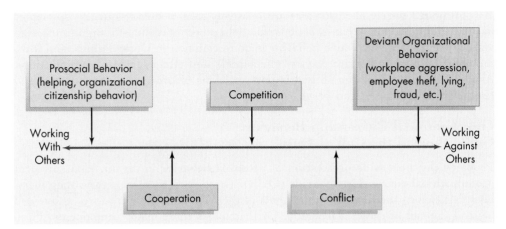

FIGURE 10.1

Working With or Against Others
Individuals and groups can choose to work with or against each other, and these contrasting strategies can result in a wide range of behaviors, which can be arranged along the continuum shown here.

The first of these processes is known as *prosocial behavior*, and it involves actions that benefit others without requiring anything obvious or immediate in return. Prosocial behavior can play an important role in organizational effectiveness, so it clearly is a topic worthy of attention. The second process, or *cooperation*, involves mutual, two-way assistance in which individuals, groups, or organizations provide benefits to each other in a reciprocal, joint manner—that is, the kind of situation described in the preview case.

The third major topic we consider is *conflict*, which often is defined as a process that develops when individuals or groups perceive that actions by others have (or will soon have) negative effects on their own interests. Such perceptions often trigger a costly spiral that produces negative outcomes for both parties. Indeed, long-standing, bitter conflicts may proceed to a point at which both sides become more concerned with harming their opponents than with maximizing their own outcomes. Conflict is not the only form of behavior that can produce negative outcomes in work settings, however. Such effects also can be produced by *deviant behavior*—that is, actions by employees that intentionally violate existing standards (of their group, organization, or society) and that result in negative consequences for their coworkers or organization. The most dramatic and visible forms of dysfunctional behavior are known as *workplace aggression*, which are instances of individuals seeking to harm other members of their organization or the organization itself. Finally, we also consider *employee theft*, another important form of dysfunctional behavior.

PROSOCIAL BEHAVIOR: HELPING OTHERS AT WORK

Is there such a thing as pure **altruism**—that is, actions by one person that benefit others under conditions in which the donor expects nothing in return? Philosophers have long puzzled over this question, and more recently, social scientists have as well.[1] Their research casts considerable doubt on the existence of totally selfless helping. People sometimes do offer help to others—even risk their lives for others—without expecting anything tangible in return. Parents who sacrifice their own lives for those of their children provide a dramatic example. Such actions appear to be quite rare, however, and in most instances when individuals help others, they tend to anticipate *some* form of compensation. This return on their investment can be quite subtle, including even the warm feeling of having "done the right thing" or the pleasure of seeing another person's joy or relief. Such reactions are very real, and they seem to provide at least a portion of the motivation behind seemingly altruistic acts.

altruism

Actions by one person that benefit others under conditions in which the donor expects nothing in return.

prosocial behavior
Actions that help other individuals or organizations in various ways.

Although purely altruistic acts are relatively rare, people frequently do engage in **prosocial behavior** — that is, actions that help other individuals or organizations in various ways. Moreover, such behavior is quite common in work settings, and it often contributes in important ways to the success and effectiveness of organizations. Accordingly, we now examine two important forms of prosocial behavior: *organizational citizenship behavior*, and *whistle-blowing*.

Organizational Citizenship Behavior: Going Beyond the Call of Duty

organizational citizenship behavior (OCB)
Actions by organization members that exceed the formal requirements of their job.

Probably the most widespread form of prosocial behavior in organizations involves **organizational citizenship behavior (OCB)**. These are actions by organization members that exceed the formal requirements of their job and, therefore, are "above and beyond the call of duty."[2] Generally, OCB involves three major components. First, the behaviors *go beyond the formal requirements* or official job descriptions. Second, the behaviors are *discretionary in nature*. In other words, individuals perform them voluntarily. Third, they are *not necessarily recognized by the formal reward structure* of the organization.[3]

What Forms Does OCB Take? Although OCB can take many forms, these behaviors generally fall into five basic categories:

know these

1. Those involving actions that help another person and appear to be *altruistic*. Have you ever offered aid to a coworker with a difficult project? If so, you have engaged in this type of OCB.
2. Those involving *conscientiousness* — that is, going well beyond the minimum requirements in areas such as attendance, obeying rules, taking breaks, and so on. If you pride yourself on never missing a day at work, you are engaging in this type of OCB (Figure 10.2).
3. Those involving participating in and showing concern about the life of the organization. Often termed *civic virtue*, this includes behaviors such as attending voluntary meetings and getting actively involved in those events (e.g., clubs, committees).
4. Those involving *sportsmanship* — that is, a willingness to tolerate less-than-ideal circumstances without complaining. If you ever followed the dictum "grin and bear it!" while at work, then you have engaged in such behavior.
5. Those involving *courtesy* — that is, being polite and behaving in a manner that prevents interpersonal problems with others.

FIGURE 10.2

Conscientiousness in Action
In September 20, 1998, Cal Ripken, Jr. — baseball's "Iron Man" — ended his historic streak of 2,632 consecutive games played when he bowed out of the Baltimore Orioles' starting line-up. After 17 seasons without missing a game, Ripkin surely is an extreme model of conscientiousness, which is a key component of OCB.

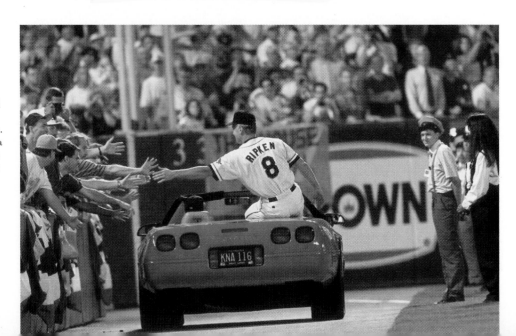

Additional examples of these types of organizational citizenship behavior are shown in Table 10.1.[4]

What Are the Determinants of OCB?   Why do employees sometimes go well beyond the call of duty in performing their jobs? Three factors appear to play a role.

One of the most important of these factors is *expected fair treatment*—that is, the belief among employees they will be treated fairly by their organization and, more specifically, by their immediate supervisors. To the extent employees believe their supervisors' decisions are made fairly (e.g., in an equitable manner; see chapter 4), the greater their trust in these supervisors. In turn, the more trust employees have, the more willing they are to engage in prosocial behavior.[5] This is especially true when it comes to trust in the fair use of punishment. Specifically, the more employees trust their bosses to dole out punishment fairly, the more likely they are to engage in OCB.[6]

People's perceptions regarding the breadth of their jobs—that is, their beliefs about which behaviors are required and which are voluntary—also affect OCB. In general, the more broadly employees define their jobs, the more likely they are to engage in OCB.[7] For example, suppose a professor is asked to take over another professor's classes while she is out of town. If that first professor believes helping other professors is a part of his job (e.g., it is the "right thing to do"), he is more likely to do so. To the extent that he believes helping a colleague in this fashion definitely is *not* part of the job and *not* his responsibility, however, he is less likely to do so.

Third, OCB is influenced by employees' attitudes about their organizations. As noted in chapter 5, such attitudes generally are known as *organizational commitment*.[8] Not surprisingly, the more strongly employees are committed to their organizations, the more willing they are to "go the extra mile" when needed, thus leading them to engage in various forms of OCB.

Does OCB Really Matter?   Clearly, OCB is important. Most of us would prefer working for an organization populated by good citizens than for one whose employees just don't care. After all, a company full of good citizens is likely to be a more enjoyable place to work than one full of unhelpful people trying to do only the minimum needed to stay out of trouble. A basic question, however, remains: Does OCB really enhance organizational performance? Answering this question is not easy, because acts of

TABLE 10.1

Organizational Citizenship Behavior: Specific Forms and Examples

Organizational citizenship behavior (OCB) can take many different forms, most of which fall into the five major categories shown here.

FORM OF OCB	EXAMPLES
Altruism	Helping a coworker with a project Switching vacation dates with another person Volunteering
Conscientiousness	Never missing a day of work Coming to work early if needed Not spending time on personal calls
Civic virtue	Attending voluntary meetings and functions Reading memos; keeping up with new information
Sportsmanship	Making do without complaint ("Grin and bear it!") Not finding fault with the organization
Courtesy	"Turning the other cheek" to avoid problems Not "blowing up" when provoked

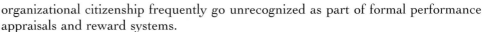

FIGURE 10.3

A Famous Whistle-Blower

Film buffs may recall the 1979 film *Norma Rae*, in which Sally Field won an Oscar for her portrayal of a textile worker who exposed the intolerable working conditions in her factory. Although the struggle faced by this character may be more extreme and dramatic than most, it probably is a relatively realistic depiction of the uphill battles most whistle-blowers face.

whistle-blowing

Disclosure by employees of illegal, immoral, or illegitimate practices by employers to people or organizations able to do something about it.

organizational citizenship frequently go unrecognized as part of formal performance appraisals and reward systems.

Recent studies, however, indicate that the greater the incidence of OCB in an organization, the higher that organization's performance. In addition, individuals who engage in prosocial behavior *are* recognized both formally and informally in many companies. Specifically, people who engage in OCB tend to be liked by their bosses and coworkers. In addition, they usually receive higher performance evaluations because of frequently behaving in a helpful, prosocial way.[9] Overall, then, OCB seems to produce the beneficial effects we would expect. Accordingly, there is good reason for managers to encourage their employees to behave in a prosocial manner.

Whistle-Blowing: Helping an Organization by Dissenting with It

Another form of prosocial behavior in organizations is known as **whistle-blowing**. This is the disclosure by employees of illegal, immoral, or illegitimate practices by employers to people or organizations able to do something about it (Figure 10.3).[10]

In many instances, whistle-blowers can protect the health, safety, or economic welfare of the general public. For example, consider the case of Bill Bush, who in 1974 blew the whistle on the National Aeronautics and Space Administration for circulating an internal memo ordering supervisors—such as himself—to not consider employees older than 54 years for promotion. Feeling this violated both legal and ethical principles, Bush exposed the memo.

Another example is the case of Robert Young, an agent for the Prudential Insurance Co. in New Jersey. He noticed agents regularly churning policies—that is, needlessly selling new and more expensive plans to existing policyholders to gain extra commissions. Young complained, but at first, nothing happened. Then, because of the stress he experienced from this situation, he went on disability leave. Shortly thereafter, he was fired. The official grounds were that Young was an abusive manager who had sexually harassed his subordinates. Young denies these charges and claims he was fired simply to "shut him up" and to punish him for being a "troublemaker."[11]

Fortunately, not all whistle-blowers are punished for doing what they believe is the right thing. For example, consider Daniel Shannon, who in 1993 was an in-house lawyer for Intelligent Electronics. After protesting the alleged misuse of marketing funds from computer manufacturers—a complaint that produced an informal SEC inquiry and lawsuits by several shareholders—Shannon was fired. He then filed a lawsuit in which he claimed wrongful termination by his former employer. The suit was settled out of court for between $500,000 and $1 million.

As you might imagine, whistle-blowers face a tough fight. As Thomas Devine, legal director of the Government Accountability Project in Washington, DC, puts it, "If there is one common denominator among whistle-blowers, it is that they face harassment, retaliation, and professional apocalypse."[12] Such persons frequently find themselves facing a long, uphill battle as they attempt to prove the wrongdoing they reported. They often lose their jobs as some companies quickly find other, seemingly legitimate grounds for dismissing them, or they may discover they have been "blackballed" in their industry or profession and cannot find another job. Clearly, whistle-blowers sacrifice a great deal to protect innocent victims.

GLOBAL MATTERS   Whistle-blowing occurs more commonly in the United States and other Western nations than in Asian or African nations. Why might this be so? ■

Does whistle-blowing really qualify as prosocial behavior, or are whistle-blowers merely disgruntled employees looking for a way to "get even" with their organizations? The latter conclusion can be ruled out in most cases. Whistle-blowers generally are motivated to correct what they perceive as acts of wrongdoing. Moreover, most try to work inside their companies before going public, which they do only after these internal efforts fail.[13] Even so, however, the situation remains complex. Whether such actions are—or are not—prosocial in nature depends on the motivation underlying them. If a whistle-blower benefits from his or her actions while the organization suffers, or if the whistle-blower's actions are part of a personal quest for vengeance, then whistle-blowing cannot be viewed as being prosocial regarding the organization.[14]

If you ever find yourself in a situation where you feel you should "blow the whistle" on your company, what should you do? For some suggestions, see the "Tips" section below.

■ How to Blow the Whistle Effectively

Suppose you someday discover a company for which you work is engaged in practices you consider to be immoral, unethical, or illegal. If you are like most people, this creates quite a conflict. On the one hand, you feel you cannot ignore the matter; on the other hand, you feel unwilling to put your own job or career in jeopardy. Is there some way to "do the right thing" both for yourself and for society at large?

Fortunately, experts have identified several ways to maximize the chances you will do some good while also safeguarding your career:

- *Document your claims scrupulously.* Never stir things up without solid documentation for your claims. Otherwise, you probably will not be taken seriously, thus leaving you ineffective for getting anything done—and, indeed, putting your job at risk.
- *Speak to your immediate supervisor first.* Make every effort to work out the problem internally. First, bring it to the attention of your boss; if that does not help, then speak to her or his supervisor. Whatever you do, do not go public with your charges until you have given all appropriate people in the company every opportunity to act.
- *Talk to a lawyer.* Thirty-five U.S. states and many countries now have laws to protect whistle-blowers. The provisions of these laws vary greatly, however, so check carefully to determine your own legal rights—and protections—before you proceed.
- *Plan for the worst.* Trusting your company and your immediate boss is good, but do not proceed unless you are prepared—financially as well as psychologically—for negative outcomes such as being put on temporary leave, probation, or even being fired. The people who are guilty of the unethical, immoral, or illegal actions you noticed will not go down without a fight, and if all else fails, they will try to take you with them. Therefore, be ready for the worst while you remain optimistic that "right" will triumph.

These suggestions may be difficult to follow, but they surely are worth the effort considering the consequences involved—both of reacting and of doing nothing at all! ■

COOPERATION: MUTUAL ASSISTANCE IN WORK SETTINGS

As described thus far, prosocial behavior is basically a one-way process: One person helps another. Many help-giving interactions in organizations, however, involve the two-way process known as **cooperation**—that is, a pattern of behavior in which assistance is mutual and two or more individuals, groups, or organizations work together

cooperation
A pattern of behavior in which assistance is mutual and two or more individuals, groups, or organizations work together toward shared goals for their mutual benefit.

toward shared goals for their mutual benefit.[15] Cooperation is a common form of co-ordination in work settings, largely because by doing so, the persons or groups involved can accomplish more than by working alone.

Given the obvious benefits of cooperation, a question arises: If it is so useful, why does cooperation often fail to occur? In other words, why do people with similar goals sometimes not join forces? Many factors are involved, but the most important in some situations, is that cooperation simply *cannot* occur because the goals sought by the individuals or groups involved cannot be shared. For example, two people seeking the same job or promotion cannot join forces to attain it. Similarly, two companies courting the same potential merger candidate cannot cooperate to reach their goal—only one company can conclude the merger. In cases such as these, an alternative form of behavior known as **competition**—that is, a pattern of behavior in which each person, group, or organization seeks to maximize its own gains, often at the expense of others—often emerges.[16] For a comparison of cooperation and competition, see Figure 10.4.

In some contexts, competition is both natural and understandable. People and groups need to compete for scarce resources and rewards, and organizations must compete for supplies, government contracts, customers, and sales. For example, consider the "cruiser wars"—that is, intense competition between the legendary motorcycle giant Harley-Davidson and several start-up companies challenging it for a share of the lucrative "cruiser" market. (*Cruisers* are upscale motorcycles equipped with windshields, luggage compartments, and other luxury features.) To compete with Harley-Davidson, which sold more than 132,000 motorcycles in 1997, young companies like Victory and Excelsior-Henderson are engineering cruisers that match a Harley-Davidson's performance but give customers even more features for their money (e.g., elaborate paint jobs, chrome parts). Will these new companies succeed? Only one thing is certain: Competition in the cruiser segment of the motorcycle market has shifted into high gear.

Competition obviously is an inevitable feature built into retail settings. In many other contexts, however, competition is *not* required but cooperation still fails to develop. This raises an interesting question: What leads people to cooperate with each other? To understand the answer, we take a closer look at the basic nature of cooperation.

The Nature of Cooperation: Situations Involving Mixed Motives

Suppose you live in a community with a strict recycling policy that requires you to separate glass, plastic, metal cans, and paper in your trash. From a purely selfish point of view, the easier thing would be to ignore the rule and mix all your trash together. If everyone in the community did do this, however, everyone would loose. Your landfill soon would become full, and you would pay much higher taxes to ship your trash elsewhere. If you were the only one to not go along with the policy, you might come out ahead in terms of convenience (at least in the short run). If all your neighbors

competition

A pattern of behavior in which each person, group, or organization seeks to maximize its own gains, often at the expense of others.

FIGURE 10.4

Cooperation vs. Competition: A Summary Comparison

When *cooperating* with each other, people contribute to attaining the same goal, which they share. When *competing* with each other, however, people attempt to attain the same goal while excluding the other.

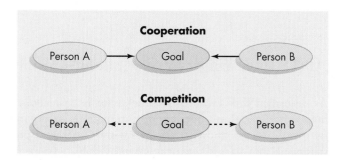

pursued their self-interest in this way, however, all of you would lose. Figure 10.5 provides another illustration of this point, but the example here describes what is known as a **social dilemma**—that is, a situation in which all parties (be they individuals, groups, or organizations) can increase their gains by acting in one way but stand to lose if all (or most) do so.[17] The parties involved in such situations must deal with *mixed motives*. In other words, there are reasons for them to cooperate (i.e., to avoid negative outcomes for all) and to *defect* (i.e., to do what is best for themselves regardless of the effect on others).

Many everyday situations are social dilemmas.[18] For example, we may obey traffic regulations willingly even if they inconvenience us, because they are necessary for the long-term well-being of all who use our roadways. Similarly, to avoid a costly trade war that could harm everyone, the nations of the world refrain from imposing tariffs on imported goods even though they would realize short-term gains by doing so.

In the situations we described, there are some individuals—as you no doubt know—who do not separate their trash for recycling or follow traffic regulations. From time to time, some nations also impose tariffs on at least some imported goods. In general terms, some parties at times fail to cooperate and take a more self-oriented course of action instead of doing something for the common good. Why is this so? What factors encourage or discourage cooperative behavior? In the next section, we consider individual factors influencing cooperation, and in the following section, we discuss cooperation across organizations.

Individual Determinants of Cooperation

Many factors determine whether individuals choose to cooperate with others in situations involving the mixed motives generated by social dilemmas. Three, however, appear to be most important: tendencies toward *reciprocity, personal orientations* concerning cooperation, and *trust*.

Reciprocity: Following the "Golden Rule"   Throughout life, all of us are urged to follow the "Golden Rule," which is to do unto others as we would like them to do unto us. This idea is drummed into us thoroughly by parents, teachers, and religious leaders as we grow up, but we still usually behave in a different manner. Most of us tend to react to others not as we would prefer to be treated ourselves but instead as we actually have been treated by those others in the past. In short, much of the time, people follow the principle of **reciprocity**—that is, the tendency for people to return the

social dilemma
A situation in which all parties (e.g., individuals, groups, or organizations) can increase their gains by acting in one way but stand to lose if all (or most) do so.

reciprocity
The tendency for people to return the kind of treatment they receive from others.

FIGURE 10.5

The Nature of Social Dilemmas

In *social dilemmas*, each person can increase her or his outcomes by acting selfishly. When many of the people involved behave this way, however, outcomes for all are reduced. Drivers of small, fuel-efficient cars (left) may be acknowledged for behaving cooperatively, because their vehicles conserve natural resources and pollute the atmosphere to a relatively small degree. Drivers of large, gas-guzzling sport utility vehicles (right), however, can be viewed as acting more selfishly, because their vehicles waste fuel and pollute to a much greater degree.

kind of treatment they have received previously from others.[19] This principle is followed carefully when choosing between cooperation and competition. In other words, when others cooperate with us and put their own selfish interests aside, we usually respond in kind. If others opt to pursue their own interests, however, we generally do the same.

Personal Orientation   Think about the many people you have known during your life. Can you remember ones who strongly preferred cooperation, who could be counted on to work together with other group members in almost every situation? Can you remember ones who usually preferred to pursue their own selfish interests and could *not* be relied on to cooperate? You probably have little difficulty naming examples of both.

Indeed, social scientists note that differences between people in their tendencies to cooperate with others are quite reliable. In turn, such differences reflect contrasting perspectives toward working with others. Individuals carry these perspectives with them from situation to situation, even over relatively long periods of time.[20] Specifically, people tend to possess one of three distinct orientations toward situations involving social dilemmas:

- People with a *cooperative* orientation prefer to maximize the joint outcomes received by all parties. They are concerned with helping themselves as well as others.
- People with an *individualistic* orientation focus primarily on maximizing their own outcomes. They do not care how much others get so long as they get as much as they want.
- People with a *competitive* orientation focus primarily on defeating others. They care less about how well they do than with obtaining better outcomes than those of others.

Research in controlled settings has confirmed these differences in personal orientation actually do account for real differences in how people behave. In other words, some people really are more competitive than others, and this is reflected in their treatment of others.

Trust   Earlier, we noted that employees are more likely to be active organizational citizens to the extent they trust their supervisors to treat them fairly.[21] Indeed, trust derives—at least in part—from perceptions that one's boss or leader has reached decisions through fair procedures (i.e., procedural justice).[22] The higher the trust, the greater the employee's commitment to the leader's decisions.

trust
An individual's confidence in the goodwill of others and the belief they will make efforts consistent with the group's goal.

Extending this idea, it should not be surprising that **trust**, which is defined as an individual's confidence in the goodwill of others and the belief they will make efforts consistent with the group's goals, also plays an important role in cooperation.[23] Specifically, the more people trust their coworkers, the more likely they are to cooperate with them.[24]

In practice, however, this relationship is a bit more complex. In particular, there are two distinct kinds of trust, each of which may relate to increased cooperation in a distinct way.[25] The first, which is known as *cognition-based trust*, refers to our beliefs about the reliability and trustworthiness of others. It is measured by the extent of agreement with items such as "Given this person's track record, I see no reason to doubt his/her competence and preparation for the job." The second, which is known as *affect-based trust*, refers to the emotional bond between individuals that involve genuine care and concern for the welfare of others. It is measured by the extent of agreements on items such as "I should say we have both made considerable emotional investments in our working relationship."

Affect-based trust is influenced by factors such as the frequency with which the managers interact with their peers and their previous help extended to these persons.[26] In turn, such trust appears to influence directly several forms of helping and cooperation and indirectly the performance of both managers and peers. In contrast, cognition-based trust does not seem to influence cooperation directly (Figure 10.6).

In sum, trust is an important determinant of cooperation. In turn, cooperation yields many beneficial effects, such as increased performance and coordination. Therefore, building high levels of trust among persons who work together is well worth the effort involved.

GLOBAL MATTERS

Trust in supervisors and coworkers generally is higher in Western nations than in Asian nations (e.g., Japan).[27] Why might this be so? What cultural or economic factors might account for this difference? ▨

Organizational Determinants of Cooperation

That organizations differ greatly in their internal levels of cooperation is obvious. Some (typically those that are quite successful) demonstrate a high degree of coordination between their various departments.[28] Others, however, contain departments whose members all too often work at cross-purposes. What accounts for these differences? Individual factors provide a partial answer, but factors relating to an organization's internal structure and function also play a role.

Reward Systems and Cooperation   Consider the following situation: A large insurance company has two major divisions: Consumer Underwriting, which issues policies for individuals; and Commercial Underwriting, which issues policies for businesses. The company also has a bonus system, in which annual awards are distributed to individuals in the more profitable division. This produces a high degree of competition between the units, which at first glance might seem beneficial.

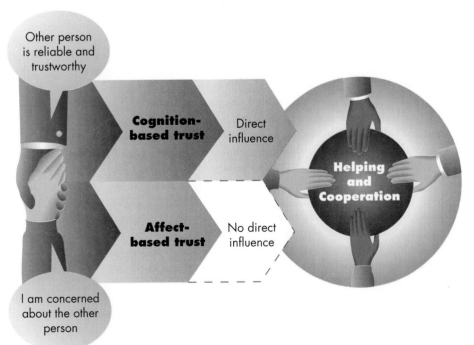

FIGURE 10.6

Two Kinds of Trust

Cognition-based trust exists when someone believes another person is reliable and trustworthy, and it directly influences helping and cooperation. In contrast, *affect-based trust* exists when someone is concerned about another person. It has no direct influence on helping and cooperation.

You may become concerned, however, that sales personnel from one division might actively interfere with the efforts of personnel from the other division. For example, while working hard to win a multimillion-dollar policy with a large manufacturing concern, agents from the Commercial Underwriting division may discourage top managers in that company from seeking individual life and property policies from their own company. After all, this would contribute to the sales of their rival division, Consumer Underwriting. The opposite pattern is true as well, with consumer agents discouraging large clients from seeking policies for their businesses from the commercial division.

This may be an extreme case, but it reflects conditions that are all too common in organizations. Many reward systems are "winner-take-all" in form, such as when various divisions of a company compete with each other for a bonus. This tends to reduce coordination between units or divisions, because each seeks to maximize its own rewards. This is not to imply such internal competition is necessarily bad or counterproductive. Far from it! Still, managers should ensure such competition does not hinder the functioning and success of the entire organization.

Interdependence Among Employees   Consider two organizations: In the first, the major tasks performed by employees can be completed alone, so there is no need for individuals to work closely with others. In the second, however, the major tasks performed by employees cannot be completed alone. Therefore, these employees must work together closely to do their jobs. In which organization will higher levels of cooperation develop? Obviously, in the second. The reason for this difference is apparent as well: The level of cooperation attained is determined by the nature of the work performed.

Specifically, the greater the interdependence among employees, the higher the cooperation among them tends to be. After all, the more that members of a team count on each other for outcomes, the less likely they are to jeopardize their own outcomes by harming others. Those whose outcomes are not linked as closely, however, may have less concern in this regard. This relationship has been verified in many studies, and it appears to be a strong and general one.[29]

Cooperation Across Organizations

Whenever we think of relations between different organizations in the same industry, *competition* is sure to come to mind. The fundamental nature of business relationships encourages us to concentrate on how organizations compete and what strategies they adopt to improve their competitive advantage in the marketplace. There also are situations, however, in which organizations coordinate their efforts for mutual gain. In short, there are important instances of what is termed *interorganizational coordination*.

Chapter 14 describes in detail how such organizational arrangements are structured. Here, we only address a fundamental question about the nature of cooperation itself: Why would organizations in the same industry agree to cooperate with one another? The answers reside in three different sets of conditions.

Partnering with Suppliers   To a growing degree, today's organizations are reaping the benefits of coordinating their efforts in a special way: by joining forces with the other organizations on which they rely for products or services. This approach is illustrated by the new relationships emerging between large manufacturing companies and their suppliers of component parts.

Traditionally, manufacturers have hammered away at their suppliers, trying to drive down their prices as much as possible. This can backfire, however, because suppliers can be pushed only so far. In addition, when large companies reduce the profit margins of their suppliers, they also reduce the ability of these companies to invest in

FIGURE 10.7

Partnering with Suppliers: An Example

AlliedSignal entered into a partnership with Baja Oriente of Ensenada, Mexico—the company from which it purchases aluminum castings. In exchange for an annual cost reduction of six percent, AlliedSignal increased its orders from $500,000 to more than $6 million. This allowed Baja to spread its fixed costs over more units and to make longer production runs, thus reducing the time spent on changeovers. This helped Baja to cut costs and meet AlliedSignal's demands. Both companies benefited from this cooperation.

equipment to make themselves more efficient, thereby enabling them to reduce their prices still more. This growing realization has led some companies to seek a partnership with their suppliers.[30] Rather than treating them as adversaries across the bargaining table, they now view suppliers as being partners whose outcomes are intimately linked with their own. Thus, they not only offer these suppliers both training and assistance, they adopt a win-win approach in which goals shared by both organizations—greater efficiency and reduced prices—are established.

Consider, for example, the case of AlliedSignal, an $11.8-billion-per-year maker of auto parts and aerospace electronics. To reduce the costs of components used in its products, this company has worked out win-win arrangements with many of its suppliers. For example, in 1993, AlliedSignal offered to double its orders from Mech-Tronics, but only if Mech-Tronics would cut its prices by 10 percent. These terms initially eliminated Mech-Tronics' profits, but with help from AlliedSignal in improving its efficiency, the higher volume soon paid off. The result? Both companies gained. (For another example, see Figure 10.7 on page 380.)

As you might imagine, AlliedSignal is not the only company to recognize the benefits of cooperative relationships with their suppliers. Honda and Toyota have long reaped both savings in cost and gains in quality from developing such relationships with their suppliers. In fact, officials of these auto-manufacturing giants credit such relationships with a key role in ensuring the steady stream of high-quality, low-cost parts so central to their missions of providing excellent value to their customers.

By partnering with each other, independent companies can reduce their costs and gain major advantages. They also, however, may make it more difficult for new, start-up companies to enter the market. Does this make it unethical for existing companies to cooperate with one another? ■

ETHICS MATTERS

Promoting Business Growth   Coordination between organizations may occur when independent companies conclude they can greatly increase their potential gains by joining forces. For example, consider the 1998 merger of Chrysler and Daimler-Benz. (In fact, Daimler-Benz purchased Chrysler for $58 billion, but the move is still viewed as a merger in many quarters.)

These two companies hope to gain quite a lot. Chrysler is strong in North America but weak in Europe, where it has less than one percent of the total market. Conversely, Daimler-Benz is strong in Europe but has only one percent of the North American market. In addition, Chrysler's line of modestly priced models will complement Daimler-Benz's array of luxury Mercedes models, and by joining forces, the two companies also can combine their financial, engineering, and marketing resources—a combination that will make them a very strong competitor. Indeed, Daimler-Benz's arch rival in Germany, Volkswagen, already is feeling the effects of the merger and is considering several major steps to help withstand the expected assault from its strengthened adversary.

Responding to External Threats   Interorganizational coordination often occurs when one or more new competitors enter a mature and previously stable market, thereby "shaking things up." This occurred in the United States during the late 1970s and early 1980s, when sales of Japanese automobiles rose to very high levels. In response to this external threat, the three major U.S. auto manufacturers joined forces to lobby for government protection. They succeeded, and legislation restricting the import of Japanese cars provided the breathing room they needed to improve their own products. Cooperation between competitors helped to protect each company from the external threat.

CONFLICT: ITS NATURE, CAUSES, AND EFFECTS

If prosocial behavior and cooperation constitute one end of a continuum describing how individuals and groups work together in organizations, *conflict* certainly lies at the other end. This term has many meanings, but in the field of OB, it refers primarily to instances when units or individuals within an organization work against rather than with one another.[31]

conflict

A process in which one party perceives another has taken (or is about to take) some action that will exert a negative effect on its major interest.

More formally, **conflict** is a process in which one party perceives that another has taken (or is about to take) some action that will exert negative effects on its major interest. The key elements in conflict, then, are:

- Opposing interests between individuals or groups.
- Recognition of such opposition.
- The belief by each side that the other will thwart (or already has thwarted) these interests.
- Actions that actually produce such thwarting.

Unfortunately, when defined in this manner, conflict is all too common in modern organizations, and its effects are far too costly to ignore. Practicing managers report they spend approximately 20 percent of their time dealing with conflict and its effects.[32] In addition, the smoldering resentment and broken relationships in the aftermath of many conflicts can persist for months or even years, continuing to exact a major toll in human resources long after the original situation has become a memory. For these reasons, organizational conflict is an important topic in the field of OB— and one deserving of our careful attention.

In this section, we provide an overview of current knowledge about this costly process. First, we examine two basic dimensions that underlie many forms of conflict. Second, we consider various causes of conflict. Finally, we examine the major effects of conflict, which you may be surprised to learn sometimes are positive as well as negative in nature.

Integration and Distribution: Two Basic Dimensions of Conflict

Consider this actual incident: Mark, a marketing expert who worked for a telephone company, persuaded two friends to start a company of their own. Because they were good friends, he was certain they would succeed. Soon, however, it became apparent his partners had goals that contrasted strikingly with his own. "They wanted the company to pay for their cars and to conduct meetings in the Bahamas," the disillusioned founder notes, "but I wanted to plow our money back into the business." Over and over, they outvoted him, until finally, drained of all resources, the company collapsed. Today, Mark doesn't even nod to his former partners when he passes them on the street. "I never thought a business relationship could overpower friendship," he notes, "but this one did." As he observes, "Where money's involved, people change."[33]

distribution

Concern with one's own outcomes.

integration

Concern with the outcomes of others.

This incident nicely illustrates two basic dimensions that play a role in many conflicts: **distribution**, which is concern with one's own outcomes; and **integration**, which is concern with the outcomes of others. Mark clearly was concerned with integration: He wanted the company—and therefore both he and his partners—to thrive. His friends, however, were more concerned with distribution: They wanted to take care of themselves. Thus, they outvoted their more conservative partner and stripped the company of its assets for their own gain.

Much evidence indicates these two dimensions are important and, moreover, are largely independent. Thus, in a given situation, it is possible to pursue actions that are high in both distribution and integration, low in both, or high in one and low in the other.[34] In fact, various combinations of these motives underlie five distinct styles of handling conflict: *competing, collaborating, avoiding, accommodating,* and *compromising*.[35] The relative positions of each of these styles or approaches regarding the key dimensions of distribution and integration are shown in Figure 10.8. As depicted, *competition* is high on distribution but low on integration, *compromise* is in the middle on both dimensions, and *avoidance* is low on both. *Accommodation* (i.e., giving others what they want) is high on integration but low on distribution, and *collaboration* is high on both dimensions.

Considering our earlier discussion of individual differences regarding preferences for cooperation and competition, you should not be surprised that individuals also differ greatly in their preferences of conflict-handling styles.[36] What you may find more unexpected, however, is that cultures differ in this respect as well. In many Western cultures, which tend to be *individualistic* in orientation (i.e., focused on one's own interests), there is a strong preference for competition. In many African and Asian cultures, which are *collectivisitic* in orientation (i.e., focused on the interests of all parties), however, preferences for accommodating and avoiding are relatively strong.[37] Such differences are worth noting, because they have important implications for conflict management (a topic we consider in detail later in this chapter).

Major Causes of Conflict

As noted, conflict involves the presence—or at least perception—of opposing interests. By itself, however, this condition is neither necessary nor sufficient for actual conflict to occur. Open confrontations sometimes fail to develop even when people's interests are incompatible, and conflict sometimes emerges even when opposing interests are not perceived to be present.

Clearly, many factors and conditions contribute to the occurrence of conflict. These can be divided in two major groups: factors relating to organizational structure or functioning, and factors relating to interpersonal relations. We now consider both.

Organizational Causes of Conflict   Perhaps the most obvious organizational cause of conflict is *competition over scarce resources*. No organization has unlimited resources, and conflicts often arise over the division or distribution of space, money, equipment, and personnel. This situation is heightened by the tendency for each side to believe it is

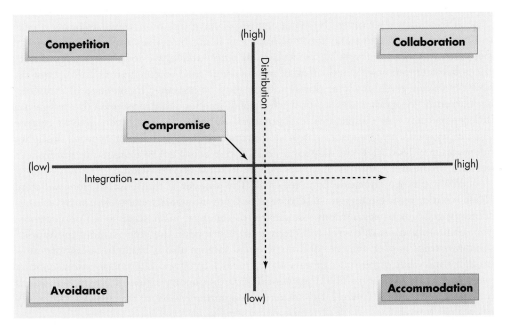

FIGURE 10.8

Basic Styles of Resolving Conflict

Different approaches to resolving conflict reflect two underlying dimensions present in most such situations: concern with one's own outcomes (i.e., *distribution*), and concern with others' outcomes (i.e., *integration*). The five major styles of resolving conflict reflect people's various positions regarding these two dimensions.

more deserving than the other, thereby justifying a larger share of the available resources. Not surprisingly, the result can be intense, prolonged conflict. If you ever vied with a coworker for the same office space or a share of the pot of raise monies, you already know only too well about the nature of the conflicts involved.

Two additional—and closely related—causes of conflict are *ambiguity over responsibility* and *ambiguity over jurisdiction*. Groups of individuals within an organization sometimes are uncertain who is responsible for various tasks or duties. When this occurs, each involved party disclaims responsibility, and conflict can quickly develop. Similarly, uncertainty over who has jurisdiction or authority also frequently exists. The more clearly organizational responsibilities are laid out, whether by formal policy or informal organizational culture, the less likely such conflicts are to arise.

Interpersonal Causes of Organizational Conflict   Our definition of conflict focuses on incompatible interests. Indeed, this is *the* defining feature of all conflicts. As you know from experience, however, conflicts do not develop automatically because both sides have incompatible interests. Conflicts sometimes occur when the two sides only *believe* they have opposing interests.[38] Clearly, the matter is a bit more complex than our definition. For conflict to occur, there must be more than just opposing interests.

Interpersonal factors may play as strong—or even stronger—role than incompatible interests in initiating conflicts. One such factor involves what have been termed *faulty attributions*—that is, errors concerning the believed causes behind others' behavior.[39] When individuals find their interests have been thwarted, they generally try to determine *why* this occurred (see chapter 2). Was it bad luck, a lack of planning on their part, or a lack of needed resources? Was it the intentional interference of another person or group? If they conclude the latter is true, then the seeds of an intense conflict may be planted—*even if these other persons actually had nothing to do with the situation*! In other words, erroneous attributions concerning the causes of negative outcomes can—and often do—play an important role in conflicts. In fact, they sometimes even cause them to occur when they could have been readily avoided.

Another interpersonal factor playing an important role in conflict is what might be termed *faulty communication*—that is, that individuals sometimes communicate with others in a way that unintentionally angers or annoys them. Have you ever been on the receiving end of criticism you felt was unfair, insensitive, and not in the least bit helpful? Feedback of this type, which is known as *destructive criticism*, can leave the recipient hungry for revenge—and thus set the stage for conflicts that, again, do not stem from incompatible interests.

A third cause involves the tendency to perceive our own views as being objective and reflecting reality but those of others as being biased by their own ideology.[40] Because of this tendency, which is known as *naïve realism*, we tend to magnify differences between our views and those of others—and also to exaggerate conflicts of interest between us. Moreover, this tendency may be stronger for groups of individuals currently in a dominant or powerful position: Such persons tend to exaggerate differences between themselves and potential opponents to an even greater degree than individuals or groups not in a dominant position.[41] In other words, this phenomenon may lead high-status people (e.g., top executives) to exaggerate differences between themselves and lower-status people in their organization.

What can we conclude from all this? The answer is that conflict does *not* stem solely from opposing interests. It also derives from interpersonal factors, such as long-standing grudges or resentment, the desire for revenge, inaccurate social perceptions, poor communication, and similar factors. (As described in the "OB Around the World" section in this chapter, the role of interpersonal factors also is likely to be important—though somewhat different—in various cultures.) In short, like cooperation, conflict has many different roots. The most central may be incompatible interests, but this is only part of the story. Clearly, the social and cognitive causes of this process definitely should *not* be overlooked. (For a summary, see Figure 10.9.)

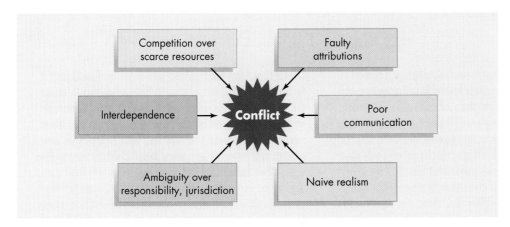

FIGURE 10.9

Organizational and Interpersonal Causes of Conflict

Many factors, including those summarized here, contribute to conflict in work settings.

The Effects of Conflict: Definitely a Mixed Bag

In everyday speech, the term *conflict* has strong negative connotations. It conjures images of angry emotions, direct confrontations, as well as harsh and damaging behavior. Conflict in work settings, however, operates like the proverbial "double-edged sword." Depending on why it occurs and how it develops, conflict can yield beneficial as well as harmful effects. (For a summary, see Figure 10.10).

The Negative Effects of Conflict   Some of the negative effects produced by conflict are so obvious they require little comment. For example, as you no doubt know from experience, conflict may yield strong negative emotions, which can be quite stressful (see chapter 6). Conflict also frequently interferes with communication between individuals, groups, or divisions, and in this way, it can all but eliminate coordination between them. In addition, it diverts attention and needed energies from major tasks and efforts to attain key organizational goals. Add it up, and conflict clearly can interfere seriously with organizational effectiveness.

Other effects are more subtle and, therefore, sometimes are overlooked. For example, conflict between groups often encourages leaders to *shift from participative styles to authoritarian styles of leadership*.[42] In other words, they shy away from encouraging others to get involved in favor of making decisions by themselves. This makes sense given that groups in conflict likely are encountering high levels of stress—and that people experiencing such conditions require firm direction if they are to succeed. Recognizing this fact, their leaders adopt more controlling tactics in these situations.

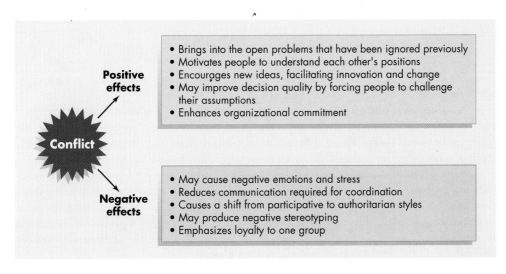

FIGURE 10.10

Positive and Negative Effects of Conflict: A Summary

In organizations, conflict can have a variety of positive and negative effects, such as those summarized here.

CONFLICT ACROSS ETHNIC AND CULTURAL BOUNDARIES

When people attempt to resolve conflicts, it is natural for them to seek outcomes favorable to themselves, such as getting a larger share of some desired resource. Inevitably, however, at least one of the parties involved may be dissatisfied with the outcomes they receive. Still, this is only part of the story. In general, disputing parties do not care only about outcomes; they also are concerned about how they are treated by each other during their interaction. In other words, whether someone is treated with dignity and respect can be at least as important to that individual as the outcomes that he or she receives.[43] In fact, this often is a key factor in determining if the relationship will continue.

On further thought, you may realize this tendency might not apply to people who are interacting with members of different cultures. After all, how we are treated by members of our own group may tell us more about how they view us — because we are more like them and can relate to them better — than how we are treated by people who outside our own culture. Furthermore, we are less confident of our ability to "read" people from other cultures, so we are less likely to rely on their treatment of us as useful information. Therefore, we may care less about the interpersonal treatment we receive when resolving conflicts with people of different cultures than we do when resolving conflicts with those from our own culture. As a result, when interacting with people from different cultures, we may pay greater attention to the outcomes received than to the nature of our interpersonal relations, and the opposite may occur when dealing with people from our own culture.

This reasoning has been supported by a survey of a large, ethnically diverse group of employees at a large university.[44] These employees were asked to describe conflicts they recently had with their supervisor and to rate both the *outcomes* received (e.g., "How favorable was the outcome to you?") and their *treatment* by this person (e.g., "How politely were you

treated?" or "How much concern was shown for your rights?"). In addition, participants also rated their willingness to accept the supervisor's decision in this dispute. Because participants and supervisors varied in ethnic background, it was possible to compare their concern over how they were treated with their concern over outcomes both when these individuals were of the same ethnic background and when they were not. The results were clear: For conflicts within the same ethnic groups, interpersonal relations were more important in determining acceptance of the supervisor's decision, for conflict with members of other ethnic groups, outcomes were more important.

These findings were replicated by a Japanese study that focused on disputes between Japanese and Western teachers of English. Again, participants rated the kind of treatment they received from a third party who mediated such disputes, the outcomes they received, and the extent to which they accepted these decisions. The results again indicated that interpersonal relations were a greater concern in disputes between persons belonging to the same cultures, whereas outcomes were more important in disputes between persons from the two cultures.

The implications of this research are critical considering that business transactions between people of different cultures are increasingly common and that conflicts are inevitable in such settings. After all, the less people take into account the personal feelings of those who are different than themselves, the more likely they are to base their interactions on stereotypes, thereby making cross-cultural conflicts potentially more difficult to resolve. Thus, training employees in the norms and values of the cultures with which they will be dealing — as commonly practiced in many multinational businesses today — seems well advised. Not only may such training make relations with people from different cultures both easier and more comfortable, it also may help to make them more sensitive to the interpersonal factors so important in resolving conflicts between them.

Because of such changes, groups experiencing conflict tend to provide less pleasant work environments than those not facing this type of stress.

Conflict also increases the tendency of both sides to *engage in negative stereotyping*. As noted earlier, members of opposing groups or units tend to emphasize the differences between them. These differences are interpreted in a negative light as well, so that each side views the other in increasingly unfavorable terms.

Finally, conflict leads each side to *close ranks and emphasize loyalty to their own department or group*. Anyone who suggests — even tentatively — that the other side's position has some merit is viewed as being a traitor and strongly censured. As a result, it becomes increasingly difficult for opponents to take each other's perspectives, which in turn sharply reduces the likelihood of an effective resolution of their differences and increases the likelihood of *groupthink* (see chapter 9).

The Positive Effects of Conflict   The picture is not entirely bleak, however. Conflict often does have a disruptive effect on organizations, but it sometimes yields benefits as well:

- *Conflict brings previously ignored problems into the open.* Because recognizing problems is a necessary first step toward their solution (see chapter 9), conflict sometimes can be very useful.
- *Conflict motivates people on both sides to understand the other position more fully.* This can foster open-mindedness and lead each side to incorporating aspects of the opposing view into their own.[45]
- *Conflict encourages consideration of new ideas and approaches, thus facilitating innovation and change.*[46] Whenever open conflict erupts, an organization or work unit cannot continue with "business as usual." As a result, the parties involved are encouraged to do whatever it takes to get things back to normal, which leads them to make the hard decisions and to establish new policies as necessary.
- *Conflict sometimes leads to better decisions.* When decision-makers receive information that is incompatible with their views—which often is the case when conflict exists—they tend to make better decisions than when controversy does not exist.[47] This only occurs, of course, when the conflict forces people to challenge their assumptions, to confront new ideas, and to consider new positions. If people resent having to engage in such activities, however, the results may be far more disruptive.[48]
- *Conflict can enhance organizational commitment.* Conflict helps to bring opposing views into the open, thus causing them to be fully discussed.[49] In turn, this allows peoples' ideas to be considered, thereby enhancing their involvement with the organization and, hence, their commitment to it. In contrast, people generally are less committed to organizations in which the free exchange of opposing views is not permitted.

In sum, conflict actually may contribute to organizational effectiveness. Note, however, that benefits occur only when conflict is managed carefully and does not get out of control. If conflict becomes extreme, rationality—and the potential benefits described—may vanish in a haze of intense, negative emotions.

CONFLICT MANAGEMENT: TECHNIQUES FOR INCREASING THE BENEFITS AND MINIMIZING THE COSTS OF CONFLICT

If conflict can yield benefits as well as costs, the key task facing organizations, then, is *managing* the occurrence of conflict. In short, the overall goal should not be to eliminate conflict but to maximize its potential benefits while minimizing its potential costs. Several techniques for reaching this goal exist.

Bargaining: The Universal Process

By far, the most common strategy for resolving organizational conflicts and managing them effectively is **bargaining** or **negotiation**.[50] In this process, opposing sides exchange offers, counteroffers, and concessions, either directly or through representatives (Figure 10.11). If the process is successful, a solution that both parties find acceptable is attained—and the conflict is resolved. Sometimes beneficial byproducts can occur as well, such as enhanced understanding and improved relations between the two sides. If bargaining is unsuccessful, however, costly deadlock may result—and the conflict may intensify.

bargaining

The process in which opposing sides exchange offers, counteroffers, and concessions, either directly or through representatives.

negotiation

See *bargaining*.

What factors determine which outcome occurs? Given the importance of bargaining and its use in virtually all spheres of life, this has been the subject of intense study for decades.[51] As a result, several key factors have been identified.

Special Tactics   First, and perhaps most obviously, the outcome of bargaining is partly determined by the specific tactics of the bargainers. Many of these tactics are designed to accomplish a key goal. For example, one such goal may be to reduce the opponent's *aspirations* so this person or group becomes convinced they cannot get what they want and should, instead, settle for something quite favorable to the other side. Tactics for accomplishing this goal include:

1. *The extreme offer.* Whether settling a lawsuit, asking for a raise, or determining the price of a house, people routinely begin negotiating with others by making an extreme initial offer — that is, one very favorable to themselves. The rationale is straightforward: Knowing you will be asked to compromise, you begin with an extreme position so that you end close to what you really desire.

2. *The big lie.* When negotiating, people often attempt to convince the other side that one's break-even point is much higher than it really is. For example, a used car salesperson may claim he or she will lose money on the deal by accepting a lower price when, in fact, this is false.

3. *Claiming an "out."* It is not unusual for negotiators to convince each other they "have an out."[52] For example, suppose you are bargaining with a salesperson about the price of a car. To get the lowest price, you may say that you can go elsewhere and get an even better deal.

4. *Misrepresenting your position on common issues.* Suppose your organization is interested in purchasing another company, and two issues are on the table: the selling price of the factory itself, and the price of the equipment inside. Suppose you also know what price the seller is asking for the factory, and it is exactly what you expected to pay. If you agree to it, however, you then have less room to negotiate the price of the equipment. Thus, by misrepresenting your true position (e.g., by saying you expected to pay much less for the building), you then can "settle" on the seller's asking price in exchange for a much better price on the equipment. This way, you come out ahead.[53]

FIGURE 10.11

Bargaining: A Major Technique for Resolving Conflicts

In *bargaining,* the two sides in a dispute trade offers, counteroffers, and concessions until an agreement is reached or the discussions deadlock.

You may find some of these tactics ethically questionable, but they have become commonplace. In fact, many people justify using them on very practical grounds: They claim that "others expect me to do this, so I have to do so just to come out even. Besides, if I don't, my opponent surely will!"

Is it ever appropriate to engage in tactics such as "the big lie," pretending to have an "out," or misrepresenting your position on common issues? Should ethical negotiators always refrain from using such tactics, even if they might be effective? ◼

Overall Orientation   A second—and very important—determinant of the outcome of bargaining involves the overall orientation of the bargainers to the process.[54] People taking part in negotiations can approach such discussions from two distinct perspectives. First, they can view negotiations as "win-lose" situations, in which gains by one side are necessarily linked with losses for the other. Alternatively, they can view negotiations as potential **win-win situations**—that is, ones in which the interests of both sides are not necessarily incompatible and in which the potential gains for both can be maximized.

Not all situations offer the potential for win-win solutions, but many that first appear to involve head-on clashes do, in fact, provide such possibilities. If the participants are willing to explore all their options carefully, they sometimes can attain what are known as **integrative agreements**—that is, ones that offer greater joint benefits than simple compromise (i.e., splitting all differences down the middle). For example, suppose two cooks are preparing recipes that call for one entire orange, but there is only one orange in their kitchen. Assuming they cannot get another, what should they do? One possibility is to divide the orange in half. That leaves each chef with less than he or she needs, however, so this is an unsatisfactory outcome for both. Now suppose one cook only requires the juice whereas the other only needs the peel. Here, a much more effective solution is possible—if they bother to discuss the matter with each other. Specifically, by comparing recipes, they may learn it is possible to share the orange, with each chef using only the needed part. As obvious as this may appear, however, people in conflict with each other may fail to recognize the possibility of an integrative solution. Many techniques for attaining integrative solutions exist, and Table 10.2 summarizes several of them.

win-win situations
Ones in which the interests of both sides are not necessarily incompatible and the potential gains for both can be maximized.

integrative agreements
Ones that offer greater joint benefits than simple compromise (i.e., splitting all differences down the middle).

TABLE 10.2

Techniques for Reaching Integrative Agreements
Several strategies can be useful for attaining integrative agreements in bargaining, including those summarized here.

TYPE OF AGREEMENT	DESCRIPTION
Broadening the pie	Available resources are broadened so that both sides can obtain their major goals.
Nonspecific compensation	One side gets what it wants, and the other is compensated on an unrelated issue.
Logrolling	Each party makes concessions on low-priority issues in exchange for concessions on issues it values more highly.
Cost-cutting	One party gets what it desires, and the costs to the other party are reduced or eliminated.
Bridging	Neither party gets its initial demands, but a new option that satisfies the major interests of both sides is developed.

Perceptual Errors   As you might imagine (especially based on the material in chapter 2), the kinds of solutions that people come up with—or don't come up with!—in bargaining situations likely is influenced by how they perceive those situations themselves. Not surprisingly, people in conflict with each other may misperceive the situations they face, and they do so in systematic ways that constitute perceptual errors.

One such error is known as the **incompatibility error**—that is, the tendency for both sides of a conflict to assume their interests are entirely incompatible. Such beliefs overlook the possibility that both parties actually may be in considerable agreement on at least some issues.[55] The more people appreciate their positions are not totally incompatible, the more willing they are to work out those areas in which they disagree.

Another error is the **fixed-sum error**, which is the tendency to assume one side of a conflict places the same importance as the other side on every issue. Again, however, this may not be the case. For example, suppose three friends are discussing which apartment to rent for the coming year. They disagree on this overall issue, but they place different weights on different variables. For one friend, rent is the most important factor. For another, location is key. For the third, the number of bathrooms is most important. If these friends are willing to juggle these priorities somewhat so that all get what they want as their top priority—or something close to it—they stand a good chance of finding an apartment satisfactory to everyone.

Bargainers also sometimes suffer from **transparency overestimation**—that is, the belief that our own goals and motives are more apparent to opponents than actually is the case.[56] This can produce serious problems when, for example, bargainers believe they have clearly signaled their intention to compromise but their opponents continue acting "tough." In fact, the other bargainers may not have noticed this signal, but we nonetheless may become angry with them for not responding.

Many other factors also determine the outcome of bargaining, but those discussed here are among the most important. Thus, all are worth considering the next time *you* must bargain with others.

Third-Party Intervention: Mediation and Arbitration

Despite the best efforts of both sides, negotiations sometimes deadlock, and when they do, the aid of a third party—that is, someone not directly involved in the dispute—often is sought. Such third-party intervention can take many forms, but the most common are *mediation* and *arbitration*.[57]

In **mediation**, a third party attempts to facilitate voluntary agreements between the parties in dispute. Mediators have no formal power, and they cannot impose an agreement. Instead, they seek to clarify the issues involved and to enhance communication between the opponents. Mediators sometimes offer specific recommendations for compromise or integrative solutions, but in other cases, they merely guide the parties toward developing such solutions themselves. Their role is primarily that of a *facilitator*—that is, someone who helps the two sides toward agreements both will find acceptable.[58]

Because it requires voluntary compliance by the disputing parties, mediation often proves to be ineffective. Indeed, when the mediation process fails, it simply underscores the depth of the differences between the two sides. As such, definite risks are associated with using mediation.

In contrast, third parties are more powerful during **arbitration**. This is a process in which third parties (i.e., *arbitrators*) have the power to impose—or at least to recommend strongly—the terms of an agreement between disputing parties. (For a comparison of mediation and arbitration, see Figure 10.12.) Four types of arbitration are most common:

- In *binding arbitration*, the two sides agree in advance to accept the terms set by the arbitrator, whatever these may be.

---

incompatibility error

The tendency for both sides of a conflict to assume their interests are entirely incompatible.

fixed-sum error

The tendency to assume one side of a conflict places the same importance as the other side on every issue.

transparency overestimation

The belief that our own goals and motives are more apparent to opponents than actually is the case.

mediation

The process of a third party attempting to facilitate voluntary agreements between parties in dispute.

arbitration

The process in which third parties (i.e., *arbitrators*) have the power to impose (or at least to recommend strongly) the terms of an agreement between disputing parties.

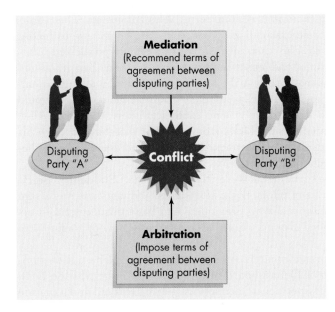

FIGURE 10.12

Mediation vs. Arbitration: The Difference

Mediation and *arbitration* are both popular techniques for resolving conflicts. Third parties known as *arbitrators* can impose terms of agreement, whereas mediators can merely recommend such terms.

- In *voluntary arbitration*, the two sides retain the freedom to reject the recommended agreement, but the personal stature and expertise of the arbitrator could make it difficult for them to do so.
- In *conventional arbitration*, the arbitrator can offer any package of terms that he or she wishes.
- In *final-offer arbitration*, the arbitrator chooses between final offers made by the disputants themselves.

These forms of arbitration have been used successfully to manage conflict in many settings. As with negotiation, however, arbitration also has its limits. In fact, four key drawbacks can be identified. First, arbitration may exert a *chilling effect* on negotiations, thereby bringing voluntary progress to a halt. Both sides know that the arbitrator will resolve the dispute for them, so they see little point in serious bargaining—which, after all, is hard work. Second, one or both sides may come to suspect the arbitrator is biased, and when this occurs, disputants tend to become increasingly reluctant to agree to arbitration. Third, arbitration tends to cost more and to take longer than mediation.[59] Finally, people also tend to be less strongly committed to arbitrated settlements than to ones they negotiate directly. After all, the decision was made for them rather than by them.

In sum, mediation and arbitration may be useful in resolving conflicts, but they are not without limitations. (For an example of a particularly ineffective way of resolving conflict, see the "Trends" section below.)

TRENDS: WHAT TODAY'S COMPANIES ARE DOING

■ **Stirring Up Conflict at Delta Airlines: "So Be It"**

Most managers—particularly high-ranking, experienced ones—usually do a respectable job of resolving conflict. Every so often, however, a high-profile executive does or says something that not only fails to resolve conflict but that actually promotes it. Just ask Ronald W. Allen, former CEO of Delta Airlines.

Delta was losing hundreds of millions of dollars per year in the early to mid-1990s, so to stem the rising tide of red ink, Allen embarked on a program of drastic

(continued)

cost-cutting that included firing thousands of long-term Delta employees. The results were predictable: Employee morale crashed, and customer complaints rose to record levels. Allen's response was, to say the least, insensitive. In a widely publicized interview, he acknowledged his actions had upset many employees, and then he added these words: "*But so be it.*" Here, in short, was the head of the company telling his employees they were unimportant and totally expendable — and that the company would get rid of them if necessary. In a sense, there was no conflict of interest between Allen and employees. Both sides wanted to save Delta from financial disaster. Through his words, however, Allen stirred up strong resentment and anger and drove a wedge between himself and his employees that had not previously existed.

To Delta employees, Allen's comments were "fighting words." Suddenly, "So Be It" buttons appeared on the chests of pilots, flight attendants, and mechanics as a sign of protest. Even union representatives, who previously had been unsuccessful in organizing Delta's employees, rallied around what they viewed as a new opportunity to unionize the company.

Allen's cost-cutting measures ultimately succeeded in pulling Delta out of its financial tailspin, but in the eyes of Delta's board of directors, the price was too high. They saw Delta's reputation for superb customer service getting trashed and a parade of senior managers heading for the exits. Finally, they took the only step they felt would bring an end to the conflict simmering within the ranks: They declined to renew Allen's contract. The reason given was that "an accumulation of abrasions over time" had undermined confidence in Allen's leadership. As a Delta flight attendant put it, however, "He got what he deserved."

As you might imagine, Delta Airlines is not the only organization with executives who triggered conflict within the ranks. Indeed, conflict-arousing behaviors have occurred in many organizations, but only the most extreme cases ever receive the publicity that brings them to our attention. Clearly, however, the fate of Allen shows Delta is so keenly sensitive to the potential costs of internal conflict that it will pay the price of ousting an otherwise effective executive just to avoid them. Fortunately, conflict-arousing behavior is more the exception than the rule within the upper echelons of corporate management, but today's companies clearly are increasingly intolerant of any potentially disruptive, conflict-arousing tactics whatsoever. ■

DEVIANT ORGANIZATIONAL BEHAVIOR: WHEN EMPLOYEES BEHAVE BADLY

Consider the following facts:

- By their own admission, fully 75 percent of employees have stolen from their employers at least once.[60]
- Seven percent of employees report having been threatened with physical violence on the job.[61]
- Authorities estimate that from one-third to three-quarters of all employees have engaged in some type of fraud, vandalism, or sabotage in their workplace.[62]
- Forty-two percent of women report they have been sexually harassed at work.[63]
- Employees steal more than $200 billion from their employers each year in the United States alone.[64]

deviant organizational behavior

Actions by employees that intentionally violate the existing norms of their group, organization, or society and that result in negative consequences for coworkers or the organization.

These statistics paint a sobering picture: They suggest that **deviant organizational behavior** — that is, actions by employees that intentionally violate the existing norms of their group, organization, or society and that result in negative consequences for coworkers or the organization — occur all too frequently today.

In our view, such behavior certainly represents another point — or cluster of points — along the continuum of working with to working against others, which is the central theme of this chapter. As suggested by the statistics presented, deviant behavior takes many different forms, ranging from petty theft and small acts of revenge to grand theft, frivolous law suits, and acts of physical violence that, in extreme circumstances, even include murder.[65] All these forms of deviant organizational behavior are important, but we focus on two of the best-understood forms: *workplace aggression*, and *employee theft*.

Workplace Aggression: Its Nature and Causes

Newspapers and magazines have been filled with recent, disturbing reports of **workplace violence**—that is, direct, physical assaults by present or former employees against others in their organization. In fact, media attention to such events at first appears to be fully justified: More than 800 people are murdered at work each year in the United States alone.[66] The United States does not appear to rank first, however, regarding the frequency of such behavior: One recent survey indicates that workplace violence is a global problem and that several countries (e.g., France, Argentina) report considerably higher rates than those in North America.[67]

    Such statistics suggest that workplaces are becoming truly dangerous locations where disgruntled employees frequently attack or even shoot one another, but two facts should be carefully noted. First, most violence occurring in work settings is performed by "outsiders"—that is, people who do not work there but who enter a workplace to commit robbery or other crimes. Second, threats of physical harm or incidents of actual harm in work settings actually are quite rare. In fact, in the United States, the chances of being killed at work by outsiders or coworkers combined are only one in 450,000 in the United States—although the odds are considerably greater in some "high-risk occupations," such as taxi drivers or police officers.[68] Thus, the picture of workplaces suggested by Figure 10.13 does not seem to be accurate: Violence between the employees of any given organization is a very rare event.

workplace violence

Direct, physical assaults by present or former employees against others in their organization.

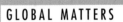

GLOBAL MATTERS

Rates of workplace violence vary greatly from country to country. Do you think that cultural factors (e.g., the extent to which a given culture condones physical aggression) play a role in these differences? ■

"We've got to get rid of some people, Cosgrove. Who are the least likely to come back and shoot us?"

FIGURE 10.13

Workplace Violence: Not as Frequent as the Media Suggest

Contrary to what newspaper articles, television programs, and this cartoon suggest, workplace violence between members of an organization is relatively rare.

(*Source*: The New Yorker Collection 1997. Leo Cullum, from cartoonbank.com. All Rights Reserved.)

workplace aggression

Any action through which individuals seek to harm others in the workplace.

Forms of Workplace Aggression   As noted, workplace *violence* occurs only rarely, but it is the dramatic extreme of a much broader form of deviant behavior known as **workplace aggression**. This behavior may be defined as any action through which individuals seek to harm others in their workplace.[69]

Growing evidence suggests that workplace aggression largely is *covert* rather than *overt* in nature. In other words, it is relatively subtle and allows aggressors to harm others while simultaneously preventing those others from identifying them as being the source of such harm. For example, someone who submits an anonymous complaint about a coworker is committing a covert aggressive act. Someone who publicly berates a coworker is committing an overt aggressive act.

As you might imagine, covert forms of aggression are more common in workplaces than overt forms for one obvious reason: Aggressors may fear retaliation from their intended victims, with whom they probably expect to have continued interaction in the future. Using covert forms of aggression is "safer," because they reduce the likelihood that victims will retaliate.

What specific forms of aggression do individuals actually use in workplaces? Most acts of workplace aggression fall into three major categories[70]:

1. *Expressions of hostility*: Behaviors that are primarily verbal or symbolic in nature (e.g., belittling others' opinions, talking behind their backs).
2. *Obstructionism*: Behaviors that are designed to obstruct or impede the target's performance (e.g., failure to return phone calls or respond to memos; failure to transmit needed information, thus interfering with activities important to the target).
3. *Overt aggression*: Behaviors that typically have been included under the heading of "workplace violence" (e.g., physical assault, theft or destruction of property, threats of physical violence).

Causes of Workplace Aggression   What causes such behavior? Many factors seem to play a role; however, one key factor appears to be *perceived unfairness*.[71] When individuals feel they have been treated unfairly by others in their organization or by their organization itself, they experience intense feelings of anger and resentment, which lead them to "even the score" by harming the people they hold responsible in some manner.[72]

Have you ever heard the phrase "going postal"? This stems from several recent instances of workplace violence among employees of the U.S. Postal Service. One important cause of such behavior is intense feelings of "unfairness" experienced by the persons involved.[73] These people believe they have been fired, passed over for promotion, or treated *unfairly* in some other way, and this belief plays an important role in their subsequent aggression. In turn, such feelings are most likely to translate into overt assaults against others in communities with high overall rates of violence outside work. In other words, employees bring norms concerning physical violence with them into their workplaces, and these norms then influence their reactions to unfairness.

Perceived unfairness is only part of the story, however. Other factors also play roles in workplace aggression. Some of these relate to recent changes in many workplaces, such as downsizing, layoffs, and increased use of part-time employees (Figure 10.14). Several recent studies indicate that the greater the extent to which such changes have occurred, the greater the aggression occurring in such workplaces.[74] Moreover, because downsizing, layoffs, and other changes that produce negative feelings among employees (e.g., increased anxiety and resentment) have occurred with increasing frequency in recent years, these changes may well be contributing to increased aggression.

Effectively Managing Workplace Aggression

Can the incidence of workplace aggression be reduced? In other words, can this process be managed effectively? Several tactics are particularly useful.

Employee Screening   First, efforts can be made to *screen* prospective employees. Those with a history of aggressive behavior or who evidence high levels of traits associated with aggression may be more prone than others to become involved in workplace aggression. Indeed, some people are more likely to "explode" aggressively than others when facing difficult, unpleasant conditions.[75]

Techniques for accurately identifying such persons primarily involve paper-and-pencil tests of personality (see chapter 3). These are far from perfect, however, and have had only mixed success in identifying potentially aggressive individuals.[76] In fact, only the most extreme cases (i.e., those individuals most highly predisposed toward violence) tend to be identified by such tests. Of course, this does not mean such individuals necessarily will behave aggressively in all situations. Even so, being able to identify those with the greatest personal predisposition toward behaving aggressively may be particularly important when screening candidates for some types of jobs (e.g., police officers).

Disciplinary Procedures   A second approach to reducing workplace aggression involves establishing clear disciplinary procedures for such behavior. Aggression cannot thrive in environments where such behavior clearly is viewed as being inappropriate and is met with swift and certain punishment. Programs of *progressive punishment* are effective in deterring other forms of behavior considered to be inappropriate in work settings (see chapter 2), and there is every reason to assume such procedures—if used carefully—can be effective in deterring at least some forms of workplace aggression.[77]

Treating People Fairly   Given that workplace aggression often stems from anger and feelings of having been treated unfairly, such behavior may be reduced by assuring high levels of *organizational justice*. People tend to behave aggressively to the extent they feel unfairly treated, particularly regarding the interpersonal treatment they have received from others. Specifically, aggressive behavior may be discouraged when people demonstrate sensitivity to one another. It also helps to explain potentially anger-inducing (e.g., unfavorable) decisions in ways that make clear these are well-considered judgments.[78] Unfavorable decisions (e.g., the decision to terminate someone) are inevitable, but it is *not* inevitable that the people who receive them will behave

FIGURE 10.14

Organizational Determinants of Workplace Aggression

Recent changes in many organizations (e.g., downsizing, layoffs, increased use of part-time help) may contribute to workplace aggression.

YOU BE THE CONSULTANT

Recently, you notice a great deal of hostility and subtle aggression coming from your organization's marketing department. The employees there appear to be starting negative rumors, are quick to speak harshly about other department members behind their backs, and even have been hoarding unneeded resources just to prevent others from getting them.

1. Without knowing anything more, what do you suspect is behind these deviant behaviors?
2. Assuming these reasons really lie at the heart of the problem (e.g., as determined in a questionnaire), how can you minimize the behavior in question?
3. What effect are these steps likely to have on OCB and other forms of deviant behavior (e.g., employee theft)?

aggressively. To the extent termination decisions are explained in a manner sensitive to the injury of job loss, aggressive actions are unlikely to occur.

Employee Training   As noted, instances of physical violence are rare, but they do occur. Therefore, employees should be trained how to respond to threats posed by present and previous employees as well as by customers. Efforts to develop systematic programs for equipping managers with the skills to recognize potentially dangerous situations and, perhaps, to defuse them are currently underway.[79]

Through these and other steps, the incidence of workplace aggression may be reduced. In our own view, workplace aggression poses a threat to the safety and well-being of individual employees as well as to the effectiveness of their organizations. Quests for vengeance and personal vendettas drain time and energy from more productive activities. Thus, we believe efforts to manage workplace aggression are worthwhile from the standpoint of ethics and from the perspective of enhanced organizational effectiveness as well.

Employee Theft: Inappropriate Appropriations

When you think of the term *employee theft*, what image comes to mind? It probably involves a shady character breaking into the company safe to abscond with the day's cash receipts, or a computer hacker diverting company funds to his own personal account. Such actions do constitute employee theft, but we tend to think of these as things only criminals do. If an office worker takes home a box of paper clips or a supermarket clerk eats food taken from the store shelves, however, these individuals are engaging in employee theft as well. What they are doing is minor, of course, and "everyone does it." Even so, technically speaking, they constitute employee theft, because the items taken are company property. As such, **employee theft** is defined as unauthorized appropriation of company property by employees for their personal use.[80]

employee theft
Unauthorized appropriation of company property by employees for their personal use.

As you might imagine, employee theft is a costly problem. In fact, the costs of employee theft are estimated to run approximately $200 billion each year (Figure 10.15). Some portion of this figure clearly comes from grand theft, but much of it also comes from petty theft—that is, items of low value that people take without thinking they are doing anything wrong. Are you a "crook" if you take home a company pen and use it to balance your personal checkbook? If you make a personal long-distance call on the company phone? Of course not, but even such trivial acts constitute "theft"—and their effects can accumulate to quite a tidy sum. Paper clip by paper clip, many employees are bleeding their companies dry, and these companies are bleeding red ink! Not surprisingly, employee theft has been cited as one of the most common reasons of small-business failures, accounting for as many as 30 to 50 percent of such failures in some industries.[81]

Why do employees engage in such behavior, and how can organizations reduce its occurrence? These are the questions to which we now turn our attention.

Why Do Employees Steal? Traditional Approaches The answer to the question of why employees steal depends on who you ask.

Experts in industrial security—or "loss prevention" or "asset management," as it frequently is called—tell us people steal because they are given opportunities to do so. Therefore, to prevent theft, these experts create elaborate security systems involving security cameras and other high-tech gadgets to deter people from stealing—and to catch them red-handed if they do.

Criminologists tell a different story. These scientists, who usually are sociologists by training, tend to focus on the various financial pressures (e.g., overcoming financial setbacks) and vice-based pressures (e.g., paying for gambling losses) that employees experience. Their approach to dealing with employee theft is using psychological tests to weed out those individuals whose personal profiles make them most inclined to steal. As with tests to predict aggressive behavior, however, those used to predict honest and dishonest behavior on the job have had mixed success.[82]

Clinical psychologists take yet another approach. These specialists focus on the tendency for people to rationalize whatever they are doing as being correct. To some extent, we all do this, but some individuals—who are known as *psychopaths*—have developed such abnormal personalities they can convince themselves that even the most extreme criminal acts are acceptable. The approach of these professionals to dealing with the criminal personality involves giving them intensive psychotherapy.

Over the years, these various approaches have provided excellent insights into employee theft. Furthermore, their solutions have put a serious dent in the problem. Another fact, however, cannot be overlooked—namely, that despite the best efforts of these professionals, employees continue to steal. Clearly, these approaches do not provide all the answers, so to shed further light on why employees steal, specialists in the field of OB also have taken a close look at the matter.

The STEAL Motive: A Managerial Approach to Employee Theft Despite their considerable differences, the approaches of the professionals just described all have one important feature in common: They take a fatalistic approach to the problem. As a practicing manager, we can have security experts place cameras throughout the facility,

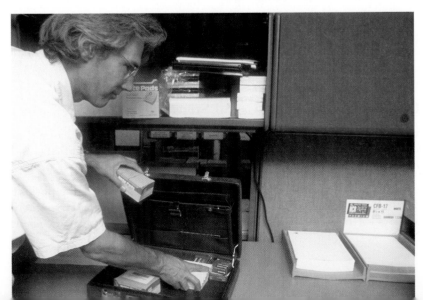

FIGURE 10.15

Employee Theft: A Serious Problem for Many Organizations

Instances of employee theft are far from rare in many organizations, and they sometimes make the difference between profit and loss.

can authorize tests to screen out individuals with criminal intent, and can arrange for psychiatrists to offer therapy to those with criminal personalities. Still, what can we, ourselves, do to avoid the problem?

The answer requires us to understand the social motives in the workplace that encourage employees to steal. In other words, what are the social dynamics in the workplace that can make even ordinary (i.e., noncriminal and nonpsychopathic) employees want to steal certain things at certain times? Scientists have identified four types of factors, which can be summarized using the acronym STEAL—that is, *Support*, *Thwart*, *Even the score*, and *ApprovaL*.[83]

In more detail, these factors can be described as follows:

- *Support* involves group norms that condone theft—that is norms suggesting it is appropriate for employees to take company property because it is part of the system or the established way of doing things. For example, it is considered acceptable by people in some companies to routinely take home certain items for personal use. To do this is to seek the *support* and acceptance of one's coworkers.

- *Thwart* describes employees' desires to resist group norms by doing whatever they want. Often, this means they "push the envelope" and steal even when group norms prohibit such behavior. Alternatively, they may take more than is condoned by these norms. For example, suppose employees at some restaurants believe it is acceptable to take food from the kitchen but taboo to take money from the cash register. Thus, if an employee in this restaurant wants to strike back at his or her coworkers, that individual purposely may violate the group standard and take money from the register—just to send the message of his or her interest in thwarting the group's values.

- *Even the score* is especially powerful and relates to employees' beliefs they have been treated unfairly. Stealing from the company is one way of getting back "their own"—that is, what they really deserve. For example, if someone feels he or she has been mistreated or underpaid, that individual might take company property to "right" the wrong created by the company.

- *Approval* refers to the fact that some supervisors not only pardon theft, they sometimes actually approve of it as an informal way to reward employees! Indeed, supervisors sometimes view theft as being part of an *invisible wage structure* that allows them to provide extra incentives to employees in an efficient manner. As a result, they turn their back on thefts or even arrange for employees to appropriate various tools or products belonging to the company. For example, a supervisor in one retail store arranged for an employee who did an especially good job of cleaning the stock room to take home a bag full of diapers for only 10 cents—far less than their actual value.[84]

Clearly, the STEAL motive represents an additional way of understanding employee theft and takes us far beyond the traditional approaches. What is particularly useful is this approach can form the basis for several important—and extremely useful—suggestions about how to manage employee theft.

Managing Employee Theft: Some Useful Steps

Given that employee theft is a major problem in many organizations, how can we, as practicing managers, deter or reduce it? Several suggestions may be identified—and unlike those from corporate security experts, these need not cost a dime:

- *Treat employees with dignity and respect.* This leads employees to develop positive attitudes toward their organization, and as one expert puts it, "It is more difficult to steal from a friend than from someone who doesn't care about you."[85]

- *Involve employees in formally defining theft.* Employees usually do not think of making personal phone calls or using the copy machine to pass along their favorite recipes as being "theft." To the extent employees are involved in producing company manuals (e.g., codes of ethics) that dictate appropriate and inappropriate behavior, however, they understand more clearly the forms of behavior that are unacceptable.

- *Openly communicate the costs of stealing.* Employees readily see the personal benefits of theft, but often do not understand clearly the scope of the problem—or the costs to their company. Explaining that theft may harm the organization—and ultimately cost them their jobs—can be a useful deterrent to such actions.

- *Use corporate hotlines.* A growing number of companies now have special phone lines that employees can use to seek answers to questions and to report misdeeds. Such a system may be used, for example, to help employees understand their organization's pay system, which in turn may reduce their feelings of being treated unfairly. Hotlines also may provide employees with a means of anonymously "blowing the whistle" on coworkers engaged in theft, and this, too, can be a useful deterrent.

- *Be a good role model.* If employees see their own managers taking company property, they eventually may take this as a sign they can do the same. A manager who is known to steal has no credibility when trying to stop others. In other words, to deter theft, managers must "walk the talk" and set high standards in their own behavior.

Through these and other steps, organizations can reduce both the incidence and the magnitude of theft by employees. In doing so, they also accomplish two important goals: enhancing their own "bottom line," and raising the internal standards of ethics by which they operate.

We invite you to visit the Greenberg page on the Prentice Hall Web site at: **www.prenhall.com/greenberg** for the monthly Greenberg update and for this chapter's World Wide Web exercise.

SUMMARY AND REVIEW OF LEARNING OBJECTIVES

1. **Define *prosocial behavior*, and distinguish it from *altruism*.**
   Prosocial behavior refers to actions that help others in various ways. Such acts are common, and take many forms in organizations. Much rarer, however, are acts of **altruism**, which refers to actions by one person that benefit one or more others under conditions in which the donor expects nothing in return. In reality, even a seemingly altruistic act (e.g., helping another in distress) may not be motivated by complete altruism, because the actor may be interested in promoting the good feelings that result from such behavior, thereby getting something in return.

2. **Describe *organizational citizenship behavior* and the major forms it takes.**
   Organizational citizenship behavior is a form of prosocial behavior in which people's actions exceed the formal requirements of their jobs. It may take forms such as aiding a coworker in need, being highly conscientious, showing concern about the organization (e.g., civic virtue), being a good sport (e.g., tolerating problems without complaint), and being courteous to others.

3. **Explain *whistle-blowing* and the dilemma faced by potential whistle-blowers.**
   Whistle-blowing is the disclosure by employees of illegal, immoral, or illegitimate practices to others who can "right the wrong." Potential whistle-blowers are interested in doing the correct thing, but they often fear retaliation by their employers for going public.

4. **Explain the nature of *cooperation*, and identify both individual and organizational factors that influence its occurrence.**
   Cooperation involves mutual assistance or coordination between two or more persons or groups. In organizations, people often confront social dilemmas in which they can increase their gains by acting in one way but will experience losses if others do the same. What people choose to do in such situations is influenced by several individual factors (e.g., strong tendencies toward reciprocity, personality orientations concerning cooperation) and by several organizational factors (e.g., reward systems, interdependence among employees).

5. **Define *trust*, and explain its relationship to organizational citizenship behavior and to cooperation.**
   Trust is defined as an individual's confidence in the goodwill of others and the belief they will make efforts consistent with the group's goals. Employees are more likely to be active organizational citizens to the extent they trust their coworkers, the more likely they are to cooperate with them.

6. **Define *conflict*, and indicate how it can produce positive as well as negative effects.**
   Conflict is a process in which one party perceives that another has taken some action (or is about to take some action) that will exert negative effects on its major interest. Often, conflict interferes with communication between individuals, groups, or divisions and all but eliminates coordination between them. It also leads people to act in an authoritarian manner and to engage in negative stereotyping. Conflict also can have beneficial effects, however. For example, it helps to bring problems into the open, motivates people to understand each other's positions, encourages consideration of new ideas, and sometimes leads to better decisions and to enhanced organizational commitment.

7. **Identify several organizational and interpersonal causes of conflict.**
   Conflict may result from organizational factors such as competition over scarce resources and ambiguity over both responsibility and jurisdiction. It also may result from interpersonal factors such as faulty attributions, faulty communication, and naive realism (i.e., the tendency to magnify differences between our views and those of others to exaggerate conflicts of interest).

8. **Describe various techniques of *managing conflict*.**
   Conflict often is managed by the process of **bargaining** (or **negotiation**), through which opposing sides repeatedly exchange offers and counteroffers until they arrive at a solution acceptable to both. This process is aided by special tactics designed to give one side an edge over the other and by efforts to seek **integrative agreements**—that is, ones that benefit both parties by offering greater benefits than simple compromise. Conflict also frequently is managed by the processes of **mediation**, in which a third party attempts to facilitate voluntary agreements

between disputants, and of **arbitration,** in which a third party is granted the power to improve or recommend terms of agreement.

9. **Distinguish** *workplace violence* **from** *workplace aggression.*

Workplace violence involves direct, physical assaults by present or former employees against other persons in their organizations. It is, however, merely one, very extreme form of a broader behavior known as **workplace aggression** — that is, any form of behavior through which individuals seek to harm others in the workplace. Many forms of workplace aggression are covert in nature.

10. **Describe causes of workplace aggression and techniques for reducing such behavior.**

Workplace aggression largely results from perceived unfairness. It also results from negative changes in the workplace (e.g., downsizing, layoffs). It can be managed through employee screening, appropriate disciplinary procedures, treating people fairly, and employee training.

11. **Describe the motives behind** *employee theft* **and techniques for reducing such behavior.**

Employee theft, which refers to the taking of company property for personal use, results from many factors, including social motives that encourage people to go along with group norms supporting theft and to "get even" with employees believed to have harmed them. To reduce theft among employees, managers should treat employees with dignity and respect, involve employees in formally defining theft, openly communicate the costs of stealing, use corporate hotlines, and serve as role models for honest behavior.

QUESTIONS FOR DISCUSSION

1. What kinds of OCBs have you observed in your own work experience? If individuals receive no direct benefit for engaging in such actions, why do they ever perform them?

2. What factors in an organization might lead to high levels of trust between employees? Would it be worthwhile to assure that these factors are present?

3. What ethical issues must one consider when deciding whether to blow the whistle on an organization suspected of some wrongdoing?

4. What steps can be taken to increase individuals' willingness to cooperate rather than to defect in situations involving social dilemmas?

5. Do you think that people differ in their preferred modes of resolving conflicts (e.g., compromise, collaboration, competition)? Do these differences show up in all situations or only in some circumstances?

6. "Conflict doesn't exist until it is recognized by the parties involved." Do you agree with this statement? Why, or why not?

7. Growing evidence indicates that conflict sometimes can produce positive results. Have you ever experienced positive results from conflict? If so, why do you think such effects occurred?

8. Suppose people in your organization are frequently in conflict with one another. How could you reduce these conflicts?

9. Do you think that acts of workplace deviance (e.g., workplace aggression, employee theft) are on the rise, remaining steady, or falling? Explain your answer.

10. Explain the following statement: "It is difficult to manage employee theft, because although just about everyone takes company property, very few of us regard what we are doing as stealing."

When Rivals Become Mortal Enemies: How Sony Used the "Ultimate Weapon" in Thailand

Price wars, as most experts agree, are a mistake. Too often, the outcome is a blood-letting for both sides, with customers being the only winners—and even then, only temporarily! In the increasingly competitive world of international business, however, some companies are using this *ultimate weapon* and are getting away with it. For example, consider how Sony assaulted its archrival Matsushita in Thailand.

When Sony first began selling its products in Thailand, Matsushita already held more than a third of the market for consumer electronics. Kazunori Somaya, Sony's head of operations in Thailand, sized up the situation and decided that pricing should be part of this business strategy. He then cut the price of Sony's 21-inch television to that of Matsushita's 20-inch set, which forced Matsushita to lower the price of its product. Sony kept up the pressure, however, lowering the price still further. The result? When the price differential between Matsushita's 20-inch set and its top-selling 14-inch set dropped to only $40, sales of this highly profitable, smaller item were threatened. Matsushita soon threw in the towel and dropped the 20-inch set from its product line, thus giving Sony the opening it needed.

This was not the only strategy Somaya used to wrest market share from his archrival, however. He also borrowed a strategy from Chairman Mao, the

famed Chinese Communist leader, and "surrounded" Matsushita. As Somaya put it, "Mao didn't attack Shanghai directly. First he captured the rice fields, and then he attacked the city." Somaya followed a similar strategy, introducing his products in stores outside the center of Bangkok—areas where Sony was not dominant. Then, once he had seized these markets, he launched the price war just described. Of course, while the battle is won for Sony, the war is far from over. Matsushita is certain to strike back, because in the battle between rival companies, only those who continue to surprise their opponents will remain on top!

CRITICAL THINKING QUESTIONS

1. What principles of competition and conflict are illustrated by this case?

2. Do you think the price-cutting tactics used by Sony were ethical? Why, or why not?

3. How could Matsushita have fought back when it discovered what Sony was doing? Was it already too late once Sony had launched its strategy?

4. Given that Matsushita has lost an important market segment to Sony, what do you think the company should do now?

VIDEO CASE

Working With—and Against—Others: Prosocial and Deviant Behavior in Organizations

SMALL BUSINESS 2000 Working with others is not always easy. Simply working in the same group—or even for the same company—does not guarantee that people will be motivated to work together. Different individuals will have different work ethics, will look to satisfy different needs from work, and will have their own ways of doing things. There is no guarantee that a work group will function either smoothly or cohesively.

Rick Presant learned about working with others when he joined his father's company, All Brand Appliance. Presant's case provides insight into a somewhat unique but not uncommon work situation. He was a family member breaking into a family-owned business. Being the boss's son or daughter probably has bad as well as good consequences, and it sounds like Presant found this out. He eventually headed off to try his own thing. Presant may have struck out on his own for any number of reasons, but we get the idea it had something to do with how things were going between himself and others at All Brand.

An interesting outcome is that Presant eventually came back to All Brand. The difference this time, however, is that he did it on his own terms. Presant was returning to run the show and to take over the business from his father. Also interesting is that although Presant had issues related to the partnership structure the first time he was there, he came back to All Brand and established a new partnership. What was different? This time, he was one of the partners. He also was taking over at a time when the company appeared to need an injection of new blood. In addition, his partner was his brother.

Presant's story is an interesting one. As you watch this video, think about how his work life has evolved from his first experience at All Brand to the way it is now. You also might want to think about some of the things Presant and his brother might be doing differently these days and the impact this has had on the company's employees, most of whom have worked at All Brand for a long time.

QUESTIONS FOR DISCUSSION

1. Rick Presant talks about his decision to join his father's business after completing college. That didn't seem to satisfy him, and he eventually left to start his own company. He mentions that part of his decision to try his own store was some issues between his father's partner and the partner's family. What types of things might have been going on there? What do you think of Presant's decision to leave the business? What else might he have done?

2. Presant eventually came back to All Brand Appliance, and he and his brother are buying the business from their father. What is different for Presant this time? What do you think the working relationship between Presant and his brother is like?

3. Rick and Jeff have several employees who have been working at the company for a long time. You saw some of these folks and heard about how they approach their jobs. Do you think they are good organizational citizens? Why, or why not?

4. The people at All Brand Appliance seem to work well together. What types of things do you see in the video that might contribute to the level of cooperation at All Brand Appliance? Do you think cooperation is important? Why, or why not?

SKILLS BANK

EXPERIENCING ORGANIZATIONAL BEHAVIOR

Personal Styles of Conflict Management

Conflict among people is a common and inescapable part of life. Thus, it is important for us to *manage* conflict effectively when it arises. How do *you* deal with such situations? What is your preferred mode of handling disagreements and conflicts with others? The following exercise should give some insights into this important issue.

Directions

1. Recall three events in which you experienced conflict with others. On a sheet of paper, describe each one briefly.

2. Answer each of the following questions with respect to each situation. (It may help to make three copies of the questionnaire.)

a. To what extent did you try to resolve this conflict through *avoidance* (e.g., sidestepping the issue, withdrawing from the situation)?

Did not do this   Did do this

| 1 | 2 | 3 | 4 | 5 | 6 | 7 |

b. To what extent did you attempt to resolve this conflict through *accommodation*?

Did not do this   Did do this

| 1 | 2 | 3 | 4 | 5 | 6 | 7 |

c. To what extent did you try to resolve this conflict through *competition* (e.g., trying to win, standing up for your rights or views)?

Did not do this   Did do this

| 1 | 2 | 3 | 4 | 5 | 6 | 7 |

d. To what extent did you try to resolve this conflict through *compromise* (e.g., finding the middle ground between your positions)?

Did not do this   Did do this

| 1 | 2 | 3 | 4 | 5 | 6 | 7 |

e. To what extent did you try to resolve this conflict through *collaboration* (e.g., working with the other person to find some solution that satisfied both of your basic needs or concerns)?

Did not do this   Did do this

| 1 | 2 | 3 | 4 | 5 | 6 | 7 |

3. Have your instructor record the scores of everyone from the class. He or she then should compute the mean score for each question.

Questions for Discussion

1. Did you note any consistencies in your responses? Did you prefer one basic mode of resolving conflict? If so, what effects will this have on your success in handling a wide range of conflicts?
2. Would you prefer different modes of handling conflicts in different situations (e.g., depending on the person with whom you are in conflict)?
3. How did your scores compare with those of others? Were they higher? Lower?
4. Can you alter your preferred mode (or modes) for handling conflicts? If so, how?

SKILLS BANK

WORKING IN GROUPS

Getting Help When You Need It: One Technique That Works

What do you do when you want a favor or some help from another person? One strategy is to come out and simply ask for what you want, but most people know that asking for help "cold" is not always the best approach. Sometimes, it is useful to wait until others are in a good mood or to put them into such a mood. This can be accomplished in several ways, such as by praising them, giving them a small gift, or exposing them to something amusing or funny. So long as their mood improves, the chances they will say "yes" increase. This exercise demonstrates the power of such effects.

Directions

1. Divide the class into two groups.
2. One group, who will serve as job applicants, reads the following information:

   Your task is to play the role of a candidate during a brief job interview. The job is a general, entry-level management position, and you are to do everything you can to come across well and to increase your chances of being selected.

3. The other group, who will serve as interviewers, is divided into two subgroups. One subgroup, who will be the favorable-evaluation condition, receives the following information:

   Your task is to play the role of an interviewer during a brief job interview. You will ask the following questions of the candidate. Supposedly, you then will evaluate this person's performance. Actually, however, you will provide a very favorable evaluation no matter what the other person says or does. Answer the five questions as follows: 1 = good, 2 = excellent, 3 = excellent, 4 = excellent, and 5 = excellent.

4. The other subgroup of interviewers, who will be the unfavorable-evaluation condition, receives the following information:

   Your task is to play the role of an interviewer during a brief job interview. You will ask the following questions of the candidate. Supposedly, you then will evaluate this person's performance. Actually, however, you will provide a very unfavorable evaluation no matter what the other person says or does. Answer the five questions as follows: 1 = poor, 2 = poor, 3 = average, 4 = poor, and 5 = average.

5. The interviewer asks the following questions:
   a. What is your major?
   b. What is your grade point average?
   c. What is your best trait?
   d. What is your worst trait or failing?
   e. How would you describe your work habits?
   f. How well do you get along with other people?

6. The interviewers then fill out the following evaluation form after the interview:
   a. Qualifications (check one):
   ____ Very Poor ____ Poor ____ Average ____ Good ____ Excellent
   b. Motivation (check one):
   ____ Very Poor ____ Poor ____ Average ____ Good ____ Excellent
   c. Interpersonal Skills (check one):
   ____ Very Poor ____ Poor ____ Average ____ Good ____ Excellent
   d. Probability of Being a Successful Employee (check one):
   ____ Very Poor ____ Poor ____ Average ____ Good ____ Excellent
   e. Overall Rating (check one):
   ____ Very Poor ____ Poor ____ Average ____ Good ____ Excellent

7. The interviewer now shares his or her evaluations with the applicant.
8. After the demonstration is over, the interviewer should ask the applicant, in a matter-of-fact manner, for a small favor, such as the loan of his or her class notes.

9. After students in both groups make their request, tabulate how many job applications in each condition agreed.

Questions for Discussion

1. Did the favorable evaluation raise the mood of persons who received it? Did the unfavorable evaluation lower the mood of persons who received it?
2. Did people in a positive mood help more than those in a negative mood?
3. How else can people be put in a good mood?
4. Have you ever used this technique or had someone use it on you?

11

INFLUENCE, POWER, AND POLITICS IN ORGANIZATIONS

LEARNING OBJECTIVES

After reading this chapter, you should be able to

1. Distinguish between *social influence, power,* and *organizational politics.*

2. Characterize the major varieties of *social influence.*

3. Describe the conditions under which various forms of *social influence* are used.

4. Identify the major types of individual *power* in organizations.

5. Explain the two major approaches to the development of subunit power in organization (i.e., the *resource-dependency model* and the *strategic contingencies model*).

6. Describe *organizational politics* as well as when and where it is likely to occur.

7. Explain the major ethical issues surrounding political behavior in organizations.

PREVIEW CASE

This Bud Rules the Airwaves

You may not have heard of Lowell Paxson, but you probably have had at least some contact with his business enterprises. In fact, if you ever bought anything from cable television's Home Shopping Network, which Paxson launched in the 1980s, or from a late-night infomercial, you may well be one of his customers. If nothing else, you may have watched one of the 55 small, UHF television stations he owns across the United States (including New York's channel 31, WPXN, and Los Angeles' channel 30, KZKI).

"Bud," as he is known, is widely reported to be a shrewd businessman. Case in point: In 1987, while running a struggling AM radio station in Clearwater, Florida, he faced an appliance-store owner who could not pay the $1,000 owed the station. Bud came up with an idea—he would take 112 electric can openers as payment. The next day, Bud went on the air and sold them all for $9.95 each, more than recovering the money owed. This episode sparked a flame in Paxson, who saw a future in selling goods over the airwaves. Thus, radio's Suncoast International Bargaineers Club was born, but he soon moved it to television as the Home Shopping Network (HSN). At its peak, HSN moved $1 billion worth of merchandise a year. Then, in 1991, Bud sold out to his partners and retired to the beach—before sales at HSN began to decline.

Paxson was too much of a workaholic to do nothing, however, and soon spotted another opportunity: A recession had left more than half the nation's television broadcast stations running in the red, thereby making them great bargains. Bud scooped up as many as he could, betting the U.S. Supreme Court would require cable companies to carry local broadcast stations. This is precisely what happened. The court's "must carry" ruling put his new stations on cable, thus increasing their exposure—and with it, a flow of advertising dollars.

You might think Paxson would be content to enjoy the millions of dollars these ventures have netted him, to drive his Rolls-Royce, to sail his 132-foot yacht, and to lounge in his 35-room, ocean-front mansion located down the beach from Donald Trump's Florida residence. You would also be wrong. As one broadcast-industry analyst characterized Bud Paxson, "It's not just the money that motivates him; he's trying to earn a place in broadcast history." Not surprisingly, the walls of his office are adorned with photos of such radio and television greats as Marconi, General Sarnoff, and Edward R. Murrow—broadcasting pioneers whose company he hopes to keep.

Should you have any doubt Paxson already has joined the ranks of these broadcasting icons, he is sure to do so in the near future. His next target? Digital television. Deals are in the works with Microsoft and Intel, so there can be no doubt the next generation of broadcast innovations will be launched with Bud Paxson's imprint.

Few individuals are as rich and powerful as Bud Paxson, but his saga illustrates a basic fact of life in organizations: People attempt to influence the actions of other individuals and companies. This occurs with a dispatcher asking a newspaper delivery person to complete the route more quickly or a board of directors pressuring a CEO to make the company more profitable. Efforts to make others behave as desired, which are known as *social influence*, are common in all social settings—and are especially so in organizations. A large part of this process involves the use of *power*—that is, the formal capacity to exert influence over others. Not only does Bud Paxson have a great deal of power, he is seeking even more. In fact, he has taken great strides to protect his own interests as well as those of his company, even if that means being ruthless with his competitors. Such efforts are known as *organizational politics*.

The processes of influence, power, and politics play key roles in organizational functioning, so in this chapter, we describe the tactics used to influence others in organizations. We carefully distinguish the concepts of influence, power, and politics, and we examine how power is attained—both by individuals and by organizational subunits—as well as used. In addition, we examine the political mechanisms used to gain power, both what they are and when they occur. As part of this discussion, we also pay special attention to the ethical aspects of organizational politics, because these activities may be of questionable morality through their potentially adverse effects on others.

SOCIAL INFLUENCE: A BASIC ORGANIZATIONAL PROCESS

Imagine you are a supervisor heading a group of 12 staff members working on an important new project for your company. Tomorrow, you will make a big presentation to company officials, but the report is not quite ready. If several staff members would work a few extra hours, the job would be done on time. There's a problem, however. Tonight, the people in your department plan on going out, so nobody wants to work late — if anything, they would prefer to leave early. How can you persuade some of your staff to work late to complete the job? In other words, how can you influence their behavior?

This question is typical of ones faced by managers everyday. To understand the dynamics of this situation, we describe the process of social influence in this section. Specifically, we identify the various forms of social influence that exist, and we describe the conditions under which they tend to be used. First, however, we describe how social influence compares with the related processes of power and politics.

Comparing Social Influence with Power and Politics

Let's return to our example — but this time from an employee's perspective. You know of your boss' predicament, but you do not want to work overtime. You have been looking forward to a night out, and you do not want anything to ruin it. At the same time, however, you do not want to anger the boss by rejecting his or her request. After all, you generally try hard to be a good citizen. What do you do? There is a simple solution: If the boss does not see you, he or she will approach someone else — and you will be spared the discomfort of dealing with the problem. Thus, when you see the boss approaching your desk, you turn away, avoid making eye contact, and walk briskly to the restroom to avoid a confrontation.

Can we say the boss influenced you in this situation? You used your stealth and cunning to duck out of the situation, but the answer is "yes." The boss has, in fact, influenced you. If this is surprising, it is because of the broad nature of social influence. Specifically, **social influence** refers to attempts to affect another in a desired fashion, whether or not these attempts are successful. In fact, we influence someone to the extent our behavior has an effect — even if unintended — on that person (Figure 11.1). In our example, the boss clearly had an effect on you. After all, you ran away

social influence
Attempts to affect another in a desired fashion.

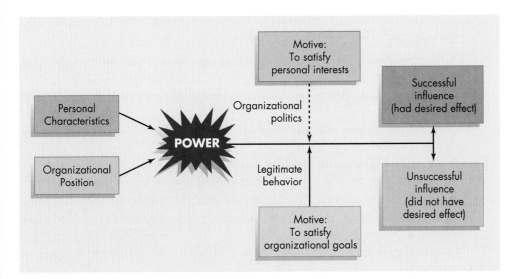

F I G U R E   1 1 . 1

Relationship Among Social Influence, Power, and Politics

When we do something that has an effect on someone else, whether or not it is successful, we exert *social influence* over that person. Our capacity to exert influence over another is known as *power*. Unofficial uses of power to enhance or protect our self-interest, which usually are at the expense of organizational goals, are known as *organizational politics*.

power

The capacity to change the behavior or attitudes of others in a desired manner.

from him or her. Thus, even though the boss did not affect your behavior as desired (i.e., by getting you to work overtime), the boss surely did influence you (i.e., by getting you to hide).

Obviously, influence is a general process, but where do power and politics fit in? As Figure 11.1 illustrates, these are narrower processes. Specifically, **power** refers to the potential to influence another successfully. More formally, it is the capacity to change the behavior or attitudes of another in a desired fashion.[1] In contrast to social influence, power is the *capacity* to have a desired effect on others. As discussed later, there are several different sources of such power, but in general, these stem from two sources: one's personal characteristics, and one's organizational position. For now, assume the boss has power over you because of access to considerable resources that enable him or her to reward you with raises (in exchange for being cooperative) or to punish you by not supporting your promotion (if you refrain from pitching in). These represent the formal actions the supervisor can take to influence you successfully — that is, they are the sources of power.

When people exercise their power, they often consider their own individual interests. For example, the supervisor in our example may be motivated by an interest in promoting — or at least saving — his or her own career by ensuring the report gets done on time. This is not to say the boss might not also recognize the value of the report to the company. It simply means the boss' actions are motivated primarily by selfish concerns.

organizational politics

Unauthorized uses of power that enhance or protect your own (or your group's) personal interests.

Actions taken to satisfy these concerns reflect **organizational politics**, which refers to unauthorized uses of power that enhance or protect one's own (or a group's) interests, usually at the expense of organizational goals.[2] It is the opposite of what is expected (i.e., using power to enhance organizational goals). If this behavior sounds negative, you are correct. In fact, organizational politics technically is illegitimate in both its means and its ends. Not surprisingly, it typically is a source of conflict as well. Later, we describe many types of political actions, or ways in which people can use their power to promote their personal interests in organizations. For now, however, we take a closer look at the process of social influence.

Tactics of Social Influence

Successful managers are those who are adept at influencing others.[3] How do they do so? Or how do *you* do so? In other words, how do you get others to do what you want them to do? Is it your style to be straightforward and tell people what you want them to do, or are you more inclined to emphasize why they should do what you say and what will happen if they do not? Is it your style to pressure people or to convince them to do what you want by getting them to like you?

Researchers have identified several techniques that people use to influence others in organizations.[4] The most typically used are[5]:

ingratiation

The process of getting someone to do what you want by putting that person in a good mood or getting that person to like you.

- *Rational persuasion*: Using logical arguments and facts to persuade another that a desired result will occur.
- *Inspirational appeal*: Arousing enthusiasm by appealing to another's values and ideals.
- *Consultation*: Asking for participation in decision making or planning a change.
- *Ingratiation*: **Ingratiation** involves getting someone to do what you want by putting that person in a good mood or getting him or her to like you.
- *Exchange*: Promising some benefits in exchange for compliance with a request.
- *Personal appeal*: Appealing to another's feelings of loyalty and friendship before making a request.
- *Coalition-building*: Seeking the assistance of others, or noting the support of others.

- *Legitimating*: Pointing out one's authority to make a request, or verifying it is consistent with prevailing organizational policies and practices.
- *Pressure*: Seeking compliance by using demands, threats, or intimidation.

When Are These Tactics Used?

As you might imagine, people are not equally likely to use all forms of influence under all circumstances. These various tactics are used based on whether one is attempting to influence someone at a higher, a lower, or an equivalent organizational level (Figure 11.2).[6] For example, leaders often use inspirational appeals to influence their subordinates, and they also may use pressure, when necessary. Subordinates, however, are unlikely to use these techniques when attempting to influence their bosses. Instead, they generally rely on consultation or ingratiation. (For a more detailed look at how people influence their own bosses, see the "Tips" section on page 412.) Finally, when attempting to influence peers, both exchange and personal appeal are among the most popularly used.

As a general rule, *open, consultative techniques are believed to be more appropriate than coercive technology*.[7] Accordingly, the most popular techniques used at all levels are consultation, inspirational appeal, and rational persuasion.[8] Each of these techniques involves getting someone else to accept a request as being highly desirable, and each is socially acceptable for influencing people at all levels. Therefore, people who use these techniques are believed to be highly effective in performing their responsibilities.

In contrast, the less socially desirable forms of influence—that is, pressure and legitimating—are used much less frequently. In fact, when used, pressure is more likely to be relied on as a follow-up technique than as a tool for one's initial attempt—and even then only for subordinates. In addition, some techniques, such as ingratiation, coalition, personal appeal, and exchange, are more likely to be used in combination with others than to be used alone.

ETHICS MATTERS

Are some forms of social influence inherently more unethical than others? If so, which ones? Explain your answer. ■

Underlying an individual's choice of technique is that person's expectations of the effects it is likely to have, and not surprisingly, this is likely to be based on the qualities of the individual being influenced. For example, people attempting to influence their bosses rely on rational persuasion when they perceive their bosses as being highly participative. After all, a participative boss should be amenable to considering a rational argument. This approach would be unlikely to work, however, on a

FIGURE 11.2

Social Influence Depends on Organizational Level

Because of their different organizational levels, this manager and subordinate are likely to use different tactics when attempting to influence each other.

highly authoritarian boss. Not surprisingly, people attempting to influence these individuals are more inclined toward highly coercive actions (e.g., going over their boss's head).[9] These findings suggest that people's use of power is not only a function of their own predispositions but also of their beliefs about the likely effects of their actions.

TIPS: DOING IT RIGHT

■ Selling Issues Upward: Ten Ways to Capture Your Manager's Attention

If you work for a large company, you can expect your firm's top executives to deal with a staggering array of issues. How will the company meet pollution standards? How should the company's image be promoted? In what community projects should the public take the greatest role? These issues—and many others—fill the plates of today's executives. In fact, there may be so much competition for their attention you probably have good reason to be pessimistic about getting them to take on one more just because you think it is important.

If you are successful, however, at "selling" this issue to the boss—that is, at getting him or her to address it—your credibility in the organization may be enhanced. This would do a great deal to improve your chances of career success as well. The question, then, is: How can you sell your issue upward in the organization? There are several possible tactics[10]:

1. *Congruence*. To enhance the credibility of your attempt, select an issue in keeping with your established expertise. If you select an issue outside your field, it probably will receive little attention.
2. *Credibility*. Make clear your interest in the issue is not based on personal gain. You have no credibility if the issue is self-serving.
3. *Communication*. Make your argument to as many people as will listen, and use as many different communication channels as possible (e.g., e-mail, presentations at meetings, memos, and so on).
4. *Compatibility*. Make sure the issue is in keeping with the principles and mission of the organization. Avoid issues that run counter to the company's culture.
5. *Solvability*. You gain attention if you present viable solutions to problems. Selecting an unresolvable issue is unlikely to capture attention.
6. *Payoff*. Identify the long-term payoff for the organization and for the manager. The greater the payoff, the more likely the issue is to be accepted.
7. *Expertise*. Explain how your issue can be addressed using the expertise of current staff.
8. *Responsibility*. Explain how your issue falls under the manager's area of responsibility, thus suggesting it is appropriate for him or her to address it. You also may point out the negative consequences of ignoring this issue.
9. *Visibility*. Sell the issue in a public forum, not in a private meeting. Doing so exposes more people to the idea, thereby enhancing the chance the boss will add it to his or her agenda.
10. *Coalition*. Bring other people on-board who support your idea. It is far more difficult to avoid a proposal backed by several people than a proposal backed by just one.

By doing these things, you will have a good opportunity to influence your boss's agenda, and in so doing, you may well affect the organization as a whole. Therefore, issue selling is a potentially important way of increasing your power within an organization. ■

INDIVIDUAL POWER: A BASIS FOR INFLUENCE

As defined earlier, *power involves the potential to influence others—both in what they do and how they feel about something.* In this section, we focus on individual bases of power—that is, on factors giving people the capacity to control others successfully.

Inevitably, some individuals have a greater capacity than others to influence people successfully. Within organizations, the distribution of power typically is unequal as well. Why is this? What sources of power do people have at their disposal? Here, consider two major categories of individual power bases: those that come with one's office, and those that come with oneself as an individual.

Position Power: Influence That Comes with the Office

Much of the power people have in organizations comes from the posts they hold. In other words, they can influence others because of the formal power associated with their jobs. This is known as **position power**. For example, the president of the United States has certain powers simply because he or she holds the office (e.g., signing bills into law, making treaties). These *formal powers remain vested in the position and are available to anyone who holds that position.* When the president's term expires, these powers transfer to the new office-holder. There are four bases of position power: *legitimate, reward, coercive,* and *information.* For a summary, see Figure 11.3.

position power
Power based on one's formal position in an organization.

Legitimate Power   The power people have because others recognize and accept their authority is known as **legitimate power**. For example, students recognize that instructors have the authority to make class policies and to determine grades, thus giving them legitimate power over the class. If someone were to challenge the teacher's decision—such as by saying, "Who are you to do that?—the answer might be, "I'm the instructor, that's who." This exchange would clarify the legitimacy of the office-holder's behavior.

legitimate power
The individual power base derived from one's position in an organizational hierarchy; the accepted authority of one's position.

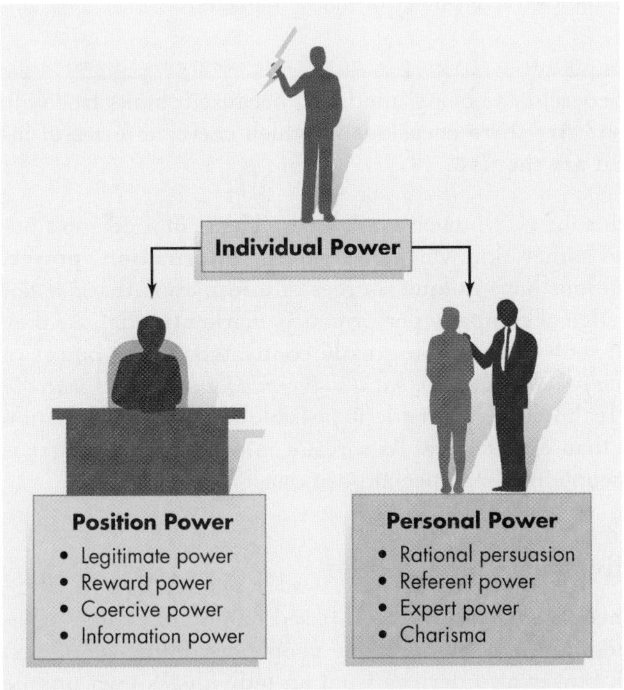

FIGURE 11.3

Types of Individual Power: A Summary

Individual power consists of two major types: *position power,* or that stemming from one's formal organizational roles; and *personal power,* or that stemming from one's personal characteristics. There are four specific types of power in each category.

Individual Power

Position Power
- Legitimate power
- Reward power
- Coercive power
- Information power

Personal Power
- Rational persuasion
- Referent power
- Expert power
- Charisma

People from nations such as the Philippines, Mexico, and India, which are said to have *high power distance*, show great respect for more powerful supervisors and would be reluctant to go above their heads. People from *low power distance* nations such as Austria, Israel, and Denmark, however, are more willing to bypass the authority of more powerful others. ■

It is important to note that *legitimate power covers a relatively narrow range of influence*, and it may be inappropriate to overstep these bounds. For example, a boss may require a secretary to type and fax a company document using his or her legitimate power to do so, but it would be an abuse of that power to ask a secretary to type his or her son's homework. This is not to say the secretary might not perform the task as a favor, but doing so would *not* be the direct result of the boss' formal authority. Legitimate power applies only to those behaviors that are recognized and accepted as being appropriate by the parties and the institution involved.

reward power

The individual power base derived from an individual's capacity to reward others.

Reward Power   Associated with holding certain jobs also comes the power to control the rewards that others receive—that is, **reward power**. Extending our previous teacher-student example, instructors have reward power over students, because they may reward students with high grades and glowing letters of recommendation. With managers, the rewards may be tangible (e.g., raises and promotions) or intangible (e.g., praise and recognition). In both cases, access to these desired outcomes gives power to the individuals who control them.

coercive power

The individual power base derived from the capacity to punish others.

Coercive Power   Power also results from the capacity to control punishments. This is known as **coercive power**. Most managers do not like threatening punishments, but many people in organizational life do rely on coercive power. If any boss has ever told you, "do what I say, or else"—or even implied it—you probably are all too familiar with coercive power. Often, people have power simply because others know they have the opportunity to punish them, even if no explicit threat is made. For example, in the military, when a commanding officer asks you to do something, you may comply if only because that request can turn into an order—with severe consequences for not obeying. In private organizations, implied threats of demotion, suspension without pay, and assignment to undesirable duties may enhance the coercive power of many managers.

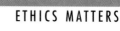

Some people regard the use of coercion as being unethical, because it limits free will. Do you agree with this position? Are there occasions in which coercive forms of influence are justified? If so, what are they? ■

information power

The extent to which a supervisor provides a subordinate with the information needed to do the job.

Information Power   The fourth source of power available by virtue of a person's position is based on data and other knowledge—that is, **information power**. Traditionally, people in top positions have unique sources of information that are not available to others (e.g., knowledge of company performance, market trends). As they say, "knowledge is power," and such information greatly contributes to the power of people in many jobs. *Information power still exists, but it is becoming a less potent source of influence in many organizations.* Technology has made it possible for more information to be available to more people than ever before. As a result information no longer is the unique property of a few people holding special positions.

Personal Power: Influence That Comes from the Individual

Thus far, the courses of influence discussed have been based on an individual's position in an organization, but these are not the only way people can influence others. As summarized in Figure 11.3, power also derives from an individual's own unique qualities or characteristics. This is known as **personal power**. There are four sources of personal power: *rational persuasion*, *referent power*, *expert power*, and *charisma*.

personal power

The power derived from a person's individual qualities or characteristics.

Rational Persuasion In the early 1990s, Apple Computer's former chairman John Scully did not like the future he saw. Apple was doing well, but computer sales threatened to flatten out in the years ahead. The real future of the company, he envisioned, involved applying Apple's user-friendly digital technology in new areas. Integrating telephones, computers, televisions, and entertainment systems was the key. Thus, Scully's first task was to get Apple's then-COO, Michael H. Spindler, and the board of directors to share his dream. After drawing on all his knowledge of the computer business and carefully studying what needed to be done to make this dream a reality, Scully thoroughly explained his plan for changing Apple from a single-product company with straightforward distribution to a multiproduct, multibusiness conglomerate. Spindler and the board were convinced, and Apple's new strategy was launched. (As we know, however, this strategy failed. With the introduction of the iMac computer in 1998, Apple returned to its core business—that is, selling simple, easy-to-use computers.)

Scully used a popular technique of social influence known as **rational persuasion**, which relies on logical arguments and factual evidence to convince others that a certain idea is acceptable. Rational persuasion is highly effective when the parties involved are intelligent enough to make their cases strongly and to understand them clearly. (There can be no doubt about this among Apple's top brass!) Based on clear logic, good evidence, and the desire to help the company, rational persuasion tends to be quite effective. (In retrospect, some critics blame Apple's recent financial problems on poor decisions by Apple executives, but these same officials certainly cannot be faulted for presenting their ideas in the rational manner they did.[11]) Not surprisingly, rational persuasion is among the most popular types of influence used in organizations.

rational persuasion

Using logical arguments and factual evidence to convince others an idea is acceptable.

Expert Power In addition to rational persuasion, Scully's ideas clearly were accepted because of his considerable expertise in the business. Thus, it can be said he also had **expert power**—that is, power based on superior knowledge of a certain field. A coach likewise has power over athletes to the extent he or she is recognized as knowing what is best. Once experts are accepted as such, their power over others can be considerable. After all, people respect and want to follow those "in the know."

Should a supervisor's expertise be lacking, any power he or she may have based on that expertise is threatened. No one is expected to be an expert on everything, but this is not necessarily problematic. A less-than-expert person simply can admit his or her shortcomings and seek guidance from others. Problems develop, however, if someone in a position of power has not yet developed a level of expertise that is acknowledged and respected by lower-ranking persons—especially when these individuals believe they are more expert than they really are! *Those who have not demonstrated their expertise clearly lack this important source of power. People whose expertise is highly regarded, however, are among the most powerful people in organizations.*

expert power

The individual power base derived from an individual's recognized, superior skills and abilities.

Referent Power As you surely know, personal qualities also form the basis of our admiration for others in organizations. Individuals who are liked and respected by others can get those others to alter their actions, which is a type of influence known as **referent power**. Senior managers with desirable qualities and good reputations may find they have referent power over younger managers who identify with and wish to emulate them.

referent power

The individual power base derived from the degree to which one is liked and admired by others.

Charisma Some people are so liked by others they are said to have **charisma**—that is, an engaging and magnetic personality. Some people also become highly influential because of their charismatic ways (see chapter 12). What makes such individuals so influential? First, highly charismatic people have definite visions regarding the future of their organizations and how to get there. Mary Kay Ash, the founder of Mary Kay Cosmetics, is widely regarded as being such a visionary. Second, people with charisma

charisma

A contagious attitude of enthusiasm and optimism; an aura of leadership.

tend to be excellent communicators, relying on colorful language and exciting metaphors to excite the crowd. They also supplement their words with emotionally expressive and animated gestures. Third, charismatic individuals inspire trust. Their integrity is never challenged, and it is a source of their strength. The late civil rights leader, Reverend Dr. Martin Luther King has been so described by many historians. Fourth, people with charisma make others feel good about themselves. They are receptive to others' feelings, and they acknowledge those feelings readily. "Congratulations on a job well done" is a phrase that may flow freely from charismatic individuals.

To summarize, people may influence others because of the jobs they have and their individual characteristics. Considering these factors, it's not difficult to understand that at any given time, in any given organization, some people are more powerful than others. For a listing of some of the most powerful women in business organizations today, see Table 11.1.[12]

TABLE 11.1

Who Are the Most Powerful Women in Corporate America?

The editors of *Fortune* magazine have identified the 50 women they consider to be the most influential in corporate America today. The top 10 are listed here. Some of these women likely are more familiar than others, but all are well known in their industries.

NAME	POSITION	EXAMPLE OF POWER WIELDED
Carly Fiorina	Group President, Lucent Technologies	Runs the core business of the largest telecom equipment company in the world.
Oprah Winfrey	Chairman and CEO, Harpo Entertainment Group	Her syndicated television show has a dramatic influence on popular culture.
Heidi Miller	CFO, Travelers Group	Controls the financial activities of the world's largest financial company
Sherry Lazarus	Chairman and CEO, Ogilvy & Mather Worldwide	Heads the seventh largest advertising agency in the world.
Sherry Lansing	Chairman, Motion Picture Group, Paramount Pictures	Boss of Hollywood's most profitable and successful movie studio.
Jill Barad	Chairman and CEO, Mattel	In charge of the world's largest toy company.
Marilyn Carlson Nelson	CEO, President, and Vice Chairman, Carlson Cos.	In charge of an empire that includes Radisson hotels, TGI Friday's restaurants, cruise ships, and travel agencies.
Andrea Jung	President and COO, Avon Products	Heads one of the largest cosmetic firms in the world.
Abby Joseph Cohen	Co-Chair, Investment Policy Committee, Goldman Sachs	Wall Street's most influential investment strategist.
Marjorie Scardino	CEO, Pearson PLC	Heads a publishing empire that includes the world's largest educational publishing unit (which, by the way, publishes this book).

Source: Based on information in Creswell, 1998; see note 12.

Power: How Is It Used?

What bases of power do you use? Chances are, you rely on several, including different types of power on different occasions. Not surprisingly, OB scientists have found that the various power bases relate closely to each other in how they are used.[13]

The more someone uses coercive power, for example, the less that person is liked — and, hence, the lower his or her referent power tends to be. Similarly, managers with expert power also are likely to have legitimate power, because people accept their expertise as a basis for having power. In addition, the higher someone's organizational position, the more legitimate power that person has, which usually is accompanied in turn by greater opportunities to use reward and coercion.[14] Clearly, *the various bases of power are completely separate and distinct. They often are used together in varying combinations* (Figure 11.4).

What bases of power do people prefer to use? The answer is quite complex, but people generally prefer using expert power the most and coercive power the least.[15] These findings are limited, however, to the power bases identified thus far. When we broaden the question and ask exactly what sources of power people have on their jobs, a fascinating picture emerges. Figure 11.5 depicts the results of a survey in which 216 CEOs of U.S. corporations were asked to rank-order the importance of specific sources of power.[16] The numbers reflect the percentage of executives who included that source of power among their top three choices. These executives not only relied on a broad range of powers but also based these powers on support from people in many other locations throughout their organizations.

Many forms of power tend to be used to influence subordinates, but *expert power is preferred to influence peers and superiors*.[17] After all, influencing others is almost always appropriate if you justify your attempt on the basis of expertise. In contrast, coercive tactics tend to be frowned on in general, and they are especially inappropriate when attempting to influence a higher-ranking person.[18] Influencing superiors is tricky because of the *counterpower* they have. When attempting to influence someone who is believed to have no power, one need not worry about retaliation. When dealing with an individual who has considerably greater power, however, one can do little other than simply comply with that person's wishes.

The situation is complicated by the fact that one party may have higher power along one dimension but lower power along another. For example, consider the case of secretaries who have acquired power because they have been with their companies for many years. They know the ropes, and they can get things done for you — if they want. They also can get you hopelessly bogged down in red tape. Their expert knowledge gives them a great sense of power over others. They may lack the legitimate power of their executive bosses, but secretaries' expertise can be a valuable source of counterpower. (To see how scientists measure different types of power — and to make

FIGURE 11.4

What Bases of Power Are Being Used Here?

People frequently rely on several bases of social power. This college instructor likely has legitimate power (by virtue of her rank), expert power (by virtue of her specialized knowledge), and several other sources of power at her disposal.

FIGURE 11.5

American CEOs: What Are Their Power Bases?

A survey of more than 200 American CEOs revealed they obtain their power primarily by cultivating the support of others at different levels of the organization.

(*Source*: Based on data appearing in Stewart, 1989; see note 16.)

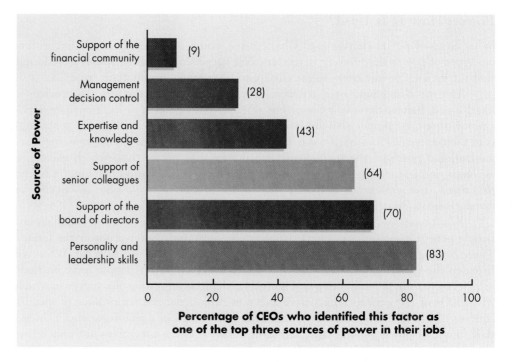

Percentage of CEOs who identified this factor as
one of the top three sources of power in their jobs

some preliminary judgments about the types of power your own supervisor uses — see the "Experiencing Organizational Behavior" exercise at the end of this chapter.)

ETHICS MATTERS

Robert Schoellhorn, the former CEO of Abbott Labs, was ousted from office after he became "drunk with power."[19] He surrounded himself with subordinates who did whatever he wanted and never challenged him. Anyone who dared not to go along with Schoellhorn was out — including three company presidents in eight years! Flexing his muscles to the end, Schoellhorn sued his former employer and eventually received a settlement of $5.2 million. The board of directors, however, considered this a small price to pay to rid themselves of this power-hungry chief executive.[20] ■

Empowerment: The Shifting Bases of Power in Today's Organizations

In a growing number of today's organizations, power is shifting from managers to employees. In fact, many of today's workers are not being "managed" in the traditional, authoritarian styles used by generations of past managers. Instead, power often is shifted down the ladder to a team of workers, who are allowed to make decisions themselves. In one survey, when asked about how much power they currently had compared with 10 years ago, only 19 percent of CEOs said they now had more power.[21] Thirty-six percent indicated they had the same amount of power. The largest group, however — 42 percent — indicated they had less power.

These figures are in keeping with the idea of **empowerment** — that is, the passing of responsibility and authority from managers to employees. For many years, workers used the excuse "I did it because my manager told me to." As employees become empowered, however, this explanation no longer is likely to be heard.

Empowerment involves more than simply giving employees leeway in determining how to carry out a leader's stated mission. It also involves sharing the appropriate information and knowledge that allows employees to do what is needed to meet the organization's goals. To underscore this point: *The key to empowering people successfully is the sharing of expert information (as opposed to the hoarding of information that has been*

empowerment

The passing of responsibility and authority from managers to employees.

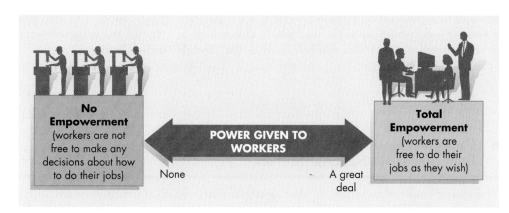

FIGURE 11.6

The Empowerment Continuum: Relinquishing Control Is a Matter of Degree

Empowering subordinate workers may take several different forms, ranging from giving workers complete power in determining how to do their jobs to giving them no power at all.

popular in the past). Today's managers are likely to be more open than their predecessors. As such, they are likely to empower their employees by widely disseminating information, thereby allowing better decisions to be made.

As you might imagine, empowerment is not a simple yes-or-no option; rather, it is a matter of degree (Figure 11.6).[22] At one end of the continuum are companies in which workers have virtually no power to determine how to do their jobs (e.g., traditional assembly lines). At the opposite end are companies in which employees have complete control over what they do and how they do it (e.g., self-managed work teams, as described in chapter 7). For example, at Chapparel Steel, managers are free to hire, train, and use new employees however they think best.[23] At W. L. Gore, the empowerment philosophy is entrenched so strongly that employees work without any fixed, assigned set of responsibilities.[24] Between these two extremes are companies whose employees have some degree of responsibility and voice in important decisions, but who are not completely free to work however they see fit. A growing number of companies fall into this category, including the General Motors Saturn plant in Spring Hill, Tennessee.[25]

When employees are empowered, their supervisors are less likely to be "bosses" who push people around (i.e., coercive power) and more likely to serve as teachers or "facilitators" who guide their teams using knowledge and experience (i.e., expert power). As John Ring, the director of Okidata (the Tokyo-based maker of printers and other office tools), says, "to influence people you have to prove you're right."[26]

Traditional managers tell people what to do, how to do it, and when to do it. Supervisors of empowered workers, however, are more inclined to ask questions to get people to solve problems and to allow them to make decisions on their own. This is precisely the approach taken by the Great Harvest Bread Company, a chain of 130 franchised bakeries in 34 states.[27] Most franchise operators must abide by standardized rules published in thick procedure manuals, at Great Harvest, franchise owners are *not* required to follow top-down regulations. Instead, as guidance, they are thoroughly exposed to the successful practices of other franchise owners (Figure 11.7). This is done through training sessions at the Dillion, Montana, company headquarters, by visiting other stores, and by hosting on-site visits from other owners. In lieu of regulations, store owners are encouraged to share recipes, management tips, and ideas about decorating and promotions over the company's intranet. Store owners are free to use, adopt, or ignore these ideas as they wish — and to try new ones, thus giving each store its own, unique, mom-and-pop feel. Acknowledging the importance of openly sharing ideas, Tom McMakin, the company's COO, refers to Great Harvest as being not only a bread company but a university.

If the practices described here do not square with your experiences, take heart. *Most managers are afraid of relinquishing control, so empowered employees remain in the minority of most organizations.*[28] Experts predict a change in that direction is coming, however, and coming fast.[29] If this prognostication is correct — as we believe it is — we can look

FIGURE 11.7

Great Power at Great Harvest

Susan and Sealie Van Raalte are preparing a loaf of bread to bake in their Great Harvest Bread Company in Larchmont, New York. Like other Great Harvest franchise owners, they receive guidance from more experienced owners but are free to run their own operation as they see fit.

forward to significant changes in how people use power in organizations. (To give you a feel for what this may look like, take a closer look at some of the empowerment practices used today, which are described in the "Trends" section below.

■ Empowerment in Action: Some Notable Success Stories

The idea of empowerment (i.e., of sharing power with others) is straightforward, but it often takes different forms in different organizations. Here are some particularly interesting examples of successful empowerment practices used by some large companies.[30]

Xerox   Since February 1992, a corporate reorganization plan has encouraged Xerox employees to take greater responsibility over their work. Nowhere has this plan been implemented more completely than in its sprawling distribution center outside Atlanta. The head of this facility considers the 24 paid-by-the-hour, union workers as being managers — and treats them as such. They are free to take responsibility for their own jobs and to solve problems as they see fit. That is just what they've done, too. For example, these employees have found ways to save money on trash removal (by recycling) and shipping costs (by using lighter-weight pallets). They even have reorganized warehousing procedures so that 99.9 percent of orders now ship on-time. Absenteeism is almost nonexistent, and productivity is up dramatically. Xerox officials now are studying the Atlanta facility in the hope of duplicating its success elsewhere in the company.[31]

Omni Hotels   In June 1990, a program called the Power of One was implemented by Omni Hotels to combat exceptionally high employee turnover and low satisfaction among guests. This involved training all employees to make independent decisions that benefit the guests — even if that meant bending the rules. Frontline employees also were empowered to listen to angry customers and to give them whatever they wanted (within reason of course).[32] After the first month, customer satisfaction surged by 16 percent, and after the first year, employee turnover fell to 42 percent (from 65 percent before the plan was introduced). This hotel chain has enjoyed higher profits ever since. In fact, it placed among the top three upscale domestic hotel chains in a 1998 survey by J. D. Power and Associates.[33]

Prudential Insurance Company   For a long time, this large insurance company's Northeastern Group Operations center was highly inefficient. Claims took too long to be filed, and managers could do nothing to resolve any problems that arose. Recognizing this, top managers agreed to relinquish power to lower-ranking employees, who were closer to the customers and had a good sense of how to make things run better. By empowering teams to process their own claims, processing time dropped from 10 days to three days at one location. In addition, operating costs fell by 12 percent, customer service measures improved, and gross revenues rose by 40 percent.[34]

These success stories of empowerment in action are not atypical. In fact, we could give many other good examples.[35] One thing that makes those examples noteworthy, however, is that they involve large companies — precisely where tall hierarchies of power tend to prevail. If empowerment strategies can be implemented successfully in these organizations, they should be even easier to introduce at smaller firms, where people have less formally defined powers. Clearly, leaders in organizations of all sizes have good reason to consider granting power to their employees. ■

GROUP OR SUBUNIT POWER: STRUCTURAL DETERMINANTS

Thus far, we have examined the use of power by individuals. In organizations, however, groups wield power as well.[36] Traditionally, organizations are divided into subunits that are given responsibility for different functions, such as finance, human resource management, marketing, and research and development. (We describe these arrangements more fully in chapter 14.) The formal departments devoted to these various organizational activities often also must direct the activities of other groups, thus requiring these departments to have power. What are the sources of such power, and how do formal organizational groups successfully control the actions of other groups?

Two theoretical models answer these questions: the *resource-dependency model*, and the *strategic contingencies model*. Reviewing these approaches helps to identify the factors responsible for subunit power and to describe how they operate.

The Resource-Dependency Model: Controlling Critical Resources

An organization can be thought of as a complex set of subunits that are constantly exchanging resources with each other. By this, we mean that formal organizational departments may be both giving to and receiving from other departments valued commodities such as money, personnel, equipment, supplies, and information. These critical resources are necessary for the successful operation of organizations.

Various subunits often depend on others for such resources. For example, imagine a large organization that develops, produces, and sells its own products. The Sales Department provides financial resources that enable the Research and Development Department to create new products. Of course, the Sales Department cannot do so effectively without having information from the Marketing Department about what consumers are interested in buying and how much they are willing to pay. The Production Department must do its part by manufacturing the goods on time, but only if the Purchasing Department can supply the needed raw materials—and at a price the Finance Department accepts as permitting the company to turn a profit.

It is easy to see how various organizational subunits are involved in a complex set of interrelationships. To the extent one subunit controls the resources on which another subunit depends, the first subunit may be said to have power over the second. After all, controlling resources allows groups to influence successfully the actions of other groups. Thus, subunits that control more resources may be considered to be more powerful in the organization. Indeed, such imbalances, or *asymmetries*, in the pattern of resource dependencies occur normally in organizations. In short, the more one group depends on another for needed resources, the less power it has (Figure 11.8).

The **resource-dependency model** proposes that a subunit's power is based on the degree to which it controls those resources required by other subunits.[37] Thus, *all subunits may contribute to an organization, but the most powerful are those that contribute the most important resources. Controlling the resources other departments need puts a subunit in a better position to bargain for the resources that it requires.*

Consider, for example, a classic study of the differences in power wielded by departments in a large university.[38] Within a university, the various academic departments may be unequal regarding the power they possess. Some may have more students, be more prestigious in reputation, receive more grants, and have more representatives on important university committees. As such, these departments would be expected to have greater control over valued resources. This was the case within the large state university examined by this study. Specifically, the more powerful departments were most successful in gaining scarce and valued resources from the

resource-dependency model

The view that power resides within subunits able to control the greatest share of valued organizational resources.

FIGURE 11.8

The Resource-Dependency Model: An Example

The *resource-dependency model* of organizational power holds that subunits acquire power when they control critical resources needed by other subunits. In this example, the accounting department would be more powerful than the production department or the marketing department.

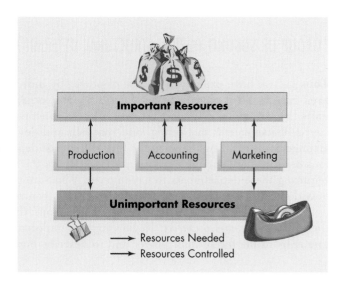

university (e.g., funds for graduate-student fellowships, faculty research grants, summer faculty fellowships). As a result, they became even more powerful, thereby suggesting that within organizations, the rich subunits get richer.

This raises another question: How do various organizational subunits become more powerful in the first place? In other words, why might certain departments control the most resources when an organization is newly formed? A fascinating study of the semiconductor industry in California provides insight.[39] Using personal interviews, market research data, and archival records, these researchers determined that *two main factors account for an organizational subunit's power: the period within which the company was founded, and the background of the entrepreneur who started the company.* For example, research and development functions were critical among the earliest semiconductor firms, so this department had the most power among the oldest firms. Hence, the importance of an area of corporate activity when the company began dictated the relative power of that area years later.

The most powerful organizational subunits also tended to be those representing the founder's area of expertise. Thus, the marketing and sales departments of companies founded by experts in marketing and sales tended to have the greatest amounts of power. This research provides an important link in our understanding of how the subunits attain power within organizations.

GLOBAL MATTERS   The tendency for the greatest corporate power to reside in the area of the founder's expertise applies throughout the world. For example, the founder of Sony (then Tokyo Telecommunications Laboratory) was an engineer—a very powerful functional area in that company to this day. ■

The resource-dependency model suggests that a key determinant of subunit power is the control of valued resources. It is not only control over resources that dictates organizational power, however. It also is control over the activities of other subunits.

The Strategic Contingencies Model: Power Through Dependence

The accounting department of a company might be expected to have responsibility over funds requested by various departments. If it does, the actions of this department greatly affect the activities of other units who depend on its decisions. In other words, other departments' operations are *contingent* on what the accounting department does. To the extent a department can control the relative power of various organizational subunits by its actions, it is said to have control over *strategic contingencies*. For example, if the accounting department consistently approves the budget requests of the production department but rejects those of the marketing department, it would be making the production department more powerful.

Where do the strategic contingencies lie within organizations? In one classic study, researchers found that power was distributed in different departments among different industries.[40] *Within successful firms, strategic contingencies were controlled by the departments most important for organizational success.* For example, within the food-processing industry, where new products are critical, successful firms have strategic contingencies controlled by the sales and research departments. In the container-manufacturing field, where the timely delivery of high-quality goods is a critical determinant of organizational success, successful firms place most of the decision-making power in the sales and production departments. Thus, successful firms focus control over strategic contingencies within those subunits most responsible for their organization's success.

What factors give subunits control over strategic contingencies? The **strategic contingencies model** suggests several key considerations.[41] These factors are summarized in Figure 11.9.

Power may be enhanced by subunits with *the capacity to reduce the uncertainty faced by others*. Thus, any department that can shed light on the murky situations organizations may face (e.g., future markets, government regulation, availability of needed supplies, financial security) can be expected to wield the most organizational power. Accordingly, the balance of power within organizations may change as the organizational conditions change.

Consider, for example, changes that have occurred in public utilities. When these companies first began, engineers tended to wield the most power. As these companies matured and began to face problems of litigation and governmental regulation (particularly over nuclear energy), however, the power shifted to lawyers.[42] A similar shift toward the legal department has occurred in the area of human resource management, where complex laws and governmental regulations have created great uncertainty for organizations. Again, powerful subunits are those that can reduce organizational uncertainty.

More powerful subunits also are those with *a high degree of centrality in the organization*. In other words, some organizational subunits perform functions that are more central and others more peripheral. For example, some departments (e.g., accounting) may need to be consulted by most other departments before any action can be taken, thus giving them a central position in their organization. Centrality also is high when a subunit's duties have an immediate effect on an organization. For example, with an auto manufacturer, the effects would be much more dramatic if the production

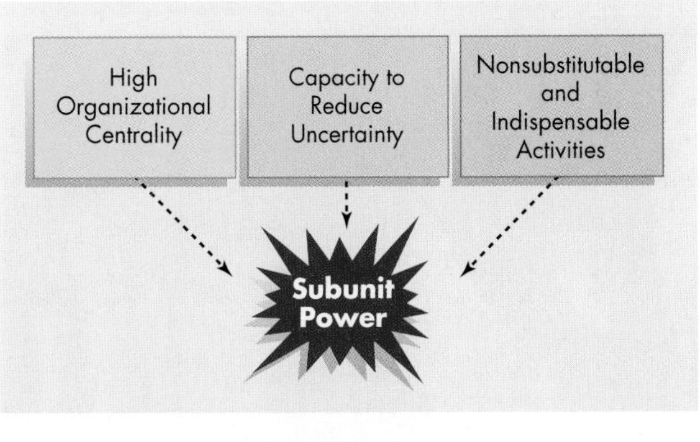

strategic contingencies model
The view that explains power in terms of a subunit's capacity to control the activities of other subunits. A subunit's power is enhanced when it can reduce the uncertainty experienced by other subunits, it occupies a central position in the organization, and its activities are highly indispensable.

FIGURE 11.9

Strategic Contingencies Model: Identifying Sources of Subunit Power

The *strategic contingencies model* explains intraorganizational power as the capacity of some subunits to control the actions of others. Subunit power may be enhanced by the factors shown here.

lines stopped than if all market research ceased. In sum, the central connection of some departments to organizational success dictates the power they wield.

In addition, a subunit controls power when its *activities are nonsubstitutable and indispensable*. If any group can perform a certain function, the subunit responsible for controlling that function may not be particularly powerful. For example, in a hospital, personnel on surgical teams certainly are more indispensable than personnel in the maintenance department, because fewer individuals have the skills needed to perform this subunit's duties. Because an organization easily can replace some employees with others, subunits composed of those individuals who are most easily replaced tend to wield very little organizational power.

The strategic contingencies model has been tested in and supported by several organizational studies.[43] For example, one investigation of several companies found that a subunit's power within an organization was higher when it could reduce uncertainty, occupied a central place in the work flow, and performed functions that other subunits could not.[44] Thus, the strategic contingencies model is a valuable source of information about the factors influencing the power of subunits within organizations.

ORGANIZATIONAL POLITICS: POWER IN ACTION

Our discussion of power thus far has focused on influencing others successfully. When this potential is realized—that is, put into action to accomplish desired goals—we no longer are talking about power but about *organizational politics*.[45] It is easy to imagine situations in which someone does something to accomplish his or her own goals, even though these goals do not necessarily agree with those of the organization. This is what *organizational politics is all about—actions not officially approved by an organization that are taken to influence others to meet one's personal goals*.[46]

If you think we are describing something a bit selfish and an abuse of organizational power, you are correct. Organizational politics does involve placing one's self-interest above the interests of the organization. Indeed, this element of using power to foster one's own interests distinguishes organizational politics from uses of power that are approved and accepted by organizations.[47]

Not surprisingly, businesspeople often look down on those who engage in organizational politics. For example, as the outspoken billionaire and former presidential candidate H. Ross Perot says, "I don't want any corporate politicians . . . some guy that wants to move ahead at the expense of others."[48] Growing numbers of people also have found organizational politics to be so intolerable they have left the corporate world altogether, venturing out on their own (Figure 11.10).

FIGURE 11.10

Organizational Politics Made Him Leave the Corporate World

Working from his home in suburban Washington, DC, Lak Vohra publishes *Party Digest*, a monthly letter about business and social networking events. This self-proclaimed "party guru" left the corporate world after complaining how very miserable he felt because of organizational politics. Mr. Vohra is one of a growing number of people becoming their own bosses because they find organizational politics intolerable.

Political Tactics: What Forms Do They Take?

To understand organizational politics, you must recognize the various forms of political behavior in organizations. In other words, what are the techniques of organizational politics? Six are used most often[49]:

Controlling Access to Information Information is the lifeblood of organizations. Therefore, *controlling who knows — and who does not know — certain things is one of the most important ways to exercise power in organizations.* Outright lying and falsifying information may be rare in organizations (in part because of the consequences of getting caught), but information can be controlled in other ways to enhance one's organizational position. For example, you might withhold information that makes you look bad (e.g., negative sales information), avoid contact with those who may ask for information you prefer not to disclose, be selective in the information you disclose, or overwhelm others with information that may not be completely relevant. All these are ways to control the nature and the degree of information people have at their disposal. Such information control can be critical.

An analysis of the organizational restructuring of AT&T's Phone Stores revealed that control was transferred through the effective manipulation, distortion, and creation of information.[50] In fact, one vice president's secret plan to feed incomplete and inaccurate information to the CEO was responsible for that vice president's winning control over these stores.

Cultivating a Favorable Impression *People who are interested in enhancing their organizational control commonly engage in some degree of image building* — that is, attempts to enhance their impressions on others. Such efforts may take many forms, such as "dressing for success," associating oneself with the successful accomplishments of others (or even taking credit for others' successes), or simply calling attention to one's own successes and positive characteristics.[51]

No one enjoys being criticized, but Saudi Arabians are particularly sensitive to negative feedback. They consider being criticized in public to be a loss of honor — one they are likely to continue suffering through private humiliation. ▪

GLOBAL MATTERS

Experts have noted that some people work hard to fit into their organizations, and these people are referred to as **organizational chameleons**.[52] Such individuals figure out what behaviors are generally appropriate in their organization and then go out of their way to make others aware they behaved in such a manner. These are ways of developing the "right image" to enhance one's individual power in organizations.

One challenge associated with doing this is making sure your actions are not perceived as being politically motivated. For example, planning ahead surely is desirable, but this same behavior may be thought of as "scheming" if it is suspected of having political intent. Similarly, documenting decisions is good management practice, but it may be thought of in less flattering terms (e.g., "covering your rear") if political motives are suspected. In other words, the most politically adept individuals need to manage impressions about how they manage their impressions.

organizational chameleons

Individuals who discern what behaviors they believe are generally appropriate in their organization and then go out of their way to make sure others are aware they behave in such a manner.

Developing a Base of Support *To influence people successfully, gaining the support of others within the organization often is useful.* For example, managers may lobby for their ideas before officially presenting them at meetings, thereby ensuring that others are committed to them in advance and avoiding the embarrassment of public rejection. Sometimes, of course, even getting an audience with high-ranking organizational officials to make your argument is difficult. Not letting this become a barrier, one particularly ingenious up-and-coming executive at Lotus Development Co. admits to having rehearsed an "elevator speech" — so he would have a chance to present his point to the company president should he ever happen to run into him in the elevator.[53]

Suppose you have lobbied for your ideas and appear to have gotten some support. Make sure, however, that those individuals will not change their minds. How can you get them to follow through on their commitment? One method involves "scattering IOUs" throughout the organization — that is, doing favors for others, who then may feel obligated to repay them in the form of supporting your ideas. This practice relies on the norm of **reciprocity**, which says that people expect to be paid back for their favors. If we consider the many popular phrases describing this norm — "You scratch my back, and I'll scratch yours," or "One good turn deserves another" — it is clear this norm generally is quite strong in organizations. After all, when someone does a favor for you, you may say, "I owe you one," thus making clear you are aware of your obligation to reciprocate that favor. In sum, "calling in" favors is a well established and widely used mechanism for developing organizational power.

reciprocity

The social norm which dictates that people expect to be paid back for the favors they grant others.

Blaming and Attacking Others   One of the most popular tactics of organizational politics involves blaming and attacking others when bad things happen. One such common tactic is finding a **scapegoat** — that is, a person who is given the blame for someone else's failure or wrongdoing. For example, a supervisor may explain the failure of a sales plan he or she designed was based on the serious mistakes of a subordinate — even if this is not entirely true (Figure 11.11). Explaining that "it's his fault" (i.e., making another "take the fall" for an undesirable event) gets the real culprit "off the hook" for it.

scapegoat

Someone who is made to take the blame for another's failure or wrongdoing.

Finding a scapegoat can allow the politically astute individual to avoid — or at least to minimize — his or her association with the negative situation. For example, when corporate performance drops, powerful chief executives often place the blame on lower-ranking individuals, thereby protecting themselves from getting fired — while their subordinates get the ax.[54]

Aligning Oneself with More Powerful Others   One of the most direct ways to gain power is by connecting yourself with more powerful others. There are several ways to accomplish this. For example, a low-power person may become more powerful if he or she has a very powerful mentor — that is, a more powerful and better-established person who can look out for and protect his or her interests (see chapter 6).

FIGURE 11.11

Finding a Scapegoat: A Widespread Tactic of Organizational Politics

Few people are as explicit about finding a scapegoat as this speaker, but the tactic of finding someone else to blame for one's misdeeds is common in organizations.

(*Source*: © The New Yorker Collection 1985. Michael Maslin from cartoonbank.com. All Rights Reserved.)

"And now at this point in the meeting I'd like to shift the blame away from me and onto someone else."

Alternatively, people may agree in advance to form *coalitions* — that is, groups that band together to achieve some common goal (e.g., overthrowing a current CEO).[55] The banding together of relatively powerless groups is one of the most effective ways these groups have of gaining organizational power.[56] Two relatively powerless individuals or groups may become stronger if they agree to act together, thereby forming a coalition (see chapter 10).

People also may align themselves with more powerful others by giving them "positive strokes" in the hope of getting those more powerful people to like and to help them, which is the process referred to earlier as *ingratiation*.[57] Agreeing with someone more powerful may be an effective way of getting that person to consider you an ally. Such an alliance may prove indispensable when you are looking for support within an organization. *To summarize, having a powerful mentor, forming coalitions, and using ingratiation all are potentially effective ways of gaining power by aligning oneself with others.*

Playing Political Games One expert in the field of organizational power and politics has likened political behavior in organizations to a collection of sets in a multiring circus.[58] In other words, many people or groups may be trying to influence many other people or groups simultaneously. What, then, are the political games that unfold in organizations? We can identify four major categories of political games: *authority*, *power base*, *rivalry*, and *change*. These are summarized in Table 11.2.

AUTHORITY GAMES Some games, which are known as *insurgency games*, are played to resist authority; others, which are known as *counterinsurgency games*, are played to counter such resistance to authority. Insurgency games can range from mild (i.e., intentionally not doing what is asked) to severe (e.g., organizing workers to mutiny or sabotage their workplaces).[59] In these cases, companies may fight back with counterinsurgency games. One specific way they might do so is by invoking stricter

TABLE 11.2

Political Games: A Summary of Some Examples

Many political games are played in organizations, each involving different individuals playing for different political goals.

GAME	TYPICAL MAJOR PLAYERS	PURPOSE
Authority Games		
Insurgency game	Lower-level managers	To resist formal authority
Counterinsurgency game	Upper-level managers	To counter resistance to formal authority
Power Base Games		
Sponsorship game	Any subordinate employee	To enhance base of power with superiors
Alliance game	Line managers	To enhance base of power with peers
Empire building	Line managers	To enhance base of power with subordinates
Rivalry Games		
Line versus staff game	Line managers and staff personnel	To defeat each other in the quest for power
Rival camps game	Any groups at the same level	To defeat each other in the quest for power
Change Games		
Whistle-blowing game	Lower-level managers	To correct organizational wrongdoings
Young Turks game	Upper-level managers	To seize control over the organization

Source: Adapted from Mintzberg, 1983; see note 3.

authority and control over subordinates. Often unproductive for both sides, such games frequently give way to the more adaptive techniques of bargaining and negotiation.

POWER BASE GAMES   These games are played to enhance the degree and the breadth of one's organizational power. For example, the *sponsorship game* is played with superiors and involves attaching oneself to a rising or established star in return for a piece of the action. For example, a relatively unpowerful subordinate may agree to help a more established person (e.g., his boss) by loyally supporting him in exchange for advice and information — as well as for some of his power and prestige. Both people benefit as a result. Similar games also may be played among peers. For example, in the *alliance game*, workers at the same level agree in advance to support each other, thereby gaining strength by increasing their joint size and power. One of the riskiest power base games is known as *empire building*, in which an individual or group attempts to become more powerful by gaining responsibility for more and more important organizational decisions. Indeed, a subunit may increase its power by gaining control over budgets, space, equipment, or any other scarce or desired organizational resource.

RIVALRY GAMES   Some political games are designed to weaken one's opponents. For example, in the *line versus staff game*, managers on the "line," who are responsible for the operation of an organizational unit, clash with those on the "staff," who are responsible for providing needed advice and information. For example, a foreman on an assembly line may ignore advice from a corporate legal specialist about how to treat one of his production workers, thereby rendering the staff specialist less powerful.

Another such game is the *rival camps game*, in which groups or individuals with differing points of view attempt to reduce each other's power. For example, an organization's production department may favor stability and efficiency, whereas its marketing department may favor growth and customer service. The result? Each side may attempt to cultivate the favor of those allies who can support it and who are less sensitive to the other side's interests. Of course, organizational success requires the various subunits to work together; therefore, such rivalries are potentially disruptive to organizational functioning. One side or the other may win from time to time, but the organization always loses.

CHANGE GAMES   Several different games are played to create organizational change. For example, in the *whistle-blowing game*, an organizational member secretly reports some wrongdoing to a higher authority in the hope of righting the wrong, thereby bringing about change. A game played for much higher stakes is known as the *young Turks game*, in which camps of rebel workers seek to overthrow the existing leadership of an organization — a most extreme form of insurgency. The change sought by people playing the game is not minor; it is far-reaching and permanent. In government terms, they are seeking a "coup d'état."

Some political activities may readily co-exist with organizational interests (e.g., the sponsorship game), whereas others clearly are antagonistic to organizational interests (e.g., the young Turks game). As such games are played, it becomes apparent that even though political activity sometimes may have little effect on organizations, it also may be quite harmful.[60] Now that we know what types of behavior reflect political activity in organizations, we are prepared to consider the conditions under which such behaviors occur.

When Does Political Action Occur?

Imagine the following situation: You are the director of a large, charitable organization that administers funds supporting many projects (e.g., saving endangered species, providing homeless shelters). A wealthy philanthropist dies, and his will leaves your organization $10 million — to be spent in any desired manner. Hearing of this generous bequest, the directors of the various projects all are interested in obtaining as much of this money as possible. Several aspects of this situation make it susceptible to triggering political activity.[61]

Conditions Triggering Political Action   First, this situation is fraught with uncertainty. After all, it is not immediately obvious where the money should be spent. If the organization has no clearly prescribed priorities about spending its funds, various groups might try to get their share by any means possible. Second, this clearly is a matter involving large amounts of scarce resources. If the size of the gift were much smaller (e.g., $500) or involved something trivial or readily available (e.g., paper clips), the incentive for political action probably would be weak.

The different groups in our example each have conflicting goals and interests. The save-our-wildlife group is intent on serving its interests, but the shelter-for-the-homeless group has very different interests. These differing goals make political activity likely. Finally, note that the potential for political activity in this situation also is great because all the different groups are approximately equal in power. If the balance of power was highly asymmetrical—that is, if one group had more control over resources than the others—political action would be futile, because the most powerful group would make the decision.

In summary, *political behavior is likely to occur when uncertainty exists, large amounts of scarce resources are at stake, organizational units have conflicting interests, or the parties involved have approximately equal power.* (Several of these conditions—especially power imbalances between employees—are likely to arise in another context: when women managers are given overseas assignments. For a look at some of the potentially political issues associated with women in international management, see the "OB Around the World" section in this chapter.)

Politics in Human Resource Management   Political behavior often centers around key human resource management activities, such as performance appraisals, personnel selection, and compensation decisions (Figure 11.12).[62] For example, given that a certain amount of ambiguity often is associated with evaluating another's performance—and that such evaluations might cultivate certain images of oneself—it follows that performance ratings may be recognized as being more reflective of the rater's interest in promoting a certain image of himself than of an interest in accurately evaluating another's behavior.[63] Similarly, when making personnel decisions, people are at least as concerned about the implications of their hires for their own careers (e.g., will this person support me or make me look bad?) as they are about doing what is best for the organization.[64]

As noted, pay raises often are politically motivated as well. Specifically, researchers conducting a management simulation exercise found that managers gave the highest raises to individuals who threatened to complain if they did not get a substantial one—particularly if these people had political connections within the

FIGURE 11.12

Human Resources: A Breeding Ground for Organizational Politics

Decisions about selecting, appraising, training, and compensating human resources are both important and inherently ambiguous. As a result, organizational politics tends to be prevalent in such situations.

THE ORGANIZATIONAL POLITICS OF SELECTING WOMEN FOR OVERSEAS ASSIGNMENTS

The practice of sending executives abroad to manage a company's overseas operations is not unusual in today's global economy. In most organizations, however, few such assignments are available at any time, and because these generally are considered to be excellent opportunities to prove oneself, they tend to be sure routes to promotion. As a result, there often is considerable competition for overseas assignments.[65] Therefore, the process of deciding who wins these jobs can be fraught with political overtones. Claims of favoritism are not unheard of in such situations, and there is good reason to believe women executives may become pawns in a political game — in which overseas assignments are the prize.

Contributing to this situation is the widespread belief that women can be passed over for such assignments because they generally are uninterested in them. For men, who tend to hold higher positions in top companies (see chapter 5), such a belief is self-serving. It also is unfounded. In fact, one survey of students graduating from seven top MBA programs found that men and women were equally interested in overseas assignments.[66] At the same time, these researchers acknowledged companies tended to send fewer women abroad. In addition, those who did go tended to be those who presented strong cases for doing so, not those who came to the minds of the decision-makers. This was found in a survey of corporate personnel practices as well: Four out of five U.S. companies are hesitant — if not altogether unwilling — to send female managers abroad.[67] The concerns they cite usually center around fears of potential mistreatment by colleagues in host countries.

The question of whether female managers actually are unsuccessful in overseas assignments, however, lends itself to being answered empirically. Indeed, this issue was examined by an in-depth survey in which managers from major North American firms were interviewed as they returned from overseas assignments.[68] The results were clear — but the opposite of what was expected: Overall, female managers were *more* successful than their male counterparts in handling overseas assignments. Almost all the female managers (97 percent) reported their international assignments were successful, which was far higher than the figure for males. Objective measures also suggested this was the case. In fact, although most of the

women sent overseas were the first ones ever sent by their companies, these same companies plan on assigning additional women overseas in the future based on these successes.

Interestingly, being a woman was not something to be overcome for a successful overseas experience. To the contrary, it actually was an advantage. There were several reasons for this:

- Most of the women's business associates were men, so the women stood out, thereby making others curious about meeting them. Their uniqueness made them more easily remembered as well.

- Women did a better job than men of putting their male counterparts at ease. Because they proved easier to talk to, they also tended to conduct business more successfully.

- Native women tended to be denied higher social status than men in the countries in which they lived. However, foreign women were not denied this status. As such, the female managers studied benefited from receiving special treatment.

- Business officials from the host country recognized it was unique for women to be sent overseas. As such, these women were assumed to be the very best, thus leading them to be given favorable treatment.

To conclude, there is every reason to suspect that women will be more successful than men in overseas assignments. Once this becomes known, what role will it play in the political nature of overseas assignments? If anything, the expectation that women will handle such assignments successfully may be threatening to men, and this may lead men to fight harder to get these assignments, thereby opening the door to political tactics. At the same time, several of the advantages women have in the world of international management appear to follow from their being so unique in that setting. Thus, as more women assume such international management positions, any such advantages resulting from their uniqueness are likely to disappear. Obviously, we can only guess at what the future holds in this regard. The only thing that is clear, however, is that we have good reason to suspect that questions about the role of women in international management positions — and, hence, the organizational politics associated with attaining such positions — are likely to grow even more important.

organization.[69] Taken together, these findings suggest that *the very nature of human resource management activities in organizations makes them prime candidates for organizational politics.*

Politics and the Organizational Life Span   The conditions leading to political activities are likely to differ as a function of an organization's life. Hence, contrasting degrees and types of political activity can be expected at different stages of an organization's life. Organizations can be distinguished as those just being started by entrepreneurs (i.e., the *birth* and *early growth* stage), those that are fully developed (i.e., the *maturity* stage), and those facing decline and dissolution (i.e., the *decline* or *redevelopment* stage). Different types of political activity are likely to occur during these various stages.[70]

When an organization is new, it may have little or no structure and be guided by the philosophy of the founder. During this stage, the entrepreneur gains political power by presenting his or her ideas to the employees as being rational. In turn, the employees accept this person's image of the corporate mission. The founder usually has complete access to information and makes decisions based on his or her own values. Explaining these decisions to subordinates is a way of inculcating these values to others in the organization and, thereby, of exercising power over them. Political activity is not particularly likely during this stage.

As organizations mature and grow more complex, however, they tend to departmentalize, thus creating conditions in which the vested interests of different groups are likely to conflict. Political means may be used to gain advantage in such situations. Indeed, *the full range of political activities noted earlier (e.g., forming coalitions, using information) likely will be employed when organizations are mature. When organizations begin to decline, however, subunits may be quite insecure, and the need for political action may be great as people and groups compete for the power to control—and, perhaps, to turn around—the organization.* A period of decline reflects a time of great uncertainty—and, thus, a period in which political activity is likely to be quite intense. For example, staff members in California school districts experiencing decline tend to have more intense, competitive interactions and to be at odds with each other more than members of similar organizations during periods of growth.[71] Clearly, use of political practices in an organization is likely to be affected by that organization's degree of maturity.

Organizational Politics: When Does It Occur?

Organizational politics is widespread, but political activity is not equally likely throughout all parts of an organization.[72] Specifically, *political activity is most likely among areas in which clear policies, such as interdepartmental co-ordination, promotions and transfers, and delegation of authority* are either nonexistent or lacking.[73] In areas with clearly defined rules and regulations, however, such as hiring and disciplinary policies, political activities are lowest.

One survey of organizational political practices revealed similar findings.[74] Specifically, organizational politics was perceived to be greatest in subunits (e.g., boards of directors, members of the marketing staff) that followed poorly defined policies, whereas political activity was perceived to be lowest in subunits

YOU BE THE CONSULTANT

The CEO of a company that operates several food processing plants comes to you with the following complaint: "Sometimes there is so much backstabbing around here that people aren't getting their work done." Company revenues have been flat for several years, and top executives blame "the politically charged atmosphere" as the main culprit.

1. How might political conflicts within the company interfere with its bottom line?

2. If there are political problems, where in the organization would you most expect to find them? Why?

3. What other forms of political behavior might you expect to find in this company?

FIGURE 11.13

Organizational Politics: More Likely at the Top

Employees believe political activity is more likely to occur at higher organizational levels, where the guiding rules are more ambiguous and the stakes are higher, than at lower levels.

(*Source*: Based on data reported by Gandz & Murray, 1980; see note 73.)

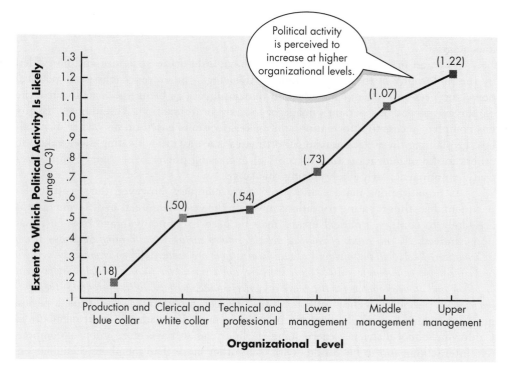

(e.g., production, accounting) in which clearly defined policies existed. Similarly, because of the inherently high levels of ambiguity associated with the tasks of human resource management (e.g., personnel selection, performance appraisal), political behavior is likely to occur when these functions are being performed.[75]

Together, these findings make an important point: *Political activity is likely to occur in the face of ambiguity.* When there are clear-cut rules about what to do, people are unlikely to abuse their power by taking political action. When people face highly novel and ambiguous situations, however, in which the rules are unclear, it is easy to imagine how political behavior results.

Where in an organization is the political climate most active? In other words, at what levels do people believe the most political activities are likely? As shown in Figure 11.13, organizations are perceived as being more political at the higher levels and as being less political at the lower managerial and nonmanagerial levels.[76] Apparently, politics is most likely to occur at the top—where, of course, the stakes are highest and power may corrupt.

THE ETHICS OF ORGANIZATIONAL POLITICS

One of the most important effects of organizational power is that it invites corruption. Indeed, *the more power an individual has, the more tempted he or she is to use that power toward some immoral or unethical purpose.*[77] Obviously, the potential for powerful individuals and organizations to abuse their power is quite real. Because such behaviors are regarded negatively, however, the most politically astute individuals—including politicians themselves—often attempt to present themselves in a highly ethical manner.

Unfortunately, the potential to behave unethically all too frequently is realized. For example, consider how greed overtook concerns about human welfare when the Manville Corporation suppressed evidence that asbestos inhalation was killing employees, or when Ford failed to correct a known defect making the Pinto vulnerable to gas-tank explosions after low-speed, rear-end collisions.[78] Companies that dump dangerous medical waste into rivers and oceans also favor their own interests over public safety and welfare.

These examples are better known than many others, but they are not unusual. In fact, they may be far more typical than we would like. One expert estimates that approximately two-thirds of the 500 largest U.S. corporations have been involved in some form of illegal and unethical behavior.[79] Given the scope of the problems associated with unethical organizational behaviors, we focus here on the ethical aspects of politics.

What, If Anything, Is Unethical About Organizational Politics?

A few years ago, more than 1,000 human resource professionals were surveyed concerning their feelings about the ethics of various managerial practices.[80] Interestingly, *among the ethical situations considered to be most serious were several practices dealing with political activities reflecting abuse of power.* These included practices such as "making personnel decisions based on favoritism instead of job performance" and "basing differences in pay on friendship." In fact, these were the two most frequently cited types of unethical situations faced by human resource managers, with almost 31 percent indicating each was among *the* most serious violation.

Another type of unethical political behavior (indicated as being most serious by more than 23 percent of the sample) was "making arrangements with vendors or consulting agencies leading to personal gain." As shown in Figure 11.14, these actions are

FIGURE 11.14

Political Antics Top the "Most Unethical List"

Among the most widely reported sources of unethical behaviors in a survey of human resources managers were those dealing with an especially inappropriate form of political behaviors: favoritism.

(*Source*: Based on data reported by the Commerce Clearing House, 1991; see note 80.)

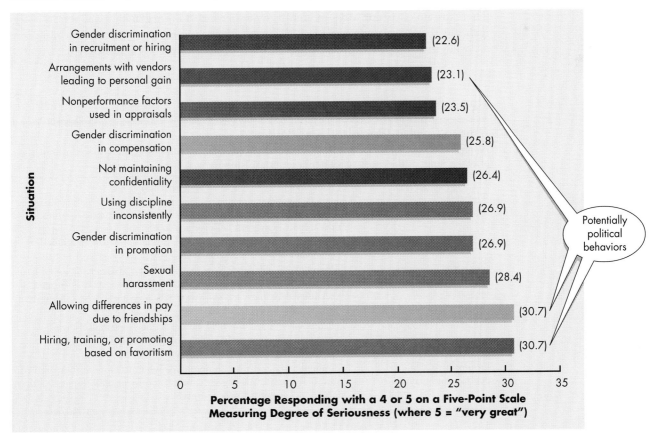

in addition to various other unethical behaviors that represent bias but that are not so clearly self-serving as to constitute political acts.

Given that so many critical ethics violations are politically motivated, self-serving actions, it is not surprising these were the very behaviors managers had the greatest difficulty addressing. In fact, only about half the managers surveyed reported any success in minimizing a problem such as hiring based on favoritism. That such behaviors benefit oneself makes them difficult to eliminate. In contrast, unethical behaviors based on insensitivity (e.g., lack of attention to privacy) are easier to combat, because these serve no beneficial functions for the person doing the violating.

Managers tend to be relatively unaware of the political biases underlying their unethical actions, however. Instead, they attribute their actions to the attitudes and behaviors of senior management. Specifically, only 10 percent of the participants attributed unethical behaviors to political pressures, but 56 percent attributed these to the attitudes and behaviors of senior management. They blamed top management most frequently for instances of unethical behavior, but they also recognized top management tends to be committed to ethical conduct. Despite such commitment, company officials tend to overlook the capacity of human resource managers to promote their company's ethical values. Too often, they concentrate on using such managers for maintaining up-to-date legal information about personnel matters.

Ethics goes well beyond mere compliance with the law, however, and society expects companies to go well beyond the ethical minimums. For these reasons—not to mention the long-term success of the companies themselves—*human resource officials must help institute policies that encourage basing personnel-related decisions on job performance instead of on favoritism.*[81] Considering the potential problems that may arise in organizations with a high amount of political activity, ways of curbing such behavior must be sought.[82] For several ways of doing so, see Table 11.3.

Assessing the Ethics of Political Behavior

There are no clear-cut ways to identify whether a certain organizational action is ethical, but there are some useful guidelines.[83] For a summary of the central questions associated with assessing the ethics of political behavior, see Figure 11.15.

TABLE 11.3

How to Combat Organizational Politics
Abolishing organizational politics completely may be impossible but managers can limit its effects. Some of the most successful tactics are summarized here.

SUGGESTION	DESCRIPTION
Clarify job expectations	Political behavior is nurtured by highly ambiguous conditions. To the extent managers help reduce uncertainty (e.g., by giving precise work assignments), they can minimize the likelihood of political behavior.
Open the communication process	People have difficulty fostering their own goals at the expense of organizational goals when the communication process is open to scrutiny. It is hard to "get away with anything" when the system is open for all to examine.
Be a good role model	Employees model the behavior of higher-ranking officials. Accordingly, an openly political manager may encourage subordinates to behave in the same way.
Do not turn a blind eye to game players	Immediately confront an employee who attempts to take credit for another's work. Managers who do not do so send a message that this kind of behavior is acceptable.

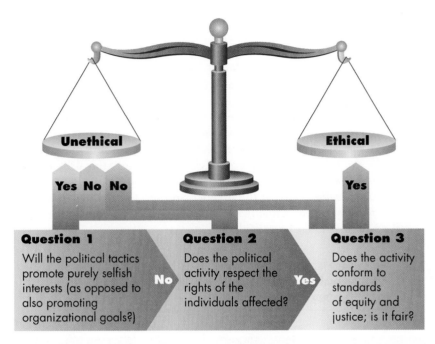

FIGURE 11.15

Guidelines for Determining Ethical Action

Assessing the ethicality of a behavior is a complex matter, but the three questions shown here can provide a good indication. This flowchart shows the path that must be taken to achieve ethical action.

(*Source*: Based on suggestions by Velasquez, Moberg, & Cavanaugh, 1983; see note 83.)

Are Only Selfish Interests Promoted?   First, will the political tactics promote purely selfish interests, or will they also help to meet organizational goals? If only one's personal, selfish interests are nurtured, political action may be unethical. Usually, but not always, political activity fails to benefit organizational goals. For example, suppose a group of top executives is consistently making bad decisions, which are leading the organization to ruin. Would political tactics to remove the power-holders from their positions be unethical in this case? Probably not. In fact, political actions designed to benefit the organization as a whole may be justified as being appropriate and highly ethical—as long as they are legal. After all, they are in the best interest of the entire organization.

Are Privacy Rights Respected?   Does the political activity respect the rights of the individuals who are affected? Generally, actions that violate basic human rights are, of course, unethical. For example, dirty political tricks that rely on espionage techniques (e.g., wiretapping) not only are illegal but also are unethical in that they violate the affected individual's *right to privacy*.

As you may know, however, police agencies sometimes are permitted by law to use methods that violate privacy rights when the greater good of the community is at stake. It is not easy to weigh the relative benefits of an individual's right to privacy against the greater societal good. Indeed, making such decisions involves a potential misuse of power in itself. Therefore, society often entrusts such decisions to high courts, which are charged with considering both individual rights as well as the rights and benefits of the community at large.

Is It Fair?   Does the activity conform to standards of equity and justice? Any political behavior that unfairly benefits one party over another may be unethical. Paying one person more than another, similarly qualified person is one example. Standards regarding the fair treatment of individuals often are unclear, however. Not surprisingly, more powerful individuals sometimes use their power to convince others (and themselves!) that they are taking action in the name of justice. In other words, they seek to implement seemingly fair rules that benefit themselves at the expense of others.[84] Of course, this represents an abuse of power.

Sometimes, however, we must consider instances in which violating standards of justice may be appropriate. For example, managers may give poorly performing employees higher pay than they deserve in the hope of stimulating them to work at higher levels.[85] The principle of equity (i.e., people should be paid in proportion to their job contributions) is violated in this case, but the manager may argue the employee and the organization benefit as a result. Of course, the result may be considered unfair by the other individuals who are not so generously treated. Obviously, we cannot settle this complex issue here. Our point is that ethical behavior involves adhering to standards of justice, but violations of these standards may be ethically acceptable in certain instances.

As you probably can tell, most matters involving moral and ethical issues are quite complex. *Each time a political strategy is considered, its potential effects should be evaluated in terms of the questions outlined here.* If the practice appears to be ethical based on these considerations, it may be acceptable in that situation. If ethical questions arise, however, alternative actions should be considered.

We invite you to visit the Greenberg page on the Prentice Hall Web site at: **www.prenhall.com/greenberg** for the monthly Greenberg update and for this chapter's World Wide Web exercise.

SUMMARY AND REVIEW OF LEARNING OBJECTIVES

1. **Distinguish between *social influence*, *power*, and *organizational politics*.**
   When someone attempts to affect another in a desired fashion, that person is said to be using **social influence**. The concept of **power** refers to the capacity to change behavior or attitudes of others in a desired manner. Behaving in a way that is not officially approved by an organization to meet one's own goals by influencing others is known as **organizational politics**.

2. **Characterize the major varieties of *social influence*.**
   Social influence may take the forms of *rational persuasion, inspirational appeal, consultation, ingratiation, exchange, personal appeal, coalition-building, legitimating,* and *pressure*.

3. **Describe the conditions under which various forms of *social influence* are used.**
   Different techniques are preferred when attempting to influence people at higher levels (e.g., consultation and ingratiation), at lower levels (e.g., inspirational appeals and pressure), and at equal levels (e.g., exchange and personal appeals). Overall, more open, consultative techniques are preferred to more coercive techniques.

4. **Identify the major types of individual *power* in organizations.**
   Position power, resides within one's formal organizational position. It includes **reward power** and **coercive power**, or the capacity to control valued rewards and punishments, respectively; **legitimate power**, or the recognized authority an individual has by virtue of his or her organizational position; and **information power**, or the power that stems from having special data and knowledge. **Personal power** resides within an individual's own unique qualities or characteristics. It includes **rational persuasion**, or using logical arguments and factual evidence to convince others an idea is acceptable; **expert power**, or the power an individual has because he or she is recognized as having some superior knowledge, skill, or

expertise; **referent power**, or influence arising because an individual is admired by others; and **charisma**, or having an engaging and magnetic personality.

5. **Explain the two major approaches to the development of subunit power in organizations (i.e., the *resource-dependency model* and the *strategic contingencies model*).**

   The **resource-dependence model** asserts that power resides within the subunits controlling the greatest share of valued organizational resources. The **strategic contingencies model** explains power in terms of a subunit's capacity to control the activities of other subunits. Such power may be enhanced by the capacity to reduce the uncertainty experienced by another unit, by having a central position within the organization, or by performing functions that other units cannot.

6. **Describe *organizational politics* as well as when and where it is likely to occur.**

   Political tactics may include blaming and attacking others, controlling access to information, cultivating a favorable impression, developing an internal base of support, and aligning oneself with more powerful others. These tactics also may involve the playing of political games, such as asserting one's authority, enhancing one's power base, attacking one's rivals, and trying to foster organizational change. Such activities typically occur under ambiguous conditions (e.g., in areas of organizational functioning without clear rules). Politics is likely to occur as well when organizational uncertainty exists, important decisions involving large amounts of scarce resources are made, and the groups involved have conflicting interests but approximately equal power. This is the case in human resource departments and during an organization's mature stage of development.

7. **Explain the major ethical issues surrounding political behavior in organizations.**

   Political behavior may be ethical to the extent it fosters organizational interests over individual greed, respects the rights of individuals, and conforms to prevailing standards of justice and fair play. The effects of organizational politics can be limited by practices such as clarifying job expectations, opening the communication process, being a good role model, and not turning a blind eye to game players.

QUESTIONS FOR DISCUSSION

1. Suppose your professor asks you to do a homework assignment again. Explain the various bases of individual social power he or she may use to influence your behavior in this situation.

2. Using the resource-dependency model and the strategic contingencies model as a basis, describe the relative power differences between groups in an organization with which you are familiar.

3. Describe the political tactics and tricks one person may use to gain a power advantage over another in an organization.

4. Suppose you are the manager of a human resources department. Are political activities more or less likely to occur in your department compared with others? Why, or why not? If more likely, what form might these actions be expected to take?

5. Argue for or against the following statement: The use of power in organizations is unethical.

6. It might not be possible to eliminate organizational politics completely, but it might be possible to effectively manage political activity. Describe some ways of coping with organizational politics.

Volkswagen's Bulldozer: Ferdinand Piëch

By all accounts, the new Volkswagen (VW) Beetle is a hit. The press and buyers alike have marveled at the advanced safety features and eye-catching style built into this modestly priced vehicle. The company's accountants cannot heap too much praise on a product that has lured customers back into VW dealerships, from which they have been driving away not only in Beetles but in all models in the showroom. On the strength of the Beetle and the highly acclaimed Passat family sedan, VW's balance sheet has soared from a loss of $1.1 billion in 1993 to earnings estimated at more than $2 billion in 1998, the year the new Beetle was launched. Industry insiders have not missed the fact that this stunning turnaround coincided with the arrival of a new CEO, Ferdinand Piëch.

Piëch has an impressive record in the German auto business. During the late 1960s, he turned Porsche into an auto-racing champion. During the 1970s and 1980s, he made Audi a technological leader by introducing innovations such as the first full-time, all-wheel-drive passenger car (i.e., the Quattro). With such impeccable credentials, you should not be surprised that Piëch's goals at VW are lofty: to reposition VW's image from a mass-marketer to one of the world's most esteemed brands. You may be surprised, however, at the highly "hands-on"—some would say, tyrannical—way he has gone about this.

Anyone at VW who questions Piëch's stance can expect to be looking for a new job. To consolidate his power, Piëch fired dozens of top executives who promised less than total support—20 in his first three years alone. Further ensuring he gets his own way, Piëch cut the management board to five members (from nine) and appointed himself its head. Almost no one speaks at meetings for fear of crossing Piëch—and getting the axe. Thus, meetings move quickly, because only "yes" men are left to make contributions.

This frees Piëch to make surprise visits to company facilities, including the sprawling Wolfsburg factory—where he keeps employees on guard by using fear as a motivator. While there, he is likely to get involved in production, research and development, and purchasing—areas over which he has assumed complete control. In contrast, at other auto companies, these functions are headed by separate directors. His grip on VW has been so intense that several years ago, company managers complained to board chairman Klaus Liesen in an open letter, which referred to Piëch as "a man with psychopathic traits."

Piëch's relations with the company's labor bosses have not been as one-sided, however. His control over them has been more a matter of give and take. Since his days at Audi, Piëch has maintained a loyal workforce by not laying off employees—even during the 1993 recession, when as many as 30,000 workers were unneeded. In exchange, the company's labor representatives—who by German law comprise half the supervisory board—back him in whatever he does, including the purchase of exotic auto companies such as Lamborghini (a move whose wisdom has been questioned).

Experts also have questioned how successful VW can remain while in the iron grip of Ferdinand Piëch. He has been called "the most brilliant and forward-looking CEO in the business today," but many think VW would be better off in the long term if Piëch would loosen his hold and allow the company to enjoy the usual checks and balances that come with more diffused power. Tell this to Piëch, however, and he'll likely dig in his heels even further—and then show you the door.

CRITICAL THINKING QUESTIONS

1. On what types of power does Ferdinand Piëch rely in running VW?

2. Is Piëch involved in any political game? If so, which ones?

3. What would happen at VW if Piëch passed away unexpectedly?

4. What conditions may have made it possible for Piëch to have such a tight hold on VW's management?

Influence, Power, and Politics in Organizations

SMALL BUSINESS 2000

If you were talking with friends on their cellular phone and they told you they were on "cloud nine," you probably would think that they were in a great mood and very happy about something. If they were calling you from San Diego, they probably would be telling you something completely different—that they were riding to the airport in a 12-passenger van. In San Diego, *Cloud 9* stands for a company that has more than 75 percent of the ground transportation market to and from the San Diego airport.

What makes Cloud 9 so interesting to us? There are several reasons, but of particular interest is how its leader took a bankrupt company with a weak image and mediocre employee morale and turned it into a market leader. John Hawkins will be the first to tell you he did not accomplish this alone. In Hawkins's words, "Our most important asset is the people." He is not referring to his customers, either; he is talking about his employees.

Hawkins has done a great deal to create a positive relationship with his employees. For example, Hawkins wanted a ride in a Cloud 9 van to be fun, so he had the whimsical company logo painted on them. He also wanted working at Cloud 9 to be a fun experience, so he put this same logo on the ties the employees wear. The idea was that these small things would encourage everyone to buy into the concept and to get as excited about their jobs as Hawkins and his managers were.

As you watch this clip, think about what you would have done if you were in Hawkins's shoes.

QUESTIONS FOR DISCUSSION

1. John Hawkins talks about what it was like to take over the Super Shuttle franchise in San Diego and transform it into what is now Cloud 9 Shuttle. Hawkins is the man in charge, and he seems to have been successful in bringing along some employees of the old company and gaining the support of new hires. What do you think Hawkins did to gain this support? On what foundation do you think Hawkins established his power base within the company?

2. Consider what you have learned about the resource-dependency and strategic contingencies models. With that in mind, identify a team in Cloud 9, and discuss how it might use one of these models to gain power for itself.

3. Cloud 9 is a company that hit bottom and came out swinging. We can assume many eyes were on this company when it emerged from bankruptcy. We also can assume the company's resources were limited. What types of political issues within the organization do you think the managers might have thought about? Do you think this was a stage of the company's development at which politics were an issue? Why, or why not?

SKILLS BANK

EXPERIENCING ORGANIZATIONAL BEHAVIOR

What Kinds of Power Does Your Supervisor Use?

One way to learn about social influence in organizations is to use questionnaires asking people to describe the behaviors of their superiors. A consistent pattern regarding how subordinates describe superiors provides strong clues about that superior's influence style. These questionnaires are similar to the one presented here. Complete this questionnaire to get an idea of the types of social influence favored by your supervisor.

439

Directions

Indicate how strongly you agree or disagree with each of the following statements in regard to your immediate supervisor. Answer using the following scale:

1 = strongly disagree
2 = disagree
3 = neither agree nor disagree
4 = agree
5 = strongly agree

For each statement, select the number corresponding to the most appropriate response. Then, score your responses following the directions below.

My supervisor can:

_____ 1. Recommend I receive a raise.
_____ 2. Assign me to jobs I dislike.
_____ 3. See I get the promotion I desire.
_____ 4. Make my life at work completely unbearable.
_____ 5. Make decisions about how things are done.
_____ 6. Provide useful advice on how to do my job better.
_____ 7. Comprehend the importance of doing things a certain way.
_____ 8. Make me want to look up to him or her.
_____ 9. Share with me the benefit of his or her vast job knowledge.
_____ 10. Get me to admire the things for which he or she stands.
_____ 11. Find out things nobody else knows.
_____ 12. Explain things so logically I want to do them.
_____ 13. Have access to vital data about the company.
_____ 14. Share a clear vision of what the future holds for the company.
_____ 15. Present the facts needed to make a convincing case about something.
_____ 16. Put me in a trance when he or she communicates to me.

Scoring

1. Add the numbers assigned to statements 1 and 3. This is the *reward power* score.
2. Add the numbers assigned to statements 2 and 4. This is the *coercive power* score.
3. Add the numbers assigned to statements 5 and 7. This is the *legitimate power* score.
4. Add the numbers assigned to statements 6 and 9. This is the *expert power* score.
5. Add the numbers assigned to statements 8 and 10. This is the *referent power* score.
6. Add the numbers assigned to statements 11 and 13. This is the *information power* score.
7. Add the numbers assigned to statements 12 and 15. This is the *rational persuasion* score.
8. Add the numbers assigned to statements 14 and 16. This is the *charisma* score.

Questions for Discussion

1. In which dimensions did your supervisor score highest and lowest? Are these consistent with what you would have predicted in advance?

2. Does your supervisor behave in ways consistent with the dimension along which you gave him or her the highest score? In other words, does he or she fit the description given in the text?

3. How would your own subordinates answer these various questions regarding yourself?

4. Which of the eight forms of social influence do you think are most common and least common? Why?

(*Source*: Adapted from Schriesheim & Hinkin, 1990; see note 4.)

WORKING IN GROUPS

Recognizing Organizational Politics When You See It

A good way to understand organizational politics is to practice different political tactics and attempt to recognize these tactics when portrayed by others. This exercise is designed with these objectives in mind. The more practiced you are at recognizing political activity, the better equipped you may be to defend yourself against it.

Directions

1. Divide the class into groups of approximately four students each.

2. Each group should select, at random, one of the six major political tactics described in this chapter, including any of the political games included in Table 11.2.

3. Meeting together for approximately 30 minutes, each group should prepare a brief skit in which the members enact the political tactic. These skits should be as realistic as possible and not written simply to broadcast the answer. In other words, the tactic should be presented much as you would expect to see it used in a real organization.

4. Each group should take a turn presenting its skit to the class. Feel free to announce the setting or context in which your portrayal occurs. Don't worry about giving an award-winning performance; it's okay to keep a script or set of notes in your hand. The important thing is depicting the political tactic in a realistic manner.

5. After each group presents its skit, the class should identify the specific tactic depicted. This should lead to a discussion of the clues suggesting that answer as well as of additional things that could have been done to depict the particular tactic.

Questions for Discussion

1. How successful was the class in identifying the various political tactics? Were some tactics more difficult to portray than others.

2. Based on these portrayals, which tactics do you believe are most likely to be used in organizations? Under what circumstances might these tactics be used?

3. Which political tactics do you believe are most negative? Why?

4. Using the suggestions in Table 11.3, how can the effects of the most negative political tactics be combatted?

LEADERSHIP IN ORGANIZATIONS

After reading this chapter, you should be able to

1. Define *leadership*, and explain how leading differs from *managing*.
2. Describe the *trait approach to leadership*, and identify what distinguishes successful leaders from ordinary people.
3. Describe various forms of participative and autocratic leadership behavior.
4. Distinguish the two basic forms of leader behavior — *person-oriented* behavior and *production-oriented* behavior — and explain how *grid training* helps to develop both.
5. Explain the *leader-member exchange (LMX) model* and the *attributional approach to leadership* in terms of the relationships between leaders and followers.
6. Describe *charismatic* leadership and how it compares with *transformational* leadership.
7. Explain the *contingency theories* of leader effectiveness.
8. Summarize the *LPC contingency theory* and the *situational leadership theory* in terms of the connection between leadership style and situational variables.
9. Explain *path-goal theory* and *normative decision theory*.
10. Describe the *substitutes for leadership approach* and what it says about the conditions when leaders are needed in the workplace.

PREVIEW CASE

Chan Suh: Not Your Typical Advertising Executive—Yet

You see them whenever you visit web sites—those flashy banner ads, beckoning for your attention with catchy text and animated graphics. You probably never think about how they get there, but this is the main thought in Chan Suh's head these days. A 37-year-old Korean who moved to New York with his mother in 1976, Suh is the founder and CEO of Agency.com, one of the largest interactive, on-line ad agencies around these days.

Interactive advertising comprises only one-half percent of a $200 billion overall market, but its potential is enormous. In 1998 alone, the four-year-old Agency.com quadrupled in size, with sales zooming from $18 million to $80 million. Its client list—including Ford, GTE, Hitachi, Metropolitan Life Insurance, and British Airways—would be the envy of any traditional, Big Six advertising agency as well. Unlike these firms, however, Agency.com is not populated by slick executives in tailored suits, luxuriating in the wood-paneled suites of New York high-rises. Instead, Agency.com's casually attired, body-pierced twenty-somethings work in a poorly ventilated room over the loading dock in Manhattan's Time-Life building.

Suh considers himself fortunate to have these 600 talented employees as well as the space itself—his first major business asset. Bankers laughed at his business plan in 1995, but Suh was determined to launch his agency. So, capitalizing on the good will he developed with his former employer, Time-Life (for whom he developed *Vibe* on-line before venturing out on his own), Suh struck a deal that got him space in exchange for completing several projects. One of these was the highly regarded web site for the 1995 *Sports Illustrated* swimsuit-edition video. On the strength of his successful experiences with Time-Life, Suh attracted more blue-chip clients for whom he struck gold. For example, the web site Agency.com developed for MetLife grew in popularity from 300,000 hits in 1996, before Suh's influence, to more than four million hits in 1997 after he took over. In addition, this web site was only one of more than two dozen for which the company won awards for various clients in 1998, including a prestigious Clio for Pacific Bell.

For Agency.com to continue to grow—or to survive the inevitable, forthcoming shakeout in the interactive advertising business—Suh realizes his company must almost double in the next 18 months. As clients grow more sophisticated, however, they are moving from being knocked-out by the novel, whiz-bang technology to demanding results—that is, a return on their advertising investment. Suh knows this will keep him busy hiring the most talented and creative people he can find—individuals who share his vision for taking technology where no advertising agency has ever been.

Having a vision—and chasing it—keeps Chan Suh navigating these uncharted waters. After all, only a true visionary and pioneer would say, "We love the fact that we get to invent the future while we live in it." If Suh's vision continues being as accurate as it has been, he should easily reach the goal of making Agency.com a $1 billion company by 2003. We have no doubt he will do so.

Name some of the most important business leaders throughout history. Who did you identify? John D. Rockefeller at Standard Oil, or Tom Watson at IBM? Alfred Sloan at General Motors, or Bill Gates at Microsoft? Indeed, these—and many others—are fine choices.

These individuals come to mind because their accomplishments as business leaders have been well publicized. Such well-known leaders, however, represent only the tip of a much larger iceberg. Mirroring their accomplishments are untold thousands of less visible individuals—such as Chan Suh—who are no less important and toil daily in businesses both large and small.

In fact, if you were to describe Chan Suh's ground-breaking accomplishments at Agency.com, you could hardly do so without referring to his impressive *leadership*. Agency.com would not exist without him, after all, and his pioneering vision is what keeps the company so successful. Suh is certainly a unique individual, but he also is one of many who have risen above the pack to make their organizations special—that is, people we refer to as **leaders**. Indeed, leadership is a key ingredient in corporate effectiveness.[1] As you might imagine, the importance of leadership is not restricted to business organizations, either. Indeed, leadership also plays a central role in politics, sports, and many other activities.[2]

leaders

Individuals within groups or organizations who wield the most influence over others.

Given its importance, leadership has been one of the most widely studied concepts in the social sciences.[3] To make the task of summarizing this wealth of information more manageable, we proceed as follows. First, we consider some basic points about leadership, such as what it is and why being a leader is not necessarily synonymous with being a manager. We then examine views of leadership that focus on the traits of leaders and on leaders' behaviors. Next, we examine several major theories of leadership, which focus on the relationship between leaders and their followers. Finally, we review several contrasting theories dealing with the conditions under which leaders are effective — or ineffective.

THE NATURE OF LEADERSHIP

In a sense, leadership resembles love: It is something most people believe they can recognize but often cannot define. So, what is leadership, and how does being a leader differ from being a manager?

Leadership: A Working Definition

Imagine you accept a new job and enter a new work group. How do you recognize its leader? One possibility, of course, is through the formal titles and assigned roles of each person in the group. In short, the individual who is designated as the department head or project manager is the one you would identify as being the group's leader.

Imagine, however, that during several staff meetings, you notice this person really is not the most influential. She or he holds the formal authority, but these meetings actually are dominated by another person — who ostensibly is a subordinate. What can you conclude about leadership now? Probably that the real leader of the group is the person who actually runs things, not the person with the fancy title and the apparent authority.

In many cases, this disparity does not exist. The individual possessing the most formal authority also is the most influential. In some situations, however, this is not so, and then we typically identify the person who actually exercises the most influence over the group as being its leader. These facts point to the following working definition of leadership, and one accepted by many experts on this topic: **leadership** is the process whereby one individual influences group members toward attaining defined group or organizational goals.[4] For a summary of the leadership process, see Figure 12.1.

leadership
The process whereby one individual influences other group members toward attaining defined group or organizational goals.

Leadership Involves Noncoercive Influence According to this definition, leadership primarily involves influence — that is, a leader changes the actions or attitudes of several group members or subordinates. As discussed in chapter 11, many techniques for exerting influence exist. These range from relatively coercive ones (i.e., the recipient has little choice but to do what is requested) to relatively noncoercive ones (i.e., the recipient can accept or reject the influence). In general, leadership refers to the use of noncoercive techniques. This is what distinguishes a leader from a *dictator*: Whereas dictators get others to do what they want using physical coercion or threats of physical force, leaders do not.[5]

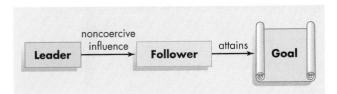

FIGURE 12.1

The Leadership Process: A Summary

Leadership is a process in which one person, the *leader*, influences a *follower* in a noncoercive manner to attain a goal.

Mao Zedong, founder of the People's Republic of China, said, "Power grows out of the barrel of a gun." This may be true regarding the power of dictators — but *not* regarding the power of leaders. At least in part, leadership rests on positive feelings between leaders and their subordinates. In other words, subordinates accept the influence of leaders because they respect, like, or admire them — not because they hold positions of formal authority.[6]

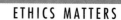

ETHICS MATTERS Leadership is founded on noncoercive influence. In actual practice, however, leaders sometimes do cross the line and use coercive means. This constitutes an abuse of leadership, and it is not the most effective way to lead people. ■

Leadership Influence Is Goal-directed   The definition presented here suggests that leadership involves the exercise of influence for a purpose — that is, to attain defined group or organizational goals. In other words, leaders focus on altering those actions or attitudes of their subordinates that relate to specific goals. They are less concerned with altering actions or attitudes that are irrelevant to such goals.

Leadership Requires Followers   By emphasizing the central role of influence, our definition implies that leadership really is a two-way street. Leaders influence subordinates in various ways, but leaders also are influenced by their subordinates. In fact, it may be said that leadership exists only in relation to followers. (After all, one cannot lead without followers!)

Leaders Versus Managers: A Key Distinction — at Least in Theory

In everyday speech, the terms *leader* and *manager* tend to be used interchangeably. We understand the temptation to do so, but these terms are not identical and must be distinguished. In essence, the primary function of a *leader* is to create the essential purpose or mission of the organization and the strategy for attaining it. In contrast, the primary function of a *manager* is to implement that vision.

Essentially, the manager's job is to put into practice the means to achieve the leader's vision. Thus, whereas management is about coping with complexity, leadership is about coping with change. Specifically, managers create plans and monitor results, but leaders establish direction by creating a vision of the future. Thus, effective leaders get people to believe in their vision — and to go along with it.[7]

These differences are simple to articulate, but the distinction between establishing and implementing a mission often is blurred in practice (Figure 12.2). This is be-

FIGURE   12.2

Leaders and Managers: Distinguishing Their Roles

Leaders primarily are responsible for establishing an organizational mission, whereas *managers* primarily are responsible for implementing that mission through others. The intermediate steps (i.e., formulating a strategy for the mission, increasing people's commitment toward it) tend to be performed by either leaders or managers. These overlapping functions blur the distinction between leaders and managers in actual practice.

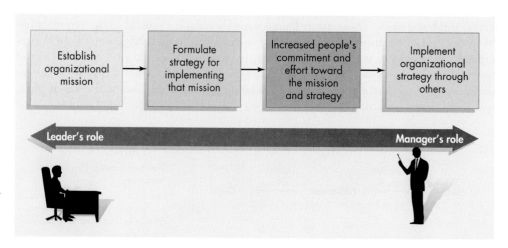

cause many leaders (e.g., top corporate executives) frequently must create a vision, formulate a strategy for implementing it, and also increase people's commitment toward that vision and plan. In contrast, managers are charged with implementing organizational strategy through others. At the same time, however, managers frequently are involved also in helping to formulate strategy and with increasing people's commitment and effort toward implementing that plan.

In summary, leaders and managers play several overlapping roles in actual practice, which makes distinguishing between them difficult. Some managers also are considered leaders, whereas others are not. Similarly, some leaders take on more of a management role than others. Thus, although these differences are not always obvious, they are real. For this reason, we distinguish carefully between leaders and managers throughout this chapter.

THE TRAIT APPROACH TO LEADERSHIP: HAVING THE RIGHT STUFF

Most people have daydreams about being a leader. They fantasize about taking charge of large groups—and about being viewed with great awe and respect. Despite the prevalence of such dreams, however, relatively few individuals become leaders. Furthermore, among those who do, only a small proportion are considered to be effective in this role.

This raises an intriguing question: What sets effective leaders apart from most others? In other words, why do some people—but not others—become effective leaders? One of the most widely studied approaches to this question suggests that effective leadership is based on the characteristics people have. In short, people become leaders because, in some special ways, they are different from others.[8] This is known as the **trait approach to leadership**.

trait approach to leadership
The idea that people become leaders because of the special traits they possess.

The Great Person Theory

Are some people born to lead? Common sense suggests they are. Great leaders of the past, such as Alexander the Great, Queen Elizabeth I, and Abraham Lincoln, do seem to differ from ordinary human beings in several respects. Contemporary leaders, such as Colin Powell, Ronald Reagan, and John Glenn, do as well. No matter what you may feel about these individuals, you have to agree they all possess high levels of ambition coupled with clear visions of precisely where they wanted to go. To a lesser degree, even leaders without such history-shaping fame seem to differ from their followers.

GLOBAL MATTERS

Because of our familiarity with leaders from our own culture, we tend to think of these individuals first when identifying "the greats." Great leaders, however, may be found throughout the world. British Prime Minister Margaret Thatcher is a prime example, as is Pope John Paul II. Can you identify several others? ■

Top executives, some politicians, and even sports figures often seem to possess an aura that sets them apart. Contemporary theorists have expressed this idea as follows:

[I]t is unequivocally clear that leaders are not like other people. Leaders do not have to be great men or women by being intellectual geniuses or omniscient prophets to succeed, but they do need to have the "right stuff" and this stuff is not equally present in all people. Leadership is a demanding, unrelenting job with enormous pressures and grave responsibilities. It would be a profound disservice to

leaders to suggest that they are ordinary people who happened to be in the right place at the right time. . . . In the realm of leadership (and in every other realm), the individual does matter.[9]

great person theory

The view that leaders possess special traits, which set them apart from others, and that these traits are responsible for their positions of power and authority.

This approach to the study of leadership is known as the **great person theory**. According to this orientation, great leaders possess key traits that set them apart from most other humans. Furthermore, the theory contends these traits remain stable over time and across different groups. Thus, it suggests all great leaders share these characteristics, regardless of when or where they lived or the precise role in history they fulfilled.

What Are the Characteristics of Great Leaders?

What are the characteristics of great leaders? In other words, in what measurable ways do successful leaders differ from people in general? Researchers have identified several such characteristics, which are listed in Table 12.1.[10] Most of these characteristics (e.g., drive, honesty and integrity, self-confidence) require no elaboration. Several others, however, are not quite as obvious.[11]

leadership motivation

The desire to influence others, especially toward attaining shared goals.

personalized power motivation

The wish to dominate others, reflected in an excessive concern with status.

socialized power motivation

The desire to cooperate with others, to work with them rather than dominate or control them.

Leadership Motivation: The Desire to Lead   Consider what has been termed **leadership motivation**, which refers to a leader's desire to influence others and, in essence, to lead. Such motivation can take two distinct forms. First, it may cause leaders to seek power as an end in itself. Leaders who demonstrate such **personalized power motivation** wish to dominate others, and their desire to do so often is reflected in an excessive concern with status. In contrast, leadership motivation also may cause leaders to seek power as a means to achieve desired, shared goals. Leaders who evidence such **socialized power motivation** cooperate with others, develop networks and coalitions, and generally work with subordinates rather than dominate or control them. Needless to say, this type of leadership motivation usually is far more adaptive for organizations.

Special Abilities   As you might expect, the most effective leaders tend to possess special abilities; however, these abilities are not always the ones you might expect. For example, consider *cognitive ability*. It should be no surprise that effective leaders are intelligent and capable of integrating and interpreting large amounts of information. Mental genius does not seem to be necessary, however, and in some cases, this quality may prove to be detrimental.[12] Thus, although the best leaders surely are smart, they tend not to be geniuses.

TABLE 12.1

Characteristics of Successful Leaders

Successful leaders possess many of the traits listed here.

TRAIT OR CHARACTERISTIC	DESCRIPTION
Drive	Desire for achievement, ambition, high energy, tenacity, and initiative.
Honesty and integrity	Trustworthy, reliable, and open.
Leadership motivation	Desire to influence others to reach shared goals.
Self-confidence	Trust in own abilities.
Cognitive ability	Intelligence; ability to integrate and interpret large amounts of information.
Knowledge of the business	Knowledge of industry and relevant technical matters.
Creativity	Capacity to come up with original ideas.
Flexibility	Ability to adapt to needs of followers and the situation.

Unfortunately, we have become aware of the morally questionable behavior of many top leaders—including U.S. President Bill Clinton, who was impeached in December 1998. Many of the most successful leaders, however, pay scrupulous attention to high moral values. ■

Another special characteristic of effective leaders is *flexibility*, which refers to the ability of leaders to recognize which actions are required and then to act accordingly. Evidence suggests the most effective leaders are not prone to behave in the same ways all the time but instead to be adaptive, matching their style to the needs of followers or the demands of the situations they face.[13]

LEADERSHIP BEHAVIOR: WHAT DO LEADERS DO?

The trait approach to leadership focuses on the appealing idea that certain characteristics distinguish effective leaders from others. In short, it focuses on *who leaders are*. As plausible as this approach may be, however, it also makes sense to consider that leaders may be distinctive in how they behave. In other words, we can supplement our focus on leadership traits by paying attention to leadership behavior—that is, by examining *what leaders do*.

The leadership approach is appealing, because it offers an optimistic view of the leadership process. All of us may not be born with "the right stuff," but we certainly can strive to do "the right things"—that is, to do what it takes to *become* a leader. The general question underlying the behavioral approach is simple: What do leaders do that make them effective? As we describe here, there are several good answers.

Participative and Autocratic Leadership Behaviors

When describing the behavior of leaders, one key variable involves how much influence they allow subordinates to have over decisions. There are two ways of describing these behaviors.

The Autocratic-Delegation Continuum Model Think about the bosses you have had in your life or career. Can you remember one who wanted to control everything—that is, someone who made every decision, told people precisely what to do, and wanted to run the entire show? Such a person is said to be **autocratic**. In contrast, can you recall a boss who allowed employees to make their own decisions? If so, this individual would be described as relying on *delegation*.

You probably know supervisors who have acted in ways that fall between these two extremes—that is, bosses who invited your input, were open to suggestions, and allowed you to perform various tasks in your own way. These individuals may be said to be using a *participative* leadership style; more precisely, they may be *consulting* with you or involving you in a *joint decision* of some sort. In either case, you were more involved than you would have been with an autocratic leader but less involved than you would have been with a leader who delegated all responsibility to you. For a summary of this **autocratic-delegation continuum model**, see Figure 12.3.

autocratic (leadership style)
A style of leadership in which the leader makes all decisions unilaterally.

autocratic-delegation continuum model
An approach to leadership describing how leaders allocate influence to subordinates. This ranges from controlling everything (i.e., *autocratic*) to allowing others to make decisions for themselves (i.e., *delegating*). Between these extremes are more participative forms of leadership (i.e., *consulting* and making *joint decisions*).

People from all cultures are not equally likely to practice participative leadership. For example, in Sweden, participation in work-related decisions is mandated by law. Not surprisingly, some of the most actively participative, openly democratic leadership styles are found there. ■

FIGURE 12.3

The Autocratic-Delegation Continuum Model

Traditionally, the amount of influence leaders give to followers has been summarized as a continuum ranging from *autocratic* behavior (i.e., no influence) to *delegation* behavior (i.e., high influence). *Consultation* and *joint decisions* are intermediate forms of *participation* in decision making.

(*Source*: Based on suggestions by Yukl, 1998; see note 2.)

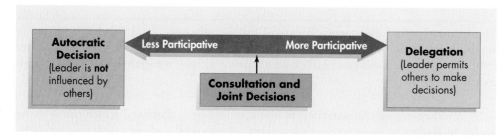

The autocratic-delegation continuum model reasonably describes the role of leaders in organizational decision making, but it also is regarded as being overly simplistic. In fact, describing a leader's participation in decision making involves two separate dimensions.[14]

two-dimensional model of subordinate participation

An approach to leadership describing the nature of how leaders influence followers. This model distinguishes between leaders who are *directive* or *permissive* toward subordinates and the extent to which they are *participative* or *autocratic* in their decision making. Individual leaders may be classified into four types by where they fall on a grid combining these two dimensions.

The Two-Dimensional Model of Subordinate Participation   Acknowledging the need for a more sophisticated approach, scientists have proposed the **two-dimensional model of subordinate participation**. As the name implies, this model describes subordinates' participation in decisions regarding two dimensions.

The *autocratic-democratic* dimension characterizes the extent to which leaders permit subordinates to take part in decisions. The autocratic extreme is marked by no participation, whereas the democratic extreme is marked by high participation. The *permissive-directive* dimension involves the extent to which leaders direct the activities of subordinates and tell them how to perform their jobs. The permissive extreme is marked by not telling subordinates how to do their jobs, whereas the directive extreme is marked by considerable attempts at doing so. Combining these two variables yields the four possible patterns described in Table 12.2:

1. The *directive autocrat.*
2. The *permissive autocrat.*
3. The *directive democrat.*
4. The *permissive democrat.*

TABLE 12.2

The Two-Dimensional Model of Subordinate Participation

Leaders can be described as having different styles based on how they involve subordinates in making decisions about how to do their jobs. Four distinct styles are summarized here.

ARE SUBORDINATES TOLD EXACTLY HOW TO DO THEIR JOBS?	ARE SUBORDINATES PERMITTED TO PARTICIPATE IN MAKING DECISIONS?	
	YES (*DEMOCRATIC*)	NO (*AUTOCRATIC*)
Yes (*directive*)	**Directive democrat** (*makes decisions participatively; closely supervises subordinates*)	**Directive autocrat** (*makes decisions unilaterally; closely supervises subordinates*)
No (*permissive*)	**Permissive democrat** (*makes decisions participatively; gives subordinates latitude in carrying out their work*)	**Permissive autocrat** (*makes decisions unilaterally; gives subordinates latitude in carrying out their work*)

Source: Based on suggestions by Muczyk & Reimann, 1987; see note 14.

Any attempt to divide human beings into discrete categories raises thorny issues, but these patterns seem to make good sense. Many managers adopt a leadership style that fits (at least roughly) within one.

Given that leaders differ along these two dimensions and, thus, can be classified as falling into one of the patterns listed, do any of these divisions have a clear-cut edge? In short, is one pattern superior to the others in many—if not most—situations? So far, evidence suggests this is doubtful. All four styles seem to involve a mixed pattern of advantages and disadvantages. Moreover—and this is crucial—the relative success of each depends heavily on the conditions within a given organization as well as on that organization's specific stage of development.

To illustrate, consider a manager who is a *directive autocrat*. This person makes decisions without consulting subordinates and supervise their work activities closely. It is tempting to view such a pattern as being undesirable, because it runs counter to the value of personal freedom. Actually, however, this approach may be highly successful in some settings, such as when employees are inexperienced or underqualified or subordinates adopt an adversarial stance toward management and must be closely supervised. As you might imagine, such managers tend to be unpopular. For an extreme example of a directive autocrat, see Figure 12.4.

In contrast, consider the *permissive autocrat*—that is, a leader who combines permissive supervision with an autocratic style of decision making. This pattern may be useful with employees who have a high level of technical skill and want to be left alone to manage their own jobs (e.g., scientists, engineers, computer programmers) but who have little desire to participate in routine decision making. The remaining two patterns—*directive democrat* and *permissive democrat*—also are most suited to specific organizational conditions. Thus, the key task for leaders is to match their own style to the needs of their organization—and to change their styles as these needs shift and evolve.

What happens when leaders lack such flexibility? Actual events in one now-defunct company—People Express—are instructive.[15] Don Burr, the founder and CEO of this airline, had a clear managerial style: He was a highly permissive democrat. He involved employees in many aspects of decision making, and he emphasized autonomy in work activities. Indeed, he felt everyone at People Express should be viewed as a "manager." While the company was young, this style worked well, but as it grew and increased in complexity, such practices created mounting difficulties. New employees were not necessarily as committed as the older ones, so permissive supervision was ineffective with them. In addition, as decisions increased in both complexity and number, a participative approach became less appropriate. Unfortunately, however, top management was reluctant to alter their style, which seemed to have been instrumental in the company's early success. Along with many other factors, this

FIGURE 12.4

Al "Chainsaw" Dunlap: A Directive Autocrat

Known for his take-no-prisoners approach to leadership, Al Dunlap is widely regarded as a "Corporate Rambo." A ferocious cost-cutter best known for orchestrating major layoffs at Scott Paper and Sunbeam, he has earned the nickname "Chainsaw." When Dunlap was fired from Sunbeam in 1998, the announcement met with cheers from the many thousands of laid-off workers he had ousted through the years.

poor match between the style of top leaders and the changing external conditions seems to have contributed to People Express' ultimate demise.

To conclude, no single leadership style is best. Recognizing the importance of differences in conditions and situations, however, can be a constructive first step toward assuring the style most suited to a given organization is, in fact, adopted. (The difference between participative and more directive styles of leadership is especially important in self-managed work teams. For suggestions regarding how to lead such units, see the "Tips" section below.

TIPS: DOING IT RIGHT

■ Self-Managed Teams: Leading People to Manage Themselves

When most people think of leaders, they think of individuals who make strategic decisions on behalf of followers, who then are responsible for carrying out these decisions. In many of today's organizations, however, the movement toward *self-managed teams* predominates. Thus, leaders are less likely than ever to be responsible for getting others to implement their orders to fulfill their visions. Instead, team leaders may be called on to provide special resources to groups that are empowered to implement their own missions in their own ways. These leaders do not call all the shots; rather, they help subordinates to take responsibility for their own work.

This suggests the role of team leader clearly differs from the traditional, "command-and-control" role discussed in this chapter.[16] Here are a few guidelines that may help you to achieve success as a team leader:

1. Instead of directing people, *team leaders build trust and inspire teamwork*. One way to do so is by encouraging interaction between all members as well as between the team and its customers and suppliers. Another key ingredient is to take initiatives to make things better. Instead of taking a reactive, "if-it-ain't-broke, don't-fix-it" approach, teams may be lead to success by individuals who set a good example for improving the quality of their efforts.

2. Rather than focusing simply on training individuals, *team leaders concentrate on expanding team capabilities*. In this connection, team leaders function primarily as coaches. These leaders help the team by providing all members with the skills needed to perform the task, remove barriers that might interfere with success, and find the necessary resources to get the job done. Likewise, team leaders work at building the confidence of team members, thereby cultivating their untapped potential.

3. Instead of managing one-on-one, *team leaders create a team identity*. In other words, leaders must help teams to understand their missions and to recognize what the leaders are doing to help fulfill it. In this connection, team leaders may help the group to set goals, point out how they may adjust their performance when they do not meet them, and plan celebrations when they do.

4. Traditional leaders work at preventing conflict between individuals, but *team leaders make the most of team differences*. Without doubt, melding a group of diverse individuals into a highly committed and productive team is a challenge, but doing so is important. This can be done by building respect for diverse points of view, by making sure all members are encouraged to present their views, and by respecting these ideas once they are expressed.

5. Unlike traditional leaders who simply react to change, *team leaders should foresee and influence change*. To the extent leaders recognize change is inevitable (a point we emphasize in chapter 16), they may be better prepared to make

the various adaptations required. Effective team leaders continuously scan the business environment for clues that changes are forthcoming, and they help teams to decide on their response.

In conclusion, leading teams is a far cry from leading individuals in the traditional directive — or even participative — manner. The special nature of teams makes the leader's job very different. Appreciating these differences is easy, but making the appropriate adjustments may be extremely challenging — especially for those individuals well practiced in traditional leadership. Given the prevalence of teams in today's work environment, however, the importance of making these adjustments cannot be overstated. Leading new teams using old methods is a sure formula for failure. ■

Person-Oriented and Production-Oriented Leaders

Think again about all the bosses you have had in your career. Now, divide them into two categories: those who were relatively effective, and those who were relatively ineffective. How do the two groups differ?

If you think about this issue carefully, your answers are likely to take one of two forms. First, you might reply, "My most effective bosses helped me to get the job done. They gave me advice, answered my questions, and let me know exactly what was expected. My most ineffective bosses didn't do this." Alternatively, you might answer, "My most effective bosses seemed to care about me as a person. They were friendly, listened when I had problems or questions, and seemed to help me toward my personal goals. My most ineffective bosses didn't do this."

A large body of research, much of it conducted during the 1950s at the University of Michigan[17] and at the Ohio State University,[18] suggests leaders differ greatly along these dimensions. Those at the high end of the first dimension, which is known as **initiating structure** (or **production-oriented**), mainly are concerned with production and primarily focus on getting the job done. They engage in actions such as organizing work, inducing subordinates to follow rules, setting goals, and making the leader and subordinate roles explicit. In contrast, other leaders are lower on this dimension, and they show less tendency to engage in these actions.

Leaders at the high end of the second dimension, which is known as **consideration** (or **person-oriented**), primarily focus on establishing good relations with their subordinates and on being liked by them. They engage in actions such as doing favors for subordinates, explaining things to them, and assuring their welfare. In contrast, other leaders are low on this dimension, and they do not really care how well they get along with subordinates.

At first glance, you might assume initiating structure and consideration are linked — that is, such people who are high on one of these dimensions automatically are low on the other. This is not the case, however. The two dimensions actually seem to be largely independent.[19] Thus, a leader may be high on both concern with production and concern for people, high on one of these dimensions and low on the other, moderate on one and high on the other, and so on (Figure 12.5).

Is any one pattern best? This is a complex issue. Both production-oriented and people-oriented leadership behaviors offer a mixed pattern of advantages and disadvantages. For showing consideration (i.e., high concern with people and human relations), the major benefits are improved group atmosphere and morale.[20] Leaders high on this dimension are reluctant to act in a directive manner toward subordinates, however, and they often shy away from presenting negative feedback. Thus, productivity sometimes suffers. For initiating structure (i.e., high concern with production), efficiency and performance sometimes are enhanced by this leadership style. If leaders focus entirely on production, however, employees soon may conclude no one cares about them or their welfare. Thus, work-related attitudes such as job satisfaction and organizational commitment may suffer.

initiating structure
Activities by a leader to enhance productivity or task performance. Leaders who focus primarily on these goals are described as demonstrating a task-oriented style.

production-oriented
See *initiating structure*.

consideration
Actions by a leader that demonstrate concern with the welfare of subordinates and establish positive relations with them. Leaders who focus primarily on this task are described as demonstrating a person-oriented style.

person-oriented
See *consideration*.

FIGURE   12.5

Two Basic Dimensions of Leader Behavior

A leader's behavior can vary from low to high regarding *consideration* (i.e., person orientation) and *initiating structure* (i.e., task orientation). Patterns of leader behavior produced by variations along these two dimensions are illustrated here.

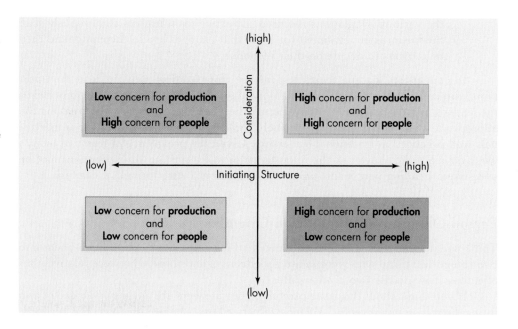

Having said this, one specific pattern may, indeed, have an edge in many settings. This is a pattern in which leaders demonstrate high concern with people *and* with production.[21] High amounts of concern with people (i.e., showing consideration) and with productivity (i.e., initiating structure) are not incompatible. In fact, skillful leaders can combine both these orientations into their overall styles to produce favorable results. Thus, although no one leadership style is best, leaders who combine these two concerns often have an important edge over those showing one or the other (Figure 12.6). In the words of U.S. Army Lieutenant General William G. Pagonis:

> *To lead successfully, a person must demonstrate . . . expertise and empathy. In my experience, both of these traits can be deliberately and systematically cultivated; this personal development is the first important building block of leadership.*[22]

Developing Successful Leader Behavior: Grid Training

How can one develop concern for production and concern for people? A technique known as **grid training** proposes a multistep process to cultivate these two important skills.[23]

The initial step consists of a *grid seminar* — that is, a session in which managers who previously have been trained in the appropriate theory and skills help organization members to analyze their own management styles. This is done using a specially designed questionnaire that allows managers to determine where they stand regarding their *concern for production* and *concern for people*. Each participant's approach on each dimension is scored using a number ranging from 1 (low) to 9 (high).

Managers who are low on both skills are scored 1,1 — that is, evidence of *impoverished management*. Managers who are highly concerned about production but show little interest in people score 9,1 — that is, evidence of *task management*. In contrast, ones who show the opposite pattern — high concern with people but little concern with production — are described as having a *country club* style of management and score 1,9. Managers with moderate concern for both dimensions are said to follow a *middle-of-the-road* management style and score 5,5. Finally, individuals who are highly concerned with both production and people score 9,9. This is the most desirable pattern and rep-

grid training

A multistep process to develop both concern for people and concern for production.

FIGURE 12.6

**Technical Skills + People Skills
= Successful Leadership**

In addition to technical expertise (i.e., knowledge about how to get the job done), successful leaders also must have "people skills." Either one can go only so far in vaulting someone to success as a leader. Someone needs to explain this to the dog depicted here.

(*Source*: © *The 5th Wave* by Rich Tennant, Rockport, MA. Email: the5wave@tiac.net.)

resents *team management*. These various patterns are charted in a diagram like that shown in Figure 12.7, which is known as the *managerial grid*.

After a manager's position on the grid is determined, training begins to improve concern over production (i.e., planning skills) and concern over people (i.e., communication skills) to reach the ideal *9,9* state. This consists of organization-wide training to help people interact more effectively with each other. Training then is expanded to reducing conflict between groups that work with each other. Further training includes identifying the extent to which the organization is meeting its strategic goals and then comparing this performance to an ideal. Next, plans are made to meet these goals,

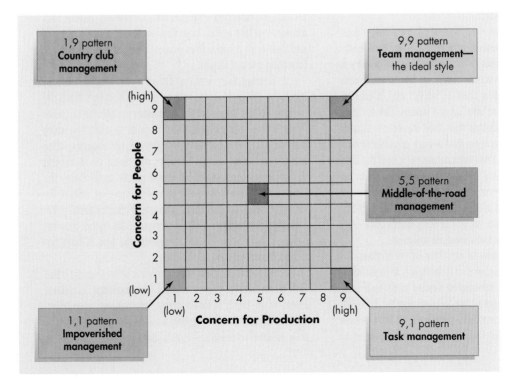

FIGURE 12.7

The Managerial Grid

A manager's standing along two basic dimensions, concern for production and concern for people, can be illustrated through a *managerial grid*. In *grid training*, people are taught to be effective leaders by demonstrating high amounts of both dimensions.

(*Source*: Based on dimensions by Blake & Mouton, 1969; see note 23.)

and these plans are implemented in the organization. Finally, progress toward these goals is assessed continuously, and any problem areas are identified.

Grid training is widely considered to be an effective way of improving leadership behaviors in organizations. Indeed, this approach has been used to train hundreds of thousands of people in developing these two key forms of leadership behavior.

LEADERS AND FOLLOWERS

Thus far, we have focused on the traits and behaviors of leaders. Followers, by and large, have been ignored. In a crucial sense, however, followers are the essence of leadership. Without them, there really is no such thing as leadership. As Lee put it, "Without followers leaders cannot lead. . . . Without followers, even John Wayne becomes a solitary hero, or, given the right script, a comic figure, posturing on an empty stage."[24] (Interestingly, although followers play an important role in the leadership process, that role is not always identical between countries. For a look at some extreme differences in this regard, see the "OB Around the World" section in this chapter.

The importance of followers and the complex, reciprocal relationship between leaders and followers is widely recognized by organizational researchers. Indeed, major theories of leadership note—either explicitly or implicitly—that leadership really

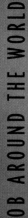

OB AROUND THE WORLD

FOLLOWING THE LEADER IN SWEDEN AND THE PEOPLE'S REPUBLIC OF CHINA

In general, followers rely on directions from their leaders. Differences in national norms, however, make reliance on a leader's influence less clear-cut than you might imagine. This difference is particularly sharp when considering Sweden and the People's Republic of China.[25]

Specifically, most Swedes (78 percent) completing a questionnaire agreed it sometimes is necessary to bypass those who are immediately above them in the organizational hierarchy to promote organizational efficiency.[26] Only one-third of the Chinese completing this questionnaire, however, felt this way. In practice, this suggests that compared with Swedish leaders, Chinese leaders may have greater influence over their immediate subordinates. Thus if a Swedish employee were to work in a Chinese company, he or she might not think twice before going over the boss' head if it appeared necessary. The Chinese manager who was bypassed surely would feel threatened by this action. In contrast, a Chinese employee working in a Swedish company likely would be viewed as lacking initiative for not seeking information from someone other than his or her immediate supervisor.

These differences may be explained by the tendency for the Chinese more than their Swedish counterparts to expect their supervisors will have the information needed to do their jobs. Specifically, only 10 percent of the Swedes reported believing it is important for their immediate supervisors to have precise answers to questions about their work, whereas 74 percent of the Chinese believed this to be the case. Thus, Swedish workers may be willing to tap the expertise of anyone in their organization, but their Chinese counterparts would be unlikely to venture away from an immediate supervisor as a source of expertise. The downside of this is that supervisors without such answers lose face in their organizations (i.e., they are shamed), and their work group suffers because alternative sources of information are not sought.

Framing these national differences in another manner, it may be said the Swedes rely on an organization's hierarchy to structure how things get done, whereas the Chinese are more likely to view hierarchy as being a guide to authority, which must be followed if harmony is to prevail. For example, when planning a project, Swedish leaders may focus on identifying the necessary functions and the best people to fill them. The Chinese may take a different approach, however, instead focusing on selecting individuals who would observe social priorities and work together most harmoniously. Doing this, they believe, not only helps the group perform the task at hand but also to promote future relationships.

We cannot say that one approach is better than the other. Each works well in its own country. The challenge, of course, comes when doing business across international boundaries, when recognizing and accepting national differences—in this case, reliance on leaders—is essential for success.

is a two-way street. We now consider two such approaches: the *leader-member exchange model*, and the *attribution approach* to leadership.

The Leader-Member Exchange Model: The Importance of Being in the "In-Group"

Do leaders treat all their subordinates in the same manner? Informal observations suggest they clearly do not, yet many theories of leadership ignore this fact. Instead, they discuss leadership behavior in terms that suggest similar actions occur toward all subordinates. The importance of potential differences in this respect is brought into sharp focus by the **leader-member exchange (LMX) model**.[27]

This theory suggests that for various reasons, leaders form different kinds of relationships with different groups of subordinates. One group, which is referred to as the *in-group*, is favored by the leader. Members of in-groups receive considerably more attention from the leader and larger shares of resources the leader has to offer (e.g., time and recognition). In contrast, other subordinates fall into the *out-group*. These individuals are disfavored by leaders, and as such, they receive fewer valued resources. Leaders distinguish between in-group and out-group members early in their relationships with them—and on the basis of surprisingly little information. Sometimes, perceived similarity in personal characteristics such as age, gender, or personality is sufficient to categorize followers in a leader's in-group.[28] Similarly, a particular follower may be granted in-group status if the leader believes this person is especially competent at his or her job.[29]

Research supports the idea that leaders favor in-group members. For example, one study found that supervisors inflated the ratings they gave to poorly performing employees when these individuals were members of the in-group but not when they were members of the out-group.[30] Given the favoritism shown toward in-group members, it follows that such individuals should perform their jobs better and hold more positive attitudes toward their jobs than members of out-groups, and in general, research has supported this prediction. For example, in-group members are more satisfied with their jobs and more effective in performing them than out-group members.[31] In-group members also are less likely to resign from their jobs than out-group members.[32] In addition, in-group members tend to receive more mentoring from their superiors than do out-group members, thus helping them to become more successful in their careers (Figure 12.8).[33]

These studies provide good support for the LMX model. Such findings also suggest attention to the relations between leaders and their followers can be very useful, because the nature of such relationships can strongly affect the morale, commitment, and performance of employees. Therefore, helping leaders to improve such relations can be extremely valuable in several respects.

The Attribution Approach: Leaders' Explanations of Followers' Behavior

As noted, leaders' relationships with individual subordinates can play an important role in determining the performance and satisfaction of those employees. One specific aspect of such exchanges serves as focus for another contemporary perspective on leadership—that is, the **attribution approach**.[34] This theory emphasizes the role of leaders' attributions concerning the causes behind their followers' behavior (and especially the causes of their job performance).

Leaders observe the performance of their followers and then attempt to understand why this behavior met, exceeded, or failed their expectations. Poor performance often poses greater difficulties than effective performance, so leaders are more likely to engage in careful attributional analysis when confronted with the former. When they are, they examine the three kinds of information described in chapter 2 (i.e., consensus, consistency, and distinctiveness) and, based on this information, form an

leader-member exchange (LMX) model

A theory suggesting that leaders form different relations with various subordinates and that the nature of such dyadic exchanges can affect subordinates' performance and satisfaction.

attribution approach

The approach to leadership focusing on leaders' attributions of followers' performance—that is, on their perceptions of its underlying causes.

FIGURE 12.8

The Leader-Member Exchange (LMX) Model: A Summary

According to the *leader-member exchange (LMX) model*, leaders distinguish between groups they favor (i.e., *in-groups*) and those they do not (i.e., *out-groups*). Members of in-groups generally enjoy higher levels of morale, commitment, and job performance than members of out-groups.

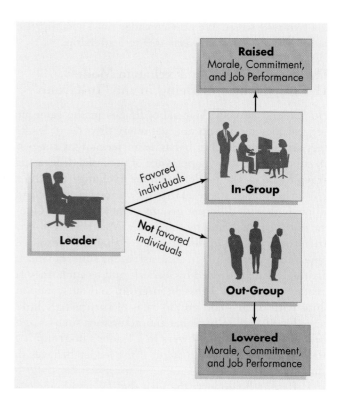

initial judgment of whether a follower's performance stemmed from internal causes (e.g., low effort, commitment, or ability) or external causes (e.g., faulty equipment, unrealistic deadlines, or illness). Then, on the basis of such attributions, they formulate specific actions to change the present situation and, perhaps, to improve the follower's performance. Attribution theory suggests such actions are determined, at least in part, by leaders' explanations of followers' behavior. For example, if leaders perceive poor performance as stemming from a lack of required materials or equipment, they may focus on providing such items. If leaders perceive poor performance as stemming mainly from a lack of effort, however, they may reprimand, transfer, or terminate the person involved. For a summary example, see Figure 12.9.

Several studies support the accuracy of these predictions.[35] For example, in one study, researchers presented supervisors with brief accounts of errors committed by nurses.[36] These incidents suggested the errors stemmed either from internal causes (e.g., lack of effort or ability) or from external causes (e.g., an overdemanding work environment). After reading about the incidents, the supervisors indicated what kind of action they would be likely to take in each situation. Results showed they were more likely to direct corrective action toward the nurses whose errors they perceived as stemming from internal causes (e.g., showing them how to do something) but toward the environment when they perceived these errors as stemming from external factors (e.g., changing schedules, improving facilities).

GLOBAL MATTERS

When attributing characteristics to leaders or followers, do not assume the general qualities of people in one culture apply to everyone in that culture. For example, Koreans in general may be more concerned with group than with individual recognition, but it would be terribly misleading to assume that a new Korean employee is disinterested in his or her individual pay level. ▪

In summary, the attribution approach suggests leaders' behavior often reflects their attributions concerning the actions and performance of followers. Thus, leader-

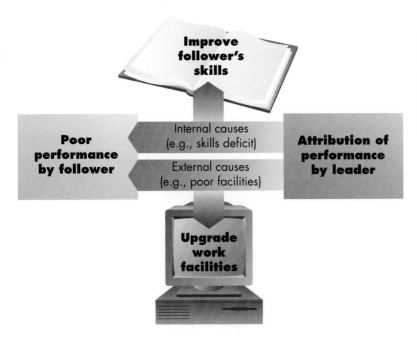

FIGURE 12.9

Leaders' Attributions of Followers' Poor Performance
How leaders respond to their followers depends on the attributions leaders make regarding their followers' performance. In this example, attributions of the causes of a subordinate's poor performance directs a leader toward very different courses of action.

ship lies as much in the perceptions of those exercising such influence as in the perceptions of those conferring the right to wield such influence over them.

CHANGE-ORIENTED LEADERSHIP: FUTURE VISIONS

For organizations to thrive—let alone *survive*—they must be led by individuals with a strong commitment to change. As such, leaders must have clear visions of what the future holds. The world's top leaders tend to agree as well. In a large-scale survey of CEOs from 20 different countries, 90 percent identified having "a strong sense of vision" as being the most important characteristic for a CEO to have. Not surprisingly, companies with the most visionary leaders tend to outperform those with less visionary leaders in all important financial respects.

The question then arises about what, precisely, is involved in giving leaders the capacity to envision the most effective changes for the future. The answers are provided by two interesting approaches to leadership: *charismatic leadership*, and *transformational leadership*.

Charismatic Leadership: That "Something Special"

In the 1970s, Chrysler Corporation was written off as being terminal by many automobile-industry analysts. Lee Iacocca, Chrysler's CEO, refused to accept this economic verdict, however. Instead, he launched a campaign to win government loan guarantees, thus paving the way for Chrysler's survival. By setting an example of personal sacrifice—taking only $1 as salary for one year during the crisis—Iacocca rallied Chrysler's tens of thousands of employees to new levels of effort and saved the day. Chrysler not only paid back all its loans ahead of schedule, it now is thriving.

Both world history and the history of organizations are replete with similar examples. Through the ages, some leaders have had extraordinary success in generating profound changes among their followers. Indeed, it is not extreme to suggest that some such people (e.g., Napoleon, Bill Gates, John Lennon) have changed entire societies

charismatic leaders

Leaders who exert especially powerful effects on followers through the attributions followers make about them. Such individuals have high self-confidence, present a clearly articulated vision, behave in extraordinary ways, are recognized as change agents, and are sensitive to environmental constraints.

through their words and actions. Individuals who accomplish such feats are referred to as **charismatic leaders**. These are individuals who exert especially powerful effects on followers by virtue of their commanding confidence and clearly articulated visions.

Qualities of Charismatic Leaders   Charismatic leaders tend to be special in several important ways. These are:

- *Self-confidence*. Charismatic leaders are highly confident in their ability and judgment, and others readily become aware of this. For example, John Bryan, the CEO of Sara Lee, is widely regarded by his employees as someone who really knows his stuff.
- *A vision*. A leader is said to have vision to the extent he or she proposes a state of affairs that improves the status quo. He or she also must articulate that vision clearly and be willing to sacrifice to make it come true. This is precisely what Lee Iacocca did when he took a $1 salary during Chrysler's troubled period. For more examples of visions stated by some well-known charismatic leaders, see Table 12.3.
- *Extraordinary behavior*. Charismatic leaders frequently are unconventional, and when successful, their quirky ways elicit admiration. For example, much of the success of Southwest Airlines is attributed to the zany antics of its CEO, Herb Kelleher.
- *Recognized as agents of change*. The status quo is the enemy of charismatic leaders, because these people make things happen. This can be said about the late Roberto Goizueta, for example, who made Coca-Cola one of the most admired—and profitable—companies in America.
- *Environmental sensitivity*. Charismatic leaders are highly realistic about both the constraints imposed on them and the resources needed to change things. Consequently, they know what they can—and cannot—do.

TABLE 12.3

Some Famous Charismatic Leaders and Their Visions

One quality that makes charismatic leaders so effective is that they share clear visions for their organizations and then help to pave the way toward attaining it. The visions of a few well-known charismatic leaders are paraphrased here.

CHARISMATIC LEADER	COMPANY	VISION
Steven Jobs	Apple Computer	To make computing simple and available to everyone.
Charles Schwab	Charles Schwab	To provide high-quality financial services to people at reasonable prices.
Herb Kelleher	Southwest Airlines	To provide excellent service and great value to the flying public.
Mary Kay Ash	Mary Kay Cosmetics	To enhance the self-esteem of women by building their financial independence while providing quality cosmetics.
Rupert Murdoch	News Corporation	To provide accurate access to news for people throughout the world.
Walt Disney	Walt Disney Co.	To provide wholesome, high-quality entertainment to families throughout the world.

Reactions to Charismatic Leaders   At first glance, it is tempting to assume charismatic leaders are special merely because of their traits. It also makes sense, however, to look at charismatic leadership as having a special relationship with their followers. In other words, leaders are considered to be charismatic because of their effects on followers. Such reactions include:

- Performance levels beyond what would normally be expected.[37]
- High levels of devotion, loyalty, and reverence toward the leader.[38]
- Enthusiasm for and excitement about the leader and his or her ideas.[39]

In short, charismatic leadership involves a special kind of leader-follower relationship. In the words of one author, the leader can "make ordinary people do extraordinary things in the face of adversity."[40]

The Effects of Charismatic Leadership   As you might imagine, charismatic leaders have dramatic effects on the behavior of their followers. Because these leaders are perceived as being so heroic, followers are very pleased with them—and this satisfaction generalizes to their perceptions of the job itself. In short, people enjoy working for charismatic leaders and do well under their guidance. On a larger scale, U.S. presidents who were believed to be highly charismatic (as suggested through biographical accounts of their personalities and reactions to world crises) received higher ratings by historians of their effectiveness.[41] In short, charismatic leadership can have some very beneficial effects.

Being charismatic, however, does not necessarily imply being virtuous. In fact, many of the most vicious dictators (e.g., Adolph Hitler) rose to power because of their considerable charisma. Indeed, it was their clear visions of different worlds— misguided though they may have been—that produced such profound effects on their followers.

Are Charismatic Leaders Always Needed?   There may not always be a place for charismatic leaders in organizations. Such leaders tend to be needed most during some crisis.[42] For example, charismatic leaders tend to emerge under wartime conditions, such as when U.S. General Norman Schwartzkopf expressed a vision of victory over Iraq and led his troops to victory in the 1991 Gulf War. The Great Depression led to the election of President Franklin D. Roosevelt, who would lead the United States out of it. In addition, as noted earlier, the economic crisis at Chrysler during the 1970s led to the emergence of Lee Iacocca, the man who saved the company.

By the same token, it is easy to imagine that under everyday conditions, leaders who approach others with such overwhelming levels of arrogance and self-confidence may be more of a liability than an asset. For example, such was the case at Borland International, the world's largest database software provider.[43] When the company faced financial crises in the late 1980s, charismatic president and CEO Philippe R. Kahn was most helpful in turning things around. Interestingly, however, Kahn's "barbarian" approach to leadership only interfered with the company's operations as it emerged from crisis.

The Liabilities of Charismatic Leaders   In closing, one particularly interesting thing about charismatic leaders is that people's reactions toward them tend to be highly polarized. In other words, people either love them (as is the case most of the time) or hate them. Thus, it is not surprising that some of the world's most charismatic leaders, such as President John F. Kennedy and Israeli Prime Minister Itzak Rabin, have fallen victim to assassination. Less visionary leaders certainly would have done little to inspire would-be assassins to leave their own marks on the world in such clearly inappropriate ways.

transformational leadership

Leadership in which leaders use their charisma to transform and revitalize their organizations.

FIGURE 12.10

Estée Lauder: A Transformational Leader

Estée Lauder, who turned 90 years old in 1998, has transformed the cosmetic business. The lines she developed and acquired during a half-century now account for more than 45 percent of the cosmetics market in U.S. department stores — three times as much as the closest competitor! Her mesmerizing ways also were influential in getting counter space in some of the most exclusive stores.

Transformational Leadership: Beyond Charisma

If you are thinking charismatic leaders are something special, we agree. Being charismatic is only the beginning, however, in getting followers to be their most effective. Theorists recognize that although charisma is important, the most successful leaders also revitalize and transform their organizations. Accordingly, their orientation is referred to as **transformational leadership**.

Characteristics of Transformational Leaders   Transformational leaders have several characteristics. First, as mentioned, they have *charisma* — that is, they provide a strong vision and a sense of mission for the company. As one leadership theorist said, "If you as a leader can make an appealing dream seem like tomorrow's reality, your subordinates will freely choose to follow you."[44] For example, consider the great visions expressed by two highly charismatic leaders: Dr. Martin Luther King, Jr., when he shared his vision of world peace in his "I have a dream" speech; and President John F. Kennedy, when he shared his vision of landing a man on the moon and returning him safely to earth before 1970.

Charisma alone, however, is insufficient for changing how an organization operates. Transformational leaders also must provide the following:

- *Intellectual stimulation*: Transformational leaders help their followers to recognize problems and solutions.
- *Individualized consideration*: Transformational leaders give their followers the support, encouragement, and attention they need to perform well.
- *Inspirational motivation*: Transformational leaders clearly communicate the importance of the company's mission and rely on symbols (e.g., pins and slogans) to help focus their efforts.

As you might imagine, transformational leaders arouse strong emotions. They also help to transform their followers by teaching them (often by serving as mentors).[45] In so doing, transformational leaders seek to elevate their followers to do "their own thing." In contrast, charismatic leaders may keep their followers weak and highly dependent. A charismatic leader may be the whole show, whereas a transformational leader inspires change in the whole organization. Many celebrities tend to be highly charismatic, but they do not necessarily have any transformational effects on their followers. As such, some people may idolize and even dress like certain rock stars, but the charisma of these musicians is unlikely to stimulate their fans into making sacrifices that revitalize the world. Thus, in short, charisma is just a part of transformational leadership.

Profile of a Transformational Leader   Jack Welch, the chairman and CEO of General Electric (GE), is a good example of a transformational leader. Under Welch's leadership, GE has undergone a series of changes regarding the way it does business.[46] At the individual level, GE has abandoned its highly bureaucratic ways and now does a better job of listening to its employees. Not surprisingly, GE consistently has ranked among the most admired companies of its industry in *Fortune* magazine's annual survey of corporate reputations — including a number-one ranking in 1998![47]

During the 1980s, Welch bought and sold many businesses for GE. His guideline was that GE would keep a company only if it placed either first or second in market share. If this meant closing plants, selling assets, and laying off personnel, he did it — and got others to follow suit. Not surprisingly, Welch earned the nickname "Neutron Jack." Did Welch transform and revitalize GE? Having added $52 billion of value to the company, there can be no doubt he did.[48] (Jack Welch is not the only transformational leader we can identify of course; for another example, see Figure 12.10).

Measuring Transformational Leadership and Its Effects   Scientists measure transformational leadership using a questionnaire known as the *Multifactor Leadership Questionnaire*. In completing this instrument, subordinates answer questions in which they describe the behavior of their superiors. The questionnaire consists of items tapping the four aspects of transformational leadership described earlier. So, for example, agreeing with an item such as "My leader makes me feel proud to be associated with him/her" is taken as an indication of the leader's transformational ways. The more subordinates agree with such statements, the more highly the leader in question is scored as being transformational. Using this questionnaire, scientists have found that transformational leaders tend to be very effective in making their organizations highly successful.

GLOBAL MATTERS

In one study, researchers gave the Multifactor Leadership Questionnaire to teachers in various secondary schools in Singapore and asked them to complete it with their school principals in mind.[49] The more highly transformational the principals were found to be, the more highly satisfied the teachers were with their jobs — and the more strongly committed they were to their schools. To a lesser degree, the principals' transformational leadership scores also predicted how well the students in their schools performed. ■

Managers at FedEx who are rated by their subordinates as being highly transformational tend to be higher performers, and they are recognized by their superiors as being highly promotable.[50] This study (as well as others) suggests the benefits of being a transformational leader may be considerable.

It certainly would be useful to consider how people might go about developing their transformational leadership skills. We summarize several key guidelines in Table 12.4 on page 464. You may find it easier to understand than to carry out some of these suggestions, but evidence regarding the effectiveness of transformational leadership suggests this effort may be worth it.

CONTINGENCY THEORIES OF LEADER EFFECTIVENESS

That leadership is a complex process should be obvious by now. It involves intricate social relationships, and it is affected by a wide range of factors. Given these complications, you may wonder why so many researchers focus such time and energy on understanding all of these intricacies. The answer, of course, is that effective leadership is essential for organizational success. With effective leadership, organizations can grow, prosper, and compete; without it, many simply cannot survive. This basic point lies behind several modern theories of leadership, which collectively are referred to as **contingency theories of leadership**.

These theories differ sharply in their content, terminology, and scope, yet all are linked by two common themes. First, all adopt a *contingency approach* — that is, they recognize that no single style of leadership is preferred and that the key task of OB researchers is determining which leadership styles are most effective under which conditions. Second, all are concerned with the issue of *leader effectiveness*. In other words, they seek to identify the conditions and factors determining whether — and to what degree — leaders enhance the performance and satisfaction of their subordinates. Several theories fall into this category.[51] The five described here are the *LPC contingency theory*, the *situational leadership theory*, the *path-goal theory*, the *normative decision theory*, and the *substitutes for leadership* framework.

contingency theories of leadership
Any of several theories recognizing that certain leadership styles are more effective in some situations than in others.

TABLE 12.4

Guidelines for Becoming a Transformational Leader
Being a transformational leader is not easy; however, by following these suggestions, leaders
may transform and revitalize their organizations.

SUGGESTION	EXPLANATION
Develop a vision that is both clear and highly appealing to followers.	A clear vision guides followers toward achieving organizational goals and makes them feel good about doing so.
Articulate a strategy for bringing that vision to life.	Don't present an elaborate plan; rather, state the best path toward achieving the mission.
State your vision clearly, and promote it to others.	Visions must not only be clear but made compelling, such as by using anecdotes.
Show confidence and optimism about your vision.	If a leader lacks confidence about success, followers will not try very hard to achieve that vision.
Express confidence in followers' capacity to carry out the strategy.	Followers must believe they can implement a leader's vision. Leaders should build followers' self-confidence.
Build confidence by recognizing small accomplishments toward the goal.	If a group experiences early success, it will be motivated to continue working hard.
Celebrate successes and accomplishments	Formal or informal ceremonies are useful for celebrating success, thereby building optimism and commitment.
Take dramatic action to symbolize key organizational values.	Visions are reinforced by things leaders do to symbolize them. For example, one leader demonstrated concern for quality by destroying work that was not up to standards.
Set an example; actions speak louder than words.	Leaders serve as role models. If they want followers to make sacrifices, for example, they should do so themselves.

Source: Based on suggestions by Yukl, 1998; see note 2.

LPC Contingency Theory: Matching Leaders and Tasks

As noted earlier, the behaviors associated with effective leadership fall into two major categories: concern for people, and concern for production. Both types contribute to a leader's success; however, a more refined look at this issue leads us to ask exactly when each type works best. In other words, under what conditions are leaders more successful when they demonstrate a concern for people compared with a concern for production?

LPC contingency theory

A theory suggesting the characteristics of leaders (i.e., their *LPC* scores) and the level of situational control they can exert over subordinates determines leader effectiveness.

LPC

Short for *esteem for least preferred coworker;* a personality variable distinguishing between individuals by their concern for people (i.e., high LPC) and for production (i.e., low LPC).

low LPC leaders

Leaders who primarily are concerned with attaining successful task performance.

The Basics of the Theory   This same question is addressed by a widely studied approach to leadership known as the **LPC contingency theory**. The contingency aspect is reflected by the assumption that a leader's contribution to successful performance by a group is determined both by his or her own traits and by the situation. Thus, different levels of leader effectiveness occur under different conditions. To understand leader effectiveness, both types of factors must be considered.

According to this theory, *esteem (i.e., liking) for the least preferred coworker* — or **LPC** for short — is the most important personal characteristic. This refers to a leader's tendency to evaluate in a favorable or an unfavorable manner the person with whom she or he finds it most difficult to work. Leaders who perceive this person in negative terms (i.e., **low LPC leaders**) primarily are concerned with attaining successful task performance. In contrast, those who perceive this person in positive terms (i.e., **high LPC leaders**) mainly are concerned with establishing good relations with subordinates. A questionnaire is used to measure one's LPC score. It is important to note, however, that this theory views LPC as being *fixed* — that is, as an aspect of an individual's leadership style that cannot be changed. As we explain later, this has important implications for applying the theory to improve leader effectiveness.

Which type of leader — one low in LPC or one high in LPC — is more effective? As suggested by the word *contingency*, the answer is: "It depends." What it depends on is the degree to which the situation favors the leader — that is, how much it allows the leader to control his or her subordinates. In turn, this is determined largely by three factors:

1. The nature of the *leader's relations with group members* (i.e., the extent to which he or she enjoys their support and loyalty).

2. The *degree of structure* in the task (i.e., the extent to which task goals and subordinates' roles are clearly defined).

3. The leader's *position power* (i.e., his or her formal capacity to enforce compliance by subordinates).

Combining these factors, the leader's situational control can range from very high (i.e., positive relations with group members, a highly structured task, and high position power) to very low (i.e., negative relations with group members, an unstructured task, and low position power).

What types of leaders are most effective under these various conditions? According to this theory, low LPC leaders (i.e., ones who are task-oriented) are superior to high LPC leaders (i.e., ones who are relations-oriented) when situational control is either very low or very high. In contrast, high LPC leaders have an edge when situational control falls within the moderate range (Figure 12.11).

high LPC leaders

Leaders who primarily are concerned with establishing good relations with subordinates.

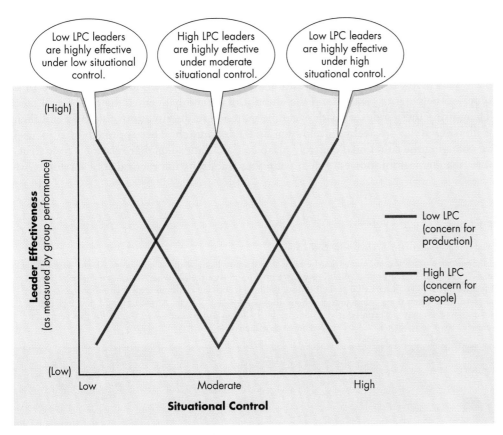

FIGURE 12.11

LPC Contingency Theory: An Overview

LPC contingency theory predicts that low-LPC leaders (i.e., ones who primarily are task-oriented) are more effective than high-LPC leaders (i.e., ones who primarily are people-oriented) when situational control is either very low or very high. The opposite is true, however, when situational control is moderate.

The rationale for these predictions is quite reasonable. Under conditions of low situational control, groups need considerable guidance to accomplish their tasks, because without such direction, nothing would get done. For example, imagine a military combat group with an unpopular platoon leader. Any chance of effectiveness this person has will result from paying careful attention to the task at hand rather than from establishing better relations with the group. (In fact, in the U.S. Army, it often is said that a leader in an emergency is better off giving wrong orders than giving no orders whatsoever.) Low LPC leaders are more likely to provide structure than high LPC leaders, so they usually are superior in such cases.

Similarly, low LPC leaders also are superior under conditions of high situational control. Indeed, when leaders are liked, their power is not challenged, and when the demands of the task make clear what a leader should do, it is perfectly acceptable for them to focus on the task at hand. Subordinates expect their leaders to exercise control under such conditions, and they accept it when their leaders do so. In turn, this leads to task success. For example, an airline pilot leading a cockpit crew is expected to take charge. This pilot is not expected to seek the consensus of others as he or she guides the plane onto the runway for a landing. Surely, the pilot would be less effective if he or she did not take charge but instead asked the co-pilot for an opinion.

Things are different, however, when situations offer leaders only moderate situational control. For example, consider a leader with good subordinate relations but an unstructured task. Suppose this leader's power is somewhat restricted as well. This generally is the case within a research-and-development team attempting to find creative, new uses for a company's products. Here, it clearly would be inappropriate for a low LPC leader to impose directives. Rather, a highly nurturant leader, who is considerate of the feelings of others, would be most effective — that is, a high LPC leader (Figure 12.12).

Applying LPC Contingency Theory   Practitioners have found LPC contingency theory to be quite useful in suggesting ways of enhancing leader effectiveness. Because this theory assumes certain kinds of leaders are most effective under certain kinds of situations — and that leadership style is fixed — the best way to enhance effectiveness is to match the right leaders with the right situations.

This involves completing questionnaires that can be used to assess both the LPC score of the potential leader and the amount of situational control he or she will face. Then, using these indexes, leaders can be matched to the situations that best suit their leadership styles — a technique known as **leader match**. This approach also focuses on changing the situational control variables (i.e., leader-member relations, task structure, leader position power) when changing leaders is impractical. For example, we

leader match

According to *LPC contingency theory*, the practice of matching leaders (based on their *LPC* scores) to situations best matching those in which they are expected to be most effective.

FIGURE 12.12

Matching Leadership Style to the Situation

LPC contingency theory recognizes that the most appropriate leadership style depends on the situation being confronted. The aircraft cockpit crew (*left*) may be most effective when its leader, the pilot, uses a highly directive (i.e., low LPC) style. So, too, military troops in a difficult battle situation (*center*) may perform best when their commanding officer adopts a low LPC style. A research-and-development team, however, may perform poorly if their leader behaved in this same way (*right*). In this setting, a less directive (i.e., high LPC) style may be more effective.

may move a high LPC leader to a job in which situational control is extremely high or extremely low. Alternatively, we may attempt to change the situation (e.g., altering relations between the leader and group members, raising or lowering the leader's position power) to increase or decrease the amount of situational control encountered.

Several companies, including Sears, have used the leader match approach with some success. In fact, several studies have found this approach to be effective—on at least some occasions—in improving group effectiveness.

Situational Leadership Theory: Adjusting Leadership Style to the Situation

Situational leadership theory also is considered to be a contingency theory, because it focuses on the best leadership style for a given situation. The scientists who developed this approach, argue that leaders are effective when they select the right leadership style for the situation they face.[52] Specifically, this depends on the *maturity* of the followers—that is, on their readiness to take responsibility for their own behavior. This, in turn, is based on two variables with which we already are familiar: *task behavior*, or the degree to which followers have the appropriate job knowledge and skills (i.e., their need for guidance and direction); and *relationship behavior*, or the degree to which followers are willing to work without taking direction from others (i.e., their need for emotional support).

As shown in Figure 12.13, if you combine high and low levels of these independent dimensions, four different types of situations can be identified, each of which is associated with a leadership style that is most effective.

Starting in the lower-right corner of the figure are situations in which followers need a great deal of direction from their leaders but do not need much emotional support from them (i.e., S1). The practice of *telling* followers what to do is most useful in such situations—that is, giving followers specific instructions and closely supervising their work may be the best approach.

situational leadership theory

A theory suggesting the most effective style of leadership (i.e., *delegating, participating, selling,* or *telling*) depends on the extent to which followers require guidance, direction, and emotional support.

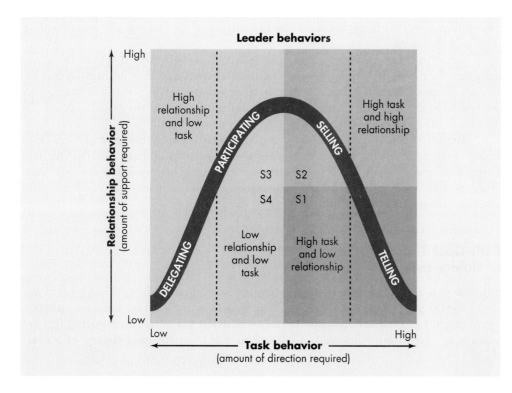

FIGURE 12.13

Situational Leadership Theory: Its Basic Dimensions

Situational leadership theory specifies that the most appropriate leadership style depends on the amount of emotional support and guidance followers require to do their jobs.

YOU BE THE CONSULTANT

The president and founder of a small tool-and-die casting firm tells you, "Nobody around here has any respect for me. The only reason they listen to me is because this is my company." Company employees report he is highly controlling and does not let anyone do anything for themselves.

1.   What behaviors should the president emulate to improve his leadership style? How may he do so?
2.   Under what conditions would you expect the president's current leadership style to be most effective?
3.   Do you think these conditions might exist in his company? If not, how might they be created?

Moving toward the upper-right corner are situations in which followers still lack the skill to succeed but require more emotional support (i.e., S2). Under these conditions, *selling* works best. Being very directive may make up for the followers' lack of ability, whereas being very supportive will help get them to go along with what the leader asks of them.

In the upper-left corner (i.e., S3) are conditions in which followers need little guidance regarding how to do their jobs but considerable emotional hand-holding and support to motivate them. In other words, low levels of task behavior but high levels of relationship (i.e., supportive) behavior are required. A *participating* style of leadership works well in such situations, because it allows followers to share their expertise and enhances their desire to perform.

Finally, in the lower-left corner (i.e., S4), followers are both willing and able to do what is asked. In other words, low levels of task behavior and low levels of relationship behavior are required. Under such conditions, *delegating* is the best way to treat followers—that is, giving them the responsibility for making and implementing their own decisions.

According to this situational leadership theory, leaders must diagnose the situations they face, identify the appropriate behavioral style, and then implement that response. Because situations may change, leaders must constantly reassess them, paying special attention to their followers' needs for guidance and emotional support. To the extent they do so, these leaders are likely to be effective.

Specialized training in these skills is quite useful. In fact, this approach has been widely used to train leaders in corporate giants such as Xerox, Mobile Oil, and Caterpillar, and even in the U.S. military. (Which style of leadership are you most prone to follow? For some insight into this question, complete the "Experiencing Organizational Behavior" section at the end of this chapter.

Path-Goal Theory: Leaders as Guides to Valued Goals

Suppose you ask 100 people what they expect from their leaders. What kind of answers would you receive? They would vary greatly, of course, but one common theme might be "I expect my leader to *help*—to assist me in reaching goals I feel are important." This basic idea plays a central role in the **path-goal theory** of leadership.[53]

path-goal theory
A theory suggesting subordinates are motivated by a leader only to the extent they perceive this individual as helping them to attain valued goals.

In general, this theory contends that subordinates react favorably to a leader only to the extent they perceive this person as helping them to progress toward various goals by clarifying actual paths to such rewards. In other words, effective leaders clarify what followers need to do to get to where they should be, and they help these followers to do so. More specifically, by clarifying the nature of tasks and reducing or eliminating obstacles, a leader increases the perceptions of subordinates that working hard leads to good performance, which in turn is recognized and rewarded. Under such conditions, this theory suggests, job satisfaction, motivation, and actual performance are enhanced.

How, precisely, can leaders best accomplish these tasks? As in other modern views of leadership, the answer here is: "It depends." (In fact, this is how you can tell it is a contingency theory.) What it depends on is a complex interaction between key aspects of *leader behavior* and certain *contingency* factors. Regarding leader behavior, path-goal theory suggests that leaders can adopt four basic styles:

1. *Instrumental (directive)*: An approach focused on providing specific guidance and on establishing work schedules and rules.
2. *Supportive*: A style focused on establishing good relations with subordinates and on satisfying their needs.
3. *Participative*: A pattern in which the leader consults with subordinates, thereby permitting them to participate in decisions.
4. *Achievement-oriented*: An approach in which the leader sets challenging goals and seeks improvements in performance.

According to this theory, these styles are not mutually exclusive. In fact, the same leader can adopt them at different times and in different situations. Indeed, showing such flexibility is one important aspect of an effective leader. (Recognizing the importance of these styles, many of today's leaders have adopted an approach to leadership known as *coaching*. For a look at this orientation, see the "Trends" section below.

■ Coaching: From Locker Room to Boardroom

If you have ever played on a sports team, you have experienced the important leadership function of a coach. What did your coach do? Chances are, he or she was actively involved with helping you in the following ways:

- Analyzing ways of improving your performance and extending your capabilities.
- Creating a supportive climate in which barriers to development are eliminated.
- Encouraging you to improve your performance (no matter how good you already may be).

Coaching has been around a long time, but only recently has coaching emerged as a philosophy of leadership in organizations.[54] Largely, this appears to have been stimulated by books in which coaches (e.g., former Notre Dame football coach Lou Holtz)[55] and executives (e.g., Green Bay Packers' executive vice president and general manager Ron Wolf)[56] have shared insight into the coaching process.

These big-time sports insiders tell us what makes coaching a unique form of leadership is the special relationship between the coach and team members. The key

continued

to this relationship is trust. Team members acknowledge the coach's expertise, and they trust the coach to have their best interests in mind. At the same time, the coach believes in the team members' capacity to profit from his or her advice. In other words, coaching is a partnership. Both the coach and the team members play an important part in achieving success.

Additional dimensions of the coach's leadership power have been described by basketball hall of famer and former U.S. Senator Bill Bradley.[57] One key to coaching, Bradley emphasizes, is getting players to commit to something bigger than themselves. In sports, this may mean winning a championship. In business, it may mean landing a huge contract or surpassing a long-standing sales record. Focusing on the goal itself — and identifying how each individual may contribute to achieving it — is the key.

Bradley also advises that the best coaches do not do all the talking when someone gets out of line. Rather, they harness the power of all team members to put pressure on the problem person. For example, consider what happened when the *Chicago Bulls'* Scottie Pippin angrily took himself out of a 1994 semifinal championship game after Coach Phil Jackson called for teammate Toni Kukoc to make the final, game-deciding shot. Naturally, Coach Jackson came down hard on Pippin during his postgame interview, but that was mostly for show. The real work of getting Pippin to see his mistake came not from the coach, however, but from his teammates. After the game, the coach left the locker room, announcing the team had something to say to Pippin. Then, one by one, the *Bulls* expressed their disappointment in Pippin for letting down the team. Seeing the error of his ways, Pippin apologized on the spot — and immediately went back to being the team player he had been all along. Had the coach not orchestrated this session, the outcome would not have been as successful.

One way coaches can support their team members and earn their trust is to refrain from bad-mouthing team members to others. Athletic coaches who use the media to send critical messages to their players live to regret it, Bradley tells us. Behind the closed doors of the locker room, however, is quite a different story. In that setting, there is no such thing as being too frank. The same applies in an office or a shop as well. A manager who complains to other managers what a poor job some employee has been doing not only makes himself or herself look bad but, more importantly, betrays that employee's trust — and as we said earlier, trust is the heart of coaching. ∎

Which of these contrasting styles is best for maximizing subordinates' satisfaction and motivation? The answer depends on two contingency factors. First, the style of choice is strongly affected by several *characteristics of subordinates*. For example, if followers are high in ability, an instrumental style of leadership may be unnecessary, and a less structured, supportive approach may be preferable. If subordinates are low in ability, however, the opposite may be true, because people with poor ability need considerable guidance to help them attain their goals. Similarly, people high in need for affiliation (i.e., those desiring close, friendly ties with others) may strongly prefer a supportive or participative style, whereas those high in need for achievement may strongly prefer an achievement-oriented style.

Second, the most effective leadership style also depends on several *aspects of the work environment*. For example, path-goal theory predicts that when tasks are unstructured and nonroutine, an instrumental approach by the leader may be best because much clarification and guidance are needed. When tasks are structured and highly routine, however, such leadership actually may impede good performance and be resented by subordinates, who think the leader is engaging in unnecessary meddling. For an overview of all these aspects of path-goal theory, see Figure 12.14.

Path-goal theory has been tested empirically in several studies.[58] In general, the results have been consistent with the major predictions derived from this theory, although not uniformly so. Thus, at present, path-goal theory appears to offer valuable insights into leadership and the many factors that determine how successful individual leaders are in this role.

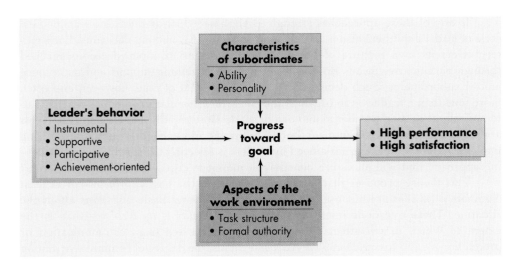

FIGURE 12.14

Path-Goal Theory: An Overview
According to *path-goal theory*, perceptions among employees that leaders are helping them to reach valued goals enhance both employee motivation and job satisfaction. In turn, such perceptions are encouraged when a leader's style is consistent with the needs and characteristics of his or her subordinates (e.g., their level of experience) and of the work environment (e.g., the requirements of the tasks being performed).

Normative Decision Theory: The Right Time for Employee Participation

As discussed in chapter 9, making decisions is one of the major tasks performed by leaders. Indeed, a defining characteristic of some leadership positions is that they are where "the buck finally stops" and concrete actions must be taken. Because the decisions reached by leaders often have far-reaching effects on subordinates, one major determinant of a leader's effectiveness clearly is the adequacy with which he or she performs this task. Leaders who make good decisions are more effective in the long run than leaders who make bad ones, but how should leaders go about making decisions? As noted earlier, participation in decision making is an important variable in many organizational settings—one with implications for job satisfaction, stress, and productivity. Thus, how leaders handle this issue can be crucial to their effectiveness.

How much participation in decisions by subordinates should leaders allow? Perhaps the most useful answer is provided by the **normative decision theory**.[59] This theory holds that leaders often adopt one of five distinct methods for reaching decisions. These methods are summarized in Table 12.5. As you can see, they range from decisions made solely by the leader in a totally autocratic manner through decisions made in a fully participative manner.

normative decision theory

A theory of leader effectiveness focusing primarily on strategies for choosing the most effective approach to decision making.

TABLE 12.5

Potential Strategies for Making Decisions
According to Vroom and Yetton, leaders making decisions often adopt one of the five basic strategies described here.

DECISION STRATEGY	DESCRIPTION
AI (autocratic)	Leader solves problem or makes decision unilaterally using available information.
AII (autocratic)	Leader obtains necessary information from subordinates but then makes decision unilaterally.
CI (consultative)	Leader shares the problem with subordinates individually but then makes decision unilaterally.
CII (consultative)	Leader shares problem with subordinates in group meeting but then makes decision unilaterally.
GII (group decision)	Leader shares problem with subordinates in a group meeting; decision is reached through discussion to consensus.

Source: Based on suggestions from Vroom & Yetton, 1973; see note 59.

Is any of these approaches strongly preferable? Just as there is no single best style of leadership, there also is no single best strategy for making decisions. Each pattern offers its own mixture of benefits and costs. For example, decisions reached through participative means stand a better chance of gaining support and acceptance among subordinates. Such decisions require a great deal of time, however, and often more time than a leader or an organization can afford. Similarly, decisions reached autocratically (i.e., by the leader alone) can be made more rapidly and efficiently, but this approach can generate resentment among followers and encounter difficulties during implementation. One major task faced by leaders is selecting the specific decision-making approach that will maximize benefits yet minimize costs. How can this be done?

This theory proposes that leaders should select the best approach—or at least eliminate ones that are not useful—by answering several basic questions about the situation. These questions relate primarily to the *quality of the decision*—that is, the extent to which it will affect important group processes (e.g., communication or production)—and to *acceptance of the decision*—that is, the degree of commitment among subordinates needed for its implementation. For example, regarding decision quality, a leader should ask questions such as: Is a high-quality decision required? Do I have enough information to make such a decision? Is the problem well structured? Regarding decision acceptance, a leader should ask questions such as: Is it crucial for effective implementation that subordinates accept the decision? Do subordinates share the organizational goals that will be reached through solution of this problem?

According to normative decision theory, answering such questions—and applying specific rules such as those shown in Table 12.6—eliminates some potential approaches to reaching a given decision. Those that remain constitute a feasible set that, at least potentially, can be used to reach the necessary decision.

To simplify this process, use a decision tree, such as the one shown in Figure 12.15. In such a diagram, a manager begins on the left side and responds, in turn, to

TABLE 12.6

Decision Rules in Normative Decision Theory

By applying the rules shown here, leaders can eliminate decision-making strategies that are likely to prove ineffective in a given situation and select those likely to be most effective.

RULES DESIGNED TO PROTECT DECISION QUALITY		RULES DESIGNED TO PROTECT DECISION ACCEPTANCE	
• Leader Information Rule	If the quality of the decision is important and you do not have enough information or expertise to solve the problem alone, eliminate an autocratic style.	• Acceptance Rule	If acceptance by subordinates is crucial for effective implementation, eliminate the autocratic styles.
• Goal Congruence Rule	If the quality of the decision is important and subordinates are not likely to make the right decision, rule out the highly participative style.	• Conflict Rule	If acceptance by subordinates is crucial for effective implementation and they hold conflicting opinions over the means of achieving some objective, eliminate autocratic styles.
• Unstructured Problem Rule	If the quality of the decision is important but you lack sufficient information and expertise and the problem is unstructured, eliminate the autocratic leadership styles.	• Fairness Rule	If the quality of the decision is unimportant but acceptance is important, use the most participatory style.
		• Acceptance Priority Rule	If acceptance is critical and not certain to result from autocratic decisions and subordinates are not motivated to achieve the organization's goals, use a highly participative style.

the questions listed under each letter (i.e., A, B, C, and so on). As the manager replies to each question, the set of feasible approaches narrows. For example, imagine a manager's answers are as follows:

- *Question A*: Yes — a high-quality decision is needed.
- *Question B*: No — the leader does not have sufficient information to make a high-quality decision alone.
- *Question C*: No — the problem is not structured.
- *Question D*: Yes — acceptance by subordinates is crucial to implementation.
- *Question E*: No — if the leader makes the decision alone, subordinates may not accept it.

FIGURE 12.15

Normative Decision Theory: An Example

By answering the questions listed here and tracing a path through this decision tree, leaders can identify the most effective approaches to making decisions in a specific situation. The path suggested by the answers to questions A through G is shown by the broken line.

(*Source*: Based on suggestions by Vroom & Yetton, 1973; see note 59.)

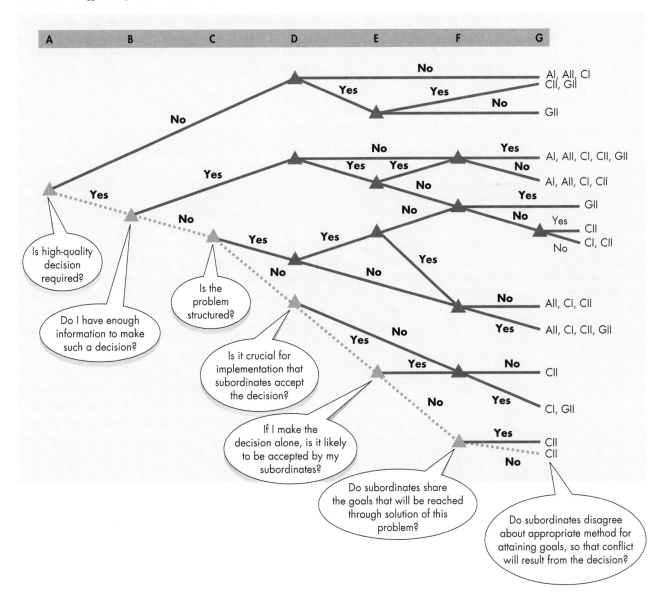

- *Question F*: No — subordinates do not share the organizational goals.
- *Question G*: Yes — conflict among subordinates is likely to result from the decision.

As you can see, these replies lead to the conclusion that only one decision-making approach is feasible: full participation by subordinates. (The path leading to this conclusion is shown by the broken line in Figure 12.15.) Of course, different answers to any of the seven key questions would have led to different conclusions.

The normative decision model is highly appealing, both because it takes full account of the importance of subordinate participation in decisions and because it offers leaders clear guidance for choosing among various methods for reaching decisions. As with any theory, however, the key question remains: Is it valid? In other words, are its suggestions concerning the most effective style under various conditions accurate? The results of several studies designed to test this model have been encouraging.

The latest version of this theory is more complex: Instead of seven contingency questions, there are twelve, and instead of answering questions with a simple "yes" or "no," there now are five options. In fact, this revised model is so complex that a computer program is used instead of a decision tree. Even so, preliminary evidence suggests the resulting theory is more valid than the original (although it is far too complex to present here).

Whether the more sophisticated version or the original version is used, this formulation clearly makes an important contribution to our understanding of leadership. Currently, there is widespread interest in allowing subordinates to participate in decision making, so normative decision theory, which gives leaders clear guidance regarding when such a move may improve task performance, is useful.

Substitutes for Leadership: When Leaders Are Superfluous

Throughout this chapter, we have emphasized that leaders are important. Their style, actions, and degree of effectiveness all exert major effects on subordinates and on organizations. Almost everyone, however, either has observed or been part of groups in which the designated leaders actually had little influence — that is, groups in which designated leaders were mere figureheads, with little impact on subordinates. One explanation for these situations involves the characteristics of the leaders in question: They simply are weak and unsuited for their jobs. Another — and in some ways more intriguing — possibility is that in some contexts, other factors actually may substitute for a leader's influence, thus making it superfluous, or may neutralize a leader's influence. This has been proposed in what is known as the **substitutes for leadership** framework.[60]

substitutes for leadership

The view that high skill levels among subordinates or certain features of technology and organizational structure sometimes substitute for leadership, thus rendering a leader's guidance or influence superfluous.

According to this conceptualization, various factors make it impossible for leaders to have any effect on subordinates — that is, these factors *neutralize* the effects of leadership. For example, people who are indifferent to the rewards a leader controls are unlikely to be influenced. Thus, the leader's influence is negated by this factor. Leadership also may be irrelevant if conditions make a leader's influence unnecessary — that is, various factors *substitute for* leadership. For example, leadership may be superfluous when subordinates have a highly professional orientation and find their work to be intrinsically satisfying. In short, when the leader's impact is either neutralized or substituted for by various conditions, his or her impact is limited at best.

Many different variables can produce such effects. Thus, we may ask: Under what conditions will leaders have only limited effects on task performance? The answers fall into three categories. First, as mentioned, leadership may be unnecessary because of various individual characteristics. For example, a high level of knowledge, commitment, or experience on the part of subordinates may render it unnecessary for anyone to tell them what to do or how to do it. Second, leadership may be unnecessary if jobs themselves are structured to make direction and influence from a leader redundant. For example, highly routine jobs require little direction, and highly interesting jobs also require little outside stimulation by leaders. Third, various characteristics of organizations also may make leadership unnecessary. For example, various work norms and strong feelings of cohesion among employees may directly affect job performance and render a leader unnecessary. Similarly, the technology associated with certain jobs may strongly determine the decisions and actions of those people performing them — and so leave little room for input from a leader.

Evidence for these assertions has been obtained in several studies.[61] One such study examined the work performance and attitudes of a broad sample of workers who completed scales measuring their perceptions of the extent to which various leadership behaviors and substitutes for leadership were exhibited on their jobs.[62] Consistent with the theory, job performance and attitudes were associated more strongly with the various substitutes than with the leadership behaviors themselves.

If leaders are superfluous in many situations, why is this so often overlooked? One possibility is that people have a strong tendency to *romanticize* leadership — that is, to perceive it as being more important and more closely linked to performance than it actually is.[63] In one study, researchers testing this possibility presented MBA students with detailed financial information about an imaginary firm, including a paragraph describing its key operating strengths. The content of this paragraph varied, however, so that four different groups of students received four different versions. These four versions attributed the firm's performance either to its top-level management team, to the quality of its employees, to changing patterns of consumer needs and preferences, or to federal regulatory policies.

After reading one of these paragraphs and examining other information about the firm, subjects rated two aspects of its overall performance: profitability and risk. It was reasoned that because of the tendency to overestimate the importance of leadership, subjects would rate the firm more favorably when its performance was attributed to top-level management. As Figure 12.16 shows, this was precisely what occurred. The

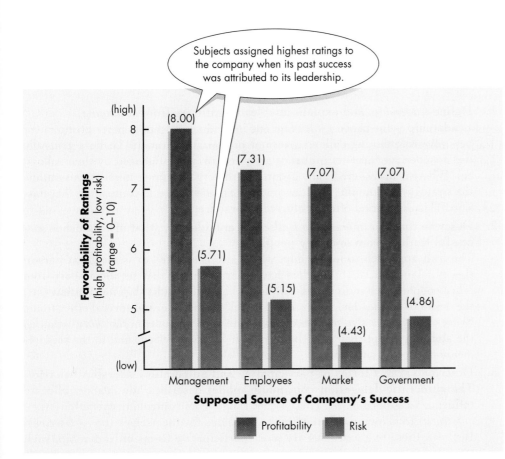

Subjects assigned highest ratings to the company when its past success was attributed to its leadership.

FIGURE 12.16

Overestimating the Importance of Leadership: Research Evidence

People who received information suggesting an imaginary company's success was attributable to its top management rated that company more favorably (i.e., higher in profitability, lower in risk) than those who received information suggesting the identical record resulted from other causes. These findings suggest people *romanticize* leadership, thereby overestimating its effect in many situations.

(*Source*: Based on data reported by Meindl & Ehrlich, 1987; see note 63.)

imaginary company was rated higher in profitability and lower in risk by subjects who read the leadership-based paragraph than by subjects who had read any of the others.

These findings (as well as others) help to explain why leaders often are viewed as being important and necessary — even when to a large degree they are superfluous. Note, however, that this in no way implies leaders usually are unimportant. On the contrary, leaders often do play a key role in work groups and organizations, but because this is not always so, their necessity should never be taken for granted.

We invite you to visit the Greenberg page on the Prentice Hall Web site at: **www.prenhall.com/greenberg** for the monthly Greenberg update and for this chapter's World Wide Web exercise.

SUMMARY AND REVIEW OF LEARNING OBJECTIVES

1. **Define *leadership*, and explain how leading differs from *managing*.**
   Leadership is the process whereby one individual influences other group members toward attaining defined group or organizational goals. Leaders generally use noncoercive forms of influence and, in turn, are influenced by their followers. Whereas *leaders* create the group's or the organization's mission and outline the strategy for attaining it, *managers* are responsible for implementing that mission. This distinction often is blurred in practice.

2. **Describe the *trait approach to leadership*, and identify what distinguishes successful leaders from ordinary people.**
   The **trait approach to leadership**, which also is referred to as the **great person theory**, claims successful leaders have characteristics that set them apart from other people. Such individuals tend to be higher in **leadership motivation** (i.e., the desire to be a leader), drive, honesty, self-confidence, and several other traits. Successful leaders also tend to demonstrate high amounts of *flexibility* — that is, the ability to adapt their style both to their followers' needs and to the requirements of specific situations.

3. **Describe various forms of participative and autocratic leadership behavior.**
   The **autocratic-delegation continuum model** describes how leaders allocate influence to subordinates. These styles range from controlling everything (i.e., *autocratic*) to allowing others to make decisions for themselves (i.e., *delegating*). Between these two extremes are more participative forms of leadership, such

as *consulting* and making *joint decisions*. A more complex approach is taken by the **two-dimensional model of subordinate participation**. It distinguishes between leaders who are *directive* or *permissive* toward subordinates and the extent to which they are *participative* or *autocratic* in their decision making. Individual leaders may be classified into four types by where they fall when these two dimensions are combined. No one style is universally successful, however, and each approach may be better suited to one given situation than to another.

4. **Distinguish the two basic forms of leader behavior — *person-oriented* behavior and *production-oriented* behavior — and explain how *grid training* helps to develop both.**

   Leaders differ regarding the extent to which they focus on attaining successful task performance, which is known as **initiating structure** (or being *production-oriented*), and in their concern with maintaining favorable personal relations with subordinates, which is known as **consideration** (or being *person-oriented*). **Grid training** is a systematic way of training managers to raise their concern for people as well as for production by training them in communication as well as planning skills.

5. **Explain the *leader-member exchange (LMX) model* and the *attributional approach to leadership* in terms of the relationships between leaders and followers.**

   The **leader-member exchange (LMX)** *model* specifies that leaders favor members of some groups (i.e., *in-groups*) more than others (i.e., *out-groups*). As a result, in-groups tend to perform better than out-groups. The relationship between leaders and followers also is the focus of the **attributional approach** to leadership. This approach focuses on leaders' assessments regarding the underlying causes of their followers' performance. Specifically, when leaders perceive the poor performance of their subordinates results from internal factors, they react by helping subordinates to improve. When poor performance is attributed to external factors, however, leaders direct their attention toward changing aspects of the work environment they believed are responsible for this performance.

6. **Describe *charismatic* leadership and how it compares with *transformational* leadership.**

   Charismatic leaders exert profound effects on the beliefs, perceptions, and actions of their followers. Such individuals have a special relationship with their followers as well, inspiring exceptionally high levels of performance, loyalty, and enthusiasm. Charismatic leaders also tend to have high self-confidence, present a clearly articulated vision, behave in extraordinary ways, are recognized as change agents, and are sensitive to environmental constraints. **Transformational leaders**, in addition to being charismatic, also transform and revitalize their organizations. These leaders provide intellectual stimulation, individualized consideration, and inspirational motivation, and they tend to be very effective.

7. **Explain the *contingency theories* of leader effectiveness.**

   Contingency theories of leadership assume there is no one best style of leadership. Instead, the most effective style of leadership is thought to depend on the specific conditions or situations faced.

8. **Summarize the *LPC contingency theory* and the *situational leadership theory* in terms of the connection between leadership style and situational variables.**

   LPC contingency theory suggests that a leader's characteristics and various situational factors determine a group's effectiveness. Task-oriented leaders (i.e., **low-**

LPC leaders) are more effective than people-oriented leaders (i.e., **high-LPC leaders**) when the leader has either high or low control over the group in question. In contrast, people-oriented leaders are more effective when the leader has moderate control. The **situational leadership theory** suggests the most effective style of leadership—*delegating, participating, selling,* or *telling*—depends on the extent to which followers require guidance, direction, and emotional support. Effective leaders diagnose the situations they face and implement the appropriate behavioral style.

9. **Explain *path-goal theory* and *normative decision theory*.**
The **path-goal theory** of leadership suggests that a leader's behavior is accepted by subordinates and enhances their motivation to the extent it helps them progress toward valued goals. A leader's behavior also is accepted when it provides guidance or clarification not already present in work settings. The **normative decision theory** focuses on decision making as a key determinant of leader effectiveness, and it specifies that different situations call for different styles of decision making (e.g., autocratic, consultative, participative) by leaders. Decisions about the most appropriate style for a given situation are based on answers to questions regarding the quality of the decision required and the degree to which followers must accept and be committed to it. Complex decision trees also are used to guide some managers to the most appropriate styles of leadership.

10. **Describe the *substitutes for leadership approach* and what it says about the conditions when leaders are needed in the workplace.**
The **substitutes for leadership** approach suggests that leaders are unnecessary when other factors can have just as much influence. For example, leaders are superfluous when subordinates have exceptionally high levels of knowledge and commitment, jobs are highly structured and routine, and the technology used strongly determines behavior.

QUESTIONS FOR DISCUSSION

1. What are the major differences between leaders, dictators, and managers? Identify some examples of each.

2. It has been said that "great leaders are born, not made." Do you agree with this statement? If so, why? If not, why?

3. Argue for or against the following statement: "The best leaders encourage participation from subordinates."

4. In your experience, do most leaders have a small in-group? If so, what are the effects of this clique on other group members?

5. Explain how the process of attribution is involved in organizational leadership.

6. Consider all the people who have been president of the United States during your lifetime. Which (if any) would you describe as being charismatic? Which (if any) would you describe as being transformational? Explain your answers.

7. Concern for people and concern for production are two recurring themes in the study of leadership. Describe how they manifest themselves in various theories of leadership.

8. Based on the material in this chapter, how can you improve your success as a leader?

Jill Barad: Barbie's Boss

Not many CEOs of $4.8 billion companies once played a beauty queen in a Dino De Laurentis film (*Crazy Joe*) or modeled bellbottom pants. Then again, no one is like Jill Barad. This 48-year-old married mother of two has been described as being "a unique blend of tough and feminine." Tough is what you must be like to make it at Mattel, the giant toy company that is well known for chewing up and spitting out those who attempt to tame it. That is precisely the kind of challenge Barad likes however, and, rising from product manager in 1981 to CEO in 1997, there can be no doubt she has more than met this challenge.

To describe Barad as a "dynamo" would be an understatement. It also would not do her justice, because the same adjective might be used to describe any ordinary mover-and-shaker in the business world. "Ordinary" is not a word you would use to describe anything about Barad, however. She is visible, vocal, and never fails to express her point of view — no matter how many toes she may step on.

She quickly worked her way up the corporate ladder at Mattel by finding out what was needed to get ahead and then making it happen. One of her biggest accomplishments was resuscitating the company's famed Barbie doll, whose sales were languishing at $200 million annually when Barad first took over the brand. By developing new dolls, outfits, and Barbie-branded products — including a digital camera children can use to put their images next to Barbie's on a computer — she grew sales to $2 billion, thereby accounting for 55 percent of Mattel's operating profits. Toy industry experts also expect this figure to rise dramatically as Mattel develops local-version Barbie dolls to be sold in countries around the world. Even before this international push, three Barbies already are being sold every second!

The hard-driving, fiercely competitive Barad has done her best to make this happen. Her sharp tongue and combative nature have made it impossible for anyone in the toy industry — let alone inside Mattel — to take her for granted. It is not only Barad's brashness that has taken her to the top, however. It also is a keen sense of style, which has led her to develop eye-catching packages that help Mattel products to fly off store shelves. These boxes are almost as attention-getting as Barad herself, whose bright, flashy clothing helps her to stand out in a navy-blue, button-down, corporate world.

Barad does not need to look flashy to call attention to herself, however. Her talent and the impressive growth of her company do all the work. There is not one aspect of the job in which Barad is not involved, either. Take a recent Barbie makeover. After the options were presented to her, she breezed around the table and made all her choices in only 5 minutes. Few CEOs take such a hands-on approach to product decisions. Then again, Barad feels a real connection to Barbie — she's a fan herself, having 52 different Barbies in her office.

Make no mistake: Beneath this hard-driving executive is a person who truly cares about her employees. She has done a great deal for them as well, such as extending insurance benefits to domestic partners and lengthening the year-end holiday break to a full 16 days. "I love you all" she openly announced to employees at one recent company meeting. If the rousing applause as she took the stage is any indication, the feeling clearly is mutual, too.

CRITICAL THINKING QUESTIONS

1. What is your opinion of Jill Barad as a leader? Would you be comfortable or uncomfortable working for her?

2. Regarding her participativeness as a leader, how would you describe Barad?

3. What characteristics have been responsible for Barad's success as a leader?

4. What behaviors have been responsible for Barad's success as a leader?

5. In what ways, if any, do you believe Barad's leadership style should change? Explain your answer.

Leadership in Organizations

SMALL BUSINESS 2000

You probably can easily think of some businesses that have been around a long time. You also probably can think of others that have not lasted very long. Why do you think some survive whereas others fail? One consideration is the leadership of the company. You also might think that if a company has survived for a long time, then it can survive forever. Although, at first, this might make sense, think about it a minute. Do you drive the same type of car that your parents did when they were your age? Is the PC you buy today the same as the one you might have bought even three years ago? The answer to these questions is probably no. Age alone does not guarantee success. Rather, it is the knowledge and experience that age provides that contributes to a company's success.

In Newark, New Jersey, Howard Kent has been running a pipe and industrial valve company for more than 30 years. The basic products he sells haven't changed much in that time, but the way that the company runs surely has. Kent takes us on a trip down memory lane and discusses the evolution of his company. Some companies change because the technology or product they sell changes. The Ironbound Supply Company changed—and still does—because of the approach Kent has to running a business.

In addition to understanding how the business has evolved over 30 years, we learn at least two other things from Kent. First, we gain an understanding of the importance of working smart. Kent talks about ef-ficiency and the importance of taking advantage of technology in running a company. Second, we learn about Kent's attitude toward the importance of the people that make up a company. Kent is no push-over, but he is concerned about being fair with his employees. As you watch this video, try to imagine how this company has changed from the day Kent started it as a one-person operation to what it is today.

QUESTIONS FOR DISCUSSION

1. Howard Kent does not run the same company that he did 30 years ago. What do you think about Kent as a leader? Do you think he is a leader? Why, or why not?

2. We met Scott Gross, an 18-year veteran at Ironbound Supply, who has worked his way up from truck driver to vice president. Kent talked about what he thought of Gross and a little bit about why he has the job he does today. What do you think this says about Kent's approach to leadership?

3. Kent talked about "backing off and relinquishing some control." Do you think this is easy for him to do? What advice might you give him on how to handle mistakes that could be made as new managers grow into their roles?

4. What do you think about Kent's attitude toward sharing the wealth and determining if raises should be given? Do you think this is a good attitude for him to have? Why, or why not?

SKILLS BANK

EXPERIENCING ORGANIZATIONAL BEHAVIOR

Determining Your Leadership Style

As noted in this chapter, *situational leadership theory* identifies four basic leadership styles. To identify and enact the most appropriate style in any given situation, you first must understand the style to which you are most predisposed. This exercise helps you to gain such insight.

Directions

Following are eight hypothetical situations in which you must make a decision affecting both you and your work group. For each situation, indicate which of the following actions you would be most likely to take.

Action A: Let the group members decide what to do.

Action B: Ask the group members what to do but make the final decision yourself.

Action C: Make the decision yourself but explain your reasons.

Action D: Make the decision yourself and simply tell the group exactly what to do.

_____ 1. Because of financial pressures, you are forced to make budget cuts for your unit. Where do you cut?

_____ 2. To meet an impending deadline, someone in your secretarial pool must work late one evening to finish typing an important report. Who will it be?

_____ 3. As coach of the company softball team, you must trim your squad to 25 players from the current 30 on the roster. Who goes?

_____ 4. Employees in your department must schedule their summer vacations to keep the office appropriately staffed. Who decides first?

_____ 5. As chair of the social committee, you must determine the theme for the company ball. How do you do so?

_____ 6. You have an opportunity to buy or rent an important piece of equipment for your company. After gathering all the facts, how do you make the choice?

_____ 7. The office is being redecorated. How do you decide on the color scheme?

_____ 8. Along with your associates, you are taking a visiting dignitary to dinner. How do you decide on a restaurant?

Scoring

1. Count the number of situations to which you responded by marking *A*. This is your *delegating* score.
2. Count the number of situations to which you responded by marking *B*. This is your *participating* score.
3. Count the number of situations to which you responded by marking *C*. This is your *selling* score.
4. Count the number of situations to which you responded by marking *D*. This is your *telling* score.

Questions for Discussion

1. Based on this questionnaire, what was your predominant leadership style? Is this consistent with what you would have predicted in advance?
2. According to situational leadership theory, in what kinds of situations would this style be most appropriate? Have you ever been in such a situation, and if so, how well did you do?
3. Do you think it is possible for you to change this style, if needed?
4. To what extent were your responses affected by the nature of the situations described? In other words, would you have opted for different decisions in different situations?

WORKING IN GROUPS

Who Are the Great Leaders, and What Makes Them so Great?

One useful way to understand the *great person theory* is to identify "great leaders" and then to consider what makes them so great. This exercise is designed to guide a class in this activity.

Directions

1. Divide the class into four equal-size groups, arranging each in a semicircle.
2. In the open part of the semicircle, one group member — the recorder — should stand at a flip chart and write down the group's responses.
3. The members of each group should identify the 10 most effective leaders they can think of — living or dead, real or fictional — in one of the following fields: business, sports, politics/government, and humanitarian endeavors. One group should cover each of these domains. If more than 10 names are mentioned, the group should vote on the 10 best. The recorder should write down the names as they are identified.
4. Examining the list, group members should identify the traits and characteristics these people have in common that distinguish them from others. In other words, what makes these people so special? The recorder should write down the answers.
5. One person from each group should present his or her group's responses to the class. This should include both the names and the underlying characteristics.

Questions for Discussion

1. How did the traits identified in this exercise compare with those described in this chapter as being important determinants of leadership? Were they similar or different? Why?
2. To what extent were the traits identified in the various groups different or similar? In other words, were different characteristics associated with success in different walks of life, or were the ingredients for success more universal?
3. Were some traits identified surprising to you, or were they all expected?
4. Is it possible to change the traits identified in this exercise, or are they immutable?

CULTURE, CREATIVITY, AND INNOVATION

LEARNING OBJECTIVES

After reading this chapter, you should be able to

1. Define *organizational culture*.
2. Distinguish *dominant organizational culture* from *subcultures*.
3. Describe the role of culture in organizations.
4. Describe the four types of organizational culture identified by the *double S cube*.
5. Identify various factors that lead to the creation of organizational culture.
6. Identify the tools through which organizational culture is transmitted.
7. Describe the effects of organizational culture on organizational functioning.
8. Identify the factors responsible for changing organizational culture.
9. Define *creativity* and describe the basic components of individual and team creativity.
10. Define *innovation* and identify the basic components of innovation and the various stages of the innovation process.

PREVIEW CASE

Behind the Scenes with Steven Spielberg

Unless you've been living under a rock somewhere in Jurassic Park, you probably recognize Steven Spielberg as the king of the Hollywood blockbusters. In an industry where many movies fail to break even, Spielberg consistently draws moviegoers to the big screen with monumental films like *E.T.*, *Jaws*, and *Raiders of the Lost Ark*. Beneath this success lies a unique individual whose cinematic magic has been nurtured—if not inspired—by more than just a little managerial magic.

All told, the Spielberg empire is estimated to have surpassed $1 billion in value. In addition to Spielberg's film, television, and animation company, Amblin Entertainment, the multifaceted entrepreneur also owns large portions of restaurants and other businesses. Among the most important of these is DreamWorks SKG, the movie studio Spielberg launched in 1994 along with record executive David Geffen and former Disney executive Jeffrey Katzenberg. If for nothing else, this venture is noteworthy because it is the only major Hollywood studio to be formed in the last 50 years!

When asked where he gets his ideas, Spielberg usually points to some personal tie that inspired him. For example, *E.T.* in many ways reflects the sadness and loneliness he felt when his parents' marriage ended during his teenage years. His interest in the Nazi Holocaust of World War II, reflected in his films *Schindler's List* (1993) and *The Last Days* (1999), may be traced to relatives lost in those atrocities and a grandmother who taught English to European Jews who survived. Will the reservoir of inspiration ever run dry? Reassuring film buffs, Spielberg explains he will never be able to capture on film all the stories he wants to tell in his lifetime.

When not on location, Spielberg travels daily to his DreamWorks office, where he always takes the time to consult with his various teams. Much initial screening is handled by the husband-and-wife team of Walter Parkes and Laurie MacDonald, who head the DreamWorks film unit. Frequently, this trusted duo updates Spielberg on potential projects as well as those already in the works. Spielberg also gets together with screenwriters and producers to discuss current DreamWorks projects. The hardworking Spielberg is always willing to consider the suggestions of team members, but he admits to sometimes overruling ideas with little or no discussion.

Still Spielberg can recognize and tap into the talent of others when he sees it. As Tom Hanks, the star of Spielberg's award-winning 1998 film *Saving Private Ryan*, notes, "It's Spielberg, so you work that much harder to please him." Other Hollywood actors such as Drew Barrymore, the child star of *E.T.*, and Whoopi Goldberg, whose first film was Spielberg's *The Color Purple*, also credit this talented director with drawing out the very best of their abilities.

Beyond the artistic realm, another area in which Spielberg has been creative is finding ways to save money. For example, Spielberg often uses bags of flour to simulate explosions before filming. In addition, when a construction crew mistakenly built a radar tower facing the sun during the filming of *Saving Private Ryan*, Spielberg chose not to have it rebuilt. Instead, he selected different angles for shooting.

Unquestionably, films are the mainstay of Spielberg's empire, but his interests also draw him into new territory. For example, he indicates that his foray into the world of cartoons (e.g., *Animaniacs*, *Tiny Toons*) may be short-lived. The family oriented entrepreneur openly admits that his animated endeavors continue largely because, as he says, "my kids think I'm cool when I do it." The child in him also inspired DreamWorks' joint venture with Sega Enterprises. Given the success of his efforts to date, most Spielberg fans hope that child will never grow up.

I f you were to use one word to capture the genius of Steven Spielberg, it would be "creative." Indeed, Spielberg brings an enormous amount of *creativity* and talent to the process of film-making. At the same time, it is not only Spielberg's creativity as an individual that makes his projects so successful but also the credibly high degree of *innovation* shown by the companies he runs. Something special is in the air at DreamWorks and other Spielberg companies, and it makes the people in them willing to go out on a limb to create entertaining products. This magical something is not the product of film-making special effects but of good management—that is, there is something unique about these companies that makes them so special.

Then again, anyone who has worked in several different organizations surely knows that in one way or another, each organization is unique. Even those concerned with the same activities or that provide similar products or services can be very different places. For example, in retailing, Wal-Mart employees have long been encouraged to be agents for the customer, thereby focusing on service and satisfaction.[1] In contrast, employees of Sears allegedly have been pressured into meeting sales quotas, thereby pushing customers to make unnecessary purchases.[2]

Both Sears and Wal-Mart are large, national chains selling a large variety of goods, but somehow, these similar businesses have taken very different approaches to customer service. Why is this? It is tempting to speculate that because people have different personalities, the organizations in which they work have different personalities as well. When you consider that entire organizations often are so consistently different from each other, however, it becomes apparent that more is involved than simple differences in the employee personalities. In fact, in many organizations, the employees are constantly changing, but despite such shifts, the organizations themselves change only slowly—if at all. In fact, it often is the new employees who change rather than the organization. In a sense, organizations have a stable existence of their own, and one that is quite apart from the unique combination of people of which they are composed at any given time.

What accounts for such stability? To a great extent, the answer involves the shared beliefs, expectations, and core values of the people in the organization—what is known as *organizational culture*.[3] Once established, these beliefs, expectations, and values tend to be relatively stable and to strongly influence both organizations and those working in them.

Among these influences lies a particularly important one—that is, an organization's tendency toward *creativity* and *innovation*. As you probably know, some people— even if they are not at the level of Steven Spielberg—regularly take novel, ingenious, and cutting-edge approaches to problems. What accounts for such differences in individual creativity, and why are some organizations more innovative than others? People in one organization are unlikely to be more creative than people in another by chance alone. Indeed, companies such as 3M, Gillette, and Rubbermaid go out of their way to breed cultures in which creativity and innovation flourish (Figure 13.1).

What makes these companies—and others like them—places where people routinely do the nonroutine? This question concerning the culture of creativity and innovation is addressed in this chapter. To set the stage, we begin by describing the basic nature of organizational culture, including the role it plays in organizations. Then, we describe the processes through which organizational culture is both formed and maintained. Following this, we review the effects of organizational culture on individual and organizational functioning, and we examine both when and how culture is subject to change. This discussion of organizational culture will prepare us for understanding the nature of creativity and innovation in organizations, which is the major topic in the second half of this chapter—that is, how this creativity can be harnessed to implement innovative ideas in organizations.

FIGURE 13.1

Gillette: A Company at the Cutting Edge

You might not think of shaving as the kind of activity that requires much innovation, but Gillette Co. has been developing breakthroughs for many years. The key, says CEO Alfred Zeien, is developing a culture that constantly inspires employees to come up with new ideas—and then brings those ideas to life.

organizational culture

A cognitive framework consisting of attitudes, values, behavioral norms, and expectations shared by an organization's members.

FIGURE 13.2

Yahoo!: A Culture of Open Communication

Timothy A. Koogle grew Yahoo! into one of the best-known brands on the Internet — and one of today's leading Web portals. His idea of making the organization a consumer-driven media company became successful largely because he created a culture in which employees communicated with each other freely and joined in whatever decisions needed to be made. This aspect of the company's culture is considered to be essential in the ultrafast-moving world of the Internet.

THE BASIC NATURE OF ORGANIZATIONAL CULTURE

To fully appreciate organizational culture, we must understand its basic nature. Therefore, we now examine three key aspects of culture; its basic characteristics, whether there generally is only one or more than one culture within organizations, and the role culture plays in organizational functioning.

Organizational Culture: A Definition and Core Characteristics

Thus far, we have discussed organizational culture in general terms, so a specific definition is in order. Accordingly, we define **organizational culture** as a cognitive framework consisting of attitudes, values, behavioral norms, and expectations shared by the organization's members.[4] At the root of any organizational culture is a set of core characteristics that are collectively valued by the members. Several such characteristics are especially important (Table 13.1).[5]

First, organizations differ regarding their *sensitivity to the needs of customers and employees*. For example, several years ago, the organizational culture at UPS was relatively rigid and inflexible in terms of customer needs. Today, however, the culture places a high value on customer service and satisfaction.

Second, organizations differ regarding their *interest in having employees generate new ideas*. Walt Disney Co. employees — or "cast members" as they are called — undergo lengthy orientation to ensure they know exactly what to say and how to behave toward guests. In contrast, people working at MCI are encouraged to be unique and to bring fresh ideas to their work. In fact, company founder Bill McGowan is so adamant about this characteristic that procedure manuals are nowhere to be found at MCI.

Third, companies differ regarding the *value placed on taking risks*. For example, Bank of America is very conservative, making only the safest investments, but buyers at The Limited are discouraged from making too many "safe" choices.

Fourth, organizations differ regarding the *openness of available communication options*. In some newer organizations such as Yahoo!, the popular Internet media company, employees are expected to make decisions freely and to communicate with whomever is needed to get the job done — even if that means going right to CEO Timothy A. Koogle (Figure 13.2). At IBM, however, the tradition is to work within the proper channels and to vest power in only a few key individuals (although this appears to be changing). These examples clearly illustrate different sets of core values that are reflected in organizational cultures.

TABLE 13.1

Core Organizational Values Reflected in Culture

Organizations may be distinguished by their basic values, such as the fundamental ones summarized here.

- Sensitivity to needs of customers and employees
- Freedom to initiate new ideas
- Willingness to tolerate taking risks
- Openness to communication options

Source: Based on suggestions by Martin, 1992; see note 5.

Cultures Within Organizations: One or Many?

Our discussion thus far has implied each organization has only a single, uniform culture—that is, one set of shared values, beliefs, and expectations. Rarely, however, is this the case. Instead, organizations—and particularly large ones—typically have *several* cultures operating within them.

In general, people tend to have more attitudes and values in common with others in their own fields or work units than with those in other fields or units of the organization. These various groups may be said to have several different **subcultures**—that is, cultures existing within parts of organizations rather than entirely throughout them. Typically, these are distinguished by functional differences (i.e., the type of work) or geographic distances (i.e., the physical separation between people). Indeed, several subcultures based on occupational, professional, or functional divisions usually exist within any large organization.

This is not to say there also may not be a **dominant culture**—that is, a distinctive, overarching "personality" of an organization and the kind of culture to which we have been referring. A dominant culture reflects its core values, its dominant perceptions that generally are shared throughout the organization. Typically, members of subcultures, who may share additional sets of values, generally also accept the core values of their organizations as a whole. Thus, subcultures should not be considered as totally separate cultures but rather as "mini" cultures operating within a larger, dominant one.

subcultures

Cultures existing within parts of an organization rather than entirely throughout it.

dominant culture

The distinctive, overarching "personality" of an organization.

A dominant culture may override the local norms within a subculture. Can you think of instances when this process may be unethical? Explain. ■

ETHICS MATTERS

Culture's Role in Organizations

As you read about the various cultural values that make organizations special, you probably realize culture is an intangible force (albeit one with far-reaching consequences). Indeed, culture plays several important roles in organizations.

Most obviously, an organization's culture provides a *sense of identity* for the members. The more clearly an organization's shared perceptions and values are defined, the more strongly people can associate themselves with the organization's mission and can feel they are a vital part of it. For example, employees at Southwest Airlines feel special because of their company's emphasis on having fun and joking around on the job—a widespread practice initiated by the founder, Herb Kelleher. Southwest's employees feel strongly associated with the company; they feel that they belong there. As a result, these employees only infrequently resign to take positions at other airlines.

This example also illustrates a second important function of culture: generating *commitment to the organization's mission*. People sometimes have difficulty in thinking beyond their own interests (i.e., how will this affect me?) When there is a strong, overarching culture, however, people feel they are part of that larger, well-defined whole and are involved in the entire organization's work. Bigger than any one individual's interests, culture reminds people what their organization is all about.

A third important function of culture is to *clarify and to reinforce standards of behavior*. This is essential for newcomers, but it also is beneficial for seasoned veterans. In essence, the culture guides the employees' words and deeds, thus making it clear what they should do or say in a given situation. In this sense, it provides stability to behavior, both what an individual might do at different times and what different individuals might do at the same time. For example, in a company with a culture that strongly supports customer satisfaction, employees have clear guidance regarding how

FIGURE 13.3

The Basic Functions of Organizational Culture

Organizational culture serves the three major functions summarized here.

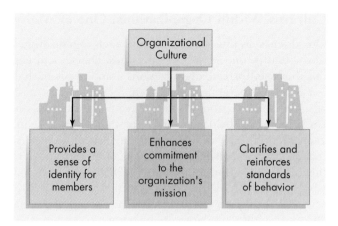

to behave: doing whatever it takes to please the customer. By serving these three important roles, culture clearly is an important force influencing behavior in organizations. (For a summary, see Figure 13.3.)

GLOBAL MATTERS   Both organizational culture and national culture strongly influence people and teams on the job. How are these two types of culture similar or different from each other? ■

IDENTIFYING ORGANIZATIONAL CULTURES: THE DOUBLE S CUBE

As you might imagine, the culture of any organization can be described in many ways. To understand and to compare organizational cultures, however, it helps to have a systematic taxonomy for organizing them. Recently, a pair of British scientists and consultants have developed a very promising system for doing precisely this.[6] We describe this system here.

Two Underlying Dimensions of Organizational Culture

double S cube

A system of categorizing four types of organizational culture by combining two dimensions, *sociability* and *solidarity*. Each of the four resulting cultural types—*networked culture, mercenary culture, fragmented culture,* and *communal culture*—can be both positive and negative in nature.

The system for categorizing varieties of organizational culture is known as the **double S cube**, and it is summarized in Figure 13.4. The name comes from the fact that the approach characterizes organizational culture along two independent dimensions, both of which begin with the letter "s" — *sociability* and *solidarity*.

By combining high and low amounts of these two dimensions, four basic types of organizational culture can be identified. In Figure 13.4, these are indicated by the large square (containing the four smaller squares) at the front of the diagram. Each of the four resulting types of organizational culture has both positive and negative qualities, however, so a third dimension is added, which extends the square into a cube. We now describe the two basic dimensions on which the four types of organizational culture are based.

sociability

A dimension of the *double S cube* characterized by the degree of friendliness among members of an organization.

The Sociability Dimension   The first dimension, **sociability**, is just as it sounds — that is, a measure of the friendliness of an organization's members. Among the first things a new employee notices about a company is its degree of sociability. Some companies are very friendly and have people who always socialize and go out together (i.e., high sociability). Others are composed of people who largely refrain from socializing and who stick to themselves (i.e., low sociability).

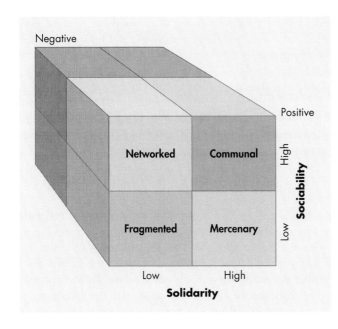

FIGURE 13.4

The Double S Cube

According to the **double S cube**, four types of organizational culture may be identified by combining two key dimensions, **sociability** and **solidarity**. Each of the four types of culture has both positive and negative aspects associated with it.

(*Source*: "Double S Cube" from THE CHARACTER OF A CORPORATION by ROB GOFFEE and GARETH JONES. Copyright © 1998 by Rob Goffee and Gareth Jones. Reprinted by permission of HarperCollins Publishers, Inc.)

Sociability has both a positive side and a negative side. On the positive side, sociability helps to promote creativity, because it encourages people to work together in teams and to share information, thereby making them open to new ideas.[7] On the negative side, sociability may cause workers to form informal cliques that can become so influential they actually subvert the usual decision-making process. In keeping with this idea, members of highly sociable groups may be reluctant to disagree or to criticize each other, thus possibly leading to the problem of groupthink (see chapter 9).

The Solidarity Dimension   The second dimension of organizational culture, **solidarity**, has nothing to do with people liking each other. Instead, it focuses on the extent to which the people share a common understanding of the organization's tasks and goals. Police officers in pursuit of a criminal and surgeons at an operating table have a high degree of solidarity, because they tend to stick together in a highly focused way to accomplish an agreed-on goal. Many times, however, people work together on tasks about which they share little common focus. Such a low-solidarity group may be seen when a committee is composed of individuals with little interest in working on the topic at hand.

It is easy to imagine how high solidarity can be beneficial in getting an important job done. The police officers who come to each other's aid and the surgeons who coordinate their efforts can accomplish a great deal because of their solidarity. At the same time, however, high solidarity can be painful to anyone who is not part of the team. For example, imagine how difficult things might be for a rookie police officer on a squad of veterans who all work together like the gears of a finely tuned clock. This newcomer might feel excluded and wonder if he or she will ever "fit in."

Four Organizational Cultures

By combining high and low levels of both sociability and solidarity, it is possible to identify four basic types of organizational culture.[8] Each is identified in Figure 13.4, and we also describe them here.

Networked Culture   Starting in the upper-left corner of Figure 13.4, we find the **networked culture,** which is characterized by high sociability and low solidarity. Networked cultures are extremely friendly and light-hearted in style. People tend to keep their doors open, and they tend to talk about business in a casual, informal

solidarity

A dimension of the *double S cube* characterized by the degree to which people share a common understanding of their organization's tasks and goals.

networked culture

In the *double S cube*, a type of organizational culture characterized by high sociability and low solidarity.

manner. They also spend a great deal of time socializing — and without getting into trouble because of it! In networked cultures, people generally get to know each other quickly and feel they are part of the group.

mercenary culture

In the *double S cube*, a type of organizational culture characterized by low sociability and high solidarity.

Mercenary Culture   At the opposite extreme, in the lower-right corner of Figure 13.4, is the **mercenary culture,** which is characterized by low sociability and high solidarity. Mercenary cultures involve people who are highly focused on pulling together to get the job done. Communication tends to be swift, direct, and handled in a no-nonsense way; a businesslike manner predominates. Idle chatter is not tolerated, because it is considered to be a waste of time. Winning is considered to be everything, and people are encouraged to put in whatever time is necessary to make that happen.

fragmented culture

In the *double S cube*, a type of organizational culture characterized by low sociability and low solidarity.

Fragmented Culture   In the lower-left corner of Figure 13.4 is the **fragmented culture,** which is characterized by low solidarity and low sociability. People working in fragmented cultures are likely to have little contact with their associates — and in many cases, they may not even know each other. Employees talk to others when it is necessary or useful to do so, but people generally leave each other alone. In fact, people go to the office only when they feel it is absolutely necessary, so absence is common. Not surprisingly, members of a fragmented culture do not identify with the organization in which they work. Instead, they tend to identify with the profession of which they are a part.

communal culture

In the *double S cube*, a type of organizational culture characterized by both high sociability and high solidarity.

Communal Culture   Finally, in the upper-right corner of Figure 13.4, we find the **communal culture,** which is characterized by high sociability and high solidarity. Members of communal cultures are very friendly with each other, and they get along well both personally and professionally. Communal cultures widely exist among many computer-related companies (Figure 13.5). Because individuals in such organizations tend to share so many things, it often is difficult to determine who is assigned to a

FIGURE 13.5

Communal Cultures Predominate in the Computer Biz

Jack Breese, Eric Horvitz, and David Heckerman developed the Troubleshooting Wizard at Microsoft's web site. Inquire as to why your printer won't print, and their program guides you through the troubleshooting process. Microsoft — and many other high-tech organizations — tend to have highly communal cultures. Computer programmers generally expect communal cultures to predominate in their industry and believe they work best under such conditions.

particular office. Communication flows easily across people at all levels of the organization and in all formats. Everyone is so friendly, in fact, that the distinction between work and nonwork times often is blurred. Employees strongly identify with communal organizations. They wear the company logo, live the company credo, and staunchly support the organization when talking about it with outsiders.

GLOBAL MATTERS

The concept of the double S cube was developed by scientists in England. To what extent do you believe it does a good job of describing organizational culture in your own national culture? Do you think the four cultural types are equally likely to be found among companies in different countries? ■

Interpreting Organizational Culture

To assess systematically people's perceptions of their organization's culture using the double S cube, many employees complete a questionnaire similar to the one shown in Table 13.2 to assess sociability and solidarity. Items such as these may help to identify which type of culture people believe their organization possesses, but it is important to remember several key points once you have this information. In other words, what, exactly, do these types of organizational culture mean? Before jumping to any conclusions, pay careful attention to the three points:

1. *Companies contain not one but several cultures.* Recall that an organization may have one dominant culture but also several distinct subcultures. For example, some large organizations have very different subcultures in different units, and one individual completing a questionnaire is most likely to tell you about his or her personal experiences — which likely are based on limited experiences. After you read about the many factors responsible for creating and maintaining culture (in the next section), you will not find this to be surprising.

2. *Organizational cultures tend to change over time.* Suppose that you create a new company. It is likely to be small and friendly — that is, to be communal. As the company changes, however, its culture can be expected to change

TABLE 13.2

Assessing Organizational Culture
Questions similar to these are used to assess the *sociability* and the *solidarity* dimensions of organizational culture. Responses take the form of indicating (on a scale ranging from 1 to 5) the extent to which the respondent agrees with each statement, with higher scores reflecting greater agreement.

The more you agree with these statements, the higher is your score with respect to . . .

SOCIABILITY	SOLIDARITY
Where I work, the people like each other a great deal.	The people in my company know their goals very clearly.
In my company, people generally get along very well.	At work, we give and get very strong guidelines about what to do.
At work, we do small favors for each other.	If someone performs poorly, we deal with it at once.
On the job, we make friends just because we want to; there is no other agenda.	Where I work, being successful is the most important thing.
We look out for each other on the job.	Every project we start, we also complete; nothing is left hanging.

Source: Based on material in Goffee and Jones, 1998; see note 6.

as well. Precisely how is difficult to say, mostly because so many factors play important roles in the process. Suffice it to say that organizational culture is fluid, not fixed. To describe this process, we rather like the analogy of a family: The relationships between its members are likely to change over time as people change, conditions change, and members come and go. If you recognize how the dynamics of your family has changed over the years, you can appreciate how the culture of an organization is likely to change.

3. *No one culture is necessarily better or worse than any other.* Is it better to have a communal culture than a fragmented culture? Is any one culture better than the others? The answer to both questions is "no." To make this point, we need only to reiterate a basic premise of the double S cube: All cultures have both positive and negative sides. Interestingly, some organizations are successful because they have particular cultures that might be completely inappropriate in other companies. The trick to an effective organizational culture is not to have any particular form of culture but rather to have the right culture for the specific conditions. Culture is complex, so what works in one company might not work in another. Even within a given company, the kind of culture that is most effective might change over time.

Clearly, identifying organizational culture is just the beginning. Interpreting what it really means for an organization to have a certain culture is important as well.

THE FORMATION AND MAINTENANCE OF ORGANIZATIONAL CULTURE

Now that we have described the basic nature of organizational culture, we consider two more important issues: how culture initially is created, and how culture is sustained (i.e., what keeps it going once it is created).

How Is Organizational Culture Created?

Why do many individuals within an organization share basic attitudes, values, and expectations? Several factors contribute to this state of affairs and, hence, to the emergence of an organizational culture.

Company Founders   Organizational culture may be traced, at least in part, to the founders of the company.[9] These individuals often possess dynamic personalities, strong values, and a clear vision of how the organization should operate. Because they are on the scene first and play a key role in hiring the initial staff, their attitudes and values are readily transmitted to new employees. The result? These views become the accepted ones in the organization, and they persist as long as the founders are on the scene.

The culture at Microsoft, for example, calls for working exceptionally long hours—largely because that is what co-founder Bill Gates has always done. Sometimes, a founder's values continue to drive an organization's culture even after that individual is no longer there. For example, the late Ray Kroc founded the McDonald's restaurant chain on the values of good food at a good price in clean, family oriented surroundings; these key cultural values persist today. Likewise, Walt Disney's wholesome family values are still cherished at the company that bears his name, largely because employees ask themselves, "What would Walt think?"[10] These individuals' values continue to permeate their companies and to be central parts of their dominant cultures.

ETHICS MATTERS

Is it unethical for the founder of a company to encourage employees to adapt to his or her views? Can you think of instances when doing so is coercive? When doing so is not coercive? ■

Experience with the Environment   Organizational culture also often develops from an organization's experience with the external environment. Every organization must find a niche in its industry and in the marketplace. As the organization struggles to do so in its early days, some values and practices may work better than others. For example, one company may determine that delivering defect-free products is its unique market niche; by doing so, it can build a core of customers who prefer it to competing businesses. Thus, this organization gradually may acquire a deep, shared commitment to high quality. In contrast, another company may find that selling moderate-quality products at attractive prices works best. The result? A dominant value centering around *price leadership* takes shape. In these—and countless other—ways, an organization's culture is shaped by its interaction with the external environment.

Contact with Others   Organizational culture develops out of contact between groups of individuals within an organization as well. To a large extent, culture involves shared interpretations of events and actions by organization members. In short, organizational culture reflects that people assign similar meaning to various events and actions. In other words, they come to perceive key aspects of the world (i.e., those relevant to the organization's work) in a similar manner (see chapter 2).

Tools for Transmitting Culture

How are cultural values transmitted between people? In other words, how do employees learn about their organization's culture? Several key mechanisms are involved: *symbols, stories, jargon, ceremonies,* and *statements of principle.*

Symbols: Objects That Say More Than Meets the Eye   First, organizations often rely on **symbols**—that is, material objects that connote meanings beyond their intrinsic content (Figure 13.6). For example, some companies use impressive buildings to convey the organization's strength and significance as a large, stable place. Other companies rely on slogans to symbolize their values. These slogans change all the time, but classic examples include General Electric's "Progress is our most important product" and Ford's "Quality is job one." Corporate cars—or even jets!—also

symbols
Material objects that connote meanings beyond their intrinsic content.

"*I don't know how it started, either. All I know is that it's part of our corporate culture.*"

FIGURE 13.6

Symbols: Important Indicators of Corporate Culture

The culture of an organization is transmitted largely by various symbols. Various slogans and objects—such as these silly hats!—are used in this connection.

(*Source*: ©The New Yorker Collection 1994. Mick Stevens from cartoonbank.com. All Rights Reserved.)

convey information about certain aspects of an organization's culture, such as who wields power.

In one interesting study, a researcher showed drawings of company reception areas to people and then asked them to evaluate what the organizations pictured were like.[11] Different types of symbols projected different images of the organizations' likely cultures. For example, firms with many plants and flower arrangements were judged to have friendly, person-oriented cultures, whereas those with awards and trophies were believed to be highly interested in achieving success. These findings suggest material symbols are potent tools for sending messages about organizational culture. (To demonstrate this phenomenon for yourself, try the "Working in Groups" exercise at the end of this chapter.)

Stories: "In the Old Days, We Used to . . ."   Organizations also transmit information about culture by the *stories* told in them, both formally and informally. Stories illustrate key aspects of an organization's culture, and telling them can effectively introduce or reaffirm those values.[12] Stories need not involve some great event, however, such as someone who saved the company with a single decision. They may be small tales that become legends because they so effectively communicate a message. For example, employees at the British confectionery firm Cadbury are purposely told stories about the company's founding on Quaker traditions to get them to appreciate — and to accept — the basic Quaker value of hard work.

Jargon: The Special Language That Defines a Culture   Even without telling stories, the everyday language used in companies helps to sustain culture. For example, the slang — or *jargon* — in a company helps its members to define their identities as members of an organization (see chapter 6). For example, employees at IBM for many years referred to disk drives as "hard files" and to circuit boards as "planar boards," terms that defined the insulated nature of their culture.

Today, someone who works in human resources may talk about the FMCS (i.e., Federal Mediation and Conciliation Service), ERISA (i.e., Employee Retirement Income Security Act), BFOQs (i.e., bona fide occupational qualifications), RMs (i.e., elections to vote out a union), and other acronyms that sound odd to the uninitiated. Over time, as organizations — or departments within them — develop a unique language to describe their work, these terms (although strange to newcomers) serve as a common factor that brings together individuals belonging to a corporate culture or subculture.

Ceremonies: Special Events That Commemorate Corporate Values   Organizations also sustain their cultures by conducting various types of *ceremonies*. Indeed, ceremonies may be seen as celebrations of an organization's basic values and assumptions. Just as a wedding ceremony symbolizes a couple's mutual commitment and a presidential inauguration ceremony the beginning of a new administration, various organizational ceremonies also celebrate some important accomplishment. For example, one accounting firm celebrated its move to better facilities by throwing a party — a celebration signifying it "had arrived" or "made it to the big time." Such ceremonies convey meaning to people both inside and outside the organization. As one expert put it, "Ceremonies are to the culture what the movie is to the script . . . values that are difficult to express in any other way."[13]

GLOBAL MATTERS

statements of principle

Explicitly written statements describing the principles and beliefs that guide an organization. Such documents can help to reinforce an organization's culture.

How might the use of symbols, stories, and ceremonies to transmit organizational culture be affected by national culture? ■

Statements of Principle: Defining Culture in Writing   Another way in which culture is transmitted is by direct **statements of principle**. Some organizations have explicitly written their principles for all to see. For example, Forrest Mars, the founder of the candy company M&M Mars, developed his "Five Principles of Mars" that still guide his company today: quality (i.e., everyone is responsible for maintaining quality), responsibility (i.e., all employees are responsible for their own actions and decisions), mutuality (i.e., creating a situation in which everyone can win), efficiency (i.e., most factories operate continuously), and freedom (i.e., giving employees opportunities to shape their futures).

Some companies also have make explicit the moral aspects of their cultures by publishing **codes of ethics**—that is, explicit statements of a company's ethical values. According to Hershey Foods' CEO Richard Zimmerman, this is an effective device: "[O]ften, an individual joins a firm without recognizing the type of environment in which he will place himself and his career. The loud and clear enunciation of a company's code of conduct . . . [allows] that employee to determine whether or not he fits that particular culture."[14]

codes of ethics
Explicit statements of a company's ethical values.

ETHICS MATTERS

To what extent to you believe codes of ethics are effective in transmitting key aspects of an organizational culture? Have you had experience with ones that worked effectively in this regard? ▪

ORGANIZATIONAL CULTURE: ITS CONSEQUENCES AND CAPACITY TO CHANGE

By now, you probably are convinced that organizational culture can play an important role in the functioning of organizations. To make this point explicit, however, we now examine how organizational culture has been found to affect organizations and the behavior of the individuals in them. Because some of these effects might be undesirable, organizations sometimes are interested in changing their cultures; accordingly, we also consider both why and how organizational culture might be changed.

The Effects of Organizational Culture

Organizational culture exerts many effects on individuals and on organizational processes. Some of these effects are dramatic, and others are more subtle. Culture generates strong pressures on people to go along—that is, to think and to act in ways consistent with the existing culture. Thus, if an organization's culture stresses the importance of product quality and excellent service, customers generally will find their complaints handled both politely and efficiently. If the organization's culture stresses high output at any cost, however, those customers may find themselves on a much rockier road. An organization's culture can strongly affect everything from how employees dress (e.g., the white shirts traditionally worn by male employees of IBM) to the amount of time allowed to elapse before meetings begin to the speed with which people are promoted.

Turning to organizational processes, considerable research has focused on the possibility of a link between culture and performance.[15] Such research has shown that to influence performance, organizational culture must be strong. In other words, approval or disapproval must be expressed to those who act consistently or inconsistently with the culture, respectively, and there must be widespread agreement on values among the members. Only if these conditions prevail is a link between organizational culture and performance observed.

This idea has important implications, both for individuals and for organizations. First, it suggests people seeking employment should examine carefully the prevailing culture of an organization before deciding to join. If they do not, they run the risk of finding themselves in a situation where their own values and those of their company clash. Second, it also suggests organizations should focus on attracting individuals with values matching their own (i.e., *person-organization fit*). This involves identifying key aspects of the organizational culture, communicating these to prospective employees, and selecting candidates for whom the person-organization fit is best (Figure 13.7). Considerable effort may be involved in completing these tasks. Given that high levels of person-organization fit can contribute to commitment, satisfaction, and low rates of turnover among employees, however, the effort appears to be worthwhile.

Why and How Does Organizational Culture Change?

Our earlier comments about the relative stability of organizational culture may have left you wondering about the following questions: If culture tends to be so stable, why and how does it ever change? Why is culture not simply passed from one generation of organizational members to the next in a totally static manner? The basic answer, of course, is that the world in which all organizations operate constantly changes (see chapter 16). External events such as shifting market conditions, new technology, altered government policies, and many other factors change over time, thereby necessitating changes in an organization's mode of doing business and, hence, in its culture.

Composition of the Workforce   Over time, the people entering an organization may differ from those already in it, and these differences may impinge on the existing organizational culture. For example, people from different ethnic or cultural backgrounds may have contrasting views about various aspects of behavior at work. They may hold dissimilar views about style of dress, the importance of being on time (or even of what constitutes "on time" behavior), the level of deference shown to higher-status people, and even what foods should be served in the company cafeteria. In other words, as people with different backgrounds and values enter the workplace, changes in the organizational culture may be expected to follow.

Mergers and Acquisitions   Another, even more dramatic source of cultural change is mergers and acquisitions—that is, when one organization purchases or otherwise absorbs another.[16] When this occurs, the financial and material assets of the acquired organization are likely to be carefully analyzed. Rarely, however, is any consideration given to the acquired organization's culture. This is unfortunate, because in several cases, the merger of two organizations with incompatible cultures has produced serious problems, which are referred to as *culture clashes*.

A classic example is the 1988 merger of Nabisco, Inc., a producer of cookies and other baked goods famous for brands such as Fig Newtons and Oreos, with RJ Reynolds, Inc., a major producer of tobacco products, to become RJR Nabisco. If you've ever seen the movie or read the book *Barbarians at the Gate*, then you already know the story.[17] Nabisco was headquartered in New York, and its executives were known for a fast-paced style in which perks such as corporate jets, penthouse apartments, and lavish parties featured prominently. Even so, company employees prided themselves on the "American-as-apple-pie" image of Nabisco, and they valued their high degree of autonomy in performing their jobs. RJ Reynolds was headquartered in Winston-Salem, North Carolina, and had a strikingly different culture. This company was characterized by a strong work ethic, much less autonomy for employees, and a deep commitment to its local community and to philanthropic activities. Corporate jets, penthouse apartments, and lavish parties definitely were *not* features of corporate life at RJ Reynolds.

When these two companies merged, sparks flew. Nabisco executives chafed under the tighter controls imposed by Tylee Wilson, CEO of Reynolds. As some put it, "You have to raise your hand to go to the bathroom!" That their company was not afforded the level of independence within the new corporation that had been promised

FIGURE 13.7

Matching People and Cultures: An Important Task

Crunch is New York City–based chain of gyms that offers unusual classes such as gospel aerobics and co-ed wrestling. Before CEO Doug Levine hired anyone on his 30-person staff, he made sure they fit in well with the company's nontraditional ways. To ignore this fit between the person and the organizational culture would be to court disaster.

before the merger upset many Nabisco employees. The result? Within a year, bitter internal feuds erupted, and these resulted in a takeover of the new company by Ross Johnson, CEO of Nabisco. Once in power, Johnson quickly purged the company of virtually all former Reynolds executives and moved the merged company's headquarters to a neutral location: Atlanta. Today, years later, the merged organization still suffers from decreased productivity in some units, increased turnover, and strong internal divisions. Clearly, when organizational cultures collide, the changes that follow can be wrenching.

ETHICS MATTERS

When two companies merge, several ethical issues are likely to arise. For example, layoffs and forced organizational change may threaten people's livelihoods. These costs may be offset, however, by the creation of a stronger, new company. What do you think of this idea? ∎

Sometimes, the story is not so intriguing as to warrant a book and a film, but the consequences can remain quite severe. For example, the 1993 merger of Mellon Bank and the Boston Company looked great on paper. The financial analysts, however, did not consider how Mellon's highly cost-conscious culture would be an affront to the Boston Company's most important asset: its talented money-management officers. Offended, a key executive left the newly merged institution—and 30 others followed suit within 3 months. The cost was staggering: Some \$3.5 billion in assets—and many of the firm's largest clients—were lost as a result.[18]

In recent years, there have been several very large mergers, particularly in the oil, banking, and telecommunications industries. For a summary at the five largest mergers occurring in just one recent year, see Figure 13.8 on page 498.[19] Although it is too soon to tell in many cases, keep an eye peeled on the business press for signs of potential culture clashes that might occur in these newly merged companies. (For some suggestions on how to avoid potential culture clashes in merging companies, see the "Tips" section below.)

**TIPS:
DOING IT RIGHT**

∎ **To Merge Cultures Effectively, Develop a New Psychological Contract**

Only about half of all mergers result in financial gains, and the main cause of failure is incompatible corporate cultures. The good news is the blending of cultures that follow mergers does not have to have an unhappy ending. For example, in 1994, the huge drug company SmithKline Beecham bought Sterling Winthrop's over-the-counter drug business from Kodak. To avoid repeating the brain-drain fiasco that occurred at Mellon Bank, SmithKline's CEO immediately wrote letters to each of Sterling's managers assuring them they would have key roles in the newly combined organization.

This gesture was effective in two ways. It alleviated any insecurities the managers may have had, and it established a foundation of open communication that would serve as the platform on which the new, integrated culture would be built.[20] The key seems to be involving people in the planning and execution of a merger so that they feel they have some control over their fate. In so doing, they also can showcase their talents to the members of their new business family.

Perhaps the main trick to integrating newly merged cultures is establishing each employee's relationship with the new company. This involves what is known as a **psychological contract**—that is, an implicit, informal understanding between an

continued

psychological contract

An implicit, informal understanding between an employee and the organization regarding what each will give to the other and what each will receive from the other.

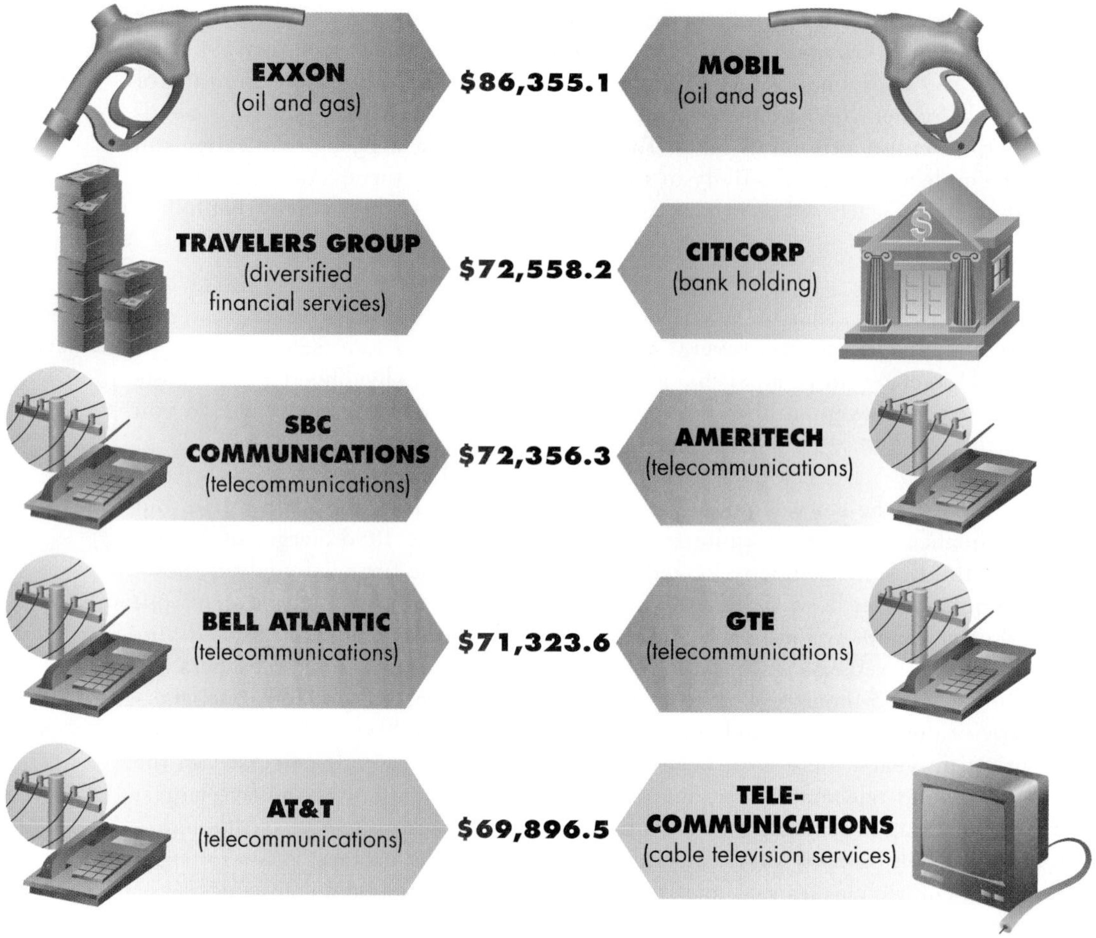

EXXON (oil and gas)	$86,355.1	**MOBIL** (oil and gas)
TRAVELERS GROUP (diversified financial services)	$72,558.2	**CITICORP** (bank holding)
SBC COMMUNICATIONS (telecommunications)	$72,356.3	**AMERITECH** (telecommunications)
BELL ATLANTIC (telecommunications)	$71,323.6	**GTE** (telecommunications)
AT&T (telecommunications)	$69,896.5	**TELE-COMMUNICATIONS** (cable television services)

FIGURE 13.8

The Five Largest Mergers of 1998

Companies have been merging at a frantic pace, and 1998 was a record year, bringing together some of the world's largest firms. The figures shown here are the values of the new companies in millions of dollars. Hopefully, culture clashes between these megacompanies will not occur and cause them to falter.

(*Source*: Based on data reported by Colvin, 1999; see note 19.)

employee and the organization regarding what each will give to the other and what each will receive from the other. Think of it as the central, reinforcing pillar of organizational culture or the context for workplace arrangements. A written contract can cover all the formal arrangements (e.g., what work will be done in exchange for what pay), but it cannot capture all the subtle, unspoken, interpersonal elements that are so important in the workplace. When companies merge, old psychological contracts are broken, and new ones must be formed. To facilitate this change, experts recommend moving through five distinct phases:

1. *Break with the past.* Explain why the change is necessary, such as by noting how the old company was not performing well and how the newly merged company promises to be more successful.

2. *Mobilize for change.* Signal that change is coming, such as by bringing in a new senior manager, changing the corporate name, or moving key units to new locations.

3. *Realize a new contract.* Line managers should be the first to forge new contracts with employees.

4. *Embed the new contract.* Make sure the new contract is consistent with the new organizational structure and reward system. For example, if a new person is in charge, make that clear. If a certain form of behavior is required, that behavior should be rewarded.

5. *Live the contract.* Everyone in the organization should send consistent messages about the new ways of doing things. These steps make it clear that organizational rewards and structure are key parts of any psychological contract. In turn, such contracts are vital aspects of organizational culture. Companies not considering such factors when merging are overlooking one of the most important determinants of any merger's success. One expert put it as follows:

> In the final analysis, the highest price of a merger is not the purchase price, but the psychological price paid by employees. The most significant is not the merger agreement, but the psychological agreements that must be replaced and redefined. Pay attention to these intangibles, and your merger has a chance for success. Ignore them, and everyone — customers, shareholders, managers and employees — will lose.[21] ■

Planned Organizational Change   Even if an organization does not change by acquiring another, cultural change still may result from other planned changes, such as conscious decisions to alter the internal structure or the basic operations (see chapter 14). Once such decisions are reached, many practices in the company that both reflect and contribute to its culture may change. For example, the company may adopt different criteria for recruiting newcomers or for promoting current employees. Similarly, managers may be directed to focus on different goals. As these shifts occur, new norms governing preferred or acceptable behavior emerge, and attitudes and values supporting these norms take shape. The result may be a considerable shift in the existing culture.

A good example of this can be seen in IBM.[22] After staggering losses, IBM realized one of its problems was that it was heavily bureaucratic, thereby making it difficult for lower-level people to make on-the-spot decisions. As a result, IBM changed the nature of its corporate structure from a steep hierarchy with many layers of management to a "delayered" hierarchy with far fewer managers. As you might imagine, the newly "rightsized" IBM developed a new corporate culture. Once known for a highly rigid, autocratic culture, in which decision making was centralized in just a few, the reorganized company is much more open and democratic in its approach.

To conclude, organizational culture clearly is generally stable, but it is not immutable. In fact, culture often evolves in response to outside forces (e.g., changes in workforce composition) as well as from deliberate attempts to change the design of organizations (e.g., mergers, corporate restructuring). An important aspect of culture that organizations frequently strive to change is the degree to which problems are approached in creative and innovative ways. Thus, we now turn to the topics of *creativity* and *innovation* in organizations.

CREATIVITY IN INDIVIDUALS AND TEAMS

You probably have no difficulty recognizing creativity when you see it, but defining creativity can be more challenging. Following several scientists, we define **creativity** as the process by which individuals or small groups produce novel and useful ideas.[23] In this section, we explain in more detail how the process of creativity operates.

creativity
The process by which individuals or small groups produce novel and useful ideas.

Components of Individual and Team Creativity

Creativity in individuals and teams involves three basic components: domain-relevant skills, creativity-relevant skills, and intrinsic task motivation.

Domain-Relevant Skills   Whether we consider the manual dexterity required to play the piano or to use a computer keyboard or the sense of rhythm and knowledge of music needed to conduct an orchestra, specific skills and abilities are necessary to perform these tasks. In fact, virtually any task requires certain talents, knowledge, or skills. Those skills and abilities we already have constitute the raw materials of creativity. After all, without the capacity to perform a certain task at even a basic level, one has no hope of demonstrating creativity on that task. For example, before a driver can even begin to create stunning automotive stunts, he or she must have the basic skills of dexterity and eye-hand coordination required to drive a car.

Creativity-Relevant Skills   Beyond the basic skills, being creative also requires additional skills—that is, special abilities that help people to approach what they do in novel ways. Specifically, when fostering creativity, it helps to do the following:

- *Break mental sets and take new perspectives*: Creativity is enhanced when people do not limit themselves to old ways of doing things—that is, when they *think outside the box*. Restricting oneself to the past can inhibit creativity. Take a fresh look at even the most familiar things. In fact, some of the most creative ideas come from people who do precisely this—that is, not limit themselves to old ways of doing things.[24] For some interesting examples, see Table 13.3.
- *Understand complexities*: Instead of making things overly simplistic, consider complex ways in which ideas may interrelate.
- *Keep options open, and avoid premature judgments*: Creative people consider all options. To do so, they consider all the angles and avoid reaching premature conclusions.
- *Use productive forgetting*: Creativity sometimes is inhibited by our becoming fixated on certain ideas we just cannot seem to get out of our heads. Thus, it helps to practice **productive forgetting**—that is, the ability to abandon unproductive ideas and temporarily put aside stubborn problems until new approaches can be considered.

productive forgetting
The ability to abandon unproductive ideas and temporarily put aside stubborn problems until new approaches can be considered.

TABLE 13.3

"Thinking Outside the Box": Some Impressive—and Famous—Results
Some of the most creative ideas come from people who take a fresh look at everyday experiences. As summarized here, some of the world's most important inventions were inspired in this manner.

INVENTOR	PRODUCT	INSPIRATION
Dr. Rene Laennec	Stethoscope	Children sending signals to each other by tapping on either end of logs
Samuel Colt	Six-shooter revolver	Spokes of a ship's wheel
John Dunlop	Rubber tires	Garden hose
James Carrier	Air conditioner	Seeing water condense on the side of a glass
Thomas Edison	Telegraph	The movements of a water pump
Charles Duryea	Spray-injection carburetor	His wife spraying herself with a perfume atomizer

Source: Based on information in Mattimore, 1994; see note 24.

TABLE 13.4

Creativity Heuristics: Some Examples

Creativity heuristics are techniques to help people approach tasks in novel ways. Some such techniques are summarized here.

TECHNIQUE	DESCRIPTION
Juxtaposing	Forcing yourself to pit one idea against another, forming a new idea from the comparison.
Blending	Taking the characteristics of several ideas and combining them to create a new idea.
Pyramiding	Coming up with a new idea by joining together bits and pieces of others in a way that combines them all together.
Encircling	Beginning with a vague new idea and then systematically narrowing the choices until one best idea results.
Imagining	Using your imagination; fantasizing to produce a new idea from an old one.

Sources: Based on suggestions by Ayan, 1997; see note 25.

- *Follow creativity heuristics*: People sometimes follow certain strategies known as **creativity heuristics** to help them come up with creative, new ideas. These are rules people follow to help them approach tasks in novel ways. They may involve techniques such as considering the counterintuitive and using analogies.[25] For more examples of creativity heuristics, see Table 13.4.[26]

creativity heuristics
Rules people follow to help them approach tasks in novel ways.

To help individuals and groups become more creative, many organizations invite employees to participate in training exercises to promote these skills. (For a look at what some of today's companies are doing in this regard, see the "Trends" section below. To partake in one such exercise yourself, see the "Experiencing Organizational Behavior" section at the end of this chapter.)

TRENDS: WHAT TODAY'S COMPANIES ARE DOING

■ How Rubbermaid Gets Employees to Think Outside the (Plastic) Box

Admittedly, few things are as mundane as ice-cube trays, food-storage containers, dish drainers, and laundry hampers. The people who develop these items, however, along with 5,000 other products at Rubbermaid, Inc., face this challenge with the same care and precision as engineers building delicate surgical instruments. Attention to quality is a well-ingrained element of this 80-year-old company's corporate culture. Company officials strive to put innovations into their products that make everyday living easier on us all. Exactly how does this company stimulate creative thinking among its employees?

For one thing, all Rubbermaid employees are asked to think about how to create new products using the company's existing technologies.[27] In other words, they are encouraged to build new ideas from existing ones. For example, a top Rubbermaid manager one day toured the company's facility where picnic coolers were made. Seeing the plastic blow-molding equipment in action gave him an idea: He could use this same process to make a line of light-weight, durable, and inexpensive office furniture. Today, the line of furniture made using this process is hugely successful.

At Rubbermaid, everyone is brought into the creative foray and encouraged to share whatever ideas they may have. The rationale is simple: Something might just work! For example, some years ago, the head of product development toured a museum and became fascinated by an exhibit of Egyptian antiquities. The kitchen utensils particularly interested him. Sure enough, the company started turning out utensils inspired by these ancient designs. People never know when they will become inspired — or by what. At Rubbermaid, employees are recognized for sharing their inspirations.

At other companies, the introduction of new products might come after several intensive months — or even years — of market testing, but not at Rubbermaid. In fact, Rubbermaid does no market testing at all! Company executives explain they do not want to give their competitors a chance to copy their products before Rubbermaid's national rollout. This is not the only reason, however. Also involved is the idea that releasing a product without testing it extensively creates pressure to do it right the first time, that creativity without a strong dose of reality may be misguided. Perhaps knowing there is no safety net to catch them helps product developers to take their tasks as seriously as they do — regardless of how mundane their products may be. ■

Intrinsic Task Motivation   The first two components of creativity, domain-relevant skills and creativity-relevant skills, focus on what people are *capable* of doing. The third component, intrinsic task motivation, focuses on what people are *willing* to do. The idea is simple: To be creative, a person must be willing to perform the task in question. After all, someone with the capacity to be creative but without the motivation to do what it takes to produce creative outcomes certainly would not be considered "creative."

Intrinsic task motivation tends to be high under several conditions. For example, when an individual has a *personal interest* in the task, he or she will be motivated to perform it — and may do so creatively. Certainly, however, anyone who does not find a task interesting surely will not perform it long enough to demonstrate any creativity. Likewise, task motivation is high whenever an individual perceives he or she has internal reasons to perform that task. People who come to believe they are performing a task for some external reason, such as high pay or pressure from a boss, are unlikely to find the work inherently interesting in and of itself, and they are unlikely to show much creativity when performing it.

Putting It all Together

As you might imagine, the components of creativity are important because they can be used to paint a picture of when people will be creative. In this connection, scientists claim people will be at their most creative when they have high amounts of all three components (Figure 13.9).

Specifically, it has been claimed there is a multiplicative relationship between these three components of creativity. Thus, if any one component is low, the overall level of creativity will be low. In fact, people will not be creative at all if any one com-

FIGURE 13.9

Components of Creativity

Scientists claim people are at their most creative when they exhibit high levels of the three factors shown here.

(*Source*: Adapted from Amabile, 1988; see note 23.)

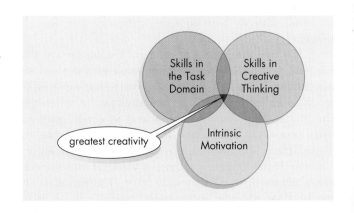

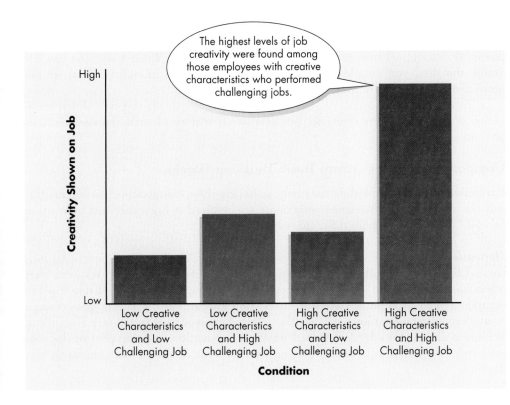

FIGURE 13.10

Individual and Environmental Characteristics: Important Determinants of Creativity on the Job

In any organization, who does the most novel work? The answer depends on both individual differences in creativity and environmental conditions. Specifically, the most creative individuals tend to come up with the most novel ideas — but only under conditions that bring out that creativity, such as being given complex and challenging jobs.

(*Source*: Based on data reported by Oldham and Cummings, 1996; see note 28.)

ponent is at zero (i.e., completely missing). This makes sense if you think about it. After all, you are unlikely to be creative at a job without the skills needed to do it, regardless of how motivated you are and how well practiced at coming up with new ideas. Likewise, creativity can be expected to be nonexistent if either creativity-relevant skills or motivation are zero. The practical implications are clear: To be as creative as possible, people must strive toward high levels of all three components of creativity.

A fascinating recent study illustrates this point.[28] Employees in two manufacturing plants were asked to complete a lengthy questionnaire that assessed the extent to which they possessed the characteristics associated with creativity (e.g., capable, clever, confident, humorous, insightful, original). The jobs these people performed then were assessed regarding how challenging and complex they were. Finally, each employee was evaluated by his or her supervisor regarding creativity — that is, the extent to which that individual performed novel and useful work. As shown in Figure 13.10, the relationship between these variables took a form that makes considerable sense. Specifically, the most creative individuals had both the individual characteristics associated with creativity and worked in an environment that brought out that creativity because of the highly complex and challenging jobs they performed. Those with jobs or personal characteristics that did not predispose them to be creative tended not to demonstrate as much creativity.

THE PROCESS OF INNOVATION

Now that we have examined the process of individual and small group creativity, we look at situations in which people implement their creative skills to improve the organization. This is the process of *innovation* to which we referred earlier. Specifically, **innovation** may be defined as the successful implementation of creative ideas within an organization. Thus, you probably suspect that some companies are far more

innovation

The successful implementation of creative ideas within an organization.

innovative than others, and indeed, this is the case: Some companies are far more effective than others in bringing new ideas to market. For the 10 most innovative companies as determined by a recent *Fortune* magazine poll, see Table 13.5.[29] As you examine this list, you should not be surprised if you can identify several of the innovations produced by these companies.

To understand this process, we review the various stages through which innovation progresses. Before doing so, however, we first must identify the various components of innovation.

Components of Innovation: Basic Building Blocks

Earlier, we depicted individual creativity as having three components: motivation, resources, and skills. These same components are involved in organizational innovation as well (albeit in somewhat different ways).

Motivation to Innovate   Just as individual creativity requires that people be motivated to do what it takes to be creative, organizational innovation requires that organizations have the kind of cultures that encourage innovation. When top executives fail to promote a vision of innovation and accept the status quo, change is unlikely. At companies such as Microsoft, however, where leaders (including president and co-founder Bill Gates) envision innovation as being part of the natural order of things, it is not surprising that innovative efforts are constantly underway.

Resources to Innovate   Again, a parallel to individual creativity is in order: Just as people must have certain basic skills to be creative, organizations must possess certain basic resources to make innovation possible. For example, to be innovative, organizations must have what it takes in terms of human and financial resources. After all, unless the necessary skilled people and deep pockets are available with which to innovate, stagnation is likely to result.

TABLE 13.5

The 10 Most Innovative Companies

According to *Fortune* magazine, the 10 companies listed here rise to the top when comparisons are made of their effectiveness in creating new products or services and bringing them to market.

RANK	COMPANY	EXAMPLE OF INNOVATION
1	Enron	Next-generation fiber optics
2	Intel	Advanced computer chips
3	Nike	Air Jordan XIV, high-performance athletic shoe
4	Herman Miller	Aeron office chair
5	Mirage Resorts	Elaborate themed hotels, such as Treasure Island in Las Vegas
6	Gillette	Mach 3 razor
7	Minnesota Mining & Manufacturing (3M)	Post-it notes
8	Motorola	Ultraportable cellular phones
9	Home Depot	Combines high levels of customer service with the prices and variety of warehouse stores
10	Charles Schwab	On-line stock trading offering service to investors

Source: Based on information reported by Brown, L. R., Kane, H., & Ayres, E., 1999; see note 29.

Innovation Management   Finally, just as individuals must hone special skills to be creative, organizations must develop special ways of managing people to encourage innovation—that is, *skills in innovation management*. Most notable in this regard is the matter of *balance*. Specifically, managers promote innovation when they show balance with respect to three key matters: goals, reward systems, and time pressure (Figure 13.11):

- Organizational innovation is promoted when *goals* are carefully linked to the corporate mission but are not so specific they tie the hands of those who put them into practice. Innovation is unlikely to result when such restrictions are imposed.

- *Reward systems* should generously and fairly recognize one's contributions, but they should not be so specific they connect every move to a bonus or monetary reward. To do so discourages people from taking the risks that make innovation possible.

- Innovation management requires carefully balancing the *time pressures* under which employees are placed. If such pressures are too great, people may be unimaginative and offer routine solutions. If such pressures are too weak, employees may have no sense of time urgency and believe the project is not important enough to warrant any creative attention on their part.

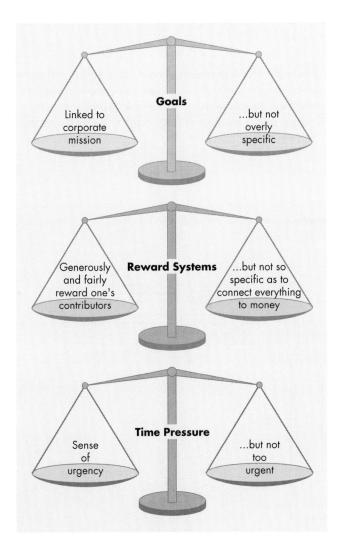

FIGURE 13.11

Skills in Innovation Management: A Careful Balancing Act

Managing innovation requires carefully balancing the three matters identified here.

(*Source*: Based on information reported by Amabile, 1988; see note 23.)

Stages of the Organizational Innovation Process

Any CEO who snaps his or her fingers one day and expects the troops to be innovative on command surely is in for a disappointment. Innovation does not happen all at once. Rather, it occurs gradually, and scientists have identified five specific stages through which the process of organizational innovation progresses.[30] We now describe each of these stages (Figure 13.12).

Stage 1: Setting the Agenda   The first stage of the innovation process involves setting the agenda for innovation. This involves creating a **mission statement** — that is, a document describing an organization's overall direction and general goals for accomplishing that movement. The component of innovation most involved here is motivation. After all, the highest-ranking officials of the organization must be highly committed to innovation before they will initiate a push toward it.

Stage 2: Setting the Stage   Once an organization's mission has been established, it is prepared to set the stage for innovation. This may involve narrowing certain broad goals into more specific tasks and gathering the resources to meet them. It also may involve assessing the environment, both outside and inside the organization, and searching for anything that may support or inhibit later efforts to "break the rules" by being creative. Effectively setting the stage for innovation requires the skills necessary for innovation management as well as the full use of the organization's human and financial resources (Figure 13.13).

Stage 3: Producing the Ideas   This stage of the process involves coming up with new ideas and testing them. It also is the stage in which individual and small group creativity enters the picture. As a result, all the components of individual creativity mentioned earlier are involved, and these may combine in important ways with various

mission statement

A document describing an organization's overall direction and general goals for accomplishing that movement.

F I G U R E   1 3 . 1 2

The Process of Innovation

The innovation process consists of the various components and steps shown here.
(*Source*: Adapted from Amabile, 1988; see note 23.)

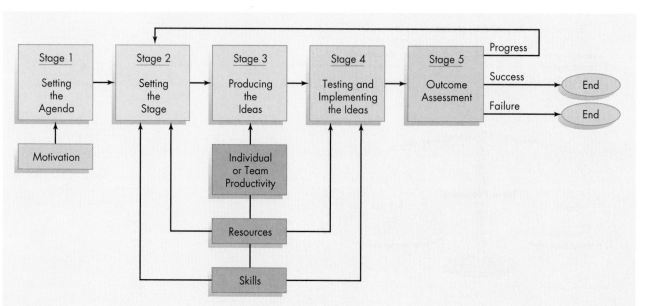

The president of your organization, a small manufacturing company, has complained that sales are stagnant. A key problem, you discover, is that the market for your products is fully developed—and that the products themselves are not very exciting. No one seems to care about doing anything innovative. Instead, the employees seem more interested in doing things the way they have always done them.

1. What factors do you suspect are responsible for the culture in this organization over the years?
2. What do you recommend to enhance the creativity of this company's employees?
3. How can the company's products be made more innovative?

organizational factors. For example, an individual with the skills and motivation to be highly creative might find this motivation waning as he or she attempts to introduce novel ideas to an organization that is not committed to innovation and that fails to make the necessary resources available. In contrast, an organization with highly innovative nature may bring out the more creative side of an individual who previously might not have been especially creative.

Stage 4: Testing and Implementing the Ideas   This is the stage of implementation. Now, after an initial group of individuals has developed an idea, other parts of the organization become involved. For example, a prototype product may be developed and tested and market research conducted. In short, input is provided by the many functional areas of the organization. As you might imagine, resources in the task domain are important at this stage. After all, unless adequate amounts of money, personnel, materials, and information are provided, the idea will be unlikely to survive.

Interestingly, even a good idea and resources are not enough to bring innovation to life. We noted in Figure 13.13 that skills in innovation management are critical

FIGURE 13.13

Louis B. Mayer: An Innovator in Motion Pictures

Louis B. Mayer (1885–1957), better known simply as "L. B.," is widely acknowledged to be an innovator in the motion-picture business. Here, the trademark MGM lion is recorded, making his trademark roar for the first time, as "talkies" emerged on the film scene. L. B. was highly creative as an individual but also was an excellent manager of the innovation process.

U.S. FIRMS LAG BEHIND JAPANESE FIRMS IN INNOVATION

When it comes to innovation, statistics reveal Japanese companies are far more innovative than their U.S. counterparts.[31] This is not surprising given that on average, U.S. companies spend significantly less (as a percentage of their gross national product) than Japanese companies on research and development. U.S. companies tend to make changes more quickly and do a good job of emulating Japanese companies, but the money they spend on innovation tends not to yield as much benefit.[32] For every dollar a U.S. firm spends on research and development, it generally gets back less in terms of profit than a corresponding Japanese firm.[33] Several important factors contribute to this state of affairs.

First, the Japanese are far more committed to product innovation. In fact, Japan made a conscientious effort in 1986 to become an innovator rather than an imitator—a commitment that has been renewed each year since.[34] We see this, for example, in the development of Kumanoto and Tsukuba Science City, the Japanese versions of California's Silicon Valley and North Carolina's Research Triangle.

The phrase "made in Japan" once implied a product was a "cheap imitation," but it now represents the latest in innovation. This is easy to see throughout Japan. For example, Sony is regarded as the world's most innovative consumer-electronics firm. You know Sony for the Walkman, the Discman, and the Mini Disc, but you may not know these are among 1,000 products it generates each year—200 of which are completely new.[35] Sony is only one Japanese company known for its innovations, however. Toyota and Hitachi are additional examples. In fact, Hitachi is so innovative it consistently ranks at or near the top of companies holding the most patents for product innovations.[36]

For another explanation, experts point to what they call *technochauvinism* in U.S. firms. This refers to the belief that all good ideas come from the United States—and that research done elsewhere should be ignored.[37] This belief is terribly misguided. If nothing else, it is inconsistent with two key facts. First, Japanese universities produce more engineers than U.S. universities, even though Japan's population is only half the size of that in the United States.[38] Second, many U.S. professors of math, science, and engineering are retiring—and are not being replaced. At the same time, more than half the doctoral students in U.S. universities are foreign nationals. These individuals also are returning to their home countries, contributing to the lack of scientists in the United States.[39] Not surprisingly, many U.S. companies now are searching abroad for scientists, and they are finding many of the best ones in Japan.[40] As this trend continues, we suspect technochauvinism will fade.

Finally, differences between Japanese and U.S. firms regarding creativity and innovation have been in effect for some time. For example, in 1985, a group of U.S. and Japanese managers were asked to indicate what percentage of their corporate profits for the next five years was expected to come from innovation. The average answer was 82 percent among the Japanese, but it was only 51 percent among the Americans.[41] This is likely, at least in part, to result from the fact that mergers and acquisitions are far more common in the United States compared to Japan—and that these tend to reduce investment in research and development.[42]

According to one expert, this state of affairs paints an unsettling picture for the future success of U.S. business: "If you consider that the ability to compete is at the heart of any business, you will recognize that the only long-term sustainable competitive advantage is innovation." He then goes on to urge U.S. businesses to be more innovative by admonishing "innovate or evaporate!"[43]

during this stage of the process. This is largely because good ideas must be "nourished" and supported throughout the organization if they are to survive. Even the best ideas may be "killed" if people in some parts of the organization are not supportive. For some astonishing examples of this, see Table 13.6.[44] When you see all the great ideas that did not quite make it at first, you will realize you are in excellent company if your own ideas are rejected.

Stage 5: Outcome Assessment The final stage of this process involves assessing the new idea. What happens to that idea depends on the results of this assessment, and three outcomes are possible. If the resulting idea (e.g., a certain product or service) has been a total success, it will be accepted and carried out in the future. This ends the process. Likewise, the process is over if the idea has been a complete failure, in which case there is no good reason to continue. If the new idea shows promise, how-

TABLE 13.6

Is Your Innovative Idea Rejected? You're in Good Company
Some of the best, most innovative ideas were rejected at first because one or more powerful people failed to see their merit. When you look at these examples, you can imagine how bad these individuals must have felt about "the one that got away."

PRODUCT	REJECTION STORY
Star Wars	Turned down by 12 Hollywood studios before finally being accepted
Photocopying process	Rejected as a viable technology by IBM, GM, and DuPont
Velcro	Victor Kiam (of Remington Razor fame) turned down the patent for $25,000
Transistor radio	In the 1950s, Sony's founder, Akio Morita, was unsuccessful in marketing this idea
The Beatles	Turned down by Decca Records in 1962 because "groups with guitars were on the way out"
Movies with soundtracks	In 1927, Harry Warner, president of Warner Brothers, said nobody wanted to hear actors talk

Source: Based on information reported by Ricchiuto, 1997; see note 31.

ever, and has made some progress toward the organization's objectives but still has problems, the process starts again at stage 2.

This five-stage process does not account for all innovations you may find in organizations, but it does a good job of identifying the major steps through which most innovations travel along their path from a specific organizational need to a product or service to meet that need. (Companies in some countries tend to be more innovative than those in others. For a close-up look at one such comparison, see the "OB Around the World" section in this chapter.)

We invite you to visit the Greenberg page on the Prentice Hall Web site at: **www.prenhall.com/greenberg** for the monthly Greenberg update and for this chapter's World Wide Web exercise.

SUMMARY AND REVIEW
OF LEARNING OBJECTIVES

1. **Define *organizational culture*.**
   Organizational culture is a cognitive framework consisting of attitudes, values, behavioral norms, and expectations shared by an organization's members.

2. **Distinguish *dominant organizational culture* from *subcultures*.**
   An organization may have a **dominant culture**—that is, a distinctive, overarching "personality" of an organization as a whole. It also is likely to have various **subcultures**, which exist only in part of the organization.

3. **Describe the role of culture in organizations.**
   Culture plays three major roles in organizations. It provides a sense of identity for the members, generates commitment to the organization's mission, and both clarifies and reinforces standards of behavior.

4. **Describe the four types of organizational culture identified by the** *double S cube***.**
   The **double S cube** identifies four types of organizational culture created by combining high and low levels of two variables, **solidarity** (i.e., the extent to which people focus together on the job) and **sociability** (i.e., the extent to which people get along with each other personally). A **networked culture** exists when solidarity is low and sociability is high. A **mercenary culture** exists when solidarity is high and sociability is low. A **fragmented culture** exists when both sociability and solidarity are low, and a **communal culture** exists when both sociability and solidarity are high. Each of these four cultures can have both positive and negative characteristics.

5. **Identify various factors that lead to the creation of organizational culture.**
   Organizational culture is created by the influence of company founders, an organization's experience with the environment, and contact between groups of people.

6. **Identify the tools through which organizational culture is transmitted.**
   Organizational culture may be transmitted through symbols, stories, jargon, ceremonies, and statements of principle.

7. **Describe the effects of organizational culture on organizational functioning.**
   Organizational culture generates strong pressures on people to go along, to think and to act in ways consistent with the existing culture. Culture has effects on organizational performance only when culture is strong; subtle nuances of organizational culture have little or no effects on organizational performance.

8. **Identify the factors responsible for changing organizational culture.**
   Organizational culture tends to be stable, but it is subject to change. The factors most responsible for changing organizational culture include the composition of the workforce, mergers and acquisitions, and planned organizational change.

9. **Define** *creativity* **and describe the basic components of individual and team creativity.**
   Creativity is the process by which individuals or small groups produce novel and useful ideas. Creativity in organizations is based on three fundamental components: domain-relevant skills (i.e., basic knowledge needed to perform the task at hand), creativity-relevant skills (i.e., special abilities needed to generate creative new ideas), and intrinsic task motivation (i.e., people's willingness to perform creative acts).

10. **Define** *innovation* **and identify the basic components of innovation and the various stages of the innovation process.**
    Innovation refers to the implementation of creative ideas in organizations. Innovation involves three components, which are analogous to the three components of creativity. These are motivation to innovate, resources to innovate, and innovation management. These components are used in a process that generally proceeds through five stages: setting the agenda, setting the stage, producing the ideas, testing and implementing the ideas, and assessing the outcome.

1. *Organizational culture* is a mushy concept. You cannot quite see it, but you know it is there. What indications are there that organizational culture really exists?

2. In which of the four types of organizational culture identified by the *double S cube* would you most like to work? Why? In which would you least like to work? Why?

3. Think of an organization in which you have worked. Was its culture predominantly *communal, mercenary, fragmented,* or *networked*? Was this an effective culture given the nature of the people employed and the type of work done?

4. Again, think of an organization in which you have worked. How was its culture transmitted to the people who worked in it and to those who remained outside (e.g., the public)?

5. Have you ever lived through a change of organizational culture? If so, what happened? What was it like?

6. Do you think of yourself as a creative person? How could you be even more creative in your work?

7. Think of an innovation you may have seen in a company in which you have worked. To what extent did it follow the steps outlined in Figure 13.12? How was it similar to or different from the general process described in this diagram?

Case in Point

3M: Where Innovation Is Everything

3M is one of those companies whose products just cannot be avoided. Whether it is Scotch Magic Transparent Tape, Post-it Notes, Scotch-Brite Scouring Pads, Scotchgard fabric protector, or O-Cel-O Sponges, the 3M name appears everywhere around the house. You might not know it, but hundreds of 3M products also are widely used in hospitals, factories, and along our roadways. In fact, there are more than 900 different varieties of Scotch tape alone!

The company was founded in Two Harbors, Minnesota, along the northwest shore of Lake Superior almost a century ago. From the beginning, 3M has produced innovative products that met customers' needs. (Among the first was 3M-Ite, a cloth abrasive that was used to help sand the contoured areas of automobile bodies without giving off harmful irritants.) It can be said that what 3M really specializes in is innovation itself.

If there is a problem, chances are 3M has developed a product to solve it. Consider these examples: 3M engineers recently have developed ways of producing large, custom signs in small numbers at prices even small businesses can afford (Scotchprint II). To help address the problem of making batteries that are powerful enough to run notebook computers but small enough to be carried around easily, 3M has developed not a new battery but a new way of making computer screens that draw less energy. If you broke a limb in recent years, chances are your orthopedic physician set your break using fiberglass-reinforced synthetic casting tape (i.e., Scotchcast Casting Tape) instead of the weaker, heavier wet-plaster casts used for hundreds of years.

What makes 3M so innovative? Among the answers is the company's "15-percent rule," which allows technical personnel to devote as much as 15 percent of their time to projects of their own choosing without getting approval from others. From the company's early days, it has been recognized that when technical people are allowed to tinker as they wish, they tend to come up with ideas that simply cannot be envisioned by management. To this day, the 15-percent rule is alive and well at 3M.

Furthering the innovative spirit within its ranks, 3M also encourages cross-pollination of ideas between departments. Thus, the company encourages both formal and informal networking among technical personnel (see chapter 6). For example, 3M divisions

(continued)

regularly hold fairs in which they show off their latest technologies to personnel from other divisions.

Management's primary objective at 3M is to foster creativity and innovation. 3M has long challenged its personnel to produce new products following a "25/5 rule"—that is, 25 percent of annual sales were to come from products that had been around for no more than five years. In 1992, chairman and CEO L. D. DeSimone noted that product life cycles were shrinking and introduced a more difficult goal: 30 percent of sales were to come from products that had been around for no more than four years. This really sparked the creative fires, and the new goal was met only two years later.

Most companies recognize their employees' accomplishments with some form of monetary reward (see chapter 3), but 3M goes a step further. It gives a variety of special, highly coveted awards to employees who have been among the most creative. For example, 3M has established the "Carlton Society," which is an honorary organization recognizing extraordinary contributions to 3M's science and technology. Among its members are those individuals who have invented such ubiquitous products as Post-it Notes, Scotch Magic Transparent Tape, and Scotchgard fabric protector. Various grants also are given to both technical and non-

technical personnel to help them develop innovations whose expenses fall outside their department's regular budget.

Obviously, 3M is a company that not only is innovative but that goes out of its way to make sure innovation occurs. To a larger degree, this focus on innovation has been responsible for the company's century-long record of success. Without doubt, 3M is very special, but it hardly is alone in its quest for innovation. Among some of the most innovative companies today are DuPont, General Electric, Pfizer, and Rubbermaid.

CRITICAL THINKING QUESTIONS

1. Recently, 3M quietly did away with the 25/5 rule. Why do you think this decision was made?

2. What is it about the culture at 3M that makes innovation occur so frequently?

3. Do you think the people who work at 3M are naturally creative, the environment brings out whatever creativity they may have, or both? Explain.

4. Would you like to work at a highly innovative firm like 3M? Why, or why not? If so, what pressures do you think you would face?

VIDEO CASE

Culture, Creativity, and Innovation

SMALL BUSINESS 2000

If someone told you to "take a hike," you might be offended. If someone told one of the Quenemoen sisters, the owners of Jagged Edge, to take a hike, they might just grab their climbing gear and go for it. Margaret and Paula Quenemoen have built a business that evolved from their love of the outdoors. Many people attempt to turn hobbies or personal interests into businesses. Some succeed and some fail. Jagged Edge, by all accounts, is a successful venture. What is really interesting about this company, however, is the working environment that has emerged.

Many things can affect the culture of a business. To understand the culture at Jagged Edge, it might be best to better understand the women who run it and what makes them tick. Margaret comes across as being a survivor. The company is oriented as an envi-

ronmentally conscious manufacturer of outdoor clothing, but Margaret founded it for a more fundamental reason: She was broke and needed to earn some money—and to earn it fast. As you will learn first hand, Margaret is not easily discouraged, and she is very committed to the things in which she believes. Paula Quenemoen is also very driven but, perhaps, in a different way than her sister. Paula joined her sister after spending several years studying in China and other parts of Asia. Paula brings to the company the spiritual influence of this experience.

Paula and Margaret do not run Jagged Edge by themselves. In building a staff, they seem to have worked hard at finding individuals who in some way are similar to themselves. This does not mean they cloned themselves, but they have sought out employees with some common interests. The obvious common interest is mountain climbing and hiking, but this is not the only possibility. As you watch this case, try to develop an understanding of the culture of this company. Think about why people would want to work at Jagged Edge—and how comfortable you might feel working in a company like this.

QUESTIONS FOR DISCUSSION

1.   You learned about Paula and Margaret's personal beliefs and some things they have done in their lives. How do you think the sisters influence the personality and culture of the company?

2.   Paula told us about a factory in China with which she does business on a handshake, without any formal contracting. She even sends cash in advance of receiving finished goods. What do you think about this practice? Why do you think Jagged Edge does business this way?

3.   It seems like the staff at Jagged Edge not only works together but, sometimes, plays together, too. What do you think are some of the advantages and disadvantages of the work/recreation commonality that many employees share? How might this affect the culture of the company?

EXPERIENCING ORGANIZATIONAL BEHAVIOR

Stimulating Creativity Using an Idea Box

One day, the marketing director of a company that makes laundry hampers was tinkering with ways of boosting sales in a stagnant, mature market. To trigger his imagination, he thought explicitly about something most of us take for granted—that is, the basic parameters of laundry hampers. Specifically, he noted they differed in four basic ways: their materials, their shape, their finish, and how they are positioned. For each dimension, he identified five different possibilities, resulting in the following chart or *idea box*.

IMPROVE DESIGN FOR LAUNDRY HAMPER

	MATERIAL	SHAPE	FINISH	POSITION
1	Wicker	Square	Natural	Sits on Floor
2	Plastic	Cylindrical	Painted	On Ceiling
3	Paper	Rectangle	Clear	On Wall
4	Metal	Hexagonal	Luminous	Chute to Basement
5	Net Material	Cube	Neon	On Door

Source: Reprinted with permission from *Tinkertoys* by Michael Michalko, Ten Speed Press, Berkeley, California.

Then, by randomly combining one item from each column—net material, cylindrical shape, painted finish, and positioning on a door—he came up with a completely new idea. It was a laundry hamper made to look like a basketball net: approximately one yard of netting attached to a cylindrical hoop hung from a backboard attached to the back of a door.

With some quick math, you can see this particular idea box generates 3,125 different combinations. This is a far greater number of ideas than you probably could generate without aid, so idea boxes make sense for situations requiring creative, new solutions. Nurture your own creativity by following the directions given here.

Directions

To generate an idea box, do the following:

1. *Specify the challenge you face.* You may not be interested in developing exciting new laundry baskets, but you must start at the same point indicated in our example—that is, identifying exactly what you are attempting to do.
2. *Select the parameters of your challenge.* Material, shape, finish, and position were the parameters of the laundry-basket problem. What are yours? To help determine if the parameter you are considering is important enough to add, ask yourself if the challenge would still exist without that parameter.
3. *List variation.* Our example shows five variations of each parameter, but you may list as many key ones as you can. As your idea box grows larger, however, it gets increasingly difficult to spot new ideas. (For example, if your idea box has 10 parameters, each of which contains 10 variations, you face 10 billion potential combinations to consider—hardly a practical task!)
4. *Try different combinations.* After your idea box is complete, work your way through it. Begin by examining the entire box and then limit yourself to the most promising combinations.

Questions for Discussion

1. Have you ever used the idea box, or something similar to it, before now? If so, how effective was it?
2. For what kinds of challenges is the idea box most useful and least useful?
3. It has been said that generating an idea box is similar to writing a poem. How is this so?

(*Source*: Based on suggestions by Michalko, 1991; see note 26.)

SKILLS BANK

WORKING IN GROUPS

What Does Your Workspace Say About Your Organizational Culture?

Newcomers' impressions of an organization's culture depend greatly on the visual images they first see. Even without knowing anything about an organization, seeing the workplace sends a message — intentional or not — regarding what that organization is like. The following exercise is designed to demonstrate this phenomenon.

Directions

1. Each member of the class should take several photographs of his or her workplace and then select the three that best capture, in his or her mind, the essence of what that organization is like.
2. One member of the class should identify the company depicted in his or her photos, describe the type of work it does, and present the photos to the rest of the class.
3. Members of the class then should rate the organization shown in the photos using the following dimensions. Circle the number that comes closest to your feelings about the company shown.

Unfamiliar	1	2	3	4	5	6	7	Familiar
Unsuccessful	1	2	3	4	5	6	7	Successful
Unfriendly	1	2	3	4	5	6	7	Friendly
Unproductive	1	2	3	4	5	6	7	Productive
Not innovative	1	2	3	4	5	6	7	Innovative
Uncaring	1	2	3	4	5	6	7	Caring
Conservative	1	2	3	4	5	6	7	Risky
Closed	1	2	3	4	5	6	7	Open

4. Take turns sharing your individual reactions to each set of photos. Compare the responses of the student whose company pictures were examined with those of the students seeing these photos for the first time.

5. Repeat this process using the photos of other students' organizations.

Questions for Discussion

1. For each set of photos examined, how much agreement or disagreement was there in the class about the companies rated?

2. For each set of photos examined, how closely did the descriptions of class members match the photographers' assessments of their own companies? In other words, how well did the photos capture the culture of the organization as perceived by an "insider"?

3. As a whole, were people more accurate in assessing the culture of companies they already were familiar with than those they did not already know? If so, why do you think this occurred?

4. Was there more agreement regarding the cultures of organizations in some types of industries (e.g., manufacturing) than in others (e.g., service)? If so, why do you think this occurred?

14

ORGANIZATIONAL STRUCTURE AND DESIGN

LEARNING OBJECTIVES

After reading this chapter, you should be able to

1. Describe *organizational structure* and how it is revealed by an *organizational chart*.

2. Explain the basic characteristics of organizational structure as revealed in an organizational chart (*hierarchy of authority*, *division of labor*, *span of control*, *line versus staff*, and *decentralization*).

3. Describe different approaches to departmentalization, including *functional organizations*, *product organizations*, *matrix organizations*, and the *boundaryless organization*.

4. Distinguish *classical* from *neoclassical* approaches to organizational design.

5. Distinguish *mechanistic organizations* from *organic organizations* as described by the *contingency approach* to organizational design, and describe the conditions under which each is most appropriate.

6. Describe the five organizational forms identified by Mintzberg: *simple structure*, *machine bureaucracy*, *professional bureaucracy*, *divisional structure*, and *adhocracy*.

7. Characterize two forms of intraorganizational design: *conglomerates*, and *strategic alliances*.

PREVIEW CASE

Ameritech and Random House Join Forces on Emerging Technology

Considering the uncertainties involved, no one company can expect to control all the technologies needed to deliver multimedia entertainment to the home market. Of the emerging key players, however, Ameritech appears to have a head start. As a regional Bell operating company, it has considerable copper-wire and fiberoptic networks throughout the Midwest. Clearly, however, Ameritech cannot blaze the path itself. There are too many undeveloped technologies and unanswered questions about market interests for any one company—even Ameritech—to go it alone.

With this in mind, Ameritech has positioned its technological skills and considerable assets alongside those of other companies with complementary skills. One such alliance involves Random House, the giant publisher of books and magazines. But why, you ask, would Ameritech join forces with a publisher when another high-tech company would make more sense? The answer is simple: The capacity to deliver multimedia information to the home is of limited use unless content delivered is desired. This is where Random House comes in. As owner of *The New Yorker* magazine and various travel guides, including Fodor's and the Arthur Frommer series, Random House brings some highly regarded content to the table.

As of this writing, you cannot yet receive Random House's content through Ameritech's networks in your home. The two firms have formed a company called Worldview Systems, however, which publishes an electronic, monthly current-events database of travel information, which is sold primarily to travel agents. It consists of information about 170 international destinations that agents can access either on-line or through a toll-free telephone number.

Ameritech's vice president of development, Thomas Thornton, is optimistic that his company can take the lead in bringing this service to the consumer market. The key, he notes, is advancing technology to the point at which a viable product emerges—and management's ultimate commitment to the project. This is always the case with any new direction for an organization, but something is special about this case. Senior managers, he cautions, must be willing to "move fast in investing, but be patient in waiting for returns." Not all companies are in a position to do this.

Two things are certain. To at least some extent, Ameritech will advance this technology and market it, but it will not—and cannot—be alone in bringing it to fruition. Experts estimate that hundreds (if not thousands) of companies already are or soon will be, joining forces to capitalize on this emerging technology. Ameritech is only one tile in the emerging multimedia mosaic, but with the help of Random House, Ameritech just might find its way.

As the preview case illustrates, careful co-ordination between organizations may be required for success—particularly in large-scale, high-tech projects. Co-ordination between individuals or departments in a single organization, however, also is required. This raises a question about how, exactly, various organizational tasks should be coordinated between the units of an organization. In this regard, it helps to think of an organization as being a large jigsaw puzzle with many different pieces. To form a meaningful whole, the various parts (i.e., the organizational units) must combine in precisely the right manner. In organizations, however, there is no one, single way they can come together. Instead, these pieces can be joined in any of several different ways. Thus, the key question is: How can the various units of an organization be combined to make it most effective?

Researchers and theorists in OB have provided considerable insight into this matter by studying what is called *organizational structure* — that is, how individuals and groups are arranged regarding the tasks they perform — and *organizational design* — that is, the process of co-ordinating these structural elements in the most effective manner. As you probably suspect, finding the best way to structure and design organizations is not simple. Because understanding the structure and design of organizations is essential to appreciate their functioning, however, organizational scientists have devoted considerable energy to this topic. We describe these efforts in this chapter.

To begin, we identify the basic building blocks of organizations, which can be identified by the *organizational chart* (i.e., a useful pictorial way of depicting key features of organizational structure). We then examine how these structural elements can be combined most effectively into productive organizational designs. Finally, we discuss the role of technology as a cause—and as a consequence—of organizational design, and in so doing, we highlight some basic facts regarding the role of the environment on organizational design.

ORGANIZATIONAL STRUCTURE: THE BASIC DIMENSIONS OF ORGANIZATIONS

Think about how a simple house is constructed. A wooden frame is positioned atop a concrete slab and is covered by a roof and siding materials. Within this basic structure are separate systems that provide electricity, water, and telephone service. Similarly, the human body is composed of a skeleton surrounded by various organ systems, muscle, and tissue serving bodily functions such as respiration, digestion, and the like. In a similar fashion, we also can identify the structure of an organization.

Consider, for example, the college or university you attend. It probably is composed of various groupings of people and departments working together to serve special functions. Individuals and groups are dedicated to tasks such as teaching, providing financial services, maintaining the physical facilities, and so on. Of course, within each group, even more distinctions can be found. For example, the instructor for your OB course is unlikely to teach seventeenth-century French literature as well. You also can distinguish between the various tasks and functions people perform in other organizations. In other words, an organization is not a haphazard collection but a meaningful combination of groups and individuals working purposefully together to meet the organization's goals.[1] The term **organizational structure** refers to the formal configuration between individuals and groups regarding the allocation of tasks, responsibilities, and authority within organizations.[2]

Strictly speaking, one cannot see the structure of an organization. It is an abstract concept. The connections between various clusters of functions within an organization, however, can be represented in a diagram known as an **organizational chart**. In other words, an organizational chart can be considered to be a representation of an organization's internal structure. As you might imagine, such charts may be useful tools for avoiding confusion within organizations regarding how various tasks or functions inter-relate. By carefully studying organizational charts, we can learn some of the basic elements of organizational structure. Thus, we now turn our attention to the five basic dimensions of organizational structure that such charts reveal.

Organizational charts provide information about the various tasks performed within an organization and the formal lines of authority between them. For example, part of a hypothetical manufacturing organization is depicted in Figure 14.1. Each box represents a specific job, and the lines connecting these boxes reflect the formally prescribed lines of communication between the individuals performing those jobs. To specialists in organizational structure, however, such diagrams reveal a great deal more.

Hierarchy of Authority: Up and Down the Organizational Ladder

In particular, an organizational chart also provides information about who reports to whom, or what is known as the **hierarchy of authority**. The diagram reveals which particular lower-level employees are required to report to which particular individuals immediately above them in the organizational hierarchy. In Figure 14.1, the various regional salespeople (at the bottom of the hierarchy and the diagram) report to

organizational structure

The formal configuration between individuals and groups regarding the allocation of tasks, responsibilities, and authorities within organizations.

organizational chart

A diagram representing the connections between the various departments within an organization; a graphic representation of organizational design, indicating who is supposed to communicate with whom.

hierarchy of authority

A configuration of the reporting relationships within organizations (i.e., who reports to whom).

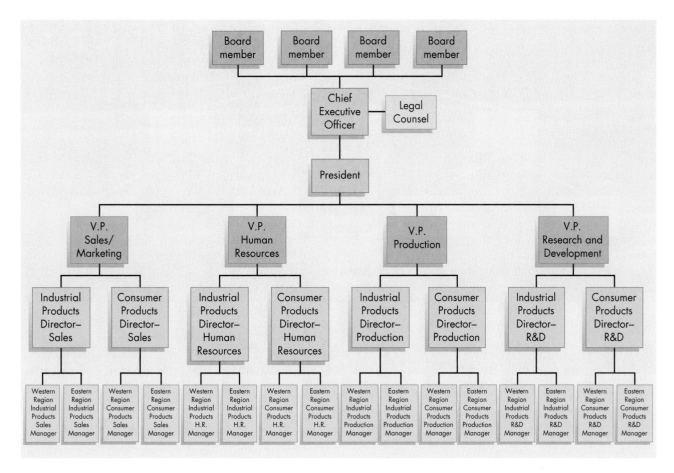

FIGURE 14.1

Organizational Chart of a Hypothetical Manufacturing Firm

An organizational chart such as this identifies pictorially the various functions performed within an organization and the lines of authority between the people performing those functions.

their respective regional sales directors, who report to the vice president of sales, who reports to the president, who reports to the chief executive officer, who reports to the board of directors. As we trace these reporting relationships, we work our way up the organization's hierarchy. In this case, the organization has six levels, but organizations may have many levels, in which case their structure is considered to be *tall*, or only a few levels, in which case their structure is considered to be *flat*.

Recently, many organizations have been restructuring their work forces by flattening them out.[3] This is what occurs as companies "downsize," "rightsize," "delayer," or "retrench" by eliminating entire layers of organizational structure (we return to this topic again in chapter 16).[4] Job losses from restructuring have hit particularly hard at the middle levels of organizations (Figure 14.2). In keeping with the trend toward getting work done through teams (see chapter 7), tall organizational hierarchies become unnecessary. The underlying assumption is that fewer layers reduce waste and enable people to make better decisions (by moving them closer to the problems at hand), thereby leading to greater profitability.

Division of Labor: Carving Up the Jobs Done

The standard organizational chart shows that many tasks within an organization are divided into specialized jobs, which is a process known as the **division of labor**. The more tasks are divided into separate jobs, the more those jobs are *specialized* and, thus,

division of labor

The process of dividing the many tasks in an organization into specialized jobs.

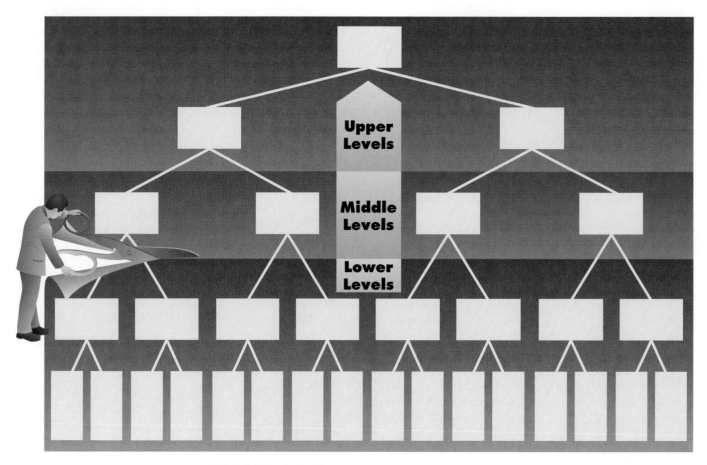

FIGURE 14.2

The Flattening of Organizational Hierarchies: A Modern Trend

As today's organizations restructure, the middle layers of organizational hierarchies tend to be removed. The result is a flatter organizational structure, which puts managers closer to the issues about which they must make decisions.

the narrower the range of activities job incumbents must perform. In theory, the fewer tasks a person performs, the better he or she may be expected to perform them, thereby freeing others to perform the tasks they do best. Taken together, an entire organization is composed of people performing a collection of specialized jobs. This probably is the most obvious feature that can be observed from the organizational chart.

As you might imagine, the degree to which employees perform specialized jobs likely depends on the size of the organization. In other words, the larger the organization, the more opportunities for specialization to exist. For example, an individual working in a large advertising agency may specialize in a highly narrow field, such as writing jingles for radio and television spots for automobiles. In contrast, someone working at a much smaller agency may do all the writing of print and broadcast ads in addition to helping out with the artwork and meeting with clients. Obviously, the larger company might reap the benefits of efficiently using the talents of the employee — a natural result of an extensive division of labor. As companies downsize, however, many managerial jobs become less specialized. For example, at General Electric, quite a few middle-management positions have been eliminated. As a consequence, the remaining managers must perform a wider variety of jobs, thereby making their own jobs less specialized.[5] You can see this relationship in the summary in Table 14.1.

TABLE 14.1

Division of Labor: A Summary
Low and high levels of division of labor can be characterized regarding the dimensions shown here.

	DIVISION OF LABOR	
DIMENSION	LOW	HIGH
Degree of specialization	General tasks	Highly specialized tasks
Typical organizational size	Small	Large
Economic efficiency	Inefficient	Highly efficient

Span of Control: Breadth of Responsibility

For how many individuals should a manager have responsibility? The earliest management theorists and practitioners (even the Roman legions) addressed this question.[6] When you look at an organizational chart, the number of people formally required to report to each individual manager is clear, and this number constitutes a manager's **span of control**. Those responsible for many individuals are said to have a *wide* span of control, whereas those responsible for few individuals are said to have a *narrow* span of control. In our organizational chart (see Figure 14.1), the CEO is responsible for only the actions of the president, thus giving this individual a narrower span of control than the president, who has a span of control of five individuals. When organization leaders are concerned they do not have enough control over lower-level employees, they sometimes restructure their organizations so that managers have responsibility for fewer subordinates. This is the case at Canada's largest bank, Royal Bank, where top managers recently recommended that area managers reduce the number of branches under their control to between seven and 12.[7]

When a manager's span of control is wide, the organization itself tends to have a flat hierarchy. In contrast, when a manager's span of control is narrow, the organization tends to have a tall hierarchy. This is demonstrated in Figure 14.3. The diagram at the top shows a tall organization — that is, one with many layers in the hierarchy and relatively narrow spans of control (i.e., the number of people supervised is low). In contrast, the diagram at the bottom shows a flat organization — that is, with only a few levels in the hierarchy and the relatively wide spans of control. Note that both organizations depicted have the same number of positions but that they are arranged differently.

The organizational chart may not reflect perfectly a manager's actual span of control. Other factors not immediately indicated by the chart may be involved. For example, managers may have additional responsibilities that do not appear (e.g., assignments on various committees). Moreover, some subordinates (e.g., new people to the job) might require more attention than others. In addition, the needed degree of supervisory control may increase (e.g., when jobs change) or decrease (e.g., when subordinates become more proficient). In fact, it is not readily possible to specify the "ideal" span of control that should be sought. Instead, consider what form of organization is best suited to various purposes. For example, supervisors in a military unit must have tight control over subordinates and get them to respond both quickly and precisely, so a narrow span of control is likely to be effective. As a result, military organizations tend to be extremely tall. In contrast, people working in a research-and-development lab must have an open exchange of ideas and typically require little managerial guidance to be successful, so units of this type tend to have very flat structures.

span of control
The number of subordinates in an organization who are supervised by managers.

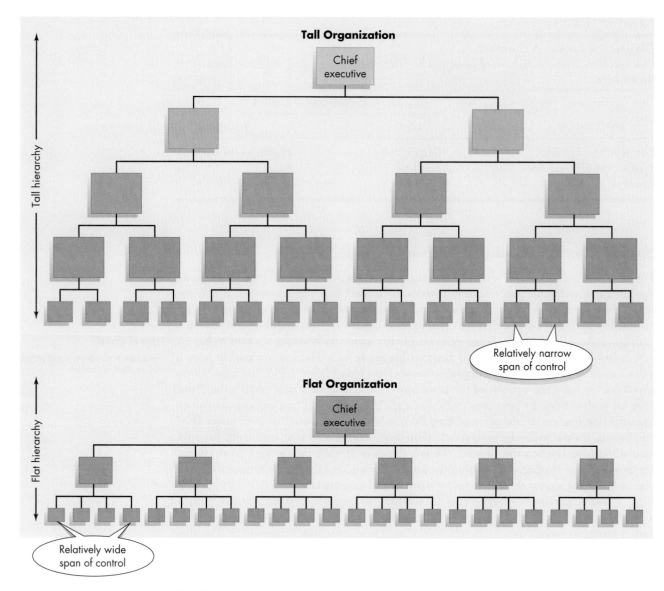

FIGURE 14.3

Tall and Flat Organizations: A Comparison

In *tall* organizations, the hierarchy has many layers, and managers have a narrow span of control (i.e., they are responsible for few subordinates). In *flat* organizations, however, the hierarchy has few layers, and managers have a wide span of control (i.e., they are responsible for many subordinates). Each organization depicted here has 31 members, but each is structured differently.

Line and Staff Positions: Decision Makers and Advisers

line positions

Positions in organizations in which people can make decisions related to basic work.

staff positions

Positions in organizations in which people make recommendations to others but are not involved in decisions concerning day-to-day operations.

The organizational chart in Figure 14.1 reveals an additional distinction — that between line positions and staff positions. People occupying **line positions** (e.g., the various vice presidents and managers) have decision-making power. Others, occupying **staff positions**, are merely advisory. For example, the legal counsel cannot make decisions; instead, he or she provides advice and recommendations to the line managers. This individual may help corporate officials decide if a certain product name can be used without infringing on copyright restrictions. In many of today's organizations, human resources managers may be seen as occupying staff positions as well, because they often provide specialized services regarding testing and interviewing procedures as well as information about the latest laws on personnel discrimination. The ultimate decisions on personnel selection, however, might be made by more senior managers in specialized areas — that is, by staff managers.

Differences between line and staff personnel are not unusual, but such differences may be conflict-arousing — or even be used to create intentional sources of conflict. For example, when Harold Green was the CEO of ITT, staff specialists in the areas of planning and strategy were regularly brought in to challenge the decisions of line managers to "keep them on their toes."[8] Sociologists have noted that staff managers tend to be younger, better educated, and more committed to their fields than to the organizations employing them.[9] Line managers might feel more committed to the organization not only because of the greater opportunities they have to exercise decisions but because they are more likely to perceive themselves as being part of a company rather than an independent specialist (whose identity lies primarily within his or her area of expertise).

Decentralization: Delegating Power Downward

As companies grew larger and larger during the first half of the twentieth century, they shifted power and authority to a few upper-echelon administrators — that is, executives whose decisions influenced the many people below them in the organizational hierarchy. In fact, during the 1920s, Alfred P. Sloan, Jr., who then was the president of General Motors, introduced the notion of a "central office," a place where a few individuals made policy decisions for the entire company.[10] As part of Sloan's plan, decisions regarding day-to-day operations were pushed lower and lower down the organizational hierarchy, thus allowing those individuals who would be most affected to make the decisions. This process of delegating power from higher to lower levels within an organization is known as **decentralization**. It is the opposite, of course, of *centralization*, which is the tendency for a few powerful individuals or groups to hold most of the decision-making power.

Recent years have seen a marked trend toward increasing decentralization. As a result, organizational charts might show fewer staff positions, because decision-making authority is being pushed farther down the hierarchy. Many organizations have moved toward decentralization to promote managerial efficiency and to improve employee satisfaction (i.e., the result of giving people greater opportunities to take responsibility for their own actions). For example, thousands of staff jobs have been eliminated at companies such as 3M, Eastman Kodak, AT&T, and General Electric as these companies have decentralized.[11]

Decentralization is not always ideal, however. In fact, for some jobs, it actually may hinder productivity. For example, consider production-oriented positions, such as assembly-line jobs. In one classic study, researchers found that decentralization improved performance on some jobs — notably, the work of employees in a research laboratory — but interfered with performance on more routine, assembly-line jobs.[12] These findings make sense considering that people in research-and-development positions are likely to enjoy the autonomy that decentralization allows, whereas people in production jobs are likely to be less interested in taking responsibility for decisions — and may enjoy not having to take such responsibility. Thus, many of today's companies that are heavily involved in research and development — Hewlett-Packard, Intel Corporation, Philips Electronics, and AT&T's Bell Laboratories — have shifted to more decentralized designs.[13]

In contrast, under some conditions, such as when only a few individuals can judge what is best for the company, highly centralized authority makes sense. For example, during the 1990 recession, Delta Airlines' then-CEO Ronald W. Allen personally approved every expenditure greater than $5,000 (except for jet fuel).[14] By so doing, he could monitor the company's expenses and keep it afloat during those difficult times. Despite the possible benefits likely to result from relieving Allen of these

decentralization

The extent to which authority and decision making are spread throughout all levels of an organization rather than being reserved for top management (i.e., *centralization*).

TABLE 14.2

Decentralization: Benefits When Low and When High
Various benefits are associated with low decentralization (high centralization) and high decentralization (low centralization) within organizations.

LOW DECENTRALIZATION (HIGH CENTRALIZATION)	HIGH DECENTRALIZATION (LOW CENTRALIZATION)
• Eliminates the additional responsibility not desired by people performing routine jobs • Permits crucial decisions to be made by individuals who have the "big picture"	• Can eliminate levels of management, making a leaner organization • Promotes greater opportunities for decisions to be made by people closest to problems

chores, he believed it was necessary to enforce decisions when the margin for error was small. To conclude, the potential exists to derive considerable benefits from decentralization, but the process should be avoided under certain conditions (Table 14.2).

The five elements of structure described thus far — hierarchy of authority, division of labor, span of control, line versus staff positions, and decentralization — are the building blocks of organizational structure. Therefore, they represent the key dimensions along which organizations differ.

DEPARTMENTALIZATION: WAYS OF STRUCTURING ORGANIZATIONS

Thus far, we have talked about "the" organizational chart. Typically, such charts — like the one shown in Figure 14.2 — divide an organization according to the various functions performed. As we explain in this section, however, this is only one option. Organizations can be divided not only by function but by product or market and even by a special blend of function and product or market, which is known as the *matrix form*. We now take a closer look at these ways of breaking organizations into coherent units — that is, at the process of **departmentalization**.

departmentalization

The process of breaking organizations into coherent units.

Functional Organizations: Departmentalization by Task

Because it is both the form organizations usually take when first created and how we usually think of organizations, the **functional organization** can be considered the most basic approach to departmentalization. Essentially, functional organizations departmentalize individuals according to the nature of the functions they perform. Thus, people who perform similar functions are assigned to the same department. For example, a manufacturing company might consist of separate departments devoted to basic functions such as production, sales, research and development, and accounting (Figure 14.4).

functional organization

The type of departmentalization based on the activities or functions performed (e.g., sales, finance).

Naturally, as organizations grow and become more complex, additional departments are added or deleted. As certain functions become centralized, resources can be saved by avoiding duplication of effort, thus resulting in a higher level of efficiency. This form of organizational structure takes advantage of economies of scale (by allowing employees performing the same jobs to share facilities and not duplicating functions) but also allows individuals to specialize, thereby performing only those tasks at which they are most expert. The result is a highly skilled work force, which is a direct benefit to the organization.

Partly offsetting these advantages, however, are several potential limitations. The most important arises because functional organizational structures encourage separate

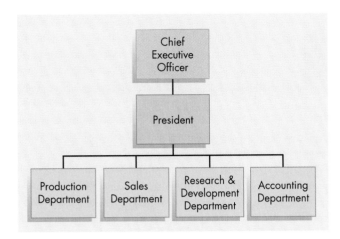

FIGURE 14.4

Functional Organization of a Typical Manufacturing Firm

Functional organizations are those in which departments are formed based on common functions. In the hypothetical manufacturing firm in this simplified organizational chart identifies four typical functional departments. (In specific organizations, the actual functions may differ.)

units to develop their own narrow perspectives and, thereby, to lose sight of overall organizational goals. For example, in a manufacturing company, an engineer might see the company's problems in terms of product reliability and lose sight of other key considerations, such as market trends, overseas competition, and so on. Such narrow-mindedness inevitably results from functional specialization—the downside of people seeing the company's operations through a narrow lens. A related problem is that functional structures also discourage innovation, because they channel individual efforts toward narrow, functional areas and do not encourage coordination and cross-fertilization of ideas between those areas. As a result, functional organizations respond slowly to challenges and opportunities (e.g., the need for new products and services). In summary, functional organizations certainly are logical in nature and useful in many contexts, but they by no means are the perfect way to departmentalize people in organizations.

Product Organizations: Departmentalization by Type of Output

Organizations—at least successful ones—do not stand still but rather constantly change in size and scope. As they develop new products and seek new customers, they might find a functional structure no longer works as well as it once did. For example, manufacturing a wide range of products using many different methods might strain the manufacturing division of a functional organization. Similarly, tracking the varied tax requirements for different businesses (e.g., restaurants, farms, real estate, manufacturing) might challenge a single financial division in a company. In response, a **product organization** might be created. This type of departmentalization creates self-contained divisions, each of which is responsible for a certain product or group of products. For a look at the structure of a product organization, see Figure 14.5.

When organizations are departmentalized by products, separate divisions are established, each of which is devoted to a certain product or group of products. Each unit contains all the resources needed to develop, manufacture, and sell its product. The organization itself is composed of separate divisions, which operate independently and the heads of which report to top management. Some functions might be centralized within the parent company (e.g., human resource management or legal staff), but on a day-to-day basis, these divisions operate as separate companies or, as accountants call them, *cost centers* of their own. A good example is the separate divisions of General Motors devoted to manufacturing different brands of cars and trucks (e.g., Chevrolet, Oldsmobile, Saturn, GMC Trucks, Pontiac, Cadillac). Still more divisions are responsible for manufacturing and selling locomotives, refrigerators, and auto parts. The managers of each division thus can devote their energies to one particular business.

product organization

The type of departmentalization based on the products (or product lines) produced.

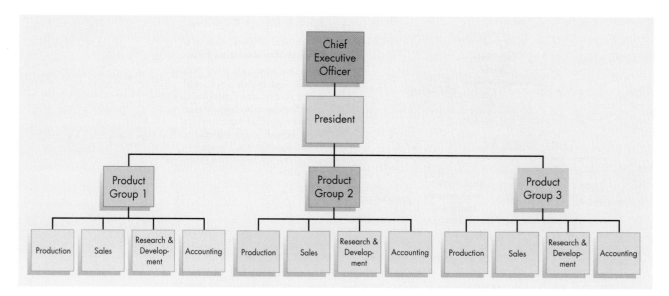

FIGURE 14.5

An Example of a Product Organization

In a *product organization*, separate units handle different products or product lines. Each of these divisions contains all the departments necessary for operating as an independent unit.

This is not to say product organizations are without limitations. Indeed, they have several drawbacks, the most obvious of which is loss of economies of scale stemming from duplication of various departments within operating units. For example, if each unit performs its own research and development, the need for costly equipment, facilities, and personnel may be multiplied. Another problem involves the organization's ability to attract — and to retain — talented employees. Because each department within operating units is necessarily smaller than a single, combined department would be, opportunities for advancement and career development may suffer. In turn, this may pose serious problems regarding long-term retention of talented employees. Finally, problems of coordination across product lines also may arise. In fact, in extreme cases, actions taken by one operating division may adversely affect the outcomes of others.

A clear example of such problems was provided by Hewlett-Packard, a major U.S. manufacturer of computers, printers, and scientific test equipment (Figure 14.6). During most of its history, Hewlett-Packard adopted a product design involving scores

FIGURE 14.6

Hewlett-Packard: Departmentalization Based on Market Segment

Rather than organizing around products, Hewlett-Packard has experienced success by departmentalizing around market segments. Different divisions are responsible for consumer items (e.g., computers, printers), business products, and scientific equipment.

of small, largely autonomous divisions, each concerned with producing — and selling — certain products. As Hewlett-Packard grew in size and complexity, however, it found itself in an increasingly untenable situation: Sales representatives from different divisions sometimes attempted to sell different lines of equipment, often to be used for the same basic purposes, to the same customers! To deal with such problems, top management decided to restructure the company into sectors based largely on the markets they served (e.g., business customers, scientific and manufacturing customers). In short, Hewlett-Packard switched from a fairly traditional, product organization to an internal structure driven by market considerations.[15] It is too soon to determine if the effects of this reorganization will be as positive as top management hopes, but the initial results are promising.

This example points out a particular variation on the basic theme of market departmentalization: Self-contained operating units also can be established based on specific geographic regions or territories or even on customers rather than different products. Thus, for example, a large retail chain might develop separate divisions for different regions of the country (e.g., Macy's New York and Macy's California) or for different customer bases (e.g., Bloomingdales by Mail and Bloomingdales Retail). Similarly, a large record company, which itself likely is a division of a larger entertainment company, may establish independent divisions — each with its own labels — to sign, develop, produce, and promote recordings of interest to people in different markets (e.g., children's, classical, Latin, pop). By departmentalizing in this fashion, a company can give artists the attention they would expect from a small company and still realize the specialization and economies of scale they would expect from a large company. Regardless of the exact basis for departmentalizing, the basic rationale remains the same — that is, to divide the organization's operations in a way that enhances efficiency.

GLOBAL MATTERS

Before selling its food-service operations, PepsiCo organized its restaurants by geographic region. One set of executives was in charge of U.S. operations, whereas another was responsible for foreign operations. ■

Matrix Organizations:
Departmentalization by Function and Product

When the aerospace industry was first developing, the U.S. government demanded each company assign a single manager to each of its projects; thus, it was immediately clear who was responsible for the progress of each. In response to this requirement, TRW Systems Group established a "project leader" for each project — that is, someone who shared authority with the leaders of the existing functional departments.[16] This temporary arrangement later evolved into what is called a **matrix organization** — that is, the type of organization in which an employee reports to both a functional (or division) manager and a specific project (or product) manager. In essence, TRW developed a complex type of organizational structure that combines both the function and the product form of departmentalization.[17] Recently, matrix organizational forms have been used in many organizations, such as Citibank and Liberty Mutual Insurance.[18] To better understand matrix organizations, look at the organizational chart shown in Figure 14.7.

Employees in matrix organizations have two bosses; more technically, they are under *dual authority*. One line of authority, as shown by the vertical arrows on Figure 14.7, is *functional*. In other words, it is managed by vice presidents in charge of various functional areas. The other, as shown by the horizontal arrows, is *product* — or a specific project or temporary business — and is managed by specific individuals in charge of certain products (or projects).

matrix organization
The type of departmentalization in which a product or project form is superimposed on a functional form.

FIGURE 14.7

A Typical Matrix Organization

In a *matrix organization*, a product structure is superimposed on a basic functional structure. This results in a dual system of authority, in which some managers report to two bosses: a project (or product) manager, and a functional (or departmental) manager.

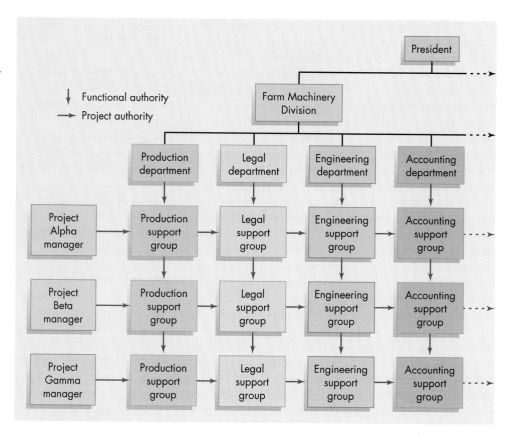

Matrix designs involve three major roles. First, there is the *top leader* — that is, the individual with authority over both lines (i.e., the one based on function and the one based on product or project). This individual's task is to enhance coordination between functional and product managers and to maintain an appropriate balance of power between them. Second, there are the *matrix bosses* — that is, people who head functional departments or specific projects. Neither functional managers nor project managers have complete authority over subordinates, so they must work together to ensure their efforts mesh rather than conflict. In addition, they must agree on issues such as promotions and raises for specific people under their joint authority. Finally, there are *two-boss managers* — that is, people who must report to both product and functional managers and attempt to balance the demands of each.

Not all organizations use the matrix structure on a permanent basis. Several partial or temporary types of matrix design have been identified.[19] First, the *temporary overlay* is a form of matrix structure in which projects are crossed with functions on a special short-term basis. This is in contrast to a *permanent overlay*, in which project teams are kept going after each project is completed. Finally, these are *mature matrix organizations*, in which both the functional and the product lines are permanent and equally strong.

Having used a matrix organization for more than twenty years, Dow Corning is an example of a mature matrix organization.[20] At this company, each functional representative reports to the leaders of his or her department while also contributing to the design and operation of the particular product line for which he or she is responsible. Because people working in this fashion have two bosses, they must have sufficient freedom to attain their objectives. As you might imagine, a fair amount of coordination, flexibility, openness, and trust is essential, thereby suggesting not everyone adapts well to such a system.

Organizations are most likely to adopt matrix designs when they confront certain conditions. These include a complex and uncertain environment (e.g., one with frequent changes) and the need for economies of scale in using internal resources. Specifically, a matrix approach often is adopted by medium-size organizations with several product lines that do not possess sufficient resources to establish fully self-contained operating units. Under such conditions, a matrix design provides a useful compromise. Some companies that have adopted this structure (at least on a trial basis) are TRW Systems Group, Liberty Mutual Insurance, and Citibank.[21]

Key advantages to matrix designs already have been suggested by our discussion.[22] First, such designs permit flexible use of an organization's human resources. Individuals within functional departments can be assigned to specific products or projects as the need arises, and they can return to their regular duties when the task is completed. Second, matrix designs offer medium-size organizations an efficient means of quickly responding to a changing, unstable environment. Third, such designs often enhance communication among managers. Indeed, they literally force matrix bosses to discuss—and to agree—on many matters.

Disadvantages of matrix designs include the frustration and stress faced by two-boss managers in reporting to different supervisors, the danger that one of the authority systems (i.e., functional or product) will overwhelm the other, and the consistently high levels of cooperation required.[23] When organizations must stretch their financial and human resources to meet challenges from the external environment or to take advantage of new opportunities, however, matrix designs often can play a useful role.

■ Horizontal Organizations: Structuring by Process

If the experts are right, tomorrow's organizations will structure work in a new way—one that involves more than just tinkering with the boxes on an organizational chart. It is called the **horizontal organization**. Advocated by many organizational experts, it is touted by consultants from McKinsey & Co. as "the first real, fundamentally different, robust alternative" to the functional organization.[24]

horizontal organization
The practice of structuring organizations by the processes performed, using autonomous work teams in flattened hierarchies.

The essence of the idea is simple: Instead of organizing jobs in the traditional, vertical fashion by having a long chain of groups or individuals performing parts of a task (e.g., one group sells the advertising job, another plans the ad campaign, and yet another produces the ads), horizontal organizations have flattened hierarchies. In other words, they arrange autonomous work teams (see chapter 7) in parallel, with each team performing many different steps in the process (e.g., members of an advertising team may bring different skills and expertise to a single team that is responsible for all aspects of advertising).

Essentially, organizations are structured around *processes* instead of tasks, and performance objectives are based on customers' needs (e.g., lowered cost, improved service). Once the core processes meeting these needs (e.g., order generation, new product development) are identified, they become the company's major components—instead of traditional departments such as sales or manufacturing.

According to consultant Michael Hammer, "In the future, executive positions will not be defined in terms of collections of people, like head of the sales department, but in terms of processes, like senior-VP-of-getting-stuff-to-customers, which is sales, shipping, billing. You'll no longer have a box on an organization chart. You'll own part of a process map."[25] Envision this structure as a whole company lying on its side

continued

and organized by process. An ardent believer in this approach, Lawrence Bossidy, CEO of Allied Signal, says, "Every business has maybe six basic processes. We'll organize around them. The people who run them will be the leaders of the business."[26] For example, in an industrial company, these processes might include new-product development, flow of materials, and the order-delivery-billing cycle. Individuals constantly will move in and out of various teams as needed, drawing from a directory of broadly skilled, in-house corporate experts available to lend their expertise.

The horizontal organization already is a reality in several organizations, including AT&T (network systems division), Eastman Chemical (a division of Kodak), Hallmark Cards, and Xerox. For example, consider General Electric's factory in Bayamón, Puerto Rico. The 172 hourly workers, 15 salaried "advisers," and a single manager manufacture "arresters" (i.e., surge protectors that guard power stations from lightning). This is the entire workforce. There are no support staff and no supervisors—and only about half as many people as in a conventional factory. Bayamón employees are formed into separate teams of approximately 10 widely skilled members who "own" such parts of the work as shipping and receiving, assembly, and so on. The teams do whatever is needed to get the job done, and the "advisers" get involved only when needed.

Carefully controlled studies have yet to assess this new approach, but those who have used it are convinced of its effectiveness. One top McKinsey & Co. consultant even claims this new approach can help companies to cut their costs by at least one-third. Some clients, they boast, have done even better. Will the horizontal organization replace the traditional pyramid of the hierarchical organization? Only time will tell. Meanwhile, those who have turned to horizontal organizational structures appear to be glad they did. ■

ORGANIZATIONAL DESIGN: COORDINATING THE STRUCTURAL ELEMENTS OF ORGANIZATIONS

organizational design

The process of co-ordinating the structural elements of an organization in the most appropriate manner.

We began this chapter by likening an organization's structure to that of a house. Now, we extend that analogy to introduce the concept of *organizational design*. Just as a house is designed in a particular fashion by combining its structural elements in various ways, so can an organization be designed by combining its basic elements in certain ways. Accordingly, **organizational design** refers to the process of coordinating the structural elements of organizations in the most appropriate manner.

As you might imagine, this is no easy task. We might describe some options that sound neat and rational, but in reality, this hardly is ever the case. Even the most precisely designed organizations face the need to change at some point, thereby adjusting to technological changes, political pressures, accidents, and so on. Organizational designs also might be changed to improve operating efficiency, such as the promise by some recent U.S. presidents to streamline the huge federal bureaucracy. Our point is simple: Because organizations operate within a changing world, their own designs must be capable of changing as well. Organizations that are poorly designed or inflexible cannot survive. If you consider the many banks and airlines that have gone out of business recently because of their inability to deal with deregulation and a shifting economy, you get a good idea of the ultimate consequences of ineffective organizational design.

Classical and Neoclassical Approaches: The Quest for the One Best Design

The earliest theorists in organizational design were not aware of the need for organizations to be flexible. Instead, they approached designing organizations as a search for "the one best way." Today, we are more aware of the need to adapt organizational designs to various environmental and social conditions, but theorists in the early and middle twentieth century sought the "universal" design.

In chapter 1, we described the efforts of organizational scholars such as Max Weber, Frederick Taylor, and Henri Fayol. These theorists believed effective organizations had a formal hierarchy, clear rules, specialization of labor, highly routine tasks, and a highly impersonal working environment. Weber referred to this organizational form as a *bureaucracy*. This **classical organizational theory** has fallen into disfavor, however, because it is insensitive to human needs and is not suited to a changing environment. Unfortunately, the ideal form of an organization, at least according to Weber, did not account for the realities of the world around it. Apparently, the "ideal" is not necessarily "realistic."

In response to these conditions—and with inspiration from the Hawthorne studies—the classical approach of the bureaucratic model gave way to more of a human relations orientation. Organizational scholars such as Douglas McGregor, Chris Argyris, and Rensis Likert attempted to improve on the classical model, which is why their approach is labeled **neoclassical organizational theory**. These theorists argued that economic effectiveness is not the only goal of an industrial organization. In their view, employee satisfaction is a goal as well.

Specifically, McGregor objected to the rigid hierarchy imposed by Weber's bureaucratic form, because this hierarchy was based on negative assumptions about people—primarily that they lacked ambition and would not work unless coerced (i.e., the *Theory X* approach).[27] McGregor argued that people desire to achieve success by working and that they seek satisfaction by behaving responsibly (i.e., the *Theory Y* approach). Argyris expressed similar ideas.[28] Specifically, he argued managerial domination of organizations blocks the basic human needs to express oneself and to accomplish tasks successfully. Such dissatisfaction, in his view, would encourage employee turnover and lead to poor performance.

Likert shared these perspectives, arguing that organizational performance is enhanced by actively promoting people's feelings of self-worth and their importance to the organization not by rigidly controlling their actions.[29] An effective organization, Likert proposed, was one in which individuals had great opportunity to participate in making organizational decisions, or what he called a *System 4 organization*. Doing this, he claimed, would enhance the employees' personal sense of worth, thereby motivating them to succeed. Likert called the opposite type of organization a *System 1*—that is, the traditional form in which organizational power is held by a few top managers who tell lower-ranking people what to do. (*System 2* and *System 3* are intermediate forms between the extremes of System 1 and System 4.)

The implications of these neoclassical approaches to organizational design are clear. The classical approach called for organizations to be designed with a rigid, tall hierarchy and a narrow span of control, thus allowing managers to maintain close supervision over their subordinates. The neoclassical approach, however, argued for designing organizations with flat hierarchical structures (minimizing managerial control over subordinates) and a high degree of decentralization (encouraging employees to make their own decisions). Indeed, such design features may well serve the underlying neoclassical philosophy.

Like the classical approach, the neoclassical approach also may be faulted, because again, it is promoted as "the one best approach" to organizational design. The benefits of flat, decentralized designs may be many, but to claim this represents the universal, ideal form for all organizations is naive. In response to this criticism, more contemporary approaches to organizational design no longer attempt to find the one best way to design organizations. Instead, they search for designs that are most appropriate to the various circumstances and contexts within which the organizations themselves operate.

classical organizational theory

Approaches assuming there is a single best way to design organizations.

neoclassical organizational theory

An attempt to improve on classical organizational theory that argues employee satisfaction as well as economic effectiveness are the goals of organizational structure.

The Contingency Approach: Design According to Environmental Conditions

contingency approach

The contemporary approach recognizing that no one approach to organizational design is best, but that the best design is the one that best fits with the existing environmental conditions.

The idea that the best design for an organization depends on the nature of the environment lies at the heart of the modern **contingency approach** to organizational design. Here, we use the term *contingency* similar to how we used it in our discussion of leadership, but rather than considering the best approach to leadership for a given situation, we are considering the best way to design an organization given the environment in which it functions.

The External Environment: Its Connection to Organizational Design   It is widely assumed the most appropriate type of organizational design depends on the organization's *external environment*. In general, the external environment is the sum of all the forces with which an organization must deal effectively if it is to survive.[30] These forces include general work conditions (e.g., the economy, geography, national resources) and specific task environment within which the company operates (e.g., competitors, customers, work force, suppliers).

Consider some examples: Banks operate within an environment highly influenced by the general economy (e.g., interest rates, government regulations) as well as a task environment sensitive to other banks' products (e.g., types of accounts) and services (e.g., service hours, access to account information by computers or telephone), the needs of the customer base (e.g., direct deposit for customers), the availability of trained personnel (e.g., individuals suitable for entry-level positions), and the existence of suppliers providing goods and services (e.g., automated teller equipment, surveillance equipment, computer workstations). Analogous examples can be found in other industries as well. For example, think about the environmental forces faced by airlines, computer companies, and automobile manufacturers. It is easy to recognize the features of their environments that must be accounted for when considering how organizations in these industries could be designed.

GLOBAL MATTERS   Governmental intervention as an element of the external environment varies greatly from country to country. U.S. business leaders often complain about the government regulations they are forced to follow, but such intervention tends to be much greater elsewhere throughout the world. Two of Europe's major auto makers, Fiat and Renault, are partially owned by the governments of their countries (Italy and France, respectively). ■

Many features of the environment may be considered when designing an organization, but a classic investigation provides some useful guidance.[31] These scientists interviewed people in 20 industrial organizations within the United Kingdom to determine the relationship between managerial activities and the external environment. In so doing, they distinguished between organizations that operated in highly *stable*, unchanging environments, and those in highly *unstable*, turbulent environments. For example, a rayon company operated in a highly stable environment. In other words, the environmental demands were predictable, people performed the same jobs in the same ways for a long time, and the organization had clearly defined lines of authority that helped to get the job done. In contrast, a new electronics development company operated in a highly turbulent environment. Conditions changed on a daily basis, jobs were not well defined, and no clear organizational structure existed.

The researchers noted many of the organizations studied tended to be described in ways that were appropriate for their environments. For example, when the environment is stable, people can do the same tasks repeatedly, thereby allowing them to perform highly specialized jobs. In turbulent environments, however, many different tasks may need to be performed, and such specialization should not be designed into the jobs. Clearly, the stability of the work environment is strongly linked to the proper organizational form. These researchers concluded that two different approaches to management existed—and that these were based largely on the degree of stability within the external environment. These two approaches are known as the **mechanistic organization** and the **organic organization**.

Mechanistic and Organic Organizations: Designs for Stable and Turbulent Conditions

If you ever worked at a McDonald's, you probably know how highly standardized each step of the most basic operation must be.[32] For example, boxes of fries are to be stored two inches from the wall in stacks one inch apart. Making those fries is another matter—one that requires 19 distinct steps, each of which is clearly laid out in a training film shown to new employees. The process is the same whether it is done in Moscow, Idaho, or in Moscow, Russia. This is an example of a highly mechanistic task. Organizations can be highly mechanistic when conditions do not change. The fast-food industry has changed a great deal in recent years (with the introduction of new, healthier menu items, competitive pricing, and the like), but the making of fries at McDonald's has not. The key to using mechanization is the lack of change. Thus, if the environment does not change, a highly mechanistic organizational form can be very efficient.

An environment is considered to be stable when there is little or no unexpected change in product, market demands, or technology. Have you ever seen an old-fashioned-looking bottle of E. E. Dickinson's witch hazel, a topical astringent used to cleanse the skin around a wound? The company has been making this product following the same distillation process since 1866, so it certainly is operating in a relatively stable manufacturing environment.[33] As described earlier, stability affords the luxury of high employee specialization, because without change, people can easily specialize. When change is inevitable, however, specialization is impractical.

Mechanistic organizations can be characterized in several additional ways (Table 14.3). Mechanistic organizations allow for a high degree of specialization, but they also impose many rules. Authority is vested in a few people at the top who give direct orders to their subordinates. Again, mechanistic organizational designs tend to be most effective under conditions in which the external environment is stable and unchanging.

Now, think about high-tech industries, such as those dedicated to computers, aerospace products, and biotechnology. Their environmental conditions are likely to be changing all the time. In fact, these industries are so prone to change that as soon as a new way of operating can be introduced, it already needs to be altered. It is not only technology, however, that makes an environment turbulent. Turbulence also can

mechanistic organization

An internal organizational structure in which people perform specialized jobs, rigid rules are imposed, and authority is vested in a few, top-ranking officials.

organic organization

An internal organizational structure in which jobs tend to be very general, there are few rules, and decisions can be made by lower-level employees.

TABLE 14.3

Mechanistic Versus Organic Designs: A Summary

Mechanistic and organic designs differ along several key dimensions identified here. These represent extremes; organizations can be relatively organic, relatively mechanistic, or somewhere in between.

| DIMENSION | STRUCTURE | |
	MECHANISTIC	ORGANIC
Stability	Change unlikely	Change likely
Specialization	Many specialists	Many generalists
Formal rules	Rigid rules	Considerable flexibility
Authority	Centralized in few top people	Decentralized, diffused throughout the organization

be high among industries that must adhere to rapidly changing regulations. For example, the hospital industry was turbulent when new Medicaid legislation passed, and the nuclear-power industry was turbulent when governmental regulations dictated many new standards to be followed. With the market dominance of foreign automobiles in the United States, the once-stable domestic auto industry has been turbulent of late. Unfortunately, because the U.S. auto industry traditionally has been highly mechanistic, the design of these companies could not rapidly accommodate the changes required by more organic forms.

The pure organic form of organization may be characterized in several different ways (Table 14.3). The degree of possible job specialization is very low; instead, a broad knowledge of many jobs is required. In addition, little authority is exercised from the top. Rather, self-control is expected, and the emphasis is placed on coordination between peers. Thus, decisions tend to be made in a highly democratic, participative manner. The mechanistic and organic types of organizational structure described here are ideal forms, however. The mechanistic-organic distinction should be thought of as opposite poles along a continuum rather than as distinct options. Certainly, organizations can be relatively organic or relatively mechanistic compared with others, but they may not be located at either extreme.

GLOBAL MATTERS   Because Swedish workers are required by law to participate in decisions affecting them on the job, organizations in that country tend to be more organic than mechanistic. ■

Finally, research supports the idea that organizational effectiveness relates to how much an organization's structure (i.e., mechanistic or organic) matches its environment (i.e., stable or turbulent). One classic study evaluated four departments in a large company, two of which manufactured containers (a relatively stable environment) and two of which dealt with communications research (a highly unstable environment).[34] One department in each pair was evaluated as being more effective than the other. For the container-manufacturing departments, the more effective unit was structured in a highly mechanistic form (i.e., roles and duties were clearly defined). In contrast, the more effective communications-research department was structured in a highly organic fashion (i.e., roles and duties were vague). In addition, the other, less effective departments were structured in the opposite manner: the less effective manufacturing department was organically structured, and the less effective research department was mechanistically structured (Figure 14.8).

These results made clear that departments were most effective when their organizational structure fit their environment. This notion of "Which design is best under which conditions?" lies at the heart of the modern orientation — that is, the contingency approach — to organizational structure. Rather than specifying *which* structure is best, the contingency approach specifies *when* each design is most effective.

Mintzberg's Framework: Five Organizational Forms

The distinction between mechanistic and organic designs is important, but it is not terribly specific regarding how, exactly, organizations should be designed. Filling this void, however, is the work of contemporary organizational theorist Henry Mintzberg.[35] Specifically, Mintzberg claims organizations are composed of five basic elements — or groups of individuals — any one of which may predominate. The one that does will determine the most effective design in that situation. These five basic elements are:

operating core

Employees who perform the basic work related to an organization's product or service.

- **The operating core**: Employees who perform the basic work related to the organization's product or service. Examples include teachers in schools and chefs and waiters in restaurants.

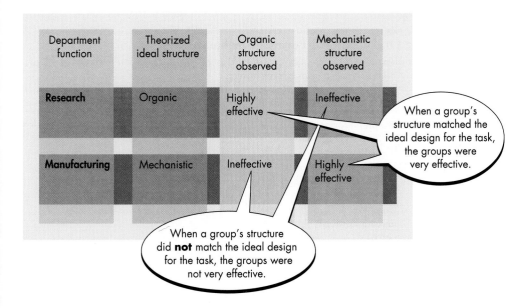

FIGURE 14.8

Matching Organizational Design and Industry: The Key to Effectiveness

In a classic study, researchers evaluated the performance of four departments in a large company. The most effective units were ones in which the way the group was structured (mechanistic or organic) matched the most appropriate form for the type of task performed (i.e., organic for research work, and mechanistic for manufacturing work).

(*Source*: Based on suggestions by Morse & Lorsch, 1970; see note 34.)

- **The strategic apex**: Top-level executives responsible for running the entire organization. Examples include the entrepreneur who runs a small business and the general manager of an automobile dealership.
- **The middle line**: Managers who transfer information between the strategic apex and the operating core. Examples include middle managers, such as regional sales managers (who connect top executives with the sales force) and the chair of an academic department (who serves as an intermediary between the dean and the faculty).
- **The technostructure**: Those specialists responsible for standardizing various aspects of the organization's activities. Examples include accountants, auditors, and computer-systems analysts.
- **The support staff**: Individuals who provide indirect support services to the organization. Examples include consultants and corporate attorneys.

strategic apex

Top-level executives responsible for running an entire organization.

middle line

Managers who transfer information between higher and lower levels of the organizational hierarchy. (See *strategic apex* and *operating core*.)

technostructure

Organizational specialists responsible for standardizing various aspects of an organization's activities.

support staff

Individuals who provide indirect support services to an organization.

What organizational designs fit best under conditions in which these five groups dominate? Mintzberg has identified five specific designs: *simple structure*, *machine bureaucracy*, *professional bureaucracy*, *divisionalized structure*, and *adhocracy* (Table 14.4).

Simple Structure   Imagine you open an antique shop and hire several people to help. You have a small informal organization in which a single individual has the ultimate power. There is little specialization or formalization, and the overall structure is organic. The hierarchy is quite flat, and as mentioned, all decision-making power is vested in a single individual—you. Such an organization, which is simple in nature and has the power residing at the strategic apex, is referred to by Mintzberg as having a **simple structure**. As you might imagine, organizations with simple structure can respond quickly to the environment and be very flexible. For example, the chef-owner of a small, independent restaurant can change the menu to suit changing tastes whenever needed without first consulting anyone else. The downside, however, is that the success or failure of the entire enterprise depends on the wisdom and health of the individual in charge. Not surprisingly, organizations with simple structure are risky ventures.

Machine Bureaucracy   If you ever worked for your state's department of motor vehicles, you probably found it to be a very large place, with numerous rules and procedures. The work is highly specialized (e.g., one person gives the vision tests,

simple structure

An organization characterized as being small and informal, with a single power individual (often the founding entrepreneur) in charge of everything.

TABLE 14.4

Mintzberg's Five Organizational Forms: A Summary

Mintzberg has identified five distinct organizational designs, each of which is likely to occur in organizations in which certain groups are in power.

DESIGN	DESCRIPTION	DOMINANT GROUP	EXAMPLE
Simple structure	Simple, informal, authority centralized in a single person	Strategic apex	Small, entrepreneurial business
Machine bureaucracy	Highly complex, formal environment with clear lines of authority	Technostructure	Government office
Professional bureaucracy	Complex, decision-making authority is vested in professionals	Operating core	University
Divisionalized structure	Large, formal organizations with several separate divisions	Middle line	Multidivision business, such as General Motors
Adhocracy	Simple, informal, with decentralized authority	Support staff	Software development firm.

Source: Based on suggestions by Mintzberg, 1983; see note 35.

another completes the registration forms), and decision making is concentrated at the top (e.g., supervisor must give permission to do anything other than exactly what is expected). This type of work environment is highly stable and does not need to change. Such an organization, in which power resides with the technostructure, is referred to as a **machine bureaucracy**. These bureaucracies can be highly efficient at standardized tasks, but they tend to be dehumanizing and very boring for employees.

Professional Bureaucracy Suppose you are a doctor at a large city hospital. You are a highly trained specialist and have considerable expertise in your field. You do not need to check with anyone else before authorizing a certain medical test or treatment; you make the decisions as they are needed, when they are needed. At the same time, however, the environment is highly formal (e.g., there are many rules and regulations to follow). Of course, you do not work alone, either. You also require the services of other highly qualified professionals, such as nurses and laboratory technicians. Organizations of this type, which also include universities, libraries, and consulting firms, maintain power with the operating core and are called **professional bureaucracies**. Such organizations can be highly effective, because they allow employees to practice those skills for which they are best qualified. Sometimes, however, specialists become so overly narrow they fail to see the "big picture," thereby leading to errors and potential conflict between employees.

Divisional Structure When you think of large organizations such as General Motors, DuPont, Xerox, and IBM, the image that comes to mind probably is closest to what Mintzberg describes as **divisional structure**. Such organizations consist of autonomous units coordinated by a central headquarters (i.e., they rely on departmental structure based on products). Because the divisions are autonomous (e.g., a General Motors employee at Buick does not consult another at Chevrolet to do his or her job), division managers (i.e., the *middle line* of Mintzberg's basic elements) have considerable control. Such designs preclude the need for top-level executives to think about day-to-day operations and, thus, frees them to concentrate on larger-scale, strategic decisions. At the same time, however, companies organized into separate divisions frequently have high duplication of effort (e.g., sep-

---

machine bureaucracy

An organizational form in which work is highly specialized, decision making is concentrated at the top, and the work environment is not prone to change (e.g., a government office).

professional bureaucracy

Organizations (e.g., hospitals, universities) with many rules to follow but with employees who are highly skilled and free to make decisions on their own.

divisional structure

The form used by many large organizations in which separate, autonomous units deal with entire product lines, thereby freeing top management to focus on larger-scale, strategic decisions.

arate order-processing units for each division). Having operated as separate divisions for the past 70 years, General Motors is considered to be the classic example of divisional structure.[36] Although the company has undergone many changes during this time—including the addition of the Saturn Corporation—it still has maintained this structure.

Adhocracy   Imagine that after graduating from college, where you spent years learning to program computers, you take a job at a small software company. Compared with your friends at large accounting firms, your professional life is much less formal. You work as a member of a team developing a new, time-management software product. There are no rules, and schedules are made to be broken. You work together, and even though someone is "officially" in charge, you would never know it. In Mintzberg's framework, you work for an **adhocracy**—that is, for an organization in which power resides with the support staff. Essentially, this is the epitome of the organic structure identified earlier. Specialists coordinate with each other not because of their shared functions (e.g., accounting, manufacturing) but because they are members of teams working on specific projects.

The primary benefit of the adhocracy is that it fosters innovation. Some large companies, such as Johnson & Johnson, nest within their formal divisional structure units that operate as adhocracies (Figure 14.9). One such unit is the New Products Division, which recently has been churning out an average of 40 products per year (see the "Case in Point" at the end of this chapter).[37] As with all other designs, however, there are disadvantages. In this case, the most serious are the high levels of inefficiency (they are the opposite of machine bureaucracies in this regard) and the great potential for disruptive conflict.

The Boundaryless Organization: A New Corporate Architecture

You hear it all the time: Someone is asked to do something but responds defiantly, saying, "It's not my job." As uncooperative as this may seem, such a comment may make sense in the traditional organizational structures—ones with layers of carefully connected boxes neatly stacked atop each other in hierarchical fashion—described earlier. The advantage of these organizational types is that they clearly define the roles of managers and employees. Everyone knows precisely what to do. The problem, however, is that such arrangements are inflexible. As a result, they do not lend themselves to the rapidly changing conditions in which today's organizations must operate.

Sensitive to this limitation, Jack Welch, the CEO of General Electric, proposed the **boundaryless organization**. This is an organization in which chains of command are eliminated, spans of control are limited, and rigid departments give way to empowered teams (Figure 14.10). Replacing rigid distinctions between people are fluid, intentionally ambiguous, and ill-defined roles. In Welch's vision, General Electric would operate like a family grocery store—albeit a $60 billion store—in which barriers that separated employees from each other and the company from its customers and suppliers would be eliminated.[38] Why? Because such barriers inhibit creativity, waste time, smother dreams, and generally slow things down. In a speech given on April 24, 1990, Welch referred to organizational boundaries as "speed bumps that slow down the enterprise."[39] General Electric has not yet become the completely boundaryless organization Welch envisions, but it has made significant strides toward removing boundaries.

So, too, have other organizations. For example, consider how Chrysler went about making the Neon.[40] In 1990, Robert P. Marcell, head of Chrysler's small-car engineering group, assembled a team of 600 engineers, 289 suppliers, and busloads of blue-collar workers. Together, they developed the inexpensive new car in a speedy 42 months—and on-budget (at $1.3 billion). Instead of working sequentially (using sep-

FIGURE 14.9

The New Products Division of Johnson & Johnson: An Adhocracy

Within its beautiful headquarters, Johnson & Johnson has a formal divisional structure. However, teams working together on developing new products operate under the informal, organic organizational form known as an *adhocracy*.

adhocracy

A highly informal, organic organization in which specialists work in teams, co-ordinating with each other on various projects (e.g., many software-development companies).

boundaryless organization

An organization in which chains of command are eliminated, spans of control are unlimited, and rigid departments give way to empowered teams.

FIGURE 14.10

Jack Welch: Making General Electric a Boundaryless Organization

It is difficult to envision one of the world's largest organizations operating without a rigid structure, but that is just what CEO Jack Welch has proposed for GE. His concept of the *boundaryless organization* entails eliminating rigid departments and having people work together in fluid teams. The company has not yet achieved this state, but the elimination of boundaries has been credited with much of the company's recent success.

modular organization

An organization that surrounds itself by other organizations to which it regularly outsources non-core functions.

arate specialists in design, manufacturing, and marketing) as typically occurs, Marcell's team worked concurrently on several tasks. People from different areas (e.g., engineering, marketing, purchasing, finance) coordinate their efforts with assembly-line workers, suppliers, and consumers. In other words, the traditional boundaries that separate people, both inside and outside the organization, were eliminated. As a result, the team was able to work quickly, unhindered by the usual restrictions of their narrow roles.

For boundaryless organizations to function effectively, they need to meet many of the same requirements as successful teams. For example, there must be high levels of trust between all parties. Everyone involved also must have high levels of skill so they can operate without much—if any—managerial guidance. In addition, because the elimination of boundaries weakens traditional managerial power bases, some executives may find it difficult to give up their authority, thus leading to political behavior. To the extent the elimination of boundaries leverages the talents of all employees, however, such limitations are worth striving to overcome.

The boundaryless organizations described thus far involve breaking down both internal and external barriers. Therefore, they sometimes are referred to as *barrier-free organizations*. There are, however, variations of boundaryless organizations that involve only the elimination of external boundaries.[41] These are known as *modular organizations* and *virtual organizations*.

Modular Organizations   Many of today's organizations outsource non-core functions to other companies while retaining full strategic control over their core business. Such companies may be thought of as having a central hub, which is surrounded by networks of outside specialists who can be added or subtracted as needed. As such, they are referred to as **modular organizations**.[42]

As a case in point, you surely recognize Nike and Reebok as being major designers and marketers of athletic shoes. You probably did not realize, however, that Nike's production facilities are limited, or that Reebok has no plants of its own. Both organizations contract all their manufacturing to companies in countries such as Taiwan and South Korea, where labor costs are less. In so doing, they avoid making major investments in facilities and can concentrate on what they do best—that is, on tapping the changing tastes of their customers. At the same time, their suppliers can focus on rapid retooling to make new products.[43] Similarly, computer companies such as Dell and Gateway buy components made by other companies and perform only the final assembly, as ordered by customers, themselves. These apparel and computer companies are examples of modular organizations.

ETHICS MATTERS   Large U.S. companies contracting with foreign manufacturers confront major ethical issues. First, by providing jobs to laborers overseas, they deny jobs to people in their own country. These companies defend their actions, however, by claiming the low wages paid abroad make it possible for them to stay competitive, which in turn, makes it possible for them to employ Americans—and to contribute to the tax base. What are your feelings about this issue? ■

Toyota, one of the world's most successful automakers, has taken the modular form to the extreme. Its network of 230 suppliers (two of which are owned by Toyota itself) do nearly everything the company needs, from making molds for machine parts to general contracting.[44] The key to the success of this arrangement is Toyota's close ties with its suppliers, which ensure they will meet Toyota's stringent quality standards. Of course, companies that outsource any proprietary work (e.g., high-tech breakthroughs) must be assured their trade secrets will not be compromised.

Virtual Organizations   Another approach to the boundaryless organization is the **virtual organization**. This type of organization is composed of a continually evolving network of companies (e.g., suppliers and customers) linked together to share skills, costs, and market access. They form a partnership to capitalize on their existing skills, and pursue common objectives. After these objectives have been met, they disband.[45] Unlike modular organizations, which maintain close control over the companies with which they outsource, virtual organizations give up some control and become part of a new organization—at least for a while. Most virtual organizations are formed on a limited basis. For example, many large rock concerts, such as the Rolling Stones' 1999 "No Security" tour, operate as virtual organizations.

virtual organization

A highly flexible, temporary organization formed by a group of companies to exploit a specific opportunity.

GLOBAL MATTERS

Corning, the giant glass and ceramics manufacturer, builds itself by developing partnerships with companies in other nations. Siemens, the German electronics firm, and Vitro, the largest glass manufacturer from Mexico, have been some of the biggest, most recent partners. ■

The underlying idea of a virtual organization is that each participating company contributes only its core competencies (i.e., its areas of greatest strength). By mixing and matching the best of what several companies can offer, a joint product—which is better than what any single company could have produced alone—is created. For example, consider the new projects from the parent company that publishes this book, Paramount Communications. In today's rapidly changing entertainment industry, no one company can do it all. Thus, Paramount has entered into partnerships with other companies that will help to create new products where none existed before. For example, Paramount has formed an alliance with Hughes Aircraft, which will allow its movies to be transferred to CDs and distributed over a satellite system. The virtual organization thus formed is not unusual in the entertainment industry. Indeed, Time-Warner also has become part of several multimedia ventures. By sharing risks, costs, and expertise, many of today's companies find the virtual organization to be a highly appealing type of organizational structure.

To summarize, the boundaryless organization is an increasingly popular organizational form. It involves eliminating all internal boundaries (e.g., those between employees) and external boundaries (e.g., those between the company and its suppliers). Variations on this organizational form involve only the elimination of external boundaries. These variations include the modular organization (in which secondary aspects of the company's operations are outsourced) and the virtual organization (in which organizations temporarily combine forces with others to form new organizations. For a summary of these three organizational structures, see Figure 14.11.

TIPS:
DOING IT RIGHT

■ When Should an Organization Go Virtual?

There can be no mistaking the current trend: More and more companies are getting smaller but also joining with other companies as needed to complete special projects. The rationale is straightforward: By reducing their own hierarchy and net-
continued

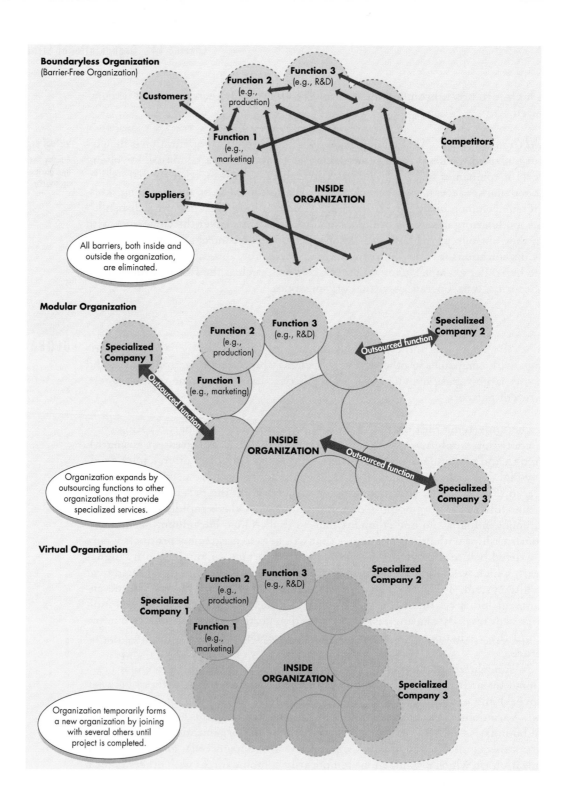

FIGURE 14.11

The Boundaryless Organization: Various Forms

The true *boundaryless organization* is free of both internal and external barriers. Variants such as the *modular organization* and the *virtual organization* eliminate only external barriers. All forms of boundaryless organizations are growing in popularity.

working with other companies on an ad-hoc basis, a given company can move faster and thus, stands a better chance of succeeding in a highly competitive environment. Under such arrangements, companies are more likely to take the risks that may help them to succeed. At the same time, however, people from different kinds of companies that form a virtual organization tend to suffer high levels of interpersonal conflict, probably because they do not share the same values and culture (see chapter 13). In addition, because they are not working together, the people involved tend to find it more difficult to coordinate their activities than if they worked within an integrated corporation. Obviously, trade-offs are associated with having a virtual organization.

This raises an important question: When should companies organize in a virtual manner? In other words, when should they perform a project within their existing organizations? Management experts answer this question based on two factors: the type of capabilities the company needs, and the type of change that will be made.[46]

First, consider the nature of the organizational changes being proposed. These may be categorized as being either *autonomous* or *systemic*. An **autonomous change** is one that is made independently of other changes. For example, an auto company that develops a new type of upholstery may do so without changing the rest of the car. A **systemic change**, however, is one that is related to other changes. For example, Polaroid's development of instant photography required changes in both film and camera technologies.

A second key distinction involves the capabilities needed to complete the project. Sometimes these exist only outside the company and, thus, must be tapped. For example, during the early 1980s, IBM developed its first personal computer in only 15 months by going completely outside itself for expertise (e.g., chips were from Intel, the operating system came from Microsoft). Other times, the capability can be found or created within the company. For example, Ford traditionally develops many of the components used in its cars, thereby making it less dependent on other companies. Many companies also do a bit of each—that is, going outside for some things but keeping other functions in house. For example, Nike relies on its partnerships with Asian companies to manufacture its footwear, but it carefully designs and markets these products itself.

By combining these factors, it becomes clear when companies should "go virtual" and when they should work exclusively within their own walls. Virtual organizations work best for companies considering autonomous changes using technologies that exist only outside their walls. For example, Motorola has developed virtual organizations with several battery manufacturers. Thus, it can focus its business on the delivery of "untethered communication" (i.e., communication anytime, anywhere, without wires) while ensuring it has the battery power to make such devices work.

In contrast, companies should keep their focus inward when the changes are systemic in nature and involve capabilities the company either already has or can create. Under such conditions, relying on outside help may be far too risky—and unnecessary. Examples of this strategy may be seen today at Intel and Microsoft, both of which are making extensive investments to enhance their current and future capabilities.

Finally, for conditions that fall between these extremes (i.e., when systemic changes are being made using capabilities that come only from outside the company, when autonomous changes are being made using capabilities that must be created), virtual alliances should be created with extreme caution. Clearly, the virtual organization has a key place in today's organizational world. The trick, however, lies in understanding precisely what that place is. These guidelines represent useful guidance in that respect. ■

autonomous change

A change in one part of an organization independent of the need for change in another.

systemic change

A change in one part of an organization that is related to change in another.

INTERORGANIZATIONAL DESIGNS: GOING BEYOND THE SINGLE ORGANIZATION

All the organizational designs examined thus far have concentrated on the arrangement of units within an organization, or on what may be termed *intraorganizational designs*. Sometimes, however, at least some parts of different organizations must operate jointly. To coordinate their efforts on such projects, organizations must create *interorganizational designs*, which are plans by which two or more organizations come together. Two such designs commonly are found: *conglomerates*, and *strategic alliances*.

Conglomerates: Diversified "Megacorporations"

conglomerate

A form of organizational diversification in which an organization (usually a very large, multinational one) adds an entirely unrelated business or product to its organizational design.

When an organization diversifies by adding an entirely unrelated business or product, it may be said to have formed a **conglomerate**. Some of the world's largest conglomerates may be found in Asia. For example, Korean companies such as Samsung and Hyundai produce home electronics, automobiles, textiles, and chemicals in large, unified conglomerates known as *chaebols*.[47] These are separate companies overseen by the same parent-company leadership. In Japan, the same type of arrangement is known as a *keiretsu*.[48] A good example is the Matsushita Group.[49] This enormous conglomerate consists of a bank (i.e., Asahi Bank), a consumer-electronics company (i.e., Panasonic), and several insurance companies (e.g., Sumitomo Life, Nippon Life). Conglomerates are not unique to Asia, of course. Many large, U.S.-based corporations, such as IBM and Tenneco, are conglomerates as well. So, too, is Johnson & Johnson, which we describe in our "Case in Point" at the end of this chapter.

ETHICS MATTERS   Some observers question whether the existence of conglomerates is ethical. Essentially, their argument is that by being so big and powerful, conglomerates can squeeze out the competition and do whatever they want. How do you feel about this issue? ■

Companies form conglomerates for several reasons. First, the parent company can enjoy the benefits of diversification. As one industry languishes, another may excel, thereby producing a stable economic outlook for the parent company. In addition, conglomerates may provide built-in markets and access to supplies, because companies typically support other organizations within the same conglomerate. For example, General Motors cars and trucks are fitted with Delco radios, and Ford cars and trucks have engines with Autolite spark plugs, which are separate companies owned by their respective parent companies. In this manner, conglomerates can benefit by providing a network of organizations that depend on each other for products and services, thus creating considerable advantages.

Strategic Alliances: Joining Forces for Mutual Benefit

strategic alliance

A type of organizational design in which two or more separate companies combine forces to develop and operate a specific business (see *mutual service consortia, joint ventures,* and *value-chain partnerships.*)

A **strategic alliance** is an organizational design in which separate firms join their competitive capabilities to operate a specific business. The goal is to provide benefits to each individual organization that could not be attained by operating separately. Forming alliances are low-risk ways of diversifying (i.e., adding new business operations) and of entering new markets. Some companies, such as General Electric and Ford, have strategic alliances with many others. Some alliances last only a short time, but others have remained in existence for more than 30 years and still are going strong.[50] In fact, it helps to think of long-term alliances as marriages (Figure 14.12).

"Do you, Scofield Industries, take Amalgamated Pipe?"

FIGURE 14.12

Strategic Alliances: The Marriage of Two or More Businesses

Companies forming strategic alliances are, in a sense, getting married. By combining their resources, each party reaps advantages they could not realize alone.

(*Source*: © The New Yorker Collection 1990. Peter Steiner from cartoonbank.com. All Rights Reserved.)

The Continuum of Alliances   A study of 37 strategic alliances throughout the world identified three types of cooperative arrangements between organizations.[51] These can be arranged along a continuum ranging from weak and distant alliances to strong and close alliances. Figure 14.13 shows, at the weak end are strategic alliances known as **mutual service consortia**. These are arrangements between similar companies from the same (or similar) industries to pool resources to receive a benefit too difficult or expensive for either to obtain alone. Often, the focus is some high-tech capacity, such as an expensive piece of diagnostic equipment that might be shared by two or more local hospitals (e.g., a magnetic resonance imager).

At the opposite end are the strongest and closest collaborations, which are referred to as **value-chain partnerships**. These are alliances between companies with complementary capabilities in different industries. Customer-supplier relationships are a prime example. In such arrangements, one company buys necessary goods and services from another so that it can do business. Because each company depends on the other, each party's commitment to their mutual relationship is high. As noted earlier, Toyota has a network of 230 suppliers with whom it regularly does business. These relationships represent value-chain partnerships.

mutual service consortia

A type of strategic alliance in which two similar companies from the same (or similar) industries pool their resources to receive a benefit too difficult or expensive for either to obtain alone.

value-chain partnerships

Strategic alliances between companies with complementary capabilities in different industries.

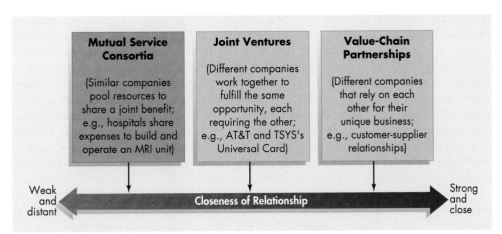

FIGURE 14.13

Strategic Alliances: A Continuum of Interorganizational Relationships

The three types of strategic alliances identified here may be distinguished by their location along a continuum from weak and distant to strong and close.

(*Source*: Based on suggestions by Kanter, 1994; see note 50.)

YOU BE THE CONSULTANT

Fabricate-It, Inc., is a medium-size manufacturing company using standard assembly lines. Its employees tend to be poorly educated and to perform monotonous work. Think-It, Inc., is a software-design firm that writes customized programs to solve its customers' problems. Its employees tend to be highly educated and to perform highly creative work. Both are reconsidering their present organizational designs.

1. What type of organizational design would best suit the needs of Fabricate-It? Explain your decision.
2. What type of organizational design would best suit the needs of Think-It? Explain your decision.
3. How might each organization benefit from strategic alliances with other organizations?

joint ventures

Strategic alliances in which several companies work together to fulfill opportunities requiring the capabilities of one another.

FIGURE 14.14

Mobil and Pertamina: A Joint Venture in Indonesia

By entering into a joint venture with state-owned Pertamina on the South Pacific island of Sumatra in Indonesia, Mobil Oil can tap the rich reserves of liquified natural gas in this region. At the same time, Pertamina profits from Mobil's vast technological and marketing resources.

Between these two extremes are **joint ventures**, which are arrangements in which companies work together to fulfill opportunities requiring the capabilities of each other. For example, two companies might enter a joint venture if one has a valuable technology and the other has the marketing knowledge to make that technology a viable commercial product (Figure 14.14).

Clearly, there are benefits to be derived from forming alliances. These benefits primarily come in the form of improved technology, widened markets, and greater economies of scale (e.g., sharing functional operations across organizations). As you might imagine, however, a high degree of coordination and fit must exist between the parties, with each delivering on its promise to the other, for those benefits to be realized.

As you also might imagine, not all strategic alliances are successful. For example, AT&T and Olivetti tried unsuccessfully to manufacture personal computers. Strong differences in management styles and organizational culture were cited as causes of their failure. Similarly, a planned alliance between Raytheon and Lexitron, a small word-processing company, failed because of clashes between the rigid culture of the larger Raytheon and the more entrepreneurial style of the smaller Lexitron. Clearly, for strategic alliances to work, the companies involved must offer each other something important and also be able to work together to make it happen.

Strategic Alliances in the Global Economy   Strategic alliances with companies in nations with transforming economies (e.g., China, Russia) provide good opportunities for those economies to develop. Given the rapid move toward economic globalization, we can expect many companies to seek strategic alliances as a means for gaining—or for maintaining—a competitive advantage. Frequently, companies form strategic alliances with foreign firms to gain entry into that country's market.[52] Such arrangements also may allow an exchange of technology and manufacturing services. For example, Korea's Daewoo receives technical information and is paid to manufacture automobiles for companies with which it has entered into alliances, such as General Motors, Germany's Opel, and Japan's Isuzu and Nissan.[53] Some companies, such as telecommunications giant MCI, are actively involved in several strategic alliances, including one in Canada and several in New Zealand.[54]

In addition to the financial incentives (e.g., circumventing trade and tariff restrictions) and marketing benefits (e.g., access to internal markets) associated with strategic alliances, direct managerial benefits also are associated with extending one company's organizational chart into another's. These benefits primarily come from im-

JOINT VENTURES IN CHINA: BEWARE OF OBSTACLES

With an enormous market now opening its doors to Western capitalism, the idea of joint ventures with Chinese companies is very appealing to organizations in other parts of the world. Some companies, such as Johnson & Johnson, have enjoyed considerable success in such joint ventures. Most, however, are finding it difficult to make these relationships work.[55]

Consider, for example, the experiences of a U.S.-based, household-products company that formed a joint venture with Shanhai Jahwa Corporation, China's largest cosmetics manufacturer. The U.S. company was looking for help introducing its products in the large Chinese market by tapping into Jahwa's distribution systems. It also was hoping for what the Chinese call *guanxi*—that is, the social and political connections required to become successful in China. In turn, Jahwa officials were looking for help in upgrading their technology and boosting their capacity to compete in the international marketplace. Unfortunately, serious disagreements over directions and resources paralyzed the two companies, thereby resulting in a failed deal. Making matters worse, joint ventures are difficult to dissolve in Chinese culture, because the relationship between the two companies is based on trust. Thus, walking away from such relationships comes at a considerable loss of face (i.e., esteem in the eyes of others).

Several factors make forming a joint venture with Chinese firms difficult at best. First, there is the obvious matter of cultural differences. Compared with Western countries, Chinese culture and traditions are profoundly different. In particular, Chinese social, governmental, and economic systems are far more complex. For example, Chinese companies are more likely to become lax after achieving success, and they are less likely to consider strategies with a long-term approach. If this were the only challenge, however, it most likely could be overcome. After all, executives interested in conducting business in various countries have learned successfully the cultural ways of their hosts.[56] In China, however, there are several more unique problems.

For one, the Chinese market is becoming extremely competitive, because many companies are attempting to be the first to introduce their products to the vast Chinese population. In fact, competition has become so fierce in some industries (e.g., construction, pharmaceuticals, electronics) that companies have been aggressively pursuing market share even if it means lowering their prices so they must sell at a loss. This is a game few companies can afford to play.

A second unique problem is that few Chinese companies have a presence throughout the country. Most operate either regionally or locally. This is a vestige of the country's planned economic system, which was in effect until 1979, that required companies to operate in very narrow market niches. Because only the earliest companies to form joint ventures with Chinese companies (e.g., Coca-Cola) managed to make contact with the few that operated nationally, finding a suitable partner is very difficult for today's foreign companies.

A third unique problem involves government intervention. Governments are involved with businesses in some way in all countries, but the connection to Chinese businesses runs deep—so much so that many companies actually are owned (in part) by government agencies. What makes this particularly frustrating is that different governmental rules operate in different territories. As a case in point, consider the difficulties that AT&T, NEC, and Siemens have had in establishing telephone service through their various Chinese partners. The problem resides in the fact that Shanghai Bell has a Chinese partner that just happens to be the Ministry of Post and Telecommunication—the government agency that controls communications. To say Shanghai Bell has a distinct advantage probably comes as no surprise.

Experts advise companies seeking joint ventures with Chinese firms to consider all their options carefully. The benefits to be received from such an enormous market may never be realized, in fact, because several important obstacles stand in the way.

proved technology and greater economies of scale (e.g., sharing functional operations across organizations). For a closer look at this process in operation in China, see the "OB Around the World" section in this chapter.

We invite you to visit the Greenberg page on the Prentice Hall Web site at: **www.prenhall.com/greenberg** for the monthly Greenberg update and for this chapter's World Wide Web exercise.

1. **Describe *organizational structure* and how it is revealed by an *organizational chart*.**

   The formal configuration between individuals and groups regarding allocation of tasks, responsibilities, and authority within organizations is known as **organizational structure**. This abstract concept can be represented by an **organizational chart**, which is a diagram indicating relationships between the various units (e.g., individuals or departments) in an organization.

2. **Explain the basic characteristics of organizational structure as revealed in an organizational chart (*hierarchy of authority*, *division of labor*, *span of control*, *line* versus *staff*, and *decentralization*).**

   Organizational charts depict five different elemental building blocks of organizational structure: **hierarchy of authority** (i.e., a summary of reporting relationships), **division of labor** (i.e., the degree to which jobs are specialized), **span of control** (i.e., the number of individuals over whom a manager has responsibility), **line** versus **staff positions** (i.e., jobs permitting direct decision-making power versus jobs in which advice is given), and **decentralization** (i.e., the degree to which decisions can be made by lower-ranking employees as opposed to a few, higher-ranking individuals).

3. **Describe different approaches to departmentalization, including *functional organizations*, *product organizations*, *matrix organizations*, and the *boundaryless organization*.**

   Within organizations, groups of people can be combined into departments in various ways. The most popular approach is the **functional organization**, which combines people in terms of the common functions they perform (e.g., sales manufacturing). An alternative approach is to departmentalize people by virtue of the specific products for which they are responsible, which is known as the **product organization**. Another form of departmentalization combines both these approaches into a single form; this is known as the **matrix organization**. In such organizations, people have at least two bosses. They are responsible to a superior in charge of the various functions and to a superior in charge of the specific product. Employees also may have to answer to high-ranking people responsible for the entire organization (i.e., the top leader). Following the lead of General Electric, many of today's companies are moving toward **boundaryless organizations**, in which chains of command are eliminated, spans of control are unlimited, and rigid departments give way to empowered teams. These organizations eliminate all internal boundaries (e.g., those between employees) and external boundaries (e.g., those between the company and its suppliers).

4. **Distinguish *classical* from *neoclassical* approaches to organizational design.**

   Organizational design is the process of coordinating the structural elements of organizations in the most appropriate way. **Classical organizational theories**, such as Weber's notion of bureaucracy, claim a universally best way to design organizations (i.e., an approach based on high efficiency) exists. **Neoclassical organizational theories**, such as those advanced by McGregor, Argyris, and Likert, also hold there is one best way to design organizations. Their approach, however, emphasizes the need to pay attention to basic human needs to succeed and to express oneself.

5. **Distinguish *mechanistic organizations* from *organic organizations* as described by the *contingency approach* to organizational design, and describe the conditions under which each is most appropriate.**

   The **contingency approach** to organizational design holds that the most appropriate way to design an organization depends on the external environment in which it operates. Specifically, a key factor is the degree to which the organization is subject to change: A stable environment is one in which business conditions do not change, whereas a turbulent environment is one in which conditions change rapidly. When conditions are stable, a **mechanistic organization** is effective. This is an organization in which people perform specialized jobs, many rigid rules are imposed, and authority is vested in a few, top-ranking officials. When conditions are turbulent, however, an **organic organization** is effective. This is an organization in which jobs tend to be very general, there are few rules, and decisions can be made by low-level employees.

6. **Describe the five organizational forms identified by Mintzberg:** *simple structure,* *machine bureaucracy, professional bureaucracy, divisional structure,* **and** *adhocracy.*
   Mintzberg identified five specific organizational forms. Organizations with a **simple structure** are small and informal, and they have a single powerful individual (often the founding entrepreneur) who is in charge of everything (e.g., a small retail store owned by a sole proprietor). In a **machine bureaucracy,** work is highly specialized, decision-making is concentrated at the top, and the work environment is not prone to change (e.g., a government office). **Professional bureaucracies** (e.g., hospitals, universities) have many rules to follow, but employees are highly skilled and free to make decisions on their own. **Divisional structure** characterizes many large organizations (e.g., General Motors) in which separate, autonomous units are created to deal with entire product lines, thereby freeing top management to focus on larger-scale, strategic decisions. Finally, the **adhocracy** is a highly informal, organic organization in which specialists work in teams, coordinating with each other on various projects (e.g., many software-development companies).

7. **Characterize two forms of intraorganizational design:** *conglomerates* **and** *strategic alliances.*
   Some organizational designs represent ways of combining more than one organization. Such interorganizational designs include the **conglomerate** (i.e., large corporations that diversify by getting involved in unrelated businesses) and the **strategic alliance** (i.e., organizations combining forces to operate a specific business). There are three major types of strategic alliances: **mutual service consortia, joint ventures,** and **value-chain partnerships**.

QUESTIONS FOR DISCUSSION

1. As organizations grow and become more complex, their designs are likely to change. Describe how size may influence organizational design. How are these changes likely to influence individuals?

2. Describe the difficulties that result from implementing a matrix organizational design.

3. Explain how traditional organizational designs are changing—and how they are expected to change in the future. What problems, if any, do you envision stemming from these trends?

4. What challenges will people face as organizations become increasingly "boundaryless"?

5. Identify contemporary organizations that are relatively mechanistic or relatively organic in nature. To what extent is each characterized by stable or turbulent outside environments (as predicted by the contingency approach to organizational design)?

6. Name a specific company you know that fits each of the five organizational forms identified by Mintzberg: *simple structure, machine bureaucracy, professional bureaucracy, divisional structure,* and *adhocracy.* On what grounds does each company qualify as an example?

7. Describe how the prevailing technology of an organization you know relates to its organizational design.

Johnson & Johnson: Separate Companies under One Umbrella

Band-Aid bandages, Johnson's Baby Oil, Mylanta, Reach toothbrushes, Retin-A acne cream, and Tylenol are well-known products found in medicine cabinets around the world. What you might not know, however, is that all these products — and many others — come from the same company: Johnson & Johnson (J&J). More precisely, they come from any of 166 separate companies belonging to J&J.

Starting in the 1930s, under the guidance of Robert Wood Johnson, longtime chairman and son of one of the co-founders, J&J went out of its way to keep the various businesses independent of each other. Believing the companies would be more manageable and responsive to their markets if they remained smaller, self-governing units, Johnson resisted pressures to merge them. He feared an enormous bureaucracy. According to J&J's Chief Executive, Ralph S. Larsen, this approach helps to create a sense of ownership and responsibility.

At the same time, Larsen realizes these benefits must be weighed against the costs — namely, excessive expenses because of redundancies. For example, at 41 percent of sales, J&J's overhead is considerably greater than that of competitors Merck & Co. or Bristol-Meyers Squib Co., whose overhead figures run no more than 30 percent of sales. Another cost arises in the area of customer service. Large retailers such as Wal-Mart and K-Mart are increasingly interested in streamlining their contacts with suppliers, and they are growing impatient with sales calls from dozens of J&J companies.

To meet these realities, J&J is centralizing some of its operations. For example, under Larsen's guidance, J&J has been pooling various administrative functions, such as payroll and benefits processing, computer services, purchasing, and accounts payable. So, too, are companies being merged — creating, for example, Ortho-McNeil Pharmaceuticals, a new drug company formed from two previously separate companies. Another innovation, code-named "Pathfinder," united customer-service and credit functions that once resided in four different departments of various companies. Now, a single phone call can handle all these needs. Streamlining J&J operations meant trimming the workforce by 3,000 in 1993, thereby leading to an annual savings of $100 million.

Not all J&J insiders have agreed with Larsen's plans. In fact, one top executive, William C. Egan, III, quit J&J after 17 years because he so strongly disagreed with Larsen's approach. In this case, the straw that broke the camel's back was the decision to merge the Baby Products Company with several others to form the Johnson & Johnson Consumer Products Company. (J&J also has many companies specializing in medical and surgical supplies, such as sutures and anesthetics.) What bothered Egan was that the decentralization he came to know at J&J was being dismantled.

Larsen believes he is simply righting an imbalance in J&J's corporate structure. For example, considering only the professional segment of the company's European business, J&J had 28 separate units, compared with the current 18. Allaying the fears of those worried he will take things too far, Larsen cautions, "We will never give up the principle of decentralization which is to give our operating executives ownership of a business." Indeed, things continue to work this way at J&J, where business strategy flows not from the top down but from the bottom up — that is, initiatives come from the individual companies themselves, not from executives in some distant corporate headquarters. In fact, although J&J employs some 84,000 people worldwide (including 40,000 in the United States alone), only 1,000 work at the company's headquarters in New Brunswick, New Jersey.

Larsen likens his job to an orchestra conductor. He gives the players direction while assuring them creative freedom to use their talents. Given the company's average annual gains in profit — 19 percent since 1980, including recent annual earnings of more than $1.5 billion — he no doubt has J&J making beautiful financial music.

CRITICAL THINKING QUESTIONS

1. What are the advantages and disadvantages of J&J becoming more highly centralized?

2. Is J&J a boundaryless organization? If so, why? If not, how could it change to become one?

3. How might J&J benefit from a strategic alliance with another company? What kind of company would be a good potential partner?

Organizational Structure and Design

SMALL BUSINESS 2000

One way to learn about a company is to look at its organizational chart. From this chart, we can learn something about a company's size (by considering the number of people it employs), how it organizes its staff, how many locations it has, how it is structured, and how it divides its work. This may sound like a lot of information, but it is only the start of understanding how a company is organized.

Another thing you might do is look at organizational charts for the same company but for different years. Why would you want to do this? It might tell you something about how the company has changed, at least in its organization. In turn, this might give you some hints as to what is important to the firm you are studying.

Analyzing organizational charts is useful, but we have more work to do. We need to understand more about the options considered and the decisions made that result in the organizations we observe. Bill Hagstrom, the CEO and president of Urocor, talks with us about how he helped transform an R&D venture with a good product but no market into a 200-employee venture with annual sales in excess of $25 million. Hagstrom discusses many aspects of the growth of Urocor, but he focuses on the importance of how the firm is organized and how sensitive people within the organization are to its growth, change, and development. This is likely to be particularly important to an early-stage venture such as Urocor, but it can be equally important to an older, more established company, too. Think about how some large companies have had to reinvent themselves to adapt to major shifts in their operating environments.

Fortunately for us, we also hear from some other key managers in his organization. Thus, we not only get Hagstrom's take on the organization, we find out what others value as well. As you watch this segment, think about what Hagstrom and his staff are telling us about the importance of planning, adaptation, synergy, and responsibility. You also might think about what Hagstrom has learned during the last five years—and about what he might be thinking about how Urocor should be organized for the next five years.

QUESTIONS FOR DISCUSSION

1. Bill Hagstrom took over a company of 12, and during the last five years, he has seen it turn into a $25-million operation with more than 200 employees. Success did not happen overnight, but it did happen quickly. What kinds of issues do you think Bill might have experienced in building a staff that quickly?

2. Think about what you have learned regarding departmentalization and boundaries within organizations. Discuss how you think Urocor might be departmentalized and the degree to which these boundaries are loose or rigid. What do you think are some reasons a company like Urocor might want either loose or rigid boundaries in its organization?

3. It seems like Urocor has carved a niche for itself in a very specialized area of medical services. It is possible, however, that Urocor may want to grow into other areas as well. How might alternative structures and strategic alliances be useful to Urocor if it decides to expand its operation?

SKILLS BANK

EXPERIENCING ORGANIZATIONAL BEHAVIOR

Which Do You Prefer—Mechanistic or Organic Organizations?

Because mechanistic and organic organizations are so different, it is reasonable to expect people will tend to prefer one form over the other. This questionnaire helps you to identify your own preferences and, in so doing, to learn about the different forms themselves.

Directions

The following questions deal with your preferences for various conditions that may exist where you work. Answer each one by checking the alternative that best describes your feelings.

1. When I have a job-related decision to make, I usually prefer to:
   ____ a. Make the decision myself.
   ____ b. Have my boss make it for me.
2. I usually find myself more interested in performing:
   ____ a. A highly narrow, specialized task.
   ____ b. Many different types of tasks.
3. I prefer to work in places in which working conditions:
   ____ a. Change a great deal.
   ____ b. Generally remain the same.
4. When many rules are imposed on me, I generally feel:
   ____ a. Very comfortable.
   ____ b. Very uncomfortable.
5. I believe governmental regulation of industry is:
   ____ a. Usually best for all.
   ____ b. Rarely good for anyone.

Scoring

1. Give yourself one point each time you answered as follows: 1 = b, 2 = a, 3 = b, 4 = a, and 5 = a. This score is your preference for *mechanistic organizations*.
2. Subtract this score from five. This score is your preference for *organic organizations*.
3. Interpret your scores as follows: Higher scores (closer to five) reflect stronger preferences, and lower scores (closer to zero) reflect weaker preferences.

Questions for Discussion

1. How did you score (i.e., which organizational form did you prefer)?
2. Think back over the jobs you have had. Were these in mechanistic or organic organizations?
3. Do you think you performed better in organizations whose designs matched your preferences than in those that did not?
4. Do you think you were more committed to organizations whose designs matched your preferences than to those that did not?

WORKING IN GROUPS

Comparing Span of Control in Organizational Charts

One of the easiest things to determine about a company from its organizational chart is the span of control. This exercise allows you to learn about—and to compare—spans of control within companies in your area.

Directions

1. Divide the class into four equal-size groups.
2. Assign one of the following industry types to each group: manufacturing companies, financial institutions, public utilities, and charities.
3. Within the industry assigned to each group, identify one company per student. Consider larger organizations, because these are more likely to have formal organizational charts. For example, if there are five students in the "financial institutions" group, name five different banks or savings-and-loan institutions.
4. Each student should search the Internet for the organizational chart for the company assigned to him or her in step 3.
5. As a group, discuss the spans of control of the organizations in your sample.
6. Gather as a class to compare the findings of the various groups.

Questions for Discussion

1. How easy or difficult was it to find organizational charts on the Internet?
2. Did you find there were differences in spans of control?
3. Were spans of control different at different organizational levels? If so, how? Were these differences the same for all industry groups?
4. How did spans of control differ for the various industry groups? Were the spans broader for some industries and narrower for others? How do you explain these differences? Do these differences make sense to you?

15

TECHNOLOGY IN ORGANIZATIONS

LEARNING OBJECTIVES

After reading this chapter, you should be able to

1. Define *technology*.
2. Describe Perrow's *matrix of technologies*.
3. Describe the various ways people respond to *automation* on the job.
4. Explain *assistive technology*, and describe how it is being used in organizations.
5. Describe *computerized performance monitoring* and its effects on people.
6. Identify how technology has been used to improve customer service.
7. Explain how *design for disassembly* is used to protect the physical environment.
8. Describe the connection between technology, organizational design, and performance.
9. Explain *work-flow integration* and how it influences organizational performance.
10. Describe *interdependence* and its connection to organizational design.

PREVIEW CASE

E-ware Wars Put the Byte on Big Business

When you need software to organize your household, to run your small business, or just to play games, you go to your local computer or office-supply store, plunk $50 on the counter, and walk out with disks in a box. When a large corporation needs software to run its operations, however, it is a very different matter. *Enterprise software* (or *e-ware*, as it is called) is used to manage and to coordinate all aspects of business operations in electronic commerce, from inventory and sales to marketing, customer service, and accounting. When you click a banner ad on the Internet and go to a company's web site where you can surf, shop, and ship, e-ware is the engine running the show.

Developing and installing state-of-the-art e-ware is not a matter of investing $50—or even several hundred dollars. In fact, a Fortune 500 company installing a full-featured enterprise system can expect to pay $30 million in licensing fees and $200 million in consulting fees—and this does not even take into account the several million dollars in computer and network hardware needed to do the work. In addition, getting the system up and running is a far cry from taking a CD-ROM out of the box, putting it into the drive, and clicking a mouse button a few times. Periods of three years or longer are not unusual for getting such systems on-line.

All the money and all the time are well worth it, companies agree, because electronic commerce (or *e-commerce*, as it is known) is the most rapidly growing segment of the market today. In fact, economists already see signs of how today's boom in e-commerce is having the same kind of devastating effects on the shopping center that the shopping center had on Main Street during the 1970s. E-ware is so important that one influential business analyst referred to it as "mission control for the largest companies on the planet."

Not surprisingly, competition in the e-ware market has been intense. More than 500 software makers are vying for this business worldwide, but five companies currently are on top of the pack: J. D. Edwards, Baan, Oracle, PeopleSoft, and SAP. You may not have heard of most of these companies. They are to e-ware today, however, what Microsoft was to the personal computer almost two decades ago. The winner of this battle stands to gain a fortune.

The latest skirmish involves venturing away from e-commerce software and toward virtually all the software used in a business. Take SAP, for example, which already sells software to Coke, Hewlett-Packard, Colgate, and other large companies. Still, it does not supply all the software these companies use in all their functions. Most companies continue using a patchwork approach, such as using Baan for manufacturing, PeopleSoft for human resources, Siebel Systems for the salesforce and SAP for financial information.

This is not because they want to; it is because they have to. The perfectly integrated suite of programs for all business operations does not yet exist. SAP's products are touted as being integrated, but they are not yet seamless. Software developers at SAP, however, are considered to have the edge in making such a product a reality. Even so, with small, upstart companies nipping at its heels by improving at least one piece of the program on which SAP cannot concentrate, the prospects of finding one-stop shopping for all corporate software needs is questionable. Given the enormous size of the market, however, growing numbers of companies no doubt will try seriously to take a "byte" out of it.

The e-ware wars will be an undeniable reality of the corporate landscape in the early twenty-first century. There can be no denying these sophisticated advances in software design take us to the cutting edge in the world of business. Curiously, however, behind it all, lies one of the oldest laws of the business world: "Build a better mousetrap, and the world will beat a path to your door." Then again, new ways of doing things have always mixed with old rules. Over the years, every change in technology has had some effect on how organizations operate. There were organizations before electricity, the steam engine, the assembly line—and even the computer. Each of these technologies has changed drastically how people work and the nature of organizations themselves. Accordingly, understanding the nature of *technology* is critical to fully understanding OB.

What image comes to mind when you think of technology? An enormous industrial robot arm? Space-shuttle astronauts repairing an orbiting telescope? The latest piece of advanced industrial equipment? How about the e-ware developed by SAP and its competitors? Technology can be all these things—and more.

technology

The physical and mental processes (e.g., knowledge, tools, procedures) used by an organization to perform its work (i.e., to transform inputs into usable outputs).

For these sophisticated images, the definition of technology is deceptively simple. Specifically, **technology** refers to the physical and mental processes used to transform inputs into usable outputs.[1] Simply put, technology deals with the activities, equipment, and knowledge used to get things done. Robots, spacecraft, and automated office equipment are all examples of technological devices, but technology also can take on abstract forms, such as ideas and formulas. Indeed, Procter & Gamble's recipe for a new household detergent is every bit as much an example of technology as the elaborate, computer-controlled equipment used to manufacture it.[2]

In just the past few years, technology has advanced at a staggering pace. The vinyl phonograph record has been replaced by the compact disc, which now is being replaced by the digital video disk. The typewriter has been replaced by the word processor, and spoken words now can be put into a computer directly, thereby bypassing the keyboard. Of course, in modern libraries, the old card catalogue has been displaced by computer terminals, and dusty reference books are being replaced by vast, on-line information services. Why are we concerned about these things in the field of OB? The answer is simple: Technology affects the behavior of people on the job as well as the effective functioning of organizations.

Advances in technology help individuals to work differently. For example, people today may conduct a videoconference instead of flying cross-country for an in-person, face-to-face meeting. They may use computerized spreadsheets instead of calculators and adding machines. They may operate a machine that does the heavy, dangerous work instead of doing that work themselves. In short, technology has changed people's relationships with machines. It appears to have closed the century-long era in which people were thought of as being part of the machinery (Figure 15.1), thereby freeing them to do work that machines cannot do—at least, not yet!

Technology also helps companies to gain advantages over their competitors, such as by finding a more effective, less expensive way of producing products or of delivering services.[3] Keeping abreast of the latest technology, however, often is needed not just to get ahead but simply to keep from falling behind. For example, in the late 1980s, having a computer might have given a company an edge over those that did not, whereas today, having a computer is an absolute necessity. In other words, sometimes using technology does not give one an advantage—it merely keeps one in the game![4]

We now turn our attention to how technology affects individual and organizational functioning. Given how wide-reaching this topic is, we already have described the effects of technology elsewhere in this book, such as in the context of communication (see chapter 8) and decision making (see chapter 9). Here, we concentrate on the more general aspects of technology. Specifically, we review the fundamental role of technology in organizations. We then explore the ways in which technology is used in today's organizations, and finally, we discuss the special connection between technology and organizational design.

THE ROLE OF TECHNOLOGY IN TODAY'S ORGANIZATIONS

To understand the role of technology in contemporary organizations, we must pay special attention to automation—and how people respond to it—in the workplace. Before doing so, however, it is necessary to describe the basic dimensions of technology in organizations.

Classifying Technology's Basic Dimensions

Many organizational theorists have described the various types of technologies that exist, but the most comprehensive scheme is that of Charles Perrow.[5] This system is useful for categorizing the technologies of both manufacturing and service organizations.

"Fertig here is one of our most reliable men."

FIGURE 15.1

Technology Changes the Nature of Work

We doubt Fertig will be at this job much longer. As reliable as he may be, he'll surely soon be replaced by an even more reliable, nonhuman "machine."

(*Source*: © The New Yorker Collection. 1938 Charles Addams from cartoonbank.com. All Rights Reserved.)

Perrow's Matrix of Technologies Perrow begins by distinguishing two basic dimensions. The first is *exceptions*—that is, the degree to which an organization uses standard inputs to turn out standard outputs (i.e., makes few exceptions) or encounters many nonroutine situations (i.e., makes many exceptions in how it operates). Perrow's second dimension is *problems*—that is, the degree to which the situations encountered are either easy to analyze, thus allowing for programmed decisions, or complex and difficult to analyze, thus requiring nonprogrammed decision making. By dichotomizing both dimensions and overlaying them onto each other, Perrow identifies four distinct technological types. The resulting **matrix of technologies** is summarized in Table 15.1.

Routine Technology The first technological type, **routine technology,** includes operations with highly standardized inputs and outcomes and problems that are easy to analyze. Examples include assembly line manufacturing (Figure 15.2) and vocational training, in both of which the product or service is clearly defined. Thus, when exceptions occur, such as when new products are to be produced or new subjects to be taught, the appropriate reaction is readily apparent.

Craft Technology Perrow's second technological type, **craft technology,** involves operations in which inputs and outputs also are standardized. Problems, however, are more difficult to analyze. For example, cabinetmakers always use wood and laminated products to create finished furniture products. Similarly, public schools focus their

matrix of technologies
Perrow's system of categorizing technologies based on two dimensions: *exceptions*, or the degree to which an organization uses standard inputs to produce standard outputs; and *problems*, or the degree to which the situations encountered are easy or difficult to analyze.

routine technology
Technology involving highly standardized inputs and problems that are easy to analyze (e.g., assembly lines, vocational training). (See *matrix of technologies*.)

craft technology
Technology involving highly standardized inputs and outputs and problems that are difficult to analyze (e.g., cabinetmakers and public schools). (See *matrix of technologies*.)

TABLE 15.1

Perrow's Matrix of Technologies

By combining two levels of exceptions (few and many) with two levels of problems (easy to analyze and difficult to analyze), Perrow identified the four technological types identified here.

EXCEPTIONS	PROBLEMS	TECHNOLOGICAL TYPE (AND EXAMPLES)
Few	Easy to analyze	Routine technology (e.g., assembly-line manufacturing, vocational training)
	Difficult to analyze	Craft technology (e.g., cabinet-making public schools)
Many	Easy to analyze	Engineering technology (e.g., heavy machinery construction, health-and-fitness club)
	Difficult to analyze	Nonroutine technology (e.g., research unit, psychiatric hospital)

Source: Perrow, 1967; see note 5.

attention on ways of teaching the average student. In either case, such as when a special order is placed or a student with a learning disability is encountered, the appropriate response is not entirely clear. Organizations of this type simply are not equipped to handle exceptional cases — ones in which the most appropriate decisions are not clearly specified in advance.

Engineering Technology   Perrow's final two technological types involve industries that are better prepared to handle exceptions. For example, organizations using **engineering technology,** such as those in heavy-machinery construction or health-and-fitness clubs, expect to encounter many exceptions in inputs or outputs, but these can be dealt with in standardized ways. For example, people come to health-and-fitness facilities in different physical conditions and with different goals. Some may be trying to lose weight. Others may be trying to regain strength and agility after an injury. Still others may be training for a major bodybuilding contest. Different types, amounts, and difficulty levels of exercise may be dictated on a case-by-case basis, but the decision regarding exactly what the client should do is relatively straightforward and is based on pre-established information about the effectiveness of different exercise regimes.

engineering technology

Technology involving many exceptions in inputs or outputs and problems that are easy to analyze (e.g., heavy machinery construction, health-and-fitness clubs). (See *matrix of technologies*.)

FIGURE 15.2

Technology Used to Mean Only the Assembly Line

For many years, simple technologies such as the assembly line made it possible for goods to be mass produced. These workers (from 1913) are making a flywheel magneto for an automobile. As unsophisticated as it may seem, the assembly line was a big advance in its day. It reduced the time required to assemble a car from 12 hours to only 93 minutes.

Nonroutine Technology Other industries also face exceptions—and more difficult decisions as well. Such organizations are said to employ **nonroutine technology**. For example, by their very existence, research units are created to tackle difficult, exceptional situations. Psychiatric hospitals also fit into this category. Not only do they encounter a wide variety of people with unique histories and combinations of mental and physical problems, the appropriate treatment is not always obvious. Despite widespread advances in psychiatric diagnoses, treatment decisions remain extremely complex and far from routine.

nonroutine technology

Technology involving many exceptions in inputs or outputs and problems that are difficult to analyze (e.g., research units, psychiatric hospitals). (See *matrix of technologies*.)

ETHICS MATTERS

Diagnosing and treating mental illness is a nonroutine technology, but doing so involves putting people into categories, thereby "routinizing" the process. This is done to aid diagnosis and treatment; however, questions have been raised about the ethics of doing so. What ethical questions may be associated with making this inherently nonroutine technology more routine? ■

Today's high-tech devices are excellent examples of nonroutine technologies. After all, the most advanced devices are designed to handle very specific problems. Interestingly, such technologies often have implications for military use. As a result, serious questions about national defense arise regarding the export of these technologies to other countries. (For a look at this fascinating issue, see the "OB Around the World" section in this chapter.)

NATIONAL DEFENSE: A CONCERN WHEN EXPORTING TECHNOLOGY

For half a century, the Export Control Act has banned the export of technology that potentially threatened the U.S. national defense. When the law was enacted in 1949, the threat came from the Soviet Union and its allies, and the United States was the only country with sufficiently advanced technology to warrant keeping it out of enemy hands. All that has changed, however. Today, the former Communist bloc countries no longer pose a security threat, and advanced technology can be found in nations throughout the world. This has led some politicians and scientists to question whether controlling technological exports still makes sense.

Those in favor of loosening export controls make several good points.[6] First, they note such restrictions are impossible to enforce, because goods easily can be re-exported from one country to another, thereby circumventing an embargo. In addition, when the technology takes the form of computer code—as it often does—it can be transmitted electronically, thus making its export virtually undetectable.

Second, they note export controls come at great cost to U.S. companies, which stand to lose billions of dollars in business. In fact, each $1 billion of exports is estimated to create 20,000 jobs. Lost business, therefore, can have serious effects on the national economy.

Third, they claim such export restrictions don't really matter given that other countries can do "dangerous" work even without the latest, cutting-edge technology. In fact, both the

United States and the Soviet Union developed nuclear weapons before supercomputers became available.

Despite these arguments, threats to national security clearly still exist. The former Soviet Union no longer is a worry, but concern now focuses on places like Libya, Iraq, and other hot spots throughout the world. It surely is not in the best interest of the United States to give enemy nations any advantages. What, then, can be done?

Experts have made several interesting recommendations. First, they argue that a key to making export controls work is not to "go it alone." Instead, governments throughout the world need to work together, tightening lax controls that currently make re-exporting loopholes possible. Second, it has been argued companies must do a better job of policing themselves, carefully screening all applications for licensing use of their technologies to foreign companies. Third, because export controls threaten the profitability of companies, they are more likely to be accepted if imposed in an equal manner—that is, in a way that does not threaten the competitive position of one company more than another. This way, the harm caused by any restrictions is spread evenly.

Controlling the export of technology is an issue that will not go away anytime soon. Experts have referred to these restrictions as "an important arrow in the quiver of national instruments to protect national and global security."[7] Thus, developing controls that are both fair and effective clearly is a challenge worth pursuing.

Automation in Today's Organizations

Traditionally, using technology on the job has involved the manual or mechanical manipulation of things. People at work used chains and pulleys to help lift heavy items and to maneuver them from one place to another. This type of work still goes on, but today's workplace is making increasing use of **high technology**—that is, of an advanced form of technology employing tools that are electronic in nature and usually rely on microprocessor chips (Figure 15.3).

High-tech devices have changed dramatically how work is done.[8] For example, typesetters once moved together pieces of metal type on wooden blocks to create plates from which documents were printed. Today, this process goes on invisibly: Compositors simply enter letters onto a keyboard, just as you do word processing at home. This is not the only example, of course. High-tech devices now are incorporated into nearly all aspects of home and work life. Some examples of very specialized high technology used by today's organizations include:

- **Advanced manufacturing technology (AMT)**: Manufacturing in which the various processes are guided by computers.
- **Computer-integrated manufacturing (CIM)**: Manufacturing processes that go beyond AMT by using computers to gather information, and then using this information to make decisions about ways in which the manufacturing process needs to be altered.
- **Computer-aided design and engineering (CAD/CAE)**: The processes of using computers to build and to simulate the characteristics of products and to test their effectiveness.
- **Industrial robotics (IR)**: Computer-controlled machines that manipulate materials and perform complex functions.
- **Flexible manufacturing systems**: Manufacturing processes relying on computer-controlled machines to produce low volumes of products at costs that rival those of mass-produced volumes.

The economics of automation are simple: As competition drives prices down, companies are forced to improve quality and to reduce labor costs. Thus, they turn to more efficient modes of operation, such as **automation**—that is, the process of using machines to perform tasks that otherwise might be done by people. Evidence of automation is all around us. Just think of automated call-menuing devices that route your phone calls to the appropriate person (if not to another computer!) and of automated teller machines that dispense currency. Such equipment certainly has reduced the need for human involvement in many activities. By substituting machines programmed to execute actions faster, more accurately, and more consistently than human beings, today's organizations seek the same kinds of increased efficiencies that factory owners sought a century ago when they introduced steam-powered machines onto their shop floors. Not surprisingly, the growth of automation has been referred to as "the second industrial revolution."[9]

high technology
Technology that is electronic in nature and usually relies on microprocessor chips.

advanced manufacturing technology (AMT)
Manufacturing in which the various processes are guided by computers.

computer-integrated manufacturing (CIM)
Manufacturing processes that go beyond *advanced manufacturing technology* by using computers to gather information, which in turn is used to make decisions regarding how the manufacturing process needs to be altered.

computer-aided design and engineering (CAD/CAE)
The processes of using computers to build and to simulate the characteristics of products and to test their effectiveness.

industrial robotics (IR)
Computer-controlled machines that manipulate materials and perform complex functions.

flexible manufacturing systems
Manufacturing processes relying on computer-controlled machines to produce low volumes of products at costs that rival those of mass-produced ones.

automation
The process of using machines to perform tasks that otherwise might be performed by people.

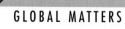

GLOBAL MATTERS　The challenge of bringing modern automation technology to the former Soviet Union and its satellite nations has proven to be difficult. Doing so, however, is necessary to strengthen the economic bases of the companies within these nations. ■

Indeed, evidence suggests today's automation vastly improves industrial efficiency. Specifically, companies using various forms of automation have reported reductions in lead time, unit cost, inventories, and labor expense as well as improvements in quality. For example, after General Electric introduced computer-integrated manufacturing in its St. Louis dishwasher factory, productivity jumped by 30 percent and warranty calls were reduced by half, thereby boosting its market share by 12 percentage points.[10] Given the high costs associated with automation, however, many corporate officials are considering carefully the wisdom of investing in highly automated facilities.

Automation is not only key to efficiency in factories and offices but in all walks of life. If you think we've seen high-tech advances thus far, experts predict what the future holds is beyond belief.[11] For a summary of some future technological advances, see Table 15.2.

Human Responses to Technology

There is more to organizations than money and machines—there also are people. Our examples show that as a result of using high technology in organizations, the kind of work people now do is different, as is the nature of the demands on them.[12] According to the U.S. Office of Technology Assessment, a main impediment to using technology effectively is its effect on people.[13]

Technology and Job Reduction   One obvious effect of automation is that it makes people so highly efficient the need for some positions is eliminated, thereby leading to unemployment. Indeed, the flip side of the effectiveness described earlier is the human cost: Automation is designed to eliminate jobs—and the more it does so, the more effective it is considered to be. Not surprisingly, many labor unions have been less than enthusiastic about automation, despite the fact it usually allows people to work in safer, cleaner, and healthier conditions while avoiding the tedious and repetitive aspects of many jobs. (A dangerous, boring job may be better than no job at all.) Fearing automation may make its members obsolete, some labor unions even have insisted on agreements with management that prohibit laying-off employees or transferring them to lower-paying jobs.[14] Indeed, statistics suggest such fears have a basis in fact: Today's companies are using high-tech tools to get more work out of fewer workers than ever before.[15]

FIGURE 15.3

Using High Tech to Make High Tech

When Blane McMichen, manager of production technologies for the information systems group at Motorola, was assigned to develop a system for producing cable modems, he was asked to do the job in only 6 weeks. Because the company's CyberSURFER modems are difficult to assemble, each step in the manufacturing process had to be documented meticulously. Instead of making elaborate engineering drawings that would take several months, McMichen took pictures of each component using an inexpensive, digital camera. Then, he posted the directions on the company's internal computer network for the assemblers to see. This "cyber-instruction process" worked so well it now is being used in other company locations as well.

TABLE 15.2

Tomorrow's Technologies: What the Future Has in Store

Technology advances so rapidly it is difficult to keep pace with the latest developments. In future years, this situation will be even more extreme. Meanwhile, experts predict we have some fascinating advances to look forward to in all walks of life.

YEAR	TECHNOLOGICAL ADVANCE	DESCRIPTION
2006	Effective hair-loss prevention	Gene therapy will prevent hair loss among men.
2010	Robot surgeon in a pill	People needing surgery will ingest a micro-robot that follows preprogrammed courses to perform surgery without exposing the body to infection.
2016	Holophone	A special telephone will use holographic technology to produce lifelike, three-dimensional images of callers.
2020	Sober-up drug	A pill will reverse alcohol's effects on the human body.
2029	Cell-repair technology	Special molecular machines will repair cells within the human body.
2043	First cryonic reanimation	Tissue that was frozen at "death" will be brought back to life.

Source: Based on information in Weiners & Pescovitz, 1996; see note 11.

Not only might fewer people be needed to do a given job, but often only those companies that can afford to invest in high-tech equipment are able to conduct business profitability. Therefore, we often see shakeouts in which many smaller companies—and their employees—find themselves casualties of the high-tech revolution. For example, as more computer-controlled machines are being used to mill lumber, fewer people are needed to flip switches and to monitor logs on video screens. Such mills operate so efficiently that smaller mills—ones that cannot afford the $15 million (or more) in automation costs—often are driven out of the market and forced to close their doors.[16]

Some people are being replaced by machines, but it also frequently is the case that people work *with* machines to help get their jobs done—and to do them better than ever before. The once-popular vision of the workerless factory, in which only white-coated technicians walked the floor to check on the machines as hoards of displaced factory workers walked the unemployment line, has not materialized. Typically, people today work side by side with robots, each doing what each does best. For example, robots play a large part in the production of automobiles, such as General Motors' highly regarded Saturn, but company officials acknowledge the technology only works because of the people.[17] Advanced technology alone will not build a successful car. In the words of the Japanese industrialist Jaruo Shimada, "Only people give wisdom to the machines."[18] The idea is that people and machines really are complementary aspects of any organization.

GLOBAL MATTERS   In the richer nations of the world, the introduction of technology may lead workers to shift from lower-level to higher-level jobs. In poorer countries, however, the introduction of modern technology (e.g., in a new factory) is likely to create new jobs that did not exist previously. ■

Technology and Job Change   If people and machines are to be cooperating elements of an organization's technology, the nature of the work performed by people must remain highly motivating. This tends to be a problem when automation so severely simplifies—or "dumbs-up"—a job that the worker becomes bored and alienated, thus leading to lower quality performance. After all, why should anyone care about doing a good job when all one needs to do is stand around and watch machines?

It would be misleading, however, to imply automation leaves only routine and boring jobs for people to perform. Indeed, new jobs created by the introduction of robots often are considered to be more demanding than the old jobs. As one employee describes his response to a robot in his manufacturing plant, "The job now requires more skills. . . . You have to learn how to program the robot and run it. . . . The job is more sophisticated."[19] Indeed, automation frequently frees people for more interesting work. For example, automatic teller machines free human bank tellers to play a more problem-solving role when dealing with bank customers.

ETHICS MATTERS   Do you believe it is unethical for companies to introduce technology that forces employees to learn new jobs? Is this inappropriately coercive? If not, is it ethically justified because it helps more people than it hurts? ■

Just because opportunities may arise for people to do interesting work (while leaving the boring work to the machinery) does not necessarily ensure this actually will happen. Thus, when introducing automation, some companies go out of their way to make the remaining human jobs as involving as possible. For example, at its heavily automated Grand Rapids, Michigan, furniture plant, Westinghouse has an elaborate network of committees and task forces to encourage employees to be highly in-

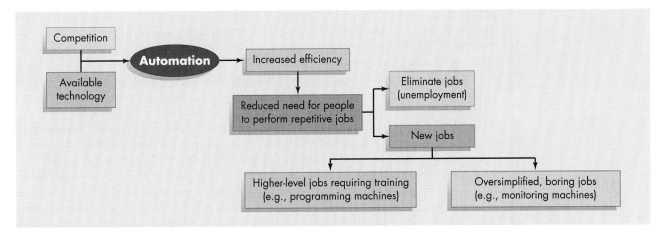

FIGURE 15.4

The Impact of Automation: A Summary

The economics of automation have a key effect on people in organizations. By making workers so efficient, automation reduces the need for as many people to perform routine jobs. Thus, jobs are either eliminated (leading to unemployment) or changed to new jobs, a few of which may be boring (e.g., monitoring machines) but many of which will be even more challenging (e.g., programming and maintaining the machines).

volved in the facility's decision making. Autonomous work teams also have been used in some organizations to ensure employees stay interested when their jobs have changed because of automation.

In other words, if people do not lose their jobs to automation, the jobs themselves certainly may change. Automation also creates new jobs as more people are needed to program and to service the high-tech equipment. Thus, automation may be seen as causing a shift in the *kinds* of jobs people do. According to an official at National Semiconductor Corporation, "We will be upgrading jobs through automation. I think we will be changing all our collars to white over the next few years."[20]

Changes of this type indicate a need for employee training if automation is to be successful. With just this in mind, Chrysler invested some 900,000 person-hours in training its employees before opening the futuristic factory used to manufacture some of its latest models.[21] For a summary of the impact of automation on people, see Figure 15.4.

Recently, we all have become aware of another important technology with profound effects on people: the Internet. As vital as it is, the Internet is not without social costs. For a look at the potential human problems arising from this vital technology, see the "Trends" section below.

**TRENDS:
WHAT TODAY'S
COMPANIES ARE DOING**

■ **Beware the Hidden Psychological Dangers of Internet Use**

Not long ago, the Internet was little more than a dream of a few computer pioneers.[22] Today, however, it is a reality of life in millions of households—and, in one way or another, in most organizations as well. Business organizations rely on Internet connections to do just about everything imaginable. Some use it to interview new employees.[23] Countless more use it to create a "virtual storefront," bringing their wares to anybody, anyplace in the world. A few even use it to keep abreast of the competition.[24] For most professionals, however, the Internet is used almost exclusively to

continued

gather research data and to communicate with others via e-mail.[25] Indeed, as of 1997, half of all professionals claimed to use the Internet daily, and this figure is rising dramatically.[26] Clearly, Internet use is not a passing fad but a powerful technological tool of today's business professional.

Considering this trend, scientists have asked an intriguing question: How does reliance on the Internet affect people's social and psychological well-being? After all, as people hunker alone over their terminals, one can argue they become more socially isolated.[27] In contrast, others contend that by releasing people from the constraints of geography, the Internet actually helps to bring people together, thereby deepening their social connections.[28] Recently, a fascinating study shed light on this issue.[29]

This investigation was an in-depth study of 169 people in 73 Pittsburgh households who were studied during their first one to two years of using the Internet. Most used the Internet primarily to communicate with others. Various psychological tests were administered to the participants before the study began and, again, afterward. The comparisons told a compelling story. The more people used the Internet in their households:

- The less they communicated with members of their families.
- The smaller was their circle of friends and acquaintances.
- The lonelier they felt in their lives.
- The more symptoms of psychological depression they displayed.

These findings clearly suggest Internet use is not without serious psychological consequences — most of which shockingly never cross our minds. We might voice concern about strain to our eyes, backs, and wrists from prolonged time at a computer, but we need to be at least as concerned about the psychological damage that may result. After all, time we spend on-line with others is likely to displace the richer social interaction that comes from face-to-face contact with people. At the same time, we cannot ignore that some people use the Internet to maintain contacts with those they otherwise might have no interaction with at all. From this perspective, things may not be all bad.

Still, in light of this evidence, it seems clear over-reliance on Internet technology in the workplace may have a hidden psychological cost to employees. It is one that might be overcome, however, by balancing the more solitary aspects of work with more opportunities for rich social encounters (e.g., social events, coffee breaks, and so on). Such contact is likely to occur naturally for most people who feel the need to get away from their computer terminals and talk with an actual colleague in person, but need to be concerned about those who are so socially withdrawn they "hide" behind the anonymity of Internet communication. Indeed, interested as they are in maintaining healthy working environments for their employees, today's companies must pay closer attention to the potential costs of keeping people tethered to their computers. ■

USING TECHNOLOGY IN MODERN ORGANIZATIONS

People use technology in various ways while performing many different jobs. In this section, we consider several of the latest ways in which technology is used in organizations. Specifically, we focus on four contemporary uses of technology. First, we describe *assistive technology* — that is, devices that help people with disabilities to take advantage of their work skills so they can be fully functioning, productive members of their organizations. Second, we present a controversial technology that allows company officials to observe — or, some would say, to "snoop" — on their employees, which is known as *computerized performance monitoring*. Third, we present ways in which computer-based technology, which often is criticized for being cold and impersonal, is being used to improve and to personalize the quality of *customer service* delivered in today's organizations. Finally, we discuss the developing trend toward using technology in an environmentally friendly manner using a process known as *design for disassembly*.

Assistive Technology: Helping People with Disabilities to Work Productively

If you've ever seen public telephones with volume controls, elevator signs with floor markings in Braille, and cutaway curbs on sidewalks, you already know that things are being done to enable people with various handicaps to function effectively in society. These accommodations, however, are just a small part of the picture when it comes to using technology to assist disabled people. In today's organizations, technology is widely used to allow skilled people to perform their jobs even though they may be challenged by some form of physical or mental condition. (For examples of technological advances used for these purposes, see Table 15.3.) As a result, people, who only a few years ago could not have done so, today perform mainstream jobs. Such technology is referred to as **assistive technology** — that is, devices or other solutions that help individuals with physical or mental problems to perform the various actions needed on their jobs.[30]

In addition to being "the right thing to do," there are several good reasons why assistive technology is so widespread today. First, the workplace is so competitive that employers cannot afford to overlook qualified employees simply because adjustments are required to how they do their jobs. According to the Job Accommodation Network, which is a clearinghouse of information on ways to accommodate people with disabilities, this process need not be expensive. In fact, they claim about half the accommodations that need to be made cost less than $50 — and almost one-third have no cost whatsoever.[31] For example, instead of investing in new plumbing to lower a drinking fountain so a person in a wheelchair can use it, simply provide a dispenser for cups.

Second, the workforce is aging, and people are living longer.[32] As people get older, even the healthiest are likely to suffer impairments in hearing, vision, and manual dexterity. If such individuals, who are likely to be highly experienced and knowledgeable, leave their jobs, probably it would be prohibitively expensive — and maybe

assistive technology

Devices and other solutions that help individuals with physical or mental problems to perform the various actions needed on their jobs.

TABLE 15.3

Assistive Technology: Some Examples

Technology can be used to assist people with various disabilities to function effectively on the job. Here are examples of devices — some sophisticated and some simple — applied to this purpose.

DEVICE	DESCRIPTION
Telephone handset amplifer	Mechanism for raising the volume of telephone earpiece, enabling hearing-impaired people to use the telephone.
Reading machine	Hardware using simulated speech to read to visually impaired people.
Sight devices	Portable sensory guides and closed-circuit TV monitors with magnification that enable people with visual impairments to navigate their physical environments.
Mouthpicks	Stylus-like tools that quadriplegics can use to operate computers.
Gooseneck telephones	Adjustable telephone headsets that can be used by people with limited physical dexterity.

Source: Tompkins, 1993; see note 30.

even impossible—to replace them. Thus, making the adjustments necessary to help these individuals to perform their jobs makes good business sense.

Another—and for some, the major—reason, however is they are required to do so by the *Americans with Disabilities Act (ADA)*. According to this law, U.S. employers must make "reasonable accommodations" for otherwise qualified disabled people so long as this can be done without imposing an undue financial burden on the company or directly threatening anyone's safety. As companies attempt to comply with the ADA, many new technologies have been developed, including car-top carriers for wheelchairs and desktops that are high enough to accommodate them.[33]

To help companies comply with the ADA, the federal government has several initiatives to encourage private companies to develop suitable assistive technologies. For example, the Disabled Access Credit Act gives small businesses a tax credit for investing in ways of meeting the ADA's requirements. Tax laws also provide credits to companies for attempting to make their facilities accessible to persons with disabilities and for hiring new employees with disabilities referred to them by state employment services.

ETHICS MATTERS

Clearly, the intent of the ADA is highly moral in tone—that is, helping people with disabilities to work in mainstream jobs. Some critics, however, have argued the ADA places an unfair burden on employers and, therefore, is unethical. What is your position on this issue? ■

Computerized Performance Monitoring: Management by Remote Control

computerized performance monitoring (CPM)

The practice of using computers to collect, store, analyze and report information about the work people are doing.

One of the most popular uses of technology in the workplace today is using computers to collect, store, analyze, and report information about the work people do, which is a practice known as **computerized performance monitoring (CPM)**. As the definition implies, CPM refers to a broad range of procedures that enable supervisors to "look in" on employees doing their jobs.[34]

With CPM, the work of employees—particularly those who work at computer terminals (e.g., phone sales agents, data-entry and word-processing personnel, airline reservation agents, telephone operators) can be observed and quantified. Not all CPM systems are the same, however. In some, employees are monitored all the time; in others, observation occurs only sometimes (but the software keeps a detailed record of their work). Regardless of their differences, all such systems make it possible to observe job performance in a constant, unblinking fashion.

Within the past decade, CPM systems have grown in popularity. More than 10 million employees are estimated to be monitored in more than 70,000 U.S. companies, representing an investment in equipment in excess of $1 billion.[35] Not surprisingly, use of CPM has aroused considerable debate.[36] Some argue it represents an invasion of employees' privacy, creates an atmosphere of distrust, and can be a source of work-related stress.[37] Proponents, however, counter CPM allows supervisors to gather more objective information about performance, thereby providing a valuable source of feedback and information for planning training programs and workloads.[38]

What does the scientific evidence reveal about these arguments? There has been only limited research on the effects of CPM, but the few results available suggest that—to some degree—*both* perspectives are correct. For example, research comparing monitored and nonmonitored employees found monitored employees were, in fact, more productive on simple tasks.[39] In keeping with the social facilitation effect (see chapter 7), however, monitoring lowers performance on complex tasks. Even if performance on simple tasks increases in response to monitoring, CPM also leads people to experience higher levels of stress and lower levels of job satisfaction. Part of the problem seems to be that working in front of video display terminals all day contributes to feelings of isolation and loneliness, which are unpleasant conditions associated with stress.[40]

Employees who are monitored regarding specific aspects of their performance might be expected to work hard to improve those measures—even if doing so comes at the expense of other, possibly more important aspects of performance. For example, in one company, supervisors monitored telephone operators to see that they did not spend longer than 22 seconds on each call.[41] As a result, operators almost always met the standard. A great many, however, did so by "cheating." For example, if customers required more than 22 seconds to help (e.g., if they had strong accents or hearing impediments), operators simply disconnected such callers so they could be rewarded for meeting their goal. Even those who did not take such drastic measures lamented they could not take the time to be as pleasant and as friendly as they wanted.

Not only do employees dislike being monitored, evidence shows many supervisors dislike the added workload of constantly reviewing incoming data about employees' work performance. The problem is that monitoring raises expectations supervisors will "say something" to employees about their performance, thus holding supervisors to a standard their busy schedules may not permit. When employee performance appears to be unexpectedly poor, however, supervisors can rely on computerized records of performance as a basis for accurately assessing the problem. Under such conditions, supervisors surely benefit from having accurate information at their disposal to help them diagnose the problem at hand.

To summarize, there may be some benefits associated with CPM, but there also may be some limitations. (For a summary, see Figure 15.5.) This particular use of technology has a long way to go before it gains widespread acceptance. By creating a new dynamic between superiors and subordinates, CPM—like many other new technologies introduced into the workplace—appears threatening. Will it ever be completely accepted?

We suspect the answer resides in how the technique is used—or is abused—in practice. If used as a tool to help improve performance, we believe CPM has a valuable role to play in organizations. If misused, however, such as for close surveillance of nonwork activities (e.g., bathroom trips) such invasions of privacy are sure to be rejected. In conclusion, it is not necessarily the technology itself that is useful or harmful but rather how people use it.

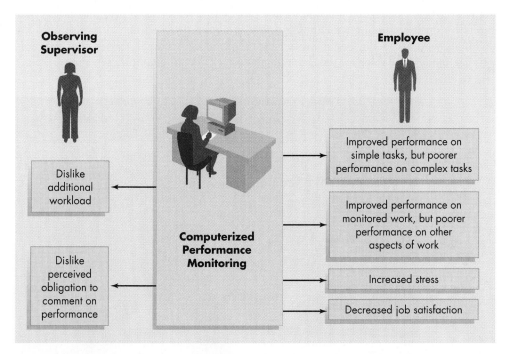

FIGURE 15.5

Computerized Performance Monitoring: A Mixed Bag of Results

Computerized performance monitoring has been introduced to improve employees' work performance, but its effects are both positive and negative.

ETHICS MATTERS   On what ethical grounds can the practice of CPM be justified? On what ethical grounds can it be rejected? Do you believe CPM is ethically appropriate? ■

Technological Aids to Customer Service

Have you ever heard someone grumble that service received today is "not like it was in the good old days"? In general, such complaints are well founded. Through the early 1950s, it was not unusual for businesses to provide high levels of courteous, personalized service. You could phone your order to Mr. Smith's corner store, and his son would deliver your groceries to your table after school—and even charge them to your account. You could go to the corner "service" station, where Gus would pump your gas, clean your windshield, check your oil, and even install a new muffler or set of tires on your car. Today, however, Mr. Smith's place probably has given way to a huge, 24-hour supermarket, and Gus most likely has been replaced by a pay-at-the-pump, self-serve operation.

Experts say the depersonalization of service has resulted from several forces. The automobile led to suburban sprawl, so cities grew and markets expanded. Increasing competition led to reduced profit margins and the need to standardize goods and services. The result? Mom's diner surely delivered more personalized service than McDonald's, but given its economic disadvantage (e.g., the higher per-unit cost of producing on a small scale), it simply could not afford to compete. As standardization became more feasible than individual attention, personal service became a casualty.

Technology, however, has made possible the revitalization of customer service in several ways never before possible.[42] For example, many organizations today employ technology aimed at *delivering personalized service*. For example, computerized systems are used to give the most appropriate coupons to shoppers who make certain purchases at the supermarket. Large chains use systems that print in-store coupons on the back of register receipts or, in some systems, on separate printers. These coupons are customized to fit the customer's profile of purchases. For example, purchasers of one brand of breakfast cereal may be given a coupon to induce them to try another brand, or purchasers of peanut butter may be given coupons for products that might go with it (e.g., bread, jelly).

These practices are not "personalized" in the same sense as Mr. Smith delivering your grocery order to your door. They represent new forms of personalization that capitalize on the computer technology now available. Interestingly, it is not only individuals who are being better served by this kind of personal service that technology has made available; so, too, have businesses. (For an example, see Figure 15.6.)

FIGURE 15.6

Business-to-Business Personalized Service

ChemStation of Dayton, Ohio, develops custom-made cleaning products for its industrial customers. Chemist Kathy Hansen and CEO George Homan are underwater to check the flow of one such concentrated custom detergent. Technology has made it possible to deliver such personalized service at a reasonable cost.

Technology also is helping to revitalize customer service by *augmenting service,* which refers to the practice of providing customers with additional support related to the product or service. How can technology help to provide "something extra"? Several companies have been fairly ingenious in this regard. Sometimes, the additional service is small — but quite helpful. For example, Hertz pioneered systems by which rental-car customers are guided to their vehicles by signs that display their names, and hand-held devices used by agents to check-in returned vehicles print customer receipts on the spot. These practices eliminate check-in and check-out lines, and such customer-friendly technology has helped Hertz to attract considerable business.

Finally, technology can help by *transforming business* — that is, by developing entirely new practices that better satisfy customers' needs. Specifically, today's advanced computer information systems allow customized goods to be made with almost the same efficiency as standardized goods. For example, Benjamin Moore paints uses a photospectrometer to identify the color of a customer's fabric sample and tell the computer how to match it by appropriately mixing the company's paints. In addition, printing technology now allows magazine publishers to tailor their advertisements and editorials to different readers. As a result, swine farmers in Iowa who subscribe to the *Farm Journal* are sent a somewhat different magazine than dairy farmers in Vermont. These examples represent how today's companies use technology to transform their businesses so they can provide improved customer service.

Some technology has led to the depersonalization of service, but clearly, technology also can be used — and, in fact, *is* being used — to improve customer service. We should not look for Mr. Smith to return to his corner grocery or Gus to his service station anytime soon, but we can expect technology to improve customer service in these — and in all — businesses in many different forms.

Environmentally Friendly Technology: Design for Disassembly

The earth's mineral deposits are being rapidly depleted, and landfills are reaching capacity. Believe it or not, 94 percent of material taken from the earth enters the waste stream only months later.[43] There is no mistaking that the industrialized world has a long history of taking riches from the earth and returning rubbish. Scientists say this cannot go on forever. If we are to rely on the earth's natural resources in the future, we must conserve them now by using them wisely. Fortunately, a movement is afoot to make manufacturers responsible for taking back their used products and for recycling them. Laws across Europe soon will require manufacturers to do this. In Germany, companies already are legally responsible for how their packaging is used, thereby encouraging them not only to recycle but to devise ingenious ways to reduce the amount of packaging.

The effect of the German legislation has been encouraging: Within the first two years, the "take-back" law has reduced the amount of packaging waste by four percent — some 600 million tons. Following this success, companies are moving to reduce the amount of product they waste, and one of the most effective processes in this regard is known as **design for disassembly (DFD).** This is the process of designing and building products so their parts can be reused several times and then safely disposed of at the end of the product's life. This means fewer parts, fewer materials, and assembly processes designed with later disassembly in mind.

design for disassembly (DFD)

The process of designing and building products so their parts can be used several times and then safely disposed of at the end of the product's life.

A good example of DFD can be seen in automobile manufacturing. For example, BMW is replacing glue and solder in bumpers with fasteners, thus making them easier to be recycled. In addition, instrument panels are made of polyurethane foam that can be recycled in one piece. Eighty percent of a BMW's weight already comes from recycled parts, and the company hopes to get this figure as high as 95 percent. Not only cars are prime candidates for DFD, however. Computers, telephones, and engines also commonly are designed with disassembly in mind.

If you've ever used a Kodak "FunSaver 35" camera, in which the camera and the film come in a single, "disposable" package, you have used a product designed for disassembly. It wasn't always this way, of course. The first such products were simply tossed away. In 1990, however, Kodak was taken to task by environmentalists for putting hundreds of thousands of used cameras into landfills. Today, these cameras are designed so they can be returned to Kodak by film processors, the plastic ground up and remolded into new parts, and the guts of the camera (i.e., the moving parts and electronics) reused as many as 10 times.

Kodak is not alone among U.S. companies using DFD. Xerox also uses recycled parts in its copiers. As you might imagine, the motivation for doing so is "green" — whether the "green" of preserving the environment or of making money. The result is the same. After retooling costs, companies find themselves saving money by using recycled parts. The Kodak FunSaver 35 camera is the company's most profitable product, and Xerox has saved approximately $500 million a year by remanufacturing and recycling parts. The bottom line: DFD is helping companies to save both money and the earth's natural environment.

GLOBAL MATTERS Clearly, DFD caught on in Europe before it did in the United States. Why do you think this is? What needs to happen for DFD to take hold in the United States? ▪

Machine Vision: Electronic Eyes Improve Quality

Traditionally, *quality control* at a factory has involved pulling a product off the assembly line and inspecting it for flaws. This still goes on, but it also is increasingly common for advanced technology to provide a higher level of measurement and inspection than ever previously imagined. Using a technology known as **machine vision,** sophisticated electronic eyes send images to a computer that interprets what it "sees" and then commands other machines to take appropriate ac-

machine vision

A sophisticated technology in which electronic eyes send images to a computer that interprets what it "sees" and then commands other machines to take appropriate action.

YOU BE THE CONSULTANT

Your company is having a difficult time retaining productive employees in the telemarketing department. Exit interviews reveal employees are dissatisfied with several things, including that their performance is closely monitored by computer and that they feel both lonely and alienated from sitting by themselves in a cubicle all day. You are asked to help address this problem.

1. Do these workers' reactions appear to be unusual, or are they to be expected? Explain.
2. What minor adjustments could be made to help alleviate these problems?
3. What arguments could be made that performance monitoring should be eliminated? If it should, under what conditions?
4. One solution you are considering involves finding a larger pool of suitable applicants. How might assistive technology be used to open the telemarketing positions to people with physical handicaps?

tion.[44] Such technology is being used for many purposes. Some of the key uses are:

- Spotting blemished vegetables before they are packaged.
- Ensuring that the right pills go into the right packages.
- Checking for ice on aircraft wings before taking off.
- Finding knots in logs.
- Identifying microscopic errors in computer chips.

One of the most impressive uses of this technology has been at Vance, Alabama, where the Mercedes Benz M-class sport utility vehicle is manufactured. In this factory, every vehicle is fully inspected for flaws—in just 45 seconds—using 38 laser cameras that take 84 key measurements. The equipment used in this process costs nearly $1 million, but the machine-vision device has done a great deal to pay for itself by ensuring a high-quality product. Given this company's reputation for quality, this investment is a small price to pay.

Do not be misled, however, into thinking machine vision is used only in industrial settings. It also has consumer applications. For example, machine-vision devices ensure quality in custom-fitted golf gloves (Figure 15.7). This same technology is now being tested to scan people's eyeballs. Soon, you will walk up to an ATM, and a machine-vision device will attempt to recognize your iris and to match it with the picture in its database. If it recognizes you, you will be allowed to access the machine—even without a card or a personal identification number. (For those of us who are forgetful, this day cannot come too soon.)

TECHNOLOGY: A MAJOR CAUSE—AND CONSEQUENCE—OF ORGANIZATIONAL DESIGN

Thus far, we have focused on technology's role in individual and group behavior. As you might imagine, however, technology is closely related to the design and performance of organizations. Clearly, technology employed by a given organization is closely linked to the work that organization performs and the major tasks it seeks to accomplish. This relationship is something of a two-way street, however. Organizations

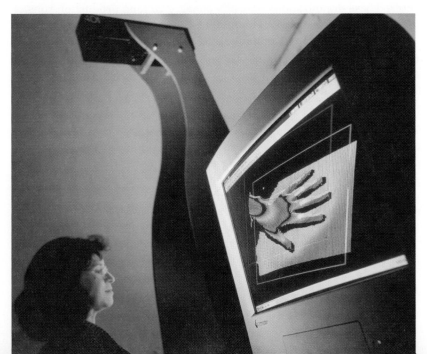

FIGURE 15.7

Machine Vision in Action
This machine-vision device is used to ensure the quality fit of a custom-made golf glove. This same technology also has many industrial uses.

not only choose the technology they employ, they also are affected by that technology once it is selected. In this section, we describe several major studies that point to this conclusion. These investigations classify technology in contrasting ways and focus on many issues. Their findings often are difficult to compare in a simple, direct manner, but they all illustrate the same point: Technology plays an important role in shaping both the design and the performance of many organizations.

Technology and Structure in Manufacturing Companies

One prominent tradition of research has examined the connection between technology and the design of manufacturing companies. Reviewing these studies helps to illustrate the complex nature of this relationship.

The Woodward Studies　Perhaps the best-known of these studies are those that were conducted in England during the 1960s by Woodward and her associates.[45] To determine the relationship between various structural characteristics (e.g., span of control, decentralization) and organizational performance (e.g., profitability, market share), Woodward gathered data about 100 manufacturing firms. In keeping with the classical approach to organizational design (see chapter 14), she initially expected organizations classified as being highly successful would share similar structural characteristics and those classified as being relatively unsuccessful would share other characteristics. Surprisingly, however, this was not the case. Instead, various aspects of organizational structure appeared to be as common in successful and in unsuccessful companies. Thus, Woodward found little — if any — support for the accuracy of universal principles of management.

Instead, Woodward found an organization's success depended on the degree to which it was structured in the most appropriate way given the technology it used. Specifically, she compared organizations using each of three different types of technology popular at the time:

small-batch production

A technology in which products are custom-produced in response to specific customer orders.

large-batch production

Technology based on long production runs of standardized parts or products.

mass production

See *large-batch production*.

continuous-process production

A highly automated form of production that is continuous in nature and highly integrated regarding component steps and processes.

- **Small-batch production:** Custom work was the norm. Machinery was simple, and the companies typically produced small batches of products to meet specific orders from customers. Firms in this category made items such as specialized construction equipment or custom-ordered electronic items. Other examples included dressmaking and printing.
- **Large-batch production (mass production):** Relied on assembly line procedures. These organizations typically engaged in long production runs of standardized parts or products. This output then went into inventory, from which orders were filled on a continuous basis.
- **Continuous-process production:** These were technologically complex companies in which production was fully automated. Firms in this category included oil refining and chemical companies.

When Woodward compared companies using these types of technology, important differences were noted. First, as expected, they demonstrated contrasting internal structures. For example, the span of control (of first-level supervisors) and centralization were higher in companies employing mass production than in companies employing small-batch or continuous-process technologies. Similarly, chains of command were longest in organizations using continuous-process production and shortest in companies using small-batch methods. In short, the specific technology used in production was an important determinant of organizational structure. As Woodward put it, "Different technologies imposed different kinds of demands on individuals and organizations, and those demands had to be met through an appropriate structure."[46]

Perhaps even more important was that the characteristics distinguishing highly successful from unsuccessful companies also varied with technology. At the low and the high ends of the technology dimension described earlier, an *organic* approach worked best (i.e., authority is decentralized and diffused throughout the organization); thus, companies using this strategy were more successful than those using a *mechanistic* approach (i.e., authority is centralized in a few people). (Recall the distinction between organic and mechanistic organizations in chapter 14.) In contrast, in the middle of the technology dimension (i.e., mass production), the opposite was true, and companies adopting a mechanistic approach tended to be more effective (Figure 15.8).

Successful firms also tended to have structures suited to their level of technology. Specifically, those with above-average performance had structural characteristics similar to those of most other firms using the same type of production methods. In contrast, those with below-average records tended to depart from the median structure of companies in the same technology category. In summary, the results of Woodward's study indicate that important links exist between technology and performance.

Contemporary Studies   As you might imagine, we have learned a great deal about organizational design since Woodward's time — if for no other reason than technology has changed so very much. In addition to the three types studied by Woodward, some organizations today produce highly customized, high-performance products in relatively small runs. This process is known as **mass customization** (Figure 15.9).[47] Because these products are technologically advanced and complex, however, they are produced by highly automated, computer-controlled equipment. Moreover, people involved in their manufacture often must possess a high level of professional or technical knowledge. In short, such companies share some characteristics with the

mass customization

The process of manufacturing goods to-order in a way that relies on mass-assembly processes.

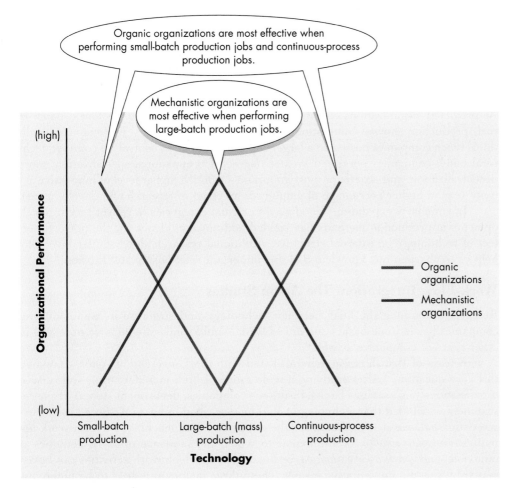

FIGURE 15.8

The Woodward Studies: The Relationship between Technology and Design

In a classic set of studies, Woodward found that organic organizations were most effective when performing small-batch and continuous-batch production jobs, whereas mechanistic organizations were most effective when performing large-batch production jobs.

(*Source*: Based on findings by Woodward, 1965; see note 45.)

FIGURE 15.9

Mass Customization: One Size Does *Not* Fit All

If you need shoes, you can buy an inexpensive, ready-made pair that may — or may not — be of the style you want and the fit you need. Alternatively, if your budget permits, you can get exactly the shoes you want custom made for you. At Custom Foot, however, advanced manufacturing techniques make it possible for customized products to be made at a mass-produced price. Here, a customer in a Connecticut Custom Foot shop is having his foot measured precisely by an electronic scanner. This information then is fed directly into the machinery to ensure delivery of a pair of perfect-fitting shoes.

traditional, small-batch firms studied by Woodward, but they also share other characteristics with the technologically advanced, continuous-process firms at the other end of her continuum.

What type of internal structure do such technical batch organizations demonstrate? In one particular study, researchers examined the internal structure of 110 separate companies operating in the United States.[48] By carefully examining these companies' methods of production, the investigators divided these organizations into four categories: traditional batch, technical batch, mass production, and process production. Then, they compared the companies' internal structures along several key dimensions (e.g., supervisory span of control, occupational specialization, decentralization, formalization). As Figure 15.10 shows, the types of organizations differed in various ways. As predicted, organizations classified as being traditional batch or technical batch in their production showed contrasting structure in several respects. For example, traditional batch companies possessed a larger supervisory span of control. In contrast, technical batch companies possessed greater degree of occupational specialization, more decentralization, and — perhaps most important — a much higher level of innovative activity (e.g., a higher percentage of employees involved in research and development).

In summary, expanding Woodward's original categories to reflect recent developments in production methods has yielded additional evidence for the powerful effect of technology on internal structure. Additional research along similar lines may help us to sharpen our knowledge of this important relationship still further.

Work-Flow Integration: The Aston Studies

Research examining the links between technology and structure in manufacturing companies has left one basic issue unresolved: Would similar findings be observed in other types of companies as well?

A team of British researchers affiliated with the University of Aston examined this very question.[49] After studying a wide range of both manufacturing and service organizations (e.g., savings banks, insurance companies, department stores), these researchers concluded that technology could be described in terms of three basic characteristics: *automation of equipment*, or the extent to which machines perform work activities; *work-flow rigidity*, or the extent to which the sequence of work activities is inflexible; and *specificity of evaluation*, or the degree to which work activities can be assessed by specific, quantitative means. These three factors appeared to be highly as-

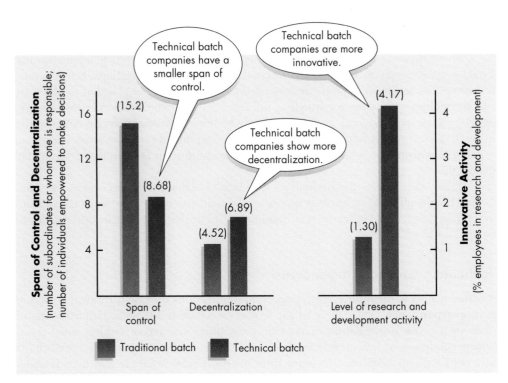

FIGURE 15.10

Technology and Structure: Evidence of Linkages

Organizations employing technical batch technology differ in several respects from those employing traditional batch technology.

(*Source*: Based on data from Hull & Collins, 1987; see note 48.)

sociated, so they were combined into a single scale labeled **work-flow integration**. The higher an organization's score on this scale, the more likely it was to employ automation, rigid task sequences, and quantitative measurement of operations. The work-flow integration scores obtained by various companies are shown in Table 15.4; as you can see, manufacturing firms generally score higher than service firms.

When these investigators related work-flow integration to structural characteristics in the organizations studied, no strong or general links were uncovered. Thus, at first glance, these findings seemed to contradict those reported by Woodward. Closer analysis, however, revealed that technological complexity *was* related to structural features — at least in some ways. For example, as work-flow integration increased, so did specialization, standardization, and decentralization of authority. The magnitude of these findings was small, however, and seemed to involve mainly those aspects

work-flow integration

A measure of technology that considers the degree of automation, work-flow rigidity, and specificity of evaluation in an organization.

TABLE 15.4

Work-flow Integration in Different Organizations

Manufacturing firms generally score higher on work-flow integration than do service organizations (e.g., banks, stores).

ORGANIZATION	CLASSIFICATION (MANUFACTURING OR SERVICE)	WORK-FLOW INTEGRATION SCORE
Vehicle manufacturer	Manufacturing	17
Metal goods manufacturer	Manufacturing	14
Tire manufacturer	Manufacturing	12
Printer	Service	11
Local water department	Service	10
Insurance company	Service	7
Savings bank	Service	4
Department store	Service	2
Chain of retail stores	Service	1

Source: Based on data from Hickson, Pugh & Pheysey, 1969; see note 48.

of structure closely connected to actual work flow. Moreover, *organizational size* exerted stronger effects than technology on several aspects of structure.

These findings (as well as those of later studies) point toward two conclusions. First, technology seems to affect the internal structure of organizations, but it is only one of several influences. Thus, the so-called *technological imperative* — that is, the view that technology always has a compelling influence on organizational structure — clearly overstates the case. Second, technology probably exerts stronger effects on structure in small organizations, where such characteristics impinge directly on work flow, than in large organizations, where structure is complex and often far removed from actual production.

Taken as a whole, the findings of the Aston studies can be interpreted as indicating that the effect of technology on organizational structure is not restricted to manufacturing concerns. Under certain conditions, it can be observed in other types of companies as well.

Technology and Interdependence

interdependence

The extent to which individuals, departments, or units in a given organization depend on each other for accomplishing their tasks.

Another aspect of technology with important implications for organizational structure is **interdependence**. This refers to the extent to which individuals, departments, or units in a given organization depend on each other for accomplishing their tasks. Under conditions of low interdependence, each person, unit, or group can perform its functions without assistance or input from others. Under conditions of high interdependence, however, such coordination is essential. A framework proposed by Thompson helps to clarify the various types of possible interdependence in organizations as well as the implications of this factor for effective structural design.[50]

pooled interdependence

A relatively low level of interdependence, in which units of an organization operate in a largely independent manner.

The lowest level within this framework is **pooled interdependence,** in which departments or units are part of an organization but work does not flow between them. Rather, each performs its tasks independently. One example of pooled interdependence is the branch stores of a clothing retailer in many large shopping malls. Each contributes to the total earnings of the parent company, but there is little — if any — contact or coordination between them.

sequential interdependence

An intermediate level of interdependence, in which the output of one department or subunit becomes the input for another.

The next higher level is **sequential interdependence,** in which the output of one department or subunit becomes the input of another. For example, the marketing department of a food company cannot proceed with promotional campaigns until it receives information about new products from the product-development unit. Similarly, in a company that manufactures electronic toys, the final assemblers cannot perform their jobs without a steady supply of component parts from other units or outside suppliers. Note that in sequential interdependence, information, products, and components flow in one direction. Thus, units farther along the chain of production depend on those preceding them, but the reverse is not true.

reciprocal interdependence

The highest level of interdependence, in which the output of one department or unit serves as the input for another in a reciprocal fashion.

The highest level in Thompson's model is **reciprocal interdependence,** in which the output of each department or unit becomes the input for other departments or units in a reciprocal fashion. Thus, the output of Department A provides input for Department B, and the output of Department B provides input for Department A. An example of such reciprocal interdependence is provided by the marketing and production departments of many companies. Through appropriate surveys, the marketing department may develop a profile of new products or product innovations that are attractive to potential customers. This profile serves as input for the production department, which considers the feasibility of actually making such products and suggests modifications. The appeal of these modifications then is assessed by the marketing department, and the results obtained serve as the basis for further planning by the production department. This process may be repeated until a plan for product innovations acceptable to both units is devised (Figure 15.11).

These forms of interdependence require varying levels of coordination between units. The need for coordination is quite low under conditions of pooled interdepen-

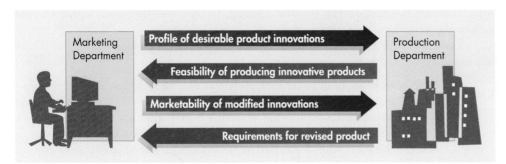

FIGURE 15.11

Reciprocal Interdependence: An Example

Under conditions of *reciprocal interdependence*, the output of two or more departments serves as the input for each other in a reciprocal fashion.

(*Source*: Based on suggestions by Thompson, 1967; see note 50.)

dence, because each department is relatively independent. Rules and standard operating procedures usually suffice. In contrast, sequential interdependence requires substantially greater coordination; formal meetings and vertical communication often are needed. Finally, reciprocal interdependence requires concerted efforts at coordination, including many meetings and a high level of horizontal communication.

The level of interdependence between various units of an organization also has important implications for that organization's internal structure. In organizational design, special attention should be directed to reciprocally interdependent departments or units, which should be grouped together so they can engage in continuous, mutual adjustment (e.g., they should be close to each other physically and fall under the authority of the same person). Specific mechanisms for ensuring a high degree of coordination between them (e.g., daily meetings, creation of special liaison positions) also should be developed. Top priority in devising internal structure should be given to reciprocal interdependence, but efforts to establish effective communication between sequentially interdependent units are important, too. These units should have ready access to one another so that work flow between them can proceed in a smooth and orderly manner. (For an example of how this is accomplished at FedEx, see the "Case in Point" section at the end of this chapter.)

In summary, the kind of work activities performed in an organization and the specific technologies it employs often determine the level of interdependence between its various units. In turn, such interdependence should be considered carefully when planning internal structure. (You may note that the various theories linking technology and structure fail to address the most modern technologies—those used in many of today's high-tech firms. For a discussion of the special organizational design considerations relevant to such firms, see the "Tips" section below.)

■ **Flexibility: The Key to Designing Successful High-Tech Organizations**

**TIPS:
DOING IT RIGHT**

It's no secret to anyone looking for a job that most of today's growth lies in high-tech fields such as telecommunications, hardware and software design, and systems analysis. Organizations specializing in these and other high-tech areas are springing up all over the world.

In many ways, these are not ordinary organizations. Their products have short life cycles (e.g., how long did you have your computer before it was replaced with a more powerful—and less expensive—model?), new products are introduced rapidly, markets change rapidly, and narrow windows of opportunity must be met. A successful product can bring rapid growth, which in turn can be eclipsed by a competitor's technical breakthrough. Thus, today's successful company can be tomorrow's bankruptcy case. In this "boom or bust" world, orderly growth and carefully considered

continued

organizational designs are just dreams. Instead, today's well-designed, high-tech firm is sporting *flexibility*—and plenty of it.

How are these high-tech firms designed to make them so highly flexible? There appear to be several key characteristics[51]:

1. High-tech firms tend to be extremely flat and have *little or no vertical hierarchy*. Because their world moves so rapidly, there is no time for the slow responses associated with seeking decisions from higher up. Instead, high-tech firms are akin to a *federation* or a *constellation* of independent business units that rely on each other for expertise, with a core leadership that orchestrates a broad strategic vision. As one high-tech executive described management's mission, it is "to support our business units in fulfilling their business goals, and perform the truly corporate services in an effective and cost efficient manner."[52] This idea that management operates as a service to the employees is typical of many high-tech firms—even very large ones, such as Apple Computer.

2. In high-tech firms, *organizational designs change frequently*. A design that works when a company is small and makes few products might be less effective when it is large and makes many. For example, consider ROLM, a telecommunications firm that operated as an independent company from 1969 to 1984 (when it was acquired by IBM). During its 15 years of existence, this company had four different organizational designs, including functional (in 1973, when revenues were only $3.6 million), divisional (in 1977, when revenues were $30 million), and various combinations of these and other designs (in the 1980s, when revenues were in hundreds of millions of dollars). ROLM's ever-changing size and technology necessitated a bewildering evolution of designs during its lifetime.

3. Competitive pressures to reduce costs have *blurred the distinction between line and staff functions*. Thus, instead of some specialists merely advising others (i.e., the traditional staff function) and others having the power to make decisions based on that advice (i.e., the traditional line function), use of teams in many high-tech work groups gives decision-making power to those individuals who need to take action.

4. Instead of dividing jobs into specific, predetermined roles and formal hierarchical relationships, many high-tech firms are characterized by *informal networks and relationships*. Continuous changes makes institutionalized roles and positions impractical. Instead, informal groupings of people based on the knowledge and skills they bring to the task determines how people work together and what they do.

High-quality performance in today's high-tech firms—or even their existence, for that matter—demands previously unheard of levels of flexibility, agility, and versatility. Key among the adjustments required to succeed in this environment is a willingness to change one's traditional thinking about organizational design. In this rapidly changing, "anything goes" environment, anything tying employees to a traditional, rigid organizational form goes down the tubes. ■

We invite you to visit the Greenberg page on the Prentice Hall Web site at: **www.prenhall.com/greenberg** for the monthly Greenberg update and for this chapter's World Wide Web exercise.

1. **Define** *technology*.
   Technology refers to the physical and mental processes used to transform inputs into usable outputs. Simply put, technology deals with the activities, equipment, and knowledge used to get things done.

2. **Describe Perrow's** *matrix of technologies*.
   Perrow's **matrix of technologies** identifies two dimensions of technology: reliance on exceptions (i.e., the degree to which an organization uses standard inputs to produce standard outputs), and difficulty of problems (i.e., the degree to which situations encountered are either easy or difficult to analyze). Combining high and low levels of these dimensions results in four different technologies: **routine technology** (i.e., few exceptions/easy problems), **craft technology** (i.e., few exceptions/difficult problems), **engineering technology** (i.e., many exceptions/easy problems), and **nonroutine technology** (i.e., many exceptions/difficult problems).

3. **Describe the various ways people respond to** *automation* **on the job.**
   Automation generally reduces the number of people required to perform jobs but also creates many new, highly challenging, white-collar jobs.

4. **Explain** *assistive technology*, **and describe how it is being used in organizations.**
   Assistive technology refers to using technology to help individuals with physical or mental problems perform the various actions needed on their jobs. It may involve high-tech solutions (e.g., using computer-aided speech) or simple solutions (e.g., lowering door handles). Such efforts are stimulated by both law (e.g., the Americans with Disabilities Act) and economic forces (e.g., the need to attract and retain qualified employees, who happen to be disabled).

5. **Describe** *computerized performance monitoring* **and its effects on people.**
   Computerized performance monitoring (CPM) refers to using technology to observe and to record the performance of employees, particularly those working at computer terminals. This practice may improve performance, but it also creates stress and generally is disliked by employees.

6. **Identify how technology has been used to improve customer service.**
   Technology is used to enhance the delivery of more personalized service (e.g., providing customized coupons at the supermarket check-out), to augment service (e.g., giving faster check-out service by auto-rental companies), and to transform business (e.g., offering computer-matched paint colors).

7. **Explain how** *design for disassembly* **is used to protect the physical environment.**
   Design for disassembly (DFD) is the process of designing and building products so their parts can be used several times and then safely disposed of at the end of the product's life. This involves using fewer parts, fewer materials, and assembly processes that ensure easy disassembly later.

8. **Describe the connection between technology, organizational design, and performance.**
   Organic organizations (i.e., those in which authority is decentralized and diffused throughout the organization) are most effective when performing small-batch production jobs (e.g., custom work) and continuous-process production jobs (e.g., fully automated work). Mechanistic organizations (i.e., those in which authority is centralized in a few people), however, are most effective when performing large-batch production jobs (e.g., assembly line work).

577

9. **Explain *work-flow integration* and how it influences organizational performance.**

   Work-flow integration is the degree to which an organization employs automation, rigid task sequences, and quantitative measurement of operations. A high degree of work-flow integration is associated with high performance more strongly in smaller organizations than in larger ones.

10. **Describe *interdependence* and its connection to organizational design.**

    Interdependence refers to the extent to which individuals, departments, or units in a given organization depend on each other in accomplishing their tasks. Under conditions of low interdependence, each person, unit, or group can perform its functions without assistance or input from others. Under conditions of high interdependence, however, such coordination is essential.

QUESTIONS FOR DISCUSSION

1. Identify three jobs with which you are highly familiar. Name the type of technology each uses as described by Perrow's matrix of technologies. Explain your answers.

2. Your company is planning to automate some processes now performed completely without intervention by machines. How would you expect the employees to respond?

3. Suppose you oversee a department of telemarketers and you have the opportunity to monitor their performance using the computer. Would you recommend doing so? What problems would you expect to encounter with computerized performance monitoring, and how might these be overcome?

4. Explain at least two ways in which technology can enhance the performance of any job you routinely perform.

5. How might assistive technology, design for disassembly, or machine vision be applied to any work process with which you are familiar?

6. Describe the relationship between technology and organizational structure as you have seen it in any organization with which you are familiar. How does this compare with the relationships described in the text?

7. For any job you know well, describe the type of interdependence that exists. Explain how this interdependence is appropriate or inappropriate for the design of the organization in which it is used.

Case in Point

FedEx: A Study in High Tech, Low Tech, and No Tech

Every day, FedEx pulls off what appears to be a logistical miracle. Using 37,000 vans and more than 550 airplanes, it delivers some three million packages to destinations in 211 countries. It also does this better than anyone else — so well, in fact, that it takes in approximately $10 billion annually. None of this would be possible, of course, without technology.

As you might expect, FedEx relies on the latest "whiz-bang" technologies to get the job done. No doubt, you've seen the optically read digits on their airbills, and you even may have used their sophisticated customer-service web site to track shipments on your own computer. What you don't see, however, also is very high tech. For example, FedEx uses the latest navigation devices to direct its planes to appropriate airports. FedEx even maintains its own staff of meterologists, who provide information to managers so they can plan accordingly for weather conditions.

Weather is always an issue, and appropriate planning is key to not letting it become a problem. A foot of snow may be on the ground in Detroit or a desert windstorm swirling in Tucson, but customers are unlikely to care about these problems when their packages don't arrive on time. After all, says FedEx Vice-president Roger Podwoski, you don't get a second chance "when the life cycle of your relationship with a customer is anywhere from 15 to 17 hours," adding that "customer service is all we have." So, this company goes out of its way to plan accordingly.

One day, for example, when FedEx's Memphis hub — through which all packages pass — was fogged in, 100 planes were diverted to surrounding airports. No amount of high-tech gadgetry was going to help. What the company did was simple — if you have the resources, at least. It called in 5,000 employees and had them drive to those surrounding airports, retrieve the packages, and get them to Memphis for processing. The technologies used obviously were not the most high tech — telephones, trucks, and lots (and lots) of people were called on to come to the rescue. As far as the customers were concerned, however, there was no behind-the-scenes problem at all. Each of these packages was just another shipment.

Holding this entire operation together is the Daily Operations Review, a fast-paced, hour-long overview of overnight performance. Each weekday at 5:00 A.M. sharp, a taped voice-mail message is made available that summarizes the previous night's performance. Between 15 and 30 representatives from various company departments (e.g., air operations, customer service, computer systems) check these messages before assembling — either in person or via conference call — with the company's Global Operations Control and Coordination Group chairs. This gives them time to review any problems they'll need to discuss at the meeting.

Using a military-style checklist, the coordinator at this meeting calls on representatives from each department. That individual then reports the status of operations in his or her area and announces any problems that may exist. If there is a problem, a plan is put into place, right then and there, to fix it — and at FedEx, it's not just talk. The plan is always carried out meticulously.

CRITICAL THINKING QUESTIONS

1. What types of technologies are used in the operations described here?

2. How do you think FedEx employees are likely to respond to these technologies? Would you expect them to be comfortable with them? Why, or why not?

3. Based on this case, what characteristics of organizational design would support the technology used at FedEx?

VIDEO CASE

Technology in Organizations

David Arnold, the founder of the King Company, tells us how he used technology to help solve a problem. Arnold says that he was "selling a lot of watches, that wasn't the problem, we just weren't making any money at it." The King Company has found that properly managed and maintained information systems can be at the heart of a company's success. The sole U.S. distributor for the Lorus line of Seiko watches, the King Company employs about 60 people and has annual sales in excess of $50 million. Customers include retailers as large as Wal-Mart and as small as your corner drug store.

How does information management fit into the King Company's operation? Not only does the company use its information systems to improve its own business performance, it interacts electronically with most of its customers. Approximately 95 percent of all

(continued)

communication, from taking an order to final payment, is handled electronically; little or no human intervention is needed. In addition, because the company has a direct electronic interface with its customers, orders, inquiries, billing, and even payment can be done without a single piece of paper being generated. The King Company also uses its information as a marketing tool. The company not only tracks what it has sold to its customers but also, in some cases, monitors its customers' sales on a daily basis. The knowledge from this activity supports short-term needs such as ordering and production planning, but it also has longer-range value. Over time, the company can track product trends and make decisions regarding product-line development based on real market input.

Companies today must deal with many issues when it comes to information and information management. You might think a simple solution is to collect everything you can and save it. On the surface, this may make sense, but think about it for a minute. How useful is information if it is not organized, if it is not stored in an easy-to-retrieve manner, if it cannot be accessed in a timely manner, and if no one has a real use for it? Remember, having volumes of useless information is not nearly as valuable as having a small pile that actually means something.

QUESTIONS FOR DISCUSSION

1. David Arnold added staff to manage information and technology in the early stages of the King Company's relationship with Seiko. What are some advantages and disadvantages of adding computer and information management processes early in a company's development?

2. You have learned about Perrow's two-dimensional matrix of technology. Considering this model, discuss the technology(s) in play at the King Company. Did you identify a single technology type, or did you identify several?

3. The King Company's operation was not always automated. How do you think David Arnold's employees feel about this automation? Use some examples from the video, and consider both valuable and threatening aspects of automation, in developing your answer.

4. The King Company collects information about its customers and the final purchasers of its products. Are there any ethical issues in establishing such information transfers between vendors and customers? Why, or why not?

SKILLS BANK

EXPERIENCING ORGANIZATIONAL BEHAVIOR

What Is Your Customer Service Orientation?

As noted, technology can enhance the quality of an organization's customer service. So long as people are still involved in the process, however, no technology — however sophisticated — will counter the effects of a poor attitude toward customer service. The following exercise is designed to help you understand your own orientation toward customer service.

Directions

Answer the following questions as honestly as possible. Use the following scale:

    1 = not at all
    2 = slightly
    3 = moderately
    4 = greatly
    5 = extremely

In general, to what extent . . .

_____ 1. Do your customers think of you as being honest and sincere?

_____ 2. Would your customers think of you as being reliable?

_____ 3. Would your customers choose to deal with you if they could deal with someone else?

_____ 4. Do your clients believe you take their best interests into consideration?

_____ 5. Do you handle customers' complaints in a satisfactory fashion?

_____ 6. Do you enjoy solving your customer's problems?

_____ 7. Are you considered to be a good source of information about the products or industry you represent?

_____ 8. Do you receive positive comments from your customers?

_____ 9. Are you interested in your customers getting the best possible deal?

_____ 10. Do you want your customers to be pleased they have been dealing with you?

Scoring

Add your individual responses to these questions. They will range from 10 through 50. Higher scores, particularly those greater than 40, reflect higher degrees of self-perceived customer-service orientation.

Questions for Discussion

1. What did this questionnaire tell you about your customer-service orientation?

2. Do you think other people would rate you the same way?

3. How did your customer-service orientation compare with those of others in the class?

4. How might technology enhance your approach to customer service?

SKILLS BANK

WORKING IN GROUPS

Identifying Types of Technology

This exercise will help you to recognize the different types of technologies when you find them.

Directions

1. Gather together a stack of recent, business-related newspapers and periodicals (e.g., *Wall Street Journal*, *Fortune*, *Business Week*). Give one issue to each student in the class.

2. Working by yourself, thumb through the newspaper or periodical you were given. When you find a story about a company, clip it out and read it. Then, based on what you read, classify the company into one of the four types of technologies identified by Perrow.

3. Assemble around a circle in small groups. Each group member should describe the company he or she selected.

4. After hearing the description, the other group members should identify the type of technology that company is using.

Questions for Discussion

1. Was there general agreement or disagreement about how the various companies should be classified?

2. What types of companies were easiest to classify? What types were most difficult?

3. What types of technologies were found most often? What types were found least often?

MANAGING ORGANIZATIONAL CHANGE: STRATEGIC PLANNING AND ORGANIZATIONAL DEVELOPMENT

LEARNING OBJECTIVES

After reading this chapter, you should be able to

1. Characterize the prevalence of the change process in organizations.
2. Understand what occurs during *organizational change* and the forces responsible for unplanned organizational change.
3. Describe *strategic planning*, and explain the types of strategic changes that organizations make.
4. Identify the 10 steps in the *strategic planning* process.
5. Explain why people resist organizational change and how this resistance may be overcome.
6. Identify and describe the major *organizational development* techniques in use today.
7. Identify both sides of the debate regarding whether organizational development is inherently unethical.

PREVIEW CASE

Lockheed Martin: A Survival Story

For most companies, the loss of even a few percentage points is considered to be a notable setback, so imagine the catastrophe of losing 60 percent of your business! That was precisely the situation in which Lockheed Corp., one of the world's largest aerospace companies, found itself in 1989. The reasons were clear: The end of the Cold War brought the U.S. government's spending on national defense to a standstill. At the same time, severe budget cuts at NASA and losses in the airline industry affected spending on aerospace as well. To say this left Lockheed in turmoil would be an understatement. To put it bluntly, the company was fighting for its life.

A decade later, Lockheed not only has survived, but with sales tripling from $10 billion to $30 billion, it is thriving. What is the basis of this survival story? First, in 1995, Lockheed joined forces with Martin Marietta Corp. to become Lockheed Martin. The idea was simple enough: Each company had some technical expertise the other did not, thus making a friendly merger a wise choice. This strategy appears to have worked, gaining Lockheed Martin a larger share of the markets in which both companies did business. In fact, Lockheed Martin is now the world-leader in building satellites and the U.S.-leader in launching spacecraft. It also is the largest provider for the U.S. Department of Defense, Department of Energy, and NASA.

Survival was based on restructuring to trim costs as well. By restructuring its workforce, Lockheed Martin reduced its plant space by 16 million square feet and its workforce by 100,000 people, thereby saving $2.6 billion annually. You can save only so much money by cutting production costs, however. Ultimately, what matters most is getting as much as possible out of the people who remain with the company. During the 1980s, when Lockheed had more business than it could handle, there was little incentive for Lockheed executives to manage smartly. Today, however, smart management is the key to Lockheed's success — and to its survival.

Lockheed Martin officials, therefore, have focused on eliminating layers of the corporate hierarchy, thus pushing decision making down the organization chart. As chairman and CEO Norman R. Augustine says, the company strives "to delegate most decision making to the lowest level at which a considered judgment can be made." For example, when NASA challenged Lockheed Martin to cut the weight of the space shuttle's fuel tank, the engineers came up 800 pounds short. No one could figure out how to shed the extra weight. Finally, an assembly line worker came up with a solution: stop painting the tank. In fact, the tank was so big that all the white paint added 800 pounds. The problem was solved not through any engineering genius but because an assembly worker was empowered to offer a solution.

Lockheed Martin officials do even more to keep the company ahead of the pack. For example, Mr. Augustine and other top executives keep an open line of communication with the company's 200,000 employees. By doing so, they hope to keep employees focused on their jobs by dispelling rumors about the company's future.

It is not only employees that Lockheed Martin strives to keep happy, however, but customers as well. For example, years ago, it was not unusual for electronics kits shipped from the company's facility in Orlando, Florida, to be missing parts. Today, a sheet of paper is packaged with each kit containing the names and phone numbers of the workers who prepared it. Missing parts are now a thing of the past.

T here can be little doubt that Lockheed Martin has changed radically. Then again, to survive, it had no choice. As Charles Darwin put it, "It is not the strongest of the species that survives, nor the most intelligent, it is the one that is most adaptable to change." Indeed, the changes at Lockheed Martin have been dramatic, but this experience is far from unique in the world of business. Think of the many changes in how businesses operate in recent years. Clearly, change has become the rule rather than the exception. For example, commerce over the Internet now occurs regularly, and small companies in most fields (especially auto manufacturers and banks) have been consolidating at a breathtaking rate. In fact, mergers are so common it now is almost impossible for old-fashioned, small, "mom and pop" businesses to stay afloat (Figure 16.1).

To say the impact of *organizational change* can be found everywhere is an understatement. To understand this important process, we examine it from several key perspectives in this chapter. First, we describe the nature of this process, including the forces that require organizations to change. Then, we focus on changes that are more

FIGURE 16.1

Organizational Change Takes a Toll on Small Business

Small, privately held businesses frequently are casualties of today's megamerger mania. Those "mom and pop" operations that manage to survive are likely to be bought out eventually by larger competitors.

(*Source*: © The New Yorker Collection 1994. Roz Chast from cartoonbank.com. All Rights Reserved.)

deliberate and describe what is known as *strategic planning*, which involves deliberately making radical changes in how an organization operates.

As you might imagine, most people have difficulty accepting they may have to change the people they work with and even the basic nature of their jobs. After all, if you're accustomed to working a certain way, sudden change can be very unsettling. In other words, for various reasons, people resist change. Fortunately, however, such resistance can be overcome. With this in mind, social scientists have developed various methods, which are known collectively as *organizational development* techniques, to implement needed organizational change in a manner that is acceptable to employees and that enhances the effectiveness of the organization.

THE PREVALENCE OF CHANGE IN ORGANIZATIONS

A century ago, advances in machine technology made farming so efficient that fewer hands were needed to plant the fields and to reap the harvest. The displaced laborers fled to nearby cities and sought jobs in newly opened factories—opportunities created by some of the same technologies that sent them away from their farms. The economy shifted thus from agrarian to manufacturing, and the Industrial Revolution began. With it also came drastic shifts in where people lived, how they worked, how they spent their leisure time, how much money they made, and how they spent it.

Today's business analysts claim we currently are experiencing *another* such revolution, driven by a new wave of economic and technological forces. As one observer put it, "This workplace revolution . . . may be remembered as a historic event, the Western equivalent of the collapse of communism."[1]

The Message Is Clear: Change or Disappear!

The business landscape is not the same as it was just a few years ago. Consider the auto industry: Recently, Volvo merged with Ford, and Chrysler merged with Daimler-Benz, the manufacturer of the Mercedes-Benz (Figure 16.2). The Volkswagen Beetle has even re-emerged. In banking, things are more extreme: Almost every small bank has been gobbled-up by a large bank in recent years—and the largest now are joining forces. No industry, no organization is immune. Change is everywhere. Those companies that fail to change when required find themselves out of business as a result.[2] In fact, in one study, support among senior managers for **organizational change** was a characteristic distinguishing the most successful organizations, in which such support occurred 94 percent of the time, from other organizations, in which such support occurred only 76 percent of the time.[3]

organizational change

Planned or unplanned transformations in an organization's structure, technology, or people.

This is important, because business failure is the rule rather than the exception. Fully 62 percent of all new ventures fail within five years, and only two percent survive as long as 50 years.[4] Thus, it is particularly impressive that some U.S. companies have beaten the odds so soundly that they have remained in business for more than 200 years (see Table 16.1 for a summary of these "corporate Methuselahs").[5] As you might imagine, these companies have undergone *many* changes during their existence. For example, the oldest U.S. company, J. E. Rhoads & Sons, now makes conveyer belts, but when it began in 1702, it made buggy whips. Another company, Dexter, in Windsor Locks, Connecticut, began in 1767 as a grist mill; it now makes adhesives and coatings for aircraft. Earlier, it manufactured specialty papers for stationery and for tea bags. Obviously, this company is very willing to change. According to Dexter spokesperson Ellen Cook, "We have no traditions, whatsoever. None."[6]

first-order change

Change that is continuous in nature and involves no major shifts in how an organization operates.

First-Order Change   As you might imagine, the changes that organizations make differ in scope. Some are minor, whereas others are major. Change that is continuous in nature and involves no major shifts in how an organization operates is known as **first-order change**. Changes of this type are apparent in the deliberate, incremental modifications Toyota has made in continuously improving the efficiency of its production process.[7] Similarly, a restaurant makes first-order changes as it gradually adds new items to its menu and gauges their success before completely revamping its concept.

second-order change

Radical change; major shifts involving many different levels of the organization and aspects of business.

Second-Order Change   As you might imagine, however, other types of organizational change are far more complex. **Second-order change** refers to more radical change, to major shifts involving many different levels of the organization and many different aspects of business.[8] For example, General Electric, Allied Signal, Ameritech, and Tenneco recently have radically altered the ways they operate, their culture, the technology they use, their structure, and the nature of their relations with employees.[9] The preview case about Lockheed Martin is another excellent example of second-order change.

FIGURE 16.2

The $94 Billion Deal of the Decade

Long considered to be one of the world's most prestigious—and expensive—cars Mercedes-Benz vehicles have never sold at high volumes. Facing losses of $3.5 billion in 1995, Jurgen Schrempp, CEO of the company that manufactures Mercedes-Benz automobiles, realized that staying ahead of the game required boosting sales dramatically. Soon thereafter, Schrempp masterminded a merger with U.S. automaker Chrysler—a megamerger that redefined the international nature of the auto business. Profits for the new Daimler-Chrysler were $2.6 billion in 1998.

TABLE 16.1

The 10 Oldest Companies in America

Very few companies continue to exist as long as the ones shown here. As you might expect, all have undergone considerable changes in their 200 to 300 years.

RANK	YEAR FOUNDED	NAME	CURRENT BUSINESS
1	1702	J. E. Rhoads & Sons	Conveyer belts
2	1717	Covenant Life Insurance	Insurance
3	1752	Philadelphia Contributorship	Insurance
4	1767	Dexter	Adhesives and coatings
5	1784	D. Landreth Seed	Seeds
6	1784	Bank of New York	Banking
7	1784	Mutual Assurance	Insurance
8	1784	Bank of Boston	Banking
9	1789	George R. Ruhl & Sons	Bakery supplies
10	1790	Burns & Russell	Building materials

Source: Reprinted from the July 26, 1993 issue of *FORTUNE* by special permission; copyright 1993, Time Inc.

Change Is a Global Phenomenon

Interestingly, the forces for organizational change are not isolated to the United States. In fact, they appear to be global in nature. Consider a survey of 12,000 managers in 25 different countries conducted a few years ago.[10] When asked to identify the changes they have experienced in the past two years, these managers reported major restructuring, mergers, divestitures and acquisitions, reductions in employment, and international expansion in their organizations.

Figure 16.3 on page 588 shows the percentage reporting each of these activities in six selected nations. Some forms of change were more common in some countries than others, but organizations in all countries were actively involved in each of these efforts. This suggests organizational change is occurring throughout the world. Different forces may be shaping change at different rates in different places, but change is a universal fact of life for organizations.

THE NATURE OF THE CHANGE PROCESS

Given that change is so common, it is important to understand the basic nature of the process. Thus, we turn our attention to two key questions: What, exactly, is changed when organizational change occurs, and what forces are responsible for unplanned organizational change?

Targets: What Is Changed?

Imagine you are an engineer responsible for overseeing the maintenance of a large office building. The property manager has noted a dramatic increase in use of the heating system, thereby causing operating costs to skyrocket. In other words, a need for change exists—specifically, a reduction in the building's heat usage. You cannot get the power company to lower its rates, so you recognize you must change the use of heat.

One possible solution is to rearrange job responsibilities so that only maintenance personnel are permitted to adjust the thermostats. Another option is to put timers on all thermostats so the building temperature is lowered automatically during periods of non-use. You also might put stickers next to the thermostats that request occupants do not adjust them. These options are good examples of the three

FIGURE 16.3

Organizational Change: An International Phenomenon

A large, cross-national survey found that various forms of organizational change occur throughout the world. Shown here are the percentages of respondents in six countries who indicated that each of four different forms of change occurred in organizations within their country during the past two years. Major restructuring was the most widely encountered form of change in most countries.

(*Source*: Based on data reported by Kanter, 1991; see note 10.)

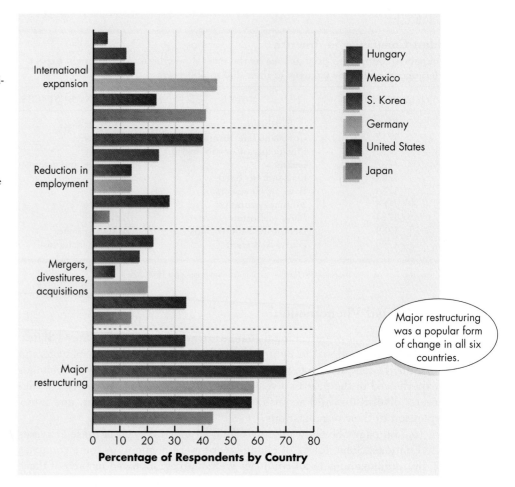

potential targets of organizational change that we consider: changes in *organizational structure*, *technology*, and *people* (Figure 16.4).

Changes in Organizational Structure   In chapter 14, we described the key characteristics of organizational structure; here, we note that altering an organization's structure may be a reasonable way of responding to a need for change. In our example, a structural solution to the heat-regulation problem comes in the form of reassigning job responsibilities. Indeed, modifying rules, responsibilities, and procedures may be an effective way to manage change. Changing the responsibility for temperature regulation from a highly decentralized system (i.e., anyone can make adjustments) to a centralized one (i.e., only maintenance personnel may do so) is one way of implementing organizational change in response to this problem. This particular structural solution called for changing the power structure (i.e., who is in charge of a particular task).

Different types of structural changes, however, may take other forms. For example, changes can be made to an organization's span of control, thereby altering the number of employees for whom supervisors are responsible. Structural changes also may take the form of revising the basis for creating departments, such as from product-based departments to functional departments. Still other structural changes may be much simpler, such as clarifying someone's job description or the written policies and procedures to be followed.

Changes in Technology   In our example, one possible solution is to use thermostats that automatically reduce the building's temperature when not in use. This is an example of a technological approach. Placement of regulating devices on the thermostats

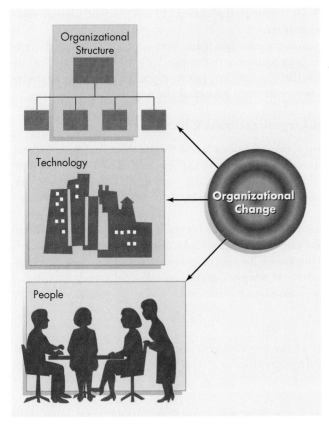

FIGURE 16.4

Organizational Change Targets: Structure, Technology, and People

To create change in organizations, one can rely on altering organizational structure, technology, or people. Changes in any one of these areas may necessitate changes in the others.

that would thwart attempts to raise the temperature also is possible. In addition, the thermostats could be encased in a locked box — or even removed altogether. A new, modern, energy-efficient furnace could be installed in the building as well. All of these suggestions represent technological approaches to the need for change.

Changes in People You've probably seen stickers next to light switches in hotels asking guests to turn off the lights when not in use. These are similar to our suggestion of affixing signs near thermostats asking occupants to refrain from adjusting them. Such efforts represent attempts to respond to the needed organizational change by altering how people behave. The basic assumption is that the effectiveness of organizations depends on the behavior of people working in them.

As you might imagine, changing people is not easy. Indeed, this process lies at the core of most of the topics discussed in this book. Theorists have identified three basic steps, however, that summarize what is involved in changing people.

The first step is known as *unfreezing*, which refers to the process of recognizing that the current state of affairs is undesirable. The realization that change is needed may be the result of some serious organizational crisis or threat (e.g., serious financial loss, strike, major lawsuit) or of growing awareness that current conditions are unacceptable (e.g., antiquated equipment, inadequately trained employees).

Some executives have gotten employees to accept the need to change while things are still good by creating a sense of urgency. They introduce the idea of an impending crisis although conditions are, in fact, currently acceptable. This approach is referred to as **doomsday management,** and it effectively unfreezes people, thereby stimulating change before it is too late to do any good.

After unfreezing, *changing* may occur. This step is some planned attempt to create a more desirable state for the organization and its members. Attempts at change may be quite ambitious (e.g., an organization-wide restructuring) or quite minor (e.g.,

doomsday management

The practice of introducing change by suggesting an impending crisis is likely.

a change in a training program). (A thorough discussion of such planned-change techniques is presented later in this chapter.)

Finally, *refreezing* occurs when the changes made are incorporated into the employees' thinking and into the organization's operations (e.g., mechanisms for rewarding behaviors that maintain the changes are put in place). Hence, the new attitudes and behaviors become a new, enduring aspect of the organizational system.

Forces Behind Unplanned Organizational Change

As technology and markets change, organizations face a formidable challenge. Indeed, organizations also must be responsive to changes that are unplanned. These can include changes in the demographic composition of the workforce, performance gaps, government regulation, and international competition.

Shifting Employee Demographics   It is easy to see how the composition of the workforce has changed—even within your own lifetime. As noted in chapter 1, the U.S. workforce now is more diverse than ever. To people concerned with the long-term operation of organizations, these are not simply curious sociological trends but rather shifting conditions that force organizations to change.

GLOBAL MATTERS   Racial and ethnic diversification of the workforce is occurring throughout the world. Accordingly, shifting employee demographics is a force for change in all nations, not just the United States. ▪

Questions regarding, for example, how many people will be working, what skills they will bring to their jobs, and what new influences they will bring to the workplace are of key interest to human-resources managers. In the words of Frank Doyle, corporate vice president for external and industrial relations at General Electric, the impending changes in workforce demographics "will turn the professional human-resources world upside down."[11]

Performance Gaps   If you ever heard the phrase "If it's not broken, don't fix it," you already have a good feel for one of the most potent sources of unplanned, internal changes in organizations—that is, *performance gaps*. A product line that is not moving, a vanishing profit margin, a level of sales that is not up to corporate expectations—these are all examples of gaps between real and expected levels of organizational performance.

Few things force change more than sudden and unexpected information about poor performance. Organizations usually stay with a winning course of action, and they usually change in response to failure. Indeed, a performance gap is a key factor providing an impetus for organizational innovation. Those organizations that are best prepared to mobilize change in response to unexpected downturns can be expected to succeed.

Government Regulation   One of the most commonly witnessed unplanned organizational changes results from government regulation. During the late 1980s, U.S. restaurant owners had to alter how they reported the income of waiters and waitresses to the federal government for the purpose of collecting income taxes. More recently, the U.S. government has imposed as well as eliminated regulations in industries such as commercial airlines (e.g., mandating inspection schedules but no longer controlling fares) and banking (e.g., restricting the amount of time checks can be held before clearing but no longer regulating interest rates). Such activities have influenced greatly how these industries conduct business.

If you want to know more, just ask Microsoft's CEO and founder, Bill Gates, about the U.S. government's influence on his company. As you probably know, there has been an on-going anti-trust case against Microsoft, with federal government alleging the company has a monopoly on fundamental aspects of the personal computer business (Figure 16.5). Regardless of the outcome, the government's hand clearly will force changes in that industry.

ETHICS MATTERS

Do you think it is ethically appropriate for governments to intervene in business operations, ostensibly to help and to protect the population? Do you think businesses should be free to operate without government intervention? If so, how would the interests of citizens be protected? ▪

Global Economic Competition   It happens every day: Someone builds a better mousetrap — or, at least, a cheaper one. As a result, companies often must fight to maintain their market share, advertise more effectively, and produce goods less expensively. This kind of economic competition not only forces organizations to change but also demands they change effectively if they are to survive.

Competition always has been crucial to organizational success, but today, competition comes from all over the world. As it has become increasingly less expensive to transport materials, the industrialized nations have found themselves competing with each other for market share in nations throughout the world. This extensive economic globalization presents a strong challenge to change and to innovate. For example, consider how the large U.S. automobile manufacturers suffered from being unprepared to meet the world's growing demand for small, high-quality cars — products their Japanese competitors were only too glad to supply. With this rapidly changing growth in globalization, one thing is certain: Only the most adaptive organizations can survive.

Advances in Technology   As described in chapter 15, advances in technology have changed how organizations operate. For example, senior scientists and engineers probably can tell you how their work altered drastically in the mid-1970s, when plastic slide rules gave way to powerful pocket calculators. Things changed again a decade later, when pocket calculators in turn were supplanted by powerful desktop microcomputers, which have revolutionized how documents are prepared, transmitted, and filed in an office.

Today, powerful hand-held devices make portable, wireless communication a reality, further changing how work is done. Companies that once thought of jumping

FIGURE 16.5

Governmental Intervention: A Force for Change

Microsoft Corporation's CEO Bill Gates is defending his company against charges from the U.S. Department of Justice that the company has monopolized certain aspects of the personal computer business. The disposition of this case will go a long way toward determining the future not only of this business but of all businesses in general.

on the technology bandwagon simply to gain competitive advantage quickly found doing so actually was a requirement just to stay in the game. Technology also has made it possible for people to develop new, web-based businesses with only limited start-up capital. Businesses started by *Internet entrepreneurs* were unheard of only a few years ago (Figure 16.6).

STRATEGIC PLANNING: DELIBERATE CHANGE

strategic planning

The process of formulating, implementing, and evaluating decisions that enable an organization to achieve its objectives.

Thus far, we have described unplanned organizational change, but not all changes that organizations make fall into this category. Indeed, organizations also make changes that are carefully planned and deliberate. This is the idea of **strategic planning,** which we define as the process of formulating, implementing, and evaluating decisions that enable an organization to achieve its objectives.[12]

Basic Assumptions About Strategic Planning

To understand the nature of strategic plans used in organizations today, it is important to highlight three fundamental assumptions about them.[13]

Strategic Planning Is Deliberate   When organizations make strategic plans, they make conscious decisions to change fundamental aspects of themselves. These changes tend to be radical (e.g., changing the nature of the business) rather than minor (e.g., changing the color of the office walls) in nature.[14] These changes also may be inspired by any of several factors, such as new competitors, new technologies, and the like.

Strategic Planning Occurs When Current Objectives No Longer Can Be Met   Generally, when a company's present strategy is bringing about the desired results, change is unlikely. When it becomes clear the current objectives no longer can be met, however, new strategies are formulated to turn things around.

New Organizational Objectives Require New Strategic Plans   Whenever a company takes steps to move in a completely new direction, it establishes new objectives—and it designs a strategic plan to meet them. Acknowledging that the various parts of an organization are interdependent, this new strategic plan is likely to involve all functions and levels of the organization. Moreover, it requires adequate resources from throughout the organization to succeed.

To illustrate how these assumptions come to life, we now describe some examples of strategic plans for change.

About What Do Companies Make Strategic Plans?

As you might imagine, organizations can make strategic plans to change just about anything. Most of the strategic planning today, however, involves changing either a company's products and services or its organizational structure.

Products and Services   Imagine you and a friend have a small janitorial business. The two of you divide the duties, each doing some cleaning, buying of supplies, and some administrative work. Before long, the business grows. You expand, add new employees, and really start "cleaning up." Many of your commercial clients express interest in window cleaning, so you and your partner decide to expand into that business as well. This decision to take on a new direction—to add a new, specialized service—will require a fair amount of organizational change. New equipment and supplies will be needed, and new personnel will have to be hired and trained. New insurance must

F I G U R E   1 6 . 6

City Boxers: Shorts in Cyberspace

Betty A. Ford is one of several *Internet entrepreneurs* who have set up small businesses on the World Wide Web. Her company, City Boxers, sells hand-tailored boxer shorts. Although the business currently is small, Ms. Ford hopes to follow many now-large companies that have found financial success in cyberspace.

be purchased as well, just as new accounts will have to be secured. In short, you have made a strategic decision to change the company's line of services—and this necessitates organizational change.

Real companies make such changes all the time. For example, in 1989, Federal Express (now known as FedEx) sought to expand its package-delivery service, which formerly had been limited exclusively to North America, into international markets. Initially, the company faced difficult challenges in this attempt, FedEx's international services now are performing well.

Organizational Structure   Companies make strategic plans about more than just changes in products and services. They also make strategic plans to change their organizational structure. For example, consider the decision by PepsiCo to reorganize.[15] For many years, PepsiCo had a separate, international food-service division, which included 62 foreign locations of the company's Pizza Hut and Taco Bell restaurants. Then, in 1990, because of the great profit potential of these foreign restaurants, PepsiCo officials decided to reorganize, and they put these restaurants under the direct control of the same executives responsible for the successful national operations of Pizza Hut, Kentucky Fried Chicken, and Taco Bell. In 1997, however, PepsiCo made another strategic decision—to get out of the restaurant business—and it spun-off these three restaurants to form a separate company: TRICON Global Restaurants.

Recently, many organizations that struggled to stay competitive have reduced the size and basic configurations of their organizational charts. The process of reducing the number of employees needed to operate effectively is known as **downsizing**. Typically, this involves more than just laying off people to save money. It is directed at adjusting the number of employees needed to work in newly designed organizations, which is why it also has been called **rightsizing**. Whatever it is called, figures from the U.S. Bureau of Labor Statistics reveal the trend toward reducing the size of the workforce reached its peak in 1992 and has been reversing ever since.[16] In fact, levels of new job losses are as low as they have been in more than a decade.

Interestingly, several organizations are finding out they have cut their workforces too deeply—and they are now struggling to re-hire many of the workers they once released. With a strong economy, however, there are many new opportunities, thereby making this a real challenge. With unemployment at its current exceptionally low level, there is a monstrous labor crunch, thus leading some prospective employees to be offered generous salaries and benefits—and even gifts in exchange for interviews (Figure 16.7).

Another way organizations are restructuring is by completely eliminating units that focus on non-core sectors of their business and then hiring outside firms to perform these functions instead, which is a practice known as **outsourcing**. For example, companies like ServiceMaster, which provides janitorial services, and ADP, which provides payroll-processing services, allow organizations to concentrate on the business functions most central to their mission, thereby freeing them from these peripheral, support functions.

Some critics fear outsourcing represents a "hollowing out" of companies—that is, a reduction of functions that weakens organizations by making them more dependent on others. Some counter, however, that outsourcing makes sense when the work is not highly critical to competitive success (e.g., janitorial services) or is so highly critical that success requires outside assistance. If you think outsourcing is an unusual occurrence, think again. One industry analyst has estimated that 30 percent of the largest U.S. industrial films outsource more than half their manufacturing?[17]

The Ten Steps of Strategic Planning

The process of strategic planning typically follows 10 ordered steps, which we now describe.[18] These steps are not immutable, and they are not always followed in perfect order. They do a reasonably good job, however, of describing how companies plan

downsizing
The process of systematically reducing the number of employees required to perform newly restructured jobs.

rightsizing
See *downsizing*.

outsourcing
The practice of eliminating parts of organizations that focus on non-core sectors of the business and hiring outside firms to perform these functions instead.

change strategically. As we describe these, you may find it useful to examine the summary of steps in Figure 16.8.

Define Goals   A strategic plan must begin with a stated goal. Typically, these goals involve a company's market (e.g., gaining certain position within it) or its financial standing (e.g., achieving a certain return on equity). Organizational goals also can involve society (e.g., to benefit certain groups or the environment) or organizational culture (e.g., to make the workplace pleasant).

A company's overall goals must be translated into corresponding goals to be achieved by the various organizational units. For example, suppose a company wants to change its market position from a manufacturer of wholesale machinery to a manufacturer of consumer products. The company identifies reaching 10 percent of the market within the first two years as its strategic goal, which then must be translated into goals for the various departments. The marketing department must have goals for reaching certain consumers in its advertising. Likewise, the production department must have goals for manufacturing certain numbers of products within a specific period of time.

Define the Scope of Products or Services   For a strategic plan to be effective, company officials must define their organization's *scope* — that is, the businesses in which it already operates and the new businesses in which it aims to participate. If the scope is defined too narrowly, the company will overlook opportunities; if the scope is defined too broadly, the company will dilute its effectiveness.

The matter of defining scope involves answering questions about what business a company is in — and what business it could be in. For example, long known for its

FIGURE 16.7

Restructuring Organizations Pay a Premium for Talented Employees

Showered with gifts from prospective employers, these two recently graduated MBA students (*left*) are finding it easy to get excellent jobs in a booming economy. Today's employers are desperate not only to attract qualified new employees but to retain those they already have. This Bell Atlantic line installer (*right*), once the victim of downsizing, was lured back to the company — and is kept working there — by being offered a generous pension.

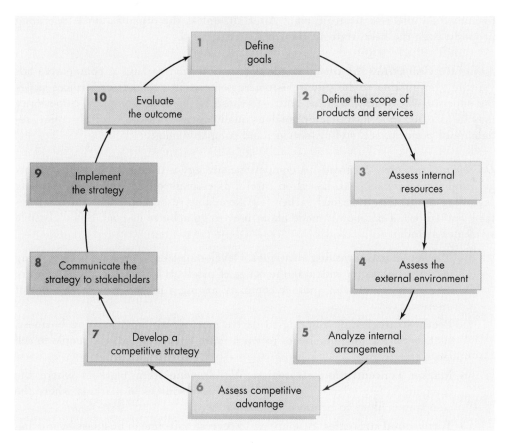

FIGURE 16.8

Strategic Planning: A 10-Step Process

Strategic planning — the process of formulating, implementing, and evaluating decisions that enable an organization to achieve its objectives — generally follows the 10 steps summarized here.

(*Source*: Based on suggestions by Christensen, 1994; see note 18.)

infant food, Beech-Nut faced a challenge created by lowered birthrates and, therefore, a smaller overall market. Then, someone recognized the company's scope could be broadened to include the elderly (i.e., another group with difficulty digesting hard food). Broadening its scope in this manner was a key part of this company's strategic plan for success.[19]

Assess Internal Resources   The question regarding internal resources is: What resources does the company have available to plan and to implement its strategy? The resources in question involve funds (e.g., money to make purchases), physical assets (e.g., required space), and human assets (e.g., workers' knowledge and skills).

Assess the External Environment   As noted throughout this book, organizations do not operate in a vacuum. Rather, they function within environments that influence their capacity to operate and to grow as desired. The extent to which the environment aids or hinders a company's growth — or even its existence — depends on several key factors. Specifically, a company has a competitive advantage over others when its resources cannot easily be imitated by others, its resources will not depreciate anytime soon, and competitors do not have better resources.[20]

Analyze Internal Arrangements   By "internal arrangements," we refer to the nature of the organization itself (as identified by the characteristics described in this book). For example, are employees paid in a way that motivates them to strive for corporate goals (see chapter 4)? Does the organizational culture encourage people to be innovative and to make changes, or does it encourage them to be stagnant (see chapter 13)? Do people communicate with each other clearly enough (see chapter 8), and do they get along well enough with each other (see chapter 10) to accomplish their goals? These and other basic questions about the organization itself must be answered to formulate an effective strategic plan. After all, unless the organization is operating properly, even the best strategic plans may not succeed.

Assess the Competitive Advantage   One company is said to have a competitive advantage over another to the extent customers perceive its products or services as being superior—in quality, cost, or both—to those of the other company. Superiority may be assessed in terms of factors such as quality, price, breadth of product line, reliability of performance, styling, service, and company image.

Develop a Competitive Strategy   A competitive strategy is the means by which an organization achieves its goal. Based on careful assessment of the company's standing regarding the factors described earlier (e.g., available resources, competitive advantage, and so on), a decision is made about how to go achieve its goal. Some possible strategies include:

- **Market-share increasing strategies**: Developing a broader share of an existing market, such as by widening the range of products or forming a joint venture (see chapter 14) with another company having a presence in the market of interest.
- **Profit strategies**: Attempting to derive more profit from existing business, such as by training employees to work more effectively or salespeople to sell more effectively.
- **Market concentration strategies**: Withdrawing from markets where the company is less effective and concentrating resources in markets where the company is likely to be more effective.
- **Turnaround strategies**: Attempting to reverse a decline in business by moving to a new product line or by radically restructuring operations.
- **Exit strategies**: Withdrawing from a market, such as by liquidating assets.

Communicate the Strategy to Stakeholders   The term **stakeholder** refers to an individual or a group in whose interest the organization is run. In other words, these are individuals with a special stake—or claim—on the company. The most important stakeholders include employees at all levels, boards of governors, and stockholders. It is essential to communicate a firm's strategy to stakeholders so they may contribute to its success, whether actively (e.g., employees who pitch in to help meet goals) or passively (e.g., investors who pour money into the company to help meet goals). Without stakeholders fully understanding and accepting a firm's strategy, that firm is unlikely to receive the full support needed to meet its goals.

Implement the Strategy   Once a strategy has been formulated and communicated, it can be implemented. When this occurs, some upheaval is likely as people scramble to adjust to new ways of doing things. As we describe later, people tend to be reluctant to change how they work, but several steps can be taken to ensure the people responsible for making the changes come about will embrace rather than reject them.

Evaluate the Outcome   Finally, after a strategy has been implemented, it is crucial to determine if the goals have been met (Figure 16.9). If so, new goals may be sought; if not, different goals may be defined or different strategies followed to achieve success next time. (The process of strategic planning as described here may strike you as being perfectly rational—so much so, in fact, that you may expect it to be universal. As we describe in the "OB Around the World" section of this chapter, however, this is not the case.)

market-share increasing strategies

A deliberate attempt by a company to develop a broader share of an existing market (e.g., widening the range of products or forming a joint venture with another company having a presence in the market of interest).

profit strategies

Attempts to derive more profit from existing business (e.g., training employees to work more effectively or salespeople to sell more effectively).

market concentration strategies

The tactic of withdrawing from markets where a company is less effective and concentrating resources in markets where the company is likely to be more effective.

turnaround strategies

Attempts to reverse a decline in business by moving to a new product line or by radically restructuring operations.

exit strategies

The tactic by which a company withdraws from a market (e.g., by liquidating its assets).

stakeholder

Any individual or group in whose interest an organization is run.

STRATEGIC VALUES: MORE AMERICAN THAN UNIVERSAL

You may not realize it, but the process of strategic planning described in this chapter has several underlying values associated with it. Specifically, the process is highly deliberate, is based on competition, assumes radical change is both possible and desirable, and assumes shareholder ownership of the company. As we outline here, however, these values are not universally held, thereby casting doubt on generalizations of the strategic planning process outside American culture.

The most obvious feature of the strategic planning process as described here is its *deliberate nature*. In the United States, the most successful companies are those that carefully analyze, plan, and implement key decisions.[21] Such a deliberate process is not used, however, in other countries. For example, in Southeast Asian countries, gut feelings and informal knowledge are used instead of deliberate analyses. In the words of one expert, companies in these countries "don't have strategies. They do deals. They respond to opportunities."[22]

Clearly, our analysis of strategic planning is strongly based on one's position relative to the competition, but outside the United States, open expressions of *competitiveness* are not as common. Japan provides a fascinating example. In that nation, almost nothing is ever said about being competitive. Rather, the good work of the company is likely to be stressed in formal company publications. Ironically, however, Japanese com-

panies tend to be fierce competitors in the international market. Thus, competitive values may not be expressed in Japan — where as a result, they are not likely to appear in any strategic plans — but they certainly exist.

Our discussion of strategic planning also is based on the idea that *radical change is not only possible but desirable*. In Vietnam and Thailand, however, experts caution that radical change is doomed to fail. Instead, minor, incremental adjustments are advised.[23]

Finally, strategic decisions in the United States tend to be made primarily in the *interest of stockholders*. In fact, it often is said the mission of a company is to raise stockholder value. Outside the United States, however, the interests of other stakeholders are given more weight. For example, in Germany and France, the interests of employees tend to be accorded far greater importance in the planning process. In Japan, companies are considered to belong to all the stakeholders, with employees taking precedence over all others.[24]

In conclusion, the values underlying the strategic planning process in the United States clearly are not equally prevalent elsewhere in the world. As a result, it appears questionable whether the strategic planning process as described here would work — or would even be worth attempting — outside of this country.

FIGURE 16.9

Continental Airlines: A Successful Turnaround Strategy
CEO Gordon Bethune is widely credited for formulating and implementing a strategic plan that took Continental Airlines from a money-losing carrier despised by travelers to one of the most successful, favored airlines today. A large part of this strategy involved paying greater attention to passengers and to employees, both of whom felt unappreciated when Bethune took over in 1994.

RESISTANCE TO CHANGE: MAINTAINING THE STATUS QUO

resistance to change
The tendency for employees to be unwilling to go along with organizational change because of individual fears of the unknown or organizational impediments (e.g., structural inertia).

People may be unhappy with the current state of affairs in their organization, but also they may be afraid any changes will be disruptive and only make things worse. Indeed, fear of new conditions is quite real, and it creates an unwillingness to accept change, which is referred to as **resistance to change**. As you might imagine, for organizations to make the changes needed to remain competitive — let alone to survive — they must tackle this problem. Therefore, we now discuss the issue of readiness for change and examine both individual and organizational barriers to change. We then conclude this section by identifying specific steps to overcome such resistance.

Readiness for Change: When Will Organizational Change Occur?

As you might imagine, there are times when change is more likely and times when change is less likely. In general, change is likely to occur when the people involved believe the benefits associated with that change outweigh the costs.[25] The factors contributing to the benefits of making a change are as follows:

- The amount of dissatisfaction with current conditions.
- The availability of a desirable alternative.
- The existence of a plan for achieving that alternative.

Theorists consider these three factors to combine multiplicatively and to determine the benefits of making a change (Figure 16.10). Thus, if any one factor is zero, the benefits of making a change — and the likelihood of change itself — also is zero. If you think about it, this makes sense. After all, people are unlikely to initiate change if they are not dissatisfied or they have no desirable alternative in mind (or any way of attaining that alternative if they do). Of course, for any organizational change to occur, the expected benefits must outweigh the likely costs involved (e.g., disruption, uncertainties).

Individual Barriers to Change

Organizational scientists recognize that resistance to change stems from both individual and organizational variables. Here, we describe several key factors that make people resistant to change in organizations.[26] Then, in the following section, we describe various organizational barriers to change.

FIGURE 16.10

Organizational Change: When Will It Occur?

Whether an organizational change is made depends on people's beliefs regarding the relative benefits and costs of that change. The benefits are reflected by the three considerations reviewed here.

(*Source*: Based on suggestions by Beer, 1980; see note 25.)

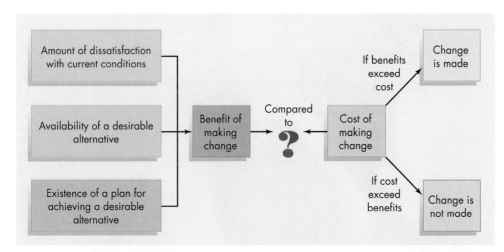

Economic Insecurity Because changes on the job may threaten one's livelihood — either by loss of job or by reduced pay — some resistance to change is inevitable.

Fear of the Unknown Employees derive a sense of security from doing things the same way, from knowing who their coworkers are and to whom they need to answer. Disrupting these well-established, comfortable patterns creates unfamiliar conditions — a state of affairs that often is rejected.

Threats to Social Relationships As people work within organizations, they form strong bonds with their coworkers. Many organizational changes (e.g., reassignment of job responsibilities) threaten the integrity of friendship groups, which provide valuable social rewards.

Habit Jobs that are well learned and become habitual are easy to perform. The prospect of changing how jobs are done challenges people to develop new skills, which clearly is more difficult than continuing to perform the job as it originally was learned.

Failure to Recognize the Need for Change Unless employees can recognize and fully appreciate the need for change in an organization, any vested interests they may have in keeping things the same may overpower their willingness to accept change.

Organizational Barriers to Change

Resistance to organizational change also stems from conditions associated with organizations themselves.[27] Several such factors can be identified.

Structural Inertia Organizations are designed to promote stability. To the extent employees are carefully selected and trained to perform certain jobs — and rewarded for doing them well — the forces acting on individuals to perform in certain ways are very powerful — that is jobs have **structural inertia**. Thus, because jobs are designed to have stability, overcoming the resistance created by the forces that create stability often is difficult.

structural inertia

The organizational forces encouraging employees to perform their jobs in certain ways (e.g., training, reward systems), thereby making them resistant to change.

Work Group Inertia Inertia to continue performing jobs in a specified way comes from the jobs themselves and from the social groups within which people work — that is, *work group inertia*. Because strong social norms develop within groups (see chapter 7), potent pressures exist to perform jobs in certain ways. Introducing change disrupts these established normative expectations, thereby leading to formidable resistance.

Threats to the Existing Balance of Power If changes are made regarding who is in charge, a shift in the balance of power between individuals and organizational subunits is likely to occur. Units that currently control the resources, have the expertise, and wield the power may fear losing their advantageous positions because of organizational change.

Previously Unsuccessful Efforts Anyone who has lived through a past disaster understandably may be reluctant to endure another attempt at the same thing. Similarly, groups or entire organizations that have been unsuccessful at introducing change may be cautious about accepting further attempts.

An Example During the past decade, General Electric (GE) has undergone a series of widespread changes in its basic strategy, organizational structure, and relationship with employees. Throughout this process, several of the barriers just identified have been encountered. For example, GE managers had mastered a set of bureaucratic traditions that kept their habits strong and their inertia moving straight ahead. The prospect of doing things differently was scary for those who were so strongly entrenched in doing things the "GE way." In particular, the company's interest in globalization triggered many fears of the unknown.

Resistance to change also was strong because it threatened to strip power from those units that traditionally had possessed most of it (e.g., the Power Systems and Lighting Division). In addition, changes were highly disruptive to GE's "social architecture"; friendship groups were broken up and scattered throughout the company. In all, GE has been a living example of the many different barriers to change—all rolled up into a single company.

How to Overcome Resistance to Organizational Change

Because organizational change is inevitable, managers should be sensitive to barriers so that resistance can be overcome. Of course, this is easier said than done, but several useful approaches have been suggested.[28]

Shape Political Dynamics   For change to be accepted, it often is useful—if not absolutely necessary—to win the support of the most powerful and influential individuals in the company. Doing so builds a critical internal mass of support for change. Demonstrating clearly that key organizational leaders endorse the change is an effective way to get others to go along, either because they share the leader's vision or because they fear the leader's retaliation. Either way, their support will facilitate the acceptance of change.

Educate the Workforce   Sometimes, people are reluctant to change because they fear what the future has in store. For example, fears about economic security may be put to rest by a few reassuring words from powerholders. As part of educating employees about what organizational change may mean for them, top management must show considerable emotional sensitivity. Doing so makes it possible for those people affected by a change to help make it work. Some companies have found that simply answering the question "What's in it for me?" can help to allay many fears (Figure 16.11).

FIGURE 16.11

Charles Schwab & Company: From Discount Broker to Full-Service Broker

Charles Schwab & Company, once the only discount brokerage firm, has faced stiff competition in recent years. Price-conscious investors now can buy and sell stocks over the Internet at deeply discounted rates. They also can get advice from full-service investment firms, albeit at a stiff price. Recently, Schwab has defined its market as being a unique blend of the two. According to the firm's president and CEO, David Potter, Schwab customers do not want to be spoon-fed investment advice; they prefer to be taught about investing while enjoying the convenience of the Internet. This shift in strategy has brought about a change in how brokers are paid—which some have found threatening. Educating brokers in the benefits involved, however, was helpful in gaining their acceptance of the firm's new strategy.

Involve Employees in the Change Efforts   People who participate in making a decision tend to be more committed to the outcome than those who are not involved. Accordingly, employees who are involved in responding to unplanned change or are made part of the team charged with planning a needed organizational change may have very little resistance to such change. Organizational changes that are "sprung" on the workforce with little or no warning, however, might encounter resistance — simply as a knee-jerk reaction — until employees can assess how the change affects them. In contrast, employees who are involved in the change process better understand the need for change and, therefore, are less likely to resist it. Says Duane Hartley, general manager of Hewlett-Packard's microwave instruments division, "I don't think people really enjoy change, but if they can participate in it and understand it, it can become a positive [experience] for them."[29]

Reward Constructive Behaviors   One rather obvious — and quite successful — mechanism to facilitate organizational change is rewarding people for behaving in the desired fashion. Changing organizational operations may necessitate changing the behaviors that need to be rewarded by the organization. This is especially critical during the transition period (i.e., when the change is introduced). For example, employees who are required to learn to use new equipment should be praised for their successful efforts. Feedback on how well they are doing not only provides a great deal of useful assurance to uncertain employees but also helps to shape the desired behavior.

Create a "Learning Organization"   All organizations change whether they want to or not, but some do so more effectively than others. Those organizations that have developed the capacity to adapt and to change continuously are known as **learning organizations**.[30] In these organizations, people set aside their old ways of thinking, freely share ideas with others, form a vision of the organization, and work together on a plan for achieving that vision. Examples of learning organizations include Ford, General Electric, Motorola, Wal-Mart, and Xerox.

learning organization
An organization that is successful at acquiring, cultivating, and applying knowledge that can be used to help it adapt to change.

As you might imagine, becoming a learning organization is no simple feat. In fact, it involves implementing many of the OB principles described in this book. Specifically, for a firm to become a continual learner, management must:

- *Establish a commitment to change*: Unless all employees clearly see top management as being strongly committed to changing and to improving the organization, they will be unlikely to make the changes necessary to bring about such improvements.
- *Adopt an informal organizational structure*: Change is more readily accepted when organizational structures (see chapter 14) are flat, when cross-functional teams are created (see chapter 7), and when formal boundaries between people are eliminated.
- *Develop an open organizational culture*: As described in chapter 3, managers play a key role in forming organizational culture. To adapt effectively to changes in their environments, organizations should have cultures that embrace risk taking, openness, and growth. Companies with leaders who are reluctant to confront the risk of failure are unlikely to grow and to develop.

These five suggestions may be easier to state than to implement, but such efforts will be well rewarded. Given the many forces that make employees resistant to change, managers should keep these guidelines in mind. (For additional suggestions on effectively changing people, based on the experiences of three of the world's most successful organizations, see the "Tips" section on page 602.)

TIPS: DOING IT RIGHT

■ Making Change Stick: Three Not-So-Simple Suggestions from Sears, Shell, and the U.S. Army

There is no mistaking that organizational change is occurring more rapidly than ever before. There also is no mistaking that three of the world's largest organizations—Sears, Royal Dutch Shell, and the U.S. Army—appear to have managed change quite well. After all, each has been in existence for more than 100 years, and each has gone through many changes.

Fortunately, analyses of these companies makes it possible to identify some of the keys to their longevity.[31] Specifically, we can learn three things from the experiences of these organizations in adapting to the environments around them. Because these practices have been followed successfully in such different organizations, we also can be confident in their applicability to a variety of organizations. These useful tips are:

1. *Fully incorporate employees into challenges faced by the organization.* This means more than simply involving employees in the organization's operations but actively engaging them at all levels in the problems being faced. For example, officials from Shell Malaysia had long been unsuccessful in getting employees to work together to beat the competition. They were far too complacent, and the competition was rapidly gaining market share. In response, Shell officials called together all 260 managers for a $2\frac{1}{2}$-day session on the problem of the rapidly encroaching competition. The managers emerged from this marathon session with a firm plan. Back on the job, regular follow-up meetings were held to make sure the plan was implemented. Finally, because the employees were brought into the problem and met the challenge themselves, Shell was successful in changing the way it operated.

2. *Lead in a way that stresses the urgency of a change.* It is not unusual for company officials to get in a rut, becoming lazy and complacent about how they operate—even if decisive action is necessary. All too often, this results in the business slipping through their collective fingers. This is *almost* what happened to Sears a few years ago. The retailing giant was losing customers rapidly as officers sat by and merely lowered sales goals. Then CEO Arthur Martinez lit a fire under everyone by stressing the importance of turning things around—or else! He generated a sense of urgency by setting very challenging goals (e.g., quadrupling market share, increasing customer satisfaction by 15 percent). Martinez did not have all the answers to Sears' problems, but he provided something even more important—straightforward, honest talk about those problems, which created a sense of urgency that got everyone moving in the right direction.

3. *Create relentless discomfort with the status quo.* After military maneuvers, the U.S. Army thoroughly debriefs all participants in what is called an After Action Review. During these sessions, careful feedback is given about what soldiers did well and where they could stand to improve. By focusing in a relentless, detailed manner on work that needs to be done, officers eventually get soldiers to internalize the need for excellence. Soldiers then return to their home bases and ask themselves how they can do something better (e.g., faster, cheaper, more accurately) or if a new and better approach can be taken. In short, the status quo is the enemy; current performance levels are never accepted. Army brass liken this commitment to continuous improvement to painting a bridge: The job is never over.

These are rather extreme measures and not always easy to implement, but they certainly warrant careful consideration. After all, they have worked well for some of the most successful organizations in the world. ■

ORGANIZATIONAL DEVELOPMENT INTERVENTIONS: IMPLEMENTING PLANNED CHANGE

Now that we have shed some light on the basic issues surrounding organizational change, we look at planned ways of implementing it, which collectively are known as techniques of **organizational development (OD)**. Formally, we may define this as a set of social science techniques to plan and to implement change in work settings for purposes of enhancing the personal development of individuals and of improving organizational functioning. By planning organization-wide changes involving people, OD seeks to enhance organizational performance by improving the quality of the work environment as well as the attitudes and well-being of employees.

Over the years, many strategies for implementing planned organizational change (i.e., *OD interventions*) have been used by specialists attempting to improve organizational functioning (i.e., *OD practitioners*).[32] All the major methods of OD attempt to produce some kind of change in individual employees, work groups, or entire organizations. This is the goal of the four interventions reviewed here.

organizational development (OD)

A set of social science techniques to plan change in organizational work settings to enhance the personal development of individuals and to improve the effectiveness of organizational functioning.

Management by Objectives: Clarifying Organizational Goals

Chapter 4 discussed the motivational benefits of setting specific goals. As you might imagine, not only individuals but entire organizations benefit from specific goals. For example, an organization may strive to "raise production" and to "improve the quality" of its manufactured goods. Well-intentioned as these goals may be, they may not be as useful to an organization as more specific ones, such as "increase production of widgets by 15 percent" or "lower the failure rate of widgets by 25 percent." After all, as the old saying goes, "It's usually easier to get somewhere if you know where you're going." When consulting for General Electric during the early 1950s, Peter Drucker was well aware of this idea. In fact, he is credited with promoting the benefits of specifying clear organizational goals—a technique known as **management by objectives (MBO)**.

As summarized in Figure 16.12, the MBO process consists of three basic steps. First, goals are selected that employees will try to attain to best serve the needs of the

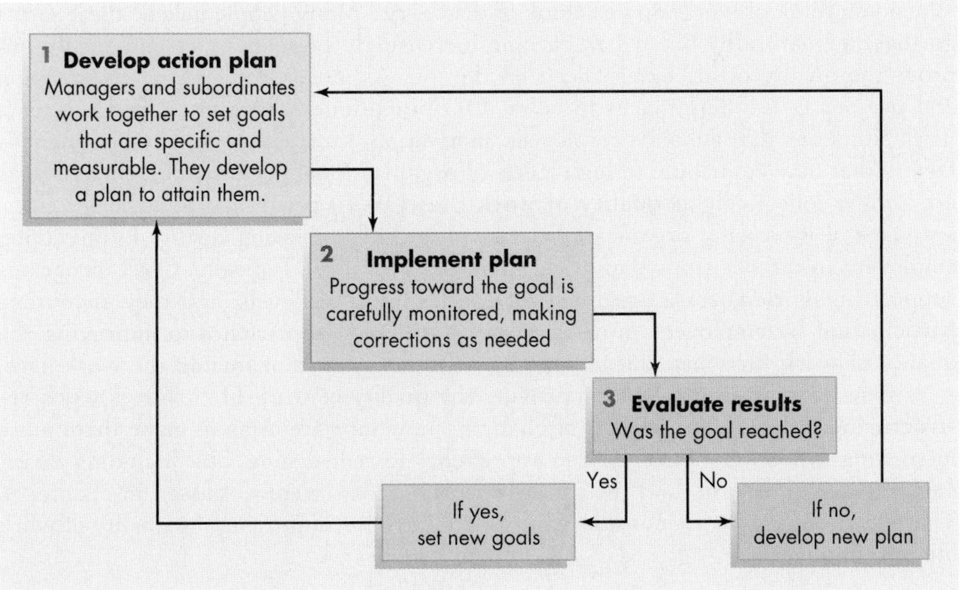

management by objectives (MBO)

The technique by which managers and subordinates work together to set and then to meet organizational goals.

FIGURE 16.12

Management by Objectives: Developing Organizations Through Goal Setting

The OD technique of *management by objectives* requires managers and subordinates to work together on setting and trying to achieve important organizational goals. The basic steps of the process are outlined here.

organization. These goals should be selected by managers with their subordinates. The goals must be set mutually by all involved, not simply imposed. These goals also should be directly measurable and have some time frame attached to them. Goals that cannot be measured (e.g., to make the company better) or that have no time limits are useless. In addition, it is crucial that managers and their subordinates work together to plan ways of attaining the goals they have selected, thereby developing an *action plan*.

Once the goals are set and the action plans developed, the second step calls for *implementation*—that is, carrying out the plan and regularly assessing its progress. Is the plan working? Are the goals being approximated? Are problems being encountered in meeting these goals? Such questions must be considered while implementing the action plan. If the plan is failing, a midcourse correction may be in order, thus changing the plan, how it is carried out, or even the goal itself.

Finally, after monitoring progress toward the goal, the third step may be instituted: *evaluation*, or assessing goal attainment. Were the organization's goals reached? If so, what new goals should be set to improve things still further? If not, what new plans can be initiated to meet the goals? Because the ultimate assessment of the extent to which goals are met helps to determine the selection of new goals, MBO is a continuous process.

As such, MBO represents a potentially effective source for planning and implementing strategic change in organizations. Individual efforts designed to meet organizational goals get the individual employee and the organization working together toward common ends. Hence, system-wide change results. Of course, for MBO to work, everyone involved must buy into it. MBO programs typically require a great deal of participation by lower-level employees, so top managers must be willing to accept—and to support—the cooperation and involvement of all.

Making MBO work also requires a great deal of time—anywhere from three to five years. Hence, MBO may be inappropriate in organizations without the time to commit to making it work. Even so, MBO has become one of the most widely used techniques for affecting organizational change. It not only is used on an ad hoc basis by many organizations but also constitutes an ingrained element of the organizational culture in some companies (e.g., Hewlett-Packard, IBM).

Quality of Work Life Programs: Humanizing the Workplace

When you think of work, do you think of drudgery? Many people believe these terms go together naturally, but it has become increasingly popular to systematically improve the quality of life experienced on the job. As more people demand satisfying and personally fulfilling places to work, OD practitioners have attempted to create work situations that enhance employees' motivation, satisfaction, and commitment—factors that may contribute to high levels of organizational performance. Such efforts are known collectively as **quality of work life (QWL)** programs. Specifically, these are ways of increasing organizational output and of improving quality by involving employees in the decisions that affect them on their jobs. Typically, QWL programs support highly democratic treatment of employees at all levels, and they encourage participation by employees in decision making. Many approaches to improving the quality of work life exist, but all share a common goal: humanizing the workplace.

One popular approach to improving the quality of work life involves **work restructuring**—that is, the process of changing how jobs are done to make them more interesting to workers. Several such approaches to redesigning jobs, including *job enlargement*, *job enrichment*, and the *job characteristics model*, were discussed in chapter 4. These techniques also are considered to be effective for improving the quality of work life for employees.

quality of work life (QWL)
An OD technique designed to improve organizational functioning by humanizing the workplace, by making it more democratic, and by involving employees in decision making.

work restructuring
The process of changing how jobs are performed to make them more interesting to workers.

Another approach to improving the quality of work life is **quality circles (QCs)**. These are small groups of volunteers (usually around 10) who meet regularly (usually weekly) to identify and to solve problems relating to the quality of their work and to the conditions under which people do their jobs. An organization may have several QCs operating at once, each dealing with the particular area about which it has the most expertise. To help QCs to work effectively, the members usually receive some form of training in problem solving. Large companies such as Westinghouse, Hewlett-Packard, and Eastman Kodak have included QCs as part of their QWL efforts. These groups have dealt with issues such as how to reduce vandalism, how to create safer and more comfortable working environments, and how to improve product quality. QCs are very effective at bringing about short-term improvements in the quality of work life (i.e., those lasting as long as 18 months), but they are less effective at creating more permanent changes.

quality circles (QCs)

An approach to improving the quality of work life in which small groups of volunteers meet regularly to identify and to solve problems related to the work they perform and the conditions under which they work.

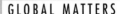

GLOBAL MATTERS

The quality circle was developed during the 1950s by an American — management pioneer W. Edwards Deming. It also was rejected at first in the United States. Only after the technique became successful in Japan was it subsequently "re-imported" back to the United States. ■

As you might imagine, a variety of benefits — even if only short-term ones — might result from QWL programs, and these fall into three major categories. The most direct benefit usually involves increased job satisfaction, organizational commitment, and reduced employee turnover. A second benefit is increased productivity, and related to these first two benefits is the third — namely, increased organizational effectiveness (e.g., profitability, goal attainment). Many companies (e.g., Ford, General Electric, AT&T) have active QWL programs and reportedly are quite pleased with the results.

Achieving these benefits is not automatic, however. Two major pitfalls must be avoided for QWL programs to be successful. First, both *management and labor must cooperate in designing the program*. Should any one side believe the program is just a method of gaining an advantage over the other, that program is doomed to fail. Second, the *plans agreed to by all concerned parties must be fully implemented*. It is too easy for action plans developed in QWL groups to be forgotten during the hectic pace of daily activities. It is the responsibility of employees at all levels — from the highest-level executive to the lowest-level laborer — to follow through on their parts of the plan.

Team Building: Creating Effective Work Groups

The process of **team building** applies the techniques and the rationale of sensitivity training to work groups. This approach attempts to get members of a work group to diagnose how they work together and to plan how this can be improved. Given the importance of group efforts in effective organizational functioning, improving the effectiveness of work groups is likely to affect an organization profoundly. If one assumes work groups are the basic building blocks of an organization, then organizational change should emphasize changing groups instead of individuals.

Team building begins when group members admit they have a problem and gather data to provide insight. The problems that are identified may come from sensitivity-training sessions or from more objective sources (e.g., production figures, attitude surveys). These data then are shared in a *diagnostic session* to develop a consensus regarding the group's current strengths and weaknesses. From this consensus, a list of desired changes is created, as are plans for implementing these changes. In other words, an *action plan* is developed — some task-oriented approach to solving the group's problems as diagnosed. The plan is performed, and its progress is evaluated

team building

An OD technique in which employees discuss problems related to their work group's performance. On the basis of these discussions, specific problems are identified, and plans for solving them are devised and implemented.

to determine whether the originally identified problems remain. If the problems are solved, the process is completed — and the team may stop meeting. If the problems remain, the process should begin again. (For a summary of these steps, see Figure 16.13.)

Work teams have been used effectively to combat many important organizational problems. For these efforts to be successful, however, all group members must participate in the gathering and evaluating of information as well as in the planning and implementing of action plans. Input from group members is especially crucial for evaluating the effectiveness of the team-building program.[33] Because the team-building approach is highly task oriented, however, interpersonal problems between group members may be disruptive and need to be neutralized by an outside party. With interpersonal strain out of the way, the stage then is set for groups to learn to solve their own problems effectively. Even so, this does not happen overnight. To be effective, team building should not be approached as a one-time exercise during a few days away from the job. Rather, it should be considered an on-going process that takes several months — or even years — to develop. Given the great impact effective teams can have on organizational functioning (see chapter 7), efforts to build effective work teams seem to be quite worthwhile.

Survey Feedback: Inducing Change by Sharing Information

For organizational change to be effective, employees must understand the organization's current strengths and weaknesses, which is the rationale behind the **survey feedback** method. This technique follows the three steps summarized in Figure 16.14. First, data are collected to provide information about matters of general concern to employees (e.g., organizational climate, leadership style, job satisfaction). This may take the form of intensive interviews, structured questionnaires, or both. Because this

survey feedback

An OD technique in which questionnaires and interviews are used to collect information about issues of concern to an organization. This information is shared with employees and is used as the basis for planning organizational change.

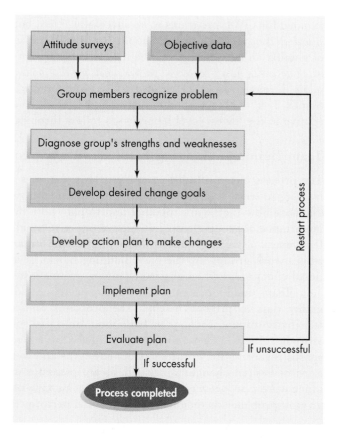

FIGURE 16.13

Team Building: Its Basic Steps

Team building, a popular technique of organizational development, follows the steps outlined here.

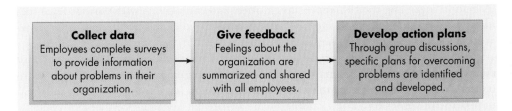

FIGURE 16.14

Survey Feedback: An Overview
The *survey feedback* technique of OD follows the three steps outlined here: collecting data, giving feedback, and developing action plans.

information must be as unbiased as possible, employees providing feedback should be assured their responses will be confidential. For this reason, the process usually is conducted by outside consultants.

The second step calls for reporting this information to the employees during small group meetings. Typically, this consists of summarizing the average scores found on the attitudes assessed by the survey. Profiles then are created of feelings about the organization, its leadership, the work done, and related topics. Discussions also focus on why the scores are as they are and on what problems the feedback reveals.

The final step involves analyzing problems dealing with communication, decision making, and other organizational processes to make plans for dealing with them. Such discussions usually are most effective when they are carefully documented and a specific plan of implementation is made—with someone also being put in charge of carrying it out.

Survey feedback is a widely used OD technique, which is not surprising considering the advantages it offers. It allows a great deal of information to be collected relatively quickly. It also is very flexible and can be tailored to the needs of different organizations facing a variety of problems. The technique can be no better than the quality of the questionnaire used, however. It must measure what really matters to employees. Of course, to derive the maximum benefit from survey feedback, it must have the support of top management as well. Plans developed by the small discussion groups also must be capable of being implemented with the full approval of the organization. When these conditions are met, survey feedback can be a very effective OD technique.

(The basic idea behind survey feedback is that employees receive information that guides them through the process of making changes. Another source of information that may be used, however, comes from finding out what competitors are doing. For a closer look at this practice, see the "Trends" section below.)

■ Competitive Intelligence: Planning Change by Learning about the Competition

Only about 10 percent of U.S. companies do it—and the other 90 percent probably should. Do what, you ask? The answer is: **competitive intelligence (CI)**—that is, the process of gathering information about one's competitors to use as the basis for planning organizational change. CI is a search for clues about what a competitor is actually doing or is considering doing. To stay competitive, some of the biggest companies—especially those in rapidly changing, high-tech fields (e.g., General Electric, Motorola, Microsoft, Hewlett-Packard, IBM, AT&T, Intel)—engage in CI all the time. In fact, Gary Costley, the former president of Kellogg Co. North America, says that managers who do not engage in CI are "incompetent" because it is "irresponsible to not understand your competitors."[34]

Before you dismiss CI as being unethical, note that we are not talking about doing anything illegal. Rather, CI usually involves gathering readily available information, such as that contained in public records. Companies are required to disclose in-

continued

competitive intelligence (CI)
The process of gathering information about one's competitors for use in planning organizational change.

formation regarding their finances, inventories, and compliance with various legal regulations. Documents containing this information are available to anyone, and growing numbers of competitors are availing themselves of these records.

Valuable information also may be obtained by interviewing people who work for competing companies. It is amazing what loose-lipped employees may tell you without any need to pry it out of them. Sometimes, all you have to do to gather information is to be observant. For example, years before he became president of Kellogg, Costley simply stood on a public street and watched as a competitor, General Foods, unloaded a new extruding machine at its Post cereal plant, which was located across the street from his own company. Costley later used what he saw as the basis for convincing his bosses to switch to that machine.

Most companies would not know what to do with CI if they stumbled on it, but a few of the more sophisticated ones go out of their way to put such information to good use. For example, during the mid-1980s, Motorola sent someone to Japan to research the budgets of companies that might compete with its electronics market in Europe. Discovering that several Japanese firms planned to sell semiconductors in Europe, Motorola immediately strengthened its business in that area (e.g., by starting strategic alliances with other companies). Thus, when the Japanese entered that market, their impact was far less than it would have been had Motorola not struck first.

Competitive intelligence also helped the Adolph Coors Co. to avoid failure in the wine-cooler market. Coors sent a team to study its competitor, Gallo, to see exactly what they did right. The team learned that Gallo could make the product for much less, because they owned their own vineyards. Deciding it could not beat Gallo, Coors dropped its plans to compete.

Knowing how effective a little detective work may be, some of the most careful companies make sure they do not become easy targets for competitors who may be trying their hands at CI. In fact, these companies sometimes hire people to crack their own security. If these counterspies get valuable information, they can plug the leak before any real harm is done. Of course, we are not talking about information that must be disclosed but rather information that was disclosed for no good reason.

Some companies, for example, provide too much information on the forms they must complete. Some executives divulge too much in speeches they give or in press releases without ever thinking that what they say may get into the wrong hands. Not surprisingly, companies that are most sophisticated in matters of CI not only engage in it but make sure they do not become targets themselves. Experts advise you to play it safe: Assume your competitors are better at CI than you are.

There is no mistaking that CI has become an important source of profit for many companies. Robert Flynn, the former CEO of the NutraSweet division of Monsanto, has claimed CI was worth some $50 million to his company (in terms of revenues gained and revenues not lost to competitors).[35] With figures like these, it is easy to make the case that companies cannot afford to *not* make CI an important part of their strategic change plans. ■

CRITICAL ISSUES IN ORGANIZATIONAL DEVELOPMENT

No discussion of OD would be complete without addressing two very important questions: Do the techniques work, and are they ethical?

The Effectiveness of Organizational Development: Does It Really Work?

Thus far, we have described some of the major OD techniques to improve organizational functioning. These techniques require a considerable amount of time, money, and effort. Accordingly, it is appropriate to ask if this investment is worthwhile. In other words, does OD really work? Given the popularity of OD in organizations, this question is very important, and most of the relevant studies show the effects of these various interventions to be beneficial — mostly in the area of improving organizational functioning.[36]

We hasten to add that any conclusions about the effectiveness of OD should be qualified in several important ways. First, OD interventions tend to be more effective among blue-collar employees than among white-collar employees. Second, these beneficial effects can be enhanced by using a combination of several techniques (e.g., four or more together) instead of any single one. Finally, the effectiveness also depends on the degree of support these techniques receive from top management: The more these programs are supported from the top, the more successful they tend to be.

Despite the importance of evaluating the effectiveness of OD interventions, a great many of them go unevaluated. Undoubtedly, there are many reasons for this, but one key factor is the difficulty of assessing change. Because many factors can cause people to behave differently in organizations and such behaviors may be difficult to measure, many OD practitioners thus avoid the problem of measuring change altogether. In a related vein, political pressures to justify OD programs may discourage some OD professionals from honestly and accurately assessing their effectiveness. After all, in doing so, you run the risk of scientifically demonstrating your own wasted time and money.

GLOBAL MATTERS

The effectiveness of OD techniques depend, in part, on the extent to which the values on which the technique is based match the underlying values of the national culture in which it is employed. For example, in the Southeast Asian nation of Brunei, the prevailing cultural value is such that problems are not confronted openly.[37] As a result, a technique such as survey feedback may be destined to fail. ■

We may conclude, however, that despite some limitations, OD shows considerable promise in its ability to benefit organizations and the individuals working within them.

Is Organizational Development Inherently Unethical? A Debate

By its very nature, OD applies powerful social science techniques to change attitudes and behavior. From the perspective of a manager attempting to accomplish various goals, such tools are immediately recognized as being very useful. From the perspec-

YOU BE THE CONSULTANT

Your company is considering merging with a competitor. This has caused great disruption in the workplace as people begin to fear for their jobs. Work is slowing down, because people are taking time off to find new jobs. Meanwhile, production is sagging badly.

1. Does it make sense to expect employees to have these fears? Why, or why not?
2. Describe how you would help to allay these fears and to return the workplace to normal. How effective do you think these steps might be?
3. If a merger did occur, how might you use an organizational development technique to smooth the transition?

tive of the individual being affected, however, several ethical issues arise (Figure 16.15).[38]

It has been argued, for example, that OD techniques impose the values of the organization on the individual without accounting for individual's own attitudes. OD is a very one-sided approach, reflecting the imposition of the more powerful organization on the less powerful individual. A related issue is that the OD process does not provide for any free choice by the employees. Therefore, it may be seen as being *coercive* and *manipulative*. When faced with a "do it, or else" situation, employees tend to have little free choice and must allow themselves to be manipulated—a potentially degrading prospect.

Another issue is that the unequal power relationship between the organization and its employees can allow the true intent of OD techniques to be misrepresented. For example, imagine an MBO technique is presented to employees as a means of allowing greater organizational participation, whereas in reality, it is a means to hold individuals responsible for their poor performance and to punish them as a result. Such an event might not happen, but the potential for abuse of this type does exist—and the temptation to misuse the technique (even if that was not the original intention) might later prove to be too great.

Despite these considerations, many professionals do not agree that OD is inherently unethical. It has been countered that such a claim is to say the practice of management is itself unethical. After all, the very act of going to work for an organization requires one to submit to the organization's values—and to the overall values of society at large. One cannot help but face life situations in which others' values are imposed. This is not to say organizations have the right to impose patently unethical values on people for the purpose of making a profit (e.g., stealing from customers). Indeed, because they have the potential to abuse their power (e.g., the MBO example), organizations have a special obligation to refrain from doing so.

Abuses of organizational power are all too common, but OD itself is not necessarily the culprit. Indeed, like any other tool—even a gun!—OD is not inherently good or evil. Instead, *whether the tool is used for good or evil depends on the individual using it*. Thus, the ethical use of OD interventions requires they be supervised by professionals in an organization that places a high value on ethics. To the extent top management embraces ethical values and behaves ethically, norms for behaving ethically

FIGURE 16.15

The Ethics of OD: A Summary of the Debate

Some claim OD is an inherently unethical practice, but others counter that it is not. The arguments for each side are summarized here.

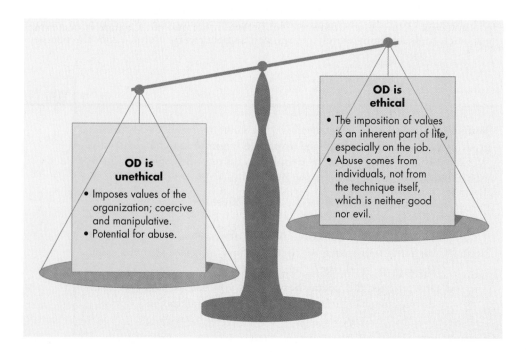

OD is unethical
- Imposes values of the organization; coercive and manipulative.
- Potential for abuse.

OD is ethical
- The imposition of values is an inherent part of life, especially on the job.
- Abuse comes from individuals, not from the technique itself, which is neither good nor evil.

are likely to develop in that organization. When an organization has a strong ethical culture, OD practitioners are unlikely to even think of misusing their power to harm individuals. The need to develop such a culture has been recognized as a way for organizations to take not only moral leadership in their communities but financial leadership as well.

Having considered these viewpoints, what is your position on the ethics of OD techniques? Are they generally ethical? If not, how could they be revised to be ethical? ■

ETHICS MATTERS

We invite you to visit the Greenberg page on the Prentice Hall Web site at: **www.prenhall.com/greenberg** for the monthly Greenberg update and for this chapter's World Wide Web exercise.

SUMMARY AND REVIEW OF LEARNING OBJECTIVES

1. **Characterize the prevalence of the change process in organizations.**
    Organizational change is very prevalent and occurring at a rapid pace. Almost all organizations are changing in one way or another to survive. Those that fail to adapt, inevitably, fail altogether. The tendency for organizational change to occur is not limited to organizations in North America, however. Change is occurring rapidly in organizations throughout the world.

2. **Understand what occurs during *organizational change* and the forces responsible for unplanned organizational change.**
    The process of organizational change involves some combination of changing organizational structure, technology, and people. Unplanned change occurs in organizations because of shifting employee demographics, performance gaps, government regulations, global economic competition, and advances in technology.

3. **Describe *strategic planning*, and explain the types of strategic changes that organizations make.**
    Strategic planning is the process of formulating, implementing, and evaluating decisions that enable an organization to achieve its objectives. Typically, strategic plans are made to change a company's products and services or its organizational structure.

4. **Identify the 10 steps in the *strategic planning* process.**
    The strategic planning process follows 10 steps: (1) define the goals, (2) define the scope of products or services, (3) assess the internal resources, (4) assess the external environment, (5) analyze the internal arrangements, (6) assess the competitive advantage, (7) develop a competitive strategy, (8) communicate the strategy to stakeholders, (9) implement the strategy, and (10) evaluate the outcome.

5. **Explain why people resist organizational change and how this resistance may be overcome.**

In general, people resist change because of individual factors (e.g., economic insecurity, fear of the unknown) and organizational factors (e.g., stability of work groups, threats to the existing balance of power). Resistance to change can be overcome in several ways, however, including shaping the political dynamics, educating the workforce about the effects of the changes, involving employees in the change efforts, rewarding constructive behaviors, and creating a learning organization.

6. **Identify and describe the major *organizational development* techniques in use today.**

Survey feedback uses questionnaires, interviews, or both as the basis for identifying organizational problems, which then are addressed in planning sessions. **Team building** involves using work groups to diagnose and to develop scientific plans for solving problems in their functioning as a work unit. **Quality of work life programs** attempt to humanize the workplace by involving employees in the decisions affecting them (e.g., through quality circle meetings) and by restructuring the jobs themselves. Finally, **management by objectives** focuses on attempts by managers and their subordinates to work together at setting important organizational goals and at developing a plan to meet those goals. The rationale underlying these techniques is that they may enhance organizational functioning by involving employees in identifying and solving organizational problems.

7. **Identify both sides of the debate regarding whether organizational development is inherently unethical.**

Some have argued OD is unethical because it can be used for illegitimate purposes. Others, however, counter that OD is just a tool and that it is people who are at fault for using it inappropriately.

QUESTIONS FOR DISCUSSION

1. Some changes in organizations are unplanned, whereas others result from strategic plans. Give examples of each variety of change, and explain their implications for organizational functioning.

2. Suppose you are having difficulty managing a small group of subordinates who work in an office 1,000 miles away from your home base. What changes in structure, technology, and people can be implemented so you can supervise these distant employees more closely?

3. Under what conditions are people most willing to make changes in organizations? Explain your answer, and give an example.

4. Suppose you are a top executive at a large organization about to undertake an ambitious restructuring that involves massive changes in job responsibilities for most employees. Explain why people might resist such changes and how to overcome this resistance.

5. Overall, how effective is organizational development in improving organizational functioning? With respect to what factors does it work or not work?

6. Argue for or against the following statement: Organizational development is inherently unethical and should not be used.

Zales Becomes a Gem of a Chain

Robert DiNicola has a history of shaking things up at the department stores he has run. Not surprisingly, it sparked curiosity when DiNicola took over as chief executive of Zale Corp., the Irving, Texas–based chain of jewelry stores (operating as Zales, Gordon's, and Bailey, Banks & Biddle) in April 1994. Zale's board of directors was not looking for someone with jewelry experience; they had that in company president Larry Pollack. Rather, they wanted someone who could help the stores to regain the glory — and the profitability — they had enjoyed before serious financial troubles caused the company to file for bankruptcy protection in 1992 (from which it emerged only 18 months later).

DiNicola wasted no time in showing he was up to the challenge. No sooner did he find his new office than he began inquiring about plans for Memorial Day sales. Store officials could barely contain their surprise at the new boss' naiveté about the jewelry business. After all, jewelry traditionally is purchased for special occasions (e.g., weddings, anniversaries) and not on impulse (e.g., in response to attractive sale prices). At least, that *was* the case. On Memorial Day 1994, Zales stores kept their doors open late to accommodate the throngs of holiday shoppers — who were lured by attractive prices for clearance goods.

Based on that experience, DiNicola completely revamped Zale's approach to doing business. He identified their 100 best-selling items (e.g., diamond tennis bracelets and anniversary bands), purchased them in large quantities, and then promoted them heavily in radio and TV ads. After only a few months, these items, which had represented 30 percent of total sales, rose to 40 percent. Advertising low prices for popular items quickly became part of how Zales did business.

In another move, DiNicola positioned Zales as a value leader. Dropping its long-standing, 60-percent profit margin, he traded lower margins for higher volume. For example, instead of selling a bracelet at $1,295 and moving only 300 of them, Zales now sells the same product at $799 and moves 10 times as many. DiNicola also has renovated Zales stores and standardized their inventory and advertising at the national level (subject to minor regional variations) following the time-tested McDonalds's formula for success.

As far as DiNicola is concerned, this is only the beginning of things to come for Zales. He has several new ideas up his sleeve, such as increasing the chain's presence by opening 250 stores during the next three years. As of 1998, Zales had 1,100 stores in the United States, Guam, and Puerto Rico. In the fall of 1995, the company also experienced success with its first mail-order campaign. Other shop-at-home ideas DiNicola is pondering include a Zales home shopping channel and a Zales Internet site. If there is jewelry to be sold, chances are good that Zales will be involved.

There can be little doubt DiNicola has made Zales a very different chain of jewelry stores than it was when he took over. It is a more profitable place as well. In 1998, Zale Corp. enjoyed an impressive 26 percent increase in operating earnings. With numbers like these, DiNicola appears to have the Midas touch.

CRITICAL THINKING QUESTIONS

1. What unplanned or planned forces were responsible for stimulating change at Zales?

2. What was DiNicola's strategic plan for the company?

3. What factors might create resistance for change at Zales? How may these be overcome?

4. What might DiNicola and other Zales officials do to help ensure the company's future as a major jewelry retailer?

Managing Organizational Change: Strategic Planning and Organizational Development

SMALL BUSINESS 2000 ▪▪▪▪▪▪▪▪▪ There is one thing most managers in today's business world can be 100 percent certain of: The environment their company operates in — and the company itself — will go through many changes over time. If the only factors a manager needed to worry about were those over which she or he had complete control, you might argue they could keep things the same and, maybe, do as they pleased. This is not the case, however.

Companies operate in environments over which they often have little control. Technology is continuously changing, competitors are trying new things, and customers change their preferences and demand different products. Internal to a company, employees change, too. Attitudes toward work are not fixed. Priorities change based on events both in the workplace and in people's lives outside the workplace.

Boardroom, Inc. knows about change. This company has grown from a family-based business in the founder's basement to a company employing more than 80 people and generating more than $100 million in annual sales. Until now, the company has been headed by its founder, Marty Edelston. Soon, however, he will step aside and hand the operation to a team made up of his three children and a gentleman who has been with the company for more than 15 years. What will this mean for Boardroom Inc.? It's hard to say. One thing is for sure: Instead of being run and guided by a single force — Edelston's — the company will now be managed by a group of four. We can expect the new leaders to have some new ideas for the company and, maybe, to manage it with different priorities than Edelston had.

As you watch this segment, think about what you would do if you were on the new management team. The company has tremendous history and appears to be strong in both financial and market terms — people want Boardroom's products. As you have learned, however, nothing stands still. Think about how the new management team, long-time employees, and customers might respond to the change in leadership at Boardroom, Inc.

QUESTIONS FOR DISCUSSION

1. Identify some things you think may be external factors that affect Boardroom, Inc. How might these things affect the company? If you were a member of the management team, how would you react? What would you do?

2. We have learned that Boardroom, Inc. will soon undergo a change in leadership. What do you think of the approach the company is taking to prepare for this transition? If you were a consultant to the company, what else might you recommend they do regarding this change in leadership?

3. We can expect some things to stay the same after the new management team takes over at Boardroom, Inc., but other things undoubtedly will change. What types of things do you think might change? How do you think the staff, many of whom have worked for Edelston for a long time, will react to changes the new managers make? What might the new management team do to help the staff understand and adjust to these changes?

SKILLS BANK

EXPERIENCING ORGANIZATIONAL BEHAVIOR

Developing a Strategic Plan

Developing a strategic plan is not easy. In fact, doing it right requires a great deal of information — and a great deal of practice. This exercise gives you a feel for some of the challenges involved in developing such a plan.

Directions

1. Suppose you are the president of a small software-development firm that for years has sold a utility that added functionality to the operating system used in most computers. Now, you suddenly face a serious problem: Microsoft has changed its operating system, and your product no longer serves any purpose.
2. Using the 10 steps outlined in Figure 16.8, develop a strategic plan to keep your company alive. Make any assumptions you need to develop your plan, but state these in the process of describing it.

Questions for Discussion

1. How easy — or difficult — was it to develop this strategic plan? What would have made the process easier or more effective?
2. Which step do you imagine would be easiest to implement? Which step do you think would be most challenging?
3. Would you use competitive intelligence in the course of implementing your plan? If so, how?
4. What special challenges, if any, would the employees of your company face as they implemented this plan? How would you overcome these challenges?

SKILLS BANK

WORKING IN GROUPS

Recognizing Impediments to Change — and How to Overcome Them

To confront the reality of organizational change, one of the most fundamental steps involves recognizing the barriers to it. Then, once these impediments have been identified, consideration can be given to ways of overcoming them. This exercise helps you to practice thinking along these lines while working in groups.

Directions

1. Divide the class into groups of approximately six, and gather each group around a circle.
2. Each group should consider the following situations:
   - *Situation A*: A highly sophisticated e-mail system is being introduced at a large university. It will replace the practice of transmitting memos on paper.
   - *Situation B*: A very popular employee who has been with the company for many years is retiring. He will be replaced by a completely new employee from the outside.
3. For each situation, discuss three major impediments to change.
4. Identify a way of overcoming each impediment.
5. Someone from the group should record the answers and present them to the class for discussion.

Questions for Discussion

1. Were the impediments to change in each situation similar or different?
2. Were the ways of overcoming the impediments in each situation similar or different?
3. How might the nature of the situation being confronted dictate the types of barriers involved and the ease with which they may be overcome?

NOTES

CHAPTER 1

Preview Case Source

Yates, R. E. (1998). *The Kikkoman chronicles*. New York: McGraw-Hill.

Chapter Notes

1. Greenberg, J. (Ed.) (1994). *Organizational behavior: The state of the science*. Hillsdale, NJ: Erlbaum.

2. Elden, M., & Chisholm, R. F. (1993). Emerging varieties of action research: Introduction to the special issue. *Human Relations, 46*, 121–142.

3. Warner, M. (1994). Organizational behavior revisited. *Human Relations, 47*, 1151–1166.

4. Kennedy, C. (1991). *Instant management*. New York: William Morrow and Company.

5. Taylor, F. W. (1947). *Scientific management*. New York: Harper & Row.

6. Drucker, P. F. (1974). *Management: Tasks, responsibilities, practices*. New York: Harper & Row (quote, p. 27).

7. Münsterberg, H. (1913). *Psychology and industrial efficiency*. New York: Houghton Mifflin.

8. Metcalf, H., & Urwick, L. F. (Eds.) (1942). *Dynamic administration: The collected papers of Mary Parker Follett*. New York: Harper & Row.

9. Bedian, A. (1976, June). Finding the one best way: An appreciation of Frank B. Gilbreth, the father of motion study. *Conference Board Record*, pp. 37–39.

10. Gotcher, J. M. (1992). Assisting the handicapped: The pioneering efforts of Frank and Lillian Gilbreth. *Journal of Management, 18*, 5–13.

11. Mayo, E. (1933). *The human problems of an industrial civilization*. London: MacMillan.

12. Roethlisberger, F. J., & Dickson, W. J. (1939). *Management and the worker*. Cambridge, MA: Harvard University Press.

13. Baron, R. A., Rea, M. S., & Daniels, S. G. (1992). Lighting as a source of environmentally-generated positive affect in work settings: Impact on cognitive tasks and interpersonal behavior. *Motivation and Emotion, 15*, 1–34.

14. Fayol, H. (1949). *General and industrial management*. London: Pittman.

15. Weber, M. (1921). *Theory of social and economic organization* (A. M. Henderson & T. Parsons, Trans.). London: Oxford University Press.

16. Flexner, S. B. (1976). *I hear America talking*. New York: Van Nostrand Reinhold.

17. Lawrence, P. R. (1987). Historical development of organizational behavior. In J. W. Lorsch (Ed.), *Handbook of organizational behavior.* (pp. 1–9). Englewood Cliffs, NJ: Prentice-Hall.

18. Gardner, B., & Moore, G. (1945). *Human relations in industry*. Homewood, IL: Irwin.

19. See note 18.

20. Gordon, R. A., & Howell, J. E. (1959). *Higher education for business*. New York: Columbia University Press.

21. Case, J. (1993, April). A company of businesspeople. *Inc.*, pp. 79–84, 86–87, 90, 92–93.

22. McGregor, D. (1960). *The human side of enterprise*. New York: McGraw-Hill.

23. Pennings, J. M. (1992). Structural contingency theory: A reappraisal. In B. M. Staw & L. L. Cummings (Eds.), *Research in organizational behavior* (Vol. 14, pp. 267–310). Greenwich, CT: JAI Press.

24. Katz, D., & Kahn, R. (1978). *The social psychology of organizations*. New York: Wiley.

25. Cascio, W. E. (1995). Whither industrial and organizational in a changing world of work? *American Psychologist, 50*, 928–939 (quote, p. 928).

26. Gwynne, S. C. (1992, September 28). The long haul. *Time*, pp. 34–38.

27. Investing in people and prosperity. (1994, May). U.S. Department of Labor, Washington, DC, p. 7.

28. See note 27.

29. Brown, L. R., Kane, H., & Ayres, E. (1994). *Vital signs*. New York: W. W. Norton.

30. Lodge, G. C. (1995). *Managing globalization in the age of interdependence*. San Francisco: Pfeifer.

31. Anonymous. (1993, March 27). A survey of multinationals. *The Economist*, p. 6.

32. "Cross-border investment is high." (1993, September 15). *Chemical Week*, p. 5.

33. Ronen, S. (1986). *Comparative multinational management*. New York: Wiley.

34. Duerr, M. G. (1986, October). International business management: Its four tasks. *Conference Board Record*, pp. 42–45 (quote, p. 43).

35. Earley, P. C., & Singh, H. (1995). International and intercultural management research: What's next? *Academy of Management Journal, 38*, 327–340.

36. Ogbonna, E. (1993). Managing organizational culture: Fantasy or reality? *Human Resource Management Journal, 3*(2), 42–54.

37. DeCieri, H., & Dowling, P. J. (1995). Cross-cultural issues in organizational behavior. In C. L. Cooper & D. M. Rousseau (Eds.), *Trends in organi-*

zational behavior (Vol. 2, pp. 127–145). New York: Wiley.

38. Hesketh, B., & Bochner, S. (1994). Technological change in a multicultural context: Implications for training and career planning. In H. C. Triandis, M. D. Dunnette, & L. Hough (Eds.), *Handbook of industrial and organizational psychology* (Vol. 4, pp. 190–240). Palo Alto, CA: Consulting Psychologists Press.

39. Janssens, M. (1995). Intercultural interaction: A burden on international managers? *Journal of Organizational Behavior, 16,* 155–167.

40. See note 37.

41. Garraty, J. A., & McCaughey, R. A. (1987). *The American nation: A history of the United States* (6th ed.). New York: Harper & Row.

42. Boyett, J. H., & Boyett, J. T. (1995). *Beyond workplace 2000.* New York: Dutton.

43. Carnevale, A. P., & Stone, S. C. (1995). *The American mosaic: An in-depth report on the future of diversity at work.* New York: McGraw-Hill.

44. See note 43.

45. Mason, J. C. (1993, July). Working in the family way. *HRMagazine,* pp. 25–28.

46. Shellenbarger, S. (1994, February 16). The aging of America is making "elder care" a big workplace issue. *Wall Street Journal,* p A1.

47. Fenn, D. (1993, July) Bottoms up. *Inc.,* pp. 57–60.

48. Martinez, M. N. (1993). Family support makes business sense. *HRMagazine,* pp. 38–43.

49. Meier, L., & Meagher, L. (1993, September). Teaming up to manage. *Working Woman,* pp. 31–32, 108.

50. Mason, J. C. (1993, July). Working in the family way. *HRMagazine,* pp. 25–28.

51. See note 50 (quote, p. 28).

52. See note 50.

53. Cohen, A. R., & Gadon, H. (1980). *Alternative work schedules.* Reading, MA: Addison-Wesley.

54. Galen, M., Palmer, A. T., Cuneo, A., & Maremont, M. (1993, June 28). Work & family. *Business Week,* pp. 80–84, 86, 88.

55. Olmsted, B., & Smith, S. (1994). *Creating a flexible workplace* (2nd ed.). New York: AMACOM.

56. Meier, L., & Meagher, L. (1993, September). Teaming up to manage. *Working Woman,* pp. 31–32, 108.

57. See note 56.

58. See note 56.

59. Greengard, S. (1994, September). Workers go virtual. *Personnel Journal,* p. 71.

60. Kugelmass, J. (1995). *Telecommuting: A manager's guide to flexible work arrangements.* New York: Lexington Books.

61. DuBrin, A. J. (1994). *Contemporary applied management: Skills for managers* (4th ed.). Burr Ridge, IL: Irwin.

62. Zuboff, S. (1988). *In the age of the smart machine.* New York: Basic Books.

63. Bridges, W. (1994). *Job shift: How to prosper in a workplace without jobs.* Reading, MA: Addison-Wesley.

64. See note 63.

65. Tomasko, R. M. (1993). *Rethinking the corporation,* New York: AMACOM.

66. Bettis, R. A., Bradley, S. P., & Hamel, G. (1992). Outsourcing and industrial decline. *Academy of Management Review, 6,* 7–22.

67. Haapaniemi, P. (1993, Winter). Taking care of business. *Solutions,* pp. 6–8, 10–13.

68. See note 67.

69. Stewart, T. A. (1993, December 13). Welcome to the revolution. *Fortune,* pp. 66–68, 70, 72, 76, 78.

70. Fierman, J. (1994, January 24). The contingency workforce. *Fortune,* pp. 30–34, 36.

71. Brotherton, P. (1995, December). Staff to suit. *HRMagazine,* pp. 50–55.

72. Aley, J. (1995, September 18). Where the jobs are. *Fortune,* pp. 53–54, 56.

73. Byrne, J. A., Brandt, R., & Port, O. (1993, February 8). The virtual corporation: The company of the future will be the ultimate in adaptability. *Business Week,* pp. 98–102.

74. Davidow, W. H., & Malone, M. S. (1992). *The virtual corporation.* New York: Harper Business.

75. See note 74 (quote, p. 99).

76. Walton, M. (1990). *The Demming management method at work.* New York: Perigree.

77. Hart, C. W. L., & Bogan, C. E. (1992). *The Baldridge.* New York: McGraw-Hill.

78. Hodgetts, R. M. (1993). *Blueprints for continuous improvement: Lessons from the Baldridge winners.* New York: AMACOM.

79. Boyett, J. H., Schwartz, S., Osterwise, L., & Bauer, R. (1993). *The quality journey: How winning the Baldridge sparked the remaking of IBM.* New York: Dutton.

80. Ferrell, O. C., & Fraedrich, J. (1994). *Business ethics: Ethical decision making and cases* (2nd ed.). Boston: Houghton Mifflin.

81. Henderson, V. E. (1992). *What's ethical in business?* New York: McGraw-Hill (quote, p. 24).

82. Verschoor, C. C. (1998). A study of the link between a corporation's financial performance and its commitment to ethics. *Journal of Business Ethics, 17,* 1509–1516.

83. See note 87 (quotes, pp. 1512–1513).

84. Embley, L. L. (1993). *Doing well while doing good.* Englewood Cliffs, NJ: Prentice-Hall.

85. DuBrin, A. J. (1994). *Contemporary applied management: Skills for managers* (4th ed.). Burr Ridge, IL: Irwin.

86. Manley, W. W., II. (1991). *Executive's handbook of model business conduct codes.* Englewood Cliffs, NJ: Prentice-Hall.

87. Treviño, L. K., & Nelson, K. A. (1995). *Managing business ethics.* New York: Wiley.

88. Skelly, J. (1995, March/April). The Caux round table principles for business: The rise of international ethics. *Business Ethics,* supplement pp. 2–5.

Case in Point Source

Material from pp. 5–34 of Special Advertising section in *Business Week.*

APPENDIX

1. Cooper, H., & Hedges, L. V. (1994). *The handbook of research synthesis.* New

York: Russell Sage Foundation.

2. Van Mannen, J., Dabbs, J. M., Jr., & Faulkner, R. R. (1982). *Varieties of qualitative research*. Beverly Hills, CA: Sage Publications.

3. Greenberg, J., & Folger, R. (1988). *Controversial issues in social research methods*. New York: Springer-Verlag.

4. Eisenhardt, K. M. (1989). Building theories from case study research. *Academy of Management Review, 14*, 532–550.

PREVIEW CASE SOURCE

Kirkpatrick, D. (1998, December 7). The e-ware war: Competition comes to enterprise software. *Fortune*, pp. 102–104, 106, 108, 110, 112.

CHAPTER 2

Preview Case Source

Barrett, A. (1997, November 17). Lessons for the tutors. *Business Week*, pp. 91, 93.

Chapter Notes

1. Schiffman, H. R. (1993). *Sensation and perception* (4th ed.). New York: Wiley.

2. Kenny, D. A. (1994). *Interpersonal perception*. New York: Guilford.

3. Weiner, B. (1995). *Judgments of responsibility*. New York: Guilford.

4. Jones, E. E., & McGillis, D. (1976). Correspondent inferences and the attribution cube: A comparative reappraisal. In J. H. Harvey, W. J. Ickes, & R. F. Kidd (Eds.), *New directions in attribution research* (Vol. 1, pp. 389–420). Hillsdale, NJ: Lawrence Erlbaum Associates.

5. Kelley, H. H. (1972). Attribution in social interaction (pp. 1–26). In E. E. Jones, D. E. Kanous, H. H. Kelley, R. E. Nisbett, S. Valins, & B. Weiner (Eds.), *Attribution: Perceiving the causes of behavior*. Morristown, NJ: General Learning Press.

6. Burger, J. M. (1991). Changes in attribution errors over time: The ephemeral fundamental attribution error. *Social Cognition, 9*, 182–193.

7. Murphy, K. R., Jako, R. A., & Anhalt, R. L. (1993). Nature and consequences of halo error: A critical analysis. *Journal of Applied Psychology, 78*, 218–225.

8. Pulakos, E. D., & Wexley, K. N. (1983). The relationship among perceptual similarity, sex, and performance ratings in manager–subordinate dyads. *Academy of Management Journal, 26*, 129–139.

9. Turban, D. B., & Jones, A. P. (1988). Supervisor–subordinate similarity: Types, effects, and mechanisms. *Journal of Applied Psychology, 73*, 228–234.

10. Dougherty, T. W., Turban, D. B., & Callender, J. C. (1994). Confirming first impressions in the employment interview: A field study of interviewer behavior. *Journal of Applied Psychology, 79*, 659–665.

11. Dearborn, D. C., & Simon, H. A. (1958). Selective perception: A note on the departmental identification of executives. *Sociometry, 21*, 140–144.

12. Waller, M. J., Huber, G. P., & Glick, W. H. (1995). Functional background as a determinant of executives' selective perception. *Academy of Management Journal, 38*, 943–974.

13. Srull, T. K., & Wyer, R. S. (1988). *Advances in social cognition*. Hillsdale, NJ: Lawrence Erlbaum Associates.

14. Mohrman, A. M., Jr., Resnick-West, S. M., & Lawler, E. E., III. (1989). *Designing performance appraisal systems*. San Francisco: Jossey-Bass.

15. Ilgen, D. R., Major, D. A., & Tower, S. L. (1994). The cognitive revolution in organizational behavior (pp. 1–22). In J. Greenberg (Ed.), *Organizational behavior: The state of the science*. Hillsdale, NJ: Lawrence Erlbaum Associates.

16. Hogan, E. A. (1987). Effects of prior expectations on performance ratings: A longitudinal study. *Academy of Management Journal, 30*, 354–368.

17. Wayne, S. J., & Liden, R. C. (1995). Effects of impression management on performance ratings: A longitudinal study. *Academy of Management Journal, 38*, 232–260.

18. Harris, P. R., & Moran, R. T. (1991). *Managing cultural differences* (3rd ed.). Houston: Gulf Publishing.

19. Fletcher, C. (1989). Impression management in the selection interview. In R. A. Giacalone & P. Rosenfeld (Eds.), *Impression management in the organization* (pp. 269–282). Hillsdale, NJ: Lawrence Erlbaum Associates.

20. Giacalone, R. A., & Rosenfeld, P. (Eds.). (1989). *Impression management in the organization*. Hillsdale, NJ: Lawrence Erlbaum Associates.

21. Jordan, M., & Sullivan, K. (1995, September 8). Saving face: Japanese can rent mourners, relatives, friends, even enemies to buff an image. *Washington Post*, pp. A1, A28.

22. Stevens, C. K., & Kristof, A. L. (1995). Making the right impression: A field study of applicant impression management during job interviews. *Journal of Applied Psychology, 80*, 587–606.

23. Garbett, T. (1988). *How to build a corporation's identity and project its image*. Lexington, MA: Lexington Books.

24. Gatewood, R. D., Gowan, M. A., & Lautenschlager, G. J. (1993). Corporate image, recruitment image, and initial job choice decisions. *Academy of Management Journal, 36*, 414–427.

25. Brown, E. (1999, March 1). America's most admired companies. *Fortune*, pp. 68–73.

26. Bongiorno, L. (1995, April 10). The duller the better: For 1994's annual reports, modesty is a virtue. *Business Week*, p. 44.

27. Wick, C. W., & Leon, L. S. (1993). *The learning edge: How smart managers and smart companies stay ahead*. New York: McGraw-Hill.

28. Atkinson, R. C., Herrnstein, R. J., Lindzey, G., & Luce, R. D. (Eds.). (1988). *Stevens' handbook of experimental psychology* (2nd ed.) (Vol. 1, pp. 218–266). New York: Wiley.

29. Skinner, B. F. (1969). *Contingencies of reinforcement*. New York: Appleton-Century-Crofts.

30. Scott, W. E., & Podsakoff, P. M. (1985). *Behavioral principles in the practice of management*. New York: Wiley.

31. Bandura, A. (1986). *Social foundations of thought and action*. Englewood Cliffs, NJ: Prentice Hall.

32. Harrison, J. K. (1992). Individual and combined effects of behavior modeling and the cultural assimilator in cross-cultural management training. *Journal of Applied Psychology, 77*, 962.

33. Goldstein, I. L. (1991). Training in work organizations. In M. D. Dunnette & L. M. Hough (Eds.), *Handbook of industrial and organizational psychology* (2nd ed.) (Vol. 2, pp. 507–620). Palo Alto, CA: Consulting Psychologists Press.

34. Schnake, M. E. (1986). Vicarious punishment in a work setting. *Journal of Applied Psychology, 71,* 343–345.

35. Carnevlae, A. P., & Gainer, L. J. (1989). *The learning enterprise.* Alexandria, VA: American Society for Training and Development.

36. Del Valle, C. (1993, April 26). From high schools to high skills. *Business Week,* pp. 110, 112.

37. Francesco, A. M., & Gold, B. A. (1998). *International organizational behavior.* Upper Saddle River, NJ: Prentice-Hall.

38. Gist, M. E., Stevens, C. K., & Bavetta, A. G. (1991). Effects of self-efficacy and post-training intervention on the acquisition and maintenance of complex interpersonal skills. *Personnel Psychology, 44,* 837–861.

39. O'Reilly, B. (1993, April 5). How execs learn now. *Fortune,* pp. 52–54, 58.

40. Argyris, C. (1991, May–June). Teaching smart people how to learn. *Harvard Business Review, 69*(3), 99–109.

41. Meister, J. C. (1998). *Corporate universities.* New York: McGraw-Hill.

42. Driskell, J. E., Cooper, C., & Moran, A. (1994). Does mental practice enhance performance? *Journal of Applied Psychology, 79,* 481–492.

43. Tracey, B. J., Tannenbaum, S. I., & Kavanaugh, M. J. (1995). Applying trained skills on the job: The importance of the work environment. *Journal of Applied Psychology, 80,* 239–252.

44. Tannenbaum, S. I., & Yukl, G. A. (1992). Training and development in work organizations. *Annual Review of Psychology, 43,* 399–441.

45. Hoffman, R. (1995, April). Ten reasons you should be using 360-feedback. *HRMagazine,* pp. 82–85.

46. Edwards, M. R., & Ewen, A. J. (1996). *360° feedback: The powerful new model for employee assessment and performance improvement.* New York: AMACOM.

47. Tornow, W. W., & London, M. (1998). *Maximizing the value of 360-degree feedback.* San Francisco: Jossey-Bass.

48. Lepsinger, R., & Lucia, A. D. (1997). *The art and science of 360-degree feedback.* San Francisco: Jossey-Bass.

49. Flannery, T. P., Hofrichter, D. A., & Platten, P. E. (1996). *People, performance, and pay.* New York: Free Press.

50. Hills, F., Bergmann, T., & Scarpello, V. (1994). *Compensation decision making.* New York: Dryden.

51. Denton, D. K. (1992, September). Multi-skilled teams replace old work systems. *HRMagazine,* 55–56.

52. Gross, S. E. (1995). *Compensation for teams.* New York: AMACOM.

53. Gross, S. E. (1996, November–December). When jobs become team roles, what do you pay for? *Compensation and Benefits Review,* pp. 48–51.

54. Novak, C. J. (1997, April). Proceed with caution when paying teams. *HRMagazine,* pp. 73–78.

55. Miller, L. (1978). *Behavior management.* New York: Wiley.

56. Brooks, S. S. (1994, April). Non-cash ways to compensate employees. *HRMagazine,* pp. 38–43.

57. Lawler, E. O. (1993, April). How MCI wrought a 100-day "miracle." *Business Marketing,* pp. 56–57.

58. Frederiksen, L. W. (1982). *Handbook of organizational behavior management.* New York: Wiley.

59. Beyer, J., & Trice, H. M. (1984). A field study of the use and perceived effects of discipline in controlling work performance. *Academy of Management Journal, 27,* 743–754.

60. Trahan, W. A., & Steiner, D. D. (1994). Factors affecting supervisors' use of disciplinary actions following poor performance. *Journal of Organizational Behavior, 15,* 129–139.

61. Oberle, R. J. (1978). Administering disciplinary actions. *Personnel Journal, 18*(3), 30–33.

62. Arvey, R. D., & Jones, A. P. (1985). The use of discipline in organizational settings: A framework for future research. In L. L. Cummings & R. M. Staw (Eds.), *Research in organizational behavior* (Vol. 7, pp. 367–408). Greenwich, CT: JAI Press.

63. Kiechell, W., III. (1990, May 7). How to discipline in the modern age. *Fortune,* pp. 179–180 (quote, p. 180).

64. Arvey, R. E., & Icancevich, J. M. (1980). Punishment in organizations: A review, propositions, and research suggestions. *Academy of Management Review, 5,* 123–132.

65. Trevino, L. K. (1992). The social effects of punishment in organizations: A justice perspective. *Academy of Management Review, 17,* 647–676.

66. Lussier, R. H. (1990, August), A discipline model for increasing performance. *Supervisory Management,* pp. 6–7.

67. Kerr, S. (1975). On the follow of rewarding "A" while hoping for "B" *Academy of Management Journal, 18,* 769–783.

68. Dechant, K., & Viega, J. (1995). More on the folly. *Academy of Management Executive, 9,* 15–16.

Case in Point Sources

Safeway workers frowning upon service-with-a-smile policy (1998, September 3). *Columbus Dispatch,* p. C1, and Kornheiser, T. (1998, September 13). Unsafe way? *Washington Post,* p. F1.

CHAPTER 3
Preview Case

Greising, D. (1998, March 23). Fast Eddie's future bank: How Crutchfield is racing to revolutionize First Union. *Business Week,* pp. 74–77.

Chapter Notes

1. Carver, C. S., & Scheier, M. F. (1992). *Perspectives on personality* (2nd ed.). Boston: Allyn & Bacon.

2. Eysenk, M. W. (1994). *Individual differences.* Hillsdale, NJ: Erlbaum.

3. Mischel, W. (1985, August). *Personality: Lost or found? Identifying when individual differences make a difference.* Paper presented at the meeting of the American Psychological Association, Los Angeles, CA.

4. Osipow, S. H. (1990). Convergence in theories of career choice and development: Review and prospect. *Journal of Vocational Behavior, 36,* 122–131.

5. Caldwell, D. F., & O'Reilly, C. A., III (1990). Measuring person-job fit with a profile-comparison process. *Journal of Applied Psychology, 75,* 648–657.

6. Allport, G. W., & Odbert, H. S. (1936). Trait names: A psycholexical study. *Psychological Monographs, 47,* 211–214.

7. Costa, P. T., & McCrae, R. R. (1992). *The NEO-PI Personality Inventory.* Odessa, FL: Psychological Assessment Resources.

8. Funder, D. C., & Colvin, C. R. (1991). Explorations in behavioral consistency. Properties of persons, situations, and behavior. *Journal of Personality and Social Psychology, 60,* 773–794.

9. Salgado, J. F. (1997). The five-factor model of personality and job performance in the European community. *Journal of Applied Psychology, 82,* 30–43.

10. Judge, T. A., Martocchio, J. J., & Thoresn, C. J. (1998). Five-factor model of personality and employee absence. *Journal of Applied Psychology, 82,* 745–755.

11. See note 10.

12. Barrick, M. R., Stewart, G. L., Neubert, M. J., & Mount, M. K. (1998). Relating member ability and personality to work-team processes and team effectiveness. *Journal of Applied Psychology, 83,* 377–391.

13. George, J. M., & Brief, A. P. (1992). Feeling good—doing good: A conceptual analysis of the mood at work-organizational spontaneity relationships. *Psychological Bulletin, 112,* 310–329.

14. Isen, A. M., & Baron, R. A. (1992). Positive affect as a factor in organizational behavior. In B. M. Staw & L. L. Cummings, eds. *Research in organizational behavior,* (Vol. 13, pp. 1–54). Greenwich, CT: JAI Press.

15. Staw, B. M. & Barsade, S. G. (1993). Affect and managerial performance: A test of the sadder-but-wiser vs. happier-and-smarter hypotheses. *Administrative Science Quarterly, 38,* 304–331.

16. George, J. M. (1990). Personality, affect, and behavior in groups. *Journal of Applied Psychology, 75,* 107–116.

17. Friedman, M., & Rosenman, R. H. (1974). *Type A behavior and your heart.* New York: Knopf.

18. Lee, C., Ashford, S. J., & Jamieson, L. F. (1993). The effects of type A be-havior dimensions and optimism on coping strategy, health, and performance. *Journal of Organizational Behavior, 14,* 143–157.

19. Schauabroeck, J., Ganster, D. C., & Kemmerer, B. E. (1994). Job complexity, "Type A" behavior, and cardiovascular disorder: A prospective study. *Academy of Management Journal, 37,* 426–439.

20. Glass, D. C. (1977). *Behavior patterns, stress, and coronary disease.* Hillsdale, NJ: Erlbaum.

21. Holmes, D. S., McGilley, B. M., & Houston, B. K. (1984). Task-related arousal of type A and type B persons: Level of challenge and response specificity. *Journal of Personality and Social Psychology, 46,* 1322–1327.

22. Jamal, M., & Baba, V. V. (1991). Type A behavior, its prevalence and consequences among women nurse: An empirical examination. *Human Relations, 44,* 1213–1228.

23. Lee, M., & Kanungo, R. (1984). *Management of work and personal life.* New York: Praeger.

24. Berman, M., Gladue, B., & Taylor, S. (1993). The effects of hormones, Type A behavior pattern and provocation on aggression in men. *Motivation and Emotion, 17,* 125–138.

25. Doktor, R. H. (1990). Asian and American CEOs: A comparative study. *Organizational Dynamics, 18*(3), 36–56.

26. Baron, R. A. (1989). Personality and organizational conflict: Effects of the type A behavior pattern and self-monitoring. *Organizational Behavior and Human Decisions Processes, 44,* 281–297.

27. Maurer, T. J., & Pierce, H. R. (1998). A comparison of Likert scale and traditional measures of self-efficacy. *Journal of Applied Psychology, 83,* 324–329.

28. Wood, R., Bandura, A., & Bailey, T. (1990). Mechanisms governing organizational performance in complex decision-making environments. *Organizational Behavior and Human Decision Processes, 46,* 181–201.

29. Kanger, R., & Kanfer, F. H. (1991). Goals and self-regulation: applications of theory to work settings. *Advances in Motivation and Achievement, 7,* 287–326.

30. Bandura, A. (1997). *Self-efficacy: The exercise of control.* New York: Freeman.

31. Judge, T. A., Locke, E. A., & Durham, C. C. (1997). The dispositional cause of job satisfaction: A core evaluations approach. *Research in Organizational Behavior, 19,* 151–188.

32. Gist, M. E., & Mitchell, T. R. (1992). Self-efficacy: A theoretical analysis of its determinants and malleability. *Academy of Management Review, 17,* 183–211.

33. Mitchell, T. E., Hopper, H., Daniels, D., George-Falvy, J., & James, L. R. (1994). Predicting self-efficacy and performance during skill acquisition. *Journal of Applied Psychology, 79,* 506–507.

34. Judge, T. A., Locke, E. A., Durhamn, C. C., & Kluger, A. N. (1998). Dispositional effects on job and life satisfaction: the role of core evaluations. *Journal of Applied Psychology, 83,* 17–34.

35. Eden, D., & Aviram, A. (1993). Self-efficacy training to speed reemployment: Helping people to help themselves. *Journal of Applied Psychology, 78,* 352–360.

36. Snyder, M. (1987). *Public appearance/private realities: The psychology self-monitoring.* San Francisco: Freeman.

37. Caldwell, D. F., & O'Reilly, C. A., III. (1982). Boundary spanning and individual performance: The impact of self-monitoring. *Journal of Applied Psychology, 67,* 124–127.

38. Kilduff, M., & Day, D. V. (1994). Do chameleons get ahead? The effects of self-monitoring on managerial careers. *Academy of Management Journal, 37,* 1047–1060.

39. Rosenbaum, J. E. (1979). Tournament mobility: Career patterns in a corporation. *Administrative Science Quarterly, 24,* 220–241.

40. Sellers, P. (1996, January 15). What exactly is charisma? *Fortune,* pp. 68–72, 74–75.

41. Friedman, H. S., & Miller-Herringer, T. (1991). Nonverbal display of emotion in public and private: Self-monitoring, personality, and expressive cues. *Journal of Personality and Social Psychology, 62,* 766–775.

42. Jamieson, D. W., Lydon, J. E., & Zanna, M. P. (1987). Attitude and activity preference simliarity: Different bases of interpersonal attraction for low and high self-monitors. *Journal of Personality and Social Psychology, 53,* 1052–1060.

43. Christie, R., & Geis, F. L. (1970). *Studies in Machiavellianism*. New York: Academic Press.

44. McHoskey, J. W., Worzel, W., & Szyarto, C. (1998). Machiavellianism and psychopathy. *Journal of Personality and Social Psychology, 74,* 192–210.

45. See note 44.

46. Wilson, D. S., Near, D., & Miller, R. R. (1997). Machiavellianism: A synthesis of the evolutionary and psychological literatures. *Psychological Bulletin, 119,* 285–299.

47. Schultz, C. J., II. (1993). Situational and dispositional predictors of performance: A test of the hypothesized Machiavellianism × structure interaction among sales persons. *Journal of Applied Social Psychology, 23,* 478–498.

48. O'Connell, L. (1997, May 6). Be set for co-workers who have it in for you. *Orlando Sentinel,* p. B1.

49. McClelland, D. C. (1985). *Human motivation.* Glenview, IL: Scott, Foresman.

50. McClelland, D. C. (1977). Entrepreneurship and management in the years ahead. In C. A. Bramletter (Ed.), *The individual and the future of organizations* (pp. 12–29). Atlanta: Georgia State University.

51. Miller, D., & Droge, C. (1986). Psychological and traditional determinants of structure. *Administrative Science Quarterly, 31,* 539–560.

52. McClelland, D. C. (1961). *The achieving society.* Princeton, NJ: Van Nostrand.

53. Lynn, R. (1991). *The secret of the miracle economy.* London: SAU.

54. Furnham, A., Kirkcaldy, B. D., & Lynn, R. (1994). National attitudes to competitiveness, money, and work among young people: First, second, and third world differences. *Human Relations, 47,* 119–132.

55. Turban, D. B., & Keon, T. L. (1993). Organizational attractiveness: An interactionist perspective. *Journal of Applied Psychology, 78,* 184–193.

56. Guthrie, J. P., Ash, R. A., & Bandapudi, V. (1995). Additional validity evidence for a measure of *morningness. Journal of Applied Psychology, 80,* 186–190.

57. Fierman, J. (1995, August 21), It's 2 A.M. Let's go to work. *Fortune,* pp. 82–86.

58. Totterdell, P., Spelten, E., Smith, L., Barton, J., & Folkard, S. (1995). Recovery from work shifts: How long does it take? *Journal of Applied Psychology, 80,* 43–57.

59. See note 56.

60. Wallace, B. (1993). Day persons, night persons, and variability in hypnotic susceptibility. *Journal of Personality and Social Psychology, 64,* 827–833.

61. Eysenk, M. W. (1994). *Individual differences.* Hillsdale, NJ: Erlbaum.

62. Neisser, U., Boodoo, G., Bouchard, T. J., Jr., Bykin, A. W., Brody, N., Ceci, S. J., Halpen, D. F., Loehlin, J. C., Perloff, R., Sternberg, R. J., & Urbina, S. (1996). Intelligence: Knowns and unknowns. *American Psychologist, 51,* 77–101.

63. Sternberg, R. J., Wagner, R. K., Williams, W. M., & Horvath, J. A. (1995). Testing common sense. *American Psychologist, 50,* 912–927.

64. Goleman, D. (1998). *Working with emotional intelligence.* New York: Bantam.

65. See note 64.

65. Baron, R. A., & Markman, G. (1998). *Social competence and entrepreneurs' financial success: Evidence for the role of group-level variables in the performance of new ventures.* Manuscript submitted for publication.

66. Reed, T. E., & Jensen, A. R. (In press). Conduction velocity in a brain nerve pathway of normal adults correlates with intelligence level. *Intelligence.*

67. See note 66.

68. Rempel, D. M., Harrison, R. J., & Barnhart, S. (1992). Work-related cumulative trauma disorders of the upper extremity. *Journal of the American Medial Association, 267,* 833–843.

69. Holweijn, M., & Lotens, W. A. (1992). The influence of backpack design on physical performance. *Ergonomics, 35,* 149–157.

70. Bloswick, D. S., Gerber, A., Sebesta, D., Johnson, S., & Mecham, W. (1994). Effect of mailbag design on musculoskeletal fatigue and metabolic load. *Human Factors, 36,* 210–218.

Case in Point Source

Tietlebaum, R. (1997, December 8). Who is Bob Kierlin — And why is he so successful? *Fortune,* pp. 245–246, 248.

CHAPTER 4
Preview Case Sources

Palmeri, C. (1997, September 8). Believe in yourself, believe in the merchandise. *Forbes,* pp. 118–119, 122, 124. Internet site: http://www.wal-mart.com/newsroom; and Vance, S. S., & Scott, R. V. (1997). *Wal-Mart: A history of Sam Walton's retail phenomenon.* New York: Twayne.

Chapter Notes

1. Kanfer, R. (1990). Motivational theory and industrial and organizational psychology. In M. D. Dunnette & L. M. Hough (Eds.), *Handbook of industrial and organizational psychology* (2nd ed.) (Vol. 1, pp. 75–170). Palo Alto, CA: Consulting Psychologists Press.

2. Blau, G. (1993). Operationalizing direction and level of effort and testing their relationships to individual job performance. *Organizational Behavior and Human Decision Processes, 55,* 152–170.

3. Jones, B. (1998, January). What future European recruits want. *Management Review,* p. 6.

4. "Work still a labor of love." (1981, April 20). *The Columbus Dispatch,* p. 1.

5. Maslow, A. H., Stephens, D. C., & Heil, G. (1998). *Maslow on management.* New York: Wiley.

6. Mudrack, P. E. (1992). 'Work' or 'leisure'? The Protestant work ethic and participation in an employee fitness program. *Journal of Organizational Behavior, 13,* 81–88.

7. Restructuring the family diet. (1995, September). *World Traveler,* p. 92.

8. Miller, A., & Springen, K. (1988, October 31). Forget cash, give me the TV. *Newsweek,* 58.

9. Porter, L. W. (1961). A study of perceived need satisfaction in bottom and middle management jobs. *Journal of Applied Psychology, 45,* 1–10.

10. Wahba, M. A., & Bridwell, L. G. (1976). Maslow reconsidered: A review of research on the need hierarchy theory. *Organizational Behavior and Human Performance, 15,* 212–240.

11. Alderfer, C. P. (1972). *Existence, relatedness, and growth.* New York: Free Press.

12. Salancik, G. R., & Pfeffer, J. (1977). An examination of need-satisfaction models of job satisfaction. *Administrative Science Quarterly, 22,* 427–456.

13. Miller, A., & Bradburn, E. (1991, July 1). Shape up—or else! *Newsweek,* pp. 42–43.

14. Tullly, S. (1995, June 12). America's healthiest companies. *Fortune,* pp. 98–100, 104, 106.

15. McLaughlin, S. (1998). Freudian chip. *Inc. Tech.,* no. 1, p. 18.

16. Cronin, M. P. (1993, September). Easing workers' savings woes. *Inc.,* p. 29.

17. Leana, C. R., & Feldman, D. C. (1992). *Coping with job loss.* New York: Lexington Books.

18. Schwartz, E. L. (1991, June 17). Hot dogs, roller coasters, and complaints. *Business Week,* p. 27.

19. Jaffe, C. A. (1990, January). Management by fun. *Nation's Business,* pp. 58–60.

20. Gunsch, D. (1991). Award programs at work. *Personnel Journal, 23*(4), 85–89.

21. Miller, A., & Springen, K. (1988, October 31). Forget cash, give me the TV. *Newsweek,* p. 58.

22. Austin, N. K. (1994, March). Why sabbaticals make sense. *Working Woman,* pp. 19, 22, 24.

23. See note 22 (quote, p. 22).

24. Kennedy, M. M. (1998, January). It's all about time. *Across the Board,* pp. 51–52 (quote, p. 51).

25. Caggiano, C. (1998, January). Can you achieve high impact with a low-cost perk? *Inc.,* p. 82.

26. See note 22 (quote, p. 24).

27. Wood, R. A., & Locke, E. A. (1990). Goal setting and strategy effects on complex tasks. In B. M. Staw & L. L. Cummings (Eds.), *Research in organizational behavior* (Vol. 12, pp. 73–110). Greenwich, CT: JAI Press.

28. Locke, E. A., & Latham, G. P. (1990). *A theory of goal setting and task performance.* Englewood Cliffs, NJ: Prentice-Hall.

29. Mento, A. J., Locke, E. A., & Klein, H. J. (1992). Relationship of goal level to valence and instrumentality. *Journal of Applied Psychology, 77,* 395–405.

30. Wright, P. M., O'Leary-Kelly, A. M., Cortinak, J. M., Klein, H. J., & Hollenbeck, J. R. (1994). On the meaning and measurement of goal commitment. *Journal of Applied Psychology, 79,* 795–803.

31. Klein, H. J. (1991). Further evidence on the relationship between goal setting and expectancy theories. *Organizational Behavior and Human Decision Processes, 49,* 230–257.

32. Harrison, D. A., & Liska, L. Z. (1994). Promoting regular exercise in organizational fitness programs: Health-related differences in motivational building blocks. *Personnel Psychology, 47,* 47–71.

33. Gellatly, I. R., & Meyer, J. P. (1992). The effects of goal difficulty on physiological arousal, cognition, and task performance. *Journal of Applied Psychology, 77,* 694–704.

34. Wright, P. M. (1992). An examination of the relationships among monetary incentives, goal level, goal commitment, and performance. *Journal of Management, 18,* 677–693.

35. Earley, P. C., & Litucy, T. R. (1991). Delineating goal and efficacy effects: A test of three models. *Journal of Applied Psychology, 76,* 81–98.

36. Latham, G. P., & Lee, T. W. (1986). Goal setting. In E. A. Locke ed. *Generalizing from laboratory to field settings* (pp. 100–117). Lexington, MA: Lexington.

37. Latham, G., & Baldes, J. (1975). The practical significance of Locke's theory of goal setting. *Journal of Applied Psychology, 60,* 122–124.

38. Locke, E. A., & Latham, G. P. (1984). *Goal setting: A motivational technique that works!* Englewood Cliffs, NJ: Prentice-Hall.

39. Wright, P. M., Hollenbeck, J. R., Wolf, S., & McMahan, G. C. (1995). The effects of varying goal difficulty operationalizations on goal setting outcomes and processes. *Organizational Behavior and Human Decision Processes, 61,* 28–43.

40. Bernstein, A. (1991, April 29). How to motivate workers: Don't watch 'em. *Business Week,* p. 56.

41. Stedry, A. C., & Kay, E. (1964). *The effects of goal difficulty on task performance.* General Electric Company, Behavioral Research Service.

42. Latham, G. P., Erez, M., & Locke, E. A. (1988). Resolving scientific disputes by the joint design of crucial experiments by the antagonists: Application to the Erez-Latham dispute regarding participation in goal setting. *Journal of Applied Psychology, 73,* 753–772.

43. Ludwig, T. D., & Geller, E. S. (1997). Assigned versus participative goal setting and response generalization: Managing injury control among professional pizza deliverers. *Journal of Applied Psychology, 82,* 253–261.

44. Folger, R., & Cropanzano, R. (1998). *Organizational justice and human resource management.* Thousand Oaks, CA: Sage.

45. Grienberger, I. V., Rutte, C. G., & Van Kippenberg, A. F. M. (1997). Influence of social comparisons of outcomes and procedures on fairness judgments. *Journal of Applied Psychology, 82,* 913–919.

46. Greenberg, J. (1997). *The quest for justice on the job.* Thousand Oaks, CA: Sage.

47. Greenberg, J. (1987). A taxonomy of organizational justice theories. *Academy of Management Review, 12,* 9–22.

48. Adams, J. S. (1965). Inequity in social exchange. In L. Berkowitz (Ed.), *Advances in experimental social psychology* (Vol. 2, pp. 267–299). New York: Academic Press.

49. Greenberg, J. (1989). Cognitive reevaluation of outcomes in response to underpayment inequity. *Academy of Management Journal, 32,* 174–184.

50. Harder, J. W. (1992). Play for pay: Effects of inequity in a pay-for-performance context. *Administrative Science Quarterly, 37,* 321–335.

51. Greenberg, J. (1990). Employee theft as a reaction to underpayment inequity: The hidden cost of pay cuts. *Journal of Applied Psychology, 75,* 561–658.

52. Skarlicki, D. P., & Folger, R. (1997). Retaliation in the workplace: The roles of distributive, procedural, and interactional justice. *Journal of Applied Psychology, 82,* 434–443.

53. Thibaut, J., & Walker, L. (1975). *Procedural justice: A psychological analysis.* Hillsdale, NJ: Erlbaum.

54. Cropanzano, R., & Greenberg, J. (1997). Progress in organizational jus-

tice: Tunneling through the maze. In C. L. Cooper & I. T. Robertson (Eds.), *International review of industrial and organizational psychology* (Vol. 12, pp. 317–372). New York: Wiley.

55. Greenberg, J. (1986). Determinants of perceived fairness of performance evaluations. *Journal of Applied Psychology, 71,* 340–342.

56. Konovsky, M. A., & Cropanzano, R. (1993). Justice considerations in employee drug testing. In R. Cropanzano (Ed.), *Justice in the workplace.* (pp. 171–192). Hillsdale, NJ: Erlbaum.

57. Parker, C. P., Baltes, B. B., & Christiansen, N. D. (1997). Support for affirmative action, justice perceptions, and work attitudes: A study of gender and racial-ethnic group differences. *Journal of Applied Psychology, 82,* 376–389.

58. Brockner, J., & Wiesenfeld, B. M. (1996). An integrative framework for explaining reactions to decisions: The interactive effects of outcomes and procedures. *Psychological Bulletin, 120,* 189–208.

59. Martin, J. E., & Peterson, M. M. (1987). Two-tier wage structures: Implications for equity theory. *Academy of Management Journal, 30,* 297–315.

60. Ross, I. (1985, April 29). Employers win big on the move to two-tier contracts. *Fortune,* pp. 82–92.

61. Lawler, E. E., III. (1967). Secrecy about management compensation: Are there hidden costs? *Organizational Behavior and Human Performance, 2,* 182–189.

62. See note 61.

63. Schaubroeck, J., May, D. R., & Brown, F. W. (1994). Procedural justice explanations and employee reactions to economic hardship: A field experiment. *Journal of Applied Psychology, 79,* 455–460.

64. Porter, L. W., & Lawler, E. E., III. (1968). *Managerial attitudes and performance.* Homewood, IL: Irwin.

65. Mitchell, T. R. (1983). Expectancy-value models in organizational psychology. In N. Feather (Ed.), *Expectancy, incentive, and action* (pp. 293–314). Hillsdale, NJ: Erlbaum.

66. Flexible-benefit plans grow. (1989, March 21) *USA Today,* p. C1.

67. Zippo, M. (1982). Flexible benefits: Just the beginning. *Personnel Journal, 17*(4), 56–58.

68. Stern, J. M., & Stewart, G. B., III. (1993, June). Pay for performance: Only the theory is easy. *HRMagazine,* pp. 48–49.

69. Ettore, B. (1998, May). The brave new world of executive compensation. *Management Review,* p. 8.

70. Schuster, J. R., & Zingheim, P. K. (1992). *The new pay: Linking employee and organizational performance.* New York: Lexington.

71. Fierman, J. (1994, June 13). The perilous new world of fair pay. *Fortune,* pp. 57, 59, 61, 63.

72. Curry, S. (1997, August 18). Surprise! Money talks loudest. *Fortune,* p. 227.

73. Schafer, S. (1997, August). Battling a labor shortage? It's all in your imagination. *Inc.,* p. 97.

74. Griffin, R. W., & McMahan, G. C. (1994). Motivation through job design. In J. Greenberg (Ed.), *Organizational behavior: The state of the science* (pp. 23–44). Hillsdale, NJ: Erlbaum.

75. Rigdon, J. E. (1992, May 26). Using lateral moves to spur employees. *Wall Street Journal,* pp. B1, B9.

76. Campion, M. A., & McClelland, C. L. (1991). Interdiscipliniary examination of the costs and benefits of enlarged jobs: A job design quasi-experiment. *Journal of Applied Psychology, 76,* 186–198.

77. Campion, M. A., & McClelland, C. L. (1993). Follow-up and extension of the interdisciplinary costs and benefits of enlarged jobs. *Journal of Applied Psychology, 78,* 339–351.

78. Gellenhammar, P. G. (1977). *People at work.* Reading, MA: Addison-Wesley.

79. Luthans, F., & Reif, W. E. (1974). Job enrichment: Long on theory, short on practice. *Organizational Dynamics, 2*(2), 30–43.

80. Steers, R. M., & Spencer, D. G. (1977). The role of achievement motivation in job design. *Journal of Applied Psychology, 62,* 472–479.

81. Goldman, R. B. (1976). *A work experiment: Six Americans in a Swedish plant.* New York: Ford Foundation.

82. Winpisinger, W. (1973, February). Job satisfaction: A union response. *AFL-CIO American Federationist,* pp. 8–10 (quote, p. 8).

83. Hackman, J. R., & Oldham, G. R. (1980). *Work redesign.* Reading, MA: Addison-Wesley.

84. Graen, G. B., Scandura, T. A., & Graen, M. R. (1986). A field experimental test of the moderating effects of growth need strength on productivity. *Journal of Applied Psychology, 71,* 484–491.

85. Hackman, J. R., & Oldham, G. R. (1976). Motivation through the design of work: Test of a theory. *Organizational Behavior and Human Performance, 16,* 250–279.

86. Johns, G., Xie, J. L., & Fang, Y. (1992). Mediating and moderating effects in job design. *Journal of Management, 18,* 657–676.

87. Orpen, C. (1979). The effects of job enrichment on employee satisfaction, motivation, involvement, and performance: A field experiment. *Human Relations, 32,* 189–217.

88. Ropp, K. (1987, October). Candid conversations. *Personnel Administrator,* p. 49.

89. Hackman, J. R. (1976). Work design. In J. R. Hackman & J. L. Suttle, (Eds.), *Improving life at work* (96–162). Santa Monica, CA: Goodyear.

90. Callari, J. J. (1988, June). You can be a better motivator. *Traffic Management,* pp. 52–56.

91. Magnet, M. (1993, May 3). Good news for the service economy. *Fortune,* pp. 46–50, 52.

92. Finegan, J. (1993, July). People power. *Inc.,* pp. 62–63.

93. See note 92 (quote, p. 62).

Case in Point Source

Ehrenfeld, T. (1993, July). Cashing in. *Inc.,* pp. 69–70.

CHAPTER 5
Preview Case Source

Faircloth, A. (1998, August 3). Guess who's coming to Denny's. *Fortune,* pp. 108–110.

Chapter Notes

1. Quarstein, V. A., McAfee, R. B., & Glassman, M. (1992). The situational

occurrences theory of job satisfaction. *Human Relations, 45,* 859–873.

2. Hulin, C. L. (1991). Adaptation, persistence, and commitment in organizations. In M. D. Dunnette & L. M. Hough (Eds.), *Handbook of industrial and organizational psychology* (2nd ed.). (Vol. 2, pp. 445–506). Palo Alto, CA: Consulting Psychologists Press.

3. Stone, E. F., Stone, D. L., & Dipboye, R. L. (1991). Stigmas in organizations: Race, handicaps, and physical unattractiveness. In K. Kelley (Ed.), *Issues, theory, and research in industrial/organizational psychology* (pp. 385–457). Amsterdam: Elsevier.

4. McGuire, W. J. (1985). Attitudes and attitude change. In G. Lindzey & E. Aronson (Eds.), *Handbook of social psychology* (3rd ed.). (Vol. 2, pp. 233–346). New York: Random House.

5. Locke, E. A. (1976). The nature and causes of job satisfaction. In M. D. Dunnette (Ed.), *Handbook of industrial and organizational psychology* (pp. 1297–1350). Chicago: Rand McNally.

6. Thornburg, L. (1992, July). When violence hits business. *HRMagazine,* pp. 40–45.

7. Page, N. R., & Wiseman, R. L. (1993). Supervisory behavior and worker satisfaction in the United States, Mexico, and Spain. *Journal of Business Communication, 30,* 161–180.

8. Quinn, R. P., & Staines, G. L. (1979). *The 1977 quality of employment survey.* Ann Arbor, MI: Institute for Social Research.

9. Weaver, C. N. (1980). Job satisfaction in the United States in the 1970s. *Journal of Applied Psychology, 65,* 364–367.

10. Eichar, D. M., Brady, E. M., & Fortinsky, R. H. (1991). The job satisfaction of older workers. *Journal of Organizational Behavior, 12,* 609–620.

11. Bedian, A. G., Ferris, G. R., & Kacmar, K. M. (1992). Age, tenure, and job satisfaction: A tale of two perspectives. *Journal of Vocational Behavior, 40,* 33–48.

12. Lambert, S. L. (1991). The combined effect of job and family characteristics on the job satisfaction, job involvement, and intrinsic motivation of men and women workers. *Journal of Organizational Behavior, 12,* 341–363.

13. Staw, B. M., & Ross, J. (1985). Stability in the midst of change: A dispositional approach to job attitudes. *Journal of Applied Psychology, 70,* 55–77.

14. Steel, R. P., & Rentsch, J. R. (1997). The dispositional model of job attitudes revisited: Findings of a 10-year study. *Journal of Applied Psychology, 82,* 873–879.

15. Smith, P. C., Kendall, L. M., & Hulin, C. L. (1969). *The measurement of satisfaction in work and retirement.* Chicago: Rand McNally.

16. Weiss, D. J., Dawis, R. V., England, G. W., & Loftquist, L. H. (1967). *Manual for the Minnesota Satisfaction Questionnaire* (Minnesota Studies on Vocational Rehabilitation, Vol. 22). Minneapolis, MN: Industrial Relations Center, Work Adjustment Project, University of Minnesota.

17. Heneman, H. G., III, & Schwab, D. P. (1985). Pay satisfaction: Its multidimensional nature and measurement. *International Journal of Psychology, 20,* 129–141.

18. Judge, T. A., & Welbourne, T. M. (1994). A confirmatory investigation of the dimensionality of the Pay Satisfaction Questionnaire. *Journal of Applied Psychology, 79,* 461–466.

19. Sutton, R. I., & Callahan, A. L. (1987). The stigma of bankruptcy: Spoiled organizational image and its management. *Academy of Management Journal, 30,* 405–436.

20. Herzberg, F. (1966). *Work and the nature of man.* Cleveland: World.

21. Machungaws, P. D., & Schmitt, N. (1983). Work motivation in a developing country. *Journal of Applied Psychology, 68,* 31–42.

22. Landy, F. J. (1985). *Psychology of work behavior* (3rd ed.). Homewood, IL: Dorsey.

23. Magnet, M. (1993, May 3). Good news for the service economy. *Fortune,* pp. 45–50, 52.

24. Sundstrom, E. (1986). *Workplaces.* New York: Cambridge University Press.

25. Locke, E. A. (1984). Job satisfaction. In M. Gruenberg & T. Wall (Eds.), *Social psychology and organizational behavior* (pp. 93–117). London: Wiley.

26. McFarlin, D. B., & Rice, R. W. (1992). The role of facet importance as a moderator in job satisfaction processes. *Journal of Organizational Behavior, 13,* 41–54.

27. Dalton, D. R., & Todor, W. D. (1993). Turnover, transfer, absenteeism: An interdependent perspective. *Journal of Management, 19,* 193–219.

28. Porter, L. W., & Steers, R. M. (1973). Organizational work and personal factors in employee turnover and absenteeism. *Psychological Bulletin, 80,* 151–176.

29. Tett, R. P., & Meyer, J. P. (1993). Job satisfaction, organizational commitment, turnover intention, and turnover: Path analyses based on meta-analytic findings. *Personnel Psychology, 46,* 259–293.

30. Mobley, W. H., Horner, S. O., & Holingsworth, A. T. (1978). An evaluation of precursors of hospital employee turnover. *Journal of Applied Psychology, 63,* 408–414.

31. Carsten, J. M., & Spector, P. E. (1987). Unemployment, job satisfaction, and employee turnover: A meta-analytic test of the Murchinsky model. *Journal of Applied Psychology, 72,* 374–381.

32. Armour, S. (1998, November 6). Workplace absenteeism soars 25%, costs millions. *USA Today,* p. 1A.

33. Iaffaldano, M. T., & Murchinsky, P. M. (1985). Job satisfaction and job performance: A metaanalysis. *Psychological Bulletin, 97,* 251–273.

34. Porter, L. W., & Lawler, E. E., III. (1968). *Managerial attitudes and performance.* Homewood, IL: Dorsey Press.

35. Weinstein, M. (1996). *Managing to have fun.* New York: Fireside.

36. O'Reilly, B. (1994, June 13). The new deal: What companies and employees owe each other. *Fortune,* pp. 44–47, 50, 52. (quote, p. 45).

37. Ko, J., Price, J. L., & Mueller, C. W. (1997). Assessment of Meyer and Allen's three-component model of organizational commitment in South Korea. *Journal of Applied Psychology, 82,* 961–973.

38. Lee, T. W., Ashford, S. J., Walsh, J. P., & Mowday, R. T. (1992). Commitment propensity, organizational commitment, and voluntary turnover: A longitudinal study of organizational entry processes. *Journal of Management, 18,* 15–32.

39. Van Dyne, L., & Ang, S. (1998). Organizational citizenship behavior of

contingent workers in Singapore. *Academy of Management Journal, 41,* 692–703.

40. Johns, G., & Xie, J. L. (1998). Perceptions of absence from work: People's Republic of China versus Canada. *Journal of Applied Psychology, 83,* 515–530.

41. Bond, M. H. (1986). *The psychology of the Chinese people.* New York: Oxford University Press.

42. Rosen, R. H. (1991). *The healthy company.* Los Angeles: Jeremy P. Tarcher (quote, pp. 71–72).

43. Stephan, W. G. (1985). Intergroup relations. In G. Lindzey & E. Aronson (Eds.), *Handbook of social psychology* (3rd ed.). (Vol. 2, pp. 599–658). New York: Random House.

44. Fernandez, J. P., & Barr, M. (1993). *The diversity advantage.* New York: Lexington Books.

45. Malone, M. S. (1993, July 18). Translating diversity into high-tech gains. *New York Times,* p. B2.

46. Yang, C. (1993, June 21). In any language, it's unfair: More immigrants are bringing bias charges against employers. *Business Week,* pp. 110–112.

47. Hawkins, C. (1993, June 28). Denny's: The stain that isn't coming out: Can a pact with the NAACP help it overcome charges of bias? *Business Week,* pp. 98–99.

48. Mason, J. C. (1993, July). Knocking on the glass ceiling. *Management Review,* p. 5.

49. Solomon, C. M. (1992, July). Keeping hate out of the workplace. *Personnel Journal,* 30–36.

50. Ornstein, S. L., Sankowsky, D. (1994). Overcoming stereotyping and prejudice: A framework and suggestions for learning from groupist comments in the classroom. *Journal of Management Education, 18,* 80–90.

51. Boyett, J. H., & Conn, H. P. (1992). *Workplace 2000.* New York: Plume.

52. Overman, S. (1993, June). Myths hinder hiring of older workers. *HRMagazine,* pp. 51–52.

53. Hassell, B. L., & Perrewe, P. L. (1995). An examination of beliefs about older workers: Do stereotypes still exist? *Journal of Organizational Behavior, 16,* 457–468.

54. Stone, E. F., Stone, D. L., & Dipboye, R. L. (1991). Stigmas in organizations: Race, handicaps, and physical unattractiveness. In K. Kelley (Ed.), *Issues, theory, and research in industrial/organizational psychology* (pp. 385–457). Amsterdam: Elsevier.

55. Yang, C., & Forest, S. A. (1993, April 12). Business has to find a new meaning for "fairness": The Disabilities Act means some workers get special treatment. *Business Week,* p. 72.

56. See note 55.

57. See note 55.

58. Fernandez, J. P., & Barr, M. (1993). *The diversity advantage.* New York: Lexington Books.

59. Yang, C. (1993, June 21). In any language, it's unfair: More immigrants are bringing bias charges against employees. *Business Week,* pp. 110–112.

60. See note 59 (quote, p. 111).

61. See note 59.

62. Martinez, M. N. (1993, June). Recognizing sexual orientation is fair and not costly. *HRMagazine,* pp. 65–68, 70, 72.

63. Williamson, A. D. (1993, July–August). Is this the right time to come out? *Harvard Business Review,* pp. 18–20, 22, 24, 26, 28.

64. See note 63.

65. See note 63 (quote, p. 22).

66. See note 63.

67. Lander, M. (1992, June 8). Corporate women. *Business Week,* pp. 74, 75–78.

68. Steinberg, R., & Shapiro, S. (1982). Sex differences in personality traits of female and male master of business administration students. *Journal of Applied Psychology, 67,* 305–310.

69. Bilmoria, D., & Piderit, S. K. (1994). Boward committee membership: Effects of sex-based bias. *Academy of Management Journal, 37,* 1453–1477.

70. Carnevale, A. P., & Stone, S. C. (1995). *The American mosaic.* New York: McGraw-Hill.

71. Towers Perrin. (1992). *Workforce 2000 today.* New York: Author.

72. See note 71 (quote, p. 1).

73. See note 71.

74. Thomas, R. R., Jr. (1992). Managing diversity: A conceptual framework. In S. E. Jackson (Ed.), *Diversity in the workplace* (pp. 305–317). New York: Guilford Press (quote, p. 310).

75. Murray, K. (1993, August 1). The unfortunate side effects of 'diversity training.' *New York Times,* pp. E1, E3.

76. Gottfredson, L. S. (1992). Dilemmas in developing diversity programs. In S. E. Jackson (Ed.), *Diversity in the workplace* (pp. 279–305). New York: Guilford Press.

77. See note 70.

78. Urresta, L., & Hickman, J. (1998, August 3). The diversity elite. *Fortune,* pp. 114–116, 118, 120, 122.

79. Johnson, R. S. (1998, August 3). The 50 best companies for blacks and Hispanics. *Fortune,* pp. 94–96, 98, 100–102, 104, 106 (quote, p. 116).

80. See note 79 (quote, p. 98).

81. See note 70.

82. Battaglia, B. (1992). Skills for managing multicultural teams. *Cultural Diversity at Work, 4,* 4–12.

83. Wright, P., Ferris, S. P., Hiller, J. S., & Kroll, M. (1995). Competitiveness through management of diversity: Effects of stock price valuation. *Academy of Management Journal, 38,* 272–287.

84. See note 75.

85. See note 76.

86. Gardenswartz, L., & Rowe, A. (1994). *The managing diversity survival guide.* Burr Ridge, IL: Irwin.

87. Rynes, S., & Rosen, B. (1995). A field survey of factors affecting the adoption and perceived success of diversity training. *Personnel Psychology, 48,* 247–270.

88. Meyer, J. P., & Allen, N. J. (1991). A three-component conceptualization of organizational commitment. *Human Resource Management Review, 1,* 61–89.

Case in Point Source

Martinez, M. N. (1995, January). Equality effort sharpens bank's edge. *HRMagazine,* pp. 38–43.

CHAPTER 6
Preview Case Source

Kaufman, J. (1998, May 5). A middle manager, 54, and insecure, struggles to adapt to the times. *Wall Street Journal*, pp. A1, A6.

Chapter Notes

1. Ornstein, S., & Isabella, L. A. (1993). Making sense of careers: A review, 1989–1992. *Journal of Management, 19*, 243–267.

2. Kahn, R. L., & Byosiere, P. (1992). Stress in organizations. In M. D. Dunnette & L. M. Hough, (Eds.), *Handbook of industrial and organizational psychology*, (2nd ed.) (Vol. 3., pp. 571–650). Palo Alto, CA: Consulting Psychologists Press.

3. Wanous, J. P. (1992). *Organizational entry: Recruitment, selection, orientation, and socialization*. Reading, MA: Addison-Wesley.

4. Kram, K. E. (1985). *Mentoring at work: Development relationships in organizational life*. Glenview, IL: Scott, Foresman.

5. Brown, D., & Brooks, L. (1996). *Career choice and development*. San Francisco: Jossey-Bass.

6. Van Maanen, J., & Schein, E. H. (1991). Toward a theory of organizational socialization. In B. M. Staw (Ed.), *Research in organizational behavior* (Vol. 12, pp. 209–264). Greenwich, CT: JAI Press.

7. Feldman, J. C. (1981). The multiple socialization of organization members. *Academy of Management Review, 6*, 309–318.

8. Fisher, C. D. (1986). Organizational socialization: An integrative review. In G. R. Ferris & K. M. Rowland (Eds.), *Research in personnel and human resources management* (Vol. 4, pp. 101–145). Greenwich, CT: JAI Press.

9. Wanous, J. P., Poland, T. D., Premark, S. L., & Davis, K. S. (1992). The effects of met expectations on newcomer attitudes and behavior: A review and meta-analysis. *Journal of Applied Psychology, 77*, 288–297.

10. Fedor, D. B., Buckley, M. R., & Davis, W. D. (1997). A model of the effects of realistic job previews. *International Journal of Management, 14*, 211–221.

11. Buckley, M. R., Fedor, D. B., Veres, J. G., Wiese, D. S., & Carraher, S. M. (1998). Investigating newcomer expec-

tations and job-related outcomes. *Journal of Applied Psychology, 83*, 452–461.

12. Bretz, R. D., Jr., & Judge, T. A. (1998). Realistic job previews: A test of the adverse-self-selection hypothesis. *Journal of Applied Psychology, 83*, 330–337.

13. Morrison, R. F., & Brantner, T. M. (1992). What enhances or inhibits learning a new job? A basic career issue. *Journal of Applied Psychology, 77*, 926–940.

14. Lancaster, H. (1998, July 14). To avoid job failure, learn the culture of a company first. *Wall Street Journal*, p. B1.

15. See note 4.

16. Whitely, W., Dougherty, T. M., & Dreher, G. F. (1991). Relationship of career mentoring and socioeconomic origin to managers' and professionals' early career progress. *Academy of Management Journal, 34*, 331–351.

17. Olian, J., Carroll, S., Giannantonio, D., & Feren, D. (1998). What do protégés look for in a mentor? Results of three experimental studies. *Journal of Vocational Behavior, 33*, 13–37.

18. Granfield, M. (1992, November). '90s mentoring: Circles and quads. *Working Woman*, p. 15.

19. Tepper, B. J. (1995). Upward maintenance tactics in supervisory mentoring and nonmentoring relationships. *Academy of Management Journal, 38*, 1191–1205.

20. Kram, K. E. (1983). Phases of the mentor relationship. *Academy of Management Journal, 26*, 608–625.

21. Kram, K. E., & Brager, M. C. (1992). Development through mentoring: A strategic approach. In D. Montross & C. Shinkman (Eds.), *Career development: Theory and practice* (pp. 221–254). Chicago: Thomas Press.

22. Ragins, B. R., & Cotton, J. (1991). Easier said than done: Gender difference in perceived barriers to gaining a mentor. *Academy of Management Journal, 34*, 939–951.

23. Thomas, D. A. (1993). Racial dynamics in cross-race developmental relationships. *Administrative Science Quarterly, 38*, 169–194.

24. Ragins, B. R., & Scandura, T. A. (1997). The way we were: Gender and the termination of mentoring relationships. *Journal of Applied Psychology, 82*, 945–953.

25. See note 18.

26. Pink, D. H. (1998, January). Free agent nation. *Fast Company*, pp. 131–137.

27. See note 26.

28. Zimmerer, T. W., & Scarborough, N. M. (1998). *Essentials of entrepreneurship and small business management* (2nd ed.). Upper Saddle River, NJ: Prentice Hall.

29. Link Resources, Inc. (1998). *Employment trends*. Marietta, GA: Author.

30. See note 1.

31. Holland, J. L. (1985). *Making vocational choices: A theory of vocational personalities and work environments*. Englewood Cliffs, NJ: Prentice-Hall.

32. Meier, S. T. (1991). Vocational behavior, 1988–1990: Vocational choice, decision-making, career development interventions, and assessment. *Journal of Vocational Behavior, 39*, 131–138.

33. Chatman, J. A. (1991). Matching people and organizations: Selection and socialization in public accounting firms. *Administrative Science Quarterly, 36*, 459–484.

34. Judge, T. A., & Bretz, R. D., Jr. (1992). Effects of work values on job choice decisions. *Journal of Applied Psychology, 77*, 261–271.

35. Monthly Labor Review. (1997, November). Bureau of Labor Statistics. (From the Internet, http://www.oohinfo @bls.gov.)

36. Stewart, T. A. (1995, March 20). Planning a career in a world without managers. *Fortune*, pp. 72–74, 75, 77, 79.

37. Fingleton, E. (1995, March 20). Jobs for life: Why Japan won't give them up. *Fortune*, pp. 119–123, 125.

38. Campion, M. A., Cheraskin, L., & Stevens, M. J. (1994). Career-related antecedents and outcomes of job rotation. *Academy of Management Journal, 37*, 1518–1542.

39. Gartner, W. B. (1990). What are we talking about when we talk about entrepreneurship? *Journal of Business Venturing, 5*, 15–28.

40. Lambling, P. A., & Kuehl, C. (1997). *Entrepreneurship*. Upper Saddle River, NJ: Prentice-Hall.

41. Venkataraman, S. (1997). The distinctive domain of entrepreneurship research: An editor's perspective. In J.

Katz & R. H. Brockhaus (Eds.) *Advances in entrepreneurship, firm emergence, and growth* (Vol. 3, pp. 119–138). Greenwich, CT: JAI Press.

42. Hatten, T. S. (1997). *Small business: Entrepreneurship and beyond.* Upper Saddle River, NJ: Prentice-Hall.

43. Tharenou, P., Latimer, S., & Conroy, D. (1994). How do you make it to the top? An examination of influences on women's and men's managerial advancement. *Academy of Management Journal, 37,* 899–931.

44. U.S. Department of Labor (1992). *Employment and earnings* (Vol. 39, No. 5; Table A022). Washington, DC: Author.

45. Glass Ceiling Commission. (1995). *Good for business: Making full use of the nation's human capital.* Washington, DC: Glass Ceiling Commission.

46. Heilman, M. E. (1995). Sex stereotypes and their effects in the workplace: What we know and what we don't know. *Journal of Social Behavior and Personality, 10,* 3–26.

47. Aluetta, K. (1998, April 20). In the company of women. *The New Yorker,* pp. 71–78.

48. See note 47.

49. Lyness, K. S., & Thompson, D. E. (1997). Above the glass ceiling? A comparison of matched samples of female and male executives. *Journal of Applied Psychology, 82,* 359–375.

50. See note 49.

51. Northwestern National Life Insurance Company. (1991). *Employee burnout: America's newest epidemic.* Minneapolis, MN: Author.

52. Lazarus, R. S., & Folkman, S. (1984). *Stress, appraisal, and coping.* New York: Springer-Verlag.

53. Selye, H. (1986). *Stress in health and disease.* London: Butterworths.

54. See note 49.

55. Shaw, J. B., & Riskind, J. H. (1983). Predicting job stress using data from the Position Analysis Questionnaire. *Journal of Applied Psychology, 68,* 253–261.

56. Monani, A. Q. (1998, June 10). Plane misbehavior: In the skies today, a weird new worry: Sexual misconduct. *Wall Street Journal,* pp. A1, A8.

57. Williams, K. J., & Alliger, G. M. (1994). Role stressors, mood spillover, and perceptions of work-family conflict in employed parents. *Academy of Management Journal, 37,* 837–868.

58. Kossek, E. E., & Ozeki, C. (1998). Work-family conflict, policies, and the job-life satisfaction relationship: A review and directions for organizational behavior-human resources research. *Journal of Applied Psychology, 83,* 139–149.

59. McGrath, J. E. (1987). Stress and behavior in organizations. In M. D. Dunnette (Ed.), *Handbook of industrial and organizational psychology* (pp. 1351–1398). Chicago: Rand McNally.

60. Peterson, M. F., Smith, P. B., Akande, A., et al. (1995). Role conflict, ambiguity, and overload: A 21-nation study. *Academy of Management Journal, 38,* 429–452.

61. Hofstede, G. (1994). Management scientists are human. *Management Science, 40,* 4–13.

62. McClean, A. A. (1980). *Work stress.* Reading, MA: Addison-Wesley.

63. Doby, V. J., & Caplan, R. D. (1995). Organizational stress as threat to reputation: Effects on anxiety at work and at home. *Academy of Management Journal, 38,* 1105–1123.

64. See note 63.

65. Bureau of National Affairs. (1994, April 6). Survey finds 31 percent of women report having been harassed at work. *Employee Relations Weekley,* pp. 111–112.

66. Felsenthall, E. (1998, June 17). Rulings open way for sex-harass cases. *Wall Street Journal,* pp. A1, A10.

67. Segal, T., Kelly, K., & Solomon, A. (1992, November 9). Getting serious about sexual harassment. *Business Week,* pp. 78, 82.

68. Gutek, B., Nakamura, C. Y., Gadart, M., Handschumacher, J. W., & Russell, D. (1980). Sexuality and the workplace. *Basic and Applied Social Psychology, 1,* 255–265.

69. McClean, A. A. (1980). *Work stress.* Reading, MA: Addison-Wesley.

70. Lind, E. A., Greenberg, J., Scott, K., & Welchans, T. (1998, August). *The winding road from employee to complainant: Situational and psychological determinants of wrongful termination lawsuits.* Paper presented at the meeting of the Academy of Management, San Diego, CA.

71. Holmes, T. H., & Rahe, R. H. (1967). Social readjustment rating scale. *Journal of Psychosomatic Research, 11,* 213–218.

72. See note 52.

73. Motowidlo, S. J., Packard, H. J., & Manning, M. R. (1986). Occupational stress: Its causes and consequences for job performance. *Journal of Applied Psychology, 71,* 618–629.

74. Schaufeli, W. B., & Brunk, B. P. (1996). Professional burnout. In M. J. Schabracq, J. A. Winnubst, & C. L. Cooper (Eds.), *Handbook of work and health psychology* (pp. 3121–3146). Chichester, England: Wiley.

75. Zohar, D. (1997). Predicting burnout with a hassle-based measure of role demands. *Journal of Organizational Behavior, 18,* 101–115.

76. Lee, R. T., & Ashforth, B. E. (1996). A meta-analytic examination of the correlations of the three dimensions of job burnout. *Journal of Applied Psychology, 81,* 123–133.

77. Golombiewski, R. T., Ninzenrider, R. F., & Stevenson, J. G. (1986). *Stress in organizations: Toward a phase model of burnout.* New York: Praeger.

78. Stelzer, J., & Numerof, R. E. (1986). Supervisory leadership and subordinate burnout. *Academy of Management Journal, 31,* 439–446.

79. Moss, L. (1981). *Management stress.* Reading, MA: Addison-Wesley.

80. Wright, T. A., & Bonnet, T. A. (1997). The contribution of burnout to work performance. *Journal of Organizational Behavior, 18,* 491–499.

81. Schaufeli, W. B. (1995). The evaluation of a burnout workshop for community nurses. *Journal of Health and Human Resources Administration, 18,* 11–40.

82. Dierendonck, D. V., Schaufeli, W. B., & Buunk, B. P. (1998). The evaluation of an individual burnout intervention program: The role of inequity and social support. *Journal of Applied Psychology, 83,* 392–407.

83. Matthes, K. (1992). In pursuit of leisure: Employees want more time off. *Human Resources Focus, 69,* 1.

84. Weitzman, M., & Eden, D. (1997). Effects of a respite from work on burnout: Vacation relief and fade-out. *Journal of Applied Psychology, 82,* 516–527.

85. Adams, G. T. (1987). Preventive law trends and compensation payments for stress-disabled workers. In J. C. Quick, R. S. Bhaghat, J. E. Dalton, & J. D. Quick (Eds.), *Work stress: Health care systems in the workplace* (pp. 67–78). New York: Praeger.

86. Quick, J. C., & Quick, J. D. (1984). *Organizational stress and preventive management.* New York: McGraw-Hill.

87. Cohen, S., & Williamson, G. (1991). Stress and infectious disease in humans. *Psychological Bulletin, 109,* 5–24.

88. North, F., Syme, S. L., Feeney, A., Head, J., Shipley, M. J., & Marmot, M. G. (1996). Psychosocial work environment and sickness absence among British civil servants: The Whitehall II study. *American Journal of Public Health, 86,* 332–340.

89. Kivimaki, M., Vahtera, J., Thomson, L., Griffiths, A., & Cox, T. (1997). Psychological factors predicting employee sickness absence during economic decline. *Journal of Applied Psychology, 82,* 858–872.

90. Schaubroeck, J., Ganster, D. C., & Kemmerer, B. E. (1994). Job complexity, "Type A" behavior, and cardiovascular disorder: A prospective study. *Academy of Management Journal, 37,* 426–439.

91. Baron, R. A. (1997). *Psychology* (4th ed.). Boston: Allyn & Bacon.

92. See note 91.

93. Sobel, D. (1993, May). Outsmarting stress. *Working Woman,* pp. 83–84, 101.

94. Benson, H. (1975). *The relaxation response.* New York: Morrow.

95. Roskies, E. (1987). *Stress management for the healthy Type A.* New York: Guilford.

96. Ferner, J. D. (1995). *Successful time management* (2nd ed.). New York: Wiley.

97. Reynolds, S., & Shapiro, D. A. (1991). Stress reduction in transition: Conceptual problems in the design, implementation, and evaluation of worksite stress management inventories. *Human Relations, 44,* 717–733.

98. See note 86.

99. Beadle, C. E. (1994, July 24). And let's save "Wellness." It works. *New York times,* p. F9.

100. Tully, S. (1995, June 12). America's healthiest companies. *Fortune,* pp. 104–106.

101. Philips, S. B., & Mushinki, M. H. (1992). Configuring an employee assistance program to fit the corporation's structure: One company's design. In J. C. Quick, K. R. Murphy, & J. J. Hurrell, Jr. (Eds.) *Stress and well-being at work* (pp. 317–328). Washington, DC: American Psychological Association.

102. Mitchell, R. (1996, November 20). Are your employees physically fit? *Amarillo Business Journal.* (From the Internet, http://www.businessjournal/net.health.)

103. Wellness Councils of America. (1998, September). (From the Internet, http://www.welcoa.org/works.)

Case in Point Source

Kirschman, E., Scrivner, E., Ellison, K., & Marcy, C. (1992). Work and well-being: Lessons from law enforcement. In J. C. Quick, L. R. Murphy, & J. J. Hurrell, Jr. (Eds.), *Stress and well-being at work.* Washington, DC: American Psychological Association.

CHAPTER 7
Preview Case Source

Cutler-Hammer Web site: http://www.ch.cutler-hammer.com/; and Hiebeler, R., Kelly, T. B., & Ketteman, C. (1998). *Best practices.* New York: Simon & Schuster.

Chapter Notes

1. Cartwright, D., & Zander, A. (1968). Origins of group dynamics. In D. Cartwright & A. Zander (Eds.), *Group dynamics: Research and theory* (pp. 3–21). New York: Harper & Row.

2. Bettenhausen, K. L. (1991). Five years of groups research: What we have learned and what needs to be addressed. *Journal of Management, 17,* 345–381.

3. Forsyth, D. L. (1983). *An introduction to group dynamics.* Monterey, CA: Brooks/Cole.

4. Long, S. (1984). Early integration in groups: "A group to join and a group to create." *Human Relations, 37,* 311–332.

5. Tuckman, B. W., & Jensen, M. A. (1977). Stages of small group development revisited. *Group and Organization Studies, 2,* 419–427.

6. Gersick, C. J. G. (1988). Time and transition in work teams: Toward a new model of group development. *Academy of Management Journal, 31,* 9–41.

7. Gersick, C. J. G. (1989). Marking time: Predictable transitions in task groups. *Academy of Management Journal, 32,* 274–309.

8. Romanelli, E., & Tushman, M. L. (1994). Organizational transformation as punctuated equilibrium: An empirical test. *Academy of Management Journal, 37,* 1141–1166.

9. Biddle, B. J. (1979). *Role theory: Expectations, identities, and behavior.* New York: Academic Press.

10. Jackson, S. E., & Schuler, R. S. (1985). A meta-analysis and conceptual critique of research on role ambiguity and role conflict in work settings. *Organizational Behavior and Human Decision Processes, 36,* 16–78.

11. Benne, K. D., & Sheats, P. (1948). Functional roles of group members. *Journal of Social Issues, 4,* 41–49.

12. Hackman, J. R. (1992). Group influences on individuals in organizations. In M. D. Dunnette & L. M. Hough (Eds.), *Handbook of industrial and organizational psychology* (2nd ed.) (Vol. 3, pp. 199–268). Palo Alto, CA: Consulting Psychologists Press.

13. Feldman, D. C. (1984). The development and enforcement of group norms. *Academy of Management Review, 9,* 47–53.

14. Watson, T. J., Jr. (1990). *Father son & co.: My life at IBM and beyond.* New York: Bantam.

15. Wilson, S. (1978). *Informal groups: An introduction.* Englewood Cliffs, NJ: Prentice-Hall.

16. Greenberg, J. (1988). Equity and workplace status: A field experiment. *Journal of Applied Psychology, 73,* 606–613.

17. Stryker, S., & Macke, A. S. (1978). Status inconsistency and role conflict. In R. H. Turner, J. Coleman, & R. C. Fox (Eds.), *Annual review of sociology* (Vol. 4, pp. 57–90). Palo Alto, CA: Annual Reviews.

18. Jackson, L. A., & Grabski, S. V. (1988). Perceptions of fair pay and the gender wage gap. *Journal of Applied Social Psychology, 18,* 606–625.

19. Torrance, E. P. (1954). Some consequences of power differences on decision making in permanent and temporary three-man groups. *Research Studies: Washington State College, 22,* 130–140.

20. Hare, A. P. (1976). *Handbook of small group research* (2nd ed). New York: Free Press.

21. Aronson, E., & Mills, J. (1959). The effects of severity of initiation on liking for a group. *Journal of Abnormal and Social Psychology, 59,* 177–181.

22. Long, S. (1984). Early integration in groups: "A group to join and a group to create." *Human Relations, 37,* 311–322.

23. Cartwright, D. (1968). The nature of group cohesiveness. In D. Cartwright & A. Zander (Eds.), *Group dynamics: Research and theory* (3rd ed.) (pp. 91–109). New York: Harper & Row.

24. George, J. M., & Bettenhausen, K. (1990). Understanding prosocial behavior, sales performance, and turnover: A group-level analysis in a service context. *Journal of Applied Psychology, 75,* 698–709.

25. Douglas, T. (1983). *Groups: Understanding people gathered together.* New York: Tavistock.

26. Geen, R. (1989). Alternative conceptualizations of social facilitation. In P. B. Paulus (Ed.), *Psychology of group influence* (2nd ed.) (pp. 15–51). Hillsdale, NJ: Erlbaum.

27. Zajonc, R. B. (1965). Social facilitation. *Science, 149,* 269–274.

28. Zajonc, R. B. (1980). Compresence. In P. B. Paulus (Ed.), *Psychology of group influence* (pp. 35–60). Hillsdale, NJ: Erlbaum.

29. Geen, R. B., Thomas, S. L., & Gammill, P. (1988). Effects of evaluation and coaction on state anxiety and anagram performance. *Personality and Individual Differences, 6,* 293–298.

30. Aiello, J. R., & Kolb, K. J. (1995). Electronic performance monitoring and social context: Impact on productivity and stress. *Journal of Applied Psychology, 80,* 339–353.

31. Aiello, J. R., & Svec, C. M. (1993). Computer monitoring of work performance: Extending the social facilitation framework to electronic presence. *Journal of Applied Social Psychology, 23,* 537–548.

32. Koelsch, F. (1995). *The informedia revolution.* New York: McGraw-Hill.

33. See note 31.

34. Band, W. A. (1994). *Touchstones.* New York: Wiley.

35. Minkin, B. H. (1995). *Future in sight.* New York: Macmillan.

36. See note 35.

37. Watson, W. E., Kumar, K., & Michaelsen, K. K. (1993). Cultural diversity's impact on interaction process and performance: Comparing homogeneous and diverse task groups. *Academy of Management Journal, 36,* 590–602.

38. Steiner, I. D. (1972). *Group processes and productivity.* New York: Academic Press.

39. Shepperd, J. A. (1993). Productivity loss in performance groups: A motivation analysis. *Psychological Bulletin, 113,* 67–81.

40. Latané, B., Williams, K., & Harkins, S. (1979). Many hands make light the work: The causes and consequences of social loafing. *Journal of Personality and Social Psychology, 37,* 822–832.

41. Kravitz, D. A., & Martin, B. (1986). Ringelmann rediscovered: The original article. *Journal of Personality and Social Psychology, 50,* 936–941.

42. Karau, S. J., & Williams, K. D. (1993). Social loafing: A meta-analytic review and theoretical integration. *Journal of Personality and Social Psychology, 65,* 681–706.

43. Latané, B., & Nida, S. (1980). Social impact theory and group influence: A social engineering perspective. In P. B. Paulus (Ed.), *Psychology of group influence* (pp. 3–34). Hillsdale, NJ: Erlbaum.

44. Earley, P. C. (1993). East meets west meets mideast: Further explorations of collectivistic and individualistic work groups. *Academy of Management Journal, 36,* 319–348.

45. Nordstrom, R., Lorenzi, P., & Hall, R. V. (1990). A review of public posting of performance feedback in work settings. *Journal of Organizational Behavior Management, 11,* 101–123.

46. Bricker, M. A., Harkins, S. G., & Ostrom, T. M. (1986). Effects of personal involvement: Thought-provoking implications for social loafing. *Journal of Personality and Social Psychology, 51,* 763–769.

47. George, J. M. (1992). Extrinsic and intrinsic origins of perceived social loafing in organizations. *Academy of Management Journal, 35,* 191–202.

48. Albanese, R., & Van Fleet, D. D. (1985). Rational behavior in groups: The free-riding tendency. *Academy of Management Review, 10,* 244–255.

49. Miles, J. A., & Greenberg, J. (1993). Using punishment threats to attenuate social loafing effects among swimmers. *Organizational Behavior and Human Decision Processes, 56,* 246–265.

50. Katzenbach, J. R., & Smith, D. K. (1993, March-April). The discipline of teams. *Harvard Business Review, 71*(2), 111–120.

51. Harari, O. (1995, October). The dream team. *Management Review,* pp. 29–31.

52. See note 51.

53. Katzenbach, J. R. (1998). *Teams at the top.* Boston: Harvard Business School.

54. Mohrman, S. A. (1993). Integrating roles and structure in the lateral organization. In J. R. Galbraith & E. E. Lawler, III (Eds.), *Organizing for the future* (pp. 109–141). San Francisco: Jossey-Bass.

55. Tuckman, B. W., & Jensen, M. A. (1977). Stages of small group development revisited. *Group and Organization Studies, 2,* 419–427.

56. Ray, D., & Bronstein, H. (1995). *Teaming up.* New York: McGraw-Hill.

57. Wellins, R. S., Byham, & Wilson, J. M. (1991). *Empowered teams.* San Francisco: Jossey-Bass.

58. Moravec, M., Johannessen, O. J., & Hjelmas, T. A. (1997, July/August). Thumbs up for self-managed teams. *Management Review,* pp. 42–47.

59. Manz, C. C., & Sims, H. P., Jr. (1993). *Business without bosses.* New York: Wiley.

60. Osburn, J. D., Moran, L., Musselwhite, E., & Zenger, J. H. (1990). *Self-directed work teams*. Burr Ridge, IL: Irwin.

61. Hackman, J. R. (1987). The design of work teams. In J. W. Lorsch (Ed.), *Handbook of organizational behavior* (pp. 315–342). Englewood Cliffs, NJ: Prentice-Hall.

62. See note 60 (quote, p. 338).

63. Sheridan, J. H. (1990, October 15). America's best plants. *Industry Week*, pp. 27–64.

64. Fisher, K. (1993). *Leading self-directed work teams*. New York: McGraw-Hill.

65. Dumaine, B. (1990, May 7). Who needs a boss? *Fortune*, pp. 52–60.

66. Ilgen, D. R., Major, D. A., Hollenbeck, & Sego, D. J. (1993). Team research in the 1990s. In M. M. Chemers & R. Ayman (Eds.), *Leadership theory and research* (pp. 245–270). San Diego: Academic Press.

67. Lawler, E. E., III, Mohrman, S. A., & Ledford, G. E., Jr. (1992). *Employee involvement and total quality management*. San Francisco: Jossey-Bass.

68. Hackman, J. R. (Ed.) (1990). *Groups that work (and those that don't)*. San Francisco: Jossey-Bass.

69. See note 68.

70. Katzenbach, J. R., & Smith, D. K. (1993). *The wisdom of teams*. Boston: Harvard Business School.

71. See note 70.

72. Pearson, C. A. L. (1992). Autonomous workgroups: An evaluation at an industrial site. *Human Relations, 45*, 905–936.

73. Wall, T. D., Kemp, N. J., Jackson, P. R., & Clegg, C. W. (1986). Outcomes of autonomous workgroups: A long-term field experiment. *Academy of Management Journal, 29*, 280–304.

74. Robbins, H., & Finley, M. (1995). *Why teams don't work*. Princeton, NJ: Peterson's/Pacesetters Books.

75. Stern, A. (1993, July 18). Managing by team is not always as easy as it looks. *The New York Times*, p. B14.

76. Smith, P. B., Peterson, M. F., & Misumi, J. (1993). Event management and work team effectiveness in Japan, Britain and USA. *Journal of Occupational and Organizational Psychology, 67*, 33–43.

77. Nahavandi, A., & Aranda, E.

(1994). Restructuring teams for the re-engineered organization. *Academy of Management Executive, 8*, 58–68.

78. See note 75.

79. See note 75.

80. See note 75.

81. See note 75.

82. See note 75.

83. Maginn, M. D. (1994). *Effective teamwork*. Burr Ridge, IL: Business One Irwin.

84. Dumaine, B. (1994, September 5). The trouble with teams. *Fortune*, pp. 86–88, 90, 92. (quote, p. 86).

85. See note 84.

86. Campion, M. A., & Higgs, A. C. (1995, October). Design work teams to increase productivity and satisfaction. *HRMagazine*, pp. 101–102, 104, 107.

87. Campion, M. A., Medsker, R., & Higgs, A. C. (1993). Relations between work group characteristics and effectiveness: Implications for designing effective work groups. *Personnel Psychology, 46*, 823–850.

88. Frangos, S. J. (1993). *Team zebra*. Essex Junction, VT: Omneo.

89. McDermott, L. C., Brawley, N., & Waite, W. W. (1998). *World Class Teams*. New York: Wiley.

Case in Point Source

Kirsner, S. (1998, April/May). "Everyday, it's a new place." *Fast Company*, pp. 130–135.

CHAPTER 8
Preview Case Sources

Digital Equipment held a state of the company meeting. (1989, June 20). *Wall Street Journal*, p. 1A; Gardner, D. (1998, April 13). Merger creates new force in networking. *EE Times*. Tech Search issue 1002; (www.techweb.com/se/directlink); and Borland, J. (1998, July 28). Compaq says no deal on alta vista domain. *Tech Web*; www.techweb.com/wire.story.

Chapter Notes

1. Fulk, J. (1993). Social construction of communication technology. *Academy of Management Journal, 36*, 921–950.

2. Roberts, K. H. (1984). *Communicating in organizations*. Chicago: Science Research Associates (quote, p. 4).

3. Weick, K. E. (1987). Theorizing about organizational communication. In F. M. Jablin, L. L. Putnam, K. H. Roberts, & L. W. Porter (Eds.), *Handbook of organizational communication* (pp. 97–122). Newbury Park, CA: Sage (quote, p. 100).

4. Barnard, C. I. (1938). *The functions of the executive*. Cambridge, MA: Harvard University Press (quote, p. 5).

5. Mintzberg, H. (1973). *The nature of managerial work*. New York: Harper & Row.

6. Baskin, O. W., & Aronoff, C. E. (1980). *Interpersonal communication in organizations*. Santa Monica, CA: Goodyear.

7. Quinn, R. E., Hildebrandt, H. W., Rogers, P. S., & Thompson, M. P. (1991). A competing values framework for analyzing presentational communication in management contexts. *Journal of Business Communication, 28*, 213–232.

8. Lengel, R. H., & Daft, R. L. (1988). The selection of communication media as an executive skill. *Academy of Management Executive, 2*, 225–232.

9. Yates, J., & Orlikowski, W. J. (1992). Genres of organizational communication: A structurational approach to studying communication and media. *Academy of Management Review, 17*, 298–326.

10. Szwergold, J. (1993, June). Employee newsletters help fill an information gap. *Management Review*, p. 8.

11. Sibson and Company, Inc. (1989). *Compensation planning survey, 1989*. Princeton, NJ: Author.

12. Brady, T. (1993, June). Employee handbooks: Contracts or empty promises? *Management Review*, pp. 33–35.

13. Anonymous. (1993, November). The (handbook) handbook. *Inc.*, pp. 57–64.

14. Level, D. A. (1972). Communication effectiveness: Methods and situation. *Journal of Business Communication, 28*, 18–25.

15. Klauss, R., & Bass, B. M. (1982). *International communication in organizations*. New York: Academic Press.

16. Daft, R. L., Lengel, R. H., & Treviño, L. K. (1987). Message equivo-

cality, media selection, and manager performance: Implications for information systems. *MIS Quarterly, 11,* 355–366.

17. Barnum, C., & Wolnainsky, N. (1989, April). Taking cues from body language. *Management Review,* pp. 3–8.

18. Malloy, J. T. (1990). *Dress for success.* New York: Warner Books (quote, p. 27).

19. Rafaeli, A., Dutton, J., Harquail, C., & Mackie-Lewis, S. (1997). Navigating by attire: The use of dress by female administrative employees. *Academy of Management Journal, 40,* 9–45.

20. Caggiano, C. (1997). Benchmark: Does anyone still wear a power tie? *Inc.,* p. 148.

21. Global businesswear trends. (1997, June). *Casual Clothing in the Workplace News,* pp. 2–4.

22. Malloy, A. (1996, June). Counting the intangibles. *Computerworld,* pp. 31–33.

23. Schwartz, G. (1976). *Queuing and waiting.* Chicago: University of Chicago Press.

24. Greenberg, J. (1989). The organizational waiting game: Time as a status-asserting or status-neutralizing tactic. *Basic and Applied Social Psychology, 10,* 13–26.

25. Greenberg, J. (1988). Equity and workplace status: A field experiment. *Journal of Applied Psychology, 73,* 606–613.

26. Zweigenhaft, R. L. (1976). Personal space in the faculty office: Desk placement and student-faculty interaction. *Journal of Applied Psychology, 61,* 628–32.

27. Greenberg, J. (1976). The role of seating position in group interaction: A review, with applications for group trainers. *Group and Organization Studies, 1,* 310–327.

28. Capowski, G. S. (1993, June). Designing a corporate identity. *Management Review,* pp. 37–40.

29. Scully, J. (1987). *Odyssey: Pepsi to Apple . . . a journey of adventure, ideas, and the future.* New York: Harper & Row (quote, p. 33).

30. Carstairs, E. (1986, February). No ivory tower for Procter & Gamble. *Corporate Design and Reality,* pp. 24–30.

31. McCallister, L. (1994). *"I wish I'd said that!" How to talk your way out of trouble and into success.* New York: Wiley.

32. See note 42.

33. Tannen, D. (1995). *Talking 9 to 5.* New York: Avon.

34. *Tannen, D. (1995, September-October). The power of talk: Who gets heard and why.* Harvard Business Review, 137–148.

35. See note 45 (quote, p. 148).

36. Munter, M. (1993, May–June). Cross-cultural communication for managers. *Business Horizons,* pp. 75–76.

37. Mellow, C. (1995, August 17). Russia: Making cash from chaos. *Fortune,* pp. 145–148, 150–151.

38. Adler, N. (1991). *International dimensions of organizational behavior* (2nd ed.). Boston: PWS/Kent.

39. Argyris, C. (1974). *Behind the front page: Organizational self-renewal in a metropolitan newspaper.* San Francisco: Jossey-Bass.

40. Hawkins, B. L., & Preston, P. (1981). *Managerial communication.* Santa Monica, CA: Goodyear.

41. Szilagyi, A. (1981). *Management and performance.* Glenview, IL: Scott, Foresman.

42. Beck, S. (1997, December 8). What to do before you say, "You're outta here." *Business Week,* pp. ENT 6–ENT 7.

43. See note 42.

44. Coulson, R. (1981). *The termination handbook.* New York: Free Press.

45. Walker, C. R., & Guest, R. H. (1952). *The man on the assembly line.* Cambridge, MA: Harvard University Press.

46. Luthans, F., & Larsen, J. K. (1986). How managers really communicate. *Human Relations, 39,* 161–178.

47. Kirmeyer, S. L., & Lin, T. (1987). Social support: Its relationship to observed communication with peers and superiors. *Academy of Management Journal, 30,* 137–151.

48. Read, W. (1962). Upward communication in industrial hierarchies. *Human Relations, 15,* 3–16.

49. Glauser, M. J. (1984). Upward information flow in organizations: Review and conceptual analysis. *Human Relations, 37,* 613–643.

50. Lee, F. (1993). Being polite and keeping MUM: How bad news is communicated in organizational hierarchies. *Journal of Applied Social Psychology, 23,* 1124–1149.

51. Tesser, A., & Rosen, S. (1975). The reluctance to transmit bad news. In L. Berkowitz (Ed.), *Advances in experimental social psychology* (Vol. 8, pp. 192–232). New York: Academic Press.

52. Kiechel, W., III. (1990, June 18). How to escape the echo chamber. *Fortune,* pp. 128–130 (quote, p. 130).

53. Rogers, E. M., & Rogers, A. (1976). *Communication in organizations.* New York: Free Press.

54. Harcourt, J., Richerson, V., & Waitterk, M. J. (1991). A national study of middle managers' assessment of organization communication quality. *Journal of Business Communication, 28,* 347–365.

55. Krackhardt, D., & Hanson, J. R. (1993, July-August). Informal networks: The company behind the chart. *Harvard Business Review,* pp. 104–111.

56. Zenger, T. R., & Lawrence, B. S. (1989). Organizational demography: The differential effects of age and tenure distributions on technical communication. *Academy of Management Journal, 32,* 353–376.

57. Ibarra, H. (1992). Homophily and differential returns: Sex differences in network structure and access in an advertising firm. *Administrative Science Quarterly, 37,* 422–447.

58. Lesley, E., & Mallory, M. (1993, November 29). Inside the Black business network. *Business Week,* pp. 70–72, 77, 80–81.

59. Brass, D. J. (1985). Men's and women's networks: A study of interaction patterns and influence in an organization. *Academy of Management Journal, 28,* 327–343.

60. Krackhardt, D., & Porter, L. W. (1986). The snowball effect: Turnover embedded in communication networks. *Journal of Applied Psychology, 71,* 50–55.

61. Duncan, J. W. (1984). Perceived humor and social network patterns in a sample of task-oriented groups: A reexamination of prior research. *Human Relations, 37,* 895–907.

62. Baskin, O. W., & Aronoff, C. E. (1989). *Interpersonal communication in organizations.* Santa Monica: Goodyear.

63. Walton, E. (1961). How efficient is the grapevine? *Personnel, 28,* 45–49.

64. Thibaut, A. M., Calder, B. J., & Sternthal, B. (1981). Using information

processing theory to design marketing strategies. *Journal of Marketing Research*, *18*, 73–79.

65. Lesley, E., & Zinn, L. (1993, July 5). The right moves, baby. *Business Week*, pp. 30–31.

66. Schiller, Z. (1995, September 11). P&G is still having a devil of a time. *Business Week*, p. 46.

67. See note 62.

68. Fiol, C. M. (1995). Corporate communications: Comparing executives' private and public statements. *Academy of Management Journal*, *38*, 522–536.

69. Alessandra, T., & Hunksaker, P. (1993). *Communicating at work*. New York: Fireside.

70. Borman, E. (1982). *Interpersonal communication in the modern organization* (2nd ed.). Englewood Cliffs, NJ: Prentice-Hall.

71. Cantoni, C. J. (1993). *Corporate dandelions*. New York: AMACOM.

72. Thornton, R. J. (1987, February 25). I can't recommend the candidate too highly: An ambiguous lexicon for job recommendations. *The Chronicle for Higher Education*, p. 42.

73. Rowe, M. P., & Baker, M. (1984, May-June). Are you hearing enough employee concerns? *Harvard Business Review*, pp. 127–135.

74. Burley-Allen, M. (1982). *Listening: The forgotten skill*. New York: Wiley.

75. Brownell, J. (1985). A model for listening instructions: Management applications. *ABCA Bulletin*, *48*(3), 38–44.

76. Austin, N. K. (1991, March). Why listening's not as easy as it sounds. *Working Woman*, pp. 46–48.

77. See note 95.

78. Seyper, B. D., Bostrom, R. N., & Seibert, J. H. (1989). Listening, communication abilities, and success at work. *Journal of Business Communication*, *26*, 293–303.

79. Penley, L. E., Alexander, E. R., Jernigan, I. E., & Henwood, C. I. (1991). Communication abilities of managers: The relationship to performance. *Journal of Management*, *17*, 57–76.

80. Brownell, J. (1990). Perceptions of effective listeners: A management study. *Journal of Business Communication*, *27*, 401–415.

81. Jones, B. (1997, July/August). Communication: Dying for information. *Management Review*, p. 9.

82. Nichols, R. G. (1962, Winter). Listening is good business. *Management of Personnel Quarterly*, p. 4.

83. See note 82.

84. McCathrin, Z. (1990, Spring). The key to employee communication: Small group meetings. *The Professional Communicator*, pp. 6–7, 10.

85. Vernyi, B. (1987, April 26). Institute aims to boos quality of company suggestion boxes. *Toledo Blade*, p. B2.

86. Taft, W. F. (1985). Bulletin boards, exhibits, hotlines. In C. Reuss & D. Silvis (Eds.), *Inside organizational communication* (2nd ed.) (pp. 183–189). New York: Longman.

87. Walter, K. (1995, September). Ethics hot lines tap into more than wrongdoing. *HRMagazine*, pp. 78–85.

88. See note 87.

89. See note 87.

90. Beck, S. M. (1997, September 7). How'm I really doing? No, really. *Business Week*, ENT 10–ENT 11.

91. Schnake, M. E., Dumler, M. P., Cochran, D. S., & Barnett, T. R. (1990). Effects of differences in superior and subordinate perception of superiors' communication practices. *Journal of Business Communication*, *27*, 37–50.

92. Whetten, D. A., & Cameron, K. S. (1995). *Developing management skills* (3rd ed.). New York: HarperCollins.

93. Aeuerback, J. G. (1997, June 16). Getting the message. *Wall Street Journal*, p. R22.

94. Creighton, J. L., & Adams, J. W. R. (1998, January). The cybermeeting's about to begin. *Management Review*, pp. 29–31.

95. Craiger, P., & Weiss, R. J. (1998, June). Traveling in cyberspace: Video-mediated communication. *The Industrial-Organizational Psychologist*, pp. 83–92.

96. Diamond, L., & Roberts, S. (1996). *Effective videoconferencing*. Menlo Park, CA: Crisp Publications.

97. Pape, W. R. (1997, March). A meeting of the minds. *Inc. Tech*, pp. 29–30.

98. Grossman, J. (1998, April). We've got to start meeting like this. *Inc.*, pp. 70–72, 74.

99. Judge, P. C., & Browder, S. (1998, February 23). Let's talk. *Business Week*, pp. 61–64, 66–68, 72, 74, 76.

Case in Point Sources

Kelly, P. (1998, April). Forget policy manuals. *Inc.*, pp. 37–38; and Kelly, P. (1998). *Faster company: Building the world's nuttiest, turn-on-a-dime, home-grown, billion dollar business*. New York: Wiley.

CHAPTER 9
Preview Case Notes

Lienert, A. (1998, December). Plowing ahead in uncertain times. Management Review, pp. 16–21. Deere & Co. General information (http://www.deere.com/aboutus/general/sheet1.htm).

Chapter Notes

1. Mintzberg, H. J. (1988). *Mintzberg on management: Inside our strange world of organizations*. New York: Free Press.

2. Allison, S. T., Jordan, A. M. R., & Yeatts, C. E. (1992). A cluster-analytic approach toward identifying the structure and content of human decision making. *Human Relations*, *45*, 49–72.

3. Harrison, E. F. (1987). *The managerial decision-making process* (3rd ed.). Boston: Houghton Mifflin.

4. Wedley, W. C., & Field, R. H. G. (1984). A predecision support system. *Academy of Management Review*, *9*, 696–703.

5. Nutt, P. C. (1993). The formulation process and tactics used in organizational decision making. *Organization Science 4*, 226–251.

6. Nutt, P. (1984). Types of organizational decision processes. *Administrative Science Quarterly*, *29*, 414–450.

7. Cowan, D. A. (1986). Developing a process model of problem recognition. *Academy of Management Review*, *11*, 763–776.

8. Dennis, T. L., & Dennis, L. B. (1998). *Microcomputer models for management decision making*. St. Paul, MN: West.

9. Fulk, J., & Boyd, B. (1991). Emerging theories of communication in organizations. *Journal of Management, 17,* 407–446.

10. Sainfort, F. C., Gustafson, D. H., Bosworth, K., & Hawkins, R. P. (1990). Decision support systems effectiveness: Conceptual framework and empirical evaluation. *Organizational Behavior and Human Decision Processes, 45,* 232–252.

11. Collyer, S. C., & Malecki, G. S. (1998). Tactical decision making under stress: History and overview. In J. A. Cannon-Bowers & E. Salas (Eds). *Making decisions under stress: Implications for individual and team training* (pp. 3–15). Washington, DC: American Psychological Association.

12. Morrison, J. G., Kelly, R. T., Moore, R. A., & Hutchins, S. G. (1998). Implications of decision-making research for decision support and displays. In J. A. Cannon-Bowers & E. Salas (Eds). *Making decisions under stress: Implications for individual and team training* (pp. 375–406). Washington, DC: American Psychological Association.

13. Stevenson, M. K., Busemeyer, J. R., & Naylor, J. C. (1990). Judgment and decision-making theory. In M. D. Dunnette & L. M. Hough (Eds.), *Handbook of industrial and organizational psychology* (2nd ed.) (Vol. 1, pp. 283–374). Palo Alto, CA: Consulting Psychologists Press.

14. Hill, C. W., & Jones, G. R. (1989). *Strategic management.* Boston: Houghton Mifflin.

15. See note 5.

16. Amit, R., & Wernerfelt, B. (1990). Why do firms reduce business risk? *Academy of Management Journal, 33,* 520–533.

17. Provan, K. G. (1982). Interorganizational linkages and influence over decision making. *Academy of Management Journal, 25,* 443–451.

18. Galaskiewicz, J., & Wasserman, S. (1989). Mimetic processes within an interorganizational field: An empirical test. *Administrative Science Quarterly, 34,* 454–479.

19. Parsons, C. K. (1988). Computer technology: Implications for human resources management. In G. R. Ferris & K. M. Rowland (Eds.), *Research in personnel and human resources management* (Vol. 6, pp. 1–36). Greenwich, CT: JAI Press.

20. Simon, H. A. (1987). Making management decisions: The role of intuition and emotion. *Academy of Management Executive, 1,* 57–64.

21. Kirschenbaum, S. S. (1992). Influence of experience on information-gathering strategies. *Journal of Applied Psychology, 77,* 343–352.

22. Simon, H. (1977). *The new science of management decisions* (2nd ed.). Englewood Cliffs, NJ: Prentice-Hall.

23. Case, J. (1995). *Open-book management.* New York: HarperBusiness.

24. Remdomo, M. G. (1995, April). Team effort at Maguire Group leads to ethics policy. *HRMagazine,* pp. 63–64, 66.

25. Rowe, A. J., Boulgaides, J. D., & McGrath, M. R. (1984). *Managerial decision making.* Chicago: Science Research Associates.

26. See note 12.

27. Murninghan, J. K. (1981). Group decision making: What strategies should you use? *Management Review, 25,* 56–62.

28. Janis, I. L. (1982). *Groupthink: Psychological studies of policy decisions and fiascoes* (2nd ed.). Boston: Houghton Mifflin.

29. Morehead, G., Ference, R., & Neck, C. P. (1991). Group decision fiascoes continue: Space shuttle Challenger and a revised groupthink framework. *Human Relations, 44,* 539–550.

30. Turner, M. E., & Pratkanis, A. R. (1998). Twenty-five years of groupthink theory and research: Lessons from the evaluation of a theory. *Organizational Behavior and Human Decision Processes, 73,* 105–115.

31. Morehead, G., & Montanari, J. R. (1986). An empirical investigation of the groupthink phenomenon. *Human Relations, 39,* 399–410.

32. Schweiger, D. M., Sandberg, W. R., & Ragan, J. W. (1986). Group approaches for improving strategic decision making: A comparative analysis of dialectical inquiry, devil's advocacy, and consensus. *Academy of Management Journal, 29,* 51–71.

33. Schweiger, D. M., Sandberg, W. R., & Rechner, P. L. (1989). Experiential effects of dialectical inquiry, devil's advocacy, and consensus approaches to strategic decision making. *Academy of Management Journal, 32,* 745–772.

34. Cosier, R. A., & Schwenk, C. R. (1990). Agreement and thinking alike: Ingredients for poor decisions. *Academy of Management Executive, 4,* 69–74.

35. Sloan, A. P., Jr. (1964). *My years with General Motors.* New York: Doubleday.

36. Tjosvold, D. (1984). Effects of crisis orientation on managers' approach to controversy in decision making. *Academy of Management Journal, 27,* 130–138.

37. Johnson, R. J. (1984). Conflict avoidance through acceptable decisions. *Human Relations, 27,* 71–82.

38. Neustadt, R. E., & Fineberg, H. (1978). *The swine flu affair: Decision making on a slippery disease.* Washington, DC: U.S. Department of Health, Education, and Welfare.

39. Adler, N. J. (1991). *International dimensions of organizational behavior.* Boston: PWS-Kent.

40. Roth, K. (1992). Implementing international strategy at the business unit level: The role of managerial decision-making characteristics. *Journal of Management, 18,* 769–789.

41. Linstone, H. A. (1984). *Multiple perspectives for decision making.* New York: North-Holland.

42. Simon, H. A. (1979). Rational decision making in organizations. *American Economic Review, 69,* 493–513.

43. March, J. G., & Simon, H. A. (1958). *Organizations.* New York: Wiley.

44. See note 29.

45. Simon, H. A. (1957). *Models of man.* New York: Wiley.

46. Shull, F. A., Delbecq, A. L., & Cummings, L. L. (1970). *Organizational decision making.* New York: McGraw-Hill.

47. Browning, E. B. (1850/1950). *Sonnets from the Portuguese.* New York: Ratchford and Fulton.

48. Mitchell, T. R., & Beach, L. R. (1990). ". . . Do I love thee? Let me count . . . "Toward an understanding of intuitive and automatic decision making. *Organizational Behavior and Human Decision Processes, 47,* 1–20.

49. Beach, L. R., & Mitchell, T. R. (1990). Image theory: A behavioral theory of image making in organizations. In B. Staw & L. L. Cummings (Eds.), *Research in organizational behavior* (Vol. 12, pp. 1–41). Greenwich, CT: JAI Press.

50. Dunegan, K. J. (1995). Image theory: Testing the role of image compatibility in progress decisions. *Organizational Behavior and Human Decision Processes, 62,* 79–86.

51. Dunegan, K. J. (1993). Framing, cognitive modes, and image theory: Toward an understanding of a glass half full. *Journal of Applied Psychology, 78,* 491–503.

52. Gaeth, G. J., & Shanteau, J. (1984). Reducing the influence of irrelevant information on experienced decision makers. *Organizational Behavior and Human Performance, 33,* 263–282.

53. Ginrich, G., & Soli, S. D. (1984). Subjective evaluation and allocation of resources in routine decision making. *Organizational Behavior and Human Performance, 33,* 187–203.

54. Levin, I. P., Schneider, S. L., & Gaeth, G. J. (1998). All frames are not created equal: A typology and critical analysis of framing effects. *Organizational Behavior and Human Decision Processes, 76,* 149–188.

55. Kahneman, D., & Tversky, A. (1984). Choices, values, and frames. *American Psychologist, 39,* 341–350.

56. Highhouse, S., & Yüce, P. (1996). Perspectives, perceptions, and risk-taking behavior. *Organizational Behavior and Human Decision Processes, 65,* 159–167.

57. Levin, I. P., & Gaeth, G. J. (1988). Framing of attribute information before and after consuming the product. *Journal of Consumer Research, 15,* 374–378.

58. Levin, I. P. (1987). Associative effects of information framing. *Bulletin of the Psychonomic Society, 25,* 85–86.

59. Meyerowitz, B. E., & Chaiken, S. (1987). The effects of message framing on breast self-examination attitudes, intentions, and behavior. *Journal of Personality and Social Psychology, 52,* 500–510.

60. Frisch, D. (1993). Reasons for framing effects. *Organizational Behavior and Human Decision Processes, 54,* 399–429.

61. Nisbett, R. E., & Ross, L. (1980). *Human inference: Strategies and shortcomings of social judgment.* Englewood Cliffs, NJ: Prentice-Hall.

62. Abelson, R. P., & Levi, A. (1985). Decision-making and decision theory. In G. Lindzey & E. Aronson (Eds.), *Handbook of social psychology* (3rd ed.) (Vol. 1, pp. 231–309). Reading, MA: Addison-Wesley.

63. Kahneman, D., & Tversky, A. (1973). On the psychology of prediction. *Psychological Review, 80,* 251–273.

64. Gaeth, G. J., & Shanteau, J. (1984). Reducing the influence of irrelevant information on experienced decision makers. *Organizational Behavior and Human Performance, 33,* 187–203.

65. Power, D. J., & Aldag, R. J. (1985). Soelberg's job search and choice model: A clarification, review, and critique. *Academy of Management Review, 10,* 48–58.

66. Soelberg, P. O. (1967). Unprogrammed decision making. *Industrial Management Review, 8,* 19–29.

67. Langer, E., & Schank, R. C. (1994). *Belief, reasoning, and decision making.* Hillsdale, NJ: Erlbaum.

68. Conlon, D. E., & Garland, H. (1993). The role of project completion information in resource allocation decisions. *Academy of Management Journal, 36,* 402–413.

69. Ross, J., & Staw, B. M. (1986). Expo '86: An escalation prototype. *Administrative Science Quarterly, 31,* 274–297.

70. Bobocel, D. R., & Meyer, J. P. (1994). Escalating commitment to a failing course of action: Separating the roles of choice and justification. *Journal of Applied Psychology, 79,* 360–363.

71. Staw, B. M. (1981). The escalation of commitment to a course of action. *Academy of Management Review, 6,* 577–587.

72. Whyte, G. (1993). Escalating commitment in individual and group decision making: A prospect theory approach. *Organizational Behavior and Human Decision Processes, 54,* 430–455.

73. Simonson, I., & Staw, B. M. (1992). Deescalation strategies: A comparison of techniques for reducing commitment to losing courses of action. *Journal of Applied Psychology, 77,* 419–426.

74. Garland, H., & Newport, S. (1991). Effects of absolute and relative sunk costs on the decision to persist with a course of action. *Organizational Behavior and Human Decision Processes, 48,* 55–69.

75. Ross, J., & Staw, B. M. (1993). Organizational escalation and exit: Lessons from the Shoreham nuclear power plant. *Academy of Management Journal, 36,* 701–732.

76. Whyte, G. (1991). Diffusion of responsibility: Effects on the escalation tendency. *Journal of Applied Psychology, 76,* 408–415.

77. Staw, B. M., Barsade, S. G., & Koput, K. W. (1997). Escalation at the credit window: A longitudinal study of bank executives' recognition and write-off of problem loans. *Journal of Applied Psychology, 82,* 130–142.

78. Heath, C. (1995). Escalation and de-escalation of commitment in response to sunk costs: The role of budgeting in mental accounting. *Organizational Behavior and Human Decision Processes, 62,* 38–54.

79. Tan, H., & Yates, J. F. (1995). Sunk cost effects: The influences of instruction and future return estimates. *Organizational Behavior and Human Decision Processes, 63,* 311–319.

80. Davis, J. H. (1992). Introduction to the special issue on group decision making. *Organizational Behavior and Human Decision Processes, 52,* 1–2.

81. Delbecq, A. L., Van de Ven, A. H., & Gustafson, D. H. (1975). *Group techniques for program planning.* Glenview, IL: Scott, Foresman.

82. Hill, G. W. (1982). Group versus individual performance: Are N + 1 heads better than one? *Psychological Bulletin, 91,* 517–539.

83. Wanous, J. P., & Youtz, M. A. (1986). Solution diversity and the quality of group decisions. *Academy of Management Journal, 29,* 149–159.

84. Yetton, P., & Bottger, P. (1983). The relationships among group size, member ability, social decision schemes, and performance. *Organizational Behavior and Human Performance, 32,* 145–149.

85. See note 84.

86. See note 84.

87. Osborn, A. F. (1957). *Applied imagination.* New York: Scribner's.

88. Bouchard, T. J., Jr., Barsaloux, J., & Drauden, G. (1974). Brainstorming

procedure, group size, and sex as determinants of the problem-solving effectiveness of groups and individuals. *Journal of Applied Psychology, 59*, 135–138.

89. Bottger, P. C., & Yetton, P. W. (1987). Improving group performance by training in individual problem solving. *Journal of Applied Psychology, 72*, 651–657.

90. Patterson, J., & Kim, P. (1991). *The day America told the truth.* New York: Plume.

91. Dubrin, A. J. (1994). *Contemporary applied management* (4th ed.). Burr Ridge, IL: Irwin.

92. Vogel, D. (1993, November/December). Is U.S. business obsessed with ethics? *Across the Board*, pp. 31–33.

93. Insider trading. (1987, March 23). *Business Week*, p. 66.

94. Nomura Securities. (1991, August 26). *Business Week*, p. 27.

95. Singer, A. W. (1991, September). Ethics: Are standards lower overseas? *Across the Board*, pp. 31–34.

96. Dalkey, N. (1969). *The Delphi method: An experimental study of group decisions.* Santa Monica, CA: Rand Corporation.

97. Van de Ven, A. H., & Delbecq, A. L. (1971). Nominal versus interacting group processes for committee decision making effectiveness. *Academy of Management Journal, 14*, 203–212.

98. See note 97.

99. Gustafson, D. H., Shulka, R. K., Delbecq, A., & Walster, W. G. (1973). A comparative study of differences in subjective likelihood estimates made by individuals, interacting groups, Delphi groups, and nominal groups. *Organizational Behavior and Human Performance, 9*, 280–291.

100. Ulshak, F. L., Nathanson, L., & Gillan, P. B. (1981). *Small group problem solving: An aid to organizational effectiveness.* Reading, MA: Addison-Wesley.

101. Harmon, J., Schneer, J. A., & Hoffman, L. R. (1995). Electronic meetings and established decision groups: Audioconferencing effects on performance and structural stability. *Organizational Behavior and Human Decision Processes, 61*, 138–147.

102. Willis, R. E. (1979). A simulation of multiple selection using nominal group procedures. *Management Science, 25*, 171–181.

103. Stumpf, S. A., Zand, D. E., & Freedman, R. D. (1979). Designing groups for judgmental decisions. *Academy of Management Review, 4*, 589–600.

104. Rogelberg, S. G., Barnes-Farrell, J. L., & Lowe, C. A. (1992). The stepladder technique: An alternative group structure facilitating effective group decision making. *Journal of Applied Psychology, 77*, 730–737.

Case in Point Sources

Meeks, F. (1995, October 23). Catering to indulgent parents. *Forbes*, pp. 148, 150, 154–155; and The Motley Fool. (1996, October 2. http://www.fool.com/EveningNews/1996/EveningNews961002.htm).

CHAPTER 10
Preview Case Source

Sapsford, J. (1998, July 8). Deadbeat days: It's Japan's paradox: Troubled banks buoy their ailing borrowers. *Wall Street Journal*, pp. A1, A10.

Chapter Notes

1. Spacapan, S., & Oskamp, S. (Eds.). (1992). *Helping and being helped.* Newbury Park, CA: Sage.

2. Organ, D. W. (1997). Organizational citizenship behavior: It's construct clean-up time. *Human Performance, 10*, 85–98.

3. See note 2.

4. Morrison, E. W. (1994). Role definitions and organizational citizenship behavior: The importance of employee's perspective. *Academy of Management Journal, 37*, 1543–1567.

5. Konovsky, M. A., & Pugh, S. D. (1994). Citizenship behavior and social exchange. *Academy of Management Journal, 37*, 656–689.

6. Ball, G. A., Trevino, K. K., & Sims, H. P., Jr. (1994). Just and unjust punishment: Influences on subordinate performance and citizenship. *Academy of Management Journal, 37*, 299–322.

7. See note 4.

8. Randall, D. M., Fedor, D. P., & Longenecker, C. O. (1990). The behavioral expression of organizational commitment. *Journal of Vocational Behavior, 36*, 210–224.

9. Allen, T. D., & Rush, M. C. (1998). The effects of organizational citizenship behavior on performance judgments: A field study and a laboratory experiment. *Journal of Applied Psychology, 83*, 247–260.

10. Near, J. P., & Miceli, M. P. (1985). Organizational dissidence: The case of whistle-blowing. *Journal of Business Ethics, 4*, 1–16.

11. Lancaster, H. (1995, July 18). Workers who blow the whistle on bosses often pay a high price. *Wall Street Journal*, p. B1.

12. Henkoff, R. (1995, September 4). So who is this Mark Whitacre, and why is he saying these things about ADM? *Fortune*, pp. 64–66, 68.

13. Yates, R. E. (1995, July 7). Whistle-blowers pay dearly for heroics. *Chicago Tribune*, p. B7.

14. Miceli, M. P., & Near, J. P. (1997). Whistle-blowing as antisocial behavior. In R. A. Giacalone & J. Greenberg, (Eds.), *Antisocial behavior in organizations* (pp. 130–149). Thousand Oaks, CA: Sage.

15. Ring, P. S., & Van de Ven, A. (1994). Developmental processes of cooperative interorganizational relationships. *Academy of Management Review, 19*, 90–118.

16. Tjosvold, D. (1986). *Working together to get things done.* Lexington, MA: Lexington Books.

17. Komorita, M., & Parks, G. (1995). Interpersonal relations: Mixed-motive interaction. *Annual Review of Psychology, 46*, 183–207.

18. Baron, R. S., Kerr, N. L., & Miller, N. (1992). *Group process, group decision, group action.* Pacific Grove, CA: Brooks/Cole.

19. Pruitt, D. G., & Carnevale, P. J. (1993). *Negotiation in social conflict.* Pacific Grove, CA: Brooks/Cole.

20. Knight, G. P., & Dubro, A. F. (1984). Cooperative, competitive, and individualistic social values: An individualized regression and clustering approach. *Journal of Personality and Social Psychology, 46*, 98–105.

21. McAllister, D. J. (1995). Affect- and cognition-based trust as foundations for interpersonal cooperation in organizations. *Academy of Management Journal*, *38*, 24–59.

22. See note 21.

23. Smith, K. G., Carrol, S. J., & Ashford, S. J. (1995). Intra- and interorganizational cooperation: Toward a research agenda. *Academy of Management Journal*, *38*, 7–23.

24. Korsgaard, M. A., Schweiger, D. M., & Sapienza, H. J. (1995). Building commitment, attachment, and trust in strategic decision-making teams: The role of procedural justice. *Academy of Management Journal*, *38*, 60–84.

25. See note 24.

26. See note 24.

27. Yamagishi, T., & Yamagishi, M. (1994). Trust and commitment in the United States and Japan. *Motivation and Emotion*, *18*, 129–166.

28. Peters, T. J., & Waterman, R. H., Jr. (1982). *In search of excellence: Lessons from America's best-run companies*. New York: Warner Books.

29. Cheng, J. L. (1983). Interdependence and coordination in organizations: A role-system analysis. *Academy of Management Journal*, *26*, 156–162.

30. Tully, S. (1995, February 20). Purchasing's new muscle. *Fortune*, pp. 75–76, 78–79, 82–83.

31. See note 3.

32. Thomas, K. W., & Schmidt, W. H. (1976). A survey of managerial interests with respect to conflict. *Academy of Management Journal*, *10*, 315–318.

33. Mamis, R. A. (1994, June). Partner wars: Six true confessions. *Inc.*, pp. 36–42.

34. Walton, R. S., & McKersie, R. B. (1965). *A behavioral theory of labor negotiations: An analysis of a social interaction system*. New York: McGraw-Hill.

35. Thomas, K. W. (1976). Conflict and conflict management. In M. D. Dunnette (Ed.), *Handbook of industrial and organizational psychology* (pp. 889–935). Chicago: Rand McNally.

36. Rahim, M. A. (1983). A measure of styles of handling interpersonal conflict. *Academy of Management Journal*, *26*, 368–376.

37. Ting-Toomey, S. (1988). Intercultural conflict styles: A face-negotiation theory. In Y. Kim & W. Gudykunst (Eds.), *Theories in intercultural communication* (pp. 213–235). Newbury Park, CA: Sage.

38. Tjosvold, D., & De Dreu, C. (1997). Managing conflict in Dutch organizations: A test of the relevance of Deutsch's cooperation theory. *Journal of Applied Social Psychology*, *27*, 2213–2227.

39. Baron, R. A. (1989). Personality and organizational conflict: The Type A behavior pattern and self-monitoring. *Organizational Behavior and Human Decision Processes*, *44*, 281–297.

40. Robinson, R., Keltner, D., Ward, A., & Ross, L. (1995). Actual versus assumed differences in construal: "Naïve realism" in intergroup perception and conflict. *Journal of Personality and Social Psychology*, *68*, 404–417.

41. Keltner, D., & Robinson, R. J. (1997). Defending the status quo: Power and bias in social conflict. *Personality and Social Psychology Bulletin*, *23*, 1066–1077.

42. Fodor, E. M. (1978b). Group stress, authoritarian style of control and use of power. *Journal of Applied Psychology*, *61*, 313–318.

43. Huo, Y. J., Smith, H. J., Tyler, T. R., & Lind, E. A. (1996). Superordinate identification subgroup identification and justice concerns: Is separation the problem, is assimilation the answer? *Psychological Science*, *7*, 40–45.

44. Tyler, T. R., Lind, E. A., Ohbuchi, K. I., Sugawara, I., & Huo, Y. J. (1998). Conflict with outsiders: Disputing within and across cultural boundaries. *Personality and Social Psychology Bulletin*, *24*, 137–146.

45. Tjosvold, D. (1985). Implications of controversy research for management. *Journal of Management*, *11*, 21–37.

46. Robbins, S. P. (1974). *Managing organizational conflict: A nontraditional approach*. Englewood Cliffs, NJ: Prentice-Hall.

47. Schwenk, C. R., & Cosier, R. A. (1980). Effects of the expert, devil's advocate, and dialectical inquiry methods of prediction performance. *Organizational Behavior and Human Decision Processes*, *26*, 409–424.

48. See note 47.

49. Cosier, R. A., & Dalton, D. R. (1990). Positive effects of conflict: A field assessment. *International Journal of Conflict Management*, *1*, 81–92.

50. Thompson, L. (1998). *The mind and heart of the negotiator*. Upper Saddle River, NJ: Prentice-Hall.

51. Thompson, L., & Hastie, R. (1990). Social perception in negotiation. *Organizational Behavior and Human Decision Processes*, *47*, 98–123.

52. Lewicki, R. J., & Litterer, J. A. (1985). *Negotiation*. Homewood, IL: Irwin.

53. Pruitt, D. G., & Carnevale, P. J. (1993). *Negotiation in social conflict*. Pacific Grove, CA: Brooks/Cole.

54. Thompson, L., & Hastie, R. (1990). Social perception in negotiation. *Organizational Behavior and Human Decision Processes*, *47*, 98–123.

55. See note 53.

56. Vorauer, J. D., & Claude, S. D. (1998). Perceived versus actual transparency of goals in negotiation. *Personality and Social Psychology Bulletin*, *24*, 371–385.

57. Thomas, K. W. (1992). Conflict and conflict management: Reflections and update. *Journal of Organizational Behavior*, *13*, 265–274.

58. Overman, S. (1993, May). Why grapple with the cloudy elephant? *HRMagazine*, pp. 60–65.

59. See note 58.

60. McGurn (1988, March 7). Spotting the thieves who work among us. *Wall Street Journal*, p. 16A.

61. Northwestern National Life Insurance Company (1993). *Fear and violence in the workplace*. Milwaukee, WI: Author.

62. Harper, D. (1990). Spotlight abuse, save profits. *Industrial Distribution*, *79*, 47–51.

63. Gruber, J. E. (1990). How women handle sexual harassment: A literature review. *Social Science Research*, *74*, 3–9.

64. Buss, D. (1993). Ways to curtail employee theft. *Nation's Business*, pp. 36–38.

65. Robinson, S. L., & Greenberg, J. (1998). Employees behaving badly: Dimensions, determinants, and dilemmas in the study of workplace deviance. In D. M. Rousseau & C. Cooper (Eds.), *Trends in organizational behavior* (Vol. 5). New York: Wiley.

66. National Institute for Occupational Safety and Health, 1993.

67. Deibel, M. (1998). Study: Workplace violence a global problem. *Albany Times Union*, July 20, 1996, p. B1.

68. Leonard, J. R., & Sloboda, B. A. (1996, April). *Workplace violence: A review of current literature.* Paper presented at the Annual Meeting of the Society for Industrial and Organizational Psychology, San Diego, CA.

69. Neuman, J. H., & Baron, R. A. (1997). Aggression in the workplace. In Giacalone, R. A., & Greenberg, J. (Eds.), *Anti-social behavior in organizations* (pp. 37–67). Thousand Oaks, CA: Sage.

70. Baron, R. A., Neuman, J. H., & Geddes, D. H. (In press). Social and personal determinants of workplace aggression: Evidence for the impact of the Type A behavior pattern and perceived injustice. *Aggressive Behavior.*

71. Neuman, J. H., & Baron, R. A. (1998). Workplace violence and workplace aggression: Evidence concerning specific forms, potential causes, and preferred targets. *Journal of Management, 24,* 391–419.

72. Greenberg, J., & Alge, B. J. (1998). Aggressive reactions to workplace injustice. In R. W. Griffin, A. O'Leary-Kelly, & J. Collins (Eds.), Dysfunctional behavior in organizations, Vol. 1: Violent behaviors in organizations. Stamford, CT: JAI Press.

73. Folger, R., Robinson, S. L., Dietz, J., McClean Parks, J., & Baron, R. A. (1998, August). *When colleagues become violent.* Paper presented at the meetings of the Academy of Management, San Diego, CA.

74. See note 84.

75. Folger, R., & Baron, R. A. (1996). Violence and hostility at work: A model of reactions to perceived injustice. In G. R. VandenBos & E. Q. Bulatao (Eds.), *Violence on the job: Identifying risks and developing solutions* (pp. 51–85). Washington, DC: American Psychological Association.

76. Griffin, R. W., O'Leary-Kelly, A., & Collins, J. M. (1998). *Dysfunctional behavior in organizations: Violent and deviant behavior.* Stamford, CT: JAI Press.

77. Arvey, R. D., & Jones, A. P. (1985). The use of discipline in organizational settings: A framework for future research. In L. L. Cummings & B. M. Staw (Eds.), *Research in organizational behavior* (Vol. 7, pp. 367–408). Greenwich, CT: JAI Press.

78. Greenberg, J. (1993). The social side of fairness: Interpersonal and informational classes of justice. In R. Cropanzano (Ed.), *Justice in the workplace: Approaching fairness in human resource management.* Hillsdale, NJ: Erlbaum.

79. Mantell, M., & Albrecht, S. (1994). *Ticking bombs: Defusing violence in the workplace.* New York: Irwin.

80. Greenberg, J. (1997). The STEAL motive: Managing the social determinants of employee theft. In R. Giacalone & J. Greenberg (Eds.), *Antisocial behavior in organizations* (pp. 85–108). Newbury Park, CA: Sage.

81. Snyder, N. H., & Blair, K. E. (1989, May-June). Dealing with employee theft. *Business Horizons,* pp. 27–34.

82. Miner, J. B., & Capps, M. H. (1996). *How honesty testing works.* Westport, CT: Quorum.

83. See note 82.

84. Altheide, D. L., Adler, P. A., Adler, P., & Altheide, D. A. (1978). The social meanings of employee theft. In J. M. Johnson & J. D. Douglas (Eds.), *Crime at the top: Deviance in business and the professions* (pp. 90–124). Philadelphia: Lippincott.

85. Greenberg, J. (1998). The cognitive geometry of employee theft. In *Dysfunctional behavior in organizations: Nonviolent and deviant behavior* (pp. 147–193). Stamford, CT: JAI Press.

Case in Point Source

Tjosvold, D. (1986). *Working together to get things done.* Lexington, MA: Lexington.

CHAPTER 11
Preview Case Notes

Gunther, M. (1997, August 18). Will Uncle Bud sell Hollywood? *Fortune,* pp. 185–186, 188.

Chapter Notes

1. Cobb, A. T. (1984). An episodic model of power: Toward an integration of theory and research. *Academy of Management Review, 9,* 482–493.

2. Mayes, B. T., & Allen, R. T. (1977). Toward a definition of organizational politics. *Academy of Management Review, 2,* 672–678.

3. Mintzberg, H. (1983). *Power in and around organizations.* Englewood Cliffs, NJ: Prentice-Hall.

4. Schriesheim, C. A., & Hinkin, T. R. (1990). Influence tactics used by subordinates: A theoretical and empirical analysis and refinement of the Kipnis, Schmidt, and Wilkinson subscales. *Journal of Applied Psychology, 75,* 246–257.

5. Yukl, G., & Tracey, J. B. (1992). Consequences of influence tactics used with subordinates, peers, and the boss. *Journal of Applied Psychology, 77,* 525–535.

6. Yukl, G., Falbe, C. M., & Youn, J. Y. (1993). Patterns of influence behavior for managers. *Group & Organization Management, 18,* 5–28.

7. Offermann, L. R. (1990). Power and leadership in organizations. *American Psychologist, 45,* 179–189.

8. Falbe, C. M. & Yukl, G. (1992). Consequences for managers of using single influence tactics and combinations of tactics. *Academy of Management Journal, 35,* 638–652.

9. Ansari, M. A., & Kapoor, A. (1987). Organizational context and upward influence tactics. *Organizational Behavior and Human Decision Processes, 40,* 39–49.

10. Dutton, J. E., & Ashford, S. J. (1993). Selling issues to top management. *Academy of Management Review, 18,* 397–428.

11. Rebello, K., Burrows, P., & Sager, I. (1996, February 5). The fall of an American icon. *Business Week,* pp. 34–42.

12. Creswell, J. (1998, October 12). Ranking the 50 most powerful women. *Fortune,* pp. 83–86.

13. Podsakoff, P. M., & Schriesheim, C. A. (1985). Field studies of French and Raven's bases of power: Critique, re-analysis, and suggestions for future research. *Psychological Bulletin, 97,* 387–411.

14. Huber, V. L. (1981). The sources, uses, and conservation of managerial power. *Personnel, 51*(4), 62–67.

15. Kipnis, D., Schmidt, S. M., Swaffin-Smith, C., & Wilkinson, I. (1984,

Winter). Patterns of managerial influence: Shotgun managers, tacticians, and bystanders. *Organizational Dynamics*, 58–67.

16. Stewart, T. (1989, November 6). CEOs see clout shifting. *Fortune*, p. 66.

17. Kahn, R. L., Wolfe, D. M., Quinn, R. P., Snoek, J. D., & Rosenthal, R. A. (1964). *Organizational stress: Studies in role conflict and ambiguity*. New York: Wiley.

18. See note 13.

19. Symonds, W. C., & Siler, J. F. (1991, April 1). CEO disease. *Business Week*, pp. 52–60.

20. Morris, S. (1990, March 13). Abbott boss's suit points to a trend. *Chicago Tribune*, Business Section, p. 1.

21. See note 17.

22. Ford, R. C., & Fottler, M. D. (1995). Empowerment: A matter of degree. *Academy of Management Executive, 9*, 21–29.

23. Dumaine, B. (1990, May 7). Who needs a boss? *Fortune*, pp. 52–54, 56, 58, 60.

24. Shipper, F., & Manz, C. C. (1991). Employee self-management without formally designated teams: An alternative road to empowerment. *Organizational Dynamics, 20*(3), 48–61.

25. Sherman, J. (1994). *In the rings of Saturn*. New York: Oxford University Press.

26. Dumaine, B. (1993, February 22). The new non-manager managers. *Fortune*, pp. 80–84 (quote, p. 81).

27. Row, H. (1998, December). Great Harvest's recipe for growth. *Fast Company*, pp. 46, 48.

28. DeGus, A. (1997). *The living company*. Boston: Harvard Business School.

29. See note 26.

30. DuBrin, A. J. (1994). *Contemporary applied management* (4th ed.). Burr Ridge, IL: Irwin.

31. Patalon, W., III. (1992, June 14). Xerox's gateway to the world. *Rochester Democrat and Chronicle*, pp. 1F–2F.

32. Lesser, Y. (1992, May). From the bottom up: A toast to empowerment. *Human Resources Forum*, pp. 1–2.

33. Omni Hotels Web site (http://www.omnihotels.com/pages/common/number.html).

34. Fleming, P. C. (1991, December). Empowerment strengthens the rock. *Management Review*, pp. 34–37.

35. Byham, W. C., & Cox, J. (1991). *ZAPP: The lightening of empowerment*. New York: Harmony.

36. Gresov, C., & Stephens, C. (1993). The context of interunit influence attempts. *Administrative Science Quarterly, 38*, 252–276.

37. Pfeffer, J., & Salancik, G. (1978). *The external control of organizations*. New York: Harper & Row.

38. Salancik, G., & Pfeffer, J. (1974). The bases and uses of power in organizational decision-making. *Administrative Science Quarterly, 19*, 453–473.

39. Boeker, W. (1989). The development and institutionalization of subunit power in organizations. *Administrative Science Quarterly, 34*, 388–410.

40. Lawrence, P. R., & Lorsch, J. W. (1967). *Organization and environment*. Cambridge, MA: Harvard University Press.

41. Hickson, D. J., Astley, W. G., Butler, R. J., & Wilson, D. C. (1981). Organization as power. In L. L. Cummings & B. M. Staw (Eds.), *Research in organizational behavior* (Vol. 4, pp. 151–196). Greenwich, CT: JAI Press.

42. Miles, R. H. (1980). *Macro organizational behavior*. Glenview, IL: Scott, Foresman.

43. Saunders, C. S., & Scarmell, R. (1982). Intraorganizational distributions of power: Replication research. *Academy of Management Journal, 25*, 192–200.

44. Hinings, C. R., Hickson, D. J., Pennings, J. M., & Schneck, R. E. (1974). Structural conditions of intraorganizational power. *Academy of Management Journal, 19*, 22–44.

45. See note 2.

46. Drory, A., & Romm, T. (1990). The definition of organizational politics: A review. *Human Relations, 43*, 1133–1154.

47. Ferris, G. R., & Kacmar, K. M. (1992). Perceptions of organizational politics. *Journal of Management, 18*, 93–116.

48. Rosen, R. H. (1991). *The healthy company*. New York: Tarcher/Perigree (quote, p. 71).

49. Mulder, M., de Jong, R. D., Koppelaar, L., & Verhage, J. (1986). Power, situation, and leaders' effectiveness: An organizational field study. *Journal of Applied Psychology, 71*, 566–570.

50. Feldman, S. P. (1988). Secrecy, information, and politics: An essay in organizational decision making. *Human Relations, 41*, 73–90.

51. Greenberg, J. (1990). Looking fair vs. being fair: Managing impressions of organizational justice. In B. M. Staw & L. L. Cummings (Eds.), *Research in organizational behavior* (Vol. 12, pp. 111–157). Greenwich, CT: JAI Press.

52. Ferris, G. R., & King, T. R. (1991). Politics in human resources decisions: A walk on the dark side. *Organizational Dynamics, 20*, 59–71.

53. Warshaw, M. (1998, April/May). The good guy's and gal's guide to office politics. *Fast Company*, pp. 156–158, 160, 162, 166, 168, 170, 172, 174, 176, 178.

54. Boeker, W. (1992). Power and managerial dismissal: Scapegoating at the top. *Administrative Science Quarterly, 37*, 400–421.

55. Cobb, A. T. (1991). Toward the study of organizational coalitions: Participant concerns and activities in a simulated organizational setting. *Human Relations, 44*, 1057–1079.

56. Feldman, S. P. (1988). Secrecy, information, and politics: An essay in organizational decision making. *Human Relations, 41*, 73–90.

57. Liden, R. C., & Mitchell, T. R. (1988). Ingratiatory behaviors in organizational settings. *Academy of Management Review, 13*, 572–587.

58. See note 3.

59. Sprouse, M. (1992). *Sabotage in the American workplace*. San Francisco: Pressure Drop Press.

60. Madison, D. L., Allen, R. W., Porter, L. W., Renwick, P. A., & Mayes, B. T. (1980). Organizational politics: An exploration of managers perceptions. *Human Relations, 33*, 79–100.

61. Pfeffer, J. (1992). *Managing with power*. Boston: Harvard Business School.

62. See note 38.

63. Wayne, S. J., & Ferris, G. R. (1990). Influence tactics, affect, and ex-

change quality in supervisor-subordinate interactions. *Journal of Applied Psychology, 75,* 487–499.

64. See note 43.

65. Adler, N. J., & Israeli, D. N. (1995). Women managers: Moving up and across borders. In O. Shenkar (Ed.), *Global perspectives of human resource management* (pp. 165–193). Englewood Cliffs, NJ: Prentice-Hall.

66. Adler, N. J. (1984). Women do not want international careers: And other myths about international management. *Organizational Dynamics, 13*(2), 66–79.

67. Moran, Stahl, & Boyer, Inc. (1988). *Status of American female expatriate employees: Survey results.* Boulder, CO: International Division.

68. Jelinek, M., & Adler, N. J. (1988). Women: World-class managers for global competition. *Academy of Management Executive, 2*(1), 11–19.

69. Bartol, K. M., & Martin, D. C. (1990). When politics pays: Factors influencing managerial compensation decisions. *Personnel Psychology, 43,* 599–614.

70. Gray, B., & Ariss, S. S. (1985). Politics and strategic change across organizational life cycles. *Academy of Management Review, 10,* 707–723.

71. Hannan, M. T., & Freeman, J. H. (1978). Internal politics of growth and decline. In M. W. Meyer (Ed.), *Environment and organizations* (pp. 177–199). San Francisco: Jossey-Bass.

72. Ferris, G. R., & King, T. R. (1991). Politics in human resources decisions: A walk on the dark side. *Organizational Dynamics, 20,* 59–71.

73. Gandz, J., & Murray, V. V. (1980). The experience of workplace politics. *Academy of Management Journal, 23,* 237–251.

74. Allen, R. W., Madison, D. L., Porter, L. W., Renwick, P. A., & Mayes, B. T. (1979). Organizational politics: Tactics and characteristics of its actors. *California Management Review, 22,* 77–83.

75. See note 72.

76. See note 73.

77. Kipnis, D. (1976). *The powerholders.* Chicago: University of Chicago Press.

78. Buchholz, R. A. (1989). *Fundamental concepts and problems in business ethics.* Englewood Cliffs, NJ: Prentice-Hall.

79. Gellerman, S. W. (1986, July-August). Why "good" managers make bad ethical choices. *Harvard Business Review,* pp. 85–90.

80. Commerce Clearing House. (1991, June 26). *1991 SHRM/CCH survey.* Chicago: Author.

81. Kumar, P., & Ghadially, R. (1989). Organizational politics and its effects on members of organizations. *Human Relations, 42,* 305–314.

82. Andrews, G. (1994, September). Mistrust, the hidden obstacle to empowerment. *HRMagazine,* pp. 66–68, 70.

83. Velasquez, M., Moberg, D. J., & Cavanaugh, G. F. (1983). Organizational statesmanship and dirty politics: Ethical guidelines for the organizational politician. *Organizational Dynamics, 11,* 65–79.

84. See note 83.

85. Greenberg, J. (1982). Approaching equity and avoiding inequity in groups and organizations. In J. Greenberg & R. L. Cohen (Eds.), *Equity and justice in social behavior* (pp. 389–435). New York: Academic Press.

CHAPTER 12
Preview Case Sources

Farrell, G. (1998, December). "My mouse is my first." *Business 2.0,* 72–74, 76, 78, 80, 82, 84 (http://www.agency.com/ourcompany/).

Chapter Notes

1. House, R. J., & Podsakoff, P. M. (1995). Leadership effectiveness: Past perspectives and future directions for research. In J. Greenberg (Ed.), *Organizational behavior: The state of the science* (pp. 45–82). Hillsdale, NJ: Erlbaum.

2. Yukl, G. (1998). *Leadership in organizations* (4th ed.). Upper Saddle River, NJ: Prentice-Hall.

3. Bennis, W. G., & Nanus, B. (1985). *Leaders: The strategies for taking charge.* New York: Harper & Row (quote, p. 4).

4. See note 1.

5. Locke, E. A. (1991). *The essence of leadership.* New York: Lexington Books.

6. Cialdini, R. B. (1988). *Influence* (2nd ed.). Glenview, IL: Scott, Foresman.

7. Kotter, J. P. (1990). *A force for change: How leadership differs from management.* New York: Free Press.

8. Geier, J. G. (1969). A trait approach to the study of leadership in small groups. *Journal of Communication, 17,* 316–323.

9. Kirkpatrick, S. A., & Locke, E. A. (1991). Leadership: Do traits matter? *Academy of Management Executive, 5,* 48–60 (quote, p. 58).

10. House, R. J., Shane, S. A., & Herold, D. M. (1996). Rumors of the death of dispositional research are vastly exaggerated. *Academy of Management Review, 21,* 203–224.

11. See note 9.

12. Lord, R. G., DeVader, C. L., & Alliger, G. M. (1986). A meta-analysis of the relation between personality traits and leadership perceptions: An application of validity generalization procedures. *Journal of Applied Psychology, 61,* 402–410.

13. Zaccaro, S. J., Foti, R. J., & Kenny, D. A. (1991). Self-monitoring and trait-based variance in leadership: An investigation of leader flexibility across multiple group situations. *Journal of Applied Psychology, 76,* 308–315.

14. Muczyk, J. P., & Reimann, B. C. (1987). The case for directive leadership. *Academy of Management Review, 12,* 637–647.

15. Chen, C. C., & Meindl, J. R. (1991). The construction of leadership images in the popular press: The case of Donald Burr and People Express. *Administrative Science Quarterly, 36,* 521–551.

16. Zenger, J. H., Musselwhite, E., Hurson, K., & Perrin, C. (1994). *Leading teams: Mastering the new role.* Homewood, IL: Business One Irwin.

17. Likert, R. (1961). *New patterns in management.* New York: McGraw-Hill.

18. Stogdill, R. M. (1963). *Manual for the leader behavior description questionnaire, form XII.* Columbus, OH: Ohio State University, Bureau of Business Research.

19. Weissenberg, P., & Kavanagh, M. H. (1972). The independence of initiating structure and consideration: A review of the evidence. *Personnel Psychology, 25,* 119–130.

20. Vroom, V. H. (1976). Leadership. In M. D. Dunnette (Ed.), *Handbook of in-*

dustrial-organizational psychology (1527–1552). Chicago: Rand-McNally.

21. See note 3.

22. Band, W. A. (1994). *Touchstones*. New York: Wiley (quote, p. 247).

23. Blake, R. R., & Mouton, J. J. (1969). *Building a dynamic corporation through grid organizational development*. Reading, MA: Addison-Wesley.

24. Lee, C. (1991). Followership: The essence of leadership. *Training, 28,* 27–35 (quote, p. 28).

25. Mead, R. (1998). *International management* (2nd ed.). Malden, MA: Blackwell.

26. Adler, N. J., Campbell, N. C., & Laurent, A. (1989). In search of appropriate methodology: From outside the People's Republic of China looking in. *Journal of International Business Studies, 12,* 61–74.

27. Graen, G. B., & Wakabayashi, M. (1994). Cross-cultural leadership-making: Bridging American and Japanese diversity for team advantage. In H. C. Triandis, M. D. Dunnette, & L. M. Hough (Eds.) *Handbook of industrial and organizational psychology* (2nd ed.) (Vol. 4, pp. 415–466). Palo Alto, CA: Consulting Psychologists Press.

28. Phillips, A. S., & Bedian, A. G. (1994). Leader-follower exchange quality: The role of personal and interpersonal attributes. *Academy of Management Journal, 37,* 990–1001.

29. Dunegan, K. J., Duchon, D., & Uhl-Bien, M. (1992). Examining the link between leader-member exchange and subordinate performance: The role of task analyzability and variety as moderators. *Journal of Management, 18,* 59–76.

30. Duarte, N. T., Goodson, J. R., & Klich, N. R. (1993). How do I like thee? Let me appraise the ways. *Journal of Organizational Behavior, 14,* 239–249.

31. Deluga, R. J., & Perry, J. T. (1991). The relationship of subordinate upward influencing behaviour, satisfaction and perceived superior effectiveness with leader-member exchanges. *Journal of Occupational Psychology, 64,* 239–252.

32. Ferris, G. R. (1985). Role of leadership in the employee withdrawal process: A constructive replication. *Journal of Applied Psychology, 70,* 777–781.

33. Scandura, T. A., & Schriesheim, C. A. (1994). Leader-member exchange and supervisor career mentoring as complementary constructs in leadership research. *Academy of Management Journal, 37,* 1588–1602.

34. Lord, R. G., & Maher, K. (1989). Perceptions in leadership and their implications in organizations. In J. Carroll (Ed.), *Applied social psychology and organizational settings* (Vol. 4, pp. 129–154). Hillsdale, NJ: Erlbaum.

35. Heneman, R. L., Greenberger, D. B., & Anonyuo, C. (1989). Attributions and exchanges: The effects of interpersonal factors on the diagnosis of employee performance. *Academy of Management Journal, 32,* 466–476.

36. Mitchell, T. R., & Wood, R. E. (1980). Supervisor's responses to subordinate poor performance: A test of an attribution model. *Organizational Behavior and Human Performance, 25,* 123–138.

37. Bass, B. M. (1985). *Leadership and performance beyond expectations*. New York: Free Press.

38. House, R. J. (1977). A 1976 theory of charismatic leadership. In J. G. Hunt & L. L. Larson (Eds.), *Leadership: The cutting edge* (pp. 189–207). Carbondale, IL: Southern Illinois University Press.

39. See note 38.

40. Conger, J. A. (1991). Inspiring others: The language of leadership. *Academy of Management Executive, 5,* 31–45 (quote, p. 32).

41. House, R. J., Woycke, J., & Fedor, E. M. (1988). Charismatic and noncharismatic leaders: Differences in behavior and effectiveness. In J. A. Conger & R. N. Kanungo (Eds.), *Charismatic leadership* (pp. 122–144). San Francisco: Jossey-Bass.

42. See note 1.

43. Zachary, G. P. (1994, June 2). How "barbarian" style of Philippe Kahn led Borland into jeopardy. *Wall Street Journal,* p. A1.

44. See note 7 (quote, p. 44).

45. See note 1.

46. Tichy, N. M. (1993). *Control your destiny or someone else will*. New York: Doubleday Currency.

47. Stewart, T. A. (1998, March 2). America's most admired companies. *Fortune,* 70–82.

48. Morris, B. (1995, December 11). The wealth builders. *Fortune,* pp. 80–84, 88, 90, 94.

49. Koh, W. L., Steers, & Terborg, J. R. (1995). The effects of transformational leadership on teacher attitudes and student performance in Singapore. *Journal of Organizational Behavior, 16,* 319–333.

50. Hater, J. J., & Bass, B. M. (1988). Superiors' evaluations and subordinates perceptions of transformational and transactional leadership. *Journal of Applied Psychology, 73,* 695–702.

51. Fiedler, F. E. (1978). Contingency model and the leadership process. In L. Berkowitz (Ed.), *Advances in experimental social psychology* (Vol. 11, pp. 60–112). New York: Academic Press.

52. Hersey, P., & Blanchard, K. H. (1988). *Management of organizational behavior*. Englewood Cliffs, NJ: Prentice-Hall.

53. House, R. J., & Baetz, M. L. (1979). Leadership: Some empirical generalizations and new research directions. In B. M. Staw (Ed.), *Research in organizational behavior* (Vol. 1, pp. 341–424). Greenwich, CT: JAI Press.

54. Whitworth, L., House, H., Sandahl, P., & Kimsey-House, H. (1998). *Co-active coaching: New skills for coaching people toward success in work and life*. Palo Alto, CA: Davies-Black.

55. Holtz, L. (1998). *Winning everyday*. New York: Harper Business.

56. Wolfe, R. (1998). *The Packer way*. New York: St. Martins.

57. Bradley, Bill. (1998). *Values of the game*. New York: Artisan.

58. Milbank, D. (1990, March 5). Managers are sent to "charm schools" to discover how to polish up their acts. *Wall Street Journal,* pp. A14, B3.

59. Vroom, V. H., & Yetton, P. W. (1973). *Leadership and decision making*. Pittsburgh: University of Pittsburgh Press.

60. Kerr, S., & Jermier, J. M. (1978). Substitutes for leadership: Their meaning and measurement. *Organizational Behavior and Human Performance, 22,* 375–403.

61. Sheridan, J. E., Vredenburgh, D. J., & Abelson, M. A. (1984). Contextual model of leadership influence in hospital units. *Academy of Management Journal, 27,* 57–78.

62. Podsakoff, P. M., Niehoff, B. P., MacKenzie, S. B., & Williams, M. L. (1993). Do substitutes for leadership really substitute for leadership? An empirical examination of Kerr and Jermier's situational leadership model. *Organizational Behavior and Human Decision Processes, 54,* 1–44.

63. Meindl, J. R., & Ehrlich, S. B. (1987). The romance of leadership and the evaluation of organizational performance. *Academy of Management Journal, 30,* 91–109.

Case in Point Source

Morris, K. (1998, May 25). The rise of Jill Barad. *Business Week,* pp. 112–116, 118–119.

CHAPTER 13

Preview Case Sources

Cortese, A. (1996, February 26). It's a wrap — with the intranet. *Business Week,* pp. 48–49, 51; and Grover, R. (1998, July 13). Steven Spielberg: The storyteller. *Business Week,* pp. 56–60, 62, 64.

Chapter Notes

1. Saporito, B. (1992, August 24). A week aboard the Wal-Mart express. *Business Week,* pp. 77–81, 84.

2. Flynn, J., Del Valle, C., & Mitchell, R. (1992, August 3). Did Sears take other customers for a ride? *Business Week,* pp. 24–25.

3. Schneider, B. (1990). *Organizational climate and culture.* San Francisco: Jossey-Bass.

4. Schein, E. H. (1985). *Organizational culture and leadership.* San Francisco: Jossey-Bass.

5. Martin, J. (1992). *Cultures in organizations.* New York: Oxford University Press.

6. Goffee, R., & Jones, G. (1998). *The character of a corporation.* New York: Harper Business.

7. Amabile, T. (1996). *Creativity in context.* Denver: Westview Press.

8. See note 6.

9. Martin, J., Sitkin, S. B., & Boehm, M. (1985). Founders and the elusiveness of a cultural legacy. In P. J. Frost, L. F. Moore, M. R. Louis, C. C. Lundberg, & J. Martin (Eds.), *Organizational culture* (pp. 99–124). Beverly Hills, CA: Sage.

10. Dobrzynski, J. H. (1993, April 12). "I'm going to let the problems come to me." *Business Week,* pp. 32–33.

11. Ornstein, S. L. (1986). Organizational symbols: A study of their meanings and influences on perceived psychological climate. *Organizational Behavior and Human Decision Processes, 38,* 207–229.

12. Martin, J. (1982). Stories and scripts in organizational settings. In A. Hastorf & A. Isen (Eds.), *Cognitive social psychology* (pp. 255–306). New York: Elsevier-North Holland.

13. Neuhauser, P. C. (1993). *Corporate legends and lore: The power of storytelling as a management tool.* New York: McGraw-Hill (quote, p. 63).

14. Manley, W. W., II. (1991). *Executive's handbook of model business conduct codes.* Englewood Cliffs, NJ: Prentice-Hall (quote, p. 5).

15. Weiner, Y. (1988). Forms of value systems: A focus on organizational effectiveness and cultural change and maintenance. *Academy of Management Review, 13,* 534–545.

16. Walter, G. A. (1985). Culture collisions in mergers and acquisitions. In P. J. Frost, L. F. Moore, M. R. Louis, C. C. Lundberg, & J. Martin (Eds.), *Organizational culture* (pp. 301–314). Beverly Hills, CA: Sage.

17. Burrough, B., & Helyar, J. (1990). *Barbarians at the gate.* New York: HarperCollins.

18. Davenport, T. O. (1998, January). The integration challenge. *Management Review,* pp. 25–28.

19. Colvin, G. (1999, January 11). The year of the mega-merger. *Fortune,* pp. 62–88.

20. See note 18.

21. See note 18 (quote, p. 28).

22. Carroll, P. (1993). *Big blues: The unmaking of IBM.* New York: Crown.

23. Amabile, T. M. (1988). A model of creativity and innovation in organizations. In B. M. Staw & L. L. Cummings (Eds.), *Research in organizational behavior* (Vol. 10, pp. 123–167). Greenwich, CT: JAI Press.

24. Mattimore, B. W. (1994). *99% inspiration.* New York: AMACOM.

25. Ayan, J. (1997). *Aha.* New York: Three Rivers Press.

26. Michalko, M. (1991). *Thinkertoys.* Berkeley, CA: Ten Speed Press.

27. Higgins, J. M. (1995). *Innovate or evaporate.* Winter Park, FL: New Management Publishing Company.

28. Oldham, G. R., & Cummings, A. (1996). Employee creativity: Personal and contextual factors at work. *Academy of Management Journal, 39,* 607–634.

29. Brown, E. (1998, March 1). America's most admired companies. *Fortune,* pp. 68–73.

30. See note 17.

31. Hayes, R. H., & Abernathy, W. J. (1980, July-August). Managing our way to economic decline. *Harvard Business Review,* pp. 67–77.

32. Hill, C. W., Hitt, M. A., & Hoskisson, R. E. (1988). *Academy of Management Executive, 2,* 51–60.

33. Dumaine, B. (1991, December 2). Closing the innovation gap. *Fortune,* pp. 57–59.

34. Gross, N. (1994, March 21). Who says science has to pay off fast? *Business Week,* pp. 110–111.

35. Schlender, B. R. (1992, February 24). How Sony keeps the magic going. *Fortune,* pp. 76–80, 82, 84.

36. Gross, N. (1992, September 28). Inside Hitachi. *Business Week,* pp. 92–94, 96, 98, 100.

37. Young, J. A. (1990, February). Myths of technology leadership lull U.S. into risky comfort zone. *Financier,* pp. 32–36.

38. Lord, L. L., & Horn, M. (1987, January 19). The brain battle. *U.S. News & World Report,* pp. 58–65.

39. Bowen, E. (1988, January 11). Wanted: Fresh, homegrown talent. *Time,* 65.

40. Moffat, S. (1991, March 25). Picking Japan's research brains. *Fortune,* pp. 84–86, 88, 90–92, 94, 96.

41. Arthur D. Little, Inc. (1985). *Management perspectives on innovation: Innovation management practices in North America, Europe, and Japan*. Cambridge, MA: Author.

42. Hitt, M. A., Hoskisson, R. E., Ireland, R. D., & Harrison, J. S. (1991). Effects of acquisitions on R&D inputs and outputs. *Academy of Management Journal, 34*, 693–706.

43. See note 27 (quote, p. 18).

44. Ricchiuto, J. (1997). *Collaborative creativity*. New York: Oakhill.

Case in Point Sources

Coyne, W. E. (1997). 3M (Minnesota Mining and Manufacturing Company). In R. M. Kanter, J. Kao, & F. Wiersema (Eds.), *Innovation* (pp. 43–63). New York: Harper Business; and Kanter, R. M., Kao, J., & Wiersema, F. (1997). *Innovation*. New York: Harper Business.

CHAPTER 14
Preview Case Source

Lubove, S. (1995, July 17). New-tech, old-tech. *Forbes*, 58, 60, 62.

Chapter Notes

1. Miller, D. (1987). The genesis of configuration. *Academy of Management Review, 12*, 686–701.

2. Galbraith, J. R. (1987). Organization design. In J. W. Lorsch (Ed.), *Handbook of organizational behavior* (pp. 343–357). Englewood Cliffs, NJ: Prentice-Hall.

3. Hendricks, C. F. (1992). *The rightsizing remedy*. Homewood, IL: Business One Irwin.

4. Swoboda, F. (1990, May 28–June 3). For unions, maybe bitter was better. *Washington Post National Weekly Edition*, p. 20.

5. Speen, K. (1988, September 12). Caught in the middle. *Business Week*, pp. 80–88.

6. Urwick, L. F. (1956). The manager's span of control. *Harvard Business Review, 34*(3), 39–47.

7. Charan, R. (1991, July–August). How networks reshape organizations — for results. *Harvard Business Review*, pp. 10–17.

8. Green, H., & Moscow, A. (1984). *Managing*. New York: Doubleday.

9. Dalton, M. (1950). Conflicts between staff and line managerial officers. *American Sociological Review, 15*, 342–351.

10. Chandler, A. (1962). *Strategy and structure*. Cambridge, MA: MIT Press.

11. Mitchell, R. (1987, December 14). When Jack Welch takes over: A guide for the newly acquired. *Business Week*, p. 93–97.

12. Lawrence, P., & Lorsch, J. (1967). *Organization and environment*. Boston: Harvard University Press.

13. Pitta, J. (1993, April 26). It had to be done and we did it. *Forbes*, pp. 148–152.

14. Dumaine, B. (1990, November 5). How to manage in a recession. *Fortune*, pp. 72–75.

15. Uttal, B. (1985, June 29). Mettle test time for John Young. *Fortune*, pp. 242–244, 248.

16. Mee, J. F. (1964). Matrix organizations. *Business Horizons, 7*(2), 70–72.

17. Bartlett, C. A., & Ghoshal, S. (1990). Matrix management: Not a structure, a frame of mind. *Harvard Business Review, 68*(3), 138–145.

18. Wall, W. C., Jr. (1984). Integrated management in matrix organizations. *IEEE Transactions on Engineering Management, 20*(2), 30–36.

19. Davis, S. M., & Lawrence, P. R. (1977). *Matrix*. Reading, MA: Addison-Wesley.

20. Goggin, W. (1974). How the multidimensional structure works at Dow Corning. *Harvard Business Review, 56*(1), 33–52.

21. See note 20.

22. Ford, R. C., & Randolph, W. A. (1992). Cross-functional structures: A review and integration of matrix organization and project management. *Journal of Management, 18*, 267–294.

23. See note 22.

24. Stewart, T. A. (1992, May 18). The search for the organization of tomorrow. *Fortune*, pp. 93–98 (quote, p. 93).

25. Byrne, J. A. (1993, December 20). The horizontal corporation. *Business Week*, pp. 76–81 (quote, p. 76).

26. See note 3 (quote, p. 96).

27. McGregor, D. (1960). *The human side of enterprise*. New York: McGraw-Hill.

28. Argyris, C. (1964). *Integrating the individual and the organization*. New York: Wiley.

29. Likert, R. (1961). *New patterns of management*. New York: McGraw-Hill.

30. Duncan, R. (1979, Winter). What is the right organization structure? *Organizational Dynamics*, pp. 59–69.

31. Burns, T., & Stalker, G. M. (1961). *The management of innovation*. London: Tavistock.

32. Deveney, K. (1986, October 13). Bag those fries, squirt that ketchup, fry that fish. *Business Week*, pp. 57–61.

33. Kerr, P. (1985, May 11). Witch hazel still made the old-fashioned way. *New York Times*, pp. 27–28.

34. Morse, J. J., & Lorsch, J. W. (1970). Beyond theory Y. *Harvard Business Review, 48*(3), 61–68.

35. Mintzberg, H. (1983). *Structure in fives: Designing effective organizations*. Englewood Cliffs, NJ: Prentice-Hall.

36. Livesay, H. C. (1979). *American made: Man who shaped the American economy*. Boston: Little, Brown.

37. See note 1.

38. GE: Just your average everyday $60 billion family grocery store. (1994, May 2). *Industry Week*, pp. 13–18.

39. Slater, R. (1993). *The new GE*. Homewood, IL: Business One Irwin (quote, p. 257).

40. Woodruff, D., & Miller, K. L. (1993, May 3). Chrysler's Neon: Is this the small car Detroit couldn't build? *Business Week*, pp. 116–126.

41. Dees, G. D., Rasheed, A. M. A., McLaughlin, K. J., & Priem, R. L. (1995). The new corporate architecture. *Academy of Management Executive, 9*, 7–18.

42. See note 41.

43. Tully, S. (1993, February 3). The modular corporation. *Fortune*, pp. 106–108, 110.

44. Taylor, A. (1990, November 19). Why Toyota keeps getting better and better and better. *Fortune*, pp. 72–79.

45. Byrne, J. (1993, February 8). The virtual corporation. *Business Week*, pp. 99–103.

46. Chesbrough, H. W., & Teece, D. J. (1996, January-February). When is virtual virtuous? Organizing for innovation. *Harvard Business Review*, 96, 65–73.

47. Nakarmi, L., & Einhorn, B. (1993, June 7). Hyundai's gutsy gambit. *Business Week*, p. 48.

48. Gerlach, M. L. (1993). *Alliance capitalism: The social organization of Japanese business*. Berkeley, CA: University of California Press.

49. Miyashita, K., & Russell, D. (1994). *Keiretsu: Inside the Japanese conglomerates*. New York: McGraw-Hill.

50. Kanter, R. M. (1994, July-August). Collaborative advantage: The art of alliances. *Harvard Business Review*, pp. 96–108.

51. See note 50.

52. Fletcher, N. (1988, December 10). U.S., China form joint venture to manufacture helicopters. *Journal of Commerce*, p. 58.

53. Bransi, B. (1987, January 3). South Korea's carmakers count their blessings. *The Economist*, p. 45.

54. Mason, J. C. (1993, May). Strategic alliances: Partnering for success. *Management Review*, pp. 10–15.

55. Vanhonacker, W. (1997, March-April). Entering China: An unconventional approach. *Harvard Business Review*, 97, 130–131, 134–136, 138–140.

56. Earley, P. C., & Erez, M. (1997). *The transplanted executive: Why you need to understand how workers in other countries see the world differently*. New York: Oxford University Press.

CHAPTER 15
Preview Case Source

1. Hulin, C. L., & Roznowski, M. (1985). Organizational technologies: Effects on organizations' characteristics and individuals' responses. In L. L. Cummings & B. M. Staw (Eds.), *Research in organizational behavior* (Vol. 7, pp. 39–86). Greenwich, CT: JAI Press.

2. Swasy, A. (1993). *Soap opera: The inside story of Procter & Gamble*. New York: Times Books.

3. Porter, M. E. (1985). *Competitive advantage*. New York: Free Press.

4. Drucker, P. F. (1992). *Managing for the future*. New York: Truman Talley Books/Dutton.

5. Perrow, C. (1967). A framework for the comparative analysis of organizations. *American Sociological Review*, 32, 194–208.

6. Czinkota, M. R., & Dichtl, E. (1998). Export controls: Providing security in a volatile environment. In M. R. Czinkota & M. Kotabe (Eds.), *Trends in international business* (pp. 43–51). Malden, MA: Blackwell.

7. See note 7 (quote, p. 51).

8. Katzell, R. (1994). Contemporary meta-trends in industrial and organizational psychology. In H. C. Triandis, M. D. Dunnette, & L. M. Hough (Eds.), *Handbook of industrial and organizational psychology* (2nd ed.). (Vol. 4, pp. 1–89). Palo Alto, CA: Consulting Psychologists Press.

9. Dean, J. W., Yoon, S. J., & Susman, G. I. (1992). Advanced manufacturing technology and organization structure: Empowerment or subordination? *Organization Science*, 3, 203–229 (quote, p. 207).

10. Valery, N. (1988). Factory of the future. In J. Gibson, J. Ivancevich, & J. Donnelly, Jr. (Eds.), *Organizations close-up* (pp. 274–301). Plano, TX: Business Publications.

11. Weiners, B., & Pescovitz, D. (1996). *Reality check*. San Francisco: Hardwired.

12. Weick, K. (1990). Technology as equivoque: Sensemaking in new technologies. In P. S. Goodman, & L. S. Sproull (Eds.), *Technology and organizations* (pp. 1–44). San Francisco: Jossey-Bass.

13. Office of Technology Assessment. (1985). *Automation of American offices, 1985–2000*. Washington, DC: Author.

14. Solomon, J. S. (1987, Fall). Union responses to technological change: Protecting the past or looking into the future? *Labor Studies Journal*, pp. 51–65.

15. Farnham, A. (1993, Autumn). Making high tech work for you. *Fortune* (Special Issue), p. 1.

16. Bayless, A. (1986, October 16). Technology reshapes North America's lumber plants. *Wall Street Journal*, p. 6.

17. Sherman, J. (1994). *In the rings of Saturn*. New York: Oxford University Press.

18. Neff, R. (1987, April 20). Getting man and machine to live happily ever after. *Business Week*, pp. 61–63.

19. Argote, L., Goodman, P. S., & Schkade, D. (1983, Spring). The human side of robots: How workers react to a robot. *Sloan Management Review*, 31–42 (quote, p. 42).

20. Carstairs, J. F. (1988, March 28). America rushes to high tech for growth. *Business Week*, pp. 84–86, 88, 90 (quote, p. 86).

21. See note 20.

22. Segaller, S. (1998). *Nerds 2.0.1*. New York: TV Books.

23. Pape, W. R. (1997). Hiring blind. *Inc. Tech.*, No. 4, pp. 31–32.

24. Face-to-face: Spies like us. (1998, March). *Inc.*, pp. 28, 20, 32.

25. Price Waterhouse EMC Group. (1997). *American Internet user survey*. New York: Author.

26. Pappas, B. (1997, August 25). Executives versus computers. *Forbes*, pp. 18, 20.

27. Turkle, S. (1996, Winter). Virtuality and its discontents: Searching for community in cyberspace. *The American Prospect*, 24, 50–57.

28. Katz, J. E., & Aspden, P. (1997). A nation of strangers? *Communications of the ACM*, 40(12), 81–86.

29. Kraut, R., Patterson, M., Lundmark, V., Kiesler, S., Mukopadhyay, T., & Scherlis, W. (1998). Internet paradox: A social technology that reduces social involvement and psychological well-being? *American Psychologist*, 53, 1017–1031.

30. Tompkins, N. C. (1993, April). Tools that help performance on the job. *HRMagazine*, pp. 84, 87, 89–91.

31. See note 30.

32. Anonymous. (1993, September). New technology and the disabled. *Information Management Forum*, pp. 1, 4.

33. See note 30.

34. See note 30.

35. French, W. L., Bell, C. H., Jr., & Zawacki, R. A. (1989). *Organization development: Theory, practice and research* (3rd ed.). Homewood, IL: BPI/Irwin.

36. Marx, G. T., & Sherizen, S. (1986). Monitoring on the job: How to protect privacy as well as property. *Technology Review, 89*, 62–72.

37. See note 36.

38. Kulik, C. T., & Ambrose, M. L. (1993). Category-based and feature-based processes in performance appraisal: Integrating visual and computerized sources of performance data. *Journal of Applied Psychology, 78*, 821–830.

39. Aiello, J. R. (1993). Computer-based work monitoring: Electronic surveillance and its effects. *Journal of Applied Social Psychology, 23*, 499–507.

40. See note 38.

41. See note 38.

42. Ives, B., & Mason, R. O. (1990). Can information technology revitalize your customer service? *Academy of Management Executive, 4*, 52–69.

43. Bylinsky, G. (1996, February 6). Manufacturing for reuse. *Fortune*, pp. 102–104, 108, 110, 112.

44. Brown, S. F. (1998, February 16). Giving more jobs to electronic eyes. *Fortune*, pp. 104[B]–104[D].

45. Woodward, J. (1965). *Industrial organization: Theory and practice.* London: Oxford University Press.

46. See note 45 (quote, p. 58).

47. Oleson, J. D. (1998). *Pathway to agility: Mass customization in action.* New York: John Wiley & Sons.

48. Hull, F. M., & Collins, P. D. (1987). High-technology batch production systems: Woodward's missing type. *Academy of Management Journal, 30*, 786–797.

49. Hickson, D., Pugh, D., & Pheysey, D. (1969). Operations technology and organization structure: An empirical reappraisal. *Administrative Science Quarterly, 26*, 349–377.

50. Thompson, J. D. (1967). *Organizations in action.* New York: McGraw-Hill.

51. Bahrami, H. (1992). The emerging flexible organization: Perspectives from Silicon Valley. *California Management Review, 34*(4), 33–52.

52. See note 51 (quote, p. 38).

Case in Point Source

Goldberg, M. (1997, April-May). How FedEx runs on time. *Fast Company*, p. 38.

CHAPTER 16
Preview Case Source

Augustine, N. R. (1997, May-June). Reshaping an industry: Lockheed Martin's survival story. *Harvard Business Review, 75*(3), 83–94.

Chapter Notes

1. Sherman, S. (1993, December 13). How will we live with the tumult? *Fortune*, pp. 123–125 (quote, p. 125).

2. Haveman, H. A. (1992). Between a rock and a hard place: Organizational change and performance under conditions of fundamental environmental transformation. *Administrative Science Quarterly, 37*, 48–75.

3. Smith, D. (1998, May). Invigorating change initiatives. *Management Review*, pp. 45–48.

4. Nystrom, P. C., & Starbuck, W. H. (1984, Spring). To avoid organizational crises, unlearn. *Organizational Dynamics*, 44–60.

5. Reese, J. (1993, July 26). Corporate Methuselahs. *Fortune*, p. 16.

6. See note 5 (quote, p. 15).

7. Miller, K. L. (1993, May 17). The factory guru tinkering with Toyota. *Business Week*, pp. 95, 97.

8. Levy, A. (1986). Second-order planned change: Definition and conceptualization. *Organizational Dynamics, 16*(1), 4–20.

9. A master class in radical change. (1993, December 13). *Fortune*, pp. 82–84, 88, 90.

10. Kanter, R. M. (1991, May-June). Transcending business boundaries: 12,000 world managers view change. *Harvard Business Review*, pp. 151–164.

11. Stewart, T. A. (1993, December 13). Welcome to the revolution. *Fortune*, pp. 66–68, 70, 72, 76, 78 (quote, p. 70).

12. David, F. R. (1993). *Concepts of strategic management.* New York: Macmillan.

13. Mead, R. (1998). *International management* (2nd ed.). Malden, MA: Blackwell.

14. Taylor, B. (1995). The new strategic leadership — driving change, getting results. *Long Range Planning, 28*(5), 71–81.

15. McCarty, M. (1990, October 30). PepsiCo to consolidate its restaurants, combining U.S. and foreign operations. *Wall Street Journal*, p. A4.

16. Bureau of Labor Statistics. (1999). Web site: http://stats.bls.gov.)

17. See note 11.

18. Christensen, H. K. (1994). Corporate strategy: Managing a set of businesses. In I. L. Fahley & R. M. Randall (Eds.), *The portable MBA in strategy* (pp. 53–83). New York: Wiley.

19. Markides, C. (1997, Spring). Strategic innovation. *Sloan Management Review*, 9–23.

20. Collis, D. J., & Montgomery, C. A. (1995, July-August). Competing on resources: Strategy in the 1990s. *Harvard Business Review, 73*, 118–128.

21. Dean, J. W., Jr., & Scharfman, M. (1996). Does decision process matter? A study of strategic decision-making effectiveness. *Academy of Management Journal, 29*, 368–396.

22. Porter, M. (1996, March 14). "It's time to grow up." *Far Eastern Economic Review*, pp. 1–2.

23. Lasserre, P., & Putti, J. (1990). *Business strategy and management: Text and cases for managers in Asia.* Singapore: Institute of Management.

24. Yoshimori, M. (1995). Whose company is it? The concept of the corporation in Japan and the West. *Long Range Planning, 28*(4), 33–34.

25. Beer, M. (1980). *Organizational change and development: A systems view.* Glenview, IL: Scott, Foresman.

26. Nadler, D. A. (1987). The effective management of organizational change. In J. W. Lorsch (Ed.), *Handbook of organizational behavior* (pp. 358–369). Englewood Cliffs, NJ: Prentice-Hall.

27. Katz, D., & Kahn, R. L. (1978). *The social psychology of organizations* (2nd ed.). New York: Wiley.

28. See note 26.

29. Huey, J. (1993, April 5). Managing in the midst of chaos. *Fortune*, pp. 38–41, 44, 46, 48 (quote, p. 40).

30. Senge, P. M. (1990). *The fifth discipline.* New York: Doubleday.

31. Pascale, R., Millemann, M., & Gioja, L. (1997, November-December). Changing the way we change. *Harvard Business Review*, pp. 127–139.

32. Collarelli, S. M. (1998). Psychological interventions in organizations. *American Psychologist, 53*, 1044–1056.

33. Vicars, W. M., & Hartke, D. D. (1984). Evaluating OD evaluations: A status report. *Group and Organization Studies, 9*, 177–188.

34. Ettorre, B. (1995, October). Managing competitive intelligence. *Management Review*, pp. 15–19 (quote, p. 18).

35. See note 34.

36. Porras, J. I., & Robertson, P. J. (1992). Organization development: Theory, practice, and research. In M. D. Dunnette & L. M. Hough (Eds.) *Handbook of industrial and organizational psychology* (2nd ed.). (Vol. 3, pp. 719–822). Palo Alto, CA: Consulting Psy-chologists Press.

37. Blunt, P. (1988). Cultural consequences for organizational change in a Southeast Asian state: Brunei. *Academy of Management Executive, 2*, 235–240.

38. White, L. P., & Wotten, K. C. (1983). Ethical dilemmas in various stages of organizational development. *Academy of Management review, 8*, 690–697.

Case in Point Source

Feldman, A. (1995, October 23). Shaking things up. *Forbes*, pp. 260–262; and the Zale Corporation Internet site (http://www.zalecorp.com/).

GLOSSARY

A

Abilities Mental and physical capacities to perform various tasks. (p. 117)

Achievement motivation The strength of an individual's desire to excel, to succeed at difficult tasks, and to do them better than others. (p. 113)

Ad hoc committee A temporary committee formed for a special purpose. (p. 254)

Additive tasks Group tasks in which the co-ordinated efforts of several people are added together to form the group's product. (p. 268)

Adhocracy A highly informal, organic organization in which specialists work in teams, co-ordinating with each other on various projects (e.g., many software-development companies). (p. 537)

Administrative model A model of decision making that recognizes the *bounded rationality* that limits the making of optimally rational-economic decisions. (p. 344)

Advanced manufacturing technology (AMT) Manufacturing in which the various processes are guided by computers. (p. 558)

Affective commitment The strength of a person's desire to work for an organization because he or she agrees with its goals and wants to do so. (p. 183)

Affirmative action laws Legislation to give employment opportunities to groups that have been underrepresented in the workforce (e.g., women, minorities). (p. 194)

Altruism Actions by one person that benefit others under conditions in which the donor expects nothing in return. (p. 371)

Analytical model of decision making A general model that describes the formulation and implementation of decisions occurring in eight steps. (p. 331)

Apprenticeship programs Formal training programs, often used in the skilled trades, involving both on-the-job and classroom training, usually over a long period. (p. 76)

Arbitration The process in which third parties (i.e., *arbitrators*) have the power to impose (or at least to recommend strongly) the terms of an agreement between disputing parties. (p. 390)

Assistive technology Devices and other solutions that help individuals with physical or mental problems to perform the various actions needed on their jobs. (p. 563)

Attitudes Relatively stable clusters of feelings, beliefs, and behavioral intentions toward specific objects, people, or institutions. (p. 170)

Attribute framing effect The tendency for people to evaluate a characteristic more positively when it is presented in positive terms than in negative terms. (p. 347)

Attribution The process through which individuals attempt to determine the causes behind others' behavior. (p. 56)

Attribution approach (to leadership) The approach to leadership focusing on leaders' attributions of followers' performance that is, on their perceptions of its underlying causes. (p. 457)

Autocratic (leadership style) A style of leadership in which the leader makes all decisions unilaterally. (p. 449)

Autocratic-delegation continuum model An approach to leadership describing how leaders allocate influence to subordinates. This ranges from controlling everything (i.e., *autocratic*) to allowing others to make decisions for themselves (i.e., *delegating*). Between these extremes are more participative forms of leadership (i.e., *consulting* and making *joint decisions*). (p. 449)

Automation The process of using machines to perform tasks that otherwise might be performed by people. (p. 558)

Autonomous change A change in one part of an organization independent of the need for change in another. (p. 541)

Availability heuristic The tendency for people to base their judgments on readily available though potentially inaccurate information, thereby adversely affecting decision quality. (p. 348)

Avoidance See *negative reinforcement*. (p. 71)

Awareness-based diversity training A type of diversity management program to make people more aware of diversity issues in the workplace and get them to recognize the underlying assumptions they make about people. (p. 196)

B

Baby boom generation The generation of children born in the economic boom period following World War II. (p. 21)

Bargaining The process in which opposing sides exchange offers, counteroffers, and concessions, either directly or through representatives. (p. 387)

Behavioral component Our predisposition to behave in a way consistent with our beliefs and feelings about an attitude object. (p. 169)

Behavioral sciences Fields such as psychology and sociology that seek knowledge of human behavior and society through the scientific method. (p. 3)

Benchmarking The process of comparing one's own products or services with the best from one's competitors. (p. 28)

Big five dimensions of personality Five basic dimensions of personality assumed to underlie may specific traits. (p. 102)

Boundaryless organization An organization in which chains of command are eliminated, spans of control are unlimited, and rigid departments give way to empowered teams. (p. 537)

Bounded discretion The practice of limiting decision alternatives to those falling within the bounds of current moral and ethical standards. (p. 344)

Bounded rationality The major assumption of the administrative model that organizational, social, and human limitations lead to making *satisficing* rather than optimal decisions. (p. 344)

Brainstorming A technique to foster group productivity by encouraging interacting members to express their ideas noncritically. (p. 353)

Bureaucracy An organizational design developed by Max Weber that attempts to make organizations operate efficiently through clear hierarchy of authority in which people perform well-defined jobs. (p. 10)

Burnout A syndrome resulting from prolonged exposure to stress and consisting of physical, emotional, and mental exhaustion as well as feelings of a lack of personal accomplishment. (p. 234)

C

Cafeteria-style benefit plans Incentive systems in which employees can select the fringe benefits they want from a menu of available alternatives. (p. 151)

Career The evolving sequence of a person's work experience over time. (p. 215)

Case method A research technique in which a particular organization is thoroughly described and analyzed to understand what occurred in that setting. (p. 52)

Channels of communication The pathways over which messages are transmitted (e.g., telephone lines, mail, and so on). (p. 293)

Charisma A contagious attitude of enthusiasm and optimism; an aura of leadership. (p. 415)

Charismatic leaders Leaders who exert especially powerful effects on followers through the attributions followers make about them. Such individuals have high self-confidence, present a clearly articulated vision, behave in extraordinary ways, are recognized as change agents, and are sensitive to environmental constraints. (p. 460)

Child-care facilities Sites either at or near company locations where parents can leave their children during work. (p. 22)

Classical organizational theory An early approach to the study of management that focused on the most efficient way of structuring organizations. (pp. 9, 531)

Code of ethics A document describing what an organization stands for and the general rules of conduct it expects from employees (e.g., to avoid conflicts of interest, to be honest, and so on). (p. 32)

Codes of ethics Explicit statements of a company's ethical values. (p. 495)

Coercive power The individual power base derived from the capacity to punish others. (p. 414)

Cognitive component What we believe, whether true or false, about an attitude object. (p. 169)

Cognitive intelligence The ability to understand complex ideas, adapt effectively to the environment, learn from experience, engage in various forms of reasoning, and overcome obstacles by careful thought. (p. 117)

Cohesiveness The strength of the members' desires to remain part of the group. (p. 262)

Collectivistic cultures Cultures whose members place a high value on shared responsibility and the collective good of all. (p. 269)

Command group A group determined by the connections between individuals who are formal members of the organization. (p. 253)

Communal culture In the *double S cube*, a type of organizational culture characterized by both high sociability and high solidarity. (p. 490)

Communication The process by which a person, group, or organization (i.e., the *sender*) transmits some type of information (i.e., the *message*) to another person, group, or organization (i.e., the *receiver*). (p. 292)

Competition A pattern of behavior in which each person, group, or organization seeks to maximize its own gains, often at the expense of others. (p. 376)

Competitive intelligence (CI) The process of gathering information about one's competitors for use in planning organizational change. (p. 607)

Compressed workweeks The practice of working fewer days each week but longer hours each day (e.g., four 10-hour days). (p. 23)

Computer-aided design and engineering (CAD/CAE) The processes of using computers to build and to simulate the characteristics of products and to test their effectiveness. (p. 558)

Computer-integrated manufacturing (CIM) Manufacturing processes that go beyond *advanced manufacturing technology* by using computers to gather information, which in turn is used to make decisions regarding how the manufacturing process needs to be altered. (p. 558)

Computerized performance monitoring The process of using computers to monitor job performance. (p. 264)

Computerized performance monitoring (CPM) The practice of using computers to collect, store, analyze and report information about the work people are doing. (p. 564)

Confirmation candidate A decision alternative considered only to convince onself of the wisdom of selecting the *implicit favorite*. (p. 350)

Conflict A process in which one party perceives another has taken (or is about to take) some action that will exert a negative effect on its major interest. (p. 382)

Conglomerate A form of organizational diversification in which an organization (usually a very large, multinational one) adds an entirely unrelated business or product to its organizational design. (p. 542)

Conjunctive statements Statements that keep conversations going by connecting remarks of one speaker with those of another. (p. 319)

Consensus In Kelley's theory of causal attribution, information regarding the extent to which other people behave in the same manner as the person who we're judging. (p. 58)

Consideration Actions by a leader that demonstrate concern with the welfare of subordinates and establish positive relations with them. Leaders who focus primarily on this task are described as demonstrating a person-oriented style. (p. 453)

Consistency In Kelley's theory of causal attribution, information regarding the extent to which the person who we're judging acts the same way at other times. (p. 58)

Contingencies of reinforcement The various relationships between one's behavior and the consequences of that behavior (e.g., positive reinforcement, negative reinforcement, punishment, and extinction). (p. 72)

Contingency approach The contemporary approach recognizing that no one approach to organizational design is best, but that the best design is the one that best fits with the existing environmental conditions. (pp. 14, 532)

Contingency theories of leadership Any of several theories recognizing that certain leadership styles are more effective in some situations than in others. (p. 463)

Contingent workforce People hired temporarily by organizations to work as needed for finite periods of time. (p. 27)

Continuance commitment The strength of a person's desire to continue working for an organization because he or she needs to and cannot afford to do otherwise. (p. 182)

Continuous reinforcement A schedule of reinforcement in which all desired behaviors are reinforced. (p. 72)

Continuous-process production A highly automated form of production that is continuous in nature and highly integrated regarding component steps and processes. (p. 570)

Convergence hypothesis A biased approach to the study of management that assumes principles of good management are universal and ones that work well in the United States apply equally well in other nations. (p. 18)

Cooperation A pattern of behavior in which assistance is mutual and two or more individuals, groups, or organizations work together toward shared goals for their mutual benefit. (p. 375)

Core competency An organization's key capability (i.e., what it does best). (p. 26)

Corporate image The impressions that people have of an organization. (p. 68)

Corporate universities Centers devoted to handling a company's training needs on a full-time basis. (p. 77)

Correlation The extent to which two variables relate to each other. (p. 46)

Correlation coefficient A statistical index indicating the nature and extent to which two variables relate to each other. (p. 46)

Correspondent inferences Judgments about people's dispositions, traits, and characteristics that correspond to what we have observed of their actions. (p. 56)

Craft technology Technology involving highly standardized inputs and outputs and problems that are difficult to analyze (e.g., cabinetmakers and public schools). (See *matrix of technologies*.) (p. 555)

Creativity The process by which individuals or small groups produce novel and useful ideas. (p. 499)

Creativity heuristics Rules people follow to help them approach tasks in novel ways. (p. 501)

Critical incidents technique A procedure for measuring job satisfaction in which employees describe incidents relating to their work they found especially satisfying or dissatisfying. (p. 173)

Cross-cultural training (CCT) A systematic way of preparing employees to live and work in another country. (p. 77)

Cross-functional teams Teams that include people from different specialty areas within organizations. (p. 275)

Cultural pluralism The idea that social harmony does not require people from various cultures to assimilate or "melt" together into one but that people's separate identities should be maintained and accepted by others. (p. 20)

Culture The set of values, customs, and beliefs people have in common with other members of a social unit (e.g., a nation). (p. 17)

Culture shock The tendency for people to become confused and disoriented when adjusting to a new culture. (p. 17)

D

Daily hassles Problems of everyday life that are important causes of stress. (p. 232)

Decentralization The extent to which authority and decision making are spread throughout all levels of an organization rather than being reserved for top management (i.e., *centralization*). (p. 523)

Decision making The process of choosing among several alternatives. (p. 331)

Decision style Differences between people regarding their orientations toward decisions.

Decision support systems (DSS) Computer programs that present information about OB to decision-makers in a manner that helps them to structure their responses to decisions. (p. 332)

Decision-style model The conceptualization according to which people use one of four predominant decision styles: *directive, analytical, conceptual,* and *behavioral.* (p. 338)

Decoding The process by which a receiver transforms a message back into the sender's ideas. (p. 293)

Defensive avoidance The tendency for decision-makers to fail to solve problems because they avoid working on them. (p. 355)

Deficiency needs The group of physiological needs, safety needs, and social needs in Maslow's *need hierarchy theory*. If these needs go unmet, people will fail to develop in a healthy fashion. (p. 135)

Delphi technique A method of improving group decisions using the opinions of experts, which are solicited by mail and then compiled. The expert consensus of opinions is used to make a decision. (p. 358)

Departmentalization The process of breaking organizations into coherent units. (p. 524)

Dependent variable The behavior that is being measured by a researcher; it is dependent on the *independent variable.* (p. 49)

Design for disassembly (DFD) The process of designing and building products so their parts can be used several times and then safely disposed of at the end of the product's life. (p. 567)

Deviant organizational behavior Actions by employees that intentionally violate the existing norms of their group, organization, or society and that result in negative consequences for coworkers or the organization. (p. 392)

Discipline The process of systematically administering punishments. (p. 84)

Discrimination The behavior consistent with a prejudicial attitude; the act of treating someone negatively because of his or her membership in a specific group. (p. 187)

Disjunctive statements Statements that are disconnected from a previous statement, thus tending to bring conversations to a close. (p. 319)

Dispositional model of job satisfaction The conceptualization proposing that job satisfaction is a relatively stable, individual disposition, that is, a characteristic that stays with people across situations. (p. 172)

Distinctiveness In Kelley's theory of causal attribution, information regarding the extent to which a person behaves in the same manner in other contexts. (p. 58)

Distribution Concern with one's own outcomes. (p. 382)

Divergence hypothesis The approach to the study of management that recognizes knowing how to manage most effectively requires a clear understanding of the culture in which people work. (p. 19)

Diversity management programs Programs in which employees are taught to celebrate the differences between people and in which organizations create supportive work environments for women and minorities. (p. 195)

Division of labor The process of dividing the many tasks in an organization into specialized jobs. (p. 519)

Divisional structure The form used by many large organizations in which separate, autonomous units deal with entire product lines, thereby freeing top management to focus on larger-scale, strategic decisions. (p. 536)

Dominant culture The distinctive, overarching "personality" of an organization. (p. 487)

Doomsday management The practice of introducing change by suggesting an impending crisis is likely. (p. 589)

Double S cube A system of categorizing four types of organizational culture by combining two dimensions, *sociability* and *solidarity*. Each of the four resulting cultural types—*networked culture, mercenary culture, fragmented culture*, and *communal culture*—can be both positive and negative in nature. (p. 488)

Downsizing The process of systematically reducing the number of employees required to perform newly restructured jobs. (p. 593)

Drive theory of social facilitation The theory according to which the pres-ence of others increases arousal, which in turn increases people's tendencies to perform the dominant response. If that response is well-learned, performance improves; if that response is novel, performance is impaired. (p. 263)

E

Elder-care facilities Facilities where employees can leave elderly relatives for whom they are responsible (e.g., parents and grandparents) during work. (p. 22)

Electronic meeting systems The practice of bringing individuals from different locations together for a meeting via telephone or satellite transmissions, either on television monitors or shared space on a computer screen. (p. 360)

Emotional intelligence (EQ) A cluster of skills relating to the emotional side life (e.g., the ability to recognize and regulate our own emotions, to influence those of others, to self-motivate). (p. 117)

Employee assistance programs (EAPs) Plans that provide employees with assistance for various problems (e.g., substance abuse, career planning, financial and legal problems). (p. 241)

Employee handbook A document that describes basic information about a company; a general reference regarding a company's background, the nature of its business, and its rules. (p. 295)

Employee theft Unauthorized appropriation of company property by employees for their personal use. (p. 396)

Employee withdrawal Actions such as chronic absenteeism and voluntary turnover (i.e., quitting one's job) that enable employees to escape adverse organizational situations. (p. 177)

Empowered decision making The practice of vesting power for making decisions in the employees. (p. 336)

Empowerment The passing of responsibility and authority from managers to employees. (p. 418)

Encoding The process by which an idea is transformed so that it can be transmitted to and recognized by a receiver (e.g., a written or spoken message). (p. 293)

Engineering technology Technology involving many exceptions in inputs or outputs and problems that are easy to analyze (e.g., heavy machinery con-struction, health and fitness clubs). (See *matrix of technologies*.) (p. 556)

Entrepreneur An individual who starts his or her own business. (p. 220)

Entry shock The confusion and disorientation experienced by many newcomers to an organization.

Equitable payment The state in which one person's outcome/input ratio is equivalent to that of another, comparison person. (p. 144)

Equity theory The theory stating that people strive to maintain a ratio of their own outcomes (rewards) to their own inputs (contributions) equal to the outcome/input ratios of others with whom they compare themselves. (p. 143)

ERG theory An alternative to Maslow's *need hierarchy theory* proposed by Alderfer that asserts there are three basic human needs: existence, relatedness, and growth. (p. 136)

Escalation of commitment phenomenon The tendency for individuals to continue supporting previously unsuccessful courses of action. (p. 350)

Esteem needs In Maslow's *need hierarchy theory*, the need to develop self-respect and to gain the approval of others. (p. 135)

Ethics audit The process of actively investigating and documenting incidents of dubious ethical value within a company. (p. 32)

Evaluation apprehension The fear of being evaluated or judged by another person. (p. 264)

Evaluative component Our liking or disliking of any particular person, item, or event. (p. 169)

Evening persons Individuals who feel most energetic and alert late in the day. (p. 115)

Executive training programs Sessions in which companies systematically develop their top leaders, either in specific skills or in general managerial skills. (p. 77)

Exit strategies The tactic by which a company withdraws from a market (e.g., by liquidating its assets). (p. 596)

Expatriates People who are citizens of one country but who live and work in another. (p. 17)

Expectancy The belief that one's efforts will influence one's performance positively. (p. 149)

Expectancy theory The theory that asserts motivation is based on people's beliefs about the probability that their effort will lead to performance (*expectancy*), multiplied by the probability that performance will lead to reward (*instrumentality*), multiplied by the perceived value of that reward (*valence*). (p. 149)

Experimental method A research technique used to determine cause-and-effect relationships between the variables of interest (i.e., the extent to which one variable causes another). (p. 48)

Expert power The individual power base derived from an individual's recognized, superior skills, and abilities. (p. 415)

External causes of behavior Explanations based on situations over which the individual has no control. (p. 58)

Extinction The process through which responses that are no longer reinforced tend to gradually diminish in strength. (p. 71)

F

Feedback Knowledge of the results of one's behavior (p. 79); knowledge about the effect of messages on receivers. (p. 293)

First-impression error The tendency to base judgments of others on our earlier impressions of them. (p. 61)

First-order change Change that is continuous in nature and involves no major shifts in how an organization operates. (p. 586)

Five-stage model (of group development) The conceptualization claiming that groups develop in five stages—forming, storming, norming, performing, and adjourning. (p. 256)

Fixed internal schedule Schedules of reinforcement in which a fixed period of time must elapse between reinforcements. (p. 72)

Fixed ratio schedule Schedules of reinforcement in which a fixed number of responses must occur between reinforcements. (p. 73)

Fixed-sum error The tendency to assume one side of a conflict places the same importance as the other side on every issue. (p. 390)

Flexible manufacturing systems Manufacturing processes relying on computer-controlled machines to produce low vol-

umes of products at costs that rival those of massed-produced ones. (p. 558)

Flextime programs Policies that give employees some discretion over when they can arrive and leave work, thereby making it easier to adapt their work schedules to the demands of their personal lives. (p. 23)

Formal communication The sharing of messages regarding the official work of the organization. (p. 303)

Formal groups Groups created by the parent organization that are designed intentionally to direct the members toward some organizational goal. (p. 253)

Formal status The prestige one has by virtue of his or her official position in an organization. (p. 260)

Fragmented culture In the *double S cube*, a type of organizational culture characterized by low sociability and low solidarity. (p. 490)

Framing The tendency for people to make different decisions based on how the problem is presented. (p. 346)

Friendship groups Informal groups that develop because their members are friends and often see each other outside of the organization. (p. 254)

Functional organization The type of departmentalization based on the activities or functions performed (e.g., sales, finance). (p. 524)

Fundamental attribution error The tendency to attribute others' actions to internal causes (e.g., their traits) while largely ignoring external factors. (p. 60)

G

Glass ceiling A barrier preventing females from reaching top positions in many organizations. (p. 223)

Globalization The process of interconnecting the world's people regarding the cultural, economic, political, technological, and environmental aspects of their lives. (p. 16)

Goal commitment The degree to which people accept and strive to attain goals. (p. 139)

Goal framing effect The tendency for people to be persuaded more strongly by information framed in negative terms than by information framed in positive terms. (p. 348)

Goal setting The process of determining specific levels of performance for workers to attain. (p. 139)

Grapevine An organization's informal channels of communication, which are based mainly on friendship or acquaintance. (p. 308)

Great person theory The view that leaders possess special traits, which set them apart from others, and that these traits are responsible for their positions of power and authority. (p. 448)

Grid training A multistep process to develop both concern for people and concern for production. (p. 454)

Group dynamics The social science focusing on the nature of groups, including the factors governing their formation and development, the elements of their structure, and their interrelationships with individuals, other groups, and organizations. (p. 251)

Group A collection of two or more interacting individuals who maintain stable patterns of relationships, share common goals, and perceive themselves as being a group. (p. 252)

Group structure The pattern of interrelationships between the individuals constituting a group; the guidelines of group behavior that make group functioning both orderly and predictable. (p. 258)

Groupthink The tendency for members of highly cohesive groups to conform so strongly to group pressures regarding a certain decision that they fail to think critically and reject the potentially correcting influences of outsiders. (p. 340)

Growth need strength The personality variable describing the extent to which people have a high need for personal growth and development on the job. The *job characteristics model* best describes people with a high growth need strength. (p. 156)

Growth needs In Maslow's *need hierarchy theory*, esteem needs and the need for self-actualization condensed as a group. Gratification of these needs helps a person to reach his or her full potential. (p. 135)

H

Halo effect The tendency for our overall impressions of others to affect objective evaluations of their specific traits, such as perceiving high correlations between characteristics that may be unrelated. (p. 60)

Heuristics Simple decision rules (e.g., rules of thumb) used to make quick decisions about complex problems. See *availability heuristic* and *representativeness heuristic*. (p. 348)

Hierarchy of authority A configuration of the reporting relationships within organizations (i.e., who reports to whom). (p. 518)

High LPC leaders Leaders who primarily are concerned with establishing good relations with subordinates. (p. 465)

High technology Technology that is electronic in nature and usually relying on microprocessor chips. (p. 558)

High-performance teams Teams whose members are deeply committed to one another's personal growth and success. (p. 273)

Horizontal organization The practice of structuring organizations by the processes performed, using autonomous work teams in flattened hierarchies. (p. 529)

Human relations movement A perspective on organizational behavior that rejects the primarily economic orientation of scientific management and instead recognizes the importance of social processes in work settings. (p. 7)

HURIER model The conceptualization that describes effective listening as having six components: *h*earing, *u*nderstanding, *r*emembering, *i*nterpreting, *e*valuating, and *r*esponding. (p. 313)

Hypervigilance The state in which an individual frantically searches for quick solutions and goes from idea to idea from desperation that one is not working and another must be considered before time runs out. (p. 355)

Hypotheses Logically derived, testable statements about the relationships between variables that follow from a theory. (p. 44)

I

Image theory A theory of decision making that recognizes deciszions are made in an automatic, intuitive fashion. In this theory, people adopt courses of action that best fit their individual principles, current goals, and future plans. (p. 345)

Implicit favorite One's preferred decision alternative, which is selected even before all the options have been considered. (p. 350)

Impression management Efforts by individuals to improve how they appear to others. (p. 66)

Improvement teams Teams whose members are oriented primarily toward increasing the effectiveness of the processes used by the parent organization. (p. 274)

Incompatibility error The tendency for both sides of a conflict to assume their interests are entirely incompatible. (p. 390)

Independent variable A variable that is systematically manipulated by the researcher to determine its effects on behavior (i.e., the *dependent variable*). (p. 49)

Individualistic cultures Cultures whose members place a high value on individual accomplishments and personal success. (p. 269)

Industrial robotics (IR) Computer-controlled machines that manipulate materials and perform complex functions. (p. 558)

Informal communication The sharing of unofficial messages that go beyond the organization's formal activities. (p. 303)

Informal groups Groups that develop naturally among people, without direction from the organization within which they operate. (p. 254)

Informal status The prestige accorded individuals with certain characteristics not formally recognized by the organization. (p. 261)

Informate The process by which workers manipulate objects through "inserting data" between themselves and those objects. (p. 26)

Information power The extent to which a supervisor provides a subordinate with the information needed to do the job. (p. 414)

Ingratiation The process of getting someone to do what you want by putting that person in a good mood or getting that person to like you. (p. 410)

Initiating structure Activities by a leader to enhance productivity or task performance. Leaders who focus primar-

ily on these goals are described as demonstrating a task-oriented style. (p. 453)

Innovation The successful implementation of creative ideas within an organization. (p. 503)

Inputs People's contributions to their jobs, such as their experience, qualifications, or amount of time worked. (p. 143)

Instrumental conditioning See *operant conditioning*. (p. 70)

Instrumentality An individual's beliefs regarding the likelihood of being rewarded according to his or her own level of performance. (p. 149)

Integration Concern with the outcomes of others. (p. 382)

Integrative agreements Ones that offer greater joint benefits than simple compromise (i.e., splitting all differences down the middle). (p. 389)

Interactional justice The perceived fairness of the interpersonal treatment used to determine organizational outcomes. (p. 147)

Interactionist perspective The view that behavior results from a complex interplay between personality and situational factors. (p. 98)

Interdependence The extent to which individuals, departments, or units in a given organization depend on each other for accomplishing their tasks. (p. 574)

Interest group A group of employees who come together to satisfy a common interest. (p. 254)

Intermittent reinforcement See *partial reinforcement*. (p. 72)

Internal causes of behavior Explanations based on actions for which the individual is responsible. (p. 58)

Invalidating language Language that arouses negative feelings about one's self-worth. (p. 318)

J

Jargon The specialized language used by a particular group (e.g., people within a profession). (p. 311)

Job characteristics model An approach to job enrichment that specifies that five core job dimensions (skill variety, task identify, task significance, autonomy, and job feedback) that produce critical psychological states that, in turn, lead to beneficial outcomes for individuals (e.g., high job satisfaction) and the organization (e.g., reduced turnover). (p. 154)

Job Descriptive Index (JDI) A rating scale for assessing job satisfaction; individuals respond to this questionnaire by indicating whether various adjectives describe aspects of their work. (p. 173)

Job design An approach to motivation suggesting that jobs can be designed to enhance people's interest in doing them (see *job enlargement, job enrichment,* and the *job characteristics model*). (p. 153)

Job enlargement The practice of expanding the content of a job to include more variety and more tasks at the same level. (p. 153)

Job enrichment The practice of giving employees a high degree of control over their work, from planning and organization through implementation and evaluating the results. (p. 153)

Job rotation Lateral transfers of employees between jobs in an organization. (p. 219)

Job satisfaction Positive or negative attitudes held by individuals toward their jobs. (p. 170)

Job sharing A form of regular part-time work in which pairs of employees assume the duties of a single job, thus splitting its responsibilities, salary, and benefits in proportion to the time each works. (p. 23)

Joint ventures Strategic alliances in which several companies work together to fulfill opportunities requiring the capabilities of one another. (p. 544)

K

K.I.S.S. principle A basic principle of communication advising that messages should be as short and simple as possible (i.e., *keep it short and simple*). (p. 312)

Kelley's theory of causal attribution The approach suggesting that people will believe others' actions to be caused by internal or external factors based on three types of information: consensus, consistency, and distinctiveness. (p. 58)

L

Large-batch production Technology based on long production runs of standardized parts or products. (p. 570)

Law of Effect The tendency for behaviors leading to desirable consequences to be strengthened and for behaviors leading to undesirable consequences to be weakened. (p. 71)

Leader match According to *LPC contingency theory,* the practice of matching leaders (based on their *LPC* scores) to situations best matching those in which they are expected to be most effective. (p. 466)

Leader-member exchange (LMX) model A theory suggesting that leaders form different relations with various subordinates and that the nature of such dyadic exchanges can affect subordinates' performance and satisfaction. (p. 457)

Leaders Individuals within groups or organizations who wield the most influence over others. (p. 444)

Leadership The process whereby one individual influences other group members toward attaining defined group or organizational goals. (p. 445)

Leadership motivation The desire to influence others, especially toward attaining shared goals. (p. 448)

Learning organization An organization that is successful at acquiring, cultivating, and applying knowledge that can be used to help it adapt to change. (p. 601)

Learning A relatively permanent change in behavior resulting from experience. (p. 70)

Legitimate power The individual power base derived from one's position in an organizational hierarchy; the accepted authority of one's position. (p. 413)

Line positions Positions in organizations in which people can make decisions related to basic work. (p. 522)

Low LPC leaders Leaders who primarily are concerned with attaining successful task performance. (p. 464)

LPC Short for *esteem for least preferred co-worker*; a personality variable distinguishing between individuals by their concern for people (i.e., high LPC) and for production (i.e., low LPC). (p. 464)

LPC contingency theory A theory suggesting the characteristics of leaders (i.e., their *LPC* scores) and the level of situational control they can exert over subordinates determines leader effectiveness. (p. 464)

M

Machiavellianism A personality trait involving a willingness to manipulate others for one's own purposes. (p. 111)

Machine bureaucracy An organizational form in which work is highly specialized, decision making is concentrated at the top, and the work environment is not prone to change (e.g., a government office). (p. 536)

Machine vision A sophisticated technology in which electronic eyes send images to a computer that interprets what it "sees" and then commands other machines to take appropriate action. (p. 568)

Malcolm Baldrige Quality Award An award given annually to U.S. companies that practice effective quality management and significantly improve the quality of their goods and services. (p. 29)

Management by objectives (MBO) The technique by which managers and subordinates work together to set and then to meet organizational goals. (p. 603)

Market concentration strategies The tactic of withdrawing from markets where a company is less effective and concentrating resources in markets where the company is likely to be more effective. (p. 596)

Market-share increasing strategies A deliberate attempt by a company to develop a broader share of an existing market (e.g., widening the range of products or forming a joint venture with another company having a presence in the market of interest). (p. 596)

Mass customization The process of manufacturing goods to-order in a way that relies on mass-assembly processes. (p. 571)

Mass production See *large-batch production.* (p. 570)

Matrix of technologies Perrow's system of categorizing technologies based on two dimensions: *exceptions,* or the degree to which an organization uses standard inputs to produce standard outputs; and *problems,* or the degree to which the situations encountered are easy or difficult to analyze. (p. 555)

Matrix organization The type of departmentalization in which a product or project form is superimposed on a functional form. (p. 527)

Mechanistic organization An internal organizational structure in which people perform specialized jobs, rigid rules are imposed, and authority is vested in a few, top-ranking officials. (p. 533)

Mediation   The process of a third party attempting to facilitate voluntary agreements between parties in dispute. (p. 390)

Meditation   A technique for inducing relaxation in which individuals clear disturbing thoughts from their minds by repeating a single syllable. (p. 238)

Melting pot   The principle that people from different racial, ethnic, and religious backgrounds are transformed into a common American culture. (p. 19)

Mentor   A more experienced employee who offers advice, assistance, and protection to a younger, less experienced one (i.e., a *protégé*). (p. 212)

Mentoring   The process of serving as a mentor. (p. 212)

Mercenary culture   In the *double S cube*, a type of organizational culture characterized by low sociability and high solidarity. (p. 490)

Middle line   Managers who transfer information between higher and lower levels of the organizational hierarchy (see *strategic apex* and *operating core*.) (p. 535)

Minnesota Satisfaction Questionnaire (MSQ)   A rating scale for assessing job satisfaction in which people indicate the extent to which they are satisfied with various aspects of their jobs. (p. 173)

Mission statement   A document describing an organization's overall direction and general goals for accomplishing that movement. (p. 506)

Modeling   See *observational learning*. (p. 74)

Modular organization   An organization that surrounds itself by other organizations to which it regularly outsources non-core functions. (p. 538)

Morning persons   Individuals who feel most energetic and alert early in the day. (p. 115)

Motivating potential score (MPS)   A mathematical index describing the degree to which a job is designed to motivate people, as suggested by the *job characteristics model*. It is computed based on the Job Diagnostic Survey (JDS) questionnaire. (p. 157)

Motivation   The set of processes that arouse, direct, and maintain human behavior toward attaining some goal. (p. 130)

Motivator-hygiene theory   See *two-factor theory*. (p. 175)

Multicultural society   A society with many different racial, ethnic, socioeconomic, and generational subgroups, each with its own culture. (p. 17)

Multinational corporations (MNCs)   Organizations with significant operations spread throughout various nations but headquartered in a single nation. (p. 16)

Multiple regression   A statistical technique used to determine the extent to which each of several different variables contributes to predicting another variable (typically where the variable being predicted is the behavior in question). (p. 47)

MUM effect   The reluctance to transmit bad news, which is shown either by not transmitting the message at all or by delegating the task to someone else. (p. 306)

Mutual service consortia   A type of strategic alliance in which two similar companies from the same (or similar) industries pool their resources to receive a benefit too difficult or expensive for either to obtain alone. (p. 543)

N

Naturalistic observation   A research technique in which people are systematically observed in situations of interest to the researcher. (p. 51)

Need for achievement   See *achievement motivation*. (p. 113)

Need hierarchy theory   Maslow's theory specifying there are five human needs (physiological, safety, social, esteem, and self-actualization) that are arranged so that lower-level, more basic needs must be satisfied before higher-level needs become activated. (p. 133)

Negative affectivity   The tendency to experience negative moods in many settings and under many different conditions. (p. 104)

Negative correlation   A relationship between two variables such that more of one is associated with less of the other. (p. 46)

Negative reinforcement   The process through which people learn to perform acts that leads to the removal of undesired events. (p. 71)

Negotiation   See *bargaining*. (p. 387)

Neoclassical organizational theory   An attempt to improve on classical organizational theory that argues employee satisfaction as well as economic effectiveness are the goals of organizational structure. (p. 531)

Networked culture   In the *double S cube*, a type of organizational culture characterized by high sociability and low solidarity. (p. 489)

Newsletters   Regularly published internal documents describing information of interest to employees regarding business and nonbusiness issues affecting them. (p. 295)

Noise   Factors capable of distorting the clarity of messages. (p. 294)

Nominal group technique (NGT)   A technique for improving group decisions in which small groups systematically present and discuss their ideas before privately voting on their preferred solution. The most preferred solution then is accepted as the group's decision. (p. 359)

Nonprogrammed decisions   Decisions made about highly novel problems for which there are no prespecified courses of action. (p. 334)

Nonroutine technology   Technology involving many exceptions in inputs or outputs and problems that are difficult to analyze (e.g., research units, psychiatric hospitals). (See *matrix of technologies*.) (p. 557)

Nonverbal communication   The transmission of messages without the use of words (e.g., gestures, use of space). (p. 295)

Normative commitment   The strength of a person's desire to continue working for an organization because he or she feels obligations from others to remain. (p. 183)

Normative decision theory   A theory of leader effectiveness focusing primarily on strategies for choosing the most effective approach to decision making. (p. 471)

Norms   Generally agreed-on, informal rules that guide the behavior of group members. (p. 259)

O

Objective tests Questionnaires and inventories designed to measure various aspects of personality. (p. 99)

Observational learning The form of learning in which people acquire new behaviors by systematically observing the rewards and punishments given to others. (p. 74)

Old-boys network A gender-segregated, informal communication network composed of men with similar backgrounds. (p. 307)

Open systems Self-sustaining system that transform input from the external environment into output, which the system then returns to the environment. (p. 15)

Operant conditioning The form of learning in which people associate the consequences of their actions with the actions themselves. Behaviors with positive consequences are acquired; behaviors with negative consequences are eliminated. (p. 70)

Operating core Employees who perform the basic work related to an organization's product or service. (p. 534)

Organic organization An internal organizational structure in which jobs tend to be very general, there are few rules, and decisions can be made by lower-level employees. (p. 533)

Organization A structured social system consisting of groups of individuals working together to meet some agreed-on objectives. (p. 4)

Organizational behavior The field that seeks knowledge of all aspects of behaviors in organizational settings by the use of the scientific method. (p. 4)

Organizational behavior management The practice of altering behavior in organizations by systematically administering rewards. (p. 83)

Organizational behavior modification (OB Mod) See *organizational behavior management*. (p. 83)

Organizational chameleons Individuals who discern what behaviors they believe are generally appropriate in their organization and then go out of their way to make sure others are aware they behave in such a manner. (p. 425)

Organizational change Planned or unplanned transformations in an organization's structure, technology, or people. (p. 586)

Organizational chart A diagram representing the connections between the various departments within an organization; a graphic representation of organizational design indicating who is supposed to communicate with whom. (pp. 304, 518)

Organizational citizenship behavior (OCB) Actions by organization members that exceed the formal requirements of their job. (p. 372)

Organizational commitment The extent to which an individual identifies and is involved with his or her organization or is unwilling to leave it (see *affective commitment* and *continuance commitment*). (p. 181)

Organizational culture A cognitive framework consisting of attitudes, values, behavioral norms, and expectations shared by an organization's members. (p. 486)

Organizational design The process of co-ordinating the structural elements of an organization in the most appropriate manner. (p. 530)

Organizational development (OD) A set of social science techniques to plan change in organizational work settings to enhance the personal development of individuals and to improving the effectiveness of organizational functioning. (p. 603)

Organizational justice People's perceptions of fairness in organizations, consisting of perceptions regarding how decisions are made concerning the distribution of outcomes (*procedural justice*) and the perceived fairness of those outcomes themselves (as studied in *equity theory*). (p. 142)

Organizational politics Unauthorized uses of power that enhance or protect your own (or your group's) personal interests. (p. 410)

Organizational socialization The process through which newcomers to an organization become full-fledged members who share its major values and understand its policies and procedures. (p. 208)

Organizational structure The formal configuration between individuals and groups regarding the allocation of tasks, responsibilities, and authorities within organizations. (pp. 304, 518)

Outcomes The rewards, such as salary and recognition, that employees receive from their jobs. (p. 143)

Outplacement services Assistance in finding new jobs that companies provide to employees they lay off. (p. 136)

Outsourcing The practice of eliminating parts of organizations that focus on noncore sectors of the business and hiring outside firms to perform these functions instead. (pp. 26, 593)

Overload The condition in which a unit of an organization becomes overburdened with too much incoming information. (p. 314)

Overpayment inequity The condition, resulting in feelings of guilt, in which the ratio of one's outcomes to one's inputs is more than the corresponding ratio of another, comparison person. (p. 143)

P

Partial reinforcement A schedule of reinforcement in which only some desired behaviors are reinforced. Types include fixed interval, variable interval, fixed ratio, and variable ratio. (p. 72)

Participant observation A qualitative research technique in which people systematically observe what occurs in a setting by becoming an insider (i.e., part of that setting itself). (p. 52)

Participation Active involvement in the process of learning (more active participation leads to more effective learning). (p. 78)

Path-goal theory A theory suggesting subordinates are motivated by a leader only to the extent they perceive this individual as helping them to attain valued goals. (p. 468)

Pay Satisfaction Questionnaire (PSQ) A questionnaire to assess employees' satisfaction with various aspects of their pay (e.g., its overall level, raises, benefits). (p. 173)

Pay-for-performance A payment system in which employees are paid differentially based on the quantity and quality of their performance. Pay-for-performance plans strengthen *instrumentality* beliefs. (p. 151)

Perception The process through which people select, organize, and interpret information. (p. 55)

Perceptual biases Predispositions that people have to misperceive others in various ways. Types include the fundamental attribution error, halo effect, similar-to-me effect, first-impression error, and selective perception. (p. 60)

Performance appraisal The process of evaluating employees on various work-related dimensions. (p. 65)

Personal communication style The consistent ways in which people communicating with others (i.e., the *Noble*, the *Socratic*, the *Reflective*, the *Magistrate*, the *Candidate*, and the *Senator*). (p. 300)

Personal power The power derived from a person's individual qualities or characteristics. (p. 415)

Personal support policies Widely varied practices that help employees to meet the demands of their family lives, thus freeing them to concentrate on their work. (p. 22)

Personality The unique and relatively stable pattern of behaviors, thoughts, and emotions shown by an individual. (p. 97)

Personalized power motivation The wish to dominate others, reflected in an excessive concern with status. (p. 448)

Person-job fit The extent to which individuals possess the traits and competencies required for specific jobs. (p. 98)

Person-oriented See *consideration*. (p. 453)

Physical abilities The capacity to engage in the physical tasks required to perform a job. (p. 120)

Physiological needs The lowest-order, most basic needs in Maslow's *need hierarchy theory*, including fundamental biological drives such as the need for food, air, water, and shelter. (p. 134)

Pooled interdependence A relatively low level of interdependence, in which units of an organization operate in a largely independent manner. (p. 574)

Position power Power based on one's formal position in an organization. (p. 413)

Positive affectivity The tendency to experience positive moods and feelings in many settings and under many different conditions. (p. 104)

Positive correlation A relationship between two variables such that more of one is associated with more of the other. (p. 46)

Positive reinforcement The process through which people learn to perform behaviors leading the presentation of desired outcomes. (p. 71)

Power The capacity to change the behavior or attitudes of others in a desired manner. (p. 410)

Practical intelligence Adeptness at solving the practical problems of everyday life. (p. 117)

Predecision A decision about which process to follow in making a decision. (p. 332)

Prejudice Negative attitudes toward the members of specific groups based solely on their membership in those groups (e.g., age, race, sexual orientation). (p. 187)

Prescriptive norms Expectations within groups regarding what is supposed to be done. (p. 259)

Procedural justice Perceptions regarding the fairness of procedures used to determine outcomes. (p. 145)

Product organization The type of departmentalization based on the products (or product lines) produced. (p. 525)

Production-oriented See *initiating structure*. (p. 453)

Productive forgetting The ability to abandon unproductive ideas and temporarily put aside stubborn problems until new approaches can be considered. (p. 500)

Professional bureaucracy Organizations (e.g., hospitals, universities) with many rules to follow but with employees who are highly skilled and free to make decisions on their own. (p. 536)

Profit strategies Attempts to derive more profit from existing business (e.g., training employees to work more effectively or salespeople to sell more effectively). (p. 596)

Profit-sharing plans Incentive plans in which employees receive bonuses in proportion to the company's profitability. (p. 186)

Programmed decisions Highly routine decisions made according to pre-established organizational routines and procedures. (p. 334)

Progressive discipline The practice of gradually increasing the severity of punishments for employees who exhibit unacceptable job behavior. (p. 84)

Proscriptive norms Expectations within groups regarding behaviors in which members are not supposed to engage. (p. 259)

Prosocial behavior Actions that help other individuals or organizations in various ways. (p. 372)

Protégé A less experienced (often new) employee whose organizational socialization is facilitated by working with a *mentor*. (p. 212)

Psychological contract An implicit, informal understanding between an employee and the organization regarding what each will give to the other and what each will receive from the other. (p. 497)

Punctuated-equilibrium model The conceptualization of group development claiming that groups generally plan their activities during the first half of their time and then revise and implement their plans in the second half. (p. 257)

Punishment Decreasing undesirable behavior by following it with undesirable consequences. (p. 71)

Q

Qualitative overload The belief among employees that they lack the skills or abilities needed to perform their jobs. (p. 228)

Qualitative research A nonempirical type of research that relies on preserving the natural qualities of the situation being studied. (p. 51)

Qualitative underload The lack of mental stimulation that accompanies many routine, repetitive jobs. (p. 229)

Quality circles (QCs) An approach to improving the quality of work life in which small groups of volunteers meet regularly to identify and to solve problems related to the work they perform and the conditions under which they work. (p. 605)

Quality control audits Careful examinations of how well a company meets its standards. (p. 29)

Quality of work life (QWL) An OD technique designed to improve organizational functioning by humanizing the workplace, by making it more democratic, and by involving employees in decision making. (p. 604)

Quantitative overload A situation requiring individuals to accomplish more work than they actually can in a given period of time. (p. 228)

Quantitative underload A situation in which individuals have so little to do that they spend much of their time doing nothing. (p. 229)

R

Rational decisions Decisions that maximize the chance of attaining an individual's, group's, or organization's goals. (p. 343)

Rational persuasion Using logical arguments and factual evidence to convince others an idea is acceptable. (p. 415)

Rational-economic model The model of decision making according to which decision-makers consider all possible alternatives before selecting the optimal solution. (p. 343)

Realistic job previews Accurate information concerning the conditions within an organization or job provided to potential employees before to their decision to join. (p. 209)

Reciprocal interdependence The highest level of interdependence, in which the output of one department or unit serves as the input for other another in a reciprocal fashion. (p. 574)

Reciprocity The social norm which dictates that people expect to be paid back for the favors they grant others; the tendency for people to return the kind of treatment they receive from others. (pp. 377, 426)

Referent power The individual power base derived from the degree to which one is liked and admired by others. (p. 415)

Relaxation training Procedures through which individuals learn to relax to reduce anxiety or stress. (p. 239)

Reliability The extent to which a test yields consistent scores on various occasions and to which all its items measure the same underlying construct. (p. 100)

Repatriation The process of readjusting to one's own culture after spending time away from it. (p. 17)

Repetition The process of repeatedly performing a task so that it may be learned. (p. 78)

Representativeness heuristic The tendency to perceive others in stereotypical ways if they appear to be typical representatives of the category to which they belong. (p. 349)

Resiliency Learning ways of minimizing the degree to which stressors adversely affect us. (p. 238)

Resistance to change The tendency for employees to be unwilling to go along with organizational change because of individual fears of the unknown or organizational impediments (e.g., structural inertia). (p. 598)

Resource-dependency model The view that power resides within subunits able to control the greatest share of valued organizational resources. (p. 421)

Reward power The individual power base derived from an individual's capacity to reward others. (p. 414)

Rightsizing See *downsizing*. (p. 593)

Risky choice framing effect The tendency for people to avoid risks when situations are presented in a way that emphasizes positive gains and to take risks when presented in a way that emphasizes potential losses. (p. 347)

Role The typical behavior characterizing a person in a specific social context. (p. 258)

Role ambiguity The confusion arising from not knowing what one is expected to do as the holder of a role. (pp. 228, 258)

Role conflict Incompatible demands on an individual made by different groups or persons. (p. 228)

Role differentiation The tendency for various specialized roles to emerge as groups develop. (p. 259)

Role expectations The behaviors expected of someone in a particular role. (p. 258)

Role incumbent A person holding a particular role. (p. 258)

Routine technology Technology involving highly standardized inputs and outputs and problems that are easy to analyze (e.g., assembly lines, vocational training). (See *matrix of technologies*.) (p. 555)

Rumors Information with little basis in fact and often transmitted through informal channels (see *grapevine*). (p. 309)

S

Safety needs In Maslow's *need hierarchy theory*, the need for a secure environment, free from threats of physical or psychological harm. (p. 134)

Satisficing decisions Decisions made by selecting the first minimally acceptable alternative that becomes available. (p. 344)

Scapegoat Someone who is made to take the blame for another's failure or wrongdoing. (p. 426)

Schedules of reinforcement Rules governing the timing and frequency of administering reinforcement. (p. 72)

Scientific management An early approach to management and organizational behavior emphasizing the importance of designing jobs as efficiently as possible. (p. 6)

Second-order change Radical change; major shifts involving many different levels of the organization and aspects of business. (p. 586)

Selective perception The tendency to focus on some aspects of the environment and to ignore others. (p. 62)

Self-actualization In Maslow's *need hierarchy theory*, the need to discover who we are and to develop ourselves to our fullest potential. (p. 135)

Self-directed teams See *self-managed teams*. (p. 274)

Self-efficacy An individual's beliefs concerning his or her ability to perform specific tasks successfully. (pp. 107, 139)

Self-managed teams Teams whose members are permitted to make key decisions about how their work is done. (p. 274)

Self-monitoring A personality trait involving the extent to which individuals adapt their behavior to specific situations, primarily to make the best possible impression on others. (p. 109)

Self-oriented role The activities of an individual in a group who focuses on his or her own good, often at the expense of others. (p. 259)

Sequential interdependence An intermediate level of interdependence, in which the output of one department or subunit becomes the input for another. (p. 574)

Sexual harassment Unwanted contact or communication of a sexual nature. (p. 230)

Shaping The process of selectively reinforcing behaviors that approach a desired goal behavior. (p. 83)

Shared-screen conferencing The process of connecting computer workstations to provide concurrent displays of information and interaction between individuals. (p. 266)

Similar-to-me effect The tendency for people to perceive in a positive light others who they believed are similar to themselves in any of several different ways. (p. 60)

Simple structure An organization characterized as being small and informal, with a single power individual (often the founding entrepreneur) in charge of everything. (p. 535)

Situational leadership theory A theory suggesting the most effective style of leadership (i.e., *delegating*, *participating*, *selling*, or *telling*) depends on the extent to which followers require guidance, direction, and emotional support. (p. 467)

Skill-based pay An innovative reward system in which people are paid based on the number of different skills they have learned relevant to performing one or more jobs in the organization. (p. 81)

Skills-based diversity training An approach to diversity management that goes beyond *awareness-based diversity training* to develop people's skills in managing diversity. (p. 197)

Small-batch production A technology in which products are custom-produced in response to specific customer orders. (p. 570)

Snowball effect The tendency for people to share informal information with others. (p. 307)

Sociability A dimension of the *double S cube* characterized by the degree of friendliness among members of an organization. (p. 488)

Social dilemma A situation in which all parties (e.g., individuals, groups, or organizations) can increase their gains by acting in one way but stand to lose if all (or most) do so. (p. 377)

Social facilitation The tendency for the presence of others to enhance an individual's performance at times and to impair it at others. (p. 263)

Social impact theory The theory that explains social loafing in terms of the diffused responsibility of each group member for doing what is expected (see *social loafing*). The larger the group, the less each member is influenced by the social forces acting on that group. (p. 268)

Social influence Attempts to affect another in a desired fashion. (p. 409)

Social loafing The tendency for group members to exert less individual effort on an additive task as the size of the group increases. (p. 268)

Social needs In Maslow's *need hierarchy theory*, the need to be affiliative that is, to have friends and to be loved and accepted by other people. (p. 135)

Social perception The process of combining, integrating, and interpreting information about others to gain an accurate understanding of them. (p. 56)

Socialized power motivation The desire to cooperate with others, to work with them rather than dominate or control them. (p. 448)

Socioemotional role The activities of an individual in a group who is supportive and nurturant of other members and who helps them to feel good. (p. 259)

Solidarity A dimension of the *double S cube* characterized by the degree to which people in an organization share a common understanding of the tasks and goals about which they are working. (p. 489)

Span of control The number of subordinates in an organization who are supervised by managers. (p. 521)

Staff positions Positions in organizations in which people make recommendations to others but are not involved in decisions concerning day-to-day operations. (p. 522)

Stakeholder Any individual or group in whose interest an organization is run. (p. 596)

Standing committees Committees that are permanent. (p. 254)

Statements of principle Explicitly written statements describing the principles and beliefs that guide an organization. Such documents can help to reinforce an organization's culture. (p. 494)

Status The relative prestige, social position, or rank given to groups or individuals by others. (p. 260)

Status symbols Objects reflecting the position of an individual within an organization's hierarchy of power. (p. 260)

Stepladder technique A technique for improving the quality of group decisions that minimizes the tendency for members to be unwilling to present their ideas. New members to a group are added one at a time and are required to present his or her ideas independently to a group that already has discussed the problem at hand. (p. 360)

Stereotypes Beliefs that all members of specific groups share similar traits and are prone to behave in the same way. (p. 62)

Strain Deviations from normal states or functioning that result from *stress*. (p. 226)

Strategic alliance A type of organizational design in which two or more separate companies combine forces to develop and operate a specific business (see *mutual service consortia*, *joint ventures*, and *value-chain partnerships*.) (p. 542)

Strategic apex Top-level executives responsible for running an entire organization. (p. 535)

Strategic communication The practice of presenting information about the company to broad, external audiences (e.g., the press). (p. 311)

Strategic contingencies model The view that explains power in terms of a subunit's capacity to control the activities of other subunits. A subunit's power is enhanced when it can reduce the uncertainty experienced by other subunits, it occupies a central position in the organization, and its activities are highly indispensable. (p. 423)

Strategic decisions Nonprogrammed decisions, typically made by high-level executives, regarding the direction the organization should take to achieve its mission. (p. 334)

Strategic planning The process of formulating, implementing, and evaluating decisions that enable an organization to achieve its objectives. (p. 592)

Stress The pattern of emotional states, cognitions, and physiological reactions resulting from *stressors*. (p. 226)

Stress management programs Systematic efforts by organizations designed to help employees reduce or prevent stress. (p. 241)

Stressors Various factors in the external environment that induce stress among people exposed to them. (p. 226)

Structural inertia The organizational forces encouraging employees to perform their jobs in certain ways (e.g., training, reward systems), thereby making them resistant to change. (p. 599)

Subculture A smaller cultural subgroup, having its own well-defined culture, operating within larger, primary culture. (pp. 17, 487)

Substitutes for leadership The view that high skill levels among subordinates or certain features of technology and organizational structure sometimes substitute for leadership, thus rendering a leader's guidance or influence superfluous. (p. 474)

Support staff Individuals who provide indirect support services to an organization. (p. 535)

Supportive communication Any communication that is accurate and honest and that builds and enhances relationships instead of jeopardizing them. (p. 317)

Survey feedback An OD technique in which questionnaires and interviews are used to collect information about issues of concern to an organization. This information is shared with employees and is used as the basis for planning organizational change. (p. 606)

Surveys Questionnaires in which people report how they feel about various aspects of themselves, their jobs, and their organizations. (p. 45)

Symbols Material objects that connote meanings beyond their intrinsic content. (p. 493)

Systemic change A change in one part of an organization that is related to change in another. (p. 541)

T

Tacit knowledge Knowledge about how to get things done. (p. 118)

Task force See *ad hoc committee*. (p. 254)

Task group A formal organizational group that is formed around some specific task. (p. 253)

Task-oriented role The activities of an individual in a group who, more than anyone else, helps that group to reach its goal. (p. 259)

Team A group whose members have complementary skills and are committed to a common purpose or set of performance goals for which they hold themselves mutually accountable. (p. 271)

Team-based rewards Innovative reward systems in which employees are paid based on their team's performance. (p. 82)

Team building An OD technique in which employees discuss problems related to their work group's performance. On the basis of these discussions, specific problems are identified, and plans for solving them are devised and implemented. (p. 605)

Teamwork The practice of working in teams (see *team*). (p. 251)

Technology The physical and mental processes (e.g., knowledge, tools, procedures) used by an organization to perform its work (i.e., to transform inputs into usable outputs). (p. 554)

Technostructure Organizational specialists responsible for standardizing various aspects of an organization's activities. (p. 535)

Telecommuting The practice of using communications technology to perform work from remote locations (e.g., the home). (p. 24)

Theory A set of statements about the interrelationships between concepts that allow us to predict and to explain various processes and events. (p. 43)

Theory X A traditional philosophy of management suggesting that most people are lazy, irresponsible, and work hard only when forced to do so. (p. 12)

Theory Y A philosophy of management suggesting that under the right circumstances, people are fully capable of working productively and accepting responsibility for their work. (p. 12)

360° feedback The practice of collecting performance feedback from multiple sources at various organizational levels. (p. 79)

Time-and-motion study A type of applied research designed to classify and streamline the individual movements needed to perform a job and so the "one best way" to perform it. (p. 7)

Top-down decision-making The practice of vesting decision-making power in superiors as opposed to their lower-level employees. (p. 336)

Total quality management (TQM) An organizational strategy of commitment to improving customer satisfaction by developing techniques to carefully manage output quality. (p. 28)

Training The process of systematically teaching employees to acquire and improve job-related skills and knowledge. (p. 76)

Trait approach to leadership The idea that people become leaders because of the special traits they possess. (p. 447)

Transfer of training The degree to which skills learned during training sessions may be applied to performance of one's job. (p. 79)

Transformational leadership Leadership in which leaders use their charisma to transform and revitalize their organizations. (p. 462)

Transparency overestimation The belief that our own goals and motives are more apparent to opponents than actually is the case. (p. 390)

Trust An individual's confidence in the goodwill of others and the belief they will make efforts consistent with the group's goal. (p. 378)

Turnaround strategies Attempts to reverse a decline in business by moving to a new product line or by radically restructuring operations. (p. 596)

Two-dimensional model of subordinate participation An approach to leadership describing the nature of how leaders influence followers. This model distinguishes between leaders who are *directive* or *permissive* toward subordinates and the extent to which they are *participative* or *autocratic* in their decision making. Individual leaders may be classified into four types by where they fall on a grid combining these two dimensions. (p. 450)

Two-factor theory A theory of job satisfaction suggesting that satisfaction and dissatisfaction stem from different groups of variables (i.e., *motivators* and *hygiene*, respectively). (p. 175)

Two-tier wage structures Payment systems in which newer employees are paid less than employees hired at earlier times who do the same work. (p. 147)

Type A behavior pattern A pattern of behavior involving high levels of competitiveness, time urgency, and irritability. (p. 105)

Type B behavior pattern A pattern of behavior characterized by a casual, laid-back style; the opposite of the Type A behavior pattern. (p. 105)

U

Unconflicted adherence The tendency for decision-makers to stick with the first idea that comes to mind without more deeply evaluating the consequences. (p. 355)

Unconflicted change The tendency for people to change their minds quickly and to adopt the first new idea that comes along. (p. 355)

Underpayment inequity The condition, resulting in feelings of anger, in which the ratio of one's outcomes to one's inputs is less than the corresponding ratio of another, comparison person. (p. 143)

V

Valence The value a person places on the rewards he or she expects to receive from an organization. (p. 149)

Validating language Language that makes people feel recognized and accepted for who they are. (p. 318)

Validity The extent to which a test actually measures what it claims to measure. (p. 100)

Value-chain partnerships Strategic alliances between companies with complementary capabilities in different industries. (p. 543)

Value theory A theory suggesting that job satisfaction depends primarily on the match between the outcomes individuals value in their jobs and their perceptions about the availability of such outcomes. (p. 176)

Valuing diversity The practice of encouraging awareness of and respect for different people in the workplace. (p. 20)

Variable interval schedules Schedules of reinforcement in which a variable period of time (based on some average) must elapse between reinforcements. (p. 73)

Variable ratio schedules Schedules of reinforcement in which a variable number of responses (based on some average) must occur between reinforcements. (p. 73)

Verbal communication The transmission of messages using words, either written or spoken. (p. 294)

Videoconferencing The practice of using technology to provide audio and video links (either limited or full-motion) between work sites, thus allowing visual communication between people who are not physically present. (p. 266)

Video-mediated communication (VMC) Conferences in which people can hear and see each other using computers. (p. 319)

Virtual corporation A highly flexible, temporary organization formed by a group of companies to exploit a specific opportunity. (p. 28)

Virtual organization A highly flexible, temporary organization formed by a group of companies to exploit a specific opportunity. (p. 539)

Voluntary reduced work time (V-time) programs Programs that allow employees to reduce the amount of time they work by a certain amount (typically 10 or 20 percent) with a proportional reduction in pay. (p. 24)

W

Wellness programs A variety of training programs (e.g., exercise, nutritional training) designed to promote healthy employees. (p. 241)

Whistle-blowing Disclosure by employees of illegal, immoral, or illegitimate practices by employers to people or organizations able to do something about it. (p. 374)

Win-win situations Ones in which the interests of both sides are not necessarily incompatible and the potential gains for both can be maximized. (p. 389)

Work restructuring The process of changing how jobs are performed to make them more interesting to workers. (p. 604)

Work teams Teams whose members are concerned primarily with using the parent organization's resources to create its results. (p. 273)

Work-flow integration A measure of technology that considers the degree of automation, work-flow rigidity, and specificity of evaluation in an organization. (p. 572)

Workplace aggression Any action through which individuals seek to harm others in the workplace. (p. 394)

Workplace violence Direct, physical assaults by present or former employees against others in their organization. (p. 393)

Work-related attitudes Attitudes relating to any aspect of work or work settings. (p. 170)

Chapter 1, page 6: Brown Brothers, page 12 (left to right): Dana Downie/Photo 20–20, Corbis-Bettmann, page 23: Bob Rowan/Progressive Image/Corbis-Bettmann, page 24: IBM Corporation/Courtesy of International Business Machines Corporation. Unauthorized use not permitted.

Chapter 2, page 55: Ken Reid/FPG International LLC, page 63 (left to right): Andrew Medichini/AP/Wide World Photos, Li-Hau/The Image Works/Michele Bergess/The Stock Market, page 82: Unisys Corporation, page 98: Howard Grey/Tony Stone Images.

Chapter 3, page 105 (left to right): Roy Morsch/The Stock Market, VCG/FPG International LLC, page 108: Mark Cardwell/Reuters/Corbis-Bettmann, page 119: Steve Chenn Photography/Westlight/Corbis, page 120: Reuters/Joe Traver/Archive Photos.

Chapter 4, page 132: The Columbus Dispatch, page 134: Mark Richards, Page 137: David M. Barron/Oxygen Group Photography, page 146: Bill Kostroun/AP/Wide World Photos, page 146: Alan Klehr/Tony Stone Images, page 147: Michael Tweed/AP/Wide World Photos, page 159: Kenneth Jarecke/Contact Press Images Inc.

Chapter 5, page 179: Richard Morgenstein/Richard Morgenstein Photography, page 187: Brian Coats/Brian Coats Photography, page 189: UPI/Corbis-Bettmann, page 190: Reed Rahn/Rahn & Associates, page 194: Louis Psihoyos/Matrix International, Inc.

Chapter 6, page 209: Keith Brofsky/PhotoDisc, Inc., page 212: David M. Jennings/ The

Image Works, page 214: Esbin-Anderson/Photo 20–20, page 222: Reuters/Toshiyuki Aizawa/Archive Photos, page 222: Jeff Mermelstein, Inc., page 234: Amy Sancetta/AP/Wide World Photos, page 239: G. Steiner/Premium/Westlight Corbis.

Chapter 7, page 261: Frank Siteman/Index Stock Imagery, Inc., page 262: Laurent Rebours/AP/Wide World Photos, page 275: The British Petroleum Company p.i.c./"© BP Amoco p.i.c. (2000)," page 280: Dilip Mehta/Contact Press Images Inc.

Chapter 8, page 292: Mark Scott/FPG International LLC, page 298: Rob Lewine/The Stock Market, page 302: Edward D. Opp.

Chapter 9, page 337: John Abbott Photography, page: 360: Bob Hower/Quadrant Photography.

Chapter 10, page 372: Mitchell Layton/Duomo Photography Incorporated, page 374: Donald Smetzer/Shooting Star International Photo Agency, page 377(left to right): Ron Kimball/Ron Kimball Photography, General Motors Corporation/Copyright 1998 General Motors Corporation. Used with permission of GM Media Archives, page 380: Churchill & Klehr Photography, page 388: Christopher Bissell/Tony Stone Images, page 395: Bob Daemmrich/The Image Works, page 397: Michael Newman/PhotoEdit.

Chapter 11, page 411: Richard Pasley/Stock Boston, page 417: Tom Levy/Photo 20–20, page 419: Larry Ford Foto, page 424: Douglas Woods Photography, page 429: Churchill & Klehr Photography.

Chapter 12, page 451: Luis M. Alvarez/AP Wide World Photos, page 462: Oberto Gili/The Condé Nast Publications/Photo by Oberto Gili. Courtesy Vogue. © 1990 by the Condé Nast Publications Inc. Vogue, 5/90, p268., page 466 (left to right): Greg Kiger/Picture Cube, Inc./Index Stock Imagery, Robin Adshead/The Military Picture Library/Corbis-Bettmann, Henning Christoph/Dan Fotoar/Black Star.

Chapter 13, page 485: Brad Trent Photography/© 1999 Brad Trent, page 486: Jamie Tanaka, page 490: Bob Sacha Photography, page 496: Sylvia Otte, page 507: Corbis-Bettmann.

Chapter 14, page 526: Andy Freeberg Photography, page 537: Jim Allor Photography/200, page 538: John Abbott/John Abbott Photography, page 544: Lincoln Potter/Liaison Agency, Inc.

Chapter 15, page 556: Henry Ford Museum & Greenfield Village/"From the collections of Henry Ford Museum & Greenfield Village," page 559: Dana Smith/Black Star, page 569: Jay Reed, page 572: Jonathan Saunders, page 566: Patrick Harbron.

Chapter 16, page 586: Plissis/SIPA Press, page 591: Doug Mills/AP/Wide World Photos, page 592: Rex Rystedt Photography, page 594 (left to right): Larry Ford Foto, David Strick Photography, page 597: Pam Francis Photography/Pam Francis Photography. Printed in "Business Week," January 13, 1997, p. 60, page 600: Mark Richards.

COMPANY INDEX

NAME INDEX

Creativity *(Continued)*
components of, 500–502
defined, 499
idea box to stimulate,
513–14
innovation process
and, 506–7
Creativity heuristics,
501, 502
Creativity-relevant skills,
500–1
Credibility, 412
Criterion standard,
defining, 83
Critical incidents
technique, 173–74
Criticism, destructive, 384
Cross-cultural conflict, 386
Cross-cultural differences.
See Cultural differences
Cross-cultural training
(CCT), 77
Cross-cultural under-
standing, 197
Cross-functional teams,
275–76
Cultural briefings, 77
Cultural differences
in absenteeism, 185
in communications, 302–3
in decision making,
342–43
ethical decisions and, 357
leadership norms and, 456
nonverbal miscommuni-
cations and, 297
in performance evalua-
tions, 66, 67
recognizing value
differences on
job, 204–5
in role ambiguity, 228
in status given cognitive
intelligence, 119
in strategic planning,
597
Culturally diverse groups,
task performance
in, 267–68
Cultural pluralism, 20
Culture(s). *See also*
Organizational culture
adjusting to foreign,
stages of, 17–18
collectivistic, 269–70,
342–43, 383
defined, 17
impact of, 17–19

individualistic, 82, 269,
342, 383
perception and, 56
Type A vs. Type B
behavior and, 106
Culture assimilator, 77
Culture clashes, 496–98, 499
Culture shock, 17, 18
Customer service,
technological aids to,
563, 566–67
Customer service
orientation, 580–81
Customization, mass, 571–72
Cybermeetings, 319
Cyberspace, groups in, 266

D

Decentralization, 181,
523–24, 531
technology and, 572
work-flow integration
and, 573–74
Decision(s)
broad spectrum of
organizational, 334–37
certain, 335–36
conflict and, 387
creative, 353–54
by expert consensus,
358–59
group, 352–54
nonprogrammed, 334–35
ownership of, 318
programmed, 334–35
rational, 343
satisficing, 344
strategic, 334
testing ethics of, 32
uncertain, 335–36
Decision frame, 345–46
Decision makers, 522–23
Decision making, 329–68
administrative model
of, 344–45
analytical model of,
331–34
assessing personal style
of, 366–68
bias toward implicit
favorites in, 349–50
broad spectrum of
organizational
decisions, 334–37
case studies of, 364–66
cultural differences in,
342–43
defined, 331

empowered, 337
escalation of commitment
phenomenon, 350–52
factors affecting, 337–43
for firing, explanation
of, 232, 305
framing effects and,
346–48
group influences on,
339–41
heuristics and, 348–49
image theory of, 345–46
imperfections in, 346–52
individual differences
in, 337–39
intuitive approach to,
336, 345–46
normative decision
theory, 471–74
organizational influences
on, 341–42
procedural justice and
fair, 145–47
rational-economic model
of, 343–44
stress caused by, 227
techniques for improving
effectiveness
of, 354–62
top-down, 336–37
Decision rules, 472
Decision style, 337–39
Decision-style inventory, 339
Decision-style model, 338–39
Decision support systems
(DSS), 332–34
Decision tree, 473
Decoding, 293
Defensive avoidance, 355
Defensive strategies against
high Machs, 112–13
Deficiency needs, 135
Degenerative diseases, stress
and, 237
Degree of structure, LPC
contingency theory
and, 465
Delegation, 468
autocratic-delegation
continuum model,
449, 450
decentralization
and, 523–24
of responsibility, 240
Delphi Technique, 358–59
Demands
inability to cope with
work, 235

stress and occupa-
tional, 227–28
stress from competing,
228
Demographics of workforce,
shifting, 19–21, 590
Departmentalization, 524–30
defined, 524
by function and
product, 527–29
by market segment, 526
by task, 524–25
by type of output, 525–27
Dependence, power
through, 422–24
Dependent variable, 49–50
Depersonalization, 235, 236,
566
Design. *See* Organizational
design
Design and engineering,
computer-aided
(CAD/CAE), 558
Design for disassembly
(DFD), 563, 567–68
Destructive criticism, 384
Deviant organizational
behavior, 371, 392–99
defined, 392
employee theft, 371, 392,
396–99
workplace aggression, 371,
393–96
Devil's advocate, role of, 341
Diagnostic session, 605
Dictator, leader vs., 445
Diet, eating proper, 239
Difficult performance goals,
assigning, 141
Difficult tasks, attraction
to, 113–14
Difficulty of implemen-
tation, 155
Diffusion of responsibility,
351
Dignity, treating employees
with, 398
Direct experience, self-efficacy
development and,
107–8
Direction (component of
motivation), 131–32
Directive autocrat, 450, 451
Directive democrat, 450, 451
Directive style, 338
Disabilities, people with
assistive technology for,
562, 563–64

Exceptions dimension on matrix of technologies, 555
Exchange, influence through, 410
Excuses, impression management using, 68
Executive training programs, 77
Exhaustion, emotional, 235, 236
Existence needs, 136
Exit strategies, 596
Expatriates, 17
Expectancy, 149, 150, 151
Expectancy theory, 149–53
  basic elements of, 149–50
  defined, 149
  managerial applications of, 151–53
Expectations
  first-impression error and, 61–62
  motivation and, 149–53
  role, 258
  social influence tactics and, 411–12
Expected fair treatment, 373
Expediency, 111
Experience
  decisions based on, 336
  direct, 107–8
  with environment, organizational culture and, 493
  job satisfaction and, 172
  openness to, 102, 104
  vicarious, 107–8
Experienced meaningfulness of task, 156
Experimental evidence on team effectiveness, 278–79
Experimental logic, 49–50
Experimental method, 48–51
Expert consensus, decisions by, 358–59
Expertise, 412
Expert power, 415, 417
Export Control Act, 557
Exposure of high Machs, 112
External causes of behavior, 58
External communications, 310–11
External environment
  assessing, 595
  organizational design and, 532–33

External threats, interorganizational coordination in response to, 381
Extinction, 71–72
Extraordinary behavior of charismatic leader, 460
Extraversion, 102, 103–4
Extreme offer, 388
Extrinsic rewards, 179

F

"Face-saving" pressure, political, 342
Face-to-face discussions, 295
Facilitation, social, 263–66, 564
Facilitation skills, 197
Facilitator, 390
Factory work, 12
Failure, resistance to change due to past, 599
Fairness, 395–96
  assessing political action for, 435–36
  expected fair treatment, 373
  motivation and, 142–48
  in pay system, 144, 179–80
  procedural justice, 142–43, 145–47
Fairness Rule, 472
Fair notice of firing, 305
Family-supportive practice, 241
Faulty attributions, 384
Faulty communication, 384
Favorites, biases toward implicit, 349–50
Favoritism, hiring based on, 433, 434
Fear of the unknown, resistance to change and, 599
Federal Clean Air Act of 1990, 24
Federation, high-tech firms as, 576
Feedback, 293–94, 315–17
  active listening and, 312
  defined, 293
  destructive criticism, 384
  effective training through, 79
  on goal attainment, providing, 141–42
  in job characteristics model, 156, 157

opening channels for, 158
survey, 606–7
360°, 79–80, 81
Field experiences, cross-cultural training with, 77
Field experiment, 50, 51
Final-offer arbitration, 391
Financial performance, commitment to ethics and, 31–32
Financial security, providing, 136–37
Firing an employee, 231–32, 305–6
First-impression error, 61–62
First-order change, 586
Five-stage model of group development, 256–57
Fixed interval schedules, 72–73
Fixed ratio schedules, 73
Fixed-sum error, 390
Flat organizational structure, 519, 520, 521, 522, 531
  horizontal organization as, 529–30
Flexibility, 197
  designing high-tech organizations and, 575–76
  of great leaders, 449
  physical, 120
Flexible manufacturing systems, 558
Flexible work arrangements, 23–26
Flexplace programs (telecommuting), 24–26
Flextime programs, 23
Flyers, 295
Followers, 446, 456–59
  leaders' attributions to, 457–59
  leadership style and characteristics of, 470
  maturity of, 467
Follow-up, 334
Forgetting, productive, 500
Formal academic knowledge, 118
Formal communication, 303–7
Formal groups, 253
Formal status, 260
Forming stage of group development, 256
Founders, organizational culture and, 492–93

Fragmented culture, 490
Framing effects, 346–48
Freedom to initiate new ideas, 486
Free riding, social loafing and, 268–71
Friendship groups, 254
Fun, making jobs, 179
Function, departmentalization by product and, 527–29
Functional organizations, 524–25
Fundamental attribution error, 60, 64

G

Games, playing political, 427–28
Gatekeepers, 314, 315
Gays, prejudice against, 192
Gender. *See also* Women
  career development and, 222–24
  communication and, 301–2
  mentoring and, 214–15
Gender stereotypes, 193
Germany, packaging laws in, 567
Glass ceiling, 188–89, 223–24
Global economy, 16–19
  competition in, 591
  strategic alliances in, 544–45
Globalization, 16–19
Global managers, 36
Goal(s)
  career, 219
  feedback on goal attainment, 141–42
  group, 252
  innovation management and, 505
  leadership and, 446
  MBO to clarify organizational, 603–4
  motivation and attainment of, 132
  path-goal theory of leadership and, 468–71
  specific, assigning, 140
  in strategic plan, 594
  team, clarity of, 281
Goal acceptance, enhancing, 141

Performance *(Continued)*
appropriate measures for teams, 281–82
criteria for telecommuters, 26
financial, commitment to ethics and, 31–32
guidelines for setting effective goals, 140–42
individual, in group, 263–71
job, 132, 150
organizational culture and, 495–96
positive affectivity and, 104
self-monitoring and work, 109
Performance appraisal, 65–66
Performance gaps, 590
Performance monitoring, computerized, 264–66, 562, 564–66
Performance problems, written records of, 305
Performing stage of group development, 256–57
Permanent overlay, 528
Permanent teams, 273, 274
"Permanent temporary" employees, 27
Permissive autocrat, 450, 451
Permissive democrat, 450, 451
Personal appeal, 410
Personal communication style, 299–301
assessing, 326–27
Personal decision style, assessing, 366–68
Personal distance, 298
Personality, 96–116, 125. *See also* Abilities
achievement motivation, 113–15
big five dimensions of, 102–4
defining, 97
Machiavellianism, 110–13, 127
measuring, 99–101
morning persons and evening persons, 115–16
positive and negative affectivity, 104–5
role in organizational behavior, 97–99
self-efficacy, 107–9, 139
self-monitoring, 109–10, 125–26

Type A behavior, 105–7, 237–38
work-related aspects of, 102–16
Personality tests, 99–101
Personalized power motivation, 448
Personalized service, delivering, 566–67
Personal orientation, 378
Personal power, 414–16
Personal stories, impression management using, 68
Personal support policies, 22
Person-job fit, 98–99, 107, 180, 216
Person-organization fit, 495–96
Person-oriented leaders, 453–54
Persuasion, rational, 410, 411, 415
Physical abilities, 117, 120–21
Physical condition, prejudice based on, 190
Physiological needs, 134, 136
Physiological stress management techniques, 238–39
Planned organizational change, 498–99
Pluralism, cultural, 20
Policies, political activity and lack of clear, 431–32
Political action, triggering of, 428–31. *See also* Organizational politics
Political dynamics, shaping, 600
Political "face-saving" pressure, 342
Political games, playing, 427–28
Pooled interdependence, 574
Pooling of resources, 339
Position power, 413–14, 465
Positive affectivity, 104–5
Positive correlation, 46
Positive effects of conflict, 385, 387
Positive reinforcement, 71, 72
Power, 408, 413–24. *See also* Organizational politics
balance of, 599
case study of, 438
centralization of, 114, 523, 570
coercive, 414, 417
defined, 410

empowerment and, 417, 418–20
ethics of organizational politics and, 432, 433
expert, 415, 417
group or subunit, 421–24
information, 414
legitimate, 413–14, 417
methods of using, 417–18
organizational development techniques and unequal, 610
personalized power motivation, 448
personal power, 414–16
position power, 413–14, 465
referent, 415
reward, 414
social influence compared to, 409–10
socialized power motivation, 448
Power base games, 427, 428
Power distance, 228, 414
Practical intelligence, 117–19
Predecision, 332
Prediction, as major goal of science, 43
Predisposition, 170
Pre-entry period, organizational socialization in, 208–11
Prejudice, 169, 186–93
based on age, 189–90
based on physical condition, 190
based on race and national origin, 190–91
based on sexual orientation, 192
defined, 187
discrimination as distinct from, 187, 188
reality of diversity and problems of, 187–89
against women, 192–93
Prescriptive (normative) approach, 344
Prescriptive norms, 259
Pressure, influence through, 411
Prestige of group membership, 260–62
Price leadership, 493
Price wars, 402
Prince, The (Machiavelli), 110–11

Priorities, setting, 240
Privacy rights, 435, 564, 565
Private reality, self-image vs., 109–10
PROACT, 136
Probability in decision making, 335–36
Problem identification, 331–32
Problems, focusing on, 317
Problems dimension on matrix of technologies, 555
Procedural justice, 142–43, 145–47
questionnaire on, 164–65
social side of, 147
structural side of, 146–47
Process, structuring by, 529–30
Procrastination, 355
Product(s)
defining scope of, 594–95
departmentalization by function and, 527–29
strategic planning for change in, 592–93
Production
continuous-process, 570
large-batch (mass production), 570
small-batch, 570
Production-oriented leaders, 453–54
Productive forgetting, 500
Productivity
Hawthorne studies of, 7–9, 531
job satisfaction and, 178–79
work as productive and pleasant, 12–13
Product organizations, 525–27
Professional bureaucracy, 536
Profitability test, 345
Profit-sharing plans, 186
Profit strategies, 596
Programmed decisions, 334–35
Progressive discipline, 84–85
Progressive punishment, 395
Proscriptive norms, 259
Prosocial behavior, 371–75
defined, 372
organizational citizenship behavior (OCB), 184, 372–74